ALPHABETICAL LIST OF SECTIONS

HANDBOOK OF
CORPORATE FINANCE

HANDBOOK OF CORPORATE FINANCE

Edited by

EDWARD I. ALTMAN
Professor of Finance
Chairman, MBA Program
Graduate School of Business Administration
New York University

Associate Editor

MARY JANE McKINNEY

WILEY PROFESSIONAL BANKING AND FINANCE SERIES

EDWARD I. ALTMAN, Editor

JOHN WILEY & SONS

New York · Chichester · Brisbane · Toronto · Singapore

GE

Library of Congress Cataloging in Publication Data:

Handbook of corporate finance.
    (Wiley professional banking and finance series)
    "A Ronald Press Publication."

    Rev. ed. of: Financial handbook. 5th ed. c1981.
    Bibliography: p.
    1. Corporations--Finance--Handbooks, manuals, etc.
    I. Altman, Edward I., 1941-   . II. McKinney, Mary
Jane. III. Financial handbook. IV. Series.

HG4026.H288 1986   658.1′5   86-15978
ISBN 0-471-81957-3

Printed in the United States of America

10 9 8 7 6 5 4 3 2 1

To my wife, Elaine, and son, Gregory

Whose love and understanding continue
to make a difference

PREFACE

The last revision of the *Financial Handbook* was published in 1981 as the fifth edition of that venerable and respected reference book. I was privileged then to be nominated by the Ronald Press Division of John Wiley & Sons to follow the earlier works of Dr. Jules I. Bogen, who edited the third and fourth editions (the original edition was vintage 1925). The fifth edition came out 14 years after its most immediate predecessor and although we all agreed that the field of finance had evolved enormously in that time span, it still was a relatively long period between editions. Nobody, however, predicted that the finance and related areas would virtually explode, in the early and mid-1980s, in terms of innovation and sophistication, requiring a rapid assessment of the need to revise again. As early as 1984, just three years after its publication, those of us involved with the *Financial Handbook*, *Fifth Edition*, decided that it was time to map out the next revision. The result is this book and its companion volume, the *Handbook of Financial Markets and Institutions*.

When we were planning for the sixth edition of the *Financial Handbook*, it became apparent that a number of new sections were needed, especially related to financial markets and institutions. The fifth edition was already "heavy" with over 1400 book pages. We knew that a single volume could not encompass our four major designated areas related to finance: (1) domestic financial markets and institutions, (2) international markets and institutions, (3) investment theory and practice, and (4) corporate finance. We decided to concentrate on markets, institutions, and investments for the sixth edition and change its title to the *Handbook of Financial Markets and Institutions*, *Sixth Edition*, which is available as a separate volume or can be obtained from the publisher as part of a two-volume package. The result is that both books are hefty compendiums since our primary objective is to be broadly eclectic in our coverage as well as comprehensive within a specific area.

A group of distinguished and respected experts in the fields chosen for discussion has been assembled. These experts represent business executives, financial economists from the academic and business worlds, government authorities—some of whom have now moved from the public to the private sector—and financial consultants. They have synthesized the latest literature and developments in their fields in order to present fairly concise yet comprehensive studies of current principles and practice. My suggestions were as before: Write about what you know best and present the material in a modern financial analytic structure. Since our audience, for the most part, consists of practitioners of the art of finance, or those who aspire to be practitioners, a premium is put on communication of essential concepts and a summary of practices.

In the fifth edition's preface, I stated that one of my objectives was "that the bulk of material presented not soon be out of date." Although it is true that the field of financial markets and institutions has developed and intensified in just a few short years, at the same time much of what was written before is still relevant. Indeed, 14 of 15 authors who wrote sections in the fifth edition return again to discuss their fields in this volume and 15 of 23 in the financial markets and institutions volume have been retained.

Once again I have been assisted by several extraordinarily talented persons. My primary debt of gratitude goes to my Associate Editor, Mary Jane McKinney. Mary Jane and I might be considered veterans by now but we really did learn a great deal more about editing, especially in our efforts to put together two volumes at the same time. We were aided by a distinguished group of Editorial Consulting Board members from business and academia. The credit for the exceptional quality of the book, in the final analysis, must rest with the contributing authors and we are so fortunate to have such a distinguished group accept the challenge. Not everyone realizes the difficulty of summarizing a field into a concise manuscript that is both comprehensive and easily read and understood in a relatively short time. Our authors have succeeded in this challenge.

My staff at New York University worked very hard and diligently in assisting in the massive logistical editing process. I would like to thank Diana Coryat, Nayan Kisnadwala, Brenda Lane, Susan Meah, Teresa Santamaria, Karen Sosnick, and Eva Wan for their tremendous contributions. Several talented individuals at John Wiley & Sons were involved in various stages of the projects and were also very helpful. Reflecting back on the process, I feel the *Handbook of Corporate Finance* is indeed a team effort.

Finally, I owe a great deal to my wife Elaine and son Gregory for their encouragement and support.

EDWARD I. ALTMAN

New York, New York
August 1986

CONTENTS

CONTRIBUTORS

EDWARD I. ALTMAN is professor of finance and chairman of the MBA program at New York University. He has been visiting professor at the Hautes Etudes Commerciales and Universite de Paris-Dauphine in France, at the Pontifica Catolica Universidade in Rio de Janeiro, Brazil, and the Australian Graduate School of Management. Altman has an international reputation as an expert on corporate bankruptcy and credit analysis. He was named *Laureate 1984* by the Hautes Etudes Commerciales Foundation in Paris for his accumulated works on bankruptcy prediction models and procedures for financial rehabilitation. Altman is editor of an international publication, the *Journal of Banking and Finance*, and two publisher series, *Wiley Professional Banking and Finance Series* (Wiley) and *Contemporary Studies in Economics and Finance* (JAI Press). Dr. Altman has published several books and over 60 articles in scholarly finance, accounting, and economic journals. He is the current editor of the *Financial Handbook* and the author of recently published books on *Corporate Financial Distress* and *Recent Trends in Corporate Finance*. His work has appeared in several languages including Portuguese, Japanese, German, and French. Altman's primary areas of research include bankruptcy analysis and prediction, credit and lending policies, corporate finance, and capital markets. He has been a consultant to several government agencies, major financial and accounting institutions, and industrial companies, has lectured to executives in North America, South America, Europe, and Asia, has testified before the U.S. Congress on several occasions, and is on the Scientific and Technical Committee of Italy's Centrale dei Bilanci.

STEVEN J. APPEL is managing director–small business/general practice of the international accounting firm Arthur Andersen & Co. He has spent his entire 21-year career providing accounting, audit, financial, and tax consulting services to owner-managed, emerging small businesses. Under Appel's direction, Arthur Andersen & Co. has developed various programs dealing with small business personal and business taxes, cash planning, management reporting requirements, and other issues related to growth, diversification, and profitability. Previously, Appel managed the small business practice of Arthur Andersen's Milwaukee office. He has also served on the Firm's Chairman's Advisory Council, Audit Advisory Council, Marketing Implementation Group, Financial Consulting Services Steering Committee, and Audit Research and Development Advisory Committee. Appel is a founding board member of the Independent Business Association of Wisconsin and participated in the 1980 White House Conference on Small Business. Appel is a member of the AICPA and has a BBA degree from the University of Wisconsin.

MOSHE BEN-HORIM is a senior lecturer in finance at the Jerusalem School of Business at Hebrew University, Jerusalem, Israel. He has held financial research positions at institutions in the United States and Israel, including the (U.S.) National Bureau of Economic Research, the Israeli Institute of Financial Research, and the Hebrew University of Jerusalem. He has taught at New York University, the University of Florida, McGill University, and Montclair (New Jersey) State College. Dr. Ben-Horim has written articles in professional journals and books in business and economics statistics (1980). He received his BA and MA degrees in economics from the Hebrew University of Jerusalem, and a PhD degree in finance and economics from the Graduate School of Business Administration, New York University.

HAROLD BIERMAN, JR. is the Nicholas H. Noyes Professor of Business Administration at the Johnson Graduate School of Management, Cornell University. He has taught at Louisiana State University, University of Michigan, and the University of Chicago. He is the author or coauthor of 17 books and over 100 journal articles, and the coordinator of the Financial Management portion of Cornell's Executive Development Program. He has been a consultant to a number of firms including Emerson Electric, Xerox, Corning Glass Works, Owens Corning Fiberglas, Exxon, and IBM. He has also testified at public utility rate cases for corporations and for public service commissions.

Bierman has served on two tax commissions for the Governor of the State of New York (his recommendations were not followed). He received his PhD from the University of Michigan.

EUGENE F. BRIGHAM is graduate research professor of finance and director of the Public Utility Research Center at the University of Florida, Gainesville. Brigham has served as president of the Financial Management Association and has written more than 40 journal articles dealing with the cost of capital, capital structure, and other aspects of financial management. The 10 textbooks on managerial finance and managerial economics of which he is author or coauthor are used at more than 1000 universities in the United States and have been translated into seven languages for worldwide use.

Brigham has testified in numerous electric and telephone rate cases at both the federal and state levels, and has served as a consultant to many utility and industrial companies and to the Federal Reserve Board, the Federal Home Loan Bank Board, the U.S. Office of Telecommunications Policy, and the Rand Corp. He received a BS degree from the University of North Carolina, Chapel Hill, and MBA and PhD degrees from the University of California, Berkeley.

THOMAS E. COPELAND is an associate professor of financial economics at the Graduate School of Management of the University of California, Los Angeles. He is coauthor of *Financial Theory and Corporate Policy* (2nd ed.), an advanced-level text, and *Managerial Finance* (8th ed.), a best-selling intermediate-level text. Copeland has published articles in numerous academic journals including *Journal of Finance*, *Journal of Financial Economics*, *Journal of Financial and Quantitative Analysis*, *Journal of Economics and Business*, *Engineering Economist*, and *Journal of Accounting, Auditing, and Finance*. He is a member of the New York Stock Exchange Arbitration Board, an associate editor of *The Financial Review*, a member of the Board of Directors of Kaloma Chemical Inc., does consulting in the area of corporate valuation, and is active in executive education. Copeland received a BA degree from Johns Hopkins University, and MBA and PhD degrees from the University of Pennsylvania's Wharton School of Finance.

MARTIN S. FRIDSON is a principal at Morgan Stanley & Co. Incorporated, where he edits *High Performance: The Magazine of High Yield Bonds*. His previous professional experience includes trading electric utility bonds and analyzing industrial and natural gas credits. He belongs to the Financial Analysts Federation and Fixed Income Analysts Society and served as chairman of those organizations' 1985 Bond Seminar. Fridson is also a member of the New York Society of Security Analysts and is a Chartered Financial Analyst. Besides contributing to *Bondweek* on such topics as credit analysis and relative valuation, he has written several humorous pieces in the *Wall Street Journal*, *The New York Times*, and *Playbill*. Fridson received his BA cum laude in history from Harvard College and MBA from Harvard Business School.

RICHARD KARL GOELTZ is vice president of finance and director of Joseph E. Seagram and Sons, Inc. as well as vice president, treasurer, and controller of The Seagram Company Ltd. His current responsibilities include treasury, controllers, tax, internal audit, credit, and risk management. He has published articles on international financial management and foreign exchange in periodicals, newspapers, and books. Goeltz has also presented speeches on the topic of international finance to numerous professional groups, including bank and corporate executives. He has appeared on panels at the

Financial Executives Institute and the Financial Management Association. Goeltz received an AB degree in Economics from Brown University and an MBA from Columbia University.

JOHN T. HACKETT is a director of Cummins Engine Company, Cummins Engine Foundation, Irwin Union Corp., the Ransburg Corp., CADEC Systems, the Indianapolis Zoological Society, the Corporation for Innovation Development, the Heritage Venture Group, and the Ohio State Development Fund and is president of the Indiana Secondary Market for Education Loans, Inc. He is a past director of the Federal Reserve Bank of Chicago. He has served on the faculties of Ohio State, Case Western Reserve, and Kent State universities. Hackett received his BS and MBA from Indiana University and his PhD from Ohio State University, where he now serves on the Alumni Advisory Council.

NED C. HILL is associate professor of finance at Indiana University School of Business. He has served as coeditor of the *Journal of Cash Management* and now serves as contributing editor. He has been actively involved in research, teaching, and consulting in the areas of cash management, credit policy, payables policy, banking, and short-term financial planning. Hill has written many articles which have appeared in such journals as *Journal of Finance*, *Financial Management*, *Journal of Financial and Quantitative Analysis*, *Journal of Bank Research*, and *Journal of Cash Management*. In 1984 he and coauthor Daniel M. Ferguson won the Fentress Prize from the Bank Administration Institute for the best paper in cash management. He also wrote, with William Sartoris and Gary Emery, *Essentials of Cash Management: A Study Guide* (National Corporate Cash Management Association, 1985). He received his MBA and PhD from Columbia University.

ROBERT W. JOHNSON is professor of management and director of the Credit Research Center, Krannert Graduate School of Management, Purdue University, Lafayette, Indiana. He was reporter–economist to the Special Committee on the Uniform Consumer Credit Code (1965–1974) and a presidential appointee to the National Commission on Consumer Finance (1969–1972). Johnson is a trustee of the National Foundation for Consumer Credit and is on the Policy Board of *Journal of Retail Banking*. During 1970 he was president of the newly formed Financial Management Association. Johnson is the author of two books, *Financial Management* (4th ed.) and *Capital Budgeting*, and coauthor of *Self-Correction Problems in Finance* (3rd ed.). He holds a PhD degree from Northwestern University, Evanston, Illinois, and was a fellow at the Institute of Basic Mathematics for Application to Business, Harvard University.

JARL G. KALLBERG is an associate professor of finance at New York University's Graduate School of Business where he has taught financial theory and working capital management since 1978. He has taught at the University of British Columbia, as well as in Stockholm and Singapore. He is a senior editor with the *Journal of Cash Management*. In addition to publishing a number of articles in journals such as *Management Science*, *Operations Research*, *Journal of Finance*, and *Financial Management*, he wrote, with Kenneth Parkinson, *Current Asset Management*. He has a BSc and MSc in mathematics, and received his PhD in business administration from the University of British Columbia.

W. CARL KESTER is assistant professor of business administration at Harvard University. The focus of his work has been the theory and practice of corporate finance with special emphasis on problems of strategic capital budgeting. He is a member of the American Finance Association, the Financial Management Association, and the American Economics Association. Kester is the author of a number of articles and cases on corporate finance topics, has been a consultant to a wide variety of firms and government agencies, and teaches in numerous executive training programs. He is also an associate editor of *Financial Management*.

HAIM LEVY is professor of finance at Hebrew University in Jerusalem, Israel. He has taught extensively in the United States as a visiting professor at the University of Illinois, the University of California, Berkeley, the University of Florida, and the University of Pennsylvania. Levy has served as consultant to many firms as well as to the government of Israel and has had almost 100 articles and books published. He is an editor of *Research in Finance*. Levy received a BA degree in economics and statistics, an MA degree in statistics and finance, and a PhD degree in economics and finance, all from the Hebrew University of Jerusalem.

MICHAEL J. MAROCCO is an associate at Morgan Stanley and Co., Inc. with primary responsibility for the credit analysis of media, communications, and gaming and hotel companies in the high yield bond market. In addition, Marocco periodically comments on current accounting issues in *Accounting Perspectives* and has contributed to the *Journal of Accountancy* on such topics. His previous professional experience was as an auditor for a Big Eight accounting firm. He belongs to the Rhode Island Society of CPAs and is an author of *The Financial Management Resource Manual for Non Profit Organizations*. He received his BS cum laude in accounting from the University of Southern Maine and his MBA from New York University.

JOHN MARTIN is professor of finance at the University of Texas (Austin) and serves as Advisor for the PhD program in Finance. He is coauthor of a number of texts including *Basic Financial Management* (3rd ed.) and *Introduction to the Theory of Finance*. He has written numerous articles in financial management and serves as finance and economics editor for the *Journal of Business Research*. He received his BA and MBA from Louisiana Tech University and his PhD from Texas Tech University, Lubbock.

ROGER F. MURRAY is professor emeritus of finance, Graduate School of Business, Columbia University, and currently serves as consultant to foundations and corporate pension funds. He is a member of the Pension Research Council, the Investment Advisory Committee of the New York State Teachers' Retirement System, the board of the Investor Responsibility Research Center, and the boards of 10 mutual funds in the Alliance Capital Management Group. Murray previously served as a public director of the Chicago Board Options Exchange, an executive officer of College Retirement Equities Fund, and director of the National Bureau of Economic Research pension study (1968). He was an original member of the Pension Benefit Guaranty Corporation's Advisory Committee and served for eight years on its Investment Policy Panel. He is a past president of the American Finance Association and originator of the individual retirement account (IRA) concept. Murray received his BA degree from Yale University, MBA and PhD degrees from New York University, and an LLD degree from Hope College.

GEORGE G. C. PARKER is director of Executive Education and senior lecturer at the Graduate School of Business at Stanford University. His primary teaching areas are commercial and investment banking and corporate financial management. Parker is a member of the board of directors of and/or consultant to various corporations and banks, including Central Pacific Corp., California Casualty Group of Insurance Companies, Citicorp, J. P. Morgan, Inc., and Haverford College. He has written and been coauthor of several articles for the *Financial Analysts Journal*, the *Harvard Business Review*, and the *Journal of Financial and Quantitative Analysis*. Parker received his BA from Haverford College and his MBA and PhD from Stanford University.

KENNETH L. PARKINSON is the executive editor of the *Journal of Cash Management*. He is also an adjunct professor at New York University's Graduate School of Business, teaching corporate cash management practices. Before founding the consulting and publishing firm Treasury Communications, he was head of worldwide treasury operations at RCA. In addition to a number of publications in journals such as *American Banker* and *Pensions and Investment Age*, he and Jarl Kallberg wrote *Current Asset Management*. Parkinson received his BSc degree from the Pennsylvania State University.

ALFRED RAPPAPORT is the Leonard Spacek Professor at the Kellogg Gradute School of Management at Northwestern University. He also serves as Chairman of the Board of The Alcar Group Inc. He has served as a consultant to numerous Fortune 500 firms on mergers and acquistions analysis, strategic financial planning, and executive compensation and incentives. He has designed two widely acclaimed executive programs (Merger Week and Strategic Financial Planning) at Northwestern University. His shareholder value approach to merger analysis, planning, and performance evaluation provides the conceptual foundation for the Alcar management education and software programs. Rappaport is a frequent contributor to many of the nation's leading business publications, including *The Wall Street Journal*, *Business Week*, and *Harvard Business Review*.

ALAN C. SHAPIRO is a visiting professor of finance at UCLA's Graduate School of Management (with a permanent teaching position at the University of Southern California) and has held teaching positions at many other universities, among them the Wharton School and the Stockholm School of Economics. Shapiro has published over 25 articles in leading finance and business journals and has written two monographs in the areas of international finance and foreign exchange risk management for the American Management Association and the Financial Management Association. In addition to his research, he is the author of the foremost textbook on the subject, *Multinational Financial Management* (2nd ed.), and a new textbook, *Modern Corporate Finance*, is scheduled for late 1986. Shapiro has taught in numerous executive education programs and has conducted in-house seminars for and consulted with various banks, corporations, and law firms.

BERNELL K. STONE is the Mills B. Lane Professor at Georgia Institute of Technology. He was the founding editor of *Journal of Cash Management*. He served as the academic administrator for the National Corporate Cash Management Association from 1980 to 1983. He has served as an associate editor for *Financial Management*, *Journal of Financial and Quantitative Analysis*, and *Journal of Financial Research*. He now serves on the editorial board for the *Journal of Business Research* and *Advances in Working Capital Research*. More than 40 of his numerous articles deal with cash management and related topics. Stone's papers won awards in the Financial Management Association's annual competitions in 1974 and 1975. Stone holds a BS from Duke University, an MS from the University of Wisconsin, and a PhD from MIT.

MARTI G. SUBRAHMANYAM is a professor of finance and chairman of the finance area at the Graduate School of Business Administration, New York University. He has taught finance and economics at the Massachusetts Institute of Technology, Cambridge, the Indian Institute of Management, Ahmedabad, and at Ecole Superieur de Science Economics et Commerce (France). Subrahmanyam has published in several leading journals in finance and economics. His research interests are in the areas of capital market theory, corporation finance, and international finance. He is coauthor of the books *Capital Market Equilibrium and Corporate Financial Decisions* and *Financial Analysis of Corporate Assets*. He serves as an associate editor of *Management Science*, the *Journal of Banking and Finance*, and the *Journal of Finance*. Subrahmanyam received a BA from the Indian Institute of Technology, an MBA degree from the Indian Institute of Technology, an MBA degree from the Indian Institute of Management, Ahmedabad, and a PhD from the Massachusetts Institute of Technology.

T. CRAIG TAPLEY is assistant professor of finance and member of the graduate faculty at the University of Florida. He has written a number of journal articles dealing with aspects of financial management and problems faced by utilities, and has been a contributing author to several handbooks. He received a BS degree from Trinity College, an MBA from the Amos Tuck School at Dartmouth College, and a DBA from Indiana University.

J. FRED WESTON is professor emeritus of managerial economics and public policy and Cordner Professor of Money and Financial Markets at the Graduate School of Management of the University of California, Los Angeles. Weston has served as president of the American Finance Association, Western Economic Association, the Financial Management Association, and has served as consultant to business firms on financial and economic policies. He has been teaching at UCLA since 1949 and received a Distinguished Teaching Award as one of the five outstanding teachers in 1978. Weston is the author of over 25 books including *Managerial Finance* and *Financial Theory and Corporate Policy*. His books have been translated into approximately 10 languages. He has written over 175 articles which have appeared in such journals as the *Journal of Finance* and the *Journal of Business* on subjects dealing with cost of capital, price behavior, antitrust policy, and mergers. Weston has testified in numerous cases for such companies as AT&T and General Motors. He received his BA, MBA, and PhD degrees from the University of Chicago.

HANDBOOK OF
CORPORATE FINANCE

1

PLANNING AND CONTROL TECHNIQUES

CONTENTS

1

PLANNING AND CONTROL TECHNIQUES

Ned C. Hill

FINANCIAL PLANNING

FINANCIAL PLANNING DEFINED. The planning process in general concerns an assessment of possible future states of the world and their impact on the firm. It is intended to enable the planner to formulate courses of action to meet those various states successfully. The description of a specific future state is called a **scenario** and may include brief or extensive assumptions about economic, social, and political events and conditions. It may also include assumptions about the firm's operations. A simple example of a scenario would be: "Assume that next year inflation is 11%, short-term interest rates 13%, and the competition has introduced a new product that will take 10% of our current market share." A more complex scenario could provide many more details of the economic, social, and political world.

Financial planning concerns the financial impact of these scenarios and leads to the development of financial plans. A **financial plan** consists of a set of intended financial actions designed to respond to possible future requirements over the **planning horizon.** Since new information about the future is continually becoming available, no financial plan can ever be considered final. It is always subject to revision.

BENEFITS OF PLANNING. Among the benefits of financial planning are:

1. *Anticipation of future decisions.* Planning requires managers to think about future financial consequences of decision alternatives. The process identifies potential problems as well as opportunities.
2. *Coordination of activities.* The planning process requires communication between the separate activity units of the firm and thereby fosters conflict resolution and efforts to achieve common goals.

3. *Goal clarification.* Planning often brings out the need to set priorities when it is seen that some goals conflict under various scenarios. For example, planning may show that the goal of 15% growth per year is incompatible with a goal of no debt financing, in which case management would have to decide which is more important.

4. *Educational benefits.* Undertaking the planning process is an excellent way to learn about the firm and its workings. Some firms train new managers by having them experiment with financial planning models.

5. *Aid in control.* As discussed later under "Budgeting," planning forms the basis for the budgeting and control process of the firm. Specific plans are translated into budgets, which are used to communicate goals and evaluate performance.

STEPS IN FINANCIAL PLANNING. Modern financial planning techniques are based on generating possible scenarios, assessing the implications of those scenarios for the firm, generating **pro forma** or future **financial statements,** and deciding from the statements how to respond with financial plans. It is a repetitive process in which the conclusions from a scenario often prompt **sensitivity analysis** or an exploration of how the conclusions would change if the scenario changed slightly. The steps illustrated in Exhibit 1 are discussed in detail below.

Scenario Generation. Planners first generate a set of scenarios that could possibly be realized in the future. Some scenarios may have a high probability of occurrence, others a low probability. Scenarios often begin with forecasts such as economic forecasts of interest rates, prices, and consumer spending, market forecasts of sales levels, and an assessment of competitive factors. The section of this *Handbook* entitled "Financial Forecasting" deals in detail with these techniques. Scenarios may also include internal factors such as credit policy alternatives or capital investment projects.

"Most likely case" forecasets usually form the basis for one scenario. Though some planners use only the most likely scenario, this neglects the real benefits of planning. Since forecasts are more or less subject to error, most planners develop several scenarios by assuming deviations from forecasts in the "most likely case."

Translating Scenarios into Concrete Numbers. Scenarios often contain vague, nonspecific terms such as "recession," "inflation," and "high level of sales." These vague notions must be translated into concrete numbers. Consumer spending levels and actions of competitors, for example, are used to generate numerical sales levels; and interest rate estimates are translated into interest costs and customer credit payment patterns. For this step, planners usually solicit guidance from many managers in the firm: marketing, production, tax, operations, and so on. Here, as in all other steps in the process, planning cannot be successful if done in a vacuum.

EXHIBIT 1   FLOW DIAGRAM FOR FINANCIAL PLANNING PROCESS

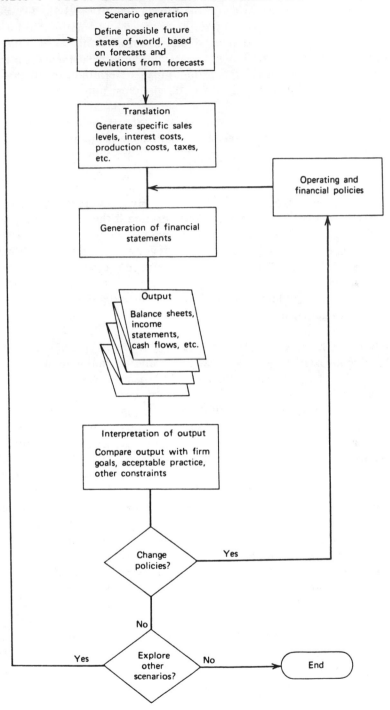

Generating Financial Statements. Once specific numbers have been generated, the impact of the scenarios on the firm is quantitatively measured and reported in a format readily understood: financial statements. **Pro forma** or future financial statements, such as balance sheets, income statements, cash flow reports, and funds statements, are generated. **Pro forma statements** provide the basis for measuring profitability, determining cash needs or surpluses, establishing potential dividend policies, and computing key financial ratios.

The generation of financial statements is often performed by a computer. The computer has made possible the examination of many more scenarios and policy variations than was possible when planning was done largely by hand.

Interpreting Output and Formulating Plans. By examining the pro forma financial statements, management can determine if the firm's policies need to be adjusted to meet firm goals and to operate under constraints imposed by prudent management practice and/or outside parties such as debtholders or regulatory agencies. For example, one firm in the midst of an excellent sales year could foresee a reduction in revenues over the next few years. It was then able to formulate plans for orderly cutbacks in operations and for financial contingencies.

PLANNING HORIZON. The time period covered by a financial plan is called the **planning horizon.** The horizon varies depending on the ability of the firm to forecast and the purpose of the specific plan. For example, in an electric utility where long lead times are required to construct power plants and forecasting is relatively good, capital financing plans extend 10 or 15 years. On the other extreme, planning for cash inflow and outflow requires a horizon of weeks or even days. To aid in planning cash needs in one firm, for example, the **corporate treasurer** calls financial heads of each operating group and gets a daily forecast of cash flows for the coming week and a weekly forecast for the coming four-week period.

Financial plans for a given planning horizon are often broken into smaller time periods, with near periods being more finely divided. One executive stated: "Many large corporations work with a five-year business plan. To accommodate short-term needs, and most importantly, to keep current, a business plan should be further broken down by year, by quarter, by month and by week, and reworked at appropriate intervals" (D.N. Judelson, *Financial Executive,* (January 1977), p. 22.

FREQUENCY OF REVISING FINANCIAL PLANS. The frequency with which financial plans are revised depends again on the ability to accurately forecast and the volatility of the economic environment. **Quarterly revision** of the annual plan is common practice, but there are many variations. One firm, for example, reexamines financial plans whenever the price of an important commodity changes by 1% or more. Another firm extends financial plans two years but updates every month to achieve a **rolling horizon.** The computer has made the planning process less onerous a task because revisions may be produced more frequently with less cost.

STRATEGIC AND TACTICAL PLANNING. Planning is often broken into strategic and tactical planning.

Strategic planning connotes a longer planning horizon and implies decisions that, if effected, are difficult to reverse. Strategic planning affects a broader segment of the firm and is more involved with overall firm goals than is tactical planning.

Tactical planning is of shorter range and the effects of its decisions are more easily reversed than is the case with strategic planning. Tactical planning focuses more on means to achieve goals than on goals themselves.

RESPONSIBILITY FOR FINANCIAL PLANNING. Strategic financial planning is best done by those who have the authority to make financial decisions in the firm. Strategic financial planning—longer range planning involving issuance of stock or debt, major capital investment projects, acquisitions or divestitures—is done by some combination of the chief executive officer, board of directors, and chief financial officer. Some firms have a planning committee and planning staff to do the background work such as setting up the scenarios, producing the forecasts, and distilling details down to essential elements. Generally, however, the more decision makers are directly involved in the process, the more effective the planning will be.

Tactical financial planning—involving cash flow projections, credit line or commercial paper usage, and short-term investments—generally comes under the direction of the **treasurer** and, in the multidivision firms, the division financial officer. The treasurer may have a cash management staff to assist in this level of planning.

GENERATING PRO FORMA STATEMENTS BY HAND. Generating pro forma financial statements is a key element of financial planning. A simple example, illustrated in Exhibit 2, using a "quick and dirty" approach will serve to illustrate the general procedure. A common method used is the **percent of sales method.** This method assumes that several balance sheet and income statement accounts vary directly with sales. For example, inventory might always be 30% of sales. When sales increase, inventory will increase by a corresponding amount to maintain the same percentage. To determine this percentage, past financial statements serve as a guide. In the example, we use only the previous year for our projections. Exhibit 2 gives the balance sheet and income statement for the year ending 19X1. The task at hand is to project financial statements for 19X2 and determine whether additional financing will be needed to support additional sales and planned plant expansion.

EXHIBIT 2   CITY CHEMICAL CO. INCOME STATEMENT AND BALANCE SHEET ($ MILLION)

	19X1	% of Sales	Pro Forma 19X2
INCOME STATEMENT			
Sales	$12.0	——	$15.0
Cost of goods sold	6.0	50%	7.5
Depreciation	1.0	——	1.0
General selling and administration	2.0	——	2.0
Operating profit	3.0	——	4.5
Taxes (40%)	1.2	——	1.8
Net income	$ 1.8	——	$ 2.7
BALANCE SHEET			
Assets			
Cash and marketable securities	$ 4.0	——	$ 5.0
Accounts receivable	6.0	50	7.5
Inventory	12.0	100	15.0
Net property plant and equipment	28.0	——	30.0
Total assets	50.0		57.5
Liabilities and Equity			
Accounts payable	4.0	33	5.0
Long-term debt	5.0	——	7.0
Common equity	30.0		30.0
Retained earnings	11.0		13.7
Total	$50.0		$55.7
Additional financing			1.8

Step 1. Using the percent of sales method, accounts are identified that are likely to vary with sales, and percentages are computed based on past data. Such accounts are cost of goods sold in the income statement and accounts receivable, inventory, and accounts payable in the balance sheet. The percentages are given next to the appropriate accounts in Exhibit 2. Note that if more years of data had been available, percentages from those years would have been averaged with consideration given to trends.

Step 2. Based on marketing projections under the "most likely" scenario, a sales increase to $15 million is forecast. Other information provided by the firm is given as follows.

1. General selling and administrative expenses will remain constant.
2. A new facility will be constructed at a cost of $3 million partly financed by a $2 million term loan. The new plant will not affect total depreciation during the coming year.
3. No existing long-term debt will be retired.
4. Dividends will not be paid.
5. Cash and marketable securities will be maintained at $5 million.

Step 3. The income statement is computed from the information given above. As shown in Exhibit 2, net income after taxes is $2.7 million.

Step 4. The balance sheet is next computed given the information above. Cash and marketable securities is set at $5 million. Accounts receivable, accounts payable, and inventory go up 25% along with the increase in sales. Net property, plant, and equipment is computed by adding the $28 million from last year to the $3 million in new investment minus $1 million for depreciation. Long-term debt goes to $7 million, since $2 million more was added and none retired. Retained earnings go up by the amount of aftertax net income, since no dividends are distributed.

Step 5. The total assets are $57.5 million, while total liability and equity are $55.7 million. Since the two sides of the balance sheet must balance, a **balancing account** is created on the liability side for $1.8 million. This represents the additional financing required.

Step 6 (Optional). To see the need for the extra $1.8 million in financing from a different perspective, it is helpful to produce a cash flow statement. Exhibit 3 shows cash inflows and outflows. A net cash outflow shows the need for additional funds. Note that some balance sheet changes have the effect of a cash flow. For example, an increase in accounts receivable has the effect of a cash outflow, since added receivables correct for the overstatement of cash inflows from sales. Combining the inflows with the outflows shows a net outflow of $1.8 million. Hence, to balance cash flows, an additional inflow of $1.8 million is needed. This is (and must be, if correct procedures have been followed) the same number as that computed in generating the pro forma balance sheet.

EXHIBIT 3   CITY CHEMICAL CO. CASH FLOW STATEMENT, 19X2 ($ MILLIONS)

CASH INFLOWS AND ADJUSTMENTS	
Sales	$15.0
New debt	2.0
Increase in accounts payable	1.0
Cash inflows	18.0
CASH OUTFLOWS AND ADJUSTMENTS	
Cost of goods sold	$ 7.5
General selling and administration	2.0
Taxes	1.8
Increase in inventory	3.0
Increase in accounts receivable	1.5
New construction	3.0
Increase in cash	1.0
Cash outflows	19.8

Net cash flow = 18.0 − 19.8 = −1.8

Sensitivity Analysis. Using this kind of procedure, future financing needs may be determined. The planner will also want to see how financing needs depend on assumptions made at the outset. For example, what if sales increased 40% instead of 25%? What would happen if sales dropped 5%? Exploring how results change as input varies is called **sensitivity analysis.** Appropriate steps in the planning process are repeated and new statements generated.

Limitations of Percent of Sales Method. The method illustrated is widely used because it is simple and easy to do. Drawbacks are that most accounts do not vary directly with sales. For example, cost of goods sold generally includes costs that are fixed, or fixed over a certain range of sales, as well as variable costs. Accounts receivable also do not depend on current sales levels alone, but on past sales and customer payment patterns, as well. Correcting these approximations introduces complexities that would make hand computations tedious. Sensitivity analysis would also be quite difficult if performed by hand. A computer is therefore almost mandatory for the generation of realistically complex pro forma statements and the performance of sensitivity analysis.

FINANCIAL PLANNING WITH A MICROCOMPUTER

ROLE OF COMPUTERS IN PLANNING. Financial planning is based on the construction of various future scenarios and the evaluation of their effects on the firm under different financial policies. The ability to efficiently generate financial statements based on these scenarios and policies is key to financial planning. The tedious task of producing financial statements—whether for the whole firm or for a small cost center—is facilitated by computers.

In the past, firms developed or purchased planning models primarily for their mainframe computers. Historical data needed in planning was available through accounting systems resident on the mainframe. Unfortunately, access to such models was often limited to a relatively small planning staff. Over the past several years, microcomputer usage has grown dramatically. This growth has brought computer power to a much wider range of management levels. With the growth of microcomputers has also come a large variety of inexpensive, easy-to-use financial statement generators. Hence, the ability to participate in financial planning is now distributed throughout almost all levels of the firm.

SPREADSHEETS AND MODEL-BASED SOFTWARE. Software refers to computer programs that consist of instructions to the computer. There are two basic types of software used by microcomputers to generate financial statements: **spreadsheets** and **model-based software.**

SPREADSHEETS. A **spreadsheet program** is essentially a computerized worksheet. The worksheet is similar to an accountant's worksheet laid out in rows and columns. Each space or cell on the worksheet may hold data. The user specifies the data in a cell (1) by manually entering the data one cell at a time, (2) by reading from a preexisting data base, or (3) by telling the computer how data is to be computed and letting it do the computations. The latter method is crucial for financial planning.

Spreadsheet programs are easy to learn and are adaptable to many different uses. Spreadsheets were the most frequently purchased business software programs in 1984. (J.W. Verity, "Upstarts Outshine the Stars," *Datamation,* November 15, 1984.) Some programs combine worksheet technology with computer graphics, word processing, and data base management features. Though spreadsheets were initially designed for the microcomputer, their popularity has led to adaptations used on mainframe computers.

Example. In Exhibit 4 we generate a set of four quarterly income statements for the year by letting the computer do much of the work. Sales for the first quarter are estimated to be $100,000. In this "normal scenario," sales in each succeeding quarter are assumed to increase by 2%. We need only enter the $100,000 and tell the computer to generate the remaining sales numbers at a growth rate of 2%. Methods for giving these instructions to the computer vary by spreadsheet. The spreadsheet program then quickly computes the remaining three sales numbers for us. Cost of goods sold, estimated to be 60% of sales, are quickly computed by telling the program that numbers in the second row are to be .6 times numbers in the first row. The gross margin is also easily computed by defining it as the difference between the first and second rows. Likewise, other cost categories may be defined until an income statement is constructed.

Sensitivity Analysis. Sensitivity analysis is the ability to generate alternative financial statements for alternative scenarios. It is key to financial planning. **Spreadsheets** are ideal for sensitivity analysis because by changing one num-

EXHIBIT 4   SAMPLE OF SPREADSHEET PROJECTIONS

	Quarter			
	1	2	3	4
Sales (2% growth)	$100,000	$102,000	$104,040	$106,121
Cost of goods sold (60%)	60,000	61,200	62,424	63,672
Gross margin	40,000	40,800	41,616	42,448
Fixed costs	20,000	20,000	20,000	20,000
Profit before taxes	20,000	20,800	21,616	22,448
Taxes (40%)	8,000	8,320	8,646	8,979
Net profit	$ 12,000	$ 12,480	$ 12,970	$ 13,469

ber, numbers in other cells may be recomputed automatically. This permits the user to easily explore the financial consequences of different scenarios. As a simple example, we will change the sales growth rate to produce a "high growth scenario" where sales increase by 4% each quarter instead of 2%. Rather than recompute each cell, we have only to change the growth rate from 2 to 4% and let the computer recompute all the remaining cells for us. Exhibit 5 shows that changing only this one number results in changes in any other numbers that depend on sales numbers.

Some spreadsheet software allows the user to save the results of various scenarios for reporting in a summary table. Exhibit 6 shows the results of annual profits as a function of four different sales growth rates. The first two scenarios come from Exhibits 4 and 5, respectively.

Uploading and Downloading. Financial planning often requires historical data from mainframe computers. Such data may be transferred (downloaded) to microcomputers by using communications software. The data can then be read into a spreadsheet program. After manipulation by a microcomputer, the results may be transferred back to the mainframe (uploaded) for storage or consolidation with other data.

Templates. Rather than constructing a spreadsheet from scratch by defining how data is computed for each cell, it is possible to purchase predefined spreadsheets or **templates** to be used with a spreadsheet program. Templates are available for general financial planning, real estate planning, and tax planning, as well as general accounting applications.

MODEL-BASED SOFTWARE. Closely related to spreadsheet programs are **model-based planning models.** Though many features are the same, model-

EXHIBIT 5   SPREADSHEET RECOMPUTATION FEATURE

THE FOLLOWING FINANCIAL REPORT WAS PREPARED BY CHANGING ONLY THE GROWTH FIGURE TO 4% FROM 2%. THE REMAINING NUMBERS WERE RE-COMPUTED BY THE COMPUTER AUTOMATICALLY.

	Quarter			
	1	2	3	4
Sales (4% growth)	$100,000	$104,000	$106,080	$108,202
Cost of goods sold (60%)	60,000	62,400	63,648	64,921
Gross margin	40,000	41,600	42,432	43,281
Fixed costs	20,000	20,000	20,000	20,000
Profit before taxes	20,000	21,600	22,432	23,281
Taxes (40%)	8,000	8,640	8,973	9,312
Net profit	$ 12,000	$ 12,960	$ 13,459	$ 13,968

EXHIBIT 6   SPREADSHEET SENSITIVITY ANALYSIS

	Scenario			
	1	2	3	4
Scenario Name	Normal	High Growth	Very High Growth	No Growth
Growth rate (quarterly)	2%	4%	6%	0%
Net profit after taxes (annual)	$50,919	$52,387	$56,970	$48,000

based programs generate data as a series of mathematical equations defined by the user. Displaying the data is accomplished through a separate report generator. In contrast, spreadsheets need no report generator, since the worksheet is the report. While more complicated to learn initially, model-based programs are potentially more powerful.

Such programs are available for linear programming optimization modeling, consolidation of multiple financial statements, internal rate of return computations, sophisticated subroutines for amortization, taxation, and so forth.

Simultaneous Equations. Model-based programs can handle **simultaneous equations.** These arise frequently in financial planning. For example, suppose a firm were trying to plan how much cash to borrow on its credit line to cover operating expenses of $40,000 for the month. The total amount borrowed should also cover additional interest expenses for the credit line. If the interest rate is 1% per month, the amount to borrow can be expressed as two simultaneous equations:

$$\text{Cash borrowed} = \$40,000 + \text{interest}$$

$$\text{Interest} = .01 * \text{cash borrowed}$$

A spreadsheet program wouldn't be able to handle this problem directly since all cells must be computed from previously defined cells. The user would have to solve the simultaneous equation separately or perform several spreadsheet iterations to set the appropriate level of cash borrowed to cover the $40,000 plus needed interest. In contrast, a model-based program recognizes the two equations as simultaneous and solves them exactly before proceeding with other computations.

Goal Seeking. Equation-generated data is also handy in financial planning that uses **goal seeking.** In goal seeking the value of a variable (such as profit) is set at a desired level. Then the model determines the level of other variables (such as sales) that must occur to reach profit goal. This cannot be accomplished automatically with spreadsheet programs.

Flexible Reporting. Since model equations are separate from report programs, model-based programs allow for more flexibility in reporting the same information in different ways. With spreadsheet programs, converting data to a new report format may require significant reworking of the worksheet.

SPECIAL PLANNING PROGRAMS. While spreadsheets and model-based programs are general purpose planning tools, other software is available for financial planning in specialized areas. Examples of such areas include:

Tax Planning. There are dozens of **tax planning programs** available for individual and corporate use. They range from simple tax preparation programs to complex tax planning models that allow the user to explore the consequences of alternative depreciation and amortization schedules. Some offer specialized programs relating to state taxes.

Real Estate Planning. These programs analyze financial decisions resulting from buying and selling real property.

Personal Financial Planning. A large number of programs are available that specialize in **personal financial planning** including insurance, estate building, taxation, retirement plans, investments, and so on.

PROFIT PLANNING AND BREAK-EVEN ANALYSIS

COST-VOLUME-PROFIT RELATIONSHIPS. Planning that focuses on the relationship between **costs, sales volume,** and **profits** (C-V-P) has often been called "profit planning." While something of a misnomer—since planning is generally done with an eye to the profitability of the firm—the label is still frequently used in finance and accounting texts. C-V-P relationships are important because they get to the heart of issues such as selling price, policies that may effect volume, different types of cost, and the profitability of the firm. C-V-P analyses are sometimes performed to determine the probable success or failure of a proposed project.

TYPES OF COST. Costs may be roughly divided into three types.
   Fixed costs remain constant regardless of the sales volume. Examples of fixed costs are executive salaries, interest expenses, depreciation, long-term leases, and insurance expense. While no costs are truly fixed for all levels of sales, many costs may be considered to be fixed for an appropriate planning range.

Variable costs change as sales volume varies. Examples of variable costs are direct labor and material costs.

Semivariable costs vary, but not in direct proportions to sales. Some costs remain fixed over some range of sales but increase when sales enter a higher range. As an example, expense for a milk delivery truck is fixed up to some level of sales, but another truck must be purchased if sales rise above that level.

DETERMINING COST TYPES. It is not easy to sort out which costs are fixed and which are variable or semivariable. There are three general ways to approximate these distinctions, however.

Department-Based Classification. Departments of a firm or division may themselves be classified as incurring fixed or variable costs. The research and development, accounting, and legal departments, for example, are generally considered to be "fixed" because the expenses they incur are less sensitive to volume changes, at least over the short run. Expenses for manufacturing and to some extent marketing departments tend more to vary with sales. Hence, classifying each department in this way will give some idea of the variable-fixed expense mix.

Statistical Methods. By regressing total costs against sales volume using past data, one can approximate fixed costs as the intercept term and variable costs per dollar as the slope of the regression line. This method is generally reliable only when the currently employed technology and operating policies are similar to those employed in the past. Care must also be taken in assuming that the same C-V-P relationships hold over volume levels outside the ranges observed in the past.

Engineered Standards. Production engineering departments often develop standard unit costs for manufactured products and overhead costs for various levels of activity. These costs from the firm's cost accounting systems may be used for classifying manufacturing costs.

BREAK-EVEN ANALYSIS. Once fixed and variable costs have been determined (semivariable costs are neglected for the moment), break-even analysis is used to determine what volume of sales will just cover total costs. The break-even graph shown in Exhibit 7 is based on fixed costs of $100,000 and variable costs of 60¢ per dollar of sales. The total costs increase at a slower rate than revenue. At a sales volume of $250,000, revenues just cover total variable plus fixed costs. This is the **break-even point.** Sales above the break-even point generate profits, while sales below that point generate losses. The break-even point may also be found by using the equation:

$$\text{break-even sales level} = \frac{\text{fixed costs}}{1 - \text{variable costs per sales dollar}}$$

EXHIBIT 7   BREAK-EVEN ANALYSIS

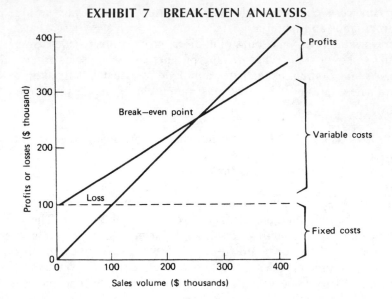

Purposes of Break-Even Analysis. Break-even analysis is useful in the following kinds of decision.

1. *Changing production methods.* Planners need to know how break-even levels change to be able to assess the likelihood that sales will be sufficient to cover costs when the firm is contemplating a switch to technology involving higher fixed costs and lower variable costs (or the reverse).
2. *New product introduction.* Firms often request a break-even analysis for a proposed new product. Combining this information with marketing data on potential sales, an assessment of likely success can be made.
3. *Expansion of operations.* When general plant expansions are considered, break-even analysis helps determine whether added fixed costs can be justified.

Limitations of Break-Even Analysis. While break-even analysis is relatively simple and can yield some useful insights into relationships between cost, volume, and profitability, it is limited as a planning tool when contrasted with planning based on financial statement generation. See Exhibit 7 for an example of break-even analysis.

1. Costs are complex: they are not only fixed and variable. While some allowances can be made in more sophisticated versions of break-even analysis, most financial statement generators are flexible enough to handle any kind of cost-volume relationship.

2. Defining "sales volume" is difficult. The same dollar sales may be generated by unlimited possible combinations of product mix. Each product mix can be associated with different fixed and variable costs.

3. **Break-even analysis** ignores many other financial considerations such as credit and borrowing needs, nonexpense-related cash flows, and capital investment. Thus break-even analysis focuses only on profitability and cannot handle issues involving overall cash flow. Financial statement generators, on the other hand, consider cash flows as well as profits.

4. Because cash flows are ignored, break-even analysis cannot reflect the **time value of money.** It is therefore an incomplete tool for capital investment decisions. Financial statement generators often have subsystems that can perform time-value **capital budgeting analysis.**

"Profit planning" or break-even analysis of cost-volume-profit relationships serves a useful function in identifying important relationships in the firm. The methodology is incomplete, however, as a financial planning or decision-making tool. The methodology was developed before the widespread availability of computer-based financial planning systems and is gradually being replaced by that more complete and versatile tool.

BUDGETING AND CONTROL

CONTROL DEFINED. While planning involves the design of a desirable future state and the effective means to achieve it, **managerial control** seeks to ensure adherence to those means or plans. Mockler (*The Management Control Process,* Appleton-Century-Crofts, New York, 1972, p. 111) defines **management control** as "a systematic effort by business management to compare performance to predetermined standards, plans, or objectives in order to determine whether performance is in line with these standards and presumably in order to take any remedial action required to see that human and other resources are being used in the most effective and efficient way possible in achieving corporate objectives." Perhaps the most widely used technique for exerting managerial control is **budgeting.**

BUDGETS: DEFINITION AND PURPOSES. The planning process generates **pro forma financial statements** under a variety of scenarios or assumptions about business policies and economic conditions. A **budget** may be considered to be a set of financial statements resulting from a particular scenario— generally the most likely or hoped for scenario. A budget therefore reflects management opinions regarding future financial circumstances.

Budgets can be applied to the firm's entire operations as in a master budget or broken down into much smaller segments as in a sales representative's expense budget. Budgets serve many functions, among which are the following.

Planning. By definition, a budget is the outcome of a more or less structured planning process. Hence, to encourage planning activities, some organizations require budgets. Such planning leads management to consider relationships between their areas of responsibility, the economy, and other activities of the firm. The planning process leads to better decision making.

Evaluating Performance. Budgets are frequently used as a yardstick against which actual performance is measured. To effectively evaluate management performance, it is desirable to consider uncontrollable events during the budget period, recalling that a budget is the expression of only one future scenario.

> Evaluating present performance in terms of past performance assumes that the company's present condition and operating environment are the same as in the past. This is rarely the case. If the purpose of the evaluation is to measure managers' operating abilities as opposed to their forecasting skills, it might also be desirable to remove the effects of uncontrollable or unforeseeable environmental changes that have occurred during the budget period. Examples of uncontrollable environmental variables might be changes in government regulations, labor unrest, and either shortages or unexpected increases in the costs of raw materials. (Barrett and Fraser, "Conflicting Roles in Budgeting for Operations," *Harvard Business Review,* July–August 1977, p. 138).

Motivating Actions. A budget formalizes and quantifies a plan of action. When appropriately designed, a budget encourages adherence to the plan. It can motivate different units in the firm toward the same goals.

Coordinating Activities. As budgets from lower levels flow to higher levels within the organization, incompatibilities between various units can be resolved. In an operating unit, budgets from marketing departments, for example, must be coordinated with budgets from the manufacturing department to efficiently utilize resources.

Authorizing Actions. Especially in government and not-for-profit organizations, budget appropriations provide authorization and spending ceilings on management.

NEED FOR BUDGETING. Budgeting is found in virtually all industries and in firms of all sizes. The computer has made budgeting a less tedious task to perform. While the volatility of the economy has given management the incentive to look ahead more, it has made forecasting the future extremely difficult. To those who despairingly give up on budgeting, Horngren admonishes (*Cost Accounting: A Managerial Emphasis,* p. 124):

> Many managers claim that the uncertainties peculiar to their business make budgets impractical for them. Yet one can nearly always find at least some

companies in the same industry that use budgets. Such companies are usually among the industry leaders, and they regard budgets as indispensable aids. The point is that managers must grapple with uncertainties, either with a budget or without one. The advocates of budgeting maintain that the benefits from budgeting nearly always exceed the costs. Some budget program, at least, will be helpful in almost every organization.

TYPES OF BUDGET. There are many kinds of budget, but most can be placed into one of three classifications (Exhibit 8).

Capital Budgets. These express planned and approved expenditures for capital investment projects one or many years into the future. The capital budget is more strategic and points out the need for long-term fund-raising activities. The main role of capital budgets is to plan and coordinate.

Operational Budgets. These express information about revenues, production costs, and general selling and administration expenses. Pro forma income statements are a type of operational budget and are often prepared for the firm, a division, a product line, and a plant.

Operational budgets focus on the tactical plans and have a horizon of a year, a quarter, or a month. They are frequently used in motivating and evaluating management, sales, and production personnel. Operational budgets also serve to coordinate various segments in the firm.

EXHIBIT 8   TYPES OF BUDGET

Capital Budgets

Operational Budgets
Budgeted income statement
Production budget
   Materials
   Direct labor
   Factory overhead
   Inventory levels
Cost-of-goods-sold budget
Selling-expense budget
Administrative-expense budget

Financial Budgets
Cash budgets
   Receipts
   Disbursements
Budgeted balance sheet
Budgeted sources and application of funds

Source: Adapted from C.T. Horngren, *Cost Accounting: A Managerial Emphasis,* Prentice-Hall, Englewood Cliffs, NJ, 1977, p. 126.

Financial Budgets. While all budgets relate to financial decisions, the term **financial budget** traditionally refers to budgets of three interrelated types: balance sheet, cash flow budget, and sources and applications of funds budget.

The **budgeted balance sheet** is derived from the budgeted income statement and is useful in controlling trends in key financial ratios.

In contrast to other types of budget, which often contain noncash items (depreciation, credit sales, and so on) that are necessary in accounting profitability measures, the **cash flow budget** focuses directly on cash generated or needed on a monthly, weekly, or daily basis. Cash flow budgets are crucial in planning credit line usage, the issuance of commercial paper, investment in short-term securities, and the establishment of credit and purchasing policies. The **sources and applications of funds budget** is useful in identifying key changes in balance sheet accounts over time.

BUDGET PREPARATION. There are two extreme approaches in budgeting. In **top-down budgeting,** the highest level of management determines the overall goals of the firm and translates these into sales and production budgets for each division. The division heads then generate sales and production budgets for each operating unit in the division, and the process continues down the organization. The advantages are easy coordination of various units, conformity of unit budgets to overall corporate goals, and speed. The main disadvantages are both motivational and operational. Lower managers who feel that the budget is imposed by others may be less motivated to implement it. In addition, since top management may lack important knowledge possessed by lower management concerning feasible operating and marketing characteristics, there is a potential for serious mistakes in the budgets. For example, unrealistic goals may be established that either are ignored or produce frustration.

At the opposite extreme, **bottom-up budgeting** begins with sales estimates from each sales district or even each sales representative. **Production budgets** are generated from each plant operation. These budgets are consolidated at higher and higher levels until the firm's master budget is produced. The process is slower and costlier and does not guarantee that unit budgets will be coordinated with each other or that they will conform to overall corporate goals. More effort is required to coordinate all the budgets at each level. There may also be a greater tendency for budget ''padding.'' On the other hand, bottom-up budgeting allows greater decentralization and more localized decision making. It places budgeting into the hands of the those more familiar with product costs and marketing potential.

In practice, most firms combine the two methods. Overall guidelines are given by top management as a framework for developing unit budgets. Once developed, unit budgets are reviewed and, if needed, revisions are suggested by top management. The process allows all levels of management to participate, each level giving feedback to other levels. The final budget may be the result of several cycles up, down, and across the management structure.

BUDGET TIME HORIZON. Capital budgets often span a period of 10 years or more. Operational and financial budgets generally cover one year, broken down into shorter periods for the near future. An annual budget is frequently segmented into months for the first quarter and presented quarterly thereafter. Cash budgeting is sometimes done on a weekly or even daily basis. The horizon of the useful budget period depends to a large degree on the firm's ability to forecast and plan future sales levels, costs, and so on. A freight firm with long-term contracts can budget for a longer period than a ski resort, which must rely on the uncertainties of the weather to forecast sales.

Because more information comes forth as the year evolves, many firms update budgets at frequent intervals. At the end of the first quarter, for example, new data will cause a revision in the budget for the next three quarters.

Continuous or **rolling horizon budgets** are also popular. In such budgets at the end of one quarter, another quarter is added to the end of the budget period. That way management is forced to plan a full year ahead at all times of the year. The time and expense required to update the budget so frequently can be drawbacks.

PROBLEMS OF BUDGETING. While budgeting provides an important tool to exert financial control in an organization, there are four major problems in the effective use of budgets.

Overbudgeting. Budgets can become so complex and detailed that the time and expense of preparing them become excessive. Overly complex budgets also tend to be ignored.

Budget Inflexibility. Because budgets are prepared in advance based on an assumed future, changing circumstances invalidate the underlying assumptions that generated the budget. It is unrealistic to measure current performance against an outdated plan. To overcome this problem, firms sometimes use flexible budgets that take into account the changed environment.

Budget Masking. Budgets based on past budgets can tend to mask inefficient operations. To overcome this problem, some firms use a **zero-base budgeting review.**

> According to a regular schedule, each ongoing activity is studied intensively, perhaps once every five years. In contrast with the usual budget review, which takes the current level of spending as the starting point, this more intensive review starts from scratch and attempts to build up, *de novo,* the resources that actually are needed by the activity. It may even challenge the need for having the activity at all. These studies are especially important when costs are of the discretionary cost type. Basic questions are raised, such as: (1) Should the function be performed at all? (2) What should the quality level be?

Are we doing too much? (3) Should it be performed in this way? (4) How much should it cost? (Anthony and Dearden, *Management Control Systems,* Irwin, Homewood, IL, 1976, p. 408.)

Budget Pressure. Budgets can sometimes be used as tools to exert pressure on subordinates. When budgets cause resentment and frustration, they have lost their purpose. To reduce this problem, firms often use **participative budgeting,** which gives subordinates an important voice in establishing the budget.

FINANCIAL CONTROL SYSTEMS

RESPONSIBILITY CENTERS. Budgeting is the chief tool for exerting **financial control** in the organization. This subsection discusses how a **financial control system** is designed. There are four basic types of financial control system, each associated with a **responsibility center.** The management of a responsibility center is charged with carrying out the financial plans associated with the budget for that center and is held accountable for performance in relation to the budget. The four types of responsibility centers differ in the scope of financial activities they are accountable for. The four types are:

- **Cost centers,** responsible for only the costs incurred by the unit.
- **Revenue centers,** responsible only for the revenues generated by the unit.
- **Profit centers,** responsible for both revenues and costs.
- **Investment centers,** responsible for revenues, costs, and the capital investment base.

Cost Centers. Dermer has provided the following definition:

A cost center is the smallest organizational segment for which costs are traced and accumulated and over which an individual has responsibility. Although every unit classified as a cost center produces some useful output, it is usually neither feasible nor desirable to measure these outputs in monetary terms. (Dermer, *Management Planning and Control Systems,* Irwin, Homewood, IL, 1977, p. 15.)

There are two types of cost center: **engineered cost centers** and **discretionary cost centers.** Engineered costs are generally associated with a manufacturing or production facility. Each unit of output has associated with it an **engineered or standard cost.** This is the "acceptable" cost that should be incurred. Engineered cost centers are responsible then for maintaining costs at or below the standard cost per unit.

The discretionary cost center produces output for which there is no readily measurable monetary value. An example of a discretionary cost center is a training staff. The output, training, is likely to be of worth to the firm, but its value and quantity cannot be easily measured in monetary terms. While the efficiency of an engineered cost center can be determined by the extent to which costs are below budgeted costs per unit, the efficiency of a discretionary cost center cannot be so measured. The discretionary cost center manager is generally held responsible for holding to a budget, while efficiency is left to other more qualitative judgments.

The **disadvantage of cost centers** is their emphasis on cost minimization per se, which is not the main goal of the firm. Revenues generated by the firm are obviously important, too.

Revenue Centers. Marketing units are typically the only revenue centers in most firms. Control is exerted through budgeted sales levels, with incentives for meeting or exceeding budget.

Revenue centers pose some problems when managers have discretion over pricing and/or credit terms. Revenues can often be increased by lowering price or by liberalizing credit terms. Steps need to be taken to ensure that profitability is maintained by restricting pricing and credit control of the center.

Profit Centers. When both costs and revenues of a unit can be measured in quantitative terms, the responsibility unit is a profit center. Since profitability is an important goal for the firm, making various units of the firm responsible for pieces of the profit is generally viewed as a desirable organizational objective. In creating an effective profit center, the management of that center is given authority to make decisions regarding operating policies, supply sources, prices, credit terms, and so on. Revenues and expenses must be clearly identifiable and controllable, or a profit center has little meaning.

Measuring the profitability of a profit center is sometimes a difficult task because of three problems:

1. The center may buy from another unit within the firm at an artificially low or high **transfer price.**
2. Revenues may be jointly generated by two or more profit centers within the firm. An allocation must be made on some reasonable basis.
3. Sometimes several profit centers consume joint services from another unit within the firm. Again, the costs have to be fairly allocated.

Anthony and Dearden (*Management Control Systems,* p. 249) describe four profitability measures, discussed briefly below.

Contribution Margin. Revenues minus the cost of goods sold. Only variable costs are considered, based on the assumption that the profit center may have little control over fixed expenses or allocated corporate expenses.

Direct Divisional Profit. Although similar to the contribution margin, this measure also contains such costs as fixed expenses and direct charges from divisions, even though these may be considered uncontrollable.

Income Before Taxes. Subtracting allocated corporate costs from direct profit gives income before taxes. General corporate expenses are allocated because it is held that the profit center benefits, if only indirectly, from expenses incurred from sources such as general corporate administration, image advertising, and annual report preparation. A profit center, it is argued, has not made a profit until all expenses have been covered.

Net Income. This measure includes all the expenses above and also subtracts out taxes. This combination serves to keep managers aware of the tax consequences of their decisions. Exhibit 9 illustrates the computation of the various profitability measures.

Investment Centers. Investment centers are responsible for revenues, costs, and also the **investment base** or the assets generating the revenues and costs. Profits themselves, it is argued, are not really an adequate basis for control unless the assets employed are considered. The profits of two divisions may be identical, but one may employ more assets to generate the profits than the other.

   Investment centers imply that management has the responsibility for increasing the investment base or decreasing it. The manager's aims are to generate adequate profits from existing assets and to expand the asset base if an adequate return is likely.

   There are two basic methods for measuring the performance of an investment center: return on investment and residual income.

Return on Investment (ROI). While ROI has long been used to evaluate investments, only in the early 1960s was the measure applied to a division

EXHIBIT 9   PROFITABILITY MEASURES USED IN PROFIT CENTERS

Revenues	$10,000
Cost of goods sold	− 5,000
Variable costs	− 1,000
Contribution margin[a]	4,000
Fixed division expense	− 1,000
Direct charges from other divisions	− 500
Direct division profit[a]	2,500
Allocation of corporate costs	− 500
Income before taxes[a]	2,000
Taxes	− 1,000
Net income[a]	$ 1,000

[a]A performance measure.

or investment center. Advantages of ROI over other performance measures discussed above are:

1. It incorporates essentially all ingredients of profitability, including the asset base.
2. It can be used to compare the performance of investment centers in the firm with outside firms.
3. It encourages management to think in terms of a broader measure of profitability.

ROI is measured as follows:

$$\text{ROI} = \frac{\text{net income}}{\text{invested capital}}$$

While the formula is simple, many difficulties arise in measuring both net income and invested capital. Among the issues that must be faced are:

1. How should total assets be measured? The alternatives are total assets and total assets minus liabilities. Some assets may not be under management control. An example is cash, which even in a **divisionalized firm** may be under highly centralized control. Most firms use total assets, even though some may be uncontrollable.
2. When should assets be measured? The options are book value at time of purchase, net book value after subtracting depreciation, and replacement value. Using depreciated value tends to overstate the performance of divisions with older equipment and may discourage beneficial upgrading of assets. **Replacement costs** may be difficult to determine and could be somewhat arbitrary. Hence the preferred method for many firms is to use the undepreciated book value.
3. How should jointly held assets be allocated? Accounts receivable, cash, and marketable securities, for example, may be maintained at corporate headquarters. An **allocation to investment centers** is generally made on some basis; for example, accounts receivable is often allocated in proportion to sales.
4. How should inventory be valued? While LIFO methods may be desirable for tax purposes, LIFO tends to understate inventory value when prices rise. Hence most firms use FIFO for computing ROI.

Similar problems are encountered in measuring the net income for the ROI computation.

1. Should expenses charged from other divisions within the firm be adjusted if these expenses are different from those that would have been

incurred in the open market? Generally **transfer prices** are set so that such adjustments will not have to be made.

2. How should general corporate expenses be allocated to investment centers? Usually some allocation base is used such as sales or fixed assets.

3. How should general corporate revenues be allocated? The marketable securities portfolio, for example, generates a return. If an investment center's asset base includes an allocation of these assets, the proportional revenues are generally also allocated.

4. How does the firm treat research and development costs (or any other cost that will be beneficial in the future)? If the costs are customarily expensed, management may be reluctant to invest in such projects.

While these are only a few of the problems encountered in measuring ROI, they serve to illustrate the kinds of difficulty faced and the caution that must therefore be used in computing and using ROI.

Shortcomings of ROI. Besides the measurement difficulties mentioned above, ROI suffers from several deficiencies. First, accounting measures of return are not cash flows and may not capture the **true economic picture of the investment center.** Second, ROI may encourage a short-term decision horizon that would be bad for the firm in the long run. For example, by selling off assets and leasing them back, the manager might immediately increase ROI; yet such a decision could be harmful over the longer run. Third, the pressure to maintain the current ROI may lead to the rejection of projects that would be beneficial. For example, if a division currently had an ROI of 20%, it would reject investments yielding 16% even if the firm's target were 14%. Fourth, focusing only on keeping ROI high may lead to projects of high risk. Modern managers recognize that ROI and risk are usually directly related.

Residual Income (RI). This performance measure also measures revenues, expenses, and assets but in a different way from ROI. RI is designed to overcome some of the problems encountered by ROI, though RI is also based on accounting measures of assets and profits. RI is defined as the dollar amount left over after subtracting from net income a capital charge for the assets employed:

$$RI = \text{revenues} - \text{operating expenses} - I \times \text{asset base}$$

where I **is the interest rate measuring the cost of providing capital** to the investment center.

The advantage of RI over ROI is that RI encourages the investment center to undertake investments as long as the return is greater than the firm's required return I. Thus a 16% investment should be pursued when the required return is 14% even if the division currently has an ROI of 20%. Another advantage is that the interest rate can be different for various classes of assets. For risky assets, a higher rate can be applied.

Shortcomings of RI. Besides similar problems of accounting measures of assets and income also encountered in ROI, RI suffers from other deficiencies. RI is a dollar measure, not a return. Hence it is **difficult to compare divisions**—especially when they are of different sizes. Furthermore, RI does not really overcome two problems associated with ROI: namely, those involving the incentives to reduce assets in the short run and to undertake risky projects with higher returns. So, while RI may be superior for investment decisions, it still has drawbacks that must be considered before it is used to evaluate management performance.

Examples of ROI and RI Computations. To illustrate the difference in ROI and RI performance measures, consider a very simple example. Assume an investment base of 100 and current net income of 20. Thus ROI for the investment center is 20%. If the rate on invested capital is required to be 14%, the residual income is:

$$RI = 20 - 0.14(100) = 6$$

Now assume that a project is under consideration that would require an investment of 50 and give an annual income of 8, with the same risk as the firm's current projects. The division's return on investment would become

$$ROI = \frac{20 + 8}{100 + 50} = 18.7\%$$

Since this is less than the current ROI of 20%, a manager seeking to maintain a high ROI would not accept the investment. On the other hand, RI = 28 − 0.14 (150) = 7. The residual income of the division of the firm increases, so a manager seeking to increase RI would accept the investment project. From the viewpoint of the firm, the investment should be accepted, since it returns 16% and the required return is only 14%.

REFERENCES

Ackoff, Russell L., *A Concept of Corporate Planning,* Wiley-Interscience, New York, 1970.

Anthony, Robert N., and Dearden, John, *Management Control Systems,* 3d ed., Irwin, Homewood, IL, 1976.

Barrett and Fraser, "Conflicting Roles in Budgeting for Operations," *Harvard Business Review,* July–August 1977, p. 138ff.

"Choosing and Using Electronic Spreadsheets," *Healthcare Financial Manager,* January 1985, pp. 39ff.

Dermer, Jerry, *Management Planning and Control Systems,* Irwin, Homewood, IL, 1977.

Donaldson, Gordon and Lorsch, J.W., *Decision Making at the Top,* Basic Books, New York, 1985.

Horngren, Charles T., *Cost Accounting: A Managerial Emphasis,* 4th ed., Prentice-Hall, Englewood Cliffs, NJ, 1977.

The Journal of Financial Software, 2811 Wilshire Blvd., Suite 640 Santa Monica, CA 90403. This journal provides reviews of financial planning software.

Judelson, David N., "Financial Controls That Work," *Financial Executive,* January 1977, pp. 22–25.

Lorange, Peter, and Vancil, Richard F., "How to Design a Strategic Planning System," *Harvard Business Review,* September–October 1976, pp. 75–81.

Mockler, J., *The Management Control Process,* Appleton-Century-Crofts, New York, 1972.

O'Connor, Rochelle, *Planning Under Uncertainty: Multiple Scenarios and Contingency Planning,* Conference Board, New York, 1978.

Perry, Robert L., "The Latest Revolution in Financial Modeling Software," *Computer Decisions,* October and November 1984 (2 parts), pp. 167–188 and pp. 139–146, respectively.

Verity, John W., "Upstarts Outshine the Stars," *Datamation,* November 15, 1984, p. 34ff.

Weston, J. Fred, and Brigham, Eugene F., *Managerial Finance,* 6th ed., Dryden Press, Hinsdale, IL, 1978.

Wheelwright, Steven C., and Clarke, Darral G., "Corporate Forecasting: Promise and Reality," *Harvard Business Review,* November–December 1976, pp. 39ff.

2

FINANCIAL FORECASTING

CONTENTS

2

FINANCIAL FORECASTING

George G. C. Parker

In recent years, financial forecasting has taken on increasing importance in the overall planning process. This has occurred primarily because of the larger role that capital has in the conduct of business and the general increase in the cost of capital. Many firms have found that both the **cost** and **availability** of funds are as important in determining growth rates as are the traditional factors of market opportunity, supply of labor, or supply of materials. Indeed, many firms are in a position to grow as fast as their financial resources will permit. Thus, good financial forecasting is often a prerequisite to the conduct of a successful business.

Inadequate attention to financial forecasting can lead to unanticipated financial emergencies that could be avoided—partially or entirely—by having **contingency plans** in place. Much as in other business decisions, the formulation of a proper plan is based on a well-formulated forecast. Without good financial forecasts, otherwise successful companies can encounter serious financial trouble in spite of record sales and profits. A good financial forecast goes hand in hand with every other part of the business plan.

This section is organized into five parts, which illustrate the financial forecasting process through the use of both description and example. Every attempt is made throughout to use general business illustrations that can be applied to a broad cross section of companies.

USES OF FINANCIAL FORECASTS

AVOIDING DAY-TO-DAY CRISES. Implicit in the need for careful financial planning is the reality that many financial opportunities in the form of loans, new equity, or investments are not available on short notice, or are not available unless advance arrangements have been made. Bank loans require prior approval, a process that is not without delay and occasionally entails uncertainty. New equity financing can require 90 days to six months or more to arrange. When cash accumulates, the time-consuming process of deciding how and where to invest excess funds can be significantly enhanced by advance planning. Understanding when and in what amounts financial resources will be required or become available is essential in the optimal securing or allocation of those resources.

Accurate estimates of the timing and amount of funds required are essential in arranging bank financing. Most bankers require that borrowers organize their financial planning before they enter into agreements. These agreements can be tailored to individual requirements if the financial plan is convincingly made and presented. An accurate balance sheet, income statement, and cash flow data for the future should be made available to the banker or other lender. Few tools of financial management are as critical to the orderly operation of the firm as the well-prepared financial forecast.

COSTS OF FORECASTING VERSUS COSTS OF "EMERGENCIES." An important part of the financial forecasting process is the balancing of the cost of forecasting with the benefits derived from it. These costs must be related to the value of the information generated. Thus in an era of low interest rates (long since past in U.S. history) and ready availability of financing, the time and expense that management devotes to forecasting should be relatively low. When funds are cheap and plentiful the real or **opportunity cost** of holding excess cash (or other liquid assets) is not high. Thus, idle resources may be held instead of establishing a tight financial plan. Indeed, financial forecasts are far more important in the 1980s than they were in the 1960s or most of the 1970s. This was true because it was less expensive to protect against uncertainty through holding large cash balances or maintaining large amounts of unused borrowing capacity.

TAX PLANNING. A further major use of financial forecasts concerns planning for an optimal tax strategy. The importance of such planning has increased as the government has expanded the use of tax incentives to stimulate certain sectors of the economy. Capital investment is encouraged through the use of investment tax credits and accelerated depreciation. Employment subsidies may take the form of added tax deductions or tax credits.

While tax subsidies can be an important part of the profit or loss of a business, they require careful financial forecasting to take advantage of available tax savings. Thus, in a year when the firm is not scheduled to be profitable, it is not wise to undertake large capital projects and possibly forfeit the investment tax credit or benefits of accelerated depreciation. Furthermore, in a year when profits are scheduled to be high, it may be advantageous to move expenses, to the extent they are discretionary, into the high-profit year. This not only has the effect of "smoothing" earnings from a reporting point of view, but it assures that tax benefits will be realized.

Finally, where capital expenditures or investments are affected by tax considerations, it is important to coordinate tax planning with cash on hand or cash available from external sources. Investment subsidies are not valuable without the resources to make the investment.

"FORECASTING" VERSUS "BUDGETING." While the terms "budgeting" and "financial forecasting" are sometimes used interchangeably, forecasting is distinct from budgeting in the sense that a forecast is more passive in its approach to what will happen. A budget, on the other hand, frequently emphasizes what ought to happen if management functions efficiently. Thus a budget is a more active document, and may include a financial forecast as one of the ingredients in its preparation. Budgets may involve a motivational dimension by defining what could happen if everything went well and everyone pulled together. These are sometimes called **"stretch budgets,"** and they are analogous to the rabbit in front of a racing greyhound—it is not expected that the budget will be achieved as much as it is expected that everyone will pursue those figures as a goal. Such budgets may involve an element of wishful thinking, but it is injected knowingly.

Forecasts, by contrast, are more objective than budgets in that they attempt to identify what will happen if normal forces are at work. Budgets and forecasts may go hand in hand in a well-managed organization, but they are quite different in their preparation and use.

A further, and final, distinction between budgets and forecasts is that budgets are usually prepared in the accounting office or controller's department, while financial forecasts are more often prepared by the treasurer's department. Of course, in many firms these two functions merge at the level of the financial vice-president. Nonetheless, the distinction remains that budgets are usually prepared by those responsible for results, while financial forecasts are the responsibility of those responsible for planning.

UNCERTAINTY. The basis of the need for financial forecasts is uncertainty about the future. Without such uncertainty, the planning process would be much simpler. In many respects financial forecasting could be renamed "coping with uncertainty."

Because uncertainty about the future is involved, and because complete resolution of this uncertainty is impossible, the end result of forecasting is never a perfectly reliable estimate. As noted above, the value of forecast financial information has increased in recent years as financial resources have become more costly. Nonetheless, managers must decide at what point they will stop analyzing data in search of a more perfect model and proceed with the model that is available at a reasonable cost. The examples used in this section are well within the bounds of reasonable cost. More complex systems of forecasting are described in several of the references.

FORECASTING SALES

IMPORTANCE OF SALES FORECASTS TO FINANCIAL PLAN. Nearly every financial forecast begins with an estimate of sales. Since this is the starting point, the accuracy or inaccuracy of this estimate will affect the dependability of all other parts of the financial forecast. Pan, Nichols, and Joy emphasized this point in a recent article on sales forecasting: "Sales forecasting is a crucial part of many financial planning activities including . . . profit planning, cash budgeting and merger analysis." They concluded: "Large industrial firms recognize the importance of sales forecasting and commit resources to these efforts on a planned, regular basis." (See Pan, Nichols, and Joy, *Financial Management,* Fall 1977, pp. 72–76).

Often the financial executive responsible for preparing the financial plan is not required to produce the sales forecast from which projected financial results are derived. Instead, the sales forecast is generated in the marketing department or in other planning groups within the company. Thus much of the treatment of the process of financial forecasting that follows presumes that a reasonably accurate sales forecast is available to the financial manager. Nonetheless, some general discussion of sales forecasting techniques is useful either to assess the reliability of the sales estimate or, occasionally, to generate a sales estimate when one is not otherwise provided.

WAYS TO FORECAST SALES. There are three basic ways to forecast sales. They are the subjective method, trend forecasts, and causal models of estimation.

Subjective Method. This essentially is the forecaster's own estimate of what sales will be, based on knowledge of the economy, industry, and generalized past experience. Subjective forecasts may be individual or a consensus of group opinion. As is true of most subjective techniques, such forecasts are "nonscientific." They are, instead, more visionary and rely on guesswork, imagination, insight, and specialized knowledge about the product and the market. While such forecasts are difficult to "prove" and equally difficult to "defend," there are numerous examples of high degrees of reliability for subjective forecasts of a forecaster whose track record has been good in the past. In most instances, subjective forecasts are enhanced by a group process, with the forecast being a weighted average of a cross section of individual judgments. However, the numerous examples of successful forecasts prepared by particularly gifted individual analysts cannot be ignored.

Trend Forecasts. This form of sales forecasting, also called time series analysis, is slightly more scientific and is a simple **extrapolation of past trends** to come up with a projection. Trend forecasts generally rely on the premise that "the best estimate for tomorrow is a continuation of yesterday's trend." Refinements of the simple extrapolation technique can include **adjustments**

for seasonal or cyclical variability in the historical data. Similarly, data from the past may be weighted more heavily toward the immediate past than toward the distant past.

The most frequently used method of extrapolation is to assemble sales data for the past four or five years, plot them on a graph, and try to "read a trend." Depending on how well the data fit along a simple trend, the reading may be easy or difficult. The obvious disadvantage of the simple extrapolation technique is that it is less than optimal in predicting turning points in sales. The prediction of turning points may be better accomplished using the subjective method noted above or the causal method that follows.

Causal Models of Estimation. Causal models of sales forecasting attempt to identify the underlying determinants of sales in a formal statistical model. In some sense, causal models are a statistical version of subjective forecasting techniques that assess determinants of sales less "scientifically." In the subjective method, the forecaster uses personal experience of the factors that affect sales to make the forecast. In the causal statistical model, the forecaster examines a variety of numerical relationships from the past to formulate a causal model. Causal models are better at predicting turning points in sales when the direction or rate of sales may change significantly in response to the external environment.

TECHNIQUE OF REGRESSION ANALYSIS. Virtually all statistically based predictive models for sales rely on the use of the statistical technique called regression analysis. Regression is a mathematical procedure that relates one variable, such as sales, to one or more other variables, such as gross national product (GNP), housing starts, or automobile sales. Regression analysis is a powerful tool that permits the forecaster to measure the statistical impact (and, by inference, the actual impact) of each independent variable on the dependent variable, sales. If there appears to be a significant correlation between the dependent variable sales and the other variables, the regression model is useful in describing the size of the relationship and its predictive value.

In a hypothetical company in the home furnishing industry, sales might be expected to correlate with such factors as:

- New marriages.
- New housing starts.
- Disposable personal income.
- General time trend.

Formulating the Equation. It is safe to say that most experienced observers, both within and outside the home furnishings field, will have certain preconceived notions about the effects of the variables listed above on sales of home furnishings. Through the regression technique, however, one can measure precisely how large and how significant each variable is in its historical relationship with sales. The overall relationship can be described by means of an industry sales regression equation:

$$S = B + B_m(M) + B_h(H) + B_i(I) + B_t(T)$$

where S = gross sales for year
$\quad\ \ B$ = base sales, or starting point from which other factors have influence
$\quad\ \ M$ = marriages during year
$\quad\ \ H$ = housing starts during year
$\quad\ \ I$ = annual disposable personal income
$\quad\ \ T$ = time trend (first year = 1, second year = 2, third year = 3, etc.)

B_m, B_h, B_i, and B_t represent the amount of influence on sales of the factors M, H, I, and T, respectively. These "B" terms, called regression coefficients, indicate the extent of the relationship between the dependent variable, sales, and each independent variable on the right-hand side of the equation.

Amount of Data Required. The estimation of the relationships suggested by the equation generally require the use of several years' data because a meaningful correlation can hardly be judged when trends are measured only for a short time. Furthermore, when more than one variable is being correlated with sales, as in the equation above, the number of years of observations should be increased to make sure the results have reasonable statistical significance.

While there is no definitive cutoff point for the minimum number of years of data that are required, a period of five years is a general rule of thumb when only one variable is being analyzed, and eight years is a minimum with two. A longer time span is necessary with three or more variables, as is the case in our example.

Testing Other Models. Regression analysis has the advantage that the basic sales equation can be augmented by the addition of other variables if the forecaster feels they would add to the predictive value of the model. It is the ability of the computer to process large quantities of statistical information that makes regression analyses feasible, since calculations that previously would have taken many, many hours to perform can be done in a matter of a few minutes. In fact, several companies now produce hand-held calculators that will test certain regression equations for those without access to large computer facilities.

Most Common Factors. The most common macroeconomic factors incorporated into regression equations for sales forecasting are:

1. *Gross national product.* This variable correlates macroeconomic activity with company sales.
2. *Demographic data.* Correlations of these factors (e.g., new households, unemployment, housing starts, and age distribution of population) may differ.
3. *Interest rates.* This factor often has a major impact on sales of higher-priced consumer and capital goods.

Numerous other variables may be selected as long as they can be expected to have a causal effect on sales.

Interpreting Results. Hewlett-Packard, Texas Instruments, and several other manufacturers of calculators provide user information for the application of regression analysis to sales forecasting. This section does not deal in detail with regression analysis as a tool, but readers are referred to the article by Parker and Segura cited in the References or to any of a number of the introductory statistics textbooks with chapters on "regression analysis" (see, e.g., Draper and Smith, *Applied Regression Analysis*. The major statistics to emerge from a regression equation are discussed next.

Coefficient of Determination (R^2). This statistic indicates the proportion of variation in observed sales in prior years that is explained by the regression equation (model). Theoretically it can range from .00 to 1.00, although, in reality, regression equations seldom demonstrate an R^2 greater than .95 or less than .50. Even the most naive models succeed in capturing some of the variation in sales on a historical basis. Systematic experimentation can improve the R^2.

"*t*-Values." These statistics measure the reliability of relationships of the individual variables with the dependent variable (sales). Usually, a *t*-value of at least ± 2.0 (assuming adequate sample size) will indicate that the variable is meaningful as a predictor. This does not mean, however, that there is not a better variable available. Only trial and error can establish that.

Standard Error of Estimate. This indicates the degree to which the estimate is a good predictor. Sales can be expected to fall within ± 2.0 standard errors of the estimate of predicted sales. Thus the smaller the standard error of the estimate, the more useful the model is as a predictor.

OTHER METHODS OF SALES FORECASTING. There are numerous other methods of forecasting sales that are variations and combinations of the subjective and statistical techniques described. It is to be stressed, however, that the financial forecaster is usually somewhat peripheral to the sales forecasting process. The output from the sales forecasting system is the "starting point" for the financial forecaster's task. The partial summary of sales forecasting techniques that follows is from J.C. Chambers, S.K. Mullick, and D.D. Smith, "How to Choose the Right Forecasting Technique."

All these methods have pitfalls and may differ vastly in cost and administration. Sales forecasting is a specialty unto itself and requires considerable expertise.

1. Subjective methods
   a. Historical judgment based on similar circumstances.
   b. Market research.
   c. Panel consensus.
   d. Delphi method (a more formal panel consensus relying on sequential questionnaires; results of each questionnaire are used to prepare the subsequent survey).
   e. Individual "guess work."
2. Time series
   a. Moving average—simple and exponentially smoothed.
   b. Box–Jenkins (a highly complex trend forecast).
   c. X-11 (designed to isolate subtrends such as seasonality).
   d. Mechanical trend line.
3. Causal methods
   a. Regression (as above).
   b. Econometric models (simultaneous regression equations).
   c. Survey of intentions to buy.
   d. Life cycle analysis.

SELECTING APPROPRIATE INTERVAL. Implicit in the sales forecasting process is selection of the appropriate time period to be forecast. Forecasts may be made **monthly** and aggregated for a **yearly forecast.** Some financial planning however, requires weekly and even daily forecasting to be maximally useful for the financial planner. Short-term sales forecasts of the weekly and daily variety are of particular relevance in cash management, whereas forecasts for planning longer-term needs may more appropriately be done monthly, quarterly, or yearly. This section emphasizes monthly sales forecasts aggregated to produce an annual sales forecast. It is sometimes observed that an excessively short forecasting interval is dangerous because it implies a degree of accuracy that may be unrealistic. Thus, a longer interval, for example a month, may be better than a daily forecast.

FORECASTING THE CASH POSITION

Often the first report prepared by the financial forecaster is the cash budget. This report attempts to estimate the cash position of the company, and, indirectly, the financing requirements over the forecast period (usually one year) presented on a monthly basis. Cash budgets, however, can be prepared on a weekly or even daily basis.

INFORMATION FOR A CASH BUDGET. Supplementing the sales forecast in preparing the cash budget are various discretionary items that affect the financial position of the firm and its cash balances. These items include:

1. Scheduled purchases or sales of assets, especially fixed assets such as buildings or equipment.
2. Scheduled new financing such as long-term debt or a new stock issue.
3. Scheduled debt repayments and interest charges.
4. Dividends.
5. Other contractual or planned receipts or disbursements that fall outside the normal operating cycle of the business such as lease payments.

The sales forecast, in combination with the other known cash inflow and outflow as noted previously, is used to produce a schedule of cash receipts and disbursements. A diagram of the relationship of the key financial accounts as they affect cash is shown in Exhibit 1.

EXAMPLE OF CASH BUDGET. To illustrate the preparation of a monthly cash budget forecast for 1985, a hypothetical example, the Taft Manufacturing Co., is presented. The example is a model for the type of data needed to prepare a cash budget in other companies.

1. *Company history.* The hypothetical Taft Co., a distributor of foreign auto parts, has experienced dramatic sales growth over the period 1982–1984, as shown in the historical income statements of Exhibit 2. While sales have been increasing, profits have decreased slightly as shown in the exhibit.
2. *Year-end balance sheets for 1982–1984.* The year-end financial position of Taft (Exhibit 3) shows a growth in assets from $247,907,000 to $382,659,000, with long-term debt increasing significantly to $96,000,000.

Cash Budget Data

1. Monthly and annual sales of Taft were estimated by the marketing staff using a **trend forecast** with subjective estimates providing for some seasonal fluctuations. The actual estimates are as follows:

1985 Estimated Monthly Sales
($000 Omitted)

January	$ 58,000
February	59,000
March	61,000
April	62,000
May	64,000
June	69,000
July	70,000
August	72,000
September	72,000
October	75,000
November	76,000
December	77,000
Total for 1980	$815,000

EXHIBIT 1   THE CASH CYCLE[a]

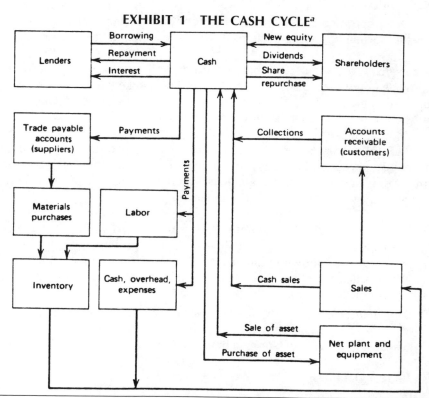

[a] Cash is normally generated by cash sales, collection of accounts receivable, borrowing, new equity, and sale of an asset. Cash is utilized by cash expenses, payment of a accounts payable, debt repayments and interest repayments, dividends or share repurchase, and purchase of an asset.

EXHIBIT 2 TAFT MANUFACTURING CO. ANNUAL INCOME STATEMENTS ($000 OMITTED)

	1982	1983	1984
Sales	432,042	504,104	653,242
Cost of goods sold	− 302,436	− 343,829	− 468,850
Gross profit	129,606	160,275	184,392
Operating expense	− 89,056	− 107,068	− 139,179
Operating profit	40,550	53,207	45,213
Interest	− 3,738	− 8,354	− 10,547
Profit before taxes	36,812	44,853	34,666
Income taxes	− 15,980	− 21,171	− 16,016
Net income	20,832	23,682	18,650
Dividends	− 800	− 800	− 800
Change in net worth	20,032	22,882	17,850

EXHIBIT 3 TAFT MANUFACTURING CO. YEAR-END BALANCE SHEETS ($000 OMITTED)

	1982	1983	1984
Assets			
Cash and securities	15,399	39,372	15,940
Accounts receivable	64,487	76,804	101,764
Inventories	117,994	154,485	177,038
Other current assets	4,871	9,724	10,801
Total current assets	202,751	280,385	305,543
Net plant and equipment	39,579	49,998	68,010
Other long-term assets	5,577	6,678	9,106
Total Assets	247,907	337,061	382,659
Liabilities and Net Worth			
Accounts payable	20,729	23,617	33,233
Notes payable	13,096	1,861	22,955
Other current liabilities	19,718	29,525	26,563
Total current liabilities	53,543	55,003	82,751
Long-term debt	31,188	96,000	96,000
Total liabilities	84,731	151,003	178,751
Common stock	48,960	48,960	48,960
Capital surplus	43,563	43,563	43,563
Retained earnings	70,653	93,535	111,385
Net worth	163,176	186,058	203,908
Total capitalization	247,907	337,061	382,659

2. Cash sales expected to account for 10% of total sales.

3. Credit terms; net 60 days. Collections made two months after the sale (i.e., January credit sales were collected in March. February credit sales collected in April, etc.) Bad debt losses were expected to be insignificant.

4. The company scheduled monthly production so that inventories did not change during the year.

5. Taft followed a policy of "direct" costing; that is, all overhead costs, including depreciation, were charged evenly throughout the year. Overhead, exclusive of depreciation, was projected at 19% of sales and was paid each month.

6. Cost of goods sold was budgeted at 70% of sales. Since 80% of Taft's production costs was for materials purchased on terms of net 30 days, the company paid for materials one month after they were used in production. All labor expenses were paid currently.

7. Depreciation expense for 1985 was scheduled to be $1.2 million per month, while new capital expenditures were planned as follows:

March	$4,500,000
June	4,600,000
September	4,800,000
December	4,900,000

8. Income taxes for each calendar year were paid in the following years, with 25% due in the first month of each calendar quarter (i.e., 25% on January 15, April 15, July 15, and October 15). Thus, 1985 the 1984 taxes of $16,016,000 were paid in equal installments. Taxes due for 1985 were accrued. For 1985, Taft assumed a tax rate of .46 of profits.

9. Taft's board of directors declared a quarterly dividend of $400,000 in 1979, paid in the second month of the quarter. Plans for 1985 included a significant increase in the dividend to $2 million quarterly, to be paid in February, May, August, and November.

10. Taft kept at least 18.8% of current monthly sales volume in cash and marketable securities at all times. This was considered a minimum acceptable level of cash for contingencies and was useful in maintaining good bank relations.

11. Interest on Taft's $96 million in long-term debt was computed at 8.5% per year. Interest rates on the company's short-term debt (notes payable) varied, but for 1980 it was projected at 14%. Interest was paid at the beginning of each calendar quarter for the three preceding months.

12. No amortization of the long-term debt was required before 1985.

13. No change in other current assets or other long-term assets was projected for 1985.

14. Interest and tax expenses accrued, but not yet paid, are entered as other current liabilities.

Interpreting Cash Budget Results. Exhibit 4a-4d indicates the monthly cash flows as well as the monthly financing needed by Taft based on the sales

EXHIBIT 4 1985 CASH BUDGET—TAFT MANUFACTURING COMPANY, BASE PLAN ($000 OMITTED). (a) SALES UP 25%; (b) SALES UP 75% VERSUS 25%; (c) SALES UP 75% VERSUS 25%, COST OF SALES 80% VERSUS 70%, SHORT-TERM INTEREST RATE 20% VERSUS 14%; AND (d) SALES 35% BELOW PLAN, COST OF SALES 80% VERSUS 70%, SHORT-TERM INTEREST RATE 20% VERSUS 14%.

Sales (a)	58000	59000	61000	62000	64000	69000	70000	72000	72000	75000	76000	77000	815000
	Jan	Feb	Mar	Apr	May	Jun	Jul	Aug	Sep	Oct	Nov	Dec	Year
CASH RECEIPTS													
Cash sales (b)	5800	5900	6100	6200	6400	6900	7000	7200	7200	7500	7600	7700	81500
Collections (c)	50882	50882	52200	53100	54900	55800	57600	62100	63000	64800	64800	67500	697564
Total receipts	56682	56782	58300	59300	61300	62700	64600	69300	70200	72300	72400	75200	779064
CASH DISBURSMENTS													
Direct labor (d)	8120	8260	8540	8680	8960	9660	9800	10080	10080	10500	10640	10780	114100
Direct materials (e)	33233	32480	33040	34160	34720	35840	38640	39200	40320	40320	42000	42560	446513
Cash oper exp (f)	12904	12904	12904	12904	12904	12904	12904	12904	12904	12904	12904	12904	154848
Int. (arrears) (g)	2780			2813			2890			2946			11429
Taxes (h)	4004			4004			4004		4004				16016
Dividends (i)		2000			2000			2000			2000		8000
Capital expend (j)			4500			4600			4800			4900	18800
Total disbursments	61041	55644	58984	62561	58584	63004	68238	64184	72108	66670	67544	71144	769706
Net cash flow	-4359	1138	-684	-3261	2716	-304	-3638	5116	-1908	5630	4856	4056	9358
Beginning cash (k)	-7015	10904	11092	11468	11656	12032	12972	13160	13536	13536	14100	14288	
End of month cash	-11374	12042	10408	8207	14372	11728	9334	18276	11628	19166	18956	18344	
Desired cash (l)	10904	11092	11468	11656	12032	12972	13160	13536	13536	14100	14288	14476	
‡‡ENDING LOAN NEEDED (m)	22278	21328	22388	25837	23497	24741	28568	23828	25736	20669	16001	12133	

Notes:
a. given
b. 10% of sales (given)
c. Jan and Feb are each 1/2 of yr.end accts. rec., then 90% of sales 2 months prior
d. 20% of sales (given)
f. 1/12 of 19% of base forecasted sales (given) paid monthly
g. Jan from 1984 bal sheet; then sum of three month prior interest from inc. statment
h. 1/4 of prior years taxes from 1984 income statement
i. given
j. given
k. sum of 1984 year end cash less 1984 year end notes payable
l. .188 of sales (given)
m. enough to bring end of month cash to zero plus desired cash balance
‡‡ THIS IS THE LOAN REQUIREMENT AND ITS SCHEDULING FOR PLANNING PURPOSES

(a)

EXHIBIT 4   CONTINUED

Sales (a)	81200	82600	85400	86800	89600	96600	98000	100800	100800	105000	106400	107800	1141000
	Jan	Feb	Mar	Apr	May	Jun	Jul	Aug	Sep	Oct	Nov	Dec	Year
CASH RECEIPTS	------	------	------	------	------	------	------	------	------	------	------	------	------
Cash sales (b)	8120	8260	8540	8680	8960	9660	9800	10080	10080	10500	10640	10780	114100
Collections (c)	50882	50882	73080	74340	76860	78120	80640	86940	88200	90720	90720	94500	935884
Total receipts	59002	59142	81620	83020	85820	87780	90440	97020	98280	101220	101360	105280	1049984
CASH DISBURSMENTS													
Direct labor (d)	11368	11564	11956	12152	12544	13524	13720	14112	14112	14700	14896	15092	159740
Direct materials (e)	33233	45472	46256	47824	48608	50176	54096	54880	56448	56448	58800	59584	611825
Cash oper exp (f)	12904	12904	12904	12904	12904	12904	12904	12904	12904	12904	12904	12904	154848
Int. (arrears) (g)	2780			3175			2999			2341			11295
Taxes (h)	4004			4004			4004		4004				16016
Dividends (i)		2000			2000			2000			2000		8000
Capital expend (j)			4500			4600			4800			4900	18800
Total disbursments	64289	71940	75616	80059	76056	81204	87723	83896	92268	86393	88600	92480	980524
Net cash flow	-5287	-12798	6004	2961	9764	6576	2717	13124	6012	14827	12760	12800	69460
Beginning cash (k)	-7015	15266	15529	16055	16318	16845	18161	18424	18950	18950	19740	20003	
End of month cash	-12302	2468	21533	19017	26082	23421	20878	31548	24962	33777	32500	32803	
Desired cash (l)	15266	15529	16055	16318	16845	18161	18424	18950	18950	19740	20003	20266	
**ENDING LOAN NEEDED (m)	27568	40629	35151	32453	23215	17955	15502	2904	-3108	-17145	-29642	-42178	

Notes:
a. given
b. 10% of sales (given)
c. Jan and Feb are each 1/2 of yr.end accts. rec., then 90% of sales 2 months prior
d. 20% of sales (given)
f. 1/12 of 19% of base forecasted sales (given) paid monthly
g. Jan from 1984 bal sheet; then sum of three month prior interest from inc. statment
h. 1/4 of prior years taxes from 1984 income statement
i. given
j. given
k. sum of 1984 year end cash less 1984 year end notes payable
l. .188 of sales (given)
m. enough to bring end of month cash to zero plus desired cash balance
** THIS IS THE LOAN REQUIREMENT AND ITS SCHEDULING FOR PLANNING PURPOSES

(b)

forecast and other information presented in items 1–14. Exhibit 3*a* indicates an increase in short-term notes payable through July to 28,569,000, then a decrease to 12,136,000 by year end. The feasibility of such financing can be negotiated with Taft's lender (probably a bank) on the basis of this systematic plan.

The reason for borrowing can be analyzed on a monthly basis in the January–December period. Here it is seen that there are wide swings in monthly cash requirements, which vary from January (the high month) with a net financing need of $4,359,000, to October (the low month), with a net positive cash flow of $5,630,000. It is noted further that the discretionary items of "capital expenditures" and "dividends" account for $28.8 million

EXHIBIT 4   *CONTINUED*

Sales (a)	81200	82600	85400	86800	89600	96600	98000	100800	100800	105000	106400	107800	1141000
	Jan	Feb	Mar	Apr	May	Jun	Jul	Aug	Sep	Oct	Nov	Dec	Year
CASH RECEIPTS													
Cash sales (b)	8120	8260	8540	8680	8960	9660	9800	10080	10080	10500	10640	10780	114100
Collections (c)	50882	50882	73080	74340	76860	78120	80640	86940	86200	90720	90720	94500	935884
Total receipts	59002	59142	81620	83020	85820	87780	90440	97020	98280	101220	101360	105280	1049984
CASH DISBURSMENTS													
Direct labor (d)	12992	13216	13664	13888	14336	15456	15680	16128	16128	16800	17024	17248	182560
Direct materials (e)	33233	51968	52864	54656	55552	57344	61824	62720	64512	64512	67200	68096	694481
Cash oper exp (f)	12904	12904	12904	12904	12904	12904	12904	12904	12904	12904	12904	12904	154848
Int. (arrears) (g)	2780			4001			5000			5554			17336
Taxes (h)	4004			4004			4004		4004				16016
Dividends (i)		2000			2000			2000			2000		8000
Capital expend (j)			4500			4600			4800			4900	18800
Total disbursments	65913	80088	83932	89453	84792	90304	99412	93752	102348	99770	99128	103148	1092041
Net cash flow	-6911	-20946	-2312	-6433	1028	-2524	-8972	3268	-4068	1450	2232	2132	-42057
Beginning cash (k)	-7015	15266	15529	16055	16318	16845	18161	18424	18950	18950	19740	20003	
End of month cash	-13926	-5680	13217	9622	17346	14321	9188	21692	14882	20401	21972	22135	
Desired cash (l)	15266	15529	16055	16318	16845	18161	18424	18950	18950	19740	20003	20266	
**ENDING LOAN NEEDED (m)	29192	50401	53239	59936	59434	63274	72510	69768	73836	73176	71207	69338	

Notes:
a. given
b. 10% of sales (given)
c. Jan and Feb are each 1/2 of yr.end accts. rec., then 90% of sales 2 months prior
d. 20% of sales (given)
f. 1/12 of 19% of base forecasted sales (given) paid monthly
g. Jan from 1984 bal sheet; then sum of three month prior interest from inc. statment
h. 1/4 of prior years taxes from 1984 income statement
i. given
j. given
k. sum of 1984 year end cash less 1984 year end notes payable
l. .188 of sales (given)
m. enough to bring end of month cash to zero plus desired cash balance
** THIS IS THE LOAN REQUIREMENT AND ITS SCHEDULING FOR PLANNING PURPOSES

(c)

of the cash flow. If Taft permits sales to grow by 25% from 1984 to 1985 as shown in the forecast, the financing requirements will be as shown in Exhibit 4*a*.

Variations in Plan and Computer-Based Systems. While the process of preparing a cash budget can be done manually, the forecast can also be prepared using a computer-based system. Many such systems are available in the form of programs or software packages from computer manufacturers and independent computer service bureaus. Many medium and large companies also develop forecasting models using their own computer staffs, most often using the LOTUS 1-2-3 program. The exhibits in this chapter have been prepared using LOTUS 1-2-3.

EXHIBIT 4 *CONTINUED*

Sales (a)	37700	38350	39650	40300	41600	44850	45500	46800	46800	48750	49400	50050	529750
	Jan	Feb	Mar	Apr	May	Jun	Jul	Aug	Sep	Oct	Nov	Dec	Year
CASH RECEIPTS													
Cash sales (b)	3770	3835	3965	4030	4160	4485	4550	4680	4680	4875	4940	5005	52975
Collections (c)	50882	50882	33930	34515	35685	36270	37440	40365	40950	42120	42120	43875	489034
Total receipts	54652	54717	37895	38545	39845	40755	41990	45045	45630	46995	47060	48880	542009
CASH DISBURSMENTS													
Direct labor (d)	6032	6136	6344	6448	6656	7176	7280	7488	7488	7800	7904	8008	84760
Direct materials (e)	33233	24128	24544	25376	25792	26624	28704	29120	29952	29952	31200	31616	340241
Cash oper exp (f)	12904	12904	12904	12904	12904	12904	12904	12904	12904	12904	12904	12904	154848
Int. (arrears) (g)	2780			2851			3856			5525			15012
Taxes (h)	4004			4004			4004		4004				16016
Dividends (i)		2000			2000			2000			2000		8000
Capital expend (j)			4500			4600			4800			4900	18800
Total disbursments	58953	45168	48292	51583	47352	51304	56748	51512	59148	56181	54008	57428	637677
Net cash flow	-4301	9549	-10397	-13038	-7507	-10549	-14758	-6467	-13518	-9186	-6948	-8548	-95668
Beginning cash (k)	-7015	7088	7210	7454	7576	7821	8432	8554	8798	8798	9165	9287	
End of month cash	-11316	16637	-3187	-5584	69	-2728	-6326	2087	-4720	-388	2217	739	
Desired cash (l)	7088	7210	7454	7576	7821	8432	8554	8798	8798	9165	9287	9409	
**ENDING LOAN NEEDED (m)	18404	8977	19618	32779	40530	51690	66570	73282	86800	96352	103422	112092	

Notes:
a. given
b. 10% of sales (given)
c. Jan and Feb are each 1/2 of yr.end accts. rec., then 90% of sales 2 months prior
d. 20% of sales (given)
f. 1/12 of 19% of base forecasted sales (given) paid monthly
g. Jan from 1984 bal sheet; then sum of three month prior interest from inc. statment
h. 1/4 of prior years taxes from 1984 income statement
i. given
j. given
k. sum of 1984 year end cash less 1984 year end notes payable
l. .188 of sales (given)
m. enough to bring end of month cash to zero plus desired cash balance
** THIS IS THE LOAN REQUIREMENT AND ITS SCHEDULING FOR PLANNING PURPOSES

(d)

The decision to use a prepackaged financial forecasting model instead of an in-house *custom-made model* frequently depends on such considerations as whether the company is operating under unusual loan covenants or experiences unusual seasonal relationships in expenses and sales. With in-house systems, individual company characteristics can be incorporated into the model in specific and highly ingenious ways. The prepackaged financial programs have the advantage of being easy to use and are generally free from errors.

"What If" Analysis. The key advantage most computer-based systems have over their manual counterparts is the ease with which **sensitivity analysis** can be performed. Sensitivity analysis is often referred to as the process of asking "what if" with regard to the impact of certain changes in the planning

assumptions or in external market conditions. For example, a computer-based cash budget can forecast the effect on funds requirements for "what if" questions such as:

1. What if sales were 50% over plan? This might be expected to change the cash requirements significantly. Exhibit 4b shows cash requirements each month for a 50% increase in sales. The acceptability of this increase can be the basis for deciding whether a relaxation of credit terms can be tolerated.
2. What if the cost of goods sold were to increase to 80% of sales with a 50% increase in sales? Exhibit 4c shows the results.
3. What if sales were to fall short of forecast by 35%, cost of goods sold were 80%, and interest on the short-term loan were to go to 20%? Results are in Exhibit 3d. Note that the amount of the ending loan needed is relatively smaller in the earlier months (i.e., January–June) and then higher in later months.

Of course numerous other possibilities might be investigated, such as an increase in sales of 50% combined with an increase in the collection period to 75 days. This would clearly increase financing requirements significantly.

Similarly, if assumptions about the fixed nature of overhead were examined, overhead might be programmed to be a variable monthly expense instead of a fixed monthly expense, as in the model presented. The number of combinations of possibilities is nearly infinite, so many forecasters arrange their forecasts into three categories: most likely, worst case, and best cases.

Most Likely. This forecast, often called the "base case," is the forecast of Exhibit 4a. It is the forecast we would expect to be most accurate.

Worst Case. This is the forecast with "everything going wrong." No "worst-case" forecast is made in the Taft example. Note: a sales increase might be considered to be a "best case" in terms of profit, but in terms of cash requirements it might be a "worst-case" event.

Best Case. This would involve a shortened collection period and modest increases in sales. If "best-case" assumptions are carried to the extreme, the financing requirements may actually drop over the period.

USES OF THE CASH BUDGET. The primary use of the cash budget is to estimate funds requirements and cash balances under a variety of circumstances. Such budgets may also be valuable in formulating financial strategy. Examples include:

1. Timing in the declaration and payment of dividends. In some cases the cash budget may even dictate the nonpayment of dividends.

2. Negotiating loan repayment terms and selecting between short-term and long-term debt. This is particularly important where short-term loans are required to be "off the books" during part of the year.
3. Evaluating the cash effects of various accounts receivable policies, including offering discounts for early payment.
4. Planning and modifying capital expenditure policy.
5. Timing short-term investments, particularly marketable securities investments.

Each of these planning decisions is made easier by the basic cash budgets in Exhibit 3 including the variations that may occur.

FORECASTING BALANCE SHEETS AND INCOME STATEMENTS

USES OF PRO FORMA STATEMENTS. Upon completion of the cash budget, the projected financial statements are prepared; the pro forma balance sheet and the pro forma income statement. These statements are used to:

1. Estimate profit (or loss) for the period (day, week, month, year).
2. Test alternate strategies and their financial effect on reported results.
3. Make estimates of asset requirements.
4. Make estimates of financing requirements, both short-term and long-term, for debt and equity.
5. Predict financial "bottlenecks" so that plans may be formulated.

INTERRELATIONSHIP OF PROJECTED STATEMENTS. Before illustrating the preparation of projected financial statements, it is important to point out that since forecasted balance sheets and income statements are mutually dependent, the process may be somewhat circular. This circularity results because it is not possible to know the amount of borrowed funds that will be needed until an estimate of profit for the period is made. On the other hand, the profit estimate will be affected by the amount of funds borrowed, and the interest paid.

Usually the circularity problem is resolved by simply ignoring the interest cost of incremental financing during the forecast period on the assumption that this amount will not materially affect the result—at least not to an extent greater than the forecast error in general.

Because changes in interest cost over the planning period are usually small, the preparation of the income statement may be a logical starting point. If the incremental interest changes are significant, usually judged by inspection, the income statement can be reformulated after the balance sheet has been partially estimated; then a closer approximation of actual interest can be incorporated into the income statement. Increased interest will increase borrowing somewhat (by the amount of the added interest), and a slightly more accurate balance sheet and income statement will result.

For the perfectionist, a set of simultaneous equations may bring the balance sheet and income statement into alignment, but this refinement is seldom worth the effort in view of other forecast errors present. Most forecasters resolve the circularity problem by accepting the small amount of imprecision that is implicit in ignoring incremental interest charges.

PREPARING PRO FORMA INCOME STATEMENTS. There are two methods commonly used to prepare projected income statements. They are:

> **Percent of Sales Method.** The percent of sales method is a simple method for forecasting the income statement where historical expense ratios are applied to the sales forecast. These historical ratios may either be based on the most recent year (or shorter period), or they may be a historical average of the most recent five years or three years. Deciding on the appropriate historical ratios to apply to the future is a subjective judgment that militates against the otherwise "objective" nature of this technique.
>
> **Budgeted Expense Method.** The budgeted expense method is most appropriate when future expenses are expected to deviate substantially from historical expenses. This may be the case when depreciation is expected to increase because of new capital expenditures or the price of labor and raw materials is expected to go up more (or less) than sales prices.

Observers differ on the merits of the two methods. Both have essentially the same results. The percent of sales method tends to be more historical in its orientation, while the budgeted revenue and expense method attempts to capture future performance where it might differ from past history. Depending on the method selected, either historical or target data may be used.

It is also possible to combine the **percent of sales method** with the **budgeted expense method.** For example, the "cost of goods sold" figure may correlate well with sales, while portions of overhead may be more discretionary, as in the amount of depreciation charged. Thus the pro forma income statement can be purely a percent of sales forecast or a modified percent of sales forecast.

PROJECTED INCOME STATEMENT DATA. The projected income statement should contain the following items, in the order given:

1. *Sales.* This forecast is taken from marketing department forecasts as in the foregoing cash budget subsection.
2. *Cost of goods sold (COGS).* Projected to be 70% of sales (for the Taft Manufacturing Co. example).

3. *Operating expenses*. From cash budget plus $1.2 million depreciation expense per month.

4. *Interest*. Based on 8.5% of long-term debt and 14% of notes payable. For monthly forecasts, one-twelfth of the annual amount is used.

5. *Income taxes*. Estimated at 46% of profit before taxes.

Exhibit 5a shows the pro forma income statement for Taft by month for 1985, with explanations for each line item. The resulting profit figures demonstrate good and consistent profit growth for 1985. Exhibits 5b and 5d show the monthly profit figures with a 20% increase in sales over forecast and a 10% decrease in sales from forecast, respectively.

PREPARING PRO FORMA BALANCE SHEETS. When the cash budget and pro forma income statements are complete, the pro forma balance sheet must be prepared. This statement incorporates the effect of the projected income statement on equity and the effect of the cash budget on the cash position. The pro forma balance sheet presents the financial condition of the firm as a result of the financial performance anticipated.

Information Required. The information for the pro forma balance sheets is primarily derived from the operating data provided for the cash budget and from certain other information as noted in the list below.

EXHIBIT 5   1985 PRO FORMA INCOME STATEMENT—TAFT MANUFACTURING COMPANY, BASE PLAN ($000 OMITTED). (a) SALES UP 25%; (b) SALES UP 75% VERSUS 25%; (c) SALES UP 75% VERSUS 25%, COST OF SALES 80% VERSUS 70%, SHORT-TERM INTEREST RATE 20% VERSUS 14%; AND (d) SALES BELOW PLAN BY 35%, COST OF SALES 80% VERSUS 70%, SHORT-TERM INTEREST RATE 20% VERSUS 14%.

		Jan	Feb	Mar	Apr	May	Jun	Jul	Aug	Sep	Oct	Nov	Dec	Year
Sales		58000	59000	61000	62000	64000	69000	70000	72000	72000	75000	76000	77000	815000
Cost of sales (a)	0.70	40600	41300	42700	43400	44800	48300	49000	50400	50400	52500	53200	53900	570500
Gross margin		17400	17700	18300	18600	19200	20700	21000	21600	21600	22500	22800	23100	244500
Operating exp (b)		14104	14104	14104	14104	14104	14104	14104	14104	14104	14104	14104	14104	169248
Interest expense (c)	0.14	944	934	935	961	968	961	991	986	969	951	894	844	11338
Profit bef. tax		2352	2662	3261	3535	4128	5635	5905	6510	6527	7445	7802	8152	63914
Tax (.46)		1082	1224	1500	1626	1899	2592	2716	2995	3002	3425	3589	3750	29400
Profit after tax		1270	1437	1761	1909	2229	3043	3189	3516	3525	4020	4213	4402	34513

Notes:
a. given at 70% of sales
b. operating expenses from cash budget plus $ 1.2 million/month of depreciation
c. one month's interest on term loan @ .085/12 plus current loan @ .14/12

(a)

EXHIBIT 5 CONTINUED

		Jan	Feb	Mar	Apr	May	Jun	Jul	Aug	Sep	Oct	Nov	Dec	Year
Sales		81200	82600	85400	86800	89600	96600	98000	100800	100800	105000	106400	107800	1141000
Cost of sales (a)	0.70	56840	57820	59780	60760	62720	67620	68600	70560	70560	73500	74480	75460	798700
Gross margin		24360	24780	25620	26040	26880	28980	29400	30240	30240	31500	31920	32340	342300
Operating exp (b)		14104	14104	14104	14104	14104	14104	14104	14104	14104	14104	14104	14104	169248
Interest expense (c)	0.14	975	1078	1122	1074	1005	920	875	787	679	562	407	261	9745
Profit bef. tax		9281	9598	10394	10862	11771	13956	14421	15349	15457	16834	17409	17975	163307
Tax (.46)		4269	4415	4781	4996	5415	6420	6634	7060	7110	7744	8008	8268	75121
Profit after tax		5012	5183	5613	5865	6356	7536	7787	8288	8347	9090	9401	9706	88186

Notes:
a. given at 70% of sales
b. operating expenses from cash budget plus $ 1.2 million/month of depreciation
c. one month's interest on term loan @ .085/12 plus current loan @ .14/12

(b)

		Jan	Feb	Mar	Apr	May	Jun	Jul	Aug	Sep	Oct	Nov	Dec	Year
Sales		81200	82600	85400	86800	89600	96600	98000	100800	100800	105000	106400	107800	1141000
Cost of sales (a)	0.80	64960	66080	68320	69440	71680	77280	78400	80640	80640	84000	85120	86240	912800
Gross margin		16240	16520	17080	17360	17920	19320	19600	20160	20160	21000	21280	21560	228200
Operating exp (b)		14104	14104	14104	14104	14104	14104	14104	14104	14104	14104	14104	14104	169248
Interest expense (c)	0.20	1115	1343	1544	1623	1675	1703	1812	1866	1877	1905	1883	1851	20195
Profit bef. tax		1021	1073	1432	1633	2141	3513	3684	4190	4179	4991	5293	5605	38757
Tax (.46)		470	493	659	751	985	1616	1695	1928	1922	2296	2435	2578	17828
Profit after tax		552	579	773	882	1156	1897	1990	2263	2257	2695	2858	3027	20929

Notes:
a. given at .80 of sales
b. operating expenses from cash budget plus $ 1.2 million/month of depreciation
c. one month's interest on term loan @ .20/12 plus current loan @

(c)

		Jan	Feb	Mar	Apr	May	Jun	Jul	Aug	Sep	Oct	Nov	Dec	Year
Sales		37700	38350	39650	40300	41600	44850	45500	46800	46800	48750	49400	50050	529750
Cost of sales (a)	0.80	30160	30680	31720	32240	33280	35880	36400	37440	37440	39000	39520	40040	423800
Gross margin		7540	7670	7930	8060	8320	8970	9100	9360	9360	9750	9880	10010	105950
Operating exp (b)		14104	14104	14104	14104	14104	14104	14104	14104	14104	14104	14104	14104	169248
Interest expense (c)	0.20	1025	908	918	1117	1291	1448	1666	1845	2014	2206	2345	2476	19259
Profit bef. tax		-7589	-7342	-7092	-7161	-7075	-6582	-6670	-6589	-6758	-6560	-6569	-6570	-82557
Tax (.46)		-3491	-3377	-3262	-3294	-3254	-3028	-3068	-3031	-3109	-3018	-3022	-3022	-37976
Profit after tax		-4098	-3965	-3830	-3867	-3820	-3555	-3602	-3558	-3649	-3543	-3547	-3548	-44581

Notes:
a. given at 80% of sales
b. operating expenses from cash budget plus $ 1.2 million/month of depreciation
c. one month's interest on term loan @ .20/12 plus current loan @

(d)

Sample pro forma balance sheets are presented in Exhibit 6. Exhibit 6*a* demonstrates the financial position under the base plan and corresponds to Exhibit 4*a* in the cash budget and Exhibit 5*a* in the pro forma income statement.

It is important to note that the notes payable account in the pro forma balance sheet should correspond to the notes payable line on the cash budget for the corresponding case of assumptions, for example, collection period and sales. If this does not occur, an error has been made in the financial forecast. The three statements, the cash budget, income statement, and balance sheet, should be consistent and should reconcile to each other. If this is not the case, an error has been made.

The items below explain the calculation of each account in the pro forma balance sheet of our example.

1. *Cash/securities*. This represents cash and short-term marketable securities and is maintained at 18.8% of current monthly sales (a historical number).

2. *Accounts receivable*. Calculated to be equal to the amount of credit sales for the current month and the previous month.

3. *Inventories*. Calculated to remain constant throughout the year.

4. *Other current assets*. Calculated to remain constant.

5. *Net plant and equipment*. Calculated after deducting the effect of 1.2 million depreciation expense per month, plus scheduled capital expenditures.

6. *Other long-term assets*. Calculated to remain constant throughout the year.

7. *Accounts payable*. Equal to the materials cost for the current month.

8. *Notes payable*. A "plug figure" that equals amount required to maintain the desired level of cash and marketable securities. Calculated after all other accounts have been computed, "notes payable" is the amount required to make the balance sheet balance.

9. *Other current liabilities*. Increases by the amount of accrued interest and taxes for the current month, and decreases by the amount of any payments that take place.

10. *Long-term debt*. The principal amount of $96 million, which is not scheduled to change in 1980.

11. *Common stock and capital surplus*. Not expected to change for 1985 because no new equity issue or share repurchase is scheduled.

12. *Retained earnings*. Increases each month by the amount of profit after taxes, less any dividends paid.

Specific Use of Pro Forma Balance Sheet. The primary use of the pro forma balance sheet is to assess the financial feasibility of the plan. Judgements

EXHIBIT 6 1980 PRO FORMA BALANCE SHEET—TAFT MANUFACTURING COMPANY, BASE PLAN ($000 OMITTED). (a) SALES UP 25%; (b) SALES UP 75% VERSUS 25%; (c) SALES UP 75% VERSUS 25%, COST OF SALES 80% VERSUS 70%, SHORT-TERM INTEREST RATE 20% VERSUS 14%; AND (d) SALES BELOW PLAN BY 35%, COST OF SALES 80% VERSUS 70%, SHORT-TERM INTEREST RATE 20% VERSUS 14%.

	1984	Jan	Feb	Mar	Apr	May	Jun	Jul	Aug	Sep	Oct	Nov	Dec
ASSETS													
Cash & mkt sec. (a)	15940	10904	11092	11468	11656	12032	12972	13160	13536	13536	14100	14288	14476
Accts. receivable (b)	101764	103082	105300	108000	110700	113400	119700	125100	127800	129600	132300	135900	137700
Inventories (c)	177038	177038	177038	177038	177038	177038	177038	177038	177038	177038	177038	177038	177038
Other curr assets (d)	10801	10801	10801	10801	10801	10801	10801	10801	10801	10801	10801	10801	10801
Total curr assets	305543	301825	304231	307307	310195	313271	320511	326099	329175	330975	334239	338027	340015
Net plant & equip (e)	68010	66810	65610	68910	67710	66510	69910	68710	67510	71110	69910	68710	72410
Other fixed assets (f)	9106	9106	9106	9106	9106	9106	9106	9106	9106	9106	9106	9106	9106
Total assets	382659	377741	378947	385323	387011	388887	399527	403915	405791	411191	413255	415843	421531
LIABILITIES & NET WORTH													
Accounts payable (g)	33233	32480	33040	34160	34720	35840	38640	39200	40320	40320	42000	42560	43120
Notes payable (h)	22955	22278	21328	22388	25837	23497	24741	28568	23828	25736	20669	16001	12133
Other curr liab (i)	26563	21805	23964	26399	22169	25035	28589	25402	29382	29349	30779	35262	39856
Total curr liab	82751	76563	78332	82947	82726	84373	91970	93169	93530	95405	93449	93824	95110
Long term debt (j)	96000	96000	96000	96000	96000	96000	96000	96000	96000	96000	96000	96000	96000
Total liabilities	178751	172563	174332	178947	178726	180373	187970	189169	189530	191405	189449	189824	191110
Common stock	48960	48960	48960	48960	48960	48960	48960	48960	48960	48960	48960	48960	48960
capital surplus	43563	43563	43563	43563	43563	43563	43563	43563	43563	43563	43563	43563	43563
retained earnings (k)	111385	112655	112092	113853	115762	115991	119034	122223	123738	127263	131283	133496	137898
Total net worth	203908	205178	204615	206376	208285	208514	211557	214746	216261	219786	223806	226019	230421
Total liab & net worth	382659	377741	378947	385323	387011	388887	399527	403915	405791	411191	413255	415843	421531

Notes:
a. .188 of monthly sales
b. beginning accts. receivable plus .90 sales less collections
c. constant, i.e. no change inventory during year; monthly production & sales
d. constant (given)
e. beginning net plant plus additions as scheduled (see cash budget) less depreciation
f. constant (given)
g. .80 of cost of goods sold for month, i.e. (.70 $ .80 $ sales)
h. plug figure, i.e. total assets less all other liabilities and net worth.
   must agree with loan on cash budget
i. beginning other current liabilities from 1984 balance sheet plus accrued taxes
   and interest less tax and interest payments from cash budget
j. constant, i.e. no payments during year.

(a)

EXHIBIT 6 *CONTINUED*

ASSETS

Cash & mkt sec. (a)	15940	15266	15529	16055	16318	16845	18161	18424	18950	18950	19740	20003	20266
Accts. receivable (b)	101764	123962	147420	151200	154980	158760	167580	175140	178920	181440	185220	190260	192780
Inventories (c)	177038	177038	177038	177038	177038	177038	177038	177038	177038	177038	177038	177038	177038
Other curr assets (d)	10801	10801	10801	10801	10801	10801	10801	10801	10801	10801	10801	10801	10801
Total curr assets	305543	327067	350788	355094	359137	363444	373580	381403	385709	388229	392799	398102	400885
Net plant & equip (e)	68010	66810	65610	68910	67710	66510	69910	68710	67510	71110	69910	68710	72410
Other fixed assets (f)	9106	9106	9106	9106	9106	9106	9106	9106	9106	9106	9106	9106	9106
Total assets	382659	402983	425504	433110	435953	439060	452596	459219	462325	468445	471815	475918	482401

LIABILITIES & NET WORTH

Accounts payable (g)	33233	45472	46256	47824	48608	50176	54096	54880	56448	56448	58800	59584	60368
Notes payable (h)	22955	27568	40629	35151	32453	23215	17955	15502	2904	-3108	-17145	-29642	-42178
Other curr liab (i)	26563	25023	30516	36419	35311	41731	49071	49576	57424	61209	67173	75589	84118
Total curr liab	82751	98063	117401	119395	116372	115122	121122	119958	116776	114549	108829	105531	102308
Long term debt (j)	96000	96000	96000	96000	96000	96000	96000	96000	96000	96000	96000	96000	96000
Total liabilities	178751	194063	213401	215395	212372	211122	217122	215958	212776	210549	204829	201531	198308
Common stock	48960	48960	48960	48960	48960	48960	48960	48960	48960	48960	48960	48960	48960
capital surplus	43563	43563	43563	43563	43563	43563	43563	43563	43563	43563	43563	43563	43563
retained earnings	111385	116397	119580	125193	131058	135414	142951	150738	157026	165373	174463	181864	191571
Total net worth	203908	208920	212103	217716	223581	227937	235474	243261	249549	257896	266986	274387	284094
Total liab & net worth	382659	402983	425504	433110	435953	439060	452596	459219	462325	468445	471815	475918	482401

Notes:
a. .188 of monthly sales
b. beginning accts. receivable plus .90 sales less collections
c. constant, i.e. no change inventory during year; monthly production & sales
d. constant (given)
e. beginning net plant plus additions as scheduled (see cash budget) less depreciation
f. constant (given)
g. .80 of cost of goods sold for month
h. plug figure, i.e. total assets less all other liabilities and net worth.
   must agree with loan on cash budget
i. beginning other current liabilities from 1984 balance sheet plus accrued taxes
   and interest less tax and interest payments from cash budget
j. constant, i.e. no payments during year.

(b)

may be made about the liquidity and debt ratios that result to determine whether the financial strength of the company will be compromised in the coming year. In the case of Taft, the pro forma balance sheet indicates that total liabilities could grow over the course of the year to over 50% of assets as shown in Exhibits 6*c* and 6*d* if sales run ahead of plan or way behind plan. Should such growth in liabilities be considered imprudent, a modified plan might include:

1. New equity financing.
2. Postponed capital expenditures.

EXHIBIT 6 *CONTINUED*

	1984	Jan	Feb	Mar	Apr	May	Jun	Jul	Aug	Sep	Oct	Nov	Dec
ASSETS													
Cash & mkt sec. (a)	15940	15266	15529	16055	16318	16845	18161	18424	18950	18950	19740	20003	20266
Accts. receivable (b)	101764	123962	147420	151200	154980	158760	167580	175140	178920	181440	185220	190260	192780
Inventories (c)	177038	177038	177038	177038	177038	177038	177038	177038	177038	177038	177038	177038	177038
Other curr assets (d)	10801	10801	10801	10801	10801	10801	10801	10801	10801	10801	10801	10801	10801
Total curr assets	305543	327067	350788	355094	359137	363444	373580	381403	385709	388229	392799	398102	400885
Net plant & equip (e)	68010	66810	65610	68910	67710	66510	69910	68710	67510	71110	69910	68710	72410
Other fixed assets (f)	9106	9106	9106	9106	9106	9106	9106	9106	9106	9106	9106	9106	9106
Total assets	382659	402983	425504	433110	435953	439060	452596	459219	462325	468445	471815	475918	482401
LIABILITIES & NET WORTH													
Accounts payable (g)	33233	51968	52864	54656	55552	57344	61824	62720	64512	64512	67200	68096	68992
Notes payable (h)	22955	29192	50401	53239	59936	59434	63274	72510	69768	73836	73176	71207	69338
Other curr liab (i)	26563	21363	23200	25403	19771	22431	25750	20252	24045	23840	22487	26805	31235
Total curr liab	82751	102523	126465	133298	135259	139209	150848	155482	158325	162189	162863	166108	169565
Long term debt (j)	96000	96000	96000	96000	96000	96000	96000	96000	96000	96000	96000	96000	96000
Total liabilities	178751	198523	222465	229298	231259	235209	246848	251482	254325	258189	258863	262108	265565
Common stock	48960	48960	48960	48960	48960	48960	48960	48960	48960	48960	48960	48960	48960
capital surplus	43563	43563	43563	43563	43563	43563	43563	43563	43563	43563	43563	43563	43563
retained earnings	111385	111937	110516	111289	112171	111327	113225	115214	115477	117734	120429	121287	124314
Total net worth	203908	204460	203039	203812	204694	203850	205748	207737	208000	210257	212952	213810	216837
Total liab & net worth	382659	402983	425504	433110	435953	439060	452596	459219	462325	468445	471815	475918	482401

Notes:
a. .188 of monthly sales
b. beginning accts. receivable plus .90 sales less collections
c. constant, i.e. no change inventory during year; monthly production & sales
d. constant (given)
e. beginning net plant plus additions as scheduled (see cash budget) less depreciation
f. constant (given)
g. .60 of cost of goods sold for month
h. plug figure, i.e. total assets less all other liabilities and net worth.
   must agree with loan on cash budget
i. beginning other current liabilities from 1984 balance sheet plus accrued taxes
   and interest less tax and interest payments from cash budget
j. constant, i.e. no payments during year.

(c)

3. Reduced dividend.
4. Increased prices to improve profits and increase retained earnings.

Throughout the process of formulating the plan, it is apparent that many interrelationships exist requiring repeated reworking of the plan according to varying assumptions and constraints, such as a debt-assets limit. Fortunately, Taft appears to be able to sustain the growth projected unless the 50% limit on total liabilities proves to be limiting.

EXHIBIT 6 *CONTINUED*

	1984	Jan	Feb	Mar	Apr	May	Jun	Jul	Aug	Sep	Oct	Nov	Dec
ASSETS													
Cash & mkt sec. (a)	15940	7088	7210	7454	7576	7821	8432	8554	8798	8798	9165	9287	9409
Accts. receivable (b)	101764	84812	68445	70200	71955	73710	77805	81315	83070	84240	85995	88335	89505
Inventories (c)	177038	177038	177038	177038	177038	177038	177038	177038	177038	177038	177038	177038	177038
Other curr assets (d)	10801	10801	10801	10801	10801	10801	10801	10801	10801	10801	10801	10801	10801
Total curr assets	305543	279739	263494	265493	267370	269370	274076	277708	279707	280877	282999	285461	286753
Net plant & equip (e)	68010	66810	65610	68910	67710	66510	69910	68710	67510	71110	69910	68710	72410
Other fixed assets (f)	9106	9106	9106	9106	9106	9106	9106	9106	9106	9106	9106	9106	9106
Total assets	382659	355655	338210	343509	344186	344986	353092	355524	356323	361093	362015	363277	368269
LIABILITIES & NET WORTH													
Accounts payable (g)	33233	24128	24544	25376	25792	26624	28704	29120	29952	29952	31200	31616	32032
Notes payable (h)	22955	18404	8977	19618	32779	40530	51690	66570	73282	86800	96352	103422	112092
Other curr liab (i)	26563	17313	14844	12499	3467	1504	-76	-9338	-10524	-15623	-21959	-22636	-23182
Total curr liab	82751	59844	48364	57494	62038	68657	80318	86352	92709	101129	105593	112402	120942
Long term debt (j)	96000	96000	96000	96000	96000	96000	96000	96000	96000	96000	96000	96000	96000
Total liabilities	178751	155844	144364	153494	158038	164657	176318	182352	188709	197129	201593	208402	216942
Common stock	48960	48960	48960	48960	48960	48960	48960	48960	48960	48960	48960	48960	48960
capital surplus	43563	43563	43563	43563	43563	43563	43563	43563	43563	43563	43563	43563	43563
retained earnings	111385	107287	101322	97493	93626	87805	84251	80649	75091	71442	67899	62352	58804
Total net worth	203908	199810	193845	190016	186149	180328	176774	173172	167614	163965	160422	154875	151327
Total liab & net worth	382659	355655	338210	343509	344186	344986	353092	355524	356323	361093	362015	363277	368269

Notes:
a. .188 of monthly sales
b. beginning accts. receivable plus .90 sales less collections
c. constant, i.e. no change inventory during year; monthly production & sales
d. constant (given)
e. beginning net plant plus additions as scheduled (see cash budget) less depreciation
f. constant (given)
g. .80 of cost of goods sold for month
h. plug figure, i.e. total assets less all other liabilities and net worth.
  must agree with loan on cash budget
i. beginning other current liabilities from 1984 balance sheet plus accrued taxes
  and interest less tax and interest payments from cash budget
j. constant, i.e. no payments during year.

(d)

COMMON-SIZE BALANCE SHEET. The "common-size" balance sheet is a financial forecasting tool that serves to identify some of the *trends* that will take place under the proposed plan. Through the common-size balance sheet, the financial forecaster can assess the *acceptability* of the plan to the company and to the outside world. The level of debt, assets, and equity is portrayed in percentage terms over the forecast period.

Exhibits 7a–7d show the forecasted balance sheets in percentage terms for the four possibilities presented. It is apparent from Exhibits 7c and 7d

EXHIBIT 7   1985 PRO FORMA COMMON SIZE BALANCE SHEET— TAFT MANUFACTURING COMPANY, BASE PLAN ($000 OMITTED). (a) SALES UP 25%; (b) SALES UP 75%; (c) SALES UP 75% VERSUS 25%, COST OF GOODS SOLD IS 80% VERSUS 70%, SHORT-TERM INTEREST RATE 20% VERSUS 14%; AND (d) SALES AT ONLY 65% OF PLAN, COST OF GOODS SOLD IS 80% VERSUS 70%, SHORT-TERM INTEREST RATE 20% VERSUS 14%.

Sales projection	58000	59000	61000	62000	64000	69000	70000	72000	72000	75000	76000	77000
	Jan	Feb	Mar	Apr	May	Jun	Jul	Aug	Sep	Oct	Nov	Dec
ASSETS												
Cash & mkt sec. (a)	2.9	2.9	3.0	3.0	3.1	3.2	3.3	3.3	3.3	3.4	3.4	3.4
Accts. receivable (b)	27.3	27.8	28.0	28.6	29.2	30.0	31.0	31.5	31.5	32.0	32.7	32.7
Inventories (c)	46.9	46.7	45.9	45.7	45.5	44.3	43.8	43.6	43.1	42.8	42.6	42.0
Other curr assets (d)	2.9	2.9	2.8	2.8	2.8	2.7	2.7	2.7	2.6	2.6	2.6	2.6
Total curr assets	79.9	80.3	79.8	80.2	80.6	80.2	80.7	81.1	80.5	80.9	81.3	80.7
Net plant & equip (e)	17.7	17.3	17.9	17.5	17.1	17.5	17.0	16.6	17.3	16.9	16.5	17.2
Other fixed assets (f)	2.4	2.4	2.4	2.4	2.3	2.3	2.3	2.2	2.2	2.2	2.2	2.2
Total assets	100.0	100.0	100.0	100.0	100.0	100.0	100.0	100.0	100.0	100.0	100.0	100.0
LIABILITIES & NET WORTH												
Accounts payable (g)	8.6	8.7	8.9	9.0	9.2	9.7	9.7	9.9	9.8	10.2	10.2	10.2
Notes payable (h)	5.9	5.6	5.8	6.7	6.0	6.2	7.1	5.9	6.3	5.0	3.8	2.9
Other curr liab (i)	5.8	6.3	6.9	5.7	6.4	7.2	6.3	7.2	7.1	7.4	8.5	9.5
Total curr liab	20.3	20.7	21.5	21.4	21.7	23.0	23.1	23.0	23.2	22.6	22.6	22.6
Long term debt (j)	25.4	25.3	24.9	24.8	24.7	24.0	23.8	23.7	23.3	23.2	23.1	22.8
Total liabilities	45.7	46.0	46.4	46.2	46.4	47.0	46.8	46.7	46.5	45.8	45.6	45.3
Common stock	13.0	12.9	12.7	12.7	12.6	12.3	12.1	12.1	11.9	11.8	11.8	11.6
capital surplus	11.5	11.5	11.3	11.3	11.2	10.9	10.8	10.7	10.6	10.5	10.5	10.3
retained earnings	29.8	29.6	29.5	29.9	29.8	29.8	30.3	30.5	30.9	31.8	32.1	32.7
Total net worth	54.3	54.0	53.6	53.8	53.6	53.0	53.2	53.3	53.5	54.2	54.4	54.7
Total liab & net worth	100.0	100.0	100.0	100.0	100.0	100.0	100.0	100.0	100.0	100.0	100.0	100.0

that equity is not keeping pace with sales growth. Thus, Taft faces the prospect of new equity financing if expense ratios or sales are worse than plan.

It is also apparent from the common-size balance sheet that the liquidity of Taft during 1985 is not in serious *short-term* jeopardy except in the case of Exhibit 7d when sales fall 35% short of plan.

A FEASIBLE FINANCIAL PLAN

ASSESSING OVERALL FINANCIAL FORECAST. One of the most frequent uses of a financial forecast is the assessment of the **feasibility of plans for growth.** The notion of feasibility stems from the fact that most firms do not

EXHIBIT 7 *CONTINUED*

Sales projection	81200	82600	85400	86800	89600	96600	98000	100800	100800	105000	106400	107800
	Jan	Feb	Mar	Apr	May	Jun	Jul	Aug	Sep	Oct	Nov	Dec
ASSETS												
Cash & mkt sec. (a)	3.8	3.6	3.7	3.7	3.8	4.0	4.0	4.1	4.0	4.2	4.2	4.2
Accts. receivable (b)	30.8	34.6	34.9	35.5	36.2	37.0	38.1	38.7	38.7	39.3	40.0	40.0
Inventories (c)	43.9	41.6	40.9	40.6	40.3	39.1	38.6	38.3	37.8	37.5	37.2	36.7
Other curr assets (d)	2.7	2.5	2.5	2.5	2.5	2.4	2.4	2.3	2.3	2.3	2.3	2.2
Total curr assets	81.2	82.4	82.0	82.4	82.8	82.5	83.1	83.4	82.9	83.3	83.6	83.1
Net plant & equip (e)	16.6	15.4	15.9	15.5	15.1	15.4	15.0	14.6	15.2	14.8	14.4	15.0
Other fixed assets (f)	2.3	2.1	2.1	2.1	2.1	2.0	2.0	2.0	1.9	1.9	1.9	1.9
Total assets	100.0	100.0	100.0	100.0	100.0	100.0	100.0	100.0	100.0	100.0	100.0	100.0
	=====	=====	=====	=====	=====	=====	=====	=====	=====	=====	=====	=====
LIABILITIES & NET WORTH												
Accounts payable (g)	11.3	10.9	11.0	11.1	11.4	12.0	12.0	12.2	12.1	12.5	12.5	12.5
Notes payable (h)	6.8	9.5	8.1	7.4	5.3	4.0	3.4	0.6	-0.7	-3.6	-6.2	-8.7
Other curr liab (i)	6.2	7.2	8.4	8.1	9.5	10.8	10.8	12.4	13.1	14.2	15.9	17.4
Total curr liab	24.3	27.6	27.6	26.7	26.2	26.8	26.1	25.3	24.5	23.1	22.2	21.2
Long term debt (j)	23.8	22.6	22.2	22.0	21.9	21.2	20.9	20.8	20.5	20.3	20.2	19.9
Total liabilities	48.2	50.2	49.7	48.7	48.1	48.0	47.0	46.0	44.9	43.4	42.3	41.1
Common stock	12.1	11.5	11.3	11.2	11.2	10.8	10.7	10.6	10.5	10.4	10.3	10.1
capital surplus	10.8	10.2	10.1	10.0	9.9	9.6	9.5	9.4	9.3	9.2	9.2	9.0
retained earnings	28.9	28.1	28.9	30.1	30.8	31.6	32.8	34.0	35.3	37.0	38.2	39.7
Total net worth	51.8	49.8	50.3	51.3	51.9	52.0	53.0	54.0	55.1	56.6	57.7	58.9
Total liab & net worth	100.0	100.0	100.0	100.0	100.0	100.0	100.0	100.0	100.0	100.0	100.0	100.0
	=====	=====	=====	=====	=====	=====	=====	=====	=====	=====	=====	=====

(b)

have unlimited access to external sources of funds; thus many of the funds they require for growth must be generated internally. Therefore, a consistent and logical financial forecast is essential. Some levels of growth are simply not sustainable without massive infusions of outside capital or significant changes in historical financial ratios. In the example that follows, the concept of "sustainable" or feasible growth is developed as a financial forecasting tool. This tool supplements the cash budget and pro forma statements in an overall financial plan.

BASIC VARIABLES. To assess the components of a financial plan, it is useful to view financial performance in terms of the basic variables that govern the financial process. Thus, beneath the apparent complexity of many financial statements a few basic financial ratios serve as the key components of overall financial results. Each of these prime variables (see Exhibit 8) encompasses several subsidiary strategy variables (see Exhibit 9).

Examining these prime variables allows for improved focus on the most

EXHIBIT 7   *CONTINUED*

Sales projection	81200	82600	85400	86800	89600	96600	98000	100800	100800	105000	106400	107800
	Jan	Feb	Mar	Apr	May	Jun	Jul	Aug	Sep	Oct	Nov	Dec
ASSETS												
Cash & mkt sec. (a)	3.8	3.6	3.7	3.7	3.8	4.0	4.0	4.1	4.0	4.2	4.2	4.2
Accts. receivable (b)	30.8	34.6	34.9	35.5	36.2	37.0	38.1	38.7	38.7	39.3	40.0	40.0
Inventories (c)	43.9	41.6	40.9	40.6	40.3	39.1	38.6	38.3	37.8	37.5	37.2	36.7
Other curr assets (d)	2.7	2.5	2.5	2.5	2.5	2.4	2.4	2.3	2.3	2.3	2.3	2.2
Total curr assets	81.2	82.4	82.0	82.4	82.8	82.5	83.1	83.4	82.9	83.3	83.6	83.1
Net plant & equip (e)	16.6	15.4	15.9	15.5	15.1	15.4	15.0	14.6	15.2	14.8	14.4	15.0
Other fixed assets (f)	2.3	2.1	2.1	2.1	2.1	2.0	2.0	2.0	1.9	1.9	1.9	1.9
Total assets	100.0	100.0	100.0	100.0	100.0	100.0	100.0	100.0	100.0	100.0	100.0	100.0
LIABILITIES & NET WORTH												
Accounts payable (g)	12.9	12.4	12.6	12.7	13.1	13.7	13.7	14.0	13.8	14.2	14.3	14.3
Notes payable (h)	7.2	11.8	12.3	13.7	13.5	14.0	15.8	15.1	15.8	15.5	15.0	14.4
Other curr liab (i)	5.3	5.5	5.9	4.5	5.1	5.7	4.4	5.2	5.1	4.8	5.6	6.5
Total curr liab	25.4	29.7	30.8	31.0	31.7	33.3	33.9	34.2	34.6	34.5	34.9	35.2
Long term debt (j)	23.8	22.6	22.2	22.0	21.9	21.2	20.9	20.8	20.5	20.3	20.2	19.9
Total liabilities	49.3	52.3	52.9	53.0	53.6	54.5	54.8	55.0	55.1	54.9	55.1	55.1
Common stock	12.1	11.5	11.3	11.2	11.2	10.8	10.7	10.6	10.5	10.4	10.3	10.1
capital surplus	10.8	10.2	10.1	10.0	9.9	9.6	9.5	9.4	9.3	9.2	9.2	9.0
retained earnings	27.8	26.0	25.7	25.7	25.4	25.0	25.1	25.0	25.1	25.5	25.5	25.8
Total net worth	50.7	47.7	47.1	47.0	46.4	45.5	45.2	45.0	44.9	45.1	44.9	44.9
Total liab & net worth	100.0	100.0	100.0	100.0	100.0	100.0	100.0	100.0	100.0	100.0	100.0	100.0

(c)

sensitive parts of the financial plan to changes in the feasible growth rate. In some sense, each of these variables is a control lever in the guidance system of the firm. Although it is often easier to identify relationships than it is to modify them, it is useful to know where attention must be focused.

SUSTAINABLE GROWTH MODEL. An internal sustainable growth model can be represented symbolically as follows:

$$P/S \quad \times \quad S/A \quad = \quad P/A \quad \times \quad A/E \quad = \quad P/E \quad \times \quad R \quad = \quad SG$$

operating profit margin after tax (ROS)	asset turnover	return on assets after tax	basic leverage	return on equity (ROE)	percent earnings retained	internally sustainable growth

EXHIBIT 7   *CONTINUED*

Sales projection	37700	38350	39650	40300	41600	44850	45500	46800	46800	48750	49400	50050
	Jan	Feb	Mar	Apr	May	Jun	Jul	Aug	Sep	Oct	Nov	Dec
ASSETS												
Cash & mkt sec. (a)	2.0	2.1	2.2	2.2	2.3	2.4	2.4	2.5	2.4	2.5	2.6	2.6
Accts. receivable (b)	23.8	20.2	20.4	20.9	21.4	22.0	22.9	23.3	23.3	23.8	24.3	24.3
Inventories (c)	49.8	52.3	51.5	51.4	51.3	50.1	49.8	49.7	49.0	48.9	48.7	48.1
Other curr assets (d)	3.0	3.2	3.1	3.1	3.1	3.1	3.0	3.0	3.0	3.0	3.0	2.9
Total curr assets	78.7	77.9	77.3	77.7	78.1	77.6	78.1	78.5	77.8	78.2	78.6	77.9
Net plant & equip (e)	18.8	19.4	20.1	19.7	19.3	19.8	19.3	18.9	19.7	19.3	18.9	19.7
Other fixed assets (f)	2.6	2.7	2.7	2.6	2.6	2.6	2.6	2.6	2.5	2.5	2.5	2.5
Total assets	100.0	100.0	100.0	100.0	100.0	100.0	100.0	100.0	100.0	100.0	100.0	100.0
LIABILITIES & NET WORTH												
Accounts payable (g)	6.8	7.3	7.4	7.5	7.7	8.1	8.2	8.4	8.3	8.6	8.7	8.7
Notes payable (h)	5.2	2.7	5.7	9.5	11.7	14.6	18.7	20.6	24.0	26.6	28.5	30.4
Other curr liab (i)	4.9	4.4	3.6	1.0	0.4	.0	-2.6	-3.0	-4.3	-6.1	-6.2	-6.3
Total curr liab	16.8	14.3	16.7	18.0	19.9	22.7	24.3	26.0	28.0	29.2	30.9	32.8
Long term debt (j)	27.0	28.4	27.9	27.9	27.8	27.2	27.0	26.9	26.6	26.5	26.4	26.1
Total liabilities	43.8	42.7	44.7	45.9	47.7	49.9	51.3	53.0	54.6	55.7	57.4	58.9
Common stock	13.8	14.5	14.3	14.2	14.2	13.9	13.8	13.7	13.6	13.5	13.5	13.3
capital surplus	12.2	12.9	12.7	12.7	12.6	12.3	12.3	12.2	12.1	12.0	12.0	11.8
retained earnings	30.2	30.0	28.4	27.2	25.5	23.9	22.7	21.1	19.8	18.8	17.2	16.0
Total net worth	56.2	57.3	55.3	54.1	52.3	50.1	48.7	47.0	45.4	44.3	42.6	41.1
Total liab & net worth	100.0	100.0	100.0	100.0	100.0	100.0	100.0	100.0	100.0	100.0	100.0	100.0

Notes to pro forma balance sheets:
a. .188 of monthly sales
b. beginning accts. receivable plus .90 sales less collections
c. constant, i.e. no change inventory during year; monthly production & sales
d. constant (given)
e. beginning net plant plus additions as scheduled (see cash budget) less depreciation
f. constant (given)
g. .80 of cost of goods sold for month
h. plug figure, i.e. total assets less all other liabilities and net worth.
   must agree with loan on cash budget
i. beginning other current liabilities from 1984 balance sheet plus accrued taxes
   and interest less tax and interest payments from cash budget
j. constant, i.e. no payments during year.
j. constant, i.e. no payments during year.

(d)

where P = profit after taxes

S = annual sales

A = total assets (current assets and fixed assets)

E = total equity (paid-in capital plus retained earnings)

R = percent of earnings retained (i.e., dividend payout ratio)

SG = sustainable rate of growth in sales without external equity

EXHIBIT 8   SUSTAINABLE GROWTH MODEL WITHOUT EXTERNAL PRIME VARIABLE[a]

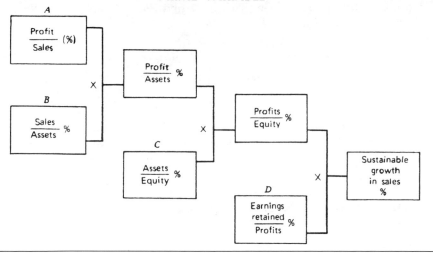

[a] The prime variables A–D may be affected by the strategy variables listed in Exhibit 9.

EXHIBIT 9   SUSTAINABLE GROWTH MODEL WITHOUT EXTERNAL FINANCING

Prime Variables	Strategy Variables
A. Profits/sales	Pricing strategy Labor expenses Materials costs Interest expense General overhead Depreciation Taxes

B. Sales/assets	Cash level
	Accounts receivable level
	Inventory level:
	  raw materials
	  work in process
	  finished goods
	Fixed assets
	Other assets

C. Assets/equity	Short-term borrowing Long-term borrowing
D. Earnings retained/profits	Dividend policy

In this series of relationships, it is possible to solve for any single variable if the others are known. For example, using the approximate projected relationships of the base plan, Taft may find its sustainable growth based on 1980 data as follows:

$$P/S \times S/A = P/A \times A/E = P/E \times b = SG$$
$$0.037 \times 1.69 = 0.062 \times 2.16 = 0.133 \times 0.68 = 0.090$$

where b is the retention rate.

The data above indicate that exclusive of outside equity financing, the sustainable rate of growth is approximately 9%. The sensitivity of Taft's sustainable growth to each of these prime variables is apparent from some further calculations.

1. **If the profit margin increases to 6%,** the revised sustainable growth rate is:

$$P/S \times S/A = P/A \times A/E = P/E \times b = SG$$
$$0.06 \times 1.69 = 0.10 \times 2.16 = 0.22 \times 0.68 = 0.15$$

2. **If the utilization of assets improves to 2.5,** along with an increase in profit margin to 6, the sustainable rate of growth is dramatically improved to 22%.

3. If leverage is increased to 2.5 along with the previous changes, the result is a sustainable growth rate of:

$$P/S \times S/A = P/A \times A/E = P/E \times b = SG$$
$$0.06 \times 2.5 = 0.15 \times 2.5 = 0.375 \times 0.68 = 0.26$$

4. Finally, if the retention rate b were increased to 0.80 (i.e., a reduction in the dividend payout ratio from 0.40 to 0.20), the sustainable growth of all the changes above would be increased to 0.30.

In inflationary times it is important to recognize that if the level of internal sustainable growth does not at least equal the inflation rate, the firm is shrinking in size in "real" terms.

ADDITION OF NEW EQUITY. It is implicit in the sustainable growth model that a one-time increase in growth is possible with the sale of new equity. Given constancy in the assets to equity ratio (leverage) and the sales to assets ratio (asset turnover) at Taft, the increase in sales possible from a new equity issue would be as follows:

increase in equity (out- side funding)		assets to equity		sales to assets		possible growth in sales
$20,000,000	×	1.5	×	2.0	=	$60,000,000

INCONSISTENT PLAN. The calculations above do not imply that it is easy or even feasible to increase profit margins or asset turnover or earnings retention in a short period of time—or even that it is desirable to do so. Rather, the relationships show that there is such a thing as an inconsistent plan or forecast, that is, a plan that is simply not feasible in terms of the basic governing financial relationships. For example, it is financially inconsistent for Taft to expect sales to go up 35% in 1980 while operating with the ratios shown in the examples in the preceding paragraphs. If, nevertheless, sales were to increase 35% in 1980 and other historical relationships were to hold, it would be possible to illustrate the infeasibility of the plan as follows:

1. Sales = $815,000,000 × 1.35 = $1,100,250,000
2. Profits at 3.7% of sales = $ 40,709,250
3. Earnings retained = 68% of profits = $ 27,682,290
4. New total equity = old equity + earnings retained = $ 251,605,290
5. Total assets at historical assets to equity of 2.16 = $ 543,467,420
6. Sales possible at historical sales to assets of 1.69 = $ 918,499,930
7. Sales deficit due to leverage and dividend constraints = $ 181,750,070

The amount in line 7 represents the infeasibility of a 35% sales revenue increase given historical ratios.

ALTERNATIVE STRATEGIES. If sales growth is to be feasible at a rate above that indicated by the initial sustainable growth model, there are only four financial alternatives.

Increase in Leverage. This is a delicate variable to manipulate for four reasons:

1. When debt levels begin to exceed industry norms, lenders begin to withdraw or charge higher interest.
2. The increased interest may adversely affect the profit margin.

3. Prior covenants or existing debt may prevent the expansion of debt beyond previously agreed levels.

4. A high debt load may affect the stock price in a negative manner.

Thus, while many firms would wish to increase debt financing, the reality is that growth through ever-increasing leverage is often not a feasible solution to the financing problem.

Increase in Asset Turnover. This option has the effect of improving the productivity of capital. Means of implementing it include operating the plant on a second shift, reducing the ratio of inventory to sales, reducing the ratio of receivables to sales, carrying fewer spare parts, and introducing numerous other strategies to make assets "work harder." While financial planners may wish to incorporate improved asset turnover into plans, it is not always feasible to do so in an operating sense. Often the guideline used is that of comparison with competitors, to determine where asset inefficiencies may be prevalent.

Improved Profit Margin. This option depends essentially on two variables: the ability to increase price, and the ability to cut operating costs. The latter ability brings up the subject of "labor productivity," about which there is much concern in the United States today. Nonetheless, emphasis on stringent cost control and optimal pricing must be maintained if profit margins are to improve or remain high enough to permit the realization of the overall financial plan.

Dividend Reduction. Few decisions are as full of complexity as the decision about the optimal dividend. Without entering the broad realm of the effect of dividends on share price, it is clear that reducing the dividend payout ratio is not popular with shareholders. Nonetheless, the concept of the feasible financial plan may indicate that unless one or more of the other basic relationships is modified, such a measure is the only way scheduled growth rates can be achieved.

INFLATION AND SUSTAINABLE GROWTH. The concept of "sustainable growth" or a "feasible financial plan" has received more attention from financial forecasters in recent years as inflation has had the effect of increasing nominal growth rates rather dramatically, creating the illusion of growth when no real growth has occurred, that is, when growth less inflation is a negative number. The need to improve profit margins to allow real growth to stay even with inflation, or ahead of it, is made clear by the sustainable growth model. Thus the sustainable growth model is of considerable value to the financial planner after the basic cash budget, income statement and balance sheet are complete. (For a more detailed description of the sustainable growth model see Higgins, "How Much Growth Can a Firm Afford?"

REFERENCES

Brigham, Eugene F., *Financial Management, Theory and Practice,* 2d ed., Dryden Press, Hinsdale, IL, 1979, Chapter 7.

Chambers, John C., Mullick, S.K., and Smith, D.D., "How to Choose the Right Forecasting Technique," *Harvard Business Review,* Vol. 49, July–August 1971, pp. 45–74.

Donaldson, G., *Strategy for Financial Mobility,* Irwin, Homewood, IL, 1969.

Draper, Norman and Smith, Harry, *Applied Regression Analysis,* Wiley, New York, 1966.

Francis, Jack C., and Rowell, D.R., "A Simultaneous Equation Model of the Firm for Financial Analaysis and Planning," *Financial Management,* Spring 1978, pp. 29–44.

Gentry, James A., and Phyrr, S.A., "Simulating an EPS Growth Model," *Financial Management,* Vol. 2, Summer 1973, pp. 68–75.

Gershefski, George W., "Building a Corporate Financial Model," *Harvard Business Review,* Vol. 47, July–August, 1969, pp. 61–72.

Higgins, Robert C., "How Much Growth Can a Firm Afford?" *Financial Management,* Fall 1977, pp. 7–16.

Helfert, E.A., *Techniques of Financial Analysis,* 3d ed., Irwin, Homewood, IL, 1977, Chapter 3.

Hunt, P., Williams, C.M., and Donaldson, G., *Basic Business Finance,* Irwin, Homewood, IL, 1974, Chapter 7.

Lyneis, James M., "Designing Financial Policies to Deal with Limited Financial Resources," *Financial Management,* Vol. 4, Spring 1975, pp. 13–24.

Merville, Larry J., and Tavis, L.A., "Long-Range Financial Planning," *Financial Management,* Vol. 3, Summer 1974, pp. 56–63.

Pan, J., Nichols, D.R., and Joy, O.M., "Sales Forecasting Practices of Large U.S. Industrial Firms," *Financial Management,* Fall 1977, pp. 72–76.

Pappas, James L., and Huber, G.P., "Probabilistic Short-Term Financial Planning," *Financial Management,* Vol. 2, Autumn 1973, pp. 36–44.

Parker, George G.C., and Segura E.L., "How to Get a Better Forecast," *Harvard Business Review,* Vol. 49, March–April, 1971, pp. 99–109.

Schall, Lawrence D., and Haley, Charles W., *Introduction to Financial Management,* 2d ed., McGraw-Hill, New York, 1980, Chapter 13.

Solomon, Ezra, and Pringle, J.J., *An Introduction to Financial Management,* Goodyear Publishing, Santa Monica, CA, 1977, Chapter 3.

Spiro, Herbert T., *Finance for the Non-Financial Manager,* Wiley, New York, 1977, Chapters 7 and 10.

Stone, B., and Wood, R.A., "Daily Cash Forecasting: A Simple Method for Implementing the Distribution Approach," *Financial Management,* Fall 1977, pp. 40–50.

Van Horne, James C., *Financial Management and Policy,* 5th ed., Prentice-Hall, Englewood Cliffs, NJ, 1980, Chapter 26.

3

FINANCIAL STATEMENT ANALYSIS

CONTENTS

3

FINANCIAL STATEMENT ANALYSIS

Martin S. Fridson, CFA
Michael J. Marocco, CPA

WHAT IS THE PURPOSE OF FINANCIAL STATEMENTS?

Financial statements play a key role in a business enterprise's task of converting resources (capital, labor, and raw materials) into finished goods and services. To attract those resources, a firm has to communicate that it offers a competitive return to those who provide them. In deciding how to communicate that information, the firm must take into account that resource providers have diverse motivations. For instance, an investor who contributes equity capital to a firm is seeking to maximize the return on that capital. The firm can often raise returns by investing in assets with a higher degree of **business risk.** That strategy, however, may conflict with the objectives of the individual who sells his or her labor to the firm. The wage earner is more concerned with the firm's ability to provide long-term employment stability. Increasing the firm's business risk, while attractive to the equity investor, is not in the laborer's interest.

Although diverse in their motivation, resource providers fall into two broad categories, based on their relationship to the business enterprise. In general, resource providers have either a direct or an indirect interest in the firm's activities. The former relationship implies a higher level of self-interest, while the latter suggests a less intense, though still important interest. Exhibit 1 lists numerous resource providers and their relationship to the firm.

To serve these numerous direct and indirect interests, the **accounting profession** has developed over many years a system of reporting financial information. Financial Accounting Standards Board (FASB) Concepts Statement No. 1, "Objectives of Financial Reporting by Business Enterprises," describes the broad purposes of financial reporting. According to FASB, financial reporting should provide:

EXHIBIT 1   PROVIDERS OF RESOURCES TO BUSINESS ENTERPRISES

Direct Interest	Indirect Interest
Owners	Financial analysts
Lenders	Investment advisers
Suppliers	Brokers
Potential investors and creditors	Underwriters
Employees	Stock exchanges
Management	Lawyers
Directors	Economists
Customers	Regulatory authorities

- Information that is useful to present and potential investors, creditors, and other users in making rational investment, credit, and similar decisions.
- Information to help investors, creditors, and others assess the amounts, timing, and uncertainty of prospective net cash inflows to the related enterprise.
- Information about the economic resources of an enterprise; the claims to those resources (obligations of the enterprise to transfer resources to other entities and owners' equity); and the effects of transactions, events, and circumstances that change resources and claims on those resources.

Concepts Statement No. 1 also gives guidance about the kinds of information that financial reporting, including financial statements, should provide:

- Information about an enterprise's economic resources, obligations, and owners' equity.
- Information about an enterprise's performance, provided by measures of earnings based on accrual accounting.
- Information about how an enterprise obtains and spends cash; about its borrowing and repayment of borrowing; about its capital (equity) transactions, including cash dividends and other distributions of enterprise resources to owners; and about other factors that may affect an enterprise's liquidity or solvency.
- Information about how management of an enterprise has discharged its stewardship responsibility to owners (i.e., stockholders) for the use of enterprise resources entrusted to it.

At the core of the system designed to implement those principles lie the basic financial statements—namely, balance sheet, income statement, and funds flow statement—to which we now turn. We shall see, however, that financial reporting goes far beyond these basic documents and that those seeking information about a firm have sources other than financial reporting available to them.

WHAT DO FINANCIAL STATEMENTS TELL US?

BALANCE SHEET. The balance sheet presents a firm's financial position at a particular point in time. It describes this position in terms of:

- *Assets.*   What the firm owns
- *Liabilities.*   The claims on the firm's assets by parties other than the owners
- *Owners' equity.*   The owners' residual claim on the firm's assets

By convention, assets appear on the left side of the balance sheet and liabilities plus owners' equity on the right. This separation enables creditors and owners to calculate whether the firm's assets are sufficient to satisfy their claims. The simple balance sheet (Exhibit 2) indicates that the imaginary firm, the Apex Popcorn Company, could sell its assets in a winding-up of business and satisfy in full both classes of claims (i.e., debt and equity) against it. That is, total assets equal the sum of liabilities and owners' equity. This equation is what balances the balance sheet. That balance continues, notwithstanding changes in assets, liabilities, and owners' equity. The relative safety of claims can change, however, even though assets remain equivalent to liabilities plus owners' equity. Exhibit 3 shows Apex Popcorn's balance sheet following an uninsured loss of half its inventory.

The owners have borne the full brunt of the calamity; their claim against the company's assets has fallen from $400 to $150. Nor has the debtholder escaped entirely unscathed. True, the claim is still $100, but it is now a first claim on $250, rather than $500 of assets. The debtholder's asset protection has declined from a ratio of 5:1 to 2.5:1 (Exhibit 4), thereby reducing the cushion against further erosion in asset value.

EXHIBIT 2   APEX POPCORN COMPANY BALANCE SHEET ($)—DECEMBER 31, 1984 ($000 OMITTED)

Assets		Liabilities and Owners' Equity	
Inventory	500	Debt	100
		Owners' equity	400
Total assets	500	Total liabilities plus owners' equity	500

EXHIBIT 3   APEX POPCORN COMPANY BALANCE SHEET—JANUARY 1, 1985 ($000 OMITTED)

Assets		Liabilities and Owners' Equity	
Inventory	250	Debt	100
		Owners' equity	150
Total assets	250	Total liabilities plus owners' equity	250

Lenders and owners are likely to want to know not only the monetary value of the assets offsetting their claims, but also the ease with which the assets can be converted to cash. Accordingly, balance sheets categorize assets by degree of liquidity. The most basic distinction is between **current assets,** which are likely to be converted into cash during the current operating cycle, and **fixed assets,** which have longer-lived usefulness to the firm. Within those categories, accountants conventionally list assets in order of decreasing liquidity, as shown in Exhibit 5.

This increased level of detail provides superior information for the claim holder. Of the total assets available to satisfy claims against the fictitious Superior Machinery Company (Exhibit 6), only half—that is $150,000—are current assets, readily convertible to cash. In a winding-up, claimholders might face delays in the full satisfaction of their claims, until land and factories could be sold. Still worse, they might have to settle for less than full satisfaction, since these fixed assets might fetch less than their stated worth in a hastily-convened "fire sale."

Claimholders can gain other useful insights into Superior Machinery from the balance sheet shown in Exhibit 6. For instance, the company's claims during the current operating cycle (**current liabilities**) are well covered by items that will be converted to cash during the current operating cycle, a fact that can be ascertained by calculating the **current ratio.**

$$\text{Current ratio} = \frac{\text{current assets}}{\text{current liabilities}} = \frac{\$150,000}{\$75,000} = 2.0$$

EXHIBIT 4   ASSET PROTECTION OF APEX POPCORN COMPANY'S DEBTHOLDER ($000 OMITTED)

December 31, 1984	January 1, 1985
$\dfrac{\text{Assets}}{\text{Debt}} = \dfrac{500}{100} = 5:1$	$\dfrac{\text{Assets}}{\text{Debt}} = \dfrac{250}{100} = 2.5:1$

EXHIBIT 5
ASSETS' LIQUIDITY CHARACTERISTICS

Current Assets	Fixed Assets
Cash	Equipment
Marketable securities	Plant
Accounts receivable	Land
Inventories	

A more stringent test of a firm's short-term financial health, as measured by its ability to meet its current cash needs, is the **quick ratio,** or **acid test,** which counts only the most liquid assets.

$$\text{Quick ratio} = \frac{\text{current assets} - \text{inventories}}{\text{current liabilities}}$$

$$= \frac{\$150,000 - \$60,000}{\$75,000} = \frac{\$90,000}{\$75,000} = 1.2$$

Analysts find it useful to look not only at the ratio of, but also the difference between current assets and current liabilities, or **working capital.**

$$\text{Working capital} = \text{current assets} - \text{current liabilities}$$
$$= \$150,000 - \$75,000 = \$75,000$$

Another way for claimholders to determine how they stand is to calculate **financial leverage.** From the equity holder's viewpoint, borrowed funds can "leverage" his or her investment, enabling the stockholder to control a larger

EXHIBIT 6   SUPERIOR MACHINERY COMPANY BALANCE SHEET— DECEMBER 31, 1984 ($000 OMITTED)

Current Assets			Current Liabilities		
Cash	15		Notes payable	35	
Marketable securities	35		Accounts payable	40	
Accounts receivable	40		Total current liabilities		75
Inventory	60				
Total current assets		150			
Fixed Assets		150	Long-term liabilities		
			Long-term debt	30	
			Deferred taxes	20	
			Total long-term liabilities		50
			Shareholders' equity		175
Total assets		300	Total liabilities		
			plus shareholders' equity		300

amount of productive assets. This potentially results in a greater return on investment, although it comes at a cost of greater earnings volatility. Financial leverage can therefore be viewed as a measure of how hard the equity holder's capital is working. The lender, however, is less concerned with return on equity than the size of the equity layer below the debt claim in the event of a winding-up. Asset protection for the lender diminishes as debt is used to finance an increasing portion of assets. Furthermore, borrowed funds tend to carry a fixed cost which, unlike dividends to equity holders, cannot easily be waived when revenues fall. Therefore, high financial leverage (i.e., a high ratio of debt to equity) implies a high risk of failure to meet financial obligations. Several different measures exist for financial leverage, each suited for particular applications. Financial institutions are particularly interested in knowing how hard their capital funds are working. A useful ratio for analyzing this is $\dfrac{\text{total assets}}{\text{equity}}$. Other types of permanent capital, such as subordinated debt, may be included in the denominator for some purposes. The **total assets-to-equity ratio** measures the extent to which the firm has leveraged its own capital through borrowed funds, as well as deposits and other liabilities. Regulators often look at the reciprocal of this leverage ratio $\left(\dfrac{\text{equity}}{\text{total assets}}\right)$ as an indicator of capital adequacy.

   To consider the adequacy of asset protection, the lender can calculate the ratio of $\dfrac{\text{total assets}}{\text{total liabilities}}$. In Exhibit 6, Superior Machinery has total assets equivalent to $\dfrac{\$300,000}{\$125,000}$, or 2.4 times total liabilities. Considered another way, the firm's assets could decline in value by 58% $\left(\dfrac{\$300,000 - \$125,000}{\$300,000}\right)$ before proceeds of a liquidation would be inadequate to satisfy lenders' claims.

   While these asset-related measures have important applications, the most frequently used measures of financial leverage compare debt to equity. The ratio of $\dfrac{\text{total debt}}{\text{total equity}}$ is often employed in analyzing financial institutions, which commonly have ratios greater than 1.0. When looking at industrial concerns, however, analysts usually find it easier to think of debt and equity as percentages of total capital. In Exhibit 6, Superior Machinery's **total debt-to-total capital ratio** is

$$\frac{\text{Notes payable} + \text{long-term debt}}{\text{Notes payable} + \text{long-term debt} + \text{shareholders' equity}} = \frac{\text{total debt}}{\text{total capital}}$$

$$= \frac{\$35,000 + \$30,000}{\$35,000 + \$30,000 + \$175,000} = 27.1\%$$

Analysts may choose to exclude short-term debt from this calculation if it clearly represents seasonal borrowing, rather than permanent capital. There are also strong arguments for including deferred taxes in the denominator as a nonborrowed form of capital, but this treatment depends on a reasonable assurance that the deferral will in fact be permanent.

INCOME STATEMENT. The income statement measures a firm's profitability over a specified period. In its simplest form, the income statement can be expressed as:

$$\text{Revenue} - \text{expenses} = \text{income}.$$

Even such a rudimentary presentation discloses important information about the firm. Revenue (or sales) is a popular measure of size, which in turn may imply a degree of strength and stability. Income (also called "earnings" or "profit") is a key variable in measuring the firm's value. Finally, enhanced with a bit of arithmetic, the three-figure income statement tells us something about the firm's viability in the event of changing business conditions. From Exhibit 7 we can calculate that the imaginary Zenith Chemical's return on sales was 5%.

$$\text{Return on sales} = \frac{\text{net income}}{\text{sales}} = \frac{\$40,000}{\$800,000} = .05$$

Viewed another way, the company's profits would fall to zero if expenses rose by just 5.3%, derived as follows: $\dfrac{\$800,000 - \$760,000}{\$760,000} = .053.$

Another safety measure derived from the income statement is **fixed charge coverage,** a popular measure of creditworthiness. The expanded Zenith Chemical income statement in Exhibit 8 provides detail on interest charges, a fixed expense that will be incurred regardless of the level of revenue. (In contrast, such items as raw material costs and hourly wages may vary with sales volume.)

EXHIBIT 7   ZENITH CHEMICAL COMPANY INCOME STATEMENT— 1983 ($000 OMITTED)

Sales	800
Expenses	760
Net income	40

EXHIBIT 8   ZENITH CHEMICAL COMPANY INCOME STATEMENT—1983 ($000 OMITTED)

Sales	800
Cost of goods sold	640
Operating expenses	76
Operating income	84
Interest expense	10
Pretax income	74
Income taxes	34
Net income	40

After paying all costs of operating its business in 1983, Zenith Chemical had $84,000 remaining to make interest payments. We derive this figure by adding pretax income and interest expense. The sum covered interest expense of $10,000 by a ratio of 8.4:1, or 8.4X.

$$\text{Fixed Charge Coverage} = \frac{\text{Pretax Income} + \text{Interest Expense}}{\text{Interest expense}}$$

$$= \frac{\$40,000 + \$34,000 + \$10,000}{\$10,000} = \frac{\$84,000}{\$10,000} = 8.4X$$

When combined with certain balance sheet items, income statement figures can tell investors how well they are being rewarded for making their capital available to the enterprise. Exhibit 9 reproduces the Zenith Chemical income statement of Exhibit 8 and adds a balance sheet. From the two statements we ascertain that equity investors earned 11.9% on their investment in 1983:

EXHIBIT 9   ZENITH CHEMICAL COMPANY—DECEMBER 31, 1983 ($000 OMITTED)

Income Statement		Balance Sheet			
Sales	800	Cash	25	Current maturities	5
Cost of goods sold	640	Accounts		of long-term debt	
		receivable	100		
Operating expenses	76	Inventory	200	Accounts payable	170
Operating income	84				
Interest expense	10	Current assets	325	Current liabilities	175
Pretax income	74	Fixed assets	275	Long-term debt	90
Income taxes	34			Shareholders' equity	335
Net income	40	Total assets	600	Total liabilities	600
				plus shareholders' equity	

$$\text{Return on equity (ROE)} = \frac{\text{net income}}{\text{shareholders' equity}} = \frac{\$40,000}{\$335,000} = 11.9\%$$

Combining income statement and balance sheet data can also give clues to the firm's efficiency in utilizing assets.

$$\text{Return on total assets} = \frac{\text{net income}}{\text{total assets}}$$

For a deeper understanding of how management has achieved its return on total assets, the analyst can study specific categories of assets more closely. The **inventory utilization ratio** or **inventory turnover ratio** measures the number of times a firm "turns" its inventory in a year. A high ratio can imply strong selling skills, elimination of slow-moving items, and avoidance of excessive buffer stocks of parts and materials. Although practitioners sometimes calculate this ratio using sales as the numerator, we define it as:

$$\text{Inventory turnover ratio} = \frac{\text{cost of goods sold}}{\text{average inventory}}$$

The advantage of this definition is that both inventory and cost of goods sold are recorded at cost, whereas sales are recorded at market. Based on a definition that uses sales in the numerator, a firm could physically turn its inventory four times in a year yet attain an inventory ratio of less than 4.0 if forced to mark its goods down to below cost. Calculating on the basis of cost of goods sold generally avoids this problem. As for the denominator, by using an average inventory level for the entire year the analyst escapes biases that could result from rising, falling or seasonally fluctuating inventories during the period. To calculate average inventory, the analyst can simply add beginning-of-period and end-of-period inventory and divide by two. If the figures are available, adding the monthly inventory balances and dividing by 12 will provide a more precise measure.

A second current asset that firms seek to utilize with maximum efficiency is accounts receivable. **Average collection period** is a powerful tool for measuring this aspect of asset utilization.

$$\text{Average collection period} = \frac{\text{accounts receivable}}{\text{sales per day}}$$

where sales per day $= \dfrac{\text{sales}}{360}$

Zenith Chemical's average collection period in 1983 was 45 days.

$$\frac{\$100,000}{\$800,000 \div 360} = 45$$

If Zenith sells its products on terms that call for payment within 30 days, a 45-day average collection period indicates that its customers are not paying their bills on time. Management may seek to tighten its collection process to achieve better asset utilization, although such action may sacrifice sales to competitors that are willing to extend more liberal payment terms.

FUNDS FLOW STATEMENT. In some circumstances, users of financial statements desire to know above all else the pattern of cash flowing in and out of a business. For instance, a lender is primarily concerned with the borrower's ability to meet scheduled interest and principal repayments. The income statement, which deducts noncash charges such as depreciation, may not present the clearest picture of that ability. Exhibit 10 presents Zenith Chemical's income statement for 1984, a loss year, along with its funds flow statement. Because of the loss, Zenith's pretax earnings failed to cover interest expense (i.e., fixed charge coverage was less than 1X).

EXHIBIT 10   ZENITH CHEMICAL COMPANY—DECEMBER 31, 1984
($000 OMITTED)

INCOME STATEMENT		FUNDS FLOW STATEMENT	
		Sources of funds:	
Revenue	750	Net income	(2)
Cost of goods sold	650	Depreciation	20
Operating expense	90	Funds provided by operations	18
Operating income	10		
Interest expense	13		
Pretax income (loss)	(3)	Sale of common stock	10
Income tax (credit)	(1)	Total sources	28
Net income	(2)		
		Uses of funds:	
		Cash dividends	5
		Capital expenditures	15
		Repayment of long-term debt	3
		Total uses	23
		Increase in working capital	5
BALANCE SHEET			
Cash	22	Current maturities	5
Accounts receivable	100	of long-term debt	170
Inventory	200	Current liabilities	175
Current assets	322	Long-term debt	85
Fixed assets	270	Shareholders' equity	332
Total assets	592	Total liabilities plus	
		shareholders' equity	592

$$\frac{\text{Net income} + \text{income tax} + \text{interest expense}}{\text{interest expense}}$$

$$= \frac{(\$2,000) + (\$1,000) + \$13,000}{\$13,000} = \frac{\$10,000}{\$13,000} = 0.77\text{X}$$

The funds flow statement, however, tells a different story by adjusting for items that affect funds flow but not reported income (dividends, capital expenditures, mandatory debt repayments, and new financings), as well as those that affect reported income but not funds flow—primarily depreciation. Expecting that 1984 would be a difficult year, Zenith eliminated or stretched out discretionary capital expenditures and decided not to raise its dividend.

To gain an additional measure of financial security, the company raised $10,000 of new equity capital. As a result, Zenith made the $13,000 interest payment shown on the income statement, repaid the $3,000 of maturing debt shown on the funds flow statement, and strengthened its working capital by $5,000 to boot.

The funds flow statement offers a variety of valuable insights into a company. For instance, the analyst can use it to categorize a company according to its stage in the business life cycle, as illustrated in Exhibit 11.

The funds flow statement is also a rich source of useful **financial ratios.** Dividing funds provided by operations by capital expenditures measures the percentage of property, plant and equipment outlays that a firm can generate internally. **Financial flexibility** is reduced to the extent that the company must fund the shortfall through external sources, that is, new debt or equity financing. In our Zenith Chemical example (Exhibit 10), the company reined in its capital spending in a difficult year and consequently succeeded in funding 120% of its budget internally.

$$\frac{\text{Funds provided by operations}}{\text{Capital expenditures}} = \frac{\$18,000}{\$15,000} = 120\%$$

The 1984 austerity capital budget represented only 75% of depreciation for the year, however.

EXHIBIT 11   TYPICAL CASH FLOW PATTERNS AT SELECTED POINTS IN THE BUSINESS LIFE CYCLE

High growth	Large Cash User—Modest profits, small depreciable asset base, large capital investment to fund growth.
Decelerating growth	Near Cash Breakeven—Large profits (reflecting scale economies achieved), substantial cash flow from depreciation, reduced capital investment requirement.
Maturity	Net Cash Generator—Moderate profits (reflecting market saturation), large cash flow from depreciation, capital investment limited to replacement spending.

$$\frac{\text{Capital expenditures}}{\text{Depreciation}} = \frac{\$15,000}{\$20,000} = 75\%$$

As such, Zenith did not fully replace its stock of capital goods during the period. While this tactic may be necessary during a business downturn, it cannot continue on a prolonged basis without impairing a firm's competitive position. Analysts should be alert to such underspending as a possible sign that management is "milking" cash from a business and that current earnings may not be sustainable.

By combining the funds flow statement and balance sheet in Exhibit 9, we can derive a handy measure of creditworthiness.

$$\frac{\text{Total debt}}{\text{Funds provided by operations}} = \frac{\$5,000 + \$85,000}{\$18,000} = 5.0$$

This measure tells us that Zenith Chemical could theoretically liquidate its entire debt burden by applying all funds generated for five years. In reality, few companies either pay off all their borrowings or direct all funds flow toward debt retirement. Nonetheless, this ratio is a valuable complement to other, better-known credit quality measures. Company-to-company comparisons based on the debt-to-equity ratio may penalize firms or industries that generate exceptionally heavy cash, which may justify above-average debt in their capital structures. **Fixed charge coverage,** on the other hand, implicitly assumes that existing debt can be rolled over, since its formula excludes current maturities.

These observations bring out the important point that no single ratio can answer our key questions about a company, such as the value of its equity or its financial strength. Later in this chapter we will describe a technique for jointly considering credit quality measures that give conflicting signals. We will also show how a financial ratio takes on greater meaning in the context of corresponding ratios computed for a peer group of companies. Now, however, let us explore the value added to a financial ratio by placing it within a single-firm time series.

HOW CAN WE DERIVE MEANING FROM RATIOS?

RATIO TREND ANALYSIS. As we have already discussed, firms vary in their ability to generate cash—and therefore to incur debt—without jeopardizing their financial integrity. In addition, a company with relatively little operating risk (noncyclical, diversified, facing moderate competition) can prudently assume greater financial risk than one with high operating risk (cyclical, single-product, facing rapid technological change). Without understanding the company's business, therefore, the analyst cannot judge whether a particular ratio is "good" or "bad." By tracking the ratio over time, however, the analyst can determine whether financial risk is increasing, stable, or declining. A convenient technique for spotting balance sheet trends is to create a **percentage balance sheet,** as shown in Exhibit 12 for Storer Communications, an actual company engaged in cable television systems. This format converts all left-hand entries into percentages of total assets and all right-hand entries into percentages of total liabilities plus shareholders' equity. While it is clear from the conventional balance sheet (Exhibit 12) that debt usage rose in absolute terms, the percentage balance sheet confirms that borrowings also rose relative to growth in assets—by definition effecting a rise in financial leverage. By adding together current maturities of long-term debt and total long-term debt for each year, we find that total debt as a percentage of total assets rose from 15.4% in 1977 to 63.5% in 1984. We can infer, at least on the basis of this one measure, that Storer's financial risk rose during the period. The analyst should regard this information as a key factor in evaluating Storer's soundness. However, it is not a sufficient basis in itself for rendering an opinion. Once the negative trend has drawn attention to possible deterioration, the analyst should inquire into its underlying causes. A debt-financed expansion program, for example, may be less troubling than a cash shortfall resulting from earnings problems.

The income statement, too, aids analysis when presented in percentage form, as in Exhibit 13. In the **percentage income statement,** all items are represented as percentages of sales. From this presentation, we can readily observe that Storer's earnings were indeed faltering at the end of the 1975–1984 period of rising financial leverage. Net income measured 10.7% of net sales in 1975, fluctuated for the next few years and then dropped sharply to 2.4% in 1982, −8.6% in 1983, and −3.1% in 1984. Analyzing the reasons for the narrowing in profit margins, we see that the cost of goods sold climbed from 35.8% to 39.3% of net sales between 1981 and 1983. Other key contributors to reduced margins were interest expense (which soared from 1.2% to 17.7% of net sales between 1977 and 1982) and depreciation expense (which climbed from 7.9% to 20.3% during the same period). The latter trends reflected much higher borrowings and depreciable assets arising from aggressive expansion. Storer's funds flow statement, which the exhibits do not show, reveals that capital expenditures began to exceed funds from operations in 1979, reaching a ratio of over 4:1 (and over 5:1, counting acquisitions) by 1982. Consequently, the rising financial leverage is attributable in part to expansion. At the same time, the downtrend in operating income as a percentage of net sales (from 34.4% in 1979 to 27.4% in 1982) shows that earnings were deteriorating even before considering the direct effects of expansion (i.e., interest and depreciation).

Declining ratio trends do not always signal deteriorating credit quality. In cyclical industries, such as automobiles, building products, and metals, profit margins fluctuate widely between periods of economic expansion and contraction. A company that prudently builds liquidity in anticipation of a

EXHIBIT 12a STORER COMMUNICATIONS INC.—YEAR ENDING: DECEMBER 31. (a) BALANCE SHEET ($000 OMITTED); (b) PERCENTAGE BALANCE SHEETS (ITEMS AS A PERCENT OF TOTAL ASSETS).

	1975	1976	1977	1978	1979	1980	1981	1982	1983	1984
Current assets:										
Cash and equivalents	7,160	17,603	8,003	5,946	24,358	27,015	22,190	12,718	20,079	16,902
Net accounts receivable	18,613	19,384	21,909	28,251	29,330	36,165	62,146	55,919	49,958	50,889
Inventory	0	8,757	12,071	10,560	0	0	0	0	0	0
Other current assets	1,431	1,255	1,488	2,199	15,956	20,136	22,952	24,439	25,907	32,937
Total current assets	27,204	46,999	43,471	46,956	69,644	83,316	107,288	93,076	95,944	100,728
Plant and equipment	157,995	109,429	124,813	146,960	202,435	367,820	668,921	996,738	1,168,919	1,286,109
Less accumulated deprecia- tion	74,423	45,977	52,019	60,817	71,339	89,661	126,892	192,793	280,528	374,362
Net fixed assets	83,572	63,452	72,794	86,143	131,096	278,159	542,029	803,945	888,391	911,747
Intangibles	37,188	57,953	55,547	75,039	62,258	98,287	123,773	147,570	156,319	167,095
Investment in subsidi- aries/others	0	7,187	6,210	4,065	5,745	8,703	27,856	10,682	9,596	6,437
Other assets	6,108	264	186	1,284	22,407	37,356	43,623	59,422	56,243	56,237
Total assets	165,298	175,855	178,208	213,487	291,150	505,821	844,569	1,114,695	1,206,493	1,242,244

Current liabilities:									
Current long-term debt	4,352	408	408	395	12,670	754	827	2,988	2,530	2,240
Accounts payable	2,063	1,544	1,907	4,146	6,254	8,061	31,253	34,976	39,688	28,356
Accrued taxes	112	8,942	4,246	6,778	3,953	460	0	0	2,239	3,265
Other current liabilities	7,406	17,407	17,505	18,532	25,765	35,991	48,848	68,828	83,522	101,133
Total current liabilities	13,933	28,301	24,066	29,851	48,642	45,266	80,928	106,792	127,979	134,994
Total long-term debt	41,348	30,308	27,150	37,540	66,369	174,259	379,048	613,707	728,708	785,095
Deferred taxes	6,951	1,559	1,943	1,893	2,916	8,454	16,461	11,223	10,903	10,848
Other liabilities	0	9,077	9,040	11,849	10,680	22,845	26,253	32,284	17,836	13,568
Total liabilities	62,232	69,245	62,199	81,133	128,607	250,824	502,690	764,006	885,426	944,505
Stockholders equity:									
Common stock	4,548	4,876	4,877	4,986	10,433	13,935	16,022	16,376	16,394	16,393
Paid in surplus	13,099	0	0	2,622	4,035	77,311	140,956	151,996	168,587	168,560
Retained earnings	85,419	101,734	111,132	124,746	148,075	163,751	184,900	182,317	136,086	112,786
Total equity	103,066	106,610	116,009	132,354	162,543	254,997	341,879	350,689	321,067	297,739
Total liabilties and equity	165,298	175,855	178,208	213,487	291,150	505,821	844,569	1,114,695	1,206,493	1,242,244

EXHIBIT 12b STORER COMMUNICATIONS INC. PERCENTAGE BALANCE SHEETS
(ITEMS AS A PERCENT OF TOTAL ASSETS) YEAR ENDING DECEMBER 31

	1975	1976	1977	1978	1979	1980	1981	1982	1983	1984
Current Assets:										
Cash and equivalents	4.3	10.0	4.5	2.8	8.4	5.3	2.6	1.1	1.7	1.4
Net accounts receivable	11.3	11.0	12.3	13.2	10.1	7.1	7.4	5.0	4.1	4.1
Inventory	0.0	5.0	6.8	4.9	0.0	0.0	0.0	0.0	0.0	0.0
Other current assets	0.9	0.7	0.8	1.0	5.5	4.0	2.7	2.2	2.1	2.7
Total current assets	16.5	26.7	24.4	22.0	23.9	16.5	12.7	8.3	8.0	8.1
Plant and equipment	95.6	62.2	70.0	68.8	69.5	72.7	79.2	89.4	96.9	103.5
Less accumulated depreciation	45.0	26.1	29.2	28.5	24.5	17.7	15.0	17.3	23.3	30.1
Net fixed assets	50.6	36.1	40.8	40.4	45.0	55.0	64.2	72.1	73.6	73.4
Intangibles	22.5	33.0	31.2	35.1	21.4	19.4	14.7	13.2	13.0	13.5
Investment in subsidiaries/other	0	4.1	3.5	1.9	2.0	1.7	3.3	1.0	0.8	0.5
Other assets	3.7	0.2	0.1	0.6	7.7	7.4	5.2	5.3	4.7	4.5
Total assets	100.0	100.0	100.0	100.0	100.0	100.0	100.0	100.0	100.0	100.0

Current Liabilities:										
Current long-term debt	2.6	0.2	0.2	0.2	4.4	0.1	0.1	0.3	0.2	0.2
Accounts payable	1.2	0.9	1.1	1.9	2.1	1.6	3.7	3.1	3.3	2.3
Accrued taxes	0.1	5.1	2.4	3.2	1.4	0.1	0.0	0.0	0.2	0.3
Other current liabilities	4.5	9.9	9.8	8.7	8.8	7.1	5.8	6.2	6.9	8.1
Total current liabilities	8.4	16.1	13.5	14.0	16.7	8.9	9.6	9.6	10.6	10.9
Total long-term debt	25.0	17.2	15.2	17.6	22.8	34.5	44.9	55.1	60.4	63.2
Deferred taxes	4.2	0.9	1.1	0.9	1.0	1.7	1.9	1.0	0.9	0.9
Other liabilities	0.0	5.2	5.1	5.6	3.7	4.5	3.1	2.9	1.5	1.1
Total liabilities	37.6	39.4	34.9	38.0	44.2	49.6	59.5	68.5	73.4	76.0
Stockholders' equity:										
Common stock	2.8	2.8	2.7	2.3	3.6	2.8	1.9	1.5	1.4	1.3
Paid in surplus	7.9	0.0	0.0	1.2	1.4	15.3	16.7	13.6	14.0	13.6
Retained earnings	51.7	57.9	62.4	58.4	50.9	32.4	21.9	16.4	11.3	9.1
Total equity	62.4	60.6	65.1	62.0	55.8	50.4	40.5	31.5	26.6	24.0
Total liabilities and equity	100.0	100.0	100.0	100.0	100.0	100.0	100.0	100.0	100.0	100.0

EXHIBIT 13a STORER COMMUNICATIONS INC., YEAR ENDING DECEMBER 31. (a) INCOME STATEMENT ($000 OMITTED); (b) PERCENTAGE INCOME STATEMENT (ITEMS AS A PERCENT OF SALES).

	1975	1976	1977	1978	1979	1980	1981	1982	1983	1984
Net sales	101,146	127,348	122,023	149,747	170,357	197,068	276,437	379,302	458,871	536,824
Cost of goods sold	27,553	37,074	43,140	50,394	59,265	71,154	98,995	144,594	180,485	198,963
Gross profit	73,593	90,274	78,883	99,353	111,092	125,914	177,442	234,708	278,386	337,861
Advertising expense	3,149	4,132	5,402	6,267	6,286	6,137	7,838	7,307	10,797	0
Research and development expense	0	1	1	1	1	0	0	0	0	0
Rental expense	9,643	4,270	4,624	5,105	5,584	6,288	9,336	13,627	0	0
Other expense	0	42,943	32,068	37,979	40,537	0	0	0	0	0
Total operating expense	42,875	51,346	42,095	49,352	52,408	64,317	93,554	130,713	151,621	165,250
Operating income	30,718	38,928	36,788	50,001	58,684	61,597	83,888	103,995	126,765	172,611
Net other income	6,490	375	306	−174	12,416	8,452	15,442	22,318	8,567	14,474
Special items	1,734	−179	−2,238	−1,263	0	0	0	0	0	0
Interest expense	2,511	2,071	1,512	2,140	5,608	11,480	32,830	67,263	78,817	91,681
Depreciation expense	11,245	8,273	9,675	11,525	15,788	23,909	41,326	69,311	92,998	108,758
Pretax income	21,718	29,138	28,145	37,425	49,704	34,660	25,174	−10,261	−36,483	−13,354
Income taxes-state	1,194	2,234	2,072	2,562	3,028	2,819	1,726	2,896	3,510	3,443
Income taxes-federal	11,255	13,799	11,414	15,742	15,390	1,476	−16,459	−17,117	0	0
Deferred taxes	644	−1,624	384	−50	1,023	5,538	8,007	−5,238	−320	−55
Total taxes	10,878	14,409	13,870	18,254	19,441	9,833	−6,726	−19,459	3,190	3,388
(Tax rate)	50	49	49	49	39	28	−27	190	−9	−25
Net income before Extraordinary expense	10,840	14,729	14,275	19,171	30,263	24,827	31,900	9,198	−39,673	−16,742
Extraordinary expense	−2,273	−7,859	0	0	0	0	0	0	0	0
Extraordinary expense	13,113	22,588	14,275	19,171	30,263	24,827	31,900	9,198	−39,673	−16,742

EXHIBIT 13b STORER COMMUNICATIONS INC. PERCENTAGE INCOME STATEMENT (ITEMS AS A PERCENT OF SALES) YEAR ENDING: DECEMBER 31

	1975	1976	1977	1978	1979	1980	1981	1982	1983	1984
Net sales	100.0	100.0	100.0	100.0	100.0	100.0	100.0	100.0	100.0	100.0
Cost of goods sold	27.2	29.1	35.4	33.7	34.8	36.1	35.8	38.1	39.3	37.1
Gross profit	72.8	70.9	64.6	66.3	65.2	63.9	64.2	61.9	60.7	62.9
Advertising expense	3.1	3.2	4.4	4.2	3.7	3.1	2.8	1.9	2.4	0.0
Research and development expense	0.0	0.0	0.0	0.0	0.0	0.0	0.0	0.0	0.0	0.0
Rental expense	9.5	3.4	3.8	3.4	3.3	3.2	3.4	3.6	0.0	0.0
Other expense	0.0	33.7	26.3	25.4	23.8	0.0	0.0	0.0	0.0	0.0
Total operating expense	42.4	40.3	34.5	33.0	30.8	32.6	33.8	34.5	33.0	30.8
Operating income	30.4	30.6	30.1	33.4	34.4	31.3	30.3	27.4	27.6	32.2
Net other income	6.4	0.3	0.3	-0.1	7.3	4.3	5.6	5.9	1.9	2.7
Special items	1.7	-0.1	-1.8	-0.8	0.0	0.0	0.0	0.0	0.0	0.0
Interest expense	2.5	1.6	1.2	1.4	3.3	5.8	11.9	17.7	17.2	17.1
Depreciation expense	11.1	6.5	7.9	7.7	9.3	12.1	14.9	18.3	20.3	20.3
Pretax income	21.5	22.9	23.1	25.0	29.2	17.6	9.1	-2.7	-8.0	-2.5
Income taxes-state	1.2	1.8	1.7	1.7	1.8	1.4	0.6	0.8	0.8	0.6
Income taxes-federal	11.1	10.8	9.4	10.5	9.0	0.7	-6.0	-4.5	0.0	0.0
Deferred taxes	0.6	-1.3	0.3	0.0	0.6	2.8	2.9	-1.4	-0.1	0.0
Total taxes	10.8	11.3	11.4	12.2	11.4	5.0	-2.4	-5.1	0.7	0.6
(Tax rate)	0.0	0.0	0.0	0.0	0.0	0.0	0.0	0.0	0.0	0.0
Net income	10.7	11.6	11.7	12.8	17.8	12.6	11.5	2.4	-8.6	-3.1
Extraordinary expense	-2.2	-6.2	0.0	0.0	0.0	0.0	0.0	0.0	0.0	0.0
Net income after Extraordinary expense	13.0	17.7	11.7	12.8	17.8	12.6	11.5	2.4	-8.6	-3.1

normal, cyclical downturn is not necessarily a worse credit risk at the low point in its operating cycle, even though ratios such as fixed charge coverage and return on sales seem to support that conclusion. Analyzing such companies requires peak-to-peak and trough-to-trough comparisons.

For example, suppose that the fluctuations in a paper company's operating margin (operating income as a percentage of net sales) have historically correlated closely with changes in gross national product (GNP). Assume also that currently, at the bottom of a recession, the company's operating margin is narrower than it was at the bottom of the last recession. Provided the present recession is no more severe than the last (i.e., the peak-to-trough percentage GNP declines are equivalent), we can infer that the company's operating decline reflects more than just a normal cyclical variation. As with other quantitative evidence, this finding indicates a need for further analysis of underlying causes. The apparent secular decline in **operating margins** might reflect either intensifying industry competition (a factor not under management's control) or failure to contain overhead costs (a problem that management can remedy).

COMPARATIVE RATIO ANALYSIS. Another helpful perspective on a company's financial ratios emerges from a comparison with its industry peers. Ratios far out of line with competitors may signal inappropriate financial policies. Underlying economic characteristics tend to promote uniformity of percentage balance sheets throughout an industry. For instance, suppose a cement producer attempts to raise its return on equity by increasing its financial leverage above the industry norm. If successful, the new financial policy could provide the company superior access to the capital markets— a valuable competitive advantage. This strategy works fine as long as cement sales remain strong, but downside earnings leverage proves substantial at the trough of the construction cycle. Faced with above-average interest costs, the company is forced to raise cash by liquidating inventories at a steep loss. Earnings, instead of merely declining, as at the other cement producers, turn negative. Obliged to cut its dividend, the company finds that its strategy has backfired—it has impaired, rather than enhanced its access to the capital markets. Chastened by the experience, the company returns to the leverage policy that generally prevails in its industry and which reflects the inherent degree of operating risk in cement.

Over time, various competitors' attempts to split from the pack reinforce the notion that there are "correct" financial ratios for an industry. If unsuccessful in achieving their objectives, the mavericks return to conventional practice; if successful, they invite imitation.

Comparative ratio analysis also furnishes information on the quality of management. A management team deserves no special credit for producing high profits in a high-profit industry. Above-average returns within a peer group, however, can indicate that a company has done better than its competitors in developing new products, exploiting attractive market niches, or

EXHIBIT 14   CABLE TELEVISION INDUSTRY—COMPARATIVE RATIO ANALYSIS (1984)

	Current Ratio	Quick Ratio	Total Debt Total Capital	Gross Margin	Operating Margin	Net Income Equity	CFITD Cash Flow Total Debt	Fixed Charge Coverage
Comcast Corp.	4.4x (1)ᵃ	4.1x (1)	56.0% (3)	57.4% (1)	23.1% (3)	14.4% (2)	26.3% (3)	2.7x (3)
Cox Communications	0.8x (4)	0.8x (4)	27.1% (1)	55.3% (3)	22.8% (4)	15.2% (1)	83.9% (1)	4.9x (1)
Jones Intercable	1.0x (2)	1.0x (2)	32.4% (2)	53.1% (4)	39.8% (1)	13.4% (3)	60.5% (2)	4.5x (2)
Storer Communications	0.7x (5)	0.7x (5)	72.6% (6)	56.6% (2)	12.7% (7)	(5.6%)(7)	10.9% (6)	0.8x (7)
Telecommunications	0.2x (7)	0.2x (7)	82.1% (7)	48.4% (6)	24.0% (2)	7.5% (5)	7.7% (5)	0.9x (6)
United Cable	0.6x (6)	0.6x (6)	68.9% (5)	42.8% (7)	18.8% (6)	5.8% (6)	19.2% (4)	1.4x (5)
Viacom International	0.9x (3)	0.9x (3)	56.6% (4)	52.5% (5)	22.6% (5)	12.5% (4)	17.0% (5)	2.0x (4)

ᵃFigures in parentheses show company rankings for each ratio. Highest ranking (1) indicate *strongest* measure, for example, the *highest* gross margin, the *lowest* total debt/total capital.

reducing costs. When using comparative ratio analysis to assess management, the analyst should focus on the factors most directly controllable by management. Operating margins, for instance, reflect management skill better than net margins do, since the latter are influenced by factors beyond management control such as interest rates and tax rates.

Exhibit 14 suggests one format for a comparative ratio analysis of the cable television industry. This presentation deepens our understanding of Storer Communications. Exhibit 14 shows that in 1984 the company ranked at or near the bottom of its peer group on all of the financial ratios shown.

HOW CAN RATIOS BE USED IN EVALUATING SECURITIES?

So far we have described techniques for assessing financial risk by analyzing raw financial statement data and for deriving greater meaning by converting the data into financial ratios. A firm's ratios, in turn, take on added significance when viewed in historical perspective or in an industry context. These findings have value in a variety of applications, such as extension of trade credit and determining whether a company being awarded a contract is likely to remain financially able to perform. In such situations, the user of financial statements often faces an all-or-none decision; the company is either creditworthy or not. All companies judged sound will receive the same terms. When we turn to securities evaluation, however, finer distinctions become necessary. As the saying goes, every security has its price. Somebody will be willing to own even the highest risk bond or stock if the prospective return is high enough. Conversely, within the universe of sound companies, securities of the lowest-risk firms will command premium prices. In an efficient market, each security will provide a return identical to that of each other security with comparable risk. Let us now see how we can apply the analytical techniques introduced previously to assign companies to specific risk categories in order to determine appropriate returns for their securities.

BOND ANALYSIS. One of the key factors in evaluating debt securities is default risk, that is, the risk that the issuer will fail to make contractual payments of principal and interest on schedule. In general, the higher a company's default risk, the higher the promised yield on its bonds. Bond pricing practices make possible exceedingly fine distinctions in credit risk. The standard unit of yield is a basis point (i.e., 1/100 of 1%) and the range of yields on lowest to highest risk companies can at times reach 1,000 basis points or more. Therefore, each of the several hundred actively traded companies in the bond market could theoretically have a unique yield premium. In practice, though, investors tend to group the hundreds of bond issuers into a smaller number of risk categories. Bond ratings provide one system of assigning risk categories. Moody's Investors and Standard & Poor's, the two best-known bond rating agencies, divide all investment grade issues into four broad categories: Aaa, Aa, A, and Baa (Moody's) or AAA, AA, A, and BBB (Standard & Poor's). Speculative grade issues are classified as Ba, B Caa, Ca, and C (Moody's) or BB, B, CCC, CC, C, and D (Standard & Poor's). The agencies make finer distinctions on bonds in categories Aa/AA through B/B with the notation 1,2,3 (Moody's) and the use of + and − at Standard & Poor's. These broad categories provide convenient pricing benchmarks for market participants.

Because a change in a company's bond rating can alter its price, investors use ratio analysis to identify companies with the potential to rise or fall from their present ratings. Ratio trend analysis (Exhibit 12) and comparative ratio analysis (Exhibit 14) are important techniques in determining upgrade or downgrade potential. In addition, the analyst can compare a company's ratios with those of its rating peers. In this approach, the analyst can make comparisons across industry lines if a sufficient sample size is not available within the industry of the company being analyzed. In no case, however, should comparative ratio analysis lump together companies from entirely different sectors of the economy. Violating this rule will produce invalid ratio comparisons between companies with dissimilar business risks. A ratio comparison by rating group might therefore mix chemical, computer, and beverage companies (industrial sector), but could not include similarly rated companies from the utility sector. Exhibit 15 uses key ratios to compare a number of double-A rated industrial companies. Those ranked near the bottom by these ratios generally face the greatest risk of downgrading to single-A. It should be noted, however, that the rating agencies also consider various qualitative factors such as operating risk and quality of management before assigning a rating.

Although ratio trend analysis and comparative ratio analysis enhance our understanding of financial data, the techniques fail to answer two important questions:

- When are deviations of a particular ratio significant?
- How do ratios offset one another?

For example, both a high current ratio and a low ratio of total debt-to-total capital generally imply strong credit quality. The techniques introduced so far, however, provide no explicit way to balance a high current ratio against a low ratio of total debt-to-total capital in assessing credit risk. In the absence of other analytical tools, one must resolve such conflicting signals subjectively.

To fill this analytical gap, Altman, in "Financial Ratios, Discriminant Analysis and the Prediction of Corporate Bankruptcy" (*The Journal of Finance,* September 1968) applied a multivariate technique known as **discriminant analysis.** This statistical approach can use any quantifiable factor to

EXHIBIT 15 DOUBLE-A INDUSTRIALS—1984 COMPARATIVE RATIO ANALYSIS

Pretax Interest Coverage		Total Debt as % of Adjusted Book Capital	
Raytheon	64.2	Whirlpool	4.6
Whirlpool	51.6	Raytheon	5.8
General Signal	26.4	SmithKline Beckman	9.1
Rockwell International	19.4	Rockwell International	9.7
American Broadcasting	17.6	American Broadcasting	10.5
USG	14.2	General Signal	11.0
SmithKline Beckman	13.2	Halliburton	16.3
Ralston Purina	12.5	General Motors	19.5
CBS	11.2	CBS	19.9
Texas Instruments	10.9	Pfizer	20.2
Unocal	10.4	Unocal	20.7
American Hospital Supply	9.8	American Hospital Supply	21.1
Motorola	9.8	Texas Instruments	21.7
Time	9.6	Squibb	21.8
Squibb	9.5	Motorola	22.0
PPG Industries	9.2	International Paper	23.0
Pfizer	9.1	R.J. Reynolds	24.2
R.J. Reynolds	8.2	PPG Industries	24.3
Times Mirror	8.0	Shell Oil	24.5
General Motors	7.8	USG	25.8
Shell Oil	7.5	Ralston Purina	26.3
Abbott Labs	7.2	Du Pont	26.7
Du Pont	6.6	Time	27.9
McDonald's	6.2	United Technolgies	28.1
Kimberly-Clark	6.1	Kimberly-Clark	29.6
Dayton-Hudson	5.6	Weyerhaeuser	30.4
Warner Lambert	5.3	Dayton-Hudson	30.5
Halliburton	5.1	Xerox	31.3
Searle (G.D.)	5.1	Times Mirror	31.5
Union Camp	5.0	Abbott Laboratories	31.7
United Technologies	4.9	Searle (G.D.)	31.8
Chesebrough-Pond's	4.4	Warner Lambert	31.8
Upjohn	4.2	Upjohn	33.3
Atlantic Richfield	4.1	Atlantic Richfield	34.1
Mobil Corp.	4.1	Pepsico	34.4
Sun Co.	3.7	Sun Co.	34.5
Weyerhaeuser	3.6	Union Camp	34.8
Xerox	3.4	McDonald's	40.4
Texaco	2.9	Chesebrough-Pond's	45.1
Pepsico	2.6	Texaco	46.4
International Paper	2.4	Mobil	48.8
Best	**64.2**	**Best**	**4.6**
Worst	**2.4**	**Worst**	**48.8**
Median	**7.5**	**Median**	**26.3**

classify members of specific populations into distinct categories. In consumer credit, loan applicants are classified as "high repayment potential" or "low repayment potential," based on personal variables such as employment, income, and owner or renter status. This is known as **credit scoring,** where each attribute is assigned an objectively determined weight and the sum of these attributes times their weights gives a credit score. Altman used the same approach to analyze firms, rather than individuals, in his original (1968) **Z-score model** of bankruptcy risk, which took the form:

$$Z = 1.4X_1 + 1.2X_2 + 3.3X_3 + 0.6X_4 + 1.0X_5$$

where X_1 = working capital/total assets (%, e.g., .20 or 20%)
  X_2 = retained earnings/total assets (%)
  X_3 = earnings before interest and taxes/total assets (%)
  X_4 = market value of equity/total liabilities (%)
  X_5 = sales/total assets (number of times, e.g., 2.0 times)

Scores below 1.81 signify serious credit problems, while a score above 3.0 indicates a healthy entity. The five ratios are indicative of liquidity, cumulative profitability, current profitability, leverage, and turnover. Discriminant analysis can analyze these ratios simultaneously; the overall score is the essence, rather than any one ratio or group of ratios.

Altman, Haldeman, and Narayanan (*Journal of Banking and Finance,* June 1977), updated and improved on Altman's 1968 model by explicitly considering such factors as lease capitalization, consolidated financial statements and other accounting changes. In addition, they applied income smoothing techniques to level out random fluctuations and trend deviations in the data. The new model was able to identify bankruptcy-prone firms very accurately (i.e., 85%) two years prior to failure and with approximately 70% accuracy for about five years prior.

As a final point on bond analysis, the reader should keep in mind that financial statements supply only a portion of the information affecting a particular issue's value at a given time. Besides the issuer's reported financial results, a bond's price responds to such factors as the general level of interest rates, expectations of future rates, and investors' risk preferences. Even within the financial results category, bond prices respond to economic and business developments both as they occur and in anticipation of their occurrence (i.e., before their impact on financial statements is reported). Speculative grade bonds, in particular, can exhibit wide price fluctuations following news reports pointing to changes in financial ratios that will be reported in the future. Therefore, in addition to applying the best available techniques for interpreting historical results, the bond analyst must also keep abreast of current developments and gain sufficient understanding of a company's business to be able to anticipate future events. In this regard, bond analysis can be viewed as part of a continuum with—rather than sharply distinct from—equity analysis. The essential unity of these two activities is explicit in contemporary financial theory, which treats various classes of securities as related claims on the firm. Since the bondholder would effectively become the firm's owner (i.e., an equity holder) in the event of bankruptcy, there is strong incentive to understand the shareholder's perspective.

EQUITY ANALYSIS. Analysis of financial statements to evaluate common stock rests on the proposition that the intrinsic value of a share equals the present value of its associated future income stream (i.e., dividends). Exhibit 16 illustrates the case of a company expected to continue earning $1 million net profit annually for the indefinite future. To calculate the value of one share of the fictitious Titan Screw, we must first calculate dividends per share.

An investor who pays $12 for a share of Titan Screw receives an annual return of a $1.80 dividend. The **dividend yield** in this case equals the required rate of return.

$$\text{Dividend yield} = \frac{\text{dividends per share}}{\text{price per share}} = \frac{\$1.80}{\$12} = 15\%$$

The value of an infinite stream of equal payments equals the size of the payment divided by the discount rate, or required rate of return. We can express this algebraically as:

$$P = \frac{D}{K}$$

where P = current stock price
   D = current dividend rate
   K = required rate of return

Applying this formula, we find that given a 15% required rate of return, the value of one share of Titan Screw is:

EXHIBIT 16   TITAN SCREW CORPORATION STOCK PRICE VALUATION

Net income = $1,000,000
Dividends to common shareholders = $450,000
Common shares outstanding = 250,000
Discount rate (investors' required rate of return) = 15%

$$\text{Dividends per share} = \frac{\text{dividends to common shareholders}}{\text{common shares outstanding}} = \frac{\$450,000}{250,000} = \$1.80$$

$$\frac{\$1.80}{.15} = \$12$$

No-growth companies are simple to analyze but rarely encountered in practice. Equity evaluation becomes more complex when earnings (and dividends) are expected to grow over time, the more typical situation faced by the analyst. To take growth into account, our dividend-based formula changes to:

$$P = \frac{D (1 + g)^1}{(1 + K)^1} + \frac{D (1 + g)^2}{(1 + K)^2} + \cdots \frac{D (1 + g)^n}{(1 + K)^n}$$

where P = current stock price
$\quad\quad D$ = current dividend rate
$\quad\quad K$ = required rate of return
$\quad\quad g$ = growth rate

If n, the number of periods considered, is infinite, this formula reduces to:

$$P = \frac{D}{K - g}$$

Let us apply this equity valuation model to Bolton Food Corp. (Exhibit 17), a fictitious company with estimated dividends over the next year of $10 million and 10 million shares outstanding. We calculate dividends per share just as we did above for Titan Screw.

Note that Bolton is expected to pay $10 million of its $30 million of available earnings to common shareholders. Its **dividend payout ratio** is therefore 33⅓%.

$$\text{Dividend payout ratio} = \frac{\text{dividends to common shareholders}}{\text{net income available to common shareholders}}$$

$$= \frac{\$10,000,000}{\$30,000,000} = 33\frac{1}{3}\%$$

If Bolton maintains a constant dividend payout ratio, it follows that the growth rate of dividends will equal the growth in earnings, which is expected

EXHIBIT 17 BOLTON FOOD CORP. STOCK PRICE VALUATION

Estimated net income available to common shareholders = $30,000,000
Estimated dividends to common shareholders = $10,000,000
Common shares outstanding = 10,000,000
Expected growth in earnings = 10% per year

to be 10% annually. Postulating the same 15% required rate of return used in the Titan Screw example, we can now calculate Bolton's current stock price:

$$P = \frac{D}{K - g} = \frac{\$1}{.15 - .10} = \frac{\$1}{.05} = \$20$$

This valuation method, the **dividend discount model,** is intuitively appealing because it considers cash flows actually received by the stockholder (i.e., dividends). It does not, however, provide a ready comparison of the values of different stocks. Investors, in continually seeking superior values, have derived a shortcut method for comparing stocks, based on the **price-earnings ratio** or **earnings multiple.** To calculate this ratio, we must first calculate earnings per share.

Earnings per share (EPS)

$$= \frac{\text{net income available to common shareholders}}{\text{common shares outstanding}} = \frac{\$30,000,000}{10,000,000} = \$3$$

$$\text{Price-earnings ratio (P/E)} = \frac{\text{stock price}}{\text{earnings per share}} = \frac{\$20}{\$3} = 6\frac{2}{3} \text{ or } 6.7X$$

To illustrate how the price-earnings ratio can help the investor compare the prices of two stocks, let us consider Bolton Food's competitor, Delicious Snax (Exhibit 18). We can observe that Delicious Snax has the same expected earnings growth rate as Bolton (10%) and can calculate that it has the same dividend payout ratio

$$\left(\frac{\$8,000,000}{\$24,000,000} = 33\frac{1}{3}\% \right).$$

Its 8.1X price-earnings ratio, however, is higher than Bolton's 6.7X ratio

---

EXHIBIT 18   DELICIOUS SNAX, INC. STOCK PRICE VALUATION

Estimated net income available to common shareholders	= $24,000,000
Estimated dividends to common shareholders	= $ 8,000,000
Common shares outstanding	= 13,000,000
Expected growth in earnings	= 10% per year
Current stock price	= $15

$$\text{Earnings per share} = \frac{\$24,000,000}{13,000,000} = \$1.85$$

$$\text{Price-earnings ratio} = \frac{\$15}{\$1.85} = 8.1x$$

An investor would regard Bolton as the better value of the two, based on its lower price-earnings ratio. The reasoning derives from Delicious Snax data via our dividend discount model.

$$P = \frac{D}{K - g} = \frac{\left(\dfrac{\$8,000,000}{13,000,000}\right)}{.15 - .10} = \frac{\$.62}{.05} = \$12.40$$

The price for Delicious Snax derived from this model is lower than the actual price of $15, implying an excessive market valuation. Observe as well that the "correct" price for Delicious Snax produces the same price-earnings ratio as that which we calculated for Bolton Foods.

$$P/E = \frac{\$12.40}{\$1.85} = 6.7X$$

Mathematically, if the market is applying the dividend discount model to two stocks with identical growth rates and requiring identical rates of return, both stocks must carry the same price-earnings ratio. Therefore, if one is available at a lower price-earnings ratio, it represents a superior value. Comparison of **price-earnings ratios** has consequently become a widespread, shorthand method for spotting undervalued and overvalued stocks within a large universe. Notwithstanding the convenience of price-earnings ratios and their consequent popularity among analysts, the reader should bear in mind that equity value ultimately derives from future dividends. Current earnings clearly cannot be the basis of stock price. If they were, a company's stock price would fall to zero if its profits were nil. In reality, based on their potential to pay dividends over the long run, corporations that produce no short-term earnings have positive stock prices.

From corporate management's viewpoint, the price-earnings ratio is significant because it provides a plan of attack for increasing shareholder value. For example, a cost-cutting program that promises higher earnings should produce a higher stock price. To demonstrate this, we first restate our price-earnings ratio definition as follows:

$$P/E = \frac{P}{EPS}$$

$$P/E \times EPS = P$$

Applying this restated form to Bolton Food, we calculate the stock price, using (1) the previous earnings estimate and then (2) a revised estimate that reflects a newly announced cost-cutting program.

$$P/E \ \times \ EPS \ = \ P$$

Old earnings estimate $6 \ 2/3 \times \$3 \quad = \$20$

New earnings estimate $6 \ 2/3 \times \$3.25 = \$21.67$

We conclude that successful cost reduction efforts will increase shareholder value.

Likewise, management can increase the price of Bolton's stock by raising the multiple assigned to its earnings. To show how a higher multiple can be achieved, we will expand our price-earnings definition by borrowing the stock price definition used above in our dividend discount model.

$$P/E \ = \ \frac{P}{EPS}$$

$$P/E \ = \ \frac{\left(\dfrac{D}{K \ - \ g}\right)}{EPS}$$

Experimentation will demonstrate that Bolton can obtain a higher multiple by paying a higher dividend (D), by reducing its required rate of return (K), or by increasing its growth rate (g). For example, suppose Bolton increases its emphasis on new products in order to raise its expected growth from 10% to 12%. The earnings multiple jumps from 6.7X to 11.1X in response to this modest increase in the growth rate.

$$\frac{\left(\dfrac{D}{K \ - \ g}\right)}{EPS} \ = \ P/E$$

$$\text{Old growth rate:} \ \frac{\left(\dfrac{\$1}{.15 \ - \ .10}\right)}{\$3} \ = \ 6.7X$$

$$\text{New growth rate:} \ \frac{\left(\dfrac{\$1}{.15 \ - \ .12}\right)}{\$3} \ = \ 11.1X$$

As for the required rate of return, it is a factor over which management has comparatively little control. This variable reflects returns available on alternative investments and investors' relative risk aversion at a particular time. Nevertheless, a company can boost its price-earnings ratio by reducing the uncertainty of its earnings. Investors will not require as high a return on a company with well-established sources of profits as they will on one relying largely on unproven products. Similarly, investors will require a higher return on (and therefore assign a lower multiple to) "low quality" earnings that depend on aggressive financial leverage or liberal accounting practices.

In applying this formula, management must avoid the error of supposing that simply raising the dividend payout ratio (and thereby increasing D) will raise the price-earnings ratio. The catch is that paying out earnings in dividends, rather than retaining them in the business, reduces the growth rate (g), which in turn reduces the price-earnings ratio. This becomes clear when one considers the following derivation of earnings per share.

Asset turnover × return on sales × leverage
$$\times \text{ book value per share } = \text{ earnings per share.}$$

$$\frac{\text{Sales}}{\text{Assets}} \times \frac{\text{net income}}{\text{sales}} \times \frac{\text{assets}}{\text{net worth}}$$

$$\times \frac{\text{net worth}}{\text{shares outstanding}} = \frac{\text{net income}}{\text{shares outstanding}}$$

Over the short run, a company can raise the productivity of its plants, but, after a while, their capacity limits asset turnover as a source of earnings per share growth. Neither can the return on sales expand indefinitely, since fat margins invite competition. Leverage cannot rise forever, since lenders will refuse to advance further funds when the company reaches some prescribed level of financial risk. Accordingly, only additions to book value per share can generate sustainable growth. We can define a company's sustainable growth rate as follows:

Sustainable growth rate = return on equity × income reinvestment rate

where
$$\text{income reinvestment rate} = 1 - \text{dividend payout rate}$$

From this definition we see that raising the dividend payout rate reduces the income reinvestment rate, which in turn cuts the sustainable growth rate. Consequently, a higher dividend rate produces a higher price-earnings ratio only if it represents a constant dividend payout applied to faster-growing earnings. Another way of looking at this analysis is to multiply the return on equity by the **dividend payout** rate, thereby yielding the firm's **dividend sustainable growth.**

The payoff for a well-managed company is increased value to its shareholders. One useful measure of value created is the **price-to-book ratio.**

$$\text{Price-to-book ratio} = \frac{\text{stock price}}{\text{book value per share}}$$

A price-to-book ratio greather than 1.0 permits a corporation to issue new shares at a price higher than was paid by its original shareholders. The original shareholders' lower average cost means that they reap a higher percentage of the company's earnings than their proportionate dollar investment in it. Conversely, an unsuccessful management, by bringing about a price-to-book lower than 1.0, may force existing shareholders to allow newcomers in on a cheaper basis. As shown in the following, management can raise the price-to-book ratio either by improving return on equity or by increasing the price-earnings ratio.

$$\frac{\text{Stock price}}{\text{Book value per share}} = \frac{\text{net income available to common shareholders}}{\text{common equity}}$$
$$\times \frac{\text{stock price} \times \text{common shares outstanding}}{\text{net income available to common shareholders}}$$

DU PONT FORMULA. The technique of disaggregating the components of a rate of return is a powerful one for analyzing equity securities. Corporate managers also find it invaluable in understanding the sources of profitability and the means of increasing it. Alfred P. Sloan, Jr., the late chairman of General Motors, recalled how GM gained financial control over its diverse operations when the company's vice president of finance, Donaldson Brown, brought with him from du Pont an elaborate system he had constructed around a basic formula for return on assets. His calculation, known as the du Pont Formula, is as follows:

$$\text{Asset turnover} \times \text{return on sales} = \text{return on assets}$$
$$\frac{\text{Sales}}{\text{Assets}} \times \frac{\text{income}}{\text{sales}} = \frac{\text{income}}{\text{assets}}$$

A variation, referred to as the **modified du Pont Formula,** incorporates financial leverage to analyze the sources of return on shareholders' investment.

$$\text{Return on assets} \times \text{financial leverage} = \text{return on equity}$$
$$\frac{\text{Income}}{\text{Assets}} \times \frac{\text{assets}}{\text{equity}} = \frac{\text{income}}{\text{equity}}$$

Exhibit 19 gives a sense of the du Pont methodology's value in analyzing the relative performance of competitors within an industry. By arraying the data in this manner, we can quickly ascertain, for example, that in 1984 Nabisco Brands achieved a higher return on equity than Carnation solely by applying greater financial leverage. Carnation surpassed Nabisco Brands

EXHIBIT 19   DU PONT ANALYSIS OF FOOD PROCESSING
INDUSTRY'S 1984 RESULTS

	Asset Turnover (X)	×	Return on Sales (%)	=	Return on Assets (%)	×	Financial Leverage (X)	=	Return on Equity (%)
Kellogg	1.56		9.62		15.02		3.42		51.42
Ralston Purina	2.48		4.87		12.10		2.00		24.33
Beatrice	1.21		3.80		4.61		4.91		22.65
Heinz (H.J.)	1.69		6.01		10.14		2.09		21.24
Nabisco Brands	1.66		4.94		8.21		2.43		20.03
Quaker Oats	1.85		4.14		7.67		2.50		19.26
General Mills	1.96		4.17		8.17		2.33		19.06
Consolidated Foods	2.51		2.61		6.55		2.80		18.32
Carnation	1.93		5.80		11.14		1.56		17.41
Pillsbury	1.60		4.07		6.51		2.49		16.23
General Foods	1.94		3.69		7.16		2.17		15.54
CPC International	1.63		4.42		7.21		2.02		14.60
Campbell Soup	1.65		5.22		8.65		1.75		14.17
Borden	1.58		4.19		6.63		2.10		13.99

on the other two components, those which measure operating skill: return on sales and asset turnover.

In wrapping up this section on equity analysis, it is helpful to remember that we began by relating the value of a common stock to future dividends. Since financial statements directly deal only with the past, the value of a stock (like the value of a bond) is affected by numerous factors that are not currently disclosed in financial statements and some that may never be. The "missing" information involves not only future events and past but not-yet-reported events, as well as facts that are not subject to mandatory disclosure under present financial reporting rules. To be complete, therefore, this chapter on financial statement analysis must discuss what is *not* in the statements, as well as what is. We now turn to some issues that reflect on how well financial statements, as currently constituted, serve the purposes outlined at the beginning of this chapter.

HOW CAN WE LOOK FORWARD WITH FINANCIAL STATEMENTS?

In both bond and equity analysis, it was necessary to make predictions about the future. The ability to continue meeting interest requirements and paying dividends determines the value of these securities, rather than the past record, per se. This does not imply that historical financial statements are irrelevant to forecasting a company's performance. While the past is not a window on the future, it does represent a basis for evaluating management's performance in implementing business objectives. Comparing the company's operating history against its business plan provides the analyst with important insights into management's effectiveness and credibility—both important factors in arriving at an investment decision. Furthermore, the historical results provide a foundation for projecting a company's future operating results and financial condition, based on its current business plan. The analyst can test the outcome's sensitivity to changes in revenue growth, operating margins, interest rates, income tax law, and investment and dividend policy. The results of this analysis help in evaluating whether management's goals are attainable, given existing market conditions and anticipated trends. Where the market discounts either a more or less favorable outlook than current conditions warrant, opportunities exist to profit on mispriced securities. We can see the value of forecasting on the basis of historical statements by returning to our study of Storer Communications.

In 1978, Storer decided to sell off the radio stations it had owned since the 1920s and to commit itself to the fast-growing business of cable television. By the end of 1984, Storer had spent approximately $1.1 billion in building cable systems with 1.4 million subscribers to the basic service. Between 1979 and 1984, the number of basic subscribers quadrupled and revenues advanced at an annual compound growth rate of approximately 61%. Unfortunately, this rapid expansion placed enormous pressure on the company's balance sheet and profitability—total cable debt increased to about $785 million, or about $560 per basic subscriber by December 31, 1984. This represented one of the highest debt loads per basic subscriber in the industry. The resulting high interest expenses and depreciation changes adversely affected Storer's profitability during the early 1980s. Consequently, in 1983 Storer reported a net loss for the first time in its history.

In July 1984, having substantially completed its cable construction, management announced an operating strategy designed to restore the company's financial and operating performance to precable expansion levels. This strategy involved consolidating existing properties, increasing subscriber rates, achieving operating efficiencies, and reducing corporate debt. Furthermore, the company's business plan took into account the planned enactment of federal legislation establishing a national cable communications policy that offered significant benefits to the industry.

Management's business plan represented an ambitious attempt to turn around the unprofitable and debt-ridden company. Certainly, the company's performance during the previous five years justified little confidence that the future was more promising.

At this juncture, there was considerable benefit in creating a financial forecast to test the likelihood that management could achieve its objectives. Through forecasting, the analyst could determine what conditions must prevail in order for the plan to succeed in restoring financial strength. The analysis consisted of a five-year projection of Storer's income statement, balance sheet, and funds flow, based on three scenarios—optimistic, most likely, and pessimistic. The assumptions underlying those scenarios are shown in Exhibit 20. The optimistic scenario was based upon forecasts supplied by the company. The pessimistic scenario assumed that the company's operating performance would remain static over the next five years—a highly unlikely development. These assumptions and historical financial data were the inputs for the five-year projection, using an **electronic spreadsheet** similar to many that are commercially available. For examples, see Section 1 (Planning & Control Techniques) in this *Handbook*.

The results indicated that Storer's capability of returning to profitability and reducing financial risk through internally generated funds was relatively high. Storer's return on equity improved to 18% in 1989 under the optimistic scenario. The 1989 return on equity (RDE) remained positive even when less optimistic assumptions were used (11% and 2% under the most likely and pessimistic scenarios, respectively).

Storer's debt ratio improved from its current level of 72% to 22% in 1989, based on the company's estimates. Likewise, its pretax interest coverage increased to 6.6 times, from a 1984 level of less than 1.0 times. Storer's downside exposure appeared to be minimal. Given a pessimistic scenario, the company's debt ratio and interest coverage still improved moderately. The former decreased to 58%, while the latter increased to 1.5 times. Finally, given a conservative growth in revenues and moderate improvements in operating margins (our most likely scenario), Storer's financial risk was reduced significantly. The company's debt ratio declined to 48% in 1989, while its pretax interest coverage improved to 2.4 times. The financial forecast can also be altered to investigate Storer's sensitivity to adverse changes in interest rates. In one scenario short-term rates were increased to approximately 14% in 1985, 16% in 1986, and 17% thereafter. These changes in interest rates had little effect on Storer's financial performance.

Storer's turnaround strategy, however, was also being closely monitored by at least one corporate raider, who, on March 19, 1985, announced a plan to gain control of the company and implement a program of liquidating Storer's assets. As a defensive response to this tender offer, management,

EXHIBIT 20   SCENARIOS USED IN STORER COMMUNICATIONS FORECAST

	Optimistic	Most Likely	Pessimistic
Annual revenue growth	7.5%	5.0%	5.0%
Operating margins (increase ratably from 1985 through 1989)	31–40%	31–35%	31%
Capital expenditures	$100 million in 1985, declining to $75 million in 1989. (Same for all scenarios.)		

in conjunction with outside investors, made an offer to take the company private in a leveraged buyout. The just-completed financial forecast showed that a **leveraged buyout** transaction would probably require asset sales of about $1 billion just to reduce debt to manageable levels. Therefore, the projected trend of improving credit quality was reversed.

In this instance, forecasting on a base of historical financial statements helped to identify an equity value that the market subsequently recognized. By the same token, the actual outcome demonstrated that unforeseen events can overwhelm the forecast's logic. This underscores the point that in addition to manipulating and forecasting financial data, the analyst who hopes to understand a company must pay careful attention to external developments that financial statements may not address.

DO FINANCIAL RATIOS REALLY MEASURE WHAT WE WANT TO MEASURE?

Up to this point, we have examined increasingly sophisticated techniques for extracting information from financial statements. We have also tacitly accepted the accuracy of the information contained in those statements. This acceptance cannot be justified, however, unless it is always true that the goals of the issuers of financial statement coincide with those of their users. In reality, a corporation has several possible motives for using all its latitude within the accounting rules to present a picture to outsiders that differs from what management sees internally. For one thing, widespread use of the standard financial ratios by securities analysts may make the ratios themselves (rather than the qualities they measure) the bogeys for management. In the case of credit quality measures, the company may try to reduce its borrowing cost by getting liabilities off-balance sheet, rather than reducing them. Likewise, a corporation may be tempted to inflate or smooth its earnings to obtain a higher price-earnings ratio for its stock. Another reason for not simply "holding up a mirror" in financial reporting is that whatever information a public corporation discloses to shareholders it discloses to its competitors, as well.

Consequently, a conflict has arisen between corporations' desire for confidentiality and investors' attempts to gain fuller understanding. In general, investors have pressed for more detailed financial statements or supplemental disclosures in the annual and quarterly reports. Resistance by corporations, however, has hindered many efforts to expand specific reporting requirements. (For insights into the tug-of-war between the status quo and expansion of financial reporting requirements, see Reiling, Henry B. and Burton, John C. *Harvard Business Review*, November-December 1972. The authors relate the pressure for fuller disclosure to wide public ownership of securities through pension funds. To facilitate decision-making by these investors and their designated managers, Reiling and Burton advocate such requirements as a breakdown of the fixed and variable components of cost and more detail on sales to indicate what percentage is likely to be recurring.)

Even without such resistance, however, the basic financial statements would lack much valuable information. Traditional accounting practice, for example, generally permits a company to recognize a gain on an asset only when a transaction occurs. Consequently, balance sheets often do not reflect the economic worth of natural resources acquired many years ago at costs substantially below their present market values. This flaw, along with distortions that may arise from management's motivations to present something other than the naked truth, have led to augmentation of the three basic financial statements with various mandatory disclosures. These "Notes to Financial Statements" sometimes provide a picture markedly different from the company portrayed by the income statement, balance sheet, and funds flow statement. The following are just a few illustrations of the importance of looking outside the three basic financial statements.

OFF-BALANCE SHEET FINANCING. While there are sometimes valid economic reasons for utilizing **off-balance sheet financing,** it is a technique that can be abused and employed to mislead investors regarding financial risk. Off-balance sheet financing, in its many guises, consists of labeling borrowings as something other than debt, so that they will appear in the Notes to Financial Statements, rather than on the balance sheet. Financial analysts have learned to recognize these financings for what they truly are and reconsolidate most off-balance sheet debt for analytical purposes. Gradually, the accounting rules, too, are moving toward putting debt by any other name onto the balance sheet. Nonetheless, off-balance sheet financing remains popular with corporations, some of which appear to believe that changes in form, rather than substance, actually enhance their creditworthiness. The following discussion describes just one form of off-balance sheet financing. (For a fuller discussion, see the article by Richard Dieter and Arthur R. Wyatt, *Financial Executive,* January 1980, which describes such techniques as sales of receivables with recourse, leases, project financing arrangements, and throughput agreements.)

Captive finance subsidiaries are commonly used by retailers, automobile manufacturers, and capital goods producers to promote sales and to remove debt from the parent companies' balance sheets. In financial terms, any manufacturer that relies on customer financing can create a captive finance subsidiary by carving out a portion of its accounts receivable and a slightly smaller amount of its debt. These assets and liabilities go into a wholly owned subsidiary, with the difference between the two representing the parent's equity. Under present accounting rules, the parent does not have to consolidate the subsidiary's debt. Without raising any new equity then, and simply by transferring debt to a subsidiary, the parent's consolidated debt-to-capital ratio has declined. (See the fictitious example in Exhibit 21). Has the parent actually reduced its financial risk, however? Because the

EXHIBIT 21 THE BIRTH OF A CAPTIVE FINANCE COMPANY ($ MILLION)

BEFORE

Empire Auto Corporation

December 31, 1984

Cash	200	Accounts Payable	25
Accounts Receivable	50	Short-Term Debt	150
Inventory	250	Long-Term Debt	200
Fixed Assets	500	Shareholders' Equity	625
	1,000		1,000

$$\text{Total Debt/Total Capital} = \frac{\$300 \text{ million}}{\$800 \text{ million}} = 37.5\%$$

AFTER

Empire Auto Corporation

January 1, 1985

Cash	200	Accounts Payable	20
Accounts Receivable	20	Short-Term Debt	50
Investment in Finance Subsidiary	195	Long-Term Debt	20
Fixed Assets	500	Shareholders' Equity	625
	915		915

$$\text{Total Debt/Total Capital} = \frac{\$215 \text{ million}}{\$715 \text{ million}} = 30.1\%$$

Empire Credit Corporation

January 1, 1985

Cash	5	Short-Term Debt	30
Accounts Receivable	100	Long-Term Debt	55
		Shareholders' Equity	20
	105		105

$$\text{Total Debt/Total Capital} = \frac{\$85 \text{ million}}{\$105 \text{ million}} = 81.0\%$$

subsidiary's debt must still be serviced if the parent is to receive revenue from the receivables, the borrowings have not really gone away. Moreover, in the event of liquidation, the parent company lenders now have only a residual claim (i.e., after captive finance subsidiary lenders have been fully paid) on the highly liquid receivables. Historically, financial assets of this sort have tended to yield a higher portion of their stated value in liquidation than have the manufacturing assets remaining at the parent. Granted, the parent may obtain a real benefit if deconsolidation of certain borrowings will reduce the danger of bumping up against covenanted restrictions on total debt. Also, the subsidiary's more liquid asset structure may enable it to borrow at a lower interest rate than its parent could, a benefit that can be passed along by permitting the parent to provide more attractive customer financing. For the user of financial statements, though, the key point is that the Notes to Financial Statements concerning captive finance subsidiaries reveal higher financial risk in the total enterprise than the consolidated statements suggest.

OVERSTATED AND UNDERSTATED ASSET VALUES. Balance sheets may mislead not only by what they omit, but also by what they show at values well above their economic worth. Such disparities arise because generally accepted accounting principles value assets almost exclusively on the basis of actual transactions. Plant and equipment, valued on initial purchase, may not be involved in another transaction until their carrying values finally reach zero through depreciation. This does not happen until years later. The economic worth of such assets may decline much faster than projected on the basis of wear-and-tear if, for example, new technology renders them obsolete. In theory, the company's books should promptly reconcile these disparities through writedowns. In practice, however, such adjustments require judgment and may lag the actual impairment of asset values. Consequently, financial statements may at any given point overestimate an enterprise's total value.

On the other side of the coin, the accounting doctrine of conservatism generally prevents assets from being written up when their dollar value rises, as through inflation. The Notes to Financial Statements now include a parallel set of financial statements meant to measure the gap between historical costs and current value resulting from a rise in the general price level. Aside from inflation, particular assets may sometimes appreciate dramatically, as in the case of oil reserves during the rapid surge in energy prices in the 1970s. Until the owner sells the reserves (either in place or as crude oil, following extraction), these assets continue to reflect merely the historical costs associated with their discovery. Real estate may be rising in value, but it does not produce income, and therefore does not affect an equity valuation based on a price-earnings ratio, until it is disposed of by the corporation. Similarly, a patent or trademark may have far more economic worth than its balance sheet valuation if it has never been sold.

Although accounting rules may not recognize such values, a special brand of financier may. Known as "**asset strippers**" or "**takeover artists,**" these individuals seek to profit from the fact that a corporation's "**breakup**" (i.e., liquidation) value may exceed its market capitalization, (i.e., the aggregate market price of its outstanding shares). By acquiring the corporation's shares at a price somewhere between the market capitalization and the breakup value, the asset stripper can sell off the pieces for more than the cost of acquiring them.

For the user of financial statements, the key point is that a corporation's financial statements may not fully reflect its equity's potential value. The share price can rise dramatically if the valuation assumption suddenly shifts from capitalization of earnings to liquidation of assets.

PARENT-SUBSIDIARY RELATIONSHIPS. Another critical factor often missing from the three basic financial statements is the relationship between a company and its parent or subsidiaries. Captive finance subsidiaries, as discussed previously, depend on arrangements for parent support to secure high credit ratings. For example, the manufacturer in our illustration might agree to sell receivables to its subsidiary at a discount calculated to yield pretax earnings sufficient to produce the minimum fixed charge coverage required by lenders. Aside from such relationships, the user of financial statements may encounter corporations that either acquire or form separately incorporated subsidiaries for a variety of purposes. If the parent irrevocably guarantees the subsidiary's debt, the subsidiary's own financial statements become inconsequential in the analysis of its debt quality. The user of financial statements should, however, generally recognize the guarantees as parent obligations, even though they do not appear on the parent's balance sheet. When a subsidiary borrows without a formal parent guarantee, judgment becomes essential. The extent to which lenders can look to the parent in the event of a subsidiary's illiquidity, and to which the parent will treat subsidiary debt as its own obligation, depends on implicit support—a difficult thing to quantify. Justifications for presuming implicit support of a subsidiary can include:

- *Strategic importance to the parent* such as vertical integration in a core business;
- *Prestige,* such as when the parent lends its name to a subsidiary engaged in a highly visible business; and
- *Demonstrated financial support* such as equity infusions, loans, or reinvestment of subsidiary earnings.

HIDDEN AND OVERSTATED EARNINGS. Although the sophisticated balance sheet reader is aware that management may have used every bit of legally allowed discretion to manipulate the figures, there is consolation in the fact that the bias will almost certainly be in the direction of making things seem rosier than they are. Not so with the income statement, for managers sometimes have an interest in making results look worse than they are, at least in the short term. This paradox arises from the stock market's practice of putting a premium on predictable earnings—a preference that managements tend to interpret as profits that rise annually in a straight line. The pursuit of steady profit gains creates an incentive for a company to understate income in an exceptionally strong year, since it might not be able to improve on the true figure in the succeeding period. This "smoothing" of earnings also permits companies to report better results in bad years by belatedly recognizing profits that were hidden in the good times. Likewise, there are ways of postponing bad news beyond a specific event, such as a planned sale of the company or retirement of present management. When examining income statements, users must be alert to the possible existence of such motives and watch for telltale signs of hidden or overstated earnings.

A common way for management to hide earnings in an unexpectedly strong year is to take discretionary, nonrecurring charges. Analysts should scrutinize financial statements for nonoperating items such as writedowns on operations that management plans to discontinue. Financial firms may add to discretionary reserves for loan losses and thereby conceal above-trendline earnings increases. Unfortunately, companies can also take smoothing actions that do not require special disclosure. For example, management may time an expensive training program—most likely a worthwhile outlay—so as to reduce extraordinarily high profits. Since such actions can often escape detection, the financial statement user should be skeptical of earnings records that slope upward in ramrod-straight fashion.

Overstated earnings frequently reflect problems swept under the rug until a subsequent reporting period. For example, management may delay a write-down of obsolete inventory to avoid a charge against earnings in the current period. To test for this type of distortion, financial statement users should look for nonseasonal declines in the inventory turnover ratio. Another category of earnings overstatement involves cutting back on expenses such as advertising and research that provide benefits in future periods. A decline in these expenses as a percentage of sales may indicate that current period earnings will prove unsustainable. Finally, financial statement users should watch for nonoperating profits taken on a discretionary basis to offset weak operating income. These items include profit-taking on securities holdings and gains on debt repurchased (other than for a current sinking fund requirement) at less than book value.

THE QUEST FOR TRUE CASH FLOW. The funds flow statement originally gained popularity partly in reaction to accounting abuses by companies that deliberately distorted their earnings per share in hopes of raising their stock prices. As emphasis shifted from earnings to cash flow, analysts sought increasingly detailed information. Their ultimate objective is to pinpoint operating cash flow, which measures a corporation's ability to generate cash from its assets by approximating actual cash received and disbursed. Going beyond the simple presentation shown in Exhibit 10, the operating cash flow model adjusts for noncash components of net income such as deferred income taxes, deferred revenues, and unremitted earnings or nonwholly owned subsidiaries. A rigorous presentation also details changes in the current asset and current liability accounts.

Although the operating cash flow model provides a more complete picture than the rudimentary format of Exhibit 10, it falls short of the ideal cash generation measure for securities valuation. For example, including 100% depreciation, calculated on the basis of historical cost, in cash flow ignores the fact that the replacement cost of a firm's assets may have risen due to inflation. In a given year, a company may reduce its income by $1 million for wear-and-tear on its equipment yet capitalize $2 million at today's costs to replace an equivalent amount of physical capacity. If the company bases its dividend payout on the net income resulting from such underdepreciation, it will eventually find itself unable to continue paying out earnings at the same level. A similar problem arises when inflation raises the nominal value of inventory. Suppose a manufacturer produces an item at a cost of $70. The item's normal *gross margin* (i.e., sales minus cost of goods sold as a percentage of sales) is 30%, implying a $100 sales price. During the time that the item remains in inventory, however, the economy's general price level rises, enabling the manufacturer to sell it for $110 and record a $40 profit. Profit margins have not really risen to 36% in this product line, however, since the manufacturer's costs, as well as the selling price, have risen with inflation. Unless adjusted for this timing illusion, net income and cash flow overstate the firm's ongoing ability to pay dividends. FASB Accounting Standard No. 33 attempted to redress problems related to changing price levels by mandating supplementary financial statements that adjust for inflationary effects. In addition, companies can voluntarily apply **accelerated depreciation** and **LIFO (last-in, first-out) inventory accounting** to avoid overstating income and cash flow.

SUPPLEMENTS TO FINANCIAL STATEMENTS. These selected examples of distortions that can arise in the three key financial statements point out the need for information outside those documents in order to understand a firm fully. Similarly, our discussion of security evaluation brought out the need for additional information—namely, information about how the future may look. Exhibit 22 shows how financial statements fit into a broader array of information sources available to analysts and others with direct and indirect interests in business enterprises.

SUMMARY

Beginning with a sketch of the fundamental purposes of financial statements, we examined the makeup of the basic statements—balance sheet,

EXHIBIT 22   SOURCES OF FINANCIAL INFORMATION

All Information Useful for Investment, Credit, and Similar Decisions

Financial Reporting

——— Area Directly Affected by Existing FASB Standards ———

——— Core Financial Reporting ———

— Foundation of Financial Analysis —

Financial Statements	Notes to Financial Statements (and parenthetical disclosures)	Supplementary Information	Other Means of Financial Reporting	Other Information
	Examples:	Examples:	Examples:	Examples:
Balance sheet	Accounting policies	Changing prices disclosures	Management discussion and	Discussion of competition and order backlog in Securities and Exchange Commission's Form 10K
Income statement	Contingencies	Oil and gas reserves	Letters to stockholders	Analysts' reports
Funds flow statement	Inventory methods			Economic statistics
	Number of shares of stock outstanding			News articles about company
	Alternative measures (market values of items carried at historical cost)			

Source: Adapted from Financial Accounting Standards Board "Statement of Financial Concepts No. 5," December 1984.

income statement, and funds flow statement—and defined financial ratios that add meaning to the raw data they contain. The ratios, in turn, revealed more about the companies being studied when manipulated with ratio trend analysis and comparative ratio analysis. Still more specialized techniques helped us to evaluate the companies' securities. In both bond and stock analysis, however, we found that financial statements lacked some information essential to determining appropriate prices. Accordingly, we discussed some of the shortcomings of financial statements and means of avoiding the resulting pitfalls. We concluded by observing that financial statements, by themselves, are valuable but not totally adequate analytical resources. In fact, statements consciously prepared with an eye toward satisfying standard ratio guidelines can seriously mislead the uncritical user. Full understanding of a company's financial strength comes only through combining the best available techniques of ratio analysis with solid knowledge of the business, its management, and the economic and competitive environment in which it operates.

REFERENCES

Altman, Edward I., "Financial Ratios, Discriminant Analysis and the Prediction of Corporate Bankruptcy," *Journal of Finance,* September 1968, pp. 589–609.

Altman, Edward I., Haldeman, R.G., and Narayanan, P., "Zeta Analysis: A New Model to Identify Bankruptcy Risk of Corporations," *Journal of Banking and Finance,* June 1977, pp. 29–54.

Bernstein, Leopold A., and Siegel, Joel G., "The Concept of Earnings Quality," *Financial Analysts Journal,* July–August 1979.

Brealey, Richard, and Myers, Steward, *Principles of Corporate Finance,* McGraw-Hill, New York, 1981.

Brigham, Eugene E., *Financial Management: Theory and Practice,* 3d ed., Dryden Press, Hindsdale, IL, 1982.

Casey, Cornelius J., and Bartczak, Norman J., "Cash Flow—It's Not the Bottom Line," *Harvard Business Review,* July–August 1984.

Dieter, Richard, and Wyatt, Arthur R., "Get It Off the Balance Sheet!" *Financial Executive,* January 1980.

Ernst, Harry B., "New Balance Sheet for Managing Liquidity and Growth," *Harvard Business Review,* March–April 1984.

Financial Accounting Standards Board, "Statement of Financial Accounting Concepts No. 5," December 1984.

Foster, George, *Financial Statement Analysis,* Prentice-Hall, Englewood Cliffs, NJ, 1978.

Hawkins, David F., "Toward the New Balance Sheet," *Harvard Business Review,* November–December 1984.

Lev, Baruch, *Financial Statement Analysis: A New Approach,* Prentice-Hall, Englewood Cliffs, NJ, 1974.

Reiling, Henry B., and Burton, John C., "Financial Statements: Signposts as Well as Milestones," *Harvard Business Review*, November–December 1972.

Reilly, Frank K., *Investment Analysis and Portfolio Management*, Dryden Press, Hinsdale, Illinois 1979.

Sloan, Alfred P., Jr., *My Years with General Motors*, John McDonald and Catharine Stevens, Eds., Doubleday, 1963.

4

RETURN ON INVESTMENT AS A DYNAMIC MANAGEMENT PROCESS

CONTENTS

4

RETURN ON INVESTMENT AS A DYNAMIC MANAGEMENT PROCESS

J. Fred Weston

INTRODUCTION

Return on investment (ROI) planning and control techniques have been used in a number of ways—some good, some bad. If used in a static or mechanical way, the ROI approach can do more harm than good. If used as a part of a dynamic management process, the ROI philosophy can contribute substantially to the achievement of excellence and outstanding performance.

ROI is most useful when used as a part of a broader **planning and control system** in an organization. It is in this broader framework that ROI will be recommended as a useful part of the planning and control process.

The defects in the application of the ROI method of planning and control result from the confusion of goals and processes. Also, ROI systems and related systems have been installed with targets and standards used bureaucratically. However, targets and standards should be viewed as instruments for achieving adaptive learning processes in an organization. The ROI system can provide information on every element of the balance sheet, income statement, and other comprehensive performance statements serving as a vehicle for dynamic communications, feedback, and creative adjustments.

ROI AND DEPARTMENTATION

Most of today's modern corporations are set up on a divisional basis. Each division is usually treated as a **profit center** and each has its own identifiable investments—current and fixed assets. Each division is expected to earn an appropriate return on the assets under its control. The corporate headquarters or central staff typically controls the various divisions by the ROI standards. The fundamental emphasis of ROI control is efficient management of a multiform organization. It aims to achieve the benefits of multidivisions without excessive use of top management time.

The ROI system was developed before World War I by Donaldson Brown at the du Pont Company. When du Pont bought 23% of General Motors' common stock in 1921, Donaldson Brown was installed as the senior financial officer in the effort to improve the performance of GM. Alfred Sloan describes in his book, *My Years with General Motors,* 1964, how the financial planning and control system installed enabled GM to put its financial house in order to provide a foundation for strategies that would overcome the approximately 65% of auto market share then held by Ford Motor Company. The successful application of the du Pont system of financial planning and control at GM resulted in subsequent recognition of its excellence as an effective implementation of ROI planning and control.

THE DU PONT SYSTEM OF FINANCIAL ANALYSIS

The du Pont system brings together the fundamental elements of a financial ratio system. It shows how these ratios interact to determine the profitability of economic resources employed by the organization. This framework of analysis is consistent with the utilization of an investment hurdle rate. In other words, the economic resources committed to a division must earn the appropriate **risk-adjusted cost of capital** for the division.

The du Pont system is simply a chart method of performing financial ratio analysis. It seeks to convey visually the interrelationships between cost control and control of investment in various forms of assets and their impact on the bottom line, the before-tax return on investment. The original use of the du Pont system was for control of individual divisions. Since individual divisions are not responsible for factors effecting corporate taxes or the degree of leverage employed by the firm, the bottom line figure was the before-tax operating income to investment. Sometimes investment is defined gross of depreciation and sometimes net of depreciation. A reason for using gross investment is that the results are then less sensitive to the age of assets. On the other hand, in some sense net investments are the actual economic resources being utilized. Also, the use of a net investment figure makes the numerical results more comparable with industry composite ratios or other financial norms or standards available.

In spirit then, ROI planning and control is a form of **financial ratio analysis.** The relationship between the financial ratios represent a measure of performance. The ratios measure the degrees of efficiency or inefficiency. The emphasis of the du Pont chart is to identify the sources of the efficiency or inefficiency reflected in the financial measures. The degree of efficiency will be a critical influence on the ultimate valuation relationships for the firm. The extent to which the market value of the firm's equity exceeds its book value particularly reflects the firm's performance as measured by key financial ratios. In the same spirit, a **prediction of bankruptcy** or failure is based on a form of financial ratio analysis. In this case, the financial ratios are employed in a sophisticated statistical procedure utilizing what is called the **discriminant analysis** as pioneered by Altman (*Journal of Finance*, 1968 in his **Z-Score model).**

The fundamental nature of ROI planning and control as utilized in the du Pont system is suggested by Exhibit 1. The data in Exhibit 1 are for a firm whose before-tax return on investment is 21%. This is the result of operating earnings of 14% of sales multiplied by a sales to investment turnover of 1.5

EXHIBIT 1   DU PONT CHART FOR DIVISIONAL CONTROL

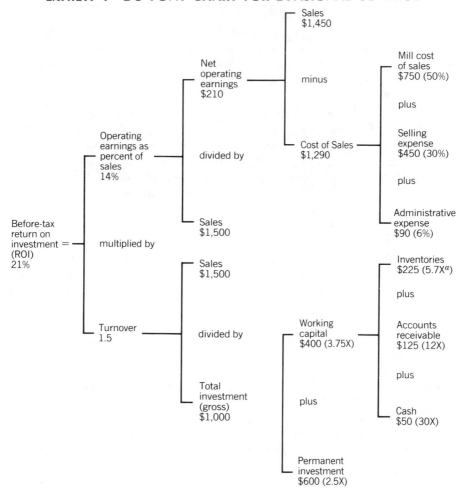

ª Cost of sales divided by inventories.

times. The net operating earnings as a percentage of sales reflect the total amount of operating earnings and the sales level. As shown in Exhibit 1, net operating earnings are the resultant of sales less the cost of sales. The cost of sales in turn represents the sum of the mill or factory cost of sales plus selling expense plus administrative expenses. Each of these items is also shown as a percentage of sales.

The turnover figure is the resultant of the relationship between sales and total gross investment. Total investment, in turn, is the sum of working capital investment plus the investment in fixed assets. **Working capital** is the sum of the major investments in cash receivables and inventories. Since investment is expressed as a turnover factor in relation to sales, each of the elements of investment is expressed in a similar fashion. The turnover of cash is shown as 30 times. The turnover of accounts receivable is shown as 12 times. The 12 times turnover of accounts receivable also represents slightly over a 30-day average collection period. The turnover of inventories is related to the cost of sales since inventories are carried on a cost basis. This contrasts with accounts receivable which are carried on the basis of the selling price of the goods sold and, therefore, more logically the turnover for accounts receivable is related to sales.

The value of the ROI planning and control method as expressed in the du Pont chart for divisional control is suggested by Exhibit 2. Here we reflect the effects when a firm develops excess inventories. The first effect is that inventories are larger than in Exhibit 1. But there are some derivative effects as well. Because inventories are excessive, this may cause selling expenses to be increased in the effort to move the growing inventory. The additional effort to push the inventories may also result in an increase in administrative expenses to some degree. Thus the cost of sales is shown to rise to $1,300.

The excess inventories may indicate some obsolescence of inventories. Also, in the effort to move the inventories there may be price reductions. As a consequence, the dollar volume of sales may decline as shown in Exhibit 2. Net operating earnings thus decline to $120. Expressed as a percent of sales the before-tax operating margin now becomes 8.28%. With the additional investment in inventories, the turnover declines from 1.5 to 1.29. The bottom line result is a decline in the before-tax return on investment from 21% to 10.68%.

Clearly, the sharp decline in the turnover ratio for inventories is the prime cause of the decline in the profit margin. The result shows up in the sharply reduced ROI. The du Pont approach provides a visual as well as analytical basis for isolating the causes of the decline in the operating margin as well as the drop in the turnover of total assets. Thus the value of the ROI approach was to provide a sophisticated form of financial ratio analysis that directed attention to the sources of a declining or low ROI.

The ROI approach as reflected in the du Pont system for divisional control has also been extended to the level of the firm as well. The success of the du Pont system as applied to managing divisions stimulated its use at the

EXHIBIT 2   EFFECT OF EXCESS INVESTMENT IN INVENTORY

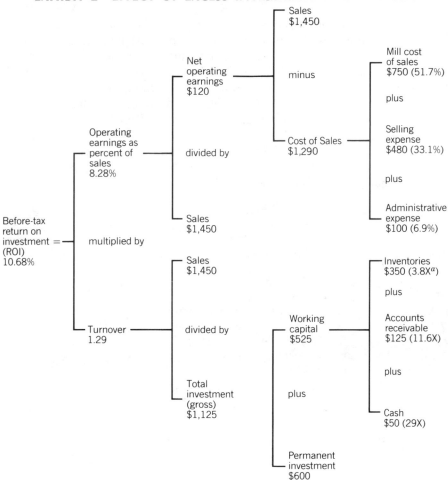

^aCost of sales divided by inventories.

overall level of the firm. When used at the level of the firm, both the effects of taxes and financial leverage are taken into account. The investment figure is then on a net basis and the income figure is net income after financial charges and taxes. Since the net income figure reflects taxes and leverage when applied to the level of the firm the emphasis then becomes the return on equity (ROE). The emphasis then shifts from ROI to ROE. A number of relationships have been developed from the standpoint of evaluation of a planning and control performance at the level of the firm as a whole. These have resulted in what are referred to as overall planning models. These will next be considered.

OVERALL PLANNING MODELS

The logic of the du Pont system for control in multidivision companies has been extended into broader overall planning models. These models provide a broad framework for understanding fundamental financial planning and control relationships. Since they generally emphasize the point of view of the firm as a whole the focus is on the return on equity after the influence of financial leverage and taxes are taken into account. To illustrate these fundamental **planning and control relationships** the following factors will be employed with numerical values that correspond to the average for all manufacturing firms in the United States in recent years. The notation will follow that found in the writings on the subject by Babcock (*Financial Analysts Journal,* January–February, 1980).

Symbol		Relationship	Numerical Value
T	=	Asset turnover	2X
m	=	Margin on sales	5%
L	=	Financial leverage	2X
b	=	Retention rate	.6
BV	=	Book value	
BVS	=	Book value per share	
EPS	=	Earnings per share	
DPS	=	Dividends per share	
G	=	Sustainable growth rate	

The ROE involves the three fundamental factors: turnover, margin, and leverage.

asset turnover × margin on sales × financial leverage
$$= \text{return on equity.}$$

These three fundamental factors are also expressed in terms of **ratios.**

$$\frac{\text{sales}}{\text{total assets}} \times \frac{\text{net income}}{\text{sales}} \times \frac{\text{total assets}}{\text{equity}} = \frac{\text{net income}}{\text{equity}}$$

In symbols we have TmL = ROE. With the numerical values suggested previously, ROE equals

$$2(.05)(2) = .20 = 20\%$$

With the knowledge of return on equity we can then calculate earnings per share (EPS):

return on equity × book value per share = earnings per share

$$\frac{\text{net income}}{\text{equity}} \times \frac{\text{equity}}{\text{number of shares}} = \frac{\text{net income}}{\text{number of shares}} = \text{EPS}$$

The earnings per share figure is widely used but reflects some arbitrary elements such as the number of shares outstanding. In order to provide a numerical illustration, we therefore need two additional items of information. One is the size of the firm. The other is the number of equity shares outstanding. It will be noted that the return on equity measure above could be calculated independent of these two additional pieces of information. Let us assume a firm with total assets of $100 million and one million shares of equity stock outstanding. The earnings per share would therefore be:

$$\frac{\$10\text{ million}}{\$50\text{ million}} \times \frac{\$50\text{ million}}{1\text{ million}} = \$10 \text{ per share}$$

Having earnings per share, it is a short step to obtain dividends per share. The additional item needed is the dividend payout. The dividend payout is 1 minus the retention rate (b) or is equal to:

$$(1 - b) = (1 - .6) = .4$$

For dividends per share we therefore have:

$$\text{earnings per share} \times \text{dividend payout} = \text{dividends per share}$$

$$\frac{\text{net income}}{\text{number of shares}} \times \frac{\text{dividends}}{\text{net income}} = \frac{\text{dividends}}{\text{number of shares}} = \text{DPS}$$

We already have all of the numerical values for making the calculation. It is simply:

$$\$10(.4) = \$4$$

   Much has been written on the concept of **sustainable dividend growth.** This can be expressed as the dollar amount of total dividends or the dollar amount of dividends per share. The concept involves nothing more than bringing together all of the factors for each of the target measures discussed to this point. The full set of factors for calculating dividends per share is now exhibited.

$$\frac{\text{sales}}{\text{total assets}} \times \frac{\text{net income}}{\text{sales}} \times \frac{\text{total assets}}{\text{equity}} \times \frac{\text{equity}}{\text{number of shares}}$$

$$\times \frac{\text{dividends paid}}{\text{net income}} = \text{dividends per share}$$

In symbols and numbers we have:

$$T \times m \times L \times BVS \times (1 - b) = DPS$$
$$2 \times .05 \times 2 \times \$50 \times .4 = \$4 \text{ per share}$$

To obtain the total amount of dividends we would use total book value rather than book value per share. In symbols:

$$T \times m \times L \times BV \times (1 - b) = \text{dividends}$$

The $50 would now represent $50 million and the total amount of dividends would be $4 million.

Related to the idea of sustainable dividends is the concept of **sustainable growth rate.** It again involves the use of factors we have already discussed arranged in a slightly different manner. The sustainable growth rate is simply the return on equity times the retention rate. Hence we have:

$$T \times m \times L \times b = \text{sustainable growth rate}$$

For our example we would have:

$$2 \times .05 \times 2 \times .6 = 12\% = \text{sustainable growth rate}$$

While the relationship appears to be simple, there is much business and financial analysis involved in the concept of sustainable growth rate. Each of the factors in the equation represents an important aspect of business decision making. Turnover refers to the effectiveness with which the firm's assets or resources are utilized. The **profit margin on sales** is an important measure of how well the firm has managed its costs in relationship to the prices received for its products. **Financial leverage** is one of the key aspects of financial decision making. The **retention rate** reflects investment requirements in relation to an important component of the firm's free cash flows.

While the above relationships are relatively simple, they provide the basic framework for highly sophisticated computerized business and **financial planning models.** No matter how bulky the computer output analysis may appear, the underlying relationships involved are the patterns which have been discussed in this section. These relationships can be calculated for business firms or segments of an operation with the use of hand calculators. They provide important insights for financial planning and control. Additional refinements and details may then be explored with the use of more elaborate computerized models.

The du Pont system as applied at the level of division has now been described and illustrated. Its extention into overall planning models for the firm has also been set forth. Next, the benefits of the ROI or ROE approach will be described after which some of the defects and pitfalls that have developed will be indicated. Finally, the potentials for ROI and ROE methodologies when they are used in a dynamic and flexible way will be explained.

THE BENEFITS OF ROI PLANNING AND CONTROL

When the du Pont system is used for **divisional control,** the process is often called ROI control. Here, return is measured by operating earnings—that is, income before interest and taxes. Sometimes the earnings figure is calculated before depreciation, and total gross assets are measured before deduction of the depreciation reserve. Measurement on gross assets has the advantage of avoiding differences in ROI due to differences in the average age of the fixed assets. Older assets are more fully depreciated and have a higher depreciation reserve and lower net fixed asset amount. This causes the ROI on net total assets to be higher when fixed assets are older.

If a particular division's ROI falls below a target figure, then the centralized corporate staff helps the division's own financial staff trace back through the du Pont system to determine the cause of the substandard ROI. Each division manager is judged by the division's ROI and rewarded or penalized accordingly. Division managers are thus motivated to keep their ROI up to the target level. Their individual actions should in turn maintain the firm's ROI at an appropriate level.

In addition to its use in managerial control, ROI can be used to allocate funds to the various divisions. The firm as a whole has financial resources—retained earnings, cash flow from depreciation, and the ability to obtain additional debt and equity funds from capital markets. These funds can be allocated on the basis of the divisional ROI's, with divisions having high ROI's receiving more funds than those with low ones.

Four major benefits of ROI planning and control are possible. First, it is a single, comprehensive measure, influenced by everything that has happened which affects the financial status of the divisions. Every item in the du Pont chart is related to its effect on either turnover or profit margin, and through either of these to its effect on ROI. If an alternative organization of the financial planning and control system is desired, the required information for doing so has been assembled.

The second advantage is that ROI measures the division manager's use of resource allocations, thereby providing a means for detailed postauditing capital investment proposals. A third advantage is that ROI is a common denominator so that comparisons can be made directly among divisions within the company, with outside companies, or with alternative investment of funds generally. Fourth, motivation will be high since the manager is evaluated on his ability to optimize ROI.

SHORTCOMINGS OF ROI CONTROL

Any system of divisional control runs the risk that executives will devise methods for "beating the system." Hence, a number of problems can arise if ROI control is used without proper safeguards. Since the divisional managers are rewarded on the basis of their ROI performance, it is absolutely essential for their morale that they feel their divisional ROI does indeed provide an accurate measure of relative performance. But ROI is dependent on a number of factors in addition to managerial competence; some of these factors are listed in the following.

1. *Depreciation.*   ROI is very sensitive to depreciation policy. If one division is writing off assets at a relatively rapid rate, its annual profits—and hence its ROI—will be reduced.

2. *Book Value of Assets.*   If an older division is using assets that have been largely written off, both its current depreciation charges and its investment base will be low. This will make its ROI high in relation to newer divisions.

3. *Transfer Pricing.*   In most corporations some divisions sell to other divisions. At General Motors, for example, the Fisher Body Division sells to the Chevrolet Division. In such cases the price at which goods are transferred between divisions has a fundamental effect on divisional profits. If the transfer price of auto bodies is set relatively high, then Fisher Body will have a relatively high ROI and Chevrolet a relatively low one.

4. *Time Periods.*   Many projects have long gestation periods, during which expenditures must be made for research and development, plant construction, market development, and the like. Such expenditures add to the investment base without a commensurate increase in profits for several years. During this period, a division's ROI can be seriously reduced; and without proper constraints, its manager may be improperly penalized. Given the frequency of personnel transfers in larger corporations, it is easy to see how the timing problem can keep managers from making long-term investments that are in the best interests of the firm.

5. *Industry Conditions.*   If one division is operating in an industry where conditions are favorable and rates of return are high, while another is in an industry suffering from excessive competition, the environmental differences may cause the favored division to look good and the unfavored one to look bad, apart from any differences in their managers. For example, Signal Companies' aerospace division could hardly have been expected to perform as well as their truck division did in 1973, when the entire aerospace industry suffered severe problems and truck

sales soared. External conditions must be taken into account when appraising ROI performance.

Because of these factors, a division's ROI must be supplemented with other criteria for evaluating performance. For example, its growth rate in sales, profits, and market share (as well as its ROI) in comparison with other firms in its own industry has been used in such evaluations. Although ROI control has been used with great success in U.S. industry, the system cannot be used in a mechanical sense by inexperienced personnel. As with most other tools, it is helpful if used properly but destructive if misused.

In summary, three major categories of defects have been found in the ROI control approach. The first category includes over-simplification of a complex decision making process, failure to distinguish the required rate of ROI in common assets used in different divisions that may have different ROI targets, and difficulties arising out of accounting methods measuring ROI. A review of these technical defects suggests that many of them are arbitrary procedures not inherent in the method. Many criticisms of this method of planning and control stem from the predilection of accounting systems for recording the expiration of historical costs, and hence reflect the limitations of traditional accounting methods.

The second category of difficulty is that of assigning responsibility. Inherently, many decision areas involve the joint participation of a number of divisions and different levels of authority. Consequently, assigning responsibility for results is difficult under a static method.

The third and most fundamental criticism is that any static control system is likely to have motivational defects. *Any* static control method will invite a wide range of practices for beating the system. In addition, there are important additional positive values not captured by the static concept. Therefore, it is important to view the du Pont or ROI system in its correct exposition—the du Pont planning and control system as a dynamic process.

ROI AS A DYNAMIC PROCESS

Too often the ROI approach has been reflected in short-term business planning. This has been referred to in the literature as "planning and control for profit," **"management by objectives" (MBO)**, or **"management information systems" (MIS).**

To be most effective the ROI method must be related to broader planning and control processes in the firm. Case study analysis and field interviews with most of the firms in the *Fortune 100,* as well as a broad sample of smaller firms, suggests three central principles to be followed in a dynamic planning and control process. These concepts, which will be discussed individually, are:

1. The necessity for an open systems approach in which administrative and operating planning are formulated within the overall framework of strategic planning.
2. An activity that is process-oriented rather than goal oriented.
3. A dynamic systems approach in which search, a review and feedback process and adaptive learning are involved.

AN OPEN SYSTEMS APPROACH IN STRATEGIC PLANNING. The environments of business firms have been changing so rapidly that a major and critical element for survival of the business firm is effective adaptation to and anticipation of changes in its environment. These environmental influences include technological, social, political, and economic changes. Accelerated research and development activities have resulted in a number of manifestations of increased technological change. Products have been obsoleted at higher rates. Individual product life cycles have been shortened. The pace at which new products have substituted for existing products has increased. New attractive growth potentials have arisen in new and diverse sectors of the economy.

Advances in communication and technology have had important social impacts. Population profiles and the rates of growth of different age groups in the population have been shifting. Product demand patterns have reflected changes in the population and income distribution patterns. The value systems of society have changed and the expectations of business firms have, therefore, altered. These, in turn, have given rise to important political and economic developments.

The increased importance of environmental influences have lead to the recognition of strategic planning as of central and critical importance to the business organization. The central aim of strategic planning is to guide resource allocation commitments so that a company "will be in the right business with the right resources to serve the world and the future."

The methodology of **strategic planning** involves a series of decision processes which can be summarized in the following outline:

1. State the firm's objective.
2. Define the nature of the firm's environment.
3. Evaluate the firm's strengths and weaknesses in relation to its environment.
4. Assess the firm's potential in its environment.
5. Compare the potential with the firm's objectives.
6. If a gap exists, search for alternatives for closing the gap between potential and objectives.
7. Select alternatives for analysis.
8. The benefits and costs of alternative policies are calculated.

9. A tentative selection from among alternatives is made (i.e., a plan is formulated).

10. The process is repeated to check the conclusions reached. Sometimes the process is gone through first from a research standpoint, from a production standpoint, from a marketing standpoint, from a financial standpoint, and finally from an over-all enterprise or systems approach.

11. Resources are committed to implement a plan.

12. A follow-up is performed to compare performance with plan.

13. The comparison of objectives and prospects is repeated.

The crucial decision point in the foregoing process is the finding of a **"strategic planning gap"**—that is, the negative gap between the prospective results and the firm's stated goals. The firm must either revise its goals downward or make important judgments on whether its present capabilities can be so altered and augmented to improve its future prospects.

This brief summary of the nature of strategic planning emphasizes two important points. One point is that while a firm might perform its administrative planning and operations effectively on a day-to-day basis, major changes in the environment coupled with inadequate strategic planning can leave such a firm with no assurance of survival—let alone achieving measures of efficiency.

The second important point is that meaningful and effective short-range budgeting, planning, and other tools of financial forecasting must be made within the broader framework of strategic planning. Articles on the du Pont experience indicated that a weakness was an over-emphasis on operating performance that appeared to be engendered by excessive preoccupation with ROI.

This failure to relate to the more dynamic aspects of strategic planning appears to have been reflected in the eight attributes of excellence chosen by Peters and Waterman (*In Search of Excellence,* 1982). These eight attributes are: (1) bias for action; (2) staying close to the competitor; (3) autonomy and entrepreneurship; (4) productivity through people; (5) hands-on value-driven; (6) stick to the knitting; (7) simple form lean staff; and (8) simultaneous loose-tight properties. These attributes appear to emphasize operating aspects of the firm.

A subsequent article by *Business Week* entitled, "Who's Excellent Now?" critiqued the Peters and Waterman book. A number of the firms that had been cited as excellent companies by Peters and Waterman subsequently encountered difficulties. The main factor causing their problems appear to be failure to promptly adjust to their changing external economic, financial, and competitive environments. This emphasizes the importance of relating both short-term plans and operating procedures to the broader framework of longer-term strategic planning.

GOAL VERSUS PROCESS ORIENTATION. An effective ROI planning and control system is not goal centered. Managers are not evaluated on the size of the return on investment earned by their division. Performance evaluation is related to the *potential* for the division, and not to any absolute standard. A manager able to hold the loss in a division to 10% in a product market characterized by severe excess capacity may be rated higher than a manager who achieves a positive 20% return on investment in a product market area where, at least temporarily, the sales/capacity relations may have made a 30% ROI possible.

Similarly, if the risks of a divisional operation are high, there will be a minimum screening standard or **investment hurdle rate** that will be higher than for a less risky division. For example, the return on investments for oil exploration will be higher than the return on the investment in the land on which a filling station is placed, because the results of the operations of the filling station are more predictable than oil exploration. A company contemplating the establishment of a manufacturing operation in a foreign country, and thus subject to a wide range of political as well as foreign exchange fluctuation risks, will require a greater return on that activity than the return on expanding its capacity to produce and sell a staple consumer nondurable good.

An important aspect of the evaluation of performance is the divergence between the actual results for a division and the projections which predominantly reflect the inputs of the responsible managers. The comparison of actual results with projected targets is more important than specific goal orientation, because errors in *either* direction result in misallocation of resources. Consider, for example, a manager who forecasts a 12% return and actually achieves a 20% return. When the corporate allocation of resources is made by the Finance Committee, the project promising a 12% return, may result in an allocation of $1 million for that investment. But if the expected return is 20%, a $2 million investment might be allocated. Hence, errors in either direction result in a misallocation of resources.

Thus, performance is related to the potentials and not to any absolute standard. Nor is it accurate to characterize the ROI planning and control system as one in which the emphasis is that results conform to budgets or projections. The philosophy of the dynamic ROI planning and control process recognizes dynamic variables exogenous to the firm (for example, economy changes, competitive conditions change, elements of costs change, and so on). These changes are taken into consideration in comparing projections with performance. To some extent it might have been expected that alert and able managers would have anticipated some of the changes.

THE SYSTEMS APPROACH. The ROI process starts with broad planning premises communicated by the corporate level office to the operating divisions. This broad planning framework is the basis for initial plans and proposals by individual operating units to the division and group levels where they receive initial review. After these initial screenings and review, plans and proposals are communicated to a corporate level group, such as the Finance Committee, for resource allocation decisions. These plans and proposals are formulated primarily from "below" and communicated upward. The initial function of the corporate level is capital allocation and rationing.

After budgets have been adopted and resource allocations made, provision is made for a feedback system through periodic reviews of performance. In a cycling procedure, a quarterly review takes place. The timing is prior to and provides a basis for another four-quarter forecast in which a new fourth quarter is forecast for the first time. The reviews and revisions of projections are more frequent for operations subject to highly dynamic influences.

A number of important aspects of this process deserve emphasis. First, it represents an information flow in a communication process. This does not represent budgets imposed on subordinates by superiors. It represents participation in the formulation of budgets. Indeed, primary responsibility is in budget formulation at the operating levels responsible for subsequent performance.

Second, the review process should be viewed as the establishment of an information and communication flow. This process does not represent top management telling subordinates what to do; it is not subordinates attempting to fool corporate level management with phony forecasts.

The process represents the establishment of a two-way information flow. In this information flow, a critical and important element is that the review is conducted by experienced, informed executives. The informed review process provides a basis for achieving increased understanding. The increased understanding provides a basis for an adaptive learning in the firm. Thus, the process provides a mechanism for a feedback process for adjusting policies. It represents a dynamic, adaptive learning process. The essence of the dynamic ROI planning and control process is to shorten reaction time to change or error and to anticipate new opportunities. It thus provides a basis for continuous improvement.

EVALUATIONS OF ROI AS A DYNAMIC PROCESS

Most criticism of the ROI control method are applicable only to the static formulation. The use of any type of static control system develops incentives in the wrong direction, leads to the development of devices for beating the system, and results in the wrong motivations. But in the dynamic management control system described, this major defect of the static ROI method is eliminated. Particularly, the informed review process and the two-way information flow system make for good communication and understanding. The process then becomes a vehicle for continued improvements and provides strong motivations in the proper directions.

A major problem in the utilization of the ROI method of control is the failure of companies to adopt its dynamic elements. One reason for this failure is that so many firms came to the method relatively late. The systematic literature on the "principles of management" developed after the mid-1950s. Particularly, the literature on long-range planning did not appear until after 1955. The emergence of second-generation computers with their increased information processing and retrieval capabilities gave impetus to formal methods of planning and control.

Widespread adoption of decentralized responsibility utilized the device to profit centers. Implementation of the profit center concept involves determination of the amount of profit and relating it to some base to determine a profitability rate. Thus, to some degree, the development of measures of performance of investment centers represents an index of the extent to which an important development in planning and control activities had taken place.

According to a survey by Mauriel and Anthony, firms were slow in adopting the ROI and profit center approach. As of mid-1965, 60% of 2658 respondents indicated the use of investment centers. Of those firms not using investment centers, about two-thirds indicated that they did not have two or more profit centers or that capital assets were relatively less significant in determining the performance of their business. It is difficult to assess whether the firms not employing profit centers should have done so for effective planning and control of their operations. Perhaps of greater significance is the timing of the adoption of investment centers in performance measures of decentralized divisions. Of 851 large American firms that responded to an inquiry with respect to how they utilized the analysis of **investment center performance,** 60% indicated that they adopted the method after 1955, and over 37% adopted the method after 1960. When the learning aspects of the dynamic control system are taken into account, it is sobering to reflect on persistent differentials in organization effectiveness that may have been caused by the lag in the adoption of modern management control methods in a large number of American corporations.

Hence, one reason why the ROI method of control is used in its static form may stem from its late installation by so many large companies. In its static form, the method is relatively mechanical in its installation and operation. Thus, it is easier to understand and easier to install. Furthermore, the review and information flow process cannot be installed as an ongoing dynamic system from the very beginning. There is an important learning element involved. This may require various forms of experimentation by companies in order to superimpose a dynamic control system on the methods of management control processes then in use.

Indeed, the difficulties of applying the ROI method in a flexible and dynamic way appear to have been experienced at the du Pont Company itself. In the early 1970s changes in the role of the Review Committee were developed. The emphasis became oriented to projections rather than to historical reviews. Another change was the recognition of adjusting the investment hurdle rate to the risks and opportunities in individual segments of the business. Another change was to more effectively integrate strategy planning with operations planning and control.

THE POTENTIAL ROLE OF ROI PLANNING AND CONTROL

After a number of years even its originator had to adapt and improve its ROI planning and control system. Even more learning was required in many firms that had adopted planning and control efforts relatively late and began with a relatively static historical accounting orientation. Direct interviews with a large number of these companies indicated three major types of difficulties that had to be overcome.

First, the most widespread errors involved a static approach to planning and control. A related error has been the reflection of the emphasis of classical management theory of a strict top-down planning approach in which the standards of performance were imposed from above. The resulting rigidity has resulted in continuing conflicts between the corporate office and the operating divisions. Second, these problems have been aggravated by the domination of short-term budgeting operations by traditional accounting practices. The third major defect was the closed systems approach in which budgeting was carried out without effective integration with strategic and long-range planning.

None of the observed errors is inherent in the ROI method. The central error is in the confusion of goals and process. But both businesspeople and theorists have committed the error of treating these objectives as ends in themselves. Without a full understanding of the dynamics of planning and control systems, business firms have installed ROI or other forms of management information systems, using the targets and standards bureaucratically.

Economists have also misinterpreted targets as goals rather than as instruments for coordination of decentralized divisions. Specific management function areas such as a marketing or engineering departments are likely to place greater emphasis on the importance of targets than the general office executives. In surveying such departments an exaggerated impression of the role of targets may be obtained.

However, the targets and standards by which managers seek to make the goals of the firm operational are not ends in themselves. Rather, they should be viewed as management instruments for engendering healthy processes in the firm. Targets and standards can be employed to contribute to an information and feedback process that is dynamic in quality, has favorable effects on the development of the firm's personnel, and can facilitate fast reaction time to change.

The ROI system of planning and control is a useful vehicle for assembling relevant information. It is not critical whether that information is focused on ROI or other "organization objectives." ROI is useful in providing information on every element of the balance sheet and income statement as a basis for further analysis. As a vehicle for a dynamic communication, feedback, and adjustment process, ROI, as well as other management information systems appropriately employed, can potentially be useful for developing healthy processes in successfully functioning firms.

REFERENCES

Altman, Edward I., "Financial Ratios, Discriminant Analysis, and the Prediction of Corporate Bankruptcy," *Journal of Finance,* September 1968, pp. 589–609.

Altman, Edward I., Haldeman, Robert G., and Narayanan, P., "ZETA Analysis: New Model to Identify Bankruptcy Risk of Corporations," *Journal of Banking and Finance,* June 1977, pp. 29–54.

Babcock, G. C., "The Roots of Risk and Return," *Financial Analysts Journal,* January–February 1980, pp. 56–63.

Babcock, G. C., "The Concept of Sustainable Growth," *Financial Analysts Journal,* May–June 1970, pp. 108–114.

Higgins, Robert C., "Sustainable Growth under Inflation," *Financial Management,* Autumn 1981, pp. 36–40.

Mauriel, John J., and Robert N. Anthony, "Misevaluation of Investment Center Performance," *Harvard Business Review,* March–April 1966, pp. 98–105.

Peters, Thomas J., and Austin, Nancy, *A Passion for Excellence: The Leadership Difference,* Random House, New York, 1985.

Peters, Thomas J., and Waterman, Robert H., Jr., *In Search of Excellence,* Harper & Row, New York, 1982.

Rappaport, Alfred, "Measuring Company Growth Capacity during Inflation," *Harvard Business Review,* January–February 1979, pp. 91–100.

Sloan, Alfred P., Jr., *My Years with General Motors,* Doubleday, Garden City, NY, 1964.

"Who's Excellent Now?" *BusinessWeek,* November 5, 1984, pp. 76–88.

Zakon, Alan J., "Capital Structure Organization," Chapter 30 in *The Treasurer's Handbook,* J. Fred Weston and Maurice B. Goudzwaard, Eds., Dow Jones-Irwin, Homewood, IL, 1976, pp. 641–668.

5

AN OPTIONS APPROACH TO CORPORATE FINANCE

CONTENTS

5

AN OPTIONS APPROACH TO CORPORATE FINANCE

W. Carl Kester

INTRODUCTION

This section provides an overview of option pricing analysis as it applies to corporate finance. A major breakthrough in finance was achieved in 1973 with the introduction of an **option pricing formula** developed by Fischer Black and Myron Scholes, (*Journal of Political Economy,* 81 (1973)). The implications of that advance go far beyond the pricing of ordinary warrants, call options, and put options, however. Specifically:

1. **Equity** and other **corporate liabilities** can be construed and valued as special types of options.
2. Discretionary opportunities to invest in real assets can be treated as options with important implications for capital budgeting.

Indeed, it can reasonably be asserted that virtually every corporate finance decision involving the issuance of securities or the commitment of capital to a project involves options in one way or another.

The advantages of approaching corporate finance from an options perspective are several:

1. Complex securities can be better understood and, in principle, valued directly using an options framework.
2. Interactions among various types of securities represented within a single capital structure can be more easily exposed and analyzed in an internally consistent manner.
3. Some shortcomings in the use of ordinary **net present value analysis** for **capital budgeting** purposes can be overcome.
4. Common ground for uniting capital budgeting and **strategic planning** can be established.

The first part of this section provides a fundamental background in option pricing principles. The applications of these principles to the pricing of corporate liabilities and capital budgeting are discussed in each of the next two parts, respectively. The final part is devoted to the problem of quantitatively estimating value when applying an options framework to corporate finance decisions.

OPTION CHARACTERISTICS

Before applying option pricing principles to corporate finance problems, it is first necessary to establish some background about option contracts. Because many people are already familiar with options on securities, this background will be developed within the context of securities and securities markets.

A complete description of options markets and instruments is provided in Section 9 of the *Handbook of Financial Markets & Institutions*, 6th ed. (Wiley, 1986). Interested readers may find this additional background helpful. However, for purposes of this section, the following condensed treatment of option contracts will provide a sufficient conceptual foundation.

DEFINITIONS

Call Option. A call option is a negotiable contract giving its owner the right (as distinct from the obligation) to purchase a specified number of shares of stock from the writer of the contract at a prespecified price on or before a prespecified date.

Put Option. The opposite of a call option, a put option is a negotiable contract giving its owner the right (but no obligation) to sell a specified number of shares of stock to the writer of the contract at a prespecified price on or before a prespecified date.

Exercise Price. The exercise price of an option is the prespecified amount that a **call option** owner must pay the writer, or that the **put option** owner will receive from the writer, for the underlying stock if the option is exercised.

Expiration or Maturity Date. The prespecified date after which the option contract is void. Options that are exercisable on or before the expiration date often referred to as **American options.** Those exercisable only on the date of expiration, and not before, are often referred to as **European options.** Calls and puts that trade on the Chicago Board Options Exchange (CBOE) are American options.

Intrinsic Value. The intrinsic value of an option is the greater of zero and the difference between the current market price of the underlying stock and the option's exercise price. In the case of a call option, this intrinsic value will be positive when the market price of the stock exceeds the exercise price of the option and zero otherwise. The opposite is true in the case of put options.

The intrinsic value can never be less than zero because option contracts entail no obligation to exercise. Rational owners of options would never exercise their rights under the option if they would incur a loss in doing so. Hence, the intrinsic value of the option has a floor value of zero.

In-the-Money and Out-of-the-Money Options. An option is said to be in the money when its intrinsic value is positive and out of the money otherwise. If the market price of the underlying stock is far above (below) the exercise price of a call (put) option, then the option is said to be "deep in the money." If the opposite is true, it is said to be "deep out of the money."

Option Premium. The option premium is the actual value or price of an option contract. The premium can never be less than zero and, for various reasons discussed in the following, will always be greater than the intrinsic value so long as some time remains before expiration.

Call Option Example. Consider a call option written for 100 shares of IBM stock with an **exercise price** of $115 per share and an expiration date six months in the future. If the market price of IBM's stock is $125 per share, then the option would be "in the money" with an intrinsic value of:

$$(\$125 - \$115) \times 100 \text{ shares} = \$1,000$$

Under reasonable assumptions, however, its premium might actually be $2,000 since there are six months before maturity and a chance that IBM will appreciate in value considerably during that time. If the price of IBM's stock was still above $115 per share six months later, then it would be worth exercising at a total cost of $11,500. If not, it would be allowed to expire worthless.

A comparable put option on IBM's stock would be "out of the money" if its exercise price is $115 per share and the market price is $125 per share. Although its intrinsic value would be zero under these conditions, its premium would probably be about $500 since there is some chance that IBM could fall in value during the next six months. If the price of IBM's stock does not drop below $115 per share during the next six months, then this premium will eventually dwindle to zero by the expiration date. However, should the put option's owner be fortunate enough to see the stock's price fall to, say, $75 per share, then the put would be "deep in the money" with an intrinsic value of $4,000.

The payoffs at expiration received by the owner of an IBM call and an IBM put with the above characteristics are shown in Exhibit 1. It is assumed that the call and put are each purchased at the aforementioned premiums and commission costs are ignored.

Note that the owner of this IBM call option is in a net loss position until the value of the IBM stock exceeds the exercise price by an amount equal to the premium paid for the call. Thereafter, net profit increases dollar for dollar as the value of the underlying stock increases.

EXHIBIT 1   PROFIT POSITIONS OF THE BUYER OF AN IBM CALL OPTION AND IBM PUT OPTION

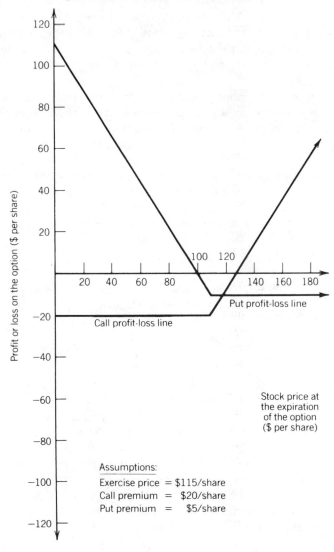

Conversely, the put option's owner is in a net loss position until the value of the IBM stock falls below the exercise price by an amount equal to the premium paid for the put. Net profit also increases dollar for dollar thereafter as the value of the stock falls, but reaches a maximum of $11,000 when the price of the stock hits zero.

BASIC DETERMINANTS OF OPTION VALUE. For a stock that receives no dividends or other types of cash disbursements, there are five basic determinants of an option's value. The effect of each on a call option, holding other factors constant, is discussed in the following.

Stock Price. The higher the price of the stock underlying the call option, the greater the option's intrinsic value and the more likely it will remain above the exercise price at expiration. Hence, the higher the stock price, the greater will be the premium of the call option.

Exercise Price. The higher the exercise price, the lower the intrinsic value of the option and the less likely it is that the option will be worth anything at maturity. Hence, the higher the exercise price, the smaller will be the premium of the call option.

Interest Rates. The higher are the interest rates, the more valuable the call option will be, if other determinants remain constant. This result occurs because higher interest rates implies a lower present value of the anticipated future exercise payment. This makes the option worth more in the present for a given fair market value of the stock.

One can gain intuition on this point by thinking of owning a call option as being tantamount to buying the underlying stock using some "free" credit. A partial payment is made now in the amount of the call option's premium, and an arrangement is simultaneously made to pay an additional amount (equal to the option's exercise price) at a future date (the maturity date). In effect, the total price paid for the stock is the cash outlay plus the future payment converted to present value dollars. The present value of this future payment declines as interest rates rise. For a given fair market value of the stock, this must mean that the initial cash outlay, which is equivalent to the option's premium, must increase.

Volatility of the Stock Price. Other determinants remaining unchanged, the more volatile the stock price, the more valuable the option. This may seem counter-intuitive since greater risk is often thought to require higher expected returns and, thus, lower present values in order to assure those future returns. The opposite result occurs in the case of options because of the asymmetry between potential upside gains and downside losses. As illustrated by the call option's payoff line in Exhibit 1, there are unlimited potential gains as the price of the stock increases. However, losses can be cut by simply not exercising the option if the stock's price falls below the exercise price. In other words, greater volatility increases the chance of realizing a large gain without equally increasing the chance of incurring a large loss. Hence, greater volatility increases option premiums.

Time to Maturity. Call options increase in value when the time remaining to maturity is further away. This positive influence derives from two sources. First, in connection with the interest rate effect, the longer the time before maturity when the exercise payment will be made, the lower the discounted present value of that payment. Second, in connection with the volatility effect, the more time there is before expiration, the more likely it is that a large price change can occur and dramatically increase the value of the option. So long as there is time remaining before expiration, an option's premium will exceed its intrinsic value, as shown in Exhibit 2. It follows that a call option should not be exercised before maturity since doing so would sacrifice the value attributable to time.

For stocks that pay a cash dividend, the **dividend yield** of the stock represents another important determinant of value. Unless the option's owner is protected against cash disbursements to shareholders, a cash dividend payout will lower the **exdividend price** of the stock and result in a loss of value to the call option. If the anticipated drop in value on the exdividend

EXHIBIT 2   CALL OPTION PREMIUM IN RELATION TO INTRINSIC VALUE

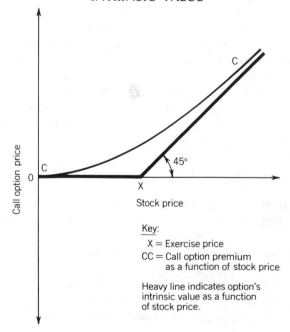

Key:

X = Exercise price

CC = Call option premium
as a function of stock price

Heavy line indicates option's
intrinsic value as a function
of stock price.

date is large enough, the option's owner might even be better off exercising the option early, thus effectively shortening the time to maturity. Because of these effects, higher dividend yields will lower a call option's premium, other things being equal.

The same factors that influence the value of a call option also influence the value of a put option, although usually in the opposite way. The two exceptions are the time to maturity and volatility. Because of the asymmetry between potential gains and losses from holding a put option (see the put option's payoff profile in Exhibit 1), high volatility continues to play a positive role in determining a put's value.

The time to maturity can be either a positive or negative influence depending on which of two effects dominate. When the put is in the money, a longer time to maturity will be a negative influence because the expected receipt of proceeds from exercising the put is delayed. However, if the put is deep out of the money, a long time to maturity will enhance value. This is because more time provides a greater opportunity for the stock price to drop far enough to make the put valuable at expiration. Of course, the stock price could rise as well, but, as in the case of call options, losses on the downside are limited relative to potential gains.

OPTION PRICING FORMULAS. A theoretical formula for valuing call options on nondividend paying stocks was developed by **Fischer Black and Myron Scholes** in 1973. The formula is presented in Exhibit 3. A more complete discussion of its derivation and underlying assumptions is provided in the mathematical appendix to this volume. For the purposes of this section, it is sufficient to note that the formula does, in fact, depend on the five major

EXHIBIT 3   THE BLACK-SCHOLES OPTION PRICING FORMULA

$$V_c = P_s N(d_1) - S e^{(t - t^*)} N(d_2)$$

$$d_1 = \frac{\ln(P_s/S) + (r + 1/2 v^2)(t^* - t)}{v\sqrt{(t^* - t)}}$$

$$d_2 = \frac{\ln(P_{s/S}) + (r - 1/2 v^2)(t^* - t)}{v\sqrt{(t^* - t)}}$$

V_c = Fair market value of the call option
P_s = Price of the underlying stock
S = Exercise price
$N(d)$ = Cumulative normal density function
r = Risk-free interest rate
t = Current date
t^* = Maturity date of the call option
v^2 = Variance rate of return on the stock
e = Natural logarithm base = 2.71828
$\ln$ = Natural logarithm

determinants of value discussed earlier, (r) being the yield on risk-free debt such as government bonds.

It is also worth noting what does not appear in the formula, however. The formula does not require special information about any one investor's attitude toward risk. Thus, it provides a purely objective, widely applicable means of determining an option's fair market value. Also, the formula does not require knowledge of expected rates of return on the underlying stock. This is useful since expected rates of return are neither directly observable nor easily estimated from past data on price movements. All the other components of the formula are observable or easily estimated. The applications of this formula and other option pricing techniques to corporate finance problems are discussed in the final part of this section.

PUT-CALL PARITY. Consider once again the example of the IBM call option and the IBM put option provided above. Because both types of options are written on the same stock and are assumed to have the same exercise price and time to maturity, it seems reasonable to suppose that their respective prices would be related to one another in a predictable way. That is, as the price of IBM's stock changes from day to day, the call option and put option prices should also change—but the change should be such that an astute investor could not buy one and sell the other so as to lock in a virtually riskless profit. Indeed, should such an **arbitrage** opportunity develop, the very act of exploiting it ought to set buy and sell transactions in motion that will ultimately ensure a kind of parity between put and call prices.

This is, in fact, the case. The precise relation between the value of a put option and the value of a call option on the same stock with the same exercise price and time to maturity is shown below.

$$V_p = V_c - P_s + Se^{r(t - t^*)}$$

or

$$V_c - V_p = P_s - Se^{r(t - t^*)}$$

V_p represents the price of the put option and the others are as defined in Exhibit 3.

Assuming exercise occurs at the expiration date, this equation says that the difference in price between a call option and put option with the same terms should equal the price of the underlying stock less the present discounted value of the exercise price. Another interpretation is that someone owning a call option, while having simultaneously written a comparable put option, should at all times be in a position equivalent to someone who bought the underlying stock with a loan equal in size to the option's exercise price and maturing at the option's expiration date. This put-call parity relation has useful implications when analyzing corporate liabilities and equities as options, as shown in the next part.

CORPORATE LIABILITIES AND EQUITY AS OPTIONS

With one exception, **warrants** are corporate liabilities that are precisely like call options on securities. The difference is that warrants are written by corporations on their own stock rather than written by other investors. An important insight was made by Black and Scholes (*Journal of Political Economy*, 81 (1973)), however, when they recognized that all types of corporate liabilities and equity could be thought of as special types of options or combinations of options. The advantage of doing so is that many complex securities can be decomposed conceptually into "parts" that are more easily recognized and valued using well established procedures. Today, many Wall Street investment banking firms hire professionals trained to analyze securities in this manner to aid their underwriting and trading operations (Donnelly, *Institutional Investor*, December 1984).

A SIMPLE EXAMPLE OF OPTIONS ON LIABILITIES AND EQUITIES. To understand how corporate liabilities and equity can be thought of as options, consider the simple, stylized balance sheet shown in Exhibit 4. Here we imagine a holding company, Company X, whose sole assets are the shares in Company Y. (Stock is used as the asset in this example for convenience only; in principle, any type of asset could be used.) It has financed the purchase of these shares by issuing bonds for $100 million cash and equity for another $100 million cash. The bonds are zero-coupon bonds maturing in five years and are priced to provide a yield to maturity of 10%. Thus, they must have an actual face value of $160 million. They are also noncallable and carry a covenant that prohibits the payment of cash dividends to the equity owners until after the bonds are repaid.

Common Equity. A moment's thought reveals that the value of Company X's equity depends heavily upon two factors: (1) the market value of its assets and (2) the face value of its debt. Thus, if Company Y's stock rises in value to $300 million, Company X's stock should rise in value to at least $140 million—the difference between $300 million (the market value of Y's stock) and $160 million (the face value of the outstanding bonds).

EXHIBIT 4   BALANCE SHEET FOR COMPANY X
($ MILLIONS)

Assets		Liabilities and Equity	
Company Y stock	$200	$100	Bonds
		$100	Equity
Total assets	$200	$200	Total liabilities plus equity

Now consider the situation that Company X's owners would face at the maturity date of the bonds. So long as its assets have a realizable market value of $160 million or more, Company X's shareholders could successfully pay off the bonds. However, if realizable market value fell below $160 million, Company X's shareholders would be unable to repay the debt completely.

Fortunately, **limited liability** would protect Company X's shareholders from having to make up the difference. They could discharge their responsibility to their company's bondholders by surrendering the company's assets at their current market value. The bondholders would then become the new owners of Company Y's stock and the value of Company X's stock would drop to zero.

This simple example helps illustrate the correspondence between call options on securities and equity as a type of call option on the assets of the firm. In effect, a company's creditors "own" the firm's assets by virtue of their senior claim and they give shareholders the right to "repurchase" the assets at a later date by paying off the debt when it matures. The **exercise price** of this "option" is the face value of the debt, and the expiration date is the debt's maturity date. Because of limited liability, the value of the equity at maturity, like that of the call option, will be worth the greater of zero and the difference between the value of the assets and the face value of the debt to be repaid.

The predicted response of equity prices to changes in those variables that are included in the option pricing framework are what one might intuitively expect, with the possible exception of risk. For example, equity should become more valuable as the value of the company's assets rise, other things being equal. If the value of the company's assets remains steady, then the value of the equity claim on those assets will increase as the size of the debt claim (i.e., the exercise price of the equity) diminishes, the maturity of the debt increases, interest rates increase, and the volatility of the business increases.

Although the positive influence of volatility on equity value may seem unusual, it is not so farfetched as might first be supposed. Companies that fall into deep financial distress, such as Chrysler in 1979 and Massey-Ferguson in 1980, often have equity prices that seem excessively high on the basis of fundamental discounted cash flow analysis. But from an option pricing perspective, the equity might be appropriately valued as an out of the money option in a highly volatile business environment as management creditors, suppliers, unions, government officials, and other corporate constituencies scramble to effect a workout. The volatility of the situation itself contributes to the value of the equity since, for firms already in deep distress, there is much more upside potential than downside risk.

The positive effect of volatility on equity value also provides a rationale for certain types of **covenants** routinely included in bond indentures. From the point of view of equity investors, companies with debt outstanding might find it advantageous to adopt a higher risk-taking posture. They might do so by approving higher risk projects and/or disposing of low risk, low return assets. Covenants that effectively (1) restrict the type of investments a company can make, (2) control the disposal of assets, or (3) secure the debt against certain assets, all serve to protect lenders from this incentive to substitute higher risk assets for low risk assets.

Debt. The analogy between securities and options does not stop with equity. Though not immediately apparent, Company X's debt also has an option-like feature to it.

To see this, note first that the total value of Company X's assets is effectively divided between the claims of bondholders and those of shareholders. It follows that the market value of the bonds (V_B), as opposed to their face value, will be the difference between the total market value of the stock owned by Company X (V_Y) and the market value of Company X's equity (V_{Eq}):

$$V_B = V_Y - V_{Eq}$$

Because the value of the debt can be equated to the difference between two quantities, one of which is possible to value as an option, it follows that the debt should also have option-like characteristics to it.

These option-like characteristics can be made still more explicit by utilizing the **put-call parity** relation described earlier. This relation can be reexpressed for the case of debt and equity as follows:

$$V_p = V_{Eq} - V_Y + Be^{r(t-t^*)}$$

where V_p, is the value of a put option on Company X's assets with an exercise price of B (the face value of Company X's bonds), and V_Y and V_{Eq} are as defined previously. Recalling that the market value of the bonds can be expressed as ($V_Y - V_{Eq}$), the put-call parity relation can be written as:

$$V_B = Be^{r(t-t^*)} - V_p$$

This equation can be quantified by using the data provided in Exhibit 4 and by assuming a yield on government securities of, say, 5%. Under these assumptions for Company X, the previous equation becomes:

$$\$100 \text{ million} = (\$160 \text{ million})e^{-.05(5)} - V_p$$

$$V_p = \$125 \text{ million} - \$100 \text{ million}$$

Thus, V_p must equal $25 million.

In words, this equation says that the current market value of Company

X's debt, V_B = $100 million, can be considered equivalent to that of a riskless, zero-coupon government bond with the same terms as Company X's debt, $Be^{r(t-t^*)}$ = $125 million, minus the price of a put option written on Company X's assets, V_p = $25 million. The value of the put option can be thought of as a **default risk discount** applied to the current market value of the riskless, **zero-coupon bond.**

Alternatively, one might note that the combination of the risky debt plus a put option on the Company X's assets with an exercise price equal to the face value of the debt, $V_B + V_p$, is equivalent to holding a riskless, zero-coupon bond. In this case, the put option can be thought of as a loan guarantee that eliminates default risk. Again, in this example, the fair price of this loan guarantee is $25 million.

The predicted response of bond prices to changes in the variables included in the option pricing framework are also what one would expect. That is, bond prices will decline as the value of the firm's assets declines, the promised payment to bondholders declines, interest rates rise, the maturity of the debt grows longer, and the riskiness of the firm's assets increases.

APPLICATIONS TO MORE COMPLEX SECURITIES. The previous example exposes the option characteristics of two very basic securities: equity and (noncallable) zero-coupon bonds. However, the options framework is widely applicable to other types of securities as well. A number of such applications and the primary insights derived are discussed in the following. Readers interested in the formal mathematics underlying these applications are encouraged to refer to the cited articles.

Coupon Bonds and Sinking Funds. The basic analysis of debt and equity as options needs to be modified only slightly if the debt receives periodic interest payments rather than having a coupon rate of zero. Under these conditions, equity ownership is like owning a call option on a dividend paying stock, except that the "stock" is really the assets of the firm and the cash "dividend" is the coupon payment to the bondholders. (An alternative characterization presented by Black and Scholes (*Journal of Political Economy,* 8.1 (1973), is that equity is like a "compound option," that is, a call option on an option, in the presence of coupon debt. By making each interest payment on schedule, the equity owners exercise their option to own the next interest period's option until the final principal repayment is made at maturity.) For the reasons presented in the first part of this section, equity will be worth slightly less and the bonds slightly more if the debt receives coupon payments, all other factors being held constant.

It may be argued by extension that regular **sinking fund** payments, which are also cash disbursements to bondholders, can be incorporated into an option pricing analysis of debt and equity in essentially the same way, except that equity must be treated as a call option with a declining exercise price over time. A discussion of how to incorporate cash payout considerations in the option pricing formula is provided by Merton (*Bell Journal of Economics and Management Science,* 4, No. 1 (1973)). He also developed a pricing formula for coupon bonds in a subsequent article (*Journal of Finance,* 19, No. 2 (1974)).

Callable Bonds. If a bond is callable, an additional adjustment must be made to the option pricing analysis of corporate securities. Specifically, the equity of the company issuing the callable bonds must be treated as an **American call option** on the assets of the firm, which can be exercised at any time prior to maturity, rather than a **European call option** that can be exercised only at maturity. Since the right to exercise a call option early should never detract from its value, it follows that the equity will be worth more, and the bonds less, if a call provision is included in the bond indenture. The value of the call provision itself may be thought of as the simple difference between the value of equity treated as an American call option and its value as a European call option, each with an exercise price equal to the par value of the bonds.

In practice most bonds are not callable at par until maturity. Rather, they are callable according to a predetermined schedule of prices that begins above par (often by an amount equivalent to a year's interest on the debt) and declines to par over time. In this case, the equity of the issuing firm can still be treated as an American call option, but one with an exercise price that changes according to the predetermined schedule.

Yet another common practice with callable bonds is to provide bondholders with 5 to 10 years of **call protection.** That is, the company is prohibited from refunding the bonds, which would expose bondholders to reinvestment risk, for a number of years. The value of the call protection can be captured in option pricing analysis by taking the difference in the value the equity as an American call option that can be exercised at any time, and an American call that can be exercised only after the call protection period.

Retractable and Extendible Bonds. Brennan and Schwartz (*Journal of Financial Economics,* 5, No. 1 (1977b)), use the option pricing framework to analyze retractable and extendible bonds. A **retractable bond** is one that can be redeemed on a prespecified date prior to expiration at the option of the bondholder. In contrast, an **extendible bond** is a short-term instrument for which the maturity can be lengthened to some predetermined date, often with a higher coupon, also at the bondholder's option.

Both these instruments are equivalent to holding an ordinary bond with an option attached. In the case of the retractable bond, the combination consists of a long-term bond with a European put option exercisable on the retraction date. For an extendible bond, the combination consists of a short-term bond with a European call option on a long-term bond exercisable on the extension date. The put option and the call option components of these instruments have exercise prices equal to the par value of the bonds. Thus, the optimal exercise strategy of the bondholder is straightforward in either case: the options should be exercised if they are in the money at the retraction/extension date.

Subordinated Debt. The preceding discussion of debt and equity as options makes the implicit assumption that only one class of debt is outstanding. Furthermore, it is assumed that if default occurs the lenders take possession of the assets of the firm and the value of the equity drops to zero.

However, subordinated debt represents a junior claim on the firm's assets that stands between senior debt claims and equity. Not surprisingly, it bears both debt and equity characteristic to some extent.

Analyzing subordinated debt within the option pricing framework requires the specification of the amount to be received by the subordinated debt at the time of its maturity. This is shown in Exhibit 5. For purposes of comparison, the amounts received by senior debt claims and equity are also shown.

It may be observed that equity, as a residual claim on the value of the firm, will be worth something only when there is more than enough value in the firm to satisfy the claims of both classes of debt. Senior debt, on the other hand, is worth whatever the firm is worth until the point is reached when it can be repaid fully. Beyond that point no additional value accrues to the senior debt holders. Subordinated debt falls between these two extremes. Once the senior debt claim is satisfied, the junior debt receives whatever is left until it can be repaid in full.

The lines shown in Exhibit 5 represent what are known as "boundary conditions" required to derive formulas for pricing each type of security as

EXHIBIT 5   THE VALUE OF VARIOUS CLASSES OF CLAIMS AS A FUNCTION OF TOTAL VALUE

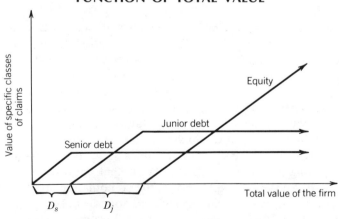

Key:
D_s = Face value of senior debt claims
D_j = Face value of junior debt claims

an option. Black and Cox (*Journal of Finance,* 17, No. 2 (1977b)), have done this for subordinated debt. An interesting feature of their results is the likely response of the subordinated debt to changes in risk, interest rates, and time to maturity. Whereas the price of senior debt should increase as these three determinants drop in value, and vice versa for the price of equity, the response of subordinated debt prices is indeterminate. When the value of the issuing company has dropped very low and is near the face value of the senior debt, the junior debt's price will behave more like equity than debt. Conversely, when the worth of the company is very high, it will behave more like ordinary debt than equity. Such a divergence in responses is consistent with the "in-between" nature of subordinated debt.

Convertible Bonds. A bond that is convertible at the holder's option into the issuing company's common stock can be decomposed into two basic parts: a bond component and a call option on the stock. The call option gives the holder a right to purchase a prespecified number of shares at an exercise price equal to the face value of the bond and with a maturity identical to that of the bond. The bond itself, rather than cash, would be surrendered to exercise the option. If the convertible bond is callable, as most are, then its value would equal that of a noncallable bond plus a warrant less the value of the call provision. Conceptually, a convertible bond would be identical to a **bond-warrant** unit in which the warrant is not detachable and the bond could be used to exercise the warrant.

An important implication for convertible bonds derived directly from call option analysis is that they should not be converted any sooner than absolutely necessary. Doing so would needlessly sacrifice the call option's premium attributable to having time to watch the course of future events before making a final decision about converting. Should the price of the issuing company's stock fall below the face value of the bonds before maturity, investors will prefer to hold the bonds rather than the stock (an exception arising if the company began paying large cash dividends to the common shareholders).

From the company's point of view, a convertible bond should be called as soon as its market price equals its call price. Doing so serves to minimize the value of the claim held by the convertible bondholders and, thus, helps to maximize the value of the equity.

Ingersoll (*Journal of Financial Economics,* 4, No. 3 (1977)), and Brennan and Schwartz (*Journal of Finance,* 32, No. 5 (1977a)), provide thorough mathematical treatments of the valuation of convertible bonds within the option pricing framework.

Rights Issues, Underwriters, and Standby Agreements. A preemptive rights issue enables a company to raise new equity without necessarily diluting the ownership position of existing shareholders. It provides shareholders of record on a given date the right, but not the obligation, to purchase newly issued shares of common stock at a predetermined price within a limited span of time. Thus, rights are essentially warrants to purchase new shares and, as such, can be correctly analyzed as call options.

The subscription price (i.e., exercise price) of the rights issue is usually placed below the common stock's current price, often by a substantial margin. This makes the rights in the money and increases the likelihood that they will still be worth exercising by the end of the subscription period.

However, there is always some chance that the market price of the stock will drop below the subscription price making it uneconomic for shareholders to exercise their rights. To guard against this possibility and ensure that equity capital will be raised as planned, most companies will execute a **standby agreement** with an underwriter. The agreement provides that the underwriter will stand ready to purchase any unsubscribed shares at the subscription price less a take-up fee. A standby fee is also paid to the underwriter independent of whether or not there are any unsubscribed shares.

In effect, the standby agreement with the underwriter functions as a put option on the newly issued shares with an exercise price equal to the subscription price less the take-up fee. The put is written by the underwriter and purchased by the company at a premium equal to the standby fee. Brealey and Myers (*Principles of Corporate Finance*) point out that many standby agreements are overpriced by underwriters relative to their value as determined by put option pricing.

Insurance and Loan Guarantees. Various types of insurance contracts are, of course, a common financial instrument possessed by corporations, banks, and households alike. Similarly, loan guarantees are a type of insurance often provided by parent companies in support of their subsidiaries' debt and, increasingly, by governments in support of favored industries or large corporations facing financial distress. Both these instruments are contingent claims in that they provide a predetermined payoff under certain prespecified conditions (e.g., loss of value due to fire, bank insolvency, or failure to meet scheduled loan obligations) so long as the policy or loan guarantee is in force. As such, they are conceptually analogous to American put options.

In fact, for relatively uncomplicated insurance policies, the correspondence with put options is exact and their premiums (or the implicit costs of the loan guarantees) can be estimated directly using option pricing techniques. The underlying "security" of the put option is the insured asset or the guaranteed loan, the exercise price is the promised payment if a legitimate claim is made, and the time to expiration is the term of the insurance policy or the maturity of the loan being guaranteed. An interesting application of put option pricing to loan guarantees and bank deposit insurance is made by Merton (*Journal of Banking and Finance*, 1 (1977), and in *Journal of Business*, 51, No. 3 (1978)). An options analysis of government loan guarantees for large scale energy projects is provided by Baldwin, Mason, and Ruback (Harvard Business School Working Paper, 83-66 (1983)).

Pension Fund Management. Sharpe (*Journal of Financial Economics*, 3 (1976)), also utilizes the correspondence between insurance and put options to analyze the implication of the **Employee Retirement Income Security Act of 1974** (ERISA) for corporate pension fund management. Briefly, a company with an insured, defined benefit pension plan can be considered to own a call option on the pension fund's assets with an exercise price equal to the promised employee benefits. Drawing upon the put-call parity relation, this is equivalent to a position in which the company owns the pension fund assets worth V_A, bears a liability equal to the present discounted value of future employee benefits, $Be^{r(t-t^*)}$, but is limited in that liability by also owning a put option on the assets, V_p, with an exercise price equal to the promised benefits. Thus,

$$V_A - Be^{r(t - t^*)} + V_p = V_c$$

where V_c is the value of a call option on the pension fund's assets with an exercise price equal to B, the promised benefits.

So long as the premium paid to the insurer of the benefits (which is the Pension Benefits Guarantee Corporation under the provisions of ERISA) is equal to the fair market value of the put option dictated by the put-call parity relation, then the company's pension funding policy can have no special effect on the value of the company's equity. However, if the insurance premiums are fixed at an inappropriate level, then an incentive is created for the company to pursue funding strategies that maximizes the difference between the value of the put option and the premium charged for it. Companies might do this by increasing their pension liabilities, decreasing pension fund assets, or increasing the riskiness of their funds' investments.

CAPITAL INVESTMENTS AS OPTIONS

A traditional analytic approach to **capital budgeting** utilizes some form of discounted cash flow analysis to provide an estimate of value that may then be used in the capital appropriation process. Typically, cash flows expected from a project are forecasted to some prespecified point in the future, and then discounted to the present using an appropriate estimate of the **cost of capital.**

Though widely used today these traditional techniques have been subjected to considerable scrutiny and criticism in recent years. One of the more important lines of criticism has been that concerned with strategic factors. Specifically, it has been claimed that ordinary **net present value analysis** tends to understate a project's value because it fails to capture adequately the benefits of operating flexibility and valuable follow-on projects that often accompany an initial investment.

Because much of what is called "flexibility" or discretionary future investment opportunities are like **contingent claims,** to be exercised under some future conditions but not under others, the potential exists for using option pricing analysis to overcome some of the aforementioned shortcomings. This potential, and other implications of option pricing analysis for capital budgeting, is the subject of this part.

OPERATING OPTIONS. When undertaking any particular project, management seldom binds itself to a single irrevocable operating strategy for that project. Should the future deviate from expectations, management generally has some degree of discretion regarding the operation of the project. Where this discretion exists, management may be said to hold some **operating options.**

One of the most significant such operating option is the **option to abandon** a project earlier than originally planned. Conventional **discounted cash flow techniques** recognize the desirability of abandonment when **salvage value** equals or exceeds the present value of future operating cash flows and fixes the terminal date of the project at that point in time. However, earlier terminations may be warranted if, for example, the project fails or a change in technology requires the substitution of a new type of equipment for the old.

The best time to abandon a project may never be known in advance with absolute certainty. But the right to abandon at any time under various circumstances is tantamount to owning an **American put option** on the project's assets. The **exercise price** of the put is the salvage value that could be received on disposal of the assets, and the time until maturity would be the physical life of the assets. Viewed this way, the true value of a project is not just the present value of cash flows forecasted to some termination date, but that present value plus the value of the option to abandon. A thorough treatment of this topic is provided by Myers and Majd (Alfred P. Sloan School of Management (August 1983)).

The option to convert assets from one use to another is a type of operating option that can be construed as a special case of the abandonment option. Again, management effectively has an American put option on the project's assets. The exercise price of the put is the assets' value in their next most productive use. Because conversion of use can, in principle, take place a number of times, this operating option might best be thought of as a **compound option,** which is an option on a series of future options.

In a similar vein, the choice of whether to operate a plant or some equipment after being placed into service represents a valuable operating option. As McDonald and Siegel (Boston University (August 1981)) point out, insofar as production might be shut down and restarted at any time, the **option to operate** is more like a large portfolio of **European call options,** each of which expires at a different date throughout the life of the assets. The underlying asset of the option to operate is the revenue that will be produced by the assets and the exercise price is the variable production costs. If revenues fall below variable production costs, then, the option to operate will be out of the money and will not be exercised.

Finally, an important operating option discussed by Mason and Merton (*Recent Advances in Corporate Finance,* (1985)) is the **option to expand or contract** the scale of operations. Many projects are engineered in such a way that output can be escalated or contracted in the future, contingent upon market conditions. This might be achieved through planned redundant capacity or built-in flexibility to alter the rate of output and length of production runs.

For most managers, the existence and value of these various types of operating options are obvious to the point of being beyond conscious consideration. Perhaps because of this fact they are so often neglected in conventional discounted cash flow analysis, which tends to be executed in such a way as to reflect a single, irrevocable operating strategy. Failure to reflect such operating flexibility, however, will understate the true value of the project.

FUTURE GROWTH OPTIONS. Capital investment projects may be more valuable than recognized by discounted cash flow analysis not only because of operating flexibility, but also because of valuable new investment opportunities that the project may create. Provided they are discretionary so there is no future obligation to invest capital, these follow-up projects can also be viewed as call options on assets, hereinafter referred to as **growth options.**

By way of analogy to ordinary call options on securities, a growth option's exercise price is the investment required to obtain the assets. The value of the assets to be acquired (i.e., the underlying security) is the present value of expected cash flow plus the value of any new growth options expected through ownership and operation of the assets. The time to maturity is the length of time that commitment of capital can safely be deferred before the opportunity ceases to exist. Clearly, this might be many years or, conceivably, just a few days depending on the nature of the opportunity.

Virtually any discretionary investment opportunity may be viewed as a growth option. An opportunity to explore for mineral deposits on a particular site within a given time frame is one obvious example of a growth option. Capacity expansion projects, new product introductions, and acquisitions are other general forms of investment that can be treated as growth options. Although outlays for advertising, basic research, and commercial development programs are typically expensed rather than capitalized, these programs may also be treated as growth options insofar as they represent investment in real assets like brand name and technical expertise that will generate long-term benefits. Even maintenance and replacement projects are in the nature of growth options since, ultimately, they can be foregone if management wishes, and their undertaking is tantamount to a decision not to shrink a business or exit from it immediately.

Growth options are of great importance to modern corporations since they account for such a large fraction of a typical firm's market value. This is illustrated in Exhibit 6, which calculates the difference between the total

EXHIBIT 6   MARKET VALUE ATTRIBUTABLE TO GROWTH OPTIONS FOR SELECTED COMPANIES

	Market Value of Equity[a] ($ Millions)	Anticipated Earnings[b] ($ Millions)	Capitalized Value of Earnings Using Various Discount Rates[c] ($ Millions)			Estimated Value of Growth Options[c] ($ Millions)	% of Market Value Represented by Growth Options
			15%	20%	25%		
Electronics							
Motorola	4,148	373	2,487	1,865	1,492	1,661 to 2,656	40 to 64
Intel	3,158	192	1,280	960	768	1,878 to 2,390	59 to 76
Harris Corp.	1,040	81	540	405	324	500 to 716	48 to 69
Chemicals							
Dow Chemical	5,812	513	3,420	2,565	2,052	2,392 to 3,760	41 to 65
du Pont	11,739	1,461	9,740	7,305	5,844	1,999 to 5,895	17 to 50
Hercules	1,821	201	1,340	1,005	804	481 to 1,017	26 to 56
Paper							
Boise Cascade	1,063	117	780	585	468	283 to 595	27 to 56
Georgia-Pacific	2,358	277	1,847	1,385	1,108	511 to 1,250	22 to 53
Weyerhaeuser	3,820	250	1,667	1,250	1,000	2,153 to 2,820	56 to 74

[a]Source: *Value Line Investment Survey;* November 1984.

[b]Anticipated earnings are treated as a perpetuity.

[c]Calculated by deducting the maximum and minimum estimates from the market value of equity.

market value of a company's equity and the capitalized value of its earnings stream treated as a perpetuity.

Although the companies represented in Exhibit 6 are only large, publicly traded companies, similar results undoubtedly hold for smaller, privately held concerns. Perhaps the most dramatic example of this was the plethora of genetic research and engineering companies that went public in the early 1980s with little or no will established cash flow. One such company, Genentech, went public with an operating cash flow of only 6 cents per share and annual revenues of $9 million. At the time of its initial public offering, its equity sold for $35 a share, implying a total market value of its equity of $262 million. Even this high figure was quickly surpassed in the immediate aftermarket for the stock. Such value can only be justified on the basis of Genentech's growth options, not its current cash flow.

GROWTH OPTION CHARACTERISTICS. Holding other factors constant, growth options will increase in value as:

- The value of the underlying assets increases
- The capital outlay required (i.e., the exercise price) decreases
- Interest rates increase
- The volatility of the underlying assets' value increases
- The length of deferrability (i.e., the time to maturity) increases

Although growth options have these characteristics in common with ordinary call options, the analogy between the two types of options is not perfect. Growth options have a number of other unique characteristics as well. Some of the more important ones are described below.

Exclusiveness of the Right to Exercise. Unlike a call option on a security, a growth option does not necessarily provide its owner with an exclusive right of exercise. Consequently, it is useful to distinguish between two types of growth options: proprietary and shared. **Proprietary growth options** do provide the owner with exclusive right of exercise. Good examples of proprietary growth options include opportunities to invest in capacity to produce a unique, patent-protected product with imperfect substitutes. The growth options possessed by Polaroid at the inception of the instant photography market were proprietary options by this definition.

Shared growth options do not provide the owner with exclusive right of exercise and are in the nature of a "collective asset" of the industry. Examples of shared growth options would be opportunities to enter a new market not yet protected by high barriers to entry (e.g., the television receiver industry in the 1950s) or to build a new plant for servicing a particular geographic market (e.g., a steel mill in the South rather than the Midwest). Cost reduction projects are also frequently in the nature of shared growth options since most companies usually can and will respond to their execution with cost reduction projects of their own, thus minimizing the benefits any one firm can expect to realize. The essential characteristic of shared growth options is that more than one industry participant or potential entrant possesses them (i.e., any competitor can undertake the same type of geographic expansion), or will come to own a similar one as soon as the opportunity is revealed to exist (i.e., all technically capable firms become potential users of a new, unpatented process).

It should be noted that the distinction between proprietary and shared growth options is more one of degree than of kind. Because of such factors as brand name awareness, locational advantages, experience curve effects, economies of scale, and so forth, different owners of a given growth option may face very different exercise prices. In some cases the difference may be so substantial as to effectively eliminate the possibility that the shared option will be exercised by more than one or two owners. For example, the expiration of Polaroid's patents in the field of instant photography converted its proprietary growth options into options that were shared with other film manufacturers. But as a practical matter, it was clear that only Kodak could be expected to exercise those options profitably.

The Dependency of Growth Options on Assets in Place. The value of growth options will not generally be independent of specific assets to which they may be "attached." Growth options may be industry specific and, frequently, even firm specific. For example, options to expand production of items whose unit costs and, thus, unit profit contributions are heavily dependent on **experience curve** effects will have different value depending upon the cumulative production experience of the firms possessing them. A capacity expansion option may be valuable in the hands of a high volume producer but be of little or no value to a potential new entrant with no production experience. Experience, in this example, is an intangible asset to which all expansion options are necessarily attached and on which their value is unavoidably dependent.

Growth Option Liquidity. Growth options will not generally be independently salable at low cost in an efficient market. Certain proprietary growth options may be purchased or sold by means of patents or licensing agreements. Such options, however, usually involve significant costs in the way of legal expenses and ongoing monitoring expenses. Many other growth options may be bought or sold only in conjunction with real assets in place, or even a specific individual, to which they may be attached. Shared growth options may not be salable at all since they are, by definition, already owned by all industry participants and potential new entrants.

This feature of growth options is significant because it means that a company cannot always avoid even anticipated erosions in a growth option's value by simply selling the option to someone else. As an example, consider again the problem of growth options whose value is tied to experience. A well-known high technology company entered into a joint venture in which it was to produce a highly complex material that it developed and learned to manufacture at a very low cost. Its partner was to market the material to industrial users. Their agreement stipulated that within one year the producer had to expand capacity to meet all new demand generated by its partner or license the technology to the marketing firm. Although the producing firm was reluctant to expand capacity because of potential regulatory and technological changes, it was equally reluctant to license the technology. The reason was that it could not easily transfer its production experience to the marketing firm. Consequently, the value of the option to build new capacity was worth much less to the buyer than the seller. In effect, the producer faced the unpleasant decision of how it preferred to lose value—that is, through adverse events that would diminish the worth of the expansion option or through the prior sale of the option at too low a price. It eventually concluded that it was better off retaining the option for itself.

Simple versus Compound Growth Options. Simple growth options create value on exercise only through the cash flows directly attributable to the specific underlying assets. Most routine cost reduction, maintenance, and replacement projects are in the nature of simple options. Their value lies principally in the effect that they will have on cash flow. As a result, they can be evaluated adequately by using conventional net present value techniques. **Compound growth options,** on the other hand, do more than simply affect cash flows. They embody valuable operating options and may generate new growth options for the firm as well. Research and development projects, a major capacity expansion project or a decision to enter a new market, are all investments likely to result in the creation of new options. Similarly, the acquisition of a company or the purchase of other real assets may bring with it additional growth options that are already attached to the assets in place, as discussed above.

CAPITAL BUDGETING IMPLICATIONS. Just as the owner of a call option exercises that option only when the value of the underlying security exceeds the exercise price, so too the owner of a growth option exercises it only when it is in the money. This, of course, is another way of saying only projects that add to a company's value should be accepted. However, recognition of operating and growth options that may be associated with projects have other implications for capital investment decisions such as those discussed by Kester (*Harvard Business Review* (March–April 1984)). These are summarized below.

An Expanded Net Present Value Rule. Projects that have a negative net present value of expected cash flows may be worth accepting if one believes they embody operating and/or growth options whose value exceeds the negative net present value incurred. In effect, the project's "expanded" net present value is made positive by consideration of the attendant options. The value sacrificed on a pure discounted cash flow basis can be considered the price paid for the options.

This principle can be illustrated using a security as an example. Consider a bond-warrant unit with a market value of $1,000. The bond component of the unit provides cash flow in the form of interest and principal repayments. The warrant component provides an option to acquire the issuing company's stock. Suppose that the unit bears interest at 5% and matures in ten years, but the appropriate yield to maturity on a conventional bond with these features is 10%. Under these conditions, the fair market value of the bond component alone is $693. Analyzed solely on a cash flow basis, the unit would appear to be a bad investment at a price of $1,000. It may be worth buying, however, if one believes that the warrant alone is worth at least $307.

Risk as a Benefit. Not only are some projects made more valuable by their attached option, their value may be still greater if they represent opportunities to invest in volatile business environments. This results from the positive effect that risk has on an option's value, other things held constant. Projects that represent **compound growth options** in risky business should have a comparative advantage in the capital budgeting process over comparable projects providing only cash flows and/or new options in less risky situations.

The Effect of High Interest Rates. The present value of future cash flows generally diminishes as interest rates (and, by implication, discount rates) rise. While such an effect should reduce the attractiveness of most capital investment projects, the severity of the effect depends to some extent on the composition of a project's value. In particular, projects that create new growth options or have lots of operating options are likely to be less severely penalized by high discount rates. This stems from the positive effect that interest rates have on an option's value, other effects being held constant. Thus, again, projects that can be considered *compound growth options* should have a comparative advantage in the capital-budgeting process when capital is tight and interest rates rise.

The Importance of Deferrability. Just as long-lived options are worth more than short-lived ones, so too are deferrable investment opportunities more valuable than nondeferrable ones. The ability to defer a final commitment of capital provides the decision maker with time to examine the course of future events and to avoid costly errors if unfavorable developments occur. More time also provides an interval in which favorable events can make a project even more profitable. Thus, even negative net present value projects can be valuable out-of-the-money growth options if they are deferrable and there is some chance that they can become more valuable in the future.

Timing Capital Commitments. A corollary of the previously discussed point is that capital ought not be committed any sooner than necessary. Doing so would needlessly sacrifice the value associated with deferrability. Referring to Exhibit 7, which replicates Exhibit 2 for the case of a growth option, this value can be represented by the vertical distance between the line GG and VV.

There are, however, two commonly encountered situations in which a commitment of capital earlier than absolutely necessary is desirable. One is when there exists an ability to preempt competitive investment that would otherwise erode a growth option's value. The other is when there is an opportunity to learn or gather relevant information from an existing project so that future investments can be made under more favorable conditions. The specific conditions under which a growth option should be exercised early for either of the above reasons will vary from one situation to the next. But in general, those growth options that are most suitable for early exercise

EXHIBIT 7   THE RELATION BETWEEN GROWTH OPTION VALUE AND THE NET PRESENT VALUE OF A PROJECT

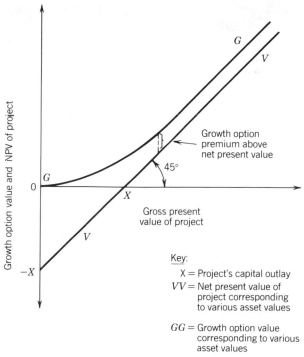

are those that are deep in the money (i.e., have high net present values), are shared with competitors, have low risk, and mature quickly.

GROWTH OPTIONS AND DEBT POLICY

The existence of valuable operating and growth options also has important implications for a company's **capital structure.** Their causes and effects are discussed at length in a seminal article by Myers (*Journal of Financial Economics,* 5, No. 2 (1977)).

Briefly, discretionary investment opportunities influence corporate capital structure because of the temptations that can arise under some future operating conditions to forego good projects. Specifically, if adverse events transpire such that the value of the firm's equity falls considerably and financial distress becomes a real possibility, a company's management seeking to act in the best interests of shareholders may sensibly forego capital investments that have a positive net present value. The reason is that further commitments of capital under such conditions will do more to "bail out" the firms creditors than to help its equity investors. Maintenance and replacement projects, for example, might be particularly susceptible to this temptation to underinvest if things go poorly. From the equity investors' point of view, such operating and growth options would be out of the money because of the seniority of the firm's debt obligations.

It is reasonable to suppose that potential lenders could foresee such contingencies (or at least intuitively grasp their possibility) and would act accordingly when setting the terms of a lending agreement. The likelihood that the company will underinvest in the future precisely when a lender would want them to maintain investment might be reflected in either a higher-than-expected cost to the debt or in loan limits. For example, lenders might choose to keep total exposure at a level no greater than the book value of the tangible assets already in place. By doing so, lenders could look to real assets for their recourse and, thus, be better assured that the value of their loans will not depend entirely on management's discretion about whether to exercise future options.

This type of rational response by lenders—and the costs it imposes on equity investors—leads to the first major implication of the growth option framework for debt policy: that is, corporate borrowing should be inversely related to the proportion of company value accounted for by options on real assets. Thus, one might expect to find higher debt ratios among profitable, capital intensive companies than among those that have little in the way of fixed asset and for which future value depends heavily on future investment decisions. An established real estate company, for instance, can be expected to use considerably more debt than a genetic engineering company or a company newly formed to explore for oil and gas.

Once again, however, the risk that characterizes a company's options plays a unique role in this situation. The riskier a firm's options relative to its assets already in place, the less well-suited the options are for purposes of bailing out creditors if and when they are exercised. Thus, in a relative sense, the temptation to underinvest is less for companies with risky options. Paradoxically, then, riskier companies may be able to borrow more than safer ones.

Other aspects of debt policy can also be better understood within the growth option framework. Because companies find it difficult and costly to borrow against growth options, it pays to tailor debt contracts to the characteristics of a particular company's assets in place. This often means **matching maturities of** the assets and liabilities such that debt is extinguished more or less in parallel with the life of the assets supporting the debt. This helps protect lenders from discovering years later that the loan is "supported" primarily by discretionary investment opportunities rather than tangible assets. A similar motive justifies the use of **sinking fund** arrangements for bonds and **covenants** restricting the sale of certain types of assets. Covenants restricting cash dividend payouts can also be viewed as an attempt to ameliorate the underinvestment problem by forcing the firm to retain cash and put it to some use. Finally, as discussed at length by Bodie and Taggart (*Journal of Finance,* 33, No. 4 (September 1978)), **call provisions** in bond indentures can provide companies with an opportunity to refund their debt under terms that would reflect the improved conditions of the company if the growth options were exercised.

IMPLEMENTING THE OPTIONS APPROACH TO CORPORATE FINANCE

An options approach to corporate finance can be a very powerful conceptual tool. In principle, securities can be valued more accurately, capital structure changes can be analyzed more completely, and capital budgeting decisions can reflect some strategic considerations more faithfully. However, these advantages are ultimately of value to practitioners only if they are quantifiable in specific situations.

In this part, the various efforts and techniques used to implement an options approach to corporate finance are discussed. Although easy, direct applications of option pricing formulas are few. Numerical approximation techniques are often possible, however. They also hold the promise of extending the application of the options framework to a wide variety of corporate finance problems.

DIRECT APPLICATION OF OPTION PRICING FORMULAS. The Black-Scholes option pricing formula has been tested and used extensively in estimating the value of ordinary call options on securities. However, its direct application to the pricing of corporate liabilities, equity, and real options is limited. Some of its limitations arise from difficulty in obtaining accurate estimates of the various variables contained in the pricing formula, although the data requirements of option pricing analysis are generally no more onerous than those of discounted cash flow analysis, and are often less so. The prevailing risk-free rate of interest and the time to maturity of, say, a bond or even a particular project are often easy to specify, and the variance surrounding an asset's value can always be estimated on the basis of past changes in value.

Problems can arise, however, when the value of the asset in question is not observable or easily estimated. The market value of a company's assets, for example, can be difficult to ascertain if some of the company's securities are not publicly traded. Similarly, the value of a unique new project might be estimated in the present, but there may be insufficient past experience upon which to gauge estimates of variance that can be used in the formula.

An interesting direct application of the Black-Scholes formula was achieved by Paddock, Siegel, and Smith (MIT Energy Laboratory Working Paper No. MIT-EL 81 (1982)) who applied it in their valuation of hydrocarbon leases. Because such leases have relinquishment requirements (i.e., time to maturity) and represent a right but not an obligation to develop hydrocarbon reserves (i.e., the underlying asset) by paying the development costs (i.e., the exercise price), there is a close analogy between such leases and call options. Furthermore, because development costs can be estimated on the basis of past experience and because claims on developed reserves are actively traded, sufficient data exists to permit use of the Black-Scholes option pricing formula.

The correspondence between variables used in the Black-Scholes pricing formula for call options cn securities and those used by Paddock, Siegel, and Smith in the valuation of an oil lease as a real option is shown in Exhibit 8. The results of their analysis indicate that many of the seemingly "high" bids for hydrocarbon leases, relative to the values estimated using discounted cash flow analysis, can be justified within the option pricing framework.

NUMERICAL METHODS OF ANALYSIS. A more common limitation on the direct application of the **Black-Scholes pricing formula** is an inability to satisfy fully the various conditions necessary to justify its use. Attempts to modify the formula to accommodate the characteristics of an actual security or investment opportunity often lead to insolvable partial differential equations.

It is at this juncture that numerical approximation techniques can be employed to estimate option values even when no simple formula exists. These techniques are complex and, depending upon the desired degree of accuracy, may entail substantial computational costs. Thorough discussions of numerical approximation techniques are provided by Schwartz (*Journal of Financial Economics,* 4 (1977)), Parkinson (*Journal of Business,* 5 (1977)), Brennan and Schwartz (*Journal of Financial and Quantitative Analysis* (Sep-

EXHIBIT 8   VARIABLES AND DATA REQUIREMENTS FOR PRICING OIL LEASES AS CALL OPTIONS ON REAL ASSETS

Call Option on a Security	Corresponding Variable for Oil Leases	Data Required
Current price of stock	Current value of developed reserves	Average prices paid for producing traded among oil companies
Variance of returns on the stock	Variance of the rate of change in the value of developed reserves	Derived from average prices paid
Exercise price	Development costs	Engineering estimates
Time before expiration	Relinquishment require- ments	Actual lease terms
Riskless rate of interest	Riskless rate of interest	Average yield to matu- rity on medium-term U.S. Treasury Notes

Source: Paddock, Siegel, and Smith, "Valuation of Corporate Bids for Hydrocarbon Leases," MIT Energy Laboratory Working Paper No. MIT-EL 81. Cambridge, MA, 1982.

tember 1978)), and Mason (Working Paper Nos. 78-52 and 79-35, Harvard Business School).

Briefly, numerical methods involve a dynamic programming approach to the determination of an option's value. This approach uses discrete time intervals such as days, weeks, months, or even years. It works by solving a system of equations that specifies the value of an option at any given period in terms of the value of the option in the next period. The method starts at the point of an option's maturity and then moves backwards in chronological time, period by period, to estimate the option's value at each stage. It begins at the time of expiration because at this point the option's fair market value is identical with its intrinsic value, which can be determined in advance once the variance in the value of the underlying assets and the number of periods before maturity is specified.

The basic idea behind numerical approximation techniques can be illustrated with a two-state option pricing formula such as that developed by Cox, Ross, and Rubenstein (*Journal of Financial Economics*, 7 (1979)), and Rendleman and Bartter (*Journal of Finance* (December 1979)). The latter's formula is shown in Exhibit 9. It assumes that the value of the underlying asset and, hence, that of a call option on the asset, can either increase or decrease by a predetermined amount in any given period.

An application of this formula to a hypothetical capital investment project that is deferrable for two years is shown in Exhibit 10. The project is assumed to have an initial present value of $9 million, which can either increase or decrease by 10% in each future year depending on whether favorable or unfavorable events transpire, respectively. It is further assumed that the project costs $10 million so its initial net present value is −$1 million.

EXHIBIT 9   A SIMPLE FORMULA FOR APPROXIMATING CALL OPTION VALUES

$$C_t = \frac{C_{t+1}^+(1 + r_f - R_{t+1}^-) + C_{t+1}^-(R_{t+1}^+ - 1 - r_f)*}{(1 + r_f)(R_{t+1}^+ - R_{t+1}^-)}$$

$C_t =$ the value of the call option in the current period, t

$C_{t+1}^+ =$ the value of the call option in the next period, assuming the underlying asset has risen in value

$C_{t+1}^- =$ the value of the call option in the next period, assuming the underlying asset has fallen in value

$R_{t+1}^+ =$ the return on the underlying asset when it rises in value (a 20% increase would be represented as 1.20)

$R_{t+1}^- =$ the return on the underlying asset when it falls in value (a 20% decline would be represented as 0.80)

$r_f =$ the riskfree rate of return

Source: Rendleman and Bartter, "Two-State Option Pricing," *Journal of Finance,* December 1979, pp. 1093–1110.

* This formula assumes that an asset's value will either increase or decrease by a known amount in the next period,

$$R_{t+1}^+ \text{ and } R_{t+1}^-$$

respectively. Hence, it is often referred to as a "two-state" option pricing formula.

Exhibit 10*a* shows the net present value of the project for each period and for all combinations of good and bad states, while Exhibit 10*b* shows the corresponding value of the project valued as a simple growth option. In year 0 (maturity), the growth option is worth the greater of zero or the project's net present value for each possible outcome. Working backwards, each pair of possible outcomes is used to estimate the possible values of the growth option with one year before maturity. These are then used in turn to estimate the value two years before maturity. Note that even though the project has negative worth in the present period, and is worth accepting in only one out of four possible outcomes two years later, it still has positive value as an out-of-the-money growth option.

Although somewhat rudimentary as a numerical method, the **two-state option pricing formula** can be used to gain insight about complex capital budgeting problems when a project's outcome can be characterized essentially as a success or failure. Kester (Working Paper No. 1-784-068, Harvard Business School) uses this technique to illustrate the conditions under which preemptive investment decisions may be justified and to determine the optimal sequence of investments when the value of one project depends upon the outcome of another within the same investment program. Preemptive

EXHIBIT 10   CALCULATING A PROJECT'S VALUE AS A GROWTH OPTION USING A SIMPLE OPTION PRICING FORMULA. (a) A DEFERRABLE PROJECT'S CHANGING NET PRESENT VALUE ($000); (b) THE PROJECT'S VALUE AS A GROWTH OPTION ($000).*

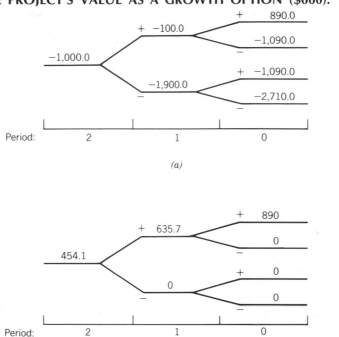

(a)

(b)

* A riskless rate of 5% was assumed in these calculations.

investment in situations where growth options are shared can be modeled in this framework by assuming a gradual erosion of project value or, alternatively, a gradual increase in required capital outlayers if a project is deferred and competitors are allowed to gain a foothold. Sequential investment decisions can be modeled by specifying the changes in value of any one project contingent on the success or failure of an earlier project, and then searching for the sequence that provides the greatest total present value.

One of the most sophisticated and extensive uses of a numerical approximation technique has been made by Jones, Mason and Rosenfeld (*Journal of Finance,* 34, No. 33 (July 1984)). They use it to predict the prices of over 300 actual bonds. Such detailed considerations as **call price** schedules, **call protection** periods, **sinking fund** payments, **seniority,** and options to redeem bonds for sinking fund purposes at par or market are incorporated in their numerical method. They find that noninvestment grade bonds (i.e., bond ratings of BB or worse) are more accurately valued by option pricing techniques than by ordinary discounted cash flow analysis, although there appears to be little advantage gained for investment grade bonds (i.e., bond ratings of BBB or better). They conclude that explicit consideration of taxes and randomly fluctuating interest rates in their numerical methods could improve the results of their numerical analysis.

At present, **numerical methods** for implementing an options approach to corporate finance problems are probably too complex and demanding in terms of computing time to warrant routine application. This is likely to change, however, as the capacity and computational efficiency of computers increases. Still, such methods are well suited to the analysis of major **capital structure** and **capital budgeting** problems. This is true particularly when such factors as restrictive covenants, interactions among securities, flexibility, or the timing of capital commitments are of importance. The options approach to corporate finance offers a comprehensive and internally consistent framework for incorporating these considerations in one's analysis that other valuation techniques cannot.

REFERENCES

Baldwin, Carliss Y., Mason, Scott P., and Ruback, Richard S., "Evaluation of Government Subsidies to Large Scale Energy Projects: A Contingent Claims Approach," Harvard Business School Working Paper, 1983.

Black, Fischer, and Cox, John C., "Valuing Corporate Securities: Some Effects of Bond Indenture Provisions," *Journal of Finance,* Vol. 17, No. 2, 1976, pp. 351–367.

Black, Fischer, and Scholes, Myron, "The Pricing of Options and Corporate Liabilities," *Journal of Political Economy,* Vol. 81, 1973, pp. 637–659.

Bodie, Zvi, and Taggart, Robert A, Jr., "Future Investment Opportunities and the Value of the Call Provision on a Bond," *Journal of Finance,* Vol. 33, No. 4, September 1978, pp. 1187–1200.

Brealey, Richard, and Myers, Stewart, *Principles of Corporate Finance,* 2d ed., McGraw-Hill, New York, pp. 438–439.

Brennan, Michael J., and Schwartz, Eduardo, S., "Convertible Bonds: Valuation and Optimal Strategies for Call and Conversion," *Journal of Finance,* Vol. 32, No. 5, 1977a, pp. 1699–1715.

Brennan, Michael J., and Schwartz, Eduardo S., "Finite Difference Methods and Jump Processes Arising in the Pricing of Contingent Claims: A Synthesis," *Journal of Financial and Quantitative Analysis* September 1978, pp. 461–474.

Brennan, Michael J., and Schwartz, Eduardo S., "Savings Bonds, Retractable Bonds and Callable Bonds," *Journal of Financial Economics,* Vol. 5, No. 1, 1977b, pp. 67–88.

Cox, John S., Ross, Stephen A., and Rubenstein, Mark, "Option Pricing: A Simplified Approach," *Journal of Financial Economics,* No. 7, 1979, pp. 229–263.

Donnelly, Barbara, "The Academic Invasion of Wall Street," *Institutional Investor,* December 1984, pp. 73–78.

Ingersoll, Jonathan E., "A Contingent Claims Valuation of Convertible Securities," *Journal of Financial Economics*, Vol. 4, No. 3, 1977, pp. 269–322.

Jones, E. Phillip, Mason, Scott P. and Rosenfeld, Eric, "Contingent Claims Analysis of Corporate Capital Structures: An Empirical Investigation." *Journal of Finance*, Vol. 34, No. 33, July 1984, pp. 611–624.

Kester, W. Carl, "Today's Options for Tomorrow's Growth," *Harvard Business Review*, March–April 1984, pp. 153–160.

Kester, W. Carl, "Turning Growth Options into Real Assets," Harvard Business School Working Paper, January 1984.

Mason, Scott P., "The Numerical Analysis of Certain Free Boundary Problems Arising in Financial Economics," Harvard Business School Working Paper, 1978.

Mason, Scott P., "The Numerical Analysis of Risky Bond Contracts," Harvard Business School Working Paper, 1978.

Mason, Scott P., and Merton Robert C., "The Role of Contingent Claims Analysis in Corporate Finance," *Recent Advances in Corporate Finance*. Edward I. Altman, ed., Irwin, Homewood, IL, 1985, pp. 7–54.

McDonald, Robert L., and Siegel, Daniel R., "Options and the Valuation of Risky Projects," Boston University, August 1981.

Merton, Robert C., "An Analytic Derivation of the Cost of Deposit Insurance and Loan Guarantees: An Application of Modern Option Pricing Theory," *Journal of Banking and Finance*, Vol. 1, 1977, pp. 3–12.

Merton, Robert C., "On the Cost of Deposit Insurance When There are Surveillance Costs," *Journal of Business*, Vol. 51, No. 3, 1978, pp. 439–452.

Merton, Robert C., "On the Pricing of Corporate Debt: The Risk Structure of Interest Rates," *Journal of Finance*, Vol. 19, No. 2, 1974, pp. 449–470.

Merton, Robert C., "The Theory of Rational Option Pricing," *Bell Journal of Economics and Management Science*, Vol. 4, No. 1, 1973, pp. 141–183.

Myers, Stewart C., "Determinants of Corporate Borrowing," *Journal of Financial Economics*, Vol. 5, No. 2, 1977, pp. 147–175.

Myers, Stewart C., and Majd, Saman, "Calculating Abandonment Value Using Option Pricing Theory," Alfred P. Sloan School of Management Working Paper, MIT, Cambridge, MA, August, 1983.

Paddock, James L., Siegel, Daniel, and Smith, James L., "Valuation of Corporate Bids for Hydrocarbon Leases," MIT Energy Laboratory Working Paper. Cambridge, MA, 1982.

Parkinson, Michael, "Option Pricing: The American Put," *Journal of Business*, Vol. 5, 1977, pp. 21–36.

Rendleman, Richard J., and Bartter, Brit J., "Two-State Option Pricing," *Journal of Finance*, Vol. 29, December 1979, pp. 1093–1110.

Schwartz, Eduardo S., "The Valuation of Warrants: Implementing a New Approach," *Journal of Financial Economics*, No. 4, 1977, pp. 79–93.

Sharpe, William F., "Corporate Pension Funding Policy," *Journal of Financial Economics*, No. 3, 1976, pp. 183–193.

6

SMALL BUSINESS FINANCE: SOURCES OF CAPITAL

CONTENTS

6

SMALL BUSINESS FINANCE: SOURCES OF CAPITAL

Steven J. Appel

INTRODUCTION

Small business decisions are guided by practical considerations—and finance is no exception. Small businesses often encounter significant financial challenges not affecting a large, established corporation. Undercapitalization, lack of ready access to capital markets, and inexperience in working with financial instruments are real problems the entrepreneur must face. With these issues in mind, entrepreneurs must take a practical approach to solving the problems of financing the business' current operations and future growth. Thus, small business finance requires the matching of specific business needs for capital with both the types of financing (i.e., instruments) and the sources of financing (i.e., institutions and markets) available.

This practical approach to finance—the matching of needs, instruments, and sources—forms the framework for this section. The materials presented here have been selected for their broad relevance to small businesses of all types. As seen in Exhibit 1, entrepreneur clearly needs to develop an individual approach to financing, based on specific business and personal objectives. For a discussion of the financial planning function, see Section 1 in this *Handbook*.

WORKING CAPITAL

Working capital is the life blood of a small business. In technical terms, working capital refers to current assets (primarily cash, inventory, and receivables) net of current liabilities (such as accounts payable, short-term debt, and income tax payable). In practical terms working capital refers to the funds used in the production cycle—starting with cash to purchase ma-

EXHIBIT 1   SMALL BUSINESS FINANCE—NEEDS VERSUS TYPES OF FINANCING

NEEDS	TYPES OF INSTRUMENTS	SOURCES
WORKING CAPITAL		
Accounts Receivable	Lines of Credit Discounting/Factoring	Banks, Finance Companies Factors
Inventory	Accounts Payable Manufacturer Financing Lines of Credit Customer Advances	Vendors Manufacturers Banks, Finance Companies Customers
FIXED ASSETS		
Equipment	Leasing Term Loans	Suppliers, Leasing Companies Banks
Real Estate	Mortgage Loans Land Contracts Industrial Revenue Bonds Urban Development Action Grants Related-Party Leasing	Banks, Insurance Companies Sellers Insurance Companies, Bank, Municipality Municipalities Owners
OTHER		
Seed Capital	Equity/Debt of Founders	Personal Funds
Start-up Capital	Venture Capital (Equity/Debt)	Venture Capitalist, SBA
Research and Development	SBIR Grants	SBIR
Acquisitions	Leveraged Buyouts Installment Sales Stock	Banks, Finance Companies Sellers Internal
Stock Repurchase Agreements	Key Man Insurance (financed before the event occurs)	Insurance Companies
GOING PUBLIC		
Any of above	Publicly Traded Securities	Capital Markets

terials and labor, through sale of products and service generating accounts receivable, and back to cash via collection of these accounts. Balancing the requirements for funds against the sources available to the small business is an essential management task. The sources of financing and instruments typically available to the small business are examined in the following.

ACCOUNTS RECEIVABLE. Accounts receivable are a significant asset on the balance sheet of most companies. Financing of receivables provides immediate funds instead of waiting 30 days or longer for collection of outstanding accounts. When a company's return on investment is greater than the cost of financing accounts receivable it may be beneficial to finance receivables in order to generate funds for business operations. Receivables may be either assigned or pledged as collateral for lines of credit or they may be sold or factored.

Assignment of Receivables. In many businesses, **receivables financing** takes the form of pledging of a security interest in accounts receivable to obtain a line of credit. Interest charges on these credit lines generally range from .5 to 4% above the lender's prime rate. The form of the transaction either can be a general assignment or a specific assignment. In a general assignment, all the receivables serve as collateral for the credit line. The amount of credit extended is based on a percentage of the total eligible receivables, usually in the range of 60 to 80%. The borrower retains full responsibility for collection. Under a specific assignment, the borrower and lender must come to terms as to which receivables will serve as collateral, who is responsible for collection of receivables, the amount of finance charge, and whether account debtors are to be notified of the assignment. Some lenders require lines of credit to be liquidated and/or renegotiated each year. Lines of credit for accounts receivable financing are offered by banks and commercial finance companies. Lines of credit are discussed in more detail in the following in relation to inventory.

Factoring Accounts Receivable. When accounts receivable are sold, the financing is usually based on a continuing agreement for advancing funds against open accounts. The factor charges a commission for its services which usually ranges from .75 to 1.5% of the net amount of receivables purchased. Customers are notified when accounts are sold so that payments can be made directly to the factor. Factoring transactions can be made without recourse or with recourse. Without recourse transactions are the most common in which the financing entity bears all the risk of the customer's default on account payment. In the case of a recourse factoring transaction, the borrower retains the risk of the customer's default. Although banks do provide factoring services, most of this activity is the province of **commercial finance companies.** These companies' main business is extending self-liquidating, collateralized credit. Because commercial finance companies are willing to assume significant levels of risk (such as the purchaser's default), they charge higher rates. (See Exhibit 2.)

INVENTORY. In addition to using customer advances, to maintain adequate levels of inventory most small businesses rely primarily on a combination of supplier and lender financing. **Trade credit** from suppliers allows payment of invoices in the normal course of business within 30 to 45 days. Since production cycles often run longer than the available trade credit, a business can then turn to lenders for additional financing. Alternatively, financing may be arranged with major manufacturers and other large vendors. Specialized inventory financing, including advances secured by **bills of lading**, the use of **trade acceptances** and **banker's acceptances**, and loans secured by **trust receipts** and **warehouse receipts**, are typical to specific industries and are rarely used by small businesses outside of those industries.

Manufacturer Financing. In addition to offering trade credit, many larger companies provide inventory financing to support the sale of their products. For example, automobile and farm equipment manufacturers routinely provide **inventory financing**, known as **floor plans**, to dealers. All types of supplier financing operate in much the same overall fashion, serving as extensions of trade credit. The terms and conditions of this financing vary widely, depending on the volume/turnaround of inventory, the business' creditworthiness, and competition among manufacturers.

EXHIBIT 2 WORKING CAPITAL CYCLE

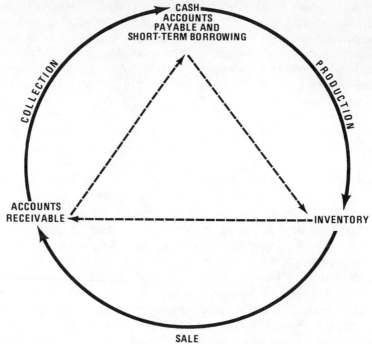

Lines of Credit. Financing inventory using a line of credit is very similar to financing of receivables. In fact, lines of credit are generally secured by a combination of receivables and inventory. The total credit limit is based on a percentage of eligible receivables as discussed previously, plus a specified percentage of qualifying inventory (usually in the 50 to 70% range).

The agreement with the lender for a line of credit contains other provisions which require careful consideration by the small business using this type of financing. Typical provisions include:

- **Fees.** In addition to the stated interest rate, the lender may charge fees that increase the effective cost of borrowing. An annual fee may be charged by the lender to audit the receivables and inventory which secure the line. A **commitment fee** (e.g., .25%) may be charged for the unused portion of the line. In cases where customers make payments on accounts receivable directly to a lockbox, the receipt may not be applied as a reduction of the outstanding line for an agreed on number of days, this lag in crediting receipts increases the effective interest rate.

- **Compensating Balances.** A compensating balance provision may require that a percentage of the outstanding borrowing (usually in the range of 10 to 20%) be deposited, in a noninterest bearing account. Compensating balance requirements also increase the effective interest rate on the debt. All of the implicit costs need to be considered when comparing the arrangements offered by different lenders.

- **Restrictive Covenants.** Provisions are included in line of credit agreements to protect the position of the lender by restricting certain actions by the borrower. The restrictions may be especially uncomfortable for a small business headed by an entrepreneur who is accustomed to running the company as he chooses. Ideally, the lender will work with the entrepreneur to waive those covenants that truly become restrictive of the growth and profitability of the business. In these situations, the covenants serve as a mechanism for keeping the lender aware of the activities of the company. Some of the common restrictive covenants include:

1. *Limitations on salaries of key employees*
2. *Limitations on the payment of dividends*
3. *Restrictions against new loans or advances, particularly to related parties*
4. *Prohibitions against creating liens on assets, or acquisition of assets in excess of a specified amount*
5. *Restrictions on leasing activity*
6. *Restrictions on sale or transfer of corporate stock*

- **Personal Guarantees.** Line of credit agreements for small businesses typically require that the owner/operator personally guarantee the debt of the company. This provision recognizes that, in practice, the personal finances of the owner are inextricably intertwined with that of the small business. Lenders include this provision, not so much for the additional security added to the loan, but for the commitment the owner feels toward the business as a result of the clause.

Exhibit 3 illustrates a line of credit.

EXHIBIT 3   LINE OF CREDIT

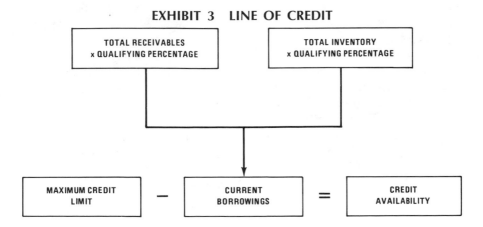

FIXED ASSETS

A small business' fixed assets are chiefly of two types: equipment and real estate. Acquisition of fixed assets typically represent a major investment for any business. Financing these assets requires a long-term commitment anywhere from 5 to 20 years, all the more reason for careful consideration of the terms of the agreement.

EQUIPMENT. Small businesses primarily rely on leasing and term loans to finance major acquisitions of equipment. Although these techniques differ in some respects, most leases are, in fact, **installment purchases**. Nonfinancial considerations such as renewal terms or the ability to obtain technological upgrades, can be a deciding factor. Some of the key aspects of leasing and term loans are reviewed below.

Leasing Arrangements. Small businesses often find leasing to be a attractive financing alternative. Leasing arrangements enable the lessee to obtain the use of property with only a modest cash down payment. When considering such factors as cash flows, equipment obsolesence, and optimizing the return on available capital, many companies—both large and small—choose leasing in lieu of purchasing. Note, however, that leasing and purchasing must be evaluated together. The choice between these financing alternatives should be made on the basis of a cost/benefit analysis entailing a variety of tax, accounting, and other business considerations. (For example, whether the investment tax credit is passed through to the lessee can be a significant factor in the lease/purchase decision.) The terms and conditions of leases vary widely. Although each lessor offers so-called standard lease agreements, these agreements can differ in many respects among lessors and types of leased property. In addition to the financial terms, lease provisions covering operating considerations—such as regular maintenance, repair and replacement, and optional upgradability (such as adding memory capacity to computers)—demand careful review. Leases are available through independent leasing companies or through the captive leasing subsidiaries of major manufactures. **Supplier financing of equipment**, which operates in much the same fashion as leasing, may offer more advantageous terms and can apply to equipment not otherwise available through leasing companies.

Leases often carry a higher implicit (i.e., built-in) interest rate than other forms of financing. Companies that can afford the higher initial cash outlay often opt for a term loan instead of a lease.

Term Loans. Under the provisions of a term loan, the full amount is borrowed at the loan's inception and is repaid over the specified number of years. Monthly, quarterly, or annual payment schedules—based on either a fixed or a floating rate of interest—may be used. Term loans are often made as part of a financing arrangement between a bank and a small business in addition to a line of credit. As such, the term loan may include restrictions on the activities of the borrower, such as limiting annual equipment purchases to a specified amount. Such restrictions are not commonly found in a lease agreement.

REAL ESTATE. The major sources of funding for small business to finance the acquisition of real estate (i.e., land, buildings, and other improvements) include: **mortgage loans**, **land contracts** (seller financing), **industrial development bonds (IDBs)**, **Urban Development Action Grants (UDAG)**, and equity-based financing. As a general rule, most small businesses make use of mortgages or, to a lesser extent, land contracts. Some municipalities make IDBs and UDAG available to stimulate industrial development for small businesses meeting specific qualifications. Related-party leasing usually in the form of a partnership, may be another technique for obtaining financing.

Mortgage Loans. Small businesses widely rely on mortgage loans to help finance expansion. With real estate as security, mortgage lenders can commit to such financing more readily than is the case for unsecured loans. Standard or conventional mortgages are financed at a fixed rate throughout the specified term. The rate on floating or **variable rate mortgage (VRMs)** are periodically adjusted on a basis set forth in the note. The use of VRMs is rapidly growing, as lenders who expect rates to rise seek to avoid "locking in" their yields for the entire term (often 10 years or more) of the mortgage. Mortgage loans often do not require the personal guarantees and do not include the restrictive convenants typical of most other forms of financing for small businesses. As such, they place fewer restrictions on operations. The primary mortgage lenders are banks, savings institutions, and insurance companies.

Land Contracts. Land contracts operate much like mortgage loans. Unlike a mortgage, however, a land contract provides that the seller retains title to the property until the last payment has been made. This provision is designed to help safeguard the seller's rights. If the purchaser fails to make payment as provided in the contract, the seller need not file for foreclosure in order to retain the title. Land contracts are the most widely used form of seller financing of real estate.

IDB Financing. Industrial development bonds (IDBs) are obligations issued by a state or local government to finance private business activity. The tax-exempt status of most IDBs is attractive to both investors and small businesses. The use of IDB financing grew rapidly through 1983. With the enactment of the Tax Reform Act of 1984, tighter restrictions were placed on the amount of such bonds that could be issued by state governments. Use of the bonds for acquisition of land and existing facilities also carries certain limitations.

Generally IDBs are designed as **mortgage bonds**, secured by the company's real estate. The state and local authorities that oversee IDB financing usually target certain economic development goals such as fostering high-technology industries or encouraging export trade. Entrepreneurs should take such preferences into account in planning to use IDB financing.

UDAG. Urban Development Action Grants (UDAGs) are funds granted to a municipality by the Department of Housing and Urban Development (HUD). The municipality, in turn, loans the funds to a borrower to finance a qualified project. To qualify for a UDAG, the project must create new jobs, meet certain ratios of private to government financing, and demonstrate the need for UDAG funding to make the project financially feasible. Interest rates on UDAG loans tend to be much lower than market, and often permit extended payback terms.

Related Party Leasing. Financing alternatives for the small business necessarily involve consideration of the personal financing position of the owners of the company. The income tax consequences of a transaction to the owners and the company often influence the form of financing. When the owners' marginal tax rate exceeds the company's marginal tax rate, financing of real estate acquisitions outside of the company may offer the owners increased tax savings and lower overall cost.

In a typical arrangement, owners of the company acquire real estate personally. The tax benefits of ownership then flow directly to the property owners. The real estate is, in turn, leased to the company. The owners can finance the acquisition or purchase the property for cash, depending on their financial position. The percentage ownership of the real estate can be different than ownership of the company's stock to accommodate the owners' differing financial needs and resources. Careful attention must be given to structuring these arrangements to comply with the tax requirements and to avoid other business problems. The rental rate, method for determining increases, purchase options, and other lease provisions must be agreed on by all parties prior to purchasing the property.

SPECIALIZED FINANCING REQUIREMENTS

In each stage of a small business' development, new requirements arise effecting (1) the need for financing, and (2) the most suitable type of instrument and source to meet those needs. Some types of financing, including most of those previously discussed, will be used throughout the life of the small business. Other financing arrangements are designed to meet needs that are more limited in terms of time or type of application. Frequently encountered by small businesses, these more specialized requirements include financing for seed capital, start-up capital, research and development activities, acquisitions, and stock repurchase agreements.

SEED CAPITAL. Although the creation of many successful companies can be traced to initial, unique ideas of their founders, good ideas do not necessarily, or even frequently, result in a successful business. All of the other ingredients required to make a business successful—organization, management, marketing, production, and capital—must also be present. Understandably, ideas alone are difficult to sell to investors.

Most often, a well-conceived and documented **business plan** is needed to attract sufficient capital to launch a business. The business plan provides the critical information required to form a judgment about the potential success of the business. Accumulating and organizing the information often involves a significant investment of time and money. Input from industry experts, an accountant, and an attorney are essential for developing the business plan.

The chief source of financing for this preliminary development effort frequently is the contribution, in the form of debt or equity, of the founder. In addition to personal savings and pledges against personal assets, entrepreneurs often rely on financing assistance from family and friends to bridge the gap until the business is able to draw on other sources of capital. Potential lenders and investors typically take a favorable view of situations where entrepreneurs have committed a substantial portion of their personal wealth to the venture.

START-UP CAPITAL. Financing the operations of a new business differs tremendously from that of a large, established company. With its limited history (if any) of success and available resources, the new business represents a much greater risk to the lender or investor than the company with a successful track record. Correspondingly, sources of finance must be geared toward dealing with this risk. Two sources of financing for new companies are venture capital and government lending programs.

Venture Capital Financing. By investing in rapidly growing businesses—and receiving, in turn, stock, debt securities, or a combination of the two—**venture capitalists** accept high levels of risk in order to share in the opportunities for significant profit. Most venture capital firms seek investments in which they expect to receive a high rate of return—often 10 to 1, or higher—in order to maintain an annual rate of portfolio return of at least 30%. Since many new ventures fail, these high rates of return are needed to offset the risk assumed by venture capitalists. Venture capital firms are generally privately owned. They are frequently formed as general or limited partnerships composed mainly of institutional investors or wealthy individuals, or as small business investment corporations licensed by the federal government. Some major corporations and lending institutions have organized venture capital firms as subsidiaries or divisions.

In addition to providing financing, the venture capitalist can be a valuable source of management and business advice for the entrepreneur. Venture capitalists often specialize in different industries, and can provide industry expertise not readily available from other sources.

The investment by the venture capitalist can take many different forms. The initial investment may be in the form of debt, equity, or debt convertible to equity at a later date. Preferred stock convertible to common stock is another possibility. The variations are endless, and require careful consideration to best achieve the objectives of the venture capitalist and entrepreneur. (See Exhibit 4.)

SBA Lending Programs. The U.S. Small Business Administration (SBA) provides financing to small businesses through direct loans and through guaranteeing loans made by private lending institutions (mainly banks). The SBA loan limits vary, depending on the type of loan and whether it is made directly or guaranteed by the SBA. Interest rates also vary. The SBA financing is only available, however, to small businesses unable to secure financing directly from private lenders. The SBA also administers specially targeted loan programs, and offers business information and assistance of far-ranging value to entrepreneurs. (Current information about these and other SBA programs can be obtained directly from the U.S. Small Business Administration, 1441

EXHIBIT 4   VENTURE CAPITAL—RETURN ON INVESTMENT

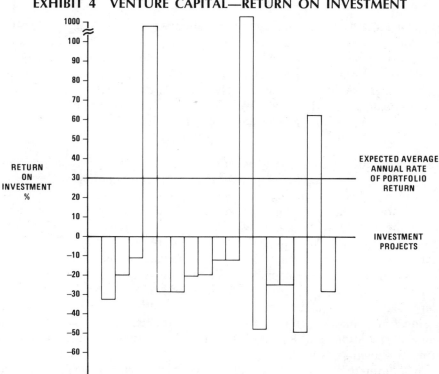

L Street, N.W., Washington, D.C. 20416, or from SBA offices in major cities.) In addition, state and local governments may also provide direct loans and loan guarantees to small businesses.

RESEARCH AND DEVELOPMENT. Small businesses with significant research and development (R&D) costs—such as high-technology companies—often need to seek outside financing for these efforts. Two important techniques of financing R&D programs are provided by federal government grants and R&D syndications, as summarized below.

SBIR Grants. In 1982, Congress established the Small Business Innovation Research Program (SBIR), enabling emerging companies with expertise in science or high technology to benefit from over $1 billion in federal grants. From 1983 to 1987, all federal agencies with R&D budgets in excess of $100 million are required to set aside a small but increasing amount of R&D funds for distribution among qualified small business. SBIR grants are integrated within a three-phase program, administered by the SBA. In the first phase, grants of up to $50,000 are awarded to evaluate the technical merits and feasibility of proposed research; such preliminary research must be completed within six months of funding. In the second phase, up to $500,000 is awarded over a one- to two-year period to fund continued development of the most promising research projects; these awards are limited to projects selected from among first-phase grantees. In the third phase, the successful development efforts of the first two phases are converted into a marketable process or product. Further information on what kinds of funds are available can be obtained from the specific federal agencies and from the SBA. (See Exhibit 5.) The National Science Foundation (NSF) began a pilot program in 1976 on which SBIR was modeled; this NSF program has been continued within the SBIR guidelines. The Department of Defense (DOD) began offering SBIR grants in 1982. Since the NSF and the DOD have the greatest experience with SBIR grants, entrepreneurs interested in applying for SBIR grants may be able to gain valuable pointers by reviewing successful NSF and DOD grants.

R&D Syndications. Research and development syndications are a recent technique developed to enable independent investors to share R&D risks and rewards and to provide alternative means of financing for companies performing research. These arrangements are typically structured by having a partnership established by investors, which in turn contracts with the sponsoring corporation to perform research. Under these R&D research partnerships, the partners claim ordinary income tax deductions for all the research payments to the contractor, retaining all rights to the technology developed under the contract. Typically, if the research is successful, the sponsoring corporation will purchase the new technology from the partners with the sale eligible for the favorable capital gains rates. From the spon-

EXHIBIT 5   SBIR GRANTS

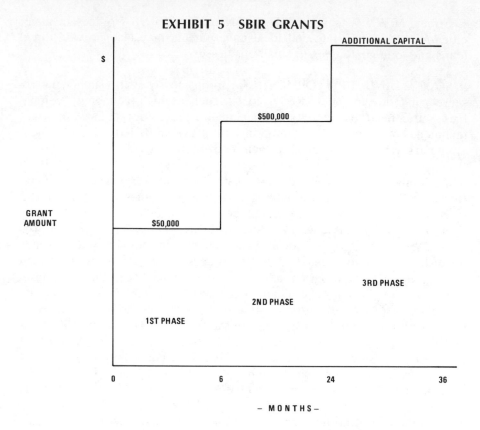

soring corporation's perspective, R&D syndications shift the risk of loss for unsuccessful research to outsiders and minimize the effect on reported earnings of the R&D efforts. They are a potentially inexpensive financing technique. Further, because the research is performed under contract it presents an opportunity to manage the base period research expenses for purposes of the R&D credit and, in many cases, increase the overall credit available to the company. In such an arrangement, the sponsoring corporation runs the risk of loss of control over its proprietary technology, which could result in more expensive overall financing of the research activities. The investors in R&D syndication typically take on significant economic risk. However, if they are successful, these arrangements offer very attractive rates of return.

ACQUISITIONS. Acquisition of one small business by another small business is a common occurrence. Unlike the much-publicized mergers of publicly traded companies, payment in the form of stock (sometimes in combination with debt securities) is rarely accepted.

Much more typically, acquisitions by small businesses are financed through a leveraged buy-out (LBO) as described in the following.

Leveraged Buyouts. The term leveraged buyout (LBO) refers to a popular form of transaction in which the purchase price is funded primarily by lenders rather than by the buyer. From the seller's perspective, it is a cash sale, but from the perspective of the purchaser, it is largely a paper transaction. In a management leveraged buyout, key members of management join or organize the buyer's equity group and must contribute their own funds or shares held in the seller's name to the transaction. The LBO transactions are more complex than most because they involve several participants (i.e., lenders, management, and the equity investors), each of which must be satisfied with the transaction. The principal qualifications for a good LBO candidate are:

- Stable cash flow
- Moderate growth prospects
- Sound management
- Ability to cover pro forma debt service and repay all debt in 10–20 years

The LBO is an evolving and expanding concept. Lenders (chiefly banks and commercial finance companies) are increasingly basing financing on cash flow rather than on the collateral value of assets, thereby making this a viable option for businesses with high cash flow but nominal physical assets. Because of the large profits that can be reaped by the equity participants, numerous leveraged buyout firms have been established, some of which specialize in smaller transactions. Note that the LBO technique also permits the seller to choose to retain a portion of the equity interest—thereby providing considerable flexibility to the seller in "cashing-out" versus sharing the future appreciation in the business' value.

Installment Sales. As opposed to a cash transaction as in the LBO, a seller may be willing to accept notes of the buyer for some part of the purchase price. Accepting paper may have several advantages to the seller:

- It may increase the number of potential purchasers and the selling price.
- It may make it possible to structure the deal as a nontaxable transaction.
- If the interest and/or dividend rate is set at an attractively high level, it may present the seller with a better-yielding investment than he could otherwise obtain. The seller may be in a better position to follow and understand this investment as well.
- If attractively yielding preferred stock is taken back, the seller will hold a preferential position over common equity holders and the risk of a decline in value may, therefore, be lessened. Conversion, participation, or other equity features may permit the seller to benefit from future appreciation of the underlying common stock.
- When marketable stock is received in a nontaxable transaction, the seller has substantial freedom in deciding when to cash in on any

realized but unrecognized gain. Future tax planning may be easier, and the shareholder may avoid bunching and alternative minimum tax problems.

- Installment sales reporting may allow for the deferral of tax payment to when the cash is received. The Tax Reform Act of 1984 reduced some of the benefits of the installment sales method by requiring recapture of depreciation at the date of sale.
- Elderly stockholders may permanently escape the payment of tax by allowing the paper to be stepped-up to current fair value in their estate on death.

Offsetting these advantages is the credit risk that the buyer will ultimately be unable to make the payments. Notes are also used in transactions where the buyer and seller may disagree on the potential for growth of the company, and, therefore, its value. A **contingent earn-out arrangement** allows the ultimate purchase price to be based on the actual earnings of the company over a period of years.

STOCK REPURCHASE AGREEMENTS. Stock repurchase agreements provide a mechanism for transferring ownership of part or all of a small business between shareholders or between the shareholder and the company itself. Transfers may be triggered by the occurrence of a specified event, such as the exercise of an option by a shareholder to withdraw or retire, or, more commonly, by the death or disability of a shareholder. In any case, the requirement to repurchase stock from a shareholder may present the need for significant capital to the small business.

To provide for the required financing of a repurchase in the event of a shareholders death, closely held companies usually carry life insurance policies on their stockholders. The life insurance proceeds are used to redeem the shareholders interest, thereby avoiding a substantial cash drain on the company and providing liquidity for the former shareholder's estate.

GOING PUBLIC

With its **initial public offering (IPO)** of stock, a small business can begin to take advantage of many associated benefits, including access to new sources of financing for the working capital, fixed assets, and specialized financing requirements summarized previously. To properly evaluate such benefits, entrepreneurs must also carefully consider the costs of going public such as the significant expenses required to prepare a company for its initial offering. The main benefits and costs of going public are reviewed in Exhibit 6.

EXHIBIT 6   BENEFITS & COSTS OF GOING PUBLIC

BENEFITS

1. *Capital:* increased access to working capital.
2. *More capital:* subsequent offerings readily accepted.
3. *Liquidity and financing alternatives:* shares provide effective means of valuing the company; makes publicly held company a fairly liquid asset; and public companies can issue many other types of securities.
4. *Wealth:* use shares as collateral or sell shares.
5. *Prestige:* recognized as significant step in corporate growth.
6. *Personnel:* offering stock benefits or options to employees

COSTS

1. *House cleaning:* review of contracts and agreements; review of capital structure; and review of accounting procedures.
2. *Expenses of offering:* underwriters, attornies, accountants, and appraisers.
3. *Ongoing expenses:* annual audit, shareholder relations, filings with the Securities and Exchange Commission.
4. *Disclosure:* all information is available to competitors, customers, employees, and the general public.

BENEFITS

Capital. The most persuasive benefit of going public is the increased access to working capital. A public offering is a good way to finance long-term capital expenditures. When a company goes public, financing is no longer limited to profits generated from operations and various types of borrowings. Even the most successful small businesses will be hard-pressed to stretch retained earnings and loans enough to finance a major new investment. Going public can give a company the funds it needs to invest in research and development, new acquisitions, plant expansions, and state-of-the-art equipment without depleting the company's store of ready cash used for daily operating expenses.

More Capital. Once an initial offering is made and the stock performs well, subsequent offerings will usually be readily accepted. Thus, additional equity capital can be raised on very favorable terms. A successful public offering also increases a company's net worth and improves its debt-to-equity ratio. This, in turn, improves the company's credibility as a borrower, making it easier for the company to borrow funds in the future on more favorable terms. A publicly held company can also use its own securities to finance acquisitions and expansions so that acquisitions can be made with equity rather than with after-tax profits.

Liquidity and Financing Alternatives. Because it is difficult to place a value on a privately held company or to establish a ready market, such companies are often an asset without liquidity. Once an offering is made, the market value of the company's share provides an effective means of valuing the company. As long as the shares are freely traded by the public, this ascertainable market value makes a publicly held company a fairly liquid asset. Liquidity and an ascertainable market value also serve to increase the company's future financing alternatives. Once a public offering is made, publicly held companies can issue other types of securities, such as **convertible debentures**. Generally, such other securities provide lower costs than traditional sources of capital because (1) they are easily converted and (2) there is an established market for the common shares.

Wealth. In most cases, a public offering also serves to increase the value of a privately held company. This higher value can translate into new-found wealth for previous owners. In addition to being able to use publicly traded shares as collateral, shareholders may elect to sell a portion of their shares during the initial offering. In recent years, this has been a popular and lucrative option for many entrepreneurs. There are, however, certain restrictions on sales of shares by management/owners and other insiders, so these sales should be planned and reviewed carefully.

Prestige. Going public is an important measure of success for many companies and is recognized as a significant step in corporate growth. Public offerings increase the company's visibility in the community and in financial circles. This new visibility can generate new interest from customers, suppliers, and financial and business associates. Executives of public companies are viewed as experts and are often asked to comment on various industry and economic factors. Carefully managed, this new prestige and higher visibility can be a real asset.

Personnel. Offering stock as a benefit or as an option for employees can be a powerful incentive for attracting and retaining key personnel. The promise of a future public offering or the success of a current offering can give an entrepreneur important bargaining power for drawing the talented executives and professionals the company will need to remain prosperous in an increasingly competitive environment.

COSTS

Planning to Go Public. The decision to go public cannot be implemented overnight. It can require as long as several years of advanced planning. Few privately held companies are structured to handle the disclosure requirements of public companies. Before a company is ready to file with the Securities and Exchange Commission (SEC), a lot of paperwork is likely to be required. Written documentation for major financial transactions and customer arrangements must be supplemented and additional documentation may have to be prepared. Companies with existing bylaws may have to amend or clarify them and those without bylaws will have to draft them. The minutes of all board meetings will have to be reviewed to ensure that the record is clear and complete. Other preparatory tasks include:

Review of Contracts and Agreements. All contracts and agreements must be scrutinized. Certain leasing and licensing arrangements with share-holders may have to be terminated or amended. Similarly, internal agreements between multiple owners or owners and key personnel on voting rights or buying and selling rights will have to be forfeited. On the other hand, the company may also be advised to draft contracts for certain key personnel to ensure their continued employment and loyalty.

Review of the Capital Structure. Some companies may also require some restructuring to accommodate the change from a private company to a public company. The capital structure must accommodate a large number of shares to be held by the public. In addition, special classes of stock that were designed to meet specific financial and estate planning objectives of family members are generally eliminated.

Review of Accounting Procedures. Accounting procedures may have to be significantly upgraded to ensure compliance with statutory reporting deadlines and increased financial statement disclosure requirements.

Reconsideration of Stock-Based Compensation Programs. Although stock oriented compensation arrangements can be a significant advantage to the company, the design of a program appropriate to furthering the company's objectives can be difficult and expensive to develop.

Expenses of the Offering. In addition to the time and effort required to prepare for the filing and offering, a company must also be prepared to incur the expenses of going public. The principal costs include the underwriters' compensation, legal and accounting fees, the cost of the appraisers and other experts, printing charges, and transfer agent and filing fees. Printing costs alone are likely to exceed $50,000 and could be as much as double that amount depending on the size and complexity of the offering circular. A company expecting to go public with a high-quality offering should anticipate spending at least $150,000, excluding underwriters' commissions that can run as much as 10% or more of the total offering. The magnitude of these costs usually make public offerings grossing less than $4 to $5 million impractical. Furthermore, entrepreneurs must remember that there is no guarantee that the offering will be a success; the costs incurred will have to be paid regardless of the outcome.

More Expenses. The expenses of going public do not end with those of the initial offer. Other costs associated with being a public company are ongoing. Management must devote time and money to such new areas as shareholder relations, public relations, public disclosures, periodic filings with the SEC, and reviewing stock activity. All of this time and the time of the personnel hired to handle these functions would be spent on other management tasks in a privately held company. It has been reported that chief executive officers of publicly held companies can spend anywhere from 25 to 50% or more of their time on such matters. In addition to the time spent by management and others on these activities, various out-of-pocket expenses must be paid, including charges for shareholder meetings, annual and quarterly reports, public relations efforts, and legal, accounting and auditing services. The total cost of these expenses varies from company to company; in most cases, they exceed $100,000 to $150,000 annually.

Disclosure. In addition to the required disclosure of results of operations and financial condition, publicly held companies must be prepared to disclose information about the company, the officers, the directors, and certain share-holders. This information might include company sales and profits by product line, salaries, and perquisites of officers and directors as well as data about major customers, the company's competitive position, any pending litigation, and related-party transactions. This information will be available to competitors, customers, employees, and the general public.

In recent years there has been some relief on the disclosure front for small businesses. In 1979, the SEC relaxed disclosure and reporting requirements for smaller offerings (i.e., those under $7.5 million) by adding Form S-18. **Form S-18** calls for narrative disclosure somewhat less extensive than required for larger offerings. This is especially true regarding descriptions of businesses and remuneration of officers and directors. Under Form S-18, the financial statement requirements for smaller offerings are less demanding than the requirements for larger offerings. A two-year profit and loss statement and statements of changes in financial condition are now sufficient rather than the three-year statements required when raising funds in excess of $7.5 million. The five-year summary of selected financial data is not necessary. Also, existing financial statements can be used if prepared in accordance with generally accepted accounting principles and practices, and do not have to be rewritten according to SEC regulations.

Pressure to Perform. The internal and external pressures publicly held company management may feel to maintain earnings and growth patterns are generally tied to the quarterly reports filed with the SEC and delivered to shareholders. Because shareholders are thus tempted to evaluate company progress quarterly rather than annually, management may, in turn, be tempted to make short-term decisions at the expense of long-term profitability. By attempting to anticipate the stock market and satisfy outside stockholders, management can begin to lose the operating flexibility it cherished before going public.

Diluted Control. Most initial public offerings will dilute entrepreneurs' and other interests by 25 to 50% or more. And, once the company is publicly held, subsequent equity offerings further dilute the owners' control of the company. As the company continues to grow and acquire other businesses with common shares, the dilution continues. If entrepreneurs are ambivalent about loss or transfer of their control, the decision to go public should be made with caution.

Market Risk. Even if entrepreneurs are willing to surrender their control, are willing to account to the shareholders, can afford the initial and ongoing expenses, and are willing to invest the upfront planning time, there is no guarantee of continued success. The marketplace is fickle, and going public means risking the vulnerability of price savings in common stock. Smaller public companies are especially vulnerable to market fluctuations because they are not generally sponsored by institutional or large investors. If small investors are the primary holders of the company's stock, the state of the economy rather than the company's performance and potential may be the primary cause and effect of changes in the market price of the shares. Behavior patterns of the consumer have a tremendous impact on the stock price and are highly unpredictable. This is especially true for companies in ''nonglamorous'' industries.

SUMMARY

Entrepreneurs almost invariably approach finance in practical terms. Specific business needs for capital must be matched with the available types of sources of financing. Most small businesses have a wide range of financing alternatives to pursue, depending on their stage of development, capital needs, and type of business. The selection and use of financing vehicles depends largely on each entrepreneur's business and personal objectives.

REFERENCES

Arthur Andersen & Co., "Cashing In On Innovation," *Small Business Forum,* 1983.

Arthur Andersen & Co., "Going Public: Milestone or Millstone," *Small Business Forum,* 1984.

7

CASH MANAGEMENT

CONTENTS

7

CASH MANAGEMENT

Bernell K. Stone

CASH MANAGEMENT PROBLEMS

DEFINITION AND CONCERNS. Cash management involves (1) the management of day-to-day cash flows, (2) short-term investment and borrowing, (3) bank system design and banking relations, (4) the performance of cash-bank support activities such as cash forecasting, cash budgeting, bank compensation management, investment accounting, and loan accounting, and (5) the design, development, implementation, and maintenance of systems for treasury-area information gathering, administrative processing, control, and decision support. The primary focus in this section is day-to-day cash flow management and the products and services that support day-to-day cash flow management.

Cash management activities can be placed in two primary categories—management and design. Design pertains to structuring a system, for example, selecting banks and money transfer methods and setting policies and procedures. Management is the day-to-day operation of the system as designed.

CONCENTRATION BANKING. Concentration banking is a technique for managing the movement of cash between a company's banks. The essence of the technique is to select one bank, the **primary concentration bank,** as the central cash pool. Adjustments to balances at all other banks are made by transferring the appropriate amount into or out of the concentration bank.

Exhibit 1 portrays the essential idea of concentration banking. It shows (1) cash moving from customers to deposit banks and then into the concentration bank and (2) cash moving out of the concentration bank to disbursement banks and then to the payees. Classifying most banks as either deposit banks or disbursement banks reflects the typical situation, that is, most banks serve either for deposits or disbursements but not both. Exhibit 1, however, does show one bank used for both deposits and disbursements.

EXHIBIT 1   CASH CONCENTRATION AND DISBURSEMENT FUNDING: FLOW OF MONEY FROM CUSTOMER TO DEPOSIT BANKS TO CONCENTRATION BANK AND OUT TO DISBURSEMENT BANKS

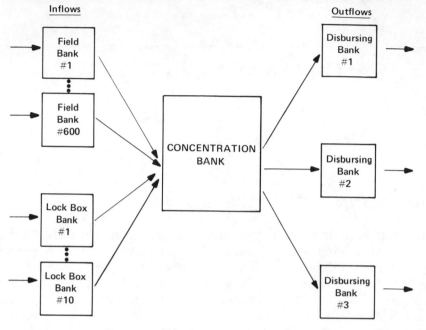

PRIMARY SUBPROBLEMS. Within the framework of concentration banking, the task of designing and managing the day-to-day cash flow system involves seven major subproblems—collection, disbursement, cash concentration, disbursement funding, aggregate cash position management, short-term portfolio management, and short-term debt position management.

A company's **collection system** is the means by which payments from customers are entered into a company's banking system. A major concern is the selection of lockbox banks for the receipt of mailed receivable payments. A second major concern is the selection of field deposit banks. In addition, there are various direct collect techniques such as preauthorized checks, drafts, and electronic debits.

The **disbursing system** is the means by which a company pays its obligations. A major design task is the selection of disbursing banks and services and the creation of policies, procedures, and information-control systems that support the day-to-day disbursement activity. With emerging concern for electronic payments, another design task is (1) the identification of payment alternatives to checks and drafts and (2) the design of systems for utilizing electronic payments.

Cash concentration is the task of moving funds from depository banks into the concentration bank. **Disbursement funding** is the task of moving funds from the concentration bank to accounts at disbursing banks. The major design problems associated with cash concentration and disbursement funding are (1) the selection of the concentration bank or banks and (2) the specification of appropriate transfer methods between banks. The primary day-to-day management problem in cash concentration and disbursement funding is **cash transfer scheduling,** deciding on the timing and amount of transfers between banks.

Aggregate cash position management (ACPM) is the task of managing the overall level of bank balances. It is also called overall cash position management. It is common in contemporary practice simply to say "cash position management," with the understanding that the concern is the overall bank balance. Once all fund transfers have been made into or out of the concentration bank to meet the target balance at all the banks other than the primary concentration bank, then managing the overall bank balance relative to an overall target is tantamount to managing the balance at the primary concentration bank relative to a company's target balance at the concentration bank. The concentration bank serves as a buffer to handle daily imbalances in cash inflows and outflows. If the balance at the concentration bank is too high or too low, then adjustments to the overall cash balance are made by borrowing or repaying and/or by short-term security sales or investments. Thus, aggregate cash position management is closely related to the management of both the short-term debt position and the short-term security portfolio, subjects treated in other sections of this *Handbook*. Exhibit 2 expands Exhibit 1 by adding links to credit banks and the money market occurring at the concentration bank.

MULTIPLE CONCENTRATION BANKS. Exhibit 2 shows only a single concentration bank. Actual systems may be more complex. A company may have several **intermediate concentration banks** (i.e., intermediate cash pools) in addition to the **primary concentration bank.**

Divisional Concentration. With divisional concentration, divisions (or other logical company subunits such as groups, subsidiaries, or geographical territories) concentrate deposits and fund disbursements from a **divisional concentration bank.** Then the balance at the divisional concentration bank is adjusted by transfers between the primary (overall corporate) concentration bank and the divisional concentration banks.

Often, headquarters serves as an internal bank for the divisions. The divisions borrow cash from and repay it to the central cash pool at the primary concentration bank. With such an arrangement, divisions are not directly involved in either borrowing or short-term investment. A close variant is that divisions may borrow (when the company is in a net borrowing position), but all short-term investment is concentrated at the corporation with any divisions in a cash surplus position being credited with a formula interest return on any funds provided by a division to the corporate cash pool.

EXHIBIT 2   DAILY CASH FLOW MANAGEMENT: CASH ALLOCATION AND AGGREGATE CASH POSITION ADJUSTMENT

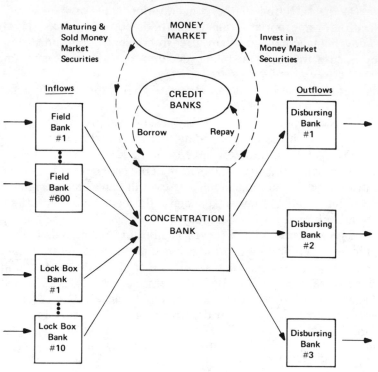

Regional Gathering. Sometimes deposits made by field units are moved first to a lockbox bank and then to the primary concentration bank. The lockbox bank serves as an **intermediate concentration bank.** In this context, it is often called a **gathering bank.** It is also called a **regional concentration bank** or simply an intermediate concentration bank.

DIRECT COLLECTIONS AND PAYMENTS. Besides the conventional collection and payment frameworks depicted in Exhibits 1 and 2, there may be collections going directly into the concentration bank from customers (e.g., from preauthorized checks, drafts, or electronic debits). Likewise, a company's vendors may make electronic payments directly to a company bank account, for example, by using the corporate trade payment feature of the **Automated Clearinghouse** (ACH) (discussed in the next subsection). Many companies disburse directly from the concentration bank, especially large payments such as taxes, major rent and lease payments, and sinking fund payments. Some also use their concentration bank to originate electronic payments.

THE PAYMENT SYSTEM

DEFINITION. The **payment system** refers to the variety of means by which funds are transferred from payor to payee. There are a number of alternative payment systems to consider.

PAYMENT ALTERNATIVES. Besides the direct exchange of coin and currency, the primary payment means are checks, payable-through drafts, credit drafts (credit card payments), wires, and **ACH transfers** (electronic check images).

Checks and Drafts. A **check** is a negotiable authorization to transfer money out of a bank account. A **payable-through draft** is also a negotiable claim on money in a bank account. However, a payable-through draft must be approved by the owner of the account before the drawee bank makes payment. In contrast, a check requires only verification of signature for the drawee bank to make payment. **Credit drafts** are commitments to pay at some future date. They usually involve a credit-granting intermediary that pays the seller and that assumes responsibility for collection from the buyer. They are primarily a means for retail payments (individual to company) rather than corporate-to-corporate payments.

Wires. A wire is a same-day movement of funds between two accounts. There are two primary domestic wire systems. **Fed wires** are wires sent via the wire network of the Federal Reserve System. **Bank wires** are transfers sent via the Payment and Telecommunications Services Corp., the wire network of a consortium of major banks. A special type of bank is a **cash wire.** The difference between a bank wire and cash wire is the settlement mechanism between the originating and receiving bank. Bank wire payments use correspondent accounts. Cash wire payments use **Federal Reserve accounts** (i.e., accounts that the originating and receiving banks have with Federal Reserve Banks). Thus, the Federal Reserve acts as a settlement intermediary for cash wires but not for bank wires.

ACH Transfers. "ACH" is the common abbreviation for **automated clearinghouse.** The ACH is a payment system that transfers funds between accounts at depository institutions (i.e., banks, savings and loans, mutual savings banks, and credit unions) via the use of computer-communication technology to transmit electronic payment information between participating depository institutions.

The ACH is organized as a system of 31 regional clearinghouse associations. The members of each regional clearinghouse association are depository institutions within a geographical area that participate in the ACH payment system. Not all commercial banks or other depository institutions participate in the ACH although 90 + % of the commercial banks and most of the large thrifts are ACH members.

The essence of fund transfer via the ACH is a set of procedures for exchanging electronic images of fund transfer instructions. There are two types of ACH transfers. **ACH credits** involve the movement of funds from a payor account to a payee account that is initiated by the payor. ACH credits are electronic analogues to check payments. An example is a direct payroll deposit. The paying company initiates ACH credit transfers that cause each employee account to receive credit for the wage amount being paid rather than providing a payroll check to these employees. **ACH debits** involve the movement of funds from a payor account to a payee account that is initiated by the payee rather than the payor. ACH debits are electronic analogues of preauthorized checks or drafts. An example is a preauthorized insurance payment in which the insurance company initiates the ACH transaction that results in a transfer of funds from its customers' accounts into its account.

Besides being electronics-based rather than paper-based, several features of the ACH system merit attention. First, the ACH provides next-day settlement throughout the entire nation. In contrast to checks, there are no geographical differences in the time required for ACH transfers. Second, the ACH is designed as a **zero-float payment** alternative in that the ACH rules call for the addition of collected funds to the payee account on the same day that funds are removed from the payor account. Third, the ACH payment message provides for the inclusion of payment addendum messages along with the fund transfer instructions. The standard CCD (**concentration and corporate debit**) transfer option provides a very limited message capability as a subset of the standard 94-character ACH fund transfer instruction. The CTP (**corporate trade payment**) transfer option provides for addendum messages in addition to the 94-character fund transfer instruction. The CTP option allows up to 4,999 addendum records. Each of the addendum records may have up to 94 characters. Thus, by packing a message into these records, a company may send a long electronic payment advice along with its ACH payment.

BANK SERVICES TO SUPPORT CASH MANAGEMENT

NONCREDIT SERVICES. Banks provide many noncredit services to support cash management. To a great extent, the design of a company's cash management system is the design of its noncredit banking system. That is, the selection of the company's lockbox banks, disbursing banks, concentration bank or banks, plus a variety of bank products and services for managing cash, short-term investment, and short-term borrowing. This subsection catalogs a number of bank and other third-party services that are critical to modern cash management.

LOCKBOX COLLECTIONS. *Lockbox collection services* are offered by many banks. The bank maintains a post office box in the company's name. Bank employees are authorized to pick up the company's mail and process its receivable payments. The essence of the service is periodic mail pickup, rapid processing, and possibly data capture and accounts receivable processing.

There are two reasons that companies use bank lockbox services. One is to accelerate the collection of mailed checks. The other is to have a bank (or other third party) provide some or all of the processing involved in updating a company's accounts receivable.

A lockbox service provides faster collection of mailed payments because of the reduction in mail time, processing time, and/or check availability time. Mail time is reduced because the services offer both more favorable locations than company processing centers and frequent, well-timed mail pickups with no post office delivery delay. Many banks specializing in lockbox services even have unique zip codes so that post office mail sorting time is also saved. Processing speedup is attributable to specialized and expeditious attention to checks including night and weekend processing. Availability can be faster to the extent that the lockbox is located nearer to the drawee banks than a company processing center. However, remote disbursing (writing the check on a bank distant from the payee address) can undo the apparent benefit of faster availability.

There are a wide variety of lockbox services. Most can be placed in two main classes—retail and wholesale.

Retail Lockbox Processing. A retail lockbox has a computer readable return document that the payors send back with their check, draft, money order, or other payment instrument. The use of a computer scannable return document is standard with most retail (i.e., consumer-to-company) payments although it also occurs in some company-to-company payments. The term "retail lockbox" arises from its primary use for consumer-to-company bill payments. Examples are credit card payments, telephone and other utility bills, and retail credit.

The essence of the processing in a retail lockbox is to verify that the amount of the payment and the amount on the return document match. Large retail lockbox services are highly automated. Often the retail lockbox service includes data capture (e.g., having a bank computer scan the return documents and prepare a tape for the payee to update accounts receivable records). Since the dollar amount of retail bills is small, the emphasis is generally on low-cost and efficient processing as much as on the acceleration of cash flow from faster processing.

Wholesale Lockbox Processing. Most wholesale (i.e., company-to-company) payments do not have a standard return document. Rather, the automated accounts payable system of the paying company creates a check and a computer-printed check addendum or payment advice that indicates the invoice(s) and other information (e.g., discounts taken, freight payments, allowances, returns, and other adjustments to the payment amount). The absence of a standard computer-readable return document means that the processing and data capture are usually much more complex for wholesale lockbox processing than for retail processing, especially when multiple invoices are paid with a single check.

Because the wholesale payments usually involve large dollar payments relative to retail, the wholesale lockbox service stresses rapid processing and collection of checks. In the simplest version, the bank acts primarily as a check processing-collection agent. A photocopy is usually made of the check. The photocopy, all other remittance documents, and possibly the envelope, are then sent to the company for its accounts receivable processing.

In many cases, the bank provides data capture and transmission services as well as the check processing and collection. There are many variations in data capture. The most complete is to convert the check data (i.e., amount, date, payor, payor account number) plus any addendum and remittance information into electronic form and deliver a tape, disk, or other electronic data storage device to the company. An alternative to sending a tape or disk to the company is computer-to-computer transmission from the bank to the company.

BALANCE REPORTING. Balance reporting is the generic term that describes the use of a computer-communication system to automate the creation and delivery of a variety of reports designed to convey balance and related transaction detail about a company's bank accounts. Cash managers have long obtained current balances and related detail by telephoning their banks and/or arranging to have their banks call them. Since the mid-1970s, major banks have put balance information on time-shared computers and provided terminal access with greatly expanded capabilities for reporting both detail and types of report.

The essence of all automated balance reporting systems is the provision of account balances and transaction detail available on a daily basis via terminal access to a time-sharing system. Differences in the various systems pertain primarily to (1) the amount of detail and the time period for which past data are available, (2) the variety of reports, and (3) the flexibility of the system in terms of user-defined reports.

A single-bank system only provides balance reports for the accounts at the bank offering the service. A multibank system allows reports for as many banks as a company can get to transmit the balance data to a bank or vendor offering a multibank balance reporting service, usually via time-shared computer. The multibank systems today generally allow only summary information and require use of fairly standard reports.

Daily Balance Information. For every account there is standard information. This includes current available balance, ledger balance, and the one-day and two-day available additions.

Average Balance Information. Reports typically indicate the average available balance for the month and possibly for longer time periods (e.g., year-to-date average).

Target Balance Report. Given the specification of a target balance, reports indicate deviation between actual average available balance and the target balance and indicate the average balance that must be maintained to meet the target (e.g., the average for the rest of the month, the rest of the year, and possibly other user-specified time periods).

Transfer Detail. Reports summarize wires received (i.e., amount, time, originating bank, and originating account identification), wires out (i.e., amount, time, receiving bank, and receiving account identification), depository transfer check (DTC) deposits, and ACH-based transfers and deposits.

Other Terminal Information. Besides reports on account status and related detail, the balance reporting systems are often used to convey other pertinent cash management information (e.g., recent quotes for a variety of money market instruments, possibly for a number of dealers).

Terminal-Initiated Money Transfers. Some of the balance reporting systems allow initiation of wire transfers, wire drawdowns, and, possibly, DTC and ACH-based transfers from the terminal in accord with a protocol for verification of the transfer amount, the identity of the initiator, and the detail on accounts to be debited and credited. Here it is important to avoid transfer initiation by unauthorized personnel and to prevent errors. It is especially important for any bank offering terminal-initiated money transfers to ensure that transfer instructions originate from an authorized user acting in accord with his or her company's policies. Terminal-initiated money transfers are usually restricted to standing transfers, that is, preauthorized accounts.

ZERO-BALANCE ACCOUNTS. **Zero-balance account** is a generic term for a set of procedures to maintain a zero balance in one or more accounts at a given bank. In the most common version, there is a set of *subaccounts* and a single *master account*. The company and its bank enter into an agreement that instructs the bank to move funds between each subaccount and the master account to achieve a zero balance in each subaccount. The company's residual balance at the bank then resides in the master account. Hence, the company can manage the balance at that bank as if there were only a single account. Therefore, a company need make at most one transfer into or out of that bank—that is, an appropriate transfer to the master account.

Zero-Balance Disbursement Accounts. When a company has several disbursing accounts at a bank, a zero-balance disbursing system has the company's disbursement bank fund each zero-balance subaccount from the master account each day. The company then funds the master account. One funding procedure is to receive a balance report via telephone or terminal indicating the master account balance and, thus, the funding requirement. Another funding arrangement is to have the disbursement bank initiate a wire drawdown in an amount that will maintain a target balance. *A wire drawdown* is the initiation of a wire request by the bank to receive the funds.

A special case of zero-balance disbursing is a single account at the disbursing bank with no subaccounts. The purpose here is to maintain an end-of-day balance of zero. The essence of the zero-balance arrangement is a report, often called a "control report," early in the day indicating total check presentments and funding requirements. The company then wire transfers the necessary funds to the disbursing bank.

Controlled Disbursing. A disbursement funding system driven by a report of each day's funding requirements is called controlled disbursing. When a zero-balance is maintained at the disbursing bank, it is controlled disbursing with a zero-balance target. A variant is controlled disbursing with a nonzero target. In this case, the control report giving each day's funding requirement tells the company's cash manager how much to transfer to maintain the given target.

Zero-Balance Lockbox Concentration. A company may have several lockbox accounts at a given bank, including different branches of the same bank. With a zero-balance system, each unit's subaccounts are set at zero with the deposits of all units consolidated into the company's master account. Thus, concentrating all lockbox deposits at a particular bank requires, at most, a single transfer from the master account. Likewise, the company can obtain a single balance report with subaccount detail rather than several balance reports. Thus, the zero-balance system saves transfers and simplifies cash management by enabling the cash manager to treat the bank and its branches as a single account for cash concentration purposes.

Zero-Balance Field Concentration. A company may have several operating units making deposits into their own accounts at a given bank, including different branches of the same bank. With a zero-balance system, each depositing unit's subaccounts are set at zero with the deposits of all units then consolidated into the company's master account at this bank. Thus, concentrating deposits from all the field units using that bank for deposits requires, at most, a single transfer from the master account rather than a transfer for each field unit. As with lockbox concentration, the zero-balance system saves transfers and simplifies cash management by enabling the cash manager to treat the bank and its branches as a single account for cash concentration purposes.

Collecting and Disbursing. Zero-balance systems may be set up at banks that are used for both collecting and disbursing. The single master account then serves to net out inflows and outflows. Both account funding and balance reporting are simplified.

Zero-Balance Benefits: Synthesis. Zero-balance systems reduce transfers and simplify cash management. The use of subaccounts also provides the company with separate activity detail for logical operating units and/or logical components of the cash flow. Therefore, the company is saved the cost of sorting account detail in its administrative processing. A system of zero-balance subaccounts and a master account provide the cash management benefits of a single account at a given bank and the administrative and control benefits of multiple accounts. These administrative benefits include forecasting and control, where unit and component detail is the logical focus.

THE COLLECTION SYSTEM

DEFINITION AND SUBPROBLEMS. The **collection system** refers to the means by which payments from customers are moved into the banking system. The collection system can be logically divided into two subproblems based on the type of payment—credit sales and noncredit sales. Most systematic design attention has been devoted to designing collection systems for credit sales, especially the design of a lockbox system to accelerate the collection of receivable payments.

COLLECTION SYSTEMS FOR NONCREDIT SALES. Noncredit sales leave money (i.e., coin, currency, checks, and credit drafts) at company field units. The term "field unit" is used as a generic term for any company entity that distributes goods and services (e.g., store, catalog showroom, service station, warehouse, branch office, and so on) and/or that receives payments from customers for deposit into bank accounts that are not the concentration account. Field receipts are usually deposited into banks near the field unit. These local deposit banks used by field units are called **field banks** or **field depositories.**

Field Collection System Design. Major field system design issues are (1) selection of field banks and field bank services, (2) deciding on the method(s) for field deposit reporting, (3) setting up a field deposit and field balance information-control system, and (4) specifying a variety of tactical issues that pertain to in-store (or in-unit) cash management, cash control, bank relations, and compensation. Many field design issues are company-specific or at least industry-specific.

Selecting Field Banks. The primary design task for the noncredit collection system is selection of the field deposit banks for receiving the deposits of the field units, specifying deposit procedures, and possibly arranging for various services from the field banks. The usual field bank selection criterion is geographical proximity to the field unit and/or convenience for the field unit manager. Hence, selecting field deposit banks is often viewed as a passive design decision and is often not given serious attention in many companies.

Multiple Units Using One Field Bank. When more than one unit uses the same field bank, should a company have separate accounts and transfers for each field unit? Or, should there be a single master account with zero-balance subaccounts? Using zero-balance subaccounts and a master account can reduce transfer costs. However, for firms relying on bank accounts for deposit control, there may be a reduction in control and/or a need for daily bank balance reports with their associated costs.

Branch Banks. In states with branch banking (e.g., California), should a company make an effort to use the branches of major banks? The tradeoffs are fewer accounts for transferring but possibly a less convenient depository location.

Compensation for Field Banks. How should field banks be compensated— *Fees, balances, or a combination?* **Compensating balances** are the standard form of compensation, primarily because information reporting and fund transfer delays make it impossible to remove all deposits as fast as they become an available balance without incurring overdrafts and/or very high administrative costs. Thus, most companies have higher field balances than necessary for field operations and decide to use these balances for compensation rather than paying fees and then also having excess field balances. For this reason, all-fee compensation is usually more costly for field banks than either all balance compensation or an appropriate combination of balances and fees.

Control. Should the branch bank play a role in a company's deposit reporting and deposit control? For instance, should the field bank call corporate headquarters if a deposit is not made by each field unit with a depository account at that bank? This would provide for improved control but most field banks are not able to provide this service except for those major corporate service banks that have a balance reporting service. Even when available, the cost is high and usually exceeds the value of improved control. Hence, most field deposit systems do not have a bank report on either field deposits or failure to make field deposits.

Coin and Currency. Arrangements must be made to provide coin and currency in some units. Frequency of replenishment and amount involve tradeoffs in management costs and effort versus higher cash balances.

Armored Car Pickup. If armored car pickup or delivery of cash is pertinent, the frequency and the time of day for both pickup and deposit are decisions that affect the cost of services and the amount of cash tied up.

DEPOSIT INFORMATION GATHERING. How should deposit information be reported—telephone calls or point-of-sale (POS) terminal transmission? If telephone calls are used, should these calls go to a central company location or should a third-party deposit information gathering service be used? Generally POS transmission is less costly than telephone calls, but it is not always available.

Deciding whether telephone call information should be gathered by the company or by an outside service is a make-or-buy decision. Most companies today use a third-party deposit information service rather than an internal system. Third-party services generally have higher variable costs but lower fixed costs than internal systems. In addition, the company avoids the burden of managing the gathering system and the cost of delivering the information to the concentration bank. The third-party service teleprocesses the deposit data to the company's concentration bank. The company receives reports on the field deposit activity from the deposit information gathering service and/or the concentration bank.

Report Timing. Most companies have their field units report the deposit amount after the deposit is made, frequently late in the day. Alternatives include more than one report per day or a midday report giving deposits (i.e., net receipts) for that morning and the previous afternoon and evening. The benefit of more frequent reporting is more information reported prior to transfer cutoff times and, therefore, faster movement of funds out of deposit banks.

Deposit Reporting Control. All the firms offering field deposit information gathering services offer a report to help control field units. This report indicates all units that have not reported by a particular time of day. Another control report may give all deposit amounts that fall outside of control limits.

THE COLLECTION SYSTEM FOR CREDIT SALES: OVERVIEW. The conventional way to pay for a purchase on credit is to send a check by mail. Hence, this is the standard assumption in designing a receivable collection system for credit sales. The essence of the design problem is to trade-off the value of faster collection of mailed checks with the cost of accelerating collection time. The term "accelerated collections" refers to reducing the time required for a mailed check to become an available balance (i.e., a collected balance) somewhere in the company's banking system. It means reducing one or more of the three components of collection time: mail time, processing time, and availability time.

There are two standard ways to process mailed receivable payments. They are company processing and lockbox processing.

Company Processing. If company processing is used, payments go to a company processing center. There, envelopes are opened, checks are removed, and administrative processing is initiated. Later, the checks, processed over some time period, are taken to a nearby bank and deposited. To avoid delays with local mail delivery, the company may direct payments to a post office lockbox. Company processing with items sent to a company-operated lockbox is often called an **internal lockbox** to distinguish it from the lockbox collection service offered by major banks.

Bank Lockbox Processing Services. Using this system, the checks are mailed directly to a company post office box maintained by a bank or other third-party offering a lockbox collection service. The bank periodically checks the lockbox and takes the envelopes to the bank's collection processing center. Alternatively, many banks now have a unique zip code. This enables these banks to receive all their lockbox mail directly from the post office without any time delay for post office sorting to individual lockboxes. These banks do their own mail sorting.

LOCKBOX NETWORKS. Until 1983, a company designing a lockbox collection system with several lockbox locations had to select a set of lockbox banks since most banks offered lockbox collections in only one state and generally only in one city within the state. Hence, having lockbox services in six cities meant dealing with six banks—and, therefore, six variants of reporting formats and processing procedures. Recently, several ways to deal with a single lockbox vendor have emerged as banks have circumvented the restriction that they take deposits only in one state. There are three generic variations: a bank consortia network, a single-bank local deposit network, and a single-bank transhipment network.

Bank Consortia Network. This format consists of a group of banks in different locations that agree to work together in a standardized service. There is a "lead service bank" with which the company deals primarily. Deposits are handled by the different banks but concentrated into a master account in the lead service bank. The company receives either a single consolidated report or multiple reports in a standard format. Hence, the consortia is a case of several banks organizing their service to provide both the organizational benefits of having a single lockbox vendor and also the acceleration benefits of multiple lockbox locations.

Single Bank Local Deposit Network. This type of network consists of a single bank with lockbox processing centers in several states. It receives the envelopes, opens them, removes checks for deposit, and does all the data capture, data transmission, and other processing associated with a given service option. Checks are deposited locally with a depository institution chartered to operate within that state. The checks are usually deposited into a correspondent account of the processing bank. These funds are then transferred to the processing bank's main office and credited to each company's account on the basis of an availability schedule for the city in which the checks were received and processed. Hence, this form of lockbox network means that a company deals with only one bank and avoids the problem of concentrating funds from the banks in each of its lockbox locations.

Single Bank Transhipment Network. A single bank offers lockboxes in many locations. However, it has neither local processing nor local deposit. Instead, the envelopes received at each lockbox location are shipped via courier to a central location for processing and deposit. This method involves the following two sources of delay relative to the alternative of local processing and local deposit: (1) the time to ship the checks via courier to the central processing location; and (2) slower availability because checks drawn on banks local to the lockbox location will be deposited at an out-of-state institution and thus receive slower availability than with local depositing. The advantage of transhipment over local processing is lower fixed cost (because there are no multiple lockbox processing sites) and, consequently, a lower price to the customer.

LOCKBOX PROCESSING: BENEFITS AND COSTS. The primary benefit of a lockbox collection service is reduced collection time (i.e., more rapid collection). The improvement in collection time arises from reducing one or more of the three components of collection time (i.e., mailing time, processing time, and availability time). A second benefit is the provision of data capture and receivable processing services.

Mail Time Improvement. Lockboxes reduce mail time because they are nearer (in mail time terms) to the customer than the company's receivable processing center. Improvements may also be achieved by avoiding the delay of moving mail from a central post office to carriers for local route delivery. Mail is also delivered to lockboxes more often than to the corporate address via local route delivery. Finally, banks with their own unique zip codes can also save some of the central post office sorting time.

Processing Time Improvement. A bank specializing in lockbox collections can generally process checks faster than a company. The time from processing initiation until deposit is less because the check is removed from envelopes, acceptability is verified, the check is photocopied (when pertinent) and deposited. Other data capture and receivable processing are usually performed subsequent to the deposit of the check. In addition, there may be benefits to specialization, including a specialized workforce and the use of special equipment for optical character recognition and for reading MICR encoding. Also, banks may have evening and weekend processing shifts and use part-time, peak-load labor more efficiently than most companies.

Availability Time Improvement. Improvements in the availability time granted a deposit are achieved in three ways. First, the lockbox bank might be closer to the drawee bank than the company's processing center. Second, the availability cutoff for lockbox deposits is often later than the availability granted over-the-counter deposits, especially over-the-counter deposits made at bank branches. Third, banks specializing in wholesale lockbox processing often have direct send programs for rapid check collection that is reflected in good availability schedules for checks.

Costs: Variable and Fixed. Lockbox processing incurs both variable and fixed costs. In addition to the usual deposit charge, there is a variable, per item cost assessed for each check processed. The fixed costs incurred reflect charges for the lockbox rental, transfer costs (arising from the need to move money into the concentration bank), and any additional account charges arising from simply having a lockbox.

LOCKBOX ECONOMICS. The essence of lockbox design is analysis of the tradeoff of the benefits of faster collection time versus incremental processing costs. Insight into this tradeoff is provided by the following example, which considers a single receivable payment of amount A processed via a lockbox rather than through a company processing center. Let i denote the interest value of funds tied up in the collection process and ΔT the acceleration in collection time at net incremental cost Δh. For a receivable of A, the net value (interest value of faster collection less incremental cost) is given by $iA\Delta T - \Delta h$. Exhibit 3 sketches the net value as a function of receivable size. For small items, the cost exceeds the benefit. Then there is a break-even size (denoted by $A^* = \Delta h/i\Delta T$). Above this size, it pays to use the lockbox in that the interest value of faster collections exceeds the incremental cost. Of course, there must also be sufficient volume of receivables that the total savings also cover the fixed cost of the lockbox.

To illustrate typical magnitudes of the break-even receivable size, consider the special case of one-day faster processing at 20 cents incremental processing cost and 0.04% interest per day (15.2% per year). In this particular case, the breakeven size is $A^* = \$0.20/(0.0004) = \$500$.

COLLECTION SYSTEM DESIGN FOR CHECK-BASED RECEIVABLES. There are two broad issues in designing a system for collecting receivables paid by check. One is deciding whether receivables should be processed by the company or by a bank (or other third-party) lockbox collection service. The second is selecting lockbox locations and assigning receivables to these locations and/or to company processing centers.

Lockbox Design. The focus of most collection systems studies is the selection of lockbox locations and the assignment of receivables to these locations. The receivables that should be processed by lockboxes are generally decided

EXHIBIT 3   BREAK-EVEN RECEIVABLE SIZE: PLOT SHOWING HOW VALUE OF ACCELERATED COLLECTIONS DEPENDS ON RECEIVABLE SIZE

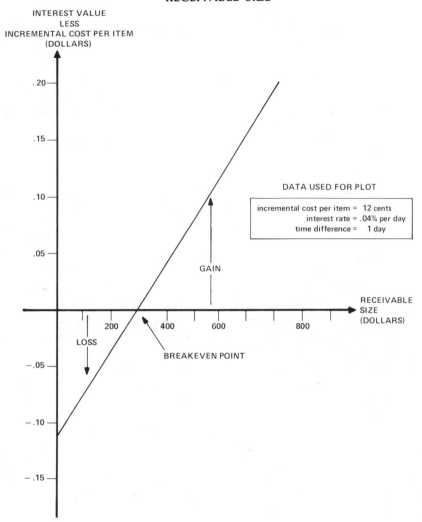

in advance, usually on the basis of some kind of break-even analysis for determining whether the receivables are large enough to justify the cost of lockbox processing.

Rather than dealing with the assignment of individual receivables, it is customary to group receivable payments into classes and to deal with the assignment of the receivable classes. The usual criterion for defining a receivable class is a zip code-based collection zone. **Collection zones** are generally defined on the basis of the first two digits of the zip code. The company generally samples its receivable payments to obtain the average check size for each class and possibly other parameters such as the current average collection time for the current mode of processing.

The Design Problem. The design task is to select lockboxes (or lockbox locations) and assign the receivable classes to the lockboxes to minimize the overall cost of processing receivables (i.e., the interest value of funds in process of collection less the processing costs). Frequently, a surrogate objective is used, generally minimizing collection time with possibly an average lockbox processing cost used to ensure an appropriate tradeoff between collection time improvement and the cost to attain it. In this case, there is no explicit distinction between lockbox processing costs at different banks.

Solution Methods. The optimization problem involved in selecting lockboxes and assigning receivables is a standard fixed-cost, assignment-location problem similar to the task of designing a warehousing system. It has been formulated in a number of articles. (See References for a listing of many of these articles.)

Using a Design Solution. The essence of arriving at an appropriate lockbox system design is deciding whether a company's current lockbox system should be changed to one of the solutions recommended by a design study. Hence, it is necessary to compare one or more alternative systems with the current system and the cost of the change.

There are three factors that must be considered in a change evaluation. First, since the data used in obtaining the new solution are based on a given sampling procedure and subject to sampling error, it is necessary to recognize that the measured improvements attributed to the alternative systems may include measurement error arising from the sampling process used to obtain input data. Second, since the company's accounts receivable compositions, the measured mail times, and the bank availability times are subject to change, it is necessary to consider how long the measured benefits are likely to be realized. Third, it is necessary to ask whether the benefits that a company can expect to realize after allowance for measurement error and instability are large enough to justify the cost of changing the system (i.e., the cost of adding or deleting lockboxes and reassigning receivables).

Because the solution of the lockbox design study is really input to a judgmental evaluation of alternative systems, the accepted industry standard in consulting studies on lockbox design involves organization of the output in a systematic way so that the reports assist the exercise of intelligent judgment. The essence of most reports is to give the best, second best, third best, and so forth, solutions for different size lockbox systems. Here, size refers to the total number of lockbox locations in the solution. Benefits for each solution are generally given as estimated improvement over the company's current system. Exhibit 4 shows how this information can be sum-

EXHIBIT 4   TOTAL COST VERSUS NUMBER OF LOCKBOXES; PLOT SHOWING TOTAL COST FOR FIVE BEST SYSTEMS OF EACH SIZE[a]

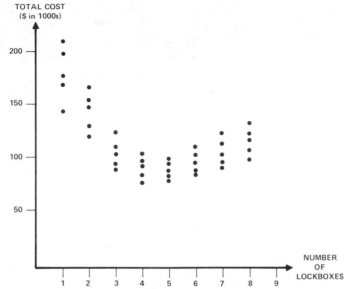

[a]The rapid improvement with size and then rather flat curve is typical of most actual situations. Having many alternatives near the optimum total cost is also typical of most actual situations.

marized graphically. In this particular case, one can tell by inspection that the minimum cost system involves five lockboxes. The increase in total cost beyond the fifth lockbox indicates that the collection time savings for additional lockboxes do not justify the additional costs associated with any additional lockboxes.

DATA ISSUES. The collection system design models require estimates of the mail time, processing time, and availability granted by the deposit bank.

Mail Time. The standard source for the mail times used by most banks in doing a lockbox study is the Phoenix-Hecht mail time data base. It measures average mail time from the downtown central post offices serving a collection zone to downtown post office boxes in lockbox cities. Actual receivable mail time is typically longer than the data base mail time because most payors do not mail receivable payments from a downtown post office. The justification for using such a sample of mail times is that there is a common bias for all lockboxes; hence, there should be no distortion in the selection of the optimal system if appropriate care is used in the design models.

Processing and Availability Times in Model Studies. The issue of how to measure processing and availability times for use in lockbox studies has been a subject of considerable controversy in lockbox design studies. In the past, the argument focused on Federal Reserve availabilities versus actual availabilities. Federal Reserve availability times were those that would be appropriate in a particular city *if* the lockbox bank used the Federal Reserve for the collection of lockbox checks. Actual availability could be better than Federal Reserve availability if the lockbox bank had a good direct send program or used correspondents and clearinghouses effectively. In "A New Industry Standard for Designing Corporate Collection Systems," (1980) Ferguson and Maier reported on a study that compared the results of a lockbox study using a standard design model based on Federal Reserve availability times and the actual availability schedules of banks. Their analysis showed that the solutions provided by the lockbox selection models depended significantly on the data source for availability times. Among the problems with Federal Reserve availability times was a bias toward too many lockbox banks in the optimal solution.

The concensus today is that the actual availability time is superior to Federal Reserve availability. However, there is still controversy over how this data should be obtained and used in a lockbox study. First, some banks offer more than one availability and price schedule. A company needs to be sure that any lockbox study its commissions uses the availability schedule (and associated the prices) that its items will actually receive. Second, there is an issue of how to measure processing time and ascertain that checks will be processed before assumed availability cut-offs. For instance, an item arriving late in the evening may not be processed until the next day if there is not a late-night processing shift or if a particular bank is not staffed to handle peak load processing. This is a particular example of processing holdover or carryover. Such holdover means much slower availability than assumed in contemporary lockbox design models. Similarly, weekends present complications and the possibility of slower processing and slower availability than usually assumed in contemporary lockbox design models. Finally, there are differences in bank processing speeds and bank availability assignment procedures that can mean not only significant differences in effective processing and availability times for banks within a particular city, but can also distort model solutions in terms of both the selected lockbox locations and the recommended number of lockbox banks. The users of lockbox studies must be very careful to ensure that data input to study models do not produce solution recommendations that do not actually reflect the best (or near best) system for their company.

BROADER DESIGN ISSUES. The conventional design of a receivable collection system assumes check payment via mail. A broader design perspective involves consideration of the means of payment.

Payment Alternatives. **Preauthorized checks (PACs), preauthorized drafts (PADS), preauthorized ACH debits,** and **wires** are alternatives to mail-based check payment. Neither the PAC nor the PAD involves mailing and they ensure timely payment. ACH debits and wires avoid not only mailing but also paper processing and thus provide even further administrative savings.

Future Collection Focus. Receiving check payments sent via the mail (with the associated problem of accelerating check collections) is the primary focus of collection system design for most companies offering trade credit. However, major opportunities for significant improvement in collection systems exist via alternative, electronic payment mechanisms that bypass the mail and provide administrative savings. Especially pertinent is the use of ACH-based payments to replace checks. The crux of electronic payment efforts is redesign of systems to achieve administrative savings with collection time being defined by the payor-payee agreement on payment terms and payment initiation time. The focus of collection system design is now shifting from check-based collection time improvements to consideration of payment form, payment terms, administrative processing systems and procedures, and overall collection system design.

Negotiated Settlement. Since incentives are often required to induce payors to use electronic payment rather than checks, negotiated settlement becomes a concern of efforts to induce payors to switch to electronic payment. *Negotiated settlement* is a generic term for ways to induce electronic payment with an agreed on date for exchange of good funds. Two forms of negotiated settlement are (1) direct agreement between payor and payee and (2) quoting of incentives (especially modified credit terms that provide either a discount for electronic payment or an extension of the nominal due date) by the payee.

THE DISBURSEMENT SYSTEM

PROBLEM DEFINITION. Within the framework of check-based payments, the primary concern of disbursement system design is deciding on (1) the number of disbursement banks, (2) their location, and (3) the assignment of checks to the particular banks. Most companies group check payments into classes and assign check classes to banks. The criteria for defining check classes include: (1) type of check (e.g., payroll, vendor payment, dividend, benefit, tax, and so on), (2) payee location (e.g., the zipcode of the payee address in a vendor payment), (3) size of check, and (4) company subunit, (e.g., a division, cost center, profit center, product group, or other logical company subunits for which the company keeps separate payment-expense records, has separate bank accounts, and/or operates separate payment systems).

The usual objective in check-based disbursement system design is the maximization of disbursement float time, that is, the time from the release of checks for mailing or delivery to payee until the checks clear the disbursement bank. A more complete and correct objective for check-based payments is to trade-off disbursement float extension and the cost of attaining it.

A broader perspective of disbursement design includes the form of payment (check versus alternatives such as wire, ACH debit, or preauthorized draft) and the overall cost of administering the disbursing system. This subsection first treats the conventional disbursement design task of selecting disbursing banks for check payments. Then treatment is expanded to broader design concerns.

DISBURSEMENT BANK LOCATION. Assume that a company has placed checks into classes and estimated the number of checks and average check size for each class. A common objective is to select disbursement banks (i.e., disbursement locations) and assign check classes to some disbursing bank to maximize either the disbursement float or the disbursement float time. A more appropriate objective is to maximize the value of disbursement float less the incremental cost of disbursing from several banks.

DISBURSEMENT FLOAT COMPONENTS. Fully understanding the issues involved in disbursement float extension requires consideration of the components of disbursement float time—that is, mail time, payee processing time, and check clearing time. Most firms do not engage in remote mailing (i.e., mailing from one or more sites that are different from the one(s) at which the checks are prepared and written, especially sites that are geographically remote from the payee). Therefore, mail time and payee processing time typically are taken as given and independent of the drawee bank location. Hence, the selection of drawee banks to maximize disbursement float time is usually tantamount to maximizing the check clearing time.

Components of Check Clearing Time. Check clearing time can be further resolved into (1) availability time and (2) clearing system slippage. Availability time is the granted availability at the depository bank. It is the time from deposit until the payee (depositor) receives credit for good funds (collected funds). Clearing system slippage is any additional time for the check to clear. For example, if the availability time were two business days and the actual clearing time were three business days, the clearing system slippage would be one business day.

Positive clearing slippage benefits the payor and may not cost the payee to the extent that the slippage is provided by the banking system and is not priced (i.e., charged for in some way). Thus, clearing system slippage is that part of the disbursement float that may be a positive-sum game between the payor and the payee; that is, the benefit for one party is not totally offset by an equivalent cost to the other party.

Views on Clearing Time Components. While most companies focus on total clearing time, there are reasons to be concerned about its source. Ferguson and Maier in "Disbursement System Design for the 1980s" (*Journal of Cash*

Management, December 1981), argue that clearing slippage is "risky float" in the sense of being more likely to be eliminated than availability time. Hence, Ferguson and Maier advocate assigning greater value to the availability component than to the clearing system slippage component of the check clearing time. A contrasting view is that the availability extension (1) is achieved at the cost of the payee (vendor), (2) is tantamount to "disguised stretching," and (3) is therefore less valuable than clearing system slippage, since availability time extension involves a cost in customer relations while clearing system slippage is a subsidy of the banking system.

Recent changes in check clearing have greatly complicated the view that clearing system slippage is a subsidy provided by the banking system. The situation depends on the source of slippage (deposit bank, Federal Reserve System, drawee bank) and the pricing policy of the deposit bank. Fed float, or delays in check clearing incurred by the Federal Reserve, may be priced in the sense of charging the deposit bank for slippage. The deposit bank may or may not actually charge a particular depositor. Thus, Fed slippage may be charged to the check depositor completely (no subsidy), fractionally (partial subsidy), or not at all (complete subsidy).

Treating Components in Disbursement System Design. Whether a company gives the conventional equal weight to availability time and clearing system slippage or gives one or the other component greater weight clearly varies from company to company since it is a matter of company policy. All cases can be handled within the framework of current disbursement design models simply by replacing total disbursement float time (or total clearing time) by a weighted float measure that assigns different weights to the components. Moreover, the standard algorithms used for maximizing total float time can be used without any change other than modifying the relative importance of the float components.

The important points here are recognition that (1) the two components of check clearing time are not necessarily of equal value and (2) variation in relative importance can be incorporated within the framework of current design methodology.

RECENT DEVELOPMENTS. The environment in which disbursing is conducted has changed significantly in recent years. Major factors include (1) Federal Reserve efforts at accelerated check processing to reduce Federal Reserve float, (2) Federal Reserve efforts to discourage remote disbursing, (3) the Depository Institution Deregulation and Monetary Control Act of 1980 (1980 Monetary Control Act), (4) evolution in payment terms, especially good funds terms, and (5) the emergence of a variety of electronic payments mechanisms that are alternatives to check-based and draft-based payments.

Federal Reserve Collection Improvements. In recent years, the Federal Reserve has made efforts to eliminate Federal Reserve float. These efforts include revising its availability schedule, changing cut-off times for receiving checks, insisting on timely check presentment by banks, arranging better processing and logistical transportation of checks, and generally improving the check processing.

Remote Disbursing. The practice of writing checks on a given bank solely to secure extended float is called "remote disbursing." Since the late 1970s, the Congress, the Federal Reserve, and the SEC have devoted considerable attention to remote disbursing. Federal Reserve float exploitation involves two major issues. First, the cost of increased Federal Reserve float is indirectly a cost to taxpayers, since the Federal Reserve remits its operating surplus to the U.S. Treasury. Second, companies not exploiting Federal Reserve float incur relatively higher net payment costs than the companies exploiting it. Therefore, they are subject to a competitive disadvantage.

Since most companies set up their disbursing system with the cooperation of their banks, the Federal Reserve discouraged remote disbursing by exerting pressure on major banks not to facilitate remote disbursing, especially via correspondent or other cooperative relationships with other banks.

Controlled Disbursing. Controlled disbursing (discussed further in connection with disbursement funding) is the practice of disbursing from banks that receive all check presentments from the Federal Reserve early in the day and are able to report the dollar volume of a company's presentments so that there is knowledge of check funding obligations early in the day. This knowledge enables a company to fund its disbursing account on a same-day basis including provision of funds by borrowing, the issuance of commercial paper, and/or the sale of short-term marketable securities. Moreover, in the case of a net surplus, controlled disbursing makes possible timely investment of any excess balances.

The Depository Institution Deregulation and Monetary Control Act of 1980. The 1980 Monetary Control Act requires that the Federal Reserve price its float. This is done by charging interest for the use of funds when the Federal Reserve grants faster check availability than its actual collection time.

Changing Payment Terms. The focus on extending disbursement float arises in part because of the traditional practice of regarding an item as paid when mailed. In recent years, the combination of remote disbursing and other stretching practices have led many companies to restate credit terms on the basis of when payment is received or when good funds (i.e., collected balances) are received, especially in the case of trade discounts. Moreover, some companies seeking to provide incentive for electronic payment might now state terms conditional on the method of payment; for example, the alternatives might be a 2% discount for check payment if mailed by the seventh day or a 2% discount for electronic payment or preauthorized draft if good funds are "received by the fourteenth day." The extended time is designed to encourage electronic payment and effectively to share savings with the payor. Such changes in credit terms mitigate the benefits of extending disbursement float. Like the Federal Reserve pricing of its clearing services and float, restatement of payment terms and/or incentives for electronic payment remove, or at least reduce, economic incentives for maximizing disbursement float.

DESIGN STRATEGY. Pricing Federal Reserve float, the economic advantages of an electronic payment over paper-based payment, and changing payment terms are all forcing companies to view the design of their disbursement systems in a broader perspective than simply trying to maximize disbursement float. In particular, it means that alternatives to mailed checks (such as ACH payments, wires, or preauthorized drafts) should be given explicit consideration.

With electronic payments (either ACH payments or wires), there is no difference in clearing time between banks and there is no mail time at all. Therefore, the issue of which bank gives the most disbursement float vanishes simply because there is no difference between disbursing banks in terms of disbursement float time. There may, however, be significant differences in terms of quality, reliability, or service costs. But, there is no float-based incentive to use multiple disbursing banks when there is no float variation across drawee banks with electronic payment.

THE BROADER PROBLEM. The new focus on disbursing systems is structuring systems for payments that are administratively efficient rather than concentrating on check float optimization. The pioneers in direct payment systems today are companies that have set up electronic payment systems with payees with whom they have a close and regular relationship, for example dealers, distributors, and franchisees.

DISBURSEMENT DESIGN: SYNTHESIS. In the 1970s, disbursement design focused on extending disbursement float time. The primary reasons for this emphasis were payment terms based on the mail initiation date, "free" Federal Reserve float, and significant geographical differences in check availabilities.

The decision focus in float extension is the selection of disbursing banks. The essence of disbursement bank selection procedures is (1) identification of candidate disbursing banks, (2) measurement of disbursement time for various classes of checks, and (3) selection of disbursing banks and assignment of checks (check classes) to the selected banks via judgment aided by rules of thumb. Others use computer-based models, often with the assistance of a bank consulting service.

Four factors now forcing a broader look at disbursement system design are:

1. An emerging trend toward changing payment terms, especially defining payment time on the basis of payment receipt and/or good funds receipt
2. A significant reduction in clearing system slippage and the geographical differences in availability times
3. A discouragement of remote disbursing by the Federal Reserve through the pricing of Federal Reserve float and clearing services and via pressure on banks
4. The economics of electronic payment relative to paper (check and draft), including the economics of electronic ordering and billing as well as electronic paying.

The short-run reaction to payment system changes has been concerned with controlled disbursing as an alternative to remote disbursing in that it preserves the structure of a company's current information system. The long-run impact, however, will be a shift away from both remote and controlled disbursing to focus disbursement design on broader issues such as (1) the method of payment, (2) systems designed to achieve savings from efficient payment, and (3) negotiation between payor and payee on payment terms and timing.

CASH CONCENTRATION

DEFINITION. Cash concentration pertains to the movement of money from deposit banks into the central cash pool at the concentration bank.

SUBPROBLEMS. Cash concentration can be broken into two major subproblems—design and management. **Cash concentration design** pertains to (1) the selection of the concentration bank (or banks), (2) the selection of transfer methods and transfer initiation times, (3) the design of a control and administrative information system, and (4) specification of a variety of policies and procedures. **Cash concentration management** involves (1) cash transfer scheduling (i.e., deciding on the time and amount of transfers), (2) the day-to-day operation of a deposit information gathering system, and (3) the operation of an administrative control system.

TYPES OF CONCENTRATION SYSTEMS. Besides the distinction between design and management, it is useful to distinguish between lockbox concentration and field concentration, the two primary types of concentration systems. **Lockbox concentration** is moving money from lockbox banks to the concentration bank. **Field concentration** is moving money from field deposit banks to the concentration bank.

Lockbox concentration is much easier than field concentration for several reasons. First, there are generally fewer lockbox banks than field banks. A large lockbox system consists of 8 to 12 lockbox banks. In contrast, 200 to 300 field banks is a small field system. Second, lockbox deposits are almost always checks and drafts rather than coin and currency. Hence, there is a time delay before a company has good funds (i.e., collected funds). Therefore, there is time to initiate the transfer of a lockbox deposit before a company has idle balances. Third, most lockbox banks can provide timely information on balances and/or assume responsibility for moving money into the concentration bank. In contrast, most field deposit banks (other than those that are also money center banks) do not provide balance reporting or provide automatic funds transfer services. Fourth, lockbox deposits do not involve the fraud-theft control problems that often arise with field deposits.

TRANSFER ALTERNATIVES. In cash concentration, funds are transferred between the accounts of the same company at two different depository institutions. Therefore, cash can be concentrated via any payment mechanism available for moving funds between bank accounts at different banks, namely wires, checks, or ACH transfers. In the case of check-based transfers, the standard method involves a specific type of check known as a **depository transfer check (DTC).** This type of check has the words "depository transfer check" written on it. With the appropriate legal agreements between a company and its banks, a DTC can be used without a signature as long as it is deposited into specified company accounts. Moreover, because it is explicitly restricted for deposit into a particular company bank account, the device of the depository transfer check simplifies administrative procedures and greatly reduces the usual problems of check control.

Banks seeking concentration business provide an **automated DTC service,** namely the automatic preparation of DTCs from deposit information or other company-provided data. Likewise, many major banks are now providing a similar service for ACH-based depository transfers, that is, an **automated ACH transfer preparation service** in which deposit information provides the basis for the automated preparation of ACH depository transfers.

The ACH-based transfer is sometimes called a **"paperless DTC"** or **"electronic DTC."** It serves the same function as a DTC but without the use of a paper check.

FIELD DEPOSIT INFORMATION: FIELD VERSUS CENTRALIZED INITIATION. While each transfer mechanism can be used in a variety of ways, field initiation and centralized initiation are the generic approaches on which transfers are based. With **field initiation,** the field unit manager or the field bank (or the lockbox bank in the case of lockbox concentration) initiates the transfer and is responsible for deciding on the amount of transfers. With centralized initiation, deposit information is gathered at a central location and the transfers are initiated at the concentration bank. Central initiation requires either a deposit information gathering system to provide the necessary deposit data at a central location, a forecast of the deposited amount, or possibly both. In contrast, field initiation takes place where the deposit data exists so that transfer preparation does not require either central gathering of deposit data or a deposit forecasting system.

Until the early 1970s, most retail field systems were field initiated with a few companies running their own centralized deposit information gathering by directing telephone calls to a central company location. Since the early 1970s, a number of third-party deposit information gathering services have been created by time-sharing firms and/or major banks. Most major banks have further facilitated central initiation by developing services to prepare and initiate transfers automatically from deposit report information. Now, more than 90% of the retail concentration systems use central initiation with a third-party deposit reporting service.

FIELD DEPOSIT REPORTING. Most field concentration systems in operation today rely on gathering deposit information in a central location. Because most of the field deposit banks cannot report field deposit data in a timely way, each field unit reports on its deposits. There are two generic ways to handle the centralized gathering of deposit data: (1) using a third-party deposit reporting service or (2) having the data sent to a central company collection point.

Deposit Information Gathering Services. Several computer service companies and at least one major bank offer services that receive, store, and later forward data on a company's field deposits. The essence of each service is a call receiving center that takes telephone calls from field unit personnel and records the information about the deposit in a computer data file. Typical information in a deposit report is (1) the dollar amount, (2) the mix of cash, checks, and credit drafts, and (3) other pertinent cash management information such as the time of day when deposits were made or predictions of future deposits. This data is stored in the information gathering service's computer and forwarded at a prearranged time to the company and/or to the company's concentration bank.

In the most common version of a third-party deposit reporting service, the entire deposit report file is typically transmitted to the concentration bank. The company only receives exception and summary reports. The two standard exception reports are (1) all units not reporting by a prespecified cut-off time, and (2) any unit that reports deposit amounts that do not fall within prespecified control limits. Often, the concentration bank will prepare the summary reports and distribute them to the company electronically via its balance reporting service.

Company-Based Information Gathering. While most companies use third-party deposit information gathering services, a few gather the information themselves. Some simply run their own call receiving centers that receive telephone calls and convert reported data into a computer data file. Then the company transmits its desired transfers to the concentration bank. Other companies use their point-of-sale terminals and the associated terminal-to-computer link to obtain, transmit, and store the deposit data. With a point-of-sale terminal system, company personnel in each field unit key appropriately coded deposit data into the unit's terminal. This data is stored in the terminal and later transmitted with other data to a central computer, which sorts out the deposit data, organizes it into a deposit file, and makes it available for use by company cash managers.

Using point-of-sale terminals generally saves telephone costs and third-party reporting charges. But it often means that the transfer preparation is slower because of delays in getting the data (1) gathered and available to the cash managers and (2) to the concentration bank.

Wire Alternatives. Traditionally, wire transfers are initiated at the depository bank. Such transfers might be initiated by a request from a field unit manager. More often, however, a company leaves standing wire instructions with the deposit bank, especially in the case of lockbox concentration. Typical instructions at the deposit bank might be, "wire out each day's deposits" or "wire all funds in excess of $5,000 whenever the balance exceeds $25,000." Such instructions are designed to maintain a target compensating balance while moving funds to the concentration bank.

It is also possible to have the concentration bank initiate wires. In this procedure, the concentration bank contacts the depository bank with wire instructions. The initiation of a wire at the request of the receiving bank is called a **wire drawdown** or simply a drawdown.

DEPOSIT CONTROL. Deposit control is primarily for field concentration. Deposit control involves (1) ensuring timely deposit execution and reporting and (2) preventing fraud and theft. Reporting controls are built into most deposit information gathering systems (e.g., an exception report listing units that have not reported).

The conventional approach to theft prevention involves the rapid removal of deposits from the field bank. An overdraft indicates both a possible failure to make reported deposits and a need for quick investigation. However, the reporting process, transfer preparation, and transfer clearing involve time delays during which theft losses can occur. Also, this process is relatively ineffective for the prevention of "skimming," that is, the taking of only a portion of the day's receipts.

Some companies use forecast-based control. These systems compare actual and/or reported deposits with pro forma predictions of deposits. Exception reports are generated whenever there are significant deviations. A variation to using forecasts simply to produce reports is to use the forecasts as the basis for transfer initiation amounts. This procedure moves money faster than deposit-report based movement. Whenever substantially less than the forecasted amount is deposited, there will be an overdraft at the field bank. To the extent that the field bank promptly reports the overdraft to company headquarters (and not the field unit personnel), the overdraft serves as a control on whether the field unit actually made the forecasted deposit. However, the problem is that forecast errors (rather than deposit problems) can also cause overdrafts with their associated costs, administrative work, and damage to banking relations if they occur too often.

TRANSFER METHOD EVALUATION. The issue of which transfer method should be used at a particular deposit bank has been traditionally viewed as an issue of cost versus transfer speed. For instance, a wire is faster but more expensive than a DTC or ACH-based transfer. Exhibit 5 summarizes typical cost ranges and availability time for various ways of using each transfer alternative.

The Break-Even Framework. The conventional framework for evaluating transfer methods is a break-even analysis comparing differences in transfer costs with the value of interest that could be earned over the difference in availability times. For instance, if the cost difference and the availability difference between a wire and DTC are $6 and one day, respectively, then the break-even transfer size at an interest rate of 0.03% per day is $20,000, since it requires $20,000 to earn $6 interest in one day at 0.03% per day.

The break-even framework is responsible for the conventional rules of thumb that dictate using DTCs for small transfers and wires for large transfers, say DTCs for transfers of less than $20,000 and wires for amounts greater than $20,000.

Limitations of Break-Even Framework. While the break-even framework and its implied rules of thumb are in wide use today, the framework is inappropriate for a variety of reasons. First, the difference in availability times for alternative transfer methods is not necessarily the effective delay, as the break-even framework assumes. For instance, a company using DTCs that knows it has $10,000 of transfers in process at a particular depository bank might remove the money tied up in the transfer process by a one-time adjusting transfer and thereby eliminate the transfer delay effect. Or, in the case of check deposits, there is typically a day or more availability delay at the deposit bank. Hence, the choice is between a DTC initiated on the day of deposit or a wire on the next business day. In this situation, since the checks deposited are removed the next day with either a DTC or wire, the effective delay difference is zero and not the one-day difference in availability time assumed in the conventional breakeven framework. The key is knowing when each instrument converts deposits into available balances at the concentration bank.

The second defect of the break-even framework pertains to differences in granted availability for the transfer at the concentration bank and the

EXHIBIT 5   DATA ON TRANSFER DELAYS AND COSTS

TRANSFER METHODS	DELAY (DAYS)	TYPICAL COST RANGE [a]	COST COMPONENTS	
WIRE	0	$12.00–$26.00	1.	Outgoing Wire
			2.	Wire Receipt
DTC: Third–Party Assisted	1–2	$ .60–$ 1.20	1.	Third–Party Charge
			2.	Deposit Charge
			3.	DTC Preparation Charge
			4.	Check Charge
DTC: Centralized Company Initiation	1–2	$ .10–$.40 plus the cost of bank and/or company preparation of either the DTCs and/or the DTC tape image and any communication costs.	1.	Deposit Charge
			2.	Check Charge
			3.	Bank Processing Charge
			4.	Company Processing Cost
			5.	Communication Cost
DTC: Mail–Based	2–7	$ .30–$.55	1.	Deposit Charge, Lockbox
			2.	Check Charge
			3.	Postage/ Envelope
ACH: Third–Party Assisted	1	$ .34–$.50 plus any bank preparation charge	1.	Third–Party Charge
			2.	Electronic Transfer Charge
			3.	Bank Preparation Charge
ACH: Centralized Company Initiation	1	$ .08–$.14 plus any bank preparation charges and/or the cost of company preparation of the EDTC tape and any communication costs.	1.	Electronic Transfer Charge
			2.	Bank Preparation Charge
			3.	Company Processing Cost
			4.	Communication Cost

[a]Cost ranges reflect variation in charges across banks and third-party information gathering services.
Source: Bernell K. Stone and Ned C. Hill, "Alternative Transfer Mechanisms and Methods: Evaluation Frameworks," Journal of Bank Research, Vol. 13, No. 1 (Spring 1982).

actual clearing time involved in removing the funds from the depository bank. For a wire, these are equal. For a DTC, the availability time may be less than, equal to, or greater than the actual clearing time. If the availability time were less by one business day, the DTC transfer would mean that the company had credit for available balances in two banks for one business day. In this case, the DTC provides the greater opportunity for interest value for any size transfer, the exact opposite to the conclusion of the break-even framework.

The third defect of the break-even framework is failure to reflect the value of balances in compensating banks for services. The fourth defect is an implicit assumption of either a one-time transfer or on-going daily transfers. Good cash transfer scheduling (discussed later in this section) means the actual situation is almost always more complicated than an automatic daily transfer of each day's reported deposits.

Cost Comparison Framework. An alternative to the incomplete breakeven framework is the cost comparison framework set forth by Stone and Hill, "Alternative Cash Transfer Mechanisms and Methods: Evaluation Frameworks" (*Journal of Bank Research,* 1981). The Stone-Hill framework is based on comparison of the total scheduling cost associated with each transfer method and the selection of the least-cost alternative. The costs consist of the direct transfer cost, the interest value of any excess balances at the deposit bank, and a measure of the value of any usable dual balances arising from differences in availability times and clearing times. Here, care is necessary to make sure that only dual balances that can be removed and/or used as compensating balances are counted. Finding the minimum value of this cost requires finding the optimal cash transfer schedule for each transfer alternative.

CASH TRANSFER SCHEDULING. Cash transfer scheduling is deciding on the timing and amount of cash transfers.

The Daily Transfer Solution. Until the mid-1970s, the conventional solution to the cash transfer scheduling problem was a daily transfer of each day's reported deposits. Stress is placed on "reported deposits" because delays in reporting and information gathering and processing could mean that transfers initiated pertained to deposits a day or so earlier than the actual transfer initiation date.

Daily transfers as soon as deposit information becomes available seem like the fastest possible mobilization of deposits. Many cash managers believe that the only way to mobilize money faster would be to reduce reporting and information processing delays. This still widespread view is incorrect. Money can be moved out faster than daily transfers of each day's reported deposits by using forecasts and/or dynamic target systems. Moreover, daily transfers can be unnecessarily expensive and can mean foregoing opportunities for cost reductions in cash concentration.

Scheduling Techniques. Beginning in the mid-1970s, a number of sophisticated cash managers recognized several ways to improve cash transfer procedures by abandoning the automatic transfer of each day's reported deposits. Several rule-of-thumb scheduling techniques were used. While there are many variants, most can be put into one of three classes: anticipation, weekend timing, and nondaily transfers.

Adjusted Target Anticipation. Anticipation is a generic term for a variety of transfer acceleration methods that use forecasts of some type to enable initiation of transfers before the company is informed of an available balance addition at the deposit bank. The most common form of anticipation is the so-called *adjusted target framework* in which a company makes a one-time removal of deposits in process. For instance, management might observe from past bank statements that deposits in process average $8,000. Hence, the cash manager removes the $8,000 and operates on company books with a target balance that is $8,000 less than the actual target balance.

Time-Varying Anticipation. A limitation on the adjusted target technique arises from time-varying deposits, especially the strong weekly cycle that is typical of field deposits at fast food companies, many soft good retailers, and food retailers. Not incurring overdrafts can mean removing only part of the average value of deposits in process. To remove more, companies may use time-varying anticipation by using deposit forecasts to determine the amount that can be anticipated at any time. In such a system deposit reports and/or balance reports provide a control on the forecast.

Availability Anticipation. For check and credit draft deposits, there is a delay before the company receives credit for an available balance. Knowledge of the ledger balance and the availability delay means that a transfer can be timed to remove deposits as they become available. For instance, a DTC with one-day clearing time might be initiated to remove tomorrow's available additions as soon as the balance report giving the ledger balance and the schedule of available additions is received. This method is also called **ledger anticipation**, since it involves predictions of the conversion of a ledger balance into an available balance. It is a special case of time-varying anticipation in which a company can forecast available additions over a one-day horizon with virtually perfect accuracy on a day-to-day basis aside from return items.

Weekend Timing. When the availability time is less than the clearing time, dual balances are created. Timing transfers to increase the amount of the dual balances over the weekend can significantly increase the amount of dual balances. For instance, with a one-day availability time and two-business day clear time, Thursday transfers provide dual balances on Friday, Saturday, and Sunday—three days rather than one. Thus, any transfer amounts shifted to Thursday can triple the dual balance creation. Hence, transferring the Wednesday deposit, the Thursday deposit, and part of the deposits expected on Friday and the weekend can significantly increase the total dollars getting the dual balance benefit.

When the availability time received is greater than the clearing time, there is a time period for which the company receives credit for an available balance in neither bank. This situation arises frequently when the deposit bank or its correspondent has an aggressive direct send program. In this case, weekend timing means avoiding weekend transfers. For instance, with one-day availability and same day clears, Friday transfers should be avoided.

Nondaily Transfers. Moving from daily to less-frequent transfers is a way to reduce direct transfer costs. There are several popular frameworks for managing nondaily transfers. A *trigger point rule* is a type of economic order quantity that initiates a transfer down to a return point whenever the balance exceeds a trigger level. A *periodic frequency* rule is a procedure involving a transfer down to a return point at periodic intervals, say every other business day, every third business day, or once a week.

The Scheduling Dilemma. The transfer schedule influences three cost factors—the direct transfer cost, the value of excess balances at the deposit bank, and the value of usable dual balances. Each of the three generic scheduling techniques focuses on different cost components. Anticipation focuses primarily on reducing excess balances. Weekend timing deals with dual balances. Nondaily transfer rules focus primarily on lowering the direct transfer cost. A good schedule should properly trade off these three cost factors and the relative emphasis placed on these techniques. Even more difficult than ensuring a good tradeoff can be resolving conflicts between some of the rule-of-thumb scheduling procedures. For instance, conventional trigger point rules preclude weekend timing and can complicate the sophisticated use of anticipation.

Optimal Cash Transfer Scheduling. Stone and Hill, in "Cash Transfer Scheduling for Efficient Cash Concentration," (*Financial Management,* Fall 1980) formulated a cost measure that properly trades off direct transfer costs and the interest value of balances. They showed that the least-cost schedule can be obtained by solving an integer scheduling problem that optimally incorporates each of the rule-of-thumb scheduling procedures in common use. Like the algorithms for lockbox design and disbursement design, the cash management consulting groups of some banks are now providing algorithms for obtaining computer-based solutions of this scheduling problem.

CASH CONCENTRATION DESIGN: SYNTHESIS. Cash concentration design pertains to specification of the structure of the cash concentration system. There are four primary design decisions: (1) selection of the concentration bank or banks, (2) assignment of concentration banks to deposit banks whenever there is more than one concentration bank, (3) selection of the set of transfer methods that a company will support, and (4) assignment of a transfer method to a deposit bank.

The primary focus of past concentration design was **transfer method as-**

signment, generally in an improperly chosen break-even framework. The systematic evaluation and selection of concentration banks and the merits of several concentration banks tend to be neglected design decisions.

CONCENTRATION BANKS: EVALUATION

PAST SELECTION CRITERIA. A company's current concentration bank or banks were selected in the past for reasons that have little to do with concentration efficiency today. In the past, selection was often based on location: namely, the headquarters city and/or New York City (the latter providing close proximity to major money markets). Another criterion used in the past was selection of the lead credit bank, or at least a major credit bank, since adjustments to the balance at the concentration bank were made primarily by bank borrowing or loan repayment.

Good communication systems and same-day money transfers mitigate the importance of location. Credit lines can be arranged at most major banks so that logic dictates first selecting the concentration bank for operational reasons and then allocating the credit lines.

CONCENTRATION SERVICES. A concentration bank must have reliable, error-free money transfer, communication, and balance reporting services. Automatic preparation of DTC transfers, ACH transfers, and possibly wire drawdowns are essential. Interface to third-party information gathering services is critical for any company using such services and is characteristic of all the banks specializing in concentration. Likewise, ability to accept company tapes or teleprocessing is critical for companies managing their own deposit information gathering. At least one concentration bank is now offering its own deposit information gathering service.

Banks not providing such services and not committed to staying at the frontiers of cash concentration services are not serious candidates for being operational concentration banks for major companies, especially those with large field deposit systems.

FAST AVAILABILITY AS A SELECTION CRITERION. The most common criterion used for systematic evaluation of alternative concentration banks is fast availability. Fastness is often measured by dollar-weighted availability time for a given region weighted by the relative dollars deposited in that region. Presumably, the best concentration bank for a particular company is the one with the fastest dollar-weighted availability.

LIMITATIONS OF DOLLAR-WEIGHTED AVAILABILITY. Dollar-weighted availability as a selection criterion has several defects, although it provides useful information. First, focusing on check availability implicitly assumes the use of DTCs for concentrating transfers. Second, granted availability is not the same as effective availability when a company uses anticipation. Third, availability (even a measure of effective availability) is only part of the overall concentration cost. There are also direct transfer charges, fixed costs, and possibly dual balance effects in the case of DTCs. For instance, a bank might grant uniform one-day availability but aggressively use direct sends, so that some DTCs clear in less than a day and the company has negative dual balances. Fourth, dollar-weighted availability implicitly assumes only a single concentration bank.

TOTAL COST CRITERION. Superior to availability-only measures are comparisons based on total concentration costs. Of course, cost comparison assumes reliable, quality services that are otherwise comparable. Measures of concentration costs should include the impact of concentration bank transfer costs, excess field balances, any dual balances, and a variety of fixed administrative costs. Incorporating factors besides availability can make measurement difficult; however, recognizing these factors is clearly superior to ignoring them.

MULTIPLE CONCENTRATION BANKS. Today, the most common reasons for multiple concentration banks are divisional concentration and regional gathering. (Regional gathering is less common.) There has been a trend in recent years to move toward fewer concentration banks and often a single bank.

The primary benefit of only one concentration bank is administrative simplicity. However, the simplicity may be incurred at some cost, especially for DTC-based concentration. Multiple banks provide ability to obtain the best of each bank's granted availability.

SYSTEMATIC DESIGN. The simultaneous consideration of concentration bank selection and transfer method selection is a complex problem. Stone and Hill, in "The Design of a Cash Concentration System" (*Journal of Financial and Quantitative Analysis,* September 1981), show that it can be structured as a fixed-cost assignment-location problem designed to minimize the overall cost of cash concentration. Once the appropriate transfer scheduling cost has been obtained, this design problem is an assignment-location problem similar to the assignment problem arising in lockbox design. Hence, analogous design algorithms can be used for systematically approaching cash concentration design.

DISBURSEMENT FUNDING

DEFINITION. Disbursement funding is the task of funding a company's disbursement accounts in a cost effective manner while also ensuring that adequate balances are maintained in a company's disbursement bank accounts. The standard way to manage disbursement funding is a daily fund transfer to active disbursement accounts in the amount of the day's net check presentments. In the case of a forecast-based funding system, the daily fund transfer amount should be the predicted net check presentment adjusted for the forcast errors from prior days.

CONTROLLED DISBURSEMENT. Controlled disbursement service is a generic term for a bank disbursement service that provides a company with both disbursement check processing and timely check presentment information that facilitates a company management of both its disbursement funding and its overall cash position management. The standard version of the controlled disbursement service assumes daily wire funding. Thus, it seeks to provide an early morning report of the check presentment amount for that day. Many cash managers want the control report no later—and ideally earlier—than 10:00 to 10:30 A.M. Eastern Time.

The reason for requiring an early morning report is daily cash position management. Disbursement funding requirements are a key part of determining a company's net cash position before balance adjustments. A company in a net investment position generally wants to invest as early in the morning as possible since the market for repurchase agreements, primary issue bank CDs, and much commercial paper is an early morning market.

The term **early morning market** refers to two key facts. First, most of the trading volume takes place before noon Eastern Time. Second, the best investment yields are usually available early in the morning. The common rule of thumb among corporate company managers is that the ability to trade at the opening of the market is worth 15–30 basis points (1% = 100 basis points) improvement in yield over trading later, say 10:00 A.M. to noon Eastern Time.

Daily Wire Funding. With daily wire funding, most firms use fees to compensate their disbursement banks. Hence, the target balance is zero and the amount of the wire transfer is the amount of each day's check presentments. This arrangement is often called a **zero balance disbursement account.**

An alternative to fee compensation is balance compensation for the disbursement bank. Based on service charges, a projection of account activity, and the disbursement bank's current earnings credit rate, the company sets a target balance that should provide the appropriate compensation. The daily funding is again the amount of the daily check presentment except that the target balance may be adjusted from time to time and these adjustments modify the amount transferred.

DTC Funding. With DTC funding, a company leaves on deposit at the disbursement bank its average daily disbursement amount at that bank plus any balances necessary for compensation. The disbursement bank creates a DTC drawn on the company's concentration bank for the amount of each day's check presentments. The DTC creation is usually part of the bank's check processing, usually late in the day. The DTC is deposited into the check collection system and will usually be presented to the company's concentration bank for collection the next business day. Therefore, a control report at the start of the next business day tells the company cash manager the amount of the DTC that will be presented for collection at the concentration bank. Thus, on the next business day, the cash manager must provide for these funds in managing the daily balance at the concentration bank. The net effect is that DTC funding provides a one day delay between check presentment and funding at the concentration bank. The basis for the one day delay is the average day's disbursement that the company maintains on deposit at the disbursement bank.

DTC funding is often called **passive funding.** The reason is that the cash manager in a company does not actually create or initiate any fund transfers. Rather he or she merely funds the disbursement account by making sure that there are adequate funds in the concentration bank to cover the amount of the DTCs created by the company's disbursement bank.

Using a DTC to fund a disbursement account is often called a **reverse DTC.** The reason is that this use of the DTC moves funds out of the concentration bank and into the disbursement bank while the conventional use of DTCs is to concentrate deposits. It involves moving funds into the concentration bank from a deposit bank.

The DTC covers the check presentments for a given day on a ledger balance basis but not on a collected funds basis. Hence, there is no ledger overdraft but the disbursement bank does not receive collected funds until at least the next business day. It therefore provides a de facto loan. This de facto loan is offset by the average day's disbursements that the company maintains on deposit at the disbursement bank in addition to any balances required to compensate the disbursement bank for its services. If the company does not maintain adequate collected balances to off-set the de facto loans, then the disbursement bank usually charges explicit interest for the loaned funds in the amount of the net loan.

ACH Debit Funding. A close variant to DTC funding of a controlled disbursement account is the use of the ACH system to fund the account. Rather than creating a DTC, the disbursement bank initiates an ACH debit transaction drawn against the company's concentration account for credit to the company's disbursement account. The ACH debit provides a ledger credit to the company's disbursement account on the day it is created and collected funds on the next business day. Funds are removed from the company's concentration account on the next business day as with DTC funding. As with DTC funding, the company usually leaves an average day's disbursements on deposit in addition to any balances required to compensate the disbursement bank for services.

EVALUATION OF FUNDING ALTERNATIVES. While wire funding is the conventional way companies now fund their controlled disbursement accounts, there are several advantages to either DTC or ACH debit funding over wire funding. The primary advantage is the one-day delay in the effective funding time at the concentration account. This provides the cash manager with funding data as early in the morning as desired. Hence, a company in an investment position can generally improve its investment yield while having more time to carry out its investments.

Additional savings can accrue because (1) DTC and ACH transfers are less costly than wire transfers, (2) balance reporting on an overnight (i.e., next day) basis may be less costly than the same-day, early morning report required for wire funding, and (3) company administrative savings may be realized because administrative effort is reduced and there is much less time pressure for quick processing and decision making and therefore less peak-load, time-critical work in cash position management.

The use of DTC or ACH funding exposes the disbursement bank to a credit risk that does not arise with wire funding. This credit risk primarily arises from the fact that DTC and ACH claims against the concentration account may not be honored if the company should go bankrupt before these items are collected. Since several days' checks or ACH debits may be returned to the disbursement bank, there is a technical risk amounting to several days' disbursements less any collected funds the company has on deposit in the disbursement bank. For this reason, most of the disbursement banks offering either DTC or ACH funding of a disbursement account make this service available only to their most creditworthy customers. Other banks levy an explicit charge for the implicit credit extension and credit risk. Many require balance compensation rather than fee compensation when a DTC or ACH funding service is provided since these balances further reduce the bank's credit risk exposure.

To evaluate DTC/ACH funding versus wire funding, a company must balance the investment benefits and other savings against any additional costs (such as a credit extension charge). If this is favorable, the company must then assess whether the net savings is large enough to justify the cost of changing its internal systems and banking services. The domniant benefit is the improved investment yield from the ability to invest earlier in the morning. Hence, this alternative is attractive primarily to companies that are large net short-term investors in traditional money market instruments, especially repurchase agreements, primary issue CDs, and short-term commercial paper.

ENVIRONMENT CHANGES. Changes in Federal Reserve check processing procedures can impact the standard controlled disbursement service (i.e., the version that provides an early morning report of that day's check presentments with the presumption of same-day wire funding by the company).

Beginning in 1983, the Federal Reserve began to phase in a program of later check presentments. Thus, disbursement banks that had previously received their final check presentment early in the morning—usually no later than 7:00–8:00 A.M. Eastern Time—were suddenly faced with noon-and-later presentments.

To enable disbursement banks to continue to provide their controlled disbursement reports, the Federal Reserve introduced a MICR capture and report service. It was called **key account reporting.** For each of the designated key accounts, the Federal Reserve would provide the disbursement bank with the total dollar amount of checks and the number of checks that it would present to the disbursement bank for collection later that day. This key report would be available between 9:00–10:00 A.M. Eastern Time and could be immediately forwarded by the disbursement bank to the company. Hence, for the incremental cost of the key account report, disbursement banks have been able to provide the early morning report for same-day funding through summer 1985. However, moving check presentment times back further could make the timely delivery of disbursement funding data technically impossible.

DTC/ACH funding with the associated one-day delay in concentration account funding is one of several ways that banks and companies may cope with these changes. Other ways include (1) an overdraft arrangement and/or (2) forecast-based funding.

DISBURSEMENT FUNDING: SYNTHESIS. For major companies, the standard approach to disbursement funding is a daily wire to cover each day's check presentments. The key to this service is a control report from the disbursement bank informing the company of the amount of that day's check presentments.

The alternative to same-day wire funding is a DTC/ACH funding service in which the disbursement bank creates the transfer and the company funds it passively by leaving the appropriate funds on deposit at the concentration bank. This alternative involves lower transfer costs, generally less administrative effort by the company, possibly less costly balance reporting, and the investment return benefits of being able to invest early in the morning. However, DTC/ACH funding involves an implicit credit risk to the disbursement bank, usually requires that companies leave collected funds on deposit at the disbursement bank, and may involve a credit extension cost.

AGGREGATE CASH POSITION MANAGEMENT

DEFINITION. Aggregate cash position management (ACPM) is the task of managing the level of the overall cash balance in all of a company's banks. This problem is also called "overall cash position management" or simply "**cash position management.**" The terms "overall" and "aggregate" stress the fact that the concern is the overall balance level.

OBJECTIVES AND CONSTRAINTS. The objective of aggregate cash position management is to manage the overall cash balance efficiently while fairly compensating the company's banks and not incurring overdrafts. Defining "efficiency" precisely usually puts most practicing cash managers in a quandary. The term is generally used to describe maximizing yield on investable cash and/or minimizing the cost of borrowing while providing adequate liquidity and at the same time recognizing that a good yield should not involve significant exposure to either default risk or interest-rate risk. The difficulty is defining "adequate liquidity," quantifying profitability-liquidity tradeoffs, and quantifying return-risk tradeoffs. In addition, for companies that borrow short-term part of the time and invest part of the time, there is the difficult task of trading off borrowing costs with investment opportunities.

DECISION FRAMEWORKS. There are several conceptual frameworks for approaching the problem of aggregate cash position management. These frameworks are: (1) daily target or daily adjustment; (2) control-limit; and (3) balance scheduling.

The Daily Target Framework. A target balance is set based on levels of tangible activity, credit lines, borrowing, and compensation aggreements with a company's banks. The cash manager adjusts the balance each day to meet this target balance, or at least to meet the balance to within an efficient money market transaction quantity (for example, $0.5 million to $1 million for a large company).

The Control-Limit Framework. The cash balance is allowed to fluctuate above and below the target as long as it stays within specified limits or is at least expected to return within the limits in a few days. Adjustments are made only if the balance falls outside the control limits rather than whenever there is a departure from the target. For a large company, the range of control limits might be plus or minus $5 million. Thus, a company with a target balance of $20 million and control limits of $5 million would not adjust the balance as long as it stayed between $15 million and $25 million.

The Optimal Scheduling Framework. The optimal balance scheduling framework uses mathematical programming to plan all cash adjustments, including purchases of short-term securities and borrowing-repayment timing. Such models have been set forth in works such as Orgler, *Cash Management: Methods and Models* (1970) and Maier and Vander Weide, "A Practical Approach to Short-Run Financial Planning" (*Financial Management,* Winter 1978). However, few firms are using this framework. One problem is the assumption that cash flows are known with certainty over a fairly long horizon, say at least 30–90 days. A second problem is the assumption that interest rates are known with certainty. Other problems are the computational complexity and the information management burden involved in solving the mathematical program required to determine the best adjustment schedule. Trying to reduce the information and computation costs means simplifying assumptions such as precluding sales of short-term securities before maturity or simply excluding a priori some of the possible decisions.

FRAMEWORK EVALUATION. The two frameworks meriting serious practitioner consideration are the two in use today, that is, the daily target framework and the control-limit framework. These two alternatives are similar in many ways: both allow for uncertainty in day-to-day flows; both separate the adjustment amount decisions from adjustment means; and both separate managing the level of the overall balance (concentration bank balance) from managing both borrowing-repayment scheduling and the short-term security portfolio. In contrast, the failure of the optimal scheduling framework is combining the decisions on adjustment and adjustment amount with the very difficult and complex problems of managing both borrowing-repayment scheduling and the short-term security portfolio. This mixing is the reason for most of the limitations of the optimal scheduling framework noted above.

THE DAILY TARGET FRAMEWORK. The daily target framework is very simple. There is always an adjustment unless the balance happens to be within an efficient transaction unit of the target. The adjustment amount is just the difference between the actual balance and the target, possibly rounded up or down for the sake of achieving efficient (i.e., round lot) transaction sizes.

Management Procedure. Typical management procedure in the daily target framework is focused on balance reporting information. First, the cash manager uses balance reports to ascertain the company's balance position after allowance for transfers in and out of the concentration bank. Second, the appropriate adjustment is made. If there is a deficiency, the cash manager makes borrowing arrangements (including the issuance of commercial paper) and/or sells short-term marketable securities. If there is a surplus, the cash manager repays debt and/or contacts a dealer to arrange investment in money market instruments.

The target balance is modified from time to time to reflect changes in bank activity that affect required compensating balances, as well as any past departure from the targets. Some balance reporting systems even include target tracking reports to facilitate this modification.

Evaluation. The merit of the daily target framework is its simplicity. However, this simplicity may incur costs relative to the control-limit framework, namely, a higher volume of money market trading with its associated trans-action costs, greater administrative effort, and lower yield on the money market portfolio and/or higher effective borrowing costs. The lower yield arises from the tendency to invest in very short marturities, especially over-night investments, which often have a lower yield than longer maturities, especially maturities beyond 10 to 15 days.

The higher effective borrowing costs reflect borrowing at one time and investing at another time at a lower rate. In contrast, averaging out the times when the balance is below target (borrowing) and the times when the balance is above target (investment) would mean less borrowing and less investing. Therefore, there would be a saving of the spread between the borrowing and investing rate on the reduced transaction amount. This saving is about 150 basis points for a prime-rate borrower. It is a bid-ask spread for a commercial paper issuer. The averaging out of cash surpluses and shortfalls relative to the target balance can be accomplished in a control-limit framework.

CONTROL-LIMIT FRAMEWORKS. The control-limit framework is based on the control-limit approach to inventories with two-way flows. Thus, the essence of this approach is to view the cash balance as an inventory able to fluctuate within control limits. No action is taken as long as the cash balance remains within the control limits.

The control-limit framework is not a single model but rather a generic approach for which there are many variations. Two key considerations are whether cash forecast information is used and how the forecast information is used.

Control Limits Without a Forecast. The use of the control-limit framework for cash management without forecasts was first set forth in Miller and Orr, "An Application of Control-Limit Models to the Management of Corporate Cash Balances," (*Financial Research and Management Decisions,* 1967) and developed in depth by Homonoff and Mullins, *Cash Management: An Inventory Control Limit Approach,* (D.C. Heath, 1975).

Without forecasts, the decision to adjust is based on whether the cash balance has moved outside the control limits on a given day. If outside, the balance is restored to a return point within the control limits. Otherwise, no action is taken.

The primary task is deciding on the control limits and possibly the return point if it is to be different from the target. The benefit of the simple control-limit framework without forecasts is a reduction in the number and volume of transactions. There may also be some smoothing value in avoiding wash transactions (i.e., investing at one time with offsetting borrowing at another time, and vice versa). However, the failure to use forecasts means that most of the potential benefits of the control-limit framework go unrealized.

Control Limits with Forecasts and Smoothing. Most cash managers using a control-limit framework would object to the exclusion of forecast data as "too simple." The primary objection would be the failure to use forecast information (including known trends and patterns) in determining the adjustment amount. In fact, most cash managers operating the control-limit framework view it as a way to use forecast information to smooth out peaks and valleys in day-to-day cash flows.

Stone, in "The Use of Forecasts and Smoothing in Control-Limit Models for Cash Management," (*Financial Management,* Spring 1972) formalized a common smoothing procedure used judgmentally by cash managers to benefit from cash forecasts. The smoothing procedure is summarized by the rules for the adjustment decision and adjustment amount.

Adjustment Decision. Do nothing if the balance is within the control limits.

Adjustment Amount. If outside the control limits, consider the position in K days, where K is the look-ahead period, typically 5 business days (1 week) to 10 business days (2 weeks). If the expected balance is still outside the control limit at the end of the look-ahead period, the adjustment amount should return the expected balance to the target at the end of the look-ahead period. However, if the cash balance returns within the control limits by the end of the look-ahead period, then make no adjustment.

Not only does the smoothing average out day-to-day flows, as done in the simple model without forecasts, but the look-ahead also smooths over anticipated future flows. Thus, if a company were at the upper limit, no action would be taken if the company anticipated significant outflows. Likewise, a company at the lower limit would take no action if it anticipated significant inflows. Because of strong weekly cycles in the cash flows of most companies, the look-ahead procedure can dramatically increase smoothing relative to no use of forecasts. Hence, it reduces "wash transactions," that is, borrowing at one time only to force borrowing at a later time and vice versa. Moreover, because it also averages out daily forecast errors, the procedure is relatively insensitive to forecast errors in the daily cash forecast as long as the net flow for a period of 3 to 10 business days is reasonably accurate.

Managing about a Target Balance. While the look-ahead smoothing rule set forth in Stone, "The Use of Forecasts and Smoothing in Control-Limit Models of Cash Management," (*Financial Management,* Spring 1972) incorporates the essence of common smoothing techniques in use today, the framework still has limitations. The crux of the problem is flat control-limit relative to a fixed target.

An alternative way to use forecast information in a control-limit framework is to determine a balance plan in which any monthly and weekly patterns are incorporated. The net result is a time-varying target balance, the average value being the target. The key to developing the plan is a measure of the minimum possible adjustment amount. It is the difference between the target balance and the average balance that would occur from a starting balance and forecasted flows without any adjustments. If positive, it indicates the average cash addition needed. If negative, it indicates the minimum average investment. Unless exposed to overdrafts, it is the minimum amount that need be transacted as long as there are not significant cumulative forecast errors.

Once a plan for transacting this amount has been determined, control limits can be set about the forecasted balance pattern. Further adjustments are necessary only if there are either significant, persistent forecast errors or large changes in the target balance itself. This approach represents an improvement insofar as it minimizes the expected total change in the cash balance on the basis of a cash forecast and uses the control limits on the forecast error, which is tantamount to time-varying limits on the planned balance. The benefits are: (1) reduction in amount transacted; (2) providing the maximum possible reduction in wash transactions; and (3) relative insensitivity to forecast error since day-to-day errors are averaged out in this system.

DAILY CASH FORECASTING

Many of the benefits to control-limit frameworks for cash position management are the balance smoothing opportunities afforded by forecasting. A framework for structuring daily cash forecasting was set forth by Stone and Miller, "A Framework for Daily Cash Forecasting," (*Journal of Cash Management,* Spring 1981). Examples of daily cash forecasting within this framework are presented in Stone and Wood, "Daily Cash Forecasting: A Simple Method for Implementing the Distribution Approach," (*Financial Management,* Fall 1977) and in Stone and Miller, "Forecasting Disbursement Funding Requirements, The Clearing Pattern Approach" (*Journal of Cash Management,* October/November 1983).

FORECAST STRUCTURING TECHNIQUES. Key ideas for organizing cash forecasting include: (1) breaking the overall cash flow into components, (2) separating major flows (i.e., tax payments, dividends, bond interest payments, sinking fund payments, major lease and rent payments, etc.) from nonmajor cash flows, and (3) recognizing that many of the major flows are known in both amount and timing and do not require a forecast.

GENERIC FORECAST APPROACHES. Besides conventional forecasting techniques (treated in Section 2 of this *Handbook* entitled "Financial Forecasting"), there are two generic forecast approaches that are particularly pertinent to daily cash forecasting. These are distribution and scheduling.

Distribution is spreading a total flow over subsequent days based on estimates of proportions of the total that will occur on each subsequent day. For instance, the total amount of payroll checks released on a particular day can be converted into predictions of when the checks will clear the disbursement bank. Or the total credit sales by month in a cash budget for a particular product line can be converted into the implied daily cash flow in subsequent months from knowledge of customer payment behavior and historical day-of-month and day-of-week patterns for receipt of customer payments.

Scheduling is using knowledge of time delays to convert information at one point in time into a forecast of cash flows at another time. For instance, knowledge of accounts payable, credit terms, and company payment policy can be converted into a schedule of planned check release amounts by day that will arise from these accounts payable.

MONTH-TO-MONTH BALANCE TARGETS AND ANNUAL SMOOTHING

Up to this point, it has been assumed that a company knows its target balance at any time in managing the aggregate balance. This may not be true and the balance might be changing over time.

DYNAMIC TARGETS. There is an opportunity to use annual smoothing by appropriately setting month-to-month target balances. The crux of the idea is to provide necessary compensating balances at the time of surplus cash to cover the balance requirement in the period of cash deficiency. The overall effects are to reduce the amount invested in periods of cash surplus and to reduce the amount borrowed in periods of cash deficiency. Hence, the net effect is to reduce the cost of short-term funding by reducing wash investment-borrowing transactions across months.

APPROACHES. The key idea is to set time-varying targets across months in the annual cash plan. Such targets can be developed by trial and error. Or, variants of linear programming approaches for borrowing-repayment scheduling set forth in articles by Stone, "Models for Allocating Credit, Planned Borrowing and Tangible Services over a Company's Banking System," (*Financial Management*, Summer 1975) and "The Design of a Company's Banking System," (*Journal of Finance*, May 1983), can be used to find the most efficient schedule of target balances for the concentration bank and each credit line bank and major operating bank as a byproduct of a period-to-period borrowing-repayment scheduling.

REFERENCES

Anvari, Mohsen, "Alternative Cash Concentration Systems in Canada: An Example of National Banking," *Journal of Cash Management*, Vol. 3, No. 3, June/July 1983, pp. 48–58.

Arthur D. Little, Inc., *The Consequences of Electronic Funds Transfer*, Arthur D. Little, Inc., Cambridge, MA, 1975.

Beehler, Paul J., *Contemporary Cash Management*, 2d ed., Wiley Interscience, New York, 1983.

Brandon, Margaret Bedford, "Contemporary Disbursing Practices and Products: A Survey," *Journal of Cash Management*, Vol. 2, No. 1, March 1982, pp. 26–39.

Calman, Robert F., *Linear Programming and Cash Management: Cash ALPHA*, M.I.T. Press, Cambridge, MA, 1968.

Carey, Kristen P., and Carr, Kevin, "ACH Transaction Processing: An Overview of Information Flows and Controls," *Journal of Cash Management*, Vol. 2, No. 3, September 1982, pp. 32–47, 59.

Carter, J. N., "Bank Evaluation," *Journal of Cash Management*, Vol. 3, No. 5, October/November 1983, pp. 10–20.

Cohen, Allen M., "Treasury Terminal Systems and Cash Management Information Support," *Journal of Cash Management*, Vol. 3, No. 4, August/September 1983, pp. 9–18.

Corrigan, E. Gerald, "Federal Reserve System Pricing: An Overview," *Journal of Cash Management*, Vol. 2, No. 3, September 1982, pp. 48–56.

Driscoll, Mary C., *Cash Management: Corporate Strategies for Profit*, Wiley Interscience, New York, 1983.

Donohue, William E., *The Cash Management Manual*, P & S Publications, Holliston, MA, 1977.

Fabozzi, Frank J., and Masonson, Leslie N., eds. *Corporate Cash Management: Techniques and Analysis*, Irwin, Homewood, IL, 1985.

Ferguson, Daniel M., and Maier, Steven F., "A New Industry Standard for Designing Corporate Collection Systems," Research Publication No. 80-07, Consulting Services Group, The First National Bank of Chicago, 1980.

Ferguson, Daniel M., and Maier, Steven F., "Disbursement System Design for the 1980s," *Journal of Cash Management*, Vol. 2, No. 4, November 1982, pp. 56–69.

Fielitz, Bruce D., and White, Daniel L., "A Two-Stage Solution Procedure for the Lock Box Location Problem," *Management Science*, Vol. 27, No. 8, August 1981.

Fielitz, Bruce D., and White, Daniel L., "An Evaluation and Linking of Alternative Solution Procedures for the Lock Box Location Problem," *Journal of Bank Research*, Vol. 13, No. 1, Spring 1982, pp. 17–27.

Gitman, Lawrence J., Forrester, D. Keith, and Forrester, John R., Jr. "Maximizing Cash Disbursement Float," *Financial Management*, Vol. 5, No. 2, Summer 1976, pp. 15–24.

Gitman, Lawrence J., Moses, Edward A., and White, I. Thomas, "An Assessment of Corporate Cash Management Practices," *Financial Management*, Vol. 8, No. 1, Spring 1979, pp. 32–41.

Haag, Leonard H., *Cash Management and Short-Term Investments for Colleges and Universities*. National Association of College and University Business Officers. Washington, D.C., 1977.

Haag, Leonard H., "Using Money Funds for Business Disbursing Accounts," *Journal of Cash Management*, Vol. 1, No. 1, October 1981, pp. 51–54.

Hausman, Warren H., and Sanchez-Bell, A., "The Stochastic Cash Balance Problem with Average Compensating Balance Requirements." *Management Science*. Vol. 21, No. 8, April 1976, pp. 849–857.

Hill, Ned C., and Riener, Kenneth D., "Determining the Cash Discount in the Firm's Credit Policy," *Financial Management*, Vol. 8, No. 1, Spring 1979, pp. 68–73.

Hill, Ned C., Sartoris, William M., and Emory, Gary W., *Essentials of Cash Management: Study Guide for Cash Management*, National Corporate Cash Management Association, Newtown, CN, 1985.

Hill, Ned C., Wood, Robert A., and Sorenson, Dale R., "Factors Influencing Corporate Credit Policy: A Survey," *Journal of Cash Management*, Vol. 1, No. 2, December 1981, pp. 38–47.

Homonoff, Richard, and Mullins, David Wiley, Jr., *Cash Management: An Inventory Control-Limit Approach*, D.C. Heath, Lexington, MA, 1975.

Johnson, Theodore O., "*Trade Credit Terms and Corporate Cash Cash Management Practices in a Changing Payments Environment*, thesis, Stonier Graduate School of Banking, Rutgers University, New Brunswick, NJ, 1978.

Johnson, Theodore O., and French, John M., "Electronic Corporate Payment Systems," *Journal of Cash Management*, Vol. 1, No. 1, October 1981, pp. 26–34.

Kallberg, Jarl G., and Parkinson, Kenneth, *Current Asset Management: Cash, Credit, and Inventory*, Wiley Interscience, New York, 1985.

Kraus, A., Janssen, C., and McAdams, A., "The Lock-Box Location Problem," *Journal of Bank Research*, Vol. 1, No. 3, Autumn 1970, pp. 50–58.

Kuhlmann, Arkadi, *Prime Cash: First Steps in the Art of Corporate Cash Management*, Institute of Canadian Bankers, Toronto, 1983.

Levy, Ferdinand K., "An Application of Heuristic Problem Solving to Accounts Receivable Management," *Management Science*, Vol. 12, No. 6, February 1966, pp. 236–244.

Maier, Steven F., and Vander Weide, James H., "A Practical Approach to Short-Run Financial Planning," *Financial Management*, Vol. 7, No. 4, Winter 1978, pp. 10–16.

Maier, Steven F., and Vander Weide, James H., "The Lock-Box Location Problem: A Practical Reformulation," *Journal of Bank Research*, Vol. 5, No. 2, Summer 1974, pp. 92–95.

Maier, Steven F., and Vander Weide, James H., "A Unified Location Model for Cash Disbursements and Lock-Box Collections," *Journal of Bank Research*, Vol. 7, No. 2, Summer 1976, pp. 166–172.

Maier, Steven F., and Vander Weide, James H., "A Decision-Support System for Managing a Short-Term Financial Instrument Portfolio," *Journal of Cash Management*, Vol. 2, No. 1, March 1982, pp. 20–25.

Maier, Steven F., and Vander Weide, James H., *Managing Corporate Liquidity: An Introduction to Working Capital Management*, Wiley, New York, 1985.

Mathur, Ike and Loy, David, "Corporate-Banking Cash Management Relationships: Survey Results," *Journal of Cash Management*, 3, No. 5, October/November 1983, pp. 35–46.

Metha, Dileep R., *Working Capital Management*, Prentice-Hall, Englewood Cliffs, NJ, 1974.

Miller, Merton, and Orr, Daniel, "An Application of Control-Limit Models to the

Management of Corporate Cash Balances,'' in *Financial Research and Management Decisions,* Alexander A., Robichek, Ed., Wiley, New York, 1967, pp. 133–151.

Miller, Tom W., and Batt, Murray W., Jr., ''The Views of Corporate Cash Managers on Cash Management Services,'' *Journal of Cash Management,* Vol. 1, No. 2, December 1981, pp. 49–58.

Miller, Tom W., and Stone, Bernell K., ''Daily Cash Forecasting and Seasonal Resolution: Alternative Models & Techniques for Using the Distribution Approach,'' *Journal of Financial and Quantitative Analysis,* Vol. 20., No. 3, September 1985.

Moyer, Jerry M., ''Implementing A Pre-Authorized ACH Payment System,'' *Journal of Cash Management,* Vol. 1, No. 1, October 1981, pp. 55–57.

Nauss, Robert M., and Markland, Robert E., ''Solving Lock Box Location Problems,'' *Financial Management,* Vol. 8, No. 1, Spring 1979, pp. 21–31.

Nauss, Robert M., and Markland, Robert E., ''Development & Implementation of An Improved Lock Box Location Analysis,'' *Review of Industrial Management & Textile Science,* Vol. 19, No.1., Spring 1980, pp. 61–80.

Nauss, Robert M., and Markland, Robert E., ''Theory and Application of An Optimal Procedure for Cash Disbursement Account and Lock Box Location Analysis,'' *Management Science,* Vol. 27, No. 8, August 1981, pp. 855–865.

Orgler, Yair E., *Cash Management: Methods and Models,* Wadsworth, Belmont, CA, 1970.

Payment and Telecommunications Services Corp., *Bank Wire II Functional Description,* Payment and Telecommunications Services Corp., New York, 1977.

Penny, Norman, and Baker, Donald I., *The Law of Electronic Fund Transfer Systems,* Warren, Gorham & Lamont, Boston, MA, 1980.

Pogue, Gerald A., Faucett, Russell B., and Bussard, Ralph N., ''Cash Management: A Systems Approach,'' *Industrial Management Review,* Vol. 11, No. 2, Winter 1970, pp. 54–74.

Richardson, Dennis W., *Electronic Money: Evolution of an Electronic Funds Transfer System,* M.I.T. Press, Cambridge, MA, 1970.

Searby, Frederick W., ''Use Your Hidden Cash Resources,'' *Harvard Business Review,* Vol. 46, No. 2, March–April 1968, pp. 71–80.

Shanker, Roy J., and Zoltners, Andris A., ''The Corporate Payment Problem,'' *Journal of Bank Research,* Vol. 3, No. 1, Spring 1972, pp. 47–53.

Simpson, H. Clay, Jr., ''International Corporate Cash Management: An Introduction to the State of Current practice,'' *Journal of Cash Management,* Vol. 2, No. 1, March 1982, pp. 40–44.

Smith, Derek V., ''Treasury Terminal Systems: A Vogue Out of Control?'' *Journal of Cash Management,* Vol. 3, No. 4, August/September 1983, pp. 23–27.

Smith, Samuel D., *An Assessment of Electronic Funds Transfer Systems to Meet the Needs of the Corporate Treasurer,* Thesis, Stonier Graduate School of Banking, Rutgers University, New Brunswick, N.J., 1980.

Smith, Samuel D., ''The Current Status of Corporate EFT,'' *Journal of Cash Management,* Vol. 2, No. 2, June 1982, pp. 28–40.

Stancil, James McNeil, Jr., ''A Lock-Box Model,'' *Management Science,* Vol. 15, No. 2, October 1968, pp. B-84 to B-87.

Stone, Bernell K., "Lock-Box Selection and Collection System Design: Objective Function Validity," *Journal of Bank Research,* Vol. 10, No. 4, Winter 1980, pp. 251–254.

Stone, Bernell K., Ferguson, Daniel M., and Hill, Ned C., "Cash Transfer Scheduling: Overview," *Cash Manager,* Vol. 3, No. 3, March 1980, pp. 3–8.

Stone, Bernell K., "The Many Facets of Integrated Systems: Fact vs Fallacy," *Journal of Cash Management,* Vol. 3, No. 4, August/September 1983, pp. 30–32.

Stone, Bernell K., and Miller, Tom W., "Forecasting Disbursement Funding Requirements: The Clearing Pattern Approach," *Journal of Cash Management,* Vol. 3, No. 5, October/November 1983, pp. 67–68, 70–78.

Stone, Bernell K., "Zero-Balance Banking and the Design of a Collection System in a Divisional Firm," *Advances in Mathematical Programming and Financial Planning,* John Guerard, ed. Greenwich, CN: JAI Press, 1986.

Stone, Bernell K., "The Design of a Receivable Collection System: Heuristic Procedures," *Management Science,* Vol. 27, No. 8, August 1981, pp. 866–880.

Stone, Bernell K., "The Use of Forecasts and Smoothing in Control-Limit Models for Cash Management," *Financial Management,* Vol. 1, No. 1, Spring 1972, pp. 72–84.

Stone, Bernell K., "Models for Allocating Credit, Borrowing, and Tangible Services Over a Company's Banking System," *Financial Management,* Vol. 4, No. 2, Summer 1975, pp. 65–83.

Stone, Bernell K., "The Design of a Company's Banking System," *Journal of Finance,* Vol. 38, No. 2, May 1983, pp. 373–389.

Stone, Bernell K., and Hill, Ned C., "Cash Transfer Scheduling for Efficient Cash Management," *Financial Management,* Vol. 9, No. 3, Fall 1980, pp. 35–43.

Stone, Bernell K., and Hill, Ned C., "The Design of a Cash Concentration System," *Journal of Financial and Quantitative Analysis,* Vol. 16, No. 3, September 1981.

Stone, Bernell K., and Hill, Ned C., "Alternative Cash Transfer Mechanisms: Evaluation Frameworks," *Journal of Bank Research,* Vol. 13, No. 1, Spring 1982, pp. 7–16.

Stone, Bernell K., and Miller, Tom W., "A Framework for Daily Cash Forecasting," *Journal of Cash Management,* Vol. 1, No. 1, Spring 1981, pp. 35–50.

Stone, Bernell K., and Wood, Robert A., "Daily Cash Forecasting: A Simple Method for Implementing the Distribution Approach," *Financial Management,* Vol. 6, No. 3, Fall 1977, pp. 40–50.

Sullivan, Craig F., "Multitier Zero Balancing—A Customized Implementation," *Journal of Cash Management,* Vol. 3, No. 5, October/November 1983, pp. 57–66.

Sullivan, Craig F., "Reviewing Bank Account Analysis: Ramada's Approach," *Journal of Cash Management,* Vol. 2, No. 4, November 1982, pp. 24–31.

White, George C., "Truncation Opportunities," *Journal of Cash Management,* Vol. 2, No. 1, March 1982, pp. 45–47.

White, George C., "EFT Opportunities for the Innovative Corporation," *Journal of Cash Management,* Vol. 2, No. 2, June 1982, pp. 42–48.

White, George C., "The Conflicting Roles of the Fed as a Regulator and a Competitor," *Journal of Bank Research,* Vol. 14, No. 1, Spring 1983. Also reprinted in *Journal of Cash Management,* Vol. 3, No. 2, April/May 1983, pp. 28–48.

8

MANAGEMENT OF ACCOUNTS RECEIVABLE AND PAYABLE

CONTENTS

8

MANAGEMENT OF ACCOUNTS RECEIVABLE AND PAYABLE

Robert W. Johnson
Jarl G. Kallberg

MANAGEMENT OF ACCOUNTS RECEIVABLE

Accounts receivable are customarily classified as current assets on a firm's balance sheet. Like any other asset, accounts receivable represent an investment of funds. Changes in policies that affect the level of the investment in accounts receivable are as much capital budgeting decisions as are investments in plant and equipment. The only difference is that accounts receivable are more liquid than plant and equipment; that is, they may be converted into cash within a few months, whereas it may take years to translate plant and equipment into cash. But the principles of capital budgeting apply. A change in investment in receivables is warranted only if the change maximizes the market value of the firm's common stock. It could also be stated that a change in investment is desirable if the aftertax rate of return resulting from that change exceeds the aftertax cost of capital.

DETERMINANTS OF LEVEL OF RECEIVABLES. The amount of accounts receivable that appears on the firm's balance sheet is a function of the average amount of sales made on credit each day and the average number of days' credit sales outstanding. The higher the average sales made on credit each day and the more days of credit sales outstanding, the larger will be the amount of receivables on the balance sheet. As illustration, if the firm has credit sales of 1,000 units per day at $60 per unit, and if the average time between the sale and collection is 60 days, outstanding accounts receivable will be $3,600,000. The relationship between days' sales and the collection period can be used to estimate receivables for pro forma balance sheets.

The daily amount of credit sales and the collection period are affected by the major credit policies of the firm, as well as by changes in the level of business activity. Since the financial manager has no control over the business cycle, this discussion centers on the credit policies that can be adjusted to affect the level of receivables. The concluding subsection shows how capital budgeting methodology can be used to evaluate proposed changes in these credit policies.

A firm's credit policy has three basic elements: credit terms, credit analysis, and selection and collection policies. These features are closely interrelated. Thus if credit terms are stringent, low-risk customers may be the only applicants to receive credit. In that case, credit analysis and collection efforts may be simple and inexpensive. The firm's collection costs may also be low if it is both effective in its credit analysis and highly selective in granting credit. Conversely, if credit terms are loose and credit analysis is cursory, collection costs and bad debt expense may be high. An optimal credit policy is one that maximizes the value of the firm as a function of credit sales and the costs of operating the credit function.

Credit Terms. Credit terms are the agreement between buyer and seller concerning the payment for goods or services. Typically, credit terms are stated on invoices or in the more formal credit agreements found in international trade. This subsection covers the features of credit or payment terms, the factors that influence credit terms, and the major types of credit terms.

Credit terms have four basic features. The credit period and the form of the credit arrangement are present in all credit transactions, while a cash discount and a cash discount period are found in most instances.

The **credit period,** or net credit period, is generally the length of time from the date of the invoice to the date on which the payment is due. (Sometimes the credit period is computed from the date on which goods are received by the customer.) For example, if a creditor offers a 2% cash discount for payment within 10 days from the date of invoice, but requires payment in full within 30 days, the credit terms are stated as 2/10, net 30 (or n/30). In this case the credit period is 30 days.

While it is generally assumed that bills should be rendered monthly, this need not be the case. For example, if some consumers' average monthly bills to a public utility amount to $6, it may be more economical for the utility to bill that group quarterly. Alternatively, if some marginal customers incur very large bills and there is some question about their ability to pay, it might be effective to bill every 20 days.

Stone ("Billing Frequency Optimization," *Journal of Systems Management,* May 1983) has provided a model for optimizing the billing period:

$$N^* = \sqrt{\frac{iX}{2f}}$$

where N^* = optimal number of bills per year
$\quad\quad\quad i$ = interest and bad debt costs as a fraction of average receivable level
$\quad\quad\quad X$ = annual bill in dollars
$\quad\quad\quad f$ = direct cost per bill

The second feature of credit terms is form of account. In the United States, most credit sales are on **open-book account.** The seller merely invoices the buyer and records the obligation on the accounts receivable ledger.

International trade and some other lines of business require more formal credit arrangements, such as trade acceptances. A **trade acceptance** is a draft drawn by the seller on the buyer. Typically, the seller sends the draft and the shipping documents to a bank. In turn, the bank delivers the shipping documents to the buyer when the buyer signs or "accepts" the draft. The bank returns the trade acceptance to the seller, who may hold it or sell it to a third party. On its due date, the trade acceptance is presented through a bank to the buyer for payment. In some instances, especially in foreign trade, the draft is accepted by the bank on behalf of the buyer, in which case it is called a **banker's acceptance.** In essence, the bank has guaranteed payment of the draft at maturity. The banker's acceptance can be held by the bank or sold in the secondary market.

Trade debt may be evidenced by a **promissory note:** an unconditional written promise to pay at some specified date. Promissory notes occur in trade credit in two main instances. They are found in lieu of open accounts in certain lines of business, such as wholesale jewelers. In other lines of business that commonly use open-book accounts, a seller may require a customer who is seriously overdue to acknowledge the debt formally with a promissory note specifying a payment date or dates. On the seller's books "notes receivable" replaces "accounts receivable."

A **cash discount** is the deduction from the face amount of the invoice that the buyer is permitted to take for payment within a specified period of time that is shorter than the credit period. In the previous illustration, if the amount of the invoice were $5000, the buyer could deduct 2% if payment were made within 10 days of the date of the invoice; thus the cash discount would be $100. The **credit discount period** is that time period within which payment must be made to earn the cash discount. In the illustration, the credit discount period is 10 days.

A number of factors influence credit terms, but the dominant factor is competition. Industry standards tend to set norms for credit periods, forms of accounts, and terms of cash discounts according to the type of product or service sold and whether the buyer is a retailer or user of the product sold. A seller who varies credit terms among buyers in the same class may be found guilty of price discrimination under the **Robinson-Patman Act.** (It also seems that this Act prohibits differential payment terms on the basis of payment mechanisms; see Johnson and Maier, "Making the Corporate Decision: Paper Checks to Electronic Funds Transfer," *Journal of Cash Management,* November/December 1985.)

Several basic economic factors play a role in setting **industry standards** for credit terms. Attributes of buyers are important. Typically, a seller does not wish to finance a buyer's entire inventory, certainly not inventory plus other assets. Thus, terms of sale are related to buyers' rates of stock turnover or marketing periods. The credit period offered by a seller will usually not exceed the time it takes the buyer to convert the inventory into cash. At one extreme are the terms offered to retail grocers on meats and dairy products. Because of the rapid turnover of such goods, the credit period allowed by wholesalers in these lines is usually a week to 10 days. At the other extreme are the terms offered on seasonal products, such as toys and textbooks. Since several months may elapse between shipment and the retailer's conversion of inventory into cash, sellers of seasonal items often extend the credit period from the invoice date to some date near or after the period of peak sales.

The risk characteristics of buyers will also affect credit terms. If individual customers of a firm are especially risky, they may be required to pay at the time of or before delivery. If an entire class of customers is risky, the credit period typically offered by the industry is likely to be short, and high cash discounts may be allowed to encourage prompt payment.

The seller's financial strength may also affect credit terms. Thus, a newly formed business may not have sufficient capital to offer extended credit terms, or even to offer credit. For example, in the early days of the automobile industry, manufacturers sold to dealers on a cash basis. A summary of credit terms offered in many transactions is illustrated in Exhibit 1.

EXHIBIT 1   CREDIT TERMS

Cash Before Delivery (CBD). Goods must be paid for before the supplier will ship them. A certified check or cashier's draft may be required. These terms are required when the customer represents such a high risk that the supplier is unwilling to extend any credit.

Cash on Delivery (COD). The goods are shipped to the customer, who must pay in cash, by certified check, or by some other assured means of payment before taking possession. These terms involve some risk to the seller, since the customer may reject the goods at the time of delivery. In this case, the seller must either absorb the round-trip shipping costs, accept a credit arrangement with a high-risk customer, or find another buyer in the same area.

Sight Draft—Bill of Lading Attached (SDBL). A bill of lading (shipping document) and a sight draft drawn on the buyer are sent by the seller to the customer's bank or a banking connection in the city. The customer may inspect the goods, but the bill of lading to release the goods from the carrier is obtained only by paying the amount demanded by the draft. The seller faces the same risks and unpleasant alternatives as in the case of COD shipments. SDBL terms are used by automobile manufacturers, meat packers, canners, and in foreign trade.

EXHIBIT 1 CONTINUED

Cash Terms. In spite of the name, cash terms involve the extension of credit for a short period of time. Other expressions are net cash, net 10 days, and bill-to-bill. Generally, all these terms mean that the buyer has a week to 10 days to make payment. Bill-to-bill requires that the bill for the previous delivery be paid at the time of a new delivery. Cash terms are found in the sale to retailers of cigars, cigarettes, and tobacco, fresh fruits and produce, meat and poultry, and dairy products.

Ordinary Terms. These most common credit terms apply to each order individually. The terms usually allow a cash discount if an invoice is paid within a specified discount period and for payment of the bill in full at the end of the credit period. Thus, ordinary terms of 2/10, n/30 require that the buyer either pay for the goods within 10 days of the invoice date, to receive a 2% discount from the invoice price, or pay the full price within 30 days. When the buyer is some distance away or the method of shipment is slow, terms may be 2/10, n/30 AOG (arrival of goods). This arrangement means that the credit period does not start until the buyer has received the goods.

Monthly Billing. Usually, under this arrangement all purchases made through the 25th of one month are paid for in a single payment in the following month. For example, wholesalers of drugs and drug sundries may sell on terms of 2%-EOM 30. Rather than require separate payments on each individual invoice, the wholesaler accumulates invoices for all shipments from the 26th of the preceding month through the 25th of the current month and sends the druggist a monthly bill for the total. If the druggist wishes to earn the 2% discount, he must pay the total (less discount) by the tenth day of the following month, that is, within 10 days from the end of the month (EOM). The full amount is due by the end of the following month. An alternative means of expressing the credit term is 2/10, prox. net 30, where "prox." stands for "proximo," meaning "the next."

Seasonal Dating. These credit terms permit the buyer to pay for goods at the end of the selling season. For example, some textbook publishers encourage university bookstores to send in their orders for fall in the early part of the summer by allowing terms of n/30 October 1. This credit arrangement allows publishers to judge their market and level out their producing and shipping activities, as well as to transfer the inventory to bookstores before the peak selling season. In return, the publisher assumes the carrying cost of the investment in the inventory through October 30, when the bookstores are to pay for the books purchased. Seasonal dating is characteristic of businesses with distinct seasons: toys, agricultural and garden supplies, and Christmas cards.

Consignment. When a sale is made on consignment, title to the goods remains with the seller, while the recipient serves as agent for the seller. The recipient is required to segregate the goods and the proceeds for their sale. Periodically, the proceeds from the sale are sent to the seller, along with reports on the remaining inventory.
Consignments are used when the buyer does not have sufficient funds to pay for goods on delivery or a credit standing high enough to warrant a credit sale. The arrangement may also be made to introduce a new product into distribution, when retailers are unwilling to assume the risk of stocking it. Consignment is common in the magazine publishing business. Retail stores grant display areas to distributors who stock the magazine racks and collect the cost of magazines sold and restock the racks weekly. Consignment terms are also characteristic of rack jobbers serving grocery stores and in the sale of photographic supplies.

Credit Terms in Practice. One of the most subjective factors in accounts receivable management is the interpretation and enforcement of trade credit terms. Surveys of corporate credit and payables policies presented in Hill, Sartoris, and Ferguson ("Corporate Credit and Payables Policies: Two Surveys," *Journal of Cash Management,* May–June 1984) show that the perception of the buyer and seller can be rather different. The credit and payable surveys received usable responses from 454 and 180 firms respectively, drawn from a wide cross-section of small to large U.S. corporations. Exhibit 2 gives the various viewpoints of the two surveyed groups on their definition of accepted payment date. A plurality of responding credit managers are interpreting the date the check is received at the lockbox as the accepted payment date (see Section 7, Cash Management); while a plurality of payables managers believe that the postmark date is the accepted date.

EXHIBIT 2   ACCEPTED PAYMENT DATE

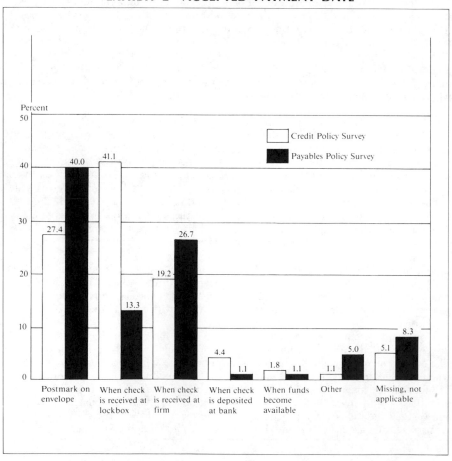

Credit Analysis and Selection. Here it is assumed that credit standards have been established by the process of analysis described in the section entitled "Changing Credit Policies" in this chapter. Given those credit standards, the issue now is whether credit applicants meet the standards and can be sold goods or services under the firm's customary credit terms.

First, the decision process requires information about the credit applicant. Second, the information must be used to judge the riskiness of the applicant. Finally, if the applicant meets the firm's credit standards, a credit limit may be established on the account.

Two types of errors can be made in assigning credit applicants to risk classes. On the one hand, an applicant who would have improved the market value of the firm by being a good customer may be rejected, because he was misclassified as a substandard risk. In the simplest case, the cost of rejection is an opportunity cost; the firm forgoes the profits that could have been made from selling to that customer. On the other hand, a "bad" customer may be accepted. The customer is "bad" in the sense that the collection costs or bad debt losses resulting from acceptance of the account reduce the value of the firm. The account is misclassified as a risk acceptable under the firm's credit standards.

Neither of these two types of error can be avoided, nor should the intent of credit policies be to minimize the total costs of these errors. It costs money to gather and to analyze information to assign credit applicants to risk classes. At some point the incremental costs of refining this information exceed the marginal benefit of avoiding misclassification errors.

The decision process is illustrated in Exhibit 3. When a purchase order is received, the credit manager may look up the applicant's credit rating in a manual such as Dun & Bradstreet's *Reference Book*. If the rating is very good or very bad, it may not be worthwhile to proceed to the next step of paying for and analyzing a credit report on the applicant. The credit manager must balance the extra cost against the expected added benefit of having and analyzing the added information. The benefit will result from correcting a misclassification error that would result from halting the credit analysis at the end of stage 1.

The benefit from further credit investigation and analysis is a product of the likelihood that a misclassification error will be corrected and the probable cost of that error. If experience shows that further investigation hardly ever changes a decision to accept or reject when the credit rating is very good or very bad, the merits of proceeding to stage 2 when these ratings are found are slight. The cost of the error is a function of the amount of credit that would have been extended and the incremental margin that will be earned (lost) if the order is accepted (rejected). On the one hand, if there is little to gain from correcting a misclassification error by proceeding to stage 2, the value of going to the next stage is small. On the other hand, if a reversal of the decision would add significantly to the value of the firm, either by gaining incremental revenues or by avoiding a substantial loss, further credit investigation and analysis may be warranted.

EXHIBIT 3   SEQUENTIAL CREDIT DECISION-MAKING FLOWCHART

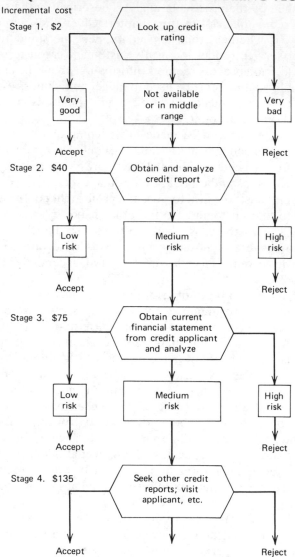

In summary, the economic advantages to a firm of incurring the costs of added credit investigation and analysis to determine the risk classification of a credit applicant are:

1. Inversely related to the added costs of the credit investigation and analysis.

2. Directly related to the probability that a misclassification error will be corrected.

3. Directly related to the costs of a misclassification error.

Sources of Credit Information. There are many sources of credit information available to assist in making credit decisions. The extent to which they are used depends on the variables discussed above, as well as the time available to make the credit decision.

Credit Grantor's Records. If the applicant has previously done business with the firm, the record of payments should be available at fairly low cost. Or the applicant may be a current customer who wishes to exceed his credit limit. Again, the firm's **ledger experience**—record of amounts owed and payment habits—should provide useful data for the credit decision.

Methods of setting **credit limits** vary widely. Cole (*Consumer and Commercial Credit Management,* pp. 616–619) notes that some firms attempt to estimate the limits set by other creditors and match those limits. Sometimes limits are set by observing the "high credit" on credit reports; in other cases the firm's share of sales to the debtor is estimated and the line of credit needed to support this level of sales is then determined. Some firms initially grant only small lines to new customers and increase lines to those who pay promptly. Other firms use "pseudoscientific" methods of setting credit limits, but these are not always based on tested historical experience, as in the case of credit scoring systems.

Modern computer techniques permit instant access to accounts receivable records. As illustration, credit analysis at Rohm and Haas can, in a matter of seconds, bring onto a cathode ray tube (CRT) for any customer "the credit line, agency rating, risk class, date of first sale, purchases this year and last year, high credit this year and last, lockbox assignment, a variety of payment statistics, the collection status, up-to-date aged balance, and a detailed listing of open items" (Stoll, "The Credit Department Goes On-Line," p. 39).

Direct Investigation. Financial statements may be obtained directly from credit applicants for analysis. In addition, personal interviews by salesmen or persons from the credit office may provide valuable information. Other creditors who have dealt with the applicant may be contacted and will customarily provide their ledger experience with the applicant, including the largest amount owed, any amount past due, and payment habits. This information is especially valuable because it can be obtained quickly and is up to date.

The applicant's commercial bank may also supply information concerning its experience with the applicant or depositor. A bank ordinarily is willing to supply such information as the length of time it has dealt with the applicant, a rough estimate of the average balance carried (e.g., "low five-figure balance"), the bank's experience with the applicant as a borrower, and a general appraisal of the firm's financial condition and reputation.

Credit Reporting Agencies. Dun & Bradstreet, Inc. (D & B) has had more than a century of experience in the field of credit reporting. Through the use of reporters, D & B gathers credit information directly from business firms, then combines these data with responses to trade inquiries sent to each firm's creditors.

Information gathered by D & B is supplied in a number of forms. The *Reference Book* is published every two months and contains ratings of the business firms on which D & B has written credit reports. Each firm is classified by a standard industrial classification (SIC) code number. Following the name of the firm is a three-character D & B rating, such as "BB2." The letters indicate the firm's estimated financial strength (measured by net worth), and the number indicates the composite credit appraisal.

If additional information is required, subscribers may request a credit report. The typical D & B business report contains credit payment records and financial statements. The payments section shows suppliers' ledger experience with the firm: the highest amount of credit extended during the previous year, the amount currently owed and past due, the credit terms, the manner of payment, and the length of time the firm has been a customer. Information is included on the firm's banking relationship and the nature of its operation, as well as a brief history of the firm.

Since 1976, TRW Business Credit Services has competed with D&B. TRW's automated data base is drawn from Standard & Poors Corp. and the regional credit files of local chapters of the National Association of Credit Management (NACM). Credit managers seeking credit information may obtain business profiles through on-line access directly to the master file or through local TRW offices. (Note: TRW has recently severed its relations with NACM; hence, the need for a change.)

There are a number of specialized credit reporting agencies that restrict their reports to a single or limited line of trade, to a particular region, or to certain types of information. For example, the **National Credit Office** provides credit rating books in such fields as textiles, leather products, mobile home and travel trailers, and chemical coatings. The **Lyons Furniture Mercantile Agency** provides credit reports on firms in furniture, interior decorating, home appliances, and related fields.

Analysis of Information. The next step in the credit granting process is to analyze the information gathered to determine whether the credit applicant falls within the acceptable credit standards of the firm. The credit decision may be based on the judgment of the credit analyst or on mathematical decision models that approximate—or may even improve on—the analyst's judgment.

Judgmental Credit Decisions. These usually rely on the "five C's of credit": character, capacity, capital, conditions, and collateral. Credit managers view character as the most important. **Character** reflects the customer's willingness or intent to pay obligations; it is an expression of honesty and integrity. It is probably best measured by reviewing the credit reports of the applicant to determine how promptly other creditors have been paid.

Capacity is a measure of the ability of the customer to pay promptly. Trade credit repayments typically are derived from the cash flow cycle from inventory to receivables to cash. (Thus, an applicant's ability to meet current obligations can best be determined by projecting future cash flows and by analyzing such measures of the applicant's current position as the current ratio and turnover of inventory and receivables.)

Capital represents the long-term financial soundness of the customer that may be relied on if cash flows are inadequate. Capital may be measured with such ratios as debt to net worth and times-interest-earned. A fuller explanation of the financial analysis necessary to judge capacity and capital may be found in the section entitled "Financial Statement Analysis."

Conditions refers to the trends in the economy or in the particular industry represented by the credit applicant. In a period of recession, credit managers are in a dilemma. On the one hand, because of slack sales, orders from new customers are desirable to fill idle capacity. On the other hand, the risks of providing credit are increased because of probable delays in collections and potential bad debt losses. Furthermore, particular industries may be depressed, even though the economy as a whole may be prosperous. For example, periodic oil crises threaten the credit standing of manufacturers of snowmobiles and recreational vehicles, even though the rest of the economy may be economically sound.

Collateral refers to the assets which explicitly are attached to the credit transaction and can be liquidated in the event of **default** on repayment. The proceeds from the liquidation go first to the creditors and any remaining proceeds are available to the general creditors of the defaulting entity.

Statistically Based Credit Decisions. Past credit experience can be used to develop a mathematical model to predict the probability that credit applicants will pay their debts satisfactorily in the future. These statistical models, or **credit scoring** systems, are widely used in consumer credit. However, this decision-making technique may also be used in commercial credit, both to evaluate new applicants and to review purchase orders from existing customers.

Credit Scoring Systems. An efficient credit scoring system offers a number of advantages to the credit grantor compared to judgmental systems. Risk management is improved, because risk can be accurately projected and adjusted by changing the minimum number of "points" needed to acquire credit. Credit scoring enhances marketing capabilities by providing a better understanding of the characteristics of customers accepted and rejected and by facilitating prompt decisions for customers. A properly designed system yields objective decisions that reduce chances of racial or gender biases leading to suits under the **Equal Credit Opportunity Act.**

To develop a credit scoring system, a credit grantor must first define a "good" account and a "bad" account. Bad loans are those that have been written off or have had major delinquency problems. Essentially, a bad account is one that left the firm worse off than if it had been rejected. Some accounts may be classified as "indeterminate" in that they cannot be clearly identified as good or bad. These should not exceed 10% of the total loan population and should be included in both the estimation and the validation sample.

Next, the population of credit applicants to be used in developing and applying the scoring model must be defined. An important assumption of the model is that the population of applicants to whom the system will be applied is as close as possible to the population from which the model was developed. Thus, a model developed for credit applicants in Minnesota may not be applicable to applicants in New York. One major retailer even has different scoring systems for different stores in the same city. Because the population evaluated with a model will usually change over time, existing credit scoring systems need to be validated and possibly revised periodically.

Once the population has been defined, random samples must then be drawn from applications of consumers who were good, bad, indeterminate, and rejected. Generally, a minimum of 800 to 1500 applicants should be available from the good, bad, and rejected loans. All data from the application blanks must be recorded and converted to machine-readable form. Missing information should be coded, as well as any other information available, regardless of whether it appears to have potential value. For example, after a mass mailing of preapproved applications for credit cards, a relevant factor in predicting risk may be the time elapsed from the mailing and the return of the application.

If the judgmental screening was biased, that bias may be partially replicated in a scoring system. For example, if all applicants under 23 years of age had been rejected under the judgmental system, no applicants in this age group will be included in the development of the scoring system. For this reason, some firms have randomly accepted all applicants and accepted somewhat higher credit losses for a period in order to develop a more efficient system.

Once coded, the data are usually examined by a process known as **multiple discriminant analysis** (MDA). This computer analysis makes it possible to identify which of the factors, in combination with other factors, distinguish significantly between good and bad accounts. In this process, MDA assigns weights to those key characteristics in order to best discriminate between the groups of accounts. Put another way, the optimal weighting system provides the greatest separation between the mean scores of the goods and bads. Techniques are available to analyze rejected applications to determine what their performance would have been had they been accepted. It may not be appropriate to assign all rejects to the "bad" category. To test the ability of the system to discriminate between these two groups, the model should be validated by applying it to a "holdout sample" (i.e., a subset of the previously drawn applications that was not included in the data base used to estimate the model).

Since a credit scoring system must be based on a creditor's historical experience with a particular group of customers, it is not possible to display a generally useful scoring model for consumer credit. *Purely as illustration* of the appearance of a credit scoring model, the final discriminant function might resemble the following. The weights assigned each variable are the coefficients of X_1, X_2, X_3, X_4.

$$S = 1.035X_1 + 1.16X_2 - 0.015X_3 + 2.345X_4$$

where X_1 = number of years at present address
X_2 = number of years at present job
X_3 = number of dependents
X_4 = rentor (0) vs. owner (1)

The resulting system of variables and their weights must be statistically valid (as demonstrated by the validation test). It should also meet all legal requirements. Hence, many credit grantors exclude the applicant's zip code from a scoring system because it might be challenged as racially biased. Finally, each factor used must have some "face validity" (i.e., it must have some economic rationale to the personnel who will apply the system and to the consumers).

Performance Scoring Models. Statistically based credit decision models may be applied to other decisions than whether to accept or reject an applicant. **Performance scoring** offers credit grantors improved ability to manage their consumer loan portfolios when there is an ongoing relationship with customers, as in the case of retail or bank credit cards. Performance scoring may be used for many decisions: targeting collection effort, changing credit limits, deciding whether to reissue a card, approving over-limit purchases, and cross-selling other financial services.

A performance scoring model may be built from the purchase and payment patterns of existing customers and their credit records. Data are collected at an observation point for the preceding 6- or 12-month observation period. Based on information from the observation period, predictions may be made about individual customer's performance during the following "outcome period." Thus, a credit manager may know that

10% of customers 30 days delinquent will roll over into the 60-day delinquent category. But this is an average. To target collection efforts, it
would be helpful to know *which* customers are most likely to extend their
delinquency. The variables required to build such predictive models are
such factors as: two or more times delinquent in last 12 months; current
dollar balance more than 10% over credit limit; two or more unsatisfactory
ratings, and so on.

As indicated, scoring systems may also be developed for trade credit—
that is, credit from a manufacturer to a wholesaler or from a wholesaler
to a retailer. For example, simplified versions of credit scoring systems
may be used to process initial orders from new customers or orders from
established customers. Analysis of experience with initial orders may
show that they may be accepted without detailed analysis if they are
below a specified amount and have a certain credit rating from Dun &
Bradstreet. Orders not falling within this blanket authorization will require
further analysis, either with a judgmental or credit scoring system.

Large firms are turning more frequently to **automated credit checking**
of orders from established customers. Under this process each customer's
order is screened by the computer against predetermined credit tests; the
firm then accepts orders that pass the test and refers others to a credit
analyst. Ideally, such a system should be based on the firm's experience
with repeat orders. Variables used to screen accounts should be those
that have been effective in segregating accounts that become bad from
those that remain good. The guidelines might include such factors as date
of last activity, type of account, date of last financial statement, an order
that exceeds a "per order" limit or the credit limit, and type of account.
Since a trade creditor would not wish to reject an order from a firm that
is past due on only one or two small invoices, tests can be developed to
permit certain levels of past due accounts. As an example, the following
"automated credit checking report" is reproduced from C. D. Whiteside
(*Credit and Financial Management,* Vol. 81, November 1979, p. 25):

Line of Credit	Allowable Past Due
All accounts under $5,000	$ 500
$5,000–$10,000 line of credit	1,000
$10,000–$25,000	3,000
Excess of $25,000	5,000

Obviously, each firm must establish its own tests from its own experience
for automated credit checking. Whiteside notes that after a few months of
operating such a system, about three-quarters of the orders are approved
by the computer.

A final step in the process of credit analysis and selection may be to set
credit lines or **credit limits.** Generally, these terms refer to the total outstanding balance permitted a debtor, although a line may also be defined as
the total amount of orders from a customer within a given period. If an order

is received that would exceed the credit limit, the account is reviewed. The order may be denied or approved as an exception, or the credit limit may be raised. The credit limit is not ordinarily a fixed barrier calling for refusal of any order that would violate the limit.

Although not all companies establish credit limits, the purpose is usually to minimize the number of orders referred to analysts. Taken in conjunction with other tests, credit limits permit a high proportion of orders to be approved automatically. Credit limits are reviewed annually or more frequently for substandard accounts. Credit lines may be set by judgment or through the use of mathematical models designed to provide automated credit checking of orders.

Collection Policies and Procedures. Once credit has been granted, the next step is to collect the amounts owed. It is worth recalling that collection policy cannot be viewed in isolation from other credit policies. A tradeoff along the following lines is frequently involved:

Restrictive credit terms and tight credit standards	Loose collection policies
Lenient credit terms and loose credit standards	Tight collection policies

The pricing of the goods or service sold on credit may also be relevant to establishing collection policies. Thus selling prices that are low relative to competitors' prices may be accompanied by generally restrictive credit policies (or cash only sales), and vice versa.

Cash outlays on collection efforts are essentially a capital investment with the objective of increasing the present value of cash inflows from collections. The present value of collections is raised either by moving them forward in time or by increasing the expected value of the amount collected. In essence, collection policies should be based on the principle of not throwing good money after bad.

As illustration, consider that a creditor is owed \$1,000 by XYZ Furniture Co. Assume that without any collection effort, the probability of collecting the amount owed at the end of six months is 0.05, but that with collection effort, the probability of collection shifts to 0.10 at the end of four months. (No collections are expected on the account in other months.) Assume that the firm's pretax cost of capital is 1% per month. The present value of the collection effort is:

$$\text{present value with collection effort} = \frac{(0.10)(1,000)}{(1.01)^4} = \$96.10$$

$$\text{present value without collection effort} = \frac{(0.05)(1,000)}{(1.01)^6} = \frac{-47.10}{}$$

$$\text{incremental present value of collection effort} = \$49.00$$

Given these data, it is apparent that the creditor should not spend more than $49 on efforts to increase the present value of expected cash collections from this customer. Estimates of collection results may be based on discriminant analysis of historical collection experience. A critical variable is the length of time that the overdue debt has been outstanding. The longer an overdue debt has been outstanding, the less likely it is for collection activity to be fruitful (Mitchner and Peterson, *Operations Research,* Vol. 5, August 1957, pp. 522–545).

For most accounts, collection procedures follow a fairly set routine. In the great majority of cases it is not necessary to proceed beyond the first few steps listed below.

Statement of Account or Duplicate of Invoice. Initially, delinquent debtors are sent a simple reminder when their account is past due a certain number of days.

Form Letters. If no response is received to the first, polite reminder, creditors may continue collection efforts with a series of form letters. Important accounts may be sent specially written letters. The later in the cycle of collection effort, the more insistent and less polite the letter.

Telephone Calls. This is often an effective collection method, especially as a means of learning the debtor's problems and obtaining a specific commitment for payments. These promises must be monitored closely, so that failure to comply will generate a quick response from the creditor.

Adjustments. If a debtor who is in serious difficulty is an important customer, there are various methods of adjusting the account. Some of these adjustments may still permit the creditor to continue to sell to the customer. In some cases shipments may be continued, provided they are paid for CBD or COD, perhaps with an additional payment to apply to the past due account. In other instances, a creditor may accept a series of promissory notes for the past due balances and continue additional shipments on a cash basis.

An **extension arrangement** should typically be agreed to by all creditors of a firm, or at least by the major creditors. Such arrangements involve a formal extension of the due date of the distressed debtors' obligations. It is binding only on the creditors who sign the agreement and may involve payment of interest for the period of extension.

Under a **composition settlement,** creditors agree to accept a partial payment in final settlement of the amounts owed. For example, creditors may agree to accept 70¢ for each dollar of debt. As in the case of the extension arrangement, the agreement applies only to the creditors who sign the contract. Both forms of settlement should be carefully handled to avoid preferential treatment of some creditors. Often these agreements may be entrusted to the adjustment bureau of the NACM.

If these voluntary settlements cannot be arranged, bankruptcy may be the only alternative (see the section entitled "Bankruptcy and Reorganization").

Third-Party Collection. If collection letters have failed and a voluntary settlement is not warranted, a creditor may turn the account over to a third party for collection. Usually this action is preceded by a final letter of warning to the delinquent customer. The NACM, Dun & Bradstreet, and many attorneys provide collection services. Collection agencies and attorneys may retain one-fourth to one-third of any amounts collected.

Credit Insurance. An adjunct to collection activities is the use of credit insurance. Just as in the case of fire insurance, credit insurance is a means of shifting the risk of extraordinary losses to a third party. Banks extending loans secured by accounts receivable may require the use of credit insurance.

Credit insurance is not designed to protect creditors against normal or primary losses. If the experience indicates that normal credit losses amount to 0.7% of credit sales, that percentage of credit sales is established by the credit insurance company as the creditor's primary loss, and that amount is not insurable.

The transfer to the insurance company of abnormal credit losses over and above the primary loss is subject to two limiting features. First, the insurance company will require the creditor to participate in 10–20% of the net loss suffered, depending on the risk involved. This **coinsurance** feature is obviously designed to prevent the careless granting of credit. Second, the insurance company will also limit coverage on individual accounts to an amount that is related to the credit rating of the customer at the time of shipment. For example, the credit insurance company may limit its coverage to $8,000 on each account receivable with a D & B rating of "EE2" at the time of shipment. Unless additional coverage is obtained by special endorsement to the insurance policy, the creditor is liable for all losses over that amount, in addition to the coinsurance share of the amount covered by the policy.

As illustration of the combined effects of the primary loss and coinsurance features, assume that the policyholder's credit sales volume was $600,000, and that the total credit loss was $7,600. The primary loss percentage is 0.7% of credit sales, and the coinsurance is 10%. Under these assumptions the net amount recoverable from the insurance company would be calculated as follows:

Total credit losses	$7,600
Amount of coinsurance (10%)	760
Net covered losses	6,840
Amount of primary loss (0.7% of covered sales)	4,200
Net recoverable from insurance company	$2,640

Delinquent accounts are filed with the insurance company within a specified time period, usually no more than 12 months from the date of shipment. The insurance company then attempts to collect the account, charging the policyholder a fee for this activity. To the extent that collection efforts are successful, the creditor receives a share equal to the coinsurance percentage.

Whether **credit insurance** is desirable depends on the premium and management's attitude toward the changed distribution of risk. The premium is evidently in the range of 0.2% of credit sales and relates directly to the risk level of accounts insured. Clearly, if credit insurance companies are to remain in business, their aggregate premiums must exceed their payments on credit losses, just as in the case of fire insurance companies. However, a creditor may wish to use credit insurance if the risk of nonpayment of the receivables is skewed to such an extent that failure of a few important accounts could jeopardize the financial stability of the firm.

Credit insurance might be used if the creditor has a concentration of sales to a few accounts, in one line of business, or in one geographical area. If adverse business, climatic, or other conditions could jeopardize repayment of a large portion of the dollar amounts of outstanding receivables, credit insurance may be desired to transfer the excess risk to the more diversified insurance company. Similarly, credit insurance may be useful if a firm is engaged in custom manufacturing or in providing services. In these situations, failure of a customer may leave the creditor with a product that is not readily salable, or with no compensation for a service provided.

Changing Credit Policies. It was observed above that the average amount of receivables outstanding is a function of the average daily credit sales and the average number of days' sales outstanding. Shifts in credit policies that affect either the level of credit sales or the average length of time between the credit sale and collection will be reflected in changes in the level of accounts receivable reported on a firm's balance sheet.

Evaluation of the desirability of a change in credit policies is a capital budgeting problem. At issue is whether a change in the firm's **investment in receivables** will maximize the market value of the owners' equity in the firm. For capital budgeting purposes it is important to distinguish between the amount of receivables as shown on the balance sheet and the investment in receivables. Assume that a wholesaler buys a product at $45 per unit and incurs direct, out-of-pocket selling and delivery costs of $5 per unit on the credit sale of each unit at $60. If credit sales average 1,000 units per day, the average day's credit sales is $60,000. If the average time between a sale and collection is 60 days, outstanding accounts receivable will average $3.6 million. However, the wholesaler's cash outlay in the sale of each unit is only $50—the purchase price of $45 plus the direct selling cost of $5. Hence the wholesaler's average investment in receivables is not $3.6 million but $3 million ($50,000 × 60 days). In summary, the firm's investment in receivables is equal to the variable costs, that is, the cash outlays that are incurred if the credit sale is made but would not be present were the credit sale not made.

The key assumption that justifies the use of variable costs to determine the firm's investment in receivables is that the changes in credit sales are incremental. To put it another way, it is assumed that without the change in policy, the existing level of credit sales would continue. For example, consider a proposed lowering of credit standards that would leave payment habits of current customers unchanged but would permit credit sales to a more risky group of customers. The added sales do not replace other credit sales that might have been made; they are entirely incremental. In this case the incremental cash investment of the firm is the variable cost of the added receivables that are outstanding as a result of the lowered credit standards. The incremental revenues are the difference between the amounts collected on the marginal accounts and the variable costs of the items sold. As a simple illustration consider that a changed credit policy results in the sale of ten more units on credit at $60 in period 1. A customer buying one unit defaults, with the result that in period 2 a cash inflow of $540 is received (9 units × $60). In summary:

Period 1. Added cash outlay = 10 units × $50 = $500
Period 2. Cash inflow before taxes = 9 units × $60 = $540.

The incremental rate of return for the one period is 8% ($40/$500).

Oh (*Financial Management,* Vol. 5, Summer 1976, pp. 32–36), argues that investment in receivables should be measured by the selling price of the items sold, not by the incremental cash outlays incurred as a direct result of the added credit sales (variable costs). Oh contends that the receivables at selling price represent an opportunity cost that could be realized if the funds were applied to alternative uses. In the example above, Oh would argue that the investment in receivables is $600 (10 units × $60), rather than $500. However, Dyl (*Financial Management,* Vol. 6, Winter 1977, p. 69) correctly points out that the difference ($100 in this case) "is simply un-collected profit and, more important, these 'funds' would be nonexistent without the change in credit standards." Put another way, were it not for the investment to gain the added credit sales of 10 units, only $500 would have been available for other investments.

In the article just cited, Dyl concluded that the opportunity cost does apply if credit policies were changed to lengthen the collection period "on existing sales." But this conclusion overlooks the basic implicit assumption in the capital budgeting approach to investment in receivables. Presumably, a wealth-maximizing firm would not change its credit policies to lengthen the collection period on existing accounts out of charity. A change in credit terms on existing accounts must be intended to retain accounts that would otherwise turn to competitors with more lenient credit terms. These credit sales are as incremental as the credit sales added as a result of relaxed credit standards. The same financial analysis must hold in both cases. Thus the investment in those accounts equals the variable cost incurred to maintain credit sales to those accounts (in this example, $500), not the receivables at their selling price ($600).

The process of evaluating a change in credit policy will now be illustrated. Assume that the firm is operating under credit policy A, but is considering becoming more lenient in granting credit. The shift toward accepting increasingly risky customers is represented by credit policies B and C. While more lenient credit policies will result in greater sales as shown in column 1 in Exhibit 4, they will also require higher accounts receivable, both because of the larger sales volume and because the more risky accounts can be expected to have a slower turnover. Estimates of the book value of receivables are shown in column 2. Additional sales will also require the ordering and stocking of more inventory. The **marginal costs** of selling the added volume of ordering and carrying the added inventory, and of collecting delinquent accounts are shown in column 4. Finally, as the firm accepts more risky classes of customers, bad debts will rise (column 5). The annual cash inflows before taxes are then equal to the revenues from sales, less the cost of goods sold (at 75% of sales), less the marginal costs, and less bad debt losses. If the tax rate is assumed to be 40% (for simplicity), the annual aftertax cash inflows are those shown in column 7.

As noted earlier, the actual cash outflow invested in accounts receivable is not equal to their book value. The data shown in column 1 of Exhibit 5 are based on the assumption that the actual cash investment in accounts receivable is equal to 80% of their book value, composed of investment in cost of goods sold (75% of sales), plus an added 5% for direct selling, handling, and collection costs. The incremental investment in inventory under

EXHIBIT 4   EFFECTS OF ALTERNATIVE CREDIT POLICIES ON REVENUES AND EXPENSES ($ THOUSANDS)

						Cash Inflows	
Credit Policy	Annual Revenues (1)	Accounts Receivable (2)	Cost of Goods (3)	Marginal Costs (4)	Bad Debts (5)	Before Tax (6)	After Tax (7)
A	$ 80	12	60	13	0.3	6.7	4.0
B	140	27	105	21	2.0	12.0	7.2
C	160	38	120	23	3.7	13.3	8.0

Assumptions
(3) Cost of goods sold = 75% of sales.
(4) Marginal cost = direct selling costs; added collection costs; added costs of ordering and carrying inventory.
(6) = (1) − (3) − (4) − (5).
(7) Tax rate = 40%.

the three credit policies is shown in column 2, with the total outlay under the three credit policies in column 3. It is assumed that the credit policies will produce incremental cash flows for perpetuity. This is not a drastic assumption, since the cash flows in years beyond the tenth year or so have little effect on the present value of flows. Thus, assuming a cost of capital of 10%, if credit policy B is adopted, the present value of its incremental cash flows will be $72,000; that is, $7,200/0.10. The net present value of credit policy B is simply the present value of aftertax cash flows ($72,000) less the initial cash outlay necessary to implement the policy ($36,300). Since credit policy B has the highest net present value, it is the optimal policy (assuming that the firm is not under capital rationing).

An alternative formulation of Exhibit 5 would be to assess the 10% cost of capital against the incremental investment and then calculate the annual net cash flow after deducting the annual change for funds invested in accounts receivable and inventory. With this approach, the analysis would conclude as shown below:

	Amounts ($ Thousands)		
Credit Policy	After Tax Cash Inflows	Capital Cost	Cash Inflows After Taxes and Capital Cost
A	4.0	1.8	2.2
B	7.2	3.6[a]	3.6
C	8.0	4.7	3.3

[a]0.10 × 36.3 (column 3 in Exhibit 5).

Policy B provides the greatest annual cash flows, net after taxes, and the cost of funds invested in accounts receivable and inventory. Thus it is the optimal policy.

EXHIBIT 5   NET PRESENT VALUES OF ALTERNATIVE CREDIT POLICIES ($ THOUSANDS)

Credit Policy	Cash Investment in		Total (1) + (2) (3)	Present Value Aftertax Cash Flows (4)	Net Present Value (5)
	Accounts Receivable (1)	Inventory (2)			
A	9.6	8.4	18.	40	22
B	21.6	14.7	36.3	72	35.7
C	30.4	16.8	47.2	80	32.8

Assumptions
(1) Cost of goods + direct selling costs = 80% of accounts receivable.
(4) Column (7), Exhibit 3, discounted in perpetuity at 10% (e.g., 4/0.10 = 40).
(5) Net present value = (4) − (3).

It is assumed in this analysis that granting credit to customers in the higher risk class acquired under credit policy B will not change the risk status of the firm. This might occur if only a few accounts were acquired or if they did not otherwise represent a diversified risk. Under such conditions, the firm might wish to insure its receivables.

Furthermore, it is assumed in this illustration that the selling price of the product or service is fixed by competition. Kim and Atkins (*Journal of Finance,* Vol. 33, May 1978, pp. 403–412) noted that a change in credit terms is, in effect, a change in the price of the goods sold. However, in a competitive market all components of price—invoice price plus credit terms—are set in the market, and additional risk classes of customers will be served only if they can be charged higher prices. In an imperfectly competitive market, changes in credit policies may increase the market value of the firm, but it is worthwhile in that case to consider the interdependence of pricing and credit policies.

EVALUATION OF MANAGEMENT OF ACCOUNTS RECEIVABLE. Once credit policies and procedures have been established, a credit manager must design a system to monitor the results. The system should avoid two types of error: (1) signaling that the accounts receivable are out of control, when in fact they are in control; and (2) failing to give a warning signal when the receivables are out of control. A system that is subject to these errors will also be deficient in predicting future levels of accounts receivable outstanding.

To compare the traditional and the more effective methods of assessing the status of receivables, we use a uniform set of data. Based on Lewellen and Johnson (*Harvard Business Review,* Vol. 50, May–June 1972, pp. 101–109), the data assume that the accounts receivable are "in control"; that is, the pattern of collections and bad debt write-offs is constant, even though credit sales vary from month to month. Specifically, it is assumed that of the credit sales in any given month, 10% are collected (or written off) during the month of sales, 30% the following month, 40% the next month, and the remaining 20% in the final month. Thus if sales of $100,000 are made in month *t,* collections and receivables outstanding at the end of each month (EOM) will appear as follows:

	Amount ($ Thousands)	
Month	Collections During Month	Receivables Outstanding EOM
t	$10	$90
t + 1	30	60
t + 2	40	20
t + 3	20	0

Effective Measures of Receivable Status. The basic demand placed on a measure of accounts receivable status is that it not be distorted by seasonal movements in credit sales. Two measures that meet this test are the receivable balance pattern and the collection pattern. One is the mirror image of the other, and there do not appear to be convincing arguments that favor one over the other, especially since such computations can readily be handled by computer.

Receivable Balance Pattern. This is the proportion of any month's sales that remains outstanding at the end of each subsequent month. The anticipated decay in outstanding receivables under the assumptions in this section is illustrated in Exhibit 6. This monitoring system is readily usable even by a small business that does not have a computer. Assume a file folder in which are placed invoices amounting to $90 for June credit sales. Invoices are removed when paid or written off as bad debts. At the end of June, one would expect about 90% of the dollar amount of invoices to still be in the folder, or about $81. When the folder is examined at the end of July, there should be about $54 of invoices left (60% × $90). At the end of August, about $18 would remain (20% × $90), and none should be left at the end of September.

The normal decay pattern can be identified by examining the firm's past experience. Obviously, there will be random variations around the norm,

EXHIBIT 6   UNCOLLECTED BALANCES AS PERCENTAGE OF CREDIT SALES

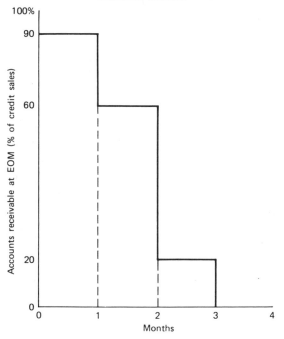

EXHIBIT 7   STATUS REPORT OF ACCOUNTS RECEIVABLE BALANCES

	Accounts Receivable Outstanding (%) at End of:				
From Sales of:	July	August	September	October	November
Same month	92	89	91	88	92
1 month before	58	61	60	58	62
2 months before	19	21	19	18	20
3 months before	0	1	2	1	0

and the norm itself may have a seasonal pattern. A control report might appear as shown in Exhibit 7. At the end of July, 92% of July's sales are still outstanding, 58% of June's sales, and so on. To track the decay pattern of receivables originating in July, the credit manager follows the percentages diagonally across the table as indicated by the arrows. Thus at the end of August, 61% of July's sales are still outstanding, at the end of September, 19%, and at the end of October, 1%. Significant variations from this decay pattern should call for investigation. If the decline in balances is more rapid than usual, credit standards may have become too high, or collections overly vigorous, with a consequent loss in sales. If the decline is less rapid than the norm established by experience, credit standards may have been lowered, or collections may have become lax.

The balance of accounts receivable at the end of some month in the future can readily be predicted, given a forecast of credit sales. Consider the projected sales for the last quarter. If the percentages for the receivable balance pattern are applied to these sales estimates, the expected receivables outstanding at year-end may be calculated as follows:

	Projected Sales		Projected Amount Uncollected (%)		Projected Balance, December 31
October	$ 20	×	20	=	$ 4
November	60	×	60	=	36
December	120	×	90	=	108
					$148

Note that this estimate is considerably above those obtained by using either DSO or the aging schedule. If the decay pattern of receivables persists, the estimate of the year-end balance is significantly more reliable than those obtained by traditional methods.

Collection Pattern. The monthly percentages of credit sales of a given month that are collected (or written off as bad debts) in each subsequent month reveal the collection pattern. Obviously, the receivables balance pattern and the collection pattern are closely related. If collections of a given month's sales are cumulated from month to month, the difference between the total credit sales for the month and the cumulated amounts collected (or written off) at the end of subsequent months must equal the receivables outstanding (EOM). The relationship between the two methods is illustrated in Exhibit 8. At the end of the first month, collections amount to 10% of the month's sales, and receivables equal 90% of the month's sales. At the end of the second month, 40% of the initial balances has been collected and 60% remains uncollected.

In the reference cited earlier, B.K. Stone favored use of the monthly collection proportions as a control mechanism for accounts receivable management. Estimates can be made of normal variation around monthly collection percentages, but this is more difficult when dealing with declining percentages of unpaid balances. Each month's unpaid balance is dependent on the balance unpaid in the previous month. Stone also argued that treatment of bad debts is facilitated by use of the monthly collection proportions.

Firms that have adopted either of these systems of monitoring receivables have found that control is most effective if maintained by lines of business, since credit terms and payment patterns vary accordingly. If receivables are aggregated for control purposes, it is not readily apparent whether collection patterns have actually changed or whether the mixture of business has changed. Diners Club has used the receivable balance pattern with excellent results, but has found that payment habits vary by region. Hence it has different control systems according to the region in which cardholders are located.

EXHIBIT 8   COLLECTIONS AS PERCENTAGE OF CREDIT SALES

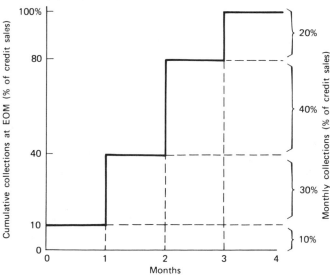

FORECASTING AND CONTROL OF ACCOUNTS RECEIVABLE. A **credit monitoring system** must be capable of assessing the status (i.e., liquidity) of the outstanding portfolio of accounts receivable and of generating reliable warning signals to alert the credit manager of potential collectability problems. Stone ("The Payments Pattern Approach to the Forecasting and Control of Accounts Receivable," *Financial Management*, Autumn 1976) conducted a survey of the primary forecasting and control techniques utilized by 150 large U.S. firms. According to the respondents, the most important control method was the **aging schedule** while the forecasting technique most utilized was ratio projection (which includes **days sales outstanding**). These and other important forecasting and control techniques are defined in the following. To facilitate comparison we use the following simple set of data: Assume that a firm has average annual sales of $30 million, all on credit terms of net 30. Exhibit 9 gives the relevant data (all in $ millions).

The accounts receivable data in Exhibit 9 have been divided into **aging categories:** a classification of the outstanding accounts receivable into those that are current, less than one month overdue, one to two months overdue, and two or more months overdue. In this categorization, at the end of each month each account (or invoice) in the outstanding accounts receivable portfolio would be classified into one of these four categories. Naturally the number of categories and the choice of aging interval (usually monthly or weekly) and so forth depend on the particular application.

Days Sales Outstanding (DSO). The most common method of computing receivable DSOs is to take the ratio of outstanding receivables at a given point to time to (forecast of) average daily credit sales. The DSO represents the number of days of credit sales currently tied up in accounts receivable. The reciprocal of this measure is the **accounts receivable turnover** which reflects the number of times that receivables will turn over in one year. For our example, we obtain

$$\text{DSO (May)} = \frac{3.5}{(30/365)} = 43$$

$$\text{DSO (June)} = \frac{4.0}{(30/365)} = 49$$

$$\text{DSO (July)} = \frac{4.1}{(30/365)} = 50$$

The fact that these three ratios are increasing seems to suggest that there is an increasing investment in accounts receivable. Whether this is due to deteriorating payment behavior or to other causes is not immediately discernable.

EXHIBIT 9   AGING DATA

Month	Total End-of-Month Accounts Receivable	Current	Days Overdue			New Bad Debts
			1–30	31–60	61–90	
May	3.5	2.2	0.4	0.3	0.4	0.2
June	4.0	2.8	0.6	0.3	0.2	0.2
July	4.1	2.7	0.8	0.4	0.2	0.1

DSO ratios can be very sensitive to the method of determining the numerator, that is, by choosing a different time period or a different approach to calculating average credit sales one can obtain very different answers. Also, in the case of a firm with seasonal sales patterns it becomes more difficult to interpret DSOs. A method described in Business International (*Global Cash Management,* Business International Corporation, 1982), together with its application at American Cyanamid Corporation, is often better in these cases. An example of this DSO calculation is as follows: using the data from Exhibit 9, the July accounts receivable figure is 4.1; this figure represents the credit sales in July (which equals the amount current at the end of July), namely, 2.7; the remainder, 1.4(4.1 − 2.7), represents 50% (1.4/2.8) of the credit sales in June. Thus,

$$DSO(July) = 31 + (1.4/2.8)30 = 46.$$

That is, at the end of July, July's credit sales plus half of June's credit sales are tied up in accounts receivable. Similarly, computing for June,

$$DSO(June) = 30 + (1.2/2.2)31 = 46.$$

These two DSOs are identical which is in contrast to the previous result. This calculation is more representative of current credit sales, as opposed to annual averages.

Ratio-Based Projections. These projections assume that the level of accounts receivable is proportional to a forecast of sales. To illustrate, assume that accounts receivable are a constant multiple, r, of sales in the current month. For our example, if one assumes $r = 1.5$ and the credit sales forecast for August is 3.0, then the forecast accounts receivable level is 4.5 (1.5 × 3.0). In general, these forecasts can be generated using more than the current month's sales figures.

Percentage of Balance. This method assumes that payments in a given month are a constant multiple of the start of the month's receivables. For example, if we estimate that we collect 80% of the past month's outstanding receivables in the current month. In this case, for August we would estimate collections of 3.28 (.8 × 4.1). See Shim ("Estimating Cash Collection Rates from Credit Sales: A Lagged Regression Approach," *Financial Management*, 1981) for a regression-based approach to forecasting cash flows from lagged credit sales data.

Collection Efficiency. This measurement of accounts receivable performance is calculated by dividing a given period's actual collections by the total amount that was due for collection, as will be clarified in the following section on Markov chain models. For our example, the amount collected in June was $1.8, thus collection efficiency for June is 51% (1.8/3.5); the July figure is 58% (2.3/4.0), suggesting better performance in the latter month.

A simple and related measure of collection efficiency commonly used is the percentage of overdue accounts. A number of firms have established guidelines for this figure.

A final and integrative approach to this problem is one that can be applied to all current assets: that of establishing asset utilization charges. Under this approach, accounts receivable are viewed as an asset that a given division (or other corporate entity) is utilizing. Management establishes an asset utilization charge and thereby the performance of accounts receivable becomes integrated into the overall asset utilization. This viewpoint is very much in keeping with modern approaches of current asset performance by taking an integrated view. See for example, Kampmeyer ("Measuring and Allocating Working Capital Usage to Operating Units: Josten's Method," *Journal of Cash Management*, 1984), Beehler ("Treasury Management Evolution," *Journal of Cash Management*, 1984), and Hill and Ferguson ("Cash Flow Timeline Management: The Next Frontier of Cash Management," *Journal of Cash Management*, 1985).

MARKOV CHAIN APPROACHES. The basic problem of separating payment patterns from sales patterns exists for the traditional performance measurement methods, that is, changing sales patterns distort the level of accounts receivable and the measurements based on this level. While ad hoc methods of seasonally adjusting performance measurement are often used in practice, a more elegant way around this problem is to use what Stone ("The Payments Pattern Approach to the Forecasting and Control of Accounts Receivable," *Financial Management*, 1976) calls the **payment pattern** approach. A closely related approach based on **receivable balance patterns** is developed in Lewellen and Johnson ("Better Way to Monitor Accounts Receivable," *Harvard Business Review*, 1972). Both of these references describe techniques that are recognized by operations researchers as being based on *Markov chain* techniques. In addition to being a fundamental modeling tool, there have been a number of applications of this technique in the area of accounts receivable management.

The Cyert-Davidson-Thompson Model. The first application in the accounts receivable area was developed by Cyert, Davidson, and Thompson ("Estimation of the Allowance for Doubtful Accounts," *Management Science,* 1962) for the problem of estimating an allowance for bad debt losses. Variations on this model have been used in financial institutions with considerable success. Cyert and Thompson ("Selecting a Portfolio of Credit Risks by Markov Chains," *Journal of Business,* 1968) later extended this basic model to develop a portfolio approach to evaluating investment in accounts receivable. Corcoran ("The Use of Exponentially-Smoothed Matrices to Improve Forecasting of Cash Flows from Accounts Receivable," *Management Science,* 1978) worked on improving this model's cash flow forecasting abilities by exponentially smoothing the estimates. Kallberg and Saunders ("Markov Chain Approaches to the Analysis of Payment Behavior of Retail Credit Customers," *Financial Management,* 1983) applied the Markov chain technique to a set of retail credit data with the goal of determining the sensitivity of payment behavior to various exogenous economic factors. Finally, statistical problems pertinent to accounts receivable applications are the focus of research papers by Karson and Wrobleski ("Confidence Intervals for Absorbing Markov Chain Probabilities Applied to Loan Portfolios," *Decision Sciences,* 1976), dealing with determining confidence intervals for cash flow forecasts, and Frydman, Kallberg, and Kao ("The Application of Markov Chains and Mover-Stayer Models to an Empirical Analysis of Credit Behavior," *Operations Research,* 1985), dealing with theoretical and empirical aspects of the testing of alternative discrete time models for credit behavior.

To characterize a Markov chain, one needs to specify a set of possible *states* (i.e., a discrete categorization, such as the particular classification of an invoice within the aging schedule) and the *transition probabilities* which dictate the probabilities of moving from one state to another in the given time period (e.g., the probability an invoice gets paid or ages another month). The basic model (similar to the Cyert, Davidson, and Thompson model cited previously) and the results of an empirical study will be described here. The illustration is deliberately kept simple; the previously mentioned references provide further details.

The essence of the technique is to examine the aging schedule and to view each of the aging categories as states into which at the end of each month (or other time period) each *invoice* can be unambiguously classified. Here let us assume all sales are made on net 30 terms and that each *invoice* at the end of each month is classified into one of the following six states:

P = paid (i.e., the invoice amount has been paid)
O = current (i.e., the invoice is not more than 30 days old)
1 = up to one month past due
2 = one to two months past due
3 = two to three months past due
B = more than three months past due: the "bad debt" state;

For simplicity, we have assumed that any debt more than three months past due is classified as a bad debt and is considered outside of the system described by the model. Note that it would be more natural to classify on the basis of each account rather than by each invoice; the latter choice is taken here to avoid a number of practical problems. To illustrate just one: some practitioners classify an account on the basis of the aging of the oldest invoice debited to the account (i.e., *oldest balance aging*), while others choose to classify partially, that is, an account would be split into a variety of aging categories according to the dollars outstanding in each category (i.e., *partial balance aging*). The implications of this difference can be significant to the Markov chain models; this is discussed in van Kuelen, Spronk, and Corcoran ("Note on the Cyert-Davidson-Thompson Doubtful Accounts Model," *Management Science*, 1981). Also, in practice, one would use more states and a more flexible write-off policy; here we are merely attempting to reveal the basic idea without a clutter of detail.

If we fix one month as the length of a period, any invoice will change states within the period, except for the states P and B which are called *absorbing states;* once an invoice enters state P or B it is no longer relevant to our application. The possible transitions between states can be described by Exhibit 10. Alternatively, they can be presented in the *probability transition matrix* given in Exhibit 11.

The rows of the matrix represent the possible originating states and the columns represent the possible ending states over the one month period. We denote by P_{ij} the probability of making the transition from state i to state j in one month. To illustrate in our example, $P_{13} = 0$ since it is impossible for an invoice to go from being less than one month overdue to more than two months overdue in one month. Note that all rows sum to one (because each invoice has to go somewhere) and that all entries are nonnegative (since they represent probabilities).

While this structure may seem complex, a little patience will reveal that this is merely a formal way of looking at how an invoice moves between the categories in an aging schedule. Applying this approach to the May and June data in Exhibit 9, shows that the 2.2 that was current in May split into 0.6,

EXHIBIT 10   POSSIBLE TRANSITIONS BETWEEN STATES

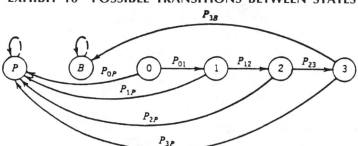

EXHIBIT 11   PROBABILITY TRANSITION MATRIX

$$P = \begin{vmatrix} 1 & 0 & 0 & 0 & 0 & 0 \\ P_{0P} & 0 & P_{01} & 0 & 0 & 0 \\ P_{1P} & 0 & 0 & P_{12} & 0 & 0 \\ P_{2P} & 0 & 0 & 0 & P_{23} & 0 \\ P_{3P} & 0 & 0 & 0 & 0 & P_{3P} \\ 0 & 0 & 0 & 0 & 0 & 1 \end{vmatrix}$$

which became the one month overdue figure for June, and the remainder, 1.6, had to be paid in June. (See Exhibit 10 to verify that these are the only two possibilities in our example.) This means that our estimates (based only on May–June data) of the transition probabilities are

$$P_{01} = \frac{1.6}{2.2} = .73$$

and

$$P_{0P} = \frac{.6}{2.2} = .27$$

Similarly,

$$P_{12} = \frac{.3}{.4} = .75$$

and

$$P_{1P} = \frac{.1}{.4} = .25$$

because the .4 that was outstanding in May during June split into .3, which is the amount that is two months overdue in June. The remainder, .1, had to be paid during June, meaning the proportion of one month overdue invoices in May that became paid in June is .25. The rest of the matrix given in Exhibit 12 is calculated in the same way. Comparing this matrix with the

EXHIBIT 12   TRANSITION PROBABILITY MATRIX FOR EXAMPLE

$$P = \begin{vmatrix} 1 & 0 & 0 & 0 & 0 & 0 \\ .73 & 0 & .27 & 0 & 0 & 0 \\ .25 & 0 & 0 & .75 & 0 & 0 \\ .33 & 0 & 0 & 0 & .67 & 0 \\ .50 & 0 & 0 & 0 & 0 & .50 \\ 0 & 0 & 0 & 0 & 0 & 1 \end{vmatrix}$$

matrix obtained from June–July data suggests that one cannot unambiguously state that payment behavior has changed: P_{1P} is higher for June–July; P_{12} is lower; P_{23} and P_{3P} are unchanged.

An Empirical Example. The following empirical example of the Markov chain approach is based on retail credit data obtained from a retail department store; the data consist of monthly records from a random sample of 200 revolving credit accounts. For each account in each month the following data are recorded: opening balance; net purchases during the month; payments received during the month; and minimum required payment.

The goal of this investigation was not to develop a cash forecasting model (although the methodology would be little changed in that case) but rather to study payment behavior. While this example is covered in detail in Kallberg and Parkinson (*Current Asset Management,* Wiley, New York, 1984), here we give a representative finding that can be obtained from this type of study. In this example, each account in each month was categorized into one of nine possible states. States P, 1, 2, and 3 are defined previously, but the current state is subdivided on the basis of outstanding balance as follows:

Oa = current account with an opening balance less than $50
Ob = current account with an opening balance between $50 and $100
Oc = current account with an opening balance between $100 and $200
Od = current account with an opening balance between $200 and $400
Oe = current account with an opening balance greater than $400

The estimated transition matrix, with the definitions of the other states as previously defined, is given in Exhibit 13. A number of conclusions can be drawn from this exhibit. For example, note that from all five current states the probability of ending up in state 1 is approximately equal. (This can be inferred from the seventh column of figures which gives the probability of ending up in state 1. The figures .176 to .194 give the respective probabilities of ending in state 1 given a starting state of Oa to Oe respectively.) Second, we can observe from the estimates for P_{12} (= .404), P_{23} (= .547), and P_{33} (= .620), that the more overdue an account is, the more difficult it becomes to collect that debt. In some applications these probabilities (P_{01}, P_{12}, P_{23}, . . .) are called **roll rates** and are effective ways to monitor payment behavior. For example, the larger these roll rates, the poorer is the payment performance. Note also that the product of these roll rates can be used to estimate the allowance for doubtful accounts.

FINANCING OF ACCOUNTS RECEIVABLE. As in the case of most other assets, funds may be raised by using accounts receivable, either as a form of collateral or by outright sale.

Asset Financing. The term "asset financing" is replacing "commercial financing" as a description of the use of assets as collateral for loans from

EXHIBIT 13 SAMPLE ESTIMATED PROBABILITY TRANSITION MATRIX

						Ending State					
		P	Oa	Ob	Oc	Od	Oe	1	2	3
	P	0.793	0.085	0.046	0.040	0.028	0.008	0.000	0.000	0.000
	Oa	0.295	0.283	0.121	0.067	0.051	0.010	0.175	0.000	0.000
	Ob	0.108	0.165	0.365	0.150	0.034	0.003	0.176	0.000	0.000
	Oc	0.043	0.041	0.151	0.413	0.145	0.023	0.184	0.000	0.000
	Od	0.025	0.010	0.023	0.155	0.544	0.078	0.165	0.000	0.000
	Oe	0.025	0.020	0.015	0.012	0.229	0.498	0.194	0.000	0.000
Beginning	1	0.087	0.084	0.108	0.147	0.090	0.081	0.000	0.404	0.000
State	2	0.070	0.047	0.086	0.117	0.078	0.055	0.000	0.000	0.547
	3	0.065	0.050	0.080	0.100	0.060	0.025	0.000	0.000	0.620

commercial finance companies or commercial banks. In this type of financing a lender is given a security interest in all or a randomly selected portion of the borrower's accounts receivable. In return, the lender agrees to supply funds equal to a percentage of the "pool" of receivables, less a reserve for returns and allowances. Additions to the pool come from new accounts receivable, and deletions occur as daily collections are charged against the pool. Also, past due accounts are usually removed from the pool.

Commercial finance companies may be willing to lend a somewhat higher percentage of the receivables in the pool than are commercial banks. Whereas commercial finance companies might be willing to advance funds in the range of 65–85% of receivables, most commercial banks operate within a range of 50–80%. The percentage of loan to receivables depends on the quality of the receivables pledged, the frequency of returns and allowances, and the payment histories and bad debt experience of the receivables.

It is important to recognize that the borrower has full responsibility for collecting the receivables. Usually the bank or finance company does not notify the customers of the borrower that their accounts have been pledged. This arrangement is known as **nonnotification financing.**

R. Goldman (*Harvard Business Review,* Vol. 57, November–December 1979, p. 210) states that "interest charges usually range from 3% to 6% above the prime rate." However, part of the interest charge is to cover the detailed handling costs required by the lender to assure the validity of the collateral. Thus the rate of charge will vary inversely with the average size and amount of accounts receivable pledged and directly with the turnover of receivables. Furthermore, the charge is based on the daily amounts borrowed, without a requirement for a compensating balance. As a result, the costs may not be significantly greater than bank loans that obligate the borrower to maintain unused funds on deposit.

A variation of asset financing is the use of **finance subsidiaries.** Many firms selling consumer goods and industrial equipment have established captive finance companies that either hold the firm's accounts receivable or lend against the receivables held by the parent. Examples of such finance subsidiaries are General Motors Acceptance Corp., J.C. Penney Financial Corp., and General Electric Credit Corp. Although the finance subsidiaries seldom pledge their receivables, they comprise most of the subsidiaries' assets. Because of the quality and liquidity of these assets, finance subsidiaries are able to borrow large amounts in relation to their assets on an unsecured basis, especially in the form of commercial paper. Proponents of finance subsidiaries argue that the consolidated firm is able to borrow more than if the accounts receivable were not segregated in a wholly owned subsidiary. In contrast, W.G. Lewellen (*Financial Management,* Vol. 1, Spring 1972, p. 30) has argued that ". . . the best circumstance is one in which parent and subsidiary have the **same** aggregate debt capacity as a combined enterprise. In many instances, a full mutual guarantee of each other's loans would be needed to accomplish even this result. Consequently, finance captives should, if anything, have a negative effect on credit standing." Empirical studies are not available to support or to refute either position.

Factoring. Factoring involves the selling or transfer of title of accounts receivable to a factoring firm, which acquires the accounts as principal, not as an agent. The receivables are sold without recourse; that is, the factor cannot turn to the seller if it is unable to collect balances owed. If a firm has borrowed against its receivables, the receivables still appear on its balance sheet. If the receivables have been sold to a factor, they disappear from the seller's balance sheet. Most factoring is **notification factoring,** whereby the seller sends invoices to the factor, who then takes over all responsibilities for collection. In nonnotification factoring, the seller collects the payments and remits them to the factor.

Factoring involves two distinct services by the factor, each with a separate fee schedule. First the factor provides credit evaluation and collection services and assumes the total credit risk and bad debt losses on accounts purchased. The factor maintains an extensive credit staff and has a diversified risk exposure that may permit it to buy accounts that the seller might not be willing to extend credit to at its own risk. A factor may, however, reject accounts offered for sale at any time. If a firm uses only the credit and collection services of the factor, the arrangement is called **maturity factoring.** The firm receives payment for the receivables sold each month on the average due date of the factored receivables.

The factor's commission for maturity factoring ranges from about 0.75 to 2%. The greater the expectancy of bad debts and the greater the amount of the handling costs involved, the higher the commission rates.

A second service provided by factors is **discount factoring.** Under this arrangement the firm selling its receivables may draw funds from the factor prior to the average maturity date. Funds available are equal to the net amount of the invoice, after cash discounts, less an allowance to cover estimated claims, returns, and other allowances. In the reference cited above, Goldman quoted the interest rates for this service as ranging from 2 to 3% above the prime rate. The interest charge is based on daily balances, and no compensating balances are required.

In addition to these two basic services, factors may provide other financing arrangements. **Daily cash balance accounts** enable firms selling to retailers "to draw against a receivable from the day it's assigned to the factor" (T.V. Pizzo, *Credit and Financial Management,* Vol. 81, December 1979, p. 18). Interest is charged from that date to the day when the receivable is collected and the advance canceled.

Overadvances permit a firm to borrow from a factor in anticipation of receivables that are yet to be generated. This type of financing permits firms to build inventories in anticipation of their peak selling season.

Factoring is particularly common in the apparel and textile industries, although it is used in a number of other fields. In the reference cited above,

Pizzo noted that to use factoring, a firm should have "annual sales of $1 million and up, with outstanding accounts receivable of $300 per invoice or more and a turnover cycle of 30 to 90 days."

MANAGEMENT OF ACCOUNTS PAYABLE

Trade credit is short-term business credit extended by a supplier to a buyer in conjunction with the purchase of goods and services. While accounts receivable are a current asset of the seller of goods and services, accounts payable are the corresponding current liability of the buyer. Thus, the forms and credit terms are the same as those discussed in connection with accounts receivable.

From an economic standpoint, trade credit arises primarily because the seller has a better access to capital than the customer-borrower. While this situation may be termed a market imperfection, it arises because the seller has a continuing relationship with the borrower. As a result, the seller has a low cost of information about the borrower and, because they are in the same line of business, good information about economic trends in the industry. Also, should the seller have to recover the inventory sold to the borrower in a bankruptcy proceeding, the seller can dispose of it with lower transaction costs than, say, a bank who acquires the collateral.

Because market imperfections affect small firms more than large ones, we would expect to find that small firms rely more heavily on trade credit as a source of funds than large businesses. This is the case. Of the $152.6 billion increase in liabilities of nonfinancial corporate business (excluding farms) in 1984, 16% was provided by trade credit (Board of Governors of the **Federal Reserve System,** Flow of Funds Accounts, September, 1985, p. 11.) Whereas corporations with positive assets under $100,000 financed 14.6% of their assets with trade credit in 1982, those with assets exceeding $250 million financed only 6.2% of their assets with trade credit.

COST OF FINANCING WITH TRADE CREDIT. The cost of trade credit depends on the credit terms offered. There are two classes of credit terms for analysis: those providing no cash discount and those that do include cash discounts.

No Cash Discount. When cash discounts are not offered, there is no explicit cost associated with the use of trade credit. Obviously, there is an implicit cost. The seller must cover the costs of providing "free" credit services in the selling price of the goods and services. If credit terms are "net 30," the credit should ordinarily be used for the full 30 days. To pay earlier means obtaining and paying for other sources of funds or foregoing the returns from investing idle funds in liquid assets.

Cash Discount. When cash discounts are available, failure to pay within the discount period bears an explicit cost. Assume that credit terms are 2/10, net 30; if the invoice is for $100, the cost of the goods purchased is really $98, and $2 will be added to the cost as a finance charge if the buyer fails to pay $98 by the tenth day. Assume that the buyer would pay by the thirtieth day in any case. The annual percentage rate charged for the use of the supplier's funds for the extra 20 days (from the tenth to the thirtieth day) is as follows:

annual percentage rate

$$= \text{rate per period} \times \text{number of periods per year}$$

$$= \frac{\text{discount percent}}{100\% - \text{discount percent}} \times \frac{365 \text{ days}}{\text{payment period} - \text{discount period}}$$

$$= \frac{2\%}{100\% - 2\%} \times \frac{365 \text{ days}}{30 \text{ days} - 10 \text{ days}}$$

$$= 0.0204 \times 18.25$$

$$= 0.3724 \text{ or } 37.24\%$$

If it were trade practice to stretch out payment to 60 days when the cash discount was missed, the annual percentage rate would be 14.9%. While it may appear that delaying final payment has the effect of lowering the annual percentage cost of missing trade discounts, this may not be the case. The cost of slow payment may be a lowered credit rating and lessened availability of trade credit from desirable suppliers.

OPTIMAL TRADE CREDIT POLICIES. Trade credit is the most important source of short-term financing between U.S. firms. Schwartz and Whitcomb ("The Trade Credit Decision," *Handbook of Financial Economics,* 1979) argue that there are three motives for a trade credit offer:

> The transaction motive reflects the fact that buyers' transaction costs are allowed to accumulate for periodic payment. . . . The financing motive exists if firms can profitably link financial intermediation to the sale of a product due to capital market imperfections. The pricing motive exists if product market imperfections make trade credit an effective means for disguised price reductions or discriminatory pricing.

The relative strengths of each of these motives in addition to industry and country specific norms, need to be considered in determining an optimal trade credit policy.

Capital budgeting approaches to the problem of determining optimal trade credit decisions have received considerable academic attention. The framework of Lieber and Orgler ("An Integrated Model for Accounts Receivable Management," *Management Science,* 1975) remains the most comprehensive (allowing variable cash discounts, variable length of discount and credit period, penalty charges for late payment, collection expenditures, and duration of past due collection effort). However, the approach of Hill and Riener ("Determining the Cash Discount in a Firm's Credit Policy," *Financial Management,* 1979) described in the following, also offers a simple yet flexible framework. For some of the many extensions to Hill and Reiner see, for example, Sartoris and Hill ("A Generalized Cash Flow Approach to Short-Term Financial Decisions," *Journal of Finance,* 1983), and Kallberg ("Discussion of Sartoris and Hill," *Journal of Finance,* 1983). Assume:

- The firm's initial trade credit policy has no discount.
- Cash payments totaling $$S$ arrive N days after sale.
- The firm is considering a credit policy with a discount of $d\%$ for early payment. This is assumed to lead to the fraction p paying on day M (to benefit from the discount) and the remainder paying on day N'.
- The relevant interest rate is i per day.

Using the net present value criterion, the discount should be offered if the net present value of the new credit policy,

$$\frac{p(1 - d)S}{(1 + i)^M} + \frac{(1 - p)S}{(1 + i)^{N'}},$$

is greater than the net present value of the initial policy,

$$\frac{S}{(1 + i)^{N'}}$$

This yields the decision rule: offer the discount if

$$d < 1 - (1 + i)^{M - N'}[(p - \{1 - (1 + i\}^{N' - N})/p].$$

While this model points out the essential tradeoffs, it is clearly too simple to reflect a number of important factors. For example, note that S and d are not connected, that is, no matter how large the discount there is no change in sales. However, this and numerous other generalizations are developed in the references mentioned previously.

EVALUATION OF MANAGEMENT OF ACCOUNTS PAYABLE. The evaluation of the management of accounts payable is the converse of the management of accounts receivable. Ultimately, failure to manage payables properly will be reflected in a firm's credit report. Since an adverse report levies costs on the firm that are implicit and difficult to measure, management of payables is an important function of financial management.

Traditional Measures of Payables Status. Just as the status of receivables is commonly measured by the use of days' sales outstanding and aging schedules, the status of accounts payable is measured by **days' purchases outstanding (DPO)** and aging schedules. The former index is calculated by dividing the dollar amount of accounts payable owed at a point in time by the average purchases per day over some preceding period of time. The reciprocal of this index is the **turnover of accounts payable.** An **aging schedule of payables** lists the percentages of outstanding payables at a point in time that are in different age classes: current, 0–30 days past due, 30–60 days past due, and so on.

When purchases vary significantly from month to month, both these measures suffer from the same deficiencies discussed with respect to DSO and aging schedules for accounts receivable. More effective monitoring procedures are available that are easy to employ.

Effective Measures of Payables Status. Either of two indexes that are not distorted by seasonal variations in purchases may be used to measure the status of accounts payable. Since both are mirror images of the effective procedures used to monitor receivables, they need not be discussed in detail. The **payable balance pattern** is calculated by determining the percentage of each month's purchases that remains outstanding at the end of each subsequent month. The **payment pattern** is shown by the monthly percentages of credit purchases in a given month that are paid in each subsequent month. Given predicted monthly purchases, either procedure can be used to predict levels of accounts payable outstanding.

Accounting for Missed Purchase Discounts. A final method of evaluating the management of accounts payable is provided by accounting procedures to isolate the cost of missed cash discounts. The cost of purchase discounts missed may be incorporated in "purchases" and carried through to "cost of goods sold." Under this procedure missed purchase discounts merely serve to lower the gross margin. A preferable procedure is to account for purchase discounts missed as a separate expense. For example, if a 2% cash discount were missed on a $100 invoice, $98 would be charged to "purchases" and carried to "cost of goods sold," and $2 would be charged to "purchase discounts missed." This account procedure highlights the cost of the failure of the financial manager to pay bills promptly.

INTEGRATION OF ACCOUNTS RECEIVABLE WITH WORKING CAPITAL MANAGEMENT. One of the most interesting developments in the accounts receivable area—and even more generally in the working capital area—has been the move towards greater integration. More specifically, the components of working capital management are increasingly being viewed in the aggregate as opposed to the traditional viewpoint in which each component (i.e., cash, accounts receivable, and inventory) was managed as a separate discipline. Cash managers in particular have begun to realize how much of the cash flow timeline can really be controlled. These points are developed in Hill and Ferguson ("Cash Flow Timeline Management," *Journal of Cash Management*, March/April 1985). For the firm, this integration offers several benefits, including

- Greater productivity
- More accurate performance measurement
- More logical incentive programs

One of the most important technological reasons for this has been the development of electronic funds transfers. These developments have altered the ways in which traditional credit terms are to be interpreted. Negotiated settlement dates (where the buyer and seller have an agreed-on settlement date when electronic payment is to made, either through a wire transfer or through an automated clearinghouse (ACH) transfer) are supplanting the more vaguely interpreted credit terms that we have previously discussed.

ELECTRONIC BUSINESS DATA INTERCHANGE. The growth in the amount of paper that corporations exchange has been explosive. One of the areas where there exists a potential to reduce this volume is in the area of corporate-to-corporate invoicing and payment. Under the usual scenario, both the buying and the selling corporations create a wide variety of paper documents to and from their respective data bases in addition to a paper item (check) to effect the purchase and eventual payment on the agreed-on date. This process is inefficient and error-prone.

The *American National Standards Institute (ANSI)* in 1979 chartered a committee to develop standards for the electronic interchange of invoice data. The perception was that there were at least three benefits to be obtained from electronic exchange of business data:

- Improved timeliness (e.g., resulting in reduced inventory investment)
- Reduction in paper processing costs and attendant errors
- Better cash availability (through certainty in the timing of cash payments and receipts)

In addition, the *National Automated Clearing House Association* (NACHA) in 1983 created a pilot program utilizing the ACH (see Section 7 on **Cash Management** for a more complete discussion) for the transmission of invoice and payment data. This program, called the *corporate trade payment program (CTP)* (and its corresponding format) thus far has met with limited success. Some of the reasons for this are documented in Johnson and Maier ("Making the Corporate Decision: Paper Checks to Electronic Funds Transfer," *Journal of Cash Management,* November/December 1985). Finally, preliminary indications from users are that a hybrid between the CTP and the *ANSI X12* format—called the *CTX* format—may prove to be the most popular. See White ("Electronic Payments Commentary: CTP, CCD, CTX: Which Format to Use?" *Journal of Cash Management,* November/December 1985) for a detailed comparison.

Johnson and Maier give the following rationale for this shift:

> Automated cash application systems already in place in many large companies provide a direct interface for updating corporate receivables based upon payment information now captured by the bank from remittance documents and then transmitted electronically to the corporation. Ideally, such a system operates without the corporation having to reexamine the paper items. In an EFT variation of this system, the bank does the translation from whatever payment format is received into the corporation's specified format for its automated cash application system. The cost to the company is very slight . . . One important advantage is that the company may be able to receive both lockbox and EFT payment data transmitted on the same file and in the same format.

The *ANSI X12* format is being increasingly utilized within the automotive industry as that group moves towards efficient working capital management via the electronic business data interchange program. One should note that these changes are causing structural shifts in working capital management, in particular, to a closer integration of these disciplines.

REFERENCES

Beehler, P.J., "Treasury Management Evolution," *Journal of Cash Management,* Vol. 4, January 1984.

Business International Corporation, *Global Cash Management,* New York, 1982.

Coffman, J.Y., and Chandler, G.G., *Applications of Performance Scoring to Accounts Receivable Management in Consumer Credit,* Working Paper No. 46, Credit Research Center, Purdue University, West Lafayette, IN, 1983.

Cole, R.H., *Consumer and Commercial Credit Management,* 6th ed., Irwin, Homewood, IL, 1984.

Corcoran, A.W., "The Use of Exponentially-Smoothed Matrices to Improve Forecasting of Cash Flows from Accounts Receivable," *Management Science,* Vol. 24, March 1978.

Cyert, R.M., Davidson, H.J., and Thompson, G.L., "Estimation of the Allowance for Doubtful Accounts," *Management Science,* Vol. 8, August 1962.

Cyert, R.M., and Thompson, G.L., "Selecting a Portfolio of Credit Risks by Markov Chains," *Journal of Business,* Vol. 1, 1968.

Dyl, E.A., "Another Look at the Evaluation of Investment in Accounts Receivable," *Financial Management,* Vol. 6, Winter 1977.

Emery, G.W., "A Pure Financial Explanation for Trade Credit," *Journal of Financial and Quantitative Analysis,* Vol. 19, September 1984.

Frydman, H.J., Kallberg, J.G., and Kao, D.-L., "The Application of Markov Chain and Mover-Stayer Models to an Empirical Analysis of Credit Behavior," *Operations Research,* Vol. 34, December 1985.

Goldman, R.L., "Look to Receivables and Other Assets to Obtain Working Capital," *Harvard Business Review,* Vol. 57, November–December 1979.

Hill, N.C., and Ferguson, D.M., "Cash Flow Timeline Management: The Next Frontier of Cash Management," *Journal of Cash Management,* Vol. 5, May 1985.

Hill, N.C., and Reiner, K.D., "Determining the Cash Discount in a Firm's Credit Policy," *Financial Management,* Vol. 8, Spring 1979.

Hill, N.C., Sartoris, W.L., and Ferguson, D.M., "Corporate Credit and Payables Policies: Two Surveys," *Journal of Cash Management,* Vol. 4, July/August 1984.

Kallberg, J.G., "Discussion of Sartoris and Hill," *Journal of Finance,* Vol. 38, May 1983.

Kallberg, J.G., and Parkinson, K.L., *Current Asset Management: Cash, Credit and Inventory,* Wiley, New York, 1984.

Kallberg, J.G., and Saunders, A., "Markov Chain Approaches to the Analysis of Payment Behavior of Retail Credit Customers," *Financial Management,* Vol. 12 Summer 1983.

Kampmeyer, J.M., "Measuring and Allocating Working Capital Usage to Operating Units: Jostens' Method," *Journal of Cash Management,* Vol. 4, May 1984.

Karson, M.J., and Wrobleski, W.J., "Confidence Intervals for Absorbing Markov Chains Probabilities Applied to Loan Portfolios," *Decision Sciences,* Vol. 7, 1976.

Kim, Y.H., and Atkins, J.C., "Evaluating Investment in Accounts Receivable: A Wealth Maximizing Framework," *Journal of Finance,* Vol. 33, May 1978.

van Kuelen, J.A.M., Spronk, J., and Corcoran, A.W., "Note on the Cyert-Davidson-Thompson Doubtful Accounts Model," *Management Science,* Vol. 27, 1981.

Lawrence, D.B., *Risk and Reward: The Craft of Consumer Lending,* New York, Citicorp, 1984.

Lewellen, W.G., "Finance Subsidiaries and Corporate Borrowing Capacity," *Financial Management,* Vol. 1, Spring 1972.

Lewellen, W.G., and Johnson, R.W., "Better Way to Monitor Accounts Receivable," *Harvard Business Review,* Vol. 50, May–June 1972.

Lieber, Z., and Orgler, Y.E., "An Integrated Model for Accounts Receivable Management," *Management Science,* Vol. 22, October 1975.

Mitchner, M.S., and Peterson, R.P., "Am Operations Research Study of the Collection of Defaulted Loans," *Operations Research,* Vol. 5, August 1957.

Oh, J.S., "Opportunity Cost in the Evaluation of Investment in Accounts Receivable," *Financial Management,* Vol. 5, Summer 1976.

Pizzo, T.V., "Factoring as a Management Tool," *Credit and Financial Management,* Vol. 81, December 1979.

Sartoris, W., and Hill, N.C., "A Generalized Cash Flow Approach to Short-Term Financial Decisions," *Journal of Finance,* Vol. 38, May 1983.

Schwartz, R., and Whitcomb, D., "The Trade Credit Decision," *Handbook of Financial Economics,* ed. J. Bicksler, North-Holland, NY, 1979.

Shim, Y., "Estimating Cash Collection rates from Credit Sales: A Lagged Regression Approach," *Financial Management,* Vol. 11, Autumn 1981.

Stoll, D.R., "The Credit Department Goes On-Line," *Credit and Financial Management,* Vol. 81, May 1979.

Stone, B.K., "The Payments-Pattern Approach to the Forecasting and Control of Accounts Receivable," *Financial Management,* Vol. 5, Autumn 1976.

Stowe, J.D., "Billing Frequency Optimization," *Journal of Systems Management,* Vol. 35, May 1983.

Whiteside, D.C., "Automated Credit Checking," *Credit and Financial Management,* Vol. 81, Nov. 1979.

BIBLIOGRAPHY

Credit Research Foundation, *Credit Limits Established by Formula and Computer,* Lake Success, NY, 1970.

———, *Present Value of Debt Settlements,* Lake Success, NY, 1979.

———, *Probability Failure Factors,* Lake Success, NY, 1979.

Lewellen, W.G., and Edmister, R.W., "A General Model for Accounts-Receivable Analysis and Control," *Journal of Financial and Quantitative Analysis,* Vol. 11, March 1973.

Lewellen, W.G., McConnell, J., and Scott, J., "Capital Market Influence on Trade Credit Policies," *Journal of Financial Research,* Vol. 1, Fall 1980.

Mehta, D.R., "The Formulation of Credit Policy Models," *Management Science,* Vol. 15, Oct. 1968.

Mehta, D.R., *Working Capital Management,* Prentice-Hall, Englewood Cliffs, NJ, 1979.

Myers, J.H., and Forgy, E.W., "The Development of Numerical Credit Evaluation Systems," *Journal of the American Statistical Association,* Vol. 58, Sept. 1963.

Schiff, M., and Lieber, Z., "A Model for the Integration of Credit and Inventory Management," *Journal of Finance,* Vol. 24, March 1974.

Smith, K.V., *Guide to Working Capital Management,* McGraw-Hill, NY, 1979.

Walia, T., "Explicit and Implicit Cost of Changes in the Level of Accounts Receivable and the Credit Policies of the Firm," *Financial Management,* Vol. 6, Winter 1977.

Wort, D.H., "The Trade Discount Decision: A Markov Chain Approach," *Decision Sciences,* Vol. 16, Winter 1985.

Wrightsman, D., "Optimal Credit Terms for Accounts Receivable," *Quarterly Review of Economics and Business,* Vol. 9, Summer 1972.

9

CAPITAL BUDGETING

CONTENTS

9

CAPITAL BUDGETING

Harold Bierman, Jr.

INTRODUCTION

Business organizations are continually faced with the problem of deciding whether the commitments of resources—time and money—are worthwhile in terms of the expected benefits. If benefits are likely to accrue reasonably soon after an expenditure is made, and if both expenditure and benefits can be measured in dollars, the solution to such a problem is relatively simple. If the expected benefits are likely to accrue over several years, the solution is more complex. A decision that involves outlays and benefits stretched out through time is called a **capital budgeting decision.** Capital budgeting is a many-sided activity that includes searching for new and more profitable investment proposals, investigating engineering and marketing considerations to predict the consequences of accepting a given investment, and making economic analyses to determine the profit potential of each investment proposal. The objective of this section is to suggest a basic approach to the evaluation of capital budgeting decisions.

CAPITAL EXPENDITURES AND FINANCIAL PLANNING

Capital expenditures should not be analyzed from a narrow or short-term point of view, but should be integrated into the strategic programs of a company. The economic justification for a capital expenditures program must be based on a long-term estimate of cash flows, which in turn requires projection of sales and costs of operation for a large number of years. **Financial control** over capital expenditures is basic to the proper administration of a business. The effects of decisions involving capital expenditures are permanent and far-reaching; frequently, they determine the success or failure of an enterprise. Once acquired, **capital assets** frequently cannot be disposed of except at a substantial loss. If increased earnings do not result from the purchase of the additional capital assets, the ability of the company to discharge its financial obligations may be impaired. The basic principles involved in evaluating investments apply to every business, regardless of size or industry.

The acquisition of capital assets and the determination of their characteristics will have an important effect on future operating costs. For example, geographical location of plants with relation to markets and sources of raw materials may result in a large difference in operating costs. A general purpose factory building rather than a specialized plant may be more adaptable to new uses in the future, and the structure may have a higher **resale value** if disposal of the plant becomes necessary later. On the other hand, a special purpose plant that costs considerably more initially and is less salable may result in substantial operating economies during the years of use. Not only must initial expenditures be balanced against estimated savings in future operating costs and estimated **residual value,** but close monitoring of construction in progress is necessary to avoid higher operating costs, delays caused by facility "bottlenecks," or the commitment of capital in idle equipment and plant and partially completed inventories.

Joel Dean (*Capital Budgeting,* 1951) prepared an extremely useful classification of investments that may be summarized as follows:

1. Replacement investments:
   a. Like-for-like replacements.
   b. Obsolescence replacements.
2. Expansion investments.
3. Product-line investments:
   a. On new products.
   b. On improving old products.
4. Strategic investments.

Replacement investments substituted for current investments will either reduce cost or increase capacity or quality. **Expansion investments** are directed toward increasing capacity rather than toward changing the operating process. Some investments combine elements of replacement and expansion. With respect to **product-line investments,** expenditures may be for purposes of developing new items or for improving those already being produced. Proposals for **strategic investment** are likely to involve basic policy such as a shift to new product lines or new geographic locations.

TYPES OF INVESTMENT

INDEPENDENT PROJECTS. Another method of classifying investments is based on the way the benefits from a given investment are affected by other possible investments. A given investment proposal may be economically independent of, or dependent on, another investment proposal. The first investment proposal is said to be economically independent of the second if the **cash flows** (or more generally the costs and benefits) expected from the first investment would be the same regardless of whether the second investment were accepted or rejected. If the cash flows associated with the first investment are affected by the decision to accept or reject the second investment, the first investment is said to be economically dependent on the second. It should be clear that when one investment is dependent on another, some attention must be given to the question of whether decisions about the first investment can or should be made separately from decisions about the second.

For investment A to be economically independent of investment B, two conditions must be satisfied. First, it must be technically possible to undertake investment A regardless of whether investment B is accepted. For example, since it is not possible to build a school and a shopping center on the same site, the proposal to build one is not independent of a proposal to build the other. Second, the net benefits to be expected from the first investment must not be affected by the acceptance or rejection of the second. If the estimates of the cash outlays and the cash inflows for investment A are not the same when B is either accepted or rejected, the two investments are not independent. Thus it is technically possible to build a toll bridge and operate a ferry across adjacent points on a river, but the two investments are not independent because the proceeds from one will be affected by the existence of the other. The two investments would not be economically independent, in the sense in which the term is used here, even if the traffic across the river at this point were sufficient to support the profitable operation of both the bridge and the ferry.

Sometimes two investments cannot both be accepted because the firm does not have enough cash to finance both. This situation could occur if the amount of cash available for investments were strictly limited by management rather than by the capital market, or if increments of funds obtained from the capital market cost more than previous increments. In such a situation the acceptance of one investment may cause the rejection of the other. But we shall not then say that the two investments are economically dependent. To do so would make all investments for such a firm dependent, and this is not a useful definition for our purposes. The cash flows of one independent investment do not directly affect the cash flows of a second independent investment. Thus, leaving out **financial constraints,** the undertaking of one investment does not affect the decision to undertake any of the other independent investments of the firm.

There is a temptation to say two investments with independent cash flows might still compete for funds, thus they are not strictly independent. While conceding that such a competition for funds can exist (in fact, we give this situation a name; it is called **capital rationing),** we still use the more restrictive definition of independent innvestments, given above. Two investments may be economically independent but their sets of cash flows may not be **statistically independent.** If knowing something about the actual level of cash flow of the one investment helps in predicting the cash flow of the second investment, there is **statistical dependency.** The level of dependency may affect a firm's willingness to undertake an investment.

MUTUALLY EXCLUSIVE INVESTMENTS. When the potential benefits to be derived from the first investment will completely disappear if the second investment is accepted, or when it would be technically impossible to undertake the first if the second were accepted, the two investments are said to be mutually exclusive. Frequently, a company will be considering two or more investments, any one of which would be acceptable, but because the investments are mutually exclusive, only one can be accepted. For example, assume that a company is trying to decide where to build a new plant. It may be that either of two locations would be profitable, but because only one new plant is needed, the company must decide which one is likely to be the more profitable. An oil company may need additional transport facilities for its products. Should it build a pipeline or acquire additional tankers and ship by water? Either of these alternatives may result in a net profit to the firm, but the company will wish to choose the one that is more profitable. In these situations, the choice is between mutually exclusive investments.

Mutually exclusive investment alternatives are common. The situation frequently occurs in connection with the engineering design of a new installation. In the process of designing such an installation, the engineers are typically faced with alternatives that are mutually exclusive. Thus a measure of investment worth that does not lead to correct mutually exclusive choices will be seriously deficient. In this light, the fact that the two discounted cash flow measures of investment worth may give different rankings to the same set of mutually exclusive investment proposals becomes of considerable importance.

TYPES OF DECISION. The primary investment decisions are (1) to accept or reject decisions involving independent investments (all the proposals can be undertaken if they are available) and (2) to choose the "best of the set" decisions involving mutually exclusive investment. Some managers think it necessary to rank independent investments; however, ranking is not defensible in an exact mathematical sense. It can be done in a subjective manner.

RANKING AND CAPITAL RATIONING

The ranking of independent investments implies that the interest rate being used to discount the future cash flows is not the correct measure of the **opportunity cost of capital** because some of the acceptable (ranked) investments will be rejected. With mutually exclusive investments, this assumption is not implicit in the calculations, since the rejected projects cannot logically be accepted given the nature of the set of mutually exclusive investments. Thus, the choice of the discount rate is not being called into question.

The ranking of independent investments implies that a form of **capital rationing** is taking place. With capital rationing there are more dollars needed for investments than there are investible funds. For one reason or another, the firm chooses not to go to the capital market to raise new capital. This assumption of not being able to raise capital is the major weakness of capital rationing analysis, since it is not clear why the firm **cannot** raise more capital at its available cost of funds. The raising of capital would be the logical move, given that the firm has more investment opportunities yielding a higher rate of return than its cost of capital (adjusted for risk) than it has available capital. Despite this apparent logical inconsistency, managers do perceive that capital rationing situations exist and want to rank investments to deal with such situations by eliminating from consideration the lower ranked investments. In fact, what managers are implying is that the costs of raising new capital are prohibitively high relative to expected returns, and that a higher cost of capital should be used.

While there are no easy calculations that would lead to useful exact rankings, there are several possible solutions. The most popular **academic solution** is a **linear programming model** that will evaluate all investments over the firm's **planning horizon.** However, this solution requires an enormous amount of information. One needs information not only about the current period's investments but also about all the investments of the future periods within the planning horizon. These information requirements tend to discourage firms from using this solution.

A second type of solution is to admit that the investment rankings are not exactly correct but to use the **internal rate of return** (sometimes adjusted for reinvestment assumptions) or the **present value index** (present value of benefits divided by present value of costs). These techniques are defined shortly. While counterexamples can be prepared to show why the resulting rankings are inexact, the rankings that are derived using these techniques probably do not introduce as much error as is introduced by faulty estimation of the cash flows or by ad hoc risk analysis.

In some very well defined situations investments can be unambiguously ranked, but these situations are not likely to occur frequently in the real world with complex cash flow patterns. Investments can be ranked in an approximate manner. Ranking cannot be done with exactness in a complex situation entailing a series of investments through time.

THE CAPITAL BUDGET

COVERAGE. The capital budget covers all proposed outlays for a specified period for the following types of investment:

1. Replacement of units (the salvage value of old items being deducted from the cost).
2. Additions and extensions to plant and equipment.
3. New plant and equipment.
4. Cost of land on which a plant is to be constructed.
5. Furniture, fixtures, and office equipment.
6. Merger decisions.
7. Make-or-buy analyses.
8. Increases in net working capital arising from the items above.

The **capital budget** is known variously as the **construction budget,** the **facilities budget,** the **capital outlay budget,** and the **budget of capital expenditures.**

ADVANTAGES OF CAPITAL BUDGETS. The administration of capital outlays is difficult without a capital budget administered by a specific manager (who may have a title such as budget director or vice-president of planning). The treasurer needs to know the capital budget to be able to plan the cash needs of the coming periods. Also, preparing a capital budget facilitates the comparison of the benefits of different projects that are competing for scarce resources.

While having a formal annual capital budget does result in a loss of flexibility of action, few companies fail to prepare formal budgets. The annual budget may be supplemented by reviews of individual requests for capital expenditures after the annual budget has been approved.

PREPARATION

Status List. It is useful to have a list that summarizes the status of all current or planned capital projects. Exhibit 1 shows a sample form that division managers or department heads would use to itemize their projects. This form lists all projects now underway, acquisitions for which **commitments have been made,** and the anticipated dates of commpletion. The final status list should be approved by the **chief financial officer** and then by the **chief executive officer** before being submitted to the **board of directors** (or one of its com-

EXHIBIT 1   SAMPLE STATUS OF PROJECTS FORM

Capital Projecting Listing

Date

	Capital Projects		Expenditures			
Division	Description	Total Amount to be Expended	Actual to Date	Amount to be Expended This Year	Estimated Date of Completion	Comments

mittees). Supporting documents for each investment itemized should be readily available for these executives.

Appropriation Request. The capital budgeting process starts with the preparation of appropriation requests for each item of capital expenditure. Individual appropriation requests are approved after review by the plant managers and then the division manager, if the size of the expenditure justifies both of these levels. These managers are required to specify the reason for the expenditure. Typical reasons for planned expenditures are:

1. New business activity.
2. Increase in capacity of present business.
3. Replacement of present equipment (nondiscretionary).
4. Replacement of present equipment (discretionary, for increased efficiency, quality, or capacity).
5. New product.
6. Cost reduction.
7. Nonrevenue-producing expenditures.
8. Mandated (by government) expenditures.

It is standard for companies to require that the following information be included in the appropriation request:

1. **Purpose of expenditure** (see list above for some general purposes).
2. **Estimated expenditures** involved in acquisition or construction.
3. **Cash flows** resulting from capital expenditure.
4. **Accounting effects** resulting from new capital assets including the loss from the write-off of any present assets.

A sample appropriation request form is shown in Exhibit 2. Forms used vary widely in detail.

Approved appropriations remain valid until the project has been either completed or canceled. Upon completion of the project, if any expended balance remains, the appropriation for it should be canceled and not be made available for other purposes. If the amount of the original appropriation does not prove adequate to cover the full cost of the project, a supplemental appropriation will be needed. A supplemental appropriation should be considered as a new investment. Normally, projects once started are eventually completed, but this should not be automatically assumed.

It is common practice to require approval of appropriation requests for each project at several managerial levels. The authority required for such approval ordinarily is governed by the size of both the request and the company. In instances involving large amounts, the project request for funds

EXHIBIT 2 SAMPLE APPROPRIATION FOR CAPITAL EXPENDITURES

Appropriation for Capital Expenditure

Appropriation No. _____

_____ _____ Date
Plant Division

==

This appropriation is to cover a capital expenditure made necessary by:

New business [ ]   Replacement [ ]

Expansion [ ]   Change in production method [ ]

Other (explain):

Description of Proposed Capital Expenditure

Estimated cost: _____
(prior to implementation)

Estimated useful life of asset: _____

Timing of expenditures (specify years and amounts):

Estimated completion date: _____

Record of Preparation and Action on This Appropriation			
Plant Record	**Date**	**Division Record**	**Date**
Prepared by _____		Received by Division Manager _____	
Approved by _____		Approved by Division Manager _____	

EXHIBIT 3   SUMMARY PROJECT ANALYSIS INFORMATION

<u>   </u>   <u>   </u>   Date:

Project title   Project no.   <u>   </u>

<u>   </u>   Purpose of project

Division   Plant

Project Description

Summary of Investment

Maximum outlays (sum)   <u>   </u>

Net present values   At 0%   <u>   </u>

                           5%   <u>   </u>

                        10%   <u>   </u>

                        20%   <u>   </u>

Internal rate of return   <u>   </u>

Payback Information

Cumulative cash flow   After 5 years   <u>   </u>

                                10 years   <u>   </u>

Payback period   <u>   </u>

Discounted payback period   <u>   </u>

Timing

    Start of expenditures   <u>   </u>

    Time of first positive flows   <u>   </u>

Cash Flows

    Time 0 (date___)   <u>   </u>

              1   <u>   </u>

              2   <u>   </u>

              3   <u>   </u>

              4 (list for all relevant years)

Major Assumptions

requires the approval of the **chief executive officer** and the **board of directors** (or one of its committees).

The Project Summary. An important tool to use in evaluating an innvestment is the project summary sheet (Exhibit 3), prepared at the site of the capital budgeting proposal. This document summarizes the primary relevant economic evaluation measures.

The **listing of cash flows** gives the person evaluating the investment a feel for the economics of the investment. The major assumption section is used to make explicit the assumptions that go into the cash flow calculations: those regarding the estimated life of the project, the residual value, changes in prices, the rate of inflation, and other important changes in economic or technological variables.

Short-Cut. The project summary sheet illustrated in Exhibit 3 includes the cash flows of each year. A possible short-cut is to compute the cash flows (after tax) before considering depreciation expense for taxes. The present value of the tax savings from depreciation expense is then computed separately.

When the assumptions about the future allow it, one might be able to bypass the year-by-year cash flow calculation completely. For example, if the cash flows before tax considerations are constant for each time period, it is not necessary to show the cash flows of each period.

EXHIBIT 4   CASH FLOW WORKSHEET: FORM

	Period 1	Period 2	Period 3
Revenues or savings (cash and receivables)			
Out-of-pocket expenses	——	——	——
Income before taxes			
Taxes (0.48)	$ ——	——	——
Income after taxes	$ ——	——	——
Plus: Net working capital decrease			
Less: Net working capital increase	——	——	——
Cash flow	$ ——	——	——
Present value factors			
Present values	══	══	══
Total present value of savings $ ——			
Cost of investment $ ——			
Less: Investment tax credit ——			
Present value of			
depreciation times tax rate ——			
Net cost ——			
Net present value ══			

EXHIBIT 5   CASH FLOW WORKSHEET: EXAMPLE

	Period 1	Period 2	Period 3
Revenues or savings (cash and receivables)	10,000	9,000	7,000
Out-of-pocket expenses	5,500	5,500	5,500
Income before taxes	4,500	3,500	2,500
Taxes (0.48)	2,160	1,680	1,200
Income after taxes	2,340	1,820	1,300
Plus: Net working capital decrease			
Less: Net working capital increase	1,000	600	1,600
Cash flow	$1,340	1,220	2,900
Present value factors	0.9091	0.8264	0.7513
Present values	1,218	1,008	1,179

Total present value of savings		$4,405
Cost of investment	$6,000	
Less: Investment tax credit	300	
Present value of depreciation times tax rate	2,464	
Net cost (6,000 − 300 − 2,464)		3,236
Net present value		1,169

Example

An investment costs $6,000 and has a life of 3 years. There is an investment tax credit of 5%. The sum of the federal and state tax rates is 0.48. The asset will earn $10,000 the first year, $9,000 the second, and $7,000 the third, and there are $5,500 of out-of-pocket expenses per year.

Working capital will be $1,000, then $1,600, then zero. The time discount rate is 10%. Using the sum-of-the-years-digits, the present value of the depreciation per dollar of asset is 0.855427, and with a cost of $6,000 it is $5,133. The tax saving is 5,133 × .48 = 2464. We assume the tax basis is not affected by the investment tax credit.

Other Forms. Detailed forms can be prepared showing how to compute the cash flows of each period. There are many equally acceptable variations. As suggested above, one useful technique is to compute the basic cash flows without including a depreciation deduction, and then treat the depreciation tax savings separately. This type of calculation is illustrated in Exhibits 4 and 5.

Many executives want to know the effect of an investment project on **accounting income.** Conceptually this is simple enough, since it merely entails doing the income statement preparation based on **pro forma information.** Accounting conventions are such that a desirable investment can depress earnings and lower return on investment for one or more of the early time periods. This result occurs because of the expensing of startup expenses that theoretically should be **capitalized** and because of large rapid deprecia-tion expense write-offs. Such a situation is the result of accounting conven-tion and does not in any way reflect on the economic measures of desirability. If the economic measures indicate that the investment is acceptable, the accounting measure (pro forma) should be consistent with the economic measures. In evaluating investments, management should either ignore the accounting measures or adjust the accounting to be consistent with the economic measures. Unfortunately this latter path is not always feasible.

CAPITAL BUDGETING PROCEDURES

OBJECTIVES OF THE FIRM. In making **capital budgeting decisions** there is implied some known and agreed on objectives for the business firm. The primary goal of the firm is assumed to be the **maximation of the net present value of the stockholders'** position. The investment decisions are made from the point of view of the stockholders, and it is assumed that their interests are best served by a procedure that systematically assigns a **cost to the capital** that is utilized in the production process.

To be consistent with the best interests of investors, a company must take into consideration a cost on the capital that is being utilized or, more generally, the time value of money. As a second step, the process must adjust for the risk of the project being considered. The investors have to be compensated both for time value of money and for risk. Since capital bud-geting decisions involve immediate outlays and uncertain benefits that are spread out through time, the primary decision problem facing management is to incorporate time value and risk considerations in such a manner that the well-being of the stockholders is maximized.

USE OF CASH FLOWS. Why use **cash flows** rather than **accounting income measures** for the capital budgeting decisions? The objective is to evaluate the investment over its entire life, and there is no need to determine the year-by-year profitability (as required for accounting) to decide whether the investment is acceptable from an economic point of view. The accountant measures yearly earnings based on complex "accrual" concepts. The cash flow calculations of capital budgeting decisions are much simpler. One needs to find the net amount of cash receipts and expenditures for each time period (an implicit cash outlay will be included when there is a relevant **opportunity cost**).

The analysis of cash flows should use the aftertax cash flows of each period as the inputs into the calculations. The results are consistent with the use of theoretically correct income measures and easier to compute, since they do not require measures of annual depreciation expense and other accounting accruals and assumptions. The primary justifications for the **use of cash flows are simplicity and theoretical correctness.**

   Debt flows (i.e., interest expense) are generally excluded from the measure of cash flows. Thus, profitability measures are obtained that are independent of the method of financing. For some purposes the decision maker may want to include all debt flows (principal and interest) to obtain **stockholder equity profitability measures.** These measures of stockholder equity cash flows must be used with care, since they are not comparable to measures that exclude the debt flows. It is a major error to include some of the effects of debt, but not all, or to include all the debt effects but not to recognize that the resulting measures pertain to the stockholders' equity, not to the entire firm.

Discounted Cash Flow Methods. The **discounted cash flow (DCF) methods** of evaluating investments are now used by almost all the largest industrial firms, and their use is spreading to the smaller firms. Thirty years ago very few firms were using DCF techniques. Users included a few chemical and oil companies and many public utilities, but otherwise DCF was considered to be too theoretical. The **payback period approach** and the **accounting return on investment** were the standard calculations.

   All firms face capital budgeting decisions for which the timing of the cash flows of an investment is a relevant factor. For many years business managers did not know how to take time value into consideration in a theoretically correct manner. Now two basic methods are widely used and they are both DCF methods. One method is to find the average return on investment earned through the life of the investment, where the average is a very special type of average. The second method is to apply a rate of discount (interest rate) to future cash flows to bring them back to the present (finding **present value equivalents**). The first method described is the **"internal rate of return"** method and the second calculation is the **"net present value."** A wide range of titles is used for these methods, and there are also variations of calculations, but these two methods are the most common and the most useful.

Time Value Calculations. A dollar in hand today is worth more than a dollar to be received a year from today. For example, if money can be invested in real assets or lent at 10% per year, $100 held today will be worth $110 a year from today. In like manner, $100 to be received a year from today has a present value now of $90.01 ($90.91 invested to earn 0.10 will earn $9.09 interest and will be worth $100 after one year).

   Assuming that we can lend and borrow at an interest of r, the following formula enables us to move cash flows back and forth through time:

$$A = (1 + r)^{-n}C$$

where r = interest rate
   C = future sum to be received in the nth period from now
   A = present value or present economic
         equivalent of C

If r, n, and C are properly specified, one is indifferent between C dollars at time n and A dollars now.

For example, assume that a firm is to receive $1 million two years from now and r is 0.10.

Then

$$A = (1.10)^{-2} \times \$1,000,000 = \$826,446$$

The firm is indifferent between an investment offering $826,444 now or an investment offering $1,000,000 in two years if money is worth 0.10. The $826,446 will grow to $909,091 after 1 year and the $909,091 will grow to $1,000,000 at the end of 2 years.

If $r = 0.10$, the present value of $1 million due in two years is $826,446. The present value of $1 due in two years is $0.826446. Tables can be prepared to give the **present value factors** for different values of r and n. To find the present value equivalent of a future value C, multiply the appropriate present value factor by C. Most **handheld calculators** can be used to determine the value of $(1 + r)^{-n}$. If the calculator has a y^x function, this is equivalent to $(1 + r)^n$, where $y = 1 + r$ and $x = n$.

METHODS OF CAPITAL BUDGETING. Many methods of capital budgeting are used by business firms, but we focus on the four that are most widely used. We consider in sequence the payback, return on investment (ROI), net present value, and internal rate of return methods. Only the latter two methods are recommended for general use.

Payback Method. Over the past 50 years the most widely used method of determining the desirability of an investment has been the "payback" method. The length of time required to recover (earn back) the initial investment is computed, and this measure is compared to maximum payback periods tolerable to the firm for this type of investment. For example, an investment costing $1 million and recovering $250,000 per year would have a payback period of four years. Well-informed managers will state that they understand the limitations of payback (not considering either the time value of money or the life of the investment after the payback period), but they use the payback measure as an indication of the amount of the investment's relative risk—that is, a payback of one year would indicate less risk than a payback of four years. Payback, however, is not a reliable risk measure.

The payback period calculation should not be used as the primary method of evaluating investments. It is, however, an effective safeguard against "game playing" in the preparation of capital budgets. A payback calculation on an investment will expose attempts to load the cash flows of the later years, making the investment appear more desirable than it actually is.

A **discounted variation of payback** is sometimes used. Assume an investment costs $379,000 and will earn a $100,000 cash flow per year. The interest rate is 10%. The **undiscounted payback period** is 3.79 years, but the discounted payback period is five years (the present values of $100,000 a year for five years are equal to the initial outlay of $379,000). This information can also be interpreted to mean that if the forecasted cash flows occur for five years, the investment will just break even economically (the investors will receive back their capital and the required return, 10%, on that capital).

Return on Investment. Another popular method of measuring profitability of an investment, though it is rapidly losing ground as the primary measure, is return on investment (ROI). The ROI of an investment is the average income divided by the average investment. Since the income and investment measures used are conventional accounting measures, the ROI measure fails to take into consideration the **time value of money.** While the conventional ROI measure is an unreliable way of evaluating investments, the error is made even worse by incorrect application of the technique. A common practice in industry is to compute the ROI of the first complete year of use. The first year's ROI, as conventionally computed, tends to be smaller than the average return. Thus its use creates a bias against accepting investments that should be accepted.

A distinction should be made between the use of ROI to measure performance of assets being used and the use of ROI to evaluate the acceptability of investments. One cannot judge the effectiveness of a manager by observing the income of a period. The amount of resources used by the manager in earning income on investments is an important variable in measuring performance. The normal procedure is to divide income by beginning of the period investment (or average investment) to obtain a return on investment for the period. If income and investment are reasonably measured, this is an extremely useful calculation. One way or another, it is necessary to measure both income and the resources used and to relate the two measures.

The use of an average ROI to evaluate investments presents problems, since ROI as conventionally computed does not consider the time value of money. A dollar of benefits added to period 10 will affect the ROI as much as a dollar of benefits added to period 1. This is neither theoretically correct nor useful in practice.

Since ROI is widely used to measure performance, **pro forma financial statements** are prepared and pro forma ROI calculations made even where ROI is not used to evaluate investments formally. This implies that in the interest of having consistency between the investment decision criteria and the performance measure calculations, considerable care and thought must be expended to make sure that the **performance measures** are theoretically sound and consistent with the DCF investment criteria being used.

Discounted Cash Flow Measures. These DCF techniques are more reliable measures of value than the payback and ROI methods described above. The discussion is limited to the internal rate of return and the net present value methods. These two measures are recommended because they are widely used and also because they will do everything that alternative methods will do and in some cases will avoid errors in application introduced by these other measures.

Net Present Value Method. The net present value method of evaluating investments has been increasing in use for the past 20 years. It is hard to find a large industrial firm that does not employ the net present value method (generally in conjunction with other measures) somewhere in its organization.

The net present value of an investment is the amount the firm could afford to pay in excess of the cost of the investment and still break even on the investment. It is also the present value of all future profits, where the profits are after the capital costs (interest on the capital) of the investments. If the net present value is positive, the investment is acceptable.

The first step in the computation of the net present value of an investment is to choose a rate of discount (this may be a required return or **"hurdle rate"**). The second step is to compute on an after tax basis the present value equivalents of all cash flows associated with the investment and sum these present value equivalents to obtain the net present value of the investment.

Example. Consider an investment costing $864,000 that promises cash flows of $1 million one period from now and $100,000 two periods from now. Using the present value factors for $r = 0.10$ we have:

Time Period	Cash Flows	Present Value Factors (0.10)	Present Value Equivalents
0	$-864,000	1.0000	$-864,000
1	1,000,000	0.9091	909,000
2	100,000	0.8264	83,000
Net present value			$ 128,000

The firm could pay $128,000 more than the $864,000 cost and break even; that is, it would just earn the 0.10 capital cost. Thus the $128,000 is in a sense the "excess" incentive to invest and is a measure of the safety margin that exists.

Let us assume the following arbitrary depreciation schedule (any other schedule would give the same present value of income):

Year	Depreciation
1	432,000
2	432,000

The following incomes then result:

Year	Revenues	Depreciation	Income Before Interest	Interest on Book Value	Income	Present Value Factors	Present Value
1	$1,000,000	$432,000	$568,000	$86,400	$481,600	0.9091	$438,000
2	100,000	432,000	−332,000	43,200	−375,000	0.8264	−310,000
	Present value of incomes						$128,000

The present value of the after interest income is $128,000, which is the amount of net present value of cash flows obtained above. This value is **independent of the method of depreciation.**

The argument is sometimes offered that the **net present value method** is difficult to use and to understand. Actually it is the simplest of the procedures to use. If the net present value is positive, the investment is acceptable. Also, the interpretation of the measure is easy and useful. The net present value is the amount the firm could pay in excess of the cost and still break even, and it is the sum of the present value of the incomes after capital costs (note the interest on the book value in the table above).

Instead of computing net present value, some managers prefer **terminal value.** Following this method, the value as of the end of a project's life is computed. The terminal value at time n is equal to the net present value times $(1 + r)^n$. The choice of method is based on preference rather than on a substantive distinction.

The terminal value of the investment being considered is $128,000 \times 1.10^2 = \$155,000$. The terminal value will always be a larger absolute value than the net present value. If the net present value is greater than zero, the terminal value will also be greater than zero. If investment A has a larger net present value than investment B, investment A will also have a larger terminal value, assuming that both investments are carried out to a common terminal date.

Internal Rate of Return Method. The net present value method gives a **dollar measure.** Some managers prefer a percentage measure that is most frequently called an investment's internal rate of return. Other terms applied to the same measure are the yield, IRR or IROR, return on investment, and time-adjusted rate of return.

The internal rate of return of an investment is the rate of discount that causes the sum of the present values of the cash flows of the investment to be equal to zero. The internal rate of return is found by a trial-and-error procedure (when the net present value is equal to zero, the rate of discount being used is the internal rate of return).

Continuing the example above, we find by trial and error that the net present value is zero using a 0.25 rate of discount. For discount rates larger than 0.25, the net present value would be negative.

Time	Present Value					
	0.00		0.10		0.25	
0	− 864,000	1.0000	− 864,000	1.0000	− 864,000	
1	1,000,000	0.9091	909,000	0.8000	800,000	
2	100,000	0.8264	83,000	0.6400	64,000	
Net present value	+ 236,000		+ 128,000		0	

The **internal rate of return** of an investment has several interesting and relevant economic interpretations. For example, it is the highest rate at which the firm can borrow using the funds generated by the investment to repay the loan. If funds were borrowed at a cost of 0.25, the following repayment schedule would apply:

Initial amount owed	$864,000
Year-1 interest (0.25)	+ 216,000
	1,080,000
Repayment using cash flows	− 1,000,000
	80,000
Year-2 interest (0.25)	+ 20,000
	100,000
Repayment using cash flows	− 100,000
Amount owed	0

The cash flows generated by the investment are just sufficient to pay the loan costing 0.25.

All **independent investments** with an internal rate of return greater than the **required return** should be accepted. This assumes that cash flows are those of a normal investment, that is, one or more periods of cash outlays followed by cash inflows.

Reinvestment Rate Assumption. It is frequently said that the net present value method assumes that funds are reinvested at the cost of money and that internal rate of return method assumes that funds are reinvested at the investment's internal rate of return. This position is not necessarily correct.

Let us consider the example above. The net present value is $128,000 if 0.10 is used as the discount rate and the investment's internal rate of return is 0.25. Both these calculations are independent of the use of the $1 million of cash flows at time 1. For example, the $1 million might be consumed at time 1 and the net present value and the internal rate of return measures remain unchanged.

Let us assume that we know that at time 1 the $1 million could be reinvested in period 2 to earn 0.30. One solution would be to assume the use of a 0.10 discount rate for period 1 and 0.30 for period 2. The net present value *NPV* of the investment is now

$$NPV = -864,000 + \frac{1,000,000}{1.10} + \frac{100,000}{(1.10)(1.30)} = \$115,000$$

The net present value is reduced from \$128,000 to \$115,000, since the time value factor of period 2 has been increased from 0.10 to 0.30.

Previously we computed an internal rate of 0.25 and compared this percentage with the time value factor of 0.10. But now there is not a single time value factor, but rather one for each time period and we cannot use the internal rate of return without an adjustment.

If the internal rate of return method is used, one solution is to compute an adjusted rate of return based on the reinvestment of the \$1 million at time 1.

Time	Cash Flow	Reinvestment	Sum: Revised Investment
0	− 864,000	—	− 864,000
1	+ 1,000,000	− 1,000,000	0
2	+ 100,000	+ 1,300,000	1,400,000

The rate of return of the basic investment is 0.25. The rate of return of the revised investment that assumes reinvestment at time 1 at 0.30 is 0.273. The 0.25 rate of return of the basic investment **is consistent** with reinvestment and earning 0.25.

Net Present Value Profile. A net present value profile can be drawn for any investment. Exhibit 6 shows the net present value profile for the example given above. On the *x*-axis are measured the different rates of discount, and

EXHIBIT 6   PROFILE OF NET PRESENT VALUE FOR AN INVESTMENT

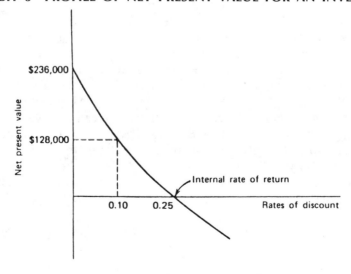

on the y-axis the net present values that result from the use of the different rates of discount. The intersection of the net present value profile and the x-axis defines the internal rate of return of the investment (the net present value is equal to zero).

Inspection of Exhibit 6 shows that for a **normal investment** (negative cash flows followed by positive flow) the net present value profile slopes downward to the right. Thus, for an investment with an internal rate of return greater than the required return, the net present value will also be positive. With conventional independent investments, the net present value method (a dollar measure) and the internal rate of return method (a percentage) will give identical accept and reject decisions.

Mutually Exclusive Investments. With mutually exclusive investments, the **internal rate of return** cannot be used to choose the best of the set without considering the rate at which the funds can be reinvested. While the basic computation of internal rate of return does not require a reinvestment assumption, the use of internal rate of return to choose the best of a set of mutually exclusive investments does require that an assumption be made.

Consider the two mutually exclusive investments A and B shown below, having internal rates of return of 0.25 and 0.30, respectively. Which of the investments should be chosen if the appropriate rate of discount is 0.10?

Investment	Period 0	Period 1	Internal Rate of Return	Present Value (0.10)
A	− 80,000	100,000	0.25	$10,910
B	− 20,000	26,000	0.30	$ 2,364

Investment B has a larger internal rate of return than A, but if the appropriate rate of discount is 0.10, investment A has a higher present value. At a 0.233 rate of interest the investor would be indifferent.

Exhibit 7 shows the net present value profiles of the two investments. The curve AA represents the net present value profile of investment A with a rate of return of r_a. The intersection of the curve with the X axis is defined to be the internal rate of return. Investment B has an internal rate of return of r_b. The present value of the investments is measured on the y-axis for a given rate of discount. Investment B has a larger internal rate of return than A. However, for all rates of discount less than i, investment A has a higher net present value than investment B. Thus if A and B are two mutually exclusive investments (only one can be undertaken), the internal rate of return criterion **incorrectly** indicates that B is to be preferred. The present value method correctly indicates that A is preferred if the appropriate rate of discount is less than i, and B is preferred if the appropriate rate of discount is greater than i.

If the investments are independent and if the firm's required return is less than r_a, both investments are acceptable. In an analysis of **independent in-**

EXHIBIT 7   TWO MUTUALLY EXCLUSIVE INVESTMENTS

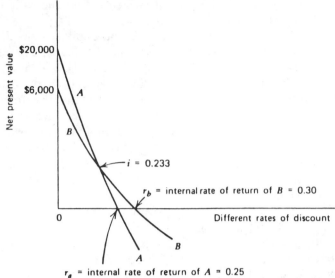

r_a = internal rate of return of A = 0.25

vestments with **conventional cash flows,** the internal rate of return and the present value procedures both **give consistent results.** If an investment's internal rate of return is larger than the firm's required return, the investment's net present value will also be positive. If the required return is greater than the internal rate of return the investment is not acceptable and the net present value is negative. Again the two methods lead to consistent decisions.

Below are two other mutually exclusive investments:

Investment	Period			Internal Rate of Return
	0	1	2	
x	− 100,000	20,000	120,000	0.20
y	− 100,000	——	144,000	0.20

Using internal rates of return, the decision maker is indifferent as to which of the two investments is accepted. The net present values of the two investments are equal if and only if .20 is used as the rate of discount. Thus if 0.20 is the appropriate time value factor, the investor is indifferent; otherwise one or the other of the two investments is preferred.

Assume that funds can be reinvested to earn some rate less than 0.20 (say, 0.10), then if the $20,000 is reinvested to earn $22,000, investment X leads to $142,000 at time 2, which is less than the $144,000 of investment Y, and Y would be prefered. However, if the reinvestment rate were greater than 0.20 (say, 0.30), with reinvestment, X leads to $146,000 at time 2, which is greater than the $144,000 of investment Y, and X is preferred.

WHAT FIRMS DO: THREE SURVEYS. In 1955, about 4% of the Fortune 500 companies were using some form of discounted cash flow calculations. These were almost all chemical and oil companies.

In 1976 Gitman and Forrester ("A Survey of Capital Budgeting Techniques Used by Major U.S. Firms," *Financial Management,* Fall 1977) conducted a survey of capital budgeting techniques used by major U.S. firms. They found that **discounted cash flow methods** were used by 79% of the respondent firms as the primary method of evaluating investments. The internal rate of return was more widely used (54%) than net present value (28%). This choice poses no problem as long as mutually exclusive investments are handled carefully. It is also interesting to note the large number of firms (25%) using the return on investment (ROI). This is also an acceptable choice as long as the ROI measures is not used as the primary decision-making technique. Unfortunately, anything that is computed is likely to be used. The extensive use of ROI is unfortunate, since it ignores the time value of money and does not adjust for risk.

Gitman and Forrester did not show the percentage of firms using each of the techniques. This information would have been interesting. For example, they reported that **payback** was used as a primary technique by 9% of the firms and as a secondary technique by 44%. It is possible, however, that some firms used payback as a "backup" procedure (a third calculation) but did not list it. The same is true with the other methods.

Gitman and Forrester also asked for the **hurdle rates** used by firms. They found that 7% of the firms used rates higher than 20%. This probably reflects either a reluctance to go to the markets for capital or a misconception of the purpose of time discounting. It is unlikely that the aftertax cost of obtaining capital in 1976 for a typical large corporation was in excess of 20%. This was no longer the case, however, in 1980, with **risk-free interest rates** exceeding 15%.

Gitman and Forrester also found that 43% of the firms responding adjusted for risk by increasing the minimum rate of return or cost of capital. Adjusting the discount rate or the required return is **not a reliable method** of adjusting for risk. The primary problem is that discount rate increases adjust for **risk and timing** in one compound interest calculation applied to the cash flow of **all** periods, when that may not be the case.

A second survey of large firms, conducted in the early 1970s, avoided some of the omissions of Gitman and Forrester (see Schall, Sundem, and Geijsbeek, "Survey and Analysis of Capital Budgeting Methods," *Journal of Finance,* March 1978). The investigators found that 86% of the firms used some form of discounted cash flow method (65% used IRR and 56% used NPV). While payback (74%) and accounting ROI (58%) were also widely used, they were usually used in conjunction with the more theoretically correct methods. For firms using a **weighted average cost of capital** as a hurdle rate (46% of the firms), 11% used a discount rate less than 10% and only 1% used a discount rate greater than 17%. Some firms (17%) used the cost of debt and a measure based on past experience (20%). It would seem that a wide range of numbers is being used at a given moment in time to accomplish time discounting and the adjustment for risk.

A third survey conducted in 1981 by Stanley and Block ("A Survey of Multinational Capital Budgeting," *The Financial Review,* March 1984), found that 81.8% of the firms surveyed (339 firms were selected from the 1,000 largest U.S. industrial corporations for 1981 as reported in *Fortune Magazine*) used a **discounted cash flow** procedure as the primary capital budgeting technique.

There is still room for improvement in capital budgeting decisionmaking, but the surveys indicate vast improvement in the past 20 years. All three of these surveys were conducted using large firms. It can be expected that **smaller firms** are using less sophisticated techniques. There is also reason to conclude that a number of the larger corporations in the United States should be concerned that the techniques they are using are not the best methods of evaluating investments.

METHODS OF CALCULATING DEPRECIATION FOR TAXES

Changes in fixed asset values can be charged off as a depreciation expense to current cost of operations by various methods. The choice of method for calculating the periodic depreciation allowance has important financial consequences, since the amount deducted directly affects the amount of taxes paid in a period.

STRAIGHT-LINE METHOD. The straight-line method is by far the easiest to compute. The basic assumption is that depreciation expense is a function of time, and that its amount is uniform with the passage of time. Thus a fixed asset with an estimated life of 10 years would be depreciated 1/10 yearly or 1/120 each month. This is usually expressed as an annual rate (e.g., 10% per annum). The expression "a 10% rate of depreciation" means that the service life of the asset is assumed to be 10 years.

DECLINING-BALANCE METHOD. The 1954 Internal Revenue Code marked a significant change from previous law in permitting liberalized depreciation methods that increased deductions in the early years of service. Its purpose was to encourage investment in plant and equipment, thereby assisting modernization and expansion of the nation's industrial capacity. In addition to the straight-line method, the 1954 Code specifically mentions the declining-balance method, with a rate not exceeding twice the rate that would have been used if the annual allowance had been computed under the straight-line procedure. Also, the sum-of-the-years-digits (SYD) method was mentioned.

In the **declining-balance method,** the annual depreciation charge represents a fixed percentage of the depreciated book value of an asset or group of assets. This method provides for heavier depreciation deductions in the early years of the life of the asset. For example, with an asset life of 4 years, the straight-line rate is 0.25 and the double declining depreciation rate is 0.50, which is then applied to the decreasing asset balance. With an investment of $100,000, the depreciation expense would be $50,000 for year 1, then the 0.50 depreciation rate would be applied to a remaining tax basis of $50,000 and the depreciation expense of year 2 would be $25,000. The firm could then switch to straight-line depreciation and the expenses of both the last two years would be $12,500. One advantage of the declining-balance method is that salvage value can be omitted in computing the tax basis that will be multiplied by the rate of depreciation.

A complexity in calculating depreciation expense is that many firms use a **half-year convention** for the first year's depreciation rather than using the exact date the asset is placed into the production stream.

SUM-OF-THE-YEARS-DIGITS METHOD. In this method, as in the declining-balance method, a larger amount is written off during the early years and a smaller amount in the later years of an asset's life. It is based on the sum of the digits that correspond to the **asset's estimated life.** Thus the numbers representing the periods of life are added and constitute the denominator of a fraction. The numerator is the same numbers in reverse order. For an 8-year asset, $1 + 2 + 3 + 4 + 5 + 6 + 7 + 8 = 36$. For the first year, the fraction would be 8/36; for the second 7/36, and so forth.

A short-cut to adding a series of numbers from 1 to n is to use the formula:

$$\Sigma = n \left(\frac{1 + n}{2} \right) ,$$

With $n = 8$, we have

$$\Sigma = 8 \left(\frac{1 + 8}{2} \right) = 36$$

The logic of the formulation is that the average number $(1 + n)/2$ is multiplied by the number of terms n.

ACRS (1981). In 1981, the tax law was changed so that firms could use the accelerated cost recovery system (ACRS) to write off assets. Assets were divided into different classes, these are:

3-Year Class. Tangible assets with a life of four years or less (tools, research and development equipment, light trucks, and autos).

5-Year Class. Most machinery and equipment and public utility property with lives between 4.5 and 18 years.

10-Year Class. Public utility property (with lives between 18.5 and 25 years).

15-Year Class. Public utility property with lives greater than 25 years.

Exhibit 8 gives the recovery schedule for assets fitting into the different classes.

The use of these classes is mandatory except for real estate, or the use of straight-line depreciation (if straight line is chosen it must be used for all assets acquired in that year in that class, except for 18-year real estate where the election may be made on a property-by-property basis).

In 1984, the tax code was again revised so that real estate was written off over 18 years (instead of 15 years) using either a 200% declining balance for low income housing or a 175% declining balance with a switch to straight line for other real estate.

There is serious discussion being given to the elimination of accelerated depreciation methods in the new tax bill likely to be enacted in 1986. This will, of course, tend to reduce the incentive for capital investments.

SENSITIVITY ANALYSIS. The objective of **sensitivity analysis** is to determine how the profitability of an investment is affected by a change in one or more of the assumptions.

EXHIBIT 8   RECOVERY SCHEDULE CLASS OF INVESTMENT

Ownership Year	3-Year (%)	5-Year (%)	10-Year (%)	15-Year Utility Property (%)
1	25	15	8	5
2	38	22	14	10
3	37	21	12	9
4		21	10	8
5		21	10	7
6			10	7
7			9	6
8			9	6
9			9	6
10			9	6
11				6
12				6
13				6
14				6
15				6
	100	100	100	100

Consider the following investment.

Time	Cash Flows
0	$-8,000
1	10,000
2	10,000

This investment has a 0.25 internal rate of return and at a discount rate of 10%, the net present value is equal to $9355 (point *A* in Exhibit 9). But now assume that we are not sure that the cost of the investment is $8000. We can test the sensitivity of the net present value to changes in the cost of the investment. We can also plot the different rates of return against the changes in cost. For example, if the initial outlay is $17,355, the rate of return is 0.10, and the present value is zero (point *B*).

A second possible step in the **risk-sensitivity analysis** would be to allow the benefits to vary as well as the cost of investment. It would be easiest to assume that the percentage error was the same both for the outlay and for the cash flows after the investment is made. The objective of the analysis is to allow the evaluator to adjust and hopefully eliminate suspected biases in the estimates of the cash flows. In addition, sensitivity analysis enables the analyst to change many of the different key variables in the analysis (e.g., sales, cost of sales, discount rates, cost of the investment) and to observe the effect on the internal rate of return or net present value. In an important article, D. Hertz ("Risk Analysis In Capital Investment," *Harvard Business Review,* Vol. 42, January–February 1964) has shown how simulation techniques can provide information on **rate of return sensitivities.**

CAPITAL BUDGETING UNDER UNCERTAINTY

Up to this point (except for the part on sensitivity analysis) it has been assumed that the cash flows were known with certainty. Now we will assume

EXHIBIT 9   CHANGE IN NPV GIVEN CHANGES IN COST

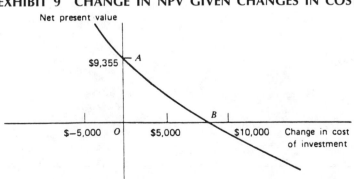

conditions of uncertainty, that is, there may be more than one outcome to the situation. The uncertainty may be in the present, as when the costs of construction are not known, or in the future when the costs of production, the selling price, or the number of units that will be sold are not known.

Four basic methods of incorporating uncertainty in the analysis are illustrated. Each of the methods has its uses and also its weaknesses. There is currently no one "correct" way of incorporating uncertainty in a capital budgeting decision. The four basic methods used are:

1. The use of **risk adjusted discount rates** applied to the expected monetary values of the cash flows.
2. The computation of the present value of the cash flows of different paths using a default-free discount rate or the borrowing rate and then applying a risk adjustment.
3. The computation of the **certainty equivalents** of the cash flows of a period, followed by discounting for time.
4. Valuing the cash flows (outcomes) for each state of nature.

Implicit in these procedures is the assumption that uncertainty gives rise to **risk aversion** on the part of the investor. That is, if there are two equally likely possible outcomes, a gain of $1 million or a zero cash flow, with an expected value of $500,000 occurring immediately, the average person would not pay $500,000, for this investment. There would necessarily be a discount for risk.

RISK-ADJUSTED DISCOUNT RATES. Let us again consider an investment costing $864,000 that promises cash flows of $1 million one period from now and $100,000 two periods from now. Using the present value factors for $r = 0.10$ we have:

Time Period	Cash Flows	Present Value Factors (0.10)	Present Value Equivalents
0	− 864,000	1.0000	864,000
1	1,000,000	0.9091	909,000
2	100,000	0.8264	83,000
Net present value			$128,000

This investment has an internal rate of return of 0.25.

Now we add the information that the cash flows of period 1 can either be $2 million or $0, with both events being equally likely (each event has a .5 probability). We will assume the $100,000 of period 2 is a certain cash flow. The expected cash flow of period 1 is $1 million. If it is decided that 0.10 is the appropriate risk-adjusted discount rate to be applied to the **expected values,** the net present value is $128,000 and the investment is acceptable. In fact, as long as the risk-adjusted rate is less than 0.25, the investment will have a positive net present value.

In the past, firms have used a **weighted average cost of capital** (see the section entitled "Long-Term Sources of Funds and the Cost of Capital") as the risk-adjusted discount rate. The same rate is used for all investments. Recent practice of some firms is to use different rates in different operating divisions. The higher the risks of the division the higher the discount rate used.

The difficulty with the application of risk-adjusted discount rates is that two factors, time value and risk, must be taken into consideration with the one calculation. The basic calculation used is to apply $(1 + r)^{-n}$ to the expected cash flow of the period, when r is the risk-adjusted discount rate and n is the number of periods in the future when the cash flows occur. Unfortunately, it is not generally true that risk compounds evenly through time; thus there is no reason to believe that $(1 + r)^{-n}$ can be applied to the cash flows of all future time periods. While 1.10^{-2} may be correct for the cash flows of period 2, the use of 1.10^{-10} for the cash flows of period 10 may not be correct.

PRESENT VALUE OF PATHS. A second procedure is to prepare a **tree diagram** showing all the possible outcomes and compute the present value of each path using a discount rate that does not reflect risk and then applying a dollar risk adjustment. Exhibit 10 shows the tree diagram for the investment being considered.

Assume that the default-free rate of interest is 0.05 (or alternatively, the cost of debt capital is 0.05). The present value of path 1 is:

EXHIBIT 10   PRESENT VALUE FOR TWO PATHS OF INVESTMENT

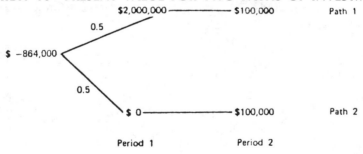

Path	Outcome	Probability	Expectation
1	1,131,000	.5	565,500
2	− 773,000	.5	− 386,500
	Expected present value		179,000

$$PV = \frac{100,000}{1.05^2} + \frac{2,000,000}{1.05} - 864,000 = \$1,131,000$$

The present value of path 2 is:

$$PV = \frac{100,000}{1.05^2} - 864,000 = -773,000$$

The expected present value of the two paths is $179,000. But we still have to adjust for the amount of risk. Assume that arbitrary estimate of the adjustment is $51,000. This amount is to be subtracted from the expected present value, that is, an adjusted present value of $128,000. If the dollar risk adjustment were $51,000, this procedure would give exactly the same result as the use of the risk-adjusted discount rate. While the net value of an investment should be independent of the method of calculation, there is no reason to think that repetitive application of the two procedures to a wide range of investments will always lead to identical value measures.

The primary difficulty with the second procedure is the determination of the dollar risk adjustments. There are no exact formulas for the determination of those risk adjustments. They are highly subjective, thus not completely satisfactory inputs into the decision process.

CERTAINTY EQUIVALENTS. The use of **certainty equivalents** is intuitively appealing. The objective is to make the decision maker indifferent to accepting either the uncertain cash flow or the "certain" one. One can estimate or compute the single cash amount (the certainty equivalent) that represents the value of the uncertain cash flows of the period and then discount the "certainty equivalent cash flows" back to the present. Since we are dealing with certainty equivalent cash flows, we use a **risk-free discount rate.**

Assume the certainty equivalent (CE) of the cash flow of period 1 is $946,000 (there is .5 probability of $2,000,000 and .5 probability of $0). The certainty equivalent cash flows and their present values are:

Year	CE	Risk-Free Discount Rate	Present Value
0	− 864,000	$(1.05)^{-0}$	− 864,000
1	946,000	$(1.05)^{-1}$	901,000
2	100,000	$(1.05)^{-2}$	91,000
	Net present value		128,000

The net present value is again $128,000. Of course, this result was dependent on the fact that the certainty equivalent of period one's uncertain cash flows is $964,000. A different certainty equivalent would have given a different net present value.

The primary weakness of this procedure is that it assumes that the **cer-**

tainty equivalents of each time period are **independent of the outcomes of the prior periods.** This assumption may not be valid. Theoretically, to compute a certainty equivalent we need to know what the prior period's outcomes are. While one might abstract from this complexity to simplify the analysis, information would be lost in the process of simplification. Managers are not likely to find the process attractive, given the amount of explicit subjective estimates necessary.

STATES OF NATURE. Initially it will be assumed that the **capital asset pricing model** applies. This assumption implies that only the mean and the variance of an investment portfolio of securities are needed for the investor (holder of the securities) to make a decision, that the securities are well diversified, and that nonsystematic, or firm specific, risk may be ignored. It is assumed that the preferences of investors in securities should determine the investment decision for real assets of the firm. The assumptions of the capital asset pricing model will later be dropped, making the capital budgeting model more general.

Conventional Net Present Value. The conventional net present value method uses present value factors to transform future cash flows into present value equivalents. Each of these present value factors implicitly defines a "price" today for the future dollar. Thus, with a time discount factor of 10%, a dollar one period from now has a price of $0.9091 and a dollar two time periods from now has a price today of $0.8264—that is, 1.10^{-2}. With the use of the present value factors derived from the formulation $(1 + r)^{-n}$, the present value of any future cash flows can be determined. The objective is to search for indifference (i.e., equal preference) amounts between certain sums today and certain future cash flows. With a 10% time discount factor, the investor is indifferent between $82.64 received today or $100 received 2 years from today.

Risk-Adjusted Present Value Factors (RAPVFs). In a world of uncertainty the counterparts of the present value factors are the RAPVFs. These factors can be used to transform future dollars back to the present taking into consideration three separate items:

1. Time value.
2. The probability of the event.
3. The risk-return preferences of the market or of the firm and the risk characteristics of the investment.

Each time period is considered as an individual investment and the value of each set of paths for a given time period is computed. It is then necessary to combine the different time periods. The recommended procedure is a

rollback technique that treats the future as a series of one-period trials. Each period is evaluated individually; then periods are combined to obtain the present value equivalents for the entire planning period. For purposes of illustration we shall consider a one-period case.

One-Period Risk Analysis. Assume a **decision tree** of one period duration with n nodes (cash flows given some event). Each node has a probability. Exhibit 11 shows the situation.

We will define r_m to be the return earned by investing in a well-diversified **"market basket" of securities.** These securities are available to all investors and are vulnerable only to overall market risk. This is referred to as the market return.

For each node there is defined a return r_{m_i} to be earned from investing in the market if node i occurs. The market return depends on the state of the world (e.g., overall economic growth) and is a **random event.** If we define the investment's dollar outcome to be equal to 1 for path 1 and zero otherwise, and if we define $s(1)$ to be the RAPVF for path 1, it can be shown that the RAPVF is:

RAPVF = time value × probability × risk preference adjustment

If a dollar at time 1 and node 1 is worth \$1.06 at time 1 (dollars are valuable, since they are in short supply), and there is 0.15 probability of

EXHIBIT 11   A ONE-PERIOD DECISION TREE

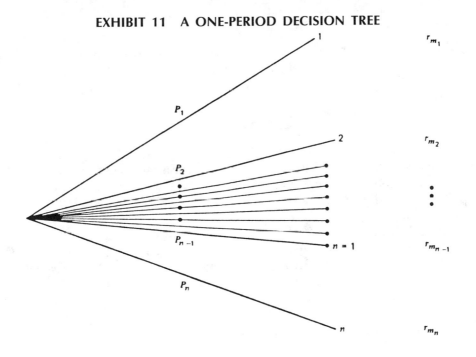

reaching node 1, and the time discount factor is 0.05, then the RAPVF for node 1 is:

$$RAPVF = 1.05^{-1} (0.15)(1.06) = 0.1514$$

If the outcome at node 1 is \$12,000, we multiply \$12,000 by 0.1514 to obtain the **risk-adjusted present value** of \$1,817. Note that the 1.06 factor incorporates the market's valuation of a dollar at node 1, not the risk preferences of the specific investor.

Using the **capital asset pricing model's** mathematical notation, if we define $s(1)$ to be the RAPVF for path 1, it can be shown that

$$s(1) = \frac{p_1}{1 + r_f} [1 - \lambda(r_{m1} - \bar{r}_m)]$$

where p_1 is the probability of path 1, r_f is the default-free or riskless discount rate, r_m is the market return and $\lambda = (\bar{r}_m - r_f)/\text{var}(r_m)$. The term $[1 - \lambda (r_{m1} - \bar{r}_m)]$ *is the* risk preference adjustment. Thus we have p_1 to take into consideration the probability of path 1, $(1 + r_f)^{-1}$ to take into consideration the one-period time value factor, and $1 - \lambda (r_{m1} - \bar{r}_m)$ for the risk return preferences of the market. We will use R_1 to represent the risk preference adjustment. Then:

$$s(1) = \frac{p_1 R_1}{1 + r_f}$$

Because an additional dollar has value, we define each $s(i)$ to be positive. If we sum the $s(i)$'s over all paths, we obtain:

$$\sum_{i=1}^{m} s(i) = \frac{1}{1 + r_f}$$

Alternatively, it can be shown that $\Sigma p_i R_i = 1$.

Thus the sum of the RAPVFs is equal to the present value factor with no risk. This is intuitively appealing, since it means that if the outcomes of all paths were \$1 (thus the outcome is certain) the RAPVF would be $1/(1 + r_f)$, as it should be.

If we define $p_i/(1 + r_f) [\lambda (r_{mi} - \bar{r}_m)]$ to be the dollar adjustment for risk to be applied to the expected present value, the sum of these dollar risk adjustment terms goes to zero if the outcomes of all the nodes are equal. There is zero risk adjustment in total if there is no uncertainty.

The risk adjusted present value may be expressed as:

risk adjusted present value = expected present value − risk adjustment

While it can be shown that this expression is equivalent to the use of RAPVF, and in some respects is easier to understand, the RAPVFs are easier to apply in practice. The RAPVFs are determined for all possible relevant events and they apply to all investments. Once determined, they can be used for any investment being evaluated.

It is necessary to define the events that are uncertain and then estimate the cash flows on those events (or nodes). This is different from defining the cash flows of the investment and then approaching the uncertainty problem.

Dropping the Capital Asset Pricing Model Assumptions. The **capital asset pricing model** (CAPM) assumptions make the application of the RAPVFs somewhat restrictive, because they are based on either an assumption of normality of outcomes or an assumption that investors have special utility functions. One can drop the assumptions of the CAPM, but retain the requirements that the RAPVF = time value × probability × risk adjustment, that is $s(i) = p_i R_i / (1 + r_f)$. This formulation assumes R_i is not a function of the amount of dollars received, but only of the time period and state of the world. A different formulation would be needed if the dollar amount of the outcomes affects their intrinsic value to the investor (i.e., a size effect).

The values of $p_i R_i$ are again constrained so that $\Sigma\ p_i R_i = 1$, where R_i equals the risk preference adjustment of the ith node and we are summing over all nodes of one time period. Constraining the $p_i R_i$ so that they add to 1 ensures that an investment with certain outcomes (giving \$1 no matter what event occurs) will be worth $(1 + r_f)^{-1}$, that is, present value of \$1 discounted at the risk-free rate.

It is important to note that a person or firm evaluating an investment can depart from the CAPM and supply subjective weights for risk adjustment. We already know that the probabilities must add to 1. Now we find the $\sum_{i-1}^{n} p_i R_i$ must also equal 1. Since $\Sigma\ P_i R_i$ equals 1, then

$$\Sigma\ s(i) = \Sigma\ \frac{p_i R_i}{1 + r_f} = \frac{1}{1 + r_f}.$$

With equal outcomes for all possible events, the cash flows are certain and it is reasonable to use a default-free discount rate. Again, the risk adjustments are constrained so that the product of the risk preference adjustments times their probabilities equals 1, and the sum of the RAPVFs over all nodes is $(1 + r_f)^{-1}$.

LIMITATION OF RISK-ADJUSTED PRESENT VALUES. The limitation of the procedure above is the determination of the values of $s(n)$. If there were markets for investments paying off in only one state of the world (say node 5), the RAPVFs for each node would be determined by market forces. In the absence of such securities and such markets, however, the implementation of the procedure is handicapped. In the certainty capital budgeting model, cash flows of each period are multiplied by present value factors. With uncertainty, the cash flows of each node are multiplied by multiperiod risk-adjusted present value factors that take into consideration three factors, the time value of money, the probability of the event, and the risk return preferences of the market (or the firm).

While the mathematical derivation tends to be complex, the basic calculations are relatively easy to understand. Most important, the sum of the RAPVFs for each node adds up to the present value factor for that time period using a default-free rate of interest. This restraint on the RAPVF tends to act as a brake preventing one's imagination (or poor intuition) from selecting factors that would give results that are not defensible. Also, the dollar risk adjustment is zero if the outcomes are certain.

The uncertainty model using the capital asset pricing model is built on several assumptions. First, it is a one-period model that assumes the investments to be well diversified. Second, the basic capital asset pricing model assumes that the mean and variance of a portfolio are the only two relevant parameters and that the outcomes are normally distributed. Third, it is assumed that an investment decision of a firm is made from the point of view of the well-diversified investors in the firm. If these assumptions are not valid, the model cannot be applied to long-lived real investments of a corporation.

The approaches involving the use of weighted average cost of capital, risk-adjusted discount rates, or payback period to adjust for risk all have known weaknesses. The procedures suggested in this section are also imperfect, and we can expect improvement in our understanding of the uncertainty problem in the future. By using more complex mathematical formulations, the academic world seems to be leaving behind the real needs of industry for feasible capital budgeting techniques. We need to build on the complex theoretical literature and well-known relationships to produce some intuitively appealing and theoretically correct ways of approaching the capital budgeting decision under conditions of uncertainty. Patience is needed as we proceed to develop more reliable methods of evaluation.

CAPITAL BUDGETING AND INFLATION

Inflation is frustrating to managers because it is beyond their immediate control. But a wide range of decisions that permit adjustment for inflation is within their control. We now consider to what extent the investment decision process of a corporation (using the **net present value** or the **internal rate of return method**) should be affected by forecasts of inflation. Corporations should be careful that the method being used to adjust for inflation does not introduce new errors into the analysis.

THE PROBLEM. Because inflation will produce price changes (sometimes dramatic) in the future, adjustments must be made in the capital budget. Four terms figure in the discussion of inflation adjustments:

Nominal Dollars. Revenue and costs are measured as they will be measured when the cash is received and disbursed.

Constant Dollars. Revenue and costs in current dollars are adjusted to reflect changes in purchasing power.

Nominal Interest Rates. The actual, out-of-pocket cost of money.

Real Interest Rate. The cost of money if there were market equilibrium and no inflation, an inflation adjustment.

Combining the wrong amount of dollars with the wrong interest rate gives rise to major errors in capital budgeting under inflationary conditions.

AN EXAMPLE. Assume that the following facts apply for an investment being considered by a firm:

Period	Nominal Dollars: Cash Flows	Price Index
0	− 18,017	100
1	10,000	112
2	10,800	125

The firm can borrow funds at a cost of 9%, and for simplicity we assume that all the capital being used is debt. Using a 9% discount rate, the investment has a net present value of $247 and the investment seems to be acceptable. The conclusion is consistent with the fact that the internal rate of return is 0.10, which is greater than the **cost of capital.**

Many firms do not use such an analysis. They prefer to express the analysis in terms of constant dollars. The initial cash flows were expressed in terms of nominal dollars. To eliminate the change in purchasing power, we convert the flows to constant dollars, which results in the following cash flows:

Period	Nominal Dollars: Cash Flows	Price Level Adjustment	Constant Dollars	Present Value Factor	Present Value
0	− 18,017	1	− 18,017	1.000	− 18,017
1	10,000	100/112	8,929	0.917	8,188
2	10,800	100/125	8,640	0.842	7,275
					($ 2,554)

Now the net present value using 9% is a negative ($2,554). When cash flows are analyzed in terms of constant dollars, the investment is not acceptable. However, it is also an error to convert to constant dollars and use the nominal interest rate of 9%.

One can use the nominal dollar cash flows and the nominal interest rates and make a decision that is consistent with maximizing the well-being of the stockholders. For example, if $18,017 is borrowed at a cost of 9%, we would have:

Time	Amount Owed	Cash Flow and Amount Paid
0	$18,017	($18,017)
1	19,639	10,000
2	10,506	10,506

After using the $10,800 cash flows of period 2 to pay the debt, there is $294 left over for the residual investors.

The **nominal dollar cash flows** do reflect the forecast of a 8% increase in the benefits of period 2 compared to the benefits of period 1. This might reflect price changes as well as other considerations.

We reach the following conclusion:

- The use of nominal dollars and nominal interest rates is a *correct* procedure.
- The use of *constant dollars* and nominal interest rates is an *erroneous* procedure in the sense that it can indicate that investment should be rejected even though stockholders benefit from undertaking the investment (see the example above).

It can be argued that the investment should be rejected because the investors will be worse off at the end of the period than at the beginning of the period. We now assume that the investors start with $18,017 of capital at time 0 and can lend to the firm and earn 9%. The 9% is accepted as a reasonable measure of the **opportunity cost of funds.** If the investment is undertaken after two periods, the investor will have:

$$\text{terminal value} = 10,000 \ (1.09) + 10,800 = \$21,700$$

But adjusted for inflation, this amount will only be worth:

$$\frac{21,700}{1.2544} = \$17,299$$

The investors started with $18,017 of purchasing power and ended with $17,299. The position of the investor at time 2 is worse than it was at time 0. However, **this is the wrong comparison.** Let us consider how the investor would have done without the investment. The amount of dollars at time 2 resulting from earning 9% would be:

$$18,017 \times 1.09^2 = \$21,406$$

and price-level adjusted this is:

$$\frac{21,406}{1.2544} = \$17,065$$

The investor is better off with the investment than without it. The fact that the **financial position** of the **investor has deteriorated** is not relevant if 9% truly represents the return from the best alternative.

USE OF CONSTANT DOLLARS. Let us define the real interest that an investor earns, in equilibrium conditions, in real terms. If $100 is invested and returns $104 in dollars of the same purchasing power one period later, this is a real interest rate of 4%. In some situations, the investor prefers not to forecast the cash flows in nominal dollars but is willing to forecast the constant dollar cash flows. This approach bypasses the necessity of forecasting the inflation rate (it can be argued that the bypassing is only approximate). If the cash flows are in constant dollars the real interest rate should be used. Unfortunately, while the nominal borrowing rate can be observed in the capital markets, the **real interest rate** cannot be so observed. Its value must be estimated using the nominal interest rate.

In equilibrium, we can hypothesize that:

nominal rate = real rate
+ inflation rate plus the product of the real and nominal rates

Thus, if the nominal rate were 0.1648 and the inflation rate were 0.12, we would earn a real rate of 0.04.

nominal rate = 0.04 + 0.12 + (0.04)(0.12) = 0.1648

Assume that $100 is invested to earn $16.48. After 1 year, the investor will have $116.48. But $116.48 converted to constant dollars with an inflation rate of 0.12 is 116.48/1.12 = $104. Thus the investor earned a real return of 0.04 on the initial investment of $100. The present value of the real cash flows ($104) discounted at the real interest rate (.04) is equal to the nominal cash flows ($116.48) discounted at the nominal interest rate (.1648). This equality will always hold.

One can observe the nominal rate and the inflation rate and compute the real return that is actually earned.

Illustrated above are a correct and an incorrect method for evaluating investments under conditions of inflation. All the possible combinations of incorrect calculations have not been illustrated. The discounted cash flow calculations are powerful tools of analysis, but if the inputs do not have a sound theoretical foundation, the output is often not useful. It is reasonable to want to adjust for inflation. The calculation of cash flows using nominal dollars does adjust for inflation in the sense that the nominal dollar forecast reflects expected price changes. While the adjustment to constant dollars is useful in evaluating whether the investor is in a better or a worse position at the end of the period than at the beginning, it is difficult to use constant dollars to make accept or reject investment decisions. The combination of constant dollars and nominal interest rates is a major error.

Further discussion on the impact of inflation on financial management is covered in the section entitled "Financial Management in an Inflationary Environment."

REFERENCES

Bierman, H., Jr., and Smidt, S., *The Capital Budgeting Decision*, 6th ed., Macmillan, New York, 1984.

Clark, J. J., Hindelang, T. J., and Pritchard, R. E., *Capital Budgeting*, Prentice-Hall, Englewood Cliffs, NJ, 1979.

Dean, Joel, *Capital Budgeting*, Columbia University Press, New York, 1951.

Gitman, L. J., and Forrester, J. K., Jr., "A Survey of Capital Budgeting Techniques Used by Major U.S. Firms," *Financial Management*, Fall 1977, pp. 66–71.

Grant, Eugene L., and Ireson, W. Grant, *Principles of Engineering Economy*, 5th ed., Ronald Press, New York, 1970.

Hirschleifer, J. H., "On the Theory of Optimal Investment Decision," *Journal of Political Economy*, August 1958.

Levy, H., and Sarnat, M., *Capital Investment and Financial Decision*, Prentice-Hall International, Englewood Cliffs, NJ, 1978.

Lutz, F., and Lutz, V., *The Theory of Investment of the Firm*, Princeton University Press, Princeton, NJ, 1951.

Quirin, G. D., and Wiginton, J. C., *Analyzing Capital Expenditures*, Irwin, Homewood, IL, 1981.

Schall, L. D., Sundem, G. L., and Geijsheek, W. R., Jr., "Survey and Analysis of Capital Budgeting Methods," *Journal of Finance*, March 1978, pp. 281–287.

Scott, D. F., and Petty, J. W., II, "Capital Budgeting Practices in Large American Firms: A Retrospective Analysis and Synthesis," *The Financial Review*, March 1984, pp. 111–123.

Solomon, E., *The Theory of Financial Management*, Columbia University Press, New York, 1963.

Stanley, M. T., and Block, S. B., "A Survey of Multinational Capital Budgeting," *The Financial Review*, March 1984, pp. 36–54.

Van Horne, J. C., Financial Management and Policy, 6th ed., Prentice-Hall, Englewood Cliffs, NJ, 1983.

Wilkes, F. M., *Capital Budgeting Techniques*, Wiley, London, 1977.

10

MERGERS AND ACQUISITIONS ANALYSIS

CONTENTS

10

MERGERS AND ACQUISITIONS ANALYSIS

Alfred Rappaport

TRENDS IN ACQUISITIONS

RECENT MERGER MOVEMENT. Over the past decade, we have been in the midst of a major wave of corporate acquisitions. In contrast to the 1960s, when acquirers were mainly freewheeling conglomerates, the merger movement in the 1970s and early 1980s includes such long-established giants of U.S. industry as du Pont, General Electric, RCA, and U.S. Steel. In 1984 and 1985 there were 42 mergers that exceeded $1 billion in value including 8 *leveraged buyouts*. Because of the greater political stability of the United States, foreign companies also have become increasingly active buyers of U.S. companies during the past few years.

Most acquisitions were accomplished with cash in the early 1980s, rather than with packages of securities as was common in the 1960s. In 1984 and 1985 however, firms have increasingly used debt securities, including low rated debt or **junk bonds, in takeovers** and **leveraged buyouts.** Finally, the current merger movement involves the frequent use of **tender offers** that often lead to contested bids and to the payment of substantial **merger premiums** above the premerger market value of the target company.

REASONS FOR TAKEOVERS. The popular explanation for the recent merger rage is that the stock market is **undervaluing** many solid companies, thus making it substantially cheaper to buy an existing company rather than to build a new one. Couple this belief with (1) the fact that many corporations are enjoying relatively strong debt capacity positions and (2) the widely held view that government regulation and economic uncertainty make internal

Revised and updated version of an article originally published in the July–August 1979 *Harvard Business Review*

growth strategies relatively unattractive, and we see why mergers and acquisitions are an increasingly important part of corporate growth strategy.

Despite all of the foregoing rationale, more than a few recent acquisitions will fail to create value for the acquirer's shareholders. After all, **shareholder value** depends not on premerger market valuation of the target company, but on the actual acquisition price the acquiring company pays compared with the selling company's cash flow contribution to the combined company.

Only a limited supply of acquisition candidates is available at the price that enables the acquirer to earn an acceptable economic return on investment. A well-conceived **financial evaluation program** that minimizes the risk of buying an economically unattractive company or paying too much for an attractive one is particularly important in today's seller's market. The dramatic increase in **merger premiums** that must be paid by a company bidding successfully calls for more careful analysis by buyers than ever before.

Because of the competitive nature of the acquisition market, companies not only need to respond wisely, but often must respond quickly as well. The growing independence of corporate boards and their demand for better information to support strategic decisions, such as acquisitions, have raised the general standard for acquisition analysis. Finally, sound analysis convincingly communicated can yield substantial benefits in negotiating with the target company's management or, in the case of tender offers, its stockholders.

FINANCIAL ANALYSIS OF TARGET COMPANIES

Salter and Weinhold outlined seven principal ways in which companies can create value for their shareholders via acquisition (*Harvard Business Reviews*, July–August, 1978). This section will show how management can estimate how much value a prospective acquisition will, in fact, create. In brief, the section will present a comprehensive framework for acquisition analysis based on contemporary financial theory—an approach that has been profitably employed in practice. The analysis provides management and the board of the acquiring company with information both to make a decision on the candidate and to formulate an effective negotiating strategy for the acquisition.

STEPS IN THE ANALYSIS. The process of analyzing acquisitions falls broadly into three stages. These are planning, search and screen, and financial evaluation.

Planning. The acquisition **planning process** begins with a review of corporate objectives and product-market strategies for various strategic business units. The acquiring company should define its potential directions for corporate growth and **diversification** in terms of corporate strengths and weaknesses and an assessment of the company's social, economic, political, and technological environment. This analysis produces a set of acquisition objectives and criteria.

Specified criteria often include statements about industry parameters, such as projected market growth rate, degree of regulation, ease of entry, and capital versus labor intensity. Company criteria for quality of management, share of market, profitability, size, and capital structure also commonly appear in acquisition criteria lists.

Search and Screen. The search and screen process is a systematic approach to compiling a list of good acquisition prospects. The search focuses on how and where to look for candidates. The screening process selects a few of the best candidates from literally thousands of possibilities according to the objectives and criteria developed in the planning phase.

Financial Evaluation. The final and most important stage is the financial evaluation process. This stage is the focus of this section. A good analysis should enable management to answer such questions as:

- What is the maximum price that should be paid for the target company?
- What are the principal areas of risk?
- What are the earnings, cash flow, and balance sheet implications of the acquisition?
- What is the best way of financing the acquisition?

CORPORATE SELF-EVALUATION. The financial evaluation process involves both a **self-evaluation** by the acquiring company and the **evaluation of the candidate** for acquisition. While it is possible to conduct an evaluation of the target company without an in-depth self-evaluation first, in general, this is the most advantageous approach (Rappapport, *Mergers and Acquisitions* (Spring 1979)). The scope and detail of corporate self-evaluation will necessarily vary according to the needs of each company.

Two fundamental questions posed by a self-evaluation are: (1) How much is my company worth? and (2) How would its value be affected by each of several scenarios? The first question involves generating a "most likely" estimate of the company's value based on management's detailed assessment of its objectives, strategies, and plans. The second question calls for an assessment of value based on the range of plausible scenarios that enable management to test the joint effect of hypothesized combinations of product-market strategies and environmental forces.

Corporate self-evaluation viewed as an economic assessment of the value created for shareholders by various strategic planning options promises potential benefits for all companies. In the context of the acquisition market, self-evaluation takes on special significance.

Vulnerability to Takeover. First, while a company might view itself as an acquirer, few companies are totally exempt from a possible takeover. From 1979 to 1983, 34 acquisitions exceeding $1 billion were completed. The recent roster of acquired companies includes such names as Cities Service, Conoco, Getty Oil, Gulf Oil, Heublein, Kennecott, and Marathon Oil. Self-evaluation provides both management and the board with a continuing basis for responding to tender offers or acquisition inquiries responsibly and quickly.

Second, the self-evaluation process might well call attention to strategic divestment opportunities. Finally, self-evaluation provides acquisition-minded companies a basis for assessing the comparative advantages of a cash versus an exchange-of-shares offer.

Exchange of Shares Analysis. Acquiring companies commonly value the purchase price for an acquisition at the market value of the shares exchanged. This practice is not economically sound, however, and could be misleading and costly to the acquiring company. A well-conceived analysis for an **exchange-of-shares acquisition** requires sound valuations of both buying and selling companies. If the acquirer's management believes the market is undervaluing its shares, then valuing the purchase price at market might well induce the company to overpay for the acquisition or to earn less than the minimum acceptable rate of return. Conversely, if management believes the market is overvaluing its shares, then valuing the purchase price at market obscures the opportunity of offering the seller's shareholders additional shares while still achieving the minimum acceptable return.

VALUATION OF ACQUISITIONS

Discounted Cash Flow (DCF) Technique. *Business Week* (December 18, 1978) reported that as many as half of the major acquisition-minded companies are relying extensively on the **discounted cash flow (DCF)** technique to analyze acquisitions and that number has increased in the early 1980s. While mergers and acquisitions involve a considerably more complex set of managerial problems than the purchase of an ordinary asset, such as a machine or a plant, the economic substance of these transactions is the same. In each case, there is a current outlay made in anticipation of a stream of future cash flows.

Thus, the DCF criterion applies not only to internal growth investments, such as additions to existing capacity, but equally to external growth investments, such as acquisitions. An essential feature of the DCF technique is that it explicitly takes into account that a dollar of cash received today is worth more than a dollar received a year from now because today's dollar can be invested to earn a return during the intervening time.

To establish the maximum acceptable acquisition price under the DCF approach, estimates are needed for (1) the **incremental cash flows** expected to be generated because of the acquisition and (2) the "discount rate" or "cost of capital"—that is, the minimum acceptable rate of return required by the market for new investments by the company.

In projecting the cash flow stream of a prospective acquisition, the cash flow contribution the candidate company is expected to make to the acquiring company should be considered. The results of this projection may well differ from a projection of the candidates' cash flow as an independent company. This is so because the acquirer may be able to achieve operating economies not available to the selling company alone. Furthermore, acquisitions generally provide new post-acquisition investment opportunities whose initial outlays and subsequent benefits also need to be incorporated in the cash flow schedule. **Cash flow** is defined as:

Cash flow = (operating profit)(1-income tax rate)
                  + depreciation and Other noncash charges
          − (incremental working capital investments + capital expenditures)

In developing the cash flow schedule, two additional issues need to be considered: (1) What is the basis for setting the length of the forecast period (i.e., the period beyond which the cash flows associated with the acquisition are not specifically projected)? (2) How is the *residual value* of the acquisition established at the end of the forecast period?

Forecasting Target's Cash Flow. A common practice is to forecast cash flows period by period until the level of uncertainty makes management too "uncomfortable" to go any farther. While practice varies with industry setting, management policy, and the special circumstances of the acquisition, five or 10 years appears to be an arbitrarily set forecasting duration used in many situations. A better approach suggests that the forecast duration for cash flows should continue only as long as the expected rate of return on incremental investment required to support forecasted sales growth exceeds the cost-of-capital rate.

If, for subsequent periods, one assumes that the company's return on incremental investment equals the cost-of-capital rate, then the market would be indifferent to whether management invests in expansion projects or pays cash dividends. This is because shareholders can in turn invest in identically risky opportunities yielding an identical rate of return. In other words, the value of the company is unaffected by growth when the company is investing in projects earning at the cost of capital or at the minimum acceptable risk-adjusted rate of return required by the market.

Thus, for purposes of simplification, we can assume a 100% payout of earnings after the end of the forecast period or, equivalently, a zero growth rate without affecting the valuation of the company. (An implied assumption of this model is that the depreciation amount can be invested to maintain the company's productive capacity.) The residual value is then the present value of the resulting cash flow perpetuity beginning one year after the horizon date. Of course, if after the end of the forecast period the return on investment is expected to decline below the cost-of-capital rate, this factor can be incorporated in the calculation.

ASSESSING ACQUISITION CANDIDATE'S RISK. When the acquisition candidate's risk is judged to be the same as the acquirer's overall risk, the appropriate rate for discounting the candidate's cash flow stream is the acquirer's cost of capital. The cost of capital or the minimum acceptable rate of return on new investments is based on the rate investors can expect to earn by investing in alternative, identically risky securities.

The **cost of capital** is calculated as the weighted average of the costs of debt and equity capital. See Section 12 on *Cost of Capital* in this *Handbook*. For example, suppose a company's aftertax cost of debt is 5% and it estimates its cost of equity to be 15%. Further, it plans to raise future capital in the following proportions: 20% by way of debt and 80% by equity. Exhibit 1 shows how to compute the company's cost of capital (i.e., the risk-adjusted, weighted average cost of debt and equity).

It is important to emphasize that the acquiring company's use of its own cost of capital to discount the target's projected cash flows is appropriate only when it can be safely assumed that the acquisition will not affect the riskiness of the acquirer. The specific riskiness of each prospective candidate should be taken into account in setting the discount rate. Higher rates should be used for more risky investments.

If a single discount rate is used for all acquisitions, then those with the highest risk will seem most attractive. Because the weighted average risk of its component segments determines the company's cost of capital, these high-risk acquisitions will increase a company's cost of capital—and thereby decrease the value of its stock.

CASE OF MITNOR CORPORATION

As an illustration of the recommended approach to acquisition analysis, consider the case of Mitnor Corporation's interest in acquiring Rano Products. Mitnor is a leading manufacturing and distributor in the industrial packaging and materials handling market. Sales for the most recent year

EXHIBIT 1   ONE COMPANY'S WEIGHTED AVERAGE COST OF CAPITAL

	Weight	Cost	Weighted Cost
Debt	.20	.05	.01
Equity	.80	.15	.12
Weighted average cost of capital			.13

totaled $600 million. Mitnor's acquisition strategy is geared toward buying companies with either similar marketing and distribution characteristics, similar production technologies, or a similar research and development orientation. Rano Products, a $50 million sales organization with an impressive new-product development record in industrial packaging, fits Mitnor's general acquisition criteria particularly well. Premerger financial statements for Mitnor and Rano are shown in Exhibit 2.

ACQUISITION FOR CASH. The Value Planner© and The Merger Planner© **microcomputer models for merger analysis** generate a comprehensive analysis for acquisitions financed by cash, stock, or any combination of cash, debt, preferred stock, and common stock. In this section, the analysis concerns only the cash and exchange-of-shares cases. In the cash acquisition case, the analysis follows six essential steps:

1. Develop estimates needed to project Rano's cash flow contribution for various growth and profitability scenarios.
2. Estimate the minimum acceptable rate of return for acquisition of Rano.

EXHIBIT 2   PREMERGER FINANCIAL STATEMENTS FOR MITNOR AND RANO ($ MILLIONS)

STATEMENT OF INCOME (YEAR ENDED DECEMBER 31)	Mitnor	Rano
Sales	$600.00	$50.00
Operating expenses	522.00	42.50
Operating Profit	78.00	7.50
Interest on debt	4.50	.40
Earnings before taxes	73.50	7.10
Provision for income taxes	36.00	3.55
Net Income	$ 37.50	$ 3.55
Number of common shares outstanding (in millions)	10.00	1.11
Earnings per share	$3.75	$3.20
Dividends per share	1.30	.64
STATEMENT OF FINANCIAL POSITION (AT YEAR-END)		
Net Working Capital	$180.00	$7.50
Marketable Securities	25.00	1.00
Other assets	2.00	1.60
Gross Property, Plant and Equipment	216.00	20.00
Less accumulated depreciation	(95.00)	(8.00)
Interest-bearing debt	$56.00	$5.10
Shareholders' equity	272.00	17.00
	$328.00	$22.10

3. Compute the maximum acceptable cash price to be paid for Rano under various scenarios and minimum acceptable rates of return.
4. Compute the rate of return that Mitnor will earn for a range of price offers and for various growth and profitability scenarios.
5. Analyze the feasibility of a cash purchase in light of Mitnor's current liquidity and target debt-to-equity ratio.
6. Evaluate the impact of the acquisition on the earnings per share and capital structure of Mitnor.

Step 1: Develop Cash Flow Projections. The cash flow formula presented earlier may be restated in equivalent form as follows:

$$CF_t = S_{t-1}(1 + g_t)(p_t)(1 - T_t) - (S_t - S_{t-1})(f_t + w_t)$$

where CF = cash flow
$\quad\quad S$ = sales
$\quad\quad g$ = annual growth rate in sales
$\quad\quad p$ = operating profit margin as a percentage of sales
$\quad\quad T$ = income tax rate
$\quad\quad f$ = incremental fixed capital investment required (i.e., total capital investment net of replacement of existing capacity estimated by depreciation) per dollar of sales increase
$\quad\quad w$ = Incremental working capital investment required per dollar of sales increase

Once estimates are provided for five variables, $g, p, T, f,$ and w it is possible to project cash flow.

Exhibit 3 shows Mitnor management's most likely estimates for Rano's operations, assuming Mitnor control; Exhibit 4 shows a complete projected 10-year cash flow statement for Rano.

EXHIBIT 3   MOST LIKELY ESTIMATES FOR RANO'S OPERATIONS UNDER MITNOR CONTROL

	Years		
	1–5	6–7	8–10
Sales growth rate (g)	.15	.12	.12
Operations profit margin as a percentage of sales (p)	.18	.15	.12
Income tax rate (T)	.46	.46	.46
Incremental fixed capital investment (f)	.20	.20	.20
Incremental working capital investment (w)	.15	.15	.15
Employing the cash flow formula for year 1:			
$CF_1 = 50(1 + .15)(.18)(1 - .46) - (57.5 - 50)(.20 + .15) = 2.96$			

EXHIBIT 4 PROJECTED 10-YEAR CASH FLOW STATEMENT FOR RANO ($ MILLIONS)

	Years									
	1	2	3	4	5	6	7	8	9	10
Sales	$57.50	$66.12	$76.04	$87.45	$100.57	$112.64	$126.15	$141.29	$158.25	$177.23
Operating expenses	47.15	54.22	62.36	71.71	82.47	95.74	107.23	124.34	139.26	155.97
Operating profit	$10.35	$11.90	$13.69	$15.74	$18.10	$16.90	$18.92	$16.95	$18.99	$21.27
Cash income taxes	4.76	5.48	6.30	7.24	8.33	7.77	8.70	7.80	8.74	9.78
Operating profit after taxes	$5.59	$6.43	$7.39	$8.50	$9.78	$9.12	$10.22	$9.16	$10.25	$11.48
Depreciation	1.60	1.85	2.13	2.46	2.84	3.28	3.74	4.25	4.83	5.49
Less incremental fixed capital investment	(3.10)	(3.57)	(4.12)	(4.47)	(5.47)	(5.69)	(6.44)	(7.28)	(8.22)	(9.29)
Less incremental working capital investment	(1.13)	(1.29)	(1.49)	(1.71)	(1.97)	(1.81)	(2.03)	(2.27)	(2.54)	(2.85)
Cash flow from operations	$2.96	$3.41	$3.92	$4.51	$5.18	$4.90	$5.49	$3.86	$4.32	$4.84

Before developing additional scenarios for Rano, we should assume certain facts about estimating some of the cash flow variables. First, the income tax rate is the cash rate rather than a book rate based on the accountant's income tax expense which often includes a portion that is deferred. Second, for some companies, it is difficult to provide a direct projection of **capital investment requirements** per dollar of sales increase. To gain an estimate of the recent value of this coefficient, simply take the sum of all capital investments less depreciation over the past five or 10 years and divide this total by the sales increase from the beginning to the end of the period. With this approach, the resulting coefficient not only represents the capital investment historically required per dollar of sales increase but also impounds any cost increases for replacement of existing capacity.

One should estimate changes in incremental **working capital investment** with care. Actual year-to-year balance sheet changes in working capital investment required for operations, may not provide a good measure of the rise or decline in funds required. There are two main reasons for this: (1) the year-end balance sheet figures may not reflect the average of normal needs of the business during the year; and (2) the inventory accounts may overstate the magnitude of the funds committed by the company.

To estimate the additional cash requirements, the increased inventory investment should be measured by the variable costs for any additional units of inventory required. Increased accounts receivable should be measured in sales dollars.

In addition to its most likely estimate for Rano, Mitnor's management developed two additional scenarios (one conservative and the other optimistic) for sales growth and operating profit margins. Exhibit 5 gives a summary of all three scenarios. Mitnor's management may also wish to examine additional cases to test, for example, the effect of alternative assumptions about the cash income tax rate, fixed capital investment, and working capital investment per dollar of sales increase.

Recall that cash flows should be forecast only for the period when the expected rate of return on incremental investment exceeds the minimum acceptable rate of return for the acquisition. It is possible to determine this in a simple yet analytical, nonarbitrary, fashion. To do so, we compute the

EXHIBIT 5   ADDITIONAL SCENARIOS FOR SALES GROWTH AND OPERATING PROFIT MARGINS

Scenario	Sales Growth (g) (Years)			Operating Profit Margins (p) (Years)		
	1–5	6–7	8–10	1–5	6–7	8–10
Conservative	.14	.12	.10	.17	.14	.11
Most likely	.15	.12	.12	.18	.15	.12
Optimistic	.18	.15	.12	.20	.16	.12

minimum incremental pretax return on sales (or **incremental threshold margin (ITM)** needed to earn the minimum acceptable rate of return on the acquisition (k) given the investment requirements for working capital (w) and fixed assets (f) for each additional dollar of sales and given a projected tax rate (T). The formula for ITM is:

$$\text{Incremental threshold margin} = \frac{(f + w)k}{(1 - T)(1 + k)}$$

Mitnor's management believes that when Rano's growth begins to slow down, its working capital requirements per dollar of additional sales will increase from .15 to about .20 and its tax rate will increase from .46 to .50. As will be shown in Step 2, the minimum acceptable rate of return on the Rano acquisition is 13%. Thus:

$$\text{Incremental threshold margin} = \frac{(.20 + .20)(.13)}{(1 - .50)(1 + .13)}$$

$$= \underline{.092}$$

Mitnor's management has enough confidence to forecast pretax sales returns above 9.2% for only the next 10 years—and the forecast duration for the Rano acquisition is thus limited to that period.

Step 2: Estimate Minimum Acceptable Rate of Return for Acquisition. In developing a company's cost of capital, **measuring the aftertax cost of debt** is relatively straightforward. The cost of equity capital, however, is more difficult to estimate.

Rational, risk-averse investors expect to earn a rate of return that will compensate them for accepting greater investment risk. Thus, in assessing the company's **cost of equity capital** (that is, the minimum expected return that will induce investors to buy the company's shares), it is reasonable to assume that investors will demand a **risk-free rate**—that is, the current yield available in government bonds plus a **premium** for accepting equity risk.

Recently, the risk-free rate on government bonds has been in the neighborhood of 8.8%. By investing in a portfolio broadly representative of the overall equity market, it is possible to diversify away substantially all of the unsystematic risk—that is, risk specific to individual companies. Therefore, securities are likely to be priced at levels that reward investors only for the **nondiversifiable market risk**—that is, the **systematic risk** in movements in the overall market.

The **risk premium** for the overall market is the excess of the expected return on a representative market index, such as the Standard & Poor's 500 stock index over the risk-free return. Empirical studies (e.g., R.G. Ibbotson and R. Sinquefield, *Financial Analysts Federation,* 1977), have estimated this market risk premium (representative market index minus risk-free rate) to average historically about 5 to 5.5%. Here, we will use a 5.2% premium for our calculations.

Investing in an individual security generally involves more or less risk than investing in a broad market portfolio. Thus, one must adjust the market risk premium appropriately in estimating the cost of equity for an individual security. The risk premium for a security is the product of the market risk premium times the individual security's systematic risk, as measured by its **beta coefficient** (stock's volatility relative to the overall market).

The rate of return from dividends and capital appreciation on a **market portfolio** will, by definition, fluctuate identically with the market. Therefore, its beta is equal to 1.0. A **beta** for an individual security is an index of its risk expressed as its volatility of return in relation to that of a market portfolio. Securities with betas greater than 1.0 are more volatile than the market and thus would be expected to have a risk premium greater than the overall market risk premium or the average-risk stock with a beta of 1.0.

For example, if a stock moves 1.5% when the market moves 1%, the stock would have a beta of 1.5. Securities with betas less than 1.0 are less volatile than the market and would thus command risk premiums less than the market risk premium. In summary, the cost of equity capital may be calculated by the following equation:

$$ke = R_f + Bj(R_M - R_F)$$

where ke = cost of equity capital
$\quad R_f$ = risk-free rate
$\quad B_j$ = the beta coefficient
$\quad R_M$ = representative market index

The acquiring company, Mitnor, with a beta of 1.0, estimated its cost of equity as 14% with the foregoing equation:

$$Ke = .088 + 1.0(.052)$$
$$= \underline{.140}$$

Since interest on debt is tax deductible, the rate of return that must be earned on the debt portion of the company's capital structure to maintain the earnings available to common shareholders is the aftertax cost of debt. The after tax cost of borrowed capital is Mitnor's current before tax interest rate (9.5%) times 1 minus its tax rate of 46%, which is equal to 5.1%. Mitnor's target debt-to-equity ratio is .30, or, equivalently, debt is targeted at 23% and equity at 77% of its overall capitalization as Exhibit 6 shows in estimating Mitnor's weighted average cost of capital. The appropriate rate for discounting Mitnor cash flows to establish its estimated value is then 12%.

EXHIBIT 6   MITNOR'S COST OF CAPITAL

	Weight	Cost	Weighted Cost
Debt	.23	.051	.012
Equity	.77	.140	.108
Cost of capital			.120

For new capital projects, including acquisitions, that are deemed to have about the same risk as the overall company, Mitnor can use its 12% cost-of-capital rate as the appropriate discount rate. Because the company's cost of capital is determined by the weighted average risk of its component segments, the specific risk of each prospective acquisition should be estimated in order to arrive at the discount rate to apply to the candidate's cash flows.

Rano, with a beta coefficient of 1.25, is more risky than Mitnor, with a beta of 1.0. Employing the formula for cost of equity capital for Rano:

$$ke = .088 + 1.25(0.52)$$
$$= \underline{.153}$$

On this basis, the risk-adjusted cost of capital for the Rano acquisition is as shown in Exhibit 7.

Step 3: Compute Maximum Acceptable Cash Price. This step involves taking the cash flow projections developed in Step 1 and discounting them at the rate developed in Step 2. Exhibit 8 shows the computation of the maximum acceptable cash price for the most likely scenario. The maximum price of $44.51 million (or $40.10 per share) for Rano compares with the current market price for Rano shares ($25). Thus, for the most likely case, Mitnor can pay up to $15 per share, or a 60% premium over current market, and still achieve its minimum acceptable 13% return on the acquisition.

Exhibit 9 shows the maximum acceptable cash price for each of the three scenarios for a range of discount rates. To earn a 13% rate of return, Mitnor can pay at maximum $38 million ($34.25 per share), assuming the conserv-

EXHIBIT 7   COST OF CAPITAL FOR RANO ACQUISITION

	Weight	Cost	Weighted Cost
Debt	.23	.054[a]	.012
Common equity	.77	.153	.118
Cost of capital			.130

[a] Before-tax debt rate of 10% times 1 minus the estimated tax rate of 46%.

EXHIBIT 8   MAXIMUM ACCEPTABLE CASH PRICE FOR RANO—MOST LIKELY SCENARIO, WITH A DISCOUNT RATE OF .130 ($ MILLIONS)

Year	Cash Flow from Operations	Present Value	Cumulative Present Value
1	$2.96	$2.62	$2.62
2	3.41	2.67	5.29
3	3.92	2.72	8.01
4	4.51	2.76	10.77
5	5.13	2.81	13.59
6	4.90	2.35	15.94
7	5.49	2.33	18.27
8	3.86	1.45	19.72
9	4.32	1.44	21.16
10	4.84	1.43	22.59
Residual value	11.48	26.02[a]	48.61

Plus marketable securities not required for current operations	1.00
Corporate value	49.61
Less debt assumed	5.10
Maximum acceptable cash price (shareholder value)	$44.51
Maximum acceptable cash price per share (Shareholder value per share)	$40.10

[a] $\dfrac{\text{Year 10 operating profit after taxes}}{\text{Discount rate}} \times \text{Year 10 discount factor} = \dfrac{11.48}{.13} \times .2946 = 26.02$

EXHIBIT 9   MAXIMUM ACCEPTABLE CASH PRICE FOR THREE SCENARIOS AND A RANGE OF DISCOUNT RATES

Scenarios	Discount Rates				
	.11	.12	.13	.14	.15
1. CONSERVATIVE					
Total price ($ million)	$48.84	$42.91	$38.02	$33.93	$30.47
Per share price	44.00	38.66	34.25	30.57	27.45
2. MOST LIKELY					
Total price ($ millions)	57.35	50.31	44.51	39.67	35.58
Per share price	51.67	45.33	40.10	35.74	32.05
3. OPTIMISTIC					
Total price ($ millions)	68.37	59.97	53.05	47.28	42.41
Per share price	61.59	54.03	47.80	42.59	38.21

ative scenario. It can pay up to $53 million ($47.80 per share) assuming the optimistic scenario. Note that as Mitnor demands a greater return on its investment, the maximum price it can pay decreases. For example, for the most likely scenario, the maximum price decreases from $44.52 million to $39.67 million as the return requirement goes from 13% to 14%.

Step 4: Compute Rate of Return for Various Offering Prices and Scenarios. Mitnor management believes that the absolute minimum successful bid for Rano would be $35 million, or $31.50 per share. Mitnor's investment bankers estimated that it may take a bid of as high as $45 million, or $40.50 per share, to gain control of Rano shares. Exhibit 10 presents the rates of return that will be earned for four different offering prices, ranging from $35 million to $45 million for each of the three scenarios.

Under the optimistic scenario, Mitnor could expect a return of 14.4% if it were to pay $45 million. For the most likely case, an offer of $45 million would yield a 12.9% return—just under the minimum acceptable rate of 13%. This is as expected, since the maximum acceptable cash price as calculated in Exhibit 8 is $44.51 million, or just under the $45 million offer. If Mitnor attaches a relatively high probability to the conservative scenario, the risk associated with offers exceeding $38 million becomes apparent.

Step 5: Analyze Feasibility of Cash Purchase. While Mitnor management views the relevant purchase price range for Rano as somewhere between $35 and $45 million, it must also establish whether an all-cash deal is feasible in light of Mitnor's current liquidity and target debt-to-equity ratio. The maximum funds available for the purchase of Rano equal the postmerger debt capacity of the combined company less the combined premerger debt of the two companies plus the combined premerger marketable securities of the two companies. (Funds beyond the minimum cash required for everyday operations of the business are excluded from working capital and classified as "marketable securities.")

In an all-cash transaction governed by purchase accounting, the acquirer's shareholders' equity is unchanged. The postmerger debt capacity is then

EXHIBIT 10   RATE OF RETURN FOR VARIOUS OFFERING PRICES AND SCENARIOS

		Offering Price			
Scenarios	Total ($ millions)	$35.00	$38.00	$40.00	$45.00
	Per Share	$31.53	$34.23	$36.04	$40.54
Conservative		.137	.130	.126	.116
Most likely		.152	.144	.139	.129
Optimistic		.169	.161	.156	.144

Mitnor's shareholders' equity of $272 million times the targeted debt-to-equity ratio of .30 (i.e., $81.6 million). Mitnor and Rano have premerger debt balances of $56 million and $5.1 million, respectively, for a combined total of $61.1 million.

The unused debt capacity is thus $81.6 million minus $61.1 million, that is, $20.5 million. Add to this the combined marketable securities of Mitnor and Rano of $26 million, and the maximum funds available for the cash purchase of Rano will be $46.5 million. A cash purchase is therefore feasible within the tentative price range of $35 to $45 million.

Step 6: Evaluate Impact of Acquisition on Mitnor's EPS and Capital Structure. Because reported **earnings per share (EPS)** continue to be of great interest to the financial community, a complete acquisition analysis should include a comparison of projected EPS both with and without the acquisition. Exhibit 11 contains this comparative projection. The EPS stream with the acquisition of Rano is systematically greater than the stream without acquisition.

The EPS standard, and particularly a short-term EPS standard, is not, however, a reliable basis for assessing whether the acquisition will in fact create value for shareholders (Rappaport, *The Journal of Business Strategy* (Spring 1983)). Several problems arise when EPS is used as a standard for evaluating acquisitions. First, because of accounting measurement problems, the EPS figure can be determined by alternative, equally acceptable methods (e.g., LIFO versus FIFO). Second, the EPS standard ignores the time value of money. Third, the standard does not take into account risk. The risk is conditioned by the nature of the investment projects a company undertakes

EXHIBIT 11   MITNOR'S PROJECTED EPS, DEBT-TO-EQUITY RATIO, AND UNUSED DEBT CAPACITY (WITHOUT AND WITH RANO ACQUISITION)[a]

Year	EPS Without	EPS With	Debt/Equity Without	Debt/Equity With	Unused Debt Capacity ($ millions) Without	Unused Debt Capacity ($ millions) With
0	$3.75	$4.10	.21	.26	$25.60	$20.50
1	4.53	4.89	.19	.27	34.44	9.42
2	5.09	5.51	.17	.28	44.22	7.00
3	5.71	6.20	.19	.29	40.26	4.20
4	6.38	6.99	.21	.30	35.45	.98
5	7.14	7.87	.24	.31	29.67	− 2.71
6	7.62	8.29	.26	.31	22.69	− 7.77
7	8.49	9.27	.27	.32	14.49	− 13.64
8	9.46	10.14	.29	.33	4.91	− 22.34
9	10.55	11.33	.31	.34	− 6.23	− 32.36
10	11.76	12.66	.32	.35	− 19.16	− 43.88

[a] Assumed cash purchase price for Rano is $35 million.

as well as by the relative proportions of debt and equity used to finance those investments.

A company can increase EPS by increasing leverage as long as the marginal return on investment is greater than the interest rate on the new debt. However, if the marginal return on investment is less than the risk-adjusted cost of capital or if the increased leverage leads to an increased cost of capital, then the value of the company could decline despite rising EPS.

Primarily because the acquisition of Rano requires that Mitnor partially finance the purchase price with bank borrowing, the debt-to-equity ratios with the acquisition are greater than those without the acquisition (see Exhibit 11). Note that even without the Rano acquisition, Mitnor is in danger of violating its target debt-to-equity ratio of .30 by the ninth year. The acquisition of Rano accelerates the problem to the fifth year. Whether Mitnor purchases Rano or not, management must now be alert to the financing problem, which may force it to issue additional shares or reevaluate its present capital structure policy.

ACQUISITION FOR STOCK. The first two steps in the acquisition-for-stock analysis—projecting Rano operating cash flows and setting the discount rate—have already been completed in connection with the acquisition-for-cash analysis developed previously. The remaining steps of the acquisition-for-stock analysis are:

1. Estimate the value of Mitnor shares
2. Compute the maximum number of shares that Mitnor can exchange to acquire Rano under various scenarios and minimum acceptable rates of return
3. Evaluate the impact of the acquisition on the earnings per share and capital structure of Mitnor

Step 1: Estimate Value of Mitnor Shares. Mitnor conducted a comprehensive corporate self-evaluation that included an assessment of its estimated present value based on a range of scenarios. In the interest of brevity, we will only consider its most likely scenario.

Management made most likely projections for its operations, as shown in Exhibit 12. Again using the equation for the cost of equity capital, the incremental threshold margin (the minimum profit margin as a percentage of sales increase needed to earn Mitnor's 12% cost of capital) is 10.9%.

$$\text{Incremental threshold margin} = \frac{(f + w)(k)}{(1 - T)(1 + k)}$$

$$= \frac{(.25 + .30)(.12)}{(1 - .46)(1.12)}$$

$$= 10.9\%$$

EXHIBIT 12   MOST LIKELY ESTIMATES FOR MITNOR OPERATIONS WITHOUT ACQUISITION

	Years		
	1–5	6–7	8–10
Sales growth rate (g)	.125	.120	.120
Operating profit margin as a percentage of sales (p)	.130	.125	.125
Income tax rate (T)	.460	.460	.460
Incremental fixed capital investment (f)	.250	.250	.250
Incremental working capital investment (w)	.300	.300	.300

Since management can confidently forecast pretax return on sales returns above 10.9% for only the next 10 years, the cash flow projections will be limited to that period.

Exhibit 13 presents the computation of the value of Mitnor's equity. Its estimated value of $36.80 per share contrasts with its current market value of $22 per share. Because Mitnor management believes its shares to be undervalued by the market, in the absence of other compelling factors it will be reluctant to acquire Rano by means of an exchange of shares.

EXHIBIT 13   ESTIMATED PRESENT VALUE OF MITNOR EQUITY— MOST LIKELY SCENARIO, WITH A DISCOUNT RATE OF .120 ($ MILLIONS)

Year	Cash Flow from Operations	Present Value	Cumulative Present Value
1	$6.13	$5.48	$5.48
2	6.90	5.50	10.98
3	7.76	5.53	16.51
4	8.74	5.55	22.06
5	9.83	5.58	27.63
6	10.38	5.26	32.89
7	11.63	5.26	38.15
8	13.02	5.26	43.41
9	14.58	5.26	48.67
10	16.33	5.26	53.93
Residual value	128.62	345.10[a]	399.03

Plus marketable securities not required for current operations	25.00
Mitnor's corporate value	424.03
Less debt outstanding	56.00
Mitnor's shareholder value	$368.03
Mitnor's shareholder per share	$ 36.80

[a] $\dfrac{\text{Year 10 profit after taxes}}{\text{Discount rate}} \times \text{Year 10 discount factor} = \dfrac{128.62}{.12} \times .32197 = 345.10$

EXHIBIT 14   CALCULATION OF LOSS BY MITNOR SHAREHOLDERS ($ MILLIONS)

Mitnor receives 87.27% of Rano's present value of $44.51 million (see Exhibit 8)	$38.4
Mitnor gives up 13.73% of its present value of $368.03 million (see Exhibit 13)	(50.5)
Dilution of Mitnor's shareholder value	$12.1

To illustrate, suppose that Mitnor were to offer $35 million in cash for Rano. Assume the most likely case, that the maximum acceptable cash price is $44.51 million (see Exhibit 8); thus the acquisition would create about $9.5 million in value for Mitnor shareholders. Now assume that instead Mitnor agrees to exchange $35 million in market value of its shares in order to acquire Rano. In contrast with the cash case, in the exchange-of-shares case Mitnor shareholders can expect to be worse off by $12.1 million.

With Mitnor shares selling at $22, the company must exchange 1.59 million shares to meet the $35 million offer from Rano. There are currently 10 million Mitnor shares outstanding. After the merger, the combined company will be owned 86.27% (i.e., $\dfrac{(10.00)}{(10.00 + 1.59)}$ — by current Mitnor shareholders and 13.73% by Rano shareholders). The $12.1 million loss by Mitnor shareholders can then be calculated as shown in Exhibit 14.

Step 2: Compute Maximum Number of Shares Mitnor Can Exchange. The maximum acceptable number of shares to exchange for each of the three scenarios and for a range of discount rates appears in Exhibit 15. To earn a 13% rate of return, Mitnor can exchange no more than 1.033, 1.210, and 1.442 million shares, assuming the conservative, most likely, and optimistic scenarios, respectively. Consider, for a moment, the most likely case. At a market value per share of $22, the 1.21 million Mitnor shares exchanged would have a total value of $26.62 million, which is less than Rano's current market value of $27.75 million (i.e., 1.11 million shares at $25 per share). Because of the market's apparent undervaluation of Mitnor's shares, an

EXHIBIT 15   MAXIMUM ACCEPTABLE SHARES TO EXCHANGE FOR THREE SCENARIOS AND A RANGE OF DISCOUNT RATES (IN MILLIONS)

Scenarios	Discount Rates				
	.11	.12	.13	.14	.15
Conservative	1.327	1.166	1.033	0.922	0.828
Most likely	1.558	1.367	1.210	1.078	0.967
Optimistic	1.858	1.630	1.442	1.285	1.152

EXHIBIT 16   MITNOR'S PROJECTED EPS, DEBT-TO-EQUITY RATIO, AND UNUSED DEBT CAPACITY-CASH VERSUS EXCHANGE OF SHARES[a]

Year	EPS		Debt/Equity		Unused Debt Capacity ($ millions)	
	Cash	Stock	Cash	Stock	Cash	Stock
0	$ 4.10	$ 3.54	.26	.21	$20.50	$25.60
1	4.89	4.37	.27	.19	9.42	35.46
2	5.51	4.93	.28	.17	7.00	46.62
3	6.20	5.55	.29	.18	4.20	48.04
4	6.99	6.23	.30	.20	0.98	46.37
5	7.87	7.00	.31	.21	−2.71	44.29
6	8.29	7.37	.31	.23	−7.77	40.90
7	9.27	8.22	.32	.24	−13.64	36.78
8	10.14	8.98	.33	.26	−22.34	29.90
9	11.33	10.01	.34	.27	−32.36	21.79
10	12.66	11.17	.35	.29	−43.88	12.29

[a] Assumed purchase price for Rano is $35 million.

exchange ratio likely to be acceptable to Rano will clearly be unattractive to Mitnor.

Step 3: Evaluate Impact of Acquisition on Mitnor's EPS and Capital Structure. The $35 million purchase price is just under 10 times Rano's most recent year's earnings of $3.55 million. At its current market price per share of $22, Mitnor is selling at about six times its most recent earnings. The acquiring company will always suffer immediate EPS dilution whenever the price-earnings ratio paid for the selling company is greater than its own. Mitnor, for example, would suffer immediate dilution from $3.75 to $3.54 in the current year. A comparison of EPS for cash versus an exchange-of-shares transaction appears as part of Exhibit 16. As expected, the EPS projections for a cash deal are consistently higher than those for an exchange of shares.

However, the acquisition of Rano for shares rather than cash would remove, at least for now, Mitnor's projected financing problem. In contrast to cash acquisition, an exchange of shares enables Mitnor to have unused debt capacity at its disposal throughout the 10-year forecast period. Despite the relative attractiveness of this financing flexibility, Mitnor management recognized that it could not expect a reasonable rate of return by offering an exchange of shares to Rano.

SUMMARY

The experience of companies that have implemented the approach to acquisition analysis described in this section indicates that it is not only an effective way to evaluating a prospective acquisition candidate but also serves as a catalyst for reevaluating a company's overall strategic plans. The results also enable management to justify acquisition recommendations to the board of directors in an economically sound, convincing fashion.

Various companies have used this shareholder value approach for evaluation of serious candidates as well as for initial screening of potential candidates. In the latter case, initial input estimates are quickly generated to establish whether the range of maximum acceptable prices is greater than the current value of the target companies. With the aid of the microcomputer model described in this section, this can be accomplished quickly and at relatively low cost.

Whether companies are seeking acquisitions or are acquisition targets, it is increasingly clear that they must provide better information to enable top management and boards to make well-conceived, timely decisions. Use of the approach outlined here should improve the prospects of creating value for shareholders by acquisitions.

REFERENCES

BusinessWeek, "The Cash-Flow Takeover Formula," December 18, 1978, p. 86.

Ibbotson, Roger G., and Sinquedfield, Rex A., *Stock, Bonds, Bills, and Inflation: The Past (1926-1976) and the Future (1977-2000),* Financial Analysts Research Foundation, New York, 1977.

Rappaport, Alfred, "Corporate Performance Standards and Shareholder Value, *The Journal of Business Strategy,* Spring 1983.

Rappaport, Alfred, "Do You Know the Value of Your Company?" *Mergers and Acquisitions,* Spring 1979.

Salter, Malcolm S, and Weinhold, Wolf A., "Diversification via Acquisition: Creating Values, July-August 1978, p. 166.

11

LEASING

CONTENTS

11

LEASING

John Martin

INTRODUCTION

IMPORTANCE OF LEASE FINANCING. Leasing has become an increasingly important source of financing during the post-World War II era. In the presidential address made to the 1984 annual meeting of the American Association of Equipment Lessors, John Giddings noted that the total dollar value of new equipment leases written in 1984 was estimated at $74.4 billion—a $13.2 billion increase over the 1983 figure. In addition, although there is no precise way to estimate the total dollar value of all equipment leases in place, this figure is thought to have been in the $200 to $250 billion range in 1984.

TYPES OF LEASE ARRANGEMENT. There are two broad categories of lease arrangement: financial leases and operating leases. Within each category there are various subcategories, and in addition there are hybrid types of lease arrangement that do not fall into either category.

Financial Leases. These are long-term or intermediate-term, noncancelable agreements. The sum of the lease payments over the term of such a lease equals or exceeds the original purchase price of the asset being leased and the **present value** of the lease equals at least 90% of the purchase price. A purchase option is often included in a financial lease agreement. The option includes a price at which the lessee can purchase the asset from the lessor at termination of the lease. The Internal Revenue Service "true" lease requirements dictate that great care be exercised in writing a purchase option. Violation of the true lease requirements results in loss of the tax deductibility of the lease payments to the lessee as well as loss of the tax deductibility of owner-related expenses (depreciation and interest) to the lessor. Financial deductibility of owner-related expenses (depreciation and interest) to the lessor. Financial leases are written by financial lease companies and commercial banks, as well as equipment dealers and manufacturers.

Sale and Leaseback Arrangements. In this special type of financial lease the lessee firm sells an asset it presently owns to a lessor and enters a financial lease agreement to "reobtain" the asset's services. For example, if a firm owns a building valued at $1 million that is fully paid for and unmortgaged, the firm might sell the building to a lessor for its full value (receiving $1 million in cash) and agree to make lease payments that fully amortize the $1 million over the next 10 years. The firm has exchanged owner financing for lease financing. In the sale and leaseback process the firm has obtained $1 million in cash, incurred a financial lease liability valued at $1 million with the lease payments reflecting the lessor's required rate of return, and in addition, maintained use of the building. Note, however, that the firm might also have borrowed the $1 million, using the building as collateral.

Leveraged Leases. Another special form of financial lease is the leveraged lease, a financial lease agreement in which the lessor borrows some portion (usually greater than 50%) of the purchase price of the leased asset. The lessor secures the loan by pledging both the asset and the stream of lease payments. The lessee is interested in determining the cost of leasing so that it can be compared with alternative sources of financing, while the lessor wants to determine a set of lease payments that will provide an acceptable return on invested funds.

Operating Leases. These differ from financial leases in two primary respects. First, an operating lease is cancelable and generally written for a shorter period of time than a financial lease. Second, with an operating lease the lessor assumes responsibility for virtually all the expenses of ownership. This type of lease is used when an asset is needed for a short period of time. The lessor captures and passes along to the lessee economics of scale in owning the asset. Operating leases are generally written by firms specializing in this type of agreement or by manufacturers.

Operating leases are an important method of providing temporary financing for the firm. Because financial leases provide a means for financing a firm's asset needs over long periods of time and also present the analyst with a unique set of problems, the balance of this section deals exclusively with financial lease arrangements.

Net Leases. These leases require the lessee to maintain the leased asset, insure it, and pay any property taxes. Most financial leases are net leases. In a gross, maintenance, or full service lease, however, the lessor has the responsibility for the costs normally associated with ownership.

Net Net Leases. This type of lease not only requires that the lessee bear the normal costs of asset ownership, but also that the asset be returned in its original condition upon the termination of the lease.

LEASING PROBLEMS FOR FINANCIAL ANALYSTS. Leasing poses two types of problems for financial analysts: "lease or purchase" (the merits of leasing versus other forms of financing) and **"lease accounting"** (the impact of leasing on the firm's financial statements).

ECONOMIC RATIONALE FOR FINANCIAL LEASING: WHY LEASE?

THE LESSOR AS FINANCIAL INTERMEDIARY. The lessor serves as a financial intermediary in the sense that he obtains funds externally from the capital markets or internally from undistributed profits and exchanges those funds for a financial lease contract. Exhibit 1 depicts the financial lease process. In the purchase process (left), funds provided by the capital markets are obtained by the purchaser through issuing stock and/or bonds. These funds are then used to obtain title to the assets whose services are being acquired.

In the leasing process (right), the lessor obtains funds from the capital market and acquires title to the asset. The lessor then provides the lessee with the "use value" of the asset in exchange for a series of lease payments as prescribed by the financial lease agreement. The lessor retains the asset's **salvage value.**

There are two fundamental differences in the lease and purchase alternatives described in Exhibit 1. First, the leasing arrangement includes an additional middleman or financial intermediary (the lessor). Second, the purchase option provides the owner with both the **use value** of the asset and its **salvage value,** whereas the lessee obtains only the use value of the asset. On the surface it appears that the lease arrangement would necessarily be more expensive than the purchase alternative, since leasing includes another financial intermediary who must be rewarded for his services. Thus, to be cost effective, the lessor must offer some saving to the lessee that he cannot obtain for himself.

POTENTIAL BENEFITS OF LEASING. To understand the potential sources of any benefits from leasing, note the following transactions involved in the purchase scenario described in Exhibit 1. First, the funds needed to acquire the asset must be raised. Second, the asset must be purchased. Third, the asset must be disposed of at the end of its useful life. These three phases of the purchase process represent the potential sources of economic benefits from leasing. That is, if the lessor can acquire funds from the capital markets on more favorable terms, or purchase the asset at a lower price or achieve a higher salvage value for the asset, then leasing offers the basis for real cost savings to the lessee. For the lessee to realize any cost saving through leasing, however, these cost savings must exceed the required profit of the

EXHIBIT 1   A COMPARISON OF PURCHASING WITH LEASING

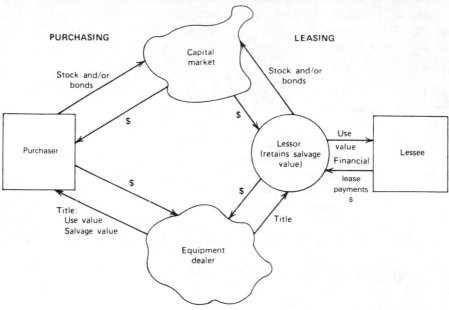

lessor and they must be passed through to the lessee in the form of reduced lease payments. Thus, although the **financial lease** may prove to be a cheaper form of financing than purchasing, there must be some underlying economic reason for those cost savings to exist.

SYNTHESIS OF TRADITIONAL "ADVANTAGES" OF LEASE FINANCING. The use of financial leases to finance the acquisition of an asset's services has several purported advantages over purchasing the asset. The term "purported" is deliberately used, since many of the advantages attributed to leasing are purely illusory and others are present only some of the time and in varying degrees. This discussion, which places the alleged advantages of lease financing into perspective so that the informed analyst can evaluate them rationally, relies heavily on the work of Martin et al. (*Basic Financial Management,* Prentice Hall, 1979).

Flexibility and Convenience.   It is often claimed that financial leases are more flexible and convenient source of financing than alternative forms of financing. For example, leasing is said to provide lessees with flexibility because it allows a firm to finance relatively small asset acquisitions in piecemeal fashion without having to sell a bond or stock issue, which is a time-consuming and expensive endeavor. Note, however, that the firm acquires this same benefit (i.e., avoiding a small security issue) by using the service of any financial intermediary, not just by leasing. Another flexibility advantage that is frequently attributed to leasing relates to the opportunity it may offer to "circumvent" cumbersome capital expenditure procedures. For example, by leasing, the preparation of a formal capital expenditure request may not be required. Thus, a lower level manager may lease just to avoid a formal capital expenditure request. Yet another flexibility advantage is that rental payments can frequently be timed to match the revenues generated by the asset. For instance, rental payments might be structured to match a seasonal pattern of cash flows.

The convenience arguments for leasing are many and varied. For example, when an asset is leased, the firm no longer has to prepare depreciation tables and maintain other bookkeeping records incident to ownership. In addition, leasing frequently eliminates the set of problems that accompany ownership, for example, servicing and selling the asset at a later point.

Many of the flexibility and convenience advantages of leasing are illusory. It is not possible, however, to generalize about their validity. For some firms and under specific sets of circumstances, some of the arguments just described may represent valid reasons for using lease financing.

Many of the flexibility and convenience arguments can be viewed in terms of the costs and benefits derived from shifting functions. That is, by leasing, the firm shifts the functions of bookkeeping and disposal of used equipment to the lessor. To the extent that the lessor can perform these functions at a lower cost than can the firm and is willing to pass these savings on to the lessee in reduced lease payments, a real advantage to leasing may exist. Unfortunately, the costs and benefits associated with flexibility and convenience are difficult to estimate. Thus, a subjective approach to evaluating the relative merits of lease financing is unavoidable.

Lack of Restrictions. It is often suggested that financial lease agreements do not include the same kinds of restrictive covenant common to bond indentures. In addition, bond indentures may not contain provisions restricting the use of financial leases, even though additional debt may be specifically prohibited or at least restricted. Kim et al. (E.H. Kim, W.G. Lewellen, and J.J. McConnell, "Sale and Leaseback Arrangements and Enterprise Valuation," *Journal of Financial and Quantitative Analysis,* Vol. 13, December 1978, pp. 871–883) demonstrate that the firm's management can exploit the absence of restrictions on its use of financial leases to the benefit of the firm's owners. For such opportunities to exist, however, the firm's creditors would have to be quite naive regarding the impact of financial leases on the firm's debt-carrying capacity.

The extent to which a firm will benefit from the lack of restrictions associated with leasing will depend on the price it must pay for lease financing. The freedom accorded the lessee translates directly into the risk underwritten by the lessor. This is not to say that a favorable set of lease terms cannot be arranged. However, lessor recognition of the lack of restrictions in the lease might result in a prohibitively expensive set of lease terms.

Avoiding Risk of Obsolescence. Leasing is often said to offer the lessee firm a means of avoiding the **risk of obsolescence.** Although cancelable operating leases may offer this advantage, a financial lease probably does not. If the lessor is aware of the risk of obsolescence, he is sure to pass the associated costs on to the lessee in the form of higher lease payments. Only when the lessor foresees lower costs associated with obsolescence than the lessee and is willing to pass these on to the lessee in lower lease payments is the risk of obsolescence even partially avoided with a financial lease. Some lessors who specialize in certain types of assets may hold an advantage over the lessee in terms of maintaining the asset in good working condition and in selling it on the lease's termination. These **economies of specialization** may allow the lessor to offer lease terms that the lessee will find to be cost effective. That is, the lessor provides **maintenance services** and **resale services** at a cost the lessee cannot duplicate. Once again, for savings to be realized by the lessee, the lessor must pass his savings along as lower lease payments. Furthermore, the lessee may obtain these benefits via the purchase of a maintenance contract from an equipment vendor.

Conservation of Working Capital. Perhaps the most commonly cited advantage of lease financing is that it provides up to 100% financing—that is, little or no cash **downpayment** is required. However, it is misleading to say that leasing should be favored over other forms of financing for this reason. For example, if bank loan financing is the alternative source of financing being compared with leasing, the downpayment itself might be borrowed. Furthermore, the fact that leasing provides 100% nonowner financing means that it used more of the firm's **debt capacity** than a less than 100% loan. Finally, the lease provides the firm with the **use value** of the asset but not its **salvage value.** If a substantial salvage value exists, its forfeiture with the lease agreement might be considered a de facto downpayment. Thus, the lease provides 100% financing of the use value of the asset only.

Tax Savings. Lease payments are fully tax deductible, whereas the interest and depreciation expense can be deducted from taxable income when an asset is purchased. A full assessment of the relative tax savings associated with leasing and owning can best be accomplished using a lease versus purchase model like the one discussed later in this section.

Ease of Obtaining Credit. It is sometimes suggested that firms with poor **credit ratings** can obtain lease financing more easily than they can obtain a loan. Since the lessor suffers the same **risk of default** as any other creditor, the lessee's credit status will be reflected in the level of the lease payments. However, the security position of the lessor is usually superior to that of other creditors.

Summary. There are a number of advantages frequently attributed to lease financing. The final decision of whether a real advantage exists depends on the particular set of lease terms being evaluated. In every instance, the advantages discussed could be converted into dollar savings capable of quantitative analysis via a lease versus purchase model. Although the associated costs and benefits pay prove difficult in many cases, the very act of attempting to evaluate the various advantages of leasing in this way should lead to better leasing decisions.

WHY LESSEES LEASE: EMPIRICAL EVIDENCE. A number of attempts have been made to survey lessees to determine their motives for leasing. Some of the recent studies include H.G. Hamel and G.C. Thompson (*Theory of Business Finance,* J.F. Weston and D.H. Woods, Eds., Wadsworth, Belmont, CA, pp. 203–213), G.L. Marrah (*Financial Executive,* Vol. 36, 1968, pp. 91–104), R.A. Fawthrop and B. Terry (*Journal of Business Finance and Accounting,* Vol. 2, 1975, pp. 295–314), and P.F. Anderson and J.D. Martin (paper presented at the Ninth Annual Meeting of the Financial Management Association, Boston, October, 11–13, 1979).

The discussion presented here is based on the study by Anderson and Martin, since it offers several methodological improvements over earlier work. Specifically, this investigation reports information regarding both the lessee–respondent's beliefs about the various "advantages" of leasing and the impact each advantage has on the decision to use lease financing.

The survey produced 191 respondents from lessee firms with sales ranging from $10 million to $300 million annually. The 1976 lease payments of the sample firms ranged from over $50 million to under $10,000. Approximately 76% of the respondents were engaged in manufacturing, 6% were mining companies, 5% were involved in transportation, communications, or public utility service, and the remainder were distributed across a wide variety of industries.

A major problem plaguing previous research efforts was the tendency to focus on the importance of leasing's purported advantages without eliciting the respondents' assessment of whether the various advantages were real or illusory. In the survey by Anderson and Martin, respondents were asked to rate each of 40 purported advantages of leasing from 1 to 5, with "1" corresponding to "strongly agree" and "5" corresponding to "strongly disagree." A second scale was used to determine the importance the respondent attached to a particular "advantage" in making leasing decisions. This scale ranged from 1 to 6 with "1" corresponding to "very important" and "6" corresponding to "not at all important."

Of the 40 potential advantages of leasing, the one with the lowest average agreement score was: "All things considered, leasing is less expensive than debt as a means of acquiring equipment." The agreement score indicates whether the respondent agreed or disagreed that the statement reflects an advantage of leasing. A low score indicates that the respondent disagreed with the statement. When the "overall" importance of the foregoing advantage was calculated, it was ranked third. The overall importance measure reflects the results obtained from the importance scale discussed above.

Thus, in this particular instance, the respondents agreed that it is important that the cost of leasing be lower than the cost of debt financing, but they disagreed with the statement that leasing is less costly than debt financing.

The inputs from the agreement scale and importance scale were combined to form an overall measure of the significance of each of the 40 alleged advantages of leasing. The various "advantages" were then arrayed from most significant to least significant, based on this overall measure.

The 10 most significant reasons for leasing appear in Exhibit 2. Note that because of the way the agreement and importance scales were formulated, a low numerical score indicates a high level of importance.

The first point to note in Exhibit 2 is the prominence of tax-related factors. Attributes ranked 1, 8, and 9 related to the potential tax benefits of leasing. This gives some credence to the view that tax considerations are indeed significant in the leasing decisions of corporations. However, Exhibit 2 also illustrates that other factors are important to the respondents. Moreover, many of these factors, as well as the tax-related factors, would be subsumed by the standard lease versus purchase models existing in the literature.

For example, attributes 1, 3, 7, 8, and 9 would all be accounted for via the discounting mechanism of a lease versus purchase model. Finally, if the problems associated with the disposal of secondhand equipment can be quantified, attribute 4 could also be included in any standard analytical model.

Since many of the most significant reasons for leasing are also reflected in the cash flows of lease-purchase models, one might expect the respondents to view leasing as a favorable alternative to debt from a cost perspective. This is suggested by evidence that corporate analysts often use models that compare leasing directly with debt financing. However, as noted previously, the statement "All things considered, leasing is less expensive than debt as a means of acquiring equipment," was rated twentieth in significance and fortieth in overall agreement. This somewhat paradoxical result suggests that perhaps other noncash-flow factors actually determine in the leasing decisions of the respondents. This view is reinforced by the growing evidence that some firms and institutions enter into lease arrangements despite rates that are far in excess of debt alternatives. See, for example, the paper by I.W. Sorensen and R.E. Johnson ("Equipment Financial Leasing Practices and Costs: An Empirical Study," *Financial Management,* Vol. 6, 1977, pp. 33–40).

Some suggestion of what these other factors might be can be seen in Exhibit 2. The respondents indicated that the problem of dilution of ownership or control (number 2), piecemeal financing (number 5), obsolescence of equipment (number 6), and maintenance of credit lines (number 10) are all significant motivations for leasing. While these "advantages" are all inconsistent with the assumption of perfect markets, it is clear that the respondents see them as real benefits of leasing. Thus many lessees apparently view themselves as operating in imperfect markets in which nontax

EXHIBIT 2   RANK ORDER OF THE 10 MOST SIGNIFICANT REASONS FOR LEASING

Rank	Advantage of Leasing	Mean Significance Score[a]
1.	Leasing provides for 100% deductibility of costs.	6.805
2.	Leasing provides the firm with long-term financing without diluting ownership or control.	8.099
3.	Leasing frees the firm's working capital for other uses.	8.508
4.	Leasing permits the firm to avoid the problems associated with the disposal of secondhand equipment.	8.626
5.	Leasing allows for piecemeal financing of relatively small equipment acquisitions for which debt financing would be impractical.	8.855
6.	Leasing protects the company from the risks of equipment obsolescence.	8.934
7.	The aftertax cost of leasing is less than the aftertax cost of equity financing.	8.994
8.	Leasing is advantageous for firms with low or heavily sheltered earnings because the lessor will be able to pass on the savings from the investment tax credit in a lower lease rate.	9.040
9.	The tax deductibility of lease payments provides a larger and more immediate cash flow than that provided by depreciation and interest deductions.	9.418
10.	Leasing leaves normal lines of credit undisturbed.	9.726

[a]The significance score was calculated as follows:

$$S_i = \sum_{j=1}^{m} B_j I_j$$

where S_i = "significance score" for ith advantage of leasing

B_j = respondent j's belief (agreement score) that leasing possesses attribute i

I_j = respondent j's importance rating for attribute i

Source: P.F. Anderson and J. D. Martin, "Financial Leases: The Corporate Viewpoint," paper presented at the Ninth Annual Meeting of the Financial Management Association, Boston, October, 1979.

and even noncash-flow factors play a role in leasing decisions. A number of authors have demonstrated the irrelevance of the advantages of financial leases under conditions of perfectly competitive capital markets. The crucial assumptions of these arguments that are violated in reality relate to their reliance on homogeneous expectations and complete and costless information to all market participants. See H. Miller and C.W. Upton, "Leasing, Buying and the Cost of Capital Services" (*Journal of Finance,* Vol. 31, June 1976, pp. 761–786) and W.G. Lewellen, M.S. Long, and J.J. McConnell, "Asset Leasing in Competitive Capital Markets" (*Journal of Finance,* Vol. 31, June 1976, pp. 787–798).

The results of the survey summarized here suggest that lessees consider more than explicit cost advantages in making leasing decisions. Indeed, the evidence indicates that a variety of cash flow and noncash-flow factors may enter into the decision process. Moreover, the respondents generally agree that leasing is more expensive than debt as a source of financing. Thus, it may be argued that "noncost" (i.e., noncash-flow) factors are important in the leasing decisions of the respondents. The lease versus purchase subsection below demonstrates that a judicious analysis of the decision to use lease financing requires quantification of many of these "non cash-flow" items.

LEASE VERSUS PURCHASE

HISTORICAL OVERVIEW. This section draws heavily on J.D. Martin and P.F. Anderson, "A Practical Approach to the Lease vs. Purchase Problem" (*International Journal of Physical Distribution and Materials Management*, Vol. 9, No. 4, 1979, pp. 150–157).

The **lease versus purchase decision** has intrigued and perplexed both the academician and the practitioner for many years. The enigmatic nature of the problem can be traced to the fact that it is a hybrid containing both financing and investment components. Unlike the related capital investment decision (where analysts and theorists have conveniently separated the financing and investment aspects of the decision through the use of a "weighted average cost of capital" concept—see the section entitled "Capital Budgeting" for a discussion of the capital budgeting decision), the lease versus purchase problem forces the analyst to consider both the feasibility of asset acquisition and whether lease financing is preferable to normal debt-equity financing.

Traditional capital budgeting procedures incorporate financing considerations into a minimum required rate of return (weighted average cost of debt and equity financing) and proceed to analyze the answer to the first of the questions above. However, when leasing is considered the firm commits itself to what is, in effect, 100% nonequity financing of an asset's acquisition. Thus traditional project analyses that relegate financial considerations to a weighted average cost of capital are not immediately amenable to the analysis. One immediate issue in lease-purchase analyses is financial risk differences between lease financing and normal purchase financing. This issue, among others, has provided the basis for a vast academic literature on the lease versus purchase questions. This subsection identifies the troublesome issues arising in lease-purchase analyses and suggests practical solutions.

At least three conflicting viewpoints on the nature of the lease-purchase decision have been expressed in the academic literature. The traditional view is that lease versus purchase analysis is appropriately considered to be a financing decision. A second, but somewhat smaller group of theorists have attempted to deal with the lease versus purchase decision in a strict investment context, devoid of financing implications. More recent theorists have approached the lease-purchase decision as a hybrid financing-investment problem.

Lease-Purchase as a Financing Decision. Those who take this approach generally view the analysis as a **lease-or-borrow** problem in which the purchase is assumed to be financed with 100% debt. Models have taken one of two basic forms. The most popular format (in terms of the sheer volume of published research) is the net present value model. Using this approach, the lease-purchase problem is evaluated by measuring the difference between the net present value of acquiring an asset through a **financial lease,** and the net present value of purchasing the asset. The net present value of leasing less the net present value of purchasing is the **net present value advantage of leasing over purchasing.** If this difference is positive, leasing is favored over purchasing; if it is negative, purchasing is preferred.

The second type of lease-or-borrow model involves use of a **rate of return** or **internal rate of return** format. This method consists of finding a rate of interest that makes the net present value advantage of leasing equal to zero. If the internal rate of return exceeds the borrowing rate, leasing is favored; if not, purchasing is favored.

Some of the better known net present value models include A.H. Cohen, *Long Term Leases—Problems of Taxation, Finance and Accounting,* University of Michigan Press, Ann Arbor, 1954; J.F. Weston and E.F. Brigham, *Managerial Finance,* 6th ed., Dryden Press, Hinsdale, IL, 1978; R.F. Vancil, "Lease or Borrow—New Method of Analysis," *Harvard Business Review,* Vol. 39, September–October 1961; R.S. Bower, F.C. Herringer, and J.P. Williamson, "Lease Evaluation," *Accounting Review,* Vol. 41, April 1966, pp. 257–265; and H. Bierman, Jr. and S. Smidt, *The Capital Budgeting Decision,* 5th ed., Macmillan, New York, 1980.

In addition, all the prominent internal rate of return models are, by definition, pure financing models (T.H. Beechy, "Quasi-Debt Analysis of Financial Leases," *Accounting Review,* Vol. 44, April 1969, pp. 375–381; T.H. Beechy, "The Cost of Leasing: Comment and Correction," *Accounting Review,* Vol. 45, October 1970, pp. 769–773; M.C. Findlay, III, "Financial Lease Evaluation: Survey and Synthesis," *Financial Review,* 1974, pp. 1–15; G.D. Quirin, *The Capital Expenditure Decision,* Irwin, Homewood, IL, 1967; and R.L. Roenfeldt and J.S. Osteryoung, "Analysis of Financial Leases," *Financial Management,* Vol. 2, Spring 1973.)

There are two practical problems associated with many of these models. First, a majority of these approaches do not properly adjust for the differential risk of the lease-purchase cash flows. This occurs in many **net present value** (*NPV*) models because the firm's aftertax cost of capital is used to discount nearly riskless contractual tax shield and operating expense flows.

On the other hand, many internal rate of return (*IRR*) models fail to adjust for risky flows such as salvage value. It has been demonstrated elsewhere that because of their failure to adjust for differential risk, the *NPV* and *IRR* approaches tend to be biased against the lease alternative (P.F. Anderson and J.D. Martin, "Lease vs. Purchase Decisions: A Survey of Current Practice and Theory," Working Paper, Virginia Polytechnic Institute and State University, July 1976).

The second problem with pure financing approaches is that many require a justification of the acquisition on a purchase basis before consideration is given to leasing. Thus the investment decision is separated from the financing decision.

The fallacy inherent in this approach has been recognized by a number of writers. As Johnson and Lewellen note, such an ex ante investment analysis can never allow a bargain lease opportunity to reverse an original negative purchase decision (R.W. Johnson and W.G. Lewellen, "Reply," *Journal of Finance,* Vol. 28, September 1973, pp. 1024–1028). Once again, a bias against the lease alternative is introduced.

A final problem associated with pure financing approaches is the basic assumption of these models that 100% debt financing is the appropriate alternative to leasing. That is, does a dollar of lease financing displace one dollar of debt capacity?

Lease-Purchase as an Investment Decision. In contrast to the pure financing approach, is the pure investment approach of Johnson and Lewellen ("Analysis of the Lease-or-Buy Decision," *Journal of Finance,* Vol. 27, September 1972, pp. 815–823; and "Reply," *Journal of Finance,* Vol. 28, September 1973, pp. 1024–1028). Johnson and Lewellen view the lease as a long-term **acquisition of services contract** that differs in timing but not in financing impact from a purchase. This view of a lease acquisition as something to be financed rather than as a source of financing led Johnson and Lewellen to apply the traditional capital budgeting framework to both the lease and purchase options. This, in turn, generated a model that excludes all consideration of interest expense and employs the **cost of capital** to discount two highly certain flows: the **depreciation tax shield** and the aftertax operating expenses covered by the lessor.

The **pure investment approach** has attracted few adherents among financial theorists. The academic community does not appear willing to accept Johnson and Lewellen's acquisition-of-services view of leasing. The consensus view appears to be that a lease does provide the firm with an alternative source of financing and that lease-purchase analyses must take this fact into account. Moreover, few writers appear willing to accept their argument that the cost of capital should be applied to flows that are nearly risk free.

Johnson and Lewellen did make an important contribution to the development of normative lease-purchase theory by challenging the pure financing approach and demonstrating the importance of the investment element. This has led to a wider recognition of the lease as a hybrid, containing elements of both investment and finance.

Lease-Purchase as a Financing and Investment Decision. The hybrid approach is best illustrated in the work of L.D. Schall ("The Lease-or-Buy and Asset Acquisition Decisions," *Journal of Finance,* Vol. 29, September 1974, pp. 1203–1214). Schall recognizes that a lease is both an investment in a revenue-generating asset and a source of debt-like financing. Moreover, he accounts for the fact that financing and investment elements are inextricably linked and cannot be separated if a meaningful choice is to be made between the lease and purchase alternatives. Thus, Schall's model considers the financing and investment decisions simultaneously. In addition, his algorithm over-comes many of the problems associated with earlier approaches.

Although Schall's model gives consideration to all the basic elements of the lease-purchase problem, it offers little insight into the differences in the impact of the alternatives on the firm's risk of illiquidity. This issue has been studied by a number of theorists, notably A. Ofer ("The Evaluation of Lease Versus Purchase Alternatives," *Financial Management,* Vol. 5, Summer 1976, pp. 67–74), L. Allen, J.D. Martin, and P.F. Anderson, ("Debt Capacity and the Lease Versus Purchase Problem: A Sensitivity Analysis," *Engineering Economist,* Vol. 24, Winter 1979, pp. 87–108), H. Levy and M. Sarnat ("Leasing, Borrowing, and Financial Risk," *Financial Management,* Vol. 8, Winter 1979, pp. 47–54), C.R. Idol ("A Note on Specifying Debt Displacement and Tax Shield Borrowing Opportunities in Financial Lease Valuation Models," *Financial Management,* Vol. 9, Summer 1980, pp. 24–29), R.G. Bowman ("The Debt Equivalence of Leases: An Empirical Investigation," *The Accounting Review,* Vol. 55, April 1980, pp. 237–253) and J. Ange and P. Peterson ("The Leasing Puzzle," *Journal of Finance,* September 1984, pp. 1055–1065). These contributions are discussed next.

ANALYZING A LEASE VERSUS PURCHASE PROBLEM. The pragmatic lease-purchase model presented here builds on the work of Schall ("The Lease-or-Buy and Asset Acquisition Decision," *Journal of Finance,* Vol. 29, September 1974, pp. 1203–1214). Specifically, this model will guide the analyst in three key areas:

1. The adjustment for risk differences in the cash flows.
2. The consideration of "bargain" lease terms that may reverse an un-favorable purchase decision.
3. The necessity for dealing with financial risk differences between leasing and purchase financing.

The model is designed to be practical. That is, it can be implemented using estimates that are both readily available and easily understood.

Schall has proposed that lease-purchase analyses be made using two net present value equations: one to measure the net present value on a project where purchase financing (composed of the firm's optimal debt-equity mix) is used, and the other reflecting the use of lease financing. The analyst, after having calculated both net present values, selects that method of financing which produces the largest positive net present value.

In the procedure discussed here a slightly different form of analysis is used. Specifically, the following two step procedure is used.

Step 1. The **net present value** (NPV) of the project is calculated for the purchase alternative. This calculation is completely analogous to that which is discussed in standard treatments of the capital budgeting problem.

Step 2. Regardless of whether NPV is found to be positive (signaling a favorable purchase decision) or negative (indicating the asset should not be purchased), the net present value advantage of leasing over purchasing (NAL) is calculated (Exhibit 4).

The decisions involved in the lease versus purchase analysis are outlined in the flowchart presented in Exhibit 3. First, the project's NPV is calculated. If that NPV is positive, the asset offers a positive contribution to the wealth of the firm's shareholders and its purchase is justified. However, even if NPV is positive, lease financing may be preferable to purchasing. Therefore, NAL is calculated. Leasing is preferred if NAL is positive; purchasing is preferred if it is negative.

EXHIBIT 3   THE LEASE VERSUS PURCHASE DECISION

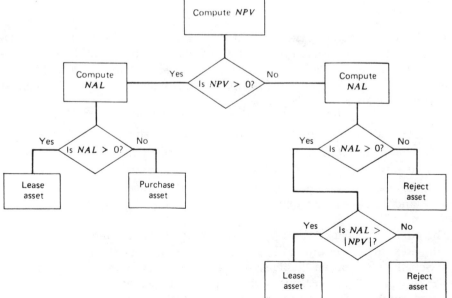

Returning to the top of Exhibit 3 where NPV is calculated, assume now that the calculated NPV is negative (e.g. −$20). Again NAL is calculated. However, this time the asset should not be purchased, since NPV is negative. Thus the only hope for the project lies in the existence of exceptionally favorable lease terms. In fact, for the asset to be worthy of acquisition (via lease), NAL must not only be positive but also greater than the absolute value of NPV. For example, if NPV is calculated to be −$20 and NAL is $10, the asset should not be leased, since the positive net present value advantage of leasing over purchasing is not large enough to offset the negative NPV associated with purchase financing.

The right-hand side of Exhibit 3 illustrates how to assess whether the firm has been offered a "bargain lease." As noted earlier, a number of lease-purchase models assume that the asset has passed an NPV hurdle before leasing is considered. This type of analysis fails to consider the possible availability of bargain lease terms. This is the objective of performing the analysis outlined on the right-hand side of the flowchart.

To demonstrate the use of the lease-purchase algorithm in Exhibit 3, an example problem is analyzed. Exhibit 4 contains both the NPV and NAL models, along with the definition of the symbols used by each. Note that NPV is calculated in the usual way. That is, first the project's expected future cash flows are estimated (i.e., the ACF_t). These cash flow estimates are then discounted back to the present, using **the cost of capital** or **required rate of return** relevant to the project. If the present value of the project's cash flows exceed the initial outlay needed to purchase the asset, purchase of the asset is justified.

Looking at the individual terms contained in NAL, we see that by leasing the asset the firm avoids certain expenses (e.g., maintenance and insurance), $O_t(1 - T)$, but incurs the aftertax rentals $R_t(1 - T)$. Furthermore, by leasing, the firm loses the tax shelters on interest TI_t, depreciation TD_t, and the interest on lost debt capacity $T\Delta I_t$. That is, if the asset were leased, there would be no equity financing, whereas, if the asset were purchased, it would be only partly debt financed. Thus, the $T\Delta I_t$ term represents the interest tax shelter on the "excess" leverage financing under the lease. Finally, the firm does not receive the salvage value from the asset V_n, but does not have to make the initial cash outlay to purchase the asset A_O. Thus we see that NAL reflects the cost savings associated with leasing net of the opportunity costs of not purchasing.

The firm's before tax borrowing or **debt rate** is employed to discount the contractual, tax shield, and operating expense flows because of their relative certainty. The contractual lease payments are relatively risk free, since they represent legal obligations of the lessee. Similarly, the various tax-shield flows are either fixed contractually as long as the firm has sufficient other income to continue paying taxes and tax rates are reasonably stable. Finally, it is assumed that the operating expenses covered by the lessor consist of predictable flows such as insurance and maintenance. Because these cash

EXHIBIT 4   THE LEASE-PURCHASE MODEL

NET PRESENT VALUE OF ASSET IF PURCHASED

Model

$$NPV = \sum_{t=1}^{n} \frac{ACF_t}{(1 + K)^t} - A_O$$

Definitions:

NPV = project net present value or expected contribution of project to wealth of firm's common shareholders

ACF_t = expected annual cash flow after taxes provided by project in year t; note that interest expense should not be deducted in arriving at ACF_t

K = firm's minimum acceptable rate of return given the project's riskiness; rate should reflect the risk attributable to the mixture of sources of funds (debt and equity) used to finance project; firm's weighted average cost of capital is often used

A_o = initial cash outlay required to purchase asset in period zero

n = productive life of asset

Note that ACF_n contains any salvage or residual value of the asset plus the *return of any working capital* invested in the project during its life.

NET PRESENT VALUE ADVANTAGE OF LEASING

Definitions:

O_t = any operating expense flows in period t that are incurred only if asset is purchased; most often this consists of maintenance and insurance expenses that would be paid by lessor

R_t = annual rental for period t

T = marginal tax rate on corporate income

I_t = tax-deductible interest expense foregone in period t if asset is leased rather than purchased; I_t is interest expenses in period t on funds that would be borrowed if asset is purchased

I_t = interest on debt that must be repaid if asset is leased to maintain firm's desired capital structure; recall that leasing entails 100% nonowner financing

D_t = depreciation expense in period t for asset

V_n = aftertax salvage value of asset expected in year n

K = discount rate used to find present value of V_n this rate should reflect risk inherent in estimated V; for simplicity, and to be consistent with computation of NPV, aftertax cost of capital is often used as a proxy for this rate

A_o = purchase price of asset, which is not paid by firm if asset is leased

r = rate of interest on borrowed funds; this rate is used to discount relatively certain contractual, tax-shield, and operating expense cash flows; note that this rate is not adjusted for taxes

streams are predictable, they can be discounted at a relatively low rate such as the firm's cost of borrowing (r). **Salvage value,** on the other hand, represents a highly uncertain cash flow and must be discounted at a higher rate. The firm's aftertax weighted average cost of capital is probably not an unreasonable approximation for this discount rate. This is particularly true if the value of V_n is based on a stream of expected earnings similar in riskiness to those of the firm as a whole. Alternatively, where V_n is simply scrap value, a certainty-equivalent approach may be employed (see M.C. Finlay, III, "Financial Lease Evaluation: Survey and Synthesis," *Financial Review*, 1974, pp. 1–15).

The two interest tax-shield terms in the NAL equation deserve mention. The first term, TI_t, represents the interest shield foregone if a lease rather than a loan is used to acquire the asset. On the other hand, the $T\Delta I_t$ term represents an adjustment for financial differences between the alternatives. Since leasing effectively involves 100% leverage financing, it "uses up" more of the firm's debt capacity than a purchase that involves a mix of debt and equity financing. For example, if the firm seeks to maintain a **target debt-equity ratio** by financing 40% of all acquisitions with owner's funds, it would have to repay outstanding debt equal to 60% of the asset's cost if it decided to lease in order to maintain its desired debt/equity mix. For simplicity, assume that $1 of lease is equivalent to $1 of loan. This is only one of several assumptions that might be used. Thus, $T\Delta I_t$ represents the lost interest shelter on the repaid debt. Of course, debt may not actually be repaid immediately. However, by leasing the asset, the firm will use more leveraged financing than the asset will support. Therefore, to maintain its target debt-equity ratio, the firm must use less leveraged financing on future projects. In other words, $T\Delta I_t$ represents the tax shield on the debt "displaced" by the lease.

Summary. The lease purchase analysis can be summarized as follows:

1. If NPV is positive, the asset should be acquired through the preferred financing method as indicated by NAL.
2. IF NPV is negative the asset's services should be acquired via the lease alternative only if NAL is greater than the absolute value of NPV. That is, the asset should be leased only if the cost advantage of lease financing (NAL) is great enough to offset the negative purchase NPV.

Thus, to evaluate a lease-purchase problem, the analyst must first calculate NPV. If NPV is positive, NAL is computed, and the appropriate method of financing for the asset can be chosen. However, NPV is negative, if NAL were greater than the absolute value of NPV.

The example discussed below is modified from the now standard problem posed by R.W. Johnson and W.G. Lewellen ("Analysis of the Lease-or-Buy Decision," *Journal of Finance*, September 1972, pp. 815–823). The B. Hilgen Manufacturing Co. (BHM) is presently involved in making a decision regarding the purchase of a new automatic casting machine. The machine will cost $15,000 and has an expected life of five years, at which time its aftertax salvage value will be $1,050. Note that the $1,050 is an after capital gain tax salvage value, where the asset is depreciated toward a zero expected

EXHIBIT 5   COMPUTING ANNUAL AFTERTAX CASH FLOWS, ACF_t

	Year, t				
	1	2	3	4	5
Annual cash revenues	$5,000	$5,000	$5,000	$5,000	$5,000
Less: Depreciation (ACRS)	(2,250)	(3,300)	(3,150)	(3,150)	(3,150)
Earnings before taxes	2,750	1,700	1,850	1,850	1,850
Less: Income taxes (46%)	1,265	782	851	851	851
Net Income	1,485	918	999	999	999
Plus: Depreciation (ACRS)	2,250	3,300	3,150	3,150	3,150
Annual aftertax cash flow (ACF_t)	3,735	4,218	4,149	4,149	4,149

salvage for tax purposes. The firm's marginal tax rate is 46%. **The Accelerated Cost Recovery System (ACRS)** is used to depreciate the asset.

The project is expected to generate net annual cash revenues of $5,000 per year over the next five years after cash operating expenses but before depreciation and taxes. BHM has a target debt ratio of 40% for projects of this type and estimates its aftertax cost of capital at 12%.

Step 1: Computing NPV. The first step in analyzing the lease-purchase problem involves computing the net present value under the purchase alternative. The relevant cash flow computations are presented in Exhibit 5.

The NPV then is found by discounting the ACF_t in Exhibit 5 back to the present at the firm's aftertax cost of capital of 12%, adding this sum to the present value of the salvage value, and subtracting the initial cash outlay. These calculations are contained in Exhibit 6. The project's NPV is a positive $237.43 indicating that the asset should be acquired. The next step is to

EXHIBIT 6   CALCULATING NPV (P)

Year, t	Annual Cash Flow (ACF_t)	+	Discount Factor for 12%	=	Present Value
1	3,735		.8929		3,334.98
2	4,218		.7972		3,362.59
3	4,149		.7118		2,953.26
4	4,149		.6355		2,636.69
5	4,149		.5674		2,354.14
5	1,050 (salvage)		.5674		595.77
Present value of ACFs and V_n					$15,237.42
NPV (P) = 15,237.43 − 15,000 =					237.43

EXHIBIT 7   TERM LOAN AMORTIZATION SCHEDULE
($6,000 LOAN AT 8%)

End of Year, t	Installment Payment, L	Interest, I_t	Principal Repayment, P_t	Remaining Balance, RB_t
1	$1,502.63	$480.00	$1,022.63	$4,977.37
2	1,502.63	398.19	1,104.44	3,872.93
3	1,502.63	309.83	1,192.80	2,680.13
4	1,502.63	214.41	1,288.22	1,391.91
5	1,502.63	111.35	1,391.28[a]	—

[a]This amount does not equal the remaining balance because of rounding errors.

determine how the acquisition should be financed. This can be determined by computing the net advantage to leasing (NAL).

Step 2: Computing NAL. To compute NAL one must first estimate the operating expenses associated with the asset that will be paid by the lessor (i.e., O_t). As discussed earlier, these cash expenses generally consist of certain maintenance expenses and insurance. BHM estimates these expenses at $1,111.11 per year over the life of the project. The annual rental payment R_t is $4,259.26.

Next, the **interest tax shelters** lost as a result of leasing the asset must be estimated. These tax shelters are lost because the firm's normal financing mix is not used and because the firm uses more than its target debt ratio allotment when it finances the asset with a lease. Determining these lost tax shelters involves the calculation of the principal and interest components of two different loans.

Exhibit 7 contains the computations for the $6,000 (0.40 × $15,000) loan used to finance the project under the purchase alternative. (The pretax debt rate is assumed to be 8%.) Note that the interest column supplies the needed information for the interest tax shelter that is lost if the asset is leased. Similarly, to compute ΔI_t the interest on that amount of debt that must be repaid to maintain the firm's target debt ratio must be determined. Since the target debt ratio is 40%, 60% of the purchase price of the asset (0.60 × $15,000 − $9,000) must be repaid. Thus, ΔI_t is found just as I_t was, except that the calculations are based on a $9,000 loan rather than a $6,000 loan. The relevant values for ΔI_t are given in the following:

Year t	Interest, ΔI_t
1	$720.00
2	596.81
3	464.17
4	321.59
5	168.65

Note that both I_t and ΔI_t constitute lost tax shelters where the asset is leased. Also, I_t and ΔI_t correspond to loans equal to 40% and 60% of the purchase price of the asset, respectively. Thus the sum of I_t and ΔI_t is the interest expense on a loan equal to 100% of the asset's purchase price A_o. A more direct and less tedious way to estimate the interest tax shelters lost through leasing would be to compute the annual interest expense on a loan equal to the full purchase price of the asset ($15,000 in the present example). Once all the necessary cash flows have been determined, they are substituted into the NAL equation. Exhibit 8 shows these computations.

To summarize the steps in the BHM Co. lease-purchase analysis, first the project's net present value was computed. This analysis produced a positive NPV of $237.43, which indicated that the asset should be acquired. However, on computing the net advantage to leasing, it was found that the financial lease is the preferred method of financing the acquisition of the asset's services. As shown in Exhibit 8, the net present value advantage to leasing is a positive $701. Thus the firm should lease the asset rather than purchase it.

This lease versus purchase model attempts to bridge the gap between financial theory and practice. It provides the practitioner with guidance on three specific issues: adjustment for risk differences in the cash flows, consideration of "bargain" lease terms, and correction for financial risk differences between the alternatives. The technique builds on the theoretical model of Schall and employs a simple debt-to-assets ratio to control for financial risk differences between leasing and purchasing. The reader interested in a more rigorous method for dealing with financial risk is directed to a similar model (C.L. Allen, J.D. Martin, and P.F. Anderson, "Debt Capacity and the Lease-Purchase Problem: A Sensitivity Analysis," *Engineering Economist,* Vol. 24, Winter 1979, pp. 87–108). This approach employs a **risk of insolvency** criterion to determine the amount of debt "displaced" by a lease.

EMPIRICAL ASSESSMENT OF INDUSTRY PRACTICE: ANALYSIS OF LEASING VERSUS PURCHASING. A survey of the "state of the art" in industry lease-purchase analysis was conducted in 1976 by Anderson and Martin (P.F. Anderson and J.D. Martin, "Lease vs. Purchase Decisions: A Survey of Current Practice," *Financial Management,* Spring 1977), using some of the 200 largest industrial firms in the United States listed by *Fortune* magazine. Each firm was given a lease versus purchase case problem and a short questionnaire. The case problem was a modified version of the example used in the well-known paper by Johnson and Lewellen, cited earlier.

A total of 48 usable responses were obtained. A distribution of respondent lease payments for 1974 is found in Exhibit 9. The majority of the responding firms were among the largest in the Fortune 200. Of the usable responses, 27 were from firms in the top 100 and 21 were from the top 150. Thus, the sample should indicate which methodologies are used by some of the most sophisticated segments of industry.

EXHIBIT 8 COMPUTING NET ADVANTAGE OF LEASING, NAL

Step 1:

Solve for: $\sum_{t=1}^{n} \dfrac{O_t(1-T) - R_t(1-T) - TI_t - T\Delta I_t - TD_t}{(1+r)^t}$

Year, t	Aftertax Operating Expenses Paid By Lessor, $O_t(1-T)$		Aftertax Rental Expense,[a] $R_t(1-T)$		Tax Shelter on Loan Interest,[a] $(TI_t + T\,I_t)$		Tax Shelter on Depreciation, TD_t	Total		Discount[b] Factor at 8% DF	Present Value PV
1	$600	−	2,300	−	552	−	1,035	−3,287	×	.9259	−3,043
2	600	−	2,300	−	458	−	1,518	−3,676		.8573	−3,151
3	600	−	2,300	−	356	−	1,449	−3,505		.7938	−2,782
4	600	−	2,300	−	247	−	1,449	−3,396		.7350	−2,496
5	600	−	2,300	−	129	−	1,449	−3,278		.6806	−2,231
											−13,703

Step 2:

Solve for: $-\dfrac{V_n}{(1+K)^n} = -\dfrac{\$1,050}{(1+0.12)^5} = -\$1,050 \times .5674 = -\$596$

Step 3: Add purchase price of asset (A_o) = +$15,000

Step 4: Net advantage of leasing, NAL = sum of (1), (2) and (3) = −$13,703 − 596 + 15,000 = $701

[a] This includes interest on the loan that is not used if the lease is undertaken plus interest on the amount of debt that must be repaid to maintain the target debt ratio. Thus for year 1 $(I_t + \Delta I_t)T = (\$480 + 720).46 = \$552$.

[b] The debt rate r equals 8%.

[c] The value of K was estimated to be the same as the firm's aftertax cost of capital, 12%.

EXHIBIT 9   DISTRIBUTION OF RESPONDENTS BY DOLLAR VALUE OF 1974 LEASE PAYMENTS

Dollar Value	Number of Firms	% of Firms
$100 million or over	2	4.3
$50–$100 million	8	17.4
$25–$50 million	12	26.1
$10–$25 million	13	28.3
Less than $10 million	11	23.9
	46[a]	100.0

[a]Note that two firms returned dual responses such that 48 lease-purchase analyses were available.

Source: Paul F. Anderson and John D. Martin, "Lease vs. Purchase Decisions: A Survey of Current Practice," *Financial Management* (Spring 1977), pp. 41–47.

Exhibit 10 contains a distribution of the methodologies employed by the respondents. The most used was the traditional internal rate of return model. For a description of the use of internal rate of return models, see, among others, T.H. Beechy, "Quasi-Debt Analysis of Financial Leases" (*Accounting Review,* Vol. 44, April 1969, pp. 375–381), R.C. Doenges, "The Cost of Leasing" (*Engineering Economist,* Vol. 17, Fall 1971, pp. 31–44), G.B. Mitchell, "After-Tax Cost of Leasing" (*Accounting Review,* Vol. 45, April 1970, pp. 308–314), G.D. Quirin, *The Capital Expenditure Decision* (Irwin, Homewood, IL, 1967).

The next most widely used model was the conventional net present value technique. For a discussion of the conventional net present value methodology, see Albert H. Cohen, *Long Term Leases—Problems of Taxation, Finance and Accounting* (University of Michigan Press, Ann Arbor, 1954), James C. Van Horne, *Financial Management and Policy,* 3rd ed., (Prentice-Hall, Englewood Cliffs, NJ, 1974). More than 70% of the respondents to the study by Anderson and Martin utilized one of these basic approaches to the

EXHIBIT 10   CLASSIFICATION OF RESPONDENTS' LEASE VERSUS PURCHASE ANALYSIS MODELS

Model	Frequency of Methodology
Traditional internal rate of return model	24
Conventional net present value model	11
Bierman and Smidt model (1966)	5
Basic interest rate model	4
Weston and Brigham model (1972)	2
Bower, Herringer, and Williamson model	2
	48

Source: Paul F. Anderson and John D. Martin, "Lease vs. Purchase Decisions: A Survey of Current Practice," *Financial Management* (Spring 1977), pp. 41–47.

analysis of the lease-purchase problem. The popularity of the internal rate of return method may well be attributable to a preference by practitioners for the use of rate of return methodology when evaluating financing cost. The relatively widespread use of the traditional net present value model might be due to its similarity to accepted capital budgeting procedures and the fact that this is one of the earliest models developed.

The third most widely used model was proposed in the second edition of *The Capital Budgeting Decision* (H. Bierman, Jr. and S. Smidt, Macmillan, New York, 1966). This model has been shown to be formally equivalent to the 1969 and 1972 Weston and Brigham models. Two of the respondents did indeed use the 1972 version of the Weston and Brigham model. The remaining respondents used either the basic interest rate method (Richard F. Vancil, "Lease or Borrow—New Method of Analysis," *Harvard Business Review,* Vol. 39, September–October 1961) or the BHW model (Richard S. Bower, Frank C. Herringer, and J. Peter Williamson, "Lease Evaluation," *Accounting Review,* Vol. 41, April 1966, pp. 257–275). The differences in these methods are slight, as noted by Findlay (M. Chapman Findlay, III, "Financial Lease Evaluation: Survey and Synthesis," *Financial Review,* 1974, pp. 1–15).

The survey findings indicate that many large industrial firms make use of lease-purchase models that produce results that are potentially biased in favor of purchasing. There are two potential sources of bias in the models used: First, a majority of the models do not properly adjust for risk differences in the cash flows attendant to the lease-purchase analysis. Second, many of the models require a justification of the investment on a purchase basis before leasing is considered.

Failure to adjust cash flows for risk differences will tend to overstate the costs of leasing in both net present value and internal rate of return models. The conventional net present value model, the basic interest rate model, and the Bower, Herringer, and Williamson models are all subject to this criticism. The source of bias against leasing is related to the use of a relatively high rate of interest, the weighted average cost of capital, to discount relatively certain contractual and tax-shield cash flows. The bias against leasing results because the cash flow benefits of a lease tend to outweigh its cash flow costs in the latter years of a project's life. Thus the use of an inordinately high rate of interest to discount these cash flows will have the effect of underemphasizing these benefits. There is no consensus among theorists on the proper discount rates; however, most agree that the cost of capital is too high a rate for discounting near riskless cash flows. For supporting arguments see R. S. Bower, "Issues in Lease Financing" (*Financial Management,* Vol. 2, Winter 1973, pp. 25–34), M. Chapman Findlay, III, "Financial Lease Evaluation: Survey and Synthesis" (*Financial Review,* 1974, pp. 1–15), Myron J. Gordon, "A General Solution to the Buy or Lease Decision: A Pedagogical Note" (*Journal of Finance,* Vol. 29, March 1974, pp. 245–250).

In the case of the traditional internal rate of return model, the discount rate bias is related to the failure of the model to consider the uncertainty of the asset's salvage value. This model enters salvage value into the internal rate of return calculation unadjusted for risk differences between the salvage value and the relatively certain tax shield and contractual cash flows. R.L. Roenfeldt and J.S. Osteryoung ("Analysis of Financial Leases," *Financial Management*, Vol. 2, Spring 1973, pp. 74–87) offer a modified internal rate of return methodology that utilizes a certainty equivalent adjustment to salvage value. However, none of the respondents cited uses this model.

The second type of bias inherent in many of the lease versus purchase models is related to the requirement that the project be adjudged worthy of purchase by the firm's capital budgeting procedure before lease financing is considered. This ex ante investment analysis fallacy has been recognized by a number of authors. See, for example, Harold Bierman, Jr., and Seymour Smidt, *The Capital Budgeting Decision,* 5th ed. (Macmillan, New York, 1980), C. Robert Carlson and Donald H. Wort, "A New Look at the Lease-vs.-Purchase Decision" (*Journal of Economics and Business,* Vol. 26, Spring 1974, pp. 199–202). A problem arises, however, because the acquisition of some projects may not be justified on a purchase basis but may be desirable when favorable lease terms are available. The Bierman and Smidt model is the only one of those used by the respondents that does not suffer from this bias.

In a follow-up survey of industry lease-purchase analysis practice, O'Brien and Nunnally (T.J. O'Brien and B.H. Nunnally, Jr., "A 1982 Survey of Corporate Leasing Analysis," *Financial Management,* Vol. 11, Summer 1983, pp. 30–36) found that some changes have occurred since the Anderson and Martin survey. First, just as in the earlier study, the 1982 respondents still required that a project clear the purchase hurdle before lease financing would be considered. Second, the cost of debt rather than the cost of capital appears to be the most widely used discount rate. Furthermore, the respondents were sophisticated in that, when the after-tax cost of debt was used to discount cash flows, the interest tax savings were properly omitted from the cash flows.

The above "true lease" requirements were effectively eliminated in 1981. In 1982 they were reinstated in a substantially modified form. We now trace these developments.

The Economic Recovery Tax Act of 1981 (ERTA) created the concept of a **"safe harbor lease."** Such a lease was not made subject to the "true lease" requirements of the Internal Revenue Service. Thus, safe harbor leases effectively opened the door for the use of financial lease agreements to sell or transfer the tax benefits accompanying asset ownership. For this reason, the safe harbor lease provision of ERTA gave rise to what became known as a **"tax benefit transfer lease"** or **"paper lease."** That is, financial leases were written only as a device for selling the tax benefits (i.e., investment tax credit, as well as depreciation and interest tax savings). However, the safe harbor lease was a highly controversial element of ERTA and it was eliminated with the passage of the **Tax Equity and Fiscal Responsibility Act of 1982 (TEFRA).** Technically, safe harbor leasing was repealed after December 31, 1983. In its place TEFRA created the **finance lease.**

A finance lease is actually a modification of the old true lease. According to TEFRA, the primary attributes of a finance lease are:

1. Equipment users have a three-month window after a new asset is placed in service to arrange lease financing. Previously the lease had to have been arranged prior to the date when the asset was placed in service.

2. The lessee may have the right to purchase the leased property at a fixed price, but not less than 10% of the property's original cost. Under the true lease requirements, the **exercise price** on a **purchase option** had to be the fair market value of the asset at the end of the lease term. Thus, the exercise price was random in the sense that neither lessee nor lessor could know its value in advance. With a fixed exercise price the lessor has the opportunity to assume the risk of fluctuation in asset's terminal value. To the extent that the lessor knows more about the asset's residual value than the lessee, and is willing to bear that risk for a price the lessee is willing to pay, this policy change promotes efficiency.

3. Under the **IRS advance ruling policy,** limited use property (i.e., property that cannot be used economically by someone other than the lessee) could not be leased. Under the modified finance lease rules, however, this property is now suitable for lease.

4. The lessor will not be able to reduce its tax liability by more than 50% due to tax benefits related to finance leases.

5. The lessor cannot carryback tax benefits in excess of 50% of its tax liability.

6. A maximum of 40% of the lessee's property can be leased using finance leases.

7. The lessor is required to spread the investment tax credit on leased property evenly over the five year period beginning with the year the asset is placed in service.

8. Public utility property and property for rehabilitation tax credits are specifically excluded from use of finance leases.

LEASING FROM THE LESSOR'S PERSPECTIVE: ANALYZING A LEVERAGED LEASE ARRANGEMENT

Leveraged Lease Arrangements. A leveraged lease arrangement can be complex. An excellent overview of the details involved in establishing a leveraged lease is found in N.B. Stiles and M.A. Walker, "Leveraged Lease Financing of Capital Equipment" (*Journal of Commercial Bank Lending,* July 1973, pp. 19–39). The essence of the arrangement need not be so complex. This discussion draws on P.R. Smith, "A Straight Forward Approach to Leveraged Leasing" (*Journal of Commercial Bank Lending,* July 1973, pp. 40–47). There are three principal participants in the typical leveraged lease arrangement:

1. The **lessee** or company that will use the leased asset.
2. The **lessor** or owner of the asset (sometimes referred to as the equity participant). The lessor is frequently a financial institution.
3. The **debt participant or lender,** which is a second financial institution.

The basic steps involved in arranging a leveraged lease are as follows:

1. The **lessee** selects the specific asset he desires and usually suggests the term over which he would like to lease it.
2. The **lessor** (owner participant) arranges for a loan of 60–80% of the asset's purchase price and supplies the balance of the funds needed to acquire the asset.
3. The **debt participant** (lender) will generally obtain a **chattel mortgage** on the full value of the leased equipment as well as an assignment of the lease payments. Note that the lender must look to the mortgaged asset's value and the assigned lease payments as the security for his loan.

In preparing a leveraged lease agreement, the lessor must be very careful to follow the guidelines of the IRS. That is, if the IRS disallows a leveraged lease on the grounds that it is in fact a **conditional sales contract,** the lessor cannot claim the tax benefits associated with ownership of the leased asset (i.e., depreciation, investment tax credit, and interest expense). The IRS has stated, "In ascertaining such intent no single test, or special combination of tests, is absolutely determinative. No general rule applicable to all cases can be laid down. Each case must be decided in light of its particular facts" (Rev. Rul. 55–540, Section 4.01). Briefly, the IRS tests of a true lease prior to the revisions to the tax code occurring in 1981 and 1982 were as follows:

1. As owner, the lessor must bear the risk of ownership, which includes the possible decline in economic value of the equipment.
2. The lessee cannot build up equity interest in the leased equipment with lease payments, nor can the lessee assume title after making a specified number of lease payments. If the equipment is sold or released at the end of the lease term, it must be at a value not less than an **"arm's-length" fair market value.**
3. Rental payments that materially exceed the fair market rental over the

lease term may be construed to be building up an equity interest in the property.

4. The lease term must be less than the economic life of the equipment so that the equipment has a residual value of at least 15% of its original value and an economic life of at least two years or 10% (whichever is greater) of the lease term.

These tests are not ironclad, and previous IRS rulings give evidence or room for flexibility. For this reason, lessors generally seek an opinion from the IRS on any new leases before consummating agreements.

Setting Lease Terms. The lessor is faced with the problem of determining lease terms (payments) every time a new lease is written. The problem is similar to that of the banker who must determine a set of installment payments that will provide the desired rate of return on a loan. The major differences in the positions of the lessor and the lender are that the lessor owns an asset that can be depreciated, whose acquisition may produce an **investment tax credit,** and the lessor will receive any **salvage value** resulting from the disposal of the asset at the termination of the lease. An interesting discussion of the risks inherent in leasing can be found in E.R. Packham, "An Analysis of the Risks of Leveraged Leasing" (*Journal of Commercial Bank Lending,* March 1975, pp. 2–29). This author notes that the greatest risks associated with lessor tax savings relate to the possibility that the IRS will rule that the lease is not a "true lease" (see previous discussion of the true lease requirements), in which case the lessor could not claim the tax shelters associated with ownership (e.g., the incremental tax credit and depreciation expense).

In general terms, the **lessor pricing model** can be characterized as follows:

$$A_O = PV[L] + PV[DTS] + ITC + PV[ITS] + PV[S]$$

where A_O represents the purchase price of the leased equipment; $PV[L]$ is the present value of the aftertax lease payments L discounted at a rate commensurate with their riskiness (it is generally recommended that the cost of borrowing be used); $PV[DTS]$ is the present value of the tax savings accruing to the lessor as a result of depreciation charges (again, the cost of borrowed funds is frequently used to discount these tax savings); ITC is the **investment tax credit** accruing to the lessor in the year in which the asset is acquired; $PV[ITS]$ is the present value of the interest tax savings realized by the lessor due to the tax deductibility of interest expense (the cost of debt is traditionally used to discount these tax savings); and $PV[S]$ is the present value of the estimated aftertax salvage value of the asset upon termination of the lease.

The discount rate used to evaluate the asset's salvage value is one that is commensurate with the risks associated with that salvage value. The determination of such a rate is difficult, and no easy solution to the problem of its estimation exists. The estimation of residual or salvage values remains one of the most difficult issues encountered in evaluating lease terms. In many instances the lessor simply assumes a zero salvage value for the sake of conservatism. This results in the setting of higher lease terms, which may make the lessor noncompetitive. In another approach that has been suggested to deal with this problem the lessor evaluates the residual value in an option pricing framework. (See W.Y. Lee, A. J. Senchack, and J.D. Martin, "The Case for Using Options to Evaluate Salvage Values in Financial Leases," *Financial Management,* Autumn 1982, pp. 33–39).

The proposed methodology involves the potential use of an **option straddle** on the **residual value** where the range of values the asset's terminal value can take on is restrained. The straddle involves the simultaneous sale of a call option and purchase of a put option on the residual value of the leased asset. The effective use of the strategy depends, of course, on the availability of a market for the needed options. A related discussion of the salvage value problem involved in setting lease terms can be found in J.K. Malernee and R.C. Witt, "Equipment Price Insurance: An Emerging Market" (*Bests Review,* Vol. 79, June 1978, pp. 22, 26, 96, 97).

The lessor's pricing problem involves the determination of a stream of aftertax lease payments L whose present value, when combined with that of the other elements on the righthand side of the lessor pricing model, will add up to A_O. This set of lease payments represents the minimum the lessor can charge the lessee and still earn his required rate of return.

There are two fundamental methods that can be used to evaluate a leveraged lease: the **net present value method** and the **internal rate of return method.** The latter had led to a great deal of discussion in the literature (see, for example, W.J. Regan, "The Dual Aspect of Leveraged Leasing," *Banker's Magazine,* Autumn 1976, pp. 75–77).

The problem of **multiple internal rates of return,** which is sometimes encountered in using this method, is related to the fact that the net cash flows to the lessor from a leveraged lease are positive during the early years, then negative in the latter years of the lease. The result is that there can be as many internal rates of return as there are changes in the sign of the project's future cash flows. Hence, for the leveraged lease with two such sign changes, there are two possible internal rates of return.

Internal rate of return methodologies are not further discussed here since the present value method is recognized as providing a more correct solution to the problem. Interestingly, Regan recognized the superiority of the present value approach but presented another rate of return criterion based on the perception that practitioners are wedded to the use of rates of return in the evaluation of new projects. No such assumption is made in the exposition presented here.

Setting Lease Terms: An Example. In this simple example a lessor uses the lessor pricing model to set terms on a leveraged lease. The details of the proposed lease are set out in Exhibit 11. Solving for the lease terms (lease payments) involves two steps:

Step 1. Rearrange the terms in the lessor pricing model as follows:

$$PV(L) = A_O - PV[DTS] - ITC - PV[ITS] - PV[S]$$

and solve for $PV[L]$.

Step 2. Having solved for the present value of the aftertax future lease payments $PV(L)$, solve for the annual lease payment annuity cash flow L, which has a present value (when discounted at the lessor's required rate of return on the lease payments) equal to the $PV[L]$ found in step 1. If these aftertax lease payments are charged, the lessor will expect to realize a rate of return equal to its required rate of return. The actual lease payments equal L (as solved above) divided by 1 minus the lessor's marginal tax rate.

Exhibit 12 contains the cash flow information required to analyze $PV[L]$ in step 1. Having solved for $PV[L]$, the analyst can solve for an annuity payment L with a 15-year term (N), which has a present value of $27,800, when discounted at the lessor's required rate of return on the lease payments.

EXHIBIT 11   LEVERAGED LEASE PROBLEM

Leased Asset

Railroad car

Cash Flow Information

Acquisition price (A_O) = $100,000
Lease term (N) = 15 years

Depreciation
Method = ACRS
Depreciable life = 11 years
Salvage value = 0.05 A_O = $5,000

Loan Information
Loan amount = 0.75 A_O = $75,000
Interest rate, r = 0.10 or 10%
Term = 15 years
Type of loan = interest only with full principal due at end of year 15

Solution
Investment tax credit = 0.10 A_O
Lessor's required rate of return on leased asset's salvage value = 0.20 or 20%
Lessor's marginal tax rate = 0.46 or 46%

EXHIBIT 12 ESTIMATING PRESENT VALUE OF LEASE PAYMENTS IN THE LESSOR PRICING MODEL ($ THOUSANDS)

Solving for $PV[L] = A_O - PV[DTS] - ITC - PV[ITS] - PV[S]$

Year	Depreciation Tax Savings, $(DTS)^a$	+	Interest Tax Savings, $(ITS)^b$	=	Sum of DTS + ITS	×	Discount Factor^c	=	Present Value of (DTS + ITS)
1	$2.19		$3.45		$5.64		.9091		$5.13
2	4.37		3.45		7.82		.8264		6.46
3	3.93		3.45		7.38		.7513		5.54
4	3.50		3.45		6.95		.6830		4.75
5	3.06		3.45		6.51		.6209		4.04
6	3.06		3.45		6.51		.5645		3.67
7	2.62		3.45		6.07		.5132		3.12
8	2.62		3.45		6.07		.4665		2.83
9	2.62		3.45		6.07		.4241		2.57
10	2.62		3.45		6.07		.3855		2.34
11	2.62		3.45		6.07		.3505		2.13
12	2.62		3.45		6.07		.3186		1.93
13	2.62		3.45		6.07		.2837		1.76
14	2.62		3.45		6.07		.2633		1.60
15	2.62		3.45		6.07		.2394		1.45

$$PV(DTS + ITS) = 49.32$$
$$ITC = 0.10 \times \$100 = \$10$$
$$PV[S]^d = \$5 \times 0.0649 = \$0.32$$
$$A_O = \$100$$

Therefore $PV[L] = \$100 - 49.32 - 10 - 0.32$
$= \$40.36$ or $\$40,360$

$^a DTS$ = depreciation expense for the year × marginal tax rate.

$^b ITS$ = interest expense for the year × marginal tax rate. Since the interest component of the assumed loan is constant at $10,000 per year, these annual tax savings equal $10,000 × 0.46 = $4,600.

^{c}Based on the cost of borrowing to the lessor ($r = 10\%$).

^{d}The present value of the asset's salvage or terminal value is calculated here by using the lessor firm's cost of capital of 20%. It is not clear that this rate is appropriate, however, since S is almost certainly more risky than the other cash flows being discounted, a rate higher than the lessor's cost of borrowing justifies.

For this example, the lessor's required return is set equal to the borrowing rate of 10%. Parenthetically, it can argued that the risks inherent in the lessor's receipt of the lease payments are the same as those involved in the lender's receipt of principal and interest on the loan that underlies 75% of the purchase price of the asset. In this case, the required rate of return of the lender on the loan ($r = 10\%$ in this instance), should be the appropriate required rate of return on the lease payments. The lessor, of course, is free to set whatever required rate he feels is commensurate with the risks associated with the lease agreement. However, setting too high a required return will produce a set of lease payments so high that the lease will be unattractive to the lessee. Nevertheless, the basic point is that the lessor must set the rate of return on the lease payments at a level that he would be happy to receive if the lease agreement were consummated. Solving for the lease payments:

$$PV[L] = \$36,540$$

or

$$L \sum_{t=1}^{15} \frac{1}{(1 + 0.10)^t} = \$40,360$$

where

$$\sum_{t=1}^{15} \frac{1}{(1 + 0.10)^t} = \text{the annuity discount factor of 10\%}$$
for 15 years (obtained from a table of discount factors)

Therefore

$$L(7.6061) = \$40,360.00$$
$$L = \$\ 5,306.27$$

The pretax lease payments are $L/(1 - T)$ or $\$5,306.27/(1 - 0.46) = \$9,826.43$.

The lessor can now set the terms of the lease at \$9,826.43 per year. Given these lease payments and the remaining estimated cash flows associated with the lease agreement, the lessor will expect to earn his required rate of return on the lease agreement.

ACCOUNTING FOR LEASES

HISTORICAL PERSPECTIVE. This section relies heavily on J.D. Martin, P.F. Anderson, and A.J. Keown, "**Lease Capitalization** and Stock Price Stability: Implications for Accounting" (*Journal of Accounting, Auditing and Finance,*

Vol. 2, Winter 1979, pp. 151–163). The debate over whether leases should be capitalized and included in the lessee's balance sheet spanned almost three decades (see, e.g., A.J. Cannon, "Danger Signal to Accountants in 'Net Lease' Financing," *Journal of Accountancy,* Vol. 85, April 1948, pp. 312–319). Throughout the debate the official accounting literature consistently supported the notion of more complete disclosure of the lessee's lease commitments; however, until recently, that literature did not support capitalization of most types of leases.

Accounting Research Bulletin (ARB) No. 38. "Disclosure of Long-Term Leases in Financial Statements of Lessees," issued by the American Institute of Certified Public Accountants (AICPA) in 1949, provided the first official pronouncement concerning the reporting of leases by lessees. This bulletin recommended disclosure of material commitments under long-term leases. In addition, leases that were in effect **installment purchases** were to be capitalized. However, only general guidelines were provided for the determination of the types of leases which should be considered installment purchases.

ARB No. 38 was also noteworthy in that it provided the basis for the legal argument for noncapitalization of leases. That is, it was argued that only leases that give rise to debt in a strict legal sense should be capitalized. The legal argument is founded on the premise that leases are **executory contracts.** In an executory contract, both parties to the contract have continuing agreements that are not fulfilled until the contract is terminated. If leases are indeed executory, it is argued, they cannot give rise to assets and liabilities as generally defined by the accounting profession and should not be capitalized. Indeed, a number of authors have argued that a lease is primarily executory. (See Donald C. Cook, "The Case Against Capitalizing Leases," *Harvard Business Review,* Vol. 41, January–February 1963, D.M. Hawkins and M.M. Wehle, *Accounting for Leases,* Financial Executives Research Foundation, New York, 1973; and Alvin Zises, "Long-Term Leases: Case Against Capitalization for Full Disclosures," *Financial Analysts Journal,* Vol. 18, May–June 1962, pp. 13–20).

Accounting Research Study No. 4. This report (John H. Myers, "Reporting of Leases in Financial Statements," AICPA, New York, 1962) concluded that certain types of financial leases give rise to "property rights" and should be capitalized. The report became one of the early pronouncements of the "economic" argument for lease capitalization, namely, that "the substance of the transaction should take precedence over its legal form" (D.M. Hawkins and M.M. Wehle, *Accounting for Leases,* Financial Executives Research Foundation, New York, 1973, p. 23). Thus, it was argued that a lease has the same basic economic consequences as debt and therefore should be treated similarly.

Specifically, Accounting Research Study No. 4 recommended lease capitalization for those leases meeting the following provisions:

1. The lease covers substantially the entire useful life of the leased property.
2. The lessee can purchase the property at the termination of the lease for a nominal price.
3. The contract is noncancelable.
4. The lessee pays fixed amounts sufficient to return to the lessor his investment in the property under lease plus a fair return.
5. The lessee pays the taxes, insurance, maintenance, and other ancillary costs associated with the leased property.

The Accounting Principles Board did not, however, adopt the recommendations of Accounting Research Study No. 4. Instead, it took the more moderate position of Accounting Research Bulletin No. 38.

Accounting Principles Board Opinion No. 5. In 1964 the AICPA issued APB Opinion No. 5, "Reporting of Leases in Financial Statements of Lessee," stating that a lease should be capitalized "only in the case in which it is in substance a purchase." In addition, this opinion further clarified the criteria to be used in determining when a lease is essentially a purchase. The opinion also added footnotes disclosure requirements for lessee balance sheets.

Accounting Principles Board Opinion No. 31 and Accounting Series Release No. 147. APB Opinion No. 31 ("Disclosure of Lease Commitments by Lessees," AICPA, New York, June 1973) further strengthened the footnote disclosure requirements of APB Opinion No. 5. Meanwhile the **Securities and Exchange Commission** issued Accounting Series Release No. 147 ("Notice of Adoption of Amendments to Regulation S-X Requiring Improved Disclosure of Leases," SEC, Washington, D.C., October 5, 1973). This document included even more stringent footnote disclosure requirements for lessees than did APB Opinion No. 31.

LEASE CAPITALIZATION. Finally, in November 1976 the accounting profession relented and for the first time called for the capitalization of most financial lease agreements. The Financial Accounting Standards Board adopted the basic premise of the "economic argument for capitalization." That is, the economic effect of the transaction should govern its accounting treatment (Financial Accounting Standards Board, Statement of Financial Accounting Standards (SFAS) No. 13, "Accounting for Leases," p. 49). The FASB took the point of view that "a lease that transfers substantially all the benefits and risks incident to the ownership of property should be accounted for as the acquisition of an asset and the incurrence of an obligation by the lessee" (SFAS No. 13, p. 49). The Statement further says that capitalized leases neet not be "in substance purchases" as was the case in Accounting Principles Board Opinion No. 5.

SFAS No. 13 specifically requires capitalization of all lessee lease agreements that satisfy one or more of the following criteria (pp. 9–10):

1. The lease transfers ownership of the property to the lessee by the end of the lease term.
2. The lease contains a bargain purchase option.
3. The lease term is equal to 75% or more of the estimated economic life of the leased property.
4. The present value of the minimum lease payments equals or exceeds 90% of the excess of the fair value of the leased property over any related investment tax credit retained by the lessor.

The last two requirements are the operational elements in the Board's statement. The first two have not been applicable to most leases for many years because of the Internal Revenue Service's **true lease** requirements (Rev. Rul. 55–540, 1955 CB 41). However, criteria 3 and 4 apply to the majority of the financial leases written in the United States. As a result, most financial leases entered into during 1977 appear in the body of the lessee's balance sheet. Moreover, the Board encouraged immediate retroactive application of the standards, and it requires such application after December 31, 1980.

SFAS No. 13 provides a landmark in terms of the accounting treatment of leases. Since the appearance of this statement, numerous refinements have been made and more are sure to come. Exhibit 13 contains a brief summary of some of these refinements.

STOCK PRICES AND LEASE CAPITALIZATION. The impact of capitalized lease disclosure on the price of the lessee's common stock has been studied by Ro (Byung T. Ro, "The Disclosure of Capitalized Lease Information and Stock Prices," *Journal of Accounting Research,* Vol. 16, Autumn 1978, pp. 315–340). The specific capitalization requirement tested was SEC Accounting Series Release No. 147 ("Notice of Adoption of Amendments to Regulation S-X Requiring Improved Disclosure of Leases," SEC, Washington, D.C., October 5, 1973, in SEC Docket October 23, 1973). ASR No. 147, which became effective as of November 30, 1973, required the disclosure of lease information that had not previously been called for by the SEC or other accounting regulatory bodies. The release required disclosure of the following items related to noncapitalized financing leases: (1) the present value (PV) of the minimum future lease commitments, (2) the interest rate(s) implicit in computing the PV, and (3) the impact on net income, i.e., the income effect (IE), if such leases were capitalized. Detailed disclosure requirements are not presented here because they are not crucial to the interpretation of the Ro test findings.

Ro developed a battery of tests to determine the impact of ASR No. 147 lease disclosure requirements on the price of common stock. These tests can be separated into two distinct groups of tests. One group tested PV disclosure firms. The second group tested firms that used both PV and IE

EXHIBIT 13   ACCOUNTING PRINCIPLES RELATED TO LEASES

STATEMENTS OF FINANCIAL ACCOUNTING STANDARDS[a]

SFAS 13	Accounting for Leases
SFAS 17	Accounting for Leases—Initial Direct Costs
SFAS 22	Changes in the Provisions of Lease Agreements Resulting from Refundings of Tax-Exempt Debt
SFAS 23	Inception of the Lease
SFAS 26	Profit Recognition on Sales-Type Leases of Real Estate
SFAS 27	Classification of Renewals or Extensions of Existing Sales-Type or Direct Financing Leases
SFAS 28	Accounting for Sales with Leasebacks
SFAS 29	Determining Contingent Rentals

FASB INTERPRETATIONS[b]

No. 19	Lessee Guarantee of the Residual Value of Leased Property
No. 21	Accounting for Leases in a Business Combination
No. 23	Leases of Certain Property Owned by a Governmental Unit or Authority
No. 24	Leases Involving Only Part of a Building
No. 26	Accounting for Purchase of Leased Asset by the Lessee During the Term of the Lease
No. 27	Accounting for a Loss on a Sublease

[a]The Financial Accounting Standards Board (FASB) was established in 1973 and had issued 34 Statements of Financial Accounting Standards (SFAS) by October 1979. SFASs are similar in scope to both the Accounting Research Bulletins and Accounting Principles Board Opinions that preceded them. The SFASs amend and supersede these existing pronouncements and establish generally accepted accounting principles in new areas.

[b]These statements represent FASB interpretations of existing pronouncements.

disclosure. Both test groups were comprised of six different tests made during six sample periods between January 1973 and September 1974.

Key dates in this period were the announcement of the proposal (June 1973), adoption of the proposal (October 1973), the effective date of the release (November 1973), and the first disclosure (March 1974). Note that all test firms had a December 31 fiscal year-end; thus the first disclosure of lease information was March 1974 for all firms. Results of the PV test group are summarized below (Byung T. Ro, "The Disclosure of Capitalized Lease Information and Stock Prices," *Journal of Accounting Research,* Vol. 16, Autumn 1978, p. 331):

> To summarize, evidence from the test results for the PV disclosure firms suggests that the disclosure of capitalized lease information as required by the SEC had no significant effect upon the pricing of securities. This implies that the PV numbers of noncapitalized financing leases, as disclosed under ASR No. 147, did not carry new information to investors for assessing the risk-return attributes of firms with such leases.

The test results for the PV and IE disclosure group were markedly different from those of the PV group. The findings suggested that the lease information disclosure did affect stock prices for five of the six subperiods tested. These results are summarized by Ro as follows (pp. 335–336):

> To summarize, the test results for the PV-IE firms suggest that the information effects of the various events of the SEC lease decision were present when the effects were measured by the changes in the expected values of return distributions. The results also reveal that the market reaction began as early as March 1973, indicating that the effects of the capitalized lease disclosure (as required by the SEC) were anticipated by the investment community prior to the disclosure of the capitalized lease numbers through accounting sources.

> The results also show that the capitalized lease disclosure did, overall, have an adverse effect on the valuation of the firms, although a slight upward readjustment of the security prices upon the disclosure of the capitalized lease data was observed for the low-risk firms. This upward readjustment may indicate that the negative effects of the PV and IE numbers (especially the latter) on various financial ratios were not as bad as investors had originally anticipated.

LEASE CAPITALIZATION AND FINANCIAL RATIOS. The capitalization of financial lease obligations can have a significant impact on computed financial ratios that involve either total liabilities or total assets. For example, the debt ratio (total liabilities divided by total assets) is increased by the inclusion of capitalized leases. Likewise the return on total assets (net aftertax profits divided by total assets) is reduced when capitalized leases are considered.

Altman et al. (E.I. Altman, R.G. Haldeman, and P. Narayanan, "ZETA™ Analysis: A New Model to Identify Bankruptcy Risk of Corporations," *Journal of Banking and Finance,* Vol. 1, 1977, pp. 29–54) report that in the sample of nonbankrupt firms analyzed, capitalized leases were 17–18% of total assets (including capitalized leases, or 20.5–22% of total assets before lease capitalization). In addition, for bankrupt firms, capitalized leases averaged 23% of total assets (or 30% of total assets before lease capitalization).

To illustrate the impact of lease capitalization on financial ratios, consider the following. Using 17.5% as the ratio of capitalized leases to total assets, a firm with a debt ratio of 50% before capitalization will have a postcapitalization ratio of 57% (i.e., using an asset base of $100 the pre-capitalization debt to asset ratio is 50/100. Now, with $17.5 in capitalized leases, the debt ratio is $(50 + 17.5)/(100 + 17.5) = .57)$. Similarly, if the firm's precapitalization return on assets were 20%, the return after capitalization would drop to 17%.

The Ro study, discussed above, found virtually no impact of lease capitalization on equity value. This result would suggest that the impact of lease capitalization on financial ratios was known to investors prior to capitalization. Before the issuance of FASB Statement of Financial Accounting Standards No. 13, which required lease capitalization of most types of financial leases, generally accepted accounting practice (APB Opinion No. 31) required substantial footnote disclosure of financial lease obligations. Lease capitalization, however, may have a detrimental effect on a firm's ability to obtain financing on favorable terms when a relatively unsophisticated lender is involved. Furthermore, some equity investors may be so naive as to be unable to properly evaluate uncapitalized leases. However, any fears that a firm may have about the unfavorable impact of capitalization of its lease obligations are based on the presumed naiveté of its financial statement users.

LEASE CAPITALIZATION AND BANKRUPTCY PREDICTION. The prediction of firm failure provides a dramatic and important testing ground for the "usefulness" of reported accounting information. R. Elam ("The Effect of Lease Data on the Predictive Ability of Financial Ratios," *Accounting Review,* January 1975, pp. 25–43) concluded that there is no evidence of improved predictability of bankruptcy that results from the use of lease data in the predictor set of financial ratios. Altman (E.I. Altman, "Capitalization of Leases and the Predictability of Financial Ratios: A Comment," Vol. 1, *Accounting Review,* April 1976, pp. 408–412) questioned Elam's findings on both conceptual and empirical grounds. In an extensive analysis of the bankruptcy prediction problem (E.I. Altman, R.G. Haldeman, and P. Narayanan, "ZETA® Analysis: A New Model to Identify Bankruptcy Risk of Corporations") provide evidence that lease data disclosed in lessee financial statements is indeed useful. The ZETA model was successful in identifying firms that would eventually become bankrupt up to five years before their actual failure. Specifically, over 90% of the firms were accurately predicted to go bankrupt or remain nonbankrupt one year before the date of failure, and 70% were correctly predicted up to five years before the failure of the bankrupt group.

A number of adjustments were made to reported accounting data before the **ZETA model** was developed. Altman et al. (1977, p. 33) made the following statement about lease capitalization: "Without doubt, the most important and pervasive adjustment made was to capitalize all noncancellable operating and finance leases." The resulting ZETA model was more accurate than the original Altman **Z-Score model** (E.I. Altman, "Financial Ratios, Discriminant Analysis and the Prediction of Corporate Bankruptcy," *Journal of Finance,* Vol. 23, September 1968, pp. 589–609) for predictions made two to five years before bankruptcy and provided roughly equivalent predictive accuracy one year before failure.

SECURITY POSITION IN BANKRUPTCY. The security position of the lessor in bankruptcy is generally considered to be superior to that of the firm's general creditors and even the mortgage lenders. If the lessee defaults on the lease payments of a realty lease, the lessor can promptly obtain a court order and taken possession of his property. In the event the lessee firm becomes bankrupt and is liquidated, the lessor's claim to damages is limited to a formula that was recently revised under the **Bankruptcy Reform Act of 1978.**

REFERENCES AND BIBLIOGRAPHY

Anderson, Paul F., and Martin, John D., "Lease vs. Purchase Decisions: A Survey of Current Practice," *Financial Management,* Vol. 6, Spring 1977, pp. 41–47.

Beechy, Thomas H., "Quasi-Debt Analysis of Financial Leases," *Accounting Review,* Vol. 44, April 1969, pp. 375–381.

———"The Cost of Leasing: Comment and Correction," *Accounting Review,* Vol. 45, October 1970, pp. 769–773.

Bierman, Harold, Jr., "Analysis of the Lease-or-Buy Decision: Comment," *Journal of Finance,* Vol. 28, September 1973, pp. 1019–1021.

———, and Hass, Jerome E., "Capital Budgeting Under Uncertainty: A Reformulation," *Journal of Finance,* Vol. 28, March 1977, pp. 119–129.

———, and Smidt, Seymour, *The Capital Budgeting Decision,* 4th ed., Macmillan, New York, 1980.

Bower, Richard S., "Issues in Lease Financing," *Financial Management,* Vol. 2, Winter 1973, pp. 25–34.

Bower, Richard S., Herringer, Frank C., and Williamson, J. Peter, "Lease Evaluation," *Accounting Review,* Vol. 41, April 1966, pp. 257–265.

Carlson, C. Robert, and Wort, Donald H., "A New Look at the Lease-Vs.-Purchase Decision," *Journal of Economics and Business,* Vol. 26, Spring 1974, pp. 199–202.

Clark, Robert A., Jantorni, Joan M., and Gann, Robert R., "Analysis of the Lease-or-Buy Decision: Comment," *Journal of Finance,* Vol. 28, September 1973, pp. 1015–1016.

Cohen, Albert H., *Long Term Leases—Problems of Taxation, Finance and Accounting,* University of Michigan Press, Ann Arbor, 1954.

Cooper, Kerry, and Strawser, Robert H., "Evaluation of Capital Investments Projects Involving Asset Leases," *Financial Management,* Vol. 4, Spring 1975, pp. 44–49.

Copeland, Thomas E. and Weston, J. Fred, "A Note on the Evaluation of Cancellable Operating Leases," *Financial Management,* (Summer 1982), pp. 60–67.

Doenges, R. Conrad, "The Cost of Leasing," *Engineering Economist,* Vol. 17, Fall 1971, pp. 31–44.

Fabozzi, Frank J. and Yaari, Uzi, "Valuation of Safe Harbor Tax Benefit Transfer Leases," *Journal of Finance,* Vol. 38, (May 1983), pp. 595–606.

Findlay, M. Chapman, III, "Financial Lease Evaluation: Survey and Synthesis," *Financial Review,* 1974, pp. 1–15.

Franks, Julian R. and Hodges, Stewart D., "Valuation of Financial Lease Contracts: A Note," *Journal of Finance,* Vol. 33, (May 1978), pp. 657–669.

Grimlund, Richard A. and Capettini, Robert, "A Note on the Evaluation of Leveraged Leases and Other Investments," *Financial Management,* (Summer 1982), pp. 68–72.

Johnson, Robert W., and Lewellen, Wilbur G., "Analysis of the Lease-or-Buy Decision," *Journal of Finance,* Vol. 27, September 1972, pp. 815–823.

———, "Reply," *Journal of Finance,* Vol. 28, September 1973, pp. 1024–1028.

Lev, Baruch, and Orgler, Yair E., "Analysis of the Lease-or-Buy Decision: Comment," *Journal of Finance,* Vol. 28, September 1973, pp. 1022–1023.

Lewellen, Wilbur G., Long, Michael S., and McConnell, John J., "Asset Leasing in Competitive Capital Markets," *Journal of Finance,* Vol. 31, June 1976, pp. 787–798.

Lusztig, Peter, "Analysis of the Lease-or-Buy Decision: Comment," *Journal of Finance,* Vol. 28, September 1973, pp. 1017–1018.

Martin, John D., Petty, J. William, Keown, Arthur J., and Scott, David F., Jr., *Basic Financial Management,* Prentice-Hall, Englewood Cliffs, NJ, 1979.

Mitchell, G.B., "After-Tax Cost of Leasing," *Accounting Review,* Vol. 45, April 1970, pp. 308–314.

Myers, Stewart C., "Interactions of Corporate Financing and Investment Decisions—Implications for Capital Budgeting," *Journal of Finance,* Vol. 29, March 1974, pp. 1–25.

———, Dill, David A., and Bautista, Alberto J., "Valuation of Financial Lease Contracts," *Journal of Finance,* Vol. 31, June 1976, pp. 799–819.

———, and Pogue, Gerald A., "A Programming Approach to Corporate Financial Management," *Journal of Finance,* Vol. 29, May 1974, pp. 579–600.

Quirin, G. David, *The Capital Expenditure Decision,* Irwin, Homewood, IL, 1967.

Roenfeldt, Rodney L., and Osteryoung, Jerome S., "Analysis of Financial Leases," *Financial Management,* Vol. 2, Spring 1973, pp. 74–87.

Sartoris, William L., and Paul, Ronda S., "Lease Evaluation—Another Capital Budgeting Decision," *Financial Management,* Vol. 2, Summer 1973, pp. 46–52.

Schall, Lawrence D., "Asset Valuation, Firm Investment, and Firm Diversification," *Journal of Business,* Vol. 45, January 1972, pp. 11–28.

———, "The Lease-or-Buy and Asset Acquisition Decisions," *Journal of Finance,* Vol. 29, September 1974, pp. 1203–1214.

Smith, Bruce D., "Accelerated Debt Repayment in Leveraged Leases," *Financial Management,* (Summer 1982), pp. 73–80.

Stapleton, Richard C., "Portfolio Analysis, Stock Valuation and Capital Budgeting Rules for Risky Projects," *Journal of Finance,* Vol. 26, March 1971, pp. 95–117.

Vancil, Richard F., "Lease or Borrow—New Method of Analysis," *Harvard Business Review,* Vol. 39, September–October 1961, reprinted in *Leasing Series,* Harvard Business Review, Cambridge, MA, n.d., pp. 72–93.

Van Horne, James C., *Financial Management and Policy,* 6th ed., Prentice-Hall, Englewood Cliffs, NJ, 1983.

Weston, J. Fred, and Brigham, Eugene F., *Managerial Finance,* 7th ed., Dryden Press, Hinsdale, IL, 1981.

12

LONG-TERM SOURCES OF FUNDS AND THE COST OF CAPITAL

CONTENTS

12

LONG-TERM SOURCES OF FUNDS AND THE COST OF CAPITAL

Thomas E. Copeland

DEFINING LONG-TERM FUNDS

LIABILITIES. The liabilities side of a firm's balance sheet can be broken down into the following broad categories:

1. Short-term liabilities:
   a. Accounts payable.
   b. Accruals.
   c. Notes payable.
   d. Current portion of long-term debt.
2. Long-term liabilities:
   a. Leasing.
   b. Long-term debt.
   c. Preferred stock.
   d. Equity:
      i. Common at par.
      ii. Common in excess of par.
      iii. Retained earnings.
      iv. Less treasury stock.

SOURCES OF FUNDS. Long-term sources of funds are recorded as long-term liabilities in item 2 above. Long-term funds are provided from both **external** and **internal sources.** The main internal source is **retained earnings,** which represents the savings of the corporation, namely, earnings not paid out to shareholders as dividends. Historically, about 35% of aggregate savings in the U.S. economy has been provided by retained earnings. The remaining 65% is the personal savings of households. The external sources of capital are debt, leasing, preferred stock, and equity.

Long-Term Debt. This is usually as any debt obligation outstanding that comes due more than one year hence. The main sources of long-term debt are **commercial banks** (although they seldom lend for maturities longer than five years), **insurance companies,** and **investment banking firms** that underwrite new issues of bonds to the public and other financial intermediaries (e.g. pension funds). Although the terms of repayment can vary widely, long-term debt is usually characterized by fixed coupon payments, predetermined schedules for the repayment of principal amount of the debt, and indenture clauses that govern the performance of the debt contract. The firm usually considers debt capital to be a favorable source of funds because interest paid is tax deductible, while preferred and common dividends are not. However, this is a complex issue that is discussed in detail later on. Investors view debt capital as less risky than preferred or common stock because debt payments have higher priority. In fact, when debt payments are not made as required by the debt contract, the provisions of the contract usually require that debt holders be given partial or full control of the firm.

Lease Financing. Lease financing provides for the use of buildings and equipment without ownership. In a number of respects leasing is similar to borrowing. It requires contractual fixed payments to the lessor and if the payments are not met, the lessor has the right to take back the leased asset. However, failure to keep up lease payments does not bankrupt the leasing firm. Lease payments, like interest on debt, are tax deductible. A description of various types of lease and a discussion of the cost of lease financing is given later.

Preferred Stock. Although more risky than debt, preferred stock is less risky than common stock. Straight preferred stock has no maturity date and promises to pay a fixed coupon rate. Almost always there is a **cumulative preferred** feature, which stipulates that whenever the firm fails to meet its promised preferred dividend payments, the firm may not make dividend payments to common shareholders until all back payments on preferred have been made. Preferred dividends are usually not tax deductible, and preferred shareholders do not have the right to force the firm into reorganization or bankruptcy if their dividends are not paid. However, if the firm does fail, preferred shareholders take precedence over common shareholders in their claim on the liquidated assets of the firm. In the event of liquidation, preferred shareholders must receive all cumulative dividends before any claim by common shareholders is settled. The main sources of capital from preferred stock are private issues with insurance companies and public issues underwritten by investment banking firms.

Common Stock. The fourth source of external capital is common stock. Shareholders of common stock are the residual claimants on the cash flows of the firm. They own whatever is left after the firm has met production costs, required payments on debt, taxes, and preferred dividends. Residual cash flows are divided into **dividends and retained earnings.** Retained earnings are reinvested in the firm and appear as equity on the long-term liabilities side of the balance sheet. Dividends, on the other hand, are paid out to shareholders as a return on their investment. Needless to say, common stock is the riskiest of the three major sources of long-term capital because it is a residual claim. Common stock has the lowest priority of payment in the event of bankruptcy. Dividends on common stock may be paid only after debtholders and preferred shareholders have received their payments.

Common stock has many different legal forms. For example, there are voting and nonvoting common stock, which are usually called class A and class B. The New York Stock Exchange has limited this practice, however, by refusing to list stocks of companies that do not give full voting power to all common stock. (This policy is currently under review.) Treasury stock refers to common stock that has been repurchased from shareholders and is held as a contraliability on the balance sheet. In other words, the dollar amount of repurchased treasury stock is subtracted from the equity account on the liabilities side of the balance sheet. Common stock may be issued to the public via investment banking firms or it may be privately held. Newly issued common stock is recorded on the balance sheet as the sum of its par value and common in excess of par. It is common practice to state a par value that is well below the market value of the common stock. However, if stock is issued for cash at less than its par value, the shareholders will be liable for the difference between the cash and par values if the firm is liquidated.

More complete descriptions of the various types of long-term source of capital are provided at the end of this section.

DEFINING THE COST OF CAPITAL

The cost of capital is the rate of return that could be earned by investors in alternative investmens of equal risk. To give greater meaning to this definition, one must consider the relationship between investment decisions and the cost of supplying the funds necessary to undertake them. For the time being it is convenient to assume that we are looking at the investment decisions made by the shareholders of an all equity firm. Suppose that the firm has $1 million of cash flow available for investment. Furthermore, suppose that it has three projects. Each costs $600,000, and the rates of return are 25, 12, and 8%, respectively. Which project should the firm undertake? It is not possible to answer this question without knowing the relative riskiness of each project; and therefore its implicit cost of capital.

Suppose that shareholders are told that the first project is very risky. In fact, if the shareholders were to invest their money elsewhere in projects of equal risk they would require at least 30% return on their investment. This is the rate of return required on alternative projects of equivalent risk. It is the **opportunity cost** of the funds employed and is the correct cost of capital for the project. Given that the cost of capital is 30% and that the project earns 25%, the investment decision is obvious. This first of the three projects should be rejected. Shareholders would be better off if they invested their money elsewhere at 30% than in this equally risky project at a 25% rate of return.

Having eliminated the first project from consideration, suppose that shareholders are told that the opportunity costs of the remaining two projects are 10 and 6%, respectively. With returns of 12 and 8%, both earn more than their cost of capital. To undertake them both, however, the firm would need $1.2 million in funds. Unfortunately, only $1 million is available. What should the shareholders do? They could undertake only one project and pay out the remaining $400,000 as dividends, but this would mean forgoing an opportunity to increase their wealth by undertaking both projects. Instead, they could invest all the firm's available cash flows as well as the additional $200,000. The extra funds could be supplied by issuing new equity.

The example above highlights the relationship between the firm's investment decision and its cost of capital. The cost of capital is the same as the **opportunity cost of funds** that can be invested elsewhere in projects of equivalent risk. The firm cannot make appropriate investment decisions unless it has a good estimate of the relevant cost of capital.

ESTIMATING THE COST OF CAPITAL: DEFINITIONS

RISK-ADJUSTED RATE OF RETURN. Any project that is undertaken must earn enough cash flow to meet the requirements of the two main sources of capital. First, creditors (debtholders) require that the project make enough to cover their required interest payments and to pay off the debt principal when it comes due. Second, shareholders require an expected rate of return on their investment that compensates them for the risk they are undertaking. If the **risk-adjusted rate of return** is high enough to meet both types of payment, the project earns its cost of capital. Any return above the cost of capital increases shareholders' wealth.

The income statement shown in Exhibit 1 summarizes the cash flows of two representative corporations. They are alike in every way except that the first carries no debt—that is, it is unlevered; the second has a reasonable amount of financial leverage. Exhibit 2 provides the current balance sheets for the representative firms. Note that the firms are of equal size, but the levered firm has less equity than its unlevered counterpart.

OPERATING CASH FLOWS AFTER TAXES. As mentioned earlier, the cost of capital is the rate of return that could be earned by investors in alternative investments of equal risk. For simplicity, suppose that the cash flows earned

EXHIBIT 1   INCOME STATEMENTS FOR REPRESENTATIVE FIRMS

Symbol	Definition	Unlevered Firm	Levered Firm
R	Revenues	1,000	1,000
$-VC$	Variable costs	−600	−600
$-FCC$	Fixed cash costs	−100	−100
$-Dep$	Noncash charge (depreciation)	−100	−100
$EBIT$	Earnings between interest and taxes	200	200
$-rD$	Interest on debt	0	−50
EBT	Earnings before taxes	200	150
$-T$	Taxes at 40% (tax rate $= t_c$)	−80	−60
NI	Net income	120	90

by the representative firms continue, without growth, forever. To maintain these perpetual cash streams, the firms must invest an amount each year equal to their depreciation. This is necessary to maintain the same level of property, plant, and equipment. Investors in the marketplace are willing to pay a price to buy claim to the cash flows of the firm. The rate at which they capitalize the perpetual cash flows is their opportunity cost, the cost of capital. For example, take the case of the unlevered firm. An investor in the unlevered firm will receive the following aftertax cash flows: earnings before interest and taxes $EBIT$; less taxes t; plus depreciation (which is a noncash charge against revenues); minus the amount of investment I, necessary to maintain the firm at its current level of operations. Algebraically, this cash flow is equal to **operating cash flows after taxes, *OCFAT*.**

$$OCFAT = EBIT - t_c(EBIT) + dep - I \tag{1}$$

COST OF CAPITAL FOR AN UNLEVERED FIRM; ITS VALUE. It is assumed that investment equals depreciation ($I = dep$), therefore,

$$OCFAT = EBIT(1 - t_c)$$
$$OCFAT = 200(1 - 0.4) = 120$$

EXHIBIT 2   BALANCE SHEETS FOR REPRESENTATIVE FIRMS

Unlevered Firm				Levered Firm			
Assets		Liabilities		Assets		Liabilities	
		Debt (D)	0			Debt (D)	500
		Equity (E)	1,000			Equity (E)	500
Total assets	1,000	Total liabilities	1,000	Total assets	1,000	Total liabilities	1,000

The theoretical value of the unlevered firm V^u is equal to these perpetual cash flows capitalized at the cost of capital appropriate for the riskiness of the firm. Call this the cost of capital for an unlevered firm, K_u. We can write the value of the unlevered firm as follows:

$$V^u = \frac{OCFAT}{K_u} = \frac{EBIT(1 - t_c)}{K_u} \tag{2}$$

Suppose that the capital market determines the market value of the unlevered firm to be \$1,200. Then, by rearranging equation 2, the cost of capital for the unlevered firm can be computed as 10%.

$$K_u = \frac{OCFAT}{V^u} = \frac{EBIT(1 - t_c)}{V^u}$$

$$K_u = \frac{120}{1,200} = 10\%$$

This example illustrates the relationship between the cash flows provided to investors in a firm, the value they are willing to pay for said cash flows, and the cost of capital. If they were willing to pay more for the same cash flows, the implied cost of capital would be lower, and vice versa. Also, note that cash flow received by investors is very different from net income NI. This is partly because not all the reported net income is available to be paid out. Some of the firm's cash flows must be reinvested to preserve the productive assets that support future cash flows.

So far the example has been fairly simple because it pertains to an all-equity firm. How does the definition of the cost of capital change when cash flows are paid out to bondholders as well as shareholders? A levered corporation makes payments to two main suppliers of capital: debtholders and shareholders. When the firm is making interest payments, the cash flow received by shareholders is equal to net income NI, plus depreciation (which was deducted from revenues as a noncash charge), minus dollars spent on investment I. Payment to bondholders is the interest on debt rD. Adding these together, total cash flows CF, paid to sources of capital in the private sector of the economy, are:

$$CF = NI + \text{dep} - I + rD$$

As before, we assume that investment equals depreciation. Therefore,

$$CF = NI + rD$$

Net income is equal to earnings before interest and taxes $EBIT$, less interest, less taxes. Using this, we can rewrite the cash flow equation as follows:

$$CF = EBIT - rD - t_c(EBIT - rD) + rD \tag{3}$$

$$CF = EBIT(1 - t_c) + t_c rD$$

Recalling that $EBIT(1 - t_c)$ is also equal to operating cash flows after taxes $OCFAT$, equation 3 may also be written as:

$$CF = OCFAT \pm t_c rD$$

VALUE OF THE LEVERED FIRM. In the preceding algebraic manipulation, the cash flows of the firm have been partitioned into two parts with different risks. The first part, operating cash flows after taxes ($OCFAT$), is exactly the same as the cash flows of the unlevered firm. It has exactly the same risk and can, therefore, be capitalized at exactly the same risk-adjusted rate, namely, the cost of equity for an all-equity firm K_u. The second part of the cash flow definition is the corporate tax rate t_c times the interest payments on debt. If the interest payments are risky, this stream of cash flows can be capitalized at a risk-adjusted rate appropriate for risky debt K_d. Capitalizing each cash flow at its risk-adjusted rate provides an expression for the **value of the levered firm.**

$$V^l = \frac{EBIT(1 - t_c)}{K_u} + t_c \frac{rD}{K_d} \tag{4}$$

Market Value of Debt. Note that the first term in equation 4 is exactly equal to the value of the unlevered firm, V^u, as given in equation 2. The second term is equal to the corporate tax rate t_c, times the **market value of debt B.** The market value of the perpetual debt is the annual interest payment rD, discounted at the cost of risky debt K_d.

$$B = \frac{rD}{K_d} \tag{5}$$

The analysis above suggests that the value of the levered firm can be written as follows:

$$V^L = V^u + t_c B \tag{6}$$

If we assume that the market-determined opportunity cost of risky debt K_d is 8%, then by using the numerical example in Exhibit 1, the value of the levered firm is found to be:

$$V^L = \frac{200(1 - 0.4)}{0.10} + \frac{0.10(500)}{0.08}$$

$$V^L = 1,200 + 0.4(526)$$

$$V^L = 1,450$$

Market Value Versus Book Value. This analysis brings out at least two important points. First, the market values of debt and equity are different from the book values as stated on the balance sheet. For example, the book value of debt is $500. However, it pays a coupon rate r of 10%, while the market required rate of return is only 8%. Consequently the bond sells for a premium of $125 because it pays a higher nominal rate of interest r than can be obtained from new bonds issued to sell for their face value. The market value of the firm's common stock S can be obtained by subtracting the market value of debt B from the market value of the firm V^L.

$$
\begin{aligned}
V^L &= S + B \\
S &= V^L - B \\
S &= 1{,}450 - 625 \\
S &= 825
\end{aligned}
\tag{7}
$$

The book value of equity is $500, while the market value is $825. One would never expect the market and book value of equity to be equal except by chance. The book value of equity is a historical number that reflects the dollars of new equity and retained earnings put into the firm by shareholders in years gone by. It has nothing to do with current market value, which is based on shareholder's expectations of the future cash flows they will receive from the firm.

WEIGHTED AVERAGE COST OF CAPITAL. A second major point is that the value of the levered firm, $V^L = 1{,}450$, is greater than the value of the same firm without any debt, $V^u = 1{,}200$. This gain from leverage arises because interest payments are deductible from earnings before taxes. Hence interest on debt is a tax shield, and the value of the firm is higher with the tax shield than without.

Up to this point we have discussed the cost of equity capital for the unlevered cash flows of the firm and the cost of debt capital. The final task is to define a single risk-adjusted cost of capital for the levered cash flows of the firm; that is, the rate of return that capitalizes the levered firm's operating cash flows after taxes so that the present value of the cash flows is equal to the market value of the firm. This capitalization rate is called the weighted average cost of capital $WACC$. The value of the levered firm is:

$$
V_L = \frac{EBIT(1 - t_c)}{WACC}
\tag{8}
$$

and the weighted average cost of capital is:

$$
WACC = \frac{EBIT(1 - t_c)}{V^L}
\tag{9}
$$

Using this definition, the weighted average cost of capital is 10% fo the unlevered firm and 8.28% for the levered firm. As before, there is an inverse relationship between the value of the firm and the capitalization rate. Holding cash flows constant, if the weighted average cost of capital decreases, the value of the levered firm goes up.

The traditional definition of the weighted average cost of capital is that it is equal to the aftertax cost of debt $K_d(1 - t_c)$, multiplied by the percentage of debt in the capital structure of the firm $B/(B + S)$, plus the cost of levered equity capital K_e, multiplied by the percentage of equity in the firm's capital structure, $S/(B + S)$:

$$WACC = K_d(1 - t_c) \frac{B}{B + S} + K_e \frac{S}{B + S} \tag{10}$$

Note that the percentages of debt and equity are computed using market value weights, not book values.

COST OF EQUITY FOR A LEVERED FIRM. To double check the consistency of this defintion of the weighted average cost of capital with that given in equation 9, we need an independent estimate of K_e, the cost of equity for the levered firm. It will be the market-determined capitalization rate for cash flows to shareholders of the levered firm. These cash flows are identified as net income NI, plus depreciation (a noncash charge against earnings), minus the amount of investment needed to replace depreciating assets. Because depreciation and investment cancel each other, we are left with net income. Thus the market value of equity S is

$$S = \frac{NI}{K_e} \tag{11}$$

and the cost of equity for the levered firm (which has no growth) is

$$K_e = \frac{NI}{S} \tag{12}$$

$$K_e = \frac{90}{825} = 10.91\%$$

Recall that the cost of equity for the unlevered cash flows K_u was 10%. As the firm takes on debt capital, the riskiness of the shareholders' claim increases. Shareholders require a higher rate of return as compensation for the risk; consequently, the cost of equity for a levered firm increases with leverage. The results above bear this out. The cost of equity has gone from 10% for the firm without any leverage to 10.91% for the firm with leverage of 43.1% of total market value.

If the cost of equity, as calculated from equation 12, is substituted into the formula for the weighted average cost of capital (equation 10), we should obtain the same answer computed earlier from equation 9, namely, that the weighted average cost of capital is 8.28%. This is worked out as follows:

$$WACC = K_d(1 - t_c) \frac{B}{B + S} + K_e \frac{S}{B + S}$$

$$WACC = 0.08(1 - 0.4) \frac{625}{1,450} + 0.1091 \frac{825}{1,450}$$

$$WACC = 8.28\%$$

This confirms the consistency of the two definitions of the weighted average cost of capital. Calculated as the market-value weighted average of the market-determined costs of debt (after taxes) and levered equity, it is the discount rate that converts the operating cash flows after taxes ($OCFAT$) into the current market value of the firm.

The next subsection goes into greater detail on the procedure for estimating the market-required rates of return for risky debt and equity for a variety of different debt and equity instruments. Before moving on, a few caveats are necessary. First, it has been assumed that cash flows to debt and equity are perpetuities without growth. This assumption must be modified, especially in the case of equity capital, to handle the more realistic situation of future cash flows that are expected to grow. Second, there has been no mention of the effect of bankruptcy costs on the market interest rate on debt. Later, it is argued that this effect, combined with the tax shield provided by interest on debt, is one possible explanation for an optimal capital structure.

ESTIMATING THE COST OF SHORT-TERM LIABILITIES

Most textbooks ignore **short-term liabilities** when estimating the cost of capital. Doing so considerably simplifies the exposition. It is argued that short-term liabilities can be ignored either because they are not part of the permanent long-term financing of the firm or because they require no explicit cash payments. For example, accounts payable and accrued taxes have no interest payments. Both the arguments against including short-term liabilities in the cost of capital of the firm are incorrect. First, while it is true that short-term liabilities are not part of the permanent financing of the firm, they still represent the utilization of scarce resources. Second, even though there are no direct interest payments, the cost of using trade credit or even deferred taxes as a short-term source of funds is not to be disregarded. The cost of noninterest-bearing liabilities, such as **trade credit,** is reflected in the income statement. Market prices in industries with generous trade credit are slightly higher to reflect the cost of extending credit. The higher prices of goods and services in these industries means lower profits for users of trade credit and in this way the cost of credit is reflected in the income statement.

The material that follows describes various short-term liabilities and provides techniques for computing their cost to the firm.

ACCOUNTS PAYABLE

Trade Credit. Accounts payable represent the trade credit being used by the firm. For example, suppose a firm purchases an average of $1,000 a day and pays its bills after 30 days. Then its accounts payable will be $30,000. If it doubles its purchases to $2,000 a day, it will automatically increase its accounts payable to $60,000, thereby creating an additional $30,000 of financing.

Credit Terms. Trade credit is usually extended with specific credit terms. As an illustration, suppose a firm has just received trade credit where the terms are 2/10 net 30. That is, if the invoice is paid within 10 days of delivery, there is a 2% discount. The cost of not taking cash discounts can be expensive. If the firm pays the bill on the eleventh day, the annualized interest cost if 730%. In general, if n is the number of days **after** the discount period and x is the percentage discount, annual cost is:

$$\text{annual cost} = \frac{365}{n} X \tag{13}$$

The more usual case if the firm forgoes the discount is to pay on the net-day, for example, the thirtieth. The annualized cost is then 36.5%.

Trade credit is a customary part of doing business in most industries. It is convenient and informal. However, as shown above, it is not costless. Even if a firm pays all its bills within the discount period, there is an implicit cost of using trade credit. Usually, the pricing policy of the lending firm is established so that prices are high enough to compensate for the discounts extended.

For an explicit calcuation of the cost of trade credit, see the Bethlehem Steel example.

NOTES PAYABLE. Notes payable usually take the form of **short-term loans** from commercial banks. For many firms, particularly small businesses, short-term debt may represent the single largest source of external financing. The costs of using various types of short-term credit are given below.

Line of Credit. This is an informal understanding between the bank and the borrower: the bank agrees to provide, upon demand, a short-term loan up to a specified amount. If the commitment on the bank's part is formalized, the arrangement is known as a **revolving credit.** Although the terms of a line of credit or revolving credit differ, it is not unusual to pay interest on the amount outstanding plus a commitment fee (e.g., 0.25%) on the unused balance. Also, the borrower is frequently required to "clean up" (reduce the balance to zero) sometime during the year.

The cost of a line of credit is the interest cost per day divided by the balance of the loan outstanding that day plus the commitment fee. Suppose, for example, a firm borrows a line of credit of $100,000 for six months at an interest rate of 12% per annum and with an annual commitment fee of 0.5%. Exhibit 3 shows how the credit arrangement would work on a month-to-month basis.

Notice that the total interest charges are $1,200 and the total commitment fees are $200. The firm used an average of $20,000 per month, and the average monthly charge (interest plus commitment fee) was $233. The effective monthly interest was approximately 1.17% (an annual rate of 14.9%). The commitment fee has the effect of raising the true interest rate on the amount borrowed. In Exhibit 3, the firm could have saved commitment fees by having requested a $70,000 line of credit rather than $100,000. The greater the unused credit line, the greater the effective interest will be.

Compensating Balances. These represent a requirement by the bank that the borrower maintain an average checking account balance of usually 15–20% of the outstanding loan. For example, suppose a firm needs to use $40,000 in debt capital and the bank makes the loan at an interest rate of 10% with a 20% compensating balance. The firm must borrow $50,000 at 10%, but it gets to use only $40,000 because the remainder is kept in a compensating balance earning no interest. If the firm has no other use for the compensating balance (e.g., using it to meet payrolls), the true cost of the loan is $5,000 ÷ 40,000 or 12.5%. In this way, compensating balances may raise the effective interest on the loan.

Regular Term Loans. When both principal and interest must be paid back on the maturity date or due date of the loan, the arrangement is called a **regular term loan.** In such cases the effective rate of interest on a 1-year

EXHIBIT 3   LINE-OF-CREDIT EXAMPLE

	Month					
	1	2	3	4	5	6
Amount use	20,000	70,000	20,000	0	0	10,000
Interest	200	700	200	0	0	100
Unused balance	80,000	30,000	80,000	100,000	100,000	90,000
Commitment fee	33	12	33	42	42	38

loan is exactly the same as the stated rate. For example, if the firm borrows $100,000 at 12% for one year, it will have to pay back $12,000 at year-end. The effective rate of interest is computed as

$$\frac{\text{interest paid}}{\text{principal amount}} = \frac{12,000}{100,000} = 12\%$$

Discount Loans. Another commonly used device, discount loans require that the interest be paid immediately upon the issue of the loan and that the principal be paid on maturity. Using the above example, the firm would have to pay $12,000 in advance. It would be able to use $100,000 - $12,000 = $88,000 during the year. Although the interest paid is the same as the term loan, the actual amount of funds that the firm can use is less. Hence the effective rate of interest is 13.64%.

$$\frac{\text{interest paid}}{\text{amount used}} = \frac{12,000}{88,000} = 13.64\%$$

The example of discount loans emphasizes the critical dependence of the effective rate of interest on the timing of cash flows as well as the amount paid.

Installment Loans. Here the loan principal must be repaid in equal install-ments over the life of the loan. Continuing with the example, suppose that the firm borrows $100,000 at a stated interest rate of 12%, but must repay the loan in monthly installments. Furthermore, assume that the annual in-terest is calcualted on the original $100,000 (this is not always the way it is done). The borrower has use of the full $100,000 only during the first month. In the second month he can use only $100,000 - (100,000 ÷ 12) = $91,667, in the third month only $83,333 and so on. After using the correct discounting procedures, we would compute that the effective rate of interest on the installment loan is not 12% as stated, but rather close to 23.75%.

For the reader who is familiar with the mathematics of discounting, the nominal rate of interest j is computed from the definition of a monthly annuity. The annuity amount b is assumed to be $1,000 in interest plus $100,000 ÷ 12 = $8,333.33 in principal. The period of payment m is monthly. The formula for present value PV is:

$$PV = 100,000 = (1,000 + 8,333.33)\left[\frac{1 - (1 + j/m)^{-m}}{j/m}\right]$$

$$j \approx 21.5\%$$

The nominal rate j, when compounded monthly, equals 23.75% per year.

Current Portion of Long-Term Debt. This short-term liability is self-explanatory. It is recorded on the short-term portion of the balance sheet to highlight the requirement that the firm repay the stated amount of principal on long-term debt during the upcoming fiscal year. Separating it in this way provides information to financial analysts about the short-term viability of the firm. If short-term liquid assets are insufficient to pay off the current portion of long-term debt, the firm can be forced into **reorganization or bankruptcy.**

Insofar as computing the cost of capital is concerned, the current portion of long-term debt is no different from the remainder of long-term debt. Therefore, further discussion of its cost is deferred until we cover the cost of long-term debt.

Commercial Paper. This consists primarily of **unsecured promissory notes** of large firms sold chiefly to other business firms. In recent years, however, mutual funds have been formed to allow individuals to hold commercial paper. Maturities of commercial paper usually vary from 2 to 6 months, and rates are typically 0.5% below the **prime rate.** Because commercial paper is sold in very large amounts, it is viable only for companies having short-term fund needs large enough to result in **economies of scale.** And because of the economies of scale, commercial paper is a "cheaper" source of funds than borrowing at the prime rate.

ACCRUALS. Accruals usually refer to accrued wages and salaries due and to accrued taxes. These are short-term obligations due in the next fiscal year. Although they have no explicit interest cost, they are not free. One might easily argue that when workers agree to receive their paychecks at an interval after the work has been performed, they will compensate for the cost of waiting by asking for a higher wage rate. In effect they are making short-term loans to the firm. Similarly, the government provides services to the economy and finances them with taxes and government debt. One can think of accrued taxes as a short-term loan to the firm by the government. If so, the opportunity cost of accrued taxes due should be taken into account in the cost of capital calculation. On the other hand, it might be argued that the cost to the firm of using accrued taxes as a source of funds is zero because government transfer payments (such as the unearned interest on accrued taxes) are a positive benefit to the private sector.

ESTIMATING THE COST OF LEASE FINANCING

Leasing is a form of **intermediate financing.** Many lease contracts last for the life of the equipment being leased. Until November 1976, there was no uniform code for accounting for lease financing, and many long-term lease commitments did not appear as liabilities on firms' balance sheets. Leasing was referred to as **off-balance-sheet financing.** However, since 1976, the accounting rules have changed.

ACCOUNTING FOR LEASING. From the point of view of the lessee, accounting for leasing is now controlled by Statement No. 13 of the Financial Accounting Standards Board (FASB). Leases are divided into two broad categories: **operating leases** and **capital leases.** A lease is defined as a **capital lease** if it meets one or more of the following four criteria: (1) ownership of the leased asset is transferred to the lessee at the end of the lease, (2) the lease contract gives the lessee an option to purchase the property at a price sufficiently below market value to make exercise of the option likely, (3) the lease term is greater than or equal to 75% of the estimated economic life of the property, or (4) the present value of the lease payments is greater than or equal to 90% of the value of the property at the beginning of the lease. **Capital leases** must be capitalized and shown on the balance sheet both as a fixed asset and a noncurrent liability. **Operating leases** meet none of the aforementioned criteria and are not capitalized on the balance sheet. The lease fees are charged as an expense on the income statement, and disclosure of the lease obligation is made in the footnotes of the firm's annual report.

DIRECT COST OF LEASING. The cost of lease financing is discussed here from the points of view of both the lessor and the lessee. For a complete discussion of the lease-buy decision, the reader is referred to Weston and Copeland (*Managerial Finance,* 8th ed., 1986) and to the section entitled "Leasing" in this *Handbook.*

There has been considerable disagreement about the appropriate cost of capital that should be used in lease financing (see, e.g., Myers, Dill and Bautista, *Journal of Finance,* June 1976; Schall, *Journal of Finance,* September 1974; and Miller and Upton, *Journal of Finance,* June 1976). Much of the confusion arises from the difficulty of separating the investment decision from the method of financing. The lessee's investment decision should be made by discounting the aftertax cash flows of the project under consideration at the appropriate **risk-adjusted weighted average cost of capital.** However, the project decision is not the main concern of this discussion. Rather, we are interested in the financing decision, namely, a comparison between the aftertax cost of lease financing and its close substitute, the aftertax cost of debt financing. Leasing and debt financing both have contractual payments that are deductible for tax purposes, both usually involve contracts of similar length, and both require an equity base. Furthermore, they have approximately the same risk.

How, then, shall we compute the aftertax cost of lease financing? First, look at the problem from the point of view of the **lessor.** The lessor receives lease payments L_t, writes off depreciation dep_t as a tax shield, and pays taxes on the net amount. In return, the lessor provides the use of an asset with current market value M. If K is the aftertax rate of return required by the lessor, we have the following relationship:

$$M = \sum_{t=0}^{T} \frac{L_t - \text{dep}_t - t_c(L_t - \text{dep}_t)}{(1 + K)^t}$$

$$M = \sum_{t=0}^{T} \frac{L_t(1 - t_c) + t_c \, \text{dep}_t}{(1 + K)^t}$$

Given the aftertax required rate of return, the depreciation schedule, and the value of the asset, the lessor can establish his required lease fee L_t. (To keep the analysis simple, it is assumed that there is no salvage value for the asset). The lessor's required rate of return K will be the interest rate on lending operations that have the same risk as leasing. The required rate is also the **lessor's weighted average cost of capital.**

From the lessee's point of view, the cost of the lease K should be compared with the aftertax cost of debt capital, which is a nearly perfect substitute. If the firm decides to take a lease, its debt capacity is reduced by the amount of the lease. Alternatively, if the lessee is already at its **optimal capital structure** prior to the lease, the lease will displace debt. The opportunity cost of the forgone debt is a cost of leasing (see Myers, Dill, and Bautista, *Journal of Finance*, June 1976).

FACTORS INDIRECTLY AFFECTING LEASING COSTS. These include (1) the riskiness of the **residual value** of the leased property, (2) the **risk of obsolescence,** (3) differences in **maintenance costs,** and (4) **economies of scale** in the leasing operation. From the point of view of the lessor, a lease contract is probably somewhat riskier than a debt contract of equal size and maturity, mainly because of the risk of having the lease terminated before its contract life. This makes leasing more expensive than borrowing. On the other hand, if there are economies of scale in maintenance or financing, or if the lessor has a higher tax rate than the lessee, leasing may be cheaper than borrowing.

ESTIMATING THE COST OF LONG-TERM DEBT

The cost of long-term debt depends on the riskiness of the debt issue, its term to maturity, its indenture restrictions, and special features such as whether it is convertible into common stock or whether it has warrants attached to it. Each of these factors is discussed in turn, beginning with the simple problem of estimating the cost of debt capital from observed market data.

YIELD TO MATURITY: DEFINITION. Consider the example presented in Exhibit 4, showing the composition of long-term debt of Bethelehm Steel in December 1976.

EXHIBIT 4   BETHLEHEM STEEL COMPOSITION OF LONG-TERM DEBT, DECEMBER 31, 1976

Issue	Rating (Moody's)	Amount	Call Price	Recent Price	Yield	Year of Issue
Consolidated, Mortgages S.F.3s, K, 1979	Aa	21,800	$100\frac{1}{8}$	NA	NA	1949
Debenture, $3\frac{1}{4}$s, 1980	Aa	3,100	100	$89\frac{1}{2}$	3.6	1955
Debenture, 5.40s, 1992	Aa	109,200	$102\frac{1}{2}$	$84\frac{3}{8}$	6.4	1967
Debenture, $6\frac{7}{8}$s, 1999	Aa	85,800	$104\frac{1}{4}$	$94\frac{1}{4}$	6.6	1969
Debenture, 9s, 2000	Aa	144,000	$105\frac{1}{2}$	$106\frac{1}{2}$	8.5	1970
Debenture, 8.45s, 2005	Aa	250,000	107.45	$103\frac{1}{2}$	8.2	1975
Debenture, $8\frac{3}{8}$s, 2001	Aa	200,000	106.63	$105\frac{1}{2}$	7.9	1976
Subordinated Debenture, $4\frac{1}{2}$s, 1990	A	94,500	102.40	$76\frac{1}{4}$	5.9	1965
Notes payable	—	30,000	—	NA	NA	NA
Subsidiary debt	—	3,200	—	NA	NA	NA
Revenue bonds, $5\frac{1}{4}$s-6s, 2002	—	100,000	—	NA	NA	NA

Source: Moody's Industrial Manual and Bank & Quotation Record, January 1977.

When trying to estimate the cost of debt capital K_d to employ in equation 10, the approppriate opportunity cost must be computed as it is determined by investors in the marketplace. This is called the **yield to maturity.** First, it is useful to discuss two rates that have little to do with the opportunity cost of debt. Nonetheless, because they are often used, it is appropriate to warn the reader against them. The first is the coupon rate, or the historical cost of debt, and the second is the simple yield, shown in column 6 of Exhibit 4.

COUPON RATE. This is the ratio of the coupon to the face value of the bond. For example, in 1955 Bethlehem Steel issued 25-year bonds with a coupon rate of 3 1/4%, due in 1980. This bond issue can be seen on line 2 of Exhibit 4. The 3 1/4% coupon rate is the **historical cost** of the bond, and it reflects the cost of long-term debt for Bethlehem Steel in 1955. This has nothing whatsoever to do with the market cost of debt for Bethlehem Steel as of December 31, 1976.

CURRENT YIELD. The **current yield** or simple yield is defined as the ratio of the coupon payment to the current **market value** of the bond. The current yield for the Bethlehem Steel 3 1/4% debentures due in 1980 is computed as follows

$$\text{current yield} = \frac{\text{coupon rate} \times \text{face value}}{\text{market value}} \tag{14}$$

$$= \frac{0.0325 \times \$1,000}{\$895} = 3.63\%$$

The current yield is the statistic published daily in the *Wall Street Journal*. It has nothing whatsoever to do with the market-determined opportunity cost of the bond that has a **finite life,** which is called the yield to maturity.

YIELD TO MATURITY: CALCULATIONS. The yield to maturity is the best measure of the correct opportunity cost of a bond. It is the rate of return an investor expects to earn if he purchases the bond today and holds it to maturity. In return for the purchase price, he receives the expected coupon payments plus the expected repayment of the principal amount (the face value) at maturity. Readers who are familiar with **capital budgeting techniques** will recognize that the **yield to maturity** is the same as the **internal rate of return** on the bond investment.

On a Consol. The yield to maturity on a **consol bond** is the easiest to compute. A consol bond is a bond that promises to pay a constant coupon at the end of each year, forever. It never repays its principal because it never matures. For this special type of bond, the yield to maturity, is computed as follows:

$$\text{yield to maturity on a consol} = \frac{\text{coupon rate} \times \text{face value}}{\text{market value}} \tag{15}$$

Note that the yield to maturity on a consol is exactly the same as the current yield described above in equation 14. The implication is that when a bond has a long time to maturity, the current yield may be a reasonable approximation for the yield to maturity. However, more often than not, a bond does not have much time left before it comes due. Therefore, one needs a more accurate way to compute a yield to maturity.

On a Finite-Lived Bond. Take the example of the **Bethlehem Steel** 3 1/4% debentures due in 1980. The coupon payments of $16.25 per $1,000 face value are made on the first day of every May and every November. The issue matures on May 1, 1980. We want to know the yield to maturity as of December 31, 1976, if an investor has to pay $895 for the bond and if he assumes that he will receive all payments with certainty. Exhibit 5 shows the payments and their timing.

The yield to maturity is the interest rate that equates the discounted present value of the cash inflows (the coupons and the face value) with the current cash price of the bond. Mathematically, this can be expressed as

$$B_0 = \sum_{t=0}^{T} \frac{E(\text{coupon}_t)}{(1 + K_d)} + \frac{E(\text{repayment of principal})}{(1 + K_d)^T} \tag{16}$$

where B_0 = current price of bond
T = maturity date of bond
$E(\text{coupon}_t)$ = **expected** coupon payment at time t

**EXHIBIT 5   PAYMENTS ON BETHLEHEM STEEL 3 1/4%
DEBENTURES DUE 1980**

Type of Cash Flow	Expected Amount	Date
Purchase price	− 895.00	December 31, 1976
First coupon	16.50	May 1, 1977
Second coupon	16.50	November 1, 1977
Third coupon	16.50	May 1, 1978
Fourth coupon	16.50	November 1, 1978
Fifth coupon	16.50	May 1, 1979
Sixth coupon	16.50	November 1, 1979
Seventh coupon	16.50	May 1, 1980
Face value	1,000.00	May 1, 1980

Source: Maturities from *Annual Report,* 1976, Bethlehem Steel Corp.

E(repayment of principal) = **expected** repayment of principal when bond matures

K_d = annual yield to maturity on bond (assumed to be constant across life of bond)

For the Bethlehem Steel example, the yield to maturity is approximately 8%. For an exact solution refer to Copeland and Weston (*Financial Theory and Corporate Policy,* 2d ed., p. 465). During December 1976 all bonds with the same risk, the same maturity, and the same payment dates had approximately the same yield to maturity, because they were nearly perfect substitutes for each other.

RISK-ADJUSTED RATE OF RETURN. One of the most important things to remember about the definition of the yield to maturity is that it is a **risk-adjusted rate of return.** Bonds of lower quality will require higher yields. Suppose, for example, that instead of being an Aa-rated bond, the Bethlehem Steel debenture had been riskier. Suppose it had a rating of Ba. Bonds of lower quality have a greater probability of delayed payment or default. This must be taken into account when estimating the yield to maturity. One way to do this is to reduce the expected coupon payments or expected repayment of principal in equation 16 to something less than the face values promised in the bond issue. To be specific, assume that the investor is willing to pay only $845 for the lower quality bond and that he expects all the coupons to be paid in full and according to schedule, but he also expects a 30% chance that the bond will repay only $600 in principal and a 70% chance that it will pay the face value of $1,000. This implies that he expects the repayment of principal to be only $880: 0.7(1,000) + 0.3(600) = 880. Under these conditions, the payments in Exhibit 5 would change. The purchase price would become $845 instead of $895, and the **expected** repayment of principal would become $880 instead of $1,000. The recomputed yield to maturity for the Ba-rated bond is approximately 9%. The higher yield is necessary to compensate the investor for the higher risk undertaken. A common error made when estimating the yield to maturity on a risky bond (junk bond, for example) is to use the promised coupon payments and face value rather than the **expected** values, as required in equation 16.

MARGINAL YIELD TO MATURITY. This is the cost of debt capital, were the firm to issue new debt in the capital market. In the previous examples we calculated the yield to maturity on a bond that had 3 1/2 years to maturity. Yet by referring to Exhibit 4 it is apparent that when Bethlehem Steel issues new debt, the maturity is typically 25 or 30 years. Therefore, the appropriate marginal cost of new debt capital for Bethlehem is the market-determined yield to maturity on new 25 (or 30) year bonds. The yield to maturity on the 8.45% debentures maturing in 2005 is approximately 8.3%. The 8.375s maturing in 2001 have a similar yield to maturity. Therefore, 8.3% should be used as the marginal cost of new long-term debt in computing the weighted average cost of capital for Bethlehem.

RIDING THE YIELD CURVE. This anachronistic concept implies that investors can earn abnormal rates of return by purchasing bonds that sell at market prices lower than their face value. For example, suppose that a bond is currently selling for $787.39, that it matures in 4 years, that it has a face value of $1,000, and that it pays an annual coupon of $50. The yield to maturity is 12%. A casual examination of the facts might lead a naive investor to believe there is an abnormally high profit to be made. After all, the investor can obtain the coupon payments, and as long as the bonds are held to maturity, the investor will also earn the difference between the face value, $1,000, and the purchase price, $787.39. Ignoring any possible tax implications, the return on investment appears to be $200 worth of coupons plus $212.61 in capital gains on an investment of $787.39. This is a 52.4% return on investment. However, this logic fails to discount the cash flows. The yield to maturity handles this problem correctly. The actual rate of return is only 12%. Assuming (for convenience) that the yield to maturity does not change over the life of the bond. The price of the bond over its life is graphed in Exhibit 6. Notice that the market price of the bond increases as it gets closer to maturity, reflecting the fact that the bond becomes more valuable as the date of the payoff of the face value draws near.

The usual convention for the payment of interest on bonds is to record interest continuously. For example, suppose that there are only six months left before the bond matures and that individual A sells to individual B. Although the final coupon is not paid until the year's end, nevertheless individual A must be compensated for the interest accrued between the six months to maturity, individual B can expect to receive $25 in interest plus the $1,000 face value. On July 1 this is worth $966.98:

$$\text{bond value on July 1} = \frac{\$25}{1 + 0.12/2} + \frac{\$1,000}{1 + 0.12/2} = \$966.98$$

EXHIBIT 6   HYPOTHETICAL PRICE OF A BOND OVER ITS LIFE

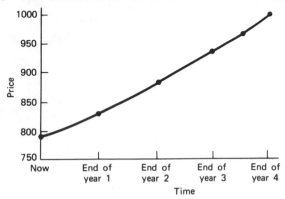

Thus, at any time to maturity, the yield to maturity will be the same, namely, 12%, even though the price rises in a predetermined fashion as shown in Exhibit 6. If the return is always 12%, no abnormal return can be earned.

ESTIMATING THE RISKINESS OF LONG-TERM DEBT. The usual method for determining the default risk of corporate long-term debt is to refer to the bond ratings supplied by various agencies. Major bond rating agencies are Moody's Investors Service Inc., Standard & Poor's Corp., and Fitch Investor Service. Moody's bond rating has seven classifications ranging from Aaa, which is the highest quality bond, down to Caa, the lowest quality. Weinstein (*Journal of Financial Economics,* December 1977) collected data on 179 new bond issues between 1962 and 1964. Exhibit 7 shows the distribution by risk class. About 40% of the new bonds qualified for the two highest quality ratings. Exhibit 8 shows the yields on bonds of different risk. Just as expected, the high-quality, low-risk bonds have lower yields than do the low-quality, high-risk bonds. A common-sense way of estimating the **marginal cost of new debt** for a firm (assuming that the new debt will not change the firm's bond rating) is to compute the yield to maturity on other bonds with the maturities and bond ratings similar to the new issue.

EXHIBIT 7   SAMPLE OF NEW ISSUES BY MOODY'S RATING OF ISSUE

Rating	Industrials	% of Total	Utilities	% of Total
Aaa	29	26.1	14	20.6
Aa	18	16.2	14	20.6
A	38	34.3	18	26.5
Baa	20	18.0	20	29.4
Ba	1	0.9	2	2.9
B	5	4.5	0	0
	111	100.0	68	100.0

Source: Adopted from Weinstein, Mark, "The Effect of a Rating Change Announcement on Bond Price," *Journal of Financial Economics,* December 1977.

EXHIBIT 8   MOODY'S INDUSTRIAL BOND YIELDS—BY RATING
1975–1984

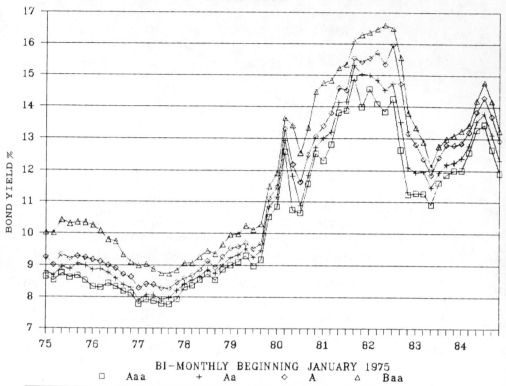

Source: Moody's Bond Record, various issues.

Of the roughly 2,000 major corporations that are evaluated by the agencies, approximately 500 are rerated quarterly because they issue commercial paper, another 500 are rerated annually (most of the utilities), and the remaining 1,000 have no established review date but are usually reviewed annually.

From an investor's point of view, one might ask the following question: Do the agencies determine the prices and interest rates paid for bonds or do investors in the capital markets? The evidence collected by Wakeman (University of Rochester, 1978) and Weinstein (*Journal of Finance,* December 1978) shows that changes in bond ratings are not treated as new information by capital market. In fact, changes in ratings usually occur several months after the capital markets have already reacted to the fundamental change in the bond's quality. Changes in agency ratings do not cause changes in required yields to maturity. It is the other way around. However, this does not imply that bond ratings are without value. On average, the ratings provide unbiased estimates of bond risk and are therefore a useful source of information.

EFFECTS OF COLLATERAL AND INDENTURE RESTRICTIONS. The riskiness of bonds, and therefore their required yield, is substantively affected by the bond covenants that are written into the bond contract. A good description of the multitude of specific provisions in debt contracts can be found in the American Bar Association compendium called *Commentaries on Model Debenture Indenture Provisions,* 1971. Bond covenants can be divided into four broad categories: (1) those restricting the issuance of new debt, (2) those with restrictions on dividend payments, (3) those with restrictions on merger activity, and (4) those with restrictions on the disposition of the firm's assets. Smith and Warner (*Journal of Financial Economics,* June 1979) examined a random sample of 87 public issues of debt registered with the Securities and Exchange Commission between January 1974 and December 1975. They observed that fully 90.8% of the bonds restrict the issuance of additional debt, 23% restrict dividend payments, 39.1% restrict merger activity, and 35.6% constrain the firm's disposition of assets.

Bond Covenants That Restrict Subsequent Financing. These are by far the most common type. The covenant provisions are usually stated in terms of accounting numbers and consequently are easy to monitor. The issuance of any new debt may carry restrictions that require all new debt to be subordinate or prohibit the creation of new debt with a higher priority unless existing bonds are upgraded to have an equal priority. All these restrictions are designed to prevent the firm from increasing the riskiness of outstanding debt by issuing new debt with a superior or equal claim on the firm's assets. Alternate restrictions may prohibit the issuance of new debt unless the firm maintains minimum prescribed ratios between net tangible assets and funded debt, income and interest charges, or current assets and current liabilities (working capital tests). There may also be "clean-up" provisions that require the company to be debt-free for limited periods.

If there is any advantage to the firm that holds debt in its capital structure, it is that bondholders can benefit by allowing new debt, but only under the condition that acquiring this obligation does not increase the riskiness of their position. Hence an outright prohibition of new debt under any condition is rare.

Other techniques that are used to protect bondholders against subsequent financing include restrictions on rentals, leases, and sale-leaseback agreements; sinking fund requirements (which roughly match the depreciation of the firm's tangible assets); required purchase of insurance; required financial reports and specification of accounting techniques; and required certifications of compliance by the officers of the firm.

Bond Covenants That Restrict Dividend Payments. These are necessary if for no other reason than to prohibit the extreme case of shareholders voting to pay themselves a liquidating dividend that would leave the bondholders holding an empty coprorate shell. Kalay (unpublished Ph.D. thesis, University of Rochester, 1979) reported that in a random sample of 150 firms, every firm had a dividend restriction in at least one of its debt instruments. Restrictions on dividend policy are relatively easy to monitor, and they protect debtholders against the unwarranted payout of the assets that serve as collateral. Appropriately, most indentures refer not only to cash dividends, but to all distributions in respect to capital stock, whether they be dividends, redemptions, purchases, retirements, partial liquidations, or capital reductions and whether in cash, in kind, or in the form of debt obligations to the company. Without such general provisions the firm could, for example, use cash to repurchase its own shares. From the bondholders' point of view, the effect would be the same as payment of cash dividends. No matter what the procedure is called, once cash is paid out to shareholders, it is no longer available in the event of **reorganization or bankruptcy.**

Most restrictions on the payout of the firm's assets require that dividends increase only if the firm's earnings are positive, if the firm issues new equity capital, or if dividends paid out since the bonds were issued have been kept below a predefined minimum level. Mathematically, the "inventory" of funds allowable for dividend payment D_T^* in quarter T, can be expressed as

$$D_T^* = K \sum_{t=0}^{T} E_t + \sum_{t=0}^{T} S_t + F - \sum_{t=0}^{T-1} D_t \tag{17}$$

where E_t = net earnings in quarter t

$\quad K$ = predetermined constant, $0 \le K \le 1$

$\quad S_t$ = net proceeds from issue of new equity

$\quad F$ = number fixed over life of bonds, known as "dip"

$\quad D_t$ = dividends paid out in quarter t

Thus the dividend covenant does not restrict dividends per se, rather, it restricts the financing of the payment of dividends with new debt or by sale of the firm's existing assets. This arrangement is in the interest of stockholders because it does not restrict the payment of earned income. It is also the interest of bondholders because it prevents any dilution of their claim on the firm's assets.

Bond Covenants That Restrict Merger Activity. These may prohibit many mergers but more often will allow mergers, provided certain conditions are met. The effect of a merger on bondholders can be beneficial if the cash flows of the merged firms are not perfectly correlated. Offsetting cash flow patterns can reduce the risk of default, thereby bettering the positions of the bondholders of both firms. Merger can also be detrimental to bondholders. For example, if firm A has much more debt in its capital structure than firm B, the bondholders of B will suffer increased risk after the merger. Or if the maturity of debt in firm A is shorter than for firm B, the bondholders of B will (for all practical purposes) become subordinate to those of firm A after the merger.

To protect against the undesirable effects that can result from a merger, it is possible to require bond covenants that allow merger only if the net tangible assets of the firm, calculated on a postmerger basis, meet a certain dollar minimum or are at least a certain fraction of long-term debt. The merger can also be made contingent on the absence of default of any indenture provision after the transaction is completed.

Bond Covenants That Restrict Production or Investment Policies. These agreements are numerous but are frequently difficult to enforce, given the impossibility of monitoring effectively the investment decisions that the managers of the firm decide not to undertake. Myers (*Journal of Financial Economics,* November 1977) suggests that a substantial portion of the value of a firm is composed of intangible assets in the form of future investment opportunities. A firm with outstanding debt may have the incentive to reject projects that have a positive **net present value** if the benefit from accepting the project accrues to the bondholders.

Direct restrictions on **investment-disinvestment policy** take the following forms: (1) restrictions on common stock investments, loans, extensions of credit, and advances that cause the firm to become a claimholder in another business enterprise, (2) restrictions on the disposition of assets, and (3) covenants requiring the maintenance of assets. Secured debt is an indirect restriction on investment policy. Assets that provide sureity cannot be disposed of under the provisions of the indenture agreement. Collateralization also reduces foreclosure expenses because the lender already has established title via the bond covenent.

EFFECTS OF TERM STRUCTURE OF INTEREST RATES. Firms always want to issue new debt, at the lowest possible cost. Frequently, long-term interest rates are observed to be different from short-term rates. Usually long-term rates are higher. The question then arises, "Why not take on shorter-term debt because it has lower interest cost?" Another aspect of the same problem is whether to issue debt currently or to wait several months until interest rates (for a given maturity) fall. The answers to these questions lie in an understanding of the term structure of interest rates.

Exhibit 9 gives an example of the term structure of interest rates on U.S. Treasury obligations on January 24, 1979. The simple yield is plotted as a function of the years to maturity. Note that in general, longer term bonds paid lower yields. This reflects the belief, current in the marketplace at that time, that short-run inflation would be worse than long-run inflation. Although the term structure is generally measured by using U.S. government obligations, other debt instruments show similar patterns.

Two major theories have been advanced to explain the term structure: the **expectations theory** and the **liquidity preference theory.**

Expectations Theory. The expectations theory predicts that any long-run rate of interest is a geometric average of today's observed short-run rate and

**EXHIBIT 9   TERM STRUCTURE OF INTEREST RATES,
JANUARY 24, 1979**

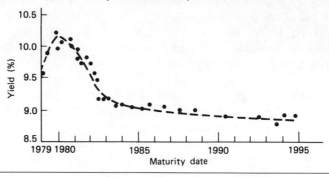

Source: *Wall Street Journal*, January 24, 1979.

expected short-term rates in the future. Mathematically, this is expressed as:

$$1 + {}_tR_N = [(1 + {}_tr_1)(1 + {}_{t+1}\bar{r}_1) \cdots (1 + {}_{t+N-1}\bar{r}_1)]^{1/N} \qquad (18)$$

where ${}_tR_N$ = average long-term rate on an N-year bond computed in year t

$\quad\;\; {}_tr_1$ = rate of return on a one-year bond as observed in year t

$\;{}_{t+1}\bar{r}_1$ = expected rate of return on a one-year bond issued in year $t + 1$

${}_{t+N-1}\bar{r}_i$ = expected rate of return on a one-year bond issue in year $t + N - 1$

For concreteness, consider the following example. The one-year interest rate on a one-year bond issued on January 1, 1979, is 15%. In addition, the expected interest rate on a one-year bond issued on January 1, 1980, is 12%, and the expected rate on a one-year bond issued on January 1, 1981, is 10%. What is the rate of return on a three-year bond issued on January 1, 1979? By substituting into equation 18, we have

$$1 + {}_{1979}R_3 = [(1 + {}_{1979}0.15_1)(1 + {}_{1980}0.12_1)(1 + {}_{1981}0.10_1)]^{1/3}$$
$$1 + {}_{1979}R_3 = [(1.15)(1.12)(1.10)]^{1/3}$$
$$1 + {}_{1979}R_3 = (1.4168)^{1/3}$$
$$1 + {}_{1979}R_3 = 1.123146$$

Thus the rate of return on the three-year bond is 12.3146%. A similar computation would show the rate of return on a two-year bond to 13.49%. For this simple example, the term structure of interest ratets would be downward sloping as shown in Exhibit 10.

EXHIBIT 10   TERM STRUCTURE FOR 3-YEAR EXAMPLE

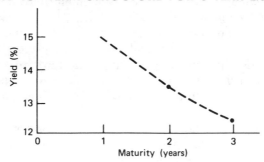

The example shows that if the expectations hypothesis is true, and if people expect future one-period interest rates to be low relative to the current one-period interest rate, the term structure will be falling. Of course if interest rates are expected to be higher in the future, the term structure will rise. Also note that it makes no difference whether the firm issues debt with a one-year maturity, in which case it rolls the debt over for two more years, or whether it issues three-year debt in the first place. The total interest payment will be the same in either case. Given the term structure of interest rates (and ignoring transactions costs), a policy of issuing short-term debt and rolling it over will have exactly the same cost as the issuance of longer term debt.

Liquidity Preference Theory. It is sometimes argued that short-term debt is more liquid than long-term debt. Consequently, long-term debt must provide investors with a higher yield than short-term debt. One explanation for the extra liquidity premium required on long-term debt is that investors are exposed to a greater danger of capital losses when interest rates change unexpectedly. The liquidity hypothesis implies (Exhibit 11) that a liquidity premium must be added to the rates of long-term bonds. Exhibit 11 assumes that all future one-period rates are expected to equal today's one-period rate; hence the expectations theory would predict a flat term structure. However,

EXHIBIT 11   LIQUIDITY PREMIUM IN THE TERM STRUCTURE

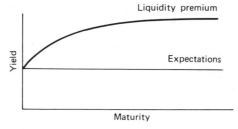

if the liquidity premium theory is correct, a premium must be added to longer term bonds to induce investors to hold them.

The expectations and liquidity theories are not mutually exclusive. In fact, empirical evidence (Roll, *The Behavior of Interest Rates,* Basic Books, 1970; Cargill, 1975; Dobson, Sutch, and Vanderford, *Journal of Finance,* September 1976) suggests that the best explanation of the term structure is unbiased expectations of future rates with liquidity premiums on longer-maturity bonds.

If the term structure reflects unbiased expectations of future rates, the implication is that it rarely pays to follow a **timing strategy for new debt issues,** or for new equity issue either. The reason is simple. Hundreds of thousands of investors and thousands of firms are constantly searching for information that would lead them to find a better forecast of future changes in interest rates. Anyone who can consistently provide a better forecast can earn large capital gains from doing so, and nearly everyone tries. The result is that market interest rates as embedded in the term structure reflect a consensus of thousands of informed forecasts. Empirical evidence has shown these forecasts to be unbiased on average. Therefore, to successfully time a new issue of debt (or equity) one's forecast has to be better than everyone else's. Attempts to "time" new issues usually fail as often as they succeed.

ESTIMATING THE COST OF PREFERRED STOCK

Preferred stock is a hybrid security. It is riskier than debt because preferred dividends are paid only after interest payments on debt have been made and because preferred has lower priority in bankruptcy than debt. On the other hand, preferred is less risky than common stock because it has higher priority in bankruptcy and because no common dividends may be paid until all **cumulative preferred dividends** have been issued. Preferred dividends are like interest payments on debt because they are contractural. Preferred shareholders may not force the firm into reorganization or bankruptcy for failure to pay preferred dividends. Finally, preferred dividends may not be deducted as an expense by the firm.

COST OF STRAIGHT PREFERRED. Usually, preferred stock is issued as a **perpetuity.** It can be retired only if the firm buys back all outstanding preferred shares in the open market. Suppose that a preferred stock was issued at a par value of $100 per share, that it pays a dividend rate of 8% on its face value, and that it is currently selling (at a discount) for $83.50 per share. What is the **cost of preferred stock** to the firm?

The discounted present value of a stream of dividend payments that never grows is given below.

$$P_0 = \frac{E(\text{preferred dividend})}{K_p}$$

where P_0 = current market value of a share of preferred stock ($83.50)

E(preferred dividend) = expected dividend rate × face value = 8% ($100) = $8

K_p = cost of preferred stock

By rearranging the formula, we can solve for the cost of **straight preferred,** K_p.

$$K_p = \frac{\text{preferred dividend}}{P_0}$$

(19)

$$K_p = \frac{\$8.00}{\$83.50} = 9.58\%$$

This is a reasonable estimate of the cost of nonconvertible preferred stock.

COST OF CONVERTIBLE PREFERRED. Approximately 40% of the preferred stock issued in recent years is convertible into common stock. For example, one share of preferred may be convertible into four shares of the firm's common stock at the option of the preferred shareholder. In this case the investor who purchases one share of convertible preferred pays a market price, P_c, in return for a stream of dividends plus the value of an option to convert, C. Mathematically, this is

$$P_c = \frac{E(\text{preferred dividends})}{K_{cp}} + C$$

If two preferred issues are alike in all respects except that one is convertible and the other is not, investors will pay more for the convertible preferred. The reader who is interested in evaluating the value of the call option, so that the cost of convertible preferred may be estimated, is referred to the section entitled "Options Markets and Instruments."

ESTIMATING THE COST OF EQUITY

The cost of equity is even more difficult to estimate than the cost of debt, mainly because future payments to shareholders are not contractual and are difficult to predict. The principle, however, is the same. The cost of equity capital is the opportunity cost forgone by not investing in an alternative investment of equal risk.

We begin by showing some of the difficulties involved in anachronistic measures of the cost of equity such as the dividend yield, the earnings-price ratio, and the **Gordon growth model.** The **capital asset pricing model** and the **Modigliani-Miller approach** are suggested as "state of the art" approaches.

Focus then shifts to problems such as how to handle flotation costs; the cost of retained earnings, the cost of retained earnings, the cost of depreciation funds, the effect of financial and operating leverage, trading on the equity, and convertible issues as a source of equity.

DIVIDEND YIELD. Why not use dividend yield or the earnings-price ratio to estimate the cost of equity capital? The dividend yield is defined as the ratio of current dividends, d_0 to the current price per share of common stock, S_0.

$$\text{dividend yield} = \frac{d_0}{S_0} \tag{20}$$

It will be equivalent to the cost of equity capital only under a special set of assumptions, namely, that the current dividend per share d_0 must be paid out at the end of each year forever and that the amount of the dividend must never change (i.e., never grow). This is an extremely unrealistic set of assumptions. Also, if the dividend yield is to be employed as a measure of the cost equity, the firm must pay a dividend. Equation 20 is useless if current dividend payout is zero. In addition low dividend yields imply a cost of equity capital that is less than the cost of debt—which is absurd.

EARNINGS–PRICE RATIO. Another incorrect definition frequently used to compute the cost of equity is the earnings-price ratio. This is the ratio of current annual accounting earnings per share e_0 to the current common stock price per share S_0. Sometimes called the earnings yield, it is computed as follows:

$$\text{earnings yield} = \frac{e_0}{S_0} \tag{21}$$

It has the advantage of being "usable" even though the firm has no dividend payout. However, it leads to a number of difficulties. Not the least among them is that it implies a negative cost of equity capital when earnings are negative. Also, it may lead one to conclude that for high price-earnings ratio firms (usually these are high-growth firms) the cost of equity is lower than the cost of debt. Equity in a levered firm, of course, being a residual claimant, is always more risky than debt. A related issue is that some firms have thought that their objective should be to maximize the price-earnings ratio because of the mistaken belief that such a policy would lower the "cost of equity" as measured by the earnings-price ratio. Exhibit 12, which demonstrates the **fallacy** of trying to maximize the firm's price-earnings ratio, shows the relationship between the rate of return on capital and the dollar amount of investment as a declining function of the amount invested. This reflects the fact that as more and more capital is invested in a given year,

EXHIBIT 12   PRICE-EARNINGS RATIO MAXIMAZATION FALLACY

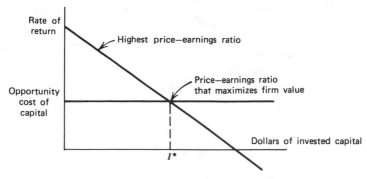

the list of good projects becomes exhausted and the rate of return on the marginal project falls. The highest price-earnings projects will be those that reflect a high **future** rate of return. The stock price is high relative to current earnings because future earnings are expected to be high. If the firm sticks to high price-earnings projects, it will fail to undertake many projects that earn more than their opportunity cost of capital. Shareholder wealth is maximized at a lower price earnings ratio. This is accomplished at I^*, where the marginal rate of return on the last investment dollar is equal to the opportunity cost of funds. Therefore, as Exhibit 12 illustrates, firms that maximize price-earnings ratios usually are not maximizing shareholder wealth.

GORDON GROWTH MODEL. The Gordon gorwth model expresses the **cost of equity capital** derived under the assumptions that the dividend per share grows at a constant rate g forever and that the risk of the firm will remain unchanged. If we designated K_e as the cost of equity, the model is:

$$K_e = \frac{d_0(1 + g)}{S_0} + g \tag{22}$$

This definition of the cost of equity is frequently employed. However, it must be used with care. First, the growth rate g is a long-run growth rate over an infinite horizon, and as such is a difficult parameter to conceptualize. Second, the long-run growth rate must, by definition, be strictly less than the cost of equity, K_e. This can be demonstrated by rearranging terms to solve for the present value of equity:

$$S_0 = \frac{d_0(1 + g)}{K_e - g} \tag{23}$$

If the long-run growth rate is equal to the cost of equity, the implied value of the firm is infinite. If $g > K_e$, the implied value is negative. Both results are impossible. Third, the parameters of the Gordon growth model (as given in equation 22) are interdependent. It would seem that a higher growth rate implies a higher cost of equity. However, this is not true because the higher rate of growth will imply a higher current value of the common stock S_0. The net effect will reduce the cost of equity. But if one estimates a higher growth rate, how much greater should S_0 become? The answer is unclear. Finally, the Gordon growth model provides no obvious answer to the question. What cost of equity should be applied when the firm is considering projects of different risk than the current operations of the firm? Because of these difficulties, it is recommended that the cost of equity be estimated by using the **capital asset pricing model** (CAPM).

CAPITAL ASSET PRICING MODEL. Modern finance theory provides an equilibrium model that can be used to estimate the cost of equity. The capital asset pricing model (CAPM) was derived by Sharpe (*Journal of Finance,* September 1964), Lintner (*Review of Economics and Statistics,* February 1965), and Mossin (*Econometrica,* October 1966).

Risks in CAPM. The CAPM is a theoretical tradeoff between the expected return on assets and their expected risk. However, the definition of risk is not the total volatility of the asset return. Rather, it is that portion of the variability of an asset's return which cannot be diversified away at virtually no cost. Hence the CAPM argues the **systematic risk,** often called **beta,** is the only relevant measure of risk because it cannot be avoided through **diversification.**

To provide a better intuitive explanation of why only undiversifiable risk is relevant, consider the following train of logic. First, investors can diversify their portfolios at very low cost. For example, one can invest in **no-load mutual funds,** which are composed of hundreds of different assets. In addition, many investors have a good portion of their wealth in pension funds, which are usually well diversified. Second, assuming that diversification costs virtually nothing, one can reduce the total variability of return on his portfolio by holding more and more assets. The portfolio with the greatest possible diversification is the economy as a whole. This portfolio would be composed of every asset (stocks, bonds, real estate, human capital, and personal property) held according to the ratio of its market value to the market value of all assets. In other words, the portfolio would be a **market portfolio,** where each asset is held according to its market value weight. Third, since one cannot escape the risk of the market portfolio, the relevant measure of the risk of an individual asset is its contribution to the risk of the market portfolio. Risk-averse investors will pay a premium to avoid that portion of an asset's **total volatility** which covaries with the market portfolio. They will pay nothing to avoid that portion of an assest's volatility which can be diversified away at no cost (i.e., that portion which is independent of the market return). Consequently, the capital asset pricing model follows from the fact that the total variance of return for every asset can be partitioned into two parts, **undiversifiable** or **systematic risk,** and **diversifiable** or **unsystematic risk:**

$$\text{total return variance} = \text{diversifiable risk} + \text{undiversifiable risk} \quad (24)$$
$$\text{total return variance} = \text{unsystematic risk} + \text{systematic risk}$$

When estimating the required rate of return on risky assets, the CAPM argues that only the systematic risk is relevant because the unsystematic risk is independent of the market portfolio and can be avoided at no cost through diversification.

For a more detailed explanation of the CAPM, the reader is referred to Modigliani and Pogue (*Financial Analysts Journal,* March–April 1974, May–June 1974) or to Copeland and Weston (*Financial Theory and Corporate Policy,* 2d. ed. Chapters 6 and 7). An example taken from Modigliani and Pogue will serve to illustrate the difference between the total variance of return and systematic risk. The actual realized rates of return, their volatility, and their systematic risk for Bayuck Cigar Co. (a NYSE-listed firm) and a randomly selected portfolio of 100 NYSE listed firms are given below. Calculations were made from monthly data between January 1945 and June 1970.

Risk and Return for Bayuck Cigar and Well-Diversified Portfolio

	Annual Return (%)	Total Volatility	Systematic Risk
100-Stock portfolio	10.9	4.45	1.11
Bayuck Cigar	5.4	7.25	0.71

Naturally one would expect the riskier asset to have a higher rate of return over the long run. Note that if total volatility is employed as a measure of risk, the "riskier" asset, Bayuck Cigar, has a lower rate of return. Part of the paradox is that we are comparing the volatility of an individual stock with the volatility of a well-diversified portfolio. Of course the portfolio has lower volatility. A better comparison, one that uses the appropriate measure of risk, is one that does not consider the diversifiable risk, and therefore compares the two alternatives on an equal basis. If one compares the systematic (nondiversifiable) risk of the alternative, the apparent paradox is resolved. Bayuck Cigar Co. is seen to have lower systematic risk and lower return. It makes sense that the low-risk asset should also have lower return in the long run.

CAPM Equation. The capital asset pricing model says that there should be a linear tradeoff between the expected rate of return on an asset and its systematic risk. This is shown in Exhibit 13 and equation 25.

EXHIBIT 13   THE CAPITAL ASSET PRICING MODEL

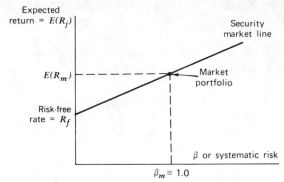

$$E(R_j) = R_f + [E(R_m) - R_f]\beta_j$$

(25)

where $E(R_j)$ = expected (or required) rate of return on jth asset
   R_f = risk-free rate (Treasury bill rate)
   $E(R_m)$ = expected rate of return on market portfolio
   β_j = cov (R_j, R_m)/var (R_m); systematic risk

Beta Defined. The statistical measure of systematic risk is β (beta). It is computed as the **covanance** between the returns of the asset with the market portfolio, standardized by the variance of the market portfolio. Mathematically, this is

$$\beta = \frac{\text{cov}(R_j, R_m)}{\text{var}(R_m)} = \frac{\sum p_t(R_{jt} - \overline{R}_{jt})(R_{mt} - \overline{R}_{mt})}{\sum p_t(R_{mt} - \overline{R}_{mt})^2}$$

(26)

where p_t = probability of observing R_j in state of nature t
   $\overline{R}_{jt}$ = mean (or average) return on asset j
   R_{mt} = return on market portfolio in state t
   $\overline{R}_{mt}$ = mean (average) return on market portfolio

By definition, the covariance of the market portfolio with itself is equal to the variance of the market portfolio. Therefore, the beta of the market portfolio, β_m is always 1.0 (see Exhibit 13).

Security Market Line. According to the theory, every risky asset traded in secondary markets will have an equilibrium required rate of return that falls exactly on the upward sloping line in Exhibit 13. This line is called the

security market line. Many empirical studies have verified that the security market line (and its variants) is a reasonably good description of reality. Without going into a long and detailed description of possible extensions and modifications of the theory, we shall proceed by assuming that the model described above is the "state of the art."

How then, can the CAPM and the security market line be used to conceptualize the cost of equity capital? According to the model (equation 25), it is necessary to estimate the **risk-free rate of return** R_f, the expected rate of return on the **market portfolio** $E(R_m)$, and the **beta** β_j of the risky asset. The rates of return R_j and $E(R_m)$ are nominal rates (they include inflationary expectations) and they are gross rates of return before taxes. Usually, the risk-free rate is interpreted to be the rate on 90-day U. S. Treasury bills.

If we return to the example of the cost of capital for Bethlehem Steel as of December 31, 1976, the 90-day Treasury bill rate was 4.6%. Next, what about the expected rate of return on the market portfolio $E(R_m)$? The expected future rate of return on the market cannot be measured. However, a good way of guessing what it might be is to add three components: (1) the long-run real rate of growth in the economy, 3–4%, (2) an adjustment for inflation next year (in December 1976 a good guess might have been 6–7%), and (3) a risk premium (above the risk-free rate) for the riskiness of the market portfolio of equity (say 4–5%). Using the mean of each of these components, we estimate the expected rate of return on the market as 14.5%. Finally, we need an estimate of the **beta of Bethlehem steel.** Many companies are in the business of estimating financial statistics. It is hard to say who provides better betas. Without revealing the source, we use an estimate of $\beta = 0.9$ for Bethlehem Steel.

Cost of Equity. Finally, using these estimates we can guess at the cost of equity of Bethlehem Steel K_e, because the required rate of return should obey the CAPM. Rewriting equation 25, we have

$$K_e = E(R_j) = R_f + [E(R_m) - R_f]\beta_j \tag{27}$$

and substituting the correct estimates gives

$$K_e = E(R_j) = 0.0467 + [0.145 - 0.0467]0.9$$

$$K_e = 13.52\%$$

This is a "state of the art" ballpark estimate for the cost of equity of Bethlehem Steel as of December 31, 1976. Note that the cost of equity will change with our estimate of expected inflation. It will also change with the systematic risk of Bethlehem. If the basic business risk of Bethlehem changes or if its long-run target capital structure changes, its systematic risk will change correspondingly.

COST OF RETAINED EARNINGS: FLOTATION COSTS. Equity capital is provided by external sources if it comes from the issue of new shares and from internal sources if provided via retained earnings. Frequently, the question arises whether these different sources of equity have different costs. The root of the controversy is the flotation cost incurred whenever new shares are issued. How should it be accounted for?

An example of a **flotation cost** is fees charged by investment banking firms for the service of underwriting a new issue to the public. Suppose common stock is issued at S_0 dollars per share, the investment banking syndicate recieves f dollars per share, and the issuing firm receives the net amount, $S_0 - f$. Some textbooks (see Weston and Brigham, *Managerial Finance,* 6th ed., p. 702) argue that the cost of external equity should be computed by adjusting the Gordon growth model, equation 22, by flotation costs as follows:

$$K_e = \frac{d_0(1 + g)}{S_0 - f} + g \tag{28}$$

This technique implies that (1) external equity is more costly than internal equity (retained earnings), (2) the firm should use up its retained earnings for investment before issuing new equity, and (3) for a given risk, the marginal cost of capital is upward sloping as shown in Exhibit 14.

Adjusting the cost of equity by flotation costs presents several problems. First, flotation costs are paid when the equity is issued, but the adjusted rate of return method spreads them out over time. Such a procedure violates discounting procedures, which require that cash outflows be recorded as they occur. Second, the cost of equity capital is an **opportunity cost** determined by the rates of return that can be earned elsewhere on projects of equivalent risk. Since flotation costs are irrelevant in determining where else to invest, they are irrelevant in determining the cost of equity.

An alternative to handling flotation costs, as suggested in equation 28, is

EXHIBIT 14   HYPOTHETICAL MARGINAL COST OF CAPITAL (MCC)

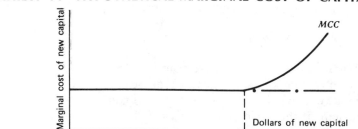

not to adjust the cost of equity at all. Rather, flotation costs can be recognized as a cash outflow to be borne by current shareholders whenever the firm needs to go to the capital markets for external capital (debt as well as equity). This cash outflow can then be combined with the other cash flows of the firm and the net cash flows should be discounted at the weighted average cost of capital determined without flotation costs. Under this recommended procedure the marginal cost of capital does not turn up, as shown by the solid line in Exhibit 14. Rather, for given risk, it stays constant and follows the dotted and dashed line. This approach implies that the cost of retained earnings and external equity are identical.

COST OF DEPRECIATION FUNDS. In their statement of sources and uses of funds, firms usually list **depreciation charges** as one of the most important sources of funds, if not the most important. Should depreciation be considered "free" capital, should it be ignored completely, or should a charge be assessed against it? The answer is that depreciation funds should be charged at their **opportunity cost,** which is the weighted average cost of capital for the firm as a whole.

Depreciation funds are part of the cash flows generated from operations (defined earlier as *OCFAT*). As such, they represent part of the total funds of the firm that are available to make payments to debtholders and shareholders. The combined opportunity cost for the total funds of the firm is the weighted average cost of capital. Finally, since the cost of depreciation-generated funds is equal to the weighted average cost of capital, depreciation does not enter separately into the calculation of the average cost of capital.

COST OF CONVERTIBLE SECURITIES. When a firm issues convertible debt (or preferred), it is really issuing a **bond plus a call option on the equity of the firm.** Convertibles are securities that are exchangeable into common stock at the option of the holder and under specified terms and conditions. The key feature is the **conversion ratio,** which determines the number of shares the holder of the convertible will receive when he surrenders his security on conversion. The **conversion price** is the **exercise price** implied by the conversion ratio. For example, suppose that the XYZ Co. issues a 20-year bond at a par value of $1,000 with a conversion feature that allows the holder to convert into 20 shares of common stock any time before the maturity of the bond. Then the conversion price X_c is

$$X_c = \text{conversion price} = \frac{\text{par value of bond}}{\text{shares received}} = \frac{\$1,000}{20} = \$50 \quad (29)$$

Sometimes the conversion ratio is stepped up over the life of the bond. For example, the ratio might be 20 shares for the first five years, 17.5 shares for the next five years, and so on. Still another factor that might affect the conversion ratio is a clause in most bonds that protects against dilution stock splits, stock dividends, and rights offerings.

Call Option. On the date of offering, the conversion price is always higher than the current stock price so that the bonds are not immediately convertible. If the conversion price is $50 as in the example above, the stock price might be $40. The coupon rate on convertibles is lower than on straight debt of equal risk and maturity because investors receive not only a bond but also a call option (the convertible feature), which allows them to gain if the stock price rises above the conversion price. The rate of return K_c received by an investor who purchases a convertible bond on the date of issue is determined by equating the price he pays for the convertible bond B_0 to the discounted value of the cash payments from the bond (coupons plus face value) plus the present value C of the **call option,** implicit in the right to convert. Mathematically the problem is to solve for K_c in the following formula:

$$B_0 = \sum_{t=0}^{T} \frac{E(\text{coupon})_t}{(1 + K_c)^t} + \frac{E(\text{face value})_T}{(1 + K_c)^T} + C \tag{30}$$

Convertible Debt. The value of the right to convert C can be determined by using the procedure suggested by Brennan and Schwartz (*Journal of Finance,* December 1977). It may be approximated by using the **European call option** pricing formula (Black and Scholes, *Journal of Political Economy,* May–June 1973), which is discussed in the section entitled "Options Markets and Instruments" of this *Handbook.* The value of the right to convert will increase with the market value of the stock S, the variable of the rate of return on the stock, the time remaining before the conversion privilege runs out, and the risk-free rate of return. It will decrease with a higher conversion price X_c.

The coupon rate on a convertible bond will be less than the coupon rate on an equivalent straight debt issue with the same par value, risk, and maturity. The actual **cost of convertible debt** K_c will also be higher than the coupon rate on the convertible issue. One of the implications is that the firm has a lower interest tax shield on convertible debt than it would have on equivalent straight debt. Thus it gives up part of its **interest tax shield** in return for lower cash coupons.

It has sometimes been argued that convertible debt is a cheap way of issuing new equity. We have **indicated** in equation 30 that the actual cost of convertible is higher than the coupon yield and not all the true cost is tax deductible. Therefore, if anything, convertible debt increases the cost of capital, not vice versa.

COMPUTING WEIGHTED AVERAGE COST OF CAPITAL: AN EXAMPLE

Cost of capital calculations are as much an art as they are a science. As seen above, this is particularly true when it comes to the problem of estimating the cost of equity. Nevertheless, we can use available methodology to reach a ballpark estimate. The example below estimates the **cost of capital for Bethlehem Steel** as of December 31, 1976. Recall that the weighted average cost of capital is defined as the cost of each type of capital multiplied by its percentage of the total capital employed by the firm.

GENERAL ALGEBRAIC EXPRESSION. The weighted average cost of capital is computed as follows:

$$WACC = K_{STD}(1 - t_c)\frac{STD}{TL} + K_{LTD}(1 - t_c)\frac{LTD}{TL}$$
$$+ K_p\frac{P}{TL} + K_c\frac{CONV}{TL} + K_e\frac{S}{TL}$$

where $WACC$ = weighted average cost of capital
K_{STD} = market value of short-term liabilities
TL = market value of total liabilities (debt and equity)
t_c = marginal corporate tax rate
K_{LTD} = cost of long-term debt
LTD = market value of long-term debt
K_p = cost of preferred stock
P = market value of preferred stock
K_c = cost of convertible deft or preferred
$CONV$ = market value of convertible debt and preferred
K_e = cost of equity
S = market value of equity

The task of estimating the $WACC$ for Bethlehem Steel is simplified because it has no convertible debt or preferred stock outstanding. Therefore the third and fourth terms in equation (31) are irrelevant.

We shall assume that Bethlehem contemplates no major changes in its capital structure over time. Consequently, the current percentages of short-term debt, long-term debt, and equity in the capital structure can be taken as the long-term weights for each capital source. Exhibit 15 gives the balance sheet for Bethlehem Steel in 1976.

COST OF SHORT-TERM LIABILITIES. This component of $WACC$ was discussed earlier. For the sake of convenience, we shall assume that the op-

EXHIBIT 15   BALANCE SHEET, BETHLEHEM STEEL, DECEMBER 1976

Assets		Liabilities	
Cash	45,600	Accounts payable	274,800
Marketable securities	355,600	Notes payable	—
Receivables	421,500	Accruals	948,600
Inventories	834,100	Long-term debt[a]	1,023,100
Long-term assets (net)	3,007,600	Common at par[b]	576,000
Total assets	4,939,100	Less Treasury stock	69,300
		Retained earnings	2,185,900
		Total liabilities	4,939,100

[a]Long-term debt is detailed in Exhibit 11.

[b]43,665,578 shares outstanding with a market price of $40.625 per share as of December 31, 1976.

Source: Moody's Industrial Manual.

portunity cost of interest-bearing short-term liabilities is the same as the interest rate on other short-term obligations of equal risk. A good approximation for Bethlehem Steel is the commercial paper rate, which in December 1976 was 4.91%.

COSTS OF LONG-TERM DEBT AND EQUITY. The **cost of long-term debt** for Bethlehem is the rate it would pay if it issued new 25–30 year Aa-rated bonds. This rate was estimated earlier to be approximately 8.3%. Finally, we used the capital asset pricing model to estimate the **cost of equity** to be 13.52% (see earlier discussion).

MARKET VALUE WEIGHTS. All that remains is to estimate the market value weights of each source of capital. For short-term liabilities (i.e., accounts payable, accruals, and notes payable) we used the book value weights. This is a reasonable approximation because there is not much chance for capital gains or losses on obligations with short lives. The only exception is the current portion of long-term debt, which may have a market value very different from book. However, since this information was not available, we were forced to use book value. Where possible, we used the market values of long-term debt as given in Exhibit 4, and when market value was unavailable we used book. The easiest source of capital to find market values was equity. Exhibit 16 gives the market value weights of the capital sources used by Bethlehem Steel. Note that non-interest-bearing liabilities (accounts payable and accruals) are not part of the weighting scheme because their cash costs are already accounted for (implicitly) in the firm's income statement. Note also, that the market values of long-term debt and equity are much lower than book values. Nevertheless, the market value weights are appropriate because they reflect the current economic value of the firm. Book value weights are irrelevant for current decision making.

EXHIBIT 16   MARKET VALUE WEIGHTS FOR CAPITAL SOURCES

	Market Value ($ Thousands)	% of Total	% of interest-bearing	Cost
Accounts payable and accruals	1,223,400	32.1	0.0	0.0
Notes payable	0	0.0	0.0	4.9%
Long-term debt	815,945	21.4	31.5	8.3%
Equity	1,773,914	46.5	68.5	13.5%
	3,813,259	100.0	100.0	

Source: Moody's Industrial Manual and Bank & Quotation Record, January 1979.

MARGINAL TAX RATE. Finally, by using equation 31 and the data given in Exhibit 16, we can estimate the weighted average cost of capital for Bethlehem Steel. The **marginal tax rate** is assumed to be 48%. TL excludes non-interest-bearing liabilities.

$$WACC = K_{STD}(1 - t_c)\frac{STD}{TL} + K_{LTD}(1 - t_c)\frac{LTD}{TL} + K_e\frac{S}{TL}$$

$$WACC = 0.049(1 - 0.48)(0.00) + 0.083(1 - 0.48)(0.315) + 0.135(0.685)$$

$$WACC = 10.61\%$$

As mentioned earlier, the weighted average cost of capital for a corporation changes from day to day as conditions in capital markets change. In recent years, one of the important causes of change has been the inflation rate. Almost every day, news arrives that changes the term structure of interest rates to reflect inflationary expectations. These changes must be taken into account when estimating the cost of capital.

OPTIMAL CAPITAL STRUCTURE

Until now we have assumed that the ratio of debt to total liabilities employed by the firm remains unchanged. It is time to turn to the question of whether the value of the firm and the weighted average cost of capital can be affected by the mixture of debt and equity financing chosen by the firm. If financing can affect the value of the firm, there is probably an optimal capital structure. Throughout the years there seem to have been empirical regularities in the capital structures employed by various industries. For example, electric utilities use a large percentage of debt, while computer firms do not. Why?

Several alternative theories have been put forward. One is that optimal capital structure results from a tradeoff between gains in value from the tax shield provided by utilizing debt capital and losses in value from potential **bankruptcy costs.** Another theory suggests that capital structure can be explained by **agency costs** that arise as bondholders and stockholders negotiate contracts. In the process of discussing these ideas, we shall also emphasize the relationship between the cost of equity capital K_e and the amount of debt in the capital structure of the firm.

DEBT, TAXES, AND BANKRUPTCY COSTS

Alternate Definition of WACC. This can be provided if we assume that the only form of taxes is corporate (no personal taxes), that there are no bankruptcy costs, that all cash flows are perpetuities, and that the firm takes on only projects that do not change its risk class. As shown in equation 4, the value of a levered firm may be written as

$$V^L = \frac{EBIT(1 - t_c)}{K_u} + t_c \frac{rD}{K_d} = V^u + t_c B$$

where V^L = market value of levered firm
$\quad V^u$ = market value of unlevered firm
$\quad EBIT$ = earnings before interest and taxes
$\quad r$ = coupon rate of debt
$\quad D$ = face value of debt
$\quad K_u$ = cost of equity for unlevered firm
$\quad K_d$ = cost of debt
$\quad B$ = market value of debt, $B = rD/K_d$

The cost of capital can be defined as the rate of return required on new investment ΔI, which is necessary to guarantee that the anticipated change in shareholders' wealth ΔS^0 will be positive. To discover a cost of capital that fits this definition, we need to examine the way in which the value of the levered firm will change as new investment is undertaken. Any change in the market value of the levered firm must come from one of four sources: the change in the value of original sharheolders' wealth ΔS^0, the change in the value of new shareholders' wealth ΔS^n, the change in the value of original bondholders' wealth ΔB^0, or the change in the value of new bondholders' wealth ΔB^n. Mathematically, this can be expressed as:

$$\Delta V^L = \Delta S^0 + \Delta S^n + \Delta B^0 + \Delta B^n \tag{32}$$

Dividing through by the amount of new investment, we have the change in the value of the firm with respect to new investment, ΔI:

$$\frac{\Delta V^L}{\Delta I} = \frac{\Delta S^0}{\Delta I} + \frac{\Delta S^n}{\Delta I} + \frac{\Delta B^0}{\Delta I} + \frac{\Delta B^n}{\Delta I} \tag{33}$$

We further assume that all new debt is subordinate to original debt and that the new project does not increase the risk of the original bondholders' claim on the firm. Therefore, $\Delta B^0/\Delta I = 0$. Also, note that the new project will be financed with new debt and new equity, therefore,

$$\Delta I = \Delta S^n + \Delta B^n \tag{34}$$

Using this fact in equation 33, we have:

$$\frac{\Delta V^L}{\Delta I} = \frac{\Delta S^0}{\Delta I} = \frac{\Delta S^n + \Delta B^n}{\Delta I} = \frac{\Delta S^0}{\Delta I} + 1 \tag{35}$$

Because shareholders are making the investment decision, we assume that they require their wealth to increase. This requirement may be stated by rearranging equation 35:

$$\frac{\Delta S^0}{\Delta I} = \frac{\Delta V^L}{\Delta I} - 1 > 0 \tag{36}$$

Equation 36 requires the value of shareholders' wealth to increase as a result of new investment ΔI. We can expand on this definition by noting that the change in the value of the firm when new investment is undertaken can be derived from equation 4:

$$\frac{\Delta V^L}{\Delta I} = \frac{\Delta EBIT(1 - t_c)}{K_u \Delta I} + t_c \frac{\Delta B^n}{\Delta I} \tag{37}$$

Note that the new investment is expected to change the earnings before interest and taxes ($\Delta EBIT$). This cash flow provides the necessary return on investment. As stated before, the cost of capital is the minimum return on investment that increases shareholders' wealth. We can obtain this definition by substituting 37 into equation 36:

$$\frac{dS^0}{dI} = \frac{\Delta EBIT(1 - t_c)}{K_u \Delta I} + \frac{\Delta B^n}{\Delta I} - 1 > 0$$

Solving for the required change in aftertax cash flows with respect to new investment, we have:

$$\frac{\Delta EBIT(1 - t_c)}{\Delta I} > K_u \left(1 - t_c \frac{\Delta B^n}{\Delta I} \right) \tag{38}$$

Equation 39 is an **alternate definition of the weighted average cost of capital.**

$$WACC = K_u \left(1 - t_c \frac{\Delta B^n}{\Delta I}\right) \tag{39}$$

Originally derived by Modigliani and Miller (*American Economic Review,* 1963), equation 39 shows the relationship between the weighted average cost of capital and the financial leverage employed in new investment. If we assume that new projects use the firm's target amount of debt and equity, equation 39 becomes:

$$WACC = K_u \left(1 - t_c \frac{B}{B + S}\right) \tag{40}$$

where $B + S$ is the sum of the market values of debt and equity. Of course, their value is identical to the value of the firm.

$$V^L = B + S \tag{41}$$

Notice that in equation 40 the cost of capital declines as the percentage of debt in the capital structure of the firm, $B/(B + S)$, increases. This reflects the fact that in a world with only corporate taxes, debt capital provides a tax shield.

Cost of Equity. Modigliani and Miller also derived an expression for the **cost of equity capital** K_e, which shows that the cost of equity rises as more and more debt is used in the firm's capital structure. Their formula is:

$$K_e = K_u + (K_u - K_d)(1 - t_c)\frac{B}{S} \tag{42}$$

Exhibit 17 shows the relationship between the weighted average cost of capital, the cost of debt, and the cost of equity as the firm increases its debt to equity ratio B/S. The cost of debt is assumed to be invariant to increases in the debt-equity ratio because new debt capital is assumed to be subordinate to old. Hence the riskiness of original debt is assumed to remain unchanged. Equity capital, on the other hand, becomes more risky as the debt-equity ratio increases. This follows because equity is the residual claimant in the cash flows of the firm. As more and more debt is undertaken, the variability of the equity position becomes greater. Shareholders will naturally require higher rates of return on equity to compensate them for their risk. Finally, the weighted average cost of capital decreases with higher financial leverage because of the tax shield provided by debt.

Sample Cost of Capital Problem. The usefulness of the theoretical results can be demonstrated by considering the following problem. The United

EXHIBIT 17 RELATIONSHIP BETWEEN CAPITAL COSTS AND LEVERAGE

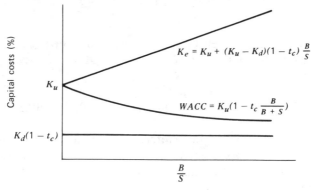

Southern Construction Co. currently has a market value capital structure of 20% debt to total assets. The company's treasurer believes that more debt can be taken on, up to a limit of 35% debt, without losing the firm's ability to borrow at 7%, the prime rate (also assumed to be the risk-free rate). The firm has a marginal tax rate of 50%. The 7% prime rate is used for instructive purposes and does not reflect recent rates. The expected return on the market portfolio next year is estimated to be 17% and the systematic risk of the company's equity β_L is estimated to be 0.5.

- What is the company's current weighted average cost of capital, and its current cost of equity?
- What will the new weighted average cost of capital be if the "target" capital structure is changed to 35% debt?
- Should a project with a 9.25% expected rate of return be accepted if its systematic risk is the same as that of the firm?

The data for this problem are all reasonably realistic. For example, the firm's systematic risk can be estimated for its current leverage of 20% by using the definition given in equation 26. Since the systematic risk is $\beta_L = 0.5$, we can use the CAPM, equation 27, to calculate the company's current cost of equity capital:

$$K_e = R_f + [E(R_m) - R_f]\beta$$

$$K_e = 0.07 + [0.17 - 0.07]\, 0.5 = 12\%$$

Equation 10, the definition of the weighted average cost of capital, can now be used to compute the firm's current cost of capital, given 20% debt in the capital structure.

$$WACC = K_d(1 - t_c)\frac{B}{B + S} + K_e\frac{S}{B + S} \qquad (10)$$

The facts of the problem tell us that the cost of debt is 7% and we have computed the cost of equity as 12%. Substituting these values into the equation, we have:

$$WACC = 0.07(1 - 0.5)(0.2) + 0.12(0.8) = 10.3\%$$

The second question is even more interesting. What will the cost of capital be if the firm increases its usage of debt up to 35% of its capital structure? We cannot directly use the traditional definition of the **weighted average cost of capital** (equation 10) because the cost of equity capital will increase with higher leverage. Only the **Modigliani-Miller approach** to the cost of capital is useful for estimating the new cost of equity and the new weighted average cost of capital. To compute the new cost of equity we can employ equation 42.

$$K_e = K_u + (K_u - K_d)(1 - t_c)\frac{B}{S}$$

All the necessary parameters are available. For example, we know that the cost of debt (up to a leverage level of 35%) K_d is 7%, the tax rate t_c is 50%, and the ratio of debt to equity will be 53.85%. With 35% debt in the capital structure, we have $B/(B + S) = 0.35$. Solving for B/S we have $B/S = 0.35/(1 - 0.35) = 53.85\%$. The only missing element is the cost of equity for the unlevered cash flow of the firm K_u. This can be estimated by using equation 40:

$$WACC = K_u\left(1 - t_c\frac{B}{B + S}\right)$$

$$K_u = \frac{WACC}{\left(1 - t_c\frac{B}{B + S}\right)} \qquad (40)$$

Substituting in the $WACC$ for 20% debt in the firm's capital structure yields:

$$K_u = \frac{0.103}{(1 - 0.5(0.2))} = 11.44\%$$

Finally, substituting all this into equation 42 gives:

$$K_e = 0.1144 + (0.1144 - 0.07)(1 - 0.5)0.5385 = 12.64\%$$

Thus we see that the cost of equity increases from 12% when leverage is 10% up to 12.64% when leverage increases to 35%. Equity holders require a higher rate of return to compensate them for the greater risk resulting from higher financial leverage.

Having computed the new cost of equity, we can estimate the weighted average cost of capital if the firm increases its debt to 35% of its capital structure.

$$WACC = K_d(1 - t_c)\frac{B}{B + S} + K_e\frac{S}{B + S}$$

$$WACC = 0.07(1 - 0.5)(0.35) + 0.1264(0.65) = 9.44\%$$

Note that the weighted average cost of capital has decreased, even though the cost of equity has increased. This happens because the firm is using a greater percentage of cheaper debt capital, which more than offsets the increased cost of equity.

One might also ask whether equity holders are better off with the new capital structure. The answer is yes—because they are able to keep the gain in the value of the firm that results from the lower cost of capital.

Finally, we are asked to decide whether a project with a 9.25% rate of return is acceptable if its sytematic risk (β) is the same as the firm's. The answer is no, because the weighted average cost of capital is 9.44%, that is, higher than the expected return on the project. A common error made in this type of problem is forgetting that the cost of equity capital increases with higher leverage. Had we estimated the weighted average cost of capital using 12% for the old cost of equity and 35% debt as the target capital structure, we would have obtained 9.03% as the cost of capital and we would have (incorrectly) accepted the project.

Effect of Personal Taxes. The results of the analysis can be considerably altered by the introduction of personal taxes. Miller (*Journal of Finance,* May 1977) has shown that under certain conditions the weighted average cost of capital may remain unchanged as the percentage of debt in the capital structure is increased. It is argued that the before-tax rate of return on corporate debt has to be "grossed up" to compensate bondholders for the personal taxes they must pay on interest received. This effect offsets the advantage of the interest tax shield the firm receives. The net result is the greater use of debt capital will have little or no effect on the firm's weighted average cost of capital.

Tax Advantage Tradeoff: Debt Financing Versus Bankruptcy Costs. This tradeoff can be used to explain the existence of an optimal capital structure for the firm. Suppose we assume that there is at least some tax benefit from carrying debt. If this were the only effect, firms would try to carry 100%

debt in their capital structures. But suppose that the tax benefit from debt is offset by a greater likelihood of incurring bankruptcy costs (defined explicitly in Section 19 on "Bankruptcy Reorganization") as the firm carries more and more debt. Bondholders bear most of the direct bankruptcy costs such as lawyers' fees, other fees, court costs, and wasted managerial time. Therefore, they require higher and higher interest rates as the firm uses greater amounts of debt in its capital structure. Exhibit 18 shows how the cost of capital changes when we consider a tradeoff between the tax benefit from using debt against the increased cost of bankruptcy. The optimal capital structure is attained at $[B/(B + S)]^*$, where the weighted average cost of capital is lowest. In practice, the choice of an optimal capital structure for a given firm is a subjective decision. Some treasurers make the decision by deciding on the lowest tolerable bond rating, say Aa; then they take on as much debt as possible without falling to the next lowest rating.

AGENCY COSTS. We have just seen that if there is a gain from financial leverage because of the tax deductibility of interest expenses, and if **bankruptcy costs** are significant, it is possible to construct a theory of optimal capital structure. One troublesome aspect of this approach is that even before income taxes existed in the United States, firms used debt in their capital structure. Furthermore, the same cross-sectional regularities in financial leverage that exist today can also be observed in data from periods before the introduction of corporate taxes. This suggests that optimal leverage (if it exists) may be explained by causes other than debt tax shields and bankruptcy costs. One possibility is a theory of agency costs as postulated by Jensen and Meckling (*Journal of Financial Economics,* October 1976).

Jensen and Meckling use the notion of **agency costs** to argue that the probability distribution of cash flows provided by the firm is not independent of ownership structure and that this relationship may be used to explain optimal leverage. First, there is an incentive problem associated with the

EXHIBIT 18   OPTIMAL COAPITAL STRUCTURE AS TRADEOFF BETWEEN BANKRUPTCY + COSTS AND TAX BENEFITS OF DEBT CAPITAL

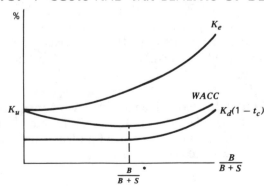

issuance of new debt. Suppose that unbeknownst to lenders, the firm has two different investment projects, both having the same systematic risk but different variances. The following are relevant probabilities and end-of-period cash flows:

Probability	Project 1	Project 2
.5	9,000	2,000
.5	11,000	18,000

Both projects cost $8,000 and both have the same expected return. Suppose the firm shows only project 1 to lenders and asks to borrow $7,000. From the lender's point of view, this request seems reasonable because project 1 will always earn enough to pay off the loan. Of course, if creditors lend $7,000 and if the owners of the firm have the abilty to switch to project 2, they will do so. The result is a transfer of wealth from bondholders to shareholders.

Agency Costs of Debt. To prevent such machinations, bondholders insist on protective covenants and monitoring devices of various types, to protect their wealth from expropriation. However, the costs of writing and enforcing such covenants may be considerable. Furthermore, these costs may increase with the percent of financing supplied by bondholders. These costs are the agency costs of debt.

Agency Costs of External Equity. Suppose, on the other hand, that a firm is owned exclusively by a single individual, the owner-manager. He will obviously take every action possible to increase his own wealth. However, if he sells a portion of the ownership rights by selling external equity to new shareholders, conflicts of interest will arise. He then becomes a co-owner with the new shareholders. If, at their expense, he can maximize his wealth by purchasing an executive jet and taking long vacations, he will do so. Co-ownership of equity implies agency problems. The new shareholders will have to incur **monitoring costs** of one form or another to ensure that the original owner-manager acts in their interest.

Jensen and Meckling (1976) suggest that given increasing agency costs with higher proportions of equity on one hand and higher proportion of debt on the other, there is an optimum combination of outside debt and equity that will be chosen because it minimizes total agency costs. In this way it is possible to argue for the existence of an optimum capital structure even in a world without taxes or bankruptcy costs.

VARIOUS FINANCING SOURCES

There are dozens of types of short-term debt, lease contracts, bonds, and preferred stock, each with a subtle difference that affects its risk and return characteristics. The purpose of this subsection is to familiarize the reader with them. The definitions that follow consist of only contracts that are undertaken by corporations.

SHORT-TERM INSTRUMENTS

Commercial Paper. This consists of any unsecured short-term promissory note issued by a corporation, a finance company, or a bank. Usually issued in denominations of $100,000 or more with maturities of 270 days or less, commercial paper is usually considered to have relatively low risk. Hence interest rates on commercial paper are only 1–2% higher than U.S. Treasury obligations of equal duration.

Bankers' Acceptances. These instruments are created as a means of financing goods in transit. The firm to which the goods are being delivered agrees to pay a given sum within a short period of time, usually 180 days or less. The bank then "accepts" this promise, obligating itself to pay the amount of the note if requested and receiving a claim on the goods as collateral. The note representing the loan becomes a liability of both the bank and the buyer of the goods and is therefore not very risky. Interest rates on bankers acceptances are usually only 1–2% above U.S. Treasury obligations of equal maturity.

LEASES

Sale and Leaseback. Such an arrangement is created when a firm owning land, buildings, or equipment sells the property to a financial institution and simultaneously enters into a contract to lease back the asset. Land leases are usually arranged with life insurance companies. The sale and leaseback of equipment could be arranged with an insurance company, a commercial bank, or a specialized leasing company. Note that the selling firm receives the value of the asset as an immediate source of cash. The lease payments are sufficient to return the purchase price plus a fair return on investment to the lessor.

Service Leases. This category includes both financing and maintenance services. The equipment involved is usually computers, automobiles, or trucks. It is the lessor's responsibility to maintian the equipment and the maintenance costs are built into the lease fee. Service leases are usually not fully amortized; that is, the payments do not recover the full cost of the equipment and the lessor maintains property rights to the residual value of the equipment when the lease period ends. Finally, many service leases have a cancellation clause that allows the lessee to stop payment and return the equipment before the lease contract ends.

Financial Leases. These are similar to sale and leaseback except that the equipment is purchased by the lessor from the manufacturer or distributor then leased out. A strict financial lease does not provide for maintenance services, is not cancelable, and is fully amortized.

Leveraged Leasing. Use of this term implies that the lessor does not have full equity interest in the leased asset. Instead, the lessor borrows a portion of the funds needed to acquire the asset for the purpose of leasing it out.

BONDS

Mortgage Bonds. These are long-term obligations that are secured by specific property. In addition, mortgage bonds are unsecured claims on the general assets of the firm. In the event of default, holders of mortgage bonds receive ownership of the mortgaged property.

Collateral Trust Bonds. Backed by other securities, usually held by a trustee, collateral trust bonds are frequently used by a parent firm when it pledges the securities of a wholly owned subsidiary as collateral.

Equipment Trust Certificates. These are backed by specific pieces of equipment or machinery. Frequently used by airlines, railroads, and shipping companies, these certificates may be issued by a trustee who holds the equipment, issues obligations, and leases the equipment to the corporation that uses it. Cash paid by the corporation is used to pay the interest and principal on the equipment trust certificates. Eventually the firm will take title to the equipment.

Debenture Bonds. Debenture bonds are general obligations of the issuing firm and are unsecured credit. They are claims on the general assets of the corporation only and are protected by their indenture restrictions. As mentioned earlier, the four most common types of indenture provision are provisions against the issuance of more debt, restrictions that limit dividend payments, provisions restricting merger activity, and restrictions on the disposition of the firm's assets.

Subordinated Debentures. Subordinated debentures are junior debt. In the event of bankruptcy, these claims against the firm will not be met unless and until the claims of senior debtholders have been fully satisfied.

Adjustment Bonds. Income bonds pay interest only when the corporation's net income is above a specified level. Occasionally they are called **adjustment bonds** because they may be issued by corporations undergoing reorganization to readjust fixed interest debt. Unfortunately, if the issue bears too many of the characteristics of equity, the Internal Revenue Service may view the interest payments as "essentially equivalent to a dividend" and taxable as such. In this event the interest payments are no longer deductible as an expense before taxes.

Guaranteed Bonds. These are bonds that are guaranteed by the assets of a corporation other than the issuing firm. Usually the guaranteeing corporation is a parent firm.

Participating Bonds. These provide fixed interest payments and, in addition, a portion of surplus earnings accruing over the life of the bond if earnings are above the fixed interest.

Joint Bonds. Obligations jointly issued by two or more corporations (usually railroads), sometimes called pooled bonds, provide joint collateral.

Voting Bonds. Usually issued in connection with reorganizations, voting bonds give holders the right to vote for directors if interest payments are not paid for a certain length of time.

Serial Bonds. Different portions of an issue of serial bonds mature at different (sometimes random) dates. A default on any portion coming due constitutes default on the entire issue.

Convertible Bonds. At the holder's option, these may be exchanged for other securities, usually common stock. The cost of capital in issuing such bonds was discussed in detail earlier.

RETIREMENT OF BONDS. One of the important features of bonds is the method of principal repayment. The various types of refunding are discussed below, followed by an economic analysis of the refunding decision.

Call Provisions. Call provisions give the firm the right to pay off a bond at any time before maturity. This provides an increased degree of flexibility, since debt can be reduced, its maturity altered via refunding, and most important, expensive debt with high interest rates may be replaced with cheaper debt if rates decline. Frequently the call price is established above par value. Nevertheless, from the investor's point of view the call provision establishes an upper limit on the amount of capital gain that can be obtained if interest rates fall. For this reason, the investor will require a higher yield to maturity on callable bonds than on straight debt of equal risk and maturity.

In effect, a callable bond is equal to an ordinary bond with an option contract. On the date of issue the bondholder equates the market price of the callable bond B_0 with the present value of the cash payments from the bond (coupons plus face value) less the present value of the call option C_0, which gives the firm the right to call in the debt early at some predetermined price. Mathematically, this may be expressed as follows:

$$B_0 = \Sigma \frac{E(\text{coupon})}{(1 + K_{\text{ca}})^t} + \frac{E(\text{face value})}{(1 + K_{\text{ca}})^T} - C_0 \tag{43}$$

where B_0 = present value of callable bond
$E(\text{coupon})$ = expected coupon payment in year t
$E(\text{face value})$ = expected face value if bond is refunded at maturity
K_{ca} = true cost of issuing a callable bond
C_0 = present value of call feature

The expression above is simlar to the earlier analysis of convertible debt except that instead of giving the bondholders something of value, namely, the right to convert, with callable bonds the firm is withholding something of value because the call provision limits the amount of capital gain the bondholder can earn.

Investors are usually given some call protection. During the first few years an issue may not be callable. In addition, a premium may be paid when a bond is called. Often this amount becomes smaller, the closer the bond is to its scheduled maturity date. Sometimes an entire issue may be called and other times only specific bonds, drawn by lot by a trustee, are called. In either case, a notice of redemption will appear in advance in the financial press.

Sinking Funds. Certain bond indenture provisions require the firm to make annual payments into a sinking fund. In this way a portion of the debt outstanding is repaid each year instead of having the entire amount come due at maturity. The corporation may pay cash to the bond trustee, who can then purchase bonds in the open market. Alternately, the firm itself may purchase the bonds, then deposit them with the trustee.

Serial bonds also allow for a portion of a debt issue to be repaid each year. The only difference is that the refunding is done at face value on a prescheduled basis.

The Refunding Decision. A careful economic analysis, which is fundamentally no different from that entailed by a project selection or capital budgeting decision, must precede the decision to refund. Usually, a firm will consider refunding if a bond has a call provision and if market interest rates have fallen below the coupon rate on the outstanding bonds. The differences of four cost components have to be contrasted against the value of the interest savings. The costs are: (1) the **call premium,** which is tax deductible, (2) the **flotation costs** on the issue of new debt, which can be deducted for tax purposes as an expense amortized over the life of the new bond, (3) the unamortized portion of the flotation cost on the outstanding issue; this may be recognized immediately as a tax-deductible expense, however, this must be netted out against the present value of the flotation costs that would have been amortized, and (4) **additional interest** paid because the old bond issue will be outstanding for a short period of time while the new bond has been issued. The present value of these costs can be subtracted from the present value of the interest savings to determine the net present value of the refunding decision. See Weston and Copeland (*Managerial Finance,* 8th ed., pp. 817–823) for a detailed example of a **bond refunding analysis.**

PRIVATE VERSUS PUBLIC PLACEMENT OF BONDS. Nearly half of all corporate bond sales are issued through private placements sold to insurance companies, pension funds, and other private holders. **Private placement** is the major alternative to underwritten issues of bonds to the public. The principal advantages of private placements are: (1) transactions costs are lower, especially for smaller issues where flotation costs on public issues would be prohibitively high, (2) indenture provisions and the timing of repayment can easily be tailored to meet the needs of both lender and borrower, (3) privately placed issues need not be registered with the **Securities and Exchange Commission,** (4) if the borrowing corporation runs into financial difficulties, the terms of the loan may be more easily renegotiated, and (5) the borrowing firm can schedule to take in funds as needed rather than all at once, as is necessary with a public issue.

The disadvantages of private placements are: (1) they lack marketablity because a market has not been established through a public offering, (2) the issuing firm loses the opportunity to repurchase the bonds through open market operations if interest rates fall, and (3) because institutional lenders are sophisticated and frequently much larger than the borrowing corporation, they can exact **indenture restrictions** that are often more restrictive than those on equivalent public offerings.

PREFERRED STOCK. Preferred stock is given preference over common stock in respect to dividends. Also, in the event of reorganization or bankruptcy, preferred stock has precedence. On the other hand, preferred stock dividends can be paid only after all interest payments on debt have been made, and in bankruptcy, preferred claims are strictly subordinate to all debt claims. Hence preferred stock is a hybrid security, riskier than debt but less risky than common stock.

Par Value. Unlike the par value of common stock, the par value of preferred stock is a meaningful quantity. First, it establishes the amount of the claim that preferred shareholders have on the assets of the firm in the event of the bankruptcy; second, preferred dividends are usually paid as a percentage of par value.

Cumulative Dividend Feature. Most preferred stock has a cumulative dividend feature. It is a protective device for preferred shareholders because it requires that all past preferred dividends must be paid before any common dividends may be paid.

As mentioned earlier, about 40% of preferred issues are convertible. For example, a share of preferred might be convertible into four shares of common at the discretion of the preferred stockholder. The conversion feature is valuable to preferred shareholders, and they are more willing to accept a lower preferred dividend rate on convertible preferred than on straight preferred. Of course, the lower coupon rate means that the firm has to pay out less cash flow.

Voting Rights. Sometimes preferred stock is given voting rights, which allow preferred shareholders to elect a minority of the company's board of directors, say two out of ten. Generally the voting privilege takes effect only when preferred dividends have not been paid for a while.

Participating Preferred. This rare type of security provides for preferred shareholders to receive a predetermined dividend, say $1 per share, for common shareholders to receive dividends up to some fixed amount, say an extra $1 per share, and then for preferred and common shareholders to share in any earnings beyond the first $2 per share.

Although preferred stock usually has no maturity date, sometimes an effective date is established by arranging a **sinking fund** requirement whereby a fixed portion of the outstanding preferred issue must be repurchased in the open market each year.

Another way of retiring preferred is to have a **call provision.** For example, the firm may be able to call in preferred stock with a par value of $100 if a **call premium** of $8 per share is paid. That is, preferred shareholders would be paid $108 per share.

COMMON STOCK. Whether publicly or privately held, common stock is the riskiest of the major forms of financing. Common shareholders are the residual claimants on the assets of the firm in the event of bankruptcy and receive dividends only after all payments on debt and preferred stock have been completed. However, common stockholders have certain **collective rights.** They elect the corporate board of directors; they may amend the charter of incorporation; they can adopt and amend the firm's bylaws; and they can authorize the sale of fixed assets, enter into mergers, change the amount of authorized common stock, and issue preferred stock, debentures, bonds, and other securities. As individual shareholders they have specific rights, which include voting for directors, selling their stock certificates, and inspecting the corporate books (within certain limits).

Cumulative Voting. The most common technique for selecting a **board of directors,** cumulative voting permits a shareholder to cast multiple votes for a single director. For example, suppose the firm has 10 directors and Mr. Jones owns 800 shares of stock. Then Mr. Jones will be given 8,000 votes, all of which may be cast for a single director instead of requiring that 800 votes be given to each of 10 nominees on the slate of directors. The significance of cumulative voting is that minority groups of shareholders can be assured of electing some directors to the board. For a more complete description of cumulative voting, see Weston and Copeland (*Managerial Finance*, 8th ed., pp. 753–755).

Par Value. For common stock, this is an arbitrary accounting designation. For example, if 1 million new shares are issued at $50 each with a $1 par value, $49 million would be recorded in the equity portion of the balance sheet as common-in-excess of par and $1 million would be recorded as common-at-par. However, the selection of a par value is arbitrary. The stock could as easily have a $5 par value or no par value at all. In fact, many corporations issue no par value common stock.

Classified Common Stock. There are voting and nonvoting classes of common stock usually called class A and class B. These designations are sometimes used by new companies seeking to acquire external equity. Class A common will be sold to the public with full voting rights and paying dividends. Class B stock will be retained by the original owners of the firm, will have voting rights, but will not pay individuals until the earnings power of the firm has been established.

Founders' Shares. These are like the class B shares except that they have sole voting rights and do not pay dividends for a predetermined number of years.

Preemptive Right. The preemptive right gives holders of common the first option to purchase additional shares of common stock. Its primary purpose is to protect shareholders against dilution of value when the new shares are issued. Shareholders of record may use their preemptive right to purchase new shares, or they can sell the right to someone else who will use it to purchase shares. A second purpose of the preemptive rights is maintain control of the firm in the hands of current shareholders. Without preemptive rights, management could theoretically issue a large number of new shares at a low price, then buy the new shares and gain control of the company.

To illustrate the use of preemptive rights, suppose that the XYZ Corp. currently has earnings of $1 million; 100,000 shares are outstanding, and the market price of a share is currently $100. Earnings per share is $10, the price-earnings ratio is 10, and the market value of the firm's equity is $10 million. Furthermore, assume that the firm wants to raise an additional $5 million in equity via a rights offering. The following questions come to mind:

- What should the terms of the right be?
- How many rights will be required to purchase a share of the newly issued stock?

- What is the value of each right?
- What effect will the rights have on the price of the existing stock?

Let us begin by assuming that the value of the firm's equity will rise $15 million. It might be higher if shareholders believe that the need to issue new equity is a signal that the company's earnings will increase as it undertakes new projects. It might be less if the firm is departing from an optimal long-run capital structure.

Furthermore, suppose that the new shares are to be sold for $62.50 each. This is a considerable discount from the current price of $100, but it ensures that the rights will have a value high enough to permit shareholders to exercise the rights and cover the transactions costs involved. If the price per share were higher, the value of rights would fall and fewer shareholders might exercise their rights.

Ex Rights Procedures. The number of new shares is determined by dividing the dollar amount of the issue by the price per share as shown below.

$$\text{number of new share} = \frac{\text{funds to be raised}}{\text{price per share}}$$

$$\text{number of new shares} = \frac{\$5,000,000}{\$62.50} = 80,000 \text{ shares}$$

Currently, there are 100,000 shares outstanding. If we divide the number of old shares by the number of new shares, we obtain the number of rights needed to purchase one new share. Each shareholder receives one right per share but needs 1.25 rights to purchase one new share. Therefore, a stockholder will have to turn in 1.25 rights and $80 to acquire a new share. We now know the number of rights per share. The terms of the rights issue will include the foregoing information and will allow a predetermined amount of time for shareholders of record to exercise their rights. Usually an **ex-rights date** represents the start of the formal rights offering. All shareholders of record as of that date will be given rights. Even though rights are valuable and should be sold or exercised, some stockholders will nevertheless neglect to do so. Therefore, rights offerings usually have an **oversubscription privilege** that allows subscribing stockholders the right to purchase all unsubscribed rights on a pro rata basis.

Next, what is the value of a right and what effect will the rights offering have on the current value of the stock? If we continue to assume that the value of equity after the offering will be $15 million, the price per share will be the total market value of equity divided by the number of shares outstanding.

$$\text{new price per share} = \frac{\text{assumed market value of equity}}{\text{total number of shares}}$$

$$\text{new price per share} = \frac{\$15,000,000}{180,000 \text{ shares}} = \$83.33$$

Therefore, after the financing is completed the price per share will have fallen from $100 to $83.33. Usually the price before the ex-rights date (i.e., $100) is referred to as the price **rights on.** After the ex-rights date the stock price will fall to $83.33 and is called the **ex-rights price.**

For an explicit mathematical derivation of the value of a right, the reader is referred to Smith (*Journal of Financial Economics,* December 1977, pp. 302–304). However, a much simpler approximation is given below. The value of one right, **ex-rights,** is equal to

$$\text{value of one right} = \frac{\text{ex-rights value of stock} - \text{subscription price}}{\text{number of rights per share}}$$

$$\text{value of one right} = \frac{\$83.33 - \$62.50}{1.25} = \$16.67$$

What is the effect of a rights offering on the wealth of a shareholder? Suppose John Doe owned 100 shares of the XYZ Corp. before the rights offering. At $100 per share, his wealth was $10,000. After the rights offering the price per share falls to $83.33, but Doe receives 100 rights, each worth $16.67 in cash. Therefore, the total value of his shares, $8,333, plus the value of his rights, $1,667, is just equal to his original wealth, $10,000. From an arithmetic viewpoint, the shareholder neither gains nor loses from the rights offering.

Underwritten Issues. There is one main alternative to rights offerings as a means of providing new equity capital to the firm: underwritten issues of stock. In fact, 90% of new equity issues are made via underwritings (see Smith, *Journal of Financial Economics,* December 1977). **Underwriting services** are provided by **investment banking firms,** which write up the required SEC registration statement, guarantee a negotiated price per share to the firm, and form a syndicate to stabilize the price of the new issue and market it.

Firm Commitment. In this type of underwriting agreement, the underwriting syndicate buys the security issue from the firm and resells it to the public. The firm is therefore guaranteed a net amount from the issue. The underwriting syndicate takes the risk of a decline in the market price between the time the investment banker transmits the money to the firm and the time the securities are placed in the hands of their ultimate buyers. In return for accepting this risk, the underwriter receives a fee that is the difference between the price at which the securities are offered to the public and the net amount received by the firm. Sometimes, part of the fee is paid by giving warrants to the investment banker.

Best Efforts. A type of underwriting less frequently used is called a **best efforts** commitment. In this case the underwriter acts only as the marketing agent for the firm. The underwriter does not agree to purchase the issue at a predetermined price, but sells the security for whatever price it will bring. The underwriter takes a predetermined spread and the firm takes the residual.

There has been a considerable amount of academic research on public issues of new equity. Two recent studies are of particular interest. Ibbotson (*Journal of Financial Economics,* September 1975) investigates the rates of return on newly issued equity and Smith compares the costs of underwritten issues with the costs of rights offerings.

The study of Ibbotson selected a random sample of 120 new issues between 1960 and 1969 (one issue each month) from among the 2,650 new issues during the time period. Using a procedure to adjust the rate of return for the riskiness of the new issue, he measured the abnormal rate of return on new issues. An abnormal rate of return is the rate above (or below) that which is required for investments in securities of equal risk. Ibbotson found that there was an abnormal rate of return during the month of issue but not thereafter. He concluded that the offering price, which is the price at which the underwriting syndicate sells to the public, is set below the equilibrium market price at the time of the issue. This abnormal rate of return does not go to the investment bankers. Rather it is "earned" by investors who buy new issues.

Smith has studied the costs of underwriting versus rights offerings. Exhibit 19 shows a cost comparison of firm commitment underwritings, rights offerings with standby underwriting, and simple rights offerings. The paradox is that although rights offerings appear to have the lowest cost as a percentage of proceeds, almost 90% of new issues are underwritten.

STOCK SPLITS AND STOCK DIVIDENDS. Stock splits and **stock dividends** do not provide any additional capital for the firm, but they do change the number of shares outstanding, hence the price per share. One often hears that the motivation for stock splits is either to increase the wealth of shareholders (because, e.g., a $100 stock that splits two for one will be worth more than $50 per share after the split) or to secure the advantage that accrues because the split moves the price per share into an ideal price range where it becomes more "affordable," and therefore more liquid. Empirical studies have examined both ideas. Fama, Fisher, Jensen, and Roll (*International Economic Review,* February 1969) investigated the rates of return for stock for 940 stock splits between January 1927 and December 1959. They found that companies that had been doing well were the ones that

EXHIBIT 19 COSTS OF FLOTATION AS A PERCENTAGE OF PROCEEDS FOR 578 COMMON STOCK ISSUES REGISTERED UNDER THE SECURITIES ACT OF 1933 DURING 1971–1975[a]

Size of Issues ($ Millions)	Underwriting				Rights with Standby Underwriting				Rights	
	Number	Compensation (% of Proceeds)	Other Expenses (% of Proceeds)	Total Cost (% of Proceeds)	Number	Compensation (% of Proceeds)	Other Expenses (% of Proceeds)	Total Cost (% of Proceeds)	Number	Total Cost (% of Proceeds)
Under 0.50	0	—	—	—	0	—	—	—	3	8.99
0.50–0.99	6	6.96	6.78	13.74	2	3.43	4.80	8.24	2	4.59
1.00–1.99	18	10.40	4.89	15.29	5	6.36	4.15	10.51	5	4.90
2.00–4.99	61	6.59	2.87	9.47	9	5.20	2.85	8.06	7	2.85
5.00–9.99	66	5.50	1.53	7.03	4	3.92	2.18	6.10	6	1.39
10.00–19.99	91	4.84	0.71	5.55	10	4.14	1.21	5.35	3	0.72
20.00–49.99	156	4.30	0.37	4.67	12	3.84	0.90	4.74	1	0.52
50.00–99.99	70	3.97	0.21	4.18	9	3.96	0.74	4.70	2	0.21
100.00–500.00	16	3.81	0.14	3.95	5	3.50	0.50	4.00	9	0.13
Total/average	484	5.02	1.15	6.17	56	4.32	1.73	6.05	38	2.45

[a]Issues are included only if the company's stock was listed on the NYSE, AMEX, or regional exchanges prior to the offering, any associated secondary distribution represents less than 15% of the total proceeds of the issue, and the offering contains no other types of securities. The costs reported are (1) compensation received by investment bankers for underwriting services rendered, (2) legal fees, (3) accounting fees, (4) engineering fees, (5) trustees' fees, (6) listing fees, (7) printing and engraving expenses, (8) Securities and Exchange Commission registration fees, (9) Federal Revenue Stamps, and (10) state taxes.

Source: C. W. Smith, Jr., "Alternative Methods For Raising Capital, Rights vs. Underwritten Offerings," *Journal of Financial Economics*, December 1977.

underwent stock splits, but there was no abnormal performance either on the split date or during the following time interval.

A more recent study by Grinblatt, Masulis, and Titman (*Journal of Financial Economics*, 1984) studied changes in equity market value on the announcement dates of stock splits and stock dividends. For 1380 stock split announcements between 1967 and 1976, they found a statistically significant announcement effect of 3.03% and for 382 stock dividends the abnormal return was 4.9% (also statistically significant). These results show that the marketplace interprets stock splits and stock dividends as favorable signals about the future of the firm.

Copeland (*Journal of Finance*, March 1979) studied the **liquidity of stocks following their splits.** He found that average trading volume declines relative to what it had been before the split, transactions costs increase as a percentage of value traded following stock splits, and bid-ask spreads as a percentage of the value traded increase following splits. Therefore, he concluded that the relative liquidity of stocks declines following splits. This is the opposite of the liquidity motive mentioned above. In sum, no one has yet discovered a good rationale for stock splits or stock dividends. When considering a stock split or stock dividend, management should consider the tradeoff between the announcement benefits documented by Grinblatt, Masulis and Titman against the liquidity costs documented by Copeland.

REFERENCES

American Bar Association, *Commentaries on Model Debenture Indenture Provisions,* Chicago, 1971.

Baranek, W., "The WACC Criterion and Shareholder Wealth Maximization," *Journal of Financial and Quantitative Analysis,* March 1977, pp. 17–32.

Baxter, N. D., "Leverage, Risk of Ruin and the Cost of Capital," *Journal of Finance,* September 1967, pp. 395–403.

Black, F., and Scholes, M. S., "The Pricing of Options and Corporate Liabilities," *Journal of Political Economy,* May–June 1973.

Brennan, M. J., and Schwartz, E. S., "Convertible Bonds: Valuation and Optimal Strategies for Call and Conversion," *Journal of Finance,* December 1977, pp. 1699–1715.

Cargill, Thomas F., "The Term Structure of Interest Rates: A Test of the Expectations Hypothesis," *Journal of Finance,* June 1975, pp. 761–771.

Copeland, T. E., "Liquidity Changes Following Stock Splits," *Journal of Finance,* March 1979.

———, and Weston, J. Fred, *Financial Theory and Corporate Policy,* 2d ed. Addison-Wesley, Reading, MA, 1983.

Dobson, Steven; Sutch, Richard; and Vanderford, David, "An Evaluation of Alternative Empirical Models of the Term Structure of Interest Rates," *Journal of Finance,* September 1976, pp. 1035–1065.

Fama, E., Fisher, L., Jensen, M., and Roll R., "The Adjustment of Stock Prices to New Information," *International Economic Review,* February 1969, pp. 1–21.

Farrar, D. E., and Selwyn, L., "Taxes, Corporate Financial Policies and Returns to Investors," *National Tax Journal,* December 1967, pp. 444–454.

Galai, D., and Masulis, R., "The Option Pricing Model and the Risk Factor of Stock," *Journal of Financial Economics,* January–March 1976, pp. 53–81.

Grinblatt, M., Masulis, R., and Titman, S., "The Valuation Effects of Stock Splits and Stock Dividends," *Journal of Financial Economics,* December 1984, pp. 461–490.

Hamada, R. S., "The Effect of the Firm's Capital Structure on the Systematic Risk of Common Stocks," *Journal of Finance,* May 1972, pp. 435–452.

Ibbotson, R., "Price Performance of Common Stock New Issues," *Journal of Financial Economics,* September 1975, pp. 235–272.

Jensen, M., and Meckling, W., "Theory of the Firm: Managerial Behavior, Agency Costs, and Ownership Structure," *Journal of Financial Economics,* October 1976, pp. 305–360.

Kalay, A., "Toward a Theory of Corporate Dividend Policy," unpublished Ph.D. thesis, University of Rochester, Rochester, NY, 1979.

Kim, E. H., "A Mean-Variance Theory of Optimal Capital Structure and Corporate Debt Capacity," *Journal of Finance,* March 1978, pp. 45–64.

Lewellen, W., Long, M., and McConnell, J., "Asset Leasing in Competitive Capital Markets," *Journal of Finance,* June 1976, pp. 787–798.

Lintner, J., "The Valuation of Risk Assets and the Selection of Risky Investments in Stock Portfolios and Capital Budgets," *Review of Economics and Statistics,* February 1965, pp. 13–37.

Miller, M., and Upton, C., "Leasing, Buying and the Cost of Capital Services," *Journal of Finance,* June 1976, pp. 761–786.

Miller, M. H., "Debt and Taxes," *Journal of Finance,* May 1977, pp. 261–275.

Modigliani, F., and Miller, M. H., "The Cost of Capital, Corporation Finance, and the Theory of Investment," *American Economic Review,* June 1958, pp. 261–297.

———, "Corporate Income Taxes and the Cost of Capital," *American Economic Review,* June 1963, pp. 433–443.

———, "Some Estimates of the Cost of Capital to the Electric Utility Industry, 1954–57," *American Economic Review,* June 1966, pp. 333–348.

Modigliani, F., and Pogue, G., "An Introduction to Risk and Return," *Financial Analysts Journal,* March–April 1974, May–June 1974, pp. 68–80, 69–85.

Mossin, J. "Equilibrium in a Capital Asset Market," *Econometrica,* October 1966, pp. 768–783.

Myers, S., Dill, DD, and Bautista, S., "Valuation of Financial Lease Contract," *Journal of Finance,* June 1976, pp. 799–819.

Myers, S. C. "Determinants of Corporate Borrowing," *Journal of Financial Economics,* November 1977, pp. 147–175.

Roll, Richard, *The Behavior of Interest Rates,* Basic Books, New York, 1970.

Rubinstein, M. E., "A Mean-Variance Synthesis of Corporate Financial Theory," *Journal of Finance,* March 1973, pp. 167–181.

Schall, L., "The Lease-or-Buy and Asset Acquisition Decisions," *Journal of Finance,* September 1974, pp. 1203–1214.

Sharpe, W. F., "Capital Asset Prices: A Theory of Market Equilibrium Under Conditions of Risk," *Journal of Finance,* September 1964, pp. 425–442.

Smith, C. W., Jr., "Alternative Methods for Raising Capital: Rights vs. Underwritten Offerings," *Journal of Financial Economics,* December 1977, pp. 273–308.

———, and Warner, J. B., "On Financial Contracting: An Analysis of Bond Covenants," *Journal of Financial Economics,* June 1979, pp. 117–161.

Stiglitz, J. E., "A Re-Examination of the Modigliani-Miller Theorem," *American Economic Review,* December 1969, pp. 784–793.

———, "On the Irrelevance of Corporate Financial Policy," *American Economic Review,* December 1974, pp. 851–866.

Wakeman, Lee M., "Bond Rating Agencies and the Capital Markets," Working Paper, Graduate School of Management, University of Rochester, Rochester, NY, 1978.

Weinstein, Mark I., "The Effect of a Rating Change Announcement on Bond Price," *Journal of Financial Economics,* December 1977, pp. 329–350.

———, "The Seasoning Process of New Corporate Bond Issues," *Journal of Finance,* December 1978, pp. 1343–1354.

Weston, J. F., and Copeland, T. E., *Managerial Finance,* 8th ed., Dryden Press, Hinsdale, IL, 1986.

13

DIVIDEND POLICY

CONTENTS

13

DIVIDEND POLICY

John T. Hackett

INTRODUCTION

In addressing the issue of dividend policy, management and the board of directors must make decisions regarding the allocation of its shareholders' returns in terms of immediate and/or future benefits. From the shareholders' standpoint, the decision as to how profits are to be divided between dividends and reinvestment is paramount. Management must be sensitive to their shareholders' concerns and aware that dividend decisions are complex.

Over the past 10 years, industrial corporations in the United States have paid out approximately 40% of their total aftertax profits as cash dividends, as shown in Exhibit 1. The remainder of industrial company earnings has been retained for investment in additional fixed assets, working capital, or acquisition of existing businesses.

This section describes the role of dividend policy in corporate financial management. **Corporate dividend policy** is not understood by a large segment of the financial community. There is a misconception that dividend policy is a straightforward and simple aspect of finance as compared with the more technical areas such as taxation, liquidity management, and cost accounting. Some observers of corporate behavior assume that dividend policy is determined easily because dividends represent only the unused portion of corporate profits available to equity investors.

Dividends represent payment to the shareholders for use of **risk capital,** as does the increase in share prices. In a sense, dividends are similar to the payments to suppliers of labor and materials and to the interest payments paid to suppliers of credit. The primary difference is that common stock dividends are not paid as a matter of contractual requirement.

Tax policies, both federal and state, discriminate between those who re-

The author acknowledges, with appreciation, the sections on "Management Views" and "Theory and Empirical Evidence" written by the editor, Edward I. Altman.

EXHIBIT 1 DIVIDEND PAYOUT

	1975	1976	1977	1978	1979	1980	1981	1982	1983	1984
STANDARD & POOR'S INDUSTRIALS										
Earnings per share	8.58	10.68	11.56	13.12	16.23	16.13	16.70	13.21	14.78	17.94
Dividends per share	3.72	4.25	4.96	5.35	5.98	6.55	7.00	7.18	7.37	7.43
Net dividend payout (%)	43	40	43	41	37	41	42	54	50	41
VALUE LINE INDUSTRIAL COMPOSITE										
Earnings per share	1.47	1.84	2.05	2.32	3.07	3.01	2.98	2.13	2.62	3.22
Dividends per share	.60	.68	.80	.88	1.01	1.11	1.17	1.19	1.19	1.29
Net dividend payout (%)	41	37	39	38	33	37	39	56	45	40

10-YEAR AVERAGE NET PAYOUTS

Value Line	40.5%
Standard & Poor's 400	43.2%

Sources: Value Line Investment Survey, New York, 1985; Standard & Poor's Corp. *Statistics*, S & P, New York, 1985.

ceive their return on investment as dividends and those who receive interest as creditors. Interest, of course, is a tax-deductible item to the corporation, whereas dividend payments to shareholders are paid from profits earned after the payment of taxes. Legislation to remedy tax treatment differentiation between dividends and interest income have been proposed, but not as a means of eliminating the difference in status between capital sources. The justification for the proposed tax reform is based on a need to increase capital formation and productivity in the United States.

There are many other interested and affected parties involved in dividend policy determination, including creditors, suppliers, and representatives of labor who seek to influence the determination of the share of current corporate earnings that will go to equity investors rather than being retained by the corporation for other purposes.

TYPES OF DIVIDEND

In describing dividends, a major distinction exists between dividends paid to **preferred shareholders** and to **common shareholders.** Although both classes represent equity investors, there are significant distinctions in terms of payment of dividends and the right of each class of shareholder with respect to claims on corporate earnings.

PREFERRED STOCK DIVIDENDS. Preferred shareholders are just that. They hold a preferred position with respect to dividend payments. In addition, there may be distinctions among preferred shareholders regarding rights to dividends. Preferred shareholders are usually entitled to a stated dividend before common shareholders receive any dividend. Unlike common stock, both the terms of dividend payment and the rate for preferred are set down in a contractual agreement between the corporation and the shareholder. Agreement regarding the amount of dividends to be received by preferred shareholders is set at the time of the issuance of preferred shares. Unlike common shares, preferred shares receive a fixed dividend rate, stated as a percentage of the face value or dollar amount of the preferred shares.

Failure to pay a preferred share dividend usually results in an obligation to pay at a later time, which is referred to as a **cumulative dividend** privilege. A cumulative clause in a preferred shareholders' agreement requires that if a corporation fails to pay a preferred share dividend, or series of dividends, the corporation incurs a liability to pay the dividend at a later time and no common share dividends may be paid as long as such cumulative dividend liabilities on preferred shares remain outstanding. If preferred share dividends are not paid for a prolonged period, preferred shareholders may assume other rights such as the right to select a number of the members of the corporate **board of directors,** approve the issuance of additional preferred shares to existing shareholders, or financial obligation rights senior to those of existing preferred shareholders in the event of corporate liquidation.

Preferred shares may also be classified on the basis of seniority with respect to receipt of dividends. Straight preferred shares usually enjoy a senior claim on dividend payments over convertible preferred shares, which carry a subordinated position both in terms of dividend payments and claim on assets in the event of liquidation. In most instances, straight preferred shares carry a higher dividend rate than convertible preferred shares. However, convertible preferred shares can be converted into a fixed number of common shares of the issuing corporation. The **conversion ratio** is part of the contract between the preferred shareholders and the corporation. In addition, there may be several classes of straight preferred shares with differing rates of dividends and claims on dividends and assets. Agreements between issuing corporations and preferred shareholders sometimes prevent the issuance of additional preferred shares with preferential or even equal dividend rights. In such instances, the corporation may have created a subordinated straight preferred issue. The differentiation of the rights of preferred shareholders are sometimes complex.

Most preferred share issues are purchased by institutional investors. The shares are frequently acquired by a **direct (private) placement** with a contract between the issuing corporation and the institutional investor. In arranging the direct placement, elaborate contracts are created to protect the investors. In isolated instances, preferred shareholders may be entitled to dividends other than cash.

The only common differentiation between the values placed on straight preferred shares and on convertible preferred shares is an increase or decrease in the value of common shares that the convertible preferred may have rights to under a convertible preferred issuance agreement. Fluctuations in common share price are normally reflected in the market price of a convertible preferred share.

COMMON STOCK DIVIDENDS. Nearly all **common stock dividends** fall into two groups: cash and shares. The most familiar form of common stock dividend is a cash payment declared by the **board of directors** and paid quarterly. However, it is not uncommon for a corporation to declare additional shares of stock as a dividend. In those instances, the dividend is referred to as a stock dividend. **Stock dividends** and **stock splits** are quite different, although they are frequently assumed to be the same.

Stock Dividends and Stock Splits. When a **stock dividend** is paid, the **retained earnings or capital surplus** of the corporation is debited and the capital shares account is credited. In addition, the company must have sufficient authorized and unissued shares available; otherwise, an amendment to the charter increasing the authorized shares will have to occur first. Such an amendment normally requires a shareholder meeting. A stock dividend requires no change in **par value.** Stock dividends are declared less frequently than cash dividends and do not follow a uniform pattern, as contrasted with cash dividends.

Unlike a stock dividend, a **stock split** does not affect the retained earnings or the capital surplus account. The capital shares account is also unaffected when a stock split is declared. A stock split does require a change in par value, but the surplus accounts remain unaffected. A corporation may also employ a **reverse stock split** to reduce the number of shares outstanding and increase the par value and market value of the remaining shares. A reverse split, for example, of 1 for 4, will reduce the number of shares outstanding by three-quarters and increase the price fourfold.

There are several reasons a management and board of directors may prefer to pay a stock dividend. For example, a very high price on existing shares, an effort to increase the number of shares outstanding, a desire to increase the number of shareholders, or a desire to retain a larger share of the earnings of the corporation are common reasons a corporation may elect to pay a stock dividend. There is widespread disagreement regarding the benefits that accrue to a shareholder as a result of stock dividends. It appears that when a shareholder receives a stock dividend, he only holds additional pieces of paper rather than receiving an actual increase in wealth. However, proponents of stock dividends contend that there is a benefit from a well-timed and well-designed stock dividend. It may signal to the investment community that the corporation is about to enter a new growth phase and, therefore, may result in an increased demand for the shares and improvement in share price. This so-called **dividend announcement effect** is discussed in a later subsection.

Common stock may also be categorized in terms of dividend payments. Some corporations issue different classes of common stock, for example, a class A and class B common stock. That is, one class of stock is given a preference with respect to dividend payments and certain liquidation rights; the remaining class may be subordinated with respect to initial dividend payments but the shareholders are entitled to voting rights and profit-sharing privileges not granted to the holders of other shares of common stock outstanding. The dividend payment declared may also differ between classes of common stock.

Other Forms of Dividend. Corporations may issue other forms of dividend, but it is uncommon. Issuance of **warrants** to existing shareholders may represent a type of dividend. Warrants give shareholders the right to purchase additional shares of stock at predetermined prices for a predetermined period of time. If a warrent permits the shareholder to buy additional shares at a price below the current market price and the warrants themselves are traded with a positive value, the shareholder can realize benefits without actually exercising the warrants and purchasing shares.

Preferred shares or debt securities may be issued by corporations as a form of dividend. These instruments are referred to as **bond or scrip dividends.** When a debt security is issued, the corporation is issuing a promise to pay rather than disbursing actual cash.

A corporation may elect to issue warrants, preferred shares, or debt at a time when it is experiencing a shortage of cash or rapid growth when earnings and cash are required to finance the growth or stability of the corporation. The shareholder may be afforded an opportunity to share in future profits by receiving **warrants** or **preferred shares as dividends.** If a corporation elects to employ these techniques for dividend policy, a careful examination of the tax impact on both the corporation and the shareholder should be determined before the actual declaration of the dividend.

Although it is uncommon, in some instances corporations distribute **property dividends.** For example, corporations might distribute products to shareholders as a dividend. Small manufacturers of consumer goods may elect to employ this technique, but it is rarely used. Again, it is important that the tax impact on both the corporation and the shareholders be carefully examined.

Corporations have declared property dividends in which shares of another corporation were distributed to shareholders. A large corporation may choose to dispose of a subsidiary by issuing the shares of the subsidiary directly to its existing shareholders. A large holding in another independent corporation may also be disposed of in this fashion; for example, **General Electric Co.** disposed of **RCA** shares in this fashion. There may be advantages to the shareholders, but the tax implications are complex.

MECHANICS OF DIVIDEND DECLARATION AND PAYMENT

The declaration of a dividend to holders of either preferred or common shares requires a resolution of the board of directors of the corporation. In addition, there may be legal requirements that must be met before a dividend is declared. The laws of the state that chartered the corporation may impose restrictions on the nature and size of dividends. Corporate laws as well as the tax laws of the state of incorporation should be considered before a dividend resolution is acted on by the board of directors. The **bylaws** of the corporation must be examined and understood by corporate management. A corporation may have adopted bylaws that place restrictions on the declaration of dividends, or it may have entered into agreements with creditors, preferred shareholders, or certain classes of common shareholders that restrict its ability to pay dividends.

Large corporations with outstanding issues of debt securities often have **covenants** within loan agreements that restrict the declaration of dividends. The most common restriction, or negative covenant, prohibits declaration of a dividend that would result in reducing the net worth of the corporation below an absolute figure or a multiple of the total debt outstanding. Other negative covenants may restrict the payment of dividends if earnings of the corporation do not equal a percentage or multiple of the corporation's past earnings. All restrictions on dividend payments are designed to protect the creditor's senior claim in the event of liquidation or dissolution.

The declaration of dividends on common shares are undertaken after preferred share dividend requirements are satisfied. A board of directors is usually unable to declare or pay a common share dividend in the event any past or present preferred share dividends remain outstanding.

Such restrictions differ according to the type of debt instrument or preference share outstanding. However, institutional lenders have attempted to adopt **uniform negative covenants.** The trend toward uniformity also reflects the influence of **investment banking firms** that act as intermediaries between institutional lenders and the corporations issuing the debt securities.

Foreign corporations are frequently subject to restrictions on dividend payments to shareholders who are not citizens or residents of the country in which the business is incorporated or the assets located. Such restrictions are usually a part of foreign exchange control legislation that is administered by a central bank or a ministry of finance. Restrictions may be placed on the actual declaration and payment of the dividend, or they may prohibit the shareholder from converting the dividend to another currency and withdrawing it from the country in which the dividend was declared. These restrictions are usually complex and are common among developing countries that experience deficits in their balance of payments or difficulty in accumulating sufficient capital to finance economic growth. For an in-depth discussion on this and other related topics, see the section "Financial Decisions for Multinational Enterprises" in this *Handbook*.

The most complex predividend declaration requirements involve the tax implications for both the corporation and the shareholders. Federal, state, and local governments may tax cash dividends as well as other dividend payments. The complexity and diversity of the tax legislation surrounding dividends is a subject that cannot be adequately treated in this section. It is sufficient to caution the reader that an understanding of the tax requirements and implications of a dividend declaration should be thoroughly understood before the actual resolution or declaration by the board of directors. Once a dividend is declared, it is a legal liability of the corporation.

Subsidiaries of corporations, both foreign and domestic, may declare dividends payable to the parent corporation as a means of transferring profits. Such dividends may be complex in terms of regulations. When a foreign corporation declares a dividend to a U.S. parent company, there must be an understanding of tax policy and the finance and foreign trade policy of the country in which the subsidiary is located. These issues play a significant role in determining the form and timing of dividends.

Before presenting a recommendation to the board of directors regarding dividends, corporate management should be thoroughly familiar with all the limitations placed on dividends by creditors, preference shareholders, and tax and economic policies of local, state, federal, and foreign governments.

Planning for dividend payments requires that in the event of the declaration of either a cash or a stock dividend, the corporation have sufficient cash or unissued shares available for payment of the dividend on the date that the board of directors selects for actual payment. A large dividend payment may require careful cash planning. Corporate management must be assured that all the laws of the state of incorporation have been satisfied regarding authorized but unissued shares in the event that a stock dividend is declared. For example, some states may prohibit issuance of **treasury shares** for a **stock dividend.** States may also require the payment of a tax on newly authorized shares before their actual issuance.

BOARD OF DIRECTORS AND DIVIDEND DECLARATIONS

State laws require a resolution of the board of directors of a corporation to declare the payment of any form of dividend to shareholders. Since the board of directors is elected by the shareholders, it is appropriate that they represent the shareholder's interest in determining what portion of a corporation's past and present earnings should be distributed to the shareholders, or if the shareholder's interests are better served by reinvesting the profits. Therefore, in addition to declaring dividend payments at regular meetings, boards of directors periodically review dividend policy. Most corporations delcare dividends **quarterly.** Corporations may schedule board of directors meetings around dividend action dates and establish regular meetings once every three months. One of the principal purposes of such a meeting may be the declaration of a dividend.

The format for dividend declaration differs among corporations and is determined in part by the technique employed by management in proposing dividend action to the board of directors. The most commonly used technique is to provide the board of directors with a draft of a formal resolution that will be voted on following discussion. The proposed resolution may be approved, amended or rejected; however, total rejection of a management recommendation is uncommon. Corporations differ widely regarding their approach to determination of dividend rate. Some corporations consider a change in dividend payments only once a year and routinely declare a quarterly dividend based on the annual determination of the dividend rate. Others prefer to evaluate the dividend rate each quarter and adjust the rate in accordance with the quarterly profit preformance of the corporation, expectations of shareholders, trends in the market price of the shares of the corporation, and other matters that the board of directors believe to be appropriate.

Dividend payments are commonly categorized as **regular, interim, extra, final, special,** and **liquidating. Regular dividends** are the cash dividends de-

EXHIBIT 2   BOARD OF DIRECTORS RESOLUTION: CASH DIVIDEND, COMMON STOCK

RESOLVED, a quarterly cash dividend of $0.50 per share on the outstanding common stock of the Company be and is declared payable on June 16, 1985, to shareholders of record on June 2, 1986.

clared at regular intervals according to a published dividend rate. **Interim dividends** are usually the quarterly dividend payments based on a stated rate. **Final and extra dividends,** the amounts paid at the close of the fiscal year, represent the regular dividend plus an extra amount. **Special dividends** are sometimes called extra dividends, but usually refer to an isolated or special event, for example, profits that result from a nonrecurring event such as the sale of an asset. **Liquidating dividends** usually refer to a return of capital to shareholders as a result of sale of all or a portion of the assets and are treated differently for tax purposes.

Despite the differences in format, a formal written resolution of the board of directors is usually required to fulfill the legal requirements, and the majority of the board must approve the action. Approval by more than a majority may be required depending on the corporate charter, corporate bylaws, or restrictions resulting from loan and preferred share agreements.

The timing of the dividend declaration is in part dictated by the size of the corporation, the number of shareholders, the number of shares outstanding, the type of dividend declared, and the legal requirements of the state of incorporation. In addition, management usually prefers that dividends be declared well in advance of actual payment to provide appropriate time for postdeclaration requirements and other administrative duties associated with dividend declarations.

Exhibit 2 is a sample resolution that a board of directors might adopt in the declaration of a quarterly cash dividend. Exhibits 3 and 4 are examples of materials that management might provide the board of directors before the actual passage of the resolution to assure that such action does not violate negative covenants in a loan agreement or a dividend policy adopted previously by the board of directors.

EXHIBIT 3   LOAN COVENANT LIMITATIONS ON CASH DIVIDENDS

Maximum current liability that may be created at this time for cash dividends **declared** but not yet paid	$ 50,000,000
Maximum retained earnings available to date that may be **paid** over time in cash dividends	$150,000,000
Total cash requirement to pay the recommended quarterly cash dividend on	$ 5,000,000

EXHIBIT 4   RECOMMENDATION FOR DIVIDEND ACTION

Management recommends that the Board of Directors, at its April 20 meeting, declare a $0.50 per share dividend, payable June 16 to holders of record June 2. This action will maintain the dividend at the $2 per share annual rate paid since December 15, 1985. The total quarterly dividend payment will be $5 million.

CURRENT DIVIDEND POLICY

Since reviewing dividend policy at the June 1984 meeting, the Board of Directors has followed the "conservative" dividend policy guidelines:

Basic Policy Guideline	Constraints to Maintain Dividend Stability
30% of previous year's earnings per share	Maximum increase of 20% in 1 year, no decreases

The conservative guideline reflects these objectives:

Retain two-thirds of earnings to capitalize on outstanding investment opportunities over the next 5 years.

Maintain a conservative payment ratio so that the dividend rate can be maintained, and perhaps even increased, during recession periods when earnings growth is restricted.

Attempt to maintain a pattern of consistent and uninterrupted growth of dividends.

REVIEW OF RECENT ACTIONS

Since the September 1985 meeting, the Board of Directors has closely adhered to the conservative dividend policy by maintaining the $0.50 per share dividend rate for three quarters. This policy was confirmed at the December 1985 meeting when the traditional practice of increasing the dividend in the fourth quarter was not followed. In 1985 dividends per share paid were $1.80, which represents a payout of 29% of 1978 earnings.

RECOMMENDATION

It would be an unusual departure from our past practices to increase the dividend rate at this time. Considering that 1986 earnings may be only equal to 1985 earnings, it would be inappropriate to declare a dividend increase. On the other hand, a reduction in the dividend rate would depart from the policy of no decreases and might suggest a poorer financial performance than expected.

We recommend maintaining the current dividend rate.

POSTDIVIDEND DECLARATION ACTIVITIES

Among publicly held corporations, the SEC requires that the declaration of a dividend be made known by a public announcement immediately following the action by the **board of directors.** Exhibit 5 is a sample public announcement to inform shareholders and other interested parties of the action taken by the board of directors regarding dividend payments. Some corporations follow a practice of having the board of directors review the press release at the time the dividend is declared, to assure that the public statement

EXHIBIT 5   SAMPLE PUBLIC ANNOUNCEMENT OF QUARTERLY DIVIDEND

For Immediate Release
April 20, 1980

COMPANY DECLARES QUARTERLY DIVIDEND

The Board of Directors of the Company, a major manufactureer of components, today declared a quarterly dividend of 50 cents per share, payable June 16, 1986, to shareholders of record on June 2, 1986.

---

reflects the intent of the board. It is important that both the resolution and the press release state clearly the date on which the dividend is to be paid, as well as the **record date,** the date on which the shareholders of record are to be the recipients of the dividend.

EX-DIVIDEND DATE. If the shares of the corporation are traded on an organized securities exchange such as the **New York Stock Exchange** or the **American Stock Exchange,** notification of a dividend declaration must be given immediately to officials of the exchange stating the nature and amount of the dividend, the date on which the dividend is to be paid, and the record date. Following notification, an **ex-dividend date** will be established. The ex-dividend date is the trading day prior to the record date on which the price of the shares will be reduced by the amount of the dividend to be paid. Shareholders who purchase shares on or after the ex-dividend date will not receive the current declared dividend because there will not be sufficient time to record the change of ownership before the record date. The seller will be the recipient because his name will still appear on the corporate books on the record date. Therefore, the buyer deducts the value of the dividend from the purchase price. The adjustment is normally at the opening of the **ex-dividend trading day.** The ex-dividend price adjustment is necessary because of the time involved in recording a change in share ownership. In determining the price of the shares, the value of the dividend is deducted, assuring that the new buyer receives the dividend in the form of a reduced price. The seller, who will receive the dividend, has the value of the dividend deducted from the proceeds of the sale of shares. Of course, there are usually tax differentials for most investors on the receipt of dividends compared with capital gains. This might affect the movement of the share price after the opening on the ex-dividend date.

TRANSFER AGENTS AND CASH MANAGEMENT. In addition to notifying the securities exchanges of the declaration of dividend, management must also maintain constant communication with the trust departments of commercial banks that act as the **shareholder registration** and **transfer agents** for the corporation. Maintenance of records of current shareholders is a difficult process, particularly among large corporations whose shares are actively traded. The dividend payment process is made more difficult by active trading of shares, as well as by the brokerage house practice of registering shares in **"street names"** (i.e., custodian names) rather than in the names of the primary owners. The trust departments of commercial banks that issue dividend checks, or additional shares in the event a stock dividend is declared, work closely with the management of the paying corporation to assure that sufficient cash is maintained as dividend checks are presented. Large corporations usually maintain recorods regarding the time lag between issuance and presentation of dividend checks. The cash management aspect of dividend payments is an important part of overall cash management procedures.

DIVIDEND CHANGES OR CANCELLATIONS. Occasionally a question arises regarding failure to pay a dividend following declaration or resolution by the board of directors. Corporate management normally has no authorization to take any action other than that prescribed in the dividend resolution. A **declared dividend** is a short-term debt of the corporation. If alternative actions are deemed necessary, the board of directors must amend the original resolution authorizing the payment of a dividend. Directors may also be held liable for declaring an illegal dividend.

When a foreign corporation or a foreign subsidiary of a U.S. corporation declares a dividend, the resolution of the board of directors may have to be approved by the central bank or the ministry of finance of the country in which the dividend-paying corporation is located or chartered before payment can be made. The foreign country authority may insist on approving the dividend action as well as the acquisition of foreign exchange associated with dividend payments of foreign shareholders. In developing countries, governmental authority may require an amendment to the dividend resolution or may even disapprove the entire action. Dividend payments and corporate dividend policy is an integral part of government economic policy among some developing nations.

WHAT IS A DIVIDEND POLICY?

Throughout most of the 1960s equity investors enjoyed a strong stock market and excellent returns in the form of capital appreciation. During this euphoric period it was popular to query whether dividend policy really mattered. During the 1970s the answer became clearer as the stock market faltered and once again dividends became more important to the investor. During the 1960s greater emphasis was placed on reinvestment of earnings on the assumption that the shareholder was better served by realizing capital appreciation on the expected increased market value of shares than by receiving increased cash dividends. However, as the market for equity issues began to deteriorate in the 1970s, dividend policy began to receive increased attention. This attention has continued in the 1980s.

A dividend policy is a decision by a corporate board of directors and the management to follow a predetermined series of actions regarding the payment of divdends to shareholders. In the case of preferred shareholders, the dividend policy is established by the legal agreement between the shareholders and the corporation. In the case of common shareholders, the board of directors has considerable discretion.

A dividend policy of a corporation may range from a mere decision regarding quarterly dividend action without attempting to define any policy beyond a quarter-to-quarter evaluation, to rather complex formal statements approved by the board of directors and reviewed on a regular basis. The review normally occurs when actions regarding dividend payments are taken by a board of directors. In addition, dividend policy may be reviewed at the **annual shareholders' meeting** or may be published in the **annual report.** Security analysts who follow a particular corporation and evaluate its performance have a strong interest in dividend policies and may ask that management discuss such policies publicly.

ANNOUNCEMENT CONSIDERATIONS. The dividend policy may also be an explicit statement that serves as a **single to the shareholders and investment community** of what may be expected in the future. Such statements attempt to establish a relationship between the earnings potential of the corporation and dividend payments. Some policies state explicitly what proportion of the corporation's earnings will be paid out as dividends to the shareholders and under what conditions the shareholders might expect either a reduction or an increase in dividends. In addition, the policy statements may cover stock dividends.

DIVIDEND CLIENTELE. Dividend policies may serve as a means of attracting and holding the type of buyer that will result in a stable shareholder base and share price. Corporations that want to attract small individual investors, as contrasted with large institutional investors, may prepare a dividend policy that places greater emphasis on a high **payout ratio,** that is, paying out a larger proportion of a corporation's aftertax earnings and dividends. In contrast, large institutional investors may be more interested in realizing appreciation in the value of their shareholdings and may concentrate their investments in corporations that reinvest a substantial proportion of earnings. Thus, corporations interested in attracting institutional investors may design a dividend policy that results in a smaller payout ratio and a higher proportion of total earnings reinvested in additional earning assets. A primary consideration, therefore, is the tax bracket of shareholders.

It is difficult to generalize regarding formulation of dividend policies. Efforts to develop a dividend policy must reflect consideration of a variety of issues. The future capital requirements of the corporation, the expected stream of earnings and cash flows and variability of these flows, shareholder expectations and attitudes, changes in corporate tax policy, the future cost and availability of capital, the strategy of the corporation with respect to investment and new product development, and the cash requirements and tax position of the corporation's shareholders all play a role in determining a dividend policy. For an excellent discussion of these determinants, see J. F. Weston and E. Brigham, *Managerial Finance*, 7th ed., Dryden Press, 1981, Chapter 17.

WHEN SHOULD A CORPORATION ADOPT A FORMAL DIVIDEND POLICY?

Not all corporations require a formal dividend policy. Closely held businesses in which the equity participants hold a position on the board of directors or maintain a working knowledge of the business probably do not require a formal policy. Formal dividend policies are normally associated with corporations that have achieved significant size in revenue and number and variety of shareholders. The complexity of financial management and planning play an important part in determining when a formal dividend policy is required. Industrial organizations that are capital intensive and must engage in long-range planning to assure adequate supplies of capital in the future may require a specific dividend policy to assure that sufficient amounts of funds are available when asset acquisition is undertaken. At the same time, it is important to achieve a balance between retained earnings and dividends to assure a market for new equity shares in the event additional equity capital is required.

COMPOSITION OF BOARD OF DIRECTORS. The composition of the board of directors may influence the need for a formal dividend policy. If a majority of the board of directors are not involved in the management of the company, there may be constrasting views of an appropriate dividend policy for the corporation. Rather than have a debate each time a quarterly dividend declaration is requiried, it is more effective to devote a significant amount of time to preparing a careful and formal statement of dividend policy on which a majority of the directors agree. Thereafter, each dividend declaration can be measured for compliance with the dividend policy. This assures continuity in dividend policy, which has become increasingly important in maintaining a strong market for equity securities.

In the past 10 years, the outside or independent members of boards of directors have emerged as a much stronger force in the direction of large corporations. It is assumed, in many cases incorrectly, that management would prefer to pay out smaller proportions of corporate earnings and retain a larger proportion for reinvestment in the corporation to finance growth and diversity. Since outside directors represent the interest of the shareholders of the corporation (although they are usually selected by management), they may require management to justify retention of earnings that otherwise would be available for the payment of dividends to shareholders.

POLICY MAINTENANCE AND REVIEW. Maintenance of a formal dividend policy is also important to institutional lenders. An erratic dividend policy may endanger the creditors' position if management or the board of directors fails to foresee substantial cash requirements associated with periods of business decline or large investments during times of rapid growth.

As with any policy of a corporation, dividend policies should be subject to periodic review by management and the board of directors to assure that dividend actions are in compliance with the policy and that the established dividend policy continues to be relevant to the needs of the corporation and the shareholders. A dividend policy adopted during a period when cash requirements are high to finance rapid growth may not be appropriate as new markets begin to mature and earnings grow significantly. Therefore, it is recommended that the dividend policy of the corporation be reviewed formally once a year with the board of directors to assure both compliance and relevance. Exhibit 6 is an example of a dividend policy review prepared for a board of directors.

Consideration should also be given to a review of dividend policy in the annual report to shareholders and at the annual meeting. At meetings with security analysts and institutional investors management should provide an explanation of dividend policy. These reviews play an important part in maintaining a good information and communication system.

DETERMINANTS OF DIVIDEND POLICY

Formulation of a dividend policy requires consideration of the major determinants of profitability and cash flow of a corporation as well as external factors that influence investors' decisions to either acquire or dispose of their investments in the company. A dividend policy refers to the percentage of a firm's earnings pair out to shareholders, although it might be expressed in absolute terms as well.

CYCLICALITY. One of the most important considerations in determining dividend policy is the impact of **business cycles** on the profitability and cash flow of the corporation. Businesses that experience little cyclicality or fluctuation in demand for their products or services are able to pursue a relatively stable dividend policy, as contrasted with businesses that experience wide fluctuations over the course of a business cycle.

Corporations that are significantly affected by business cycles often elect to pay out a lower proportion of their total profits during the recovery portion of a business cycle, but strive to maintain the dividend rate during business recessions to provide the shareholder with stability of income. Corporations

EXHIBIT 6   A REVIEW OF COMPANY DIVIDEND POLICY

The Board of Directors has approved the following dividend policy:

> The Company should continue to increase dividends gradually while direct-ing the bulk of its retained earnings toward maintaining and increasing planned growth as a most effective means of maximizing the stock price. Each dividend recommendation should:
>
> > Be viewed in terms of what is most desirable for Company shareholders.
> > Consider the amount of funds required for planned expansion.
> > Reflect the Company's view of the future.
> > Incorporate the use of strategic increases in critical years.
>
> Inherent in the goals above is the direction to:
>
> > Strive to increase our effective cash dividend rate by 15% annually as a means of demonstrating management's commitment to a 15% average annual growth rate.
> > Retain an average of 70% of our aftertax earnings for reinvestment (i.e., a payout ratio of 30%).

At the last meeting of the Board of Directors the Directors requested a study out-lining all relevant factors to be considered in dividend policy formulation. This study identified three factors of paramount importance in determining our dividend policy:

> The market premium that may or may not exist for different payout percent-ages for firms with similar circumstances to the Company.
> The preference of the Company's shareholders for capital gains versus divi-dend income.
> The requirement for funds to fulfill the investment opportunities available to the Company.

The study also concluded that the Company's payout ratio was well below its in-dustry and national averages and that a higher payout would likely produce a higher P/E ratio. However, a higher payout could not be achieved without a re-duction in capital expenditures and future growth and additional equity financing.

At the last meeting, the Board reaffirmed its policy of gradually increasing divi-dends on an annual basis while retaining the bulk of the Company's earnings to carry out planned growth. The Board expressed its acceptance of the following goals:

> Cash dividends should be increased in line with earnings growth, approxi-mately 15% per annum.
> An average of 70% of aftertax profits should be retained for reinvestment in internal projects.

The Board further expressed its intent to be guided by three additional factors in deciding appropriate dividend action.

> Near- and longer-term capital requirements to fund the Company's growth,
> Near- and longer-term expectations of the Company's profitability.
> The possible importance of strategic increases in dividends during years when shareholder expectations require reinforcement.

EXHIBIT 6 CONTINUED

WHAT FACTORS SHOULD WE CONSIDER IN EVALUATING COMPANY DIVIDEND POLICY?

1. What is an appropriate dividend policy at this stage in the Company's growth?
2. How have investors' attitudes toward dividends changed?
3. Should stability of dividend rate be emphasized?
4. What dividend policy is in the interest of the Company's various stakeholders?
5. What can the Company afford to pay?

HAVE INVESTOR ATTITUDES CHANGED?

Investors are focusing more on dividends than in the past. Why?

They are in a more conservative, defensive mood.

Higher absolute dividend yields are available.

Value placed on $1 paid out has increased more than value on $1 retained.

What does this increased interest in dividends say about the Company policy?

The individual shareholders' interest will still be best served by a low payout if the Company can invest retained funds at a higher return than a shareholder can receive through reinvesting dividends.

However, if this issue is in doubt, the Company should now lean more toward dividends than retention.

STABILITY OF DIVIDEND RATE

Dividends are meaningful to investors in two ways.

1. Dividends are part of the return on their investment. They prefer to have this cash flow grow steadily and never decline, except in extreme circumstances.
2. Dividends are one of the best indicators of the Board of Directors' outlook for the Company's power to generate earnings and cash flows over the long term. This insight into the Board's outlook is particularly informative to investors when the following factors are all markedly cyclical:

The economies in which the Company operates.

The industries to which it sells.

Its sales.

Its earnings.

Its financial condition.

Given the Company's cyclicality and its historical pattern of steady dividend growth, it is reasonable to assume that investors are relying heavily on the dividend rate as a proxy for the Board's long-term outlook for the Company.

Management recommends continuation of a steady dividend growth pattern reflective of the Company's earning power.

OTHER STAKEHOLDERS

In addition to common stockholders, the interests of other stakeholders should be considered:

Lenders.

Employees.

EXHIBIT 6 CONTINUED_____

Suppliers.

Customers.

Communities in which the Company operates.

Their interest is in having the Company remain strong financially. A key element of a strong financial position is an equity base adequate to support the current level of operations.

It matters little to these stakeholders how an adequate equity base is maintained. Since dividend policy is only one of several influences on the corporation's equity base, dividend policy in and of itself is of little concern to these stakeholders as long as the combined effect of dividend policy and other influences is maintenance of an adequate equity base.

WHAT FACTORS SHOULD WE CONSIDER?

1. What is an appropriate dividend policy at this stage in the Company's corporate life?

   > As long as the Company remains in the "established growth" phase, a payout below 40% with steady growth of dividend rate is appropriate.

2. How did investors' attitudes toward dividends change in the 1970s?

   > Investors became more interested in dividends; if the decision is not clear, we should lean toward higher payout.

3. Should stability of dividend rate be emphasized?

   > Yes, as it has been in the past.

4. What dividend policy is in the interest of the Company's various stakeholder groups?

   > They are indifferent as long as an adequate equity base is maintained.

WHAT CAN THE COMPANY AFFORD TO PAY?

There are three alternative policy guidelines.

	Basic Policy Guidelines	Constraints to Maintain Dividend Rate Stability
Conservative	30% of previous year's primary EPS	Maximum increase of 20% in 1 year; no decreases
Moderate	35% of previous year's primary EPS	Maximum increase of 35% in 1 year; no decreases
Aggressive	50% of previous year's primary EPS	Maximum increase of 100% in 1 year; no decreases

AN EXAMPLE

This example applies the conservative policy guideline to the present situation:

Annual Dividend Per Share

EXHIBIT 6 CONTINUED

Basic Policy Guideline	$3.00–$4.50
30% of estimated primary EPS of $10–$15	$1.50

Constraints

Maximum increase of 20% of present $1.50 dividend	
No decrease from present $1.50 dividend	$1.50

Rate Prescribed by Guideline	$1.80

RECOMMENDED POLICY GUIDELINE

Until the Board of Directors has approved the long-term operating, capital, and financing plan, a cautious dividend policy is appropriate.

Consequently, we recommend that the conservative dividend policy guideline be adopted, to be reviewed, and affirmed or revised, after a long-term financing plan has been adopted.

Since this guideline is mechanistic, it should be viewed as a guideline only.

RECOMMENDED COMMON DIVIDEND ACTION

In keeping with the cautious approach recommended pending completion of our financing plan, we suggest that the dividend be raised from 37.5¢ quarterly to 45¢ (from $1.50 annually to $1.80).

---

that experience little change in revenue patterns during the entire course of a business cycle usually require less retention of earnings and are able to pay out a higher proportion of total earnings during recovery and recession periods. Highly cyclical businesses may be capital intensive, requiring a larger proportion of their earnings for reinvestment purposes. Therefore, they may be doubly affected by (1) a reduction in cash and profitability during a recession and (2) an increased demand for cash to establish additional manufacturing capacity and working capital requirements in preparation for the forthcoming recovery phase of the business cycle.

STAGES OF GROWTH. Business operations, like other institutions, experience different stages of growth during an entire **life cycle.** The number of growth stages in the life of a business has been the subject of several academic studies. Some scholars attribute a three-phase life cycle to the growth of a business corporation, while others believe that there are five phases. Assuming a three-phase life cycle of formation, gestation, and maturity, each of these phases of a business life cycle creates a set of circumstances that may have a major influence on the formulation of a dividend policy.

During the **formation stage,** the typical business enterprise is least profitable and requires its limited profits for reinvestment purposes. Therefore, ability to pay dividends is limited and the emphasis is focused on providing support and growth opportunities to assure survival and protect the shareholders' initial investment. Such a strategy is of far greater value to the shareholders than any limited dividends that might be received during the first phase of the **business life cycle.**

The second phase of growth occurs when a business is succeeding and growing rapidly. This phase may also represent a period of high risk in the growth of a business in that the opportunities for major errors or strategic mistakes are greatest. The phrase "growing to death" refers to businesses that experience growth rates so rapid that the internally or externally generated capital or cash flow is insufficient to finance them. As a consequence, management may lose control of its operation and the business may falter or even fail. During the period of gestation it may be difficult for a corporation to pay significant dividends to its shareholders, particularly if shareholders require cash dividends. If the business is experiencing substantial success but requires large additions of capital, it may be appropriate to issue stock dividends rather than cash dividends without denying the corporation the cash required to finance required additions to fixed assets and working capital.

In addition, during the gestation period the business may utilize borrowed capital to a greater extent. Therefore, creditors may prefer a conservative dividend policy to assure that the corporation reinvests a large proportion of earnings, thus assuring continued growth and profitability for the protection of the creditors.

During the next stage of business growth, the **maturity stage,** profitability may increase and needs for cash decrease sufficiently to permit the corporation to pursue a more generous dividend policy and reward the shareholders for forgoing their dividend returns during the earlier stages of growth. In this stage management may discover that opportunities are diminished because of a high penetration of the markets in which they compete and fewer opportunities to serve new markets and develop new products.

It is at this stage in the life cycle of a business that its management and board of directors may face a critical decision, one that will have a major effect on dividend policy. Management and the board of directors may elect to accept the maturation of the business and pay out a large proportion of total earnings to the shareholders, in which case the stock may become a valuable income investment, attractive to those investors who seek immediate income opportunities. On the other hand, management may not be satisfied with such a conservative strategy and may seek new growth opportunities. The latter strategy may lead to **diversification, acquisition, or merger** with other companies, to realize a faster growth rate. Many shareholders may approve of a reconstituted growth strategy because they prefer to realize their returns in the form of ever-increasing appreciation in the market value of the stock as opposed to dividend income. Regardless of which strategy is selected, the impact on dividend policy will be significant, and the policy should be carefully reviewed to be sure that it complements the business strategy.

PROFITABILITY. Profitability is uneven among different businesses and over the life cycle of an individual business enterprise. Some businesses are characterized by narrow profit margins resulting from strong competition and little value added to the products they distribute (e.g., food merchandising). However, many businesses with narrow profit margins are the most stable. Public utilities are characterized by narrow profit margins; however, they are usually quasi-monopolies, and state and local governments limit their profitability and return on investment by means of rate regulation. Public utilities, like food merchandising firms, experience only small fluctuations in demand for their services over the course of a business cycle.

Predictability and the level of profits play important parts in determining the dividend policy of a corporation. Although food merchandising enterprises and public utilities are similar with respect to cyclicality of profitability, they are dissimilar in terms of the amount and type of capital required to generate profits. In food merchandising a relatively large share of total capital is devoted to inventory or working capital, whereas public utilities require significant investments in fixed assets to generate energy or communication services. Thus the profitability pattern of the corporation and the industry in which it competes must be taken into consideration in determining a dividend policy.

CASH GENERATION. A dividend policy must also recognize differences that may exist between reported profits and actual cash generation. Given the complexity of modern accounting principles, many corporations show wide variations between profitability and cash flow. High profitability is no assurance of adequate cash from which dividends may be paid. On the other hand, a low level of reported accounting profits is not always indicative of insufficient cash to pay dividends.

Numerous factors that influence reported profits may not affect the cash generation of the corporation. For example, increased market penetration resulting from an extension of credit terms to customers and maintenance of larger inventories may result in higher reported profits but may deplete the cash reserves of the corporation so greatly that the dividend rate cannot be maintained. In such instances, a corporation may experience cash deficits as it attempts to finance its increasing accounts receivable and inventory levels. On the other hand, a corporation suffering a declining profit level may actually be experiencing surpluses of cash as inventories and receivables are reduced and depreciation of fixed assets exceeds the amount invested in new or replacement assets. Accounting for foreign exchange is a more recent phenomenon that has resulted in major changes in corporate profits that may have no impact on cash flow.

   In determining the impact of profitability and cash flow on dividend policy, management and the board of directors must evaluate whether the corporation is experiencing a period of temporary or permanent profit growth or decline as well as the ability to maintain or improve the current level of cash flow. John Brittain (*Corporate Dividend Policy*, Wash. D.C., Brookings, 1966) found that post-World War II accelerated depreciation standards and added cash flow accounted for a substantial increase in cash dividends paid by U.S. corporations.

TIMING OF DIVIDEND POLICY

All the foregoing determinants of dividend policy must be evaluated in terms of the length of time these conditions are expected to prevail. Management and the board of directors should attempt to forecast as far as is reasonably possible the impacts of cyclicality, growth, profitability, and cash generation in evaluating dividend policy and to provide shareholders and the investment community with an evaluation of these issues and a statement of how they are expected to influence dividend policy.

INVESTOR EXPECTATIONS AND NEEDS

OWNER VERSUS MANAGER CONTROL. Thus far the discussion of dividend policy has centered on the characteristics and requirements of the business enterprise as opposed to the needs and expectations of the shareholders. Various factors influence investors' needs and expectations regarding dividends. If a corporation is owned by a relatively small number of shareholders, the dividend policy may be quite different from that of a publicly held corporation whose shareholders are more dependent on dividends as a means of realizing a return on their investment. If the shareholders of a corporation are restricted to a few individuals, all of whom participate in the operation of the business, the policy may be to avoid the payment of dividends and to emphasize reinvestment of earnings to realize faster growth and greater capital appreciation.

   The **Internal Revenue Service** (IRS) may evaluate the performance of privately held corporations to determine whether the restriction of dividend payments is being used by the shareholders as a means of avoiding federal income tax. If the IRS believes that abuses have occurred, the corporation may be required to pay taxes as if dividends had been paid by the corporation to the shareholders. This is referred to as an **accumulated earnings tax.**

   Investor expectations and needs are difficult for corporate management and the board of directors to evaluate, particularly for a large corporation with a wide spectrum of shareholders with differing investment objectives. The dividend policy of a large corporation should be determined by the needs of the corporation. Once dividend policy is determined, management may undertake programs to attract equity investors with investment objectives that coincide with the firm's dividend policy. This requires that management communicate its dividend policy to existing and potential shareholders and the financial community to establish a broad and stable market for equity capital.

TAX CONSIDERATIONS. Investor expectations and needs are determined largely by income requirements and federal income tax policy. Investors who do not need immediate income and who have high tax exposure prefer equity investments with high potential for rapid growth, outstanding opportunities for reinvestment of earnings, and promise of continued capital appreciation.

Investors who require immediate income are less attracted to growth stocks and may elect to invest in companies with less potential for future capital appreciation that offer more generous immediate cash dividends. In many instances investors are represented by institutions such as insurance companies and pension funds that must satisfy demands for immediate income as well as future capital appreciation. Investors who place greater emphasis on capital appreciation may favor corporations that periodically provide stock dividends, particularly if the corporation continues to demonstrate growth potential and superior profit margins.

DIVIDEND REINVESTMENT PLANS. The use of dividend reinvestment plans is a technique employed by many large corporations that pay a relatively generous dividend, but seek to reinvest a larger share of profits. Dividend reinvestment programs have had limited success. On average, they have been able to attract less than 15% of dividend payments as reinvestments, and they are expensive to administer. They offer the shareholder an opportunity to acquire additional shares without paying brokerage fees. However, the inability to select the purchase price is an unattractive aspect of dividend reinvestment plans. In addition, there is the risk that the IRS will adopt the view that brokerage fees avoided constitute a transfer of value to shareholders, and will levy a tax on the estimated value.

MANAGEMENT VIEWS

An extensive research study was conducted by Baker, Farrelly, and Edelman (*Financial Management*, Autumn 1985) to survey management views on the major determinants of corporate dividend policy. The three main objectives of the study were:

1. To test Lintner's behavioral model
2. To examine if management was aware of the **signaling** and **clientelle effects**
3. To investigate the industry influence on dividend policy

SURVEY FINDINGS

Lintner's Model. The results show that the major determinants of dividend policy appear strikingly similar to Lintner's behavioral model. Lintner's study (*American Economic Review*, May 1956) found that in the short run, dividends are smoothed in an effort to avoid frequent changes. Exhibit 7 provides the summary statistics of the major determinants of corporate dividend policy. The most highly ranked determinants are the anticipated level of a firm's future earnings and the pattern of past dividends.

Signaling and Clientele Effects. Miller and Modigliani (*American Economic Review*, October 1961) suggest that dividend policy has no effect on the value of the corporation if we assume that there are **no taxes, transaction costs,** or other **market imperfections**. However, dividend may be relevant to the extent that market imperfections exist. Signaling and clientele effects are the explanation being provided currently.

Empirical studies indicate that dividend changes signal some unanticipated information to the market. The respondents from all three industry groups agreed that dividend payments provide a signaling device of the future prospects of the company and that the market uses dividend announcements as information for assessing security value.

The research evidence on the clientele effects is mixed. Respondents from all three industry groups thought that investors are not indifferent between dividend and capital gain returns. Yet, there was a slight agreement on whether management should be responsive to its shareholders' dividend preference.

Industry Influence. The opinion of respondents from **public utility** firms differ markedly from those of the **manufacturing** and **retail industries**. Thus, the managers of regulated firms definitely have a somewhat different view of the world than managers operating in a competitive environment. The difference in the opinion may be mainly due to regulation. For example, utilities, due to its monopoly position in the market, have a smaller risk of an unexpected decline in earnings to affect the dividend payout.

This survey was completed, however, prior to the nuclear plant problems that have caused significant problems to certain electric public utilities, resulting in reduced earnings and cash flows, lower bond ratings and reduced ability to payout cash dividends. See the section in this Handbook on **Public Utility Finance** for a more complete discussion.

EXHIBIT 7 MAJOR DETERMINANTS OF CORPORATE DIVIDEND POLICY

Determinant	Level of Importance					Mean	Rank	Industry[a]
	None 0	Slight 1	Moderate 2	Great 3	Maximum 4			
1 Anticipated level of firm's future earnings		3.40%	6.80%		89.80%	3.20	1	Mfg
		1.75	14.04		84.21	3.12	1	W/R
		1.75	7.89		90.35	3.21	1	Util
9 Pattern of past dividends		6.12	29.25		64.63	2.73	2	Mfg
		1.75	29.82		68.42	2.86	2	W/R
		2.63	25.44		71.93	2.94	3	Util
8 Availability of cash		14.29	22.45		63.27	2.70	3	Mfg
		22.81	21.05		56.14	2.42	4	W/R
		21.24	34.51		44.25	2.35	4	Util
7 Concern about maintaining or increasing stock price		13.61	44.22		42.18	2.30	4	Mfg
		15.79	28.07		56.14	2.47	3	W/R
		3.51	22.81		73.68	2.96	2	Util

Source: ''A Survey of Management Views on Dividend Policy,'' *Financial Management*, (Autumn 1985) by Kent H. Baker, Gail E. Farrelly, Richard B. Edelman.

[a]Mfg = manufacturing; W/R = wholesale/retail; Util = utility.

CAPITAL STRUCTURE AND DIVIDEND POLICY

One of the most important decisions in financial management involves the determination of the appropriate capital structure for the corporation, i.e., the mix between debt and equity. Corporations that have relatively large and stable cash flows may undertake the risks of using larger proportions of debt, while corporations that tend to be more significantly affected by the business cycle and interruptions in cash flow usually pursue a more conservative capital structure and rely more heavily on equity.

The more extensively a corporation uses debt or fixed cost capital, the greater the opportunity for equity investors to realize an increasing share of the profits. However, leverage may work against the common shareholder as profits decline. Therefore, equity investors may be less attracted to highly leveraged companies if they surmise the possibility of a cyclical downturn.

A discussion of the appropriate **capital structure** for a corporation is too extensive to pursue in this section and can be found in the section entitled "Long-Term Sources of Funds and the Cost of Capital." However, it must be realized that dividend policy is an important outgrowth of the decisions regarding capital structure. If a corporation decides to establish a capital structure that emphasizes equity over debt, the dividend policy may be more conservative, to assure that a large proportion of the aftertax profits is retained to build a sufficient equity base. If management elects to pursue a liberal dividend policy and to increase equity simultaneously, new equity issues may be required periodically to replace what otherwise would have been achieved by a greater retention of earnings.

Similar decisions are required with respect to the composition of equity investment (i.e., mix of preferred and common shares). Preferred shares, like debt issues, carry a fixed dividend rate. Thus the use of preferred equity in the capital structure may also offer common shareholders the opportunity to acquire a greater share of the corporation's profits as preferred dividends claim a smaller proportion of increases in aftertax profits.

When management selects the policy regarding capital structure, the mix of debt and equity becomes a principal determinant of the corporate dividend policy. As with dividend policy, it is important that corporate management and the board of directors enunciate clearly the policy regarding capital structure. Information of this kind provided to the shareholders and the financial community is beneficial insofar as it helps attract a stable and supportive group of permanent shareholders who provide continuing markets for additional equity issues.

INSOLVENCY TESTS AND CORPORATE DISTRIBUTIONS

Corporate distributions to shareholders involve (1) the transfeer of money or other property (except a corporation's own shares) or (2) the incurrence of indebtedness, whether by **cash dividend** or **share repurchase.** The revised **Model Business Corporation Act (1979)** specifies that the board of directors may authorize the corporation to make distributions except when (*a*) the corporation would be unable to pay its debts as they became due in the usual course of business, or (*b*) the corporation's total assets would be less than its total liabilities. The former test describes **equity insolvency** and the latter describes **bankruptcy insolvency.** No longer are the terms **par value, stated value,** and **capital surplus** relevant to a firm's payment of dividends or share repurchase.

Determination of whether a firm would be insolvent as a result of a proposed distribution is to be rendered by the board of directors based on its collective business judgment. This stipulation forces the firm to analyze the future course of its business, including its ability to generate sufficient funds from operations or from the orderly disposition of its assets, and to satisfy its existing and anticipated obligations as they come due.

Discussion of these and other provisions can be found in "Changes in the Model Business Corporation Act—Amendments to Financial Provisions" (*Business Lawyer*, Vol. 34, July 1979). The question of corporate solvency may be important in determining shareholder return on investment.

THEORY AND EMPIRICAL EVIDENCE

THEORETICAL CONTROVERSY. A major issue concerning dividend policy is whether decisions by corporate management as to the amount of dividends paid actually affect the wealth of shareholders. Several determinants of dividend policy have been discussed, but the question of the decision's effect on share prices is difficult to answer.

Conventional corporate finance wisdom specifies that the dividend decision does matter and that the time and effort spent by management and the board of directors on this decision is justified. Such variables as income stability, investment opportunities, cost of alternative financing, and tax bracket of stockholders help to guide management in this important decision. The fact that dividends paid today have more value than those received tomorrow must be considered in the payout decision. In other words, traditional financial theorists and most practitioners feel that dividends do matter. Arbitrary changes in dividends, especially dividend cuts, must be carefully considered.

The opposite point of view is advocated by the "irrelevance school" led by Miller and Modigliani. In their article "Dividend Policy, Growth, and the Valuation of Shares" (*Journal of Business*, October 1961), they argued that the sole determinant of share price is the rate of return earned on investment opportunities and that how these returns are eventually passed through to the owners is irrelevant. Firms that prefer to pay out a greater percentage of earnings to stockholders can finance the investments that are expected to earn a return greater than the firm's cost of capital by other means, such as external equity or debt securities. Firms that finance investments all or in part from current earnings, in other words those that pay out small dividends or no dividends, will save the financing "costs" of interest payments on debt or common stock equity dilution.

After many years of controversy, the academic world continues to debate dividend relevancy. The great majority of practitioners presume that the dividend decision is relevant and important and pay little attention to the academic studies. Whenever a theory is uncertain, the empirical evidence must be examined to help answer the remaining questions. Such evidence and related theoretical constructs are discussed below.

CONCEPTUAL MODELS AND EMPIRICAL EVIDENCE. Researchers have frequently attempted to categorize, explain, and measure the different types of observed corporate dividend behavior. Even before the most recent theoretical controversy was articulated in the early 1960s, models to explain corporate behavior were attempted, some with considerable success. Behavioral models were developed that attempted to measure and explain several of the subjects discussed earlier in this section, namely, clinetele effects and information and announcement effects of dividend declarations on share values. Only a few of the well-known models are reviewed here. For an excellent discussion entitled "Dividend Policy: Empirical Evidence and Applications," see Copeland and Weston, *Financial Theory and Corporate Policy* 2nd ed., Addison Wesley, 1985, Chapter 15.

Behavioral Models. A classic attempt to explain corporate dividend behavior was made in the article by Lintner entitled "Distribution of Incomes of Corporations Among Dividends, Retained Earnings and Taxes" (*American Economic Review*, May 1956). After conducting interviews with the personnel of numerous large, well-established firms, Lintner concluded (1) that the primary determinants of changes in dividends paid out were the most **recent earnings** and the **past dividends** paid, (2) that management focused on the change in dividends rather than the amount, (3) that changes were made only when management felt secure that the new level of dividends could be maintained, and firms very reluctantly cut or eliminated dividends, (4) that there was a propensity to move toward some **target payout ratio** for most firms, but the speed of adjustment toward that level differed greatly among companies, and (5) that investment requirements generally had little effect on dividend behavior. The last point implies that dividend policy and changes in policy constitute an active policy variable of the firm—at least in the opinion of management in the 1950s.

Fama and Babiak, in "Dividend Policy: An Empirical Analysis" (*Journal of the American Statistical Association*, December 1968), found that Lintner's model continued to explain dividend behavior quite well and that a slightly different model with lagged earnings (last period's) as well as lagged dividends did a slightly better job in that it had higher explanatory power.

Brittain (*Corporate Dividend Policy* Wash. D.C., Brookings, 1966) found that accelerated depreciation, increased cash flows, and external cost of financing, among other factors, explained quite well the dividend payout behavior of corporations in the post-World War II period up to the mid-1960s. His study postulated that the key determinant is cash flows, rather than earnings. After all, dividends must be paid from cash.

While these studies all had impressive statistical results, the question of why firms pay out the amount of dividends they do was not addressed directly. The following are some empirical attempts to explain this.

Clientele Effect Models. Do corporations attract a specific type or types of stockholder, and can this phenomenon be measured? Most theoreticians would probably agree that the payout ratio and the dividend yield of companies do attract individuals, although the tradeoff between dividend income versus capital gains is a complex one. The clientele effect is probably one of the reasons for the reluctance of management to make extreme changes in dividend policy, especially when this entails cutting the dividend. Disgruntled shareholders could always sell their shares, although this could possibly lead to unfortunate share price movement and certainly would result in transaction costs for those who sold their shares.

Probably the most important clientele effect variable is the tax bracket of investors. As mentioned earlier, investors in higher tax brackets should prefer returns in the form of capital gains, not cash dividends. Do stockholders act rationally in this respect? One of the difficulties in translating this conceptual ganeralization into policy-related action is the problem of determining the tax bracket of a large mass of stockholders of the corporation being managed. Even knowledge of the average tax bracket would be helpful in this respect.

A number of researchers have attempted to "observe" the average tax bracket of stockholders without actually asking them—which would be costly and probably subject to a great deal of bias. Estimates of average tax brackets of all U.S. corporation shareholders, usually weighted by proportional stock ownership of individuals, have ranged from 36 to 54%. Most of these estimates were made in the 1960s and early 1970s, and with the increase in state and local taxes in many locations, one would guess that the average is higher in 1980.

A study by Elton and Gruber, "Marginal Stockholders' Tax Rates and the Clientele Effect" (*Review of Economics and Statistics*, February 1970) approached the marginal tax bracket question by examining the ex-dividend behavior of common stocks. The authors found that the average price decline of common stocks at the close on the ex-dividend date was lower than the amount of the dividend and postulated that this could be explained by the tax bracket or clientele effect. They did find evidence that firms that suffered the greatest decline on the ex-dividend date were those with higher dividend yields, which implied a lower tax bracket. The average tax bracket of all stockholders implied by this ex-dividend price behavior was 36.4%. Copeland and Weston (*Financial Theory and Corporate Policy,* Addison Wesley, 1985) argued, however, that this anomaly in the market (i.e., differential expected movement in share prices dependent on stockholder tax brackets) could not exist. If it did arbitrageurs would be able to trade on this information. None of these studies of counterarguments, however, took transaction costs into consideration.

Pettit ("Taxes, Transaction Costs, and Clientele Effect of Dividends," *Journal of Financial Economics*, December, 1977) examined portfolios of a large number of individuals and found that stocks with low dividend yields tended to be held by investors with high income, by younger investors (higher risk tolerance), by individuals whose normal versus capital gains tax rates differed greatly, and by those whose portfolios had relatively high systematic risk, or market-related (high-beta) risk.

Information and Announcement Effects. One of the more difficult complexities of empirical research is to be confident that when the association between one variable (dividends) and another (share price change) is being measured, significant results indicate direct association between the two. In fact, most theorists and empiricists now believe that it is not the added current cash flow to investors that explains share price increase when dividends increase, but that the dividend declaration conveys information about future cash flows.

It is also possible that information about future investment opportunities and cash flows could be provided from other sources, although there is a strong intuitive feeling that dividend declarations are clear and not likely to be "window dressing." Unfortunately, the evidence to date is not conclusive.

Pettit, in "Dividend Announcements, Security Performance and Capital Market Efficiency" (*Journal of Finance*, December 1972), found evidence that the market does in fact use dividend announcements as important information for assessing security values. He reported that most of the significant price adjustment takes place very quickly, either on the dividend announcement date or on the following day. Unfortunately, since no trading rules were tested inclusive of transaction costs it is not clear whether consistent profits could be made by insiders, that is, those who had information not available to the public about dividend announcements.

Watts, in "The Information Content of Dividends" (*Journal of Business,* April, 1973), on the other hand, noted a positive dividend announcement effect but concluded that the price movements of shares were not sufficient to earn **abnormal returns,** that is, returns adjusted for the overall market movement and the individual stock's **systematic risk,** that are significantly greater than zero.

REFERENCES

Altman, E., and Subrahmanyam, M., *Recent Advances in Corporate Finance,* Irwin, Homewood, IL, 1985.

Baker, H. Kent, Forrelly, Gail E., and Edelman, Richard, "A Survey of Management Views on Dividend Policy", *Financial Management*, Autumn 1985, pp. 78–84.

Black, F., and Scholes, M., "The Effects of Dividend Yield and Dividend Policy on Common Stock Prices and Returns," *Journal of Financial Economics*, May 1974, pp. 1–22.

Brigham, E., *Financial Management Theory and Practice*, 2nd ed., Dryden Press, Hinsdale, IL, 1979, Chapter 17.

Brittain, J. A., *Corporate Dividend Policy*, Brookings Institution, Washington, D.C., 1966.

Copeland, T., and Weston, J. F., *Financial Theory and Corporate Policy*, Addison-Wesley, Reading, MA, 1979.

Elton, E. J., and Gruber, M. J., "Marginal Stockholders' Tax Rates and the Clientele Effect," *Review of Economics and Statistics*, February 1970, pp. 68–74.

Fama, E., "The Empirical Relationships Between the Dividend and Investment Decisions of Firms," *American Economic Review.*, June 1974, pp. 304–318.

——, and Babiak, H., "Dividend Policy: An Empirical Analysis," *Journal of the American Statistical Association*, December 1968, pp. 1132–1161.

Kalay, A., *Essays in Dividend Policy*, Ph. D. thesis, University of Rochester, Rochester, N.Y., 1977.

Khoury, N., and Smith, K., "Dividend Policy and the Capital Gains Tax in Canada," *Journal of Business Administration*, Spring 1977.

Lintner, J., "Distribution of Incomes of Corporations Among Dividends, Retained Earnings and Taxes," *American Economic Review*, May 1956, pp. 97–113.

Miller, M., and Modigliani, F., "Dividend Policy, Growth, and the Valuation of Shares," *Journal of Business*, October 1961, pp. 411–433.

Pettit, R. R., "Dividend Announcements, Security Performance, and Capital Market Efficiency," *Journal of Finance*, December 1972, pp. 993–1007.

——, "The Impact of Dividend and Earnings Announcement: A Reconciliation," *Journal of Business*, January 1976, pp. 86–96.

——, Taxes, Transactions Costs, and Clientele Effect of Dividends," *Journal of Financial Economics*, December 1977, pp. 419–436.

Sorter, D., "The Dividend Controversy—What It Means for Corporate Policy," *Financial Executive*, May 1979, pp. 38–43.

Van Horne, J., and McDonald, J. G., "Dividend Policy and New Equity Financing," *Journal of Finance*, May 1971, pp. 507–520.

Walter, J. E., *Dividend Policy and Enterprise Valuation*, Wadsworth, Belmont, CA. 1967.

Watts, R., "The Information Content of Dividends," *Journal of Business*, April 1973, pp. 191–211.

——, "Comments on the Informational Content of Dividends," *Journal of Business*, January 1976, pp. 81–85.

Weston, J. F., and Brigham, E., *Managerial Finance*, 6th ed., Dryden, Hinsdale, IL, 1978, Chapter 24.

14

PENSION AND PROFIT-SHARING PLANS

CONTENTS

14

PENSION AND PROFIT SHARING PLANS

Roger F. Murray

NATURE OF THE COMMITMENT

One aspect of **corporate policy,** personnel and salary administration, and employee relations that extends far beyond the corporate finance function is the provision of retirement income supplemental to Social Security benefits. Related to overall corporate objectives are effective recruiting, good employee motivation and morale, systematic retirement rules to facilitate orderly advancement of career employees, and recognition of employees' contributions to the company. These objectives can be met by different means, and the choices among alternatives have distinct financial implications. In collectively bargained **pension plans,** the negotiating of benefits or contributions involves a wide range of financial considerations.

The nature of the retirement income commitment affects the firm's financial position and cost structure. For example, a **profit-sharing retirement plan** involves a cost contingent on profitability, but avoiding a "fixed charge" may turn out to be an expensive method of providing benefits perceived to be of less value by the employee because of their contingent nature. A defined contribution plan, common among multiemployer union pension programs, appears to limit liability to the negotiated pension benefits. The problems of such plans in declining industries may result, however, in obstacles to withdrawal, or to the assumption of liabilities of other participants who do fail. The defined benefit plan involves a specific commitment and the **Employee Retirement Income Security Act of 1974 (ERISA)** requires systematic funding and corporate backing of the plan. Defined benefits are desirable to employees because of the financial security provided.

The other financial dimension associated with retirement income benefits is, of course, the investment of funds set aside for providing them. This is entirely the financial officer's responsibility. Accordingly, investment management is the major topic of this section. Before discussing corporate policies with respect to pension plans, some definitions are supplied and the evolution of pension plan reporting is covered briefly.

EVOLUTION OF PENSION PLAN REPORTING AND ISSUES

DEFINITIONS AND PENSION PLAN REPORTING. Pension plans were first defined in an official reporting context in Accounting Report Bulletin (ARB) No. 47, 1956. and reprinted in *Financial Accounting Standards, Original Pronouncements as of July 1978* (Commerce Clearing House, 1978, p. 77) as follows:

> A formal arrangement for employee retirement benefits, whether established unilaterally or through negotiation, by which commitments, specific or implied, have been made which can be used as the basis for estimating costs. It does not include profit sharing plans or deferred-compensation contracts with individuals. It does not apply to informal arrangements by which voluntary payments are made to retired employees.

ARB No. 47 only indicated guides that are acceptable for dealing with costs of **pension plans** in the accounts of companies that already have plans. It was not concerned with how these plans should be funded. It was the opinion of the committee that past service benefit costs, that is, costs related to services rendered by employees prior to adoption of a plan, "should be charged to operations during the current and future periods benefited, and should not be charged to earned surplus at the inception of the plan." If the plan already exists, it is appropriate to charge to earned surplus the amount that should have been accumulated by past charges to income since the inception of the plan. The bulletin also states that for accounting purposes it is reasonable to assume that the plan, though modified or renewed, will continue for an indefinite period. The costs based on current and future services should be systematically accrued during the expected period of active service of the covered employees. Costs incurred for past services (i.e., those services rendered prior to adoption of particular benefit provisions of the plan) should be amortized over some reasonable period. The allocation should be made on a "systematic and rational" basis and not cause distortion of the operating results in any one year. The bulletin concluded that since the general opinion of accounting for pension costs had not been "crystallized sufficiently," differences in methods and procedures would be expected to continue.

PENSION PLAN PRINCIPLES AND LEGISLATION. Because of the lack of any standardized accounting method, lack of a definition of "vested," and an increased significance of pension costs in relation to the financial position of many companies, pension costs were reviewed again in 1966 in an Accounting Principles Board document, APB Opinion No. 8. This opinion was mainly concerned with the determination of **pension costs for accounting purposes.** It pointed out that the actual pension cost to be charged to expense is not necessarily the same as the amount to be funded for the year. The Board recognized that companies limit their "legal obligation by specifying that pensions shall be payable only to the extent of the assets in the pension fund . . . that plans continue indefinitely and that termination and other limitations of liability are not invoked while the company continues in business" (p. 152). Thus, companies are liable for the funded part only as long as they stay in business. The Board states that the ultimate costs of the plan will ultimately be charged to income and should not be charged directly to retained earnings at any time. The amortization of the ultimate costs will be a yearly provision between the minimum and maximum limits.

ERISA became law in September 1974. It was concerned with the funding of pension plans, the conditions for employee participation and for vesting of benefits, and the protection of employees' pension rights. All pension plans adopted after January 1, 1974, are subject to the requirements of ERISA. To protect employees' benefits, ERISA imposes an obligation on employers to make annual contributions, as determined by a recognized actuarial method, in amounts that will be sufficient over time to pay all pension benefits. ERISA also established the **Pension Benefit Guaranty Corp. (PBGC),** a federal corporation, to administer terminated plans and to guarantee the basic benefits of all participants who have vested rights under a pension plan. If a plan is terminated, the PBGC can obtain a lien against the employer's assets for the excess of any present value of guaranteed benefits over plan assets, which is limited to 30% of the fair value of corporate net worth. This lien has the same status as a federal tax lien in the event of bankruptcy; it has priority over the claims of all but those of secured creditors. We will return to this point shortly.

In December 1974, the Financial Accounting Standards Board (FASB) issued Interpretation No. 3, "Accounting for the Cost of Pension Plans Subject to the Employees Retirement Income Security Act of 1974." Although it stated that no change was necessary in the minimum and maximum limits for the annual provision for pension costs, the **FASB** did not believe that the Act created a legal obligation for unfunded pension costs that warrants accounting recognition as a liability. There are two exceptions:

1. A company must fund the minimum requirement yearly unless it receives a waiver from the Treasury. The amount not funded shall then be a liability.
2. In the event of termination, or when there is convincing evidence of possible termination, **ERISA** imposes a liability of the excess of prior accruals over funded assets, that is, the unfunded vested benefits.

In March 1980 FASB issued Statement of Financial Accounting Standards No. 35, "Accounting and Reporting for Defined Benefit Pension Plans" to deal with plan financial reports as made to the **Internal Revenue Service** (IRS) and the Labor Department on Form 5500. Such reports are designed to inform plan participants and investors in the sponsoring employer as to the ability of the plan to provide promised benefits. Net assets available for benefits are compared with the actuarial present value of accumulated plan benefits. Changes in net assets and in factors affecting liabilities are reported for each plan year.

Of greater interest and more widespread use are those financial reports which provide information as to the pension costs being incurred by the plan sponsor and the status of the funding of pension commitments. The issuance in May 1980 by FASB of Statement No. 36, "Disclosure of Pension Information" required in footnotes disclosure of the actuarial present value of accumulated plan benefits (both vested and nonvested), the value of plan assets, and the assumed rate of return employed, in addition to the information required by Opinion 8.

Under current consideration and debate is the issue of whether a corporate plan sponsor's balance sheet should include a net pension liability or asset calculated according to FASB 36, adjusted to reflect projected changes in compensation. Changes in asset values, plan provisions, and interest and actuarial assumptions would all give rise to fluctuations in a measurement valuation allowance and its amortization. Opponents of the inclusion in the plan sponsor's balance sheet fear that such accounting presentation will unduly influence companies to favor assets having more stable prices over variable assets which could provide lower pension costs by reason of their higher average returns. The present type of footnote disclosure is seen as entirely adequate for informing creditors, investors, and plan participants.

Reviewing this evolution of accounting and reporting requirements for defined benefit plans is a reminder of the evolutionary process by which pension commitments have changed from a form of modest gratuity to a major corporate liability. The calculation of that liability is based on as many assumptions as may determine the expected returns from the assets segregated for funding purposes. It is a truism to observe that the 30–40 year cost of a pension plan cannot be accurately determined until that length of time has elapsed. Interim recognition of expense, therefore, resembles an educated guess.

VESTED BENEFITS. Vested benefits are the benefits that have been accrued to date and are not contingent on the employee's continuing in the service of the employer or on the plan's termination. They are a legal obligation of the firm. Nonvested benefits have been earned but are not a legal liability because the employee has not yet fulfilled the age and service requirements of the plan.

Vesting liabilities can be triggered if a firm's plant is closed or a division sold, resulting in the reduction of its labor force, even if the firm itself continues. The unfunded present value of vested benefits will not appear on the plan sponsor's balance sheet as a liability. Nevertheless, the value of the company—for example in a merger or acquisition—will obviously be affected by the size of this item, since it is essentially an expense of the firm which will have to be met in future periods.

INSURED PENSION BENEFITS. In the event of a pension plan's discontinuance, employees' vested benefits are insured through the **Pension Benefit Guaranty Corp. (PBGC).** The employing company is liable to the PBGC for pension claims paid by the latter with a maximum liability of 30% of its net worth. "Net worth" is not defined clearly in the legislation except that it refers to the "fair value" of stockholders' equity. "Fair value" appears to refer to economic value, not to the firm's book value or market value; therefore, it is not directly measurable. In addition, the amount and seniority status of the PBGC claim is not clear. In any event, creditors and potential lenders take account of such contingent liabilities in their appraisal of firm credit worthiness.

For single employer plans, the annual assessment at $2.60 per participant soon proved totally inadequate. Congressional action is required to increase it to the requested $7 and higher in order to spread the cost of pension benefit guarantees across the current generation of plans.

RECOGNIZING COSTS AND LIABILITIES. Retirement income expectations should not, according to public policy, be created without steps taken to assure their realization. Government-approved plans must provide for systematic funding of prospective benefits and must keep the funds independent of the plan sponsor's financial position. The PBGC ensures a minimum level of benefit payments to participants in defined benefit plans, but only at the expense of solvent plans.

Determining the cost of a plan is a primary objective of financial management. At the time of adopting a plan, only estimates are available. No one really knows what the plan costs until the last employee has retired, perhaps 40 years later. Even then, postretirement pension adjustments may add to costs.

Company policies dictate some of the assumptions about the future. For example, pension planners and actuaries rely on projections of the numbers, types, age, sex distribution, and turnover characteristics of the workforce to help estimate future costs. Other decisions relate to early retirement incentives, death and disability benefits, vesting provisions, and benefit formulas.

A plan that is successful in providing a standard of living in retirement commensurate with that achieved in a person's active years is almost inevitably a final pay plan. For example, a formula that provides 1.5% of the highest five of the last 10 years' compensation for each year of service up to 30 years, less half the Social Security benefit (less for shorter service), would be expected to produce the following fractions of the final year's compensation in the case of an employee with 30 years' service:

Final Year's Compensation ($)	Fraction Replaced By Benefits (%)
9,000	61
15,000	53
25,000	48
50,000	45

Because of the reduced expenses and taxes applicable to retired persons, 10–15% can be added to the fractions above to arrive at the level of replacement in terms of disposable income.

The cost of the plan will depend on salary levels and other factors that will prevail far into the future. Actuaries can estimate with some reliability such factors as mortality, turnover, early retirements, disability cases, and other characteristics of the workforce. But the major cost elements are changes in Social Security, the effects of price level fluctuations on wages and salaries, and the rates of return that financial pension assets will earn.

Estimating the **cost of a pension plan** given such uncertainties is an elusive goal. The best that the financial manager can do is to insist on realistic assumptions and regular revisions in light of unfolding developments. A series of successive approximations will then result, rather than a single cost projection. Reasonable stability in the percentage of payroll attributable to pension costs is the primary goal for this aspect of financial management. Since the past has an appealing certainty, the inclination is strong to use the present workforce distribution, past turnover rates, and historical investment returns as the basis for calculating future costs. The assumption that the future will mirror the past, however, is seldom, if ever, valid. The financial manager, therefore, must insist that cost estimates be forward-looking, not simply retrospective views of a retirement program that will never again be in operation. The minimum level of cost recognition (regardless of the rate of funding) for a defined benefit plan is the normal cost for the period plus interest on any unfunded prior service cost and amortization of such costs over 40 years (30 years for newly created plans or new past service liabilities). This is also the minimum funding standard under ERISA.

The familiar emphasis on consistency in reporting requires footnote explanations of any changes in actuarial methods and assumptions. In the past, companies used variable cost recognition methods to "manage" or smooth reported earnings. Present and prospective reporting and disclosure rules are designed to make clear what methods of cost recognition and changes to them the firm has adopted.

To avoid transitory variations in cost, pension managers should spread actuarial gains and losses over a relatively long period of time (e.g., 15 years). The logical objective is to come as close as possible to recognizing the true cost of retirement benefits so that decisions on pricing products and services are made on the basis of reasonably reliable information.

RECAPTURE OF EXCESS ASSETS. There has been a wave of terminations of overfunded defined benefit plans in order that the plan sponsor may recapture the excess of assets over the value of accrued vested benefits. Such recaptures have been the subject of widespread controversy. In some instances, employees have sued or negotiated for additional benefits. The PBGC has had to make sure that the termination procedure has fully discharged existing liabilities and that the creation of a new plan will not expose it to new risks as a guarantor of benefits.

A plan sponsor responsible for making up funding deficiencies resulting from actuarial and investment losses, it is argued, ought to be able to withdraw excess assets created by gains. Denial of the right to recover what turn out to be excess contributions, moreover, will be another deterrent to defined benefit plans. Safeguards, rather than denials, are advocated.

Contrary views are held by those who regard prospective benefits as deferred compensation and the employees as having an ownership interest in excess assets. Discounting future benefit liabilities at interest rates which include a premium for anticipated inflation may not be fair if plan termination freezes benefits at existing levels.

In view of the uncertainties surrounding recapture of excess assets and the taxability of such recoveries, good financial management in many instances dictates avoidance of overfunding by the downward adjustment of contribution rates as rapidly as justified by experience. In any event, it is always possible that future events may bring about the disappearance of any excess.

DEFERRED PROFIT-SHARING PLANS. The financial reporting and disclosure necessary to comply with the standards of the accounting profession, the **Securities and Exchange Commission (SEC)** and **ERISA** have undoubtedly discouraged some firms, especially those that have not yet established stable earning power, from establishing defined benefit pension plans. **Profit-sharing plans** in which the amounts credited to each individual's account are deferred until retirement have more appeal because they create no past service liability. From the standpoint of the employee, however, there are serious deficiencies in such plans. Length of service is not fully recognized until many years after adoption of a plan, and there is no firm expectation of retirement benefits on which the employee may rely.

Profit-sharing plans have become more advantageous since the provision of ERISA under which the employee has the option of deferring the capital gains tax on a lump-sum distribution by placing the proceeds in an **Individual**

Retirement Account (IRA) for accumulation until retirement. In essence, this is a type of forced saving-investment plan with tax benefits.

Whatever the plan formula, whether fixed or contingent on profits, the extent to which provision has already been made for employees' retirement income is a measure of financial position. If future periods will be burdened with greater cost contributions than in the case of competitors, for funding a comparable level of benefits, the firm will be at a cost disadvantage. The higher percentage of payroll represented by contributions will be one measure. Another indicator is the size of the unfunded (pension benefits not specifically set aside by the firm) commitment. As financial reporting and disclosure practices become more complete, it will be possible for the financial officer to compare his firm's situation with that of competitors in terms of the adequacy, cost, and funding status of benefits.

TAX BENEFITS. To qualify for special treatment under the Internal Revenue Code, a plan must not discriminate in favor of higher paid employees, must include the total workforce, and must accumulate funds for the sole benefit of the pensioners and their beneficiaries. If the plan qualifies, the employer contributions are not recognized as income to covered employees until received as pension benefits. In addition, the funds accumulate without taxes on income or capital gains. The employer contribution, like any other expense, is deductible for income tax purposes. The funding requirements of **ERISA** are consistent with the favorable tax treatment afforded a qualified plan.

The tax treatment of pension fund investments makes them an attractive alternative to direct investment in the business (i.e., retained earnings), where profits are subject to the corporate income tax. The lower the marginal aftertax rate of return on new direct investment, the greater the overall advantage of fully funded pension benefit commitments.

For the self-employed individual, **Keogh plans,** established in 1962 and subsequently amended, permit taxpayers to deduct from taxable income the lesser of 25% of earned, nonsalaried, income or $30,000 in any year if contributions are segregated in an insurance contract or trust account. Individuals can set aside up to 100% of compensation but not more than $2,000 ($2,250 in certain cases) in an **Individual Retirement Account (IRA).** The tax benefit is the reduction of taxes on the contributions and the deferral of taxes on investment earnings until retirement.

Internal Revenue Code section 401(k) provides that within defined limits contributions to an employee's retirement program can be made without their being recognized as compensation. Typically, the employee asks the employer for a reduction in salary for this purpose. Such contributions, related to salary and length of service, can be invested in annuity contracts and mutual fund custodial accounts under the control of the employee. Comparable results in providing retirement income security can be obtained by incentive savings plans. The employer typically matches 50 to 100% of employee contributions of 2 to 6% of compensation, with an additional 4% of pay permitted but not matched. The tax sheltered investment may be bond or stock investment pools as selected by the employee, but the company's contribution is most frequently made in the form of its own shares.

PLAN OBJECTIVES

FINANCIAL VERSUS NONFINANCIAL FACTORS. Recruiting key personnel, particularly older employees, is facilitated by a wide range of personal incentives, of which pension benefits are only one. However, it is desirable to have retirement plans equal to or better than those of others in the industry and/or community. The financial management objective of incurring only costs that are moderate and stable relative to payrolls may have to be compromised in the interest of competing effectively for talent and commitment to the firm.

Early Retirement Costs. From a financial cost standpoint, the actuarial reduction for early retirement is about one-eleventh per year; for example, at age 62, the employee would be entitled to 75% of what the benefit would be at age 65. To encourage early retirement, many plans provide for no reduction or one of 3 or 4% for each year prior to age 65, provided the employee has 10 or 15 years of service. Our 62-year-old employee would receive 91% or retirement benefits under a 3% reduction plan. The questions to be raised are:

- How many employees will elect early retirement?
- Which kinds of employees will they be?
- What will be the advantages to the company?
- Can these advantages be quantified and compared with the additional expense?

Disability benefits are a similar analytical problem, although generally not as expensive as a retirement plan.

Post-retirement Benefit Adjustments. Post-retirement adjustments are included in benefits to take some account of inflation and higher living costs. They can easily add one-third to one-half to costs even if a limit is placed on the extent of indexing. Companies have made periodic ad hoc adjustments since the increase in the rate of inflation, thereby incurring only known costs and not committing in advance for an escalation in benefits of unknown size and duration. Such adjustments have been well received by employees and their unions and are requested with increasing frequency at the bargaining table.

Death benefits may be included in the pension plan or dealt with separately through group life insurance plans. The latter are simpler, more readily communicable, and therefore more effective, especially during service prior to retirement. Small death benefits for retirees are sometimes included at modest cost to take care of funeral and final illness expenses. The important benefit, required under ERISA, is the joint and survivor annuity option. Typically, this is 50% of the deceased employee's accrued or projected pension.

Coverage under health plans is frequently provided to retirees. These benefits, along with life insurance, are typically expensed on a current basis. Accountants have raised this question: since such supplementary retirement benefits are firm employer commitments, should they not be funded just like a pension plan? Recognition of the huge past service liability already incurred would materially set back the funding progress made in the last decade. In November 1984, the **FASB** issued Statement No. 81 requiring footnote disclosure of postretirement health care and life insurance benefits, funding policies, and costs recognized in the current period.

Vesting Standards. The minimum **vesting standards** for individuals established by **ERISA** is **one** of the following:

1. 100% vesting after 10 years of service after age 22.
2. Graduated vesting beginning with 25% after five years of service after age 22, increasing 5% a year for the next five years, and 10% a year for each year after 10, to 100% after 15 years.
3. 50% vesting after the earlier of 10 years of service or when the combination of years of service (at least five) and the employee's age total 45, increasing 10% a year for the next five years to 100%. Years of service before age 22 count.

In a typical case, the cost element in choosing among these three standards is not substantial; but patterns of turnover, both timing and extent, should be examined thoroughly. There is little advantage and some unnecessary expense in creating small vested benefits for relatively young groups of employees to whom more immediate forms of compensation would be more appreciated.

ALTERNATIVES TO DEFINED BENEFITS. Given the uncertainties as to the costs of a **defined benefit final pay plan** and the liabilities it creates for the plan sponsor, alternative approaches have been developed. A **money purchase plan,** for example, produces whatever pension benefit the sum in each employee's individual account will buy on retirement. The **defined contribution,** usually a fixed percentage of payroll, produces an accumulation that reflects capital market returns and the quality of investment management applied to it. The employer has fulfilled all obligations in making the defined contribution. All subsequent gains and losses affect only the participating employee.

There are several deficiencies in this approach, especially in a sustained period of rising wages and prices. The contributions invested for the longest periods are those based on the earliest, lower salaries; while those related to the highest years' earnings just prior to retirement are invested only for short periods. A rate of contribution that will produce a satisfactory level of benefits for young entrants will not yield adequate benefits for older entrants.

A special form of **money purchase pension plan** is provided by a **variable annuity.** The pioneer plan was that of the **College Retirement Equities Fund (CREF),** launched in 1952 as a companion to the fixed-dollar annuity benefits provided by **Teachers Insurance & Annuity Association (TIAA)** for the faculties and staffs of colleges, universities, independent schools, and their related associations. During the period of accumulation, the employer and employee contributions are invested in a portfolio of common stocks. At retirement, the accumulation units are used to acquire annuity units in the dollar equivalent of which benefits are paid. The level of retirement income is adjusted to reflect changes in the market value of the stock portfolio each year.

The **variable annuity concept** is essentially that the total return on equities across extended periods of time will, as in the past, equal a basic rate, such as 4%, plus the rate of inflation and possibly plus the rate of improvement in the general standard of living. There is the potential, then, for maintaining the real **purchasing power of pension benefits.** Variable annuities using assets other than common stocks are possible. The major problem with variable annuities during the 1970s was the long lag of security returns in reflecting price-level changes.

Some of the same disadvantages relate to **deferred profit-sharing plans** designed to provide retirement income. If the plan provides that forfeitures (i.e., the interests of employees who leave before full vesting) accrue to the benefit of those who stay, the result may be to produce a good salary replacement level for career employees.

Profit-sharing plans serve two purposes, which may be partially in conflict. One is to provide long-term financial security without burdening the firm with a fixed commitment. This argues for a conservative investment program, to ensure that a sufficient level of benefits is generated from profitable operations. The other purpose is to strengthen the employees' interest in the growth and profitability of the enterprise. This may be magnified by investing the fund, or a major portion of it, in company stock. The result is not a diversified portfolio, well designed to assure the payment of benefits. In fact, the employment risk has been compounded by the equity risk. The combination of a profit-sharing plan with a fixed benefit pension plan, however, has the incentive advantages without the exposure to serious shortfall in retirement income.

An **incentive savings plan** under which the employer matches, say, 50% of the employees' savings with shares of company stock is another approach to creating an interest in the enterprise among employees.

Finally, there is the least acceptable course of providing benefits, namely, on a pay-as-you-go basis. There is no liability for prior service to be amortized when each pension is voted on an ad hoc basis. (Any systematic treatment would be a defined benefit plan.) The employee lacks financial security and the employer lacks expense control, since this cost rises each year with a maturing workforce. This is the classic case of failure to match costs and revenues, which is rapidly disappearing from the scene in the corporate world, although still characteristic of some public programs and the Armed Services Retirement System.

None of the alternatives has, in effect, the simplicity, clarity, and assurance to the employee of a defined benefit plan. Such a pension program is relatively easy to communicate and has high value as an employee benefit. For this reason, companies seek to establish such plans as soon as their earning power warrants assuming such long-term obligations. Smaller and newer firms may substitute deferred profit-sharing plans, until they feel secure enough to provide a defined benefit plan.

ROLE OF THE ACTUARY

PLAN DESIGN. Deciding on the terms of a pension plan is important because once provisions have been established, it is virtually impossible to revise them downward. To be sure, a new plan can be adopted for new employees and for the future service of existing plan participants, but prospective changes take decades to become fully effective. The permanence of a plan, then, justifies obtaining at the outset **professional counsel** from pension planning experts and consulting actuaries. Based on complete information (age, sex, length of service, compensation, etc.) about the workforce, **actuaries** can provide crucial insights on the relative costs of different provisions. They can also describe prevailing and competitive plans.

Actuaries, with legal assistance at certain points, are the principal resource for assuring the qualification of plans under the **Internal Revenue Code** and the requirements of **ERISA.** The corporate financial officer may find himself the named fiduciary under the Act, which means that he must take all necessary steps to avoid both corporate and personal liability.

ESTIMATING COSTS. As observed earlier, the total cost of a pension plan, especially in the case of a defined benefit final pay plan, cannot be determined for 30 or 40 years after its adoption. But cost estimates are required year by year to satisfy the rules on funding in accordance with acceptable standards.

Within limits it is possible to change the timing of the incidence of costs. **Front-end loading** tends to anticipate that wage rates will continue to rise and that plan provisions will increase the level of benefits. **Back-loading** assumes that such events will occur gradually, that employees will elect later retirement (especially if **Social Security payments** changed in that direction), that growth in the employee group will long delay the maturing of the plan, and that the current period's costs should not be burdened with costly provisions adopted in future periods. A neutral stance is to seek a level percentage of payroll for the present and the future based on reasonable actuarial assumptions and projections.

Complete actuarial valuations every three years at a minimum, supplemented by annual reviews, provide the necessary support for the deduction of contributions for tax purposes, for ascertaining the current level of contributions for satisfying ERISA standards, making expense projections for financial planning, for an analysis of gains and losses, and the reporting of funding status. The certification that normal costs are being met and that prior service liabilities are being amortized is an essential statement for all purposes.

The key variables for discussion with the actuary are (1) the maturing of the work force, (2) the trend toward or away from early retirement, (3) priorities in collective bargaining demands, (4) competitors' plans and cost recognition, and (5) any other factors peculiar to the firm that might differentiate its position from the typical case in the actuary's experience. On the basis of these specifics and corporate expectations about the future economic environment (stability, inflation levels, industry developments, tax policy, etc.), actuarial assumptions have to be made. None of these questions about the future is easy to answer with confidence, but each is as germane to the elements of cost recognition and pace of funding as to the corporate capital budgeting decision on a major investment in plant and equipment or a new product development. Integration of the actuarial considerations with all other elements of financial planning is both logical and essential. The financial executive must fight against treating the pension decisions as a mysterious world apart from the firm's basic long-term strategic plans.

Apart from the assumptions as to salary progression and investment return, which are discussed below, the specific cost factors the actuary provides are mortality rates, employee turnover, incidence of disability, and retirement ages. These reflect general trends as modified by company experience. Also, the actuary must make an assumption about the future of the Social Security wage base and benefits. The financial officer has little reason to challenge these estimates when they are carefully made. He should save his principal questions for, and apply his experience to, the assumptions regarding investment returns and salary progression. These, in turn, should be derived from the investment objectives carefully defined as a matter of corporate policy.

DEFINING INVESTMENT OBJECTIVES

PURPOSE. In the past, corporate managements have given an investment manager such a vague statement of *objectives* as "seek the maximum return consistent with an acceptable level of risk." Since such a statement provides no measurable standard of performance expectations, the appraisal of results becomes a matter of hindsight and subjective judgment rather than objective appraisal. In addition, the term "risk" has so many meanings that its precise definition in this context is essential.

Beyond the question of holding an investment manager accountable for results is the major question of determining corporate policy thoughtfully and analytically. Some consistency with other policies is desirable, and stability of attitudes and expectations is essential. Absent this kind of measured consideration, decisions will be reached on the spur of the moment under the overwhelming influence of the euphoric or doomsday atmospheres that periodically invade the boardroom. Evidence of the reality of such distortions of expectations in reflection of events of the most recent past is found in the dismal record of corporate pension funds over an extended period. After a long period of excellent equity returns in the 1950s and 1960s, when stock prices were peaking in the early 1970s, corporate pension funds sold bonds to put more than 100% of new money in common stocks. By the middle and late 1970s, when stocks had been revalued downward some 50% in relation to earning power, new money was directed predominantly into bonds on the eve of the worst bond market experience in history. After the five-year favorable experience of common stocks, (1975–1979), stocks regained favor once again.

Human and peer pressures are so powerful in the direction of sharing the expectations for the future derived from yesterday's events that only a clearly thought out and understood definition of objectives can keep the investment program on a course consistent with maximizing its productivity over a 30-year funding span. Business executives who commit resources to the launching of new products, the building of new plants, and the opening of new markets with full recognition of the risks involved sometimes shrink from investing in a well diversified portfolio of seasoned companies. This paradoxical behavior was illustrated in the 1970s and 1980s when companies that were increasing the bond component of their pension funds at the same time were bidding 30, 40, and 50% premiums over market prices to make major acquisitions.

A clear and explicit statement of **objectives,** constantly reviewed and reaffirmed, is the best available antidote to the loss of perspective and the emotional reactions to transitory events that periodically influence the investment decision-making process. A measured framing of objectives and expectations that can be adhered to across time will do more to enhance the productivity of pension fund assets than any other single step.

NATURE OF THE INVESTMENT PROBLEM. The investment management of a pension fund has certain important characteristics that are favorable to the achievement of excellent results:

1. *Absence of tax considerations.* None of the usual differentiations among capital gains and ordinary income, short-term and long-term gains, or forms of holding period returns has any significance.

2. *Absence of distinctions between principal (capital) and income.* The total return or productivity of the invested assets is what matters; that is, the interest and dividend flow plus or minus changes in capital values, whether realized or not.

3. *Absence of liquidity needs.* With rare exceptions, the fund is not subject to unanticipated withdrawals that require emphasis on stability of market values or substantial assets readily convertible into cash on short notice without material risk of loss. (An exception would be a profit-sharing plan covering few members.)

4. *A long time horizon.* Results over a 20- or 30-year period are what really matter. Short-term aberrations from good long-term rates of return are not important. The long view of investment strategy can be taken.

These favorable dimensions of the investment problem must be exploited to the fullest because the achievement of the desired solution is so difficult. The provision of a standard of living that is comparable to today's standard in real terms at some far distant date implies that reasonably constant purchasing power can be delivered by earning a real rate of interest plus an inflation premium. There is substantial evidence that a continuous investment in U.S. Treasury bills will earn the inflation rate over long periods of time. By giving up the price stability and liquidity of a Treasury bill, positive real returns have been earned historically. The long record of real returns (i.e., nominal returns minus changes in the Consumer Price Index) has been tabulated as follows by Ibbotson and Sinquefield, in *Stocks, Bonds, Bills, and Inflation: The Past and the Future* (Financial Analysts Research Foundation, 1982, p. 15):

Geometric Mean Total Return, 1926–1981

	Nominal Return (%)	−	Inflation Rate (%)	=	Real Return (%)
U.S. Treasury bills	3.0		3.0		0
Long-term government bonds	3.0		3.0		0
Long-term corporate bonds	3.6		3.0		0.6
Common stocks	9.1		3.0		6.1

Each of these asset categories, except Treasury bills and bonds, provided an incremental return over inflation rates as a form of reward for accepting price variability and illiquidity. For the same period, Ibbotson and Sinquefield calculated the standard deviation of nominal returns (a widely accepted measure of variability) for Treasury bills at 3.1%, while long-term corporate bond returns showed a standard deviation of 5.6% and common stocks one of 21.9%. Although stocks provided a significantly higher average return, it was very erratic, fluctuating between − 12.8% and + 31.0% about two-thirds of the time during this 56-year period.

The logic and economic underpinnings of a **positive relationship between rate of return and the variability of that return** support the expectation that the historical risk, variability, and illiquidity premiums will persist in the future, even though their size may vary with capital market conditions. A pension plan sponsor is in a good position to accept such generally undesirable attributes of investment experience and to earn those premiums. Indeed, it would be poor judgment to give up a return increment to secure the price stability and liquidity that a pension fund does not require.

CORPORATE FACTORS. Capital market expectations are not the only factors to be considered in defining investment objectives. The characteristics of the pension plan, as we have seen, affect the timing of cash flows and the nature of the employer's commitments and liabilities. Even more relevant are the characteristics of the firm. A young firm in a period of strong growth can accept a level of variability in pension fund returns that would be undesirable for a mature company in a cyclically sensitive industry. The pension fund should be looked on as a major capital investment to be compared with corporate direct investments in production facilities for particular lines of business. If those areas of activity are profitable and stable, there are fewer reasons to emphasize stability in the returns sought from the pension fund portfolio.

A major asset on a defined pension plan's balance sheet is the present value of future contributions. The stronger the plan sponsor (i.e., the higher the credit rating for that long-term "receivable"), the greater the proportion of variable, risky assets the plan can hold to earn a higher return. At the other extreme, if the viability of the company is open to question, the assets on hand should logically be exposed to less variability and possible loss.

Financial leverage is another useful measure for setting objectives consistent both with corporate financial policy and protection of the interests of present and future pensioners. If the plan sponsor, as a matter of policy, creates a highly leveraged capital structure that results in variability of earnings, the funding of pension benefits with variable assets might be restricted. There are, indeed, some who advocate borrowing by corporations to repurchase equity while concentrating the pension plan investments in fixed return assets, like high-quality bonds. The validity of this approach depends on a series of assumptions about which serious questions can be raised; but there can be no challenge to the logic of taking an integrated view of the combined financial position of the pension fund and the plan sponsor.

The previously described characteristics of pension funds, especially the absence of liquidity needs and the long time horizon, suggest that the pension fund is a better holder of variable, illiquid assets like common stocks than is the sponsoring corporation. If such assets are described as "risky" because of the uncertainty of the timing of the realization of returns, it is clear that a typical defined benefit pension plan of a growing enterprise is an almost ideal holder of "risky" assets. This type of risk must be clearly distinguished from what can be thought of as the risk of permanent or nonrecoverable losses of the kind that are sustained when a company goes bankrupt, scales down its obligations, and retains little if any of its equity. This **default risk** can result in losses that are subtractions from the total returns realized across time, not just temporary fluctuations.

While stable costs are a normal corporate objective, stability is not necessarily to be valued more highly than lower average costs. In the case of regulated industries and defense contractors, however, the stable return that produces a stable percentage of payroll in the cost structure may have advantages in the setting of rates and the determination of allowable expenses. Whatever the tradeoff between return and variability, the actuarial methods applied can dampen short-run variations significantly by the use of average rather than single-point market values and by spreading investment gains and losses over future periods.

THE ASSET MIX DECISION. The decision as to the allocation of pension fund assets among different classes of securities is the most important single choice to be made by the financial officer and his board. Even the selection of a single manager to whom complete discretion is granted does not provide escape from responsibility for this decision. The selection of that single manager must be made with full knowledge of how he will diversify the portfolio, so that the act of selecting the manager is the act of determining the asset mix. The situation is even clearer when two or more managers are employed because then each allocation of cash flow to a manager is a choice of that person's style and an asset mix decision.

Portfolio theory commends as one type of **"efficient" portfolio** that which produces the best expected return for a given level of variability. If the best estimate is that the variability of an equity portfolio is equal to the market's (a **beta** of 1.00, in the popular jargon), one might well accept the lower return commensurate with 10% less variability (a beta of 0.90). The economic theorist would describe this whole process as determining the **corporate utility function**. This is a useful formal concept: a way to think about the question. For example, at what point will corporate management value increments of stability and predictability more highly than units of additional expected return? In most instances, such risk-return tradeoffs cannot be derived by observation and discussion with money managers but an asset allocation model will help.

Investment simulations that answer the question "what if?" are widely available from pension consultants and investment managers. These exercises are designed to estimate the probability of a pension portfolio failing to earn an assumed rate of total return over a 10-year period with various **bond-stock ratios** and with various expected returns from each type of security. These models permit the decision maker to insert his own judgments as to future trends in inflation, bond yields, and stock returns. Relating these factors to the estimated rate of increase in wages and salaries will indicate whether expected returns will be at least equal to, preferably greater than, the progression in pay scales and vested pension benefits.

The use of **asset allocation models** for determining the specific investment objectives at a single point in time may lead to bad decisions. The asset allocation model's application assumes an equilibrium relationship between, say, bond and stock expected returns. If, on the contrary, either class of asset is materially over- or undervalued relative to the other, the results will be disappointing. In other words, asset allocation models are no substitute for an informed, careful judgment of prospective returns from the different asset types. This difficulty of making infallible judgments about future capital market trends is another reason for diversifying the portfolio among different types of assets.

However reached, the decision regarding asset mix is the most important one for the plan sponsor in addressing the question of acceptable levels of return and variability. For example, the decision might be to define investment objectives in terms of the following asset mix:

	Proportion Normal (%)	Authorized Range (%)
Long-term bonds	25	10–30
Common stocks	65	50–75
Real estate	5	0–10
Cash equivalents	5	5–40

Such an asset mix expresses the following conclusions about the future:

1. Variable returns are not a cause of concern and the plan sponsor will accept them to earn a higher return across time. **Liquidity and price stability** are portfolio characteristics of little value relative to their cost in the form of total return forgone.

2. While skeptical about the ability of investment managers to make consistently successful market timing decisions, the plan sponsor provides scope for significant shifts to **cash equivalents** when managers consider prices for any asset class excessive and vulnerable to correction.

3. A relatively high positive correlation between bond and stock returns is expected in the future. As a result, aggregate returns cannot be materially stabilized by shifts between long-term bonds and common stocks. The assumption is that only cash equivalents (money market instruments) will serve that purpose.

The asset mix decision can be translated into a total return expectation by another set of assumptions regarding inflation, capital market relationships, and resulting nominal and real rates of return. An example might be:

	Proportion (%)	Expected Real Return (%)	Expected Inflation Rate (%)	Expected Nominal Return (%)	Expected Portfolio Return (%)
Long-term bonds	25	2.5	6	8.5	2.13
Common stocks	65	7.5	6	13.5	8.78
Real estate	5	8.0	6	14.0	0.70
Cash equivalents	5	0.5	6	6.5	0.32
					11.93

Return expectations, therefore, can be expressed to investment managers in either real or nominal terms (e.g., approximately 12% nominal or 6% real in the example). Ideally, the **portfolio manager** will add enough to the fund's asset value to pay for this services and other portfolio expenses. Measures like the standard deviation of returns can be specified to frame expectations more precisely. The time span for any such measurements of returns and variability should not be shorter than a full market cycle.

The resulting statement of expectations as to asset mix, returns, and variability comprises the statement of investment objectives. Some additional specifications can be provided to control the rate of permanent losses from investments in companies that prove to have marginal creditworthiness. Illustrations would be the setting of quality standards in terms of **Moody's** or **Standard & Poor's ratings,** and specifying limits on the concentration of investments and measures of diversification, yield targets for common stocks, and a range of beta coefficients as a measure of sensitivity to broad market fluctuations. Other guidelines might include the extent of international diversification or the authorization of option activity.

However defined, investment objectives must be reviewed regularly and revised to take account of changes in plan or corporate factors, changes in attitudes toward different types of risk, and fundamental changes in the capital markets that materially affect expected returns and differentials among them. Frequent review and reexamination also serve to keep stable the plan sponsor's commitment to basic policy.

SELECTING INVESTMENT MANAGERS

THE ACTIVE MANAGEMENT DECISION. Since security markets are highly efficient in pricing individual issues, some argue that a market fund will perform as well as a fund that is actively managed. **Market or index funds** seek to replicate a market index, like Standard & Poor's 500 Stock Index, by owning a very broadly diversified portfolio of stocks in the index in proportion to the market values of their capitalizations. Such a **passive portfolio** will presumably exceed the average performance of all actively managed portfolios by the saving in transaction costs. Engaging in **active management** to secure superior returns (after adjustment for relative variability) is often referred to as a **zero sum game**; that is, the winners' gains are equaled by the losses of unsuccessful managers.

The plan sponsor's decision to employ active management for part or all of the pension fund's assets presumes that he can identify managers who will produce superior returns across a market cycle. These returns must be sufficiently better than the market returns available from a passive market portfolio to pay the cost of transactions and a return warranted by the level of specific risk.

Some plan sponsors select a compromise by having a **"core" market portfolio** that is passively managed while having **specialist managers** who seek to add return by their skills in selecting stocks from such market sectors as emerging companies, growth stocks, basic value issues, and yield stocks.

The financial officer, in identifying active managers likely to add value by **active management**, must satisfy himself that the prospective manager has a style, a discipline, and a quality control system to support the marketing presentation. The term "style" refers to the general approach or strategy of an investment manager. It may be the development of expertise in selecting growth or basic value stocks, in rotating from one market sector to another, in timing bond and stock market changes, or in identifying small-capitalization stocks with strong growth potential.

But a portfolio manager's style is not meaningful unless it is reinforced by a well-defined discipline that assures a systematic and consistently applied analytical valuation approach to security selection. This must be a valid and tested decision-making process or there can be no assurance that past results will be achieved in the future.

Finally, the investment management function must be able to track performance, identify aberrations from expected results, and determine on a current basis whether the product being delivered in the form of a portfolio has uniformly defined characteristics. Active management without these safeguards may turn out to be unreliable and unpredictable.

SINGLE-MANAGER CASE. For passive management, only a single qualified manager is required. **For active management,** the plan sponsor has a choice.

The simplicity, convenience, and lower cost of working with a single manager are appealing but not persuasive reasons for selecting a single manager. Most organizations have special strengths, and the best results will always be achieved by hiring managers to do what they do best. A good bond manager may not be good at equities, and vice versa. Placing a balanced portfolio with a single manager requires separate analyses of capabilities in each area.

The commingled fund run by banks, **life insurance company separate accounts,** and **mutual funds** managed by investment advisers permit having **multiple portfolio managers** with specialized skills for funds of equal market size. Small size is, then, no longer a reason for using a single manager.

The principal arguments against the employment of a single manager are the need to obtain specialized skills and to reduce manager selection risk. Since organizations change, professionals leave, ownership shifts, leadership becomes complacent, and past performance is a thoroughly unreliable guide to future results, even the most careful process of selecting managers can fail. If the plan sponsor's perception of a manager proves to be inaccurate, too long a time may elapse before the situation is fully realized and action taken. That period is likely to be one of underperformance. Diversifying the manager risk is, therefore, worth considering.

MULTIPLE-MANAGER STRUCTURE. If the goal is not merely to diversify, but more affirmatively to obtain the benefit of superior skills in different market sectors, the plan sponsor can consider a **multiple-manager structure** for active management. If the managers add value by actively managing portfolios in their several styles, they will produce aggregate results superior, after adjustment for variability, to **a market fund**.

Active bond portfolio managers also differ in their styles. Some rely almost exclusively on the anticipation of **interest rate changes**. Others give emphasis to **"sector swaps"**; that is, seeking additional returns by shifting from a relatively fully valued market sector to a relatively undervalued one on the basis of yield spreads between them. Another approach is to use **credit analysis** to select issues that are about to be upgraded and avoid those whose credit rating is about to be downgraded. There are also substantial differences in the aggressiveness with which a manager will back his interest rate forecasts.

Guaranteed Investment Contract. Another form of fixed income management is the **guaranteed investment contract (GIC)** issued by life insurance companies. Some minimum rate of return is guaranteed by the issue for a specified period in the future. The GIC, for accounting and actuarial purposes at least, is presumed to have a **fixed value**. Typically the funds are invested in a broadly diversified portfolio of corporate direct placements.

Immunization. Investment managers have designed and offer a **bond "immunization" program** (see several sections on bond immunization and fixed income strategies in our companion volume, *Handbook of Financial Markets and Institutions,* Wiley, 1986.) The bond portfolio is invested so that for a specific period (e.g., 7 years) the return will not vary significantly from what was initially projected. This **immunity from interest rate changes** is accomplished by resetting the portfolio periodically to meet the calculated objective. Funding benefits promised to retired employees through a GIC or an immunization program is designed to fix the cost of those benefits by reducing the interest rate risk. Buying **immediate annuity contracts** from insurers would shift the mortality risk in addition.

Contracts that are designed to shift the uncertainties of future interest levels and fluctuations to an insurer must, of necessity have limited lives. In relation to a 30-year funding period for long deferred benefits, a five- or 10-year period of protection is helpful but still leaves the plan sponsor carrying the bulk of the risk.

Real Estate Pools. Life insurance companies also offer participations in **pools of real estate equity investments,** providing a degree of diversification not otherwise available to any but the largest funds. Since inflows and outflows of funds occur at appraised values, as distinguished from prices set in an active trading market, participation in **real estate separate accounts** may be more or less advantageous depending on the extent to which the valuation smoothing of appraisals brings unit values into line with the effects of interest rate and other capital market factors.

Independent real estate investment advisors periodically make available closed-end pools for pension funds, which typically last for a decade before orderly liquidation. They avoid the problem of interim valuations but do not have the advantage of a continuing cash flow for new investments.

Experience suggests that real estate is a good diversifying asset, one that responds to an increase in the price level more promptly than do corporate common stocks. **Real estate investments** need to be well diversified because of the uniqueness of each property and the factors which may affect its holding period return. Comparable data are not available for the long history of real estate investing. In recent years, however, the major organizations investing for pension funds have contributed data through the National Council of Real Estate Investment Fiduciaries to compute the **Fiduciary Real Estate Council (FRC) Property Index of returns** from income properties, diversified by location and by type and held in tax-exempt portfolios. The index has gradually added properties since the base date of December 31, 1977 until it is now comprised of more than 900 properties valued at more than $7.3 billion by the end of 1984. The principal property types by value consist of office buildings (49.6%), industrials (25.6%), and retail (19.2%). Returns have been as follows:

FRC Property Index

Year	Annual time-Weighted Rate of Return (%)
1978	15.9
1979	20.6
1980	17.9
1981	16.6
1982	9.3
1983	13.3
1984	12.9

Source: Frank Russell Company (by permission). These returns were achieved substantially without the use of financial leverage.

Managing the Managers. Once the **multiple-mnager structure** has been established, the **plan sponsor** has the task of managing it. **Managing the managers,** obviously, is not managing the portfolios. The principal tasks of the sponsor are now (1) the review and revision of investment objectives in light of changes in the external environment, plan factors, and corporate factors, (2) the allocation of new money among managers in accordance with a plan consistent with defined objectives, (3) the analysis of and rationalization for the performance of managers across a market cycle (typically three or four years), and (4) effective communication with corporate executives and investment managers of progress in and prospects for realizing the defined objectives.

The worst hazards to successful management of managers are (1) lack of effective communication and understanding, (2) impatience and hasty reactions to capital market developments, and (3) turnover in personnel without adequate transitional guidance. There is a strong tendency to increase attention to this investment pool when it is performing poorly, perhaps because of temporary capital market factors. Vastly superior rates of returns may, in fact, be a better reason for more careful analysis because they may be due to an unsustainable aberration in the relationships among asset values.

Finally, the corporate sponsor must fight the managers' tendency to hold diversified portfolios. Managers must be prodded in the direction of concentrating in their market sector of expertise, avoiding broad diversification and overlap with other managers. Only the plan sponsor should look at the total result and test the adequacy of its diversification, to prevent either seriously disappointing results or exposure to large permanent losses of capital. Related questions are, of course, whether a different mix of styles is more likely to serve the objectives better in the future and whether more specific guidelines should be furnished to individual managers to assure the uniform character of their output. The plan sponsor must be sure that what he is asking of a manager is drawing on that manager's deepest reservoir of experience, conviction, and skill.

MANAGER SELECTION. With such a wide range of alternatives (and so-called unconventional assets have not even been mentioned here), it is evident that the plan sponsor has important choices to make in selecting the combination of investment management styles and skills that is most likely to achieve the firm's defined objectives for the pension fund. Internal resources for making these decisions can be usefully supplemented by counsel from consultants. Their role is to provide information about the styles and disciplines of individual managers and to assist in the analysis of the suitability of any combination of them for matching the defined investment objectives. Whether a particular manager should be hired is, of course, the decision of the plan sponsor. If the "chemistry" of the relationship is not good, no style or discipline, however appropriate for the task, should dictate the selection.

Regardless of whether outside consultants are employed to assist in the **manager selection process,** the corporate financial officer and the **board of directors** must arrive at independent judgments and make informed decisions. Screening the very large number of capable investment managers to identify those who have the potential of performing a particular function in the manager mix is the most useful function of the consultant. The consultant's role is also helpful in preparing the questionnaire, if one is used, or the interview materials needed to ensure that time is productively employed. The consultant should also help in interpreting the interview results, sample portfolios and performance records, and to assess the effects on total portfolio characteristics of different manager mixes.

Those involved from the corporate side and the portfolio manager who is being considered for the account must meet and discover the "chemistry," good or bad, of the relationship. Before any final choice is made, a visit to the working quarters of the manager is essential, to observe this element of the firm's style. Proprietary information involving financial position, ownership, compensation, management of growth, turnover in employees and accounts, and so on, is relevant and suitable for discussion. The extensive survey of alternatives and the intensive study of individual candidates is very cost effective because of the **high costs of changing managers:** both the loss of continuity and the high transaction costs of extensive portfolio shifts.

PERFORMANCE MEASUREMENT

The appropriate measurement for **investment management performance** is the **time-weighted total rate of return** with or without adjustment for variability. The measure is of the **productivity of capital** for the periods of time under management. The manager has no control over the timing of contributions and should be neither benefited nor penalized for decisions beyond his control. The method essentially involves calculating total returns for each period in which there is no fund inflow or outflow. A simple example follows:

A fund has $1 million market value of assets on January 1.
It earns interest and dividends of $40,000 during the first six months.
Assets increase in value $60,000 during the period.
On July 1, $500,000 is added to the fund.
During the second half of the year, the fund earns $60,000 but has a decrease in market value of $100,000, with the result that the fund's December 31 value is $1,560,000.
What was the time-weighted rate of return?
The total return for the first half of the year was

$$\frac{\$40,000 + \$60,000}{\$1,000,000} = 10\%$$

For the second half of the year, the total return was

$$\frac{\$60,000 - \$100,000}{\$1,600,000} = -2.5\%$$

At the end of June, each dollar at the start of the year had a value of $1.10.
Each July 1 dollar was worth only $0.975 at the end of the year. For the year as a whole, therefore, a dollar grew to $1.0725, making the **time-weighted total return** 7.25%, compounded semiannually.

When inflows and outflows do not neatly coincide with valuation dates as in the example, approximations can be made without serious distortions of results. (The authoritative and widely accepted study on this subject is the **Bank Administration Institute's** "Measuring the Investment Performance of Pension Funds," 1968.)

The more conventional **dollar-weighted rate of return** would be lower in the example because more dollars were invested during the period of inferior returns. However, for the evaluation of progress toward funding a liability, this **internal rate of return** is the correct measure and will be used in actuarial valuations to determine investment gains and losses, that is, realized and unrealized returns across time compared with the assumed interest rate.

The **adjustment of time-weighted returns** to reflect their **variability** is a logical step, especially if (1) the data are used to make comparisons with other funds or (2) the variability is greater or less than comtemplated in the definition of investment objectives. Frequently, the **beta coefficient** (the historical sensitivity of the portfolio's returns to those of market indexes) is used for such adjustments. Ratios of return to variability are also useful to determine whether the investment manager is realizing adequate rewards for risk assumed in the form of the variability of returns.

When a manager's performance lags, he may be tempted to "play catch-up ball"—to buy lower quality, volatile securities in the hope that a positive

market environment will produce returns far above average. The plan sponsor's task is to make sure that such a strategy is not placing fund assets at
a higher than contemplated level of risk. Conversely, a manager may seek
an unnecessarily **defensive position** in terms of price stability and liquidity
at material sacrifice in return to avoid exposure to possible client disap-
pointments resulting in the loss of investment management business.

Refinements in the measurement of portfolio characteristics have made
it possible to describe a risk-return profile with a fair degree of precision.
The use of **fundamental betas** (those that take account of earnings, size,
growth, and financial leverage factors in addition to historical price variability
relative to the market) has increased the visibility of investment styles and
the sources of superior or inferior returns. **Measures of portfolio diversification** like the R^2 (percent of the variance of return explained), and measures
of **variability** like the **standard deviation** also guide the corporate financial
officer in determining whether a **multiple-manager structure** can be expected
to be productive of superior returns.

Such data on the sources of performance results permit **diagnostic analysis:**
the analysis of performance for the purpose of identifying the strategies and
tactics that added to or subtracted from realized returns. This should not be
just an exercise in hindsight. Diagnostic analysis extends to the review of
defined objectives and the corporate factors in their influence on investment
management policies. The effective use of this analytical step is not grounds
for recriminations but as an early warning of any misperceptions of the basic
asset management plan. For an in-depth discussion of portfolio performance
evaluation, see the section entitled "Performance Measurement" in *Handbook of Financial Markets and Institutions*, E. Altman, editor, Wiley, 1986.

LESS CONVENTIONAL INVESTMENTS

THE PRUDENCE CONSTRAINT. In addressing the question of whether less
conventional or even **unconventional investments** are eligible for pension
funds, the corporate financial officer must recognize that Section 404(a)(1)
of ERISA has not been definitively interpreted by the courts. Nevertheless,
the language is fairly explicit:

> . . . a fiduciary shall discharge his duties with respect to a plan solely in the
> interest of the participants and beneficiaries and (A) for the exclusive purpose
> of: (i) providing benefits to participants and their beneficiaries; and (ii) defraying
> reasonable expenses of administering the plan; (B) with the care, skill, prud-
> ence, and diligence under the circumstances then prevailing that a prudent
> man acting in a like capacity and familiar with such matters would use in the
> conduct of an enterprise of a like character and with like aims; (C) by diver-
> sifying the investments of the plan so as to minimize the risk of large losses,
> unless under the circumstances it is clearly prudent not to do so. . . .

Undivided loyalty, prudence, and diligence are not new requirements for a fiduciary; but the standard of "a prudent man acting in a like capacity and familiar with such matters" appears to call for specific expertise in managing pension funds. Being informed about the terms of the plan, the investment alternatives, and risks of loss implies some specialized knowledge of the field.

The traditional personal trust standard of prudence, which treats each investment as an individual case, does not recognize a gain on one as an offset to a loss on another. The emerging definition of prudence in pension fund asset management appears to recognize the effects of diversification and to apply the standard to a portfolio rather than to single securities. As is well known in portfolio theory, a well-diversified portfolio of risky securities may have very little exposure to large losses. Individual securities might not be clearly prudent—shares of new and unseasoned companies, for example—but a well-diversified portfolio of them could be quite acceptable.

In short, the prudent expert constraint appears to be more analytically grounded by relating investment decisions to the characteristics of a growing pool of assets with a long time horizon. The range of investment alternatives appears to have been broadened, provided the decision maker systematically studies their place in and effects on the characteristics of a total asset mix.

The other reassuring phrase is "under the circumstances then prevailing." This says that decisions will be judged not based on hindsight but on the basis of the reasonableness of judgments reached in the environment in which the investments were made.

INTERNATIONAL DIVERSIFICATION. Diversifying bond and stock portfolios across the world's capital markets is both logical and consistent with the objective of creating the most efficient portfolio, that is, securing the best return at a given level of variability. Since securities returns in different markets, including the effects of currency fluctuations, are not likely to show high positive correlations, distributing investments among the half-dozen largest markets has typically resulted in a higher return and less variability than a portfolio invested in domestic markets.

International diversification has, therefore, become widely adopted by corporate pension funds but on a modest scale. Some funds invest in a portfolio that mirrors an **international market index** while others opt for active management. **Commingled funds** are available from banks and investment advisory organizations. For a discussion on this and other related factors, see the section entitled "International Portfolio Diversification and Foreign Capital Markets" in *Handbook of Financial Markets and Institutions*, E. Altman, editor, Wiley, 1986.

OPTION AND FUTURES CONTRACTS. The purchase and sale of **option contracts** by themselves raise questions as to prudence because options have no claim on assets or earning power, provide no current return, and have a very short life. It is generally thought that the purchase of such a contract is pure **speculation** on an unpredictable price change or a device to provide high leverage without borrowing.

When combined with other assets, however, options can become risk-reducing instruments. Writing (selling) calls on stocks in the portfolio, for example, is recognized as a prudent step in reducing volatility. The premium received for writing the call is a cushion (hedge) against the loss from a decline in the stock price. A portfolio of stocks on which calls are regularly written will typically have the variability of its return reduced by 30–40% at a modest sacrifice of total return. The simultaneous purchase of stocks and writing of calls may produce an asset with no more variability than a portfolio of long-term bonds but with a higher total return.

Less widely recognized is an essentially similar strategy of buying **"protective puts"** covering some or all of a portfolio of stock positions. Prospective returns are reduced by adding the cost of the protective puts to the cost of the shares, but the exposure to loss is absolutely limited to the difference between the combined cost and the exercise value of the put contract.

Some fund managers have purchased what are sometimes called **"fiduciary calls."** The amount of the exercise price is earmarked in cash equivalents tied to the purchased call. The combination of the calls and the money market instruments provides the upside potential of owning the shares but with possible loss limited to the value of the calls. It is a **fiduciary call** because the exercise price is fully funded in riskless investments that earn interest and are highly liquid. The combination of calls and cash equivalents is also an attractive substitute for convertible securities of the same companies.

Still in the experimental stage is writing puts against assured future cash flows on stocks the manager plans to buy as soon as the funds are available. The premium received for writing the put in effect reduces the cost of acquiring the selected stocks. Earmarking cash reserves or expected cash flows to the extent of the exercise prices of the puts makes them **"fiduciary puts."**

In contrast to option contracts that may or may not be exercised, **financial futures contracts** are firm commitments to pay for or deliver Treasury bills, Teasury bonds, **Government National Mortgage Association** securities (GNMAs), or other financial instruments at a fixed price on a specified date. Entering into such contracts without the securities to make delivery or the funds to accept delivery cannot be considered prudent. However, the use of financial futures to hedge positions or in arbitrage transactions is entirely appropriate.

Timing risks in the bond market are among the major exposures to loss of earnings. Futures contracts can be used to reduce such risks and to compensate for arbitrary fluctuations in the flow of contributions to the pension fund. If investment managers use financial futures as a tool of portfolio management, the plan sponsor should establish some specific guidelines for the extent of use and for the provision of coverage for contracts with liquid or maturing assets. Such guidelines will prevent exposure to losses from forward commitments.

These rapidly developing markets in options and futures afford investment managers new tools for modifying the risk-return characteristics of a portfolio in ways not achievable by converting a proportion of it into cash. The markets in such contracts are, however, highly sophisticated. The authorization for using these tools should be given only after the corporate financial officer has satisfied himself that the manager is fully qualified.

TANGIBLE ASSETS. The ownership of gold, silver, and other precious metals is no longer "unthinkable" for a pension fund. But the time-tested measures of prudence imply or perhaps even demand that the asset have some form of earning power or contractual return. Is an expected appreciation in value sufficient? The same question applies to paintings, rare coins and stamps, and the vast array of articles that have come to be known as collectibles.

A security has value because it promises to pay a contractual rate of interest or represents a share in the earning power of an enterprise. It has an intrinsic value derived from these qualities. Precious metals and collectibles, on the other hand, depend for their return entirely on the owner's ability to sell them to someone else at a higher price. Ownership is not productive of return but only of expense for storage and insurance. When time is a source of expense instead of revenue, the question arises as to whether these classes of assets fit the basic characteristics of a pension fund. Perhaps only a period of persistent inflationary pressures could bring them to serious consideration.

SOCIAL AND CORPORATE RESPONSIBILITIES

SOCIAL RESPONSIBILITIES. Because of the large and growing ownership of American companies by corporate pension and profit-sharing plans, representatives of organized labor, government officials, employees, and the public are asking insistent questions as to how or whether plan sponsors address questions about how portfolio companies deal with a wide range of "social responsibility" concerns. Equal employment opportunities, labor practices, environmental protection, product quality and safety, deportment in South Africa and other countries, and participation in community affairs are a few examples of such concerns.

The asset allocation decisions of plan sponsors are also being questioned. For example:

- Could funds be channeled into housing and community services beneficial to employees without such sacrifices of return and safety as might call into question the decision maker's undivided loyalty to pensioners and their beneficiaries?

- What about venture capital investments which might stimulate area economic growth?
- Especially in **multiemployer jointly administered plans,** can investments be selected which will be favorable, or at least not unfavorable, to employment opportunities for the covered group?

State and local government retirement systems are regularly subjected to such questions. Corporate plans are not, but they should be because they are recognized as recipients of tax benefits in the public interest. Whatever policies a plan sponsor adopts in these matters, it is essential that they be addressed and that the conclusions be carefully documented and reviewed at regular intervals.

Unless there are some concessions in the return demanded or the safeguards required, it is difficult to see how "targeted" investments can bring about results materially different from those produced by market forces. Acting solely in the interest of plan participants, however, does not appear to permit a compromise of investment selection criteria. Court decisions have not yet clearly resolved these issues.

CORPORATE RESPONSIBILITIES. Pension asset managers are perceived, in the language of the later Professor A.A. Berle, Jr., to have "power without property." They are also thought of as silent partners of entrenched corporate managements because they have not exercised the rights and assumed the responsibilities of share ownership. Their traditional approach was known as the **Wall Street Rule:** If you can't support the management, sell the stock. Voting for management's positions was regarded as almost automatic. In taking such passive roles, asset managers progressively delegated to directors more and more of their rights of ownership.

Despite some questions being raised along the way regarding incentive compensation programs and the creation of large amounts of additional shares to which shareholders regularly relinquished their preemptive rights, no significant reaction to these trends emerged until corporate takeover activity developed on an unprecedented scale. A whole array of anti-takeover measures followed, creating a new vocabulary of staggered boards, super-majorities, fair pricing, scorched earth defenses, poison pill preferred stocks, greenmail, and golden parachutes.

The U.S. Labor Department and other observers have suggested that plan sponsors and asset managers have a shared fiduciary duty to address corporate governance issues. A case in point would be anti-takeover measures which might reduce the value of a company. Since the issues are complicated and conclusions debatable, the plan sponsor must make certain that they are fully and fairly addressed.

REFERENCES AND BIBLIOGRAPHY

Allen, Everett, J., Jr., Melone, Joseph J., and Rosenbloom, Jerry J., *Pension Planning*, 4th ed., Irwin, Homewood, Il, 1981.

Altman, Edward I., editor, *Handbook of Financial Markets and Institutions*, Wiley, New York, 1986.

Baldwin, Stuart A., et al., *Pension Funds and Ethical Investment: A Study of Investment Practices and Opportunities, State of California Retirement Systems*, Council on Economic Priorities, New York, 1980.

Bank Administration Institute, *Measuring the Investment Performance of Pension Funds*, Park Ridge, Il, 1968.

Cottle, Sidney, et al., *Pension Asset Management: The Corporate Decisions*, Financial Executives Research Foundation, New York, 1980.

DeMong, Richard F., Gray, William S. III, and Milne, Robert D., editors, *Broader Perspectives on the Interest of Pension Plan Participants*, Financial Analysts Research Foundation, Charlottesville, VA, 1985.

——— and Peavy, John W. III, editors, *Takeovers and Shareholders: The Mounting Controversy*, Financial Analysts Research Foundation, Charlottesville, VA, 1985.

Employee Benefit Research Institute, *Fundamentals of Employee Benefit Programs*, 2nd ed., Washington, D.C., 1985.

Financial Analysts Research Foundation, *Evolving Concepts of Prudence: The Changing Responsibilities of the Investment Fiduciary in the Age of ERISA*, Charlottesville, VA, 1976.

Graebner, William, *A History of Retirement: The Meaning and Function of an American Institution, 1885–1978*, Yale University Press, New Haven, CT, 1980.

Gray, Hillel, *New Directions in the Investment and Control of Pension Funds*, Investor Responsibility Research Center, Washington, D.C., 1983.

Ibbotson, Roger G. and Sinquefield, Rex A., *Stocks, Bonds, Bills, and Inflation: The Past and the Future*, Financial Analysts Research Foundation, Charlottesville, VA, 1982.

Kotlikoff, Laurence J. and Smith, Daniel E., *Pensions in the American Economy*, National Bureau of Economic Research, University of Chicago Press, IL, 1983.

Langbein, John H., Schotland, Roy A., and Blaustein, Albert P., *Divestment: Is It Legal? Is It Moral? Is It Productive?* National Legal Center for the Public Interest, Washington, D.C., 1985.

Leo, Mario, Bassett, Preston C., and Kachline, Ernest S., *Financial Aspects of Private Pension Plans*, Financial Executives Research Foundation, New York, 1975.

Maginn, John L. and Tuttle, Donald L., *Managing Investment Portfolios: A Dynamic Process*, Warren, Gorham & Lamont, New York, 1983.

McGill, Dan M., **Fundamentals of Private Pensions,** 5th ed., Richard D. Irwin for Pension Research Council, Homewood, IL, 1984.

———, ed., *Social Investing*, Richard D. Irwin for Pension Research Council, Homewood, IL, 1984.

Mennis, Edmund A. and Clark, Chester D., *Understanding Corporate Pension Plans*, Financial Analysts Research Foundation, Charlottesville, VA, 1983.

Munnell, Alicia H., *The Economics of Private Pensions*, Brookings Institution, Washington, D.C., 1982.

Pension Benefit Guaranty Corporation, *Annual Reports*, Washington, D.C., 1977–1984.

——, *Guidelines on Voluntary Termination*, Washington, D.C., 1978.

Regan, Patrick J., "Pension Fund Perspective," bimonthly, *Financial Analysts Journal*, 1983–1985.

Salisbury, Dallas L., ed., *Why Tax Employee Benefits?* Employee Benefit Research Institute, Washington, D.C., 1984.

Treynor, Jack L., Regan, Patrick J., and Priest, William W., Jr., *The Financial Reality of Pension Funding under ERISA*, Dow Jones-Irwin, Homewood, IL, 1976.

Williams, Arthur III, *Managing Your Investment Manager*, Dow Jones-Irwin, Homewood, IL, 1980.

15

FINANCIAL MANAGEMENT IN AN INFLATIONARY ENVIRONMENT

CONTENTS

15

FINANCIAL MANAGEMENT IN AN INFLATIONARY ENVIRONMENT

Moshe Ben-Horim
Haim Levy

INFLATION IN RECENT YEARS

The rate of increase in the price level of goods and services—the **inflation rate**—has had a marked impact on financial management in the United States in recent years. During the 1950s and 1960s the rate of inflation was low enough to be ignored or to draw the marginal attention of the financial manager. But Exhibit 1 shows that the rate of inflation in the 1970s was high and reached an annual double digit rate in some cases. The U.S. Consumer Price Index was about 33% higher at the end of 1970 compared to the end of 1960. But at the end of 1980, it was about 112% higher relatively to the end of 1970. Although inflation subsided in the mid-1980s, it remains a threat and an important consideration to corporate financial management. Relative to the other countries whose recent inflation history is shown in Exhibit 1, the United States has experienced the lowest average rates of inflation for the period 1961–1983. Indeed, the effect of inflation on financial management in other countries was often more significant. Two obvious examples are Brazil and Israel (not indicated).

Inflation normally reduces investment profitability and often slows down investment, which is what happened in the 1970s. In an attempt to reactivate the economy and offset inflation losses to firms, some governments have introduced **investment incentives.** For example, in the United States, firms may elect to use the **LIFO method of inventory** accounting, which relieves them of some of the tax on inflationary profits. Other incentives are **accelerated depreciation**, introduced by the Eisenhower administration, and the reduced asset lives system for tax purposes, introduced by the Kennedy and Nixon administrations. The investment tax credit, which first appeared in 1962, is another important incentive. In 1981, the Reagan administration

EXHIBIT 1 INFLATION RATES IN SELECTED COUNTRIES, 1961–1983

Year	United States	Canada	United Kingdom	Australia	Brazil	The Netherlands
1961	1.0	0.0	3.9	1.0	43.3	2.9
1962	1.0	1.9	2.8	0.0	60.8	0.0
1963	1.9	1.0	1.8	1.0	82.0	4.7
1964	0.9	1.8	4.5	3.7	84.4	5.4
1965	1.8	3.7	5.1	4.9	41.0	6.0
1966	3.6	3.5	4.1	2.6	46.0	4.0
1967	3.8	3.5	2.4	5.0	32.8	3.4
1968	4.1	4.1	4.6	2.6	22.0	3.8
1969	5.3	4.4	5.4	2.8	22.5	7.4
1970	5.9	3.4	6.3	3.9	22.0	3.6
1971	4.3	2.7	9.4	6.1	20.0	7.5
1972	3.2	4.7	7.1	5.8	16.1	7.8
1973	6.3	7.5	9.2	9.4	12.8	7.9
1974	10.8	10.9	16.0	14.5	27.0	9.8
1975	9.1	10.7	24.2	24.2	28.8	10.5
1976	5.8	7.5	16.5	16.5	41.9	8.8
1977	6.5	8.0	15.8	15.8	43.7	6.4
1978	7.6	9.0	8.3	8.0	38.8	4.2
1979	11.2	9.0	13.5	9.0	52.8	4.2
1980	13.5	10.2	17.9	10.1	82.8	6.5
1981	10.4	12.4	11.9	9.7	105.6	6.7
1982	6.1	10.9	8.6	11.1	98.0	5.9
1983	3.2	5.8	4.6	10.1	142.0	2.8
1984	4.3	4.3	5.0	4.0	196.7	3.3
Average						
1961–1972	3.1	2.9	4.8	3.2	41.1	4.7
1973–1983	8.2	9.2	13.3	12.6	61.3	6.7
1961–1983	5.5	5.9	8.5	7.7	50.7	5.7
1975–1984	7.8	8.8	12.7	10.3	83.1	6.0

Source: Based on price indexes published in various issues of the International Monetary Fund, *International Financial Statistics*, 1985.

introduced the **Accelerated Cost Recovery System** (ACRS) which adapts tax laws to an inflationary environment. Although most countries have amended their tax laws to compensate firms for inflation losses, legislation usually lags behind economic developments. The new tax legislation currently being debated in the U.S. Congress in 1986, would significantly change depreciation guidelines, making them far less attractive for companies.

INFLATION AND THE FIRM'S FINANCIAL POSITION

Changes in price levels have important implications for the relationships between the financial position of a firm, as reflected in its financial statements, and the firm's real financial position. Perhaps a reasonable point of departure for making this distinction is the measurement of income. A firm's economic income is defined as the income that it can distribute during the period, so that at the end of the period it is left with sufficient physical assets to carry on the same level of activity as at the beginning of the period.

Corporate income as reported under **generally accepted accounting practices (GAAP)** usually deviates from economic income. In the absence of inflation, however, the two measures of income are quite closely related, and income reported under GAAP gives a fair idea of both the trend of a firm's economic income and the way it compares with the economic income of other firms in the industry. The same holds for related measures such as earnings per share and the price-earnings ratio. Under inflation, however, the relationships between reported and economic incomes are often substantially distorted. In addition, because assets are recorded at historical cost, while revenues and expenses are recorded in current dollars, some of the financial ratios traditionally used to analyze a firm's financial position are affected by inflation and must consequently be carefully analyzed at periods of rapid price increase. After a long debate about inflation accounting by the Financial Accounting Standards Board (FASB), the Statement of Financial Accounting Practices No. 33, which required large public companies to report the effects of inflation on their financial statements, was issued. The FASB decided to retain historical cost recording in the primary financial statements, but Statement No. 33 specifies requirements for supplementary information in annual reports to reveal the effects of the changing price level. The effect of inflation is reported in two different ways: (1) using **constant dollar accounting** which reflects an adjustment for the general change in the price level; and (2) on a **current cost basis,** a method that employs specific price changes for each asset.

Inflation accounting is at an experimental stage. The bulk of financial reporting is still on a historical cost basis. Let us then examine the main problems and some consequences of the GAAP rules during times of inflation.

INVENTORY. The accounting treatment of inventories can affect the firm's reported earnings, tax bill, and cash position. The magnitude of the effect depends particularly on whether the firm uses the **first-in first-out** (FIFO) or the **last-in first-out** (LIFO) formula. To demonstrate this point in detail, consider a firm that has revenues of $200 million and for simplicity assume that there are no costs or expenses except the cost of goods sold. Additional information about the firm is:

	Units (Millions)	Cost per Unit
Inventory at the beginning of the year	100	$1.0
Inventory bought during the year	100	$1.5
Sales during the year	100	
Inventory at the end of the year	100	

The cost of goods sold is equal to:

inventory at beginning of year + new purchases during year
$\qquad\qquad\qquad\qquad\qquad$ − inventory at end of year

It is therefore clear that the method by which we evaluate the end-of-year inventory affects the cost of goods sold. The tax and profit will be affected as follows:

	Amount ($ Millions)	
	FIFO	LIFO
Revenue	200	200
Cost of goods sold	100	150
Net profit before tax	100	50
Tax (50%)	50	25
Net profit after tax	50	25

(The tax rate of 50% is used for purposes of illustration. In practice it would be different.)

Under FIFO, the units sold during the year are the ones bought by the firm at $1 each. Thus the end-of-year inventory is $150 million (i.e., 100 million units at $1.5 each). Under LIFO, the units sold are those bought during the year at $1.5 so that the end of year inventory is $100 million (i.e., 100 million units at $1.0).

What are the implications for a firm of switching from FIFO to LIFO? As illustrated, the FIFO method allows the firm to show a higher profit than that shown by using LIFO ($50 million vs. $25 million in the example). Thus switching will reduce reported earnings. Nonetheless, economic analysis reveals that switching from FIFO to LIFO is advantageous to the firm. Recall that the cash outlay for the materials purchased during the year was $150 million; thus the total cash flow under the two alternative methods is:

	Firm's Cash Flow ($ Millions)	
	FIFO	LIFO
Revenue	+ 200	+ 200
New purchases	− 150	− 150
Tax	− 50	− 25
Net cash flow	0	+ 25

Switching from FIFO to LIFO increases the net cash flow of the firm by $25 million because of the lower tax burden. Since the replacement cost of the 100 million inventory units sold during the year is $150 million, the firm's true pretax profit is $50 million, no matter how the firm records the inventory. LIFO reveals the true economic profit **when inflation is neutral.** However, with nonneutral inflation, neither LIFO nor FIFO measures precisely the true economic profit.

The LIFO procedure results in a tax bill of $25 million, or a 50% tax on real earnings, but, in this illustration, FIFO results in a tax bill of $50 million, or an effective tax rate of 100% i.e., as a percentage of economic income. Despite the advantage of LIFO over FIFO in terms of its effect on economic profit, only about one-third of the companies in the United States use LIFO. The main reason for this is probably that firms must use the same method both for tax purposes and for financial reporting. Along with a lower tax rate and a higher real profit, switching from FIFO to LIFO would reduce reported profit. Many financial managers hold the view that the performance of a firm is evaluated and judged largely on the basis of reported earnings per share, even if they are partly illusory, which accounts for the willingness to pay more tax than called for under LIFO, merely to keep the level of reported profit high. In particular, financial managers hesitate to switch to LIFO because the firm might report a lower profit than other firms in the same industry.

DEPRECIATION. If a firm invests $100 million in depreciable assets with a 10 year lifetime, **straight-line depreciation** comes to $10 million per annum. If the inflation rate is 20%, the first year's depreciation (i.e., one year after purchasing the assets) should be $12 million on the basis of purchasing power. However, the existing federal income tax code admits only historical cost depreciation; it does not permit replacement cost depreciation, nor does it permit adjustment for the price level. Thus although the $12 million represents the first year's depreciation in current dollars, the tax code recognizes only $10 million of this for tax purposes. Clearly, if inflation persists, depreciation adjusted for purchasing power will continue to increase while the amount recognized for tax purposes will remain constant. In the tenth year adjusted depreciation will come to $61.9 million $[= 10(1.2)^{10}]$, but it will still only be $10 million at historical cost. It is in this way that historical cost depreciation creates illusory profits and the consequently high effective tax rates and low cash flow. A number of investment incentives have been introduced over the years of rectify this situation, among them **accelerated depreciation** and the **investment tax credit.** These incentives, discussed below, are often insufficient to fully compensate firms for their inflation losses.

THE EFFECT OF INFLATION ON EARNINGS: AN EXAMPLE. Financial reporting is subject to distortions due to inflation. When inflation is low, say up to 5% a year, the distortion is not very serious. However, when the rate of inflation is higher, the distortion could be serious.

Although one example is clearly an inadequate way of examining the effect of inflation on financial reporting, it nevertheless gives a feel for how significant the effect may be. Exhibit 2 presents the impact of inflation on sales, net earnings, and net earnings per share of Fairchild Industries. In addition to the ordinary reporting, Exhibit 2 shows Fairchild's data adjusted for the general inflation (constant dollars) and to changes in specific prices (current cost). The data clearly show a marked difference between the unadjusted reported values and the inflation-adjusted values. Whereas net earnings declined an average of 9.6% per year according to reported figures, the average decrease was more than 20% per year when inflation adjustment is incorporated. On the basis of current cost dollars, the decrease has reached an average of close to 27% annually. The average decrease in earnings per share for the period was 18.4% on the basis of reported earnings, but as much as 28.6% or 33.9% on the basis of inflation-adjusted data, depending on the specific measure used.

INFLATIONARY HOLDING GAINS ON ASSETS

Unlevered Firm. An increase in the price level creates **holding gains** on assets by increasing the nominal value of the assets. Consider the effect of such holding gains on the **earnings per share** (EPS) of a no-growth and unlevered firm. Suppose the price level is stable up to time 0, when a **fully anticipated neutral inflation** starts at a rate h. For simplicity, assume that the price level becomes stable again a year later, at time 1. Since the inflation is neutral, it increases revenues, costs, expenses, asset values, and so on, in the same

EXHIBIT 2 THE IMPACT OF INFLATION ON SALES, NET EARNINGS AND NET EARNINGS PER SHARE OF FAIRCHILD INDUSTRIES, 1979–1983

(millions of $, except per share)

	Year					Average growth rate (%)
	1979	1980	1981	1982	1983	
Net sales as reported	709	906	1,339	1,093	892	6.2
constant dollars	963	1,096	1,467	1,128	892	−1.9
Net earnings						
as reported	42	55	64	35	28	−9.6
constant dollars[a]	56	63	66	27	22	−20.8
current cost	56	64	67	25	16	−26.9
Net earnings per share ($)						
as reported	3.41	4.02	3.48	1.90	1.51	−18.4
constant dollars[a]	4.51	4.67	3.57	1.47	1.17	−28.6
current cost	4.50	4.70	3.62	1.37	0.86	−33.9

[a]The constant dollar earnings measurements are obtained from adjusting sales and all costs and expenses items to the rate of inflation on an item-by-item basis. It therefore does not represent a direct application of a price deflator to the reported net earnings figures.

Source: Fairchild Industries, *1983 Annual Report*, p. 32.

proportion. Denote before-tax income at time 0 by X, the corporate tax rate by T, and the number of common shares outstanding by n; then the EPS at time 0, EPS_0, is:

$$EPS_0 = \frac{(1 - T)X}{n}$$

One period later, at time 1, the nominal EPS is

$$EPS_1 = \frac{(1 - T)X(1 + h)}{n} = EPS_0(1 + h)$$

The value of EPS is constant dollars at time 1, EPS_1^c, is obtained by discounting EPS_1 at rate h.

$$EPS_1^c = \frac{EPS_1}{1 + h} = \frac{EPS_0(1 + h)}{1 + h} = EPS_0$$

Denote the value of the firm's assets at time 0 by V; the firm gets an amount hV of holding gains on these assets, and it is assumed that these gains are spread over all the firm's assets in equal proportions. This assumption is made for simplicity, but it does not impair the generality of the discussion. The holding gains hV, however, do not represent real gain, since to keep the profitability in real terms unchanged, the value of assets at time 1 must be $V(1 + h)$. As Hicks put it (*Value and Capital*, 2nd ed., Clarendon Press, Oxford, 1957, p. 174), "income . . . must be defined as the maximum amount of money which the individual can spends this week, and still expect to be able to spend the same amount in real terms in each ensuing week." Thus holding gains should not be added to income for the EPS calculations.

Levered Firm. Consider now a levered firm. With no inflation, the situation is quite simple. Denote the market value of the debt by D and the interest rate paid on the firm's debt by r; the EPS is then

$$EPS_0 = \frac{(1 - T)(X - rD)}{n}$$

For the case of inflation, it is assumed that the market value of the debt is not affected by it, but the interest rate rises from r to $(1 + r)(1 + h) - 1 = r + h(1 + r)$. In other words, we assume that bondholders are compensated for inflation by the increase in their interest to a level equal to the sum of the no-inflation interest (rD) plus compensation for the decrease in the value of the principal (hD) plus compensation for the decrease in the value of the no-inflation interest (hrD). Interest on long-term bonds does not actually adjust fully to current inflation rates, since it is largely a function of bondholders' long-term inflation expectations. Also note that personal taxes are ignored in this analysis. All the interest is assumed to be tax deductible for the firm. Nominal EPS at time 1 excluding holding gains is

$$\text{EPS}_1 = \frac{(1 - T)[X(1 + h) - rD - hD(1 + r)]}{n}$$

$$= \frac{(1 - T)[(X - rD)(1 + h) - hD]}{n} = \text{EPS}_0(1 + h) - \frac{(1 - T)hD}{n}$$

and EPS at time 1 in constant dollars is

$$\text{EPS}_1^c = \frac{\text{EPS}_1}{1 + h} = \text{EPS}_0 - \frac{(1 - T)hD}{n(1 + h)}$$

In this case, inflation appears to have reduced the value of EPS. However, this is not so, since the holding gains on the levered firm's assets have thus far been ignored. Unlike the pure equity firm, a part of the holding gain for a levered firm is real income for the stockholders.

When calculating EPS_1^c, holding gains were not considered, although just as with the unlevered firm, there is a gain of hV. Since the holding gain "belongs" only to the equity, it is in excess of what is needed to create future income for stockholders that is equal in real terms to their past income. To see this, start with the identity $V = E + D$ (where E denotes equity), which implies that $hV = hE + hD$. As long as D is positive, the (nominal) holding gains exceed hE, that is, there are **excess holding gains** in the amount hD.

Suppose that the excess holding gains are distributed (the firm liquidates some of the fixed assets) and are subject to the tax rate T. In this case, the aftertax income (including the excess holding gains) available to stockholders is

$$(1 - T)[(X - rD)(1 + h) - hD + hD]$$

so that

$$\text{EPS}_1 = \frac{(1 - T)[(X - rD)(1 + h)]}{n} = \text{EPS}_0(1 + h)$$

This implies that EPS should be adjusted for the excess holding gains and for inflation to obtain the **real** value of EPS at time 1, EPS_1^R:

$$\text{EPS}_1^R = \frac{\text{EPS}_0(1 + h)}{1 + h} = \text{EPS}_0$$

Note the distinction between constant and real EPS: EPS^c is the deflated value of the unadjusted nominal EPS, whereas EPS^R is the deflated EPS, adjusted for excess holding gains.

It has so far been assumed that the excess holding gains on the equity are distributed to stockholders. If this amount hD is distributed by liquidating assets worth hD, the firm's debt-equity ratio will change and EPS in the year after the inflation year will not be the same (in real terms) as in the year before inflation. However, this would happen whatever the reason for the alteration in the capital structure, since in general, EPS varies with it. Denoting the preinflation debt-equity ratio by D/E, the postinflation ratio is $D/[E(1 + h) + hD]$ before the distribution of holding gains and $D/[E(1 + h)] < D/E$ after it. Since the debt-equity ratio has declined, we expect a decrease in EPS.

It is now shown that if the debt-equity ratio in the postinflation year at time 2 is restored to its original level by issuing additional debt hD, the EPS in real terms will revert to its original level.

The nominal value of the assets is $V(1 + h) = (E + D)(1 + h)$ and earnings before interest and tax (EBIT) is $X(1 + h)$. The interest rate is back at r, since it is assumed that there is no inflation in the postinflation years; after additional debt of hD has been issued, total outstanding debt is $D(1 + h)$, and total interest is then $rD(1 + h)$. Therefore nominal EPS is given by:

$$EPS_2 = \frac{(1 - T)X(1 + h) - rD(1 + h)}{n} = EPS_0(1 + h)$$

However, the earnings per share in constant preinflation dollars is given by:

$$EPS^c = \frac{EPS_2}{1 + h} = \frac{EPS_0(1 + h)}{1 + h} = EPS_0$$

That is, the distribution of excess holding gains at the end of the inflation year leaves the real EPS in the following year the same as before inflation.

The discussion has assumed a one-year period of inflation followed by a period of stable prices. However, the same result holds if prices continue to rise. Note also that if the excess holding gains are not realized, they are not taxed, and the real EPS of a levered firm will rise with inflation.

Numerical Illustration. To begin, assume the absence of leverage. Suppose that the total value of the firm's assets is $100 at the beginning of the period, EBIT is $20, the tax rate is 50%, and there are 10 shares outstanding. Exhibit 3 presents the data for the current and the next year, assuming a 10% (neutral) inflation.

Disregarding depreciation, there is a holding gain of $10, since the value of assets has risen to $110 by the beginning of the second year from $100 at

EXHIBIT 3   EXAMPLE SHOWING EFFECT OF 10% NEUTRAL INFLATION ON EPS OF UNLEVERED FIRM ($)

	First Year	Second Year
Assets	100	110
EBIT	20	22
Tax	10	11
Net income	10	11
Number of shares	10	10
EPS	1	1.1
EPS^R	1	1

the beginning of the first year. However, the gain is only nominal. The real value of the assets at the beginning of the second year is $110/1.1 = \$100$. If the firm did not have $110 worth of assets at the beginning of the second year, it could not end up with EBIT of $22. Thus there is no real holding gain, and the result is that real EPS has not changed. Looking at it in another way, suppose that the real discount rate is 10%. Then, before inflation, $V = 10/1.1 + 10/(1.1)^2 + \cdots + 10/(1.1)^\infty = \$100$; after the 10% inflation (which occurs only in the first year), the nominal value is $11/1.1 + 11/(1.1)^2 + \cdots + 11/(1.1)^\infty = \$110$, and its real value is $100.

Consider now a levered firm. Assume that the leverage is 50% at the beginning of the first year, and the firm pays 10% interest on its debt. Assume also that the inflation rate is 10% and the interest rate in the second year is 21%, to compensate bondholders for the inflation. Earnings per share calculations that do not consider holding gains are EPS expressed in constant dollars EPS^c, as shown in Exhibit 4. Thus EPS^c has declined when the stockholders' excess holding gains are not considered. However, the equity value in the example has risen beyond what is needed to keep up with inflation: with 10% inflation, the $50 of equity has to rise to $55 to keep up

EXHIBIT 4   EXAMPLE SHOWING IMPACT OF 10% NEUTRAL INFLATION ON EPS^c OF LEVERED FIRM ($)

	First Year	Second Year
Assets	100	110
Debt	50	50
Equity	50	60
EBIT	20	22
Interest	5	10.5
Taxable income	15	11.5
Tax	7.5	5.75
Net income	7.5	5.75
Number of shares	5	5
EPS	1.5	1.150
EPS^c	1.5	1.045

with inflation; but in the example it has risen to \$60; hence there is an excess holding gain hD of \$5 ($= 0.10 \times 50$), and stockholders have had a real gain.

From the debt side, it is seen that the value of the debt remains unchanged at \$50, and there is a decrease in the real value of the debt that generates \$5 of excess holding gain on the equity. If the \$5 holding gain is subject to 50% tax, the net profit available for stockholders is \$8.25 ($= 5.75 + 0.5 \times 5$), and EPS_1 is \$1.65 ($= 8.25/5$) or in real terms, EPS_1^R is \$1.50 ($= 1.65/1.1$). Thus $EPS_1^R = EPS_0 = \$1.50$, since a neutral inflation should not affect the EPS^R as long as the appropriate adjustments are carried out. No such correction should be made for unlevered firms, since for them $hD = 0$.

If the \$5 excess holding gain is subject to a lower tax rate, the real EPS is even higher. Suppose, for example, that the holding gain is not realized. In this case, $EPS_1 = \$2.15$ [$= (5.75 + 5.00)/5 = 10.75/5$], and $EPS_1^R = \$1.955$ ($= 2.15/1.1$).

While the standard EPS calculation, which ignores holding gains, shows a decline in EPS^c as a result of inflation, the correction for holding gains shows that EPS^R increases as a result of inflation. This, of course, has implications for the way EPS growth and the firm's cost of capital are to be measured. Modigliani and Cohn ("Inflation, Rational Valuation and the Market," *Financial Analysts Journal*, March–April 1979, pp. 24–44) have also described the effect of inflation on earnings. However, in their model the stockholders' gain originates in the decline in the market value of the debt. This notion is debated in an entire section devoted to inflation in Altman and Subrahmanyam, *Recent Advances in Corporate Finance*, Irwin, Homewood, IH, 1985.

LIQUIDITY. It has been demonstrated that the EPS of an unlevered firm will not be affected by inflation, whereas the EPS of a levered firm will increase. However, the negative effect of the treatment of inventory and depreciation on the firm's net income was ignored in arriving at these conclusions. When it is taken into consideration, the unlevered firm may experience reduced profitability in times of rising prices. While the levered firm would incur inflationary losses on its inventory and depreciation, it would benefit from excess holding gains on its debt. Thus the net effect of inflation on a levered firm is unclear. Both unlevered and levered firms are bound to find themselves in a **liquidity crunch** if the inflation is severe enough.

The reduced economic earnings of the unlevered firm will not necessarily be reflected in reported earnings. Consequently, **dividend payout ratios** computed on the basis of economic earnings will tend to rise. Coupled with the high effective tax rate, the firm is likely to find that its cash flow is insufficient for new investments.

Levered firms will find themselves in a similar situation. Although the levered firm's excess holding gains improve its profitability, they must be realized if they are to provide liquidity relief. The liquidity problem is illustrated in Exhibit 4 above, where a 10% anticipated inflation reduces net income from $7.5 in the first year to $5.75 in the second. The levered firm gets a $5 excess holding gain, but since it is not realized, it does not affect the firm's cash flow or its liquidity. To overcome the liquidity problem, the firm can either liquidate some of its assets or raise additional debt. The latter choice is more likely. Note that the illustration of the unlevered firm under inflation (Exhibit 3) shows no decrease in the firm's net income.

Most firms cope with the liquidity problem by issuing more debt. For example, in 1975 du Pont tripled its outstanding debt to $793 million, and in late 1979 IBM issued $1 billion of notes and debentures for financing investments and growth, the largest single debt issue by an industrial company in the United States. Kepcke ("Current Accounting Practices and Proposals for Reform," *New England Economic Review*, Federal Reserve Bank of Boston, September-October 1976, p. 23), shows that the debt-equity ratio of U.S. nonfinancial corporations rose from 0.97 to 1.34 in the period 1965–1975. However, on the basis of current value (rather than conventional) reporting, the ratio hardly changed during the period: it was 0.91 in 1965 and 0.92 in 1975.

CREDIT TERMS AND INFLATION

Sales terms specify the period for which credit is extended and the discount, if any, given for early payment. If for example, the terms are "2/10 net 30," a 2% discount is granted if payment is made within 10 days, and the full sales price is due within 30 days from the invoice date if the discount is not taken. To get the percentage **opportunity cost** if the discount is not taken, we can calculate the annual percentage cost (APC):

$$APC = \frac{\text{discount \%}}{100 - \text{discount \%}} \times \frac{360}{\text{days credit outstanding} - \text{discount period}}$$

The effective annual rate is in fact even higher, since the formula given here disregards compound interest during the year. Considering the compound interest we set $\lambda = 360/(\text{days credit outstanding} - \text{discount period})$. The rate that takes this effect into account is $APC = [1 + (\text{discount \%})/(100 - \text{discount \%})]^{\lambda} - 1$, and for "2/10 net 30" this comes to $0.438 = (1 + 0.0204)^{18} - 1$, or 43.8%.

Ignoring the compound interest we find that for "2/10 net 30" the APC is:

$$APC = \frac{2}{100 - 2} \times \frac{360}{30 - 10} = 0.367$$

or 36.7%. This is an **opportunity cost for missing a cash discount**. It can also be derived as follows. Suppose that XYZ Corp. has annual purchases of

$367.2 million. If the 2% discount is taken, the daily purchases are 367.3 × (0.98)(1/360) = $1 million. Since each bill will be paid on the tenth day, accounts payable will be $10 million. Most accountants record payables net of discount, then report the higher payments that result from not taking discounts as an additional expense. If the discount is not taken, the bills will be paid on the thirtieth day and payables will amount to $30 million, an increase of $20 million. A 2% discount on the annual sales then amounts to $7.344 million, which is 36.7% of the $20 million.

Under inflation, the discount becomes less advantageous, since the real difference between the discounted price and the full price paid at the end of the period is reduced by the decline in the purchasing power of the dollar during the credit period.

To see how the gain from the discount changes with inflation, consider a firm that purchases P dollars worth of materials per day. Consider now the credit policy "α/t_1 net t," and assume a daily inflation rate h. If the discount is taken, the purchases are paid for after t_1 days and the purchase price in real terms is $(1 - \alpha)P/(1 + h)^{t_1}$; if the discount is not taken, the bill will be paid after t days, the real purchase price is $P/(1 + h)^t$, and the real benefit from the discount is:

$$\text{Real benefit} = \frac{P}{(1 + h)^t} - \frac{(1 - \alpha)P}{(1 + h)^{t_1}}$$

Expressing the benefit as a proportion γ of the real purchase price if the discount is taken, we obtain:

$$\gamma = \frac{\dfrac{P}{(1 + h)^t} - \dfrac{(1 - \alpha)P}{(1 + h)^{t_1}}}{\dfrac{(1 - \alpha)P}{(1 + h)^{t_1}}} = \frac{1}{(1 - \alpha)(1 + h)^{t_2}} - 1$$

where $t_2 = t - t_1$. The benefit γ is obtained over t_2 days. On an annual basis, it is

$$(1 + \gamma)^\lambda - 1 = \frac{1}{[(1 - \alpha)(1 + h)^{t_2}]^\lambda} - 1$$

where $\gamma = 360/t_2$

It can be shown that the derivative of γ with respect to h is negative, which means that the percentage benefit decreases as inflation increases. Moreover, if h is sufficiently large, the expression $(1 - \alpha)(1 + h)^{t_2}$ could be greater than 1, in which case γ would be negative, and it certainly would be advantageous for the purchasing firm to forgo the discount.

CHANGING THE DISCOUNT PERCENTAGE. The financial manager who wants to get the greatest cash flow possible from the firm's sales and to exploit the firm's credit to the utmost should take the effect of inflation on γ into account and should consider an increase in the nominal rate of discount to maintain a desired level of γ, the **real** percentage benefit resulting from the discount. It is thus of interest to determine the discount rates that will yield the same real benefit as a given discount in the absence of inflation. To do so, note first that in the absence of inflation ($h = 0$), $\gamma_0 = 1/(1 - \alpha) - 1$. Given an inflation rate $h = 0$, put

$$\frac{1}{(1 - X)(1 + h)^{t_2}} - 1 = \frac{1}{1 - \alpha} - 1 = \gamma_0$$

and solve for X, the rate of discount that makes the real percentage benefit equal the noinflation rate γ_0:

$$X = 1 - \frac{1 - \alpha}{(1 + h)^{t_2}}$$

A numerical example will illustrate this. Suppose the credit policy is "2/10 net 30" and the inflation rate is zero. Then $\alpha = 0.02$ and $\gamma_0 = 1/(1 - 0.02) = 0.0204$, which translates into 0.438 on an annual basis. Now with a 12% per annum inflation rate, $(1 + h)^{t_2} = 1.0063 \, (= 1.12^{1/18})$; that is, over 20 days the inflation comes to 0.63%. Substituting $(1 + h)^{t_2} = 1.0063$ in the expression for X, we obtain $X = 0.0262$; that is, a 2.62% discount at 12% per annum inflation will yield the same real percentage benefit as a 2% discount in the absence of inflation. In other words, the discount rate must be raised significantly if it is to provide the same real percentage benefit. If this is not done, the selling firm can expect the number of cash-paying purchasers to decline, with adverse effects on the seller's liquidity.

Exhibit 5 shows the values for X for different credit terms and for a variety of annual inflation rates. Exhibit 6 portrays the ratio X/α for selected inflation rates and credit periods.

CHANGING THE CREDIT PERIOD. Instead of changing the percentage discount and keeping the credit period unchanged, the selling firm may adjust its credit terms to inflation by shortening the credit period, keeping the discount percent unchanged. The opportunity cost of forgoing the discount is given by

$$APC = \frac{1}{[(1 - \alpha)(1 + h)^{t_2}]^{\lambda}} - 1$$

If $h = 0$, this reduces to $1/(1 - \alpha)^{360/t_2} - 1$. When $h > 0$, t_2 may be shortened to some value t_2^* such that

EXHIBIT 5 INFLATION-ADJUSTED DISCOUNT PERCENTAGE FOR SELECTED CREDIT TERMS AND INFLATION RATES

Annual Infl. Rate	Net 30 Days					Net 60 Days					Net 90 Days				
	1/10	2/10	3/10	4/10	5/10	1/10	2/10	3/10	4/10	5/10	1/10	2/10	3/10	4/10	5/10
5%	1.27	2.27	3.26	4.26	5.26	1.67	2.66	3.66	4.65	5.64	2.07	3.06	4.05	5.04	6.03
6	1.32	2.32	3.31	4.31	5.31	1.80	2.79	3.79	4.78	5.77	2.28	3.27	4.26	5.24	6.23
7	1.37	2.37	3.36	4.36	5.36	1.93	2.92	3.91	4.90	5.89	2.49	3.47	4.46	5.44	6.43
8	1.42	2.42	3.41	4.41	5.41	2.06	3.05	4.04	5.03	6.02	2.69	3.68	4.66	5.64	6.62
9	1.47	2.47	3.46	4.46	5.45	2.18	3.17	4.16	5.15	6.14	2.90	3.88	4.86	5.84	6.82
10	1.52	2.52	3.51	4.51	5.50	2.31	3.30	4.28	5.27	6.26	3.10	4.08	5.05	6.03	7.01
11	1.57	2.57	3.56	4.56	5.55	2.43	3.42	4.41	5.39	6.38	3.30	4.27	5.25	6.23	7.20
12	1.62	2.62	3.60	4.60	5.60	2.56	3.54	4.53	5.51	6.50	3.49	4.47	5.44	6.42	7.39
13	1.67	2.67	3.66	4.65	5.65	2.68	3.66	4.65	5.63	6.61	3.69	4.66	5.63	6.61	7.58
14	1.72	2.71	3.71	4.70	5.69	2.80	3.78	4.77	5.75	6.73	3.88	4.85	5.82	6.79	7.77
15	1.77	2.76	3.75	4.75	5.74	2.92	3.90	4.88	5.86	6.84	4.07	5.04	6.01	6.98	7.95
20	2.00	2.89	3.98	4.77	5.96	3.51	4.48	5.46	6.43	7.41	5.01	5.97	6.93	7.89	8.85
25	2.23	3.21	4.20	5.19	6.18	4.07	5.04	6.01	6.97	7.94	5.91	6.86	7.81	8.76	9.71
30	2.44	3.43	4.41	5.40	6.38	4.61	5.57	6.53	7.50	8.46	6.77	7.71	8.65	9.59	10.54
35	2.65	3.63	4.62	5.60	6.58	5.13	6.08	7.04	8.00	8.96	7.60	8.53	9.46	10.40	11.33
40	2.85	3.83	4.81	5.79	6.78	5.62	6.58	7.53	8.48	9.44	8.40	9.32	10.25	11.17	12.10
45	3.04	4.02	5.00	5.98	6.96	6.11	7.06	8.00	8.95	9.90	9.16	10.08	11.00	11.92	12.84
50	3.23	4.21	5.13	5.16	7.14	6.57	7.52	8.46	9.40	10.35	9.91	10.82	11.73	12.64	13.55
60	3.58	4.56	5.53	6.51	7.43	7.46	8.39	9.33	10.26	11.20	11.32	12.22	13.11	14.01	14.90
70	3.92	4.89	5.86	6.83	7.80	8.29	9.22	10.14	11.07	11.99	12.65	13.53	14.41	15.29	16.18
80	4.23	5.20	6.17	7.13	8.10	9.07	9.99	10.91	11.83	12.75	13.89	14.76	15.63	16.50	17.37
90	4.53	5.49	6.46	7.42	8.39	9.81	10.72	11.64	12.55	13.46	15.07	15.93	16.79	17.64	18.50
100	4.81	5.77	6.73	7.70	8.66	10.52	11.42	12.32	13.23	14.13	16.19	17.03	17.88	18.73	19.57

EXHIBIT 6 RATIO BETWEEN INFLATION-ADJUSTED DISCOUNT PERCENTAGE X AND NO-INFLATION PERCENTAGE

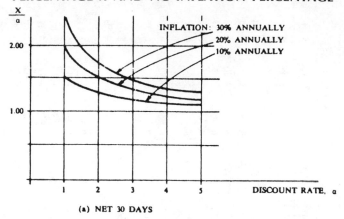

(a) NET 30 DAYS

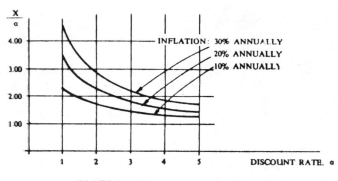

(b) NET 60 DAYS

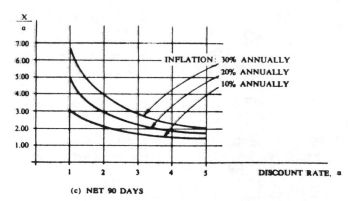

(c) NET 90 DAYS

$$\frac{1}{[(1 - \alpha)(1 + h)^{t_2^*}]^{360/t_2^*}} - 1 = \frac{1}{(1 - \alpha)^{360/t_2}} - 1$$

Solve for t_2^* to get

$$t_2^* = \frac{t_2[\log(1 - \alpha)]}{\log(1 - \alpha) - t_2[\log(1 + h)]}$$

Values of t_2^* can be derived from this expression for various combinations of t_2, α, and h. Note that the derivative of t_2^* with respect to h is negative, which means that other things being equal, the higher the inflation rate, the shorter should be the credit period for a constant real opportunity cost. Note that $t_2^* = t_2$ when $h = 0$, and when h approaches infinity, t_2^* approaches zero. Exhibit 7 gives the values of $t^* = t_1 + t_2^*$ (to the nearest whole day) for a variety of combinations of t, α, and h. For example, a credit policy "2/10 net 30" in the absence of inflation gives the same real percentage benefit as "2/10 net 24" with annual inflation of 15%. Exhibit 8 presents the ratios t^*/t for selected combinations of t, α, and h.

INFLATION, DEPRECIATION, INCOME TAX, AND CAPITAL BUDGETING

A characteristic of investment in a **fixed asset** is that the cash flow derived from it is obtained long after the asset was acquired. For both financial reporting and income tax calculations, the asset's cost is spread over its lifetime so that the depreciation expense can be matched with the revenues. Although **indexation of depreciation expense** has received serious consideration in Washington D.C. lately, the method allowed today is still based on historical cost of the asset, which is less than replacement cost during periods of inflation. Over the years, various tax incentives have been introduced. The most important of these are accelerated depreciation and investment tax credit.

ACCELERATED COST RECOVERY SYSTEM (ACRS). The **Economic Recovery Tax Act** of 1981 (**ERTA**) specifies the accelerated depreciation method currently in use and as we shall see, it provides a strong incentive for investment in plant and equipment. The reader is cautioned, however, that changes in the tax law are under consideration. Most depreciable property is eligible for **ACRS**. The acceleration of the depreciation expense under the ACRS is based on the recovery periods allowed under the law and on the accelerated depreciation method used. The recovery period itself depends in part on the **asset depreciation range (ADR)** of the asset. The ADR provides upper and lower limits for recommended lifetimes of broad classes of assets

EXHIBIT 7 INFLATION-ADJUSTED CREDIT PERIOD BY SELECTED CREDIT TERMS AND INFLATION RATES

Annual Infl. Rate	Net 30 Days					Net 60 Days					Net 90 Days				
	1/10	2/10	3/10	4/10	5/10	1/10	2/10	3/10	4/10	5/10	1/10	2/10	3/10	4/10	5/10
5%	26	28	28	29	29	40	47	51	53	54	48	62	69	73	76
6	25	27	28	29	29	38	46	49	52	53	45	59	66	71	74
7	25	27	28	28	29	36	44	48	51	52	42	56	63	68	72
8	24	27	28	28	28	34	43	47	50	51	39	53	61	66	70
9	24	26	27	28	28	33	41	46	49	50	37	51	59	64	68
10	23	26	27	28	28	31	40	45	48	50	36	49	57	62	66
11	23	26	27	27	28	30	39	44	47	49	34	47	55	61	65
12	22	25	27	27	28	29	38	43	46	48	33	45	54	59	63
13	22	25	26	27	28	28	37	42	45	47	31	44	52	58	62
14	22	25	26	27	28	28	36	41	44	47	30	42	51	56	61
15	21	24	26	27	27	27	35	40	44	46	29	41	49	55	60
20	20	23	25	26	27	24	32	37	41	43	26	36	44	50	54
25	19	22	24	25	26	22	30	35	38	41	23	33	40	46	50
30	18	22	23	25	26	21	28	33	36	39	21	30	37	42	47
35	17	21	23	24	25	20	26	31	34	37	20	28	35	40	44
40	17	20	22	24	25	19	25	29	33	36	19	27	33	38	42
45	17	20	22	23	24	18	24	28	32	35	18	25	31	36	40
50	16	18	21	23	24	17	23	27	31	33	18	24	30	34	38
60	16	19	21	22	23	16	22	26	29	32	17	22	27	32	35
70	15	18	20	22	23	16	20	24	27	30	16	21	26	30	33
80	15	18	20	21	22	15	20	23	26	29	15	20	24	28	32
90	14	17	19	21	22	15	19	22	25	28	15	19	23	27	30
100	14	17	19	20	21	15	18	22	24	27	15	19	22	26	29

EXHIBIT 8.   RATIO BETWEEN THE INFLATION-ADJUSTED NET (*t**)
AND THE NO-INFLATION NET PERIOD (*t*) FOR SELECTED NET
PERIODS AND DISCOUNT PERCENTAGES

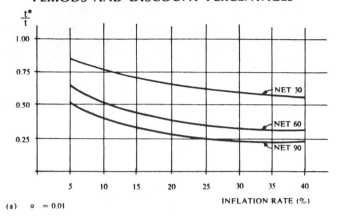

(a) $\sigma = 0.01$

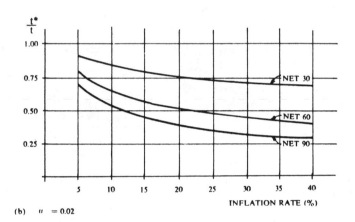

(b) $\sigma = 0.02$

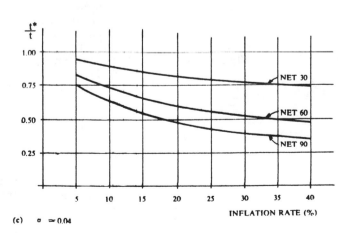

(c) $\sigma = 0.04$

so that the firm may not need to work with more than one lifetime for a class of assets. Exhibit 9 presents the recovery periods that have been established. The accelerated depreciation rates for the various ACRS classes of property are shown in Exhibit 10.

To give an example consider an asset whose depreciable value (i.e., total cost minus salvage value) is $100,000 and is qualified to a 5-year accelerated depreciation. The **depreciation of this asset under the ACRS** is as follows:

Year	Depreciation
1	$ 15,000
2	22,000
3	21,000
4	21,000
5	21,000
Total	$100,000

EXHIBIT 9 RECOVERY PERIODS UNDER THE ECONOMIC RECOVERY TAX ACT OF 1981

Economic Life	Recovery Period Under the ACRS	Description of Assets
5 to 12 years	3 years	Autos, light duty trucks, R&D equipment and certain manufacturing tools
12 to 25 years	5 years	Most other equipment, including public utility property with a current ADR life of 18 years or less, single-purpose agriculture structures and petroleum storage facilities designated as Section 1245 property
25 to 35 years	10 years	Public utility property with an ADR midpoint life greater than 18 years but not greater than 25 years, railroad tank cars and real property with an ADR midpoint life of 12.5 years or less
35 to 45 years	15 years	Public utility property with an ADR midpoint life exceeding 25 years and real property with an ADR midpoint life of over 12.5 years.

EXHIBIT 10 ACCELERATED DEPRECIATION RATES OF THE VARIOUS PROPERTY CLASSES UNDER THE ACRS[a]

Recovery Year	Class			
	3-year	5-year	10-year	15-year
1	25	15	8	5
2	38	22	14	10
3	37	21	12	9
4		21	10	8
5		21	10	7
6			10	7
7–10			9	6
11–15				6

[a]Not applicable to real estate.

EFFECT OF INFLATION ON A PROJECT'S NET PRESENT VALUE. The **net present value (NPV)** of an investment project is a widely accepted measure of investment profitability and is used extensively in **capital budgeting**. As with other measures of profit and profitability, special care is required in applying the NPV criterion to a cash flow in conditions of inflation—a project that would be accepted in the absence of inflation could very well be rejected when inflation makes it riskier. Investment incentives are ignored for the time being.

Neutral inflation. The analysis begins by assuming **neutral inflation**, in which all prices (i.e., all cash flow components) increase at the same rate h.

Suppose that the cost of capital in real terms is k, say 10% per year, so that an investment of $100 will be attractive only if the cash flow at the end of the year is at least $110 in real terms. If the cash flow is exactly $110, the net present value (NPV) of the investment is 0 ($= -100 + 110/1.1$). If the real cash flow exceeds $110, the project's NPV is positive and it will be accepted.

With a 20% neutral inflation, the minimum nominal cash flow required is $132, since

$$NPV = -100 + \frac{\$132/1.2}{1.1} = -100 + \frac{\$132}{1.32} = 0$$

The proper cost of capital adjusted for inflation deduced from this example is 32%. More generally, if k is the **real cost of capital**, the **nominal rate** k_N is

$$k_N = (1 + k)(1 + h) - 1$$

Should an investment project be evaluated in current or constant dollars? Since all cash flow components are affected proportionally by inflation, either method of evaluation will lead to the same investment decision, provided that in current dollars the cash flow is discounted by the **nominal cost of capital** k_N and in constant dollars it is discounted by the **real cost of capital** k. To see this, ignore depreciation for the moment and assume that the real annual net cash flow in year t is S_t, and with a neutral inflation rate h, the current annual net cash flow is $S_t(1 + h)^t$. Applying the nominal discount rate to the nominal annual net cash flow, the NPV computed from current amounts is

$$\text{NPV} = -I + \sum_{t=1}^{n} \frac{S_t(1 + h)^t}{[(1 + k)(1 + h)]^t} = -I + \sum_{t=1}^{n} \frac{S_t}{(1 + k)^t}$$

where I is the initial investment outlay and $(1 + k)(1 + h) = 1 + k_N$. The real cost of capital can also be applied to the real cash flow to obtain the second summation directly.

It is clear that when all cash flow items are affected by inflation in the same proportion, applying the nominal cost of capital to the current cash flow yields the same NPV and the same accept-reject decisions that would be reached if the analyst applied the real cost of capital to the cash flow in constant dollars.

In practice, not all the cash flow items are affected by inflation in the same way; and thus the two evaluation methods do not generally yield the same results. To demonstrate this, let T be the tax rate and let D_t be the depreciation in year t. In the absence of inflation, the cash flow for year t is

$$(1 - T)(S_t - D_t) + D_t = (1 - T)S_t + TD_t$$

and the project's NPV is

$$\text{NPV}_0 = -I + \sum_{t=1}^{n} \frac{(1 - T)S_t}{(1 + k)^t} + \sum_{t=1}^{n} \frac{TD_t}{(1 + r)^t}$$

where the subscript zero denotes "no inflation," k is the firm's cost of capital, and r is the riskless interest rate. Note that the firm may consider the **tax shelter** TD_t, a nonrisky cash flow (the firm can carry a loss backward and forward, thereby reducing its tax bill in years of profit), and discount it using the riskless rate r.

While S_t will be affected by inflation, the tax shelter is computed on the basis of book value so that its nominal value will be unchanged. The NPV with inflation NPV_{inf} is

$$\text{NPV}_{\text{inf}} = -I + \sum_{t=1}^{n} \frac{(1 - T)S_t(1 + h)^t}{[(1 + k)(1 + h)]^t} + \sum_{t=1}^{n} \frac{TD_t}{[(1 + r)(1 + h)]^t}$$

$$= -I + \sum_{t=1}^{n} \frac{(1 - T)S_t}{(1 + k)^t} + \sum_{t=1}^{n} \frac{TD_t/(1 + h)^t}{(1 + r)^t}$$

Three main conclusions follow from the comparison of NPV_0 and NPV_{inf}.

1. Since NPV_{inf} is the correct net present value under inflation, the firm can separate its cash flow into two components. The part of the cash flow whose nominal value changes proportionally to the price level will not be affected by inflation. The depreciation tax shelter, however, will be reduced in value. For both components, though, it is true that **one can apply either the real rate of discount to the constant dollar cash flow or the nominal rate of discount to the nominal value of the cash flow.**

2. It can be seen that $NPV_0 > NPV_{inf}$, which means that other things being equal, investment projects become less attractive under inflation. The higher the inflation rate, the greater the gap between NPV_0 and NPV_{inf}. Moreover, it is quite possible that $NPV_0 > 0$ while $NPV_{inf} < 0$, so that a project that would be accepted in the absence of inflation may be rejected when there is inflation.

3. Firms having fixed obligations (such as lease contracts) may gain from inflation, since the NPV of their fixed commitments decreases in real terms.

Nonneutral Inflation. In reality, inflation is rarely neutral. The price of oil, for example, has risen in recent years much faster than the price of larger cars, the prices of food products do not change at the same rate as the prices of durable goods, and so on. If stockholders consume a well-mixed basket of goods and services, it is only reasonable to assume that their required rate of return on investment will change proportionally to the average price change. Thus the firm's cost of capital changes from k to $(1 + k)(1 + h) - 1$ with inflation. The firm that produces only a limited number of products may increase its prices by a rate h^*, which generally differs from h. Thus under inflation, a project's NPV will be

$$NPV_{inf} = -I + \sum_{t=1}^{n} \frac{(1 - T)S_t(1 + h^*)^t}{[(1 + k)(1 + h)]^t} + \sum_{t=1}^{n} \frac{TD_t}{[(1 + r)(1 + h)]^t}$$

Under neutral inflation, the real cost of capital k can be considered constant. Since h^* differs from h, however, inflation introduces a new dimension of risk to the firm. The differential inflation rates increase the business risk of all firms, and this may increase the real cost of capital, thus reducing NPV.

Riskless Interest Rate. In the absence of inflation the tax shelter TD_t is assumed to be riskless, and the riskless discount rate r applies to it. In the presence of inflation that includes unexpected elements, the depreciation tax shelter is no longer riskless, and a rate $r^* > r$ should be applied to it. The difference between the two, $r^* - r$, is the risk premium for the uncertainties of inflation. Both neutral and nonneutral inflation increase the riskiness of the cash flow. The result is higher discount rates and lower NPV.

RANKING MUTUALLY EXCLUSIVE INVESTMENT PROJECTS: INCENTIVES NOT CONSIDERED.

To simplify the discussion of the ranking of mutually exclusive investment projects, without any loss of generality, the same cost of capital k is used to discount the uncertain component of the cash flow and the certain depreciation tax benefit.

Nelson ("Inflation and Capital Budgeting," *Journal of Finance*, Vol. 31, No. 3, June 1976, pp. 923–931) has examined some of the implications of inflation for the ranking of investment projects. Among other things he demonstrated that the NPV ranking of **mutually exclusive investment projects** depends, in general, on the rate of inflation. He showed that at higher rates of inflation, ranking will usually change in favor of projects with shorter duration. Nelson also showed that inflation generally affects replacement policy: the higher the rate of inflation, the greater the likelihood of replacement being deferred.

When projects with unequal lifetimes are compared, their net present values are not adequate as a measure of relative profitability, since the length of time over which a given amount of profit is generated must be taken into account. For example, if projects A and B have $\text{NPV}_A = \$100$ and $\text{NPV}_B = \$200$, respectively, project B should not automatically be preferred to A without regard to the project's lifetime. If, for example, the lifetimes are 2 and 10 years for A and B, respectively, project A might very well be preferred. In particular, it will be preferred if it can be assumed that other equally profitable investments will become available in years 3–10. If so (such an assumption is common in replacement chain analyses), the profitability of investments can be compared on the basis of their **uniform annuity series** (UAS), which is defined as the annuity whose present value equals the NPV:

$$\text{NPV} = \frac{\text{UAS}}{(1 + k)} + \frac{\text{UAS}}{(1 + k)^2} + \cdots + \frac{\text{UAS}}{(1 + k)^n}$$

Thus if a project's net present value is \$200 and its lifetime 10 years, its UAS, assuming a 9% cost of capital, is \$31.16, since

$$200 = \frac{31.16}{1.09} + \frac{31.16}{(1.09)^2} + \cdots + \frac{31.16}{(1.09)^{10}}$$

EXHIBIT 11 PROJECTS A–E CASH FLOWS, NPV AND UAS

	Project					
	A	B	C	D	E	F
n	1	2	5	10	20	∞
I	1,000	1,000	1,000	1,000	1,000	1,000
S_t	1,380	837	514	412	369	380
D_t	1,000	500	200	100	50	0
$(1 - T)S_t + TD_t$	1,190	668	357	256	210	190
NPV	92	176	390	642	913	1,111
UAS	100	100	100	100	100	100

Similarly, if the NPV is $100 and the lifetime is two years, the UAS is $56.85. The UAS criterion leads to selection of the second project, and this is justified if it can be assumed that an equally profitable investment will appear in two years' time.

Exhibit 11 compares six investment projects; the UAS is the basis for **capital budgeting of projects** with unequal lifetimes, the cost of capital is taken as 9% and the tax rate is assumed equal to 50%. The five projects have two things in common: they all require the same initial outlay, and in all six the UAS is $100.

Assume now an inflation of 20% per year. The cost of capital is $(1.09)(1.20) - 1 = 0.308$, the (book value) depreciation is unchanged, and inflation rises by 20% per annum starting in the first year. Exhibit 12 illustrates the cash flow of project B with and without inflation.

EXHIBIT 12 PROJECT B's CASH FLOW, WITH AND WITHOUT INFLATION

	Year		
	0	1	2
	NO INFLATION		
I	−1,000	—	—
S_t	—	836.95	836.95
D_t	—	500.00	500.00
$(1 - T)S_t + TD_t$		668.48	668.48
	WITH INFLATION		
I	−1,000	—	—
S_t	—	1,000.34	1,205.21
D_t	—	500.00	500.00
$(1 - T)S_t + TD_t$		752.17	852.61

The real NPV of project B in the presence of 20% per year inflation is:

$$\text{NPV}_\text{B} = -1{,}000 + \frac{752.17}{1.308} + \frac{852.61}{1.308^2} = 73.40$$

The UAS_B is then derived by solving $73.40 = \text{UAS}_\text{B}/1.09 + \text{UAS}_\text{B}/1.09^2$, where $1.09 = 1.308/1.2$; this UAS_B, which equals \$41.72, is thus a real value, its nominal value being $(41.72)(1.2) = \$50.06$ in the first year, and (41.72) $(1.2^2) = \$60.08$ in the second. The real NPV and UAS of the six projects, A–F is as follows:

	A	B	C	D	E	F
n	1	2	5	10	20	∞
NPV	15.28	73.39	239.87	472.15	765.42	1,111.11
UAS	16.65	41.72	61.67	73.57	83.85	100.00

With no inflation, the UAS of all six projects is \$100; thus the table shows that a project's UAS is reduced by inflation (unless, as with project F, the project's lifetime is infinite); moreover, the shorter the lifetime, the greater the decrease. It is clear from the example that when mutually exclusive investment projects with different lifetimes are ranked by NPV or UAS, inflation could change the ranking because it affects the real value of the tax shelter differently in each case.

The effect of inflation on the **internal rate of return** (IRR) can now be examined. Exhibit 13 lists the **no-inflation cash flow** of six investments as well as their nominal IRR (IRR_N) and real IRR (IRR_R) in the face of a 20% inflation rate. In the absence of inflation, the IRR of all six projects (IRR_O) is 10%. The project's real IRR, given an inflation rate h, is

$$\text{IRR}_\text{R} = \frac{1 + \text{IRR}_\text{N}}{1 + h} - 1$$

EXHIBIT 13   PROJECTS F–J CASH FLOWS AND IRR_N AND IRR_R

	Project					
	G	H	I	J	K	L
n	1	2	5	10	20	∞
I	1,000.00	1,000.00	1,000.00	1,000.00	1,000.00	1,000.00
S_t	1,200.00	652.38	327.59	225.49	184.92	200.00
D_t	1,000.00	500.00	200.00	100.00	50.00	0.00
$(1 - T)S_t + TD_t$	1,100.00	576.19	263.80	162.75	117.46	100.00
IRR_N	22.00	22.76	24.77	27.12	29.45	32.00
IRR_R	1.70	2.30	3.98	5.93	7.88	10.00

where IRR_N is the nominal value of IRR; the last two lines of Exhibit 13 presents the values of IRR_N and IRR_R of the six projects. To show their derivation, consider project H, in Exhibit 14. The project's IRR_N is 22.76%, since

$$-1,000 + \frac{641.43}{1.2276} + \frac{719.72}{1.2276^2} = 0$$

and

$$IRR_R = \frac{1.2276}{1.20} - 1 = 2.3\%$$

Comparison of the IRR_R of the six projects shows that the profitability of short-lived projects is more adversely affected by inflation, and project L with infinite lifetime, is not affected at all. Thus inflation may alter the IRR ranking of projects.

EFFECTIVENESS OF INVESTMENT INCENTIVES. We will not present a comprehensive study of the effectiveness of investment incentives against inflation here. Nevertheless it is useful to consider a number of examples. To simplify, we will deal with the effect of **accelerated depreciation** under **ERTA** only, leaving out the often substantial effect of the investment tax credit which will be discussed below.

Consider investment projects D and E of Exhibit 11. As we saw, the NPV of D equals $642 in the absence of inflation and only about $472 (in real terms) when inflation is 20% per year. Project E's NPV is $913 in the absence of inflation and about $765 with 20% annual inflation. To examine the effect of the accelerated depreciation, we have recalculated the NPVs and the UASs of projects D and E assuming that project D is qualified to be depreciated over a three-year period and project E is qualified to be depreciated over a five-year period, as outlined in Exhibits 9 and 10. The results are summarized in Exhibit 15. The effect of the accelerated depreciation on the

EXHIBIT 14   CASH FLOW DATA FOR PROJECT H

	Year 0	Years 1,2, No Inflation	20% Inflation	
			Year 1	Year 2
I	−1,000			
S_t		652.38	782.86	939.43
D_t		500.00	500.00	500.00
$(1 - T)S_t + TD_t$		576.19	641.43	719.72

EXHIBIT 15   EFFECTIVENESS OF INVESTMENT INCENTIVES: AN EXAMPLE OF THE EFFECT OF ACCELERATED DEPRECIATION

	Project (dollars)	
	D	E
NPV		
No inflation, no incentives	$642	$913
20% inflation, no incentives	472	765
20% inflation, accelerated dep.	611	916
UAS		
No inflation, no incentives	$100	$100
20% inflation, no incentives	74	84
20% inflation, accelerated dep.	95	100

profitability of both projects is very significant. The NPV and UAS of project D are only 5% below their no-incentives and no-inflation level. The NPV and UAS are essentially at the same level as in the absence of inflation.

There are three points that must be noted. First projects in the lifetime range of 10 to 30 years are perhaps the primary beneficiaries of the accelerated depreciation method existing under the ERTA. Second, the example assumes 20% inflation rate, way above the 3 to 4% annual rate experienced in the United States in the mid-1980s. With such low rates of inflation and the accelerated depreciation as it is, the incentive clearly overcompensates for inflation by substantial amounts. Third, the investment tax credit further increases the profitability of investments, an element that was not taken into account in the calculation on which Exhibit 15 is based.

Accelerated depreciation. To complete the analysis, however, we have examined the effect of the **accelerated depreciation** schedule on the **Internal Rate of Return (IRR)** of investment projects. We found that the IRR of investments J and K, are as follows: (for a discussion of the IRR technique, see the section on **Capital Budgeting** in this Handbook).

	Project	
	J	K
Real IRR, no inflation, no incentives (IRR$_O$)	10%	10%
Real IRR, 20% inflation, no incentives	5.9%	7.9%
Real IRR, 20% inflation, accelerated dep.	15.8%	13%

The effect of inflation on the projects' IRR is very significant. However, one must recall that the calculations were carried out under the assumption of 20% inflation rate, much above the rate experienced in the mid-1980s. The striking result is the effect of accelerated depreciation on the IRRs, particularly on that of project J. Clearly, an inclusion of the **investment tax**

credit in the analysis would lead to an even higher IRRs, leading to the conclusion that for projects similar to J and K the effect of investment incentives is very significant.

Investment Tax Credit. The investment tax credit was first incorporated into the federal income tax law in 1962. Under its provisions, business firms could claim a specified percentage of the dollar amount of new investment in certain assets as a credit against their income tax. Originally, the credit was 7% of new investment in assets with a lifetime of eight or more years: two-thirds of 7% for assets with six or seven years of life, and one-third of 7% for assets with four or five years of life; no credit could be claimed for assets with a lifetime of less than four years. The tax credit was twice suspended and reinstated as Congress used it to encourage investment when economic conditions required it. In 1975, the basic credit rate was raised from 7 to 10%. The investment tax credit supplements the accelerated depreciation methods as a major incentive for capital investments.

The original **Reagan tax proposal**, now (1986) being debated in Congress, specified the elimination of the investment tax credit. This could have a dampening effect on investments since it effectively increases the investment cash outflow at the outset of the project.

INFLATION AND COMMON STOCK RETURNS

The determinants of stock prices and returns have long been a target of theoretical and empirical research by students of finance and capital markets. The **capital asset pricing model** (CAPM) developed by Sharpe, Lintner, and Mossin in the early 1960's, which is an extension of the portfolio selection framework suggested by Markowitz (1959), has opened the way to a better understanding of capital assets. This model distinguishes between **diversifiable** and **nondiversifiable risk,** and shows that as the number of securities in a portfolio increases, the relative importance of the nondiversifiable risk increases while the importance of each security's own risk diminishes. The model was developed on a set of restrictive assumptions but, as Lintner ("Inflation and Security Returns," *Journal of Finance*, Vol. 30, No. 2, May 1975) asserts, "subsequent work has shown that the essential structure of the model is remarkably robust to generalizations" (p. 263).

Nevertheless, most of the studies to date have been concerned with nominal rather than **real returns on capital assets.** With the persistent inflation of recent years, it must be asked how stock returns and price react to inflation. Here, classical as well as recent findings must be considered.

CLASSICAL THEORY AND COST OF CAPITAL UNDER INFLATION. The **classical model of the effect of inflation** on the cost of capital and stock prices advanced by Irving Fisher (*The Purchasing Power of Money,* Macmillan,

New York, 1920) and John Burr Williams (*Theory of Investment Value*, Harvard University Press, Cambridge, MA, 1938) reaches three major conclusions. First, the real return on capital assets is invariant to the price level, since the returns depend on production functions that are not affected by the general price level. Second, the real rate of interest is also invariant to the price level. Third, the real market value of claims against capital assets is equal to the real return on capital goods capitalized at the real rate of interest. Since the real return as well as the real rate of interest are invariant to the price level per se, it is clear that the real market value is also invariant.

In this classical framework where the stock price in the present is invariant to a future neutral inflation, one can derive the cost of capital in the simple case of an all-equity firm that distributes all its earnings as dividends (an assumption that can be relaxed without altering the results of the analysis). In the absence of inflation, the cost of capital k of such a firm is given by

$$P_0 = \sum_{t=1}^{\infty} \frac{d_t}{(1 + k)^t} = d \sum_{t=1}^{\infty} \frac{1}{(1 + k)^t} = \frac{d}{k}$$

and

$$k = \frac{d}{P_0} = \frac{e}{P_0}$$

where P_0 denotes the present market price of the stock, and d_t is the dividend per share in year t, which by assumption is equal to e_t, the earnings per share in year t. Note also that it is assumed for simplicity that earnings, hence dividends, are constant over time. Assume now a fully anticipated neutral inflation, prices being expected to rise at a rate h per annum, and that the firm's revenues and expenses, and therefore its earnings, are also expected to grow at the same rate. Since the firm distributes all its earnings as dividends, its **nominal cost of capital** k_N is given by

$$P_0 = \frac{d(1 + h)}{1 + k_N} + \frac{d(1 + h)^2}{(1 + k_N)^2} + \frac{d(1 + h)^3}{(1 + k_N)^3} + \cdots$$

$$= \frac{d(1 + h)}{k_N - h}$$

and $k_N = d(1 + h)/P_0 + h$. Comparing this result with the zero inflation case in which $k = d/P_0$, it is clear that

$$k_N + 1 = (1 + h)(1 + k)$$

or

$$k_N = k(1 + h) + h = k + h + kh$$

where k is the **real cost of capital** and k_N is the nominal cost of capital.

This approach can be clarified by considering a simplified numerical example. Suppose that in the absence of inflation, the minimum required real rate of return on investment is 10%; that is, the firm requires a minimum return of $110 on a $100 investment with a duration of 1 year. What will be the effect of an expected rate of inflation of, say, 10% on the nominal cost of capital k_N? Using $k_N = h(1 + k) + h$, the result is $k_N = 0.10(1.10) + 0.10 = 21\%$.

STOCK PRICES AND INFLATION IN THE CLASSICAL FRAMEWORK. The relationship between stock prices and inflation has been the source of some confusion. Consider a simple case of **no growth,** that is, a firm with constant earnings per share, e, which distributes all these earnings as dividends so that $e = d$, the price of the stock in period t is given by

$$P_t = \frac{d}{1 + k} + \frac{d}{(1 + k)^2} + \cdots = \frac{d}{k}$$

The price of the stock one year later, in period $t + 1$, is the same $P_{t+1} = P_t$.

Now assume a fully anticipated neutral inflation. Today's stock price is given by the capitalization of the new stream of dividends (= earnings) which, by the definition of neutral inflation, will rise at the inflation rate (k_N denotes the new nominal cost of capital):

$$P_t = \frac{d(1 + h)}{1 + k_N} + \frac{d(1 + h)^2}{(1 + k_N)^2} + \cdots = \frac{d(1 + h)}{k_N - h} = \frac{d(1 + h)}{k(1 + h)} = \frac{d}{k}$$

There is no immediate impact on the stock price, since $k_N - h = k(1 + h)$. However, the price of the share one year later is given by:

$$P_{t+1} = \frac{d(1 + h)^2}{1 + k_N} + \frac{d(1 + h)^3}{(1 + k_N)^2} + \cdots = \frac{d(1 + h)^2}{k_N - h}$$

or, $P_{t+1} = P_t(1 + h)$, so that the end-of-point share price rises at the inflation rate. Thus, under the assumptions made, common stocks do provide a **hedge against inflation.**

In the classical framework, the return to the stock of a levered firm increases when the inflation rate over the remaining life of the outstanding debt increases above its expected value. Since the total real value of the firm is invariant to the price level, the loss of real market value of such debt is accompanied by a gain in the real market value of the stock.

Lintner ("Inflation and Common Stock Prices in a Cyclical Context," in National Bureau of Economic Research, 53rd Annual Report, September 1973) points out that subsequent works in the classical framework have replaced leverage by the concept of **net debtor position** (financial liabilities in excess of financial assets). Firms in a net debtor position will enjoy real capital gains when inflation rates rise above the expected rates over the remaining life of their debt.

Since the consolidated balance sheet of U.S. nonfinancial corporations has consistently been in the net-debtor position since 1945 (see Lintner, 1973, op. cit.), the classical theory would predict that the current market value of their stocks should show a more than proportionate capital gain in current money terms to the rates of inflation.

EMPIRICAL EVIDENCE. The accumulated empirical evidence on the relationship between inflation and stock prices does not confirm the classical view. While the classical theory concludes that common stocks provide a hedge against inflation, the empirical evidence is that they fail to do so.

Lintner has examined the relationship between annual stock price changes and annual changes in the general price level. His main findings are as follows:

1. A simple regression between the annual percentage change in stock prices and the annual percentage change in the wholesale price index over a 70-year period showed no correlation between these two variables. This result is obtained largely because high inflation rates and serious deflation tend to reduce stock returns. Lintner found that a 10% deflation would reduce stock prices by 15% and a 10% inflation would reduce them by 4.1%.

2. When percentage changes in earnings and interest rates were added to the equation, the explained variance of stock price changes (i.e., the dependent variable) rose to about 33%. Deflation was the most powerful explanatory variable in the equation. A 10% price fall was estimated to reduce prices by 33%. A 10% inflation, on the other hand, was estimated to reduce stock prices by about 6.7%. Since these are estimates in a multiple regression analysis where percentage changes in earnings and interest rates are included as explanatory variables, these effects on stock prices are **net** of the effect of earnings and interest rates.

Lintner concluded that the classical theory of the relationship between changes in the price level and stock prices is not valid. He noted that the classical theory will hold if (*a*) the **real** returns to ownership of capital goods and (*b*) the real interest rate are invariant to inflation; but there is a good reason to believe that neither premise holds.

Additional evidence contradicting the classical theory is provided in the work of Zvi Bodie ("Common Stocks as a Hedge Against Inflation," *Journal of Finance*, Vol. 31, No. 2, May 1976, pp. 459–470). Bodie's approach to the question of common stock returns and inflation is essentially a portfolio approach. He focuses on the variance of a bond free of default. The risk of such a bond originates solely from the **inflation uncertainty**. Bodie tried to find out to what extent an investor can reduce the uncertainty of the real return on such a nominal bond by combining it with a well diversified portfolio of common stocks.

Consider Exhibit 16 which shows the expected return and standard deviation of a **default-free bond** and (B) a **well-diversified portfolio** of common stocks (S). Elementary portfolio theory shows that B and S can be combined into a portfolio whose expected return and standard deviation lie along the curve BS. The precise location of the portfolio depends on the proportion of investment allocated to B and S, and Bodie was concerned with the proportions that bring the portfolio's variance (or standard deviation) to a minimum. If a combination of B and S can result in a portfolio such as H in Exhibit 16, where the standard deviation of H (σ_H) is smaller than the standard deviation of B (σ_B), equities do provide (at least some) hedge against inflation. Common stocks provide a perfect hedge against inflation when $\sigma_H = 0$ and a partial hedge when $\sigma_H > 0$. The **cost of hedging** is defined as the difference between the mean real return on the nominal bond (μ_B) and the mean real return on the minimum variance portfolio (μ_H). In Exhibit 16, $\mu_B - \mu_H < 0$. The cost is negative because combing a well-diversified portfolio of common stocks with B not only decreases the risk from σ_B to σ_H, it also increasees the return from μ_B to μ_H.

The situation described by Exhibit 16 is not the only possible one, however. In Exhibit 17 the minimum variance portfolio H is not located between the points B and S, but on the extension of the curve SB beyond B. **Portfolio theory** advises that to attain portfolio H, B must be held long and S short. If empirical findings indicate that the minimum variance portfolio includes

EXHIBIT 16.   EFFICIENT FRONTIER BETWEEN S AND B: STOCK PORTFOLIO S IS HELD LONG AT MINIMUM VARIANCE PORTFOLIO H

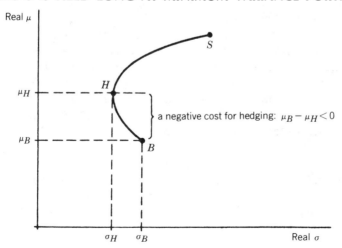

EXHIBIT 17.   EFFICIENT FRONTIER BETWEEN S AND B: STOCK PORTFOLIO S IS HELD SHORT AT MINIMUM VARIANCE PORTFOLIO H

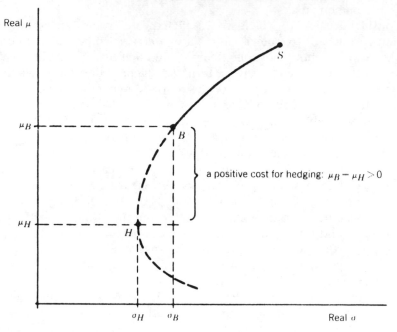

the well-diversified stock portfolio S with a negative proportion, that is, S is held short, the situation corresponds to Exhibit 17, and the conclusion is that stocks do not provide a hedge against inflation (when held in long position). The cost of hedging in Exhibit 17 is positive; $\mu_B - \mu_H > 0$, so that one can reduce the variance below σ_B, but only at the cost of reducing the expected value below μ_B.

Using data for 1953–1972, Bodie found that the minimum variance portfolio could indeed be attained only when the common stock portfolio was held short (!), not long. To attain the **minimum variance portfolio**, the investor must sell short about $0.03 worth of equity for every $1.03 invested in nominal bonds. By doing so, the hedger can eliminate roughly 18% of the variance of the real return on the bonds. The cost of such a hedge is a reduction in expected return of 0.34.

Furthermore, Bodie found not only that the real return on equity is negatively correlated with unanticipated inflation, it is also inversely related to anticipated inflation. The estimate he obtained was that an increase of 1% in the expected rate of inflation is associated with a decline of 4% in the real return on equity.

Fama and Schwert ("Asset Returns and Inflation," *Journal of Financial Economics,* Vol. 5, 1977, pp. 115–146) have examined the relationship between realized rates of return on various assets and the inflation rate. Their study concerned both expected and unexpected inflation and involved the return to stock portfolios, U.S. Treasury bills, longer term U.S. government bonds, return to privately held residential real estate, and nominal income from human capital. The period covered by their empirical study is 1953–1971.

The main tests in the study involve time series regression analyses, separate for each asset. The dependent variable in such a regression is the asset's nominal rate of return, and the two explanatory variables are measures of **expected and unexpected inflation.** The variable that was used as a proxy for the expected inflation was the Treasury bill nominal rate of interest, since if the expected real return on the bill is constant through time, and if the bill market is efficient, the nominal rate on the bill will be equal to a constant expected real return plus the expected inflation rate. The unexpected inflation was measured by the difference between the **ex post** realized inflation rate and the **ex ante** expected inflation rate. Denoting the expected inflation proxy by X_1, the unexpected inflation by X_2, and the nominal rate of return on an asset by R, the regression used for each asset of interest was

$$R_t = \beta_0 + \beta_1 X_{1t} + \beta_2 X_{2t}$$

where the subscript t denotes value for period t.

A coefficient $\beta_1 = 1.0$ in the regression would mean that when anticipated inflation rises by one percentage point so does ("on the average") the nominal rate of return on the asset, indicating that the asset is a **hedge against anticipated inflation.** Similarly, a coefficient $\beta_2 = 1.0$ means that when unanticipated inflation rises by 1% so does ("on the average") the nominal rate of return on the asset, and the asset is a hedge against unanticipated inflation.

Fama and Schwert reached the following main conclusions:

1. Of all assets, only **private residential real estate** was a complete hedge against both expected and unexpected inflation during 1953–1971.

2. Government debt instruments (i.e., bonds and bills) are a complete hedge against expected inflation, but not against unanticipated inflation.

3. Common stock returns are negatively related to expected and unexpected inflation. They are also negatively related to changes in expected inflation.

Irwin Friend and Joel Hasbrouck ("Effect of Inflation on the Profitability and Valuation of U.S. Corporations," unpublished paper, Wharton School) have examined the relationship between **rates of return on equity** and the rates of inflation. They found that the negative correlation between these two variables is attributable to two main factors: a decline in **real dividends**

and earnings of the firms, and an increase in the **real required rates of return** on stocks. They found that a 1% increase in steady-state inflation is accompanied by a 5% decline in dividends and about a 10% decline in real economic earnings per share. Thus inflation tends to decrease economic earnings per share more sharply than cash dividends, implying that the payout ratio increases under inflation. The decrease in dividends and the increase in risk depress stock prices and cause the negative relationship between rates of return on stocks and inflation.

EXPLAINING THE EMPIRICAL EVIDENCE. Lintner ("Inflation and Security Returns," *Journal of Finance*, Vol. 30, No. 2, May 1975, pp. 259–280) advanced a new theory to explain the negative relationship between inflation and stock prices. He assumes **neutral inflation** so that the firm's input and output prices all rise proportionally. He further assumes that capital stock and current rates of real investment are proportional to physical output, depreciation is taken at replacement cost for tax purposes, corporate profits are taxed at a fixed rate, and dividends are a fixed fraction of aftertax profits. With these assumptions, the excess of current dollar outlays for fixed investment over gross funds retained from operations (retained earnings plus depreciation) is a fixed fraction of current dollar sales. These excess outlays are denoted by bS_t, where b is a constant fraction of sales S_t.

Because sources of funds must equal their application, Lintner believes that additional external financing is needed to cover increases in **cash and accounts receivable.** Assuming that cash balances are a fixed ratio of current dollar sales, that a fixed proportion of sales is made on credit, and that the collection period of receivables is not affected by inflation, Lintner argues that the additional demands for external funds is a fixed fraction a of the increase in current dollar sales. The total demand for external funds is therefore $F_t = bS_t + aS_t$.

Exhibit 18 presents a numerical example to demonstrate that in these circumstances the ratio of external funds to sales F_t / S_t increases with infla-

EXHIBIT 18 NEED FOR EXTERNAL FUNDS UNDER CONSTANT INFLATION RATE AND UNDER INCREASING INFLATION RATE

	Year 1	Year 2	Year 3 Case 1	Year 3 Case 2
Inflation rate per annum	—	10%	30%	10%
S_t	1,000	1,100	1,430	1,210
ΔS_t	—	100	330	110
$bS_t = 0.1S_t$	100	110	143	121
$a\Delta S_t = 0.6\Delta S_t$	—	60	198	66
$F_t = (3) + (4)$	—	170	341	187
$F_t / S_t(\%)$	—	15.4	23.8	15.4

tion rates. The assumptions are: 10% inflation from year 1 to year 2, 30% inflation from year 2 to year 3, $a = 0.6$, and $b = 0.1$. As can be seen, the ratio of external financing to sales increases from 15.4% in year 2 to 23.8% in year 3. Since by assumption profits before and after taxes rise proportionally to sales, and since dividends are a fixed proportion of net profit, it follows that the **ratio of external to internal financing** (retained earnings plus depreciation) **also increases with inflation.** It is important to note that the dependence on external financing increases when inflation **rates** increase, that is, when the price level rises at an increasing rate. If the price level rises at a constant rate, external funds will be proportional to sales and internal funds; if inflation rates decline, the dependence on external funds will decrease. The case of constant inflation rates is illustrated in the last column of Exhibit 18, in which the inflation rate is assumed to be 10% from year 3 as well as from year 1 to year 2. As can be seen, $F_t / S_t = 15.4\%$, as in the year 1 column.

This analysis led Lintner to conclude ("Inflation and Security Returns," *Journal of Finance*, Vol. 30, May 1975, pp. 273–274) that under the assumptions made, the real value of the firm's profits will not change with inflation, but more external financing will be required with rising inflation. Consequently, the share of the **outstanding stock** in the firm's profits (whose real value is unchanged) is reduced. This in turn reduces the **outstanding** equity value.

When we examine the relationship between stock returns and inflation we often ignore changes in the real economic activity which may prove to be an important factor in determining stock return. In a recent analysis, Pindyck, (*American Economic Review*, June 1984, pp. 335–351) suggests that the uncertainty in real economic activity dominates the uncertainty in inflation. Namely the inflation uncertainty becomes insignificant in explaining stock return once the uncertainty of real economic activity is introduced as explanatory variable.

Hasbrouck (*Journal of Finance*, December 1984, pp. 1293–1310) recently investigated the relationship between stock return and inflation and found that the uncertainty of real economic activity is positively related to stock returns. The higher the uncertainty, the higher the returns. Decomposing the inflation to expected and unexpected inflation (using the Treasury Bill rate as the expected inflation proxy), the expected inflation coefficient is found to be negative and significant. Also the regression coefficient of the unexpected inflation is significantly negative. The most important of Hasbrouck's finding is that when both expected risk and expected inflation are used as explanatory variables for stock returns, the former is significantly positive, while the latter turns to be insignificantly different from zero. Thus, it suggests an explanation for the stock-return-inflation dilemma. In other words, when expected risk is incorporated into the model, the nagging negative relationship between stock returns and expected inflation vanishes.

IS INDEXATION THE ANSWER TO ALL INFLATION PROBLEMS?

In a number of countries, among them some Latin American countries and Israel, indexation has been tried as a way of coping with inflation. The procedure involves price level adjustment of such items as depreciation, inventory, and wages. Theoretically, applying complete indexation would allow firms to avoid the negative effects of inflation. In practice, complete indexation is virtually impossible to achieve. One difficulty is that inflation is not neutral. It affects various revenue and cost items differently. For example, suppose that wages and other cost items fluctuate proportionally to the Consumer Price Index. The firm's product price may rise more slowly, significantly reducing the firm's profit. Indexation theoretically reduces the uncertainty about future prices, thus encouraging investment and lowering the real cost of capital. In some cases, however, indexation may create uncertainty. For example, an exporting firm may suffer losses if exchange rates do not fully adjust to changes in the price level. Indexation (say, of wages) would only reduce the firm's flexibility. The history of indexation shows that in fact it does not provide an effective means of fighting inflation. Its mere existence, moreover, often creates the illusion that a way has been found, and this illusion prevents the search for an effective solution.

REFERENCES

Altman Edward and Subrahmanyam Marti, *Recent Advances in Corporate Finance*, R.D. Irwin, Homewood, Illinois, 1985.

Bodie, Zvi, "Common Stocks as a Hedge Against Inflation," *Journal of Finance*, Vol. 31, No. 2, May 1976, pp. 459–470.

Brigham, Eugene F., *Financial Management*, Dryden Press, Hinsdale, IL, 1977.

Fama, Eugene F., and Schwert, William G., "Asset Returns and Inflation," *Journal of Financial Economics*, Vol. 5, 1977, pp. 115–146.

Fisher, Irving, *The Purchasing Power of Money*, Macmillan, New York, 1920.

Friend, Irwin, and Hasbrouck, Joel, "Effect of Inflation on the Profitability and Valuation of U.S. Corporations" (unpublished working paper, Wharton School, University of Pennsylvania, 1979).

Hale, David, "Inflation Accounting and Public Policy Around the World," *Financial Analysts Journal*, November-December 1978, pp. 28–40.

Hasbrouck, Joel "Stock Returns, Inflation, and the Economic Activity: The Survey Evidence," *Journal of Finance* December 1984, pp. 1293–1310.

Hicks, John R., *Value and Capital*, 2nd ed., Clarendon Press, Oxford, 1957.

Kepcke, R. W., "Current Accounting Practices and Proposals for Reform," *New England Economic Review*, Federal Reserve Bank of Boston, September-October 1976.

Landskroner, Yoram, and Levy, Haim, "Inflation, Depreciation and Optimal Production," *European Economic Review*, Vol. 12, 1978, pp. 353–367.

Lintner, John, "Inflation and Security Returns," *Journal of Finance*, Vol. 30, No. 2, May 1975, pp. 259–280.

——, "Inflation and Common Stock Prices in a Cyclical Context," in National Bureau of Economic Research, 53rd Annual Report, September 1973.

Modigliani, Franco, and Cohn, Richard A., "Inflation, Rational Valuation and the Market," *Financial Analysts Journal*, March-April 1979, pp. 24–44.

Nelson, Charles R., "Inflation and Capital Budgeting," *Journal of Finance*, Vol. 31, No. 3, June 1976, pp. 923–931.

Pindyck, R. S., "Risk, Inflation and the Stock Market," *American Economic Review*, 74 (June 1984), pp. 335–351.

Williams, John Burr, *Theory of Investment Values*, Harvard University Press, Cambridge, MA, 1938.

16

PUBLIC UTILITY FINANCE

CONTENTS

16

PUBLIC UTILITY FINANCE

Eugene F. Brigham
T. Craig Tapley

BACKGROUND

Other sections of this *Handbook* deal with such topics as cash management, dividend policy, and capital budgeting techniques. However, the application of these techniques varies somewhat from firm to firm and from industry to industry, depending upon each entity's characteristics and operating environment. This is especially true of the public utilities, defined here to include electric, gas, telephone, and water companies, and, in certain respects, some of the transportation companies.

The utilities' prices are controlled by regulatory agencies, and the companies are required to provide a specified level of service as a condition for maintaining their operating franchises. This combination of controlled prices and required new investment has had a profound effect on the financial policies of utilities vis-à-vis the policies of unregulated industrial corporations. For example, the decision of an industrial company to invest or not to invest in a new plant would depend on whether the present value of the expected cash flows from the plant exceeded the cost of building it. Utilities, however, have traditionally proceeded by (1) deciding that a new plant would be needed 10 or 12 years down the road, (2) building the plant, and (3) then trying to persuade the regulatory authorities to permit the company to set prices (on the entire utility's system's output) sufficient to both cover costs and provide a fair and reasonable return on invested capital. If an industrial company's profits were "too low" and its cash flows "inadequate," it would raise prices, cut back on its investment, or even close down the operation and redeploy capital into more profitable areas. A utility, on the other hand, must go before its **regulatory commission** and seek permission to raise prices to correct financial problems.

Because of the critical—indeed, dominant—importance of regulation, this section begins with a discussion of regulatory practices and their effects on the financial posture of the utility industries. Then, building on this background, we consider the following aspects of financial policy: capital budgeting, cost of capital determination, capital structure decisions, and dividend policy. For the other aspects of financial management, which are less influenced by regulation, see the appropriate sections of this *Handbook*.

THE REGULATORY ENVIRONMENT

Utility companies are, to a large extent, **natural monopolies**—one firm can provide service to a particular territory more efficiently than could two or more companies. Thus, to minimize total operating costs, **utilities** are granted **franchises**, which give them exclusive rights within a given region. Because each firm is a monopoly, and because the service supplied is a necessity, utilities have the potential for earning excessive profits. As a result, utilities are subject to price regulations designed to limit them to a "fair" rate of return on invested capital. However, they are also required to provide service on demand, so they must build facilities to meet anticipated demand or face penalties for being unable to do so. Such penalties are very real. As an example, in the 1970s, Consolidated Edison of New York was found liable for damages resulting from blackouts.

A SIMPLIFIED VIEW OF REGULATION. In theory, regulatory procedures call for first estimating demand and cost schedules under "normal" conditions, then using these schedules to produce estimates of profits at various prices. These relationships are illustrated in Exhibit 1, where for simplicity

EXHIBIT 1   HYPOTHETICAL DEMAND-COST RELATIONSHIPS FOR A UTILITY COMPANY

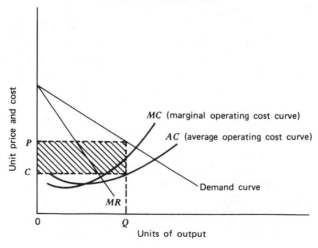

we assume that the utility provides but one type of service. At a price, P, Q units are demanded. The cost per unit at Q units of output is C. The profit per unit is P − C, and this unit profit, multiplied by Q units, gives total profits, the shaded area in the graph. If the company operated without regulation, it would set **marginal revenue** (MR) equal to **marginal cost** (MC), set a **monopoly price** higher than P, sell fewer units of output, and earn larger operating profits in spite of its lower level of operations. Clearly, some type of regulation is desirable to prevent this result.

In a simple world, regulators would (1) determine the assets necessary to supply a given level of service (the **rate base**), (2) recognize that money capital of the same amount is required to acquire the **rate base assets**, and (3) authorize a price for the utility's service such that the company's operating profits were just sufficient to cover its **cost of capital**. For example, if the required level of assets and capital were $100 million, and if the cost of capital were 12 percent, the *target operating profit level* would be $12 million. Service rates would have to be set at a level that would provide sufficient revenues to cover fuel, operating and maintenance (O&M) costs, and taxes, and still leave $12 million to compensate the investors who supplied capital to the utility enterprise.

Obviously, the real world is much more complex than this. First, it is impossible to determine the cost and demand schedules exactly. Second, utilities serve several classes of customers, which means that a number of different cost and demand schedules, with varying elasticities, are involved, so that any number of different rate schedules could be used to produce the desired level of profits. Third, the actual size of the rate base is subject to dispute, and it is not necessarily equal to the capital supplied by investors. For example, if demand has not grown as rapidly as the utility's original forecast, then some of its assets may represent excess capacity and may be excluded from its rate base. Also, as discussed in detail later, part of the capital supplied by investors is invested in operating assets, on which a cash return is earned and part is invested in **construction work in progress,** which is generally not in the rate base and consequently does not provide a current cash return.

Furthermore, utility regulation is not and should not be nearly as rigid as the example in Exhibit 1 suggests. For one thing, such rigidity, even if it were possible, would leave little or no room for managerial incentive: the profit motive for efficiency would be totally removed if the companies were simply guaranteed a specified profit. Consequently, it is often argued that rates should be set sufficiently low so that companies must strive to keep costs down and demand up to attain the profit goal. Furthermore, rates are changed with a lag, so if a particular company were especially efficient and were thus able to keep its costs lower than those that had been estimated when the rate schedule was set, it would be able to earn a higher than prescribed rate of return—at least until the regulatory agency ordered a rate reduction. Conversely, if costs rose and profits fell, there would be a lag before a rate increase could be obtained. These lags provide a powerful stimulus for utilities to operate efficiently.

To summarize, regulators in theory are supposed to do the following: (1) determine the amount of investment the company has made in facilities to serve the public, which in general is close to the amount of capital investors have supplied, (2) determine a "fair rate of return," which is based on the cost of capital, and (3) set prices that result in profits just high enough to actually provide that "fair return."

As they typically operate, commissions establish a **target rate of return** equal to the **weighted average cost of capital** and then, implicitly or explicitly, establish upper and lower bounds around this target. Exhibit 2 illustrates this concept. Even under reasonably stable economic conditions, actual earned rates of return could be expected to vary somewhat from year to year depending on weather conditions and other random factors. Furthermore, it would not be feasible to hold a rate case every time the actual rate of return varied even slightly from the target. Thus, upper and lower control limits (implicit or explicit) are set, and rate cases are held only if the actual earned rate exceeds these bounds (or if changes in capital market conditions suggest that the appropriate target return has changed).

DEVELOPMENT OF RECENT PROBLEMS. When the electric and telephone industries began, back in the late 19th century, operating costs were high. As their technology improved, these costs fell. In addition, expanding markets produced economies of scale which led to further cost reductions. Since their output prices were fixed but their costs were declining, the utilities' profits and earned rates of return tended to rise over time. Eventually, returns

EXHIBIT 2   TYPICAL RATE OF RETURN SITUATION FOR ELECTRIC AND TELEPHONE UTILITIES, 1880–1985

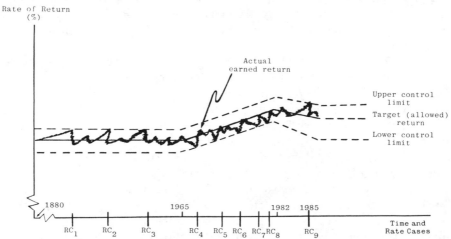

would hit the upper control limit (which was generally not explicitly stated but which existed nonetheless), triggering a reduction in service rates which lowered the earned rate of return back toward the target cost of capital.

The situation changed in the mid-1960s. **Inflation** increased, and both the rate of technological improvement and the benefits of **economies of scale** decreased. Since productivity improvements could no longer offset inflation, costs began to rise, and rising costs in the face of fixed output prices drove the earned rate of return down below the cost of capital. Further, money costs increased along with inflation from about 1965 to about 1982, which increased the cost of capital even as earned rates of return were decreasing. Therefore, from the mid-1960s to the early 1980s, the utilities tended to earn less than their costs of capital, and they were forced to seek rate increases frequently, often annually.

The electric companies' problems were further compounded during the 1970s by fuel price increases. Coal, oil, and gas were the primary fuels until the 1960s. Then, during the 1960s, pollution problems associated with coal led the federal government to force many utilities to convert to oil, gas or nuclear. However, oil prices quadrupled in 1973, and then rose further during the remainder of the 1970s, going from less than $2 per barrel in 1972 to over $30 in the 1980s. Since most electrics have **fuel adjustment clauses** which allow them to pass fuel costs on to customers without going through a rate case, customers' bills were rising steadily, even when the companies were between rate cases, all during the 1970s. The upward trend in prices reversed itself dramatically in 1985 and 1986 falling below $20 per barrel in early 1986. Many electrics, however, had already contracted to purchase oil into the future at high prices. The volatility of fuel prices increased the riskiness of utilities because it made their construction planning and demand forecasting, as described below, even more difficult.

Another problem which developed during the 1970s had to do with electric utility **construction programs.** Prior to the 1970s, a company could design and build a plant in just a few years, and plants cost about what they had been projected to cost. Further, demand could be forecast with great accuracy—for most companies, demand grew by 7% per year, and it rarely deviated from that figure by more than 1/2 of 1%. All of this changed dramatically in the 1970s. First, companies were prohibited from building new oil and gas generating plants because of shortages of those fuels, so new construction was generally for **coal** or **nuclear plants**, which are more capital intensive, more complex, and take longer to build. Second, both the time and the costs of construction increased because of increasing pollution and/or safety requirements, and because of delays in getting all the approvals necessary to build plants. The average time required to construct a coal plant increased from about four years to approximately 10 years, and nuclear plant construction increased from the five-year range to between 12 and 15 years. In addition, general cost inflation and increased safety/pollution control costs caused the labor and materials costs of plants to rise between 100 to 400%

above original forecasts. These increases were exacerbated by higher money costs. For example, if \$1 were spent on a plant in 1975, but the plant did not go into service until 1983, and if money costs rose from an average of 7.5% to an average of 13% over the eight-year construction period, then the \$1 would end up with a cost of $\$1(1.13)^8 = \$2.66$ in comparison to $\$1(1.075)^4 = \$1.33$ in prior years when the construction only took four years. Thus, the money cost/construction time increases compounded an already serious plant construction cost problem.

Furthermore, back in the late 1960s and early 1970s, before the oil price increases and before inflation had really impacted the industry, *demand* was growing by about 7% per year. Construction times had already lengthened quite a bit. Therefore, a utility with a peak load requirement of 1 megawatt and a 25% actual and target reserve margin (for a total of 1.25 megawatts of capacity) would anticipate capacity requirements of $1.25(1.07)^8 = 2.15$ megawatts in eight years. Therefore, if it used an eight-year construction period in its forecasts, it would have to commit, in, say, 1972, to build $2.15 - 1.25 = 0.90$ megawatts, or 72% of its 1972 capacity, to meet its projected 1980 demand. Of course, it would normally be committing to build some new plant each year, but the point is that the typical utility, in 1972, had to have "plant in the pipeline" equal to 70-75% of its existing plant to meet *forecasted requirements*. Because of their *obligation to serve*, the utilities believed that they had no choice but to build the plant they expected to need in the future.

Growth forecasts made in the late 1960s and early 1970s were based on historical patterns. Up to that time, prices had been declining. Electric appliances, including furnaces and air conditioners, were being used in more and more homes, and industry had been converting to electrical power. When the oil price increases began to be reflected in electric bills, residential consumers and industry both began to conserve energy. It took a while, but more energy-efficient appliances, better insulation, and the like, combined to slow down and then stop completely the increased usage of power. As a result, *load growth* from 1973 to 1985 averaged about 1 1/2% per year for the typical utility, down from 7% in prior years, and the typical forecast is about 2% for the future.

These basic structural changes have had some important effects on the utilities. If our illustrative company with a 72% capacity expansion in the pipeline in 1972, based on a 7% load growth, had an actual growth of only 1.5% per year, then its 1980 load would be only $(1.015)^8 = 1.13$ times the 1972 level, so its 1980 reserve margin would be over 90%:

$$\frac{\text{Reserve}}{\text{margin}} = \frac{1.25(1.07)^8}{1.0(1.015)^8} - 1 = \frac{2.1477}{1.1265} - 1$$

$$= 1.9066 - 1.00 = 0.9066 \text{ or } 90.66\%$$

Thus, it would have excess capacity of 90.66% − 25.00% = 65.66%. This assumes that the company correctly anticipated the slowdown in demand in 1973 and committed to build no new plant beyond that date, and that it was unable to cancel any of the plant committed in 1972 and earlier. By 1985, even with no new plants started after 1973, the company's excess capacity would still be over 50%:

$$\frac{\text{Reserve}}{\text{margin}} = \frac{2.1477}{1.0(1.015)^{13}} - 1 = \frac{2.1477}{1.2136} - 1$$

$$= 1.7698 - 1.00 = 0.7698 \text{ or } 76.98\%$$

$$\text{Excess capacity} = 76.98\% - 25.00\% = 51.98\%$$

Of course, plant retirements and/or faster load growth could change the situation, but these facts still remain:

1. Most utilities developed excess capacity during the 1970 to early 1980 period, and excess capacity still exists in 1986. Indeed, most companies have sufficient generating capacity to last to the mid-1990s, and many will not have to add capacity until the 21st century.

2. Excess capacity is expensive: depreciation, return on invested capital, and income taxes generally amount to about one-third of revenues, so if a company's capacity is 50% above its needs, its revenues—hence its customers' bills—are about 17% above what they would be if no excess capacity existed. That figure probably represents an understatement, because the plant added in recent years had a much higher cost per unit of capacity than older plant, and while new plant is often more efficient than older plant, efficiency generally does not offset the higher capital costs.

POLITICAL EFFECTS. Until the mid-1960s, utilities generally enjoyed very good public relations—they provided high quality service, and prices were falling even as quality and reliability improved. Thus, both the companies and their regulators were well regarded by the public. Things began to change in the late 1960s. There were capacity shortages and other problems in both the electric and telephone industries in several regions. Costs began to rise dramatically, and utility service rates rose in response. Consumer groups picketed utility companies and regulatory commissions to protest rising rates, and both state and federal governments provided financial and other support for the consumer groups. For example, by the mid-1970s virtually every state had set up an "Office of the Consumer Counsel," or the like, with a specific duty to intervene in rate cases on the side of residential consumers. Utility rates became a major factor in state politics, and in a number of elections, the candidate who seemed most likely to hold down rates won the election. Consumers never like higher prices, but the only prices that are directly controlled by elected officials, or people appointed by elected officials, are utility service rates. Therefore, utility regulation and politics are inextricably intertwined.

Because of regulation and political factors, utilities are in a unique and in many respects undesirable position. When times are good, or if managers make particularly good decisions, their profits will be limited because earned returns cannot exceed the cost of capital by very much or for very long. (New York has actually had a law since 1981 that requires refunds if earned returns exceed authorized levels, but no additional charges are imposed if profits fall below the allowed level.) Thus, the companies are in what amounts to a "heads I win, tails you lose position." If things go well, they earn their cost of capital. If something goes wrong, they earn less than the cost of capital. Accordingly, on average, one would expect them to earn less than the cost of capital. This has some interesting financial implications which will be discussed shortly.

DATA ON UTILITY COMPANIES' FINANCIAL PERFORMANCE. Exhibit 3 provides some information on money costs, returns, and stock prices for the electric utility industry. The situation was similar for telephone companies and gas distribution companies. Columns 1 and 2 show trends in the

EXHIBIT 3 MONEY COSTS, RETURNS, MARKET/BOOK RATIOS, AND BOND RATINGS (1965–1985)

Year	A-Rated Utility Bond Yields (1)	Cost of Common Equity (2)	Earned ROE (3)	Ratio: ROE to Equity Cost (4)	Market to Book Ratio (5)	Average Bond Rating (6)
1965	4.9	8.1	12.2	1.51	2.02	AA
1970	8.4	10.8	11.9	1.10	1.54	AA
1975	9.6	14.0	11.2	0.80	0.88	A+
1980	13.4	17.6	11.4	0.65	0.70	A+
1981	15.7	17.7	12.5	0.71	0.76	A
1982	12.2	16.3	13.6	0.83	0.91	A
1983	13.0	16.0	14.2	0.89	0.89	A −
1984	12.4	15.2	14.4	0.95	0.93	A −
1985	11.6	14.7	15.2	1.03	1.10	A

Sources: Data for Column 1 are from Standard & Poor's *Security Price Index Record*; information for Columns 3, 5, and 6 is from the S&P Compustat tapes; and data for Column 2 are from E.F. Brigham, D. Shome, and S. Vinson, "The Risk Premium Method of Estimating a Utility's Cost of Equity," *Financial Management*, Spring 1985, update to mid-1985.

cost of money: interest rates and equity costs rose dramatically during the 1970s, peaked in 1981, and then declined, but they are still close to twice the 1960s levels. Column 3 shows earned returns on equity. Column 4 gives the ratio of return on equity (ROE) to the cost of equity. Column 5 lists market/book ratios and Column 6 the average bond rating of the utility. In theory, utilities should earn their cost of capital, and if they do and are expected to do so in the future, then their stock prices will equal their book values, so their market/book ratios will be equal to 1.0 (actually, just over 1.0 to cover flotation expenses, as we will explain shortly).

Exhibit 3 shows that in 1965 and 1970 utilities were earning more than their costs of equity and consequently were selling at prices above book values. For the reasons discussed above, this situation changed during the 1970s. Until 1985, the average utility earned less than its cost of capital and sold below book. That situation was reversed in 1985, and the latest available data shows the average utility earning slightly more than its cost of equity and selling slightly above its book value.

There is reason to doubt that utilities will, as an industry, ever earn substantially more than their cost of capital and consequently sell at substantial multiples of book value. This is because there has been a change in the method used to estimate the companies' costs of equity. Prior to the late 1960s, regulators generally used the **comparable earnings method** to establish authorized returns on equity. Under this method, commissions calculate the average ROE on a set of unregulated companies deemed to be of equal risk as the utility in question and then allow the utility to earn that rate of return. The serious problems with this procedure—finding truly comparable-risk unregulated companies whose earnings are reported on a similar basis, and being sure that these "comparable" companies are not actually oligopolists which are earning "too much"—led to the adoption of the **discounted cash flow (DCF) method** of estimating the cost of equity. (The DCF method will be discussed later in this section.) Today the DCF method is used almost universally, and, if the DCF cost of equity is estimated correctly and used as the allowed return, then the company's stock must sell at approximately its book value.

ACCOUNTING POLICIES UNDER REGULATION. Utility financial managers must be concerned with both profits and cash flows—profits are nice and are necessary for a viable operation, but profits are not synonymous with cash, and cash is necessary for the payment of interest and dividends, as well as for making purchases of all types. Furthermore, the accounting policies used by regulators to determine costs have a significant effect on cash flows—two accounting policies can produce the same reported profits but vastly different cash flows. The three major areas in which utility accounting practices differ from those of unregulated firms are listed and then discussed:

1. The reporting of tax liabilities
2. The capitalizing of financing costs during construction periods
3. The phasing in of new generating plants rather than allowing them to be placed in the rate base as soon as they have been completed and gone on line.

Tax Accounting. Most corporations, utility and nonutility alike, use **accelerated depreciation** for tax purposes but charge depreciation to cost of goods sold on a **straight-line basis**. The result, for a company whose net assets are growing (as most are, because of inflation if not as a result of **real growth**), is a relatively low current tax bill combined with the certain knowledge that taxes will rise, assuming stable tax rates, at some future time when accelerated tax depreciation is less than straight-line book depreciation (see E.F. Brigham and T. Nantell, "Normalization versus Flow Through for Utilities," *Accounting Review*, July 1974, pp. 436–477). Industrial companies are required, as a condition for an **unqualified audit report**, to report as a charge against income the difference between taxes currently paid and the taxes that would have been paid if the company had used straight-line depreciation for both tax and book purposes—this charge is the item **deferred taxes**, which is shown on the income statements and balance sheets of most industrial firms.

The theory of deferred taxes is straightforward and logical—accelerated tax depreciation postpones, or defers, federal income taxes. However, these deferred taxes will someday have to be paid; hence they should be shown as a cost. This is called normalizing the effects of accelerated depreciation. Not to normalize understates costs, overstates profits, and can be construed as providing misleading information to investors. This is why the accounting profession (and the Security and Exchange Commission (SEC) implicitly) requires corporations to show deferred taxes as a cost, that is, to normalize.

Although many utilities do follow the standard practice of reporting profits after deferred taxes, in about half the states regulators forbid this practice. The result is a relative understatement of costs and a corresponding overstatement of current profit. The benefits of accelerated depreciation are, in effect, "flowed through" to current ratepayers, and hence this practice is called **flow through**.

Advocates of **flow-through accounting** argue that a growing company will never have to "pay off the deferred taxes." Opponents point out that:

1. Under all conceivable conditions, the use of flow through shifts the tax burden associated with current operations from current customers to future customers, hence creates an intergenerational inequity.
2. Flow-through utilities are forced to request rate increases more often, and if these increases are delayed because of regulatory lag, the problem of rate of return attrition is compounded.

3. The **cash flows of flow-through companies** are lower than those of normalizing utilities, forcing the flow-through firms to raise more money in the capital markets.
4. Flow-through companies' cash coverages of interest and dividends are lower than those of similar normalizing utilities.

The net effect of all this is to raise the cost of debt and equity to flow-through companies vis-à-vis normalizing ones.

If there are so many conceptual problems with the use of flow through, why do almost one-half the utilities use it? The reason seems to be political: the use of flow through postpones a cost—that is, income taxes— to some future date; hence it shifts the cost of utility service from today's customers to future ones. Apparently, a number of politicians involved in regulation are more concerned with today's customers than with those of future years.

Construction Accounting. Another major distinction between public utility accounting and accounting for unregulated firms relates to construction projects. Visualize a situation in which an electric utility has net assets of $4 billion, represented by generating plant and transmission facilities. The company has a capacity of 10 million kilowatts (kW) at a book cost of $400 per kilowatt of capacity. The company now decides that it must expand generating capacity by 20% or by two million kW. Under current federal regulations, any new capacity must be either coal or nuclear. A new coal plant started in 1985 would probably have a cost of close to $2,000 per kilowatt of capacity; nuclear would cost about $4,000. Thus, a 20% capacity expansion would call for the expenditure of about $4 billion (100% of existing assets) for a coal plant or $8 billion (200% of existing assets) for a nuclear one.

As mentioned previously, the **construction time for a new coal plant** is 8 to 10 years, and it takes at least 12 years to build a **nuclear plant**. The funds invested in the new plant will accumulate over the construction period, and, of course, any increase on the asset side of the balance sheet must be matched by an increase on the liability-capital side. Thus, to pay for the cost of constructing the plant, securities (that is, stocks and bonds) would have to be sold years ahead of the time the facility will be put into service.

The investors who supply the new capital must be compensated for the use of their money, both during the construction period and after the plant goes into service. The compensation for capital used during construction—interest on debt plus dividends and retained earnings on equity—has long been recognized as a legitimate cost that should be borne by the utility's customers. However, it is traditional to handle this element as follows:

1. **Construction work in progress (CWIP)** is segregated from plant-in-service.

2. Only plant-in-service is included in the rate base on which customer bills are based.

3. An **allowance for funds used during construction (AFUDC)** is calculated by multiplying CWIP by a figure approximately equal to the firm's weighted average cost of capital.

4. AFUDC is reported as income.

5. AFUDC is added to beginning-of-period CWIP (this is called *capitalizing AFUDC*).

6. Customers end up paying, and the company receiving, a cash return on capitalized AFUDC when the new plant is completed and added to the rate base.

This procedure is logical because it requires current customers to pay only for plant that is currently "used and useful," while future customers, who will receive the output of the new plant, will pay its full cost, including the financing costs incurred during its construction phase.

Although capitalizing AFUDC does have the significant merit of requiring those who receive the services of a plant to pay all costs associated with the plant, it also has some severe financial drawbacks. These stem from the fact that, as in the example at the beginning of this section, a utility can have a very large fraction of its assets invested in CWIP, hence be earning a great deal of AFUDC relative to cash income. For example, The Southern Company had over 25% of its assets in CWIP in 1985, and AFUDC represented 57% of the company's net income to common. The AFUDC-net income percentage has been declining for most companies in recent years as construction programs have been completed—after averaging over 50% for the industry during the latter half of the 1970s through 1983 (54.7% in 1983), it dropped to 32% in 1984 and to an estimated 25% in 1985. Further declines are anticipated until the industry-wide excess capacity is worked down and major new construction programs are started up sometime in the 1990s. The recent and even current situation is quite different from that before the 1970s—in the 1960s and earlier, before new plants became so expensive, the AFUDC-net income ratio generally was about 5% for the average electric utility, so AFUDC income then was not significant.

AFUDC is not cash, but interest and dividends must be paid in cash. Therefore, if a utility obtains a large fraction of its income as AFUDC, it has a *cash flow problem.* Such a company can be forced to sell new bonds and stock to raise the cash necessary to pay interest and dividends on its old bonds and stock. Some security analysts have likened this to a **Ponzi** or **Pyramid scheme,** and research has shown very clearly (1) that AFUDC income is regarded as being of low "quality" and (2) that utilities that have significant amounts of AFUDC tend to have **lower rated bonds**, hence higher costs of both debt and equity capital (see E.F. Brigham, et al., "The Treatment of CWIP," University of Florida, Public Utility Research Center, December 1982).

The potential problems with AFUDC have been realized in the case of a number of utilities with major nuclear construction programs. For example, on January 1, 1984, while Public Service of Indiana (PSI) was building a nuclear plant at Marble Hill, Indiana, it's CWIP was $2.7 billion. Further, PSI reported net income of $255.8 million in 1983, and $221.5 million, or 87% of that amount was AFUDC. Similar percentages have applied in other recent years. The Marble Hill plant has now been cancelled, and PSI's $2.7 billion investment in the plant abandoned. Since the plant will never go into service, the accumulated AFUDC associated with it will probably never be recovered, or certainly will not be recovered in the manner that was anticipated. Thus, it now appears that PSI's income as reported in 1983 and earlier was vastly overstated. A number of other utilities in New York, Michigan, Arkansas, Missouri, Louisiana, Mississippi, Pennsylvania, and Ohio, among others, are faced with similar problems.

Several lawsuits have been filed by stockholders against utilities and their accountants, claiming that the reporting of AFUDC as income was misleading, and that it has led to losses on stock purchases. As a result, the Accounting Standards Board is currently considering a new rule that would restrict the reporting of AFUDC income and that would also require writedowns of assets such as PSI's Marble Hill investment. (In 1985, PSI is still carrying the full cost of Marble Hill as an asset in spite of the fact that the Company has essentially a zero probability of recovering all of this investment and a fairly high probability of recovering none of it. Indeed, under the very best of conditions, whatever recovery is allowed will be stretched out over many years, and hence the present value of possible future cash flows is bound to be far less than the $2.7 billion carrying value.) However, if restrictions are imposed on reporting AFUDC as income, then utilities could have very low earnings during major construction periods, which would make it difficult for them to finance those programs.

Phase-Ins of Completed Plants. Approximately one-half of all utilities were engaged in nuclear construction programs in 1980. Because of changes in Nuclear Regulatory Commission requirements, general inflation, and interest rate increases, the final costs of the plants involved were many times higher than the original estimates. A number of the plants were cancelled—Marble Hill, for example—but many others were completed. It is not unusual for a nuclear plant coming on line in the 1980s to add 10–15% to the capacity of a utility yet have a cost equal to 50% of the utility's assets. Just before completion, when these plants are still carried as CWIP, AFUDC represents a large percentage of reported income available to common stockholders— 75–80% is not unusual. Then, when the plant is completed, AFUDC income is no longer earned, and depreciation must also be taken on the plant. To maintain the same rate of return, customer bills must be increased by an amount sufficient (1) to cover depreciation plus operation and maintenance costs, (2) to make up for lost AFUDC income, and (3) to cover additional income taxes (AFUDC income is not taxable, so when "regular" income is substituted for AFUDC, taxes increase). The addition of nuclear plant does result in lower fuel costs, but the fuel cost savings are not generally anywhere close to the added costs of the new plant placed in the rate base, so huge base rate increases—often 40% or more—are required to keep earned rates of return stable. The effect of these increases on consumers has been termed **rate shock**.

Rate shock is disruptive to residential consumers, and it can also have adverse effects on employment in the company's service area. Therefore, a utility's customers are likely to put pressure on its commission to mitigate rate increases. One direct way of doing this is to simply not allow a company to recover all of the money it invested in the plant—New York has announced plans to do this with Long Island Lighting's Shoreham plant and with other nuclear units in the state, while Kansas, Ohio, Louisiana, Arkansas, Missouri, and other states, have done likewise. Generally, when such outright *disallowances* are imposed, the ruling is coupled with an allegation of some type of imprudence in the construction of the plant.

If no imprudence is found, yet rate shock would still occur if all associated costs were billed to customers as soon as a plant is completed, then a commission may decide to **phase the plant into rate base** rather than add it in immediately. For example, if a plant has a cost of $3 billion, a commission might decide to phase it in over a five-year period, putting one-fifth of the plant into rate base each year for five years. The portion of the plant not in rate base would be held in an account similar to CWIP, and it would earn income similar to AFUDC. Utility managers and investors do not generally favor phase-ins—they prefer cash income—but political and economic reality does at times necessitate such actions.

Economic Depreciation. Another accounting issue that has arisen in recent years relates to the use of **economic depreciation** rather than traditional depreciation. Under traditional procedures, straight line depreciation is used— that is, the plant's cost, less its estimated salvage value, is written off each year in equal amounts over the estimated life of the plant. Note that the rate base—defined as original cost less accumulated depreciation—is highest immediately after the plant goes into service, and declines thereafter. Therefore, revenue requirements are high initially and decline thereafter, thus increasing the rate shock problem when new plant comes on line.

Economic depreciation is calculated differently. To use it, one estimates the value of the plant each year and then defines economic depreciation as the change in value from one year to the next. Value tends to decline due to physical wear and tear, and obsolescence, but these declines may be offset by inflation. Therefore, economic depreciation could be either positive or negative, and it would tend to vary from year to year depending on inflation rates.

Economic depreciation has intuitive appeal, but it is subject to implementation problems. First, the value of utility property depends on regulators' actions—that is, if a commission allows a company to earn a higher or lower return, then its properties will have a higher or lower value. Therefore, the use of economic depreciation for regulated companies has an element of circularity. Second, if value is defined in terms of replacement cost in order to avoid the first problem, then there is still the matter of estimating replacement cost. Variances of 50% or even 100% could easily arise, primarily because of changes in technology and environmental restrictions. Third, if replacement cost estimates were made annually, then there would almost certainly be major changes in cash flows from year to year, which would make financial planning difficult, while if costs were estimated over a longer period, huge errors would almost certainly arise. Fourth, the depreciation calculation would necessarily be more judgmental than the present procedure, and the greater the degree of judgment, the greater the potential for political pressures toward determinations that would hold down customers' bills this year and postpone payments to future years, which increases the probability that full recovery will never occur.

Economic depreciation is conceptually sound, but it does have serious implementation problems. If the inflation rate remains at current levels (about 5%), then the benefits of economic depreciation are probably not worth the costs. However, if inflation again increases to the double digit level, then it should and probably will be adopted in some form.

CAPITAL BUDGETING

Conceptually, the correct method of **capital budgeting by unregulated firms** calls for

1. Estimating the investment cost associated with a project
2. Estimating the net cash flows each year over a project's life
3. Determining the cost of capital required to complete the project
4. Using these data to calculate the project's net present value (NPV)
5. Accepting the project if its NPV is positive or rejecting it if NPV is negative.

It is not a simple matter to obtain accurate estimates of the input data, but from a conceptual standpoint this procedure is correct because it is market oriented and because it optimizes the welfare of both customers and investors within the constraints of a market economy.

TRADITIONAL UTILITY CAPITAL BUDGETING. The utilities have traditionally operated in a different manner. Before the mid-1970s, their capital budgeting process was as follows: (1) demand for service (electricity, gas, telephone service, and so on) was estimated, largely by extrapolating past trends, (2) the plant capacity needed to meet this projected demand was determined, (3) alternative plant designs (for example, coal versus oil-powered plants, or electric versus manual switching for telephone service) were considered, and (4) the plant design that would provide the needed service at the lowest present value of expected future costs was chosen. The discount rate used to find the present values was generally taken to be the *authorized rate of return*.

The whole process was dominated by engineers, who forecasted demand, designed the plants, estimated capital requirements, and generally ran the companies. The role of the financial officer was mainly to raise the capital the engineers indicated they needed. Regulatory involvement was minimal: because of technological improvements and economies of scale, when new plants went on line costs were generally lowered, so rate increases were not required. Indeed, periodic rate reductions to keep the earned rate of return within reasonable bounds were common in the electric, telephone, and gas distribution industries.

Although this procedure worked well for decades, it contained four fatal flaws, all of which surfaced in the 1970s:

1. The electric utilities' demand forecasts did not take adequate account of the relationship between the prices charged and the amount of service demanded (price elasticity).

2. It was assumed that customers wanted the highest quality service (essentially, close to zero probability of power failures, power shortages, filled telephone lines, and so on) and were willing to pay the costs for such systems, regardless of the level of these costs.

3. The relationships between the amount of capital raised and the cost of this capital, between the riskiness of cash flows associated with a project and the project's cost of capital, and between the marginal and average costs of capital, were not adequately recognized and dealt with.

4. The companies assumed that public utility commissions would authorize rate increases to cover the cost increases that would necessarily occur when new plants, whose costs under inflation were far higher than the costs of existing plants, were put on line.

With 20–20 hindsight, it is easy to see that the assumptions embodied in the utilities' capital budgeting procedures were incorrect. Experience during the 1970s taught us that **price elasticity** does indeed exist for utility services— higher prices result in reduced demand, and this demand reduction increases over time as customers adapt to higher prices by insulating houses better, buying more energy-efficient appliances, and the like. Similarly, it is now clear that, while customers may have been willing to pay the cost of carrying a 30% reserve margin to assure uninterrupted electric service when capacity cost only $200/kW and when the cost of carrying this spare capacity was based on 5% interest rates, they prefer lower reserve margins when capacity costs $2,000/kW and carrying costs are based on 15% interest rates. The utilities have also learned that during periods of high inflation, the marginal cost of raising new capital can be much greater than the embedded cost of capital, resulting in an increase in both business and financial risks. Finally, every utility in the country has found that commissions will not automatically pass the costs of new, high-cost plants on to customers without an argument and without delays.

CAPITAL BUDGETING IN THE FUTURE. Even though 20–20 hindsight suggests that the traditional method of capital budgeting by utilities, and especially by electric utilities, had major shortcomings, it is not at all clear that this methodology produced incorrect decisions during the 1960s and early 1970s. In retrospect, it appears that, although many utility companies started plants that probably should have been deferred for several years, most of these decisions would have been made under any capital budgeting procedure, given the information available at the time the decisions were actually made. Nevertheless, the methodology employed earlier should not be used during the future. The essential elements of a viable capital expenditure decision system for the future are outlined next.

Demand Forecasting. The most important element of a good capital budgeting system is a good demand forecast. The demand forecast must recognize price elasticity. This means that a utility must forecast all the elements of cost that will go into service rates, hence influence demand. Furthermore, the utilities today are subject to competition, so companies must forecast not only total market demand but also their own share of the market.

To illustrate, consider the telephone companies. They have a monopoly for local residential service, but strong competition exists in the long distance market. Different companies generally provide local versus long distance service. Under pre-1984 conditions, before the AT&T divestiture, rates were set well above costs on long distance service, and excess profits there were used to subsidize local service. After the breakup, there was a separation between local and long distance providers, and competition also lowered long distance profits. Thus, the former subsidy was largely eliminated, and local rates rose. This raised political concern. Soon, partly on sound economic grounds, but also for political reasons, the concept of the **access charge** was developed. An access charge is a sum paid to a local telephone company for the use of its lines to gain access to a long distance network. For example, New York Telephone Company receives access charges from AT&T, MCI, and other long distance providers for providing access to their networks.

Under Federal Communications Commission (FCC) regulations developed in the wake of the AT&T breakup, the long distance companies initially paid access charges, but these charges will eventually be paid by telephone subscribers at a monthly rate of about $2 per residential phone and $5 per business phone. There have, naturally, been objections that these charges are unfair, because they are too low for people who make frequent use of long distance and too high for people who seldom or never use long distance. That has led to a call for access payments tied more directly to long distance usage, and Congress has seriously entered the debate.

The access issue is made especially difficult as a result of **bypass potential**—if access charges are increased too much, then large users of long distance service will bypass the local telephone company. For example, even before the currently scheduled access charges were fully implemented, Merrill Lynch, several major banks, and numerous other companies had set up their own networks. In New York, a number of companies have banded together to establish a teleport on Staten Island. Microwave and fiber optic cables are used to carry signals from Manhattan offices to Staten Island, where an earth station is used to transmit voice and data via satellite all over the world. Similar systems are being used by companies such as Westinghouse and IBM for their own long distance service. AT&T has announced plans to send lines directly to major long distance users and thus to bypass New York Telephone and other local providers.

Obviously, the higher the access charges, the greater the incentive to bypass. Therefore, if access charges are set high enough to provide a meaningful subsidy to local service, users will be more likely to bypass the local system and thus defeat the purpose of the access charge. Two other points are significant: (1) Once a customer has installed the equipment necessary for bypass, it is not likely to return to the local system for access to long distance service. (2) When bypass occurs, revenues to the local company fall much more than its costs (which are largely fixed), so profits fall. If the local company attempts to make up the lost profits by charging the remaining customers more, this very action could stimulate further bypass, thus setting off a vicious cycle.

We do not have the answer to the problems presently faced by the telephone industry and its regulators. The breakup of AT&T is, in many respects, like the opening of Pandora's box—we simply don't know where it will lead. In any event, though, the telephone companies do have a difficult time with their capital budgeting, because as a result of potential bypass they must add uncertainty about their market share to their traditional uncertainty about the size of the total market, and all of these uncertainties are exacerbated because many of the key decisions are political and thus largely out of the hands of the companies themselves.

The electric utilities face a problem that is similar to bypass—namely, **cogeneration.** Cogeneration is the term used to describe the situation that occurs when a user of electricity builds a generating unit to (1) supply its own power, and (2) sell power to the utility. Cogeneration has been used for many years in certain areas, for example, by paper companies which had plants to make steam for use in their manufacturing process and then also generated electricity as a byproduct. During the 1970s, when conservation, energy independence, and energy efficiency were first being stressed, cogeneration was pushed very hard. It was a major part of the **Public Utility Regulatory Policies Act (PURPA)**, passed in 1978. PURPA decreed that utilities must purchase cogenerated power, with the purchase price being set at their avoided cost.

Cogeneration increases the *planning problems* of the electric companies in two ways: the electric companies cannot be sure either how much of their own power their potential customers will generate for themselves, or how much power their customers will want to sell. Several factors are relevant here, including future technological developments in power generating equipment, relative fuel costs, and regulatory policies. For example, if generators that are more efficient than those currently in use by the utilities are developed, and if utilities attempt to recover the costs of now-obsolete plants through higher service rates, then customers may find it cost-effective to generate their own power. The same situation could exist if a utility which uses coal as its primary fuel learns that **acid rain legislation** has been enacted requiring it to make huge capital and operating expenditures, and its customers consequently find that they can lower their costs of electricity by installing gas-fired generating units. Similarly, there is little question but that attempts to recover all the costs sunk in some of the nuclear fiascos could drive some customers to cogeneration. Further, as with the telephone companies and bypass, if some customers reduce their demand and the company attempts to offset these losses by imposing higher charges on other customers, the result could be to drive off still more customers.

It should be noted that such well capitalized companies as General Electric, Boeing, and General Motors are making major investments in the development of cogeneration technology. Wall Street too is developing mechanisms to provide low-cost, tax-shelter based financing to installers of such units. No one knows how things will turn out, but when one considers that the planning-construction-operating period involved in a coal or nuclear plant is at least 40 years, and that highly efficient fuel cells or other methods for generating electricity could be developed in 40 years, it is obvious that cogeneration increases the uncertainty inherent in utility demand forecasting for capital budgeting purposes.

Cost Forecasting. The utility must forecast the cost of building new facilities as well as the fuel, operating, maintenance, and capital costs that will be incurred after the plant goes into service. Since plants of alternative types can be built (for example, coal versus nuclear power plants, or satellite versus microwave telecommunication transmission systems), it is necessary to forecast the construction, fuel, and operating and maintenance costs of alternative systems to be able to build the least-cost (lowest present value of future cost) system to meet a given forecasted demand. If these cost forecasts are incorrect, the result will be a relatively high-cost, inefficient system, and if a company attempts to pass these high costs on to consumers in the form of higher service rates, then demand may be reduced, further compounding the problem.

Cost of Capital Considerations. Although many utilities apparently use their authorized rates of return as their *discount rates* for capital budgeting, this procedure is incorrect and can lead to substantial errors. The first major problem is that authorized rates of return are based on the *historic average cost of debt and preferred stock,* not on *marginal costs;* hence the authorized rate of return understates the cost of the capital used today to finance capital projects. Second, the authorized rate of return on equity may not correctly reflect the *current cost of equity.* Third, the cost of capital raised during a period depends (1) on the amount of capital raised and (2) on the perceived riskiness of the investment being made, whereas the authorized rate of return, to the extent that it reflects actual conditions at all, reflects average conditions in the past, not marginal conditions at the present time. Thus electric utilities have at times used the same cost of capital to evaluate nuclear and coal plants, even though far more capital must be raised to construct a nuclear plant, and though nuclear plants are generally regarded as being riskier than coal plants from an investment standpoint. The use of the same cost of capital for these two types of plant would tend to *bias the decision toward nuclear* and, possibly, would lead to costly mistakes.

Current Environment of Capital Budgeting Decision Making. No forecasting methodology is or can possibly be perfect. Therefore, a utility may, on the basis of the best available data, forecast its future demand at a given level, build a plant to meet forecasted demand, and find, 10 years or so later when the plant is completed, that the plant is not needed because demand has grown more slowly than had been anticipated. Or, fuel and other cost elements may have changed, or a new design may not have worked out as anticipated, making the newly completed plant's costs higher than they would have been if some other type of plant had been built. Of course, such mistakes may be identified before a plant is completed. For example, during the latter half of the 1970s, many utilities recognized that conditions were changing, and they slowed down or canceled plant construction, or converted partially completed plants from one fuel to another, but generally at substantial costs. And, of course, the costs of all new plants have tended to exceed original expectations because of inflated construction costs. The opposite situation existed in the 1960s, when actual demand often exceeded forecasted demand, and electric utilities were forced to generate power with high-cost peaking units because they could build these units and get them on line quickly.

Regulatory Approval. Since it is clear that not all capital budgeting decisions will turn out to be good ones, it is important that major investment decisions be made with the best information available. Furthermore, if consumers are expected to pay for plants, inputs from the public should enter the decision process. This leads to the conclusions, discussed in more detail below, that (1) prior commission approval should be obtained for all major projects as an integral part of the capital budgeting process, and (2) commissions should be kept apprised of new developments during the construction of a major facility and should participate in decisions to slow down, speed up, cancel, or modify projects. Utility companies may resist what they consider to be "commission interference," and commissions may resist being asked to give prior approval to major investment decisions, but commission involvement appears to be an essential ingredient in a viable capital budgeting system.

COMMISSION PARTICIPATION IN THE DECISION PROCESS. In some states, commissions have long had the authority to approve or reject major capital expenditure programs, and in most other states commissions have the right to approve or deny security issues, which gives them de facto authority to block projects. However, utility managements have traditionally regarded choosing the level and composition of the construction program as a management prerogative, hence have not actively solicited commission inputs into the process, while commissions have not sought active involvement or responsibility. Utilities have, for the most part, simply designed and built facilities (but obviously with the full knowledge of their commissions) and then, when the plants were completed, asked their commissions to put them into **rate base**.

As noted previously, in the pre-1970s era, this procedure worked well because costs were generally declining and demand increased at a steady, predictable rate. During the 1970s and 1980s however, costs rose dramatically, and demand has generally fallen short of the projections that were made at the time construction was begun. As a result, many electric utilities began plants, expecting their output to have a given cost and to be demanded in full, only to complete the project and find the cost per kilowatt-hour much higher than was originally forecasted and the plant not really needed because of lower than expected demand. As we noted earlier, consumer advocates have argued, often successfully, that these plants should not go into rate base, or that the company should be "punished" in some other way for having made a mistake. Even if plants are not excluded from rate base, questions of excess capacity or higher than required costs may delay rate case decisions, result in low authorized returns or phase-ins, or hurt the company and its investors in other ways.

In view of the very long construction periods for electric utility plants, and the volatile nature of both construction and fuel costs, planning is obviously difficult, and some mistakes will necessarily be made. In other words, risks are high. If the utilities were unregulated, then (1) the cost of *ex-post* errors would be borne by investors in the form of lower profits for some companies in some years, but (2) these risks would be priced into the cost of capital and would be reflected in both service rates and earned returns on investment. Manufacturing companies, for example, sometimes build excess capacity, or the wrong type of capacity, and suffer losses (or low rates of return) as a result; but over time these risks are compensated in the form of high (but variable) average returns. The customers of these firms pay for the inherent business risks through product prices.

Since utility plant is built for the benefit of customers, it has been argued that the customers should pay the costs associated with these plants, including the costs associated with "mistakes." These costs can be assessed in two different ways: (1) by permitting all plant to go immediately into rate base and to earn the cost of capital, or (2) by excluding certain plant, but recognizing the additional risk burden this throws on investors by allowing a higher rate of return on investment. Under the first procedure, the risks associated with a construction program would be borne directly by the utility's customers; under the second procedure, these risks would be borne directly by investors, who would be compensated for bearing them by a higher allowed and earned (on average) rate of return on invested capital.

It is debatable whether it would be better if construction risks were borne directly by investors or by customers. However, three things are clear:

1. Authorized and earned rates of return in earlier years were set by commissions, and accepted by investors, on the premise that customers would bear construction risks.

2. If it is decided that construction risks are to be allocated differently in the future, this decision should be reflected in authorized *"normal times" returns*. If failure is to be penalized, then success should be rewarded, and average returns over time should reflect the risk exposure of investors.

3. To the extent that the choice has not been explicitly made, a utility company's management is taking a tremendous chance if it goes forward with a major construction program, particularly one that involves new and unproved technology of any type. If the plant is built on time and at or under the projected cost, and if it operates at or better than expected efficiency, then the company's customers will benefit. If things do not work out well, the company's investors may be the ones who suffer. In other words, the company is taking a chance that the commission will end up playing "heads I win, tails you lose."

JOINT FACILITIES PLANNING. Some of the uncertainties inherent in construction planning could be reduced by cooperative planning and *joint ownership of facilities,* especially among the smaller utilities. For example, an electric company and its customers are exposed to increased risks if the utility relies on only one type of fuel. However, economies of scale are such that it would be inefficient for smaller utilities to have a good mix of plants that utilized different types of fuel. For instance, many utilities could not utilize all the output from several large coal and nuclear units, and unless they had several units of each type, they would be exposed to the risk of power shortages in the event of unscheduled plant outages. Similarly, to guard against plant failures, a smaller utility would have to have larger reserve margins than would a larger company with more units. Both types of problems can be reduced by cooperative planning, joint construction and ownership of plants, and **inter-tie arrangements** whereby utilities can buy or borrow power from neighboring companies. Cooperative arrangements of all types increased dramatically during the 1970s and 1980s, and it can be anticipated that this trend will continue in the years ahead.

COST OF CAPITAL

A utility must estimate its cost of capital for two major purposes: (1) as the requested rate of return in rate cases, and (2) as the discount rate for use in capital budgeting decisions. Each of these is discussed below.

COST OF CAPITAL IN RATE CASES. The **weighted average cost of capital**, k_a, set forth in Equation 1 below, is generally used as the basis for setting service rates in a rate case:

$$k_a = w_d k_d (1 - t) + w_p k_p + w_s k_s \tag{1}$$

Here, k_d is the cost of debt, k_p is the cost of preferred stock, and k_s is the cost of equity, while w_d, w_p, and w_s are the weights used for each of these items respectively in the firm's capital structure. The $(1 - t)$ term adjusts the cost of debt for taxes. For example, a utility with a capital structure containing 50% debt, 10% preferred, and 40% equity, and with costs of 10%, 12%, and 15% for these items respectively, assuming for simplicity that no taxes applied, would have a weighted average cost of capital of 12.2%:

$$\begin{aligned} k_a &= 0.5(10\%) \, (1 - 0) + 0.1(12\%) + 0.4(15\%) \\ &= 0.05 + 0.012 + 0.06 \\ &= 12.2\% \end{aligned}$$

The weights are generally based on the book value fractions of investor-supplied, long-term capital, although sometimes total debt rather than long-term debt is used. The costs of debt and preferred stock are the weighted averages of the historic costs of the outstanding debt and preferred, and they can be estimated precisely, and generally without much controversy. However, it is more difficult to estimate the cost of equity, and this is often a controversial issue in rate cases.

A landmark case decided by the U.S. Supreme Court in 1944 (*FPC v. Hope Natural Gas Co.*, 320 U.S. 591, 603 (1944)) established the general criteria for setting the rate of return on equity:

> The return to the equity owner should be commensurate with returns on investments in other enterprises having corresponding risks. That return, moreover, should be sufficient to assure confidence in the financial integrity of the enterprise, so as to maintain its credit and to attract capital.

The following procedures can be used to implement the Hope case requirements.

Comparable Earnings Method. The Hope decision did not specify how the return on equity should be measured. However, the method used at the time the case was tried was the comparable earnings method, whereby one calculates the average rate of return on book equity for a sample of companies that have risks comparable to those of the utility in question, and then allows the utility to earn a return equal to that average. The comparable earnings approach has two major problems:

1. Other utilities are more comparable, but their actual earned returns may be quite different from the rate of return that is required by investors; see Exhibit 3 for an example.
2. If nonutilities are used for the comparison, it is virtually impossible to establish comparability with regard to risk.

DCF Method. To avoid the very difficult problems associated with the comparable earnings approach, analysts in the mid-1960s began to use the constant growth discounted cash flow (DCF) method in order to estimate k_s, the cost of equity capital.

$$k_s = \frac{D_1}{P_0} + g \tag{2}$$

where D_1 is the dividend expected during the coming 12 months, P_0 is the current stock price, and g is the expected (constant) future growth rate in earnings, dividends, and the stock price. (See Brigham, *Financial Management: Theory and Practice*, 4th ed., Chapter 5, for an extended discussion of the **constant growth model**.)

The constant growth DCF model is, of course, appropriate only if the expected future growth rate is a constant. If growth is not expected to remain constant in the near future, a *nonconstant model* should be used. One such model that has been used in rate cases and is widely applied by **security analysts** in the investments business is the following:

$$P_0 = \sum_{t=1}^{n} \frac{D_t}{(1 + k_s)^t} + \left(\frac{D_n(1 + g)}{k_s - g}\right)\left(\frac{1}{1 + k_s}\right)^n \tag{3}$$

Here, n is a period during which growth is not expected to be constant, and g is the normal (and constant) growth rate expected to exist beyond Year n.

To illustrate both the constant and the nonconstant DCF models, we can use data on The Southern Company. Southern's stock has traded recently in the range of $19 to $21 (down from a 1965 high of over $36), and its expected dividend during the next 12 months is $2.00. Its past compound growth rates have been as follows:

	Dividends	Earnings	Stock Price	Book Value
1974–1984	2.7%	7.8%	8.2%	1.1%
1979–1985	3.5	14.7	10.4	2.0

Southern's **DCF dividend yield**, using $20 as P_0, is 10.0%:

$$\frac{D_1}{P_0} = \frac{\$\ 2.00}{\$20.00} = 10.0\%$$

The proper value for Southern's expected future growth rate is not obvious from the data shown above. Indeed, the only conclusions we can reach from examining the historic growth rates are that (1) they certainly are not constant, and (2) by selecting data series and time periods, many different growth rates can be calculated. Thus, most objective analysts have come to follow the lead of Myron Gordon, the man who pioneered the DCF model (often called the **Gordon model**) in a rate case involving AT&T heard before the Federal Communications Commission. That is, they estimate the expected future growth rate as $g = b(ROE)$, where b is the fraction of earnings the utility will probably retain in the future and ROE is the expected future return on equity. If Southern earns 15% on equity and retains 30% of its earnings (these values are good ballpark figures and are consistent with most analysts' expectations), its future growth rate will be 4.5%. Indeed, the consensus long-run growth rate forecast of security analysts as reported by the Institutional Brokers Estimate System (IBES) is 5%.

Combining the expected dividend yield with the expected growth rate gives an indicated DCF cost of capital of about 14.5%:

$$k_s = \frac{D_1}{P_0} + g = 10.0\% + 4.5\% = 14.5\%$$

The nonconstant growth model is a bit more complicated to utilize. It requires estimates of dividends on an individual year basis during the period of nonconstant growth, as well as the expected constant growth rate beyond the nonconstant period, and it requires that one solve an equation to obtain the value of k. The best and most objective sources of data for the nonconstant model are reports published by security analysts. Using data on The Southern Company from the report of **Value Line**, a major investment advisory service, we can illustrate Equation 3:

Projected retention rate in 1989:   b = 30.00%
Projected ROE in 1989 (and assumed
    constant beyond 1989):   ROE = 15.00%
Derived long-run growth rate: g = b(ROE) =   4.50%

Dividend projections (shown in the following equation):

$$\$20.00 = \frac{\$2.00}{(1+k_s)^1} + \frac{\$2.15}{(1+k_s)^2} + \frac{\$2.30}{(1+k_s)^3} + \frac{\$2.45}{(1+k_s)^4} + \left(\frac{\$2.45(1.045)}{k_s - 0.045}\right)\left(\frac{1}{1+k_s}\right)^4$$

This equation has but one unknown, k_s, so it can be solved to determine the value of k_s. The solution value, obtained by using the internal rate of return function on a hand-held financial calculator, is 15.12%. This is an estimate of Southern's DCF cost of equity based on the nonconstant growth model.

Risk Premium Method. Equity is riskier than debt, and investors must be compensated for bearing the additional risks of holding stock rather than bonds. Recognizing this fact, analysts frequently estimate the cost of equity by adding to a bond rate an estimated **risk premium**:

$$k_s = \text{Riskless (or low-risk) rate} + \text{Risk premium} \qquad (4)$$
$$= R_F + RP$$

The company's own bond rate, or else the yield on long-term U.S. Treasury bonds, can be used for R_F. The risk premium term (RP) is more difficult to estimate. (See E.F. Brigham, D. Shome, and S. Vinson, "The Risk Premium Approach to Measuring a Utility's Cost of Equity," *Financial Management*, Spring 1985, for a discussion.) Research suggests that the risk premium over Treasury bonds is in the range of 4-5 percentage points for most electric and telephone companies, and that it is 3-4 percentage points over the companies' own current bond yields. Thus, when the Treasury bond rate is 10.5% and its subsidiaries' bonds are yielding about 11.5%, The Southern Company's cost of equity would be estimated to be in the range of 14.5 to 15.5%.

Capital Asset Pricing Model (CAPM). The CAPM is a special, rigorous version of the risk premium method. To use the CAPM, this formula is applied:

$$k_s = R_F + b(k_M - R_F) \qquad (5)$$

Here R_F is a **risk-free rate,** k_M is the expected rate of return on an average stock (the market), and b is a stock's **beta coefficient.** Beta measures the relative volatility of stocks, with average stocks having betas equal to 1.0, less volatile stocks having betas less than 1.0, and more volatile stocks having betas greater than 1.0. (The concept of the CAPM is discussed at length in Chapter 6 of *Financial Management* 4th edition, by Brigham, Dryden Press, 1985.)

The CAPM is a great favorite among many academicians, and it has been applied fairly often in rate cases. However, most authorities who have actually tried to apply the CAPM in rate cases have concluded that while it appears to be quite precise, objective, and free of biases and judgments, it is actually highly judgmental, though the judgments are well hidden.

The vast amount of literature available on the **CAPM** (see References and Bibliography at the end of the section) makes clear the dangers lurking in the CAPM for use in rate cases, but one example can be used to illustrate the point. A witness, who shall remain nameless, testified against some 15 to 20 utilities, including The Southern Company's subsidiary, Georgia Power, in the late 1970s. His recommendations were adopted, or at least given heavy weight, by a number of commissions, including that of the State of Georgia. He used the 30-day Treasury bill rate for R_F, a beta that was generally very close to 0.7 for electric and telephone companies, and a market risk premium $(k_M - R_F)$ equal to about 7.8% based on data going back to 1926. When he began testifying, Treasury bills generally had yields in the 4.5 to 6.5% range, so his CAPM cost of capital estimates for companies such as Georgia Power generally fell into the range of 10 to 12%:

$$k_s = 4.5\% + 0.7(7.8\%) = 4.5\% + 5.5\% = 10\%$$

$$k_s = 6.5\% + 0.7(7.8\%) = 6.5\% + 5.5\% = 12\%$$

These numbers were quite satisfactory to many consumer groups, and the witness was in great demand to testify in rate cases. However, the application of his methodology in 1980, when Treasury bill rates were quite high, produced cost of equity estimates of over 23%:

$$k_s = 17.9\% + 0.7(7.8\%) = 17.9\% + 5.5\% = 23.4\%$$

Other methods put Georgia Power's 1980 cost of equity in the 17 to 18% range. To most observers, this demonstrates a basic problem in the CAPM approach when applied to public utilities.

ADJUSTMENT FOR FLOTATION COSTS. The **DCF, risk premium,** and **CAPM methods** produce **market value** or **bare bones** cost estimates which must be increased somewhat to recognize the **flotation expenses** and **market pressure** associated with new stock offerings. Underwriting costs and expenses average about 4% of gross proceeds for utility stock offerings (see R.H. Pettway, "A Note on Flotation Costs of New Equity Capital Issues of Electric Companies," *Public Utilities Fortnightly*, March 18, 1982, pp. 68–69), while market pressure (the temporary decline in a stock's price when the company adds to the supply of shares through a new offering) amounts to about 1%. Thus, total issuance costs amount to about 5% of gross proceeds.

There has been a great deal of controversy regarding both the size and the proper treatment of issuance costs. First, while all studies we have ever seen indicate the existence of pressure, on average, when new stock is sold, stock prices are influenced by many factors, so it is difficult to determine statistically the precise effects of new issues. Commissions are reluctant to allow companies to recover costs that cannot be measured with precision, so they have been disinclined to allow recovery of the market pressure portion of issuance costs. Second, there has been a great deal of confusion regarding the recovery of issuance costs by utilities that have not issued stock recently and which have no plans for issuing stock in the foreseeable future. Still, if a company issued stock in the past, incurred costs when that stock was issued, and was not allowed to recover those costs as an expense at the time of the issuance, then some procedure is required for recovery, or else stockholders will simply incur a loss.

To illustrate this point, assume that a newly formed utility sells $10 million of stock, incurs issuance costs of 5%, and then nets $9.5 million. Assume further that the DCF bare-bones cost of equity is $k = D_1/P_0 + g = 10\% + 5\% = 15\%$. Investors expect a 15% return on the $10 million they put up, not on the $9.5 million the company nets from the sale. If the company earns only 15% on $9.5 million, then its market value will drop to $9.5 million, and investors will have taken an immediate loss equal to the $500,000 of flotation expenses.

Three procedures could be used to offset this result:

1. The $500,000 could be treated as an expense in the year the issue was sold and be recovered from customers in that year. However, that would produce a mismatch between the beneficiaries of the cost (that is, future customers, because equity is used to buy assets which in turn provide service to customers in the indefinite future) and those required to pay for the cost. Hence, this procedure would represent poor regulatory policy and is not typically used.

2. The **flotation costs** could be capitalized and included in rate base. Under this procedure, the company would receive a return of $0.15(\$500,000) = \$75,000$ in perpetuity on its investment in flotation costs. This is probably the most rational policy, but it has not been used in the past.

3. The cost of equity could be adjusted by use of this formula:

$$k_{adjusted} = \frac{D_1}{P_0(1-F)} + g = \frac{D_1/P_0}{1-F} + g \qquad (6)$$

where F is the percentage flotation expense (including market pressure). In our example, $k_{adjusted}$ would be 15.53%:

$$k_{adjusted} = \frac{10\%}{0.95} + 5\% = 10.53\% + 5\% = 15.53\%$$

The stock would have a book value of $9.5 million, but its market value would be $10 million, the amount investors put up in the first place. The adjusted rate of return must be applied to all equity, including retained earnings. This point can be demonstrated mathematically, but we know of no easy, intuitive way to explain it. Perhaps the most comforting statement we can make is that revenue requirements under this procedure are identical to those that occur under the capitalization procedure. (See Brigham, Aberwald, and Gapenski, "Common Equity Flotation Costs and Rate Making," *Public Utilities Fortnightly*, May 2, 1985, for a further discussion.)

These points have been discussed at length in rate cases, and also in generic proceedings before the Federal Energy Regulatory Commission and the Federal Communications Commission. Although commissions do occasionally follow theoretically correct procedures, many simply ignore flotation costs unless a company is expected to sell new stock in the near future. As a result, there has been a systematic underrecovery of flotation costs in the utility industries.

COST OF CAPITAL FOR CAPITAL BUDGETING. The discount rate used to evaluate capital expenditure proposals, which is different from the cost of capital for ratemaking purposes, is estimated as follows:

1. The proper debt component is the **after-tax cost of new debt,** not the weighted average (or "embedded") interest rate on outstanding debt. Thus, for a company whose embedded cost of debt is 8%, whose effective tax rate is $t = 40\%$, and whose interest rate on new debt is 12%, the cost of debt for capital budgeting purposes is $k_d(1-t) = 12\%(0.6) = 7.2\%$.

2. The preferred stock component is the **flotation-adjusted yield on new preferred,** not the embedded cost of preferred. Thus, for a company whose embedded cost of preferred is 10% but whose preferred currently has a yield of 11%, and assuming that flotation costs of new preferred would be 3%, the cost of preferred for capital budgeting purposes is $k_p = 11\%/(1-0.03) = 11.34\%$.

3. The proper cost of equity is the flotation-adjusted cost of equity as calculated above.

4. A weighted average cost of capital should then be developed, using as weights the actual percentages of each type of capital, including deferred taxes, that the company expects to raise in the future, not the balance sheet capital structure. For example the balance sheet might show 50% debt, 10% preferred, and 40% common equity, but the company might have a target capital structure of 45% debt, 10% preferred, and 45% common, and it might be planning to raise capital in the future in these proportions. Then, with the numbers shown above, its basic cost of capital for capital budgeting purposes would be

$$
\begin{aligned}
k_a &= 0.45(k_d)(1 - t) + 0.10(k_p) + 0.45(k_s) \\
&= 0.45(7.2\%) + 0.10(11.3\%) + 0.45(15.5\%) \\
&= 11.4\%
\end{aligned}
$$

Several other points should be noted in connection with the cost of capital for capital budgeting purposes. First, since actual market costs are used, they can be expected to vary substantially over time, causing significant changes in the estimated average cost of capital, k_a. This may mean, for example, that a decision to build a nuclear plant made when the cost of capital was low may not look good later on if the cost of capital rises. This problem can be alleviated by the use of **futures** contracts, which can, to a large extent, enable companies to hedge against changes in money costs during a construction cycle.

Second, **depreciation** is a major source of funds for capital budgeting, yet no mention was made of it above. The reason is that the cost of depreciation, for a nonliquidating company, is approximately equal to the weighted average cost of capital as calculated above (see Brigham, *Financial Management*, 4th ed., Dryden Press, Chapter 7).

Third, the cost of capital is often an increasing function of the amount of capital raised during a given period of time. This means that if a company undertakes an exceptionally large construction program (relative to its "normal" situation), its cost of capital will be higher than normal, other things held constant. From this it follows that when comparing two major mutually exclusive projects with radically different capital costs (for example, a nuclear plant and a coal-fired plant), it may be appropriate to evaluate the larger project using a higher cost of capital.

Fourth, different types of projects often differ in risk, and it is appropriate to evaluate riskier projects using a somewhat higher cost of capital. Unfortunately, there is no precise method of measuring relative project risk, nor is there a precise way of estimating just how project risk affects the cost of capital. Still, if management judges one project to be riskier than another, then the riskier project should be evaluated with a somewhat higher cost of capital.

CAPITAL STRUCTURE

Establishing the **target capital structure** for a utility is a major task, and a highly controversial one. The academic and professional literature offers quite a bit of advice on the subject, but, unfortunately, different advisors frequently offer conflicting advice, and no one can prove his position. To complicate the matter still further, most of the theoretical academic work on capital structure has been implicitly addressed to unregulated industrial concerns, and major changes are required to apply the theory to utilities.

CAPITAL STRUCTURE THEORY. The theory of capital structure is based on **valuation:** the relationship between the value of a firm and its capital structure is set forth, and then, based on this value/capital structure relationship, the relationship between capital structure and the cost of capital is established. For an **unregulated firm,** value increases with debt because interest on debt is tax deductible: therefore, the greater the use of debt, the larger the proportion of operating income that goes to investors, and hence the greater the value of the firm. However, there are offsets to the tax advantage of debt:

1. The probability of bankruptcy, with its attendant costs, increases with leverage.
2. Firms that have high levels of debt are cut off from the capital markets during credit crunches, thus impairing operations.
3. Managements of firms with an excessive amount of leverage are often more preoccupied with raising capital, or even with survival, than with operations, and therefore efficiency suffers.
4. Both the monetary and the nonmonetary costs associated with debt and preferred stock rise sharply if the use of leverage is excessive.

These considerations give rise to value/capital structure and cost of capital/capital structure relationships like those shown in Exhibit 4. Note particularly that the capital structure that maximizes the firm's value also minimizes its weighted average cost of capital; this particular capital structure is defined as the **optimal capital structure.**

The situation is conceptually different for a public utility. Theoretically, a utility should be allowed to earn its cost of capital, no more and no less. Furthermore, if it does earn its cost of capital, its stock will sell at just over book value. Therefore, a utility's stock price should remain constant regardless of its capital structure. There are, of course, tax benefits from the use of leverage, but these benefits accrue to ratepayers, not to stockholders. Therefore, for a utility, the "net addition of leverage to value" in Exhibit 4 should be relabeled "net value of leverage to ratepayers," and the value of a utility should remain constant at the level V_0. The "cost of capital" section of the exhibit remains unchanged.

EXHIBIT 4   RELATIONSHIP AMONG STOCK PRICE, COST OF CAPITAL, AND LEVERAGE

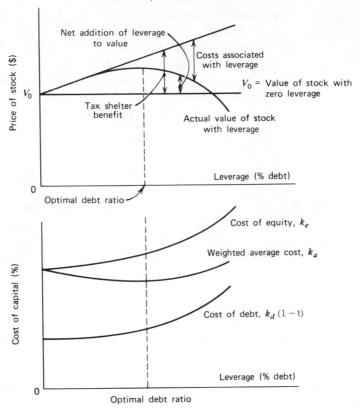

Under any reasonable set of circumstances, a utility's management would have no reason to establish any capital structure other than the one that minimizes its weighted average cost of capital and thereby minimizes customers' charges, for stockholders would not be helped or hindered by the selection of one capital structure or another.

CAPITAL STRUCTURE IN RATE CASES. Utilities' equity ratios have been rising in recent years. After hitting a low of 31.7% in 1974, the industry average equity/assets ratio was up to 40% in 1984, and most analysts expect the average ratio to continue increasing. There are three basic reasons for these changes: (1) In the 1960s and earlier, interest rates were low relative to earned returns on equity, thus permitting interest coverages of about four times (which is necessary for an A or better bond rating) to be achieved with a relatively low equity ratio. Since then, interest rates have risen much more than returns on equity, so a higher equity ratio is now required for any specified **interest coverage ratio.** (2) Utilities' business risks have increased due to increased competition, greater forecasting difficulties, nuclear problems, and the like. As business risk increases, logic suggests that financial risks associated with the use of debt should be reduced, and this, in turn, suggests that equity ratios should be increased. (3) For most of the 1970s and early 1980s, most utilities were engaged in major construction programs which required large amounts of external capital. Further, their stocks were selling at prices substantially below book value, which made stock sales unattractive, and their earned ROEs were low, which held down retained earnings. Those conditions led to a heavy use of debt. Lately, with construction programs winding down, stock prices up, and earned ROEs at historically high levels, the utilities have had the ability to build their equity ratios toward the levels required as a result of (1) and (2) just above.

In rate cases, utilities' opponents are increasingly arguing that the capital structure employed by the company is nonoptimal. They then state an opinion as to the **optimal capital structure,** calculate an average cost of capital based on this hypothetical capital structure, and recommend that the company be allowed to earn this hypothetical return rather than a return based on its actual capital structure. Invariably, the hypothetical capital structure calls for the use of more debt than the company actually uses, and the resulting average cost of capital is always lower than what the company requests.

In looking at the application of these hypothetical capital structures, observers could be struck with two thoughts:

1. The utilities' opponents have little or no basis for asserting that the companies' capital structures have too little debt. However, the companies' positions are not much stronger.
2. The adjustments (increases) in the cost of both debt and equity that would be necessary if the capital structure were changed either are not made or are arrived at in some unsupported and essentially arbitrary manner.

In truth, it is impossible to identify and to prove the existence of an optimal capital structure (see Brigham, Aberwald, and Gapenski, ''Effects of Capital Structure on Utilities' Costs of Capital and Revenue Requirements''). *Academicians* can offer advice about the factors that enter into the determination of the optimal structure, and **investment bankers** and other professionals can give their opinions on what type of financing a company should employ, but nobody can truly prove his position. This being the case, how should a company and its commission approach the capital structure issue? Probably the best solution would be for a company and its commission to meet (outside of the pressures of a rate case), discuss the company's long-term financial plans, and decide jointly what the company will do and how the commission will treat the capital structure in future rate cases. Obviously, as conditions change, plans will need to be modified; so periodic meetings would be necessary.

Commissions and managements may resist the preceding suggestion on the grounds that financing decisions are a management prerogative, and also that regulatory commissions have little expertise in these matters. This may be true, but if a commission is going to get into the business of making de facto capital structure decisions, this ought to be done outside the framework of a rate case, and the regulated company ought to have time to adjust to the mandated capital structure before this capital structure is used as a basis for ratemaking decisions.

PARENT–SUBSIDIARY ISSUES. If an operating utility is a subsidiary of a holding company, three complications may arise. First, the subsidiaries may have capital structures and component costs somewhat different from one another, or from that of the consolidated company. Second, the parent company may have its own debt, and some of this debt may have been used to acquire the equity of the subsidiaries—this is the **"double leverage"** issue. Third, if the utility has unregulated subsidiaries, the two previously mentioned problems may be exacerbated.

Differences among Subsidiaries. The **Holding Company Act of 1934** does not permit electric utility holding companies to issue long-term debt for the purpose of injecting equity into a subsidiary. However, the different subsidiaries of a utility holding company can and often do have significantly different capital structures, embedded costs of debt and preferred, and different costs of equity. To illustrate, in 1980 two Southern Company subsidiaries, Georgia Power and Alabama Power, had ratios of equity to total capital of 32.0 and 27.7% respectively, bonds with different ratings, and different embedded costs of debt and preferred stock. Southern's consolidated figures are an average, lying between those of the subsidiaries.

There is precedent in rate cases for treating each subsidiary independently and also for using the consolidated capital structure and the systemwide embedded cost of debt. Either procedure can be justified, and the results are not generally materially different regardless of which approach is used, *provided all jurisdictions use the same procedure.* However, if one procedure is used in one jurisdiction and the other in another state, the result can be either an overstatement or an understatement of costs for the system. For example, suppose a holding company's consolidated capital structure and component costs are as follows:

Holding Company

		Weight	×	Cost	=	Product
Debt	$100	50%		9%		4.5%
Preferred	20	10		10		1.0
Common	80	40		15		6.0
	$200	100%				11.5% = k_a

Its two subsidiaries each have the same structure and both are assigned the parent's cost of equity. But, because its recent growth has been quite rapid, Subsidiary B has sold most of its debt and preferred in the recent high-rate market, so its embedded costs of debt and preferred are relatively high:

Subsidiary A

		Weight	×	Cost	=	Product
Debt	$50	50%		8%		4.0%
Preferred	10	10		9		0.9
Common	40	40		15		6.0
	$100	100%				10.9% = k_a

Subsidiary B

		Weight	×	Cost	=	Product
Debt	$50	50%		10%		5.0%
Preferred	10	10		11		1.1
Common	40	40		15		6.0
	$100	100%				12.1% = k_a

If Subsidiary A is allowed to earn 10.9% and Subsidiary B earns 12.1%, the parent company will earn its 11.5% cost of capital. The parent would also earn its required return if both subsidiaries earned 11.5%. However, if the commission in Subsidiary A's state used the individual company method and authorized 10.9%, while B's commission adopted the consolidated method and authorized 11.5%, then the parent company would earn only $0.5(10.9\%) + 0.5(11.5\%) = 11.2\%$, which is below its cost of capital.

Similar, but more complex, problems can arise if the different subsidiaries have different capital structures, and if different equity capital costs are assigned to the various subsidiaries. These problems can become quite severe if a large number of subsidiaries are involved, as is the case in the **telephone industry.** The only rational solution to this situation is through some type of agreement among commissions on how the **multistate holding companies** are to be regulated, but at present no such agreement exists, and this has contributed to the telephone companies' financial problems.

Double Leverage. Double leverage exists whenever a holding company has outstanding, at the parent company level, debt that has been used to buy the equity of the subsidiaries. The double leverage situation is trivial in the electric industry because of the Holding Company Act's prohibition of parent company debt, but it does exist in the telephone industry. To illustrate, consider the following tabulation of assets versus claims for a parent company with two subsidiaries.

Parent Company

Assets		Claims	
Investment in operating companies	$200	Debt (10%)	$100
		Equity (15%)	100
	$200		$200

$$k_a = 0.5(10\%) + 0.5(15\%) = 12.5\%$$

Subsidiary A (Wholly Owned)

Operating assets	$200	Debt (10%)	$100
		Equity (all from parent)	100
	$200		$200

Subsidiary B (Wholly Owned)

Operating assets	$200	Debt (10%)	$100
		Equity (all from parent)	100
	$200		$200

Consolidated

Operating assets	$400	Debt (parent)	$100
		Debt (subs)	200
		Equity	100
	$400		$400

Now assume that all debt has a cost of 10%, and that the parent's cost of equity is 15%. The cost of capital to the subsidiaries for ratemaking purposes could be calculated in any of the following ways, but only the first two are correct:

1. Based on consolidated data:

$$k_a = 0.75(10\%) + 0.25(15\%) = 11.25\%$$

2. Double leverage: Use parent's average cost of capital as the cost of equity for the subsidiary:

$$k_{a(parent)} = 0.5(10\%) + 0.5(15\%) = 12.5\%$$
$$k_{a(sub)} = 0.5(10\%) + 0.5(12.5\%) = 11.25\%$$

3. Wrong. Use parent's cost of equity and subsidiary's own capital structure:

$$k_a = 0.5(10\%) + 0.5(15\%) = 12.5\%,$$

which is too high.

This is all simple enough as long as the two subsidiaries have identical capital structures, and as long as the parent company has no assets except its investment in subsidiaries. However, subsidiaries generally do not have identical capital structures; most of the major telephone companies, where double leverage concepts are especially important, do have substantial amounts of other assets; and much of the parent company's debt is used to support the investment in these other assets rather than to buy the equity of the subsidiaries. Because the subsidiaries do have different capital structures, the utilities' opponents can attempt to "whipsaw" the companies by using whatever combination of capital structure and embedded costs produces the lowest calculated return for the jurisdiction in question, regardless of practices in other jurisdictions, and regardless of whether, in total, the parent can earn its overall cost of capital. Similarly, but more important, utility opponents can make the implicit assumptions that (1) all assets owned by the parent company are equally risky and (2) parent company debt is used to acquire stock in subsidiaries rather than in other types of assets, and, on the basis of these assumptions, they can develop a weighted average cost of capital and then use it as the cost of equity for the subsidiaries as was done in Method 2, **double leverage,** above. Although much has been written about double leverage in the literature, these issues are far from resolved.

DIVIDEND POLICY

Electric, gas, and telephone utilities generally pay out 65 to 75% of their earnings as dividends in comparison to about 40% for the average industrial company. The utilities' high **payout ratios** were, prior to the 1980s, something of an anomaly in the eyes of some academicians, who suggested that companies that need large amounts of new equity capital should have low payout ratios. (See Brigham, *Financial Management*, Chapter 13, and the section entitled "Dividend Policy" of this *Handbook* for a discussion.) This difference between what these academicians say the companies ought to be doing and what they actually were doing has two possible causes: (1) utility company managements are misguided, or (2) there is something wrong with the academic theory as applied to utilities.

HIGH PAYOUT RATIOS: THEORY AND PRACTICE. It is impossible to prove which position is correct, and a case can be made for each of them. The academic position, set forth in most basic textbooks, in essence is this:

1. There are reasons that would lead some investors to prefer **dividends** to **reinvestment and capital gains** (a need for current cash income, and possibly less risk in cash-in-hand dividends versus hoped-for-capital gains). On the other hand, there are reasons for some investors to prefer reinvestment and capital gains (primarily the lower tax rate on capital gains income). It is impossible to decide on a theoretical basis how these two opposing forces offset one another, and empirical investigations of the issue have been inconclusive.

2. However, it does seem clear that because of **flotation costs** involved with the issuance of new stock, the greater the need of a company for new equity capital, the lower its dividend payout ratio should be. Therefore, since utilities needed large amounts of new equity in the 1970s, they should have had low payout ratios. Since their actual payouts were high, management was acting contrary to the basic principles of financial theory.

On the other hand, knowledgeable investment bankers have asserted that academic theory simply does not hold in the case of the utilities. Their argument goes like this:

1. Traditionally, the utilities were regarded as being safe, "widow and orphan" stocks that were suited for retirees and others who needed safe, assured income. Because of their "clientele" of stockholders who wanted high current income, the utilities paid out a high percentage of their earnings as dividends.

2. In the 1970s, because of **regulatory lag** and other problems, the utilities' perceived risk vis-à-vis the industrials rose, yet their ROEs did not rise to keep pace with their increasing costs of capital. This caused the prices of their stocks to decline, and most of them have sold below book value during most of the 1970s. (See Exhibit 3.)

3. The more sophisticated investors (especially institutional investors) have largely abandoned the utility stocks. (Approximately 95% of the utilities' stocks are presently owned by individuals and only 5% by institutions, in comparison to 60% of the industrials' stocks owned by individuals and 40% by institutions.) The current owners of utility stocks are (1) very much income oriented, (2) generally retirees or others on relatively low fixed incomes, hence in low tax brackets, and (3) not very sophisticated.

4. To an unusually large degree, utility stocks are "sold" rather than "bought"; that is, stockbrokers must solicit purchasers of utility stocks rather than having potential investors come to them with buy orders.

5. The major competition for utility investors' capital includes bonds, bank certificates, and other securities that are oriented toward yield (as opposed to growth).

6. Therefore, if a utility needs to raise new equity capital, the investment bankers find it easier to interest purchasers if the stocks pay a high dividend, and thus compete well with bonds in terms of current income, than if the stocks paid lower dividends but promised higher future growth rates. In other words, to sell to the people who buy utility stocks, brokers find it easier to base their pitch on dividend yield than on total return.

There is probably some truth in both the academic and the investment banking positions—the academic position is logical, but it may not hold because the sophisticated investors who are needed to make markets efficient have deserted the utility stocks. This desertion has occurred because of the decade-long experience of the utilities with regulatory problems, returns less than the cost of capital, declining stock prices (both absolute and relative to the industrials), and other problems. Thus, one may conclude that the utilities' dividend policy is probably not the one they should be following, nor the one they would be following if they had been earning their costs of capital, but it was the only policy they could follow under the conditions they faced.

DIVERSIFICATION. Because construction programs are currently low as a result of excess capacity, many utilities currently have cash flows in excess of funds needed for construction and other internal uses. As noted in an earlier section, some of these excess funds are being used to pay off debt and thus to raise equity ratios, but there are limits to that usage. Increasingly, utilities are investing surplus cash flows outside the utility industry, in unregulated businesses. This is commonly called **diversification.**

Diversification raises several important financial issues. First, it makes estimation of the cost of equity more difficult. A DCF analysis necessarily focuses on the entire company— we can find a DCF cost of capital for a publicly owned company, but such a cost reflects the riskiness inherent in the company as a whole. Now suppose a utility owns unregulated subsidiaries (or suppose the utility is part of a holding company which also owns unregulated subsidiaries). The publicly owned company whose DCF cost of equity is found has a risk which is a weighted average of the risks of its major subsidiaries. If utility operations are less risky than the unregulated operations, then the DCF cost of equity will overstate the cost of equity that should be earned on the equity portion of the utility's capital, and vice versa if the utility's risks are greater than the corporate average. Further, the utility may have a different capital structure than the other subsidiaries, so *the weighted average cost of capital might be different for the utility, the diversified subsidiaries, and the consolidated corporation.*

A second problem, or at least a potential problem, created by diversification involves *cost allocations*. If its profits are limited by regulation for the utility portion of its business, a holding company system that owned both utility and unregulated subsidiaries could maximize total corporate profits by assigning joint costs to the utility to the greatest possible extent. Those costs would then be passed on to the utility's customers, while the unregulated part of the business would enjoy high profits because costs which should have been assigned to it are actually being borne by the utility's customers. This problem could be controlled by a good audit system, but without controls it could be a serious problem.

The third problem with diversification is the reverse of the second. It has been argued by a number of security analysts that if a utility diversifies and loses money (or earns subnormal returns), its regulators will allow it to keep the losses, but if it is successful and earns high returns, its regulators will attempt to expropriate those returns for the benefit of the utility customers. Such **expropriation** could occur, indirectly, by the commission's simply authorizing low returns on utility operations. The business as a whole would still be healthy, as subnormal returns on utility operations would be offset by high returns on unregulated assets.

Expropriation could also occur directly. For example, the Staff of the New York Public Utility Commission recommended that the higher of (1) 25% of net income or (2) 1% of gross sales of diversified subsidiaries be paid as "royalties" to the utility and used to reduce rates. The Staff's logic in support of this procedure was that (1) costs would be allocated to the utility improperly in spite of audits designed to prevent such actions and (2) since utilities' subsidiaries could capitalize on the good names of the affiliated utilities, the royalty payments should compensate the utilities for these benefits. Both the legal and the factual basis for the Staff's position is currently being debated in a proceeding before the New York Commission, but the very fact that the Staff has taken such a position does point out the dangers faced by a utility that diversifies into unregulated businesses.

UTILITY OPERATIONS IN THE FUTURE

The utility industry is today in transition. The electrics, after facing steadily increasing demand and a persistent need to expand from their inception in the late 1900s to the 1970s, now face relatively slow growth and a substantial amount of excess capacity. Most companies will not, under currently forecasted demand conditions, need new generating capacity until the year 2000 or thereabouts, so they will not need to spend much money on construction until the mid-1990s. In the meantime, cash flows (net income plus depreciation) from existing operations will exceed funds needed for operations. These surplus funds can be used (1) to build liquid assets, at least up to a point, (2) to increase dividends, although utilities already have very high payout ratios, (3) to retire debt, at least until capital structures become topheavy with equity, and (4) to invest in unregulated subsidiaries. Our guess is that all four actions will occur, especially the latter, although it remains to be seen how successful utility executives will be at running unregulated enterprises and, if they are successful, to what extent the profits from these investments will accrue to stockholders.

The electric companies will probably be quite strong—with relatively low debt ratios, high coverages, and good liquid asset positions—going into the 1990s. Then times may start to get tougher. The next generation of plants will have a much higher cost per unit of capacity than plants now in use. Therefore, when those plants go into service in the late 1990s, the situation could be similar to that faced by the companies building nuclear units today. Further, the companies will probably see a need to start building in the early 1990s, but because of the uncertainties of demand forecasting, including those caused by cogeneration, they cannot be sure the plants will actually be needed when they are scheduled for completion. The companies will try to get regulators to agree that the plants are needed, and to agree to allow them in rate base when they are completed. The companies will also seek to avoid rate shock by putting some CWIP into rate base during the construction phase (and thus produce some rate increases before the plants are completed) and by phasing that part of the plants not covered by CWIP-in-rate-base in after they are completed.

If the commissions do not agree in advance to do something to reduce the risks of construction and rate shock, then the utilities may have difficulty raising the capital needed to finance the next generation of plants. Investors were badly burned during the 1970s, and they may remember that experience and resist supplying capital to the industries, or supply it only at a very high cost.

We also foresee increased competition in the electric industry, and greater **price elasticity** than has existed in the past. Depending on how technology develops, large industrial and commercial customers may be able to generate their own power at costs comparable to those of the utilities. There may also be sales of power from utilities in one region to customers in another region, with the utility in the customer's area **"wheeling"** the power through its transmission lines. This has been happening in the gas industry, where large customers have lined up their own low-cost gas supplies and then used pipelines as common carriers to bring in the gas.

The telephone industry is in an equal or greater state of flux. The long distance market is essentially unregulated, and no one knows how that business will end up. The local telephone companies are receiving subsidies in the form of access fees, but those fees lead to bypass if they are set too high, and possibly to inadequate profits and/or rates that are politically "too high" if they are set too low. The telephone companies—especially the Bell regional companies—are generating cash much like the electric companies, and they are building equity ratios and diversifying as fast as or faster than the electrics. They do not face the same future construction problems as the electrics, but due to the threat of **bypass,** their future is just as cloudy.

In conclusion, only three things are certain: death, taxes, and the fact that utility stocks aren't for widows and orphans anymore, even though they may look good now.

REFERENCES AND BIBLIOGRAPHY

BankAmeriLease Group, *On-the-Spot Leasing for Utilities*, BankAmeriLease Group, San Francisco, 1978.

Bierman, Harold, Jr., and Hass, Jerome E., "Equity Flotation Cost Adjustments in Utilities' Cost of Service," *Public Utilities Fortnightly*, March 1, 1984, pp. 46–49.

Bower, Richard S., "The Capital Recovery Question: An Overview," Dartmouth College, April 1984.

Bowyer, J.W., and Yawitz, J.B., "The Effect of New Equity Issues on Utility Stock Prices," *Public Utilities Fortnightly*, May 22, 1980, pp. 25–28.

Brigham, Eugene F., *Financial Management: Theory and Practice*, Dryden Press, Hinsdale, IL, 4th ed., 1985.

———, Aberwald, Dana, and Gapenski, Louis C., "Common Equity Flotation Costs and Rate Making," *Public Utilities Fortnightly*, May 2, 1985, pp. 28–36.

———, ———, and ———, "Effects of Capital Structure on Utilities' Costs of Capital and Revenue Requirements," University of Florida, Public Utility Research Center, June 1986.

———, and Crum, Roy L., "On the Use of the CAPM in Public Utility Rate Cases," *Financial Management*, Summer 1977, pp. 7–15.

———, and Nantell, T.J., "Normalization versus Flow Through for Utilities," *Accounting Review*, July 1974, pp. 436–477.

———, and Pappas, James L., *Liberalized Depreciation and the Cost of Capital*, Michigan State University, Institute of Public Utilities, 1970.

———, Shome, D.K., and Vinson, Steve R., "The Risk Premium Approach to Measuring a Utility's Cost of Equity," *Financial Management*, Spring 1985, pp. 33–45.

———, ———, ———, and Balakrishnan, C., "The Treatment of CWIP," University of Florida, Public Utility Research Center, December 1982.

Brown, L.D., and Rozeff, M.S., "The Superiority of Analyst Forecasts as Measures of Expectations," *Journal of Finance*, March 1978, pp. 1–16.

Deloitte, Haskins, and Sells, *Public Utilities Manual*, Public Document No. 8003, Government Printing Office, Washington, D.C., 1980.

Easterbrook, F.H., "Two Agency-Cost Explanations of Dividends," *American Economic Review*, September 1984, pp. 650–659.

Evans, Robert E., "On the Existence, Measurement, and Economic Significance of Market Pressure in the Pricing of New Equity Shares," Ph.D. thesis, Department of Economics, University of Wisconsin, 1978.

Gordon, Myron J., *The Cost of Capital to a Public Utility*, Michigan State University, Institute of Public Utilities, 1974.

Harrington, Diana R., "The Capital Asset Pricing Model and Regulated Utility Cost of Equity Estimation," D.B.A. dissertation, University of Virginia, 1978.

Ibbotson, R.G., and Sinquefield, R.A., *Stocks, Bonds, Bills, and Inflation: 1985 Yearbook*, Ibbotson Associates, Capital Markets Research Center, Chicago, IL.

Kahn, Alfred E., *The Economics of Regulation: Principles and Institutions*, vols. I and II, Wiley, New York, 1970.

Linke, C.M., "Estimating Growth Expectations for AT&T: A Survey Approach," Washington, D.C., Advanced Seminar on Earnings Regulation, November 1981.

Luftig, Mark D., and Enholm, G.B., *Nuclear Power Plants under Construction*, New York, Salomon Brothers, September 1985.

Lynch, Jones, and Ryan, Institutional Brokers Estimate System, *Monthly Summary Data*, New York, 1985.

Morin, Roger A., *Utilities' Cost of Capital*, Public Utility Reports, Arlington, VA, 1984.

Myers, Stewart, C., "The Application of Finance Theory to Public Utility Rate Cases," *Bell Journal of Economics and Management Science*, Spring 1972, pp. 58–97.

Patterson, Cleveland S., "Flotation Cost Allowance in Rate of Return Regulation: A Comment," *Journal of Finance*, September 1983, pp. 1335–1338.

——, "Flotation Cost Allowances Revisited," Working Paper.

Peseau, Dennis E., et al., "Utility Regulation and the CAPM: A Discussion," *Financial Management*, Autumn 1978, pp. 52–76.

Pettway, Richard H., "A Note on the Flotation Costs of New Equity Capital Issues of Electric Companies," *Public Utilities Fortnightly*, March 18, 1982, pp. 68–69.

——, "The Effects of New Equity Sales upon Utility Share Prices," *Public Utilities Fortnightly*, May 10, 1984, pp. 35–39.

——, and Radcliffe, Robert C., "Impacts of New Equity Sales upon Electric Utility Share Prices," *Financial Management*, Spring 1985, pp. 16–25.

Pomerantz, Lawrence S., and Suefflow, James E., *Allowance for Funds Used during Construction: Theory and Application*, Michigan State University, Institute of Public Utilities, 1975.

Reeser, Marvin P., *Introduction to Public Utility Accounting*, American Gas Association, Washington, D.C., 1976.

Salomon Brothers, Inc., *Electric Utility Quality Measures*, New York, 1980.

Value Line, *Value Line Investment Survey*, New York, 1985.

17

FINANCIAL DECISIONS FOR MULTINATIONAL ENTERPRISES

CONTENTS

17

FINANCIAL DECISIONS FOR MULTINATIONAL ENTERPRISES

Alan C. Shapiro
Richard Karl Goeltz

WORKING CAPITAL MANAGEMENT

INTERNATIONAL CASH MANAGEMENT. International money managers attempt to attain worldwide the traditional domestic objectives of cash management: (1) bringing the company's cash resources within control as quickly and efficiently as possible and (2) achieving the optimum conservation and utilization of these funds. Accomplishing the first goal requires establishing accurate, timely forecasting and reporting systems, improving cash collections and disbursements, and decreasing the cost of moving funds among affiliates. The second objective is achieved by minimizing the required level of cash balances, making money available when and where it is needed, and increasing the risk-adjusted return on the funds that can be invested.

The principles of **domestic and international cash management** are identical, except that international cash management is a more complicated exercise because of its wider scope and the need to recognize the customs and practices of other countries. When considering the movement of funds across national borders, a number of external factors inhibit adjustment and constrain the money manager.

The most obvious is a set of restrictions that impede the free flow of money into or out of a country. Numerous examples exist, such as former U.S. **Overseas Foreign Direct Investment** (OFDI) restrictions. Germany's **Bardepot**, and the requirements of many countries that their exporters repatriate the proceeds of foreign sales within a specific period. Many observers have argued that floating exchange rates would permit the global dismantling of capital controls. Although these regulations have become somewhat less prevalent and more relaxed, they continue to impede the free flow of capital and thereby hinder an **international cash management** program.

There is really only one generalization that can be made about this type of regulation: controls become more stringent during periods of crisis, precisely when financial managers want to act. Thus a large premium is placed on foresight, planning, and anticipation. Aside from a broad statement that borders on being a truism, the basic rule is that government restrictions must be scrutinized on a country-by-country basis to determine realistic options and limits of action.

This section is divided into five key areas of international cash management: organization, cash planning and budgeting, collecting and disbursing of funds, setting an optimal level of worldwide corporate cash balances, and investing excess funds. Currency risk management and netting are covered in the section of this *Handbook* entitled "Exchange Rates and Currency Exposure": see also "Cash Management."

Organization. Compared with a system of autonomous operating units, a fully centralized international cash management program offers a number of advantages.

- The corporation is able to operate with a smaller amount of cash; pools of excess liquidity are absorbed and eliminated. Each operation maintains transactions balances only and does not hold speculative or precautionary ones.
- By reducing total assets, profitability is enhanced and financing costs reduced.
- The headquarters staff, with its purview of all corporate activity, can recognize problems and opportunities that an individual unit might not perceive.
- All decisions can be made using the overall corporate benefit as the criterion.
- Greater expertise in cash and portfolio management exists if one group is responsible for these activities.
- The corporation's total assets at risk in a foreign country can be reduced. Less will be lost in the event of an expropriation or the promulgation of regulations restricting the transfer of funds.

The foregoing and other benefits have long been understood by many experienced multinational firms. Today, the combination of volatile currency and interest rate fluctuations, questions of capital availability, increasingly complex organizations and operating arrangements, and a growing emphasis on profitability virtually mandates a highly centralized international cash management system. There is also a trend to place much greater responsibility in corporate headquarters. This trend applies to European as well as American firms: see *New Techniques in International Exposure and Cash Management* (Business International Corporation) and *Foreign Exchange Markets Under Floating Rates* (The Group of Thirty).

It should be recognized that centralization does not necessarily imply control by headquarters of all facets of cash management. Instead, it requires a concentration of decision making at a sufficiently high level within the corporation so that all pertinent information is readily available and can be used to maximize the firm's position.

Cash Planning and Budgeting. Cash receipts and disbursements must be reported and forecast in a comprehensive, accurate, and timely manner. If the headquarters staff is to utilize fully and economically the company's worldwide cash resources, they must know the financial positions of affiliates, the forecast cash needs or surpluses, the anticipated cash inflows and outflows, local and international money market conditions, and likely movements in currency values. The form of these reports will vary, depending on the characteristics of the individual firm. Exhibit 1 shows the reporting format of one multinational firm.

As a result of rapid and pronounced changes in the international monetary arena, the need for more frequent reports has become acute. Firms that had been content to receive information quarterly are now requiring monthly, weekly, or even daily data. Key figures are often transmitted by telex or telecopier instead of by mail.

Collection and Disbursement of Funds. Accelerating collections both within a foreign country and across borders is a key element of international cash management. Potential benefits exist because long delays often are encountered in collecting receivables, particularly on export sales, and in transferring funds among affiliates and corporate headquarters. Allowing for mail time and bank processing, delays of 8–10 business days are common from the moment an importer pays an invoice to the time when the exporter is credited with funds available for use. Given high interest rates, wide fluctuations in the foreign exchange markets, and the periodic imposition of credit restrictions that have characterized financial markets in recent years, cash in transit has become more expensive and more exposed to risk.

With increasing frequency, corporate management is participating in the establishment of an affiliate's credit policy and monitoring of collection performance. The principal goals of this intervention are to minimize **float** (the transit time of payments), to reduce the investment in **accounts receivable**, and to lower banking fees and other transaction costs. By converting receivables into cash as rapidly as possible, a company can increase its portfolio or reduce its borrowing, earning a higher investment return or saving interest expense.

Considering either national or international collections, accelerating the receipt of funds usually involves: (1) defining and analyzing the different available payment channels. (2) selecting the most efficient method (which can vary by country and customer), and (3) giving specific instructions regarding procedures to the firm's customers and banks.

EXHIBIT 1 FORM OF CASH FLOW STATEMENT FOR A MULTINATIONAL FIRM

| | 1st Month | | 2nd Month | | 3rd Month | | | 12th Month | |
	Plan	Actual	Plan	Actual	Plan	Actual	...	Plan	Actual
Receipts									
Collections									
Domestic									
Export to nonaffiliates									
Export to affiliates									
Discounted trade bills									
Other Receipts									
Total cash receipts									
Disbursements									
Wages, salaries, and benefits									
Capital expenditures									
Maturing inventories									

Other inventories
Payments to affiliates
Advertising and marketing expenses
Import duties and excise taxes
Circulation tax (sales tax)
Income and capital taxes

Interest
External
Intracompany
Other expenses
    Total disbursements
Net receipts/(disbursements)
Cash, beginning of period
Plus:
    External borrowing
    Intracompany borrowing
Less: Repayments
    External borrowing
    Intracompany borrowing
Cash, end of period

Memo: Short-term borrowing, end of period

In addressing the first point, the full costs of using the various methods must be determined and the inherent delay of each calculated. There are two main sources of delay in the collections process: the time between the dates of payment and of receipt and the time for the payment to clear through the banking system. Inasmuch as banks will be as "inefficient" as possible to increase their float, understanding the subtleties of **domestic and international money transfers** is requisite if a firm is to reduce the time funds are held and extract the maximum value from its banking relationships. A number of multinational banks, particularly U.S. ones, now offer to corporations consulting services that focus on accelerating collections and utilizing funds within a country, the transnational movement and employment of money, or both. Even sophisticated industrial firms are likely to find these services valuable, particularly when they are applied to collections within a country.

Turning to international cash movements, having all affiliates transfer funds by telex enables the corporation to plan better because the vagaries of mail time are eliminated. Third parties, too, are asked to use wire transfers.

To cope with the transmittal delays associated with checks or drafts, customers are instructed in some cases to remit to "mobilization" points, which are centrally located in important regions with large sales volumes. The funds are managed centrally or transmitted to the selling subsidiary. For example, all European customers may be told to make all payments to Switzerland, where the corporation maintains a staff specializing in cash and portfolio management and collections. A variation is to intercept all collections within a country and forward them to a central corporate point. Intra-country collection methods vary, but they are usually constrained by prevailing trade customs.

Sometimes customers are asked to pay directly into a designated account at a branch of the bank that is mobilizing the funds of the multinational corporation internationally. This is particularly useful when banks have large branch networks. Another technique that is used both domestically and internationally is to have customers remit funds to a designated **lock box,** which is a postal box in the company's name. A local bank or branch of a multinational bank takes and opens the mail received at the lock box one or more times daily. Any deposit or transfer made is immediately reported to the national or regional mobilization office. Credit for the funds is then given to the company, usually on the same day. The period spent in transit can thereby be reduced from up to a week to one or two days.

To reduce clearing time, some companies set up accounts in their customers' banks, a useful device if there are only a few large customers or the check clearing time is quite lengthy. Some firms have gone one step further and directly debit their customers. In **direct debiting,** or preauthorized payment, the customer allows its account to be charged periodically by the supplier or the supplier's bank up to a maximum amount. With this method, there is no customer payment delay, intentional or inadvertent, and mail delay is eliminated. Clearing time can also be reduced by initiating debiting the correct number of days before the due date.

Regarding disbursements, most European banks operate on a **debit transfer** basis, whereby the customer's account is charged immediately, giving the bank, as opposed to the payer, the advantage of the float. By contrast, U.S. banks operate on a **credit transfer** basis, granting the payer the benefit of the float until the check clears. Furthermore, on international transactions, European banks will debit a company's account two days before foreign funds are made available. American banks, though, usually provide a firm with **value compensation;** that is, the firm does not give up domestic funds until the foreign funds are provided.

Optimal Worldwide Cash Levels. Centralized cash management typically involves the transfer of an affiliate's cash in excess of minimal operating requirements into a central account (pool) where all corporate funds are managed by corporate staff. Some firms have established a special corporate entity that collects and disburses funds through a single bank account.

With **cash pooling,** each affiliate need hold locally only the minimum cash balance required for transaction purposes. All precautionary balances are held by the parent or in the pool. As long as the demands for cash by the various units are reasonably independent of each other, centralized cash management can provide an equivalent degree of protection with a lower level of cash reserves. For example, assume that each of a multinational's three foreign affiliates has the following probability distribution of cash demands during the next month: a 70% chance of needing $100,000, a 25% chance of needing $250,000, and a 5% chance of needing $500,000. If cash management is decentralized, each of the three units must hold $250,000 (or a total of $750,000) to achieve a safety level of 95%, that is, to ensure that the probability that a given affiliate will run short of cash is no greater than 5%. However, on a worldwide basis, the likelihood that all three affiliates will require at least $250,000 simultaneously is only $.30^3 = .027$, provided these cash demands are independent of each other. Unless funds can be shifted, the probability that at least one unit will run short of cash is $1 - .95^3 = .1426$, even though $750,000 is being held overall (i.e., the overall safety level is only 85.74%). With centralization, only $600,000 need be held to achieve a safety level of 84.16% for the corporation as a whole because funds are no longer restricted as to use. Cash reserves of $750,000 will increase the overall safety level to 93.09%, while $850,000 will reduce the probability of a cash shortage anywhere in the firm to less than 2%.

The derivation of these probabilities is shown in Exhibit 2. Events A, B, and C denote cash requirements, of $100,000, $250,000, and $500,000, respectively. The various possible event sets, their probabilities, and the funds required to satisfy the demand associated with each event are listed in order of ascending cash requirements. For instance, the event AAB refers to any

EXHIBIT 2   CASH FLOW POOLING PROBABILITIES: A FORECASTING EXAMPLE

Event	Probability	Cumulative Probability	Cash Requirement
AAA	$.7^3 = .343$	.343	$ 300,000
AAB	$3(.7)^2(.25) = .3675$	.7105	450,000
ABB	$3(.7)(.25)^2 = .13125$	.84175	600,000
AAC	$3(.7)^2(.05) = .0735$	.91525	700,000
BBB	$.25^3 = .015625$	.930875	750,000
ABC	$6(.7)(.25)(.05) = .0525$	.983375	850,000
BBC	$3(.25)^2(.05) = .009375$	.99275	1,000,000
ACC	$3(.7)(.05)^2 = .00525$	.998	1,100,000
BCC	$3(.25)(.05)^2 = .001875$	.999875	1,250,000
CCC	$.05^3 = .000125$	1.0	1,500,000
Event A	cash requirement of $100,000		
Event B	cash requirement of $250,000		
Event C	cash requirement of $500,000		

two affiliates facing cash demands of $100,000 and one unit needing $250,000, for a total funds requirement of $450,000 with probability $3(.7)^2(.25) = .3675$.

Management of the Short-Term Investment Portfolio. A major task of international cash management is to determine the levels and currency denominations of the multinational group's investment in cash balances and money market instruments. Firms with seasonal or cyclical cash flows have special problems such as arranging investment maturities to coincide with projected needs.

To manage this investment properly requires a forecast of future cash needs based on the company's current budget and past experience as well as an estimate of a minimum cash position for the coming period. These projections should take into account the effects of inflation and anticipated currency changes on future cash flows.

Common-sense guidelines for managing the marketable securities portfolio globally include:

1. The instruments in the portfolio should be diversified to minimize the risk for a given level of return or to maximize the yield for a given level of risk. Government securities should not be used exclusively. Eurodollar and other instruments may be nearly as safe.
2. The portfolio must be reviewed daily to decide which securities are to be liquidated and what new investments made.
3. In revising the portfolio, care should be taken to ensure that the incremental interest earned more than compensates for added costs such as clerical work, the income lost between investments, fixed charges,

such as the foreign exchange spread, and commissions on the sale and purchase of securities.

4. If conversion to cash rapidly is an important consideration, the marketability (liquidity) of the instrument should be carefully evaluated. Ready markets exist for some securities but not others.

5. The maturity of the investment should be tailored to the firm's projected cash needs or a secondary market with high liquidity should exist.

6. Opportunities for **covered** or **uncovered interest arbitrage** should be carefully considered.

Some observers have attributed a major portion of the turbulence in foreign exchange markets to multinational corporations and their aggressive (or defensive) international cash management programs. Corporations do exercise control over massive amounts of liquidity and clearly possess the power to disrupt markets. Their activities, particularly in **leading** and lagging payments, have contributed on occasion to a sharp appreciation or depreciation of individual currencies, but whether they are primarily responsible for the tumult of recent years is a more difficult question to answer. In May 1971 the U.S. Department of Commerce stated, "major multinational corporations . . . played only a limited role in recent massive movements of dollars into foreign central banks." More recently, an article in the Federal Reserve Bank of Boston's *New England Economic Review* (March-April 1979) examined the role of corporations and banks as foreign exchange speculators. Admitting that only a tentative conclusion was possible, the author said, "the foreign exchange market activity reported by U.S. firms is not demonstrably destabilizing."

ACCOUNTS RECEIVABLE MANAGEMENT. Multinational corporations (MNCs) and domestic firms face the same decisions regarding the appropriate level of accounts receivable. In the multinational firm, though, this exercise is complicated by the existence of different rates of inflation, **foreign exchange fluctuations,** and restrictions within a market or on currency transfers.

Credit Management. Firms grant trade credit to customers, both domestically and internationally, because they expect the investment in receivables to be profitable, either by expanding sales volume or by retaining sales that otherwise would be lost to competitors. Some companies also earn a profit on the financing charges they levy on credit sales.

The need to scrutinize credit terms is particularly important in countries experiencing rapid rates of **inflation.** The incentive for customers to defer payment, liquidating their debts with less valuable money in the future, is great. Furthermore, **credit standards** abroad are often more relaxed than in the home market, especially in countries lacking alternative sources of credit for small customers. To remain competitive, MNCs may feel compelled to loosen their own credit standards. Finally, the compensation system in many companies tends to reward higher sales more than it penalizes an increased investment in accounts receivable. Local managers frequently have an incentive to expand sales even if the corporation overall does not benefit.

Credit Extension. The easier credit terms are, the more sales are likely to be made. Generosity is not always the best policy. The risk of default, increased interest expense on the larger investment in receivables, and the deterioration through **currency devaluation** of the dollar value of accounts receivable denominated in the buyer's currency must be balanced against higher revenues. These additional costs may be partly offset if liberalized **credit terms** enhance a firm's ability to raise its prices.

Another factor that tends to increase accounts receivable in foreign countries is an uneconomic expansion of local sales, which may occur if managers are credited with dollar sales when accounts receivable are denominated in the local currency (LC). Sales managers should be charged for the expected depreciation in the value of local currency accounts receivable. For instance, if the current exchange rate is $LC_1 = \$0.10$ but the expected exchange rate 90 days hence (or the three-month forward rate) is $0.90, managers providing three-month credit terms should be credited with only $0.90 for each dollar in sales booked at the current spot rate.

Whether judging the implications of inflation, devaluation, or both, it must be remembered that when a unit of inventory is sold on credit, a **real asset** has been transformed into a **monetary asset.** The opportunity to raise the local currency selling price of the item to maintain its dollar value is lost. This point is obvious but frequently disregarded.

Assuming that both buyer and seller have access to credit at the same cost and reflect in their decisions anticipated currency changes and inflation, it should normally make no difference to a potential customer whether he receives additional credit or an equivalent cash discount. The MNC may benefit by revising its credit terms, however, in three circumstances:

1. The buyer and seller hold different opinions concerning the future course of inflation or currency changes, leading one of the two to prefer term-price discount tradeoffs (i.e., a lower cost if paid within a specified period).

2. Because of market imperfections, the MNC has a lower risk-adjusted cost of credit than does its customer. In other words, the buyer's higher financing cost must not be a result of its greater riskiness.

3. During periods of credit restraint in a country, the affiliate of an MNC may, because of its parent, gain a marketing advantage over its competitors through having access to funds that are not available to local companies. Absolute availability of money, rather than its cost, may be critical.

The following analytical approach enables a firm to compare the expected benefits and costs associated with **extending credit internationally.** The same analysis can also be used in domestic credit extension decisions, with inflation rather than currency fluctuations being the complicating factor. Let ΔS and ΔC be the incremental sales and costs respectively, associated with an easing of credit terms. If the expected credit cost per unit of sales revenues R is expected to increase to $R + \Delta R$ because of a more lenient credit policy, terms should be eased if, and only if, incremental profits are greater than incremental credit costs or

$$\Delta S - \Delta C \geq S\Delta R + \Delta S(R + \Delta R)$$

It should be noted that ΔR reflects forecast changes in currency values as well as the cost of funds over the longer collection period. This analysis can be used to ascertain whether it would be worthwhile to tighten credit, accepting lower sales but at the same time reducing credit costs.

To illustrate the use of this approach, suppose that a subsidiary in France currently has annual sales of $1 million with 90-day credit terms. It is believed that sales will increase by 6% ($60,000) if terms are extended to 120 days. Of these additional sales, the cost of goods sold is $35,000. Monthly (30-day) credit expenses are 1% in financing charges. In addition, a 1.5% depreciation of the franc is expected over the next 90 days.

Ignoring currency changes for the moment but considering financing costs, the value today of $1 of receivables to be collected at the end of 90 days is approximately $0.97. Taking into account the 1.5% expected franc devaluation, this value declines to $0.97(1 - 0.015)$ or $0.955. Similarly, $1 of receivables collected 120 days from now is worth $[1 - (0.01)4][1 - (0.015 + d_4]$ today or $0.945 - 0.96d_4$, where d_4 (unknown) is the amount of currency change during the fourth month. Then, the cost of carrying French franc receivables for 3 months is 4.5%, while the incremental cost for the fourth month equals $0.955 - (0.945 - 0.96d_4)$ dollar or $1\% + 96d_4\%$.

Using the formula previously presented. $\Delta S - \Delta C = \$25,000$, $S\Delta R = \$1,000,000 (0.01 + 0.96d_4) = \$10,000 + \$960,000d_4$, and $\Delta S(R + \Delta R) = \$60,000 (0.045 + 0.01 + 0.96d_4) = \$3,300 + \$57,600d_4$. Then, credit extension is worthwhile only if the incremental profit, $25,000, is greater than the incremental cost, $13,300 + \$1,017,600d_4$ or

$$d_4 < \frac{11,700}{1,017,600} = 1.15\%$$

One potential problem when evaluating the desirability of extending credit to obtain greater sales is the reaction of competition. It is likely that in an oligopoly, if one firm cuts its effective price by granting longer payment terms, its competitors will be forced to follow to maintain their market positions. The result could well be no incremental sales and profits for any firm, but only greater accounts receivable for all.

INVENTORY MANAGEMENT. Although conceptually the inventory management problems faced by multinational firms are not unique, they may be exaggerated in the case of foreign operations. For instance, MNCs typically have greater difficulty in controlling their overseas inventory and realizing inventory turnover objectives for a variety of reasons, including long and variable transit times if ocean transportation is used, lengthy customs proceedings and possibilities of dock strikes, import controls, supply disruption, anticipated changes in currency values, and higher customs duties.

Advance Inventory Purchases. In many developing countries, forward contracts for foreign currency are limited in availability or nonexistent. In addition, restrictions often preclude free remittances, making it difficult if not impossible to convert excess funds into a hard currency. One means of **hedging** is anticipatory purchases of goods, especially imported items. The tradeoff involves owning goods for which local currency prices may be increased, thereby maintaining the dollar value of the asset even though inflation and devaluation are virulent, versus forgoing the return on local portfolio investments or not being able to take advantage of potentially favorable fluctuations in the specific prices of these materials. (The attractiveness of holding investments in local currency money market instruments is frequently overlooked; the aftertax dollar yield, adjusted fully for devaluation, may be positive, sometimes spectacularly so.)

Inventory Stockpiling. The problem of supply failure is of particular importance for any firm dependent on foreign sources because of long delivery lead times, the often limited availability of transport for economically sized shipments, and currency restrictions. These conditions may make the knowledge and execution of an optimal stocking policy under a threat of a disruption to supply more critical in the MNC than in the firm that purchases domestically.

The traditional response to such risks has been advance purchases. According to Business International (*Decision-Making in International Operations*): "If sourcing from a risky area for international corporations, stockpile goods outside the country and plan for and cultivate alternative supply sources." Holding large quantities of inventory can be quite expensive, though. In fact, the high cost of stockpiling inventory, including financing, insurance, storage, and obsolescence, has led many companies to identify low inventories with effective management. In contrast, production and sales managers typically desire a relatively large inventory, particularly when a cutoff in supply is anticipated.

It is obvious that as the probability of disruption increases or as holding costs go down, more inventory should be ordered. Similarly, if the cost of a stockout rises or if future supplies are expected to be more expensive, it will pay to stockpile additional inventory. Conversely, if these parameters move in the opposite direction, less inventory should be stockpiled.

MANAGING INTRACORPORATE FUND FLOWS

THE MULTINATIONAL FINANCIAL SYSTEM. The ability to adjust intra-corporate fund flows and accounting profits on a global basis is potentially of great advantage to the multinational corporation. However, inasmuch as most of the gains derive from the MNC's proficiency at taking advantage of openings in tax laws or regulatory barriers, conflicts between a government and the firm are quite likely.

Financial transactions within the MNC result from the internal transfer of goods, services, technology, and capital. These product and factor flows range from intermediate and finished goods to less tangible items such as management skills, trademarks, and patents. The transactions not liquidated immediately give rise to some type of financial claim such as royalties for the use of a patent or accounts receivable for goods sold on credit. In addition, capital investments lead to future flows of dividends and/or interest and principal repayments. Some of the myriad financial linkages possible in the MNC are depicted in Exhibit 3.

Although all the links portrayed in Exhibit 3 can and do exist among independent firms, as pointed out by Lessard ("Transfer Prices, Taxes, and Financial Markets," in Robert G. Hawkins, Ed., *The Economic Effects of Multinational Corporations*, JAI Press, Greenwich, CT, 1979), the MNC has greater control over the mode and timing of these financial transfers.

Mode of Transfer. The MNC has considerable freedom in selecting the **financial channels** through which to move funds, allocate profits, or both. For example, patents and trademarks can be sold outright or transferred in return for a contractual stream of royalty payments. By varying the prices at which transactions occur, profits and cash can be shifted within the worldwide organization. Similarly, funds can be moved from one unit to another by adjusting **transfer prices** on intracorporate sales and purchases of goods and services. With regard to **investment flows,** capital can be sent overseas as debt with at least some choice of interest rate, currency of denomination, and repayment schedule, or as equity with returns in the form of dividends. The multinational firm can use these various channels, singly or in combination, to transfer funds internationally, depending on the specific circumstances encountered. Furthermore, within the limits of various national laws and with regard to the relations between a foreign affiliate and its host government, these flows may be more advantageous than those that would result from dealings with independent firms.

EXHIBIT 3   FINANCIAL LINKAGES FOR THE MNC[a]

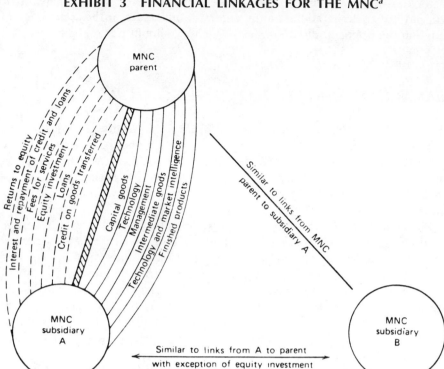

[a]Solid lines, real flows; dotted lines, financial flows.
Source: Reprinted with permission from Donald R. Lessard, "Transfer Prices, Taxes, and Financial Markets," in Robert G. Hawkins, Ed., *The Economic Effects of Multinational Corporations,* JAI Press, Greenwich, CT, 1979.

Timing Flexibility. Some of the internally generated financial claims require a fixed payment schedule; others can be accelerated or delayed. This leading and lagging is most often applied to **interaffiliate trade credit** where a change in open account terms from, say, 90 to 180 days, can involve massive shifts in liquidity. (Some nations, both developed and less developed, have regulations concerning the repatriation of the proceeds of export sales. Thus, typically, there is not complete freedom to move funds by leading and lagging.) In addition, the timing of fee and royalty payments may be modified when all parties to the agreement are related. Even if the contract cannot be altered once agreed upon, the MNC generally has latitude when the terms are established initially.

In the absence of **exchange controls,** firms have the greatest amount of flexibility in the timing of equity claims. The earnings of a foreign affiliate can be retained or used to pay dividends which, in turn, can be deferred or paid in advance.

Value. Lessard also points out that the ability to transfer funds and to real-locate profits internally presents multinationals with three different types of arbitrage opportunity:

1. *Tax arbitrage*. By shifting profits from units located in high-tax nations to those in lower tax nations or from those in a taxpaying position to those with tax losses. MNCs can reduce their burden.
2. *Financial market arbitrage*. By transferring funds among units. MNCs may be able to circumvent exchange controls, earn higher risk-adjusted yields on excess funds, reduce their risk-adjusted cost of borrowed funds, and tap previously unavailable capital sources.
3. *Regulatory system arbitrage*. Where **subsidiary profits** are a function of government regulations (e.g., where a government agency sets al-lowable prices on the firm's goods) or union pressure, rather than the marketplace, the ability to disguise true profitability by reallocating profits among units may provide the multinational firm with a negoti-ating advantage.

There is also a fourth arbitrage opportunity—the ability to permit an affiliate to negate the effect of credit restraint or controls in its country of operation. If a government limits access to additional borrowing locally, the firm with the ability to draw on external sources of funds not only can achieve greater short-term profits, but it may also be able to attain a more powerful market position over the long term.

INTRACORPORATE FUND FLOW MECHANISMS. The MNC can be visu-alized as **unbundling** the total **flow of funds** between each pair of affiliates into separate components, which are associated with resources transferred in the form of products, capital, services, and technology. For example, dividends, interest, and loan repayments can be matched against capital invested as equity or debt, while fees, royalties, or corporate overhead can be charged for various corporate services, trademarks, or licenses.

As part of the analysis of these transfer techniques of multinationals, it is useful to look first at the historical remittance patterns of U.S. firms. Exhibit 4 contains a breakdown of earnings repatriated as either fees and royalties or dividends and interest during the years 1966 through 1976. It also shows the percentage of overseas earnings actually remitted.

The most noticeable point is the stable relative contribution of each com-ponent. On average, dividend and interest payments account for approxi-mately 75% of these flows with fees and royalties making up the remaining 25%. The data suggest a slight growth in the relative importance of fees and royalties. One can also conclude that the earnings payout rate (the ratio of remitted to total earnings) has been declining somewhat over time, from 85.5% in 1966 to 77.6% in 1976.

EXHIBIT 4 AGGREGATE REMITTANCE PRACTICES OF U.S. MULTINATIONALS, 1966—1976 ($ MILLIONS)

Year	Total Earnings	Total Remittances	% of Total Earnings	Dividends and Interest	% of Total Remittances	Fees and Royalties	% of Total Remittances
1966	5,259	4,497	85.5	3,467	77.1	1,030	22.9
1967	5,605	4,983	88.9	3,847	77.2	1,136	22.8
1968	6,592	5,431	82.4	4,152	76.4	1,279	23.6
1969	7,449	6,501	87.3	4,819	74.1	1,682	25.9
1970	8,169	6,911	84.6	4,992	72.2	1,919	27.8
1971	9,159	8,143	88.9	5,983	73.5	2,160	26.5
1972	10,949	8,845	80.8	6,416	72.5	2,429	27.5
1973	16,542	11,222	67.8	8,384	74.7	2,838	25.3
1974	19,156	14,449	75.4	11,379	78.8	3,070	21.2
1975	16,615	12,110	72.9	8,567	70.7	3,543	29.3
1976	18,841	14,648	77.6	11,126	76.0	3,522	24.0

Source: U.S. Department of Commerce, *Survey of Current Business*, various issues.

These data present only a partial description, however, in that MNCs have a large degree of flexibility in shifting funds by means other than the traditional dividend or fee remittance routes. The most important additional channels include transfer price adjustments, leading and lagging, and intracorporate loans.

Transfer Pricing. The pricing of goods and services traded internally is one of the most sensitive of all management subjects, and executives are typically reluctant to discuss it. Each government normally presumes that multinationals use transfer pricing to the detriment of the host country. For this reason, a number of home and host governments have set up policing mechanisms to review the **transfer pricing policies of MNCs.**

The most important uses of transfer pricing include:

1. Diminishing taxes.
2. Reducing tariffs.
3. Avoiding exchange controls.

To illustrate the **tax effects** associated with a change in transfer price, suppose that subsidiary A is selling 100,000 circuit boards annually to subsidiary B at a unit price of $10. A change in price to $10.50 would simultaneously increase A's income by $50,000 and reduce B's income by the same amount. Assuming that the marginal tax rates on income for A and B, respectively, are 0.35 and 0.50, this transfer price change will increase A's taxes by $17,500 (0.35 × $50,000) and lower B's taxes by $25,000 (0.5 × $50,000) for a net corporate tax saving of $7,500 annually. In effect, profits are being shifted from a higher to a lower tax jurisdiction. In the extreme case, an affiliate may be in a loss position because of high startup costs, heavy depreciation changes, or substantial investments that are expensed. The MNC would forecast when that affiliate would pay taxes and determine the net present value tax rate, which by definition must be less than the statutory one.

With respect to tariffs, companies will usually set a relatively low price on goods exported to countries with high *ad valorem* duties. This practice will enable the purchasing affiliate to price the goods competitively with no loss of revenue to the corporation overall.

Most countries have specific regulations governing transfer prices. For instance, **Section 482 of the U.S. Revenue Code** grants the Secretary of the Treasury the following powers:

> In any case of two or more organizations, trades, or businesses (whether or not incorporated, whether or not organized in the United States, and whether or not affiliated) owned or controlled directly or indirectly by the same interests, the Secretary or his delegate may distribute, apportion, or allocate gross income, deductions, credits, or allowances between or among such organizations, trades, or businesses, if he determines that such distribution, apportionment,

or allocation is necessary in order to prevent evasion of taxes or clearly to reflect the income of any of such organizations, trades, or businesses.

The regulations specify three methods of pricing, which are to be applied in the following order: (1) comparable uncontrolled price, (2) resale price, (3) cost plus (Fuller, "Section 482 Revisited," *Tax Law Review*, Vol. 31, 1976). The government's strong and stated preference is for **arm's-length prices**, those that a willing buyer and a willing, unrelated seller would freely accept.

In light of Section 482, the U.S. government's willingness to use it, and similar authority in most other nations, the current practice by MNCs appears to be set standard prices for standardized products. However, the innovative nature of the typical multinational ensures a continual stream of new products for which no market equivalent exists. Some flexibility is possible in setting transfer prices. Furthermore, many of the items sold internally are components and subassemblies for which no external market exists. Firms also have a great deal of latitude in setting prices on rejects, scrap, and returned goods.

Based on their detailed interviews with 39 U.S.-based MNCs, Robbins and Stobaugh (*Money in the Multinational Enterprise*), concluded that although tax minimization is a principal goal of transfer pricing, reducing the effect of **exchange controls** is also quite important. For example, the MNC may raise the intracompany price for sales to an affiliate with blocked funds, accepting a larger global tax liability but reducing the affiliate's funds exposed to devaluation and other types of loss. To determine the attractiveness of this step, the effective income tax rates of the selling and purchasing subsidiaries, the probable duration of the blocking, and alternative investment opportunities for the affiliate with the excess funds must be known or estimated.

Fees and Royalties. Management services such as headquarters advice, allocated overhead, patents, and trademarks are often unique and, therefore, without a reference market price. The consequent difficulty in pricing these corporate resources makes them suitable for use as additional routes for international fund flows by varying the fees or royalties charged for the use of these intangible factors of production.

Transfer prices for services have the same tax and **exchange control** effects as transfer prices on goods do, but they are often subject to even greater scrutiny. However, host governments often look with more favor on payments for industrial know-how than for **profit remittances**. Restrictions that do exist are more likely to be modified to permit a fee for technical knowledge rather than dividends.

Leading and Lagging. A highly favored means of shifting liquidity between affiliates is an acceleration or delay (leading and lagging) in the payment of interaffiliate accounts by modifying the credit terms extended by one unit to another. For example, suppose affiliate A sells goods worth $1 million monthly to affiliate B on 90-day credit terms. On average, A has $3 million of accounts receivable from B and is, in effect, financing $3 million of working capital for B. If the terms are changed to 180 days, there will be a one-time shift of an additional $3 million to B. Conversely, a reduction in credit terms to 30 days will involve a flow of $2 million from B to A. This is shown in Exhibit 5.

Inasmuch as incremental accounts receivable are financed typically by short-term debt, the costs of leading and lagging are evaluated in the same way as any other use of different sources of borrowing, that is, by considering relevant interest and tax rates and the likelihood of changes in currency value.

A 1977 survey by Business International (*New Techniques in International Exposure and Cash Management*) indicates how prevalent leading and lagging is. According to that survey, over 65% of all European and U.S.-based multinationals engage in this direct form of intracompany lending. Some firms prefer not to use this technique because they feel it compromises discipline. The attitude that invoices should be paid on time, not before or after, seems to be more prevalent among European companies. To the extent that greater control is concentrated in corporate headquarters, this technique can be used more readily and effectively.

Intracorporate Loans. A prinicpal means of financing foreign operations and moving funds internationally is intracorporate lending activities. Although a variety of types of intracorporate loan exist, the most important methods currently are **direct loans, back-to-back financing, parallel loans,** and **currency**

EXHIBIT 5   FUND TRANSFER EFFECTS OF LEADING AND LAGGING: SUBSIDIARY A SELLS $1 MILLION IN GOODS MONTHLY TO SUBSIDIARY B

	Credit Terms		
Balance Sheet Accounts	Normal (90 days)	Leading (30 days)	Lagging (180 days)
Subsidiary A Accounts receivable from B	$3,000,000	$1,000,000	$6,000,000
Subsidiary B Accounts payable to A	3,000,000	1,000,000	6,000,000
Net Cash Transfers From B to A	—	$2,000,000	—
From A to B	—	—	$3,000,000

swaps. The first is a straight extension of credit from the parent to an affiliate or from one affiliate to another. The others typically involve an intermediary.

Back-to-back loans (also called **fronting loans** or **link financing**) are often employed to finance affiliates located in nations with high interest rates or restricted capital markets, especially when there is a danger of **currency controls**, or when different rates of withholding tax are applied to loans from a financial institution. In the typical arrangement, the parent company deposits funds with a bank in country A, which in turn lends the money to a subsidiary in country B. In effect, a back-to-back loan is an **intracorporate loan** channeled through a bank. From the bank's point of view, the loan is risk-free because the parent's deposit fully collateralizes it. The bank just acts as an intermediary or a "front": compensation is provided by the margin between the interest received from the borrowing unit and the rate paid on the parent's deposit.

A back-to-back loan may offer several potential advantages compared with a direct intracorporate loan. Two of the more important are:

1. Certain countries apply different withholding tax rates to interest paid to a foreign parent and to a financial institution. A cost saving in the form of lower taxes may be available with a back-to-back loan.

2. If currency controls are imposed, the government will usually permit the local subsidiary to honor the amortization schedule of a loan from a major multinational bank: to stop payment would hurt the nation's credit rating. Conversely, local monetary authorities would have far fewer reservations about not authorizing the repayment of an intra-company loan. In general, back-to-back financing provides better protection against expropriation and/or exchange controls than does an intracompany loan.

Some authors argue that a back-to-back loan conveys another benefit. The subsidiary seems to have obtained credit from a major bank on its own, possibly enhancing its reputation. This appearance is unlikely to be significant in the highly informed international financial community.

A **parallel loan** is a method of effectively repatriating **blocked funds** (at least for the term of the arrangement), circumventing exchange control restrictions, avoiding a premium exchange rate for investments abroad, or obtaining foreign currency financing at attractive rates. It consists of two related but separate, or parallel, borrowings and usually involves four parties in two different countries. The parent A will extend a loan in its home country and currency to a subsidiary of B, whose foreign parent will lend the local currency equivalent in its country to the subsidiary of A. Drawdowns, repayments of principal, and payments of interest are made simultaneously. The differential between the rates of interest on the two loans is determined in theory by the cost of money in each country and anticipated changes in currency values.

A **currency swap** achieves an economic purpose similar to a **parallel loan** but generally is simpler, involving only two parties and one agreement. Two companies sell currencies to each other and undertake to reverse the exchange after a fixed term. Unlike parallel loans, interest is not paid by both parties; in a currency swap, a fee or commission is paid by one to the other. This commission in effect is equivalent to the **forward foreign exchange premium or discount**, which in turn should reflect interest rate differentials. The **spread** is fixed for a number of years and consequently does not fluctuate as a forward discount or premium will.

Depending on the tax positions of the parent and its affiliate, the commission in a currency swap may offer some benefits to the corporation overall compared with the alternative of interest income and expense involved in a parallel loan arrangement. In addition, the **right of offset** may be more firmly established in a currency swap.

For both transactions, an exchange adjustment, or **topping-up,** clause may be sought. If one currency were to depreciate sharply, the borrower of it would be required to advance additional funds to the other party so that both amounts would remain roughly equivalent in value at the spot rates prevailing throughout the term of the agreement. This convenant provided protection against credit risk; see Suhar and Lyons, ''Choosing Between a Parallel Loan and a Swap'' (*Euromoney*, March 1979).

Since the **currency swap** is not a loan, it is not reflected as a liability on the parties balance sheets. Whether a parallel loan appears in a corporation's consolidated financial statements depends on whether a **right of offset** exists. If one does, the net of the asset and liability need be shown; this will, of course, be zero when the loans receivable and payable in U.S. dollars are identical, as they will be if currency values do not change or a topping-up provision exists. If a right of offset is not one of the provisions in the agreement, the asset and liability are shown gross (SEC Staff Accounting Bulletin Topic 10-E, paragraph 7805).

Dividends. This is by far the most important means of transferring funds from foreign affiliates to the parent company, accounting for over 50% of all remittances to U.S. firms in 1977. Among the various factors that MNCs consider when deciding on dividend payments by their affiliates are taxes, financial statement effect, exchange risk, currency controls, financing requirements, availability and cost of funds, and the parent's dividend payout (dividends-earnings) ratio. Firms differ, though, in the relative importance they place on these variables, as well as on how systematically they are incorporated in an overall remittance policy.

A major consideration in the dividend decision is the effective tax rate on payments from different affiliates. By varying payout ratios among its foreign subsidiaries, the corporation can reduce its total tax burden. Total tax payments are dependent on the regulations of both the foreign and home nations. The foreign country ordinarily has two types of tax that directly affect tax costs: **corporate income taxes** and **withholding taxes on dividend remittances**. In addition, several countries, such as Germany and Austria, **tax retained earnings** at a higher rate than earnings paid out as dividends. Many nations, such as the United States, tax dividend income received from abroad at the regular corporate tax rate. When this rate is higher than the combined foreign income and withholding taxes, the receipt of dividend income will normally entail an incremental tax cost. A number of countries, including Canada, Holland, and France, do not impose any additional taxes on dividend income from subsidiaries in which the parent holds more than a certain percentage ownership. The United States also taxes certain unremitted profits known as **Subpart F income**, including dividends paid to holding companies located in tax havens. Canada has similar tax regulations known as **FAPI** (foreign accrual property income).

As an offset to these additional taxes, most countries, including the United States, provide tax credits for taxes already paid by affiliates in countries of operation. For example, if a foreign subsidiary has $100 in pretax income, pays $40 in local income taxes, and a $6 dividend withholding tax and then remits the remaining $54 to its U.S. parent in the form of a dividend, the IRS will impose a $46 tax (0.46 × $100) but will provide a dollar-for-dollar tax credit for the $46 already paid in foreign taxes, leaving the parent with no U.S. income tax bill. **Foreign tax credits** from other remittances may be used in certain cases to offset these additional taxes. There are also a number of tax treaties between countries, established to avoid the double taxation of the same income and to provide for reduced dividend withholding taxes.

Some caution is in order. The determination of the full corporate tax cost of dividends is not as straightforward as the preceding paragraph may imply. U.S. income tax law (Regulation 1.861-8 of the Internal Revenue Code) limits the amount of foreign tax credits that can be used each year.

Putting aside qualitative considerations (which nevertheless may be quite important), the policy regarding dividends from affiliates to the parent is essentially a pure financial decision. The funds employed to make the remittance must be replaced to leave the affiliate whole. The economic effects of this substituion must be evaluated carefully. Unless constrained, once the firm has determined the amount of dividends to be received from its foreign operations, it will withdraw funds from the locations with the lowest comprehensive transfer costs.

Currency controls are another major factor in the dividend decision. Nations with balance of payments problems are likely to restrict the payment of dividends to foreign companies. These controls vary by country, but, generally, they limit the size of **dividend remittances** either in absolute terms or as a percentage of earnings, equity, or registered capital.

A number of firms attempt to reduce the danger of such interference by maintaining a record of consistent dividends that is designed to show that these payments are part of an established financial program rather than an act of speculation against the host country's currency. Dividends are paid every year, regardless of whether justified by financial and tax considerations, just to demonstrate a continuing policy to the local government and central bank. Even when they cannot be remitted, dividends are sometimes declared for the same reason, namely, to establish grounds for making future payments when these controls are lifted or modified.

Some companies even set a uniform **dividend payout ratio** throughout the corporate system to set a global pattern and maintain the principle that affiliates have an obligation to pay dividends to their stockholders. If challenged, the firm can then prove that its French or Brazilian or Italian subsidiaries must pay an equivalent percentage dividend. MNCs are often willing to accept higher tax costs to maintain the principle that dividends are a necessary and legitimate business expense. According to many executives, a record of consistently paying dividends (or at least declaring them) is a contributing factor in getting approval for further dividend disbursements.

FOREIGN INVESTMENT ANALYSIS

CAPITAL BUDGETING FOR MULTINATIONAL CORPORATIONS. The standard capital budgeting analysis involves calculating the expected aftertax values of all cash flows associated with a prospective investment, then discounting those cash flows back to the present using the firm's **weighted average cost of capital**. If the **net present value** of those cash flows is positive, the investment should be undertaken; if negative, it should be rejected. Formally, this net present value equals

$$NPV = -I_0 + \sum_{i=1}^{n} \frac{X_i}{(1+k^*)^i}$$

where NPV = net present value of project
  I_0 = net present value cost of investment
  X_i = aftertax project cash flow in year i (no financial costs included)
  n = anticipated life of project
  k^* = required rate of return

The **analysis of a foreign project** raises three issues in addition to those encountered in domestic project analysis:

1. Should cash flows be measured from the viewpoint of the project or the parent?
2. How should the availability of subsidized loans be reflected in the project analysis?
3. Should the additional economic and political risks that are uniquely foreign be reflected in cash flow or discount rate adjustments?

Parent Versus Project Cash Flows. A substantial difference can exist between the cash flow of a project and the amount that is remitted to the parent because of tax regulations and exchange controls. Furthermore, many project expenses, such as management fees and royalties, are returns to the parent company. In addition, the incremental revenue contributed to the parent MNC by a project can differ from total project revenues if, for example, the project involves substituting local production for parent company exports or if transfer price adjustments shift profits elsewhere in the system. Given the differences that are likely to exist, the relevant cash flows to use in project evaluation must be determined.

One position suggested by Rodriguez and Carter (*International Financial Management*, p. 409) is that "to the extent that the corporation views itself as a true multinational, the effect of restrictions on repatriation may not be severe." Shapiro (*Financial Management*, Spring 1978, pp. 7–16), however, claims that according to economic theory, the value of a project is determined by the net present value of future cash flows back to the investor. Thus the parent MNC should value only the cash flows that are or can be repatriated, less any transfer costs (such as taxes), because only accessible funds can be used to pay dividends and interest, to amortize the firm's debt, and for reinvestment. (This principle also holds, of course, for a domestic firm. For example, only 15% of dividends received by a U.S. firm from a domestic subsidiary that is not consolidated for tax purposes are taxed: hence this earning stream has a value of 91.9% of the original dividend paid.)

To simplify **project evaluation**, a three-stage analysis is recommended. In the first stage, project cash flows are computed from the subsidiary's standpoint, exactly as if it were a separate, national coroporation. The perspective then shifts to the parent company. The second stage of analysis requires specific forecasts concerning the amounts, timing, and form of transfers to headquarters. It reflects the taxes and other expenses that will be incurred by the remittances. Finally, the firm must take into account the indirect benefits and costs that this investment confers on the rest of the system, such as an increase or decrease in export sales by another affiliate. In general, incremental cash flows to the parent can be found only by subtracting worldwide parent company cash flows (without the investment) from postinvestment parent company cash flows.

Financial Incentives. As a means of attracting foreign investment into a country to a region or for a specific purpose, many governments offer low-cost or subsidized loans. This type of incentive may be available in the United States as well, but it is much more likely to be encountered in less developed countries. If such a loan is granted, how should the benefit be incorporated in the project analysis? Some suggest that the amount of the subsidized loan be subtracted from the total investment and the anticipated cash flows compared with the net commitment. This approach does not seem valid; the corporation's total **debt capacity** is consumed as much by a low-cost loan as by one at the market rate of interest. (This is true in accounting terms: in an economic sense, the prinicpal amount of the debt would be reduced to reflect recognition that the terms of the subsidized borrowing lower the true value of the liability compared with value at market rates.) Rather, a credit should be taken in the cash flow for the differential between the rates of interest on the incentive financing and that available on a commercial basis.

Another inducement often provided to attract foreign investment is tariff protection. Many multinational firms have learned to their dismay that an investment predicated wholly or even partially on trade barriers that promise insulation against external competition is extremely risky. This protection may be withdrawn or diminished substantially once the investment is in place; the anticipated returns vanish. Furthermore, when this type of incentive is necessary, the underlying economic attractiveness of the project is suspect. Extreme caution and skepticism are generally warranted.

Political and Economic Risk Analysis. All else being equal, firms prefer to invest in countries with stable currencies, healthy economies, and minimal political risks such as expropriation. But since all else is usually not equal, firms must devote resources to evaluating the consequences of various political and economic risks for the viability of potential investments.

Four principal methods exist for incorporating the additional political and economic risks, such as currency fluctuations and expropriation, that are encountered overseas.

1. Shortening the minimum payback period.
2. Raising the investment's required rate of return.
3. Adjusting cash flows for the costs of risk reduction, for example, charging a premium for political risk insurance.
4. Adjusting cash flows to reflect the specific impact of a given risk.

The two most prevalent approaches among multinationals are to use a higher discount rate for foreign operations and to require a shorter **payback period** (Wickes, "A Comparative Analysis of the Foreign Investment Evaluation Practices of U.S.-Based Multinational Companies"). For instance, if exchange restrictions are anticipated, a normal required return of 15% might be raised to 20% or a five-year payback period may be shortened to three years.

Neither approach, however, lends itself to a careful evaluation of the potential impact of a particular risk on investment returns, although the use of payback may be appropriate if the political environment is so uncertain that the possibility of a total loss is high. Thorough analysis requires an assessment of the magnitude and timing of risks and their implications for the projected cash flows. For example, an **expropriation** five years hence is likely to be much less threatening than one expected next year, even though the probability that the event will occur later may be higher. Thus using a uniformly higher discount rate just distorts the meaning of a project's present value by penalizing future cash flows relatively more heavily than current ones without allowing for a careful risk evaluation. Furthermore, the choice of a **risk premium** (or premiums, if the discount rate is allowed to vary over time) is an arbitrary one, whether it is 2 or 10%. Instead, adjusting cash flows makes it possible to incorporate fully all available information about the impact of a specific risk on the future returns from an investment.

In the sophisticated cash flow adjustment technique known as **uncertainty absorption**, each year's flows are charged a premium for **political and economic risk insurance**. Political risks such as currency inconvertibility or expropriation could be covered by insurance bought through the **Overseas Private Investment Corporation**, a U.S. government agency. The premiums that would be charged are a notational expense for the project. (If insurance is actually purchased, the premium is a cost, and uncertainty absorption is not really used.) This solution, however, does not really measure the effect of a given political risk on a project's present value. In the case of expropriation, political risk insurance normally covers only the book value, not the economic value of expropriated assets. The relationship between the book value of a project's assets and the project's economic value as measured by its future cash flows is tenuous at best. It is worthwhile, of course, to compare the cost of political risk insurance with its expected benefits. Insurance is the third step, however, in a sequential process of, first, identifying and quantifying risks, and second, taking any steps that can be cost justified to reduce them. It is not a substitute for a careful evaluation of the political risk for a given project.

Economic risk, such as currency fluctuations, could be hedged in the **forward exchange market**. In this case, the uncertainty absorption approach would involve adjusting each period's dollar cash flow X_i by the cost of an exchange risk management program. Thus if D_i is the expected forward discount in period i, the value of period i's cash flow is $X_i (1 - D_i)$. The uncertainty absorption technique is particularly useful if local currency cash flows are fixed, as in the case of interest on a bond denominated in a foreign currency. Where income is generated by an ongoing business operation, local currency cash flows will vary with the exchange rate. As indicated in section 11 of the *Handbook* entitled "Exchange Rates and Currency Exposure," there is a set of equilibrium conditions tending to hold in efficient financial markets that generally cause exchange rate changes and inflation to have only a minimal impact on real cash flows. The recommended approach is to adjust a project's cash flows to reflect the specific impact of a given risk, primarily because there is normally more and better information on the specific impact of a given risk on a project's cash flows than on its required return.

Although the suggestion that cash flows from politically risky areas should be discounted at the rate that ignores those risks is contrary to current practice, the difference is more apparent than real. As Lessard ("Evaluating Foreign Projects," in Donald R. Lessard, Ed., *International Financial Management*), points out, most firms evaluating foreign investments discount most likely (modal) rather than expected (mean) cash flows at a **risk-adjusted rate**. If an **expropriation** or **currency blockage** is anticipated, the mean value of the probability distribution of future cash flows will be significantly below its mode. From a theoretical standpoint, of course, cash flows should always be adjusted to reflect the change in expected values caused by a particular risk, but only if the risk is systematic should these cash flows be further discounted. This **adjusted cash flow approach** is illustrated for the case of currency controls.

Currency Controls. Cash flow adjustments must take into account the likelihood that the effect of currency controls will vary over the life of the investment. Often the impact is initially advantageous and only gradually becomes unfavorable when the venture turns into a net generator of cash. In the early phase of an investment, a corporation may be able to import capital goods at a favorable exchange rate if the equipment is assigned a high priority by the host nation. (By using **multiple exchange rates**, many governments effectively subsidize the import of products deemed essential.) Moreover, the company's foreign affiliate may be able to arrange local currency financing at attractive rates by borrowing **blocked funds** held by other foreign-owned companies. It is only when a project is generating a substantial amount of cash that restrictions on profit repatriation are likely to be onerous, until then, controls may be advantageous.

When faced with the possibility of exchange controls, the parent company may find that probability **break-even analysis** is necessary to ascertain under what risks the project would be worth undertaking. By applying break-even analysis, the firm will not have to pinpoint the exact likelihood of risk but merely to determine whether it is smaller or larger than the benchmark figure. Probability analysis may indicate that a project generating large sums of blocked cash is still acceptable, particularly if the funds are likely to be blocked only temporarily and can be invested in local money market instruments and have their dollar value preserved.

Consider, for example, a project that requires an initial outlay of $1 million, with expected annual cash flows to the parent of $375,000, all to be remitted in equal installments over five years. The net present value of the investment, discounted at 20%, is $121,250—a positive sum that means that the project is acceptable. But what if exchange controls are imposed before the second remittance, and full repatriation occurs at the end of the fifth year? Assuming either that the blocked funds cannot be reinvested locally or that they can be invested only at a rate of interest that maintains and does not augment their dollar value, the investment's net present value becomes −$84,625 (Exhibit 6A).

EXHIBIT 6 PRESENT VALUE CALCULATIONS UNDER DIFFERENT CONDITIONS OF REINVESTMENT AND EXCHANGE CONTROLS

				Present Value	
Year	Project Cash Flow	Cash Flow to Parent	20% Present Value Factor	Without Exchange Controls	With Exchange Controls

A. NO REINVESTMENT: (EXCHANGE CONTROLS IMPOSED DURING YEAR 2)

Year	Project Cash Flow	Cash Flow to Parent	20% PVF	Without Exchange Controls	With Exchange Controls
0	−$1,000,000	−$1,000,000	1.0	−$1,000,000	−$1,000,000
1	375,000	375,000	0.833	312,375	312,375
2	375,000	0	0.694	260,250	0
3	375,000	0	0.579	217,125	0
4	375,000	0	0.482	180,750	0
5	375,000	375,000 × 4	0.402	150,750	603,000

Net present value $\quad\quad\quad\quad\quad\quad\quad\quad\quad\quad$ \$ 121,250 $\quad$ \$ −84,625

Year	Project Cash Flow	Cash Flow to Parent	20% Present Value Factor	Present Value With Controls

B. WITH 5% REINVESTMENT RATE: (EXCHANGE CONTROLS IMPOSED DURING YEAR 2)

Year	Project Cash Flow	Cash Flow to Parent	20% PVF	Present Value With Controls
0	−$1,000,000	−$1,000,000	1.0	−$1,000,000
1	375,000	375,000	0.833	312,375
2	375,000	0	0.694	0
3	375,000	0	0.579	0
4	375,000	0	0.482	0
5	375,000	375,000 × $(1 + 1.05 + 1.05^2 + 1.05^3)$	0.402	649,732

Net present value $\quad\quad\quad\quad\quad\quad\quad\quad\quad\quad\quad\quad\quad\quad\quad$ −\$ 37,893

Break-even probability calculation

$$-37{,}893p + 121{,}250(1 - p) > 0$$

or

$$p < \frac{121{,}250}{37{,}893 + 121{,}250} = 0.76$$

Year	Project Cash Flow	Cash Flow to Parent	20% Present Value Factor	Present Value With controls

C. NO REINVESTMENT: (EXCHANGE CONTROLS IMPOSED DURING YEAR 3)

Year	Project Cash Flow	Cash Flow to Parent	20% PVF	Present Value With controls
0	−$1,000,000	−$1,000,000	1.0	−$1,000,000
1	375,000	375,000	0.833	312,375
2	375,000	375,000	0.694	260,250
3	375,000	0	0.579	0
4	375,000	0	0.482	0
5	375,000	375,000 × 3	0.402	452,250

New present value $\quad\quad\quad\quad\quad\quad\quad\quad\quad\quad\quad\quad\quad\quad\quad$ \$ 24,875

If p is the probability that controls will be imposed in the second year or not at all, the project's expected net present value equals $-\$84,625p +$ $\$121,250(1 - p)$. As long as $-\$84,625p + \$121,250(1 - p) > 0$, or $p < .59$, the expected net present value is positive. Hence, from the standpoint of its expected value, the project is worth undertaking only if the probability is less than 59% that exchange curbs will be imposed during the second year and not lifted until the end of the fifth year.

If the funds can be reinvested to yield an annual dollar rate of return of 5%, the net present value rises to $-\$37,893$, and to \$12,006 if the rate is 10%. The respective break-even probabilities are .76 and 1. Thus, with a dollar reinvestment rate of 5%, the expected net present value will be positive if the probability of controls in the second year is no greater than 76%; with a dollar reinvestment rate of 10%, net present value will be positive even if it is certain that currency controls will be imposed during the second year. (The computations for a 5% reinvestment rate are presented in Exhibit 6B.)

Probability break-even analysis is useful, since normally fewer data are required to ascertain whether p is smaller or larger than the benchmark needed to determine the absolute value of p. For instance, if the break-even level is 76%, it is unnecessary to spend time determining whether the chance of currency curbs is 30 or 40%, because the project's net present value will be positive in either case.

If exchange restrictions are not anticipated until just before the third remittance, the net present value with no reinvestment equals \$24,875 (see Exhibit 6C). That means that regardless of either the likelihood of currency controls after the second year or the magnitude of the rate of return on blocked funds, the investment can be undertaken, provided all funds can be repatriated at the end of the fifth year.

Exchange Rate Changes and Inflation. Projected cash flows can be stated in nominal (current) or real (constant) domestic or foreign currency terms. Ultimately, to ensure comparability between the various cash inflows and home currency outlays today, all cash flows must be expressed in real terms (i.e., units of constant purchasing power). Nominal cash flows can be converted to real cash flows by adjusting either the cash flows or the discount rate. Both methods yield the same results.

Let C_t be the nominal expected foreign currency cash flow in year t, e_t the nominal spot exchange rate in t, and i_h the home currency inflation rate. Then $C_t e_t$ is the nominal home currency value of this cash flow in year t and $C_t e_t / (1 + i_h)^t$ is its real value in current units of home currency.

Discounting at the real required rate of return k, which equals the real interest rate plus a risk premium, the present home currency value of this cash flow is:

$$\frac{C_t e_t}{(1 + k)^t (1 + i_h)^t}$$

Usually, however, the nominal cash flow in home currency terms, $C_t e_t$, is discounted at the nominal required rate of return k^*, which equals the nominal interest rate plus a premium for risk. But according to the **Fisher effect**, the nominal interest rate incorporates a premium for anticipated inflation or $1 + k^* = (1 + k)(1 + i_h)$. Therefore,

$$\frac{C_t e_t}{(1 + k^*)^t} = \frac{C_t e_t}{(1 + k)^t(1 + i_h)^t}$$

or discounting nominal cash flows using a nominal discount rate is identical in equilibrium to discounting real cash flows using a real rate of return. These possibilities are summarized in Exhibit 7.

If **purchasing power parity** holds

$$e_t = \frac{e_0(1 + i_h)^t}{(1 + i_f)^t}$$

where e_0 is the current spot rate and i_f is the foreign currency inflation rate. Then:

$$\frac{C_t e_t}{(1 + k)^t(1 + i_h)^t} = \frac{\overline{C}_t e_0}{(1 + k)^t}$$

where $\overline{C}_t = C_t /(1 + i_f)^t$ is the expected foreign currency cash flow expressed in real terms.

This demonstrates again that to evaluate foreign cash flows, it is necessary to abstract from offsetting inflation and exchange rate changes. It is worthwhile, however, to analyze each effect separately because there is often a lag between a given rate of inflation and the implied exchange rate change to maintain international equilibrium. This is particularly true when government intervention occurs, such as in a **fixed rate system** or a **managed float**. Furthermore, local **price controls** may not permit or may even retard the effect of internal price adjustments. The possibility of relative price changes within the foreign economy can be incorporated easily by altering nominal

EXHIBIT 7   EVALUATING FOREIGN CURRENCY CASH FLOWS

	Real	Nominal
Cash flow	$\dfrac{C_t e_t}{(1 + i_h)^t}$	$C_t e_t$
Discount rate	k	$k^* = k + i_h + k i_h$
Present value	$\dfrac{C_t e_t}{(1 + k)^t(1 + i_h)^t}$	$\dfrac{C_t e_t}{(1 + k^*)^t} = \dfrac{C_t e_t}{(1 + k)^t(1 + i_h)}$

project cash flows (the C_i's). Thus the present value of future cash flows can be calculated by converting nominal foreign currency cash flows into nominal home currency terms, then discounting them at the nominal domestic required rate of return. This is identical to converting nominal foreign currency cash flows into real home currency terms and discounting them at the real domestic required rate of return.

COST OF CAPITAL FOR FOREIGN INVESTMENTS. The cost of capital for a given investment is the minimum risk-adjusted return required by shareholders of the firm undertaking that investment. As such, it is the basic measure of financial performance. Unless the investment generates sufficient funds to compensate the suppliers of capital adequately, the firm's value will suffer. This return requirement is met only if the net present value of future project cash flows, using the corporation's cost of capital as the discount rate, is positive.

Discount Rates for Foreign Projects. A key issue for the MNC is whether a higher rate of return should be required of foreign projects than of domestic ones with comparable commercial risks. Many firms believe that the additional risks associated with foreign investments—currency controls, exchange risk, expropriation, and other forms of government intervention—mean that the greater a firm's international involvement, the riskier its stock should be, hence the greater its cost of equity capital.

In fact, there is good reason to believe that being international may actually reduce the riskiness of a firm. To understand this assertion, it is necessary to realize that risk is generally measured by the total variability of returns. The less variable a security's returns, the lower the risk of that security. **The capital asset pricing model** assumes that the total variability of an asset's returns can be attributed to two sources: (1) marketwide influences such as the state of the economy that affect all assets to some extent, and (2) developments or aspects that are specific to a given firm. The former is usually termed a **systematic**, or **nondiversifiable risk**, and the latter an **unsystematic**, or diversifiable risk.

By holding a portfolio of stocks whose returns are not all subject to the same risks, an investor can eliminate some of this return variability. The risk of a portfolio of stocks will be less than the average riskiness of its component securities. Thus unsystematic risk is largely irrelevant to the holder of a highly diversified share portfolio; the effects of disturbances can be expected to be offset on average in the portfolio. On the other hand, no matter how well diversified a stock portfolio is, systematic risk, by definition, cannot be eliminated; the investor must be compensated for bearing that risk.

The importance of this theory for the international company is that the relevant component of risk in pricing a firm's stock is its systematic risk, in other words, that portion of return variability that cannot be eliminated by diversification. Most of the systematic, or general, market risk is related to the cyclical nature of the national economies in which the firm operates. The **diversification effect** that comes from dealing in a number of countries whose economic cycles are not perfectly synchronous should reduce the variability of an MNC's earnings.

In fact, less developed countries (LDCs), where **political risks** are greatest, may provide the maximum diversification benefits. They are less likely to be closely linked to the U.S. or other major economies, whereas the business cycles of developed countries tend to be closely correlated with each other. Thus investments in LDCs could be regarded as a plus, rather than a minus, for a company.

Of course, the systematic risk of projects even in relatively isolated LDCs is unlikely to be too far below the average for all projects; these countries are still tied into the world economy. The important point is that the ratio of systematic risk to total risk may be quite small in those countries, not necessarily that the systematic risk itself is small.

Even if a nation's economy is not closely linked to the world economy, the systematic risk of a project located in that country might still be rather large. For example, a mining venture in a foreign nation, whether in Canada, Chile, or Zaire, will probably have systematic risk that is very similar to that of an identical investment in the United States. The major element of systematic risk in any extractive project is related to variations in the price of the mineral being mined, which is set in a world market. The global price in turn is a function of worldwide demand, which itself is systematically related to the state of the world economy.

By contrast, a market-oriented project in an LDC, whose risk depends largely on the evolution of the domestic demand in that country, is likely to have a systematic risk that is small both in relative and absolute terms.

Empirical Evidence on MNC Risk. An analysis of the available evidence on the impact of foreign operations on firm riskiness suggests that if there is an effect, it is generally to reduce both actual and perceived riskiness. Both Cohen (*Multinational Firms and Asian Exports*, Yale University Press, New Haven, CT, 1975) and Rugman (*Journal of International Business Studies*, Fall 1976, pp. 75–80) have shown that there is little correlation between the earnings of the various national components of MNCs. To the extent that foreign cash flows are not perfectly correlated with those of domestic investments, the overall risk associated with variations in total corporate retuns might be reduced. Thus the greater riskiness of individual projects overseas could well be offset by beneficial portfolio effects. Furthermore, it is generally assumed that most of the economic and political risks specific to the multinational corporation are nonsystematic and can, therefore, be eliminated through diversification.

The **benefits of international diversification** should reduce the cost of equity for an MNC. However, if international portfolio diversification can be accomplished as easily and cheaply by individual investors, the required rates of return on an MNC's securities should reflect only their contribution to the systematic risk of a fully diversified world portfolio. In fact, though, very little foreign portfolio investment is actually undertaken by U.S. investors.

Restrictions on International Portfolio Diversification. The limited amount of **investment in foreign securities** is normally explained by a lack of information and the various legal and economic barriers that serve to segment national capital markets. Currency controls, specific tax regulations, relatively less efficient and less developed capital markets abroad, exchange risk, and the paucity of adequate, readily accessible, and comparable information on potential investments in foreign securities increase the perceived riskiness of foreign securities and deter investors. Furthermore, no other country in the world has the breadth or depth of industry that the United States has. Hence, to diversify adequately in a foreign economy, it will usually be necessary to acquire shares of multinational firms in industries operating in nations where indigenous firms do not exist. Diversifying into the computer industry in Venezuela, for example, means buying the shares of IBM or some other multinational computer manufacturer with operations there. Thus U.S. investors may be able to achieve low-cost international diversification by acquiring the shares of the U.S.-based MNCs. Moreover, when countries impose restrictions on overseas portfolio investment, investors may be able to achieve international portfolio diversification only by purchasing shares in the multinational corporations domiciled in their own nations.

The value of international diversification appears to be significant. Lessard (*Financial Analysts Journal*, January-February 1976, pp. 32–38) and Solnik (*Financial Analysts Journal*, July-August 1974, pp. 48–54) have presented evidence that national factors have a strong impact on security returns relative to that of any common world factor. In addition, they find that returns from the different national equity markets have relatively low correlations with each other. These results imply that international diversification may be able to reduce significantly the risk of portfolios. In fact, the variance of an internationally diversified portfolio appears to be as little as 30% of that of individual securities. Moreover, as Solnik's data indicate (Exhibit 8), the benefits from international diversification are significantly greater than those that can be achieved solely by adding more domestic stocks to a portfolio.

Evidence from the Stock Market. The ability of MNCs to provide an indirect means of international diversification may be an important advantage to investors. However, for foreign activities to affect an MNC's **cost of equity capital**, the market must be able to distinguish between the international and domestic operations of firms.

In the first study to address this issue directly, Agmon and Lessard (*Jour-*

EXHIBIT 8   BENEFITS OF INTERNATIONAL PORTFOLIO DIVERSIFICATION

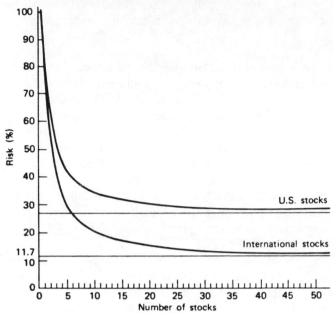

Source: Reprinted from Bruno H. Solnik, "Why Not Diversify Internationally Rather Than Domestically?" *Financial Analysts Journal,* July–August 1974, p. 51, by permission of the publisher.

nal of Finance, September 1977, pp. 1049–1055) examined the price behavior of U.S.-based multinational corporations listed on the **New York Stock Exchange**. Their analysis supports the hypothesis that investors recognize international diversification.

In a related work, Jacquillat and Solnik (*Journal of Portfolio Management*, Winter 1978, pp. 8–12) concluded that although multinational firms do provide some diversification for investors, they are poor substitutes for **international portfolio diversification**. Their results indicate that an internationally diversified portfolio leads to a much greater reduction in variance than does a portfolio comprising firms with widespread international activities. For a detailed discussion of international portfolio diversification, see the section entitled "International Portfolio Diversification and Foreign Capital Markets."

Despite the limitations of MNCs as vehicles for international diversification, they evidently have some value as is indicated by the most careful study to date of the effects of foreign operations on the **cost of equity capital**. In that study, Fatemi (*Journal of Finance*, December 1984, pp. 1325–1344) compared the performance of two carefully constructed stock portfolios: A portfolio of 84 MNCs, each with at least 25% of their annual sales generated from international operations, and a portfolio of 52 purely domestic firms. Monthly performance comparisons were made over the five-year period 1976–1980.

Although the validity of the study is limited by the relatively short time period involved and the difficulty in properly matching MNCs with their purely domestic counterparts (most firms do business in more than one industry) and in calculating the volume of foreign sales (e.g., consider the **transfer pricing** problem), its conclusions are nonetheless of interest:

1. The rates of return on the two portfolios are statistically identical; ignoring risk, MNCs and uninational corporations (UNCs) provide shareholders the same returns.

2. Consistent with our expectations, the rates of return on the MNC portfolio fluctuate less than those on the UNC portfolio. Thus, corporate international diversification seems to reduce shareholders' total risk and may do the same for the firm's total risk.

3. The **betas** of the **multinational portfolio** are significantly lower and more stable than those of the purely domestic portfolio; this indicates that corporate international diversification reduces the degree of systematic risk, at least if systematic risk is calculated relative to the domestic portfolio. It was also found that the higher the degree of international involvement, the lower the beta.

Management Implications of MNC Investment. Corporations should continue investing abroad as long as profitable opportunities exist. Retrenching based on a belief that investors desire less extensive or smaller international operations will lead to forgoing both profitable foreign investments and valuable diversification; the firm's shareholders would be penalized, not rewarded. At the very least, executives of multinational firms should seriously question whether a premium rate of return should be employed to account for the added political and economic risks of overseas operations when evaluating prospective foreign investments. The use of any such premium ignores the fact that the risk of an individual overseas investment within the context of the firm's other investments, domestic as well as foreign, will be less than that project's total risk. How much less depends on how highly correlated the outcomes of the firm's different investments are. Thus the automatic inclusion of a premium when evaluating a foreign project is not necessarily an element of conservatism. Before additional conclusions can be reached, more empirical testing of investor perceptions of the riskiness of MNCs is required. These perceptions are likely to be affected by the location as well as the percentage of foreign source earning (e.g., developed versus less developed countries).

POLITICAL RISK ANALYSIS AND MANAGEMENT. Rising nationalism both in developing and developed countries and in economic blocks has increased the political risks to which MNCs have been exposed historically. These take many forms, from currency controls to expropriation, from a change in tax laws to requirements for additional local production or expensive pollution control equipment. Their common denominator is government action that adversely affects the value of the firm. Despite the potentially severe consequences of political risk, surveys of how firms view and respond to this exposure reveal a pattern of few attempts at systematic analysis. The findings of these surveys, which are remarkably consistent, are summarized by Kobrin (*Journal of International Business Studies*. Spring-Summer 1979, p. 75) as follows:

> First, it is clear that managers consider political instability or political risk, typically quite loosely defined, to be an important factor in the foreign investment decision. Second, it is just as clear that rigorous and systematic assessment and evaluation of the political environment is exceptional. Most political analysis is superficial and subjective, not integrated formally into the decision-making process and assumes that instability and risk are one and the same. The response frequently is avoidance: firms simply do not get involved in countries, or even regions, that they perceive to be risky. Last, managers appear to rely for environmental information primarily on sources internal to the firm. When they look for outside data, they are most likely to go to their banks or the general and business media.

Measuring Political Risk. The characteristics of each company will, to a large extent, determine the susceptibility to political risk and the effects on the present value of its foreign investment. Governments, even revolutionary ones, rarely **expropriate foreign investments** indiscriminately. This assertion is supported by studies by Truitt (*Journal of International Business Studies*. Fall 1970, pp. 21–34) and Hawkins, Mintz, and Provissiero (*Journal of International Business Studies*. Spring 1976, pp. 3–15) on the post-World War II experiences of U.S. and British MNCs. The data clearly show that except for the countries in which Communist goverments gained control, companies differ in their susceptibilities to political risk, depending on the industry, size, composition of ownership, level of technology, and degree of vertical integration with other affiliates. For example, expropriation, overt or creeping, is more likely to occur in the extractive, utility, and financial service sectors of an economy than in manufacturing. Moreover, some firms may be benefited by the same event that harms other firms. A company that relies on imports will be hurt by trade restrictions, whereas an import-competing firm may well be helped.

In general, the greater the perceived benefits provided by a subsidiary to the host economy and the more expensive its replacement by a purely local operation, the smaller the degree of risk to the MNC. The implication is that goverments select their expropriation targets according to nonpolitical criteria. This degree of selectivity suggests that companies can take actions to control their exposure to political risk.

Avoiding Political Risk. The easiest way to **manage political risk** is to avoid it, which many firms do by screening out investments in politically uncertain nations. However, inasmuch as all governments make decisions that influence the profitability of business, all investments, including those made in the United States, face some degree of political risk. For example, American steel companies have had to cope with stricter environmental regulations requiring the expenditure of billions of dollars for new pollution control devices, and American oil companies are beleaguered by so-called windfall profit taxes, price controls, and mandatory allocations. Risk avoidance is impossible.

The real issue is the degree of political risk a company is willing to tolerate and the return required to bear it. A policy of avoiding countries considered to be politically unstable ignores the potentially high returns available and the extent to which a firm can control the risks. After all, companies are in business to take risks, if these are recognized, intelligently managed, and provide compensation.

Political Risk Insurance. Most developed countries sell political risk insurance to cover the foreign assets of domestic companies. The coverage provided by the U.S. government through the **Overseas Private Investment Corporation** (OPIC) is typical. By insuring assets in unstable areas, firms can concentrate on managing their businesses and forget about this risk—or so it appears.

The OPIC program provides U.S. investors with insurance against loss due to the specific political risks of expropriation, currency inconvertibility, war, revolution, or insurrection. To qualify, the investment must be a new one or a substantial expansion of an existing facility and must be approved by the host government. Coverage is restricted to 90% of equity participation. For very large investments or for projects deemed especially risky, OPIC coverage may be limited to less than 90%. The only exception is institutional project loans to unrelated third parties, which may be insured for the full amount of principal and interest. The cost of the coverage varies by industry and risk insured (Exhibit 9). It is apparent that the costs are not based solely on objective criteria but also reflect certain political aims, such as fostering development of additional energy supplies.

There are two fundamental problems associated with relying on insurance as a protection against political risk. First, as previously mentioned, the economic value of an investment is the present value of its future cash flows, but only the investment in assets is covered by insurance. Thus, although insurance can provide some insulation against political risk, it falls far short of being a comprehensive solution. Second, there is an asymmetry involved. If an investment proves unprofitable, it is unlikely to be expropriated. Since business risk is not covered, any losses must be borne by the firm itself. On the other hand, if the investment is successful and then is expropriated, the firm is compensated only for the value of its assets, not for the lost future earnings.

EXHIBIT 9 OPIC INSURANCE FEES (%) (AS OF 1980)

Coverage	Manufacturing and Services Projects	Natural Resource Projects (Other Than Oil and Gas)	Oil and Gas Projects		Institutional Loans
			Exploration	Production	
Inconvertibility	0.30	0.30	0.10	0.30	0.25
Expropriation	0.60	0.90	0.40	1.50	0.30
War revolution, insurrection (WRI)	0.60	0.60	0.60	0.60	0.60
Interference with operations	—	—	0.40	0.40	—
Inconvertibility, expropriation (combined)	—	—	—	—	0.50
Inconvertibility, expropriation, WRI (combined)	—	—	—	—	0.90

Source: Overseas Private Investment Corporation, *Investment Insurance Handbook*.

Modifying the Environment. As an alternative to insurance, therefore, some firms try to reach an understanding with the host government before undertaking the investment, defining the rights and responsibilities of both parties. Such a concession agreement, in effect, specifies the rules under which the firm can operate locally.

Concession agreements were quite popular among firms investing in less developed countries, especially in colonies of the home country. They often were negotiated with weak governments. In time, many of these countries became independent or their governments were overthrown. Invariably, the new rulers repudiated the old concession agreements, arguing that they were a form of exploitation.

Concession agreements are still being negotiated today, but they seem to carry little weight among the LDCs and are observed usually only in developed countries. Their high rate of obsolescence has led many firms to pursue a more active policy of political risk management.

Structuring Foreign Investment. Once a firm has decided to invest in a country, it can try to minimize its exposure to political risk by adjusting its operating policies in the areas of production, logistics, exporting, and technology transfer, and its financial policies.

One key element of such a strategy is to keep the local affiliate dependent on sister companies for markets and/or supplies. Similarly, by concentrating research and development facilities and proprietary technology, or at least key components thereof, in the home country, a firm can raise the cost of nationalization. To be effective, other multinationals with licensing agreements must be unable to service an affiliate if nationalized, or must be forbidden to do so. Another element of this strategy is to establish single, global trademarks that cannot be legally duplicated by a government. In this way, the incentive for a government to expropriate a local subsidiary of a consumer products company would be reduced significantly because the use of the recognized brand name would be precluded.

Control of transportation, including shipping, pipelines, and railroads, has also been used at one time or another by the United Fruit Co. and other MNCs to gain leverage over governments. Similarly, diversifying production among multiple plants changes the balance of power between government and firm by reducing the government's ability to hurt the worldwide firm by seizing a single facility.

Involving external financial stakeholders in the venture is another defensive measure that may be particularly useful in extractive industries. Capital for a venture is raised from the host and other governments, international financial institutions, and customers (with payment to be provided out of production) rather than employing funds supplied or guaranteed by the parent company. In addition to spreading risks, an international response will be elicited by any expropriation move or other adverse action by a host government. This protection is not necessarily free, and it may be obtained only by accepting expensive capital. As an example, **project financing** to develop mineral and hydrocarbon resources has been used extensively by multinational firms. By placing international banks between the company and the host government, a degree of insulation is obtained.

A last approach, particularly for extractive projects, is to obtain unconditional **host government guarantees** for the amount of the investment, which enable creditors to threaten or to institute legal action in foreign or international courts against harmful (to the MNC) commercial transactions between the host country and third parties if a subsequent government repudiates the nation's obligations. Such guarantees provide investors with potential sanctions against a foreign government without having to rely on the uncertain support of their home government. In reality, these guarantees are difficult to enforce.

Planned Divestment. Once the multinational has invested in a project, its ability to influence the susceptibility to political risk is greatly diminished but not ended. Planned divestment involves the orderly sale by a multinational firm of all or a majority of its ownership of a foreign investment to local investors. Such an arrangement, however, may be difficult to conclude to the satisfaction of all parties involved. If a *buyout price* has been set in advance on an investment that turns out to be unprofitable, the host government probably will not honor the purchase commitment or permit local investors to honor it. Moreover, with the constant threat of expropriation present during the bargaining, it is unlikely that a fair price can be negotiated.

This disadvantageous position for the multinational firm is not restricted to cases of danger of full expropriation. Legislation in a number of countries requires certain percentages of local ownership. Often these laws were enacted after the investments had been made, and grandfather clauses may not be available. For example, the **Andean Pact** nations agreed to limit foreign ownership in commerical (i.e., wholesaling and retailing) companies to 20%.

Short-Term Profit Maximization. Confronted with the need to divest itself wholly or partially of an equity position, the multinational corporation may respond by attempting to withdraw the maximum from the local operation. By deferring maintenance expenditures, cutting investment to the minimum necessary to sustain the desired level of production, curtailing marketing expenditures, producing lower quality merchandise, setting higher prices, and eliminating training programs, cash generation will be maximized for the short term, regardless of the effects of such actions on longer run profitability and viability. This policy, which almost guarantees that the company will not be in business locally for long, is a response of desperation. Of course, the behavior is likely to accelerate expropriation if such is the government's intention (and perhaps even if it was not originally).

The firm must select its time horizon for augmenting cash outflow and consider how this behavior will affect government relations and actions. The secondary implications of the short-term profit maximization strategy must be evaluated as well. The unfriendly government could be replaced by a new government more receptive to foreign investment, or the multinational firm may want to supply the local market from affiliates in other countries. In either case, an aggressive tactic of withdrawing as much as possible from the threatened affiliate probably will be considered a hostile act and will vitiate all future dealings between the multinational firm and the country.

One alternative to this indirect form of divestment is to do nothing, hoping that even though the local regime could, at a minor cost, take an affiliate over, it will choose not to do so. This is not necessarily a vain wish, since it rests on the premise that the country needs foreign direct investment and will be unlikely to receive it if potential investors fear that existing operations may be expropriated without fair and full compensation. Whether this passive approach will succeed is a function of the host country's dependence on foreign investment to realize its own development plans and the degree to which economic growth will be sacrificed for philosophical, religious, or political reasons.

Changing the Ratio of Cost to Benefit. If the government's objectives in an **expropriation** are rational (i.e., based on the belief that economic benefits will more than compensate for the costs), the multinational firm can initiate a number of programs to reduce the perceived advantages of local ownership and thereby diminish the incentive to expel foreigners. These steps include establishing local research and development facilities, developing export markets for the affiliate's output, training local workers and managers, expanding production facilities, and manufacturing a wider range of products locally as substitutes for imports. It should be recognized that many of the foregoing actions simultaneously lower the cost of expropriation and, consequently, reduce the penalty for the government. A delicate balance must be considered.

Realistically, however, it appears that the countries most prone to expropriate view the benefits (real, imagined, or both) of local ownership as more important than the cost of replacing the foreign investor. Although the value of a subsidiary to the local economy can be important, its worth may not be sufficient to protect against political risk. Thus one aspect of a protective strategy must be to raise the cost of expropriation by increasing the negative sanctions that would be exerted. This includes achieving and maintaining control over export markets, transportation, technology, trademarks and brand names, and components manufactured in other nations. Some of these tactics may not be available once the investment has been made, but others may still be implemented.

Developing Local Stakeholders. A more positive strategy is to cultivate local individuals and groups who have a stake in the affiliate's continued existence as a unit of the parent multinational. Potential stakeholders include consumers, suppliers, the subsidiary's local employees, local bankers, and joint venture partners.

Consumers worried about a change in product quality or suppliers concerned about a disruption in their production schedules (or even a switch to other suppliers) brought about by a government takeover may have an incentive to protest. Similarly, well-treated local employees may lobby against expropriation. Local borrowing could help give local bankers a stake in the health of the MNC's operations if any government action threatened the affiliate's cash flow and jeopardized loan repayments.

Having local private investors as partners would appear to provide protection. In fact, this shield is likely to be of limited value because the local investors will be deemed to be tainted by association with the multinational. A government probably would not be deterred by the existence of local shareholders from expropriation or enacting discriminatory laws. Moreover, the action could be directed solely against the foreign investor. The local partners even could be the genesis of a move to expropriate, to enable them to acquire the whole of a business at little or no cost.

Adaptation. A more radical approach to political risk management is being tried by some firms today. Rather than resisting potential expropriation, this policy entails adapting to the inevitability of it and trying to earn profits on the firm's resources by entering into **licensing and management agreements**. Oil companies whose properties were nationalized by the Venezuelan government received management contracts to continue their exploration, refining, and marketing operations. These firms have recognized that it is not necessary to own or control an asset such as an oil well to earn profits. This form of arrangement is likely to be more common in the future as countries develop greater management abilities and decide to purchase from foreign firms only the skills that remain in short supply at home. Firms unable to surrender control of their foreign operations because of the integration of these operations in a worldwide production planning system or some other form of global strategy are also those least likely to be troubled by the threat of property seizure. An expropriated automobile assembly plant is of little value in the absence of facilities for producing engines, transmissions, and body stampings.

FINANCING FOREIGN OPERATIONS

MULTINATIONAL FINANCIAL STRATEGY. In selecting an appropriate strategy for financing its worldwide operations, the availability of different sources of funds and their relative costs and effects on the multinational firm's operating risks must be considered. Some of the key variables in the evaulation are rates of interest and taxes, exchange risk, diversification of fund sources, the freedom to move funds across borders, and a variety of **government credit and capital controls and subsidies.** The eventual funding strategy selected must reconcile a variety of potentially conflicting objectives such as minimizing expected financing costs, reducing economic exposure to foreign exchange fluctuations, providing protection against **currency controls** and other forms of **political risk**, and assuring availability of funds in times of tight credit.

A general framework by Lessard and Shapiro (*Midland Corporate Finance Journal*, 1984, pp. 68–80), separates the financing of international operations into three facets and offers the following directions.

1. Seek to profit from market distortions. This includes:
    a. Taking advantage of deviations from equilibrium exchange or interest rates that may exist because of government controls and subsidies.
    b. Speculating based on forecasts divergent from those held by the market in general.
    c. Exploiting the company's unique position vis-à-vis taxes, exchange controls and other restrictions, based on its ability to adjust **intracompany fund flows.**
2. Arrange financing to reduce the riskiness of the operating cash flows. This includes:
    a. Offsetting the firm's projected economic exposure by borrowing, if cost justified, in appropriate currencies.

b. Reducing various political risks, either by giving lenders a vested interest in the continuing viability of the firm's operations or by decreasing the firm's assets that are exposed.

c. Selling the output from the plant or project in advance to customers to decrease sales uncertainty and then using the sales contracts to obtain funds.

d. Securing a continuing supply of financing for corporate activities worldwide by diversifying sources of funds and, possibly, borrowing in anticipation of needs.

3. Meet the financial structure goals of the multinational corporation overall. This includes:

a. Establishing a worldwide capital structure that balances the aftertax costs and benefits of leverage.

b. Selecting the appropriate affiliate capital structures.

FINANCING FOREIGN SUBSIDIARIES. The following factors should be considered when selecting the method of financing affiliates abroad.

Debt Versus Equity Financing. Interest payments on debt, extended by either the parent or a financial institution, generally are deductible by an affiliate for its local tax purposes, but dividends are not. In addition, the repayment of borrowing usually does not attract taxes. Thus an incentive exists to employ leverage.

Government Credit and Capital Controls. Governments intervene in their financial markets for a number of reasons: to restrain the growth of lendable funds, to make certain types of borrowing more or less expensive, and to direct funds to certain favored economic activities. When access to local funds markets is restricted, interest rates in them are usually below the risk-adjusted equilibrium level. There is often an incentive to borrow as much as possible where nonprice credit rationing is used.

Restraints on overseas borrowing, or incentives to promote it, are often employed as well. There are numerous examples of this. Certain countries have limited the amount of local financing obtainable by the subsidiary of a multinational firm to that required for working capital purposes; any additional needs must be satisfied from abroad. A precondition for obtaining official approval for a new investment or acquisition often is a commitment to inject external funds. Conversely, when a nation is concerned about excess capital inflows, a portion of any new foreign borrowing might have to be placed on deposit with the government, thereby raising the effective cost of external debt.

The multinational firm with access to a variety of sources and types of funds and the ability to shift capital with its **internal transfer system** has more opportunities to secure the lowest risk-adjusted cost of money and to circumvent credit restraints. These attributes should give it a substantial advantage over a purely domestic company.

Government Subsidies. Despite the often hostile rhetoric directed against the multinational firm, many governments offer a growing list of incentives to MNCs to influence their production and export sourcing decisions. Direct investment incentives include interest rate subsidies, loans with long maturities, guarantees of repatriation, grants related to project size, favorable prices for land, corporate income tax holidays, accelerated depreciation, and a reduction in or elimination of the payment of other business taxes and import duties on capital equipment and raw materials. Governments sometimes make the infrastructure investments as well, thereby providing the base to support a new industrial project.

In addition, all governments of developed nations have some form of export financing agency whose purpose is to boost exports by providing loans with long repayment periods at rates of interest below the market level and low-cost political and economic risk insurance. These **export credit programs** can often be employed advantageously by multinationals. The use depends on whether the firm is seeking export or import goods or services, but the basic strategy remains the same—examining the various incentives for the best possible financing arrangement.

Import Financing Strategy. If sizable imports are part of an investment, it may be possible to finance these purchases on attractive terms. A number of countries, including the United States, make credit available to foreign purchasers at low (below market) interest rates and with long repayment periods. These loans are tied to procurement in the agency's country; thus the firm must compile a list of goods and services required for the project and relate them to potential sources, country by country. Where there is overlap among the potential suppliers, the purchasing firm may have leverage to extract more favorable financing terms from the various export credit agencies involved.

Diversification of Fund Sources. A key element of any MNC's global financial strategy should be to gain access to a broad range of fund sources to lessen its dependence on any one financial market. An ancillary benefit is that the firm broadens its sources of economic and financial information, providing a useful supplement to its domestic resources and aiding in its financial decision-making process.

Worldwide Financial Structure. The multinational firm, like a purely domestic one, has as one of its key objectives a capital structure which minimizes the overall aftertax cost of capital. This determination is complicated when a firm is operating in more than one country because the laws and regulations of other nations must be considered. The worldwide capital structure, however, need not be just a residual of the decisions made for individual subsidiaries. The parent does have the ability to offset a highly leveraged overseas financial structure with a more conservative one elsewhere to maintain a target **debt-equity mix** for the firm as a whole. The focus is on the consolidated financial structure because suppliers of capital to a multinational firm associate the risk of default with the MNC's worldwide debt ratio. Shareholders look to the entire corporation for their dividends and the **cost of equity capital** is a function of the enterprise's overall profitability.

Subsidiary Financial Structure. Once a decision has been made regarding the appropriate mix of debt and equity for the entire corporation, questions about individual operations can be raised. What factors are relevant in establishing foreign affiliates' capital structures? Should they:

· Conform to that of the parent company?
· Reflect the capitalization norms in each foreign country?
· Vary to take advantage of opportunities to minimize the MNC's cost of capital?

Disregarding public and government relations and legal requirements for the moment, the parent company could decide to raise funds in its own country and inject sufficient amounts of equity to satisfy fully all subsidiaries' financial requirements. The overseas operations would then have a zero debt ratio. Alternatively, the parent could avoid the direct financial burden on itself. It would hold only one dollar of share capital in each affiliate and require all to borrow locally or internationally, with or without guarantees. In this instance, the debt ratios approach 100%. Or, the parent could itself borrow from external markets and relend the moneys as **intracompany advances.** Here again, the affiliates' debt ratios would be close to 100%. In all these cases, the total amount of borrowing and the **debt-equity mix** of the consolidated corporation are identical. Thus the question of an optimal capital structure for a foreign affiliate is completely distinct from the corporation's overall debt-equity ratio. Assets in a foreign country are to be financed; how is it to be done?

Adler (*Journal of Finance*, March 1974, pp. 119–132), moreover, has argued that any accounting rendition of a separate capital structure for the subsidiary is wholly illusory **unless** the parent is willing to allow its affiliate to default on its debt. As long as the rest of the MNC group has a legal or moral oligation or sound business reasons for preventing the affiliate from defaulting, the individual unit has no independent capital structure. Rather, its true debt-equity ratio is equal to that of the consolidated group.

The irrelevance of **subsidiary financial structures** when considering the entire corporation seems to be recognized by multinationals. A survey of eight U.S.-based MNCs by Business International (*Business International*

Money Report, September 21, 1979, pp. 319–320) reported that most of the firms expressed little concern with the debt-equity mixes of their foreign affiliates; the primary focus was on the worldwide, rather than individual, capital structure. (Admittedly, for most of the firms interviewed, the debt ratios of affiliates had not significantly raised the MNC's consolidated indebtedness.) The third option of manipulating affiliate financial structures to take advantage of local financing opportunities appears to be the preferred choice. Thus, within the constraints set by foreign statutory or minimum equity rules, the need to appear to be a responsible and a good guest, and the requirements of a worldwide financial structure, a multinational corporation should finance its affiliates to minimize its total **weighted average cost of capital.**

A subsidiary with a capital structure similar to its parent may forgo profitable opportunities to lower its cost of funds. For example, rigid adherence to a fixed debt-equity ratio may not allow a subsidiary to take advantage of government-subsidized debt or low-cost loans from international agencies. Furthermore, it may be worthwile to raise funds locally if the country is politically risky. If the affiliate were expropriated, for instance, it would default on all loans from local financial institutions. Similarly, borrowing funds in the country will decrease the company's vulnerability to exchange controls. On the other hand, forcing a subsidiary to raise funds locally to meet parent norms may be quite expensive in a country with a high-cost capital market.

The cost-minimizing approach would be to direct subsidiaries in low-cost countries to exceed the parent company capitalization norm, while affiliates in high-cost nations would have lower target debt-equity ratios. This assumes that capital markets are at least partially segmented. Although there are no definite conclusions on this issue at present, the variety and degree of governmental restrictions on capital market access lend credence to the segmentation hypothesis. In addition, the behavior of MNCs in lobbying against regulations such as the OFDI restrictions indicates that they believe that capital costs vary substantially among countries.

A counterargument by Stonehill and Stitzel (*California Management Review,* Fall 1969, pp. 91–96) is that a **subsidiary's financial structure** should conform to local norms. Then, because German and Japanese firms are more highly leveraged than, say, companies in the United States and France, the Japanese and German subsidiaries of an American firm should have much higher debt-equity ratios than the U.S. parent or a French subsidiary. There are two problems with this argument. First, according to Naumann-Etienne (*Journal of Financial and Quantitative Analysis,* November 1974, pp. 859–870), it ignores the strong linkage between U.S.-based multinationals and the U.S. capital market. Since most of their stock is owned and traded in the United States, it follows that the firms' **target debt-equity ratios** are dependent on U.S. shareholders' risk perceptions. Similar arguments hold for multinationals that are not based in the United States. Furthermore, the level of

foreign debt-equity ratios is usually determined by institutional factors that have no bearing on foreign-based multinationals. For example, **Japanese and German banks** own much of the equity as well as the debt issues of local corporations. Combining the functions of stockholder and lender may reduce the perceived risk of default on loans to captive corporations and increase the desirability of substantial leverage. This would not apply to a wholly owned subsidiary. However, a **joint venture** with a corporation tied to the local banking system may enable an MNC to lower its local cost of capital by leveraging itself, without a proportional increase in risk, to a degree that would be impossible otherwise.

Second, for purposes of capital budgeting and intercorporate comparisons, delevered cash flows must be used. To prescribe a financial structure as Stonehill and Stitzel suggest seems close to violating this tenet.

Parent Company Guarantees and Consolidation. Multinational firms are sometimes reluctant to guarantee explicitly the debt of their subsidiaries, even when a more advantageous interest rate can be negotiated. First, they argue, affiliates should be able to stand alone. In the case of a joint venture when the other partner is unable or unwilling to provide a valuable counterguarantee, a penalty rate of interest may be accepted to avoid overfinancing other shareholders. A cost is incurred to maintain a principle and avoid a dangerous precedent. Second, the protection against **expropriation** provided by an affiliate's borrowing may be lost if the parent guarantees those debts. Third, many corporations believe lenders should be reasonable, requesting a guarantee when the affiliate is operating at a loss or with a debt-heavy capital structure and lending without one when the borrower itself is creditworthy. Fourth, providing explicit support for one operation could lead to lenders' demands in other cases.

The issue of whether to issue guarantees may be more important in theory than in fact. It is likely that a parent company would "keep lenders whole" if a subsidiary defaulted even if it had no legal obligation to do so. A survey by Stobaugh (*Journal of International Business Studies,* Summer 1970, pp. 43–64) showed that not one of a sample of 20 medium and large multinationals (average foreign sales of $200 million and $1 billion annually, respectively) would allow their subsidiaries to default on debt that did not have a parent company guarantee. (There have been, however, two instances involving major multinational firms in which the parent refused to honor its subsidiaries' defaulted obligations.) Of the small multinationals interviewed (average annual sales of $50 million), only one out of 17 indicated that it would allow a subsidiary to default on its obligations under some circumstances. The previously cited study by Business International (*Business International Money Report,* September 21, 1979, pp. 319–320) had similar findings. The majority of firms interviewed said they would make good the nonguaranteed debt of a subsidiary in the event of a default. This attitude is not the result of benevolence nor, possibly, even a sense of morality. A multinational firm relies on financial institutions in many countries. In a real sense, it could rarely, if ever, function without them. Any action that jeopardizes these relations, such as allowing an affiliate to become bankrupt, has an extremely high cost. Multinational firms also may distinguish between international and local banks. The former could be kept whole and the latter directed to their own government for repayment if an affiliate were expropriated and unable to pay its debts.

If an explicit guarantee will reduce a subsidiary's borrowing costs, it is usually in the parent's best interest to give this support, provided there is an actual commitment to satisfy the subsidiary's obligations. An overseas creditor may not be as certain regarding the firm's intentions, and its ties to the multinational may be less substantial. The fact that the parent does not guarantee its subsidiaries' debt may then convey some information, namely, that the commitment to subsidiary debt is not strong.

The Internal Revenue Service recently argued that by guaranteeing foreign affiliates' debts, a U.S. corporation is providing a valuable service for which it should be compensated. The IRS, therefore, has begun imputing income to the guarantor and levying a tax. This additional tax cost should be incorporated in the determination of whether parent support should be given to an overseas subsidiary's borrowing.

SOURCES OF FUNDS FOR MNC AFFILIATES. A distinctive feature of the financial strategy of multinational firms is the wide range of internal and external sources of funds available to them. Those external sources include commercial banks, export financing agencies, public (government) financial institutions, development banks, insurance companies, pension plans, private and public bond placements, and lease financing.

Short-Term Financing. Like most domestic firms, affiliates of multinational corporations generally attempt to finance their **working capital requirements** locally both for convenience and for exposure management purposes. Commerical banks are the prime source of short-term financing. This usually takes the form of overdrafts and discounting facilities, but may be a straight loan for a set period such as 90 days or longer. Nonbank sources of funds include export financing and factoring and commercial paper.

In countries other than the United States, banks tend to lend through **overdrafts.** An overdraft is simply a line of credit against which drafts (checks) can be drawn (written), up to a specified maximum amount. These overdraft lines are often extended and expanded year after year, thus providing, in effect, a form of medium-term financing. The borrower pays interest on the debit balance only. **Commitment fees** on the unused portion of the credit line may be required, but unlike the practice in the United States, **compensating balances** (required minimum balances) are rarely requested.

The **discounting of trade bills** is the preferred short-term financing technique in many developed and less developed countries. It is popular because these bills often can be rediscounted with the central bank at a rate that does not fully reflect all the commercial risks involved (i.e., at a subsidized rate). Discounting usually results from the following set of transactions. A manufacturer selling goods to a retailer on credit draws a bill on the buyer, payable in, say, 30 days. The buyer endorses (accepts) the bill, or his bank accepts it on his behalf (at which point it becomes a **banker's acceptance**). The manufacturer gives the bill to his bank, which accepts it for a fee if the buyer's bank has not done so already. The bill is then sold at a discount to the manufacturer's bank or to a money market dealer. The rate of interest varies with the term of the bill and the general level of local money market interest rates.

Medium-Term Financing. Loans with maturities between one and seven years constitute medium-term financing. Customarily, these take the form of **renewable overdrafts** or discounting facilities (revolving acceptance credits) with the rate of interest fluctuating. They are used as a continuing source of funds or as **bridge financing** while the borrower obtains medium- or long-term fixed rate financing, usually from a financial institution other than a commercial bank. Banks that extend bridging loans also may act as agents in syndicating the subsitute financing that is used to repay the bank debt. Such arrangements are common in Germany and Italy.

Medium-term loans typically are made on the basis of cash flows expected to be generated by the borrower's investments. Thus the repayment schedule is geared to the borrower's estimated operating cash flows. A formal agreement is involved, which often contains collateral requirements as well as **restrictive covenants,** such as limits on working capital, debt-equity ratios, and dividends. Medium-term credits are available in Australia and a number of European countries including the United Kingdom, Belgium, France, Germany, the Netherlands, and Switzerland. Elsewhere, they are difficult to arrange; bankers in Japan, for example, generally prefer to provide medium-term credits by rolling over short-term loans.

Long-Term Financing. Long-term debt is normally used to purchase fixed assets, leading lenders to focus on the firm's ability to generate cash flows to service these liabilities rather than on its liquidity position. Security is often required, but the lender's principal concern remains the borrower's earnings prospects and the various technological, managerial, and market resources that affect these prospects. The major forms of long-term debt financing include loans from banks and other financial institutions (e.g., pension funds), bonds, and leasing.

In contrast to U.S. banks, commercial banks or their affiliates in many other countries, including Germany, Japan, the United Kingdom, France, Italy, Belgium, the Netherlands, and Australia, supply long-term credits to industry. The type of collateral required varies with the borrower's credit rating but often takes the form of a mortgage or a bank or parent company guarantee.

Funds from pensions and insurance plans are an important source of long-term financing in the United States, the United Kingdom, Germany, the Netherlands, and a number of other countries; such funding is growing in importance in Japan. In France and Italy, however, where private pension plans virtually do not exist, no separate pool of investable funds is available.

Compared with the United States, **leasing** is in the embryonic stage in most countries. The implicit cost tends to be quite high. Its value and use depends on the tax regulations relating to **depreciation write-offs** in a particular country and the importance of these tax shields to companies contemplating fixed asset acquisitions.

Bond placements are closely controlled in most countries, either directly by the government or by the major commercial and merchant banks. Public offerings are relatively rare in countries such as France and Italy where government agencies dominate the capital markcts with thcir own issucs or high rates of local inflation make lenders unwilling to commit their funds for extended periods. The weakness of Japan's capital market seems to stem both from investor preferences for bank deposits, which may be related to the lack of a strong secondary market and to the strength of banking institutions, and from strict government regulations. **New bond issues in Japan** are sold mainly to financial institutions, although there is currently a large demand for yen-denominated bonds from non-Japanese sources.

Unrestricted by a local counterpart of the **Glass-Steagall Act,** commercial banks outside the United States play a major role in the underwriting and placement, both public and private, of long-term debt issues. They usually form syndicates to market the securities, filling the role that only investment banks are allowed to perform in this country.

Development Banks. To help provide the huge financial resources required to promote growth in less developed areas, the United States and other countries have established a variety of development banks whose lending is directed to investments that would not otherwise be funded by private capital. The projects include dams, communication systems, roads, and other infrastructure items whose economic benefits could not be completely captured by private investors, as well as investments such as steel mills and chemical plants whose value lies in perceived political or social advantages to the host nation (or at least to its leaders). The loans generally are medium- to long-term and carry concessionary rates. Even though most lending is done directly to a government, this type of financing has two implications for the private sector. First, the projects require goods and services that corporations can provide. Second, once an infrastructure has been established, new investment opportunities become available for multinational corporations.

There are three different types of development bank: the **World Bank Group,** regional development banks, and national development banks.

The **World Bank Group,** a multinational financial institution, was established after World War II to facilitate provision of long-term capital for the reconstruction and development of member countries. It comprises three related financial organizations: the **International Bank for Reconstruction and Development (IBRD),** also known as the **World Bank,** the **International Finance Corporation (IFC),** and the **International Development Association (IDA).**

The **World Bank** makes loans at nearly conventional terms to countries for projects of high economic priority. To qualify for financing, a project must have costs and revenues that can be estimated with reasonable accuracy. A **government guarantee** is a necessity for World Bank funding. The bank's main emphasis has been on large infrastructure projects such as roads, dams, and power plants, and educational and agricultural activities. Besides its members' subscriptions, the World Bank raises funds by issuing bonds.

The **IFC** finances various projects in the private sector through loans and equity participations. In contrast to the World Bank, the IFC does not require government guarantees and emphasizes providing risk capital for firms in the manufacturing field that (*a*) have a reasonable chance of earning the investors' required rate of return and (*b*) will provide economic benefits to the nation.

The World Bank concentrates on projects that have a high probability of being profitable; consequently, many of the poorest of the less developed countries are unable to gain access to its funds. **IDA** was founded in 1960 to remedy this shortcoming. As distinguished from the World Bank, IDA is authorized to make "soft" (highly concessionary) loans with maturities to 50 years and no interest. It does require a government guarantee, however. The establishment of IDA illustrates a major unresolved issue for the **World Bank Group:** should its emphasis be on making sound loans to developing countries, or should it concentrate on investing in projects most likely to be of benefit to the host country? It is not clear, of course, that these goals are in conflict.

The past two decades have seen a proliferation of **national and regional development banks,** with the Middle East being a recent spawning ground for many new ones. The functions of a development bank are to offer debt and equity financing to aid in the economic growth of underdeveloped areas. This includes extending intermediate- to long-term capital directly, strengthening local capital markets, and supplying management consulting services to new companies. The professional guidance helps to safeguard, and thereby encourage, investments in a firm.

National and regional **development banks** have the same basic function: to provide funds for the financing of manufacturing, mining, agricultural, and infrastructure projects considered important for growth. The characteristics for success are the same for both types of organization. They must attract capable, investment-oriented management and they must propose enough economically viable projects to enable management to select a reasonable portfolio of investments.

As the names imply, a difference does exist in the orientation of these institutions. National development banks may focus on particular industries or geographical areas in a country. Regional banks tend to support projects that promote regional cooperation and economic integration. The loans typically have a 5–15 year term and carry a favorable rate of interest.

The list that follows includes some of the leading regional development banks:

1. *European Investment Bank (EIB).* Founded in 1958, it offers funds for certain public and private projects in European and other nations associated with or linked to the Common Market by cooperative agreements for financial aid. Loans to less developed areas are emphasized.

2. *Inter-American Development Bank (IADB).* The IADB is one of the key sources of long-term capital in Latin America. Founded in 1959 by the United States and 19 Latin American countries, the IADB had granted a net total of 1,022 loans with a total value of $11.9 billion through 1977. It lends to joint ventures, both minority and majority foreign owned.

3. *Atlantic Development Group for Latin America (ADELA).* Formed in 1964, this international private investment company, incorporated in Luxembourg, is dedicated to the socioeconomic development of Latin America. Its objective is to strengthen private enterprise by providing capital and entrepreneurial and technical services. The 230-odd shareholders are many of the leading industrial and financial companies of Europe, South American, Japan, and Latin America.

4. *Asian Development Bank (ADB).* Its 42 members include the countries of the UN Commission for Asia and the Far East, Canada, the United Kingdom, and the United States, and Germany, and several other West European countries. It guarantees or makes direct loans to private ventures in Asia-Pacific countries and helps develop local capital markets by underwiriting securities issued by private enterprises.

5. *African Development Bank (ADB).* Founded in 1964 by member states of the Organization of African Unity, the bank's primary purpose is to promote the economic and social development of its member states. It makes or guarantees loans and provides technical assistance in the preparation, financing, and implementation of development projects. Beneficiaries of ADB loans and activities are normally governments or government-related agencies.

6. *Arab Fund for Economic and Social Development (AFESD).* Oldest of the multilateral Arab funds (established in 1968), the AFESD has $1.4 billion (1979) in capital paid in by its members, which are all Arab League states. It actively seeks projects in Arab League countries and assumes responsibility for project implementation by conducting feasibility studies, contracting, controlling quality, and supervising the work schedule.

EVALUATING FOREIGN CURRENCY BORROWING. Firms continually face the choice of financing their overseas affiliates with dollars or with foreign currencies. Even if markets are efficient in the sense of equating pretax expected dollar financing costs, the impact of taxation of foreign exchange gains or losses on loans will generally cause aftertax costs to diverge. Thus tax effects can be a significant determinant of the financing decision when firms have the option of raising funds in several different currencies. Other important factors involved in the borrowing decision include relative interest rates, anticipated currency changes, and exposure management considerations.

Methodology. Folks and Advani ("Alternative Methods for Analyzing the Currency of Denomination Decisions for Long-Term Bonds," University of South Carolina Working Paper, April 1977) give the following steps for evaluating the appropriate currency for a loan or a bond issue:

1. Determine the effective cost (yield) of dollar (or other base currency) financing.
2. For each currency under consideration, estimate the future exchange rates, period by period.
3. Use these forecasts to convert into dollars the projected foreign currency cash outflows needed to service and repay the foreign currency debt.
4. Calculate that discount rate (the internal rate of return) that equates the present dollar value of these outflows with the dollar value of the proceeds from the financing.
5. Select that financing source with the lowest dollar cost.

Several variations on this basic methodology are possible. One is to determine the interest rate on a foreign currency borrowing that after adjustments for taxes and currency changes, provides the same yield as on dollar debt. If the projected **foreign currency interest rate** is above this break-even level, dollar debt would be preferred; the foreign currency should be borrowed when its anticipated dollar cost is below the break-even rate.

Another approach is to compute the annualized rate of currency appreciation or depreciation that would just equate the aftertax borrowing costs of dollar and foreign currency debt. The forecast devaluation or revaluation is then compared with the break-even rate and the less expensive option selected.

Short-Term Financing Cost Calculations. The aftertax U.S. dollar cost of a local currency loan at an interest rate of r_L by a foreign affiliate when the expected local currency (LC) **exchange rate depreciation** versus the dollar is d equals the aftertax interest expense less the exchange gain on principal payment:

interest cost − exchange gain

$$r_L(1 - d)(1 - t_i) - d$$

where t_i is the affiliate's marginal tax rate on interest expense. The first term is the aftertax dollar interest cost paid at year-end after an LC devaluation of d; the second is the exchange gain in dollars of repaying the local currency loan worth $1 - d$ dollars at the end of the year. The gain has no local tax effect for the affiliate because the same amount of local currency was borrowed and repaid. In the case of a forecast revaluation, a loss is entailed by local currency borrowing, and $1 + d$ is substituted for $1 - d$ and $+d$ for $-d$.

The aftertax cost of a dollar loan is the difference between the aftertax interest expense and the tax deduction (expense) arising from the effect of the currency change on the principal repayment:

interest cost
− tax gain (loss) due to change in local currency value of principal amount

$$r_{U.S.}(1 - t_i) - dt_x$$

where t_x is the affiliate's marginal tax rate on exchange gains and losses. The first term is the aftertax interest expense of borrowing dollars. The second reflects the fact that if the exchange rate fluctuates, the local currency units required to repay a dollar loan will increase (with a devaluation) or decrease (with a revaluation). Depending on the country involved and whether exchange losses or gains on a capital transaction are a taxable event, the affiliate's local tax burden may be smaller or greater.

One approach to determining whether local currency or dollar financing is less expensive is to equate the costs of each and calculate the break-even rate of LC depreciation or appreciation, that is, the value for d at which the firm is indifferent to borrowing in one currency or the other. This is given by:

$$d = \frac{(1 - t_i)(r_L - r_{U.S.})}{(1 - t_i)r_L + (1 - t_x)}$$

There are two special cases that are frequently of interest:

· When $t_i = t_x$ (which is true for many countries).

$$d = \frac{r_L - r_{U.S.}}{r_L + 1}$$

· When $t_x = 0$ (which is true, e.g., in the United Kingdom).

$$d = \frac{(1 - t_i)(r_L - r_{U.S.})}{(1 - t_i)r_L + 1}$$

The foregoing analysis can be applied when the dollars are provided by an intracompany advance from the United States rather than obtained directly by the affiliate from a financial institution. In this case:

$$d = \frac{(1 - t_p)(r_{U.S.} - I_c) + (1 - t_i)(r_L - I_c)}{(1 - t_i)r_L + (1 - t_x)}$$

where t_p is the parent company's marginal tax rate(s) on interest income and expense, and I_c is the parent company's interest charge to the affiliate. (It should be noted that $r_{U.S.}$ here is the parent's, not the affiliate's cost of dollar debt.)

With this **break-even analysis**, the treasurer can readily see the amount of foreign currency fluctuation necessary to make one type of borrowing cheaper than the other. He will then compare the firm's actual forecast, determined objectively or subjectively, of currency change with this benchmark.

For example, a Brazilian subsidiary requires funds to finance working capital for one year. It can borrow cruzeiros at a cost of 45% or dollars from a bank at 12%. The tax rates for calculating the effective cost of interest expense and a devaluation loss are identical. Then, the break-even value of d is $(0.45 - 0.12)/1.45 = 22.76\%$. If the cruzeiro is expected to devalue by less than this amount over the course of the next year, dollar debt will be less expensive. Conversely, a more rapid rate of devaluation renders cruzeiro debt preferable.

It is imperative to recognize that the devaluation is measured by the decline in the value of the local currency versus the dollar, not by the increased number of local currency units required to purchase the dollar. To illustrate, if the exchange rate at the beginning of the year was NCr 20/U.S.$ and NCr 30/U.S.$ at the end, the devaluation is 33.3%, that is, (NCr 30 − NCR20)/NCr 30. Initially, one cruzeiro was worth $0.0500 and declined in value over 12 months to $0.0333. Its devaluation in dollar terms was $0.0167; this is the reduction in worth that is to be compared with the initial value.

The error of determining the rate of devaluation by dividing the change in local currency units to one dollar by the initial exchange rate is readily apparent if one remembers that a 100% devaluation is virtually impossible. When Uruguay devalued its peso some years ago from pesos 100/U.S.$ to pesos 200/U.S.$, many newspapers and business magazines referred to the event as a 100% devaluation. If in fact the devaluation had been of that magnitude, the Uruguayan peso would have been worthless by definition. Yet, it retained a value. The amount of the devaluation in the case was 50% because the currency had lost one-half its value in U.S. dollar terms.

The logic of the foregoing break-even analysis can be extended to **financing options** other than those cited here, for example, having the parent extend interest-free financing through adjustments in the intracompany merchandise account. In all situations, the cost of each source of funds must be calculated in terms of the relevant variables (interest rates, tax rates, and future exchange rates) and the expense compared with that of all other possibilities.

Long-Term Financing Cost Calculations. Assume that a firm can borrow dollars abroad or the local (foreign) currency for n years at fixed interest rates of $r_{U.S.}$ and r_f, respectively. Interest is to be paid at the end of each year and the principal in a lump sum at the end of year n. Suppose that the foreign currency undergoes a cumulative devaluation (revaluation) of d_i between now and the end of year i, with $d_i = (e_0 - e_i)/e_0$ (d_i is negative for a revaluation), where e_0 is the current exchange rate ($\$e_0 = LC1$). e_i is the exchange rate at the end of period i, and t is the foreign tax rate. Then it can be shown that the **aftertax yield on a foreign currency-denominated bond** issued by a local affiliate can be found as the solution r to:

$$-1 + F_1(1 - t) + \sum_{i=1}^{n} \frac{r_f (1 - d_i)(1 - t)}{(1 + r)^i} + \frac{1 - d_n}{(1 + r)^n} = 0$$

Similarly, the effective aftertax cost of dollar debt is the solution k to:

$$-1 + F_2(1 - t) + \sum_{i=1}^{n} \frac{r_{U.S.}(1 - t)}{(1 + k)^i} + \frac{1 - d_n t}{(1 + k)^n} = 0$$

The terms F_1 and F_2 are the flotation costs for issuing the foreign currency and dollar bonds, respectively. It is assumed that these costs are tax deductible as soon as they are incurred.

To illustrate the application of these formulas, suppose that Global Industries, Inc., is planning to float a seven-year $30 million bond issue. It has the choice of having its Swiss subsidiary borrow U.S. dollars at a coupon rate of 9.625% or Swiss francs at 3.5%. Both bond issues are sold at par. The flotation costs are 3% for the Swiss franc and 1.2% for the dollar issue, leading to effective pre-tax rates of 4% for the Swiss franc debt and 9.87% for the dollar debt. Repayment is in a lump sum at the end of year seven.

The current exchange rate is SFr 1.75 to the dollar. Thus global Industries' subsidiary can either borrow $30 million or SFR 52.5 million. Assume that the Swiss tax rate is 45%. Exhibits 10 and 11 contain the year-by-year Swiss franc cash flows and dollar cash flows associated with both issues. The projected exchange rates for the coming seven years are listed in Exhibit 11. On the basis of these data, the effective aftertax yield on the Swiss franc issue is 8.40% and on the dollar debt issue 8.02%.

EXHIBIT 10 AFTERTAX CASH FLOWS ASSOCIATED WITH SWISS FRANC DEBT

Year	Cash Flow Category	Swiss Franc Cash Flows (1)	÷	Rate of Exchange (2)	×	Aftertax Factor (3)	=	Aftertax Dollar Cash Flows (4)
0	Bond sale	− 52,500,000		1.75		1		− $30,000,000
	Flotation charge	1,575,000		1.75		0.55		495,000
1	Interest	1,837,500		1.665		0.55		606,981.98
2	Interest	1,837,500		1.580		0.55		639,636.09
3	Interest	1,837,500		1.495		0.55		676,003.35
4	Interest	1,837,500		1.410		0.55		716,755.33
5	Interest	1,837,500		1.325		0.55		762,735.88
6	Interest	1,837,500		1.240		0.55		815,020.14
7	Interest	1,837,500		1.155		0.55		875,000.01
	Principal repayment	52,500,000		1.555		1		$43,454,545.45

EXHIBIT 11 AFTERTAX CASH FLOWS ASSOCIATED WITH DOLLAR DEBT

Year	Cash Flow Category	Dollar Cash Flow (1)	×	Aftertax Factor (2)	=	Aftertax Dollar Cash Flows (3)
0	Bond sale	− $30,000,000		1		− $30,000,000
	Flotation charge	360,000		0.55		198,000
1	Interest	2,887,500		0.55		1,588,125
2	Interest	2,887,500		0.55		1,588,125
3	Interest	2,887,500		0.55		1,588,125
4	Interest	2,887,500		0.55		1,588,125
5	Interest	2,887,500		0.55		1,588,125
6	Interest	2,887,500		0.55		1,588,125
7	Interest	2,887,500		0.55		1,588,125
	Principal repayment	$30,000,000		1		$30,000,000
	Capital gain recognized by Swiss tax authorities	$15,454,545*		0.45		$6,954,545.30

*At $0.87, 17,850,000 Swiss francs.

Such detailed currency projections are generally not made, given the uncertainties involved. Instead, it is simpler to project an average rate of currency change over the life of the debt and to calculate effective aftertax dollar costs on that basis. For example, if a steady appreciation of the foreign currency at a rate of g per annum is anticipated, the effective aftertax dollar yield on the foreign currency bond issued by a local affiliate can be found by solving the following equation for r:

$$-1 + \sum_{i=1}^{n} \frac{r_f (1 + g)^i (1 - t)}{(1 + r)^i} + \frac{(1 + g)^n}{(1 + r)^n} = 0$$

The solution r equals $r_f (1 + g)(1 - t) + g$, the same as in the one-period case.

Assuming a nominal yield r_f equal to 6%, $t = 45\%$, and $g = 3\%$, the effective cost of foreign currency borrowing is $0.06 \times 1.03 \times 0.55 + 0.03$ or 6.4%. In the absence of taxes, this cost would be 9.18% ($0.06 \times 1.03 + 0.03$).

Exposure Management Considerations.   These approaches all assume that firms are interested only in minimizing expected costs. However, foreign currency borrowing can be used to reduce the variance of total corporate cash flows and as a hedge against economic exposure. This aspect of long-term financing is important to most managers, who usually are concerned with total as opposed to systematic risk, regardless of shareholder perceptions and academic advice.

It is necessary to recognize, however, that if firms have the option of neutralizing in the **forward foreign exchange market** any exposure resulting from financial decisions, the **currency of denomination of corporate debt** may not be as important in exposure management as the role sometimes assigned to it. If a sufficiently broad and deep forward market does exist, the hedging possibilities provided by debt that is denominated in foreign currency can be replicated by forward exchange contracts. (In the absence of capital controls and other impediments to the free functioning of the forward market, arbitrage will operate to ensure that spot and future exchange rates reflect perfectly the home and foreign interest rate structures.)

At times, however, forward contracts in a particular currency are either nonexistent or unavailable in the quantity required. From the standpoint of exchange risk management, therefore, a firm may wish to borrow another currency even if it is not the theoretically least expensive form of financing on an expected value basis. The formulas above can be used to estimate the expected cost of deviating from the cost-minimizing alternative. This penalty is the benchmark for gauging foreign exchange risk management benefits.

Borrowing Cost Comparisons and Market Efficiency.   Implicit in the various approaches used to compare borrowing costs is an assumption that interest differentials among currencies do not efficiently incorporate all available information concerning future exchange rates. These interest differentials can, however, be used in an efficient market to provide relatively unbiased forecasts of currency changes. Thus substituting one's own judgment about the future course of exchange rates is questionable, unless there is reason to believe that one of the following conditions holds:

1. Certain barriers (e.g., controls on capital flows), distortions (e.g., credit rationing with interest ceilings), or interventions in the marketplace (e.g., massive government sales or purchases of securities) are likely to push the interest differential out of line with generally held exchange rate expectations.
2. The individual's forecasts are superior to the market's because of inside information or the more effective use of publicly available information.

The probability of the first condition holding is undoubtedly much greater than the probability of the second one.

SWAPS. A **swap** may be defined as an agreement between two parties to exchange one or a series of cash flows over a defined period. This financial technique originated in the foreign exchange markets and is now being applied to a broad variety of financial problems and situations. The flexibility and potential advantages offered by swaps has led to burgeoning of their application. They are now an integral tool of **liability management** for most major industrial corporations and financial institutions.

There are three major types of swaps:

- *Interest rate* to change debt from fixed into floating rate or vice versa. Typically, principal is not exchanged; only the interest is actually paid by each party.
- *Foreign currency* to transform an obligation in one currency to one in another.
- *Interest rate/foreign currency* to convert a liability in one currency with a stipulated type of interest payment into one denominated in another currency with a different type of interest payment.

The following is an illustration of an **interest rate/foreign currency swap,** the most complex of the three kinds. Corporation A has not tapped the Swiss franc public debt market because of concern about a likely appreciation of that currency and only wishes to be a floating rate dollar borrower which it can be at the **London Interbank Overnight Rate (LIBOR)** plus 3/8 of 1%. Supranational agency B has a strong preference for fixed rate Swiss franc debt and has floated such a large number of issues that investors are sated; they will accept more only if B is willing to pay a premium rate of interest, for example, 1/2 of 1% higher than the coupon which A's notes would carry.

B, however, retains essentially unlimited access to the **Eurodollar market** where it can obtain funds at LIBOR flat. An opportunity exists for each working in tandem to realize a saving.

- A issues Swiss Franc (SF) 100 million of five-year 5 1/4% bonds publicly in Switzerland. Interest is paid annually on these instruments which, after deducting issuance fees, provide SF 98,189,725 of net proceeds.
- This sum is given to the counterparty B in return for US $45,955,882 at the spot rate of SF 2.176/US$ prevailing on the date of the initial exchange, January 1, 19XX.

The flows throughout the term of the agreement are:

	B delivers to A	A delivers to B
January 1, 19XX	$45,955,882	SF 98,189,725
July 1, 19XX		Six-month LIBOR on US dollar principal
January 1, 19X1	SF 5,504,203	"
July 1, 19X1	—	"
January 1, 19X2	SF 5,504,203	"
July 1, 19X2	—	"
January 1, 19X3	SF 5,504,203	"
July 1, 19X3	—	"
January 1, 19X4	SF 5,504,203	"
July 1, 19X4	—	"
January 1, 19X5	SF105,629,203	Six-month LIBOR plus $45,955,882

The annual interest payments from B to A gives the latter yearly excess Swiss francs of:

Received by A	SF 5,524,203
Less: Interest on notes	(5,250,000)
Paying agency fees	(13,125)
Net Annual Excess	SF 241,078

The final payment by B provides A with:

Received by "A"	SF 105,629,203
Less: Repayment of notes	(100,000,000)
Less: Interest on notes	(5,250,000)
Less: Paying agency fees on interest and principal	(138,125)
Net Excess of Final Payment	SF 241,078

By selling forward the annual and final surplus Swiss francs that A receives, it can lock-in an effective **floating rate dollar loan** at LIBOR minus 25 basis points. This example is illustrated in Exhibit 12.

For swaps to provide a real economic benefit to both parties, a barrier generally must exist to prevent **arbitrage** from functioning fully. This impediment can take the form of legal restrictions on spot and forward foreign exchange transactions, different perceptions by investors of risk and creditworthiness of the two parties, appeal or acceptability of one borrower to a certain class of investor, and so forth. If the world capital market were fully integrated, the incentive to swap would be reduced because fewer arbitrage opportunities would exist. It must be acknowledged, however, that even in the United States where capital and money markets function freely, **interest rate swaps** are extremely popular.

EXHIBIT 12   INTEREST RATE/FOREIGN CURRENCY SWAP

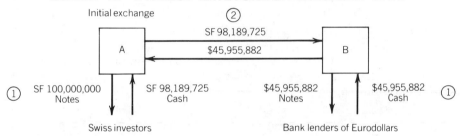

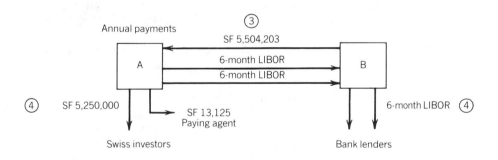

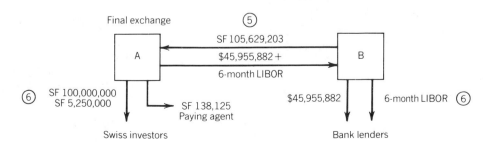

REFERENCES

Adler, Michael, "The Cost of Capital and Valuation of a Two-Country Firm," *Journal of Finance*, March 1974, pp. 119–132.

Agmon, Tamir, and Lessard, Donald R., "Investor Recognition of Corporate International Diversification," *Journal of Finance*, September 1977, pp. 1049–1056.

Arnold, T. S., "How to Do Interest Rate Swaps," *Harvard Business Review*, September–October 1984.

Business International, *Decision-Making in International Operations*, Business International Corp., New York, 1970.

———, *New Techniques in International Exposure and Cash Management, Vol. I, The State of the Art*, Business International Corp., New York, 1977.

Cohen, Benjamin I., *Multinational Firms and Asian Exports*, Yale University Press, New Haven, CT, 1975.

Fatemi, Ali M., "Shareholder Benefits from Corporate International Diversification," *Journal of Finance*, December 1984, pp. 1325–1344.

Fieleke, Norman S., "Foreign Exchange Speculation by U.S. Firms: Some New Evidence," *New England Economic Review*, March–April 1979, pp. 5–17.

Folks, William R., Jr., and Advani, Ramesh, "Alternative Methods for Analyzing the Currency of Denomination Decision for Long-Term Bonds," University of South Carolina Working Paper, presented at the Eastern Finance Association meeting, Boston, April 1977.

Grant, Charles, "How Treasurers Are Swapping Swaps," *Euromoney*, April 1985.

Group of Thirty, *Foreign Exchange Markets Under Floating Rates*, Group of Thirty, New York, 1980.

Hawkins, Robert G., Mintz, Norman, and Provissiero, Michael, "Government Takeovers of U.S. Foreign Affiliates," *Journal of International Business Studies*, Spring 1976, pp. 3–15.

Jacquillat, Bertrand, and Solnik, Bruno H., "Multinationals Are Poor Tools for Diversification," *Journal of Portfolio Management*, Winter 1978, pp 8–12.

Kobrin, Stephen J., "Political Risk: A Review and Reconsideration," *Journal of International Business Studies*, Spring-Summer 1979, pp. 67–80.

Lessard, Donald R., "World, Country, and Industry Relationships in Equity Returns: Implications for Risk Reduction Through International Diversification," *Financial Analysts Journal*, January–February 1976, pp. 32–38.

———, "Evaluating Foreign Projects—An Adjusted Present Value Approach," in Donald R. Lessard, Ed., *International Financial Management*, Warren, Gorham & Lamont, Boston, 1979.

———, "Transfer Prices, Taxes, and Financial Markets: Implications of Internal Financial Transfers within the Multinational Firm," in Robert G. Hawkins, Ed., *The Economic Effects of Multinational Corporations*, JAI Press, Greenwich, CT, 1979.

———, and Shapiro, Alan C., "Guidelines for Global Financing Choices," *Midland Corporate Finance Journal*, Winter 1984, pp. 68–80.

McGoldrick, Beth, "The Wild, Wild World of Interest Rate Swaps," *Institutional Investor*, November 1984.

Naumann-Etienne, Ruediger, "A Framework for Financial Decisions in MNCs," *Journal of Financial and Quantitative Analysis,* November 1974, pp. 859–874.

"Policies of MNCs on Debt/Equity Mix," *Business International Money Report,* September 21, 1979, pp. 319–320.

Reier, Sharon, "The Rise of Interest Rate Swaps," *Institutional Investor,* October 1982.

Robbins, Sidney M., and Stobaugh, Robert B., *Money in the Multinational Enterprise,* Basic Books, New York, 1973.

Rodriguez, Rita M., and Carter, E. Eugene, *International Financial Management,* 2d ed., Prentice-Hall, Englewood Cliffs, NJ, 1979, Chapter 10.

Rugman, Alan M., "Risk Reduction by International Diversification," *Journal of International Business Studies,* Fall–Winter 1976, pp. 75–80.

Shapiro, Alan C., "Evaluating Financing Costs for Multinational Subsidiaries," *Journal of International Business Studies,* Fall 1975, pp. 25–32.

———, "Capital Budgeting for the Multinational Corporation," *Financial Management,* Spring 1978, pp. 7–16.

———, "The Impact of Taxation on the Currency-of-Denomination Decision for Long-Term Foreign Borrowing and Lending," *Journal of International Business Studies,* Spring/Summer 1984, pp. 15–25.

Solnik, Bruno H., "Why Not Diversify Internationally Rather than Domestically?" *Financial Analysts Journal,* July–August 1974, pp. 48–54.

Stobaugh, Robert B., "Financing Foreign Subsidiaries of U.S.-Controlled Multinational Enterprises," *Journal of International Business Studies,* Summer 1970, pp. 43–64.

Stonehill, Arthur I., and Stitzel, Thomas, "Financial Structure and Multinational Corporations," *California Management Review,* Fall 1969, pp. 91–96.

Suhar, V., Victor, and Lyons, Douglas D., "Choosing Between a Parallel Loan and a Swap," *Euromoney,* March 1979, pp. 114–119.

Truitt, J., Frederick, "Expropriation of Foreign Investment: Summary of the Post-World War II Experience of American and British Investors in the Less Developed Countries," *Journal of International Business Studies,* Fall 1970, pp. 21–24.

Wickes, M. E., "A Comparative Analysis of the Foreign Investment Evaluation Practices of U.S.-Based Multinational Companies," unpublished doctoral dissertation, Pennsylvania State University, March 1980.

BIBLIOGRAPHY

Aharoni, Yair, *The Foreign Investment Decision Process,* Harvard Graduate School of Business Administration, Division of Research, Cambridge, MA, 1966.

Arpan, Jeffrey S., *International Intracorporate Pricing,* Praeger, New York, 1972.

Bavishi, Vinod, "Capital Budgeting for U.S.-Based Multinational Corporations: An Assessment of Theory and Practice," University of Connecticut Working Paper, Storrs, CT, 1979.

Bradley, David, "Managing Against Expropriation," *Harvard Business Review,* July–August 1977, pp. 75–83.

Business International, *Financing Foreign Operations,* Business International Corp. New York, various issues.

Choi, Frederick, D. S., and Mueller, Gerhard G., *An Introduction to Multinational Accounting,* Prentice-Hall, Englewood Cliffs, NJ, 1978.

Eiteman, David K., and Stonehill, Arthur I., *Multinational Business Finance,* 2nd ed., Addison-Wesley, Reading, MA, 1979.

Folks, William R., Jr., "Analysis of Short-Term, Cross-Border Financing Decisions," *Financial Management,* Autumn 1976, pp. 19–27.

Giddy, Ian H., "The Demise of the Product Cycle Model in International Business Theory," *Columbia Journal of World Business,* Spring 1978, pp. 90–97.

Goeltz, Richard K., "The Composition of Parent Financial Assistance to Foreign Subsidiaries," unpublished Esso Memorandum, 1968.

———, "Managing Liquid Funds Internationally," *Columbia Journal of World Business, ness,* July–August 1972, pp. 59–65.

Kobrin, Stephen J., "When Does Political Instability Result in Increased Investment Risk?" *Columbia Journal of World Business,* Fall 1978, pp. 113–122.

Levy, Haim, and Sarnat, Marshall, "International Diversification of Investment Portfolios," *American Economic Review,* September 1970, pp. 668–675.

Rutenberg, David P., "Maneuvering Liquid Assets in a Multi-National Company," *Management Science,* June 1970, pp. B-671–684.

Shapiro, Alan C., "Optimal Inventory and Credit-Granting Strategies Under Inflation and Devaluation," *Journal of Financial and Quantitative Analysis,* January 1973, pp. 37–46.

———, "International Cash Management—The Determination of Multicurrency Cash Balances," *Journal of Financial and Quantitative Analysis,* December 1976, pp. 893–900.

———, "Financial Structure and Cost of Capital in the Multinational Corporation," *Journal of Financial and Quantitative Analysis,* June 1978, pp. 211–226.

Stobaugh, Robert B., "How to Analyze Foreign Investment Climates," *Harvard Business Review,* September–October 1969, pp. 100–108.

Stonehill, Arthur, and Nathanson, Leonard, "Capital Budgeting and the Multinational Corporation," *California Management Review,* Summer 1968, pp. 39–54.

Wasserman, Max J., Prindle, Andreas R., and Townsend, Charles C., Jr., *International Money Management,* American Management Association, New York, 1973.

Weston, J. Fred, and Sorge, Bart W., *Guide to International Financial Management,* McGraw-Hill, New York, 1977.

Zenoff, David B., "Remitting Funds from Foreign Affiliates," *Financial Executive,* March 1968, pp. 46–63.

———, "International Cash Management: Why It Is Important and How to Make It Work," *Worldwide Projects and Installations Planning,* July–August 1973.

———, and Zwick, Jack, *International Financial Management,* Prentice-Hall, Englewood Cliffs, NJ, 1969.

18

INTERNATIONAL CASH MANAGEMENT

CONTENTS

18

INTERNATIONAL CASH MANAGEMENT

Jarl G. Kallberg
Kenneth L. Parkinson

INTRODUCTION

This chapter deals with the problems, techniques, and opportunities that comprise the current sphere of international cash mangement. While a number of the concerns of domestic (U.S.) cash management are shared by the international cash manager, a number of other complexities are involved in international cash management.

The traditional, and rather circumscribed, view of cash management has been that of **float management. Float** is defined as the lag between a buyer's initiation of payment and the seller's receipt of good funds. Float is typically thought of as being comprised of three components:

Mail Float. Delays created by mailing payments
Processing Float. Delays by the receiving entity in depositing the payment
Clearing Float. Delays caused by bank check or draft clearing

On the domestic U.S. side, these delays can create a float of up to 10 days; on the international side, the total float can often exceed a month. Thus, the incentives and possible gains from international cash management are large, but, as we shall describe, difficult to realize. Some of the reasons for this lie in the very fundamental differences between United States and international cash management practices. These include some practices (described in the following parts) that may be unfamiliar to the U.S. cash manager:

- Value dating conventions
- Overdraft banking
- Interest on credit balances
- Restrictions on cross-border funds transfer and information flows

In addition, foreign banking structures and financial practices often present barriers to implementation of techniques that are applicable to the U.S. situation. Finally, the added complexity of foreign currencies necessitates a thorough understanding of modern **treasury vehicles: pooling, netting, reinvoicing,** and so forth. A recent Business International Study (*New Directions in European Cash Management,* 1985) points out that recognition of the importance of international cash management is increasing; 98.6% of their 312 respondents stated that cash mangement would continue or increase in importance over the next two to three years. These respondents also said that they were pursuing the following objectives through improved cash management:

- Minimizing borrowing needs and costs
- Minimizing currency risks and costs
- Minimizing idle bank balances
- Minimizing customer delays and bad debts

Other surveys have echoed this increasing emphasis on international cash management practices. As well, advances in technology have provided new tools with which to achieve these and other financial objectives.

This section is organized into three major parts. The first describes the international cash management spectrum; this will provide insights into the problems likely to be encountered by the international cash manager. The second part provides an analysis of modern tools and techniques. Finally, the third subsection integrates the material described previously by illustrating how existing tools and techniques can be applied to overcome the formidable challenges of international cash management.

THE SPECTRUM OF INTERNATIONAL CASH MANAGEMENT

As shown in Exhibit 1, the spectrum of international cash management extends further than its domestic (U.S.) counterpart. The **international cash manager** is typically involved in more facets of the financial function than the domestic cash manager, dealing with different currencies and banking systems as well as overseas personnel accustomed to little oversight or direction from a central point. Of course, the **foreign exchange** area provides a great deal of complexity to this already difficult function. The major functions of international cash management can be broken down into four major categories:

    1. *Banking System Administration.* Entails the establishment, review and control of the overall banking structure or network and the variety of bank-supplied services for the corporation.

EXHIBIT 1   THE INTERNATIONAL CASH MANAGEMENT SPECTRUM

Features \ Functions	Banking system administration	Information management	Liquidity management	Foreign exchange
Business characteristics	Retail vs. manufacturing Sales, market share Need for bank-supplied services	Seasonality Exports and local sales Types of transactions	Net borrowing/investing position Discountable receivables Strength of market Sources of debt, investments	Billing and paying currencies Size of overseas exposure Governmental regulations
Organization	Overseas locations Local and central responsibilities Accounting influences	Local sources Planning and forecasting Routine reporting	Credit line responsibility Parent guarantees, global facilities Corporate guidelines, policies, reporting Inter-subsidiary loans	Parent vs. local control Corporate guidelines and policies Accounting influences
Funds flow	Accounts receivable/payable management Size and frequency of flows Intra-country and cross border flows Cash position management	Size and frequency of flows Cash mobilization Bank compensation	Types and frequency of borrowing, investing Cash concentration Funds movement	Spot, forward contracts Foreign exchange conversions Foreign currency receipts and payments
Standard techniques	Individual country studies/bank profiles Pooling Netting systems Lockbox/foreign intercepts Export collection reviews Funds transfer services	International balance reporting Bank reports, statements International cash forecasting Same day balance reporting Netting (somewhat) Service cost analyses	Leading and lagging Pooling Reinvoicing Center Finance Company Global credit facilities Portfolio systems	Exposure management models Leading and lagging Hedging Reinvoicing center, finance company Outstanding foreign exchange contracts reporting Netting (somewhat)
Typical problems	Unavailable services Local bank control Excessive value dating	Lack of information Time delays Absence of management mentality	Limited debt/investment sources Credit limits Competing organizational autonomies	Government controls Competing organizational autonomies

2. *Information Management*. Deals with the collection and dissemination of different types of treasury-related information throughout the firm.
3. *Liquidity Management*. Involves the short-term borrowing and/or investing activities of the corporation, as well as the establishment or guarantee of credit facilities for foreign subsidiaries.
4. *Foreign Exchange*. Distinguishes international from domestic cash management. It entails the procurement of foreign currencies for international transactions, the monitoring of foreign exchange exposures and related hedging programs.

Each of these functions is heavily influenced by several basic basic features of international cash management. As Exhibit 1 shows, the features exert a great deal of influence on each of the functional areas with considerable interaction. These basic, influencing features include:

Business Characteristics. The general size and nature of the overseas business mix of the corporation.

Organization. The structure of domestic home office treasury staff and the various overseas subsidiaries, as well as the relative influences, interactions, and responsibilities of each.

Funds Flow. The relative size, frequency, and sources of funds flows throughout the firm.

Standard Techniques. The common, basic tools and techniques available to the international cash manager.

Typical Problems. The various types of problems likely to be encountered in the international cash management environment.

BUSINESS CHARACTERISTICS. The business characteristics of the firm, especially those of the various overseas subsidiaries, will have a heavy influence on all functions of international cash management. They will largely determine the types of banking products and services that are needed by or even offered to any individual subsidiary. Important features are characteristics, such as the retail or manufacturing nature of the operation. For example, manufacturers in many countries depend on the **commercial banks** for collection services. In such cases, administering the banking system and selecting efficient bank services is critical. In addition, the relative strength, or market share, commanded by the individual operation can determine both the availability of bank services and, perhaps, their relative costs. The latter are highly negotiable items in many countries. Seasonality and the mix of exports versus local sales can affect the types of information reported from overseas operations. Again, the type of business will also affect this function as it will determine the various types of transactions.

In many countries, various forms of short-term borrowing may depend on the type or types of business in which the overseas subsidiary is engaged and the perceived quality of this business mix. The size of the business can also be a determining factor in the available forms of credit or in the attractiveness of short-term investment opportunities. This determining influence of the business characteristics of overseas subsidiaries carries over into the foreign exchange area as well. The larger the operation is, relative to local competitors, the greater will be the flexibility in determining billing currencies, payment terms, and collection procedures. Also, if the subsidiary is engaged in a business that is favorably viewed by the local government, then it may be able to obtain cheaper long-term financing or exemptions from governmental financial regulations. This is particularly true in developing countries.

In summary, then, the business characteristics of the home office as well as the individual overseas subsidiaries help establish the framework or environment for cash management overseas. Different types of industries essentially formulate their own set of products and services, and, in many countries, the providers of financial and banking services are very sensitive to relative market share or overall industrial importance.

ORGANIZATIONAL STRUCTURE. The organizational structure of overseas subsidiaries can greatly affect the various functions of international cash management, depending on the degree of decentralization and the relative autonomies of central treasury staff and local financial managers. The organizational structure can affect the banking system administration function to the extent that (1) the subsidiaries determine their local banking arrangements or (2) they are subject to review and/or approval by a central or regional treasury staff. Just as obvious an influence is the global dispersion of the overseas locations. The more widespread these operations are, the more banking services will be required—not to mention the possible need for cross-border funds transfer services.

The structure and relative responsibilities help determine the sources of information and what can or will be reported routinely. Exhibit 2 shows the contents of a sample monthly reporting "package" with descriptions of the four basic components. These include a **short-term cash forecast,** data showing bank balances and transaction costs, any changes in banking relations or services, and an open-ended banking problem reporting.

Responsibility for **credit facilities** and the establishment of intersubsidiary loans will be affected by the type of organization and which party (home office or local operation) has the authority to set up such arrangements. This carries over to the foreign exchange area as well with the potential for frequent conflicts as local and centralized approaches to exposure management may differ markedly. One other key organizational influence is the typical background of most overseas cash management staff members—that is, the accounting area. Since most, if not all, overseas staff members have been trained in the accounting function before moving to the **treasury function**

EXHIBIT 2   CONTENTS OF SAMPLE MONTHLY REPORTING PACKAGE

Short-Term Cash Forecast
  Typically balance sheet numbers
  Month-end figures of dubious value
  Need to focus on full cash flows
  Estimated investment/borrowing levels

Bank Balance and Transaction Cost Data
  Some form of average balance levels
  Full bank statements (optional or not every month)
  Bank costs paid (schedule or bank invoices)
  Schedule of value dating for very large items (optional)

Changes in Banking Relationships/Services
  Update(s) to master banking relationship "log"
  Cost/value date changes
  Standard forms

Banking Problems
  Ad hoc or free-form report on major problems
  Summary of resolution of problems (if resolved)
  "Pleas for help"

(if it is even a discrete function), their approach to treasury and banking will be greatly affected. This requires a major reorientation and usually involves substantial training. All too often, organizational impediments translate into significant problems for the international cash manager.

These problems involve the organizational impediments created by the characteristics of the company. These impediments may be as simple as the absence of any definite responsibility for international cash management, but usually they go much further. For example, there is almost always a conflict between the headquarters treasury staff and the local financial line officer over responsibility for local treasury matters. Local financial officers have historically had both responsibility for and autonomy over local banking and treasury practices; they are naturally reluctant to relinquish this authority. However, as noted since these officers have tended to be more accounting and/or control oriented, a full-fledged treasury function has usually not been implemented. Cash management activities have typically been at best a part-time activity. This organizational deficiency has created a number of educational problems, and, in turn, these difficulties create major obstacles in establishing an effective international cash management program.

These educational problems manifest themselves in many forms. First of all, local managers are usually unaware of actual (available) bank balances; they typically manage only their book (ledger) cash position. This book balance focus suggests that local managers are also unaware of the local cash management practices, available bank services, and the more advanced banks that can respond to corporate needs. This lack of awareness is heightened by the lack of interest in cash management displayed by the local banks. As a result, major educational barriers have arisen.

FUNDS FLOW. Cross-border transactions involve export collections, funds and data transfer between overseas points, and payments between the company's foreign subsidiaries. Collecting export sales can be very difficult because the export process typically involves many company areas, for example, the financial, marketing, and operations organization. The cash manager must gather payments and obtain good funds as soon as possible. This problem is analogous to the domestic U.S. collection problem, but with several new complexities. Since the geographic spread of customers may be extremely broad, mail times for receiving check payment can be incredibly long. Exhibit 3 summarizes some of the estimated mail times; the data were

EXHIBIT 3 TYPICAL MAIL TIMES (DAYS)

Sent From:	To: New York City	Brussels	Zurich	London
London	7	4.5	4.5	1.5
Paris	6	4	2.5	3.5
Brussels	5	2	3	4.5
Rome	10	10	7	9
Zurich	5	3	1.5	4
Amsterdam	7	3	3	3.5
Milan	8	3.5	4	4.5
Frankfurt	7.5	3.5	4	4.5
Stockholm	6.5	4	3.5	5
Athens	10	5.5	3	9

	New York City	Miami	Panama
Sao Paulo	7	6.5	7.5
Rio De Janeiro	6.5	6.5	7
Buenos Aires	12.5	9.5	5.5
Lima	9.5	8	6.5

	New York City	San Francisco	Hong Kong	Tokyo
Taipei	11	7	6	5
Kuala Lumpur	11	7	5.5	6
Hong Kong	6.5	4	2.5	5
Singapore	11.5	6	9	4.5
Tokyo	7.5	4	5	2.5

Source: Various interviews and compliations by the authors.

obtained from a recent independent study. Mail times of this magnitude discourage the use of checks for large payments. Therefore, many corporations have instructed their customers to wire transfer large payments. This procedure can be expensive if not controlled carefully. In addition to the direct wire transfer costs, it is rather common for **international transfers** to go astray with a resulting loss in the use of the funds. In addition, prices of international transfers are often based on the amount of the transfer and there can be an additional cost for cross-border transfers. (The mechanics of funds transfers are discussed later in this section.)

Some residual level of check (or check-like) payments generally remains in most companies. The timely, effective collection of these checks can pose a major challenge to the cash manager. While many checks are fairly "clean" in that they are drawn on or through a U.S. bank, many others are not. For example, a customer in West Germany will merely strike out the deutsche mark symbol of the check and write in the U.S. dollar symbol. This check, however, must be cleared back to the local West German bank to obtain good funds. Assuming that the receiver used a U.S. bank to collect the item, this process can take several weeks. This illustrates why the control of export collections can be extremely complex and can present many problems not confronted in domestic check collection.

Another problem concerns **electronic funds transfers**. Whether or not a foreign exchange transaction is also involved, the timely and accurate movement of funds can be complicated for the corporate cash manager. Because there are many steps in the process that require manual intervention, the possibility of a processing error is enhanced. Further hampering the transfer are the many interrelationships among domestic and foreign correspondent banks, usually making the actual transfer route unknown to the corporate cash manager. Also impairing the ability to predict the transfer path is the fact that the corporation's domestic concentration bank may not always use the same correspondent bank to move funds to or from the same country. The incurrence of circuitous funds transfer paths frequently means the loss of vital transaction data, especially when several banks in different locations are involved.

The potential for **wire transfer** problems on the receiving side is just as great as the sending side for many of the same reasons. For instance, if incoming receipts are in U.S. dollars, the final transfer will probably be made to the corporate concentration account through the **Clearing House Interbank Payment System** (CHIPS). This final CHIPS transfer may only be the last in a sequence of many interbank transfers. This can lead to misrouted transfers, delays in timely transfers, or the loss of important descriptive information about the transfers. Some companies have attempted to alleviate this situation by maintaining numerous points for receiving transfers. Rather than solving the problem, however, this process only creates a massive monitoring burden in establishing a system to gather information rapidly and to anticipate receipts at any of the possible receiving points.

Another cross-border problem involves the handling of payments between various **foreign subsidiaries** of the same company, as well as to and from domestic locations. Problems arise in making these payments on a routine, timely basis. If more than one transfer is required, it can be difficult to establish a pipeline for transfers that can minimize the related float. Problems may also arise due to the need for foreign currency purchase or sale and related transfer commissions.

International cash managers may be unable to monitor or even to determine the approximate size of intersubsidiary obligations. Moreover, given their role as a settlement intermediary, they are often forced to intercede between local units to settle disputes. The cash manager may also wish to optimize cash balances or positions among cash rich or cash poor units by leading and lagging payments between units. The cash manager cannot do so without timely and accurate information and an efficient funds transfer mechanism. These payments can also be affected by the value dating conventions of local banks or by local bank processing delays. These subjects are discussed further in the next subsection.

TRANSBORDER DATA FLOW. According to Greguras (Impact of Transborder Data Flow Restrictions on Cash Management Services, *Journal of Cash Management,* September/October 1985), there are two basic types of restrictions on transborder data flows: (1) those affecting access to telecommunications facilities and (2) those that restrict the types of information that can be transmitted. Prior to 1980, most transborder data flow restrictions were based on concerns for the privacy of the information of persons and of legal entities. Countries with these types of restrictions include France, West Germany, Luxembourg, Sweden, and Switzerland. Of particular relevance to the international cash manager are those countries that restrict access to corporate information; these countries include Austria, Canada, Denmark, Luxembourg, Norway, and South Korea.

In addition to these types of restrictions, foreign governments are also legislating the types of hardware, software, and data bases that can be used. As Buss (Legislative Threat to Transborder Data Flow, *Harvard Business Review,* May–June 1984) mentions, American banks have been prevented from using U. S. computers in Brazil because they were not produced locally; Control Data and Tymshare are unable to offer their information services in Japan because of legal restrictions.

BANKING SYSTEMS. There are many types of problems associated with foreign banking systems including ineffective or unavailable bank cash management services, the absence of timely bank account information, bank operating problems, value dating conventions, negotiable bank charges, and so forth. A number of these issues are discussed in more detail in the following sections.

Many of the "classical" cash management services available in the United States as part of an overall **integrated cash management system** do not exist or are difficult to obtain overseas. Such services as concentration accounts with numerous zero-balance subaccounts are rare. In countries where checks are heavily utilized for corporate payments, lockboxes are not generally available.

Bank processing errors and delays can also be major problems. In many countries, for example, bank systems are essentially manual. Thus, processing delays and inconsistencies occur with great frequency. Bank transactions affecting the company seem to be completed quickly if it involves the disbursement of funds. The transaction, however, that may benefit the company because it involves the receipt of funds seems to be completed more slowly. There is virtually universal agreement that the handling of **bank errors** in many overseas locations is not only complex, but costly as well.

The interest and involvement of the local financial staff can significantly help or hinder the resolution of these problems. As mentioned earlier, local managers must monitor their balances daily. They cannot be afraid to challenge the local bank on delays or errors in postings and transfers. Likewise, they must insist on adherence by the local bank to agreed-on value dating practices and negotiated levels of bank fees and commissions. This local involvement is difficult to establish and maintain for the many reasons cited previously.

VALUE DATING. Value dates are assigned by the bank for all items deposited as a form of deferred credit. This **forward valuing** means that a deposited check will be credited one to four business days later. They are charged on all items disbursed as a form of **back value.** For example, a **wire transfer** may be back valued by one day meaning that the account would have been debited for the amount of the transfer the previous business day. In some countries, only the deferred credit portion may be common. In others, both types are prevalent. Exhibit 4 illustrates typical value dating arrangements for a sample of countries. Note the wide range of values for the same type of item within a country. Amazingly, these ranges hold even within the same city. This demonstrates a major problem with the value dating concept—its arbitrary and highly negotiable nature. This, in turn, makes it extremely difficult to monitor bank balances at different banks, since negotiated values must be remembered for each bank.

The value dating practice on checks in Italy is worthy of special comment. As noted in Exhibit 4, checks are back valued to the date printed on the check. This is true regardless of when the check clears, which, given the manual nature of much of Italian check processing, can be an extended period. Checks in Italy must bear a date even though many companies do post-date their checks somewhat (a practice that is often considered improper).

LOCAL BANK PROBLEMS. In addition, charges by the local banks for non-credit services are highly negotiable and are often used as incentives for

EXHIBIT 4   TYPICAL VALUE DATING ARRANGEMENTS (DAYS)

Receipts	Checks		Notes/Drafts	
Country	Local	Outside	Local	Outside
Italy	1	2–3	7–13	10–14
United Kingdom	1–3	1–3	N/A	N/A
France	1–2	3–5	2–4	4–5
Brazil	0–1	0–1	7	N/A
Malaysia	1	2	N/A	N/A

Disbursements	
Country	Checks
France	1–2
United Kingdom	1–2
Italy	Back valued to check date
Spain	1–2, or back valued to check date
Switzerland	1–2
Belgium	1–2
Brazil	0–1

new business or disincentives for using other banks. Most bank transfers are based on a percentage of the amount being transferred, but this practice is generally subject to negotiation. The negotiation is often based on whether or not the sending bank was being used for foreign exchange in those cases where another currency is required.

Thus, the banking system area offers many imposing barriers for the cash manager in coming to grips with the day-to-day workings of overseas cash management. The mystique surrounding many local banking systems and practices has also contributed to the lack of development in this area. Also, as we have seen from the previous discussion, the different types of cash management problems overseas are interrelated; relatively few problems arise from a single, easily identifiable cause. Accordingly, potential solutions of these problems require changes that can encompass broad aspects of the problem area for the company and the banking system.

STANDARD TOOLS AND TECHNIQUES

POOLING. Pooling is one of the simplest international cash management techniques, but it is not offered in many countries. Essentially, it is a procedure whereby the potential overdrafts and excess balances of the various operating units of one corporation are netted against one another before any interest is charged (for overdrafts) or credited (for excesses). It is ideal for the company with numerous operating entities in the same country, such as the United Kingdom, Canada, or Australia. In its basic form it functions as a type of zero-balance account without the automatic transfer and clearance typical of such accounts in the United States. The bank performs the calculation daily and notifies the company of its resulting position. The key drawback is that many banks may require all accounts in the pool to be located at a specific branch, and the computation tends to be manual; that is, it may take longer than ordinary and thereby delay the reporting of daily bank balances. However, in cases where no other viable alternatives are possible, pooling can be an effective cash management technique.

NETTING. In most cases, the coordination of payments between foreign subsidiaries has been haphazard at best. There has been little planning and/or organization in the making of these payments. Accordingly, payments are initiated on a semirandom basis and the float loss between banking systems (to the corporation) has been significant—usually being measured in several days or weeks. Many foreign subsidiaries have waited until the right time to make the transfers of funds with little regard for the "big picture." As large U.S. multinationals have addressed the problem of control of foreign exchange they have turned to netting.

A netting system is based on the premise that different operating entities periodically owe each other funds. Each month, for example, it is possible to establish the gross amounts owed by individual units to the other units. These amounts are compared and the net amounts are transferred to the individual units. This eliminates unnecessary delays and redundant funds transfer costs. The netting computation can be done more frequently than monthly, but monthly settlement is usually established.

The system can be either bilateral or multilateral, depending on the number of intersubsidiary flows. If such flows are only between two entities, then each location may be able to net cash flows with each other, thereby establishing a **bilateral system.** If there are many cross-flows, a **multilateral system** is appropriate. After determining the feasibility of such systems, the corporation must decide whether it wishes to operate the system itself augmented by a common bank transfer system, or whether it wants to have a bank administer the system. The establishment of a netting system for internal company payments among several foreign locations can offer many significant benefits to a large multinational firm. Even for firms without a large international exposure, a netting system affords much greater control over intracompany obligations. It also enables the international cash manager to influence the cash positions of local units. The netting system can be utilized to lead and lag payments (described later), for example, in order to optimize cash holdings over several units. Thus, even if the savings seem modest, superior control will be very desirable.

A **netting center** is normally established to handle the transactions as the volume and number of subsidiaries and country locations grow. This center can be a regional treasury group or a large **multinational bank.** Each participating subsidiary notifies the center as to its intentions to pay with supporting data on appropriate currencies, lead times, and so forth. It is customary for the transactions to be in local currencies (i.e., the currency of the subsidiary), but most systems can handle multiple currencies. This notification is usually made one or two weeks prior to the final settlement date.

Once the netting transactions for the month have been received, the net flows are computed at the netting center. Each subsidiary is then advised as to whether it is a net sender or receiver of funds on the settlement date. The center secures all necessary foreign exchange contracts so that the actual settlement is fairly routine. Each subsidiary usually maintains a separate bank account to send or receive funds for netting.

Exhibit 5 gives a simple numerical example which presents some of the advantages of a multilateral netting operation. Here there are four countries with a total of 12 payments and 660 in total cash flows (Panel A), prior to the establishment of a netting system. The currency can be from any nation. For example, the West German subsidiary owes Hong Kong 80, the US 20,

EXHIBIT 5   (a) INTERCOMPANY CASH FLOWS AND (b) MULTILATERAL CLEARING CENTER

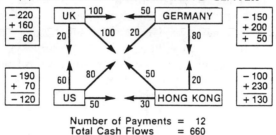

Number of Payments = 12
Total Cash Flows   = 660

(Payments in Currencies of Exporters)

(a)

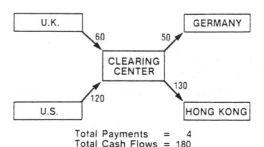

Total Payments   =   4
Total Cash Flows = 180

(b)

and the UK 50. It expects to receive 100 from the UK, 20 from Hong Kong, and 80 from the US. After netting (as shown in the second panel), the West German subsidiary receives one payment of 50 from the netting center. Note that the system now has only four payments and cash flows totalling 180 (Panel B).

The basic limiting factor is government regulation of foreign exchange transactions. In many countries, foreign exchange transactions must be approved and documented beforehand. Thus, only regular trade payments are normally handled via netting as they can be routinely processed. Payments for royalties, dividends, and so on usually require other types of approvals and are not handled through the netting system. In some countries, the ability to net transactions may require central bank approval and, accordingly, must be negotiated on an individual basis.

Another limiting factor may be the local banking system. To work effectively, netting systems move funds in a controlled manner, utilizing, for example, the overseas branch network of a large **multinational bank.** It becomes cumbersome if more than one bank is involved, and the possibility of lost or delayed funds transfers is increased. Again, this should be investigated on an individual basis although it is not a problem in most developed countries.

There are significant costs in the establishment and operation of a netting system. Many large banks offer consulting services that can study and propose a system, or a study can be done by in-house staff if the expertise exists. The benefits of a netting system can be substantial. The reduction in **float** from intercountry payments alone often justifies the system. Additional savings result from eliminating bank fees and commissions from international transfers and foreign exchange contracts. Related costs and availability can be negotiated and controlled by dealing with one bank. The final benefit, and sometimes the most desirable, is the establishment of control over cross-border payments. Local financial managers will no longer need to be continually in the foreign exchange market and the volume of international payments is drastically reduced. For the longer run, major third-party transfers can be added to the netting system to establish further centralized control. In summary, **multilateral netting systems** can offer the large multinational firm an opportunity to establish effective controls over its cross-border flows and foreign exchange risk.

LEADING AND LAGGING PAYMENTS. Another common international cash management technique is leading and lagging. Essentially this technique is used to optimize the cash positions within the overall corporation globally, moving funds to cash-poor subsidiaries from cash-rich locations. This provides needed funding at little or no external cost. The mechanics of leading and lagging are simple: the cash-rich subsidiary transfers funds sooner than normal to the cash-poor subsidiary. The firm's multilateral netting system (if one exists) is the most common means of effecting such transfers unless, of course, funds are needed sooner than the typical monthly period for netting transactions.

There are a few limiting factors that must be considered in deciding to use this technique. First of all, the use of this technique may create additional **foreign exchange exposures** as the acceleration of funds and delay of payments can significantly alter the relative positions of the paying and receiving subsidiaries. Consequently, such effects must be investigated thoroughly prior to initiating the leading/lagging transactions. In addition, governmental exchange controls may prohibit the acceleration of funds as much as is needed. Such controls tend to affect only the longer term leading and lagging decisions, not the shorter term. Again, this aspect should be thoroughly investigated, country by country, before deciding to use this technique. Finally, changing payment terms to accomodate the leading and lagging transactions must be carefully reviewed so that terms are consistent with those offered other competitors. In some cases, changing terms may accidentally offer delayed payment terms to competitors. Overall, leading and lagging represents a flexible mechanism for moving funds within the total corporation without tapping external financing sources.

BALANCE AND TRANSACTION REPORTING. In many countries, banks and companies are satisfied with the production and delivery (normally by mail) of a daily bank statement. In some instances the statements are prepared and delivered only when there is activity. Some improvement over the delay in obtaining information is gained by companies that use couriers to pick up their daily bank statements. But unless few banks are involved and major distances are not traversed, this cannot lead to significant improvements. Internal country balance reporting largely consists of telephone calls, usually from the company to the bank, in those locations that it exists. With the extensive use of value dating, the problems of balance reporting are intensified as the cleared balance is normally subject to negotiation and is not usually reported to the company. Cash managers often attempt to compute the available balance, or as is more often the case, to take a very conservative estimate of what may be available.

Cross-border balance reporting involves all the within-country obstacles, plus others including:

- The existence of government regulations prohibiting the dissemination of bank information outside the country
- The lack of readily available mechanisms to report balances routinely

An increasingly popular service is **international balance and transaction detail reporting.** For many years this service has been possible but now a wide variety of banks are offering it. Exhibit 6 illustrates available electronic banking services in 11 European countries, Japan, Canada, and the United States. In discussing this recent phenomenon, Williams (Electronic Banking

EXHIBIT 6   ELECTRONIC BANKING SYSTEMS IN EUROPE

BANK NAME/SYSTEM NAME	NETWORK	SOFTWARE DESIGN	FREQUENCY			TERMINAL				LEVEL OF DETAIL		AVAILABLE INFORMATION										OTHER			COMPENSATION METHOD				
			Real-time	Intra-day	Previous Day	Dumb terminal	Smart terminal	Mainframe	Videotex	Summary	Detail	Ledger Balances	Available Balance	Money Transfers	Deposits	Collections	Trade transaction	Forex transaction	Investments	Securities	Loan/Credit line	Days History	Consolidated	Transaction initiation	Set fees	Balances	Time-sharing	Usage access fee	Varies
Belgium																													
Banque Bruxelles Lambert / *Tele-Link*	PTT	Proprietary	•	•	•	•				•	•	•	•	•	•	•	•					30	•	•				•	•
Societe Generale de Banque[1] / *G-Line*	Proprietary	Proprietary		•		•	•	•		•	•	•	•	•	•					•	•	40	•	•					
Canada																													
Bank of Montreal[2] / *DirectLine*	ADP	Proprietary	•	•	•				•	•	•	•	•	•	•	•	•	•	•	•	NA							•
Canadian Imperial[3] Bank of Commerce / *CommCash*	NDC, CSC	NA	•	•	•	•	•	•	•	•	•	•	•	•	•	•	•				1-30	•	•					•
Royal Bank of Canada / *CashCommand*	GEISCO	NDC	•	•	•	•				•	•	•	•	•	•	•	•	•		•	45				•	•		•
France																													
Bank of Credit and Commerce[4]	PTT	Proprietary	NA		•					•	•	•	•	•	•	•	•	•			60		•					•
Credit Agricole[5] / *IBIS*	NA	NA	•			•				•	•	•	•	•	•	•	•	•	•	•	30	•					NA	
Credit Lyonnais[6] / *Telelyon* (domestic) / *LyonCash* (international)	PTT Transback GEISCO	Proprietary BankLink	•	•	•	•	•			•	•	•	•	•	•						NA	•						
Societe Generale / *SociCash*	GEISCO	GEISCO, Proprietary	•	•		•	•	•	•	•	•	•	•	•	•						3	•						
Germany																													
Commerzbank / *.COBRA*	GEISCO	BankLink	•	•		•	•			•	•	•	•	•	•	•	•				60	•	•			•	•	
Dresdner Bank / *DreCam*	GEISCO, PTT	NDC GEISCO	•	•	•					•	•	•	•	•	•					•	63	•						•
Italy																													
Banca Nazionale Del Lavoro	Proprietary NDC	Proprietary		•	•	•				•	•	•	•	•							5	•						•
Banca Nazionale Dell'Agricoltura / *ADP International*	ADP	ADP	•	•	•	•				•	•	•	•	•	•	•	•	•	•	•	90	•	•					•
Credito Italiano / *MasterCash*	GEISCO	BankLink	•	•	•					•	•	•	•	•	•						35	•			•			
Japan																													
Bank of Tokyo / *Toh Cash*	IDC, NDC	IDC, NDC	•	•						•	•	•	•	•	•						7-30	NA	•	•	•			
Mitsui Bank / *MitsuiLink*	GEISCO	BankLink	NA	•	•					•	•	•	•	•	•	•				•	63	•	NA		•			
Sumitomo Bank / *Brain*	GEISCO	NDC	•		•	•				•	•	•	•	•	•	•	•	•	•	•	60	•			NA			
The Netherlands																													
Algemene Bank Nederland[7]	GEISCO ADP	Proprietary	•	•	•	•				•	•	•	•	•	•	•	•			•	NA	•				NA		
Amsterdam-Rotterdam Bank[8]	GEISCO or ADP	Proprietary leased vendor	•	•						•	•	•	•	•	•						30	•				NA		
Bank Mees and Hope	PTT	Proprietary	•	•						•	•	•	•	•	•						0		•				•	

[1] Payment information is not available.
[2] Canadian system is real-time. European system is previous day.
[3] Pricing based on number of accounts provided and on balances in accounts.

[4] Charges on client-by-client basis
[5] System will be available in 1985. Network and pricing methods have not been decided.
[6] Telelyon is available only over Videotex; it does not consolidate information from other reporting systems. Fees paid monthly.

[7] System will be available in 1985. Pricing method has not been decided.
[8] System will be available in 1985. Pricing method has not been decided.

Comes of Age in Europe, *Journal of Cash Management,* May/June 1985) points out:

> Only recently has increasing corporate demand and competitive pressure from U.S. banks finally forced the major European institutions into action. But ironically, as more systems come on-line it is the companies that are offering continued resistance to electronic banking. The issue is the lack of facilities for consolidating data for multibank reporting. . . .

EXHIBIT 6   CONTINUED

BANK NAME/SYSTEM NAME	NETWORK	SOFTWARE DESIGN	FREQUENCY			TERMINAL				LEVEL OF DETAIL		AVAILABLE INFORMATION										OTHER			COMPENSATION METHOD				
			Real-time	Intra-day	Previous Day	Dumb terminal	Smart terminal	Mainframe	Videotex	Summary	Detail	Ledger Balances	Available Balance	Money Transfers	Deposits	Collections	Trade transaction	Forex transaction	Investments	Securities	Loan/Credit line	Days History	Consolidated	Transaction initiation	Set fees	Balances	Time-sharing	Usage access fee	Varies
Scandinavia																													
Copenhagen Handelsbank *Nordicash* (international) *Telebank* (domestic)	GEISCO PTT	NDC, Proprietary		•	•	•		•		•	•	•	•	•	•	•	•	•	•	•	5	•		•	•			
Den Danske Bank *Danske Bank Service*	PTT	Proprietary	•		•	•		•		•	•	•	•			•		•	•	NA			•	•			
Nordic Bank *Nordicash*	GEISCO	NDC		•	•	•		•		•	•	•	•			•	•	NA							
Skandinaviska Enskilda Banken (SEB)[1] *SEBLink*	GEISCO	BankLink Proprietary		•	•			•	•	•	•	•	•	•	•	•	•	•	7	•		•	•			
Svenska Handelsbanken *Nordicash*	GEISCO	NDC		•	•			•	•	•	•	•	•	•	•	•	•	•	•	5	•		•			•
Union Bank of Finland[2] *Telesyp-System*	NA	NA	NA		•	•	•	•	NA	•	•		•	•		•	NA			•			•
Switzerland																													
Credit Suisse *CS-Infaccount*	PTT, Telemet Timenet FIDES	Proprietary FIDES		•	•			•		•	•	•	•	•	•	•	•	•	3	•		•			
Swiss Bank Corp *SwisCash*	GEISCO	Proprietary		•	•			•		•	•	•	•	•	•	•	•	•	•	10	•		•			•
UK																													
Bank of Scotland *ScotLink*	GEISCO	BankLink		•	•	•		•		•	•		•		•	•	60	•	•				•
Barclays Bank *BarCAM*	GEISCO Telecom Minietel	Proprietary, BankLink		•	•			•		•	•	•	•	•	•	•	•	NA	•	•	•	•	
Lloyds Bank[3] *Cash Call*	ADP	ADP		•	•	•	•			•	•	•	•	•	60	•			NA
Midland Bank *Midland Bank Cash Management*	ADP	Proprietary		•	•	•			•	•	•	•	•	•	•	•	60 NA			•
National Westminster Bank *Natwest Network Available Funds Reporter*	GEISCO	NDC, Proprietary	•		•	•			•	•	•	•	•	•	30	•	•	•	•
Standard Chartered Bank *International Cash Management*	GEISCO	Proprietary		•	•	•	•			•	•	•	•	•	•	15	•		•	•
US																													
Bank of America[4] *Global Account Reporting*	Timenet RSCS Link, IBM	Proprietary		•	•	•	•			•	•	•	•	•	•	5	•	•		•
Bank of New York[5] *Scan International*	Timenet,	Proprietary/ Arbat		•	•	•			•	•	•	•	•	•	•	7- 30	•	•	•
Bankers Trust *CashConnector*	Proprietary	Proprietary		•	•	•		•		•	•	5	•	•	
Chase Manhattan Bank[6] *InfoCash*	Proprietary	Proprietary		•	•	•	•		•		•	•	•	5- 60	•	•	•
Chemical Bank *ChemLink*	GEISCO	Proprietary		•	•	•	•		•		•	•	•	•	60	•	•	•
Citibank *Citicash*	Proprietary, Telenet, Timenet	Proprietary	•		•	•		•	•	•	•	•	•	•	45	•	•	•	•

[1] Limited information on transfers, deposits, and collections in Sweden. Some real-time reports.

[2] Can use teletype, microcomputer, or Videotex on system called MicroTELESYP

[3] Pricing information not available.

[4] Methods of charging vary

[5] Only domestic transaction initiation

[6] Annual fees and time-sharing charge when used with micros.

FUNDS TRANSFER MECHANISMS. A recent survey by Collins and Frankle (International Cash Management Practices of Large U.S. Firms, *Journal of Cash Management,* July/August 1985), reports the usage of international cash management techniques, notably funds transfer techniques. Their sample of 200 of the Fortune 1000 firms gave the following results:

EXHIBIT 6   CONTINUED

BANK NAME/SYSTEM NAME	NETWORK	SOFTWARE DESIGN	FREQUENCY	TERMINAL	LEVEL OF DETAIL	AVAILABLE INFORMATION	OTHER	COMPENSATION METHOD
US (continued)								
Continental Illinois Bank *ConFirm*	Proprietary	Proprietary					5	
Fidelity Bank *GEMMS*	GEISCO	NA					NA	
First City National Bank of Houston *Time-Net*	GEISCO	BankLink					2-65	
First National Bank of Boston[1] *BostonLink*	GEISCO	BankLink					60	
First National Bank of Chicago *FirstCash*	GEISCO	Proprietary					29	
First Interstate Bank of California *CashLink*	GEISCO Telenet	BankLink					NA	
Harris Bank *Harris Cash Manager*	GEISCO	BankLink					60	
Inter First Bank *FirstLine*	GEISCO	BankLink					59	
Manufacturers Hanover Trust *Transend*	GEISCO, Geonet	Proprietary					45	
Manufacturers National Bank of Detroit *AM Report II*	GEISCO	BankLink					60	
Mellon National Bank *Multibank Balance Reporting*	NDC, IDC, ADP	Proprietary					4-30	
Morgan Guaranty *MARS*	GEISCO	Proprietary					5	
North Carolina National Bank *Express-Link*	GEISCO	BankLink					90	
Northern Trust *InterClear*	GEISCO	Proprietary					7 NA	
Philadelphia National Bank[2] *PhilaReport*	GEISCO	Proprietary					60	
Pittsburgh National Bank *PerformaLink*	GEISCO	BankLink					60	
Seattle First National Bank *SeaFirst Balance Reporting*	NDC	Proprietary					63	
Security Pacific Bank[3] *Spacifics*	Telenet, Timenet PTT	Proprietary/ Tandem Software	NA				30	
Southeast Bank[4] *Action-Link I and II*	GEISCO	BankLink					NA	
US National Bank of Oregon *US Money Matrix*	ADP	ADP					5-60	

[1] Reports loans but not credit lines available.
[2] Reports loan/borrowing but not available credit lines.

[3] Loans and credit line information available on separate module.

[4] Trade transactions reporting available on another system called Quantum. Loan information reported but not credit lines.

Source: Reprinted with permission from Business International Corporation.

Technique	Percent Utilizing
Wire transfer	82.8
Mail/cable transfer	51.5
Intracompany netting	35.6
Funds concentration	23.3
Lockbox	18.4
Delayed payments	16.6
Giro payment system	11.0

Given their obvious importance, we first describe the electronic means of international funds transfer.

Internal bank networks, **independent timeshare** or telex networks, and S.W.I.F.T. (**Society for Worldwide Interbank Financial Telecommunications,** the international bank administered communications system) have all been utilized to some extent in this area. S.W.I.F.T., which is owned by its member banks, began operation in 1978 with 239 banks in 15 countries, essentially in Western Europe and North America. Since then it has expanded to Latin America and Asia; there are now over 1000 banks in more than 50 countries in the system, S.W.I.F.T. provides a standardization of funds transfer instructions and other bank information (such as letters of credit). This permits the execution of international transactions almost instantaneously and at relatively low cost. In New York, S.W.I.F.T. transactions are typically cleared through **CHIPS (Clearing House Interbank Payments System);** in London, clearing is through **CHAPS (Clearing House Automated Payments System).** While S.W.I.F.T. is primarily used for international transfers, it is also important for intercountry transfers. This is certainly true in countries like the Philippines that have a poor telecommunications capability. In general, S.W.I.F.T. can offer a relatively inexpensive domestic transfer mechanism in many countries.

While these transfers are used for large value transactions, smaller value and retail transactions can often be effectively done through **giro systems.** Most European countries have a single girobank to operate direct credits and debits. For example, a corporation may instruct the girobank to debit its account and to credit another account; the payer must know the account number of the payee. These Giro transactions are typically done by punch cards although corporations use computer disks or tapes to provide giro payments. Oosthoek (European Girobanks: What They Are and How To Use Them, *Journal of Cash Management,* January/February 1985), provides details and illustrations of corporate applications.

Check payments remain an important international payments mechanism. This is despite the inherent inefficiencies in international check clearing. Exhibit 7 depicts the stages involved in a dollar check to be paid to a U.S. exporter drawn on the bank of a West German importer. The key feature of check payments is that settlement must occur in the country of the payment currency, that is, for settlement to occur, the check must be issued on a bank located in the country of the payment currency. The 10 major steps in this process are numbered on the exhibit and are as follows:

1. The West German importer on receipt of a US $ invoice, requests its bank to issue a US $ check.
2. The importer's DM account is debited.
3. The importer's bank mails the check.
4. Exporter deposits the check.
5. Since the check cannot be cleared locally, the exporter's bank must present the check to the West German bank for payment.

EXHIBIT 7   DOLLAR CHECK DRAWN ON IMPORTER'S BANK

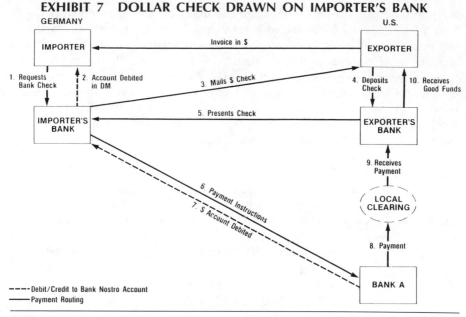

Source: Developed by Parkinson for Manufacturers Hanover Trust in New York.

6. After receipt of the check, the West German bank sends payment instructions for a US $ transfer to its U.S. correspondent (Bank A).

7. Bank A creates a US $ debit to the importer's bank.

8. Bank A pays the exporter's bank through the local clearing system.

9. Exporter's bank receives payment.

10. Exporter (finally) receives good funds.

This provides one example of this process. While in this example the importer's bank retains the float, this may not always be the case.

The situation when the check is drawn in a foreign currency, and so on is discussed in Giannotti and Smith (*Treasury Handbook,* 1981). For a good discussion of local clearing practices and payment systems in 11 countries, see *Payment Systems in Eleven Developed Countries* (Bank for International Settlements, 1985).

REINVOICING. Multinationals use *reinvoicing* (or trading) companies to achieve a wide variety of long- and short-term operating and financial objectives. These typically relate to centralization of marketing and sales. More recently, reinvoicing centers have been used to improve cash management practices.

The function of a **reinvoicing center** is to take title (without taking physical possession) of goods manufactured by the company, either the parent or its manufacturing subsidaries. These goods are then resold by the reinvoicing center to other marketing subsidaries or to third parties. The advantages of a reinvoicing center are:

- **Centralization of Foreign Exchange Exposure.** Since the reinvoicing center deals with the manufacturing and marketing subsidaries in their local currencies, it bears the foreign exchange risk. This allows for centralized exposure management and foreign exchange trading, as well as the possibility of netting.
- **More Efficient Cash Management.** Similar to the benefits of netting, reinvoicing can reduce the number of transactions.
- Improved Liquidity Management. Reinvoicing centers may assist in financing trade among the subsidaries. As well, it can allow the centralization of investment and borrowing. Finally, it may permit leading and lagging of intercompany accounts.

Balancing these advantages are a number of potential difficulties:

- **Cost.** The cost of establishing and maintaining a reinvoicing company is significant; Giannotti and Smith (*Treasury Management,* 1981) suggest a minimum threshold of $100 million in intercompany trade flows.
- **Location.** Reinvoicing centers must be established in countries with minimal foreign exchange controls and favorable tax rates. These include Switzerland, Hong Kong, Singapore, and the United Kingdom. (See Business International, *The BIMR Handbook on Global Treasury Management,* 1984, for a description of Rhone-Poulenc's network of over 50 reinvoicing companies located in the United Kingdom, Italy, Indonesia, Japan, West Germany, and so forth.)
- **Organization.** Reinvoicing requires a high degree of centralization and organization. This may be very awkward to implement in multinationals with a decentralized structure.

In summary, reinvoicing companies can offer the multinational a powerful treasury tool. However, the complexity and expense have led to rather few having been implemented.

COLLECTION SYSTEMS. A few banks (both from the United States and the United Kingdom) have begun to establish **lockbox services** comparable to those offered throughout the United States, however, the volume handled is still miniscule. The most commonly cited reason for this lack of development of **corporate lockbox services** in the overseas banking environment is the efficiency of the local postal services. (In addition, the U.S. postal service offers continuous processing of mail (rather than once per day which is generally the case); this means that there is a substantial advantage to the

lockbox bank's capability of multiple mail pickups in a day.) In addition, the fragmented nature of U.S. branch banking creates an awkward settling mechanism which is greatly inferior to those encountered in a number of developed countries, such as Canada, the United Kingdom, or West Germany. It is this check clearing float that has led to the widespread acceptance of lockboxes within the United States.

The use of noncheck means of payment (i.e., notes or drafts) is also common in many overseas locations. Extensive use of notes and drafts is often cited as a major deterrant to the development of typical U.S. cash management services. There is considerable validity to this viewpoint, especially when coupled with the lack of sophisticated corporate banking systems. Many banks, both United States and foreign, have apparently not realized that noncredit services can be profitably offered to corporate customers. Hence, until very recently, there has been little bank effort to establish or develop effective cash management services for multinational companies.

PROBLEM SOLUTIONS

The problems of international cash management can seem formidable. Yet there are many possible solutions to the various types of problems, although we note that "solution" does not generally mean elimination of the problem, but rather improvement relative to current practice. The changes required tend to be relatively simple and straightforward; sophisticated techniques have not yet evolved for dealing with these problems. Changes that are not fundamental are more apt to be applicable to a very few exceptional cases and attempting to use such approaches too broadly can have extremely frustrating results.

COMPANY-RELATED PROBLEMS. In dealing with company-related problems, the key aspects on which to focus are information-gathering and staff education. This is true for both the home office and the local overseas personnel.

The first major gap to be closed is in the documentation of existing worldwide bank relationships. International cash managers in large multinational firms, particularly those that are just beginning to address this area, often have no current, detailed descriptions of existing banking relationships. Consequently, they are at a loss as to where to begin in studying their overseas cash management activities. Through the use of simple questionnaires, the cash manager can achieve considerable success in building a wide base of useful information. Exhibits 8 and 9 give examples of these types of questionnaires. It begins with very basic information designed to enable the cash manager to understand the basic outline of worldwide banking relations and to identify fundamental inconsistencies of questions regarding local practice.

EXHIBIT 8   INTERNATIONAL CASH MANAGEMENT PROFILE

Country _____

Bank _____

Average Annual Sales _____

Average Cash—Balance Sheet _____

Daily Bank Balance _____

Bank Relations

Major banks and services provided (list contracts)

Credit facilities

Compensation methods: Fees, Balances (amounts of each as applicable).

Transactions

Average bank balances

Investments

Bank borrowings

System Descriptions

Major method of collecting receipts + approximate percentage of total

Checks via mail

Checks via messenger pick-up

Electronic transfer

Paper transfer

Drafts/receivable paper through own collectors

Drafts/receivable paper through banks

Other (specify)

Methods of Disbursement

Paper transfer

Electronic transfer

Check mail pick up

Drafts

Other (specify)

Giro (payrolls, etc.)

Short-term credit facilities

Overdrafts

"Term" loans—fixed periods

Unsecured line of credit

Receivable discounting

Promissory note financing

Commercial paper

Other (specify)

Interest rates (investments and/or credit)

Samples of recent rates for representative items (above)

Various types of "prime" borrowing rates

Source(s) of historical and future rates

Float and Fees

Float (value dating)

General comments on postal system

Value dating for domestic deposited items by location

Value dating on international transfers (in and out)

Value dating on disbursements (bank valuing)

Any available mail times (typical times)

Fees—schedule for all services (credit and noncredit)[a]

Miscellaneous

Legal controls such as those over currency or foreign exchange. Describe briefly.

Various special features of banking system. Describe items that are unique to the country (e.g., Belgian two-tier system).

---

[a]Substitute compensating balances for fees if applicable.

EXHIBIT 9 INTERNATIONAL BANKING SYSTEM PROFILE

Country ————————————————————————————
Bank ————————————————————————————

Mechanics of System

Major method(s) of payments/receipts
> Check
> Paper transfer
> Electronic transfer
> Draft
> Giro
> Other (specify)

> *Noncredit banking services available*
>> Collections of receivable drafts
>> Check "intercept"/air freight consolidation
>> Consolidation/concentration of local branch deposits
>> Zero balance accounts disbursements or deposits (tied to master concentration account)
>> Automatic investment of funds
>> Automatic overdraft available
>> Check reconcilement
>> Domestic wire transfer
>> International cable transfers
>> Other (specify)

> *Normal methods of bank compensation (for all services)*
>> Compensating balances
>> Fees
>> Commissions
>> Other (specify)

Credit Features of System

> *Short-term investment vehicles*
>> Interest on demand deposits
>> "Call" deposits
>> Time deposits—variable rate &/or time
>> Time deposits—fixed rate &/or time
>> Certificate of deposit
>> Commercial paper
>> Government securities
>> Bankers acceptances
>> Other (specify)

> Alternative investments used (indicate frequency and volume)
>> Time deposits—overnight, term (specify)
>> Interest on checking accounts
>> Commercial paper
>> Certificates of deposit
>> Swaps, loans
>> Foreign investment vehicles (specify)
>> Other (specify)

> Alternative credit facilities
>> Overdrafts
>> Term loans
>> Commercial paper
>> Other (specify)
>> Receivable or draft discounting

EXHIBIT 9   CONTINUED

Foreign exchange
  Who is used, how often?
  How are rates obtained?
Balance monitoring
  Do you set targets? If so, what are they?
  Frequency of bank statements
  Frequency of bank balances
  Sample of some form of daily cash report.
Float Analysis
  Value dating (you receive) on deposits (if any), i.e., when can funds be used?
    Show for different currencies, if applicable.
  Is there a ''disbursement float,'' in the U.S. sense? If so, how is it utilized?
  Indicate degree of flexibility or negotiability in value dates.

For instance, the cash manager may discover a location that has an abnormal number of banks for its size or one that is dealing only with small local banks rather than one or more of the large clearing banks. This initial overview survey can then be supplemented by more detailed banking profiles that are tailored to each location and request such information as credit facilities, bank charges, value dating arrangements, and historical bank balances. This information will provide a fuller picture of local cash management operations and agreements, and can help determine the priorities in conducting more detailed reviews of local units.

Whether aided by outside consultants or not, on-site reviews with local operating units are mandatory. Such visits and reviews should have as their primary objectives the further defining of existing cash management practices and the provision of a forum for mutual education. The cash manager can learn a great deal about local customs and practices from company personnel and local bankers. The manager must begin educating overseas personnel in sound cash management principles and practices and reorienting the local financial staff away from a strictly accounting approach. Another method of maintaining an effective education program is possible in cases where the company is blessed with a large international staff and/or presence overseas. In these instances, the rotating of personnel between corporate staff and the local operating units can be very beneficial.

CROSS-BORDER PROBLEMS. In dealing with export-related problems, the cash manager has a few more techniques available. If the cash manager is unable to convert most of the company's collections to an electronic medium, the use of overseas lockboxes is a new and attractive alternative.

Cross-border funds transfer problems can be alleviated through the use of **terminal-based initiation systems** that most large banks currently offer their corporate customers. In cases where these services are not available or cannot be effectively accessed, establishing additional manual procedures may be of some help, especially for internal company transfers. Here prenotification of pending transfers—often called closing the loop—can eliminate many problems associated with late or improper notification of transfers received at local units (see Exhibit 10). By instructing local personnel to act on the prenotification, regardless of whether or not the local bank has given notice of the transfer, instances of lost transfers or failures to notify become banking problems rather than company problems. Many firms have enjoyed a great deal of success by using these procedures. Of course, as more banks begin to utilize the S.W.I.F.T. system for transfers, the need for using this internal prenotification procedure will be lessened.

BANKING SYSTEM PROBLEMS. These types of problems are being addressed more and more as international cash management becomes more familiar to banks and large corporations. Recent surveys and research projects

EXHIBIT 10   CLOSING THE LOOP ON INTERNATIONAL TRANSFERS

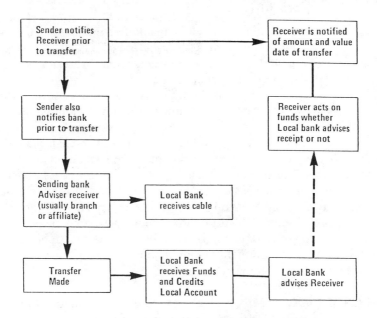

- Transfer information communicated prior to actual transfer of funds (within banking system and corporate system)

- Receiver of funds acts independently of local bank advice

- Transfer failures become bank to bank problems, not the corporation's problems

have documented the practices and services available at overseas locations. This begins to provide the cash manager with fundamental descriptions of foreign banking systems and related cash management opportunities. Such reports, when used in conjunction with basic documentation such as that described previously, can provide an effective framework for dealing with banking system problems. Individual country studies, usually conducted by outside banks or independent consultants, are useful in helping the company deal with banking system problems. Outside experts provide an objective appraisal of current practices and estimated benefits from improvements in value-dating arrangements, bank service charges, and other possible improvements.

Pooling. Typical recommended improvements are procedural in nature in that local practices will be modified without necessarily altering banking arrangements. One other technique or service that is commonly instituted, in countries like Canada and the United Kingdom where it is available, is **pooling.** Pooling permits a company to offset the balances in numerous accounts with the same bank to avoid overdrafts and excesses occurring simultaneously. Funds are not actually transferred; the bank merely computes the net balance. **Pooling banks** may require all accounts to be maintained at the same branch to simplify the computations.

SYSTEM DESIGN.   Balance reporting services can be relatively expensive from overseas locations and should be established judiciously. Many corporations will find it useful and effective to consider establishing a system for reporting and monitoring overseas cash management activities that combines the customized documentation process described previously with available balance reporting capabilities. Such a system is depicted in Exhibit 11. The main advantages of such a system are its modularity and flexibility. For instance, a location may not be able to provide all necessary data at the start, but it can be included on the overall system and can gradually add different types of cash management reports. The reports themselves can be customized to the needs and capabilities of each location (in terms of both cash flow and staff) and can be expected to provide more information than smaller ones. The locations can provide bank balance reports initially by working with their own bank statments. For locations in more developed countries and where banks are able to report balances, this manual activity can be replaced by balance reporting services directly. This may also be an effective alternative for locations that do not have sufficient staff to prepare comprehensive manual reports.

In any case, the **central cash manager** is the central recipient of these reports and must devote adequate time and effort to analytical activities. Comparisons within the same country can be made to evaluate the effectiveness of each bank used by the local unit. Such comparisons can consider bank costs, the effects of value dating, and the average balance maintained

EXHIBIT 11   GLOBAL TREASURY REPORTING SYSTEM

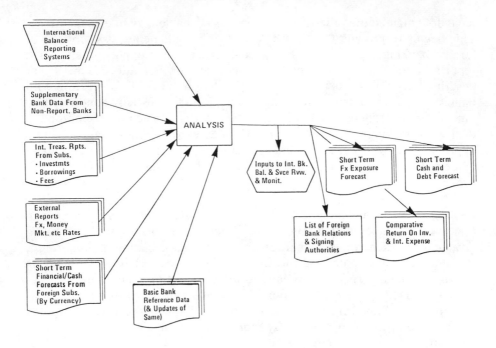

EXHIBIT 12   INTERNATIONAL BANK BALANCE AND SERVICE CHARGE MONITORING

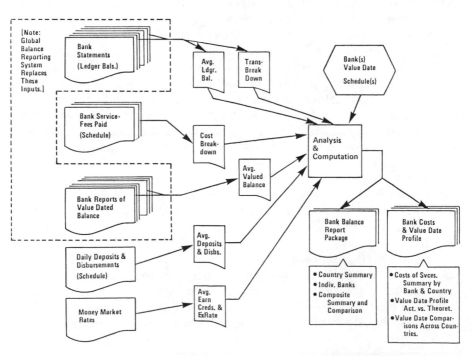

at each bank. These comparisons can also be made across countries, but definitive conclusions as to the respective performance of each bank will be difficult to form, given the vast differences in banking systems and related problems discussed previously. The flow of information to cash managers will expand their knowledge of local cash management activities. Exhibit 12 presents an overview of these information flows. On subsequent local visits, the reports can serve as topics for review with local financial managers. These reviews should also result in further customization of the system to include additional information in future reports.

SUMMARY AND CONCLUSIONS

The rate of progress in the internationalization of cash management depends on the interest and emphasis placed on this area by corporate managers and their banking counterparts. The rate of development of international cash management capabilities should increase for three reasons.

1. There is the transfer of both knowledge and technology from domestic U.S. experience. While there are many differences between international and domestic cash management, there are also important similarities. Since many of the persons now involved in the development of international cash management gained their experience in the U.S. environment, the learning curve for international cash mangement should be much shorter than the U.S. experience.
2. The services offered U.S. companies abroad by U.S. banks will force foreign banks to compete and innovate.
3. Improvements in international communications networks now in place will facilitate the information transfer that is central to innovative cash management.

International cash management is finally moving from a largely static position to one with more promise and activity. The internationalization of cash management will continue at an accelerated rate.

REFERENCES

Arntz, Klaus H., "Cash Management in the Ruhrgas Treasury: An Integrated Approach to Profitable Cash Management," *Journal of Cash Management,* Vol. 5, No. 5, September/October 1985.

Bank for International Settlements, *Payment Systems in Eleven Developed Countries,* Washington, D.C., February 1985.

Business International, *New Directions in European Cash Management,* Business International Corp., New York, 1984.

————, *The BIMR Handbook on Global Treasury Management,* Business International Corp., New York, 1984.

————, *Cutting Costs through International Cash Management,* Business International Corp., New York, 1986.

Buss, Martin D.J., "Legislative Threat to Transborder Data Flow," *Harvard Business Review,* May–June 1984.

Collins, J.M., and Frankle, A.W., "International Cash Management Practices of Large U.S. Firms," *Journal of Cash Management,* Vol. 5, No. 4, July/August 1985.

Giannotti, John B., and Smith, Richard W., *Treasury Management: A Practitioner's Handbook,* Wiley, New York, 1981.

Greguras, Fred M., "Impact of Transborder Data Flow Restrictions on Cash Management Services," *Journal of Cash Management,* Vol. 5, No. 5, September/October 1985.

Griffiths, Susan H., and Robertson, Nigel J., "Global Cash: Corporate Treasury Management in Europe—Harmonization or Standardization?" *Journal of Cash Management,* Vol. 5, No. 2, March/April 1985. September/October 1985.

————, "Global Cash: The Propensity for Change," *Journal of Cash Management,* Vol. 5, No. 6, November/December 1985.

Kallberg, Jarl G., and Parkinson, Kenneth L., *Current Asset Management: Cash, Credit, and Inventory,* Wiley Interscience, New York, 1984.

Oosthoek, Willem N., "European Girobanks: What They Are and How to Use Them," *Journal of Cash Management,* Vol. 5, No. 3, January/February 1985.

Parkinson, Kenneth L., "Dealing with the Problems of International Cash Management," *Journal of Cash Management,* Vol. 3, No. 1, February/March 1983.

Roberts, E.G., "Benefits of Export Cash Management Studies," *Journal of Cash Management,* Vol. 4, No. 5, September/October 1984.

Williams, Michael J., "Electronic Banking Comes of Age in Europe," *Journal of Cash Management,* Vol. 5, No. 3, May/June 1985.

Willis, Stephen, "Evolution of the International Treasury Function," *Journal of Cash Management,* Vol. 5, No. 6, November/December 1985.

19

BANKRUPTCY AND REORGANIZATION

CONTENTS

19

BANKRUPTCY AND REORGANIZATION

Edward I. Altman

INTRODUCTION

Business failure, including the legal procedures of **corporate bankruptcy liquidation and reorganization,** is a sobering economic reality reflecting the uniqueness of the American way of corporate death. The business failure phenomenon received a great deal of exposure during the 1970s and this attention heightened as the nation moved into the 1980s. Between 1975 and 1979, 29,500 to 35,200 firms a year petitioned the courts to liquidate or to reorganize under the protection of the nation's bankruptcy laws. In the 1980–1984 period, the number of filings exploded to between 36,433 in 1980 to a peak of 69,818 in 1983. The number dropped slightly in 1984 to 62,170 but rose again to 66,657 in 1985, (see Exhibit 1). Business failures also increased dramatically in the 1980s. Although business failure and bankruptcy are worldwide phenomena, this section concentrates on events, data, and commentary on bankruptcy in the United States.

Corporate failure is no longer the exclusive province of the small, undercapitalized entity but is increasingly found among large industrial and financial corporations. The 1970s was a watershed in this respect, from the $5 billion **Penn Central bankruptcy** (in 1970), heralding the new wave of larger firm failures, to the $12 billion all-but-bankrupt **Chrysler Corporation** problem and subsequent government bailout beginning in 1980. Exhibit 2 lists the largest U.S. bankruptcies—all of which have taken place during or since 1970. The list does not include financial organizations, such as commercial banks and savings and loan associations, but does include real estate investment trusts (REITS). Certainly, inflation accounts for the increase in size of all firms, including those that go bankrupt, but the astounding increase in the average liability of business failures (next subsection) goes beyond inflationary influence.

EXHIBIT 1 NUMBER OF BANKRUPTCY CASES FILED AND NUMBER OF BUSINESS FAILURES AND FAILURE RATES REPORTED SINCE 1950

Year	Number of Business Bankruptcies[a]	Business Failures[b]	Business Failure Rate per 10,000 Firms	Average Liability per Failure[b] ($)
1950	8,352	9,162	34	27,099
1951	7,387	8,058	31	32,210
1952	6,542	7,611	29	37,224
1953	6,772	8,862	33	44,477
1954	8,888	11,086	42	41,731
1955	9,185	10,969	42	40,968
1956	9,748	12,686	48	44,356
1957	10,144	13,739	52	44,784
1958	11,403	14,964	56	48,667
1959	11,729	14,053	52	49,300
1960	12,284	15,445	57	60,772
1961	15,241	17,075	64	63,843
1962	15,644	15,782	61	76,808
1963	16,303	14,274	56	94,100
1964	16,510	13,501	53	98,454
1965	16,910	13,514	53	97,800
1966	16,430	13,061	52	106,091
1967	16,600	12,364	49	102,332
1968	16,545	9,636	39	97,654
1969	15,430	9,154	37	124,767
1970	16,197	10,748	44	175,638
1971	19,103	10,326	42	185,641
1972	18,132	9,566	38	209,099
1973	17,490	9,345	36	245,972
1974	20,747	9,915	38	307,931
1975	30,130	11,432	43	383,150
1976	35,201	9,628	35	312,762
1977	32,189	7,919	28	390,872
1978	30,528	6,619	24	401,270
1979	29,500	7,564	28	353,000
1980	36,433[c]	11,742	42	394,744
1981	47,415[c]	17,041	61	414,147
1982	56,423[c]	24,908	89	626,304
1983	69,818[c]	31,334	110	512,953
1984	62,170[c]	52,078	107[d]	562,015
1985	66,651[c]	57,067	114[d]	584,854

[a]From the U.S. Administrative Bankruptcy Courts, Washington, D.C., 1984. Statistical year ends June 30.

[b]From Dun & Bradstreet, **Failure Record,** 1983 and D&B, Inc., N.Y. Failures include businesses that ceased operations following assignment or bankruptcy, ceased with loss to creditors; voluntarily withdrew, leaving unpaid obligations, or were involved in court actions such as receivership, reorganization, or arrangement. Certain industries such as financial enterprises, railroads, insurance, real estate companies, and many small services are not represented.
Failure liabilities do not include publicly held debt, nor most long-term liabilities and as such underestimate average liabilities.

[c]Does not include joint husband and wife filings of 9,308 (1980), 18,592 (1981) 21,080 (1982), 25,621 (1983), and 22,567 (1984).

[d]Author's calculation.

[e]Revised larger data base.

EXHIBIT 2 LARGEST UNITED STATES BANKRUPTCIES IN TERMS OF DOLLAR LIABILITIES AS OF DECEMBER 1985[a]

Company Name	Total Liabilities ($ Millions)	Bankruptcy Petition Date	Filed Under
Penn Central Transportation Co.	3300	06/1970	Section 77
Wickes	2000	04/1982	Chapter 11
Itel	1700	01/1981	Chapter 11
Baldwin—United[c]	1600	09/1983	Chapter 11
Global Marine Inc.	1800	01/1986	Chapter 11
GHR Energy Corp.[b]	1200	01/1983	Chapter 11
Bell National	1203	08/1985	Chapter 11
Manville Corp.	1116	08/1982	Chapter 11
Braniff Airlines	1100	05/1982	Chapter 11
Continental Airlines[c]	1100	09/1983	Chapter 11
W.T. Grant	1000	10/1975	Chapter XI
Charter Co.	976	04/1985	Chapter 11
North American Car Corp.	841	12/1984	Chapter 11
Seatrain Lines	785	02/1981	Chapter 11
A.H. Robins	775	08/1985	Chapter 11
Storage Technologies	695	10/1984	Chapter 11
Coral Petroleum[b]	682	05/1983	Chapter 11
Nucorp Energy	615	07/1982	Chapter 11
Continental Mortgage Investors	607	03/1976	Chapter XI
Evans Products	600	03/1985	Chapter 11
United Merchants & Manufacturing	552	07/1977	Chapter XI
AM International	510	04/1982	Chapter 11
OPM Leasing[b]	505	03/1981	Chapter 11
Bevill Bresler Schulman	498	04/1985	Chapter 11
Saxon Industries	461	04/1982	Chapter 11
Commonwealth Oil Refining Co.	421	03/1978	Chapter XI
W. Judd Kassuba	420	12/1973	Chapter XI
Erie Lackawanna Railroad	404	06/1972	Section 77
White Motor Corp.	399	09/1980	Chapter 11
Investors Funding Corp.	370	10/1974	Chapter XI
Sambo's Restaurants	370	06/1981	Chapter 11
Amarex	348	06/1982	Chapter 11
Food Fair Corp.	347	10/1978	Chapter XI
Buttes Oil & Gas	337	11/1985	Chapter 11
Great American Mortgage & Trust	326	03/1977	Chapter XI
McLouth Steel	323	12/1981	Chapter 11
MGF Oil	304	12/1984	Chapter 11
U.S. Financial Services	300	07/1973	Chapter XI
Hunt International	295	04/1985	Chapter 11
Chase Manhattan Mortgage & Realty Trust	290	02/1979	Chapter XI
Daylin, Inc.	250	02/1975	Chapter XI
Guardian Mortgage Investors	247	03/1978	Chapter XI
Waterman Steamship Corp.	242	12/1983	Chapter 11
Revere Copper & Brass	237	10/1982	Chapter 11
Chicago, Rock Island & Pacific	221	03/1975	Section 77
Air Florida System	221	07/1984	Chapter 11
Hellenic Lines, Ltd.	216	12/1983	Chapter 11
Wilson Foods	213	04/1983	Chapter 11

EXHIBIT 2   CONTINUED

Company Name	Total Liabilities ($ Millions)	Bankruptcy Petition Date	Filed Under
Lion Capital Group	212	04/1984	Chapter 11
KDT Industries	203	08/1982	Chapter 11
Equity Funding Corp. Of America	200	04/1973	Chapter X
Interstate Stores, Inc.	190	05/1974	Chapter XI
Fidelity Mortgage Investors	187	01/1975	Chapter XI
HRT Industries	183	11/1982	Chapter 11
Terex Corp.	176	11/1983	Chapter 11
Omega, Alpha Corp.	175	09/1974	Chapter X
Marion Corp.	175	03/1983	Chapter 11
Lionel Corp.	165	02/1982	Chapter 11
Thatcher Glass	165	12/1984	Chapter 11
U.N.R. Industries	165	07/1982	Chapter 11
Towner Petroleum	163	09/1984	Chapter 11
Dreco Energy	161	06/1982	Chapter 11
Reading Railroad	158	11/1971	Section 77
Anglo Energy	155	11/1983	Chapter 11
Boston & Maine Railroad	148	12/1975	Section 77
Westgate-California	144	02/1974	Chapter X
Cook United, Inc.	143	10/1984	Chapter 11
Pizza Time Theatre	143	03/1984	Chapter 11
Colwell Mortgage & Trust	142	02/1978	Chapter XI
Phoenix Steel Corp.	137	08/1983	Chapter 11
Pacific Far East Lines	132	01/1978	Chapter XI
Allied Supermarkets	124	06/1977	Chapter XI
Penn-Dixie Industries	122	04/1980	Chapter 11

[a]*Does Not Include Commercial Banking Entities.*
[b]*Privately held firm.*
[c]Subsidiary of Texas Air Corp. Estimate of long-term debt only.

Among the 64 largest bankruptcies, in terms of liabilities, are 11 retailers, 6 REITS, 4 railroads, 9 oil and gas companies, and 2 airlines. A noticeable dearth of large manufacturers is evident, but even this sector appears increasingly vulnerable with the near failure of Chrysler and International Harvester and the recent Penn Dixie Co., White Motor Co., A.M. International, Revere Copper and Brass, Johns Manville, Wheeling Pittsburgh Steel, Storage Technologies, and Wickes Companies cases—the latter is the largest bankruptcy filed thus far under the **Bankruptcy Reform Act of 1978,** which went into effect in October 1979.

BANKRUPTCY AND REORGANIZATION THEORY

In any economic system, the continuous entrance and exit of productive entities are natural components. Since there are costs to society inherent in the failure of these entities, laws and procedures have been established:

1. To protect the contractual rights of interest parties
2. To provide for the orderly liquidation of unproductive assets
3. When deemed desirable, to provide for a temporary moratorium on certain claims, in order to give the debtor time to become rehabilitated and to emerge from the process as a continuing entity.

Both **liquidation** and **reorganization** are available courses of action in most countries of the world and are based on the following premise. If an entity's intrinsic or economic value is greater than its current liquidation value, then from both the public policy and entity ownership viewpoints, the firm should attempt to reorganize and continue. If, however, the firm's assets are worth more dead than alive—that is, if liquidation value exceeds economic value— liquidation is the preferable alternative.

The **theory of reorganization in bankruptcy** is basically sound and has potential economic and social benefits. The process is designed to enable the financially troubled firm to continue in existence and maintain whatever goodwill it still possesses, rather than liquidate its assets for the benefit of its creditors. Justification of this attempt is found in the belief that continued existence will result in a healthy going-concern operation worth more than the value of its assets sold in the marketplace. Since this rehabilitation process often requires several years, the **time value of money** should be considered explicitly through a **discounted cash flow procedure.** If, in fact, economically productive assets continue to contribute to society's supply of goods and services above and beyond their **opportunity costs,** the process of the reorganization has been of benefit, to say nothing of the continued employment of the firm's employees. These benefits should be weighed against the **costs of bankruptcy** to the firm and to society.

The primary groups of interested parties are the firm's creditors and owners. The experience of these parties is of paramount importance in the evaluation of the bankruptcy-reorganization process, although the laws governing reorganization reflect the legislators' concern for overall **societal welfare.** The primary immediate responsibility of the reorganization process is to relieve the burden of the debtor's liabilities and realign the capital structure so that financial problems will not recur in the foreseeable future.

COSTS OF BANKRUPTCY

From the firm's standpoint, bankruptcy includes direct and indirect costs. **Direct bankruptcy costs** are the tangible, out-of-pocket expenses of either liquidating or attempting a reorganization of the ailing enterprise. These include bankruptcy filing fees and legal, accounting, and other professional service costs. Some analysts, such as J. Warner ("Bankruptcy Costs: Some Empirical Evidence," *Journal of Finance,* May 1977), include in the direct cost category the costs involved with **lost managerial time,** a difficult "expense" to measure empirically. We prefer to include lost managerial time with other **intangible opportunity costs** or **indirect costs.** The primary **indirect cost** is the lost sales and profits of the firm due to the perceived potential bankruptcy-primarily from customer reluctance to buy from a firm that may fail. This cost was dramatically illustrated when sales of Chrysler products dropped during the 1978–1980 financial crisis.

Continuing research in this area centers on trying to quantify the **magnitude** of these direct and indirect costs to permit their comparison with the **tax benefit** that a firm receives from additional leverage. Many theorists believe that the increasing bankruptcy possibility due to increased leverage and the attendant costs of bankruptcy help explain why firms seek some **optimal capital structure;** in other words, an optimal mix of debt and equity capital. While Warner did not find bankruptcy costs to be large relative to the value of the firm, Altman ("A Further Empirical Investigation of the Bankruptcy Cost Question," *Journal of Finance,* September 1984) found much higher amounts when the indirect costs are included.

DEFINING CORPORATE PROBLEMS

The unsuccessful business enterprise has been defined in numerous ways in attempts to depict the formal process confronting the firm and/or to categorize the economic problems involved. Three generic terms that are commonly found in the literature are **failure, insolvency,** and **bankruptcy.** Although these terms are sometimes used interchangeably, they have distinctly different meanings.

FAILURE, BY ECONOMIC CRITERIA. This means that the realized rate of return on invested capital, with allowances for risk considerations, is significantly and continually lower than prevailing rates on similar investments. Somewhat different economic criteria have also been utilized, including insufficient revenues to cover costs and cases of the **average return on investment** being below the firm's **cost of capital.** These economic situations make no positive statements about the existence or discontinuance of the entity. Normative decisions to discontinue operations are based on expected returns and the ability of the firm to cover its variable costs. It should be noted that a company may be an **economic failure** for many years, yet never fail to meet its current obligations because of the absence or near absence of legally enforceable debt. When the company can no longer meet the legally enforceable demands of its creditors, it is sometimes called a **legal failure.** The term "legal" is somewhat misleading because the condition, as just described, may exist without formal court involvement.

The term "business failure" has also been adopted by Dun & Bradstreet (D&B)—a leading supplier of relevant statistics on unsuccessful enterprises—to describe various unsatisfactory business conditions. **Business failures** include businesses that (1) cease operation following assignment or bankruptcy, (2) cease with loss to creditors after such actions as execution, foreclosure, or attachment, (3) voluntarily withdraw leaving unpaid obligations or have been involved in court actions such as **receivership, reorganization,** or **arrangement,** and (4) voluntarily **compromise with creditors.** In actuality, business failures as defined by D&B are a fraction, although a significant one, of the enterprises that are discontinued each year.

INSOLVENCY is another term depicting negative firm performance and is generally used in a more technical fashion. The state of **technical insolvency** exists when a firm cannot meet its current obligations, signifying a **lack of liquidity.** Another term used to describe the same situation is **insolvency in an equity sense.** Walter ("Determination of Technical Insolvency," *Journal of Business,* January 1957, pp. 30–43) discussed the measurement of technical insolvency and advanced the theory that net cash flows relative to current liabilities should be the primary criterion used to describe technical insolvency, not traditional working capital measurement. **Technical insolvency** may be a temporary condition, although it often is the immediate cause of formal bankruptcy declaration.

INSOLVENCY IN A BANKRUPTCY SENSE. This is more critical and indicates a chronic rather than temporary condition. A firm finds itself in this situation when its total liabilities exceed a fair valuation of its total assets. The **real net worth** of the firm is, therefore, **negative.** Technical insolvency is easily detectable, whereas the more serious bankruptcy insolvency condition requires a comprehensive valuation analysis, which is usually not undertaken until **asset liquidation** is contemplated. Insolvency, as it relates to the **formal bankruptcy process,** is defined explicitly in Section 101 (26) of the **Bankruptcy Reform Act of 1978.**

BANKRUPTCY. One type of bankruptcy (described previously) refers to the net worth position of an enterprise. A second more observable type, is a firm's formal declaration of bankruptcy in a federal district or bankruptcy court, accompanied by a petition to either liquidate its assets or attempt a recovery program. The latter procedure is legally referred to as a **bankruptcy-reorganization** and is discussed later. The judicial reorganization is a formal procedure that is usually the last measure in a series of attempted remedies.

INSOLVENCY TESTS AND CORPORATE DISTRIBUTIONS

Corporate distributions to shareholders involve the transfer of money or other property (except its own shares) whether by **cash dividend** or **share repurchase.** The revised **Model Business Corporation Act** specifies that the **board of directors** may authorize and the corporation may make distributions except where (1) the corporation would be unable to pay its debts as they become due in the usual course of its business, or (2) the corporation's total assets would be less than its total liabilities (this is sometimes known as the

balance sheet test). The former test describes **equity insolvency** and the latter describes **bankruptcy insolvency.** No longer are the terms **par value, stated value,** or **capital surplus** of any relevance to a firm's payment of dividends or share repurchase.

Whether a firm would be insolvent as a result of a proposed distribution is to be determined by the board of directors based on its collective business judgment. This is stipulated to involve judgments as to the future course of the corporation's business, including an analysis of the firm's ability to generate sufficient funds from operations or from the orderly disposition of its assets in order to satisfy its existing and reasonably anticipated obligations as they come due.

Discussion of these and other provisions can be found in "Changes in the Model Business Corporation Act-Amendments to Financial Provisions" (*Business Lawyer,* Vol. 34, July 1979). The question of **corporate solvency** is now explicit and fundamental to the concept of shareholder return on investment.

EVOLUTION OF THE BANKRUPTCY PROCESS IN THE UNITED STATES

The Constitution empowers the U.S. Congress to establish uniform laws regulating bankruptcy. By virtue of this authority, various acts and amendments have been passed, starting with the **Bankruptcy Act of 1898.** Several bankruptcy acts have been passed in this century, and in 1978 Congress enacted the **Bankruptcy Reform Act of 1978,** which is the current standard. To appreciate the bankruptcy process, it is necessary to review the previous statutes and codes that have helped to form the present system.

EQUITY RECEIVERSHIPS. The Bankruptcy Act of 1898 provided only for a company's liquidation and contained no provisions allowing corporations to reorganize and thereby remain in existence. Reorganization could be effected, however, through **equity receiverships.** Although the basic theory of corporate reorganization is sound, the equity receivership procedure proved to be ineffective. It was developed to prevent disruptive seizures of property by dissatisfied creditors who were able to obtain liens on specific properties of the financially troubled concern. Receivers were appointed by the courts to manage the corporate property during financial reorganization. This procedure presented serious problems, however, and essentially was replaced by provisions of the **Bankruptcy Acts of 1933 and 1934. Receivership in equity** is not the same as **receivership in bankruptcy.** In the latter case, a **receiver** is a court agency that administers the bankrupt's assets until a trustee is appointed. While receivership is still available to companies, it has been almost entirely replaced by reorganization under the new Bankruptcy Act.

Equity receivership was extremely time-consuming and costly, as well as susceptible to severe injustices. The courts had little control over the reorganization plan, and the committees set up to protect security holders were usually made up of powerful corporate insiders who used the process to further their own interest. The initiative for equity receivership was usually taken by the company in conjunction with some friendly creditor. There was no provision made for independent, objective review of the plans that were invariably drawn up by a biased committee or friendly receiver. Since ratification required majority creditor support, it usually meant that companies offered cash payoffs to powerful dissenters to gain their support. This led to long delays and charges of unfairness. Because of these disadvantages, the procedure was ineffective, especially when the number of receiverships skyrocketed during the Depression years.

THE CHANDLER ACT OF 1938. In 1933 a new bankruptcy act with a special Section 77 (for railroad reorganizations) was hastily drawn up and enacted. The following year, Section 77B was enacted to provide for general corporate reorganizations. The Act was short-lived: in 1938 it underwent a comprehensive revision and was thereafter known as the **Chandler Act.** This legislation was the result of the joint efforts of the National Bankruptcy Conference, the **Securities and Exchange Commission** (SEC), which had embarked on its own study of reorganization practices, and various other interested committees and associations.

Chapter XI. We will first discuss the two chapters under the Chandler Act that dealt with corporate reorganizations. These have been replaced by Chapter 11 under the 1978 Bankruptcy Code. **Chapter XI arrangements** applied only to the unsecured creditors of corporations and removed the necessity to get all creditor types to agree on a plan of action. A Chapter XI arrangement was a **voluntary proceeding** that could be initiated by corporate or noncorporate entities or persons. The court had the power to appoint an **independent trustee or receiver** to manage the corporate property or, in many instances, to permit the old management team to continue its control during the proceedings. The bankrupt's petition for reorganization usually contained a preliminary plan for financial relief. The prospect of continued management control and reduced financial obligations made **Chapter XI** particularly attractive to present management. During the proceedings, a referee called the creditors together to go over the proposed plan and any new amendments that had been proposed. If a majority in number and amount of each class of unsecured creditors consented to the plan, the court could confirm the arrangement and make it binding on all creditors. Usually, the plan provided for a scaled-down creditor claim, **composition of claims,** and/or **extension of payment over time.** New financial instruments could be issued to creditors in lieu of their old claims.

In addition to the advantages noted, **Chapter XI** placed the bankrupt's assets strictly in the custody of the court and made them free from any prior pending court proceeding. Also, the debtor could borrow new funds that had preference over all unsecured indebtedness. Although the interest rate on such new credit was expectedly high, it still enabled the embarrassed firm to secure an important new source of financing. As in all corporate reorganizations, the assets were protected by the court during these proceedings. Also the Chapter XI arrangements, if successful, were of relatively short duration compared to the more complex Chapter X cases, since administrative expenses were a function of time. Chapter XI was usually less costly than proceedings that involved all security holders. Successful **out-of-court settlements,** however, were usually even less costly. Finally, the arrangement was binding in all states of the country.

Chapter X. The least common but most important type of corporate bankruptcy-reorganization was the **Chapter X proceeding.** The importance of this bankruptcy form is clearly illustrated by the dollar amount of liabilities involved, the size and importance of the petitioning companies, and the fact that most of the empirical data utilized in bankruptcy analysis involved Chapter X bankrupts.

Chapter X proceedings applied to publicly held corporations except railroads, and to those that had **secured creditors.** This bankruptcy process could be initiated voluntarily by the debtor or involuntarily by three or more creditors with total claims of $5000 or more. It was generally felt that Section 77B of the 1934 Act was too liberal to the small creditors, since only $1000 in claims was required. The bankruptcy petition had to contain a statement of why adequate relief could not be obtained under Chapter XI. The aim of this requirement was to make Chapter X proceedings unavailable to corporations having simple debt and capital structures. On the other hand, the court had the right (and exercised it on several occasions) to refuse to allow a Chapter XI proceeding and to require that a reorganization be processed under Chapter X. This usually happened when a substantial public interest was deemed present by the court or by the SEC, and the firm had originally filed a Chapter XI voluntary petition. The SEC on particular occasions filed motions in Chapter XI proceedings to force companies into Chapter X because Chapter XI could not adequately handle the case when a substantial public interest was involved.

In most cases, a Chapter XI was preferred by the debtor because Chapter X automatically provided for the appointment of an independent, disinterested trustee or trustees to assume control of the company for the duration of the bankruptcy proceeding. Actually the Act provided for the appointment of the independent trustee in every case in which indebtedness amounted to $250,000 or more. Where the indebtedness was less than $250,000, the judge could either continue the **debtor in possession** or appoint a disinterested trustee. The only prescribed qualification of the trustee, in addition to disinterestedness, was competence to perform the duties.

The **independent trustee** was charged with the development and submission of a reorganization plan that was "fair and feasible" to all parties involved. The **Interstate Commerce Commission** (ICC) was charged with this task in the case of railroad bankruptcies. Invariably, this plan involved all the creditors as well as the preferred and common stockholders. This important task was in addition to the day-to-day management responsibilities, although the trustee usually delegated the latter authority to the old management or to a new management team. New management was often installed since management incompetence, in one form or another, was by far the most common cause of corporate failure. In most Chapter X bankruptcies, the trustee was aided by various experts in the development and presentation of **reorganization plans,** as well as by committees representing the various creditors and stockholders. This practice continues under the new Bankruptcy Code of 1978 when a trustee is appointed. At the outset, the creditors, indenture trustees, and stockholders were permitted to file answers controverting the allegations of a voluntary or involuntary petition. While bankruptcy initiation action was curtailed by the 1938 Act, the ability to answer was enhanced.

SECURITY AND EXCHANGE COMMISSION. Another extremely important participant in **Chapter X** proceedings was the **SEC.** This is clearly not the case under the current Code, which all but eliminates the role of the SEC. Although the SEC did not possess any decision-making authority, its involvement, via the **SEC Advisory Reports,** was in our opinion a powerful objective force in the entire process. The **SEC** was charged with rendering its Advisory Report if the debtor's liabilities exceeded $3 million, but the court could ask for SEC assistance regardless of liability size.

The advisory reports usually took the form of a critical evaluation of the reorganization plan submitted by the trustee and an opinion on the **fairness and feasibility** of the plan. This involved a comprehensive valuation of the debtor's existing assets in comparison with the various claims against the assets. In the event of a discrepancy between the SEC evaluation and that of the trustee, the former usually suggested alternative guidelines. Ultimately, the decisions on (1) whether the firm was permitted to reorganize, and (2) the submission of the plan for final acceptance, rested with the federal judge.

The Chandler Act provided that the reorganization plan, after approval by the court, be submitted to each class of creditor and stockholder for final approval. Final ratification required approval of two-thirds of each class of stockholder. Of course if the plan, as accepted by the court, completely eliminated a particular class, such as the common stockholders, this excluded group had no vote in the final ratification, although it could always file suits on its own behalf. Common stockholders were eliminated when the firm was deemed **insolvent in a bankruptcy sense,** that is, when the liabilities exceeded a fair valuation of the assets. Regardless of whether the old stockholders were permitted to participate in the reorganized enterprise, the plan invariably entailed a restructuring of the old capital accounts as well as plans for improving the productivity of the debtor. This will no doubt be the case in the future, as well.

The entire bankruptcy reorganization process, including those relevant features and conditions of the Bankruptcy Code of 1978, is summarized in Exhibit 3.

LIQUIDATION. If, either through a court petition or a trustee decision, it is deemed that there is no hope for rehabilitation or if prospects are so poor as to make it unreasonable to invest further efforts, costs, and time, the only alternative remaining is liquidation. Economically, **liquidation** is justified when the value of the assets sold individually *exceeds* the capitalized value of the assets in the marketplace. Usually, the key variables are time and risk. For instance, it may be estimated that the absolute economic value of the firm will exceed the liquidation value, but the estimation of economic benefits is more difficult because subjective time and probability estimates result in a lower discounted value. In this case, final liquidation may take the form of an assignment or a formal bankruptcy liquidation.

An **assignment** is a private method whereby assets are assigned to a trustee who is usually selected by the creditors, to be liquidated. The **net liquidation value** realized is equal to the funds received less the creditor claims against the company. Rarely are the funds sufficient to pay off all creditors in full. All creditors must agree to the settlement. Since the assignment is generally handled in good faith, it is customary for the creditors to release the debtor from further liability. This process is usually faster and less costly than the more rigid bankruptcy procedure, but it is not feasible when the debtor has a complicated liability and capital structure.

The expanded Act (1938) continued to provide for the orderly liquidation of an insolvent debtor under court supervision. Regardless of who filed the petition, liquidations were handled by referees who oversaw the operation until a trustee was appointed. The latter liquidated assets, made a final accounting, and paid the liquidating dividends—all subject to referee approval. Payments of receipts usually entailed the so-called **absolute priority doctrine,** under which claims with priority must be paid in full before less prior, or subordinated claims, can receive any funds at all.

The **liquidation** fate is primarily observed in the small firm. The large bankrupt firm is more likely to attempt a reorganization and/or a merger with another entity. Sometimes, however, the basis for merger terms while a corporation is in bankruptcy is based on the **net liquidating value** of the company, not its **capitalized income value.** This was precisely the basis for negotiation in the ICC hearings on the **Penn Central-New York New Haven & Hartford Railroad merger in 1968.**

Although larger firms usually attempt to reorganize or merge in bankruptcy, the result is often not successful, and liquidation eventually occurs. An earlier study (Altman, **Corporation Bankruptcy in America,** Lexington

Books, 1971 Chapter 6) showed that a large percentage of firms are not successfully reorganized and as much as 56% of the cases resulted in a total loss to common stockholders. A glaring example of a recent failure to reorganize successfully was the $1 billion **W.T. Grant** case. The firm filed under Chapter XI in 1975 and attempted to reorganize, but was forced to liquidate several months later in 1976. This is in contrast to several more recent, large successful reorganizations, including the $1 billion Wickes Companies, Itel, AM International, and United Merchants & Manufacturing. The latter firm was reorganized and emerged as a going concern in less than one year.

The delays caused by court action to determine whether a firm should file under Chapter X or Chapter XI were often costly and took time to settle because of the ambiguity in the Chandler Act. One could argue that in both the W.T. Grant and United Merchants & Manufacturing cases, a large **public interest** was involved and parties other than unsecured creditors were affected. Still, persuasive pressures were brought to bear by the debtors and their legal counsels, and the courts ruled that these cases could be handled more efficiently, without adverse effects to other interested parties, under Chapter XI. **Under the New Bankruptcy Code,** the old Chapters X and XI are combined under a new reorganization title, **Chapter 11,** and this no longer is an issue.

THE BANKRUPTCY REFORM ACT OF 1978

RATIONALE FOR THE NEW ACT. Forty years after the passage of the Chandler Act, Congress enacted the **Bankruptcy Reform Act of 1978** (the Code), which revised the administrative and, to some extent, the procedural, legal, and economic aspects of corporate and personal bankruptcy filings in the United States. The complete text of the new Act can be found in **Bankruptcy Law Reports,** No. 389, October 26, 1978, Part II, published by the **Commerce Clearing House, Chicago, Illinois.**

The following reasons were presented *in 1970* in a joint Congressional resolution to create a commission to look into the nation's bankruptcy laws (S.J.R. 88, 91st Congress, 1st Session, July 24, 1970). An accompanying report from the Committee on the Judiciary, Report No. 91-230, strongly endorsed the proposal. Charles Seligson, a member of the Commission on the Bankruptcy Laws of the United States, enumerated some current problems in "Major Problems for Consideration By the Commission on the Bankruptcy Laws of the United States" (*American Bankruptcy Law Journal*, Winter 1977, pp. 73–112).

1. In the 30 years since the last major revision, there has probably been even greater change in the social and economic conditions of the country than in the 40 years prior to the enactment of the 1938 Act.

EXHIBIT 3 SUMMARY OF FINANCIAL REHABILITATION PROCEDURES

Function	Chapter X	Chapter XI	Section 77 (1933 Act)	Chapter 11 (New Code)
1. Initiation of proceedings	1. *a.* Voluntary by the debtor *b.* Involuntary-three or more creditors with claims totaling $5000 or more	1. *a.* Voluntary only *b.* Noncorporate and corporate *c.* Affects only unsecured creditors	1. *a.* Railroad only *b.* Voluntary *c.* Involuntary by creditors representing 5% or more of total indebtedness	1. *a.* Voluntary by debtor *b.* Involuntary-by three creditors with claims of at least $5000 (where more than 12 creditors exist): fewer than three creditors with $5000 or more in claims where less than 12 creditors exist
2. Custody of property	2. Court appoints disinterested trustee (mandatory if debts exceed $250,000) *a.* Cannot be officer or employee *b* Cotrustee from previous management to aid in operation	2. Court may or may not appoint receiver or trustee	2. Trustees appointed who act as operating managers	2. Court may or may not appoint a trustee: trustee may or may not act as operating manager
3. Creditor protection	3. Committees representing each class of creditors and stockholders are formed	3. Court conducts meetings; may use advisory creditors' committee	3. Committee for each class of creditor	3. Creditors committee comprised of seven largest creditors plus any others sanctioned by the court
4. Reorganization plan submission	4. *a.* Trustee creditors, or creditors' committee prepares plan; confers with committees *b.* Court hearings on plan *c.* SEC renders advisory report (mandators	4. Debtor proposes arrangement	4. Presented by one of the following: *a.* Trustee *b.* Debtor *c.* Holders of 10% or more of each security	4. Debtor proposes plan within 120 days; adequate approval required within 180 days of petition; if deadline not met, any interested party may submit a plan

	Chapter X	Chapter XI	Section 77	Chapter 11
5. Court review	5. Court approves plan if it is: a. Fair b. Feasible	5. Court holds hearings	5. a. Hearings before Interstate Commerce Commission b. ICC submits plan to court c. Court approval	5. Court holds hearings on the plan and will approve if fair and feasible.
6. Reorganization plan provision	6. Provides for: a. Provision for exchange of securities b. Provision for selection of new management c. Adequate means for execution of plan	6. Composition-claims of unsecured creditors scaled down, or extension in time of payment, or both	6. Same as Chapter X	6. Provides for any or all aspects of old Chapters X, XI, and XII
7. Approval	7. Two-thirds of each class of creditors by value; majority of stockholders (unless total liabilities exceed total assets)	7. Majority in number and amount of each class	7. Same as Chapter X	7. Two-thirds in amount and one-half in number of the allowed claims. Where an equity exists, two-thirds in amount of outstanding shares actually voted; "Cramdown" provision possible (i.e. court may approve plan despite dissatisfied creditors). In all cases, creditors must receive an amount that is greater than if the firm was liquidated
8. Execution plan	8. Court confirms plan	8. Receiver, trustee, or disbursing agent to carry out arrangement	8. Plan executed by ICC	8. Plan is confirmed by the court and executed by U.S. Trustee or by the court

2. Population has increased by 70 million people, while installment credit has skyrocketed from about $4 billion to $80 billion. The number of total bankruptcies has risen to an annual rate of more than 200,000 from a rate of 110,000 in 1960. By far, the major increase has been in personal bankruptcies.

3. More than one-quarter of the referees in bankruptcy have problems in the administration of their duties and have made suggestions for substantial improvement in the Act.

4. There is little understanding by the federal government and the commercial community in evaluating the need to update the technical aspects in the Act.

In 1979 the problems under the old Act were even more acute. The long-term worldwide problems of **inflation and recession** had further increased the number of bankruptcy filings in the U.S. court system. Transitions in credit policies—for example, greater reticence to delay default proceedings in large corporations and other not so definable changes—have contributed to making the old bankruptcy laws awkward and the 1978 Code desirable. Whether the structure of the new Code will alleviate pressures and make the system more efficient will be determined empirically as the new Code gains experience. One thing is certain, the new Code was tested immediately as the number of filings increased in the face of the 1980–1982 recession and credit restraints due to inflation.

The new Act, which went into effect on October 1, 1979, is divided into four titles, with Title I containing much of the procedural law of bankruptcy. This part, known as "the Code," is divided into eight chapters: 1, 3, 5, 7, 9, 11, 13, 15. The number and their function are: Chapter 1 (General Provisions), Chapter 3 (Case Administration), and Chapter 5 (Creditors, the Debtor, and the Estate), apply generally to all cases, and Chapter 7 (Liquidation), Chapter 9 (Adjustment of Municipality Debt), Chapter 11 (Reorganization), Chapter 13 (Adjustment of Debts of Individuals with Regular Income), and Chapter 15 (U.S. Trustee Program). For an informative review of the new code, see Duberstein, "A Broad View of the New Bankruptcy Code" (*Brooklyn Barrister,* April 1979). The major provisions of the new Act are discussed in the subsections that follow.

BANKRUPTCY FILINGS. The debtor must reside or have a domicile or place of business or property in the United States. Liquidation cases of banks and insurance companies engaged in business in this country are excluded. A foreign bank or foreign insurance company that is not engaged in business in the United States but does have assets here may become a debtor under the Code, but an involuntary petition cannot be filed against a foreign bank even if it has property here. The debtor may file a petition for liquidation or reorganization. The filing of the petition constitutes what is known as "an order for relief." An involuntary case may be commenced only under Chapter 7, dealing with liquidation, or Chapter 11, dealing with reorganization. This route is not permitted for municipalities under Chapter 9, nor in Chapter 13 cases. An involuntary petition is prohibited against farmers, ranchers, and charitable institutions.

CLAIMS AND PROTECTIONS. The provision for an involuntary Chapter 11 case is a change from the old law: involuntary cases were permitted under Chapter X, dealing with corporate reorganization, and Chapter XII, dealing with real property arrangements, but not under a Chapter XI arrangement. **Acts of bankruptcy** are no longer the criteria for the commencement of an involuntary case. Instead, it is necessary to show that (1) the debtor is generally not paying its debts as such debts become due, or (2) within 120 days before the filing of the petition, a custodian (e.g., an assignee for the benefit of creditors) was appointed and took possession of the debtor's assets. If the debtor has more than 12 creditors, three creditors must join in the **involuntary petition** whose claims must aggregate at least $5000. If there are fewer than 12 creditors, two creditors or a single creditor holding claims of at least $5000 may file. An **indenture trustee** representing the holder of a claim against the debtor may be a petitioning creditor.

Section 10 (4) of the Code defines "**claim.**" The effect of the definition is a significant departure from the old Act, which never defined "claim" in straight bankruptcy. The term was simply used, along with the concept of provability, to limit the kinds of obligations that were payable in a bankruptcy case. The new definition adopts a broader meaning: a claim is any right to payment, whether or not reduced to judgment, liquidation, unliquidated, fixed, contingent, matured, unmatured, disputed, undisputed, legal, equitable, secured, or unsecured. The definition also includes as a claim an equitable right to performance that does not give rise to payment. The use of the term throughout the Act seems to imply that all legal obligations of the debtor, no matter how remote or contingent, will be dealt with in a bankruptcy case.

One of the most important parts of the Code deals with stays of secured and unsecured creditor action and the right of the debtor to continue to use the creditor's collateral in his or her business. The **automatic stay** is one of the fundamental debtor protections provided by the bankruptcy laws. It gives the debtor a breathing spell from creditors. It stops all collection efforts, all harassment, and all foreclosure actions. It permits the debtor to attempt a repayment or reorganization plan, or simply to be relieved of the financial pressures that drove the firm into bankruptcy.

Section 361 (64) removes some of the uncertainty concerning the **rights of secured creditors.** The basic requirement that secured creditors be afforded "adequate protection" is not formally defined, but some guidelines are offered in Section 361, which suggests that such protection might include cash payments, additional collateral, or replacement collateral, but would not include the simple giving of any **priority.**

EXECUTORY CONTRACTS. Most debtors enter bankruptcy as parties to various contracts, one of which is executory. **Executory contracts** are those contracts under which the obligations of both the debtor and the other party are unperformed at the time of filing the petition and the failure of either to complete the obligation would constitute breach of the contract. Common types include leases, employment and collective bargaining contracts, licenses, franchises, and purchase options. In general, the Code gives the debtor the right to reject or assume such contracts in its entirety, subject to the court's approval.

The Code generally provides no standards for deciding which contracts to assume and which to reject. The courts usually base their decisions on whether the rejection or assumption will benefit the estate. However, the Code prohibits the assumption of contracts which require the personal performance of the other party to the contract or in which the other party has contracted to extend credit or other financial assistance to the debtor.

Timing of rejection or assumption of contracts depends on the type of bankruptcy. In a **Chapter 7 liquidation,** any executory contract is deemed rejected unless the debtor assumes it within 60 days of filing. In **Chapter 11 reorganizations,** leases of nonresidential real property must be assumed within 60 days of filing or they are deemed rejected. However, other types of contracts may be assumed or rejected at any time before confirmation of the plan of reorganization. Furthermore, the plan of reorganization may reject a contract that the debtor had previously assumed. In either a liquidation or a reorganization, if the firm rejects a contract, the rejection is deemed to have occurred the day before the debtor filed for bankruptcy. Such timing gives the other party to the contract a prepetition, secured claim against the debtor.

In order to assume a contract, the debtor must: (1) promptly cure all defaults, (2) compensate the other party for any actual pecuniary losses suffered by the debtor's previous breach of the contract, and (3) provide adequate assurance of future performance under the contract. Once the firm has assumed a contract, it may with court approval, assign the contract to a third party, regardless of any clauses prohibiting such an action.

VOIDABLE PREFERENCES AND FRAUDULENT TRANSFERS. The debtor can enlarge its estate by regaining control of property delivered to creditors before the bankruptcy petition was filed. This is done through a legal process called avoidance, which declares the previous transfer to be void. Only certain types of transfers may be avoided by the court. The most common are the preference and **fraudulent transfers.**

The Code outlines seven criteria that a transfer must meet in order for the court to avoid it as a **voidable preference**. It defines a preference as a transfer of the debtor's property made to or for the benefit of a creditor for or on the account of a debt in existence before the bankruptcy petition was filed. To be a preference, it must be made while the debtor was insolvent during the 90 days before the petition was filed. The effect of the preference is to allow the creditor to receive more of its total claim than it would receive if the debtor's property were distributed to creditors under a Chapter 7 liquidation.

With respect to the insolvency requirement, it is not necessary to determine if the debtor's liabilities actually exceed assets because the Code deems the firm to be insolvent during the 90 days before it files for bankruptcy. With regard to the timing requirement, the 90-day period before filing during which the transfer must have occurred is extended to one year before filing if the transferee is an insider. The debtor or other creditors may claim that a creditor should be considered an insider because it has been involved in the operation of the debtor's business during the period before the filing of the petition. A creditor will receive a certain amount on its claims if the debtor is liquidated. If the transfer in question is larger than that liquidation amount, the transfer is probably a preference. If it is smaller, then there is room for argument as to the preferential nature of the transfer.

The Code limits the effect of its broad definition of preference by declaring that certain types of transfers which meet all criteria are not preferences. Since these transfers are not preferences, they are not avoidable. Such nonavoidable transfers include:

1. Transfers that are made according to the usual terms of the industry and paid in the ordinary course of business.
2. Loans made by a creditor to enable the debtor to purchase assets that will secure the loan. These are often called **enabling loans.**
3. **Contemporaneous exchanges** in which the creditor extends new value to the debtor. Payments by check, which are usually considered credit transfers, are considered to be contemporaneous for this exception to the defintion of preference.
4. **Extensions of new value,** made within the 90 days before filing, when such extensions are part of a mutual exchange between the creditor and debtor in which the creditor extends new value while the debtor makes repayments on old debt.
5. **Security interests** that are made in the 90 days before filing that are fully perfected before the petition was filed.
6. **Reclamation of goods**, if the supplier was unaware of the bankruptcy and the reclamation is made within 10 days of delivery of the goods.
7. **Margin of settlement payments** made by a stock or commodity broker before the petition was filed. This is especially relevant in today's broker failures environment.

Fraudulent Conveyances. These are another type of avoidable transfer. There are two kinds. One occurs when the debtor makes a transfer, within a year before filing, with actual intent to hinder, delay, or defraud a past or future creditor. The other arises when the debtor receives less than a reasonably equivalent value for the property transferred within a year before filing and is, therefore, left with insufficient capital to carry on its ordinary course of business.

Other types of avoidable transfers include transfers made during the period between the filing of an involuntary petition and the entering of an order for relief. Both of these types of transfers can only be avoided to the extent that the transfer is greater than any extension of new value by the creditor.

LESSOR CLAIMS. Under the old Bankruptcy Act, a lessor was entitled to a claim on unpaid rents of a maximum of one year of lease or rental payments in a **straight bankruptcy liquidation** and a maximum of three years in a **reorganization.** Under the new Code's Section 502(b)(7), a formula replaces the one-to-three year rule for both liquidations and reorganizations. In essence the claim for damages resulting from the termination of a lease of real property is now **the greater** of one year of payments, or 15%, not to exceed three years of the remaining term of the lease, plus any unpaid rent due under such lease. Such terms start the earlier of (1) the petition date or (2) the date on which the lessor repossessed the leased property, or the lessee surrendered it.

Section 365 of the Code deals with **executory contracts** and **unexpired leases** and specifies under what provisions a trustee, or the court, can assume continuance of a lease while in reorganization. Essentially, the Code specifies that lessors must be cured or compensated for their claims or that **adequate assurance** of prompt compensation be given. The trustee must assume a lease or executory contract within 60 days of the petition date.

PRIORITIES. The concept of provability of claims, apparently troublesome under the previous Act, has been discarded in favor of simple sections (501–503), dealing with the allowance of claims. Among other things, these sections require that contingent or unliquidated claims be estimated. Many of the familiar priorities for claims remain, but significant changes have been made to protect employees. The new Act expands and increases the **wage priority.** The amount entitled to priority is raised from $600 to $2000. The priority is expanded to cover fringe benefits (Section 507). A new priority has been established for consumer creditors who have deposited money in connection with the purchase, lease, or rental of property, or the purchase of services, for their personal, family, or household use, when such properties or services are not delivered or provided.

BANK SETOFFS. Banks may specify that in the event of bankruptcy all existing balances of the debtor will be setoff against the outstanding claim of the bank and the balance of the loan will be included among general creditor claims. One can argue that this is unfair to the debtor, since once a loan is made the proceeds can be used in any manner that the borrower chooses.

Conversely, the banks can argue, that the balances are a type of "security" against repayment of the loan. In any event, the new Act provides for the continuation of the setoffs, but the court must ratify them in a manner that is more formal than in the past.

As in the old law, the **right of setoff** is unaffected except when the creditor's claim is disallowed by the court or the creditor has acquired the claim, other than from the debtor, during a 90-day period preceding the case at a time when the debtor was insolvent. An exception to the right of setoff is the **automatic stay** provided for in Section 362 of the Code. The automatic stay refers to an injunction against the creditor and prohibits any action to further set off the loan after the petition is filed.

The Code does contain an additional limitation on the rights of creditors who have offset a mutual debt on or within 90 days before the filing of a petition when the creditor receives a **preferential payment.** For example, assume that a debtor owes a bank $150,000 and had $50,000 on deposit 90 days prior to the filing, when the debtor owed $75,000. The bank will recover all but $75,000 of the amount owed to it by the debtor. If the bank had setoff the amount 90 days before bankruptcy, on the other hand, it would have received $50,000. Thus by waiting 60 days before exercising its right of setoff, the bank recovered an additional $25,000 and therefore improved its position by that amount. This $25,000 is the amount that the trustee may recover for the debtor under Section 553(b).

The setoff section operates only in the case of **prefiling setoffs,** thus encouraging creditors to work with the debtor rather than attempting to recover as much as appears possible at the time. In any case, **a default** must exist before there is a setoff right. It appears that the **right of setoff** is somewhat constrained under the new Code compared to the old law. Still, we can expect that financial institutions and others will continue the practice and it will be up to the trustee to recover the funds.

CHAPTER 11 REORGANIZATIONS. An extremely important change in the new Act appears in Chapter 11, which is a consolidated chapter for business rehabilitations. It adopts much of the old **Chapter XI arrangement** and incorporates a good portion of the public protection of the old **Chapter X** and also a major part of **Chapter XII real property arrangements.**

Under Chapter 11, the debtor continues to operate the business unless the court orders a **disinterested trustee** for cause shown, or if it would be in the best interest of the creditors and/or the owners. "Cause" includes fraud, dishonesty, incompetence, or gross mismanagement, either before or after commencement of the case.

Creditors' and Other Committees. After the petition for a Chapter 11 rehabilitation has been filed, the court, or a U.S. trustee, where available, appoints a committee of unsecured creditors. Chapter 11 is permitted to affect secured debts and equity security holders and, on request of a party in interest, the court may order the appointment of additional committees of creditors or of equity security holders. Ordinarily, committees consist of the holders of the seven largest claims or interests to be represented, if they are willing to serve. The Code permits continuation of a committee selected before the case is filed if the committee is fairly chosen and is representative of the different kinds of claims to be represented. A designated committee of equity security holders ordinarily consists of the persons willing to serve who hold the seven largest amounts of shares of the debtor. On the request of a party in interest, the court is authorized to change the size of membership of the creditors of the equity security holders' committee if the membership is not representative of the different claims or interests.

The committee of unsecured creditors must meet at least once within 20- to 40-day period after the debtor has filed for bankruptcy. The debtor is required to appear at this meeting to answer questions about its operations and financial condition.

The Code gives several powers and duties to committees. The first is to consult with the debtor about the administration of the case. This task includes overseeing the periodic filing of operating statements, the payment of taxes, and various procedural matters, such as opening bank accounts. The second is to conduct the primary investigation into the debtor's financial condition and business operations before and after the filing and the plausibility of continuing the business through reorganization. The third responsibility is to participate in the formulation of a plan of reorganization and make recommendations about the plan or plans to the creditors. A committee may support a plan proposed by the debtor or develop one itself.

Reorganization Plan Filing. The essence of the reorganization process is the **plan of reorganization** for financial and operating rehabilitation. The new Code gives the debtor, or its trustee if appointed, the exclusive right for 120 days to file a plan. The debtor has up to 180 days after the reorganization petition is filed to receive the requisite consents from the various creditors and owners (if relevant). The court, however, is given the power to increase or reduce the 120- and 180-day periods. If the debtor fails to meet either of these deadlines or others established by the court, creditors, and other interested parties may file a plan for approval.

Role of the SEC. The SEC may raise and be heard on any issue but may not appeal from any judgment order or decree. Greater expediency for completing reorganization and alleged uneven performance of the SEC in past cases are reasons that have been given for the exclusion of the SEC. Although any interested party can still petition the courts and appeal any perceived inequities, the role of the SEC as the public's representative has been greatly diminished. For example, the SEC had often petitioned to change a Chapter XI arrangement to a Chapter X reorganization. There is no need for such a petition under the new Code. Despite the SEC's performance in Chapter X cases, it has issued some rather excellent commentary and suggestions in its reorganization reports, particularly in the valuation process.

Reorganization Valuation. The reorganization plan has as its centerpiece the valuation of the debtor as a continuing entity. Traditionally, valuation is based on the capitalization of future earnings flows, which involves a forecast of expected after tax earnings and the attachment of an appropriate **capitalization rate** (discount rate). The capitalized value can then be adjusted for excess working capital, tax, and other considerations. If the resulting value is greater than the liquidation value of the assets, reorganization is justified. If the value is less than the allowed claims, the firm is **insolvent in a bankruptcy sense** and the old shareholders are usually eliminated. Typically, the creditors become the new shareholders along with any shareholders that might purchase new shares.

Absolute Priority of Claims. Since the inception of the bankruptcy laws, most reorganization plans have been guided by the so-called **absolute priority doctrine.** This doctrine stipulates that creditors should be compensated for their claims in a certain hierarchical order and that the more senior claims must be paid in full before a less senior claim can receive anything. In fact, however, plans are often based on a combination of absolute and relative priorities whereby lesser claimants receive partial payment even though a claim that is more senior is "not made whole" (i.e., not paid off completely). This arrangement is often expedient, and it permits compromise with creditors who are likely to vote against the plan unless some satisfactory payment to them is forthcoming.

Creditors are frequently compensated for their claims with a combination of cash and securities different from the original securities. It is common for the old debtholders to become the new stockholders. For example, the old debtholders of the **Penn Central Transportation Co.** received a combination of new series debt securities, new preferred stock, and shares of the common stock, while the old stockholders received but a fraction of their old shares (one for each 25 shares owned).

The objective of the reorganization plan is to provide for a **fair and feasible rehabilitation.** The term "fair" refers to the priority of claims; the term "feasible" implies that the recapitalized company will be structured so that the new fixed cost burden will realistically be met without a recurrence of default. The reorganization plan must therefore provide the cash flow analysis necessary to make that assessment. The costs involved with negotiations for restructuring—both in bankruptcy or what takes place out of reorganization—are referred to as **agency costs** and represent a **deadweight loss** to the firm (i.e., a loss that is not someone else's gain in society).

Priorities are spelled out in Section 507 of the Code. Expenses and claims have priority in the following order:

1. Administration expenses of the bankruptcy, such as legal and accounting fees and trustee fees.
2. **Unsecured claims** arising in the ordinary course of the debtor's business or financial affairs after the commencement of the case, for example, supplier claims on goods delivered and accepted, with some exceptions as spelled out in Section 502(f).
3. Unsecured claims for wages, salaries, or commissions, including vacation, severance, and sick leave pay (a) earned by an individual within 90 days before the filing of the petition or the date of the cessation of the debtor's business but only (b) to the extent of $2000 per individual.
4. Unsecured claims for contributions to employee benefit plans, with the same limitations noted in item 3.
5. Unsecured claims to individuals up to $900 arising from the deposit, before bankruptcy, of money in connection with the future use of goods or services from the debtor.
6. Unsecured claims of governmental units, that is, taxes on income, property, and employment, and excise and tax penalties.

Secured debts, that is, debt that has specific assets as collateral, has priority over the funds received in the liquidation of that asset. To the extent that the funds received are insufficient to cover the entire allowed claim, the balance is owed by the debtor and is considered part of the remaining unsecured claims. **Senior debt** has priority over all debt that is specified as **subordinated** to that debt but has equal priority with all other unsecured debt. The terms of most loan agreements spell out these priorities.

After the unsecured claims are satisfied, the remaining "claimants" are the equity holders of the firm-preferred and common stockholders, in that order. As noted earlier, these individuals should not receive any payment or securities in the new firm if the value of the firm's assets is less than the allowed claims.

Cramdown and Post-Petition Interest. Even if a particular class of impaired creditors or stockholders does not accept a reorganization plan proposed to the court, the plan may nevertheless be confirmed by the court if (1) the plan's proponent requests confirmation and (2) the court finds that the plan is "fair and equitable" to the dissenting class (11 U.S.C. and 1129(b) Supp. IV 1980). This is the procedure known as **cramdown.** Recall that the concept of fair and equitable was discussed in the context of old Chapter X. Under the new Chapter 11, the court will rule on the fairness and equity issue only in the event of a dissenting class of impaired security holders. Hence, the public watchdog role of the SEC under the old Act, which revolved around its mandatory advisory capacity on fairness as well as feasibility questions, is now considered irrelevant especially since the Code specifies guidelines for determining the plan's fairness (Section 1129(b)(2)). These guidelines are that (1) the plan must provide holders of unsecured claims with property equal in value to the "allowed" amount of their claims or (2) no class junior to the dissenting class is to receive any distribution until the allowed claim is totally compensated. Hence, if these guidelines are met, a plan may be confirmed by the court over the objection of a creditor or equity class and in essence have the plan crammed down.

A key element in this controversial result is the term "allowed claim." The courts interpreted the new 1978 Code to permit them to rule on allowed claims even, it appears, if the ruling was contrary to the historical principle of **absolute priority.** An excellent example of this new interpretation is given in the commentary by Fortgang and King (*New York Law Review,* Nov.-Dec. 1981, pp. 1148–1165) which also considers the case of post-petition interest.

Post-petition interest involves the contractual interest payment claim resulting from a moratorium on such payments during reorganization or waiting for the liquidation. Post-petition interest can be substantial, especially in long, drawn-out cases involving large debtors and sizable liabilities. Under early case law and court interpretations of the original Bankruptcy Act of 1898, interest payments on claims ceased to accrue as of the bankruptcy petition date primarily as a matter of convenience. Under the new Code of 1978, the case law interpretation is codified and post-petition interest, or unmatured interest, is not allowable (Section 502(b)(2)). Also disallowed is **prepaid interest** to the debtor that represents "an original discounting of the claim." Since such claims are not allowed, even if the relevant creditor class dissents, that group may be forced to accept the plan pursuant to the **cram-down** provision.

The only exceptions to this interpretation are where (1) a **secured claim** involves **collateral** whose **liquidation value** at the time of plan confirmation is equal to or in excess of the claim, including the post-petition interest (Section 506(b)). In this case, the secured creditor will be entitled to post-petition interest. If the secured asset is critical to the continued operation of the firm, the claimholder will not receive the proceeds from the collateral (since it is not sold) but will receive assurance of **adequate protection** of the principal plus accrued interest (2) the debtor is found to be solvent with sufficient assets to pay all claims including accrued interest. This latter point emanates from Chapter 7 (liquidation). Since all creditors in a Chapter 11 reorganization must receive at least as much as they would be entitled to in a liquidation, it follows that post-petition interest can be paid where the liquidation value exceeds all claims. We are not, however, referring to the **going concern solvency** test applicable under the old Act.

The new Code is certainly less flexible on post-petition interest than the old Act. Under the latter, the courts could provide for such payments if the debtor was shown to be solvent (liberally defined) and it was not inconvenient to recompute interest claims at the time of settling the estate. This was in keeping with the historical doctrine of **absolute priority.** The new Code simply disallows such payments even if going concern solvency is clearly demonstrated.

Fortgang and King argue that Congress did not intend to do away with absolute priority although that is what precisely happens if junior creditors or equity holders retain an interest in the solvent debtor at the same time that post-petition interest is disallowed to a senior creditor. They claim that the construction of this part of the new Code was not considered carefully. They also argue that the Code's discussion of **unimpaired creditors** discriminates against those who do not receive post-petition interest. For example, if a class of bonds is offered compensation which continues the outstanding bonds at the same interest rate and other terms, their rights are considered unaltered. Similarly, if the reorganization plan provides for cash payment equal to 100% of the claim as of the petition date, then it too is "unimpaired" and can have a plan "crammed-down" over its objection. In essence, Fortgang and King argue that the new Code's consequences of cramdown and post-petition interest is unwise and could lead to abuse.

Recent events demonstrate that certain abuses of the Code can indeed occur especially when it is clear at the time of petition that the debtor was not insolvent. Under the new Code, it is not compulsory to argue that the debtor is insolvent or cannot pay its bills as they come due. The celebrated **Manville Corporation** case demonstrates an arguably solvent situation whereby neither post-petition interest nor any principal was paid for over two-and-a-half years (August 1982 to early 1985) leading to arguments that creditors as well as other claimants in this case have been discriminated against. It is not clear whether post-petition interest, and certainly interest on interest, will ever be paid in this case. While it is very uncommon, it is possible for a modern Chapter 11 to include both of these post-petition claims in the reorganization plan. **Wilson Foods Corp.** (filed April 22, 1983 and settled April 30, 1984) provided for such payments to general creditors and since no class of interested parties objected, the plan was accepted. Certainly, in noncontested plans, any amount of payment is possible.

Execution of the Plan. A plan must provide adequate means for its execution. It may provide for the satisfaction or modification of any lien, the waiver of any default, and the merger or consolidation of the debtor with one or more entities. The issuance of nonvoting equity securities is prohibited, and the plan must provide for distribution of voting powers among the various classes of equity securities. The plan may impair, or leave unimpaired, a class of secured or unsecured claims, provide for the assumption or rejection of **executory contracts** or unexpired leases not previously rejected, and propose the sale of all or substantially all of the estate property and the distribution of the proceeds among creditors and equity security holders, making it a **liquidating plan.**

Confirmation of the Plan. A plan may place a claim in a particular class if such claim is substantially similar to other claims of the class. Confirmation of a plan requires that every claimant or holder of an interest accept the plan or if it is not accepted by all classes, the creditors must receive or retain under the plan an amount that is not less than the amount that they would receive or retain if the debtor were liquidated on the date of the plan. At least one class of creditors must accept the plan. Thus, for example, if the only class affected by the plan is comprised of a mortgagee, the plan cannot be confirmed without the mortgagee's consent. A plan is deemed accepted by a class of creditors if at least two-thirds in amount and more than one-half in number of the allowed claims of the class that are voted are cast in favor of the plan. Shareholders are deemed to have accepted the plan if at least two-thirds in amount of the outstanding shares actually voted are cast for the plan. These terms are reviewed in Exhibit 3.

The Code deals with the **impairment of claims,** which is a new concept. An impaired claim is one where compensation is less than the total allowed claim. A plan may be confirmed over the dissent of a class of creditors. If all the requirements for confirmation of the plan are satisfied, except that a class of impaired claimants or shareholders has not accepted it, the court may nevertheless confirm the plan if the plan does not discriminate unfairly and is "fair and equitable" with respect to each class of claims or interests impaired.

This is the new Code's version of the **cramdown** clause, which appeared in Chapters X and XII. The test for what is "fair and equitable" with regard to a class of secured claimants impaired under a plan is met, in general, if the plan provides:

1. That said class will retain its lien on the property whether the property is retained by the debtor or transferred.
2. That the property will be sold and the lien transferred and the secured creditor will receive deferred cash payments of at least the allowed amount of the claims of the value on the date of confirmation
3. That the secured class will realize the "indubitable equivalent" of its claims under the plan. If a class of unsecured claims that are impaired under the plan will receive property or payment equal to the allowed amount of the claims or if the holders of the claims junior to such class will receive nothing under the plan, the plan has met the fair and equitable test of the Code.

Reorganization Time in Bankruptcy. One of the important goals of the new Act is to reduce the time it takes for a firm to go through the reorganization process and devise a plan for restructuring its capital financing and rehabilitating its operation. The new Code in and of itself will certainly not provide any novel **solutions to the typical problems** that cause firms to fail. But the requirement that the debtor submit a reorganization plan within 120 days was intended to speed up the initial process.

The attempt to reduce reorganization time is important since there is a positive correlation between the time spent in reorganization and the direct costs of bankruptcy. The latter include legal and accounting fees, trustee and filing fees, and any other tangible costs involved with the bankruptcy process. In a study of almost 90 reorganizations, we found that the average industrial reorganization took 27 months, with the median period being 20 months (Altman, *Corporate Financial Distress,* Wiley, 1983 Chapter 9). That same source concentrated on more complex **railroad bankruptcies** and concluded that the average and median **Section 77 reorganization** took slightly more than seven years. Another study (Warner, "Bankruptcy Costs: Some Empirical Evidence," *Journal of Finance,* May 1977), found that railroad reorganizations took even longer.

One of the objectives of the new 1978 Code was to accelerate the reorganization process by mandating time constraints on such items as plan filing deadlines. Since these deadlines can always be extended on appeal by the debtor-in-possession, it was not clear if the new Code would achieve its timing goal. In a special analysis for this *Handbook,* we looked at the recent experience of a sample of large firm bankruptcies that have taken place since 1978. The results are reported in Exhibit 4. We found that the average time spent from the petition date to the plan's confirmation was 22.8 months for those plans completed and about 26 months for those completed and pending, combined. The latter time span, over two years, is probably more indicative of the expected value. If anything, it underestimates the time since nine of the 26 sample cases were still not confirmed as of February 1985.

The more recent experience of over two years (at least) in reorganization is very similar to the pre-Code experience and it does not appear that the new Code has accelerated the process very much. Of course, these results are for a small sample of recent bankruptcies and we cannot, as yet, generalize for all reorganizations.

Changes in the Judiciary and Procedure. The Code creates a U.S. bankruptcy court in each of the present districts where there is a U.S. district court. **The bankruptcy judges** are appointed by the President, with the advice and consent of the Senate, for a term of 14 years. The established bankruptcy courts were to continue from October 1, 1979, to March 31, 1984. The **1984 Amendments to the Code** are discussed below.

The Code eliminates the present jurisdictional dichotomy between summary and plenary jurisdiction; the bankruptcy court is given exclusive jurisdiction of the property of the debtor wherever it is located. All cases under the Code and all civil actions and proceedings arising from its enforcement will be held before the bankruptcy judge unless the judge decides to abstain from hearing a particular proceeding that is already pending in the state court or in another court that he believes to be more appropriate.

Appeals from the bankruptcy judge will go to the **district judge** except if the circuit counsel of the circuit court so orders the chief judge of the circuit

EXHIBIT 4 LARGE[a] COMPANY BANKRUPTCY REORGANIZATION STATUS UNDER CHAPTER 11

Company	Filing Date	Reorganization Confirmation Date[b]	Months in Bankruptcy	Reorganization Results[d]
AM International	April 14, 1982	October 30, 1984	31	PC
Braniff Airlines	May 13, 1982	December 15, 1983	20	PC
Itel Corp.	Jan. 19, 1981	Sept. 19, 1983	33	PC
White Motor	Sept. 4, 1980	Sept. 1, 1981	12 (38)[c]	Sold off and liquidated
Wickes Co.	April 24, 1982	Jan. 26, 1985	33	PC
Wilson Foods	April 22, 1983	April 30, 1984	12	PC
Lionel Corp.	Feb. 19, 1982	—	35[d]	PS Major Asset Sold
Revere Copper & Brass	Oct. 28, 1982	Dec. 30, 1984	31	NPS
HRT Industries	Nov. 23, 1982	Feb. 10, 1984	15	PC
KDT Industries	Aug. 5, 1982	March 28, 1984	20	PC-Merged into Ames Dept. Store
Baldwin United	Sept. 25, 1983	—	16[d]	NPS
Manville Corp.	Aug. 262, 1982	—	29[d]	PS
Continental Airlines	Sept. 24, 1983	—	16[d]	PS
Seatrain Lines	Feb. 11, 1981	—	48[d]	PS
Nucorp Energy	July 27, 1982	—	30[d]	NPS
Saxon Industries	April 13, 1982	—	33[d]	PS
Sambo's Restaurants	Nov. 27, 1981	—	38[d]	NPS, Trustee is liquidating
Amarex Corp.	Dec. 2, 1982	—	26[d]	PS
McLouth Steel	Dec. 8, 1981	Dec. 11, 1984	36	PC, Assets Sold
Terex Corp.	Nov. 7, 1983	—	15[d]	NPS
Marion Corp.	March 1983	—	23[d]	NPS
UNR Industries	July 1982	—	31[d]	NPS
Dreco Energy	June 27, 1982	—	31[d]	NPS
Phoenix Steel Corp.	Aug. 12, 1983	—	18	NPS—Outline Circulate
Osborne Computer	Sept. 19, 1983	January 18, 1985	16	PC
Penn Dixie Industries	April 7, 1980	March 12, 1982	23	PC, now (Penn Dixie, Continental Steel
Average Reorganization Period—Confirmed Plans			22.8	
Average Reorganization Period—All filings			26.0	

[a]Companies with liabilities greater than $120 million; PC = Plan Confirmed.
PS = Plan Submitted but not confirmed as of February, 1985.
NPS = No Plan Submitted. Filing dates from October 1979-December 1983.

[b]Liquidation decision date, if applicable.

[c]Liquidation proceeded until December 1, 1983 when creditors were paid off from proceeds.

[d]As of February 1, 1985.

to designate panels of three bankruptcy judges to hear appeals in the bank-ruptcy court. The panel may not hear an appeal from an order entered by a panel member. An appeal can go directly from the bankruptcy court to the court of appeals if the parties so agree.

U.S. Trustee Program. To aid bankruptcy judges in avoiding involvement in many administrative functions and to allow them to devote more time to the area of judicial determination, the Code established a five-year trial pilot program of U.S. trustees. The program was operative in only 10 geographic areas of the country covering 18 present judicial districts. It included the Southern District of New York (but not the Eastern District), the District of New Jersey, the Central District of California (which includes Los An-geles), and the Northern District of Illinois (which includes Chicago). The program, which initially ran to April 1, 1984, was extended to September 30, 1986, at which time Congress will decide whether to fully implement the U.S. trustee system. The U.S. trustees will not be serving the bankruptcy courts either as assistants to the bankruptcy judges or as arms of the court, but will be under the supervision of the attorney general who will appoint them.

1984 AMENDMENTS TO THE BANKRUPTCY CODE

On June 29, 1984, the U.S. Congress approved the adoption of Bankruptcy Amendments to the 1978 Code. The **Bankruptcy Amendments and Federal Judgeship Act** of 1984 (Pub. L. 98–353, 98 Stat. 333 (July 10, 1984)) provided for a number of substantive and procedural changes to the 1978 legislation. The areas of major change and concern involve **collective bargaining agree-ments, consumer debts, grain elevator liquidations,** and the status and juris-diction of **bankruptcy judges.** Indeed, at issue was the bankruptcy court's jurisdiction over not only the bankrupt's estate but also over all proceedings (e.g., lawsuits) and procedures arising from a bankruptcy case.

The Bankruptcy Court's rather extensive jurisdiction was challenged in the *Northern Pipeline Construction Co. v. Marathon Pipe Line Co.* case (458 U.S. 50 (1982)) whereby the Supreme Court held that the jurisdiction over nonbankrupt issues was unconstitutional. This created a virtual void in bankruptcy proceedings since the Court did not have the right to act on many important issues. The *Marathon* decision also questioned the very status of **bankruptcy judges.** The latter needed, but did not have, so-called **Article III powers** (i.e., life tenure and no salary reductions) necessary for independence and protection in order to rule on a wide range of issues.

The *Marathon* decision required the Congress to define exactly what are the powers and jurisdiction of bankruptcy judges. This limbo state, whereby all pervasive powers were in theory relegated to the **federal district court judges,** lasted until the 1984 Amendment Act. As the bankruptcy judge status was being debated, a number of important and topical "riders" were included in this controversial piece of legislation. A summary and critique of these revisions can be found in various bankruptcy related newsletters and articles (e.g., *American Bankruptcy Institute* Newsletter (Spring 1984), and legal memoranda, for example, Murphy, Weir & Butter (New York, August 3, 1984)).

BANKRUPTCY JUDGE STATUS AND COURT STRUCTURE. The 1984 Amendments did not give Article III powers to bankruptcy judges and specified that those "noncore" proceedings which the *Marathon* decision challenged cannot be ruled on in the Bankruptcy court. Bankruptcy judges will conduct hearings and submit proposed findings to the district court judge who shall enter a final order of judgment after a de-novo review of objected-to matters. The district court can withdraw all or any part of a bankruptcy proceeding from the bankruptcy court. Certainly the de-novo review process will both lengthen and make more expensive any litigation and contentious issues that oftentimes arise.

The 1984 Amendment does, however, remove the uncertainty about the judges' status. This was a fiercely contested and heavily lobbied issue for two years. In essence, the emergency rules system incorporated after the *Marathon* decision have now been formally codified.

EXECUTORY CONTRACTS AND COLLECTIVE BARGAINING AGREE-MENTS. Executory contracts have been a significant issue in recent bankruptcies as pertains to collective bargaining issues. These include the Chapter 11 filings of Wilson Foods, Continental Airlines, Braniff Airlines, and the threatened filing by Eastern Airlines. In these bankruptcies one of the major uses of the filing was the unilateral abrogation of union contracts by the debtor.

Court decisions have been unanimous in holding that collective bargaining contracts are executory contracts subject to rejection under section 365(a) of the Code. The controversial aspect of abrogation in bankruptcy is the ability of management to unilaterally reject **collective bargaining agreements** immediately after the bankruptcy petition but prior to the court's sanction of this rejection.

The precedent for unilateral abrogation by management was set in the controversial case of *National Labor Relations Board (NLRB) v. Bildisco and Bildisco* 1983. The case was argued in federal bankruptcy court, U.S. Court of Appeals, and ultimately the U.S. Supreme Court in 1984. Bildisco, a small partnership selling building supplies, unilaterally rejected the terms of a collective bargaining agreement it had entered into several months prior to its seeking reorganization under Chapter 11. Prior to obtaining court permission it stopped remitting union dues and employee benefits. It then refused to make wage increases as provided in the contract.

It was ultimately ruled by the Supreme Court in February 1984 that the firm could abrogate its labor contract in Chapter 11 under the provisions for executory contracts. It was further ruled that the employer could do this unilaterally prior to obtaining a formal ruling from a bankruptcy judge. Underlying both rulings was the Supreme Court's desire to give the debtor the maximum amount of flexibility in reorganizing the company into a solvent position.

Congress amended the Bankruptcy Code to reverse the portion of the Bildisco ruling that permitted unilateral violations of collective bargaining contracts without court approval and modified the portion of Bildisco that permitted judicial rejection of such contracts. Debtors were still permitted to reject labor contracts under some circumstances, however, the unilateral rejection would no longer be permitted. The law now mandated an expedited form of collective bargaining and required a stronger showing that the changes sought are necessary for survival and fair to all parties. Meetings with employees' representatives are required. The representative must be provided with necessary relevant information, such as accounting data.

BANKRUPTCY TAX ISSUES

The Bankruptcy Reform Act of 1978 completely rewrote the laws that govern bankruptcy procedures and principles but was essentially silent with respect to tax considerations. In bankruptcy proceedings, the government acts both as a creditor and as a force to aid in the rehabilitation of an entity. The two roles are not easy to reconcile, and the tax laws that are relevant present considerable problems and are the subject of much debate. A proposed tax bill contemporaneous with the new Bankruptcy Code was so controversial, for solvent as well as nonsolvent firms, that it never was voted by Congress; instead, the **Bankruptcy Tax Bill of 1980** (H.R. 5043) was evaluated by the House Ways and Means Committee and passed by the House of Representatives on March 24, 1980. As a consequence, the nation was governed for a period of time by a Bankruptcy Code that had **no relevant tax law.** The Tax Bill of 1980 was finally passed and went into effect in early 1981.

The new bill deals with all aspects of bankruptcy and reorganization and, indeed, affects solvent firms as well, especially on the **repurchase of outstanding debt.** Three issues of the reorganization process will be discussed: (1) the discharge or reduction in outstanding debt;(2) exchange of equity for debt; and (3) tax loss carry-forwards. All are common to almost every bankruptcy reorganization and are often important elements in the estimation of the value of an emerging company on an aftertax basis.

DISCHARGE OF INDEBTEDNESS. In Public Law 95–598, Congress repealed provisions of the old Bankruptcy Act governing income tax treatment of a **discharge of indebtedness** in bankruptcy for cases filed on or after October 1, 1979. The Bankruptcy Tax Bill of 1980 fills this vacuum by providing that no amount of debt discharge is to be included in income for federal income tax purposes if the debtor is insolvent. Instead, the amount of debt reduction can be applied at the debtor's election first to reduce the debtor's depreciable asset basis. This policy can, however, affect reported income in the future, and the government will eventually be rewarded for its "generosity" if the firm becomes a profitable, going concern. In essence, the government is helping to provide a fresh start but is not totally forgiving the benefits for all time.

If the debtor does not choose to apply the reduction to depreciable assets, the amount is applied to reduce the taxpayer's tax attributes in the following order:

1. Net **operating losses and carryovers**
2. Carryovers of **investment tax credits** and other tax credits
3. **Capital losses** and carryovers
4. The basis of the **taxpayer's assets**

The reduction in each category of carryovers is made in the order of taxable years in which the items would be used, with the order based on the year of discharge and the taxes that would have been paid. After reduction of the specified carryover, any remaining debt discharge is applied to reduce the debtor's asset basis, but not below the amount of the taxpayer's remaining **undischarged liabilities.** Finally, any remaining debt discharge is disregarded (see page 10 of the Bankruptcy Tax Bill of 1980, as reported in *Bankruptcy Law Reports*).

For example, assume that a debtor borrows $1 million on a short-term note and later issues $600,000 worth of stock in cancellation of the note. Under the old bankruptcy law, the creditor recognized a $400,000 loss, but the debtor neither recognized income nor reduced tax attributes. Under the new bill, the creditor can still recognize the loss, but the debtor corporation must account for a **debt discharge** of $400,000. This ruling, which applies to all corporations, was the subject of heated debate because it was viewed as an attempt by the Treasury Department to eliminate an alleged tax loophole and recover an estimated $500 million a year in taxes (B. Greene, "What Big Teeth You Have, Grandma," *Forbes*, February 4, 1980). Therefore, **solvent companies** will have to pay income taxes on profits made when they buy back their own bonds at a discount. For companies being reorganized in bankruptcy, the gain on an exchange of the type noted previously will be treated as a **debt discharge** and will be subject to the tax rules as specified above.

RECAPTURE RULE. The new bill attempts to ensure that the **debt discharge** amount eventually will result in ordinary income. The bill provides that any gain on a subsequent sale of an asset that had been reduced in value, by virtue of the provisions of the bill, will be subject to "recapture" under rules similar to standard **recapture tax law.**

EXCHANGE OF EQUITY FOR DEBT. One of the most common provisions of a recapitalization plan in a bankruptcy reorganization is a **compensation arrangement** involving the exchange of stock in the reorganized firm for all or part of the outstanding indebtedness of the debtor-bankrupt. In essence, the old creditors become the new owners. If a debtor issues stock to its creditor for an outstanding security, such as a bond, there is no debt discharge amount. Thus, there are no consequences of the type discussed previously. There will be no recognition of gain or loss for the creditors. If stock is issued for other debts, such as a supplier claim or short-term note, the debtor is treated as having satisfied the claim with an amount of money equal to the stock's value. A value can be placed on the stock either by the bankruptcy court in a proceeding in which the Internal Revenue Service had the right to intervene or in an **out-of-court agreement** in which the debtor and creditor had adverse interests in the tax consequences of the valuation. The new tax bill provides that the special limitations on **net operating loss carryovers** generally will not apply to the extent that creditors receive stock in exchange for their claims. (See Section 382 of the Internal Revenue Code for more details.)

If both stock and other property are issued to satisfy a debt, the stock is treated as issued for a proportion of the debt equal to its proportion of the total value exchanged. For example, if $20 million of cash and $30 million in stock are issued for a claim of $100 million, the cash is to be treated as satisfying $40 million of the debt and the stock for the other $60 million, with no income resulting nor attribute reduction required.

Some recent stock for debt exchanges in large firm reorganization plans involved **Equity Funding of America** (1976), **Interstate Stores** (1978), **King Resources** (1978), and **Daylin Corporation** (1979). Debt is not always totally replaced by equity, however, as witnessed by the reorganization plans of **Penn Central Co.** (1978), **United Merchants and Manufacturing** (1978) and **Itel Corporation** (1983) (combination of debt and equity but mostly debt) (For a discussion and evaluation of the postbankruptcy performance of reorganization plan securities, see the subsection entitled "A Caveat on Successful Reorganization," especially Exhibits 7 and 8.)

TAX LOSS CARRY-FORWARDS

Importance. **Tax loss carry-forwards** are an extremely important element in any reorganization, especially if the value of the new firm is relevant, as it almost always is. Tax loss questions are irrelevant, of course, in a straight liquidation. Theoretically, the **value of a firm** is equal to the discounted present value of its future earnings after taxes. Since tax loss carrybacks or carry-forwards will affect taxes paid, they have a potentially powerful impact on the earnings to be discounted. The most appropriate procedure is to discount the expected aftertax earnings projection and then add the **present value of tax loss carry-forwards** to arrive at the net overall value.

The Old Tax Laws. Under the Chapter X, **tax-free transfers** of corporate assets to a successor corporation were generally provided for. But no reference was made to the carryover of tax losses, and this caused considerable confusion. Certain cases established the **clean-slate rule,** which held that a firm emerging from bankruptcy that had discharged its old debts was precluded from using losses from the "old" business.

Other cases ruled on the so-called continuity of business doctrine, and allowed carryovers of losses when there was a continuity of interest and of the business. When the principal purpose of a merger (in or out of bankruptcy) was **tax avoidance,** carryovers were disallowed (see Section 269 of the Code). In practice, this has come to mean that the tax loss carryover is not allowed when a greater than 50% change in ownership or a change in business occurs ater the transfer of assets. This highly subjective test probably has not been very effective in curbing takeovers for tax purposes. In addition, the debtor or creditor could petition for a favorable IRS ruling in a bankruptcy-merger reorganization plan that was the only feasible alternative to liquidation.

The New Tax Bill and Reorganization. The bill introduces a new category of **tax-free reorganization,** known as a **"G" reorganization,** which is more flexible than other types and is, in the belief of the Congress, a means to facilitate the rehabilitation of a problem firm. For instance, a "G" does not require a **statutory merger** (type A), nor does it require that the financially distressed corporation receive solely stock of the acquiring corporation in exchange for its assets (type C), and former shareholders do not have to be in control of a "split-off" company (type D). This new type of reorganization is intended to facilitate the reorganization of bankrupt companies. In light of the debt discharge rules of the bill, which adjust tax attributes of a reorganized corporation to reflect changes in debt structure, the statutory rule regarding **loss carryovers** will apply in "G" reorganizations.

Since "G" reorganizations are subject to the same rules on security exchanges for shareholders and other security holders that apply generally to reorganizations, any party receiving new securities whose principal value is greater than that of the securities surrendered is taxed on the excess and vice versa. Money or other property received in a "G" will be subject to the dividend equivalency tests (as to whether the property is a **return on capital**), which apply to reorganizations generally. Likewise, securities transferred to creditors based on claims attributable to accrued or unpaid interest on securities surrendered, will be subject to tax as if interest income were received.

TRIANGULAR REORGANIZATION. The new bill permits a firm to purchase a company in bankruptcy in exchange for stock of the parent company of the acquiring firm rather than its own stock. This is known as a **triangular reorganization.** In addition, the creditors of the insolvent company are permitted to exchange their claims for voting stock of the surviving company when the stock received equals at least 80% of the value of the debts of the insolvent firm.

MODIFICATION OF THE ABSOLUTE PRIORITY RULE. The House Ways and Means Committee Report made it clear that the continuity of interest rule would be clarified with regard to creditors. The report also advised that the **absolute priority rule** should be modified to permit junior creditors and shareholders to retain an interest in the reorganized business even when senior creditors do not receive full settlement; that is, it favored **relative priority rules.** Junior and senior claims should be considered as **proprietary interests** for purposes of the continuity of interest test.

BUSINESS FAILURE

BANKRUPTCY AND BUSINESS FAILURE STATISTICS

Sources of Data. The two primary sources of aggregate business failure and bankruptcy statistics in the United States are Dun & Bradstreet and the Administrative Office of the U.S. Courts, Division of Bankruptcy. Dun & Bradstreet has been compiling failure statistics since 1857 and presents annual data in the *Business Failure Record* publication and monthly data in *News from D&B, Monthly Failures.* The Bankruptcy Division source assembles summary reports from the 96 U.S. district courts and breaks down bankruptcy filings by chapter filed, whether business or personal, and by sector of the economy.

Exhibit 1 combines information from the two sources just named, presenting data for 1950–1984. Column 2 indicates that the number of business bankruptcy filings has increased dramatically since 1950, with the major increases registered in 1975 and 1976 and most dramatically in 1980s. The aftermath of the 1974–1975 recession saw bankruptcy filings rise to a record, over 35,000. This record was recently surpassed with a great increase in 1983 to almost 70,000 individual company filings.

The most continuous time series bankruptcy statistic is D&B's **business failure rate.** This index, which records the **number of failures** recorder **per 10,000 firms** that D&B covers, is an excellent barometer of relative changes in business "exiting" in the United States and Canada. Column 4 of Exhibit 1 shows that the failure rate has been relatively low in years prior to 1980, with less than 0.5% of the firms followed actually ceasing operations in a given year, following assignment or bankruptcy, loss to creditors, receivership, reorganization, or arrangement. However, D&B data do not include certain industries, including railroads, most financial enterprises, real estate companies, and many small service firms. The data are also less than comprehensive, since far fewer business failures (column 3) are recorded than business bankruptcy filings (column 2). Of course, the most recent data show that the failure rate has averaged around 1%, or 100 per 10,000, with 1983's rate of 110 being the highest since 1932 when the rate was 152 per 10,000.

The three final columns of Exhibit 1 show that although there has not been a noticeable trend in business failures or failure rates, the **average liability per failure** has been moving steadily upward since 1950, with a peak of over $600,000 in 1982. This can be explained only partially by inflation, since the average size of U.S. firms, and the consequent liabilities, have grown with price level increases. As noted earlier, however, it is felt that the major change in the profile of business failures in the United States is the susceptibility of the larger firm to total demise. The last column of Exhibit 1, i.e., the average liability per failure, does not include any long-term publicly held debt and primarily reflects short-term claims. As such, it understates failure claims.

Bankruptcy Filings by Chapter and Occupation. Exhibit 5 lists the nation's bankruptcy filings by chapter of the Bankruptcy Act (prior to 1980) and Bankruptcy Code (post 1979). "Straight bankruptcy," whether voluntary or involuntary, means that the firm had to liquidate its assets and repay its creditors in some manner reflecting their priorities. This filing, now known as **Chapter 7** straight bankruptcies, encompasses individuals as well as companies. Personal bankruptcies are discussed at the end of this section in the context of the new Bankruptcy Code.

If we compare the number of Chapter X and XI filings and the new Chapter 11's with the total number of business bankruptcies, it appears that the combined total is a small percentage (slightly over 10%) of all business filings and is relatively insignificant. Nothing could be further from the truth, however: the size, complexity, and public policy issues involved far outweigh the relatively large number that represents the remaining bankruptcies. To our knowledge, no accurate combined or separate compilation of Chapter X and XI liabilities existed.

The breakdown of filings by sector indicates that merchants and professional service firms account for a large proportion, but the total is dominated by "Others in Business." Certain financial and real estate firms make up the bulk of the "other" category. This explains why the **number of bankruptcy filings** exceeds D&B's **number of business failures,** since the latter source does not include them. A more complete breakdown of failures by sector can be found in D&B's Business's *Failure Record,* published annually.

AGGREGATE INFLUENCES ON BUSINESS FAILURE. Most analysts of business failures and bankruptcies concentrate their efforts on microecon-

EXHIBIT 5 FILINGS BY CHAPTER OF THE (OLD) BANKRUPTCY ACT SINCE 1950 AND NEW BANKRUPTCY CODE

Fiscal Year	Total	Voluntary Straight Bankruptcy	Involuntary Straight Bankruptcy	Chapter IX	X	XI	XII	XIII	Section 77 (1933 Act)
1950	33,392	25,263	1,369	4	134	583	31	6,007	0
1951	35,193	26,594	1,099	3	88	459	22	6,924	0
1952	34,873	25,890	1,059	15	74	413	21	7,397	0
1953	40,087	29,815	1,064	0	86	437	15	8,670	0
1954	53,136	41,335	1,398	2	104	649	12	9,634	0
1955	59,404	47,650	1,249	1	73	547	19	9,864	0
1956	62,086	50,655	1,240	1	40	597	15	9,535	0
1957	73,761	60,335	1,189	0	65	599	24	11,549	0
1958	91,668	76,048	1,417	2	67	720	23	13,391	0
1959	100,672	85,502	1,288	3	78	787	21	12,993	0
1960	110,034	94,414	1,296	0	90	622	12	13,599	0
1961	146,643	124,386	1,444	0	112	947	31	19,723	0
1962	147,780	122,499	1,382	1	77	903	37	22,880	0
1963	155,493	128,405	1,409	0	128	1,188	33	24,329	0
1964	171,719	141,828	1,339	0	125	1,088	47	27,292	0
1965	180,323	149,820	1,317	0	88	1,022	49	28,027	0
1966	192,354	161,840	1,173	2	93	909	75	28,261	1

					7[a]	11[a]		13[a]	
1967	208,329	173,884	1,241	1	138	1,033	68	31,963	1
1968	197,811	164,592	1,001	3	128	953	69	31,065	0
1969	184,930	154,054	946	0	87	867	66	28,910	0
1970	194,399	161,366	1,085	0	115	1,262	58	30,510	3
1971	201,352	167,149	1,215	2	179	1,782	120	30,904	1
1972	182,869	152,839	1,094	1	105	1,361	92	27,374	3
1973	173,197	144,929	985	0	101	1,458	92	25,632	0
1974	189,513	156,962	1,009	1	163	2,172	172	29,019	15
1975	254,484	208,064	1,266	0	189	3,506	280	41,178	1
1976	246,549	207,926	1,141	2	141	3,235	525	33,579	0
1977	214,399	180,062	1,132	1	96	3,046	640	29,422	0
1978	202,951	167,776	995	2	75	3,266	650	30,185	2
1979	226,476	182,344	915	1	63	3,042	669	39,442	0
					7[a]	11[a]		13[a]	
1980	210,364	209,428	936		157,743	4,473		48,143	
1981	360,329	358,997	1,331		265,718	7,827		86,778	
1982	367,866	366,331	1,535		255,095	14,058		98,705	
1983	374,734	373,064	1,670		251,319	21,206		102,201	
1984	344,275	342,828	1,447		232,991	19,913		91,358	

[a]Only relevant to new Bankruptcy Code starting in fiscal 1980.

Source: U.S. Bankruptcy Courts, Administrative Office of the President, Table of Bankruptcy Statistics, 1984.

omic causes and indicators. The relatively large number of studies that have attempted to classify and predict bankruptcy (see References, and the discussion on predicting bankruptcies) have obscured the relevance and influence of **macroeconomic influences on the failure phenomenon.** It can be shown, however, that in addition to individual firm inefficiencies, certain aggregate conditions are closely associated with the causes of business failures and contribute to the explanation of why marginally continuing enterprises are forced to declare bankruptcy or to simply close down.

A recent book (Altman, *Corporate Financial Distress,* Wiley, (1983)), explores several macroeconomic influences on the **business failure rate** from 1950 to 1978. Utilizing a first-difference, distributive lag regression model, it was found that the following time series helps to explain cyclical movements in business failures:

1. Percentage change in real growth in the gross national product (GNP)
2. Percentage change in the money supply (M-IB)
3. Percentage change in the Standard & Poor's 500 stock market index
4. Percentage change in new business incorporations

It is intuitively clear why overall economic activity changes and failure rates are negatively correlated, since the aggregate performance of individual firms comprises the overall GNP index.

It can also be shown that changes in the availability of credit (money supply) and in capital market expectations (stock market index) are inversely associated with the business failure rate. A firm will continue to exist as long as it can pay its bills, either through internal generation of funds or from external sources. When the money and capital markets are increasingly stringent or when credit is essentially unavailable to the marginal firm, pressures can be expected to build and failures to start increasing among all firms, particularly the most vulnerable entities. One type of vulnerable firm is the young company.

NEW BUSINESS FORMATION AND AGE OF BUSINESS FAILURE. The rate of business formation can affect the failure rate in subsequent periods, since it is well documented that there is a greater propensity for younger firms to fail than for more mature companies. Exhibit 6 shows this propensity and breaks down failures by age for different sectors and for all concerns. Note that more than 49% of all firms that failed did so in the first five years of their life. This percentage has been remarkably stable over the years.

Although almost 23% of the firms that failed did so in their first three years, only about 1% failed in the first year. This is not surprising: it takes time to fail! Even when a firm is in its worst competitive situation (i.e., when it starts out), there is usually sufficient capital to keep it going for a period of time and default on loans is usually not immediate. Because of this phe-

EXHIBIT 6   AGE OF FAILED BUSINESSES BY FUNCTION, 1981

Age(Years)	Mfg.	Wholesale	Retail	Contruction	Service	All Concerns
1 or less	1.5%	0.9%	1.8%	0.8%	1.5%	1.4%
2	7.2	6.4	10.3	4.0	8.3	7.9
3	12.1	13.3	16.4	9.4	12.6	13.5
Total 3 years or less	20.8	20.6	28.5	14.2	22.4	22.8
4	12.2	13.5	15.7	12.8	14.2	14.1
5	11.5	11.3	12.4	12.6	12.1	12.2
Total 5 years or less	44.5	45.4	56.6	39.6	48.7	49.1
6	8.4	7.5	9.6	11.9	9.7	9.7
7	7.6	7.7	6.3	8.5	7.4	7.2
8	5.9	4.5	5.0	6.6	6.0	5.5
9	4.5	4.7	3.9	5.2	4.5	4.4
10	4.8	3.8	3.1	4.7	4.0	3.9
Total 6–10 years	31.2	28.2	27.9	36.9	31.6	30.7
Over 10	24.3	26.4	15.5	23.5	19.7	20.2
TOTAL	100.0%	100.0%	100.0%	100.0%	100.0%	100.0%
Number of Failures	2,223	1,709	6,882	3,614	2,366	16,794

Source: Dun & Bradstreet, Business Failure Record, 1981, p. 10. These percentages have remained relatively stable since 1981.

nomenon, a model observing the association between **new business formation** and changes in **failure rates** could attempt to exploit this sequence.

In fact, there is a very definite positive relationship between new business formation change in some quarter **t** and the change in failures in the subsequent 4-14 quarters. That is, a lagged relationship is observed, and when the various lagged quarterly rates have differential influences, the **distributed lagged** relationship (differential importance of the same phenomena over time, e.g. new business formation) helps to explain and predict subsequent failures. For example, with new business formation declining in the first two quarters of 1980, we could expect a reduction in the business failure rate starting some time in 1981 or 1982—everything else held equal. Unfortunately, everything else rarely stays the same, and the negative economic performance of the overall economy, in 1981, had a countervailing adverse effect on failure rates.

CAUSES OF BUSINESS FAILURE. The overwhelming cause of individual firm failures is **managerial incompetence.** In 1983 over 92% of all failures were identified with the lack of experience or unbalanced experience (51%), or just plain incompetence (44%). The remaining causes are categorized as neglect (0.8%), fraud (0.4%), and reasons unknown (3.5%). These statistics represent the opinions of informed creditors and information from D&B reports for over 6000 business failures. Of course, if debtors' management were asked why business fail, the category of inexperience and incompetence would receive much lower significance.

PREDICTING CORPORATE BANKRUPTCY

PREDICTING BANKRUPTCY: WHY? The corporate bankruptcy phenomenon has intrigued researchers and practitioners for several decades because it presents an event that is clearly defined and promises significant rewards to the forecaster who supplies accurate, timely predictions. Ever since the late 1960s, the established methodology has been to classify and predict bankruptcy by combining traditional financial analysis techniques with rigorous statistical procedures. Essentially, analysts have attempted to build **early warning systems** for this negative, but extremely important, event. The References at the end of this section contains a fairly complete bibliography of these warning technique studies, and this discussion highlights some of the attempts and comments on their effectiveness.

The reasons for constructing and implementing bankruptcy prediction models are fairly obvious. They involve:

1. Credit analysis for financial institutions and firms
2. Investment analysis for capital market participants
3. Audit risk analysis for accounting firms
4. Failing company analysis and prudent man considerations for legal and antitrust issues
5. Various diverse applications, such as loan guarantees, government subsidy programs, and merger analysis

Credit Analysis. The objective of credit analysis is to determine the repayment probability of a potential or existing customer, to assist in the **accept-reject decision** and the pricing policy, and to aid in the **loan review evaluation.** Most of these applications are primarily related to the operations of financial institutions which have a large number of loan requests and portfolio clients that need to be evaluated quickly and effectively. A related application is in the **accounts receivable management function** of a firm providing goods and services.

In all cases, the optimal decision criterion should be to extend credit up to the point at which the marginal expected return from the lowest credit risk is equal to the marginal expected loss from taking on the account. Marginal returns and losses are a function of pricing (i.e., interest rates on loans) and costs of **default** or **delinquency** on outstanding credits. For an analysis of these costs for commercial banks, see Altman ("Commercial Bank Lending: Process, Credit Scoring and the Costs of Lending Errors," *Journal of Financial and Quantitative Analysis,* November 1980). The expected return variable is derived from the probability of failure or nonrepayment and its inverse, the probability of successful repayment, hence the significant importance of techniques that seek to quantify failure probabilities.

Investment Analysis. At a later point we discuss the investment performance **of securities of bankrupt firms** that went through the reorganization process. An extension of that investigation is to analyze the investment implications of models for predicting bankruptcy. The sale of securities of firms that have a high propensity to fail is one implication. More aggressive strategies might include **short sale** or **option trades,** since precipitous drops in price always accompany a firm's path toward failure.

Audit Risk Analysis. One of the more controversial issues in the accounting profession is the auditor's responsibilities toward **going-concern qualifications.** If there is a substantial likelihood that a firm will no longer be operating as a continuing entity, the auditor is obliged to state this **contingency** in the opinion attached to the audited financial statement. Several firms view their responsibility as mainly expressing their expert opinion on the firm's ability to realize asset values and determine whether these values are sufficient to cover outstanding liabilities. Most accountants do not believe that they should be responsible for assessing the **probability of failure.** At the same time, however, most would agree that it is important to counsel clients when the outlook is grim and failure is not an insignificant possibility.

A recent exposure draft of the American Institute of Certified Public Accountants (Accounting Standards Board, Exposure Draft, "The Auditor's Considerations When a Question Arises About an Entity's Continued Existence," March 24, 1980), attempts to specify auditor responsibilities in high-risk situations. The draft identifies several pieces of information that may indicate solvency problems, including "negative trends and adverse key financial ratios, recurring operating losses, working capital deficiencies, and negative cash flows." The subsequent **Financial Analysis Standards Board** report (1981) confirmed these objectives.

Regardless of the position accountants take toward the future viability of their clients, both existing and potential ones, the value of an **early warning financial system** is obvious. For a specialized reading list on this subject, see the References.

Legal Issues of Bankruptcy Prediction. Legal applications of models that attempt to classify firms as having financial profiles similar to bankrupt companies involve two controversial issues. These are the Failing Company Doctrine and fiduciary responsibility.

Failing Company Doctrine. The **failing company doctrine** is an **antitrust defense** whereby an otherwise illegal merger could be allowed because one of the partners is a failing entity and no other good-faith purchaser exists. This doctrine was first applied in the **International Shoe Co. v. FTC** (280 U.S. 291 (1930)), and has been infrequently and inconsistently applied ever since. It has been argued that such mergers should be sanctioned only if the costs of bankruptcy to society exceed the costs to society from the anticompetitive effects of the merger (Altman and Goodman, "An Economic and Financial Analysis of the Failing Company Doctrine," Salomon Brothers Center Working Paper No. 196, New York University, 1980).

The application of bankruptcy prediction models in failing company cases could provide an objective test for whether the so-called failing company is indeed on the verge of serious financial problems (Blum, "Failing Company Discriminant Analysis," *Journal of Accounting Research,* Vol. 12, No. 1, Spring 1974). For example, the merger in 1978 between two large companies, whose principal subsidiaries were **Youngstown Sheet & Tube** and **Jones & Laughlin Steel** (of Lykes Corp. and LTV Corp.), was sanctioned by the U.S. attorney general over the objection of his own staff. The degree of seriousness of the steel companies' problems was questioned, as well as the economic justification of permitting the nation's seventh and eighth largest steel manufacturers to merge. We believe that such models, as will be described, can be helpful in understanding the situation. The steel merger was consummated and, indeed, one of the failure classification models (Z-Score) did show that Lykes was a definite candidate for insolvency. Incidentally, the **going-concern qualification** that Youngstown Sheet & Tube received from its auditor in 1977 was removed in the year following the merger.

Fiduciary Responsibility. A second area of legal application concerns the investment manager's **fiduciary responsibility** to examine each individual security in his portfolio for its expected return and risk. Portfolio theorists and some legal commentators have argued (see Langbein and Posner, "Market Funds and Trust Investment Law," *American Bar Foundation Research Journal,* December 1975) that the primary responsibility of the **portfolio manager** is to maximize the overall return of the portfolio; individual firm performance is of no relevance. (These authors do concede however, that an inexpensive screen for assessing security risk would probably be worthwhile to minimize legal risk. On the contrary, one can argue that the manager can and should assess insolvency risk of the securities combined into a portfolio and that companies that possess significant failure potential should not be purchased or, if owned, should be sold (see Altman, "Bankruptcy

Identification: Virtue or Necessity," *Journal of Portfolio Management,* Spring 1977).

The application of an **early warning screen** of investment securities is particularly applicable to index fund management. **Index funds** are portfolios of securities comprised of the entire list of some established stock market index such as the **Standard & Poor's (S&P's) 500** or **Industrial 400.** The theory is that portfolio managers have rarely, if ever, consistently outperformed the indexes, so why try and in the process incur substantial personnel and transaction costs. In fact, however, index funds rarely invest in the entire index; rather, they select a subgroup of the index in which to concentrate funds. For example, a fund might hold the highest 200 stocks in terms of market capitalization instead of the entire S&P 500.

This situation is ideal for application of failure prediction models. Instead of investing in the top 200 or 300, why not, for example, screen out of that group of 200 the stocks whose companies possess significant failure risk, substituting other stocks that are part of the overall index. Indeed, several **index funds** are utilizing bankruptcy prediction screens in their analysis today. Portfolio management companies are concerned that the stockholders of index and other **mutual funds** will sue management for negligence and mismanagement. This is not likely to occur very often, but one investment manager estimated that a single lost lawsuit could wipe out five or six years of profits on a $25 million fund (see McWilliams, "Failure Models and Investment Management," in *Financial Crises: Institutions and Markets in a Fragile Environment,* Altman and Sametz, Eds. Wiley-Interscience 1977).

Diverse Applications. Other applications for failure models include (1) criteria for **loan guarantees** or other **subsidy programs,** (2) **merger target** analysis, and (3) **bond rating analysis.** In all cases, the aim is to assess creditworthiness and insolvency risk in such a manner as to objectively analyze opportunities and risks.

PREDICTING BANKRUPTCY: HOW? Since the late 1960s there has been considerable interest among researchers in the development and testing of models for classifying and predicting business failures. Two of the most influential works were by Beaver (1967) and Altman (1968) (references to this topic are listed together at the end of this section), who presented a methodology that has been replicated and modified for many different types of firms. **Beaver** segregated for analysis a sample of bankrupt firms and a matched sample of nonbankrupt firms and studied the two samples' financial performance indicators for up to five years before failure. Beaver's work was a type of **univariate analysis** whereby each measure or ratio was analyzed separately and the **optimal cutoff point** was selected so that the number of accurate classifications was maximized for that particular sample. When his analysis is evaluated based on the original samples, the technique is known as classification analysis. When a model is tested on a sample of firms other than the original one, preferably from a period after the original model's data source, the analysis takes on a predictive flavor.

Beaver tested 14 ratios and found that the cash flow to total debt ratio was the best classifier of corporate bankruptcy. Other important financial measures found by Beaver were the debt to total assets and net income to total assets ratios, and the "no credit interval."

The Z-Score Model. Altman (1968), was the first to apply the technique known as **discriminant analysis** to failure classification problem. The analysis is multivariate in that a number of variables are combined simultaneously to analyze a firm for its failure potential. That particular technique, known as the **Z-Score model,** applied to manufacturing entities, has been used by many practitioners to problems of **credit analysis, investment analysis,** and **going-concern evaluation,** among others. The Z-Score model is expressed as follows:

$$Z = 1.2x_1 + 1.4x_2 + 3.3x_3 + 0.6x_4 + 0.99x_5$$

where: x_1 = working capital/total asssets
x_2 = retained earnings/total assets
x_3 = earnings before interest and taxes/total assets
x_4 = market value of equity/total liabilities
x_5 = sales/total assets

x_1, *Working Capital/Total Assets.* The ratio of working capital to total assets, frequently found in studies of corporate problems, is a measure of the **net liquid assets** of the firm relative to the total capitalization. **Working capital** is defined as the difference between current assets and current liabilities. Liquidity and size characteristics are explicitly considered. Ordinarily, a firm experiencing consistent operating deficits will have shrinking current assets in relation to total assets.

x_2, *Retained Earnings/Total Assets (RE/TA).* This is a measure of **cumulative profitability** over time. The age of a firm is implicitly considered in this ratio. For example, a relatively young firm will probably show a low RE/TA ratio because it has not had time to build up its cumulative profits. Therefore, it may be argued that the young firm is somewhat discriminated against in this analysis, and its chance of being classified as bankrupt is relatively higher than that of another, older firm. But this is precisely the situation in the real world. As we have shown, the incidence of failure is much higher in a firm's earlier years.

x_3, *Earnings Before Interest and Taxes/Total Assets.* This ratio is calculated by dividing the earnings before interest and tax deductions into the total assets of a firm. In essence, it is a measure of the *true productivity of the firm's assets,* abstracting from any tax of leverage factors. Since a firm's ultimate existence is based on the earning power of its assets, this ratio appears to be particularly appropriate for studies dealing with corporate failure. Furthermore, insolvency in a bankruptcy sense occurs when the total liabilities exceed a fair valuation of the firm's assets, with the value determined by the earning power of the assets, This is the most important measure of the five ratios, based on *univariate tests*.

x_4, *Market Value of Equity/Book Value of Total Liabilities.* Equity is measured by the combined market value of all shares of stock, preferred and common, whereas debt includes both current and long-term obligations. The measure shows how much the firm's assets can decline in value (measured by market value of equity plus debt) before the liabilities exceed the assets and the firm becomes insolvent. For example, a company with a market value of its equity of $1,000 and debt of $500 could experience a two-thirds drop in asset value before insolvency. However, the same firm with $250 in equity will be insolvent if its drop is only one-third in value. The ratio adds a market value dimension. It appears to be a more effective predictor of bankruptcy than a similar, more commonly used ratio, the net worth to total debt (book values).

x_5, *Sales/Total Assets.* This capital turnover ratio is a standard financial ratio illustrating the sales-generating ability of the firm's assets. It is one measure of management's capability in dealing with competitive conditions. This final ratio is interesting because it is the least significant ratio on an individual basis. Because of its unique relationship to other variables in the model, however, the **sales/total assets ratio** ranks second in its contribution to the overall discriminating ability of the model.

Any firm with a **Z-Score below 1.8** is considered to be a prime candidate for bankruptcy, and the lower the score, the higher the failure probability. This model was over 90% accurate in classifying bankrupt firms correctly one statement prior to failure and over 80% accurate in subsequent prediction tests (see Altman, *Corporate Financial Distress* (Wiley 1983).

With the many important changes in reporting standards since the late 1960s, the **Z-Score model** is somewhat out of date in the 1980s. A second-generation model known as Zeta Analysis (Altman et al., 1977) adjusts for these changes, primarily the **capitalization of financial leases.** The resulting linear Zeta discriminant model is extremely accurate for up to five years before failure. Since this analysis is a proprietary one, the exact weights for the model's seven variables cannot be specified here but more information can be derived from Zeta Services, Inc. (see the following list).

Failure Prediction Services. There are at least four statistical services that seek to assess the **insolvency risk of industrial companies:**

1. The **Gambler's Ruin Model.** Developed by J. Wilcox (1971, 1976). Available from Advantage Financial Systems, Boston.
2. **Prognostic Technologies, Inc.** Developed by J. Lowenhar (New York).
3. **QES.** Available from the Trust Division of the First Union Bank, Charlotte, North Carolina.
4. **The Zeta Model.** Available from Zeta Services, Inc. Hoboken, New Jersey. Developed by R. Haldeman with E. Altman and P. Narayanan (1977).

INVESTING IN BANKRUPT SECURITIES

VALUATION AND INVESTING. Not only is the reorganization valuation process critical to the debtor, it is also an important determinant of the potential investment opportunities for those interested in **bankrupt securities.** Although a majority of bankrupt firms end in total liquidation or are evaluated as insolvent in bankruptcy (i.e., liabilities are greater than an assessed value of the assets), the firms that are reorganized successfully present potentially excellent investment returns, especially on debt securities. A study performed in 1969 (Altman, "Corporate Bankruptcy Potential, Stockholder Returns and Share Valuation," *Journal of Finance*, December 1969) showed that equity investors of bankrupt firms tend to do as well as all other equity investors if the reorganized firm lasted at least five years after its initial bankruptcy petition. Admittedly, the percentage (33%) of the firms studied that did last five years was relatively small.

The trick is to determine which firms are likely candidates for a successful reorganization and then to wait at least one month after the petition date to purchase the securities. It was found (Altman, 1969, op.cit.) that the price of bankrupt firm equities **falls on average 25%** from one month before failure to one month after. Clark and Weinstein ("The Behavior of the Common Stock of Bankrupt Firms," *Journal of Finance*, May 1983) corroborated these findings with even more dramatic evidence pertaining to common stock price declines (35–50% on the news of bankruptcy declaration). Altman and Nammacher (1985) found that the drop in price on **defaulting debt securities** was 27% from one year prior to the end of the month that the default took place and 17% from one month prior to just after default ("The Default Rate Experience on High Yield Debt," **Morgan Stanley, and Co., Incorporated** *Fixed Income Research Report,* March 1985). This drop in price, sometimes referred to as the **bankruptcy information effect,** implies that the market was not totally anticipating the bankruptcy, or else the price would have been fully discounted.

INVESTING IN RECENT BANKRUPTS. The postbankruptcy price movement of both the equity shares and debt claims for a number of recent, sizeable business failures have been observed. Exhibit 7 lists 11 recent fail-

EXHIBIT 7 INVESTMENT PERFORMANCE OF DEBTHOLDERS AND STOCKHOLDERS OF BANKRUPT FIRMS

Original Company and (Reorganization Filing Date)	Total Liabilities ($ Millions)	Security of Bankrupt Company	Prebankruptcy Market Value of 1 Bond or 100 Shares	New Company and (Date Reorganization Completed)	Securities in New Company or Cash Received in Reorganization or Liquidation for 1 Bond or 100 Shares	Value Based on Recent Market (June 30, 1980)
Penn Central Transportation Co., (June 1970)	$3,600	New York Central 6% bonds due 1980	$720	Penn Central Corp., (October 1978)	0.275 Series A and 0.164 Series B mortgage bonds + 21.98 shares B preferred + 9.91 shares common + $147	$837.25
Penn Central Co. (100% Owner of P.C.T.C.) (July 1976)	$125	Common	$150		4 Shares Common	$80
W.T. Grant Co., (October 1975)	$1,031	4¾% Sinking fund debentures due 1978	$360	Company is in liquidation	$1,000	$1,000
		4% Convertible subordinated debentures due 1990	$317.50		14% of Face value (judge's approval February 1980 pending 90% agreement of recipients)	$140
		4¾% Convertible subordinated debentures due 1966	$235		14% of face value (judge's approval February 1980 pending 90% agreement of recipients)	$140
		Common stock	$338		Probably none	—
Equity Funding Corp. of America, (April 1973)	$594	9½% Debentures due 1990	$1,098	Orion Capital Corp., (March 1976)	71.2 Shares common	$961.20

EXHIBIT 7 CONTINUED

Original Company and (Reorganization Filing Date)	Total Liabilities ($ Millions)	Security of Bankrupt Company	Prebankruptcy Market Value of 1 Bond or 100 Shares	New Company and (Date Reorganization Completed)	Securities in New Company or Cash Received in Reorganization or Liquidation for 1 Bond or 100 Shares	Value Based on Recent Market (June 30, 1980)
		5½% Convertible subordinated debentures due 1991	$800		25.5 Shares common	$344.25
		Common stock	$2,538		28.7 Shares common	$387.45
Interstate Stores, Inc., (May 1974)	$208	4% Convertible subordinated debentures due 1992	$220	Toys "R" Us, Inc., (April, 1978)	117 Shares common	$4,168.13
		4½% Convertible subordinated debentures due 1981	$450		1 Share per $10 claim, total claims unavailable	At least $4,562
		Common stock	$163		66.7 Shares common	$2,376.18
King Resources Co., (August 1971)	$117	5½% Convertible subordinated debentures due 1988	$90	Phoenix Resources Co., (January 1978)	55.5 Shares B common + $2.83	$2,070.20
		Common stock	$181		1 Share B common + $2.13	$39.38
Bowmar Instrument Corp., (February 1975)	$51	No public debt		Bowmar Instrument, (April, 1977)	—	—
		Common stock	$438		66.7 Share common	$268
Miller-Wohl Co., Inc., (September 1972)	$32	No public debt		Miller-Wohl Co., Inc., (November 1973)		
		Common stock	$675		100 shares common	$18,800

Company (July 1977 etc.)		Security		Company (exchange)	Consideration	Value
United Merchants & Manufacturing, Inc., (July 1977)	$380	9½% Sinking fund debentures due 1995	$890	United Merchants & Manufacturers, Inc., (June 1978)	50% of Principal + accrued interest, 9½% interest on remainder to be retired 1989	$760
		4½% Convertible subordinated debentures due 1990	$502.50		All interest and principal pursuant to original indenture	$350
		Common stock	$538		100 Shares common	$675
Unishops, Inc., (November 1973)	$112	No public debt		Unishops, Inc., (April 1975)		
		Common stock	$163		66.7 Shares common	$217.75
Neisner Bros., Inc., (December 1977)	$46	No public debt		Merged with Ames Department Stores, Inc., (October 1978)		
		Common stock	$325		25 Shares Ames convertible preferred (convertible to 1.25 shares common)	$437.50
Daylin, Inc., (February 1975)	$250	8.35% Debentures due 1997	$700	Daylin, Inc., (November 1976). merged with W R Grace, (March 1979)	$158 + 0.121 "A" notes + 0.558 "A" debentures + 54 shares common	$1,053
		5% Subordinated debentures due 1989	$220		0.085 Class "B" notes + 0.032 class "B" debentures + 290 shares common	$1,327.63
		Common stock	$150		100 Shares common—Received $4.0625 a share in Grace merger	$406.25

ures, the terms of the reorganization (if any), the price of the debt and equity one month prior to bankruptcy, and the value of these securities as of June 30, 1980. The June 30 value has not been discounted back to the bankruptcy date to adjust for opportunity costs over the period, nor have intermediate values for these securities between the bankruptcy date and the most current date been noted. One who is interested in these adjustments and additions can pursue the matter in as detailed a fashion as is desired. Our purpose for showing these values is to highlight the overall investment potential.

A more recent study published by Morgan Stanley & Co., Incorporated, (M. Fridson, "How Much Value in Asset Values," **High Performance,** March 1985) illustrated the post filing experience of investors in straight debt (non-convertible) securities. He tracked the effective rate of return on six recent, large bankrupt firm debentures. In every case (see Exhibit 8), the investor who bought the debt security one month after the filing date received a positive return as of the reorganization confirmation date. The returns varied, however, from 5.34% on White Motor's debt to over 50% of **Itel Corp.** and **Wickes Companies'** debt. Clearly, the profit potential is present on bankrupt debt securities. Again, the key is following the company closely, assessing **reorganization success** potential, estimating **liquidation values,** and of course, timing.

Some of the **investment returns on debt securities** have been enormous and would be even more impressive if the investor had waited until after

EXHIBIT 8   RETURNS ON BANKRUPT DEBT SECURITIES A SAMPLE OF BANKRUPTCIES, 1980-1982

Original Company and Filing Date	Security of Bankrupt Co.	Market Value 1 Month After Filing Date	Market Value at Issue Date[a]	Annual Effective Internal Rate of Return	Total Percent of Initial Purchase
AM International	9.375%	$290.00	$612.90	38.81%	211%
4/14/82	SF Deb 6/30/95	4/30/82	10/30/84		
Braniff Air	9.125%	$382.50	$691.47	46.82%	181%
5/13/82	SEN SF Deb 1/1/97	5/30/82	12/15/83		
Itel Corp.	10.50%	$250.00	$799.53	54.65%	320%
1/29/81	SF Deb 12/1/98	2/30/81	9/19/83		
White Motor	7.25%	$420.00	$495.17	5.34%	118%
9/4/80	SF Deb 12/1/93	9/30/80	12/1/83		
Wilson Foods	7.875%	$655.00	$747.50	15.47%	114%
4/22/83	SF Deb 3/1/97	5/30/83	4/30/84		
Wickes Companies	7.875%	$270.00	$806.71	52.76%	299%
4/30/82	SF Deb 5/1/98	5/30/82	1/28/85 (WI)		

Source: Fridson, Martin, "How Much Value in Asset Values," **High Performance,** Morgan Stanley & Co. Incorporated, February 1985, (follow-up in March, 1985 High Performance).
[a]"Market Value at Issue Date" does not include coupons paid before the filing date. It does include all distributions (including cash) awarded by the plan of reorganization to holders of the pre-petition issue. Issue Date is the first day of trading of the reorganized securities.

the bankruptcy to purchase the bonds. For example, United Merchants & Manufacturing's 9 1/2%, 1995 debentures dropped to $420 per bond in the wake of the July 1977 bankruptcy, and subsequently the price rose to almost par value. Several other debt securities received common stock in the reorganization and the subsequent price rise in the common shares helped make the "investment" look very good indeed. For example, Interstate Stores' successful transition to Toys "R" Us showed a $220 value, before failure, increase to over $4,168 on the 1992 convertibles and over $3,500 compared to a prebankrupt $450 value on the 1981 convertible debt. King Resources also showed a large increase as well as several securities listed in Exhibit 8.

DEFAULT RATE EXPERIENCE ON CORPORATE DEBT. A situation that is always present when a firm that files for bankruptcy has publicly traded debt outstanding is a **legal default** on these securities. The entire **par value** amount of the debt plus accrued interest becomes due and payable upon default, and a claim in reorganization. Public debtholders are represented by their **indenture trustee** during the reorganization process. It is possible for a bond issue to default without a formal bankruptcy and on a number of occasions that firm, or a subsequent purchasing firm, has renewed payments of interest and principal. Usually, however, default and bankruptcy occur simultaneously.

What has been the default rate experience on corporate debt? This is an important question to be assessed especially by the investment community. The classic **Hickman study,** (W.B. Hickman, *Corporate Bond Quality and Investor Experience,* NBER, 1958) analyzed debt securities through World War II and T. Atkinson, *Trends in Corporate Bond Quality,* NBER, 1967, updated that report through 1957. Both concluded that the **default rate** (the percentage of outstanding debt that defaults in any given calendar year) was extremely low, although during the depression years the rate on total corporate debt exceeded 3%. During recent years (1970–1984), the default rate on total corporate debt was about .08%.

A more relevant question to ask is what is the default rate, not in total corporate debt, but in the classes of debt that actually do default. Indeed, in modern times, only Johns Manville defaulted (1982) when its debt was rated investment grade by the rating agencies, Moody's and Standard & Poor's. **Investment grade debt securities** are those rated BBB- (S&P and Fitch) or Baa3 (Moody's) or above. Those bonds rate below investment grade are sometimes called **high yield bonds** or **"junk" bonds.** The term junk was given to those issues which fell from investment grade status to the lower-rated junk category.

Junk Bonds. In recent years, the so-called junk or high yield debt segment of the market has grown tremendously. Estimates are that the total high yield debt market is about $80 billion (July 1985) with over $50 billion in rated, straight debt securities. The latter comprised 11–13% of the total straight debt market at the end of 1984, depending upon if one includes high yield debt that for some reason is not rated by the agencies. Estimates are that an additional 20% of high yield debt is not rated. High yield debt has become an attractive investment alternative with **yield spreads** (yields to maturity on debt minus the equivalent maturity government bond issue) averaging 250–500 basis points (2.5% to 5.0%) over the period 1978–1984. **Realized return spreads** have also been very impressive, further fueling the enormous growth and interest in this market-place.

The high yield market is comprised of three types of issuers: (1) new emerging companies who are too young and risky to attain investment grade status; (2) those seasoned issues which have been downgraded from investment grade—the so-called **"fallen-angels";** and (3) securities of firms which have become increasingly risky due to the amount of debt issued in **exchange offers** such as **leverage buyouts** (taking a firm private by investors and usually also managers) and **hostile merger takeovers.** The latter event is currently being debated in all walks of business and government with no fewer than nine congressional committees looking into the impact of such mergers on the economy in 1985.

Default Rate on High Yield Debt. Since in almost all cases when a default takes place it is on a high yield debt security, it seems appropriate to measure the default rate on this set of bonds alone. Altman & Nammacher, ("The Default Rate Experience on High Yield Debt," *Financial Analysts Journal,* July-August 1985) documented the rate on straight, high yield debt and concluded that over the period of 1974–1984, the default rate averaged 1.52% per year. The rate ranged from as low as 0.15% in 1981 to over 4.0% in 1977 and again in 1982. The latter year saw the largest number and amount of defaulted debt until 1985 when the amount defaulting reached almost $ 1 billion. Since defaulting debt securities are not worthless, it is necessary to measure what percentage of par value was retained after default. The authors analyzed over 50 straight debt issues and found that, on average, the securities sold for 41% of par value, just after default. If the retention value and also the loss of one interest payment are considered, Altman & Nammacher concluded that the average loss of defaulting straight debt was about 1.0% per annum.

This rate is disputed by those who claim that fallen-angels should not be included in the statistics but that non-rated, high yield debt should. If these modifications are considered, the default rate drops to between 0.5–0.6%. Regardless of which rate you consider, the rate of return on high yield debt, net of defaults, has been very impressive over the most recent six–seven years with return spreads above long term government bonds averaging 400–500 basis points (4–5%).

A CAVEAT ON SUCCESSFUL REORGANIZATIONS. This exercise should not be construed as an endorsement of **investment strategies** that concentrate on bankrupt securities. On the other hand, bankruptcy does not automatically mean a loss of one's total investment. The key, again, is the successful reorganization potential of the debtor, which is usually a function of sound valuation analysis during bankruptcy and favorable economic performance after reorganization.

Most bankrupt entities attempt to recover by liquidating, or selling to another firm, the parts of the business that caused most of the problems in the past and by concentrating on building up the parts that have the greatest earnings potential. Of course, management should have been following this strategy while solvent, but usually the "crisis principle" that is, when a crisis is imminent, is the motivating force for change. Unfortunately, drastic changes are often attempted too late to keep a bankrupt from liquidating. For firms that emerge successfully, however, the **reorganization process** is critical to all interested parties, including past and future investors.

PERSONAL BANKRUPTCY

THE NEW PERSONAL BANKRUPTCY RULES. The **Bankruptcy Reform Act of 1978** made sweeping changes in the rules that govern the personal bankruptcy filings in the United States. In fact, the changes were so dramatic that the number of filings jumped considerably after the Act went into effect on October 1, 1979. For the first six months of 1980, the number of personal bankruptcies increased more than 75% over the comparable period in 1979. **Total bankruptcy filings** in 1980 exceeded 360,000, with 314,875 filings in the personal sector. Exhibit 9 shows the trend in personal filings since 1950 (see also Exhibit 5). Since 1980, the number of filings has remained very high and motivated an intense lobby in Washington to modify the alleged leniency to debtors. This lobby was quite successful and resulted in several adjustments in 1984 (see below).

Note that, as expected, the number of personal filings increases during recessionary periods and, in all but the 1974–1975 recession, the increase tends to continue for a short time after the recession has ended. Also, with the exception of 1968–1969, 1972–1973, and 1976–1978, the number of filings has been consistently increasing, and we can probably expect the trend to continue.

There are two reasons for the great increase in personal filings under the 1979 Code: (1) the recession and the attendant credit restraints, which had harsh effects on the individual, and (2) the increased liberality of new Code, particularly in the **exemptions** that are available. (See "The New Rules About Bankruptcy," *Changing Times,* May 1979 for details of the new Code related to personal filings.)

Personal bankruptcy rationale is based on the premise that individuals should have the opportunity to work out a liquidation or repayment schedule that is feasible and be able to get a fresh start on a new life. The new Code

EXHIBIT 9   PERSONAL BANKRUPTCY FILINGS IN THE UNITED STATES, 1950–1984

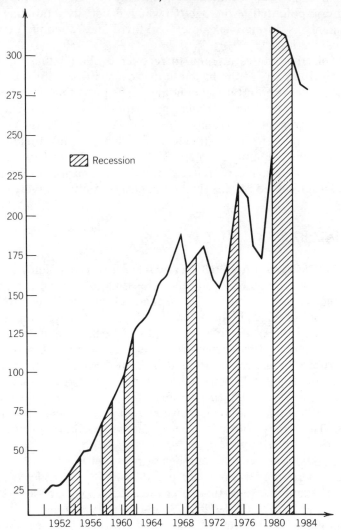

Source: Administrative Office of the U.S. District Courts. Statistical Analysis and Reports Division, Washington, D.C.

creates a broad set of federal **exemptions** that normally apply to debtors in all states. In states that provide more liberal allowances, a debtor can opt for them. Also, states can pass laws prohibiting the use of federal exemptions, and many of them have done so since the new act went into effect.

EXEMPT PROPERTY.   The following property was exempted by the 1979 Act:

1. Up to $7,500 in equity in a home or burial plot. Some states (e.g., New York) permit up to $10,000.
2. An individual's interest up to $1,200 in a **motor vehicle.**
3. An individual's interest up to $200 for **any single item** in household goods, furnishings, clothes, appliances, books, animals, crops, and musical instruments.
4. Up to $500 in jewelry.
5. Any property worth up to $400 plus any unused part of the household exemption (item 1 above).
6. Up to $750 worth of implements, books, or tools of trade.
7. Any professionally prescribed health aids.
8. Protection includes social security and veterans' benefits, unemployment compensation, alimony and child support, and pension and profit-sharing payments.

If husband and wife file for bankruptcy jointly, the dollar limit doubles. The new Code was far more liberal in its exemptions. For example, under the old act the **federal homestead exclusion** was only $2,000.

Just because property falls into an exempt category, however, a bankrupt cannot necessarily keep it. The property can only be kept if a person owns the property completely. Property that is security for a purchase or a loan can be repossessed, regardless of whether it is exempted. Once repossessed, the property is sold to satisfy the debt; if there is something left over, in the case of exempt property, the debtor can then list the asset's value under the exclusion categories noted above (e.g., $7,500 for a home). The court might, however, invalidate certain repossessable property in favor of the debtor for such items as furniture, tools of trade, and other necessities. In addition, the law limits a **creditor's claim** against certain property to the value of the property, regardless of how much still owed. So if a washing machine that cost $500 on credit has $300 still outstanding but the repossessed value was only $200, the debtor could pay the store the $200 and the remaining $100 of the debt would be eliminated.

CHAPTER 13 REPAYMENT PLANS. Chapter 13 of the new Bankruptcy Code deals with the small business debtor and the individual. Whereas previously this chapter was limited to *wage earners,* now it is possible for any individual with regular income to file a Chapter 13 if that individual has unsecured debts of less than $100,000 and secured debts of less than $350,000.

The debtor has the right to propose a *repayment plan* that may provide for payments over a period of up to three years, with the court having the power to extend a repayment period up to five years. The debtor may make payments from future income only or from a combination of future income and a liquidation of assets. A repayment plan may modify the rights of secured creditors, but not claimants who hold a security interest in real property that is the debtor's principal residence. A plan may not be confirmed unless each **secured creditor** accepts the plan or the plan provides that the creditor's claim is retained by a secured lien. There is no requirement that unsecured creditors vote on or accept a plan.

The key aspect of a **Chapter 13 repayment plan** is the monthly budget, listing expected revenues and expenses for the debtor. Any surplus then becomes the basis for the repayment schedule over the three-five year repayment period. It is not uncommon for the debtors to petition for and receive confirmation on very low repayment schedules including the so-called 1% (of liabilities) or $5 (a month) plans.

Chapter 13 offers several advantages over straight bankruptcy liquidation (Chapter 7) filings. The major one is that people can discharge, or obtain release from a wide range of debts. Student loans as well as loans obtained through false financial statements can be discharged depending on expected disposable income available. **Nondischargeable debts,** however, still include alimony and child support and long-term debts such as mortgages.

CODEBTOR CLAUSE AND REFILING RESTRICTIONS. The court also extended its protection to codebtors or guarantors of a loan. Under the old Act, if a person filed a Chapter XIII plan, a creditor had no problem in seeking repayment from a loan guarantor. The new code stipulates that creditors cannot try to collect from a codebtor as long as the repayment plan is in effect. Under **Chapter 13,** there is no limit to when one may file again for bankruptcy as long as the debtor repays at least 70% of the debts. Under Chapter 7 (liquidation), however, one must wait six years before filing for bankruptcy again.

CHAPTER 7: STRAIGHT BANKRUPTCY LIQUIDATION. Chapter 7 of the Code deals with liquidation procedures, which are similar to those that existed under the old Act. The new Code provides for the court, or the U.S. Trustee, to appoint an interim trustee to liquidate the debtor's assets and pay off the claims in their order of priority (see the material on absolute priority, above). At the first meeting, creditors holding at least 20% in amount of claims may elect a trustee. At least 20% in amount of claims must actually vote, and the candidate who receives the majority of the amount of the claims is elected. A creditors' committee is comprised of no fewer than three nor more than 11 creditors for the purpose of consulting with the trustee and making recommendations to him respecting the administration of the estate.

Section 727 of the Code provides for the discharge of all remaining debts of the estate, unless certain infractions of the individual debtor preclude it. Essentially, when one goes bankrupt, the court takes the property, sells it, splits the proceeds among the creditors, and erases any remaining debt. The broad set of exemptions discussed earlier for Chapter 13 apply for the most part to Chapter 7 as well.

1984 CONSUMER AMENDMENTS. The **Bankruptcy Reform Act of 1978** greatly increased the relief available to debtors. This resulted in a series of strong protests and specially commissioned studies by the consumer lending industry which argued that gross abuses of the Code were being perpetrated which, among other things, manifested in higher finance charges to everyone. The lobbying effort was quite successful in that the consumer amendments of the 1984 Act not only reversed a number of changes in the 1978 Code but also represented changes from the 1898 Act. These changes include the following:

1. Addition of a new clause 1325(b) providing that a *Chapter 13 Plan* cannot be approved in the face of an objection by a creditor or the trustee unless claims are paid in full or all of the debtor's "projected disposable income" for the next three years will be applied to make payments. Disposable income is defined to mean income not reasonably necessary for maintenance or support of the debtor or dependents or for operation of the debtor's business.

2. Limitation in the aggregate debtor amount of federal exemption, including household goods claimed as exempt and a reduction of the "grubstake" exemption to a maximum of $4,150 (11 U.S.C. Sections 522(d)(3) and (5)).

3. Provision that certain debts incurred within forty days before the petition date in a voluntary case are non-dischargeable.

4. Repeal of the ability of a husband and wife to split exemptions by respectively electing state and federal exemptions.

5. Requirement that a debtor file a statement of intention with respect to consumer collateral coupled with a direction to the trustee that the debtor perform his intention.

6. Provision for the court's right to dismiss a Chapter 7 case "on its own motion and not at the request or suggestion of any party of interest" based on "substantial abuse" by the debtor in seeking relief. Debtor could attempt to rebut this dismissal.

7. Requirement that the debtor commence making payments to the trustee within thirty days after filing the plan, whether or not it is confirmed. If the plan is not confirmed, payments are returned to the debtor after payment of administrative expenses.

8. Requirement that the trustee ensure that the debtor commences making payments under the plan coupled with grounds for dismissal where there has been a failure to commence payments. This is to combat Chapter 11 noncompliance—allegedly a major complaint of creditors. In favor of the debtor are the provisions that:

   (*a*) Prohibition of employment termination by private employers of an individual debtor or an "individual associated with a debtor or bankrupt'' by reason that the individual had sought bankruptcy relief.

    (b) Liberalization of the ability to obtain reaffirmation of dischargeable debts, particularly where the debtor is represented by counsel.

FILING COSTS AND LAWYER FEES. Personal bankruptcy is not costless. The filing fee for individuals is $60, up from $50 under the old Act. In 1984 the range of lawyer fees was usually $200–$500. Although the majority of individuals hire a bankruptcy lawyer, this is not necessary: the requisite forms can be purchased in stationery stores.

REFERENCES

BOOKS

Altman, Edward I., *Corporate Bankruptcy in America,* Heath, Lexington, MA, 1971.

———, *Corporate Financial Distress: A Complete Guide to Predicting, Avoiding & Dealing with Bankruptcy,* John Wiley & Son, New York, 1983.

———, and Sametz, A.W., *Financial Crises, Institutions and Markets in a Fragile Environment,* Wiley-Interscience, New York, 1977.

———, Avery R., Eisenbeis R., & Sinkey J., *An Analysis of Classification Techniques in Business, Banking & Finance,* JAI Press, Greenwich, CT, 1981.

———, and Nammacher, Scott A., *Investing in Junk Bonds: Inside the High Yield Debt Market,* John Wiley & Sons, 1986.

Argenti, John, *Corporate Collapse: The Causes and Symptoms,* McGraw-Hill, London, 1976.

Bibeault, Donald, *Corporate Turnaround,* McGraw-Hill, New York, 1982.

Dimancescu, Dan, *Deferred Future: Corporate World Debt and Bankruptcy,* Ballinger, Cambridge, MA, 1983.

Newton, Grant W., *Bankruptcy and Insolvency Accounting,* 2nd ed., John Wiley, New York, 1981.

Sinkey, Joseph, *Problems and Failed Institutions in the Commercial Banking Industry,* JAI Press, Greenwich, CT, 1979.

Stanley, David, and Girth, Marjorie, *Bankruptcy: Problem, Process of Reform,* Brookings Institution, Washington, D.C., 1971.

PERIODICALS AND OCCASIONAL PAPERS

Administrative Office of the U.S. Courts, Bankruptcy Division, *Annual Reports,* Washington, D.C.

American Institute of Certified Public Accountants, Exposure Draft, ''The Auditor's Considerations When A Question Arises About An Entity's Continued Existence,'' AICPA Accounting Standards Board, New York, March 24, 1980.

Bankruptcy Reform Act of 1978, *Bankruptcy Law Reports,* No. 389, October 26, 1978, Part II, *Commerce Clearing House,* Chicago.

Bankruptcy Tax Bill of 1980 (H.R. 5043), Commerce Clearing House, Chicago.

Business Week, "The Economic Case Against Government Bailouts," March 24, 1980, pp. 104–107.

Chapter 11 *Reporter,* Business Laws, Inc., Chesterfield, OH, monthly.

Collier on Bankruptcy, 15th ed., 1980, Matthew Bender, New York, annual.

Dun & Bradstreet, *The Failure Record,* D&B, New York, annual.

———, Record of Business Closings, monthly.

———, *News From D&B, Monthly Business Failure Record,* D&B, New York, monthly.

———, The D&B Record of Business Closings, monthly and weekly.

Federal Reserve bank of Atlanta, "Warning Lights For Bond Soundness," November 1983.

Green, B., "What Big Teeth You Have, Grandma," *Forbes,* February 4, 1980.

Herzog, Asa, and King, Lawrence, P., *Bankruptcy Code: With Legislative History and Explanatory Comment on Bankruptcy Reform Act, 1978,* 1979 Collier pamphlet ed., Matthew Bender, New York, 1979.

National Bankruptcy Reporter, Andrews Communications, Edgemont, PA.

"New Rules About Bankruptcy," *Changing Times,* May 1979.

Security and Exchange Commission, *Corporate Reorganizations Releases,* Chapter X cases, periodic, SEC, Washington, D.C.

Zeta Services, Inc., Credit Evaluation Reports, monthly update, (Hoboken N.J.).

Journal Articles: Failure Prediction Studies

Altman, Edward I., "Financial Ratios, Discriminant Analysis and the Prediction of Corporate Bankruptcy," *Journal of Finance,* September 1968, pp. 589–609.

———, "Corporate Bankruptcy Prediction and Its Implications for Commercial Loan Evaluation," *Journal of Commercial Bank Lending,* December 1970, pp. 8–22.

———, "Predicting Railroad Bankruptcies in America," *Bell Journal of Economics and Management Science,* Vol. 4, No. 1, Spring 1973, pp. 184–211.

———, "The Z-Score Bankruptcy Model: Past, Present, and Future," in *Financial Crises* (E.I. Altman and A.W. Sametz, Eds.), Wiley-Interscience, New York, 1977, pp. 89–139.

———, "Predicting Performance in the Savings and Loan Association Industry," *Journal of Monetary Economics,* October 1977, pp. 443–466.

———, "Company & Country Risk Models: An International Examination," *Journal of Banking & Finance,* special issue, June 1984.

———, Haldeman, R.G., and Narayanan, P., "Zeta Analysis: A New Model to Identify Bankruptcy Risk of Corporations," *Journal of Banking and Finance,* June 1977, pp. 29–54.

Beaver, W.H., "Financial Ratios as Predictors of Failure," *Empirical Research in Accounting: Selected Studies 1966,* January 1967, pp. 71–111.

———, "Alternative Accounting Measures as Predictors of Failure," *Accounting Review,* January 1968, pp. 113–122.

————, "Market Prices, Financial Ratios, and the Prediction of Failure," *Journal of Accounting Research*, Autumn 1968, pp. 179–192.

Blum, M., "Discussion: The Z-Score Bankruptcy Model," in *Financial Crises* (E.I. Altman and A.W. Sametz, Eds.), Wiley-Interscience, New York, 1977, pp. 120–129.

Deakin, E.B., "A Discriminant Analysis of Predictors of Business Failure," *Journal of Accounting Research*, Spring 1972, pp. 167–179.

————, "Business Failure Prediction: An Empirical Analysis," in *Financial Crises* (E.I. Altman and A.W. Sametz, eds.), Wiley-Interscience, New York, 1977, pp. 62–88.

Edmister, R.O., "An Empirical Test of Financial Rati Analysis for Small Business Failure Prediction," *Journal of Financial and Quantitative Analysis*, March 1972, pp. 1477–1493.

Elam, R., "The Effect of Lease Data on the Predictive Ability of Financial Ratios," *Accounting Review*, January 1975, pp. 25–43.

Frydman, H., Altman, E.I., and Kao, D., "Introducing Recurcive Partitioning Analysis in Financial Classification: The Case of Financial Distress," *Journal of Finance*, March, 1985, pp. 269–291.

"How to Figure Who's Going Bankrupt," *Dun's Review*, October 1975, pp. 63, 64, 107, 108.

Korobow, L., and Stuhr, D.P., and Martin, D., "A Probabalistic Approach to Early Warning of Changes in Bank Financial Condition," *Monthly Review*, Federal Reserve Bank of New York, July 1976, pp. 187–194.

Martin, D., "Early Warning of Bank Failure: A Logit Regression Approach," *Journal of Banking and Finance*, November 1979, pp. 249–276.

Meyer, P.A., and Pifer, H.W., "Prediction of Bank Failures," *Journal of Finance*, September 1970, pp. 853–868.

Mullin, R.A., "The National Bank Surveillance System," in *Financial Crises* (E.I. Altman and A.W. Sametz, Eds.), Wiley-Interscience, New York, 1977, pp. 49–55.

Sinkey, Joseph, "Problem and Failed Banks, Bank Examinations, and Warning Systems: A Summary," in *Financial Crises* (E.I. Altman and A.W. Sametz, Eds.), Wiley-Interscience, New York, 1977, pp. 24–47.

————, "The Collapse of Franklin National Bank of New York," *Journal of Bank Research*, Summer 1977, pp. 113–122.

————, "A Multivariate Statistical Analysis of the Characteristics of Problem Banks," *Journal of Finance*, March 1975, pp. 21–36.

Stuhr, D.P. and Van Wicklen, R., "Rating the Financial Condition of Banks: A Statistical Approach to Bank Supervision," *Monthly Review*, Federal Reserve Bank of New York, September 1974, pp. 233–238.

Wilcox, J.W., "A Gambler's Ruin Prediction of Business Failure Using Accounting Data," *Sloan Management Review*, Spring 1971, pp. 1–10.

————, "A Prediction of Business Failure Using Accounting Data," *Journal of Accounting Research* (Supplement), October 1973, pp. 163–171.

————, "The Gambler's Ruin Approach to Business Risk," *Sloan Management Review*, Fall 1976, pp. 33–46.

Journal Articles: Other

Altman, Edward I., "Corporate Bankruptcy Potential, Stockholder Returns and Share Valuation," *Journal of Finance*, December 1969, pp. 886–900.

———, "Bankruptcy Identification: Virtue or Necessity?" *Journal of Portfolio Management*, Spring 1977, pp. 63–67.

———, "A Further Empirical Investigation of the Bankruptcy Cost Question," *Journal of Finance*, September 1984, pp. 1067–1094.

———, "Accounting Implications of Failure Prediction Models," *Journal of Accounting, Auditing & Finance*, Fall 1982.

———, "New Bankrupt Strategies: International Harvester & Manville Corp.," *Journal of Business Strategy*, Fall 1983.

———, and McGough, T., "Evaluation of a Firm as a Going Concern," *Journal of Accountancy*, December 1974, 50–57.

———, and LaFleur, J., "How To Manage A Financial Turnaround," *Journal of Business Strategy*, Summer 1981, pp. 31–38.

———, and Goodman, L., "An Economic and Statistical Analysis of the Failing Company Doctrine," Salomon Brothers Center, Working Paper No. 196, New York University, 1980.

———, and Nammacher, S., "The Default Rate Experience on High Yield Debt," Morgan Stanley & Co., Incorporated, Fixed Income Research, March 1985.

Blum, Marc, "Failing Company Discriminant Analysis," *Journal of Accounting Research*, Spring 1974.

Clark, T. and Weinstein, M., "The Behavior of the Common Stock of Bankrupt Firms," *Journal of Finance*, May 1983, pp. 489–504.

Committee on Corporate Laws, "Changes in the Model Business Corporation Act–Amendments to Financial Provisions," *Business Lawyer*, Vol. 34, July 1979, pp. 1867–1881.

Duberstein, Conrad, "A Broad View of the New Bankruptcy Code," Reprint from *Brooklyn Barrister*, April 1979, pp. 1–19.

Fridson, Martin, "How Much Value in Asset Values," *High Performance*, Morgan-Stanley & Co., Incorporated, February and April, 1985.

Langbein, J., and Posner, R., "Market Funds and Trust Investment Law," *American Bar Foundation Research Journal*, December 1975.

Seligson, Charles, "Major Problems for Considerations by the Commission on Bankruptcy Laws of the United States," *American Bankruptcy Law Journal*, Winter 1977, pp. 73–112.

Walter, James, "Determination of Technical Insolvency," *Journal of Business*, January 1957, pp. 30–43.

Warner, Jerold, "Bankruptcy Costs, Some Empirical Evidence," *Journal of Finance*, May 1977, pp. 337–348.

White, Michelle, "Economics of Bankruptcy: Liquidation & Reorganization," New York University Working Paper, 1981.

———, "Bankruptcy Costs and the New Bankruptcy Code," *Journal of Finance*, May 1983, pp. 477–488.

———, "Public Policy Toward Bankruptcy: Me First and other Priority Rules," *Bell Journal of Economics*, Autumn 1980.

APPENDIX A

MATHEMATICS OF FINANCE

CONTENTS

APPENDIX A

MATHEMATICS OF FINANCE

Marti G. Subrahmanyam
With the assistance of William Prado

INTRODUCTION

This appendix presents the concepts and computational methods in **interest rate mathematics**. In order to better illustrate the material, we first compute example problems with the aid of tables. Since most practitioners in the field of finance now use calculators and since microcomputer spreadsheet programs are becoming increasingly popular, we include calculator and spreadsheet solutions as well.

There is a vast array of pocket financial calculators on the market today. They span the broad spectrum from simple calculators that have, in addition to basic function keys, a few financial keys to powerful programmable calculators that can handle most financial computations. The calculator solutions that are presented are intended to provide a feel for the use of a pocket calculator, rather than an exhaustive listing of programs for a wide variety of models. Thus, solutions are restricted to the Hewlett-Packard 12C.

Spreadsheets appear on the computer screen as a series of rows and columns. They automatically calculate and total rows, columns, and cells. Any changes, additions, or deletions to existing data can be instantly recalculated. As with calculators, there are many spreadsheet programs available. They vary in power, speed, and in the number of "built-in" financial functions (these make problem-solving easier). Generally, however, built-in functions handle only simple computations; one must write-in equations to solve financial problems of any complexity. Until software developers create more sophisticated built-in functions, we suggest you use built-ins whenever possible and, when these are not enough, that you conult the writer's manual and/or after-market publications (e.g., *1-2-3 for Business*—Lotus product) for spreadsheet approaches. Solutions that appear are for the Lotus 1-2-3.

INTEREST RATE MATHEMATICS

DEFINITIONS. Interest is ordinarily defined as consideration paid for the use of money. To the borrower it represents the cost of the loan, to the lender it is a source of income. The amount of interest depends on three factors: principal, rate, time.

Principal. The principal is any sum of money on which interest is to be computed. It may represent invested capital, as in the instance of partnership equities, or a loan in the form of notes or more formal bond indentures.

Rate. The interest rate is usually expressed as a percentage of the principal per unit of time; for example, 14% per annum, 7% semiannually.

Time. The time refers to the period for which interest is to be calculated. Unless otherwise stated, interest formulas use the year as a unit.

BASIC TYPES OF INTEREST. There are two basic types of interest, simple and compound. These may be represented as follows:

1. Simple interest.
   a. Ordinary.
   b. Exact—commercial practice.
   c. Exact—government securities.
2. Compound.

Simple interest refers to interest that is always computed on the original principal. If the interest is not paid when due, it is not added to the principal. Thus the amount of interest is always proportional to the time.

Ordinary interest represents a type of simple interest computed on a 360-day year, commonly referred to as the **commercial year**. Under this method the year is divided into 12 months of 30 days each. Although the method is used in many commercial transactions, modifications are often introduced. For example, in discounting commercial paper, ordinary interest is calculated, but it is based on the exact number of days in the discount period.

Exact interest is interest based on a 365-day year, or 366 days in leap years. It is generally employed by banks in allowing interest on daily balances, and also in governmental calculations other than interest on government securities. In the latter instance special tables are available from which the accrued interest may be read.

Compound interest is discussed below.

Ordinary Interest. Ordinary interest is the product of the principal, the rate, and the time:

where:

$$I = Pit$$

I = amount of interest
P = principal
i = rate
t = time (years)

For example, to find the ordinary interest on $12,148.72 for 153 days at 14% (per year), the formula yields:

$$12{,}148.72 \times \frac{14}{100} \times \frac{153}{360} = \$722.85$$

Exact Interest

Nature of Exact Interest. A given amount of principal earns in 365 days as much exact interest as the same principal earns in 360 days at ordinary interest. For 360 days therefore the exact interest is only 360/365 of the amount of ordinary interest. For practical purposes it is easier to compute ordinary interest first and then to adjust the result to get exact interest. Since 360/365 = 72/73, it is evident that exact interest is 72/73 of ordinary interest; therefore to calculate exact interest, figure ordinary interest and subtract 1/73.

Example. Municipal taxes in the town of X are due November 1 and may be paid without penalty up to and including November 30. Thereafter an interest penalty is charged at 7% per annum from the first due date. (November 1). For a tax bill of $4,850, find the total paid to the town, if payment is made on December 11 of the same year.

Solution. Elapsed time November 1–December 11, 40 days.

7% ordinary interest	$ 37.722
Less 1/73	0.517
Exact interest, 7%	$ 37.21
Amount of bill	4,850.00
Total paid	$4,887.21

Interest on U.S. Government Securities. Interest on bonds or notes issued by the U.S. government is computed on the basis of exact interest for the exact number of days falling within the interest period. Exhibit 1 shows that the length of an interest period may vary from 181 days to 184 days. The daily accrual of interest may be computed as follows. First determine the number

EXHIBIT 1   EXACT NUMBER OF DAYS IN
6-MONTH INTEREST PERIOD

Ending Dates	Ordinary Year	Leap Year
January 1 or 15	184	184
February 1 or 15	184	184
March 1 or 15	181	182
April 1 or 15	182	183
May 1 or 15	181	182
June 1 or 15	182	183
July 1 or 15	181	182
August 1 or 15	181	182
September 1 or 15	184	184
October 1 or 15	183	183
November 1 or 15	184	184
December 1 or 15	183	183

of days in the interest period. Then, compute the accrual after adjusting for the number of days and the principal amount.

Anticipation. This is a customary term used in connection with purchase invoices that have extra dating where interest is allowed if payment is made before the expiration of the final due date of the invoice. The effect of the extra dating is to extend the time within which a proffered **cash discount** may be taken. Thus, if merchandise is purchased at 2%, 10 days, 90 days extra, with anticipation at 6%, a discount of 2% is allowed for payment any time within 100 days. In addition, the purchaser may deduct interest for the number of days before the final due date. The exact procedure is first to find the amount payable on the last day of the discount period. From this amount is deducted **exact interest** at the stipulated anticipation rate for the number of days anticipated.

Example. An invoice is dated April 12, 1987, for $5,653.75, terms 2%, 10 days, 60 days extra, f.o.b. destination, anticipation at 6%. The purchaser paid $45.60 freight. What was the amount due if payment was made on May 22, 1987?

The number of days from April 12 to May 22 is 40. Hence payment is anticipated 30 days. The calculation appears as follows:

Invoice	$5,653.75
Less: Freight paid	45.60
Net invoice	$5,608.15
Less: 2% discount	112.16
Balance subject to anticipation	$5,495.99
Anticipation for 30 days at 6% per annum (exact)	27.10
Amount payable on May 22, 1987	$5,468.89

It is the custom of some stores to compute the discount on the face of the invoice and the anticipation on the net amount after deducting the discount, finally deducting the freight charges. This plan, which favors the purchaser, is illustrated below:

Invoice	$5,653.75
Less: 2% discount	113.08
Balance	$5,540.67
Anticipation for 30 days at 6% per annum	27.33
Balance	$5,513.34
Less: Freight paid	45.60
Amount of check	$5,467.74

Extra dating is sometimes secured by stores as a result of certain trade customs. Invoices are frequently dated, say, 2%, 10 days, e.o.m. (end of month). This means that if an invoice is dated June 17, it is due 10 days after the end of June (i.e., July 10). Both discount and anticipation would then be allowed if payment is made before July 10.

Again, purchase orders sometimes contain conditional clauses in which "the seller agrees that merchandise shipped on or after the twenty-fifth of a month, will be billed as of the first of the following month." Thus, merchandise shipped on April 26, terms 2%, 10 days, is billed as of May 1, with discount and anticipation available until May 10. Ordinarily the anticipation may not amount to much because of the short time. However, if the above-quoted clause is coupled with e.o.m. dating, the effect is to secure an extra month's dating. In short, if goods are shipped on April 26, terms 2%, 10 days, e.o.m., and the purchase order contains the billing clause above, the invoice becomes due on June 10, that is, 10 days after the first of the month in which the invoice would otherwise fall due.

BANK DISCOUNT

Loans and Discounts. One of the important functions of a commercial bank is the making of loans, which produce a source of income for the bank and fulfill a necessary function in the economic life of the community served by the bank. Technically **loans** are distinguished from **discounts** chiefly by the fact that in the case of loans, interest is paid periodically, during the existence of the loan or at its maturity, whereas in the case of discounts the interest or "discount" is deducted at the time the advance is made. Thus, in the case of a $1,000 loan at 8% for 6 months, the borrower receives $1,000 and pays back $1,040 at the end of 6 months. On the other hand, if he discounts a $1,000 note at 6%, he receives $970.87 and pays back $1,000 at the end of the 6-month term. In short, bank discount is the consideration deducted by the bank from the face of a note or draft prior to its maturity date.

Since the 1930s, finance companies and banks have been making **long-term loans,** especially in the field of **home financing**. These loans are usually amortized, principal and interest, through equal monthly payments. They are dealt with later in this Section in connection with annuities.

Types of Note. Notes may be variously classified, but for computation purposes it is necessary only to know whether a note is **interest bearing** (see, e.g., Exhibit 2) or **noninterest bearing** (Exhibit 3).

In discounting a note, the bank pays only what the note is worth at the time of discount. Thus, a **noninterest-bearing note** is worth its face value at maturity and not before. Any time before maturity the note is valued at less than face value by the amount of interest the bank charges. An **interest-bearing note,** however, provided the interest and discount rates are the same, is worth approximately its face value on the date of issue and thereafter increases in value each day by the amount of interest earned until maturity.

The amount that a bank pays for a note or that it credits to a borrower's account is called the **proceeds** of the note.

Basis for Calculating Proceeds. Ordinarily, banks use the actual number of days in figuring the discount period on short-term notes, but interest or discount is computed on the basis of a 360-day year (ordinary interest). In the case of the Federal Reserve System, **exact interest** is used.

Due Date of Notes. Promissory notes are payable at a stated number of days or months after date. **Drafts** may be payable so many days **after date** or **after sight**. If days are specified, the exact number of days is counted. Thus, if the note states "60 days after date . . ." and is dated May 14, it is due July 13. However, when months are specified, the note falls due in the month of

EXHIBIT 2   INTEREST-BEARING PROMISSORY NOTE

$ 3,400 00/100   New York April 2 19–

    Two (2) months   AFTER DATE   I   PROMISE TO PAY TO

THE ORDER OF   Barrows & Co.

Thirty-four hundred and 00/100   ∿∿∿∿∿∿∿∿∿∿∿∿∿∿∿∿∿∿∿   DOLLARS

AT   Irving Trust Co. with interest @ 15%

VALUE RECEIVED
No.   1   DUE   June 2 19–   J. Doe

EXHIBIT 3   NONINTEREST-BEARING PROMISSORY NOTE

```
$ 500 00/100                                    New York May 15 19–

      Twenty (20) days          AFTER DATE  I  PROMISE TO PAY TO

THE ORDER OF                         J. Doe

Five hundred and 00/100  ~~~~~~~~~~~~~~~~~~~~~~~~~~~~~~  DOLLARS

AT                          Irving Trust Co.

VALUE RECEIVED
No.    273                                        R. Roe
```

maturity on the same date as is specified in the date of the note. For example, a note dated May 14 due in 2 months is due on July 14.

If a note is dated on the last day of a 31-day month, and falls due in a 30-day month, the due date would be the last of the 30-day month. To illustrate, a note dated May 31, due in four months, matures on September 30. But a note dated May 31, due in 120 days, is payable September 28.

Computing Proceeds and Discount on Noninterest-Bearing Paper. Three steps are necessary to calculate the proceeds or deposit credit:

1. Calculate the time from the discount date to maturity.
2. Compute the interest to maturity for the time computed in step 1. This is the discount.
3. Deduct the discount from the face value.

Example 1. Find the proceeds or deposit credit on a note for $1,875, dated July 5, for 30 days, discounted at 14% per annum on the date of issue. The note is due August 4, that is, 30 days from July 5.

Face value of note	$1,875.00
Discount, 30 days, 14% on $1,875	− 21.87
Proceeds	$1,853.13

Example 2. Find the proceeds on a note for $2,863.79 dated February 8, 1986, due in 60 days, discounted on March 2 at 14 1/2% per annum. The maturity date is April 9, 1986, and the time to maturity (March 2 to April 9) 38 days.

Face value	$2,863.79
Discount on above for 38 days at 14 1/2%	− 43.83
Proceeds	$2,819.96

Discounting Interest-Bearing Paper. The general rule in discounting interest-bearing paper is to compute and then discount the maturity value. In calculating the maturity value, the interest from the date of the note to maturity is added to the face value. Next the discount is computed for the discount period and deducted from the maturity value.

Example. Find the proceeds of a 5% note for $5,350, dated August 12, 1988, due in 3 months, and discounted on September 27, 1988, at 4%.

Maturity value	
Face value	$5,350.00
Interest August 12 to November 12	205.08
(92 days on $5,350 at 15%)	
Maturity value	$5,555.08
Discount from September 27 to	
November 12 (46 days, 14%)	− 99.37
Proceeds	$5,455.72

Finding Principal to Yield Given Proceeds. Occasionally it becomes necessary to reverse the process above; that is, a debtor wishes to borrow enough so that the proceeds will exactly cover the net amount of an invoice that is to be paid. Thus the face value of the note is unknown. If the note is **noninterest bearing,** the face value to yield the given proceeds is found by dividing the given proceeds by the proceeds of $1. The expression "proceeds of one dollar" means one dollar minus the interest or discount on $1.

Example. A merchant arranges to pay for a shipment by borrowing the exact amount required to pay the invoice. The net amount of the invoice is $5,960.34 and the bank agrees to discount the merchant's note at 4% for 120 days.

Proceeds of $1 for 120 days at 4% = $1 − $0.01 1/3 = $0.98 2/3

$$\frac{\text{given proceeds}}{\text{proceeds of \$1}} = \frac{\$5,960.34}{.98\ 2/3} = \frac{\$17,881.02}{2.96} = \$6,040,89$$

Face value	$6,040.89
Interest for 120 days at 4%	80.55
Proceeds	$5,960.34

Computation of Interest Under Partial Payment Plans. When a short-term indebtedness is reduced through periodic payments, the interest is computed upon either one of two bases. The basis used commonly in business is known as the **"merchant's rule."** This method gives the results more quickly but not as accurately as the computation under the other, the **"United States rule."**

Merchant's Rule. In following the merchant's rule, the interest is computed on the total indebtedness from the date of inception to the date of maturity, and from this total is deducted the interest earned from the date that each partial payment is made to the date of maturity of the debt.

Example. The following payments were made on a $16,500, 6% note, dated June 22, 1986, due in 6 months:

October 20, 1986	$ 300
November 15, 1986	3,500

What is the amount due at maturity?

Solution

June 22	Face value		$16,500.00
December 22	Interest at 6% on above, June 22 to December 22 = 183 days		503.25
	Maturity value of note		$17,003.25
October 20	First payment	$ 300.00	
	Interest on above October 20 to December 22 = 37 days	3.15	
November 15	Second payment	3,500.00	
	Interest on above November 15 to December 22 = 37 days	21.58	
	Total credits		3,824.73
December 22	Maturity: balance due		$13,178.52

United States Rule. Under the United States rule, each installment is first applied against the interst due at the date the partial payment is made, and the balance of the installment is then applied to reduce the principal. Interest is always computed on the reduced principal. In the event that a partial payment is insufficient to cover the accrued interest, it is held in suspense. There is no reduction of principal until the suspended payment together with subsequent payments exceeds the accrued interest. Using the same figures as in the example for the merchant's rule, the solution appears as follows:

June 22	Face value		$16,500.00
October 20	First payment	$ 300.00	
	Interest on $16,500 for		
	120 days (June 22 to		
	October 20)	330.00	
	Reduction of principal		—0—
November 15	Second payment	$3,500.00	
	Add first payment	300.00	
	Total	$3,800.00	
	Interest on $16,500 for		
	146 days (June 22 to		
	November 15)	401.50	
	Reduction of principal		3,398.50
	Balance due		$13,101.50
December 22	Maturity		
	Interest on $13,101.50 for		
	37 days (November 15 to		
	December 22)		80.79
	Balance due		$13,182.29

Bank Discount Versus True Discount. In a discounting operation, the interest charge, as in the case of noninterest-bearing notes, is taken out in advance. Thus the borrower receives the maturity value minus the discount. He is paying interest calculated on the maturity value for the use of a smaller sum, the proceeds. A 60-day note for $1,000, discounted at 18%, yields $970 proceeds. The borrower pays $30 for the use of $970, which is therefore more than 18%. The discount calculated as above is called **bank discount**. So-called true discount is an interest charge based on the **present value** of the note, that is, on a sum that at the discount rate would produce the face value of the note. To find the present value of a note, merely divide the maturity value by the amount of $1 (at the given rate and for the given time). The "amount of $1" means one dollar plus the interest on $1.

Example. Find the proceeds and present value of a note for $5,632.50, dated June 22, 1986, due in 90 days, and discounted at 18% per annum on July 27, 1986. The note is due September 20, 1986.

Proceeds

Maturity value (since this is a	$5,632.50
noninterest-bearing note)	
Discount at 18% for 55 days; (i.e., from	
July 27–September 20)	154.89
Proceeds	$5,477.61

Present Value

Maturity value	$5,632.50
Amount of $1 at 18% per annum for each of 55 days	1.0275
Present value	$5,632.50 ÷ 1.0275 = $5,481.75

In this example, the **bank discount** is $154.89 but the **true discount** is $150.75 ($5,632.50 - $5,481.75).

Relation of Bank Discount Rate to True Discount Rate. Since the bank discount is based on a larger sum than the borrower receives, he evidently pays more than the indicated rate of interest. To discover the true interest rate, it is necessary to express the bank discount as a percentage of the proceeds, assuming the loan ran for 1 year. Actually, the amount is immaterial, since the calculation can be put on a unit dollar basis.

Example. A note for $10,000, due in 12 months, is discounted at 16% per annum. What is the equivalent annual interest charge?

Solution a. Here it is necessary to compute the annual discount:

Maturity value	$10,000.00
Discount 16%, one year	1,600.00
Proceeds	$ 8,400.00

The borrower, in effect, pays $1,600 for the use of $8,400 for a year. Hence the interest rate is

$$\frac{1,600}{8,400} = 0.1905 = 19.05\%$$

Solution b. By putting the calculation on a unit dollar basis a general formula may be derived as follows:

Maturity value	$1.00
Discount	0.16
Proceeds	$0.84

$$\text{Interest rate} = \frac{0.16}{0.4} = 0.1905 = 19.05\%.$$

Let d = discount rate. Then

$$1 - d = \text{proceeds of \$1 due in 1 year}$$
$$r = \text{interest rate}$$

Hence

$$r = \frac{d}{1 - d} \times 100$$

In the problem above substitution in the formula yields;

$$\frac{0.16}{0.84} \times 100 = 19.05\%$$

Thus a discount rate of 16% per annum is equal to an annual interest charge of 19.05% approximately.

CHAIN DISCOUNTS

Definition. Chain discounts are two or more discounts that are applied in succession to a quote price. The latter is usually referred to as the **list price,** that is, the price at which the item is listed in the manufacturer's or jobber's catalog. Each discount is applied to the net amount remaining after the previous discount has been taken. For example, an article quoted at $25 less 30 and 10 means $25 less 30%, and then less 10% on the diminished amount.

List price	$25.00
Less: First discount—30%	7.50
Balance	$17.50
Less: Second discount—10%	1.75
Net price	$15.75

If many chain discounts are involved in connection with a given list price, this method may be cumbersome. An alternative method is to multiply the list price by the net cost factors, that is, the percentage remaining after deducting the chain discount from 100%. Thus, in the example above, the purchaser pays

$$\$25 \times 70\% \times 90\% = 25 \times 0.63 = \$15.75$$

Finding Equivalent Single Discount. It is often convenient to convert chain discounts into equivalent single discounts. To find an equivalent single discount rate equal to two chain discounts, add the discounts and subtract their product.

Examples. Find single discounts equal to chain discount of:

1. 40 and 30.
2. 20 and 20.

3. 15 and 10.

4. 10 and 5.

5. 10 and 5.

1	2	3	4	5
0.40	0.20	0.15	0.20	0.10
+0.30	+0.20	+0.10	+0.05	+0.05
0.70	0.40	0.25	0.25	0.15
−0.12	−0.04	−0.015	−0.01	−0.005
0.58	0.36	0.235	0.24	0.145
58%	36%	23.5%	24%	14.5%

In practice, the decimal points are omitted to speed up the work. Thus problem 5 would be solved: $10 + 5 = 15$, minus $0.5 = 14.5\%$. In fact, these problems can and should be done mentally.

The same rule may be applied to three or more chain discounts, provided only two discounts are taken at a time. The order in which the discounts are taken is immaterial.

COMPOUND INTEREST

Definitions. In compound interest calculations, the interest is computed at the end of each fiscal period and added to the principal at the beginning, the total representing the new principal on the basis of which a new interest calculation is made. Compound interest may therefore be defined as that form of interest in which the interest for each period is added to the principal. Because interest is added to the principal, and interest for the next period is calculated on the new total, interest sometimes is said to be **converted** into principal.

The time for which interest is calculated and converted is known as the **conversion period.** It represents the elapsed time between two successive interest dates. The time—that is, the conversion period—may be a month, or a quarterly, semiannual, or annual period, or any other convenient time period.

The conversion period is sometimes referred to as an **accumulation period** because the principal accumulates—that is, it increases by the amount of interest added to the principal. No such term was necessary in the instance of simple interest, because the interest was not converted but always computed on the original principal. But in compound interest, the interest is computed on an ever-increasing amount, because of the repeated addition to the existing principal.

Finding the Compound Amount. The principle behind the method of compound interest calculations can be illustrated by reference to an example.

Example. Find the compound amount on $1,500 for 3 years at 6% per annum, compounded semiannually (or at 3% per 6 months).

Investment	$1,500.00
Interest 6 months, $1,500 at 3%	45.00
Amount at end of first 6 months	$1,545.00
Interest 6 months, $1,545 at 3%	46.35
Amount at end of second 6 months	$1,591.35
Interest 6 months, $1,591.35 at 3%	47.74
Amount at end of third 6 months	$1,639.09
Interest 6 months, $1,639.09 at 3%	49.17
Amount at end of fourth 6 months	$1,688.26
Interest 6 months, $1,688.26 at 3%	50.65
Amount at end of fifth 6 months	$1,738.91
Interest 6 months, $1,738.91 at 3%	52.17
Compound amount at end of 3 years	$1,791.08

If the principal amount is reduced to say $1, the tabulation above can be restated as follows:

Investment	$1.00
Interest 6 months, $1 at 3% or	0.03
Amount at end of first 6 months	$1.03
Interest 6 months, $1.03 at 3%	0.0309
Amount at end of second 6 months	$1.0609
Interest 6 months, $1,0609 at 3%	0.031827
Amount at end of third 6 months	$1.092727
Interest 6 months, $1.092727 at 3%	0.032782
Amount at end of fourth 6 months	$1.125509
Interest 6 months, $1.125509 at 3%	0.033765
Amount at end of fifth 6 months	$1.159274
Interest 6 months, $1.159274 at 3%	0.034778
Compound amount at end of 3 years	$1.194052

It is obvious therefore that if the rate of interest per period is represented by i, the statement immediately above may be recast as follows:

Compound amount at end of first 6 months	$1.03	$= (1 + i)$
Compound amount at end of second 6 months	1.0609	$= (1 + i)^2$
Compound amount at end of third 6 months	1.092727	$= (1 + i)^3$
Compound amount at end of fourth 6 months	1.125509	$= (1 + i)^4$
Compound amount at end of fifth 6 months	1.159274	$= (1 + i)^5$
Compound amount at end of sixth 6 months	1.194052	$= (1 + i)^6$

Thus the compound amount of $1,500 for 3 years at 6%, converted semiannually, is

$$\$1,500 \times 1.194052 = \underline{\$1,791.08}$$

The difference between the compound amount and the original principal is the compound interest.

Compound amount, end of 3 years	$1,791.08
Principal at beginning	1,500.00
Compound interest	$ 291.08

Similarly for n periods the compound amount for $1 is $FVIF_{i,n} = (1 + i)^n$. In this formula

$$FVIF_{i,n} = \text{compound amount of } \$1$$
$$i = \text{interest rate}$$
$$n = \text{number of periods}$$

The compound amount of any given number of dollars can then be found easily by multiplying the principal by the value of $(1 + i)^n$. In general terms,

$$A = P(1 + i)^n = P \times FVIF_{i,n}$$

where: A = compound amount
          P = principal (i.e., initial investment)

Computing Compound Value Using Tables. The arithmetical method for finding the compound amount is obviously too cumbersome. The formula may be solved either through the use of prepared tables or by use of a calculator. Exhibit 4 gives the compound amount of $1 for periods from 1 to 60 for various interest rates. The use of the table is illustrated below.

Example. Find the compound amount of $2,634.56 for 12 years at 5% annually.

$$A = P \times (1 + i)^n$$
$$= \$2,634.56 \times 1.05^{12}$$

Locate the 5% column in Exhibit 4, run down the column to the twelfth period. The figure on that line represents the compound amount of $1 for 12 years at 5%; in short, 1.05^{12}. Hence,

$$A = \$2,634.56 \times 1.7959$$
$$= \underline{\$4,731.41}$$

EXHIBIT 4 FUTURE VALUE OF $1 AT THE END OF n PERIODS $FVIF_{i,n} = (1 + i)^n$

Period	1%	2%	3%	4%	5%	6%	7%	8%	9%	10%	12%	14%	15%	16%	18%	20%	24%	28%	32%	36%
1	1.0100	1.0200	1.0300	1.0400	1.0500	1.0600	1.0700	1.0800	1.0900	1.1000	1.1200	1.1400	1.1500	1.1600	1.1800	1.2000	1.2400	1.2800	1.3200	1.3600
2	1.0201	1.0404	1.0609	1.0816	1.1025	1.1236	1.1449	1.1664	1.1881	1.2100	1.2544	1.2996	1.3225	1.3456	1.3924	1.4400	1.5376	1.6384	1.7424	1.8496
3	1.0303	1.0612	1.0927	1.1249	1.1576	1.1910	1.2250	1.2597	1.2950	1.3310	1.4049	1.4815	1.5209	1.5609	1.6430	1.7280	1.9066	2.0972	2.3000	2.5155
4	1.0406	1.0824	1.1255	1.1699	1.2155	1.2625	1.3108	1.3605	1.4116	1.4641	1.5735	1.6890	1.7490	1.8106	1.9388	2.0736	2.3642	2.6844	3.0360	3.4210
5	1.0510	1.1041	1.1593	1.2167	1.2763	1.3382	1.4026	1.4693	1.5386	1.6105	1.7623	1.9254	2.0114	2.1003	2.2878	2.4883	2.9316	3.4360	4.0075	4.6526
6	1.0615	1.1262	1.1941	1.2653	1.3401	1.4185	1.5007	1.5869	1.6771	1.7716	1.9738	2.1950	2.3131	2.4364	2.6996	2.9860	3.6352	4.3980	5.2899	6.3275
7	1.0721	1.1487	1.2299	1.3159	1.4071	1.5036	1.6058	1.7138	1.8280	1.9487	2.2107	2.5023	2.6600	2.8262	3.1855	3.5832	4.5077	5.6295	6.9826	8.6054
8	1.0829	1.1717	1.2668	1.3686	1.4775	1.5938	1.7182	1.8509	1.9926	2.1436	2.4760	2.8526	3.0590	3.2784	3.7589	4.2998	5.5895	7.2058	9.2170	11.703
9	1.0937	1.1951	1.3048	1.4233	1.5513	1.6895	1.8385	1.9990	2.1719	2.3579	2.7731	3.2519	3.5179	3.8030	4.4355	5.1598	6.9310	9.2234	12.166	15.916
10	1.1046	1.2190	1.3439	1.4802	1.6289	1.7903	1.9672	2.1589	2.3674	2.5937	3.1058	3.7072	4.0456	4.4114	5.2338	6.1917	8.5944	11.805	16.059	21.646
11	1.1157	1.2434	1.3842	1.5395	1.7103	1.8983	2.1049	2.3316	2.5804	2.8531	3.4785	4.2262	4.6524	5.1173	6.1759	7.4301	10.657	15.111	21.198	29.439
12	1.1268	1.2682	1.4258	1.6010	1.7959	2.0122	2.2522	2.5182	2.8127	3.1384	3.8960	4.8179	5.3502	5.9360	7.2876	8.9161	13.214	19.342	27.982	40.037
13	1.1381	1.2936	1.4685	1.6651	1.8856	2.1329	2.4098	2.7196	3.0658	3.4523	4.3635	5.4924	6.1528	6.8858	8.5994	10.699	16.386	24.758	36.937	54.451
14	1.1495	1.3195	1.5126	1.7317	1.9799	2.2609	2.5785	2.9372	3.3417	3.7975	4.8871	6.2613	7.0757	7.9875	10.147	12.839	20.319	31.691	48.756	74.053
15	1.1610	1.3459	1.5580	1.8009	2.0789	2.3966	2.7590	3.1722	3.6425	4.1772	5.4736	7.1379	8.1371	9.2655	11.973	15.407	25.195	40.564	64.358	100.71
16	1.1726	1.3728	1.6047	1.8730	2.1829	2.5404	2.9522	3.4259	3.9703	4.5950	6.1304	8.1372	9.3576	10.748	14.129	18.488	31.242	51.923	84.953	136.96
17	1.1843	1.4002	1.6528	1.9479	2.2920	2.6928	3.1588	3.7000	4.3276	5.0545	6.8660	9.2765	10.761	12.467	16.672	22.186	38.740	66.461	112.13	186.27
18	1.1961	1.4282	1.7024	2.0258	2.4066	2.8543	3.3799	3.9960	4.7171	5.5599	7.6900	10.575	12.375	14.462	19.673	26.623	48.038	85.070	148.02	253.33
19	1.2081	1.4568	1.7535	2.1068	2.5270	3.0256	3.6165	4.3157	5.1417	6.1159	8.6128	12.055	14.231	16.776	23.214	31.948	59.567	108.89	195.39	344.53
20	1.2202	1.4859	1.8061	2.1911	2.6533	3.2071	3.8697	4.6610	5.6044	6.7275	9.6463	13.743	16.366	19.460	27.393	38.337	73.864	139.37	257.91	468.57
21	1.2324	1.5157	1.8603	2.2788	2.7860	3.3996	4.1406	5.0338	6.1088	7.4002	10.803	15.667	18.821	22.574	32.323	46.005	91.591	178.40	340.44	637.26
22	1.2447	1.5460	1.9161	2.3699	2.9253	3.6035	4.4304	5.4365	6.6586	8.1403	12.100	17.861	21.644	26.186	38.142	55.206	113.57	228.35	449.39	866.67
23	1.2572	1.5769	1.9736	2.4647	3.0715	3.8197	4.7405	5.8715	7.2579	8.9543	13.552	20.361	24.891	30.376	45.007	66.247	140.83	292.30	593.19	1178.6
24	1.2697	1.6084	2.0328	2.5633	3.2251	4.0489	5.0724	6.3412	7.9111	9.8497	15.178	23.212	28.625	35.236	53.108	79.496	174.63	374.14	783.02	1802.9
25	1.2824	1.6406	2.0938	2.6658	3.3864	4.2919	5.4274	6.8485	8.6231	10.834	17.000	26.461	32.918	40.874	62.668	95.396	216.54	478.90	1033.5	2180.0
26	1.2953	1.6734	2.1566	2.7725	3.5557	4.5494	5.8074	7.3964	9.3992	11.918	19.040	30.166	37.856	47.414	73.948	114.47	268.51	612.99	1364.3	2964.9
27	1.3082	1.7069	2.2213	2.8834	3.7335	4.8223	6.2139	7.9881	10.245	13.110	21.324	34.389	43.535	55.000	87.259	137.37	332.95	784.63	1800.9	4032.2
28	1.3213	1.7410	2.2879	2.9987	3.9201	5.1117	6.6488	8.6271	11.167	14.421	23.883	39.204	50.065	63.800	102.96	164.84	412.86	1004.3	2377.2	5488.8
29	1.3345	1.7758	2.3566	3.1187	4.1161	5.4184	7.1143	9.3173	12.172	15.863	26.749	44.693	57.575	74.008	121.50	197.81	511.95	1285.5	3137.9	7458.0
30	1.3478	1.8114	2.4273	3.2434	4.3219	5.7435	7.6123	10.062	13.267	17.449	29.959	50.950	66.211	85.849	143.37	237.37	634.81	1645.5	4142.0	10143.
40	1.4889	2.2080	3.2620	4.8010	7.0400	10.285	14.974	21.724	31.409	45.259	93.050	188.88	267.86	378.72	750.37	1469.7	5455.9	19426.	66520.	—^a
50	1.6446	2.6916	4.3839	7.1067	11.467	18.420	29.457	46.901	74.357	117.39	289.00	700.23	1083.6	1670.7	3927.3	9100.4	46890.	—^a	—^a	—^a
60	1.8167	3.2810	5.8916	10.519	18.679	32.987	57.946	101.25	176.03	304.48	897.59	2595.9	4383.9	7370.1	20555.	56347.	—^a	—^a	—^a	—^a

^a $FVIF > 99999$.

Computing Compound Value Using a Financial Calculator. The calculator is very accurate and can handle larger ranges of both interest rates and number of time periods. For the example just discussed, the keystrokes are:

Keystroke	Display	Comment
f FIN	0.00	Clear
f REG	0.00	Clear
2634.56	2,634.56	Principal

Keystroke	Display	Comment
PV	2,634.56	—
5	5	—
i	5.00	Interest rate
12	12	—
n	12.00	Number of periods
FV	− 4,731.29	—
CHS	4,731.29	Compound amount

Computing Compound Value Using a Microcomputer Spreadsheet. Spreadsheet solutions are presented in three columns. The first column gives the cell reference; the second column presents the cell's content; the third column is reserved for explanations. Illustrations of what the screen should look like immediately follow instructions

Cell Address	Cell Content	Explanation
A1	'Principal	Label
C1	2634.56	Principal
A2	'Interest	Label
C2	0.05	Interest
A3	'# of Periods	Label
C3	12	Number of Periods
A4	'Compound Value	Label
C4	@Round (C1*(1+C2)^C3,2)	Compound Value Equation

Illustration

		A	B	C	D
	1	Principal		2634.56	
	2	Interest		0.05	
	3	# of Periods		12	
	4	Compound Value		4731.29	
	5				
	6				

where A = given sum (i.e., the compound amount, the end value after n conversion periods)

P = present value (the initial investment)

PRESENT VALUE. The general formula $A = P(1 + i)^n$ may be used to find any of the variables contained in it. The most common converse case is finding the present value [P]. This is the value at the present moment of money due at a future time. It is the reciprocal of the compound amount, and may also be defined as that sum of money that, when placed at compound interest for the full number of periods involved, will amount to the given sum.

Example. $1,500 at compound interest for six periods at 3% per period will amount to $1,791.08. Hence the present worth of $1,791.08 due six periods hence at 3% per period compounded is $1,500.

The formula for the present value of $1 is:

$$PVIF_{i,n} = \frac{1}{(1 + i)^n}$$

where $PVIF_{i,n}$ = present value of $1
i = interest rate
n = number of periods

The formula for the present value of any number of dollars (A) is:

$$P = A \frac{1}{(1 + i)^n}$$

that is,

$$A \times PVIF_{i,n}$$

This formula is used whenever prepared present value tables are available. When, because of table limitations, direct calculation must be used, the formula is more convenient for computation when written in the form

$$P = \frac{A}{(1 + i)^n}$$

Computing Present Value Using Tables. Exhibit 5 shows the present value of $1 for a number of interest rates from 1 to 60 periods. The use of the table is illustrated below.

Example. Find the present value of $6,975 received 5 years from now at 10% per annum. Locate the 10% column in Exhibit 5 and run down the column

EXHIBIT 5 PRESENT VALUE OF $1

$$PVIF = 1/(1 + i)^n$$

Period	1%	2%	3%	4%	5%	6%	7%	8%	9%	10%	12%	14%	15%	16%	18%	20%	24%	28%	32%	36%
1	.9901	.9804	.9709	.9615	.9524	.9434	.9346	.9259	.9174	.9091	.8929	.8772	.8696	.8621	.8475	.8333	.8065	.7813	.7576	.7353
2	.9803	.9612	.9426	.9246	.9070	.8900	.8734	.8573	.8417	.8264	.7972	.7695	.7561	.7432	.7182	.6944	.6504	.6104	.5739	.5407
3	.9706	.9423	.9151	.8890	.8638	.8396	.8163	.7938	.7722	.7513	.7118	.6750	.6575	.6407	.6086	.5787	.5245	.4768	.4348	.3975
4	.9610	.9238	.8885	.8548	.8227	.7921	.7629	.7350	.7084	.6830	.6355	.5921	.5718	.5523	.5158	.4823	.4230	.3725	.3294	.2923
5	.9515	.9057	.8626	.8219	.7835	.7473	.7130	.6806	.6499	.6209	.5674	.5194	.4972	.4761	.4371	.4019	.3411	.2910	.2495	.2149
6	.9420	.8880	.8375	.7903	.7462	.7050	.6663	.6302	.5963	.5645	.5066	.4556	.4323	.4104	.3704	.3349	.2751	.2274	.1890	.1580
7	.9327	.8706	.8131	.7599	.7107	.6651	.6227	.5835	.5470	.5132	.4523	.3996	.3759	.3538	.3139	.2791	.2218	.1776	.1432	.1162
8	.9235	.8535	.7894	.7307	.6768	.6274	.5820	.5403	.5019	.4665	.4039	.3506	.3269	.3050	.2660	.2326	.1789	.1388	.1085	.0854
9	.9143	.8368	.7664	.7026	.6446	.5919	.5439	.5002	.4604	.4241	.3606	.3075	.2843	.2630	.2255	.1938	.1443	.1084	.0822	.0628
10	.9053	.8203	.7441	.6756	.6139	.5584	.5083	.4632	.4224	.3855	.3220	.2697	.2472	.2267	.1911	.1615	.1164	.0847	.0623	.0462
11	.8963	.8043	.7224	.6496	.5847	.5268	.4751	.4289	.3875	.3505	.2875	.2366	.2149	.1954	.1619	.1346	.0938	.0662	.0472	.0340
12	.8874	.7885	.7014	.6246	.5568	.4970	.4440	.3971	.3555	.3186	.2567	.2076	.1869	.1685	.1372	.1122	.0757	.0517	.0357	.0250
13	.8787	.7730	.6810	.6006	.5303	.4688	.4150	.3677	.3262	.2897	.2292	.1821	.1625	.1452	.1163	.0935	.0610	.0404	.0271	.0184
14	.8700	.7579	.6611	.5775	.5051	.4423	.3878	.3405	.2992	.2633	.2046	.1597	.1413	.1252	.0985	.0779	.0492	.0316	.0205	.0135
15	.8613	.7430	.6419	.5553	.4810	.4173	.3624	.3152	.2745	.2394	.1827	.1401	.1229	.1079	.0835	.0649	.0397	.0247	.0155	.0099
16	.8528	.7284	.6232	.5339	.4581	.3936	.3387	.2919	.2519	.2176	.1631	.1229	.1069	.0930	.0708	.0541	.0320	.0193	.0118	.0073
17	.8444	.7142	.6050	.5134	.4363	.3714	.3166	.2703	.2311	.1978	.1456	.1078	.0929	.0802	.0600	.0451	.0258	.0150	.0089	.0054
18	.8360	.7002	.5874	.4936	.4155	.3503	.2959	.2502	.2120	.1799	.1300	.0946	.0808	.0691	.0508	.0376	.0208	.0118	.0068	.0039
19	.8277	.6864	.5703	.4746	.3957	.3305	.2765	.2317	.1945	.1635	.1161	.0829	.0703	.0596	.0431	.0313	.0168	.0092	.0051	.0029
20	.8195	.6730	.5537	.4564	.3769	.3118	.2584	.2145	.1784	.1486	.1037	.0728	.0611	.0514	.0365	.0261	.0135	.0072	.0039	.0021
25	.7798	.6095	.4776	.3751	.2953	.2330	.1842	.1460	.1160	.0923	.0588	.0378	.0304	.0245	.0160	.0105	.0046	.0021	.0010	.0005
30	.7419	.5521	.4120	.3083	.2314	.1741	.1314	.0994	.0754	.0573	.0334	.0196	.0151	.0116	.0070	.0042	.0016	.0006	.0002	.0001
40	.6717	.4529	.3066	.2083	.1420	.0972	.0668	.0460	.0318	.0221	.0107	.0053	.0037	.0026	.0013	.0007	.0002	.0001	—[a]	—[a]
50	.6080	.3715	.2281	.1407	.0872	.0543	.0339	.0213	.0134	.0085	.0035	.0014	.0009	.0006	.0003	.0001	—[a]	—[a]	—[a]	—[a]
60	.5504	.3048	.1697	.0951	.0535	.0303	.0173	.0099	.0057	.0033	.0011	.0004	.0002	.0001	—[a]	—[c]	—[a]	—[a]	—[a]	—[a]

[a]The factor is zero to four decimal places.

to the sixth period: the present value of $1 and 6 periods is seen to be $0.5645:

$$P = A \times \frac{1}{(1 + i)_n}$$

$$P = 6,975 \times 0.5645 = \$3,937.21$$

The difference between the present value and the given compound amount is sometimes called the **compound discount**. In the illustration above, the compound discount is

$$\$6,975 - \$3,937.21 = \$3,037.79$$

The compound discount represents the amount of interest that $3,937.21 would earn in 6 years at 10% per annum.

Computing Present Value Using a Financial Calculator. The keystrokes for the calculator to compute the present value in the example above would be:

Keystroke	Display	Comment
f FIN	0.00	Clear
f REG	0.00	Clear
6975	6,975	—
FV	6,975.00	Future value
10	10	—
i	10.00	Interest rate
6	6	—
n	6.00	Number of periods
PV	−3,937.21	—
CHS	3,937.21	Present value

OTHER CONVERSE CASES. Occasionally it becomes necessary to find how long it will take for a given sum to amount to another sum at some future time; or what interest rate is being realized on a given principal. In short, the problem is to find n or i in the general formula. These may be found either by interpolation in a table or by using a spreadsheet.

Finding Value of n. These are two methods of finding n. These are illustrated to solve the following problem: how long will it take for $765 to amount to $1,350 if money is worth 8% per annum?

Computing Present Value Using a Spreadsheet (Built-in NPV Function)

Cell Address	Cell Content	Explanation
A1	'Payments	Label
C1	'Rate	Label
E1	'NPV	Label
A2	0	Payment
C2	0.1	Interest Rate
E2	@NPV (C2,A2..A7)	Present Value
A3	0	Payment
A4	0	Payment
A5	0	Payment
A6	0	Payment
A7	6975	Payment

Illustration

	A	B	C	D	E
1	Payments		Rate		NPV
2	0		0.1		3937.21
3	0				
4	0				
5	0				
6	0				
7	6975				

Note: Alternatively, the NPV equation can be used in place of the built-in function; the @ NPV function can be cumbersome when used for a single future payment. However, the Lotus product at present does not include a built-in function to handle this type of calculation directly.

Computing n Using a Spreadsheet

Cell Address	Cell Content	Explanation
A1	'Future Value	Label
C1	1350	Future Value
A2	'Present Value	Label
C2	765	Present Value
A3	'Interest Rate	Label
C3	0.08	Interest Rate
A4	'Number of Periods	Label
C4	@Log (C1/C2)/@Log(1+C3)	Number of Periods

Illustration

	A	B	C
1	Future Value		1350.0
2	Present Value		765.0
3	Interest Rate		0.08
4	Number of Periods		7.38
5			
6			

Computing n Using Tables. In Exhibit 4, in the 8% column, locate the number of periods for which $FVIF_{i,n}$ is closest to 1,350/765 = 1.7647. It is between 7 and 8 years. By **linear interpolation,** the period n can be computed as follows:

Year	$FVIF_{i,n}$
7	1.7138
8	1.8509
?	1.7647

$$n = 7 + \frac{1.7647 - 1.7138}{1.8509 - 1.7138}$$

$$= \underline{\underline{7.37 \text{ years}}}$$

This calculation is only approximate, since the true relationship between $FVIF_{i,n}$ and n is nonlinear, not linear as assumed here.

Computing n Using a Financial Calculator. The number n can be determined exactly (without rounding errors) using the financial calculator without resorting to the linear interpolation approximation method, above. The keystrokes for this example would be:

Keystroke	Display	Comment
f FIN	0.00	Clear
f REG	0.00	Clear
1350	1,350	—
FV	1,350.00	Future value
765	765	—
CHS	− 765.00	—
PV	− 765.00	Present value
8	8	—
i	8.00	Interest rate
n	7.38	Number of periods

Finding Value of i. The methods of the solution by interpolation and using a calculator are illustrated below.

Example. Find the yield on U.S. government bonds sold at $18.75 redeemable in 10 years for $25.

Computing i Using Tables. Proceed as in the previous solution.

$$(1 + i)^{10} = \frac{25}{18.75} = 1.3333$$

Now look in Exhibit 4 on the tenth period line and find values on that line just above and below 1.3333. The value is evidently between 2% and 3%. The computation is as follows:

Interest Rate	$FVIF_{i,n}$
2	1.2190
3	1.3439
?	1.3333

$$i = 2 + \frac{1.3333 - 1.2190}{1.3439 - 1.2190}$$

$$= 2.92\%$$

Again, the foregoing calculation is only approximate because a linear relationship has been assumed, rather than a nonlinear relationship, between $FVIF_{i,n}$ and i.

Computing i Using a Spreadsheet

Cell Address	Cell Content	Explanation
A1	'Present Value	Label
C1	18.75	Present Value
A2	'Future Value	Label
C2	25	Future Value
A3	'Number of Periods	Label
C3	10	Number of Periods
A4	'Interest	Label
C4	$((C2/C1)\wedge(1/C3) - 1)*100$	Interest Rate

Illustration

	A	B	C
1	Present Value		18.75
2	Future Value		25.0
3	Number of Periods		10
4	Interest		2.92
5			
6			

Computing i Using a Financial Calculator The keystrokes for the calculation are:

Keystroke	Display	Comment
f FIN	0.00	Clear
f REG	0.00	Clear
18.75	18.75	—
PV	18.75	Present value
25	25	—
CHS	−25	—
FV	−25.00	Compound value
10	10	—
r	10.00	Number of years
i	2.92	Interest rate

ANNUITIES

Definitions. An annunity is the payment of a fixed sum of money at uniform intervals of time. An example of an annuity rent on the use of property. Payments of annuities are commonly called **rents.**

Ordinary Annuity. An ordinary annuity is a series of equal payments each of which is made at the end of a period of time.

Annuity Due. An annuity due is one in which the payments are due at the beginning of each payment period. A life insurance premium is an example of an annuity due, since such premiums are always payable in advance.

Deferred Annuity. A deferred annuity is one in which payments are due after a number of periods have elapsed.

Amount or Final Value of Annuity. The total of all annuity payments made, together with the interest earned by these payments, is the amount of annuity. It is technically referred to as the final value of an annuity.

Perpetuity. An annuity in which the payments continue without end is a perpetuity. An example of this type is to be found in the payments made from endowment funds.

Life Annuity. An annuity whose duration depends on the life expectancy of one or more persons is called a contingent or life annuity.

Annuity Certain. This is an annuity that has a definite number of periods to run.

Example. A mortgage on a piece of property is to be paid off through 20 equal quarterly payments beginning 4 years from the present time. This is an ordinary annuity deferred 4 years; it is certain because it runs for 5 years, once it becomes effective.

Final Value of Ordinary Annuity. The total accumulation of an annuity may be illustrated by reference to the following example:

Example. What is the **accumulated value** of an annuity of $200 per year for 5 years if the annual interest rate is 14% and the annuity is paid **at the end** of each year?

Payment end of first year	$ 200.00
Interest second year (14%)	28.00
Payment end of second year	200.00
Total end of second year	$ 428.00
Interest third year	59.92
Payment end of third year	200.00
Total end of third year	$ 687.92
Interest fourth year	96.31
Payment end of fourth year	200.00
Total end of fourth year	$ 984.23
Interest fifth year	137.79
Payment end of fifth year	200.00
Total accumulation (final value)	$1,322.02

In effect, the final value of an annuity is the sum of the compound amounts of the individual payments. Thus as shown below, the first payment made at the end of the year bears interest for 4 years, the second for 3 years.

	1	2	3	4	5
Payments (end of each year)	$1	$1	$1	$1	$1
Compound amount (end of fifth year)	1.14^4	1.14^3	1.14^2	1.14	1
Total value (Exhibit 5)	1.6890	+ 1.4815	+ 1.2990	+ 1.140	+ 1 = $6.6095

Assuming money is worth 14%, the compound amount of each $1 payment is shown underneath the payments. When the values are totaled, it is found that an ordinary annuity of $1 per ycar annually for 5 years at 14% amounts to $6.6101. For an annuity of $200 under these conditions, the final amount is

$$200 \times 6.6095 = \underline{\$1,322.02}$$

Instead of laboriously calculating the compound amount of each payment, recourse may be had to prepared annuity tables (Exhibit 6). Thus in the illustration above, the answer may be found directly in the 14% column of line 5 of Exhibit 6.

Formula for Compound Value of an Annuity. The symbol for the final value of an ordinary annuity of $1 per annum is $FVIFA_{i,n}$*

$$FVIFA_{i,n} = (1 + i)^{n-1} + (1 + i)^{n-2} + \cdots + (1 + i) + 1$$

$$= \sum_{t=1}^{n} (1 + i)^{n-t}$$

$$= \frac{(1 + i)^n - 1}{i}$$

where i = interest rate
    n = number of periods

The numerator of the fraction is evidently the compound interest for n periods.

$$FVIFA_{i,n} = \frac{\text{compound interest}}{\text{interest rate}}$$

The final value for any number of dollars is expressed by the following formula:

$$A = R \times FVIFA_{i,n}$$

where A = final value of annuity
    R = amount of each payment

Example. Find the final value of an annuity of $2,000 received quarterly for 5 years when invested at 8% per annum.

Computing Compound Value of Annuity Using Tables. Proceed as follows:

$$A = R \times FVIFA_{i,n}$$

$$A = 2,000 \times FVIFA_{2,20}$$

Note that interest is at 2% per period for 20 periods; hence look for the value in the 2% column, line 20 of Exhibit 6. Therefore,

$$A = \$2,000 \times 24.297 = \underline{\underline{\$48,594}}$$

Computing Compound Value of Annuity Using a Financial Calculator. The keystrokes are as follows:

Keystroke	Display	Comment
f FIN	0.00	Clear
f REG	0.00	Clear
2000	2,000	—
CHS	−2,000	—
PMT	−2,000	Annuity amount
2	2	—
i	2.00	Interest rate
20	20	—
n	20.00	Number of periods
FV	48,594.74	Compound amount

Computing Compound Value of Annuity Using a Spreadsheet (built-in function)

Cell Address	Cell Content	Explanation
A1	'Payment	Label
C1	2000	Payment
A2	'Interest	Label
C2	0.02	Interest Rate
A3	'Term	Label
C3	20	Term
A4	'Future Value	Label
C4	@FV(C1,C2,C3)	Future Label

Illustration

	A	B	C	D
1	Payment		2000	
2	Interest		0.02	
3	Term		20	
4	Future Value		48594.73	
5				
6				

SINKING FUND CALCULATIONS. Sinking funds are commonly used to accumulate, by periodic contributions, sufficient amounts for the extinction of a debt or the replacement of an asset. In the latter event, the fund is more generally referred to as a **replacement fund**. In either instance the periodic payments are annuity rentals. Many bond issues of both private and municipal corporations are of the sinking fund type. The payments are usually turned over to a trustee or municipal sinking fund commission that invests these amounts and accumulates them to maturity or uses them to retire some of the bonds each year. In some issues, no part of the debt is extinguished

EXHIBIT 6 SUM OF AN ANNUITY OF $1 PER PERIOD FOR n PERIODS

$$FVIFA_{i,n} = \sum_{t=1}^{n} (1 + i)^{n-t} = \frac{(1 + i)^n - 1}{i}$$

Number of Periods	1%	2%	3%	4%	5%	6%	7%	8%	9%	10%	12%	14%	15%	16%	18%	20%	24%	28%	32%	36%
1	1.0000	1.0000	1.0000	1.0000	1.0000	1.0000	1.0000	1.0000	1.0000	1.0000	1.0000	1.0000	1.0000	1.0000	1.0000	1.0000	1.0000	1.0000	1.0000	1.0000
2	2.0100	2.0200	2.0300	2.0400	2.0500	2.0600	2.0700	2.0800	2.0900	2.1000	2.1200	2.1400	2.1500	2.1600	2.1800	2.2000	2.2400	2.2800	2.3200	2.3600
3	3.0301	3.0604	3.0909	3.1216	3.1525	3.1836	3.2149	3.2464	3.2781	3.3100	3.3744	3.4396	3.4725	3.5056	3.5724	3.6400	3.7776	3.9184	4.0624	4.2096
4	4.0604	4.1216	4.1836	4.2465	4.3101	4.3746	4.4399	4.5061	4.5731	4.6410	4.7793	4.9211	4.9934	5.0665	5.2154	5.3680	5.6842	6.0156	6.3624	6.7251
5	5.1010	5.2040	5.3091	5.4163	5.5256	5.6371	5.7507	5.8666	5.9847	6.1051	6.3528	6.6101	6.7424	6.8771	7.1542	7.4416	8.0484	8.6999	9.3983	10.146
6	6.1520	6.3081	6.4684	6.6330	6.8019	6.9753	7.1533	7.3359	7.5233	7.7156	8.1152	8.5355	8.7537	8.9775	9.4420	9.9299	10.980	12.135	13.405	14.798
7	7.2135	7.4343	7.6625	7.8983	8.1420	8.3938	8.6540	8.9228	9.2004	9.4872	10.089	10.730	11.066	11.413	12.141	12.915	14.615	16.533	18.695	21.126
8	8.2857	8.5830	8.8923	9.2142	9.5491	9.8975	10.259	10.636	11.028	11.435	12.299	13.232	13.726	14.240	15.327	16.499	19.122	22.163	25.698	29.731
9	9.3685	9.7546	10.159	10.582	11.026	11.491	11.978	12.487	13.021	13.579	14.775	16.085	16.785	17.518	19.085	20.798	24.712	29.369	34.895	41.435
10	10.462	10.949	11.463	12.006	12.577	13.180	13.816	14.486	15.192	15.937	17.548	19.337	20.303	21.321	23.521	25.958	31.643	38.592	47.061	57.351
11	11.566	12.168	12.807	13.486	14.206	14.971	15.783	16.645	17.560	18.531	20.654	23.044	24.349	25.732	28.755	32.150	40.237	50.398	63.121	78.998
12	12.682	13.412	14.192	15.025	15.917	16.869	17.888	18.977	20.140	21.384	24.133	27.270	29.001	30.850	34.931	39.580	50.894	65.510	84.320	108.43
13	13.809	14.680	15.617	16.626	17.713	18.882	20.140	21.495	22.953	24.522	28.029	32.088	34.351	36.786	42.218	48.496	64.109	84.852	112.30	148.47
14	14.947	15.973	17.086	18.291	19.598	21.015	22.550	24.214	26.019	27.975	32.392	37.581	40.504	43.672	50.818	59.195	80.496	109.61	149.23	202.92
15	16.096	17.293	18.598	20.023	21.578	23.276	25.129	27.152	29.360	31.772	37.279	43.842	47.580	51.659	60.965	72.035	100.81	141.30	197.99	276.97
16	17.257	18.639	20.156	21.824	23.657	25.672	27.888	30.324	33.003	35.949	42.753	50.980	55.717	60.925	72.939	87.442	126.01	181.86	262.35	377.69
17	18.430	20.012	21.761	23.697	25.840	28.212	30.840	33.750	36.973	40.544	48.883	59.117	65.075	71.673	87.068	105.93	157.25	233.79	347.30	514.66
18	19.614	21.412	23.414	25.645	28.132	30.905	33.999	37.450	41.301	45.599	55.749	68.394	75.836	84.140	103.74	128.11	195.99	300.25	459.44	700.93
19	20.810	22.840	25.116	27.671	30.539	33.760	37.379	41.446	46.018	51.159	63.439	78.969	88.211	98.603	123.41	154.74	244.03	385.32	607.47	954.27
20	22.019	24.297	26.870	29.778	33.066	36.785	40.995	45.762	51.160	57.275	72.052	91.024	102.44	115.37	146.62	180.68	303.60	494.21	802.86	1298.8
21	23.239	25.783	28.676	31.969	35.719	39.992	44.865	50.422	56.764	64.002	81.698	104.76	118.81	134.84	174.02	225.02	377.46	633.59	1060.7	1767.3
22	24.471	27.299	30.536	34.248	38.505	43.392	49.005	55.456	62.873	71.402	92.502	120.43	137.63	157.41	206.34	271.03	469.05	811.99	1401.2	2404.6
23	25.716	28.845	32.452	36.617	41.430	46.995	53.436	60.893	69.531	79.543	104.60	138.29	159.27	183.60	244.48	326.23	582.62	1040.3	1850.6	3271.3
24	26.973	30.421	34.426	39.082	44.502	50.815	58.176	66.764	76.789	88.497	118.15	158.65	184.16	213.97	289.49	392.48	723.46	1332.6	2443.8	4449.9
25	28.243	32.030	36.459	41.645	47.727	54.864	63.249	73.105	84.700	98.347	133.38	181.87	212.79	249.21	342.60	471.98	898.09	1706.8	3226.8	6052.9
26	29.525	33.670	38.553	44.311	51.113	59.156	68.676	79.954	93.323	109.18	150.33	208.33	245.71	290.08	405.27	567.37	1114.6	2185.7	4260.4	8233.0
27	30.820	35.344	40.709	47.084	54.669	63.705	74.483	87.350	102.72	121.09	169.37	238.49	283.56	337.50	479.22	681.85	1388.1	2798.7	5624.7	11197.9
28	32.129	37.051	42.930	49.967	58.402	68.528	80.697	95.338	112.96	134.20	190.60	272.88	327.10	392.50	566.48	819.22	1716.0	3583.3	7425.6	15230.2
29	33.450	38.792	45.218	52.966	62.322	73.639	87.346	103.96	124.13	148.63	214.58	312.09	377.16	456.30	669.44	984.06	2128.9	4587.6	9802.9	20714.1
30	34.784	40.568	47.575	56.084	66.438	79.058	94.460	113.28	136.30	164.49	241.33	356.78	434.74	530.31	790.94	1181.8	2640.9	5873.2	12940.	28172.2
40	48.886	60.402	75.401	95.025	120.79	154.76	199.63	259.05	337.88	442.59	767.09	1342.0	1779.0	2360.7	4163.2	7343.8	22728.	69377.	—[a]	—[a]
50	64.463	84.579	112.79	152.66	209.34	290.33	406.52	573.76	815.08	1163.9	2400.0	4994.5	7217.7	10435.	21813.	45497.	—[a]	—[a]	—[a]	—[a]
60	81.669	114.05	163.05	237.99	353.58	533.12	813.52	1253.2	1944.7	3034.8	7471.6	18535.	29219.	46057.	—[a]	—[a]	—[a]	—[a]	—[a]	—[a]

[a] $FVIFA > 99999.00000$

until maturity even if the trustee invests his receipts in the bonds to be redeemed. In the latter case, he merely collects the coupons and adds the interest to the sinking fund just as in the case of investment in any other bonds.

There are two mathematical problems involved in the **flotation** of sinking fund bond issues. The first is one of determining what sum shall be set aside periodically to provide the required amount of maturity. The other problem is concerned with determining the life span of the bond issues once the size of the periodic sinking fund payment the corporation can afford to make is known. These are presented below.

Finding Amount of Sinking Fund Installments. Determination of the installment or rent necessary to be set aside periodically is equivalent to finding R in the annuity formula.

$$R = \frac{A}{FVIFA_{i,n}}$$

The value of $FVIFA_{i,n}$ can be obtained from Exhibit 6. Its reciprocal represents the periodic payment of an annuity that will amount to $1 in n periods.

Example. A corporation on June 1, 1981, issued bonds due June 1, 1987 to the amount of $200,000. Provision was made to set up a sinking fund to retire the entire issue by means of semiannual payments. If the fund earns 6% semiannually, what is the size of each installment? There are 12 payments compounded at 6% every 6 months.

Computing Value of Annuity Using Tables. From Exhibit 6, in the 6% column, line 12, the value of $FVIFA_{i,n}$ can be obtained.

$$R = \frac{200,000}{16.869} = \$11,856.07$$

Schedule of Sinking Fund Installments. The schedule below shows the periodic amounts set up and the interest earned on the accumulated balances in the sinking fund. The total semiannual installments plus the accumulated interest earned by the sinking fund equal $200,000, the accumulated amount in the sinking fund on June 1, 1987, the date of maturity of the bonds. Note that the last figure in the last column contains a rounding error.

Computing Value of Annuity Using a Spreadsheet

Cell Address	Cell Content	Explanation
A1	'Compound Value	Label
C1	200000	Compound Value
A2	'Number of Periods	Label
C2	12	Number of Periods
A3	'Interest Rate	Label
C3	0.06	Interest Rate
A4	'Annuity Amount	Label
C4	$+C1*C3/((1+C3)^{\wedge}C2-1)$	Annuity Equation

Illustration

	A	B	C
1	Compound Value		200000.0
2	Number of Periods		12
3	Interest Rate		0.06
4	Annuity Amount		11855.41
5			
6			

Date	Semiannual Installment	Interest at 6% on Accumulated Sinking Fund	Total Additions to Sinking Fund	Accumulated Amounts in Sinking Fund
June 1, 1981	—	—	—	—
December 1, 1981	11,856.07	—	11,856.07	11,856.07
June 1, 1982	11,856.07	711.36	12,567.43	24,423.50
December 1, 1982	11,856.07	1,465.37	13,320.73	37,742.85
June 1, 1983	11,856.07	2,264.57	14,119.97	51,862.82
December 1, 1983	11,856.07	3,111.77	14,967.17	66,829.99
June 1, 1984	11,856.07	4,009.80	15,865.20	82,695.19
December 1, 1984	11,856.07	4,961.71	16,817.11	99,512.30
June 1, 1985	11,856.07	5,970.74	17,826.13	117,338.44
December 1, 1985	11,856.07	7,040.31	18,895.71	136,234.15
June 1, 1986	11,856.07	8,174.05	20,029.45	156,263.60
December 1, 1986	11,856.07	9,375.82	21,231.22	177,494.81
June 1, 1987	11,856.07	10,649.69	22,505.09	199,999.90

Computing Value of Annuity Using a Financial Calculator. The keystrokes are as follows:

Keystroke	Display	Comment
f FIN	0.00	Clear
f REG	0.00	Clear
200000	200,000	—

Keystroke	Display	Comment
CHS	− 200,000	—
FV	− 200,000.00	Compound value
12	12	—
n	12.00	Number of years
6	6	—
i	6.00	Interest rate
PMT	11,855.41	Annuity amount

Finding Number of Payments in a Sinking Fund. A corporation floating a sinking fund bond issue needs to prepare a long-range budget to determine what it can spare for sinking fund payments. Once that is known, the time to build up the proper size sinking fund can easily be calculated. This involves finding the number of payments (n in the formula) from which the maturity of the bonds may be determined. The simplest solution is through interpolation using Exhibit 6.

Example. A corporation wishes to raise $300,000 through the issuance of sinking fund bonds paying 5% semiannually. It can spare $50,000 a year for sinking fund purposes and interest on the bonds. If the fund earns 4% semiannually, when should the bonds be made to mature?

Computing Number of Years Using a Spreadsheet

Cell Address	Cell Content	Explanation
A1	'Compound Value	Label
C1	300000	Compound Value
A2	'Interest Payment	Label
C2	0.05	Interest Payment
A3	'Annual Payment	Label
C3	50000	Annual Payment
A4	'Interest Rate	Label
C4	0.04	Interest Rate
A5	'Number of Periods	Label
C5	@Log((((C1*C4)/(C3 − (C1*C2))+1)/Log(1 + C4)	Number of Periods

Illustration

	A	B	C
1	Compound Value		300000
2	Interest Payment		0.05
3	Annual Payment		50000
4	Interest Rate		0.04
5	Number of Periods		7.52
6			

Computing Number of Years n Using Tables. This task is straightforward:

Total annual payment	$50,000.00
Annual interest charge (300,000 × 0.05)	15,000.00
Sinking fund contribution	$35,000.00

$$FVIFA_{i,n} = 300,000 \div 35,000$$

$$FVIFA_{i,n} = \underline{8.5714}$$

Now look in Exhibit 6 in the 4% colum for the amounts directly above and below the given figure. The time is evidently between 7 and 8 periods. Since the results are approximations in any event, only four decimals are used.

Years	$FVIFAi_1n$
7	7.8983
8	9.2142
?	8.5714

$$n = 7 + \frac{8.5714 - 7.8983}{9.2142 - 7.8983}$$
$$= \underline{7.52 \text{ periods}}$$

Since bond maturities such as this are practically unknown, the borrower must decide whether the bonds are to mature in 3 or 4 years. If $50,000 represents the limit of what the borrower can spare, the maturity must be extended to 4 years and the exact amount of R (sinking fund contribution) recalculated. If a maturity of 3 years is more desirable, the total annual burden will be greater than $50,000 and can easily be found by the formula for R.

Computing Number of Years n Using a Financial Calculator. The keystrokes on the calculator are as follows:

Keystroke	Display	Comment
f FIN	0.00	Clear
f REG	0.00	Clear
300000	300,000	—
CHS	− 300,000	—
FV	− 300,000.00	Compound value
35000	35,000	—
PMT	35,000.00	—

Keystroke	Display	Comment
4	4	—
i	4.00	Interest rate
n	7.52	Number of years

Final Value of Annuity Due. In the case of an annuity due, the payments are made at the end of the period, i.e., the last payment earns interest for the last period. The symbol for final value of an annuity due of $1 is $FVIFAB_{i,n}$. The simplest formula for it is:

$$FVIFAB_{i,n} = (1 + i)^n + (1 + i)^{n-1} + \ldots$$
$$+ (1 + i)^2 + (1 + i)$$
$$= \sum_{t=1}^{n} (1 + i)$$
$$= \sum_{t=1}^{n+1} (1 + i)^{n+1-t} - 1$$
$$= FVIFA_{i,n+1} - 1$$

Example. Find the final value of an annuity due to $6,500 for 10 years at 12%.

Computing Final Value of Annuity Due Using Tables. Start with the following formula:

$$\text{annuity due} = R \times FVIFAB_{i,n}$$
$$= \$6,500 \times (FVIFA_{i,n+1} - 1)$$
$$= \$6,500 \times 19.654$$
$$= \$127,751$$

In looking up $FVIFAB_{i,n}$ start in the 12% column in Exhibit 6, read the figure on the eleventh line, and subtract $1: that is, look up $FVIFA_{i,n+1}$ and decrease this value by $1, to get 19.654.

Computing Final Value of Annuity Due Using a Financial Calculator. The keystrokes are as follows:

Keystroke	Display	Comment
f FIN	0.00	Clear
f REG	0.00	Clear
6500	6,500	—
CHS	− 6,500	—
PMT	− 6,500.00	Annuity amount due

Keystroke	Display	Comment
12	12	—
i	12.00	Interest rate
10	10	—
n	10.00	Number of periods
FV	12,7754.79	Compound amount

Present Value of Ordinary Annuity. The present value of an annuity is an amount that represents the sum of the discounted or present values of a series of equal payments made at uniform time intervals. Note that the future payments are equal, but are discounted. Hence, each payment represents in part principal and in part interest on the remaining debt. This is a contrast to final value problems, where payments are accumulated to wipe out a future debt at maturity. Hence, wherever the annuity payments represent principal and interest, the problem is one of present value.

The symbol to represent the present value of a single dollar per annum payable at the end of each year (i.e., an ordinary annuity of $1) is $PVIFA_{i,n}$. The formula is as follows:

$$PVIFA_{i,n} = \frac{1 - 1/(1 + i)^n}{i}$$

$$= \frac{1 - PVIF_{i,n}}{\text{interest rate}}$$

Exhibit 7 shows the present values represented by the formula above and may therefore be used to solve present value problems. The present value of any number of dollars is represented by the following formula:

$$A = R \times PVIFA_{i,n}$$

where A = present value of R dollars
R = amount of each annuity payment

Example. A lumber company signs a contract with a syndicate that owns a large tract of timber land. The company agrees to cut 20,000,000 feet of timber a year for 3 years and to pay $360,000 every 6 months for the cut timber. The syndicate, desiring to anticipate the payments under its contract, applies to its bankers for the cash value of the contract, offering as security the contract itself and a mortgage on the timber land. What is the present worth of the contract if the interest rate is 8% per annum, compounded semiannually?

EXHIBIT 7 PRESENT VALUE OF AN ANNUITY OF $1 PER PERIOD FOR n PERIODS

$$PVIFA_{i,n} = \sum_{i=1}^{n} \frac{1}{(1+i)^n} = 1 - \frac{1 - 1/(1-i)^n}{i}$$

Number of Payments	1%	2%	3%	4%	5%	6%	7%	8%	9%	10%	12%	14%	15%	16%	18%	20%	24%	28%	32%
1	0.9901	0.9804	0.9709	0.9615	0.9524	0.9434	0.9346	0.9259	0.9174	0.9091	0.8929	0.8772	0.8696	0.8621	0.8475	0.8333	0.8065	0.7813	0.7576
2	1.9704	1.9416	1.9135	1.8861	1.8594	1.8334	1.8080	1.7833	1.7591	1.7355	1.6901	1.6467	1.6257	1.6052	1.5656	1.5278	1.4568	1.3916	1.3315
3	2.9410	2.8839	2.8286	2.7751	2.7232	2.6730	2.6243	2.5771	2.5313	2.4869	2.4018	2.3216	2.2832	2.2459	2.1743	2.1065	1.9813	1.8684	1.7663
4	3.9020	3.8077	3.7171	3.6299	3.5460	3.4651	3.3872	3.3121	3.2397	3.1699	3.0373	2.9137	2.8550	2.7982	2.6901	2.5887	2.4043	2.2410	2.0957
5	4.8534	4.7135	4.5797	4.4518	4.3295	4.2124	4.1002	3.9927	3.8897	3.7908	3.6048	3.4331	3.3522	3.2743	3.1272	2.9906	2.7454	2.5320	2.3452
6	5.7955	5.6014	5.4172	5.2421	5.0757	4.9173	4.7665	4.6229	4.4859	4.3553	4.1114	3.8887	3.7845	3.6847	3.4976	3.3255	3.0205	2.7594	2.5342
7	6.7282	6.4720	6.2303	6.0021	5.7864	5.5824	5.3893	5.2064	5.0330	4.8684	4.5638	4.2883	4.1604	4.0386	3.8115	3.6046	3.2423	2.9370	2.6775
8	7.6517	7.3255	7.0197	6.7327	6.4632	6.2098	5.9713	5.7466	5.5348	5.3349	4.9676	4.6389	4.4873	4.3436	4.0776	3.8372	3.4212	3.0758	2.7860
9	8.5660	8.1622	7.7861	7.4353	7.1078	6.8017	6.5152	6.2469	5.9952	5.7590	5.3282	4.9464	4.7716	4.6065	4.3030	4.0310	3.5655	3.1842	2.8681
10	9.4713	8.9826	8.5302	8.1109	7.7217	7.3601	7.0236	6.7101	6.4177	6.1446	5.6502	5.2161	5.0188	4.8332	4.4941	4.1925	3.6819	3.2689	2.9304
11	10.3676	9.7868	9.2526	8.7605	8.3064	7.8869	7.4987	7.1390	6.8052	6.4951	5.9377	5.4527	5.2337	5.0286	4.6560	4.3271	3.7757	3.3351	2.9776
12	11.2551	10.5753	9.9540	9.3851	8.8633	8.3838	7.9427	7.5361	7.1607	6.8137	6.1944	5.6603	5.4206	5.1971	4.7932	4.4392	3.8514	3.3868	3.0133
13	12.1337	11.3484	10.6350	9.9856	9.3936	8.8527	8.3577	7.9038	7.4869	7.1034	6.4235	5.8424	5.5831	5.3423	4.9095	4.5327	3.9124	3.4272	3.0404
14	13.0037	12.1062	11.2961	10.5631	9.8986	9.2950	8.7455	8.2442	7.7862	7.3667	6.6282	6.0021	5.7245	5.4675	5.0081	4.6106	3.9616	3.4587	3.0609
15	13.8651	12.8493	11.9379	11.1184	10.3797	9.7122	9.1079	8.5595	8.0607	7.6061	6.8109	6.1422	5.8474	5.5755	5.0916	4.6755	4.0013	3.4834	3.0764
16	14.7179	13.5777	12.5611	11.6523	10.8378	10.1059	9.4466	8.8514	8.3126	7.8237	6.9740	6.2651	5.9542	5.6685	5.1624	4.7296	4.0333	3.5026	3.0882
17	15.5623	14.2919	13.1661	12.1657	11.2741	10.4773	9.7632	9.1216	8.5436	8.0216	7.1196	6.3729	6.0472	5.7487	5.2223	4.7746	4.0591	3.5177	3.0971
18	16.3983	14.9920	13.7535	12.6593	11.6896	10.8276	10.0591	9.3719	8.7556	8.2014	7.2497	6.4674	6.1280	5.8178	5.2732	4.8122	4.0799	3.5294	3.1039
19	17.2260	15.6785	14.3238	13.1339	12.0853	11.1581	10.3356	9.6036	8.9501	8.3649	7.3658	6.5504	6.1982	5.8775	5.3162	4.8435	4.0967	3.5386	3.1090
20	18.0456	16.3514	14.8775	13.5903	12.4622	11.4699	10.5940	9.8181	9.1285	8.5136	7.4694	6.6231	6.2593	5.9288	5.3527	4.8696	4.1103	3.5458	3.1129
25	22.0232	19.5235	17.4131	15.6221	14.0939	12.7834	11.6536	10.6748	9.8226	9.0770	7.8431	6.8729	6.4641	6.0971	5.4669	4.9476	4.1474	3.5640	3.1220
30	25.8077	22.3965	19.6004	17.2920	15.3725	13.7648	12.4090	11.2578	10.2737	9.4269	8.0552	7.0027	6.5660	6.1772	5.5168	4.9789	4.1601	3.5693	3.1242
40	32.8347	27.3555	23.1148	19.7928	17.1591	15.0463	13.3317	11.9246	10.7574	9.7791	8.2438	7.1050	6.6418	6.2335	5.5482	4.9966	4.1659	3.5712	3.1250
50	39.1961	31.4236	25.7298	21.4822	18.2559	15.7619	13.8007	12.2335	10.9617	9.9148	8.3045	7.1327	6.6605	6.2463	5.5541	4.9995	4.1666	3.5714	3.1250
60	44.9550	34.7609	27.6756	22.6235	18.9293	16.1614	14.0392	12.3766	11.0480	9.9672	8.3240	7.1401	6.6651	6.2402	5.5553	4.9999	4.1667	3.5714	3.1250

Computing Final Value of Annuity Due Using a Spreadsheet

Cell Address	Cell Content	Explanation
A1	'Annuity Amount Due	Label
C1	6500	Annuity Amount Due
A2	'Interest	Label
C2	0.12	Interest
A3	'Number of Periods	Label
C3	10	Number of Periods
A4	'Annuity Due	Label
C4	+Cl*((((1 + C2)^(C3 + 1) − 1)/C2) − 1)	Annuity Due

Illustration

	A	B	C
1	Annuity Amount Due		6500
2	Interest		0.12
3	Number of Periods		10
4	Annuity Due		127754.7
5			
6			

Computing Present Value of Annuity Using a Spreadsheet

Cell Address	Cell Content	Explanation
A1	'Payment	Label
C1	360000	Payment
A2	'Iterest	Label
C2	0.04	Interest
A3	'Term	Label
C3	6	Term
A4	'Present Value	Label
C4	@PV(C1,C2,C3)	Present Value (built-in function)

Illustration

	A	B	C
1	Payment		360000
2	Interest		0.04
3	Term		6
4	Present Value		1887169
5			
6			

Computing Present Value of Annuity Using Tables. The number of periods is 6 and the interest rate is 4% per period. The present value annuity factor $PVIFA_{i,n}$ can be determined from Exhibit 7.

$$A = 360,000 \times PVIFA_{i,n}$$

$$= \$360,000 \times 5.2421$$

$$= \underline{\underline{\$1,887,156}}$$

Computing Present Value of Annuity Using a Financial Calculator. The keystrokes are:

Keystroke	Display	Comment
f FIN	0.00	Clear
f REG	0.00	Clear
360000	360,000	—
CHS	− 360,000	—
PMT	− 360,000.00	Annuity amount
6	6	—
n	6.00	Number of periods
4	4	—
i	4.00	Interest rate
PV	1,887,169.27	Present value

This answer represents the amount the syndicate can borrow on its contract. This means that six annual payments of $360,000 will pay off the loan and the interest on the outstanding balances. The amortization of the loan is illustrated below:

Year	Amount Outstanding at Beginning of Period	Interest at 4% on Outstanding Balance	Annuity Payment	Principal Repaid
1	$1,887,169.28	$ 75,486.77	$ 360,000.00	$ 284,513.23
2	1,602,656.05	64,106.24	360,000.00	295,893.76
3	1,306,762.29	52,270.49	360,000.00	307,729.51
4	999,032.78	39,961.31	360,000.00	320,038.69
5	678,994.09	27,159.76	360,000.00	332,840.24
6	346,153.85	13,846.15	360,000.00	346,153.85
		$272,830.72	$2,160,000.00	$1,887,169.28

Annuity That $1 Will Buy. The annuity that $1 will buy is equivalent to a series of annuity payments the sum of whose present values is $1. This type of problem is found where the size of the annuity rent (*R*) is to be determined. The formula is as follows:

$$R = A_n \times \frac{1}{PVIFA_{i,n}}$$

The fraction is the reciprocal of the present value of $1 and represents the annuity that $1 will purchase. The annuity factors can be obtained by taking the reciprocals of the numbers in Exhibit 7, as illustrated below.

Example 1. Mr. X buys a property for $150,000 agreeing to pay $50,000 down and the balance in 25 equal annual installments that include interest at 14% What is the size of each installment?

The debt amounts to $100,000 after deduction of the down payment.

Computing an Annuity Amount Using Tables. From Exhibit 7, $PVIFA_{i,n}$ is found to be 6.8729 for $i = 14\%$ and $n = 25$.

$$R = A \times \frac{1}{PVIFA_{i,n}}$$

$$= \$100,000 \times \frac{1}{6.8729}$$

$$= \$14,549.90$$

Computing an Annuity Amount Using a Financial Calculator. The keystrokes for the problem are:

Keystroke	Display	Comment
f FIN	0.00	Clear
f REG	0.00	Clear
100000	100,000	—
CHS	− 100,000	—
PV	− 100,000.00	Present value
25	25	—
n	25.00	Number of periods
14	14	—
i	14.00	Interest rate
PMT	14,549.90	Annuity amount

Example 2. The Steel Wire Co. floated a $300,000, 12% bond issue on May 1, 1985, due May 1, 1989. Interest is payable quarterly; the bonds are in denominations of $1,000, and callable at par and accrued interest. What is the standard rent that will wipe out the debt and interest?

$$R = A \times \frac{1}{PVIFA_{i,n}}$$

$$= \$300{,}000 \times \frac{1}{12.5611}$$

$$= \underline{\$23{,}883.26}$$

Exhibit 8 is a table of bond retirements. Since the bonds are issued in fixed denominations, the total semiannual charge cannot be exactly as stated above, but should be kept as near that figure as possible. Thus on August 1, 1985, $9,000 of the $23,883.26 is due as interest and the balance of $14,883.26 can be applied against principal outstanding. But the bonds must be retired in even amounts; in this case 15 bonds are retired. As a result, the first quarter involves an expenditure of $24,000 instead of $23,883. The excess payment is reflected in the column showing the excess of deficiency of any one period. A cumulative column is also provided; the purpose is to keep the cumulative error as low as possible. In the case of a $1,000 bond the maximum deviation from the standard charge should not exceed ±$500, that is half the value of the bond. In case the cumulative error threatens to become more than $500, it is best to redeem one bond more or less, so as to keep the error within the stated limits.

Computing an Annuity Amount Using a Microcomputer Spreadsheet

Cell Address	Cell Content	Explanation
A1	'Principal	Label
C1	100000	Principal
A2	'Interest	Label
C2	0.14	Interest
A3	'Term	Label
C3	25	Term
A4	'Payment	Label
C4	@PMT(C1,C2,C3)	Annuity Amount (built-in function)

Illustration

	A	B	C
1	Principle		100000
2	Interest		0.14
3	Term		25
4	Payment		14549.84
5			
6			

Finding Number of Payments to Amortize a Loan. If the amount that can be spared for principal and interest is known, the borrower must also know how long it will take to amortize the debt. This involves finding n, that is, the number of payments to be made.

EXHIBIT 8   SCHEDULE OF INTEREST PAYMENTS AND BOND RETIREMENTS FOR SERIAL BOND ISSUE

Date	Outstanding	Interest at 3%	Amount Retired	Amount to Pay Interest and Retire Bonds	Number of Bonds Retired	Over (+) and Short (−) Current	Cumulative
May 1, 1985	$300,000	—	—	—	—	—	—
August 1, 1985	300,000	$ 9,000	$ 15,000	$ 24,000	15	+117	+117
November 1, 1985	285,000	8,550	15,000	23,550	15	−333	−216
February 1, 1985	270,000	8,100	16,000	24,100	16	+217	+1
May 1, 1986	254,000	7,620	16,000	23,620	16	−263	−262
August 1, 1986	238,000	7,140	17,000	24,140	17	+257	−5
November 1, 1986	221,000	6,630	17,000	23,630	17	−253	−258
February 1, 1987	204,000	6,120	18,000	24,120	18	+237	−21
May 1, 1987	186,000	5,580	18,000	23,580	18	−303	−324
August 1, 1987	168,000	5,040	19,000	24,040	19	+157	−167
November 1, 1987	149,000	4,470	20,000	24,470	20	+587	+420
February 1, 1988	129,000	3,870	20,000	23,870	20	−13	+407
May 1, 1988	109,000	3,270	20,000	23,270	20	−613	−206
August 1, 1988	89,000	2,670	21,000	23,670	21	−213	−419
November 1, 1988	68,000	2,040	22,000	24,040	22	+157	−262
February 1, 1989	46,000	1,380	23,000	24,380	23	+497	+235
May 1, 1989	23,000	690	23,000	23,690	23	−193	+42
		$82,170	$300,000	$382,170	300		

Example. The Brass Fixture Co. on July 1, 1986 issued $300,000, 12% bonds, interest payable semiannually. The bonds are in denominations of $1,000 and are to be redeemed at par and accrued interest. How long will it take to pay them off if the corporation has budgeted $30,000 each period for interest and bond redemption?

Computing Period n Using Tables. First do the following calculations:

$$r = 6\%, \text{ semiannually}$$

$$R = A \times \frac{1}{PVIFA_{i,n}}$$

$$PVIFA_{i,n} = \frac{A}{R} = \frac{300,000}{30,000} = 10$$

Now look for the values in the 6% column of Exhibit 7 and interpolate. Evidently, n lies between 15 and 16 periods.

Years	$PVIFA_{i,n}$
15	9.7122
16	10.1059
?	10.0

$$n = 15 + \frac{10.0 - 9.7122}{10.1059 - 9.7122}$$

$$= \underline{\underline{15.73 \text{ periods} \approx 8 \text{ years}}}$$

Computing Period n Using a Financial Calculator. The keystrokes are as follows:

Keystroke	Display	Comment
f FIN	0.00	Clear
f REG	0.00	Clear
300000	300,000	—
PV	300,000.00	Present value
30,000	30,000	—
CHS	− 30,000	—
PMT	− 30,000.00	Annuity
6	6	—
i	6.00	Interest rate
n	15.73	Number of Periods

Present Value of Annuity Due. The symbol for the present value of an annuity due of $1 per period is $PVIFAB_{i,n}$. The formula is as follows:

$$PVIFAB_{i,n} = 1 + \frac{1}{1 + i} \cdots + \frac{1}{(1 + i)^{n-2}} + \frac{1}{(1 + i)^{n-1}}$$

$$= 1 + PVIFA_{i,n-1}$$

This means that the present value tables for ordinary annuities (Exhibit 7) may be used in computing the present value of an annuity due. For instance, if $PVIAB_{12,10}$ is wanted, it can be found by looking in the 12% column of Exhibit 7 on line 9 and adding $1. In this case the answer is 6.3282.

Example. What is the cash value of a lease that has 5 years to run and that calls for rentals of $1,365 quarterly, payable in advance? Assume money is worth 16% per annum, compounded quarterly.

The lease has 20 periods to run and is discounted at 4% per period. Since payments are made in advance, it is an annuity due.

Computing Period n *Using a Spreadsheet*

Cell Address	Cell Content	Explanation
A1	'Payment Amount	Label
C1	30000	Payment amount
A2	'Compound Value	Label
C2	300000	Compound Value
A3	'Interest	Label
C3	0.06	Interest
A4	'Number of Periods	Label
C4	@Log(1/(1 − C2*C3/C1))/ @Log(1+C3)	Number of Periods

Illustration

	A	B	C
1	Payment Amount		30000
2	Compound Value		300000
3	Interest		0.06
4	Number of Periods		15.73
5			
6			

Computing Present Value of Annuity Due Using Tables. The value of $PVIFAB_{4,20}$ can be obtained from Exhibit 7:

$$AD = R \times PVIFAB_{i,n}$$

$$= R \times (1 + PVIFA_{i,n-1})$$

$$= \$1,365 \times 14.1339$$

$$= \underline{\underline{\$19,292.77}}$$

Computing Present Value of Annuity Due Using a Financial Calculator. The keystrokes are as follows:

Keystroke	Display	Comment
f FIN	0.00	Clear
f REG	0.00	Clear
g BEG	0.00	Set payment line
1365	1,365	—
CHS	−1,365	—
PMT	−1,365.00	Annuity amount due
4	4	—
i	4.00	Interest Rate
20	20	—
n	20.00	Number of periods
PV	19,292.83	Present value

BOND VALUATION: DEFINITIONS AND CALCULATIONS

Bond Definitions. A bond may be defined as a long-time **promissory note** under "seal." It promises to pay to the owner of the bond a specified principal sum called the face value on a definite date in the future, called the maturity date. It also promises to pay the interest based on the face value on the interest dates as called for in the bond indenture.

The **par value** of a bond is the amount stated on its face. The **redemption value** is the price at which the bond will be redeemed. In many issues this is the same as the par value; in others, premiums are paid when bonds are redeemed before maturity.

Premium and Discount on Bonds. When bonds sell at a price greater than par, they are said to sell at a **premium,** and when at a price less than par they are said to sell at a **discount.**

Nominal and Effective Interest Rates. The **nominal rate,** also known as the **coupon rate** or the cash rate, is the rate, based on the par value, stipulated in the bond.

The **effective rate,** also called the **yield** or **market rate,** is the return that the bonds earn on the price at which they are purchased if they are held to maturity. Note that the yield is based on the price paid for the bond, not on its par value. When the nominal rate is in excess of the yield rate, that is, in excess of what in the opinion of the market is considered a fair rate of return for that type of security, the bond sells at a **premium.** When the bond rate is less than the yield rate, the bond sells at a **discount.** The amount of the premium or discount can be mathematically determined and is based on principles of compound interest and annuities.

Determining Basis Price of Bonds. The price at which a bond will sell on the open market depends on a number of factors:

1. The security for the payment of the principal and interest.
2. The bond rate.
3. The rate realized by like investments, or to be realized by the investor.
4. The time to the maturity of the bond.
5. The price at which the bond will be redeemed.
6. The tax status of the principal and interest.

From a purely mathematical point of view, once the desired yield is known, the basis price, that is, the purchase price, of a bond depends on two factors:

1. The present value of the principal.
2. The present value of the interest payments.

The sum of these two present values represents the basic price of the bond. The first factor represents the present value of a lump sum, the second the present value of an annuity.

Example. What is the price paid by Mr. X on November 1, 1986, for 100 bonds, par value $100,000, paying 16% nominal to yield 14%? The bonds pay interest May 1 and November 1, through coupons, and mature November 1, 1989.

The nominal rate per period is 8%, the effective rate 7%.

Computing the Price Using Tables. The present value of the principal six periods from now is

$$P = A \times PVIF_{i,n}$$
$$= A \times PVIF_{7,6}$$
$$= \$100,000 \times 0.6663 \text{ (Exhibit 5)}$$
$$= \underline{\$66,630}$$

The present value of the coupons is calculated by means of the annuity formula. The size of each coupon is determined from the nominal rate. In this example, the semi-annual coupons have a face value of $8,000 (i.e., $100,000 × 8%). Their present value is then found:

$$A = R \times PVIFA_{i,n}$$
$$= R \times PVIF_{7,6}$$
$$= \$8,000 \times 4.7665 \text{ (Exhibit 7)}$$
$$= \underline{\$38,132}$$

Basis price of bonds:

$$\$66,630 + 38,132 = \underline{\underline{\$104,762}}$$

Note that the yield rate is always used except for calculating the amount of cash coupon.

Short Method for Finding Basis Price. Since the difference between the coupon and yield rates gives rise to premium or discount on bonds, it is possible to compute the premium, and hence the basis price, directly from such difference. This method is illustrated below, using the same example as above.

	Rate (%)	Amount
Nominal interest	8	$8,000
Effective interest	7	7,000
Excess interest		$1,000

The bonds pays $8,000 interest per period. It should pay $7,000 to sell at par. There is, therefore, $1,000 excess interest per period. The excess interest constitutes an annuity for the life of the bond. The present value of this annuity represents the premium to be paid.

$$A = R \times PVIFA_{7,6}$$
$$= \$1,000 \times 4.7665 \text{ (Exhibit 7)}$$
$$= 4,766.50$$
$$\text{Par value} = \$100,000$$
$$\text{Basis price} = \underline{\underline{\$104,766.50}}$$

Computing the Price Using a Financial Calculator. The keystrokes are as follows:

Keystroke	Display	Comment
f FIN	0.00	Clear
f REG	0.00	Clear
8	8	—
ENTER	8.00	Nominal interest
7	7.00	Effective interest
—	1.00	—
100000	100,000.00	Par value
STO	100,000.00	—
1	100,000.00	—

Keystroke	Display	Comment
×	100,000.00	—
100	100.00	—
÷	1,000.00	Excess interest
CHS	− 1,000.00	—
PMT	− 1,000.00	—
7	7.00	—
i	7.00	Interst rate
6	6.00	—
n	6.00	Number of periods
PV	4,766.54	—
RCL	4,766.54	—
1	100,000.00	—
+	104,766.54	Basis price

Computing the Price Using a Microcomputer Spreadsheet

Cell Address	Cell Content	Explanation
A1	'Par Value	Label
D1	100000	Par Value
A2	'Face Value Coupons	Label
D2	8000	Face Value Coupons
A3	'Number of Periods	Label
D3	6	Number of Periods
A4	'Interest Rate	Label
D4	0.07	Interest Rate
A5	'Basis Price	Label
D5	+ D1*1/(1 + D4) ^ D3 + D2*(1 − (1/(1 + D4) ^ D3))/D4	Basis Price

Illustration

	A	B	C	D
1	Par Value			100000
2	Face Value Coupons			8000
3	Number of Periods			6
4	Interest Rate			0.07
5	Basis Price			104766.5
6				

Amortization Schedule. Although an investor may have paid a premium for the bond, generally speaking, he collects only the par value at maturity. This shrinkage in value takes place gradually during the life of the bond. It means that each coupon collection represents two things:

1. Return on the investment at the yields rate.
2. Partial return of the premium paid.

That this is the case can be shown by a so-called amortization table. Exhibit 9 is based on the premium bond illustrated in the last example.

The coupon income is 8% a period based on the par value of the bonds. The effective income or yield is 7% based on the remaining investment. Thus, on May 1, 1987, 7% is earned on $104,766.54 or $7,333.66. This is the true income for the period. The balance of the $8,000 coupon interest collected on that day represents a partial liquidation of the investment. Hence, the book value is reduced on May 1, 1987, by $666.34. Six months later, the effective income is 7% of the new book value of $104,100.20, and so on.

Short-Cut Method for Discount Bonds. The short-cut method just illustrated works equally well for bonds selling at a discount, as shown in the example below.

Example. Find the basis price of $10,000 bond paying 10% nominal interest on February 1 and August 1, to yield 12%. The bond was purchased February 1, 1985, and matures August 1, 1987.

	Rate (%)	Amount
Nominal interest	5	$500
Effective interest	6	$600
Deficiency of interest		$100

$$A = R \times PVIFA_{i,n}$$

$$= \$100 \times PVIFA_{6,5}$$

$$= \$100 \times 4.2124 \text{ (Exhibit 7)}$$

$$= \$421.24$$

$$\text{par value} = \$10,000.00$$

$$\text{basis price} = \$\ 9,578.76$$

EXHIBIT 9   AMORTIZATION SCHEDULE

Date	Coupon Income 8%	Effective Income 7%	Amortization	Remaining Book Value
November 1, 1986	—	—	—	$104,766.54
May 1, 1987	$8,000	$7,333.66	666.34	104,100.20
November 1, 1987	8,000	7,287.01	712.99	103,387.21
May 1, 1988	8,000	7,237.10	762.90	102,624.32
November 1, 1988	8,000	7,183.70	816.30	101,808.02
May 1, 1989	8,000	7,126.56	873.44	100,934.58
November 1, 1989	8,000	7,065.42	934.58	100,000.00

Schedule of Accumulation. A bond purchased at a discount approaches par or other redemption value gradually. The increase in value is spread over the life of the bond. Hence, the **true income** each period consists of:

1. Coupon interest.
2. Increase in book value, known as the accumulation.

Exhibit 10 is an accumulation table for the last illustration, under the short-cut method for discount bonds.

The figures in the effective interest column are obtained by taking 6% of the last book value. Thus on August 1, 1985, 6% of $9,578.76 yields $574.73. Six months later 6% of $9,653.49 amounts to $579.21, and so on. In each instance, the difference between coupon and yield interest is **added** to the previous book value.

Bond Valuation Tables. Bond tables have been devised to simplify the labor involved in determining:

1. The price to be paid when the yield is known.
2. The yield when the cost is known.

Thus it is possible to read the basis price of a bond directly from the table. The **standard bond tables** usually give the value of a million dollar bond correct to the nearest cent for a great variety of nominal and effective interest rates and for periods ranging from 6 months to 50 years at 6-month intervals, and at longer intervals thereafter. However, with the easy availability of pocket calculators, these tables are virtually obsolete.

Basis Price for Bonds Bought Between Interest Dates. The basis price of a bond changes from day to day. Hence, if a bond is bought between interest dates, its basis price must be computed by interpolation between the basis prices of the last preceding and next succeeding interest dates. In addition,

EXHIBIT 10   ACCUMULATION TABLE FOR $10,000 BOND

Date	Coupon Interest 5%	Effective Interest 6%	Accumulation	New Book Value
February 1, 1985	—	—	—	$ 9,578.76
August 1, 1985	$500	$574.73	$74.73	9,653.49
February 1, 1986	500	579.21	79.21	9,732.69
August 1, 1986	500	583.96	83.96	9,816.66
February 1, 1987	500	589.00	89.00	9,905.66
August 1, 1987	500	594.34	94.34	10,000.00

the purchaser will have to pay **accrued interest** on the bond to the seller for the time since the last interest date.

Bonds may be quoted either "and interest" or "flat." The **"and-interest" price** is the quoted price plus the accrued interest. The **"flat" price** includes the accrued interest in the quotation. To find the value of a bond between interest dates, proceed as follows:

1. Find the basis price on the preceding interest day and on the succeeding interest day, and thus determine the decrease or increase in book value for the entire period.
2. Find the fractional part of the period that has elapsed to the day of purchase. Find this fractional part of the period's change in book value.
3. Add to the book value of the preceding interest day the increase found in step 2 or subtract from it the decrease found in step 2 for the part of the period that has elapsed. The result is the "and-interest" price or "ex-interest" price.
4. Add to the ex-interest price in either instance the accrued interest, or seller's share of the current period's bond interest. The result is the **total price** or flat price.

Example. Find the "and-interest" and "flat" prices for a $1,000 bond, due February 1, 1991, bearing interest at 14% per annum, payable February 1 and August 1, if purchased April 1, 1981, to yield 12%.

The life of the bond on the last interest date (February 1, 1981) was 10 years; at the next interest date it has 9 1/2 years to run. The basis prices on these two dates can be found by the methods presented earlier (determining the basis prices of bonds) by using tables or a financial calculator.

Computing Bond Prices Using Tables. The values of the bond to yield 12% are as follows:

Step 1	10 years (February 1, 1981)	$1,114.70
	9 1/2 years (August 1, 1981)	$1,111.58
	Amortization for 6 months	$ 3.12
Step 2	From February 1 to April 1 is one-third of a period. Therefore the basis price decreased	

$$1/3 \times \$3.12 = \$1.04$$

Step 3	"And-interest" price April 1, 1981 = $1,114.70 − $1.04 = $1.113.66	
Step 4	Accured interest	
	14% per annum on $1,000 for 2 months	23.33
	Flat price	$1,136.99

It is possible also to determine the flat price directly. The seller is entitled to the book value on the preceding interest day, plus interest on this value at the yield rate, for the time elapsed since that day. The procedure is as follows:

1. Find the basis price on the preceding interest day.
2. Find the time elapsed since the last interest day, and add to the basis price on the preceding interest day interest on it at the yield rate for the elapsed time on a 360-day year basis. The result is the **total price.**
3. From the total price **subtract** the accrued interest. The result is the and-interest price or the ex-interest price.

Using the same illustration as above, the method works out as follows:

Step 1	February 1, 1981, basis price	$1,114.70
Step 2	Interest at 12% per annum for 2 months on above	22.29
Step 3	April 1, 1981, flat price	$1,136.99

If only the total price to be paid by the purchaser or to be received by the seller is wanted, this method offers a short-cut. For the purpose of setting up a schedule of amortization or accumulation, the and-interest price must be used. The first four lines of the amortization table for the bond above appear as follows:

Date	Bond Interest 14%	Effective Interest 12%	Amortization	Book Value
April 1, 1981	—	—	—	$1,113.66
August 1, 1981	$46.67	$44.59	$2.08	1,111.58
February 1, 1982	70.00	66.69	3.31	1,108.28
August 1, 1982	70.00	66.50	3.50	1,104.77

The figures for August 1, 1981, are obtained as follows:

1. Bond interest. The total coupon interest for a period is $70, one-third of which ($23.33) was paid over to the vendor on April 1. Hence, the net interest collected on August 1 is $46.67.
2. Effective interest. This must be calculated on the basis price as of the last interest date (February 1, 1981) for 4 months. In this case $1,114.70 at 12% for 4 months is $44.59.
3. Amortization. Difference between the two preceding columns. $46.69 - $44.54 = $2.08. It could also be found by taking the amortization for the full 6-month period ($3.12) and subtracting the amortization from February 1 to April 1 ($1.04).

4. Book value. Book value April 1, 1981, less current amortization. $1,114.70 − $2.08 = $1,112.62.

Computing Bond Prices Using a Financial Calculator. The keystrokes are as follows:

Keystroke	Display	Comment
f FIN	0.00	Clear
f REG	0.00	Clear
0.07	0.07	—
ENTER	0.07	—
1000	1,000.00	—
×	70.00	Coupon interest
STO	70.00	—
1	70.00	—
CHS	−70.00	—
PMT	−70.00	—
6	6.00	—
i	6.00	Yield
20	20.00	—
n	20.00	Number of periods
PV	802.89	—
0	0.00	—
PMT	0.00	—
1000	1,000	—
CHS	−1,000	—
FV	−1,000.00	—
PV	311.80	—
+	1,114.70	Bond base price, n = 20
STO	1,114.70	—
2	1,114.70	—
19	19.00	—
n	19.00	—
PV	330.51	—
RCL	330.51	—
1	70.00	—
CHS	−70.00	—
PMT	−70.00	—
0	0.00	—
FV	0.00	—
PV	781.07	—
+	1,111.58	Bond base price, n = 19
RCL	1,111.58	—
2	1,114.70	—
$x \gtreqless y$	1,111.58	—
−	3.12	—
2	2.00	—
×	6.24	—

Keystroke	Display	Comment
6	6.00	—
÷	1.04	Decrease in base price
CHS	− 1.04	—
RCL	− 1.04	—
2	1,114.70	—
+	1,113.66	"And-interest" price
STO	1,113.66	—
3	1,113.66	—
RCL	1,113.66	—
1	70.00	—
3	3.00	—
÷	23.33	Accrued interest
RCL	23.33	—
3	1,113.66	—
+	1,136.99	Flat price

Accruing Bond Interest Between Interest Dates. The interest accrued at time of purchase or sale depends on whether the bond is a corporate or a government bond. For corporate bonds delivery must be made on the fourth working day after the sale and interest is accrued on the basis of a 360-day year up to and including the day before delivery. In the case of government bonds, delivery is on the next working day, and the seller receives interest up to and including the day of the sale.

The rules are further clarified by the Committee on Securities of the New York Stock Exchange as follows:

Interest at the rate specified on a bond dealt in "and-interest" shall be computed on a basis of a 360-day year, i.e., each calender month shall be considered to be 1/12 of 360 days, and each period from a date in one month to the same date in the following month shall be considered to be 30 days.

Note: The number of elapsed days shall be computed in accordance with the examples given in the following table:

From	To
30th to 31st	1st of the following month to be figured as 1 day
30th or 31st	30th of the following month to be figured as ´30 days
30th or 31st	31st of the following month to be figured as 30 days
30th or 31st	1st of the second following month to be figured as one month one day

Thus if a January and July 15 bond were bought on March 15, 2 months are said to have elapsed since January 15. If a June and December 1 bond were bought on January 16, following the above rule there are:

From December 1 to January 1	30 days
From January 1 to January 16	15 days
Elapsed time	45 days

Determining Profit or Loss on Sale of Bonds. When bonds that have been purchased as an investment are subsequently sold, the profit or loss on the transaction is determined by comparison of the book value (i.e., the and-interest price) on the date of sale with the selling price.

The profit or loss figure represents the capital gain or loss for tax purposes and is of course exclusive of the coupon interest less amortization regularly reported as income.

Finding Yield Between Interest Dates. The calculation by tables of yield between interest dates is complex, since it requires a double interpolation, once for the basis price of the bond and then for the yield.

Example. A price of $102 is quoted for a bond with 26 semiannual coupon payments remaining. The coupon rate is 12.75%. The current coupon period contains 183 days, and the settlement date is 60 days into the period. Assuming that the bond is redeemable at par, what is the yield?

The steps in the calculation are as follows:

1. Compute the yield ignoring the adjustment in the basis price of the bond.
2. Compute the adjusted basis price of the bond to take into account the time away from the settlement date.
3. Repeat steps 1 and 2 iteratively, till the change in yield between iterations is negligible.

The keystrokes for the financial calculator are as follows:

Keystroke	Display	Comment
f FIN	0.00	Clear
f REG	0.00	Clear
59	59	Days to settlement
ENTER	59.00	—
183	183	Days in coupon period
÷	0.32	—
STO	0.32	—
5	0.32	—
6.375	6.375	Coupon
×	2.06	—
STO	2.06	—
6	2.06	—
6.375	6.375	—
CHS	−6.375	—
PMT	−6.38	—

Keystroke	Display	Comment
100	100	Future value
CHS	− 100	—
FV	− 100.00	—
STO	− 100.00	—
4	− 100.00	—
102	102.00	—
PV	102.00	Present value
STO	102.00	—
1	102.00	—
124	124.00	Days from previous settlement
÷	0.82	—
25	25.00	Coupon payments remaining other than present
+	25.82	—
n	25.82	—
STO	25.82	—
2	25.82	Coupon payments remaining including fraction of present
i	6.22	Iteration 1
0	0.00	—
PV	0.00	—
RCL	0.00	—
5	0.32	—
n	0.32	—
FV	2.01	—
CHS	− 2.01	—
RCL	− 2.01	—
6	2.06	—
+	0.04	—
PV	0.04	—
RCL	0.04	—
1	102.00	—
+	108.22	—
PV	108.22	—
RCL	108.22	—
4	− 100.00	—
FV	− 100.00	—
RCL	− 100.00	—
2	25.82	—
n	25.82	—
i	5.76	Iteration 2
0	0.00	Continue to iteration 3
PV	0.00	—
.	.	
.	.	
.	.	
i	5.79	Iteration 5

OPTION PRICING MATHEMATICS

THE BLACK-SCHOLES FORMULA. The most commonly used formula for pricing call options is one developed by **Black and Scholes** in "The Pricing of Options and Corporate Liabilities" (*Journal of Political Economy*, May–June 1973). It is often used, with minor variations, to determine the gap between the market price of a **call option** and its **intrinsic value.**
    The key assumptions of the **Black-Scholes model** are:

1. The short-term interest rate is known and is constant through time.
2. The stock price follows a random walk in continuous time with a variance rate proportional to the square of the stock price.
3. The distribution of possible stock prices at the end of any finite interval is log normal.
4. The variance rate of return on the stock is constant.
5. The stock pays no dividends and makes no other distributions.
6. The option can be exercised only at maturity.
7. There are no commissions or other transaction costs in buying or selling the stock or the option.
8. It is possible to borrow any fraction of the price of a security to buy it or to hold it, at the short-term interest rate.
9. A seller who does not own a security (a short seller) will simply accept the price of the security from the buyer and will agree to settle with the buyer on some future date by paying him an amount equal to the price of the security on that date. While this short sale is outstanding, the short seller will have the use of, or interest on, the proceeds of the sale.
10. The tax rate, if any, is identical for all transactions and all market participants.

The assumption that the distribution of the stock price at the end of any finite time interval be log normal is equivalent to saying that the distribution of the stock's returns in each instant will be normal with a constant variance. Under these assumptions and using the hedging arguments outlined in the section entitled "Option Markets and Instruments," the price of a call option is determined by:

$$P_o = P_s N(d_1) - \frac{E}{e^{rt}} N(d_2)$$

where $\quad d_1 = \dfrac{\ln(P_s/E) + (r + \frac{1}{2}\sigma^2)t}{\sigma\sqrt{t}}$

$$d_2 = \frac{\ln (P_s/E) + (r - \frac{1}{2}\sigma^2)t}{\sigma\sqrt{t}}$$

where P_o = current value of option
P_s = current price of stock
E = exercise price of option
e = 2.71828
t = time remaining before expiration (years)
r = continuously compounded riskless rate of interest
σ = standard deviation of continously compounded annual rate of return on the stock
$\ln (P_s/E)$ = natural logarithm of (P_s/E)
$N(d$ = probability that a deviation less than d will occur in a normal distribution with a mean of 0 and a standard deviation of 1

Example. Suppose the price of a share of XYZ Corp. is $36 and the exercise price of the call option is $40. The option has 3 months to maturity (i.e., 0.25 of a year). If the riskless rate of interest is 5% per year, and the standard deviation of the continously compounded annual return is 50%, determine the price of the option, using the following data:

P_s = $36
E = $40
t = 0.25 (i.e., one-fourth of a year, or 3 months)
r = 0.05 (i.e, 5% per year, continously compounded)
σ = 0.50 (i.e., the standard deviation of the continously compounded annual return is 50%)

Using the formula, we write:

$$d_1 = \frac{\ln (36/40) + [0.05 + \frac{1}{2}(0.50^2)]0.25}{0.50\sqrt{0.25}} \approx -0.25$$

$$d_2 = \frac{\ln (36/40) + [0.05 - \frac{1}{2}(0.50^2)]0.50}{0.50\sqrt{0.25}} \approx -0.50$$

From Exhibit 11, which furnishes values of the $N(d)$, the standard normal-variate for various values of d, we see that

$$N(d_1) = N(-0.25) = 0.4013$$
$$N(d_2) = N(-0.50) = 0.3085$$

Thus:

$$P_o = (36 \times 0.4013) - \left(\frac{40}{e^{0.05 \times 0.25}} \times 0.3085\right) \approx \$2.26$$

Only a hand calculator is needed to estimate the value of an option using the Black-Scholes formula. In fact, a pocket calculator can be programmed

EXHIBIT 11   (VALUES OF N(d) FOR SELECTED VALUES OF d

d	N(d)	d	N(d)	d	N(d)
		-1.00	.1587	1.00	.8413
-2.95	.0016	-0.95	.1711	1.05	.8531
-2.90	.0019	-0.90	.1841	1.10	.8643
-2.85	.0022	-0.85	.1977	1.15	.8749
-2.80	.0026	-0.80	.2119	1.20	.8849
-2.75	.0030	-0.75	.2266	1.25	.8944
-2.70	.0035	-0.70	.2420	1.30	.9032
-2.65	.0040	-0.65	.2578	1.35	.9115
-2.60	.0047	-0.60	.2743	1.40	.9192
-2.55	.0054	-0.55	.2912	1.45	.9265
-2.50	.0062	-0.50	.3085	1.50	.9332
-2.45	.0071	-0.45	.3264	1.55	.9394
-2.40	.0082	-0.40	.3446	1.60	.9452
-2.35	.0094	-0.35	.3632	1.65	.9505
-2.30	.0107	-0.30	.3821	1.70	.9554
-2.25	.0122	-0.25	.4013	1.75	.9599
-2.20	.0139	-0.20	.4207	1.80	.9641
-2.15	.0158	-0.15	.4404	1.85	.9678
-2.10	.0179	-0.10	.4602	1.90	.9713
-2.05	.0202	-0.05	.4801	1.95	.9744
-2.00	.0228	0.00	.5000	2.00	.9773
-1.95	.0256	0.05	.5199	2.05	.9798
-1.90	.0287	0.10	.5398	2.10	.9821
-1.85	.0322	0.15	.5596	2.15	.9842
-1.80	.0359	0.20	.5793	2.20	.9861
-1.75	.0401	0.25	.5987	2.25	.9878
-1.70	.0446	0.30	.6179	2.30	.9893
-1.65	.0495	0.35	.6368	2.35	.9906
-1.60	.0548	0.40	.6554	2.40	.9918
-1.55	.0606	0.45	.6736	2.45	.9929
-1.50	.0668	0.50	.6915	2.50	.9938
-1.45	.0735	0.55	.7088	2.55	.9946
-1.40	.0808	0.60	.7257	2.60	.9953
-1.35	.0885	0.65	.7422	2.65	.9960
-1.30	.0968	0.70	.7580	2.70	.9965
-1.25	.1057	0.75	.7734	2.75	.9970
-1.20	.1151	0.80	.7881	2.80	.9974
-1.15	.1251	0.85	.8023	2.85	.9978
-1.10	.1357	0.90	.8159	2.90	.9981
-1.05	.1469	0.95	.8289	2.95	.9984

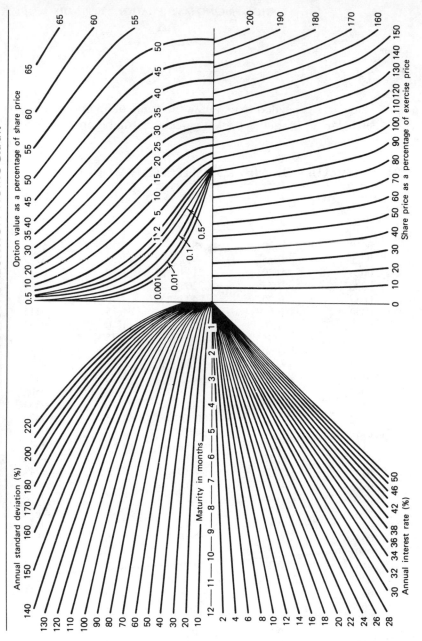

EXHIBIT 12 THE CALL OPTION VALUATION NOMOGRAM

Annual standard deviation (%)

Option value as a percentage of share price

Maturity in months

Annual interest rate (%)

Share price as a percentage of exercise price

Instructions for use:

1. Draw vertical line through maturity.

2. Draw horizontal lines from intersections with standard deviation and interest rate

3. Draw vertical line from intersection of horizontal with share price/exercise price.

4. Interpolate option value from the intersecting lines in the positive quadrant.

Source: E. Dimson, ''Instant Option Valuation,'' *Financial Analysts Journal*, May–June 1977.

EXHIBIT 13 EXAMPLE OF THE USE OF CALL OPTION VALUATION NOMOGRAM

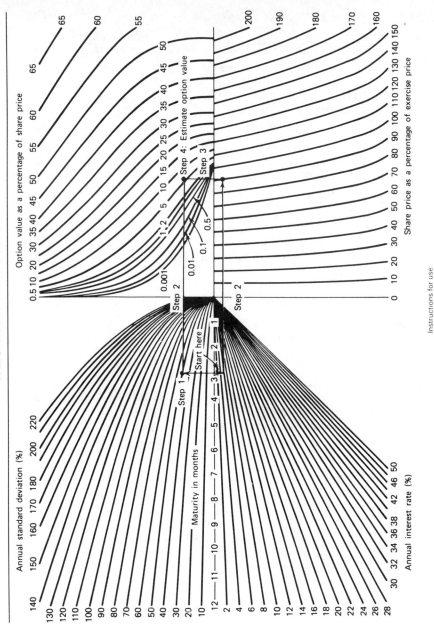

Instructions for use:

1. Draw vertical line through maturity

2. Draw horizontal lines from intersections with standard deviation and interest rate

3. Draw vertical line from intersection of horizontal with share price/exercise price

4. Interpolate option value from the intersecting lines in the positive quadrant

Source: E. Dimson, "Instant Option Valuation," *Financial Analysts Journal*, May–June 1977.

to make the calculations directly. The details of such a program are furnished in Rubinstein (1977) or Rubinstein and Cox (1981).

NOMOGRAMS FOR OPTION VALUATION. An alternative method using a **nomogram** is illustrated in Exhibit 12. To value an option, it is necessary to construct a box. The position on the left-hand side is determined by the maturity of the option. The top of the left-hand side is determined by the standard deviation of the stock's annual return and the bottom by the annual interest rate. The position of the right-hand side of the box is determined by the ratio of the current stock price to the exercise price (here, based on the location of the upper right-hand corner). In this case, the nomogram indicates that the option value is somewhat more than 5% of the exercise price, or $2(0.05 × $40); see Exhibit 13.

Exhibit 12 shows that, other things equal, an option is generally more valuable:

- The **higher** the current stock price relative to the exercise price.
- The **longer** the time remaining before expiration.
- The **higher** the riskless rate of interest.
- The **greater** the risk of the underlying stock.

Only the last of these factors requires estimation but, as the nomogram shows, it is of crucial importance.

A more detailed description, as well as nomograms for estimation of the value of put options, are available in Dimson's articles in the *Financial Analysts Journal*.

REFERENCES

Black, F., and Scholes, M., "The Pricing of Options and Corporate Liabilities, "*Journal of Political Economy*, May–June 1973, pp. 637–654.

Cox, J.C., and Rubinstein M., *Options Markets*, Prentice-Hall, Englewood Cliffs, NJ, 1985.

Dimson, E., "Instant Option Valuation," *Financial Analysts Journal*, May–June 1977, pp. 62–69.

———, "Option Valuation Nomograms," *Financial Analysts Journal*, November–December 1977, pp. 71–75.

Greynolds, E.B., Jr., Aronofsky, J.S., and Frame, R.J., *Financial Analysis Using Calculators: Time Value of Money*, McGraw-Hill, 1980.

Rubinstein, M., "How to Use the Option Pricing Formula, "University of California, Berkeley, Working Paper, 1977.

APPENDIX **B**

SOURCES OF FINANCIAL AND INVESTMENT INFORMATION

CONTENTS

APPENDIX **B**

SOURCES OF FINANCIAL AND INVESTMENT INFORMATION

ONLINE DATA BASES

Analystics
Chase Econometrics/Interactive Data Corp., Waltham, Massachusetts

Consists of 22 data bases covering a wide range of securities and financial statement data. Includes detailed security descriptions, daily price and volume data, market indicators, stock splits and dividends, commodities, international bonds and securities, and much more.

Commodities
Data Resources, Inc., Lexington, Massachusetts

Focuses on price and trading activity information for all major commodities traded in the United States, Canadian, and London markets.

Compustat
Standard & Poor's Compustat Services, Englewood, Colorado

Contains income statement, balance sheet, sources and applications of funds, line of business, and market information for publicly held U.S. and some non-U.S. corporations. Annual data are included for about 6000 industrial and nonindustrial companies. Quarterly data are available for 2800 companies.

Corporate Earnings Estimator
Zacks Investment Research, Chicago, Illinois

Reports on projected earnings of 3000 major U.S. companies. Based on a consensus of financial analysts.

Corporation Records Online
Standard & Poor's Corporation, New York, New York

Electronic version of the *Corporation Records* published in six volumes by Standard & Poor's. Includes detailed corporate descriptions. The "News Online" data base provides daily news supplements.

DRI-FACS
Data Resources, Inc., Lexington, Massachusetts

Coverage of interest rates, commercial bank assets and liabilities, and thrift institution activity. Interest rate information includes domestic money and bond markets, U.S. government security issues, and international money and foreign exchange rates.

DRI-SEC
Data Resources, Inc., Lexington, Massachusetts

Daily pricing and current fundamental information for equity, debt, and government agency issues listed on the New York, American, over-the-counter, regional, and Canadian exchanges. Includes market and industry indicators, and bond yields.

Disclosure II
Disclosure, Inc., Bethesda, Maryland

Contains information from all companies that file reports with the Securities and Exchange Commission (SEC). General descriptive information includes location and description of business, list of SEC reports filed, and more. Extracts from forms filed (10K, 10Q, 20K, 8K, proxy and registration statements) provide shareholder information, lists of subsidiaries, balance sheet and income statement data, and other financial information.

Disclosure/Spectrum Online
Disclosure, Inc., Bethesda, Maryland

Detailed and summary corporate ownership information for approximately 5000 public companies. Includes number of shares held by institutions, 5% owners, and corporate insiders.

Exstat
Extel Statistical Services, Ltd., London, England

Balance sheet and income statement account items for more than 3200 international corporations. Includes 10 years of historical annual data as well as current information.

Ford Data Base
Ford Investor Services, San Diego, California

Furnishes data on 1400 leading common stocks. Information includes earnings per share, projected earnings, debt/equity ratio, beta, quality rating, and more.

IBES
Lynch, Jones & Ryan, New York, New York

Provides earnings estimates on listed equity securities. Estimates are supplied by security analysts who follow specific stocks.

Investex
Business Research Group, Boston, Massachusetts

Provides complete text of more than 7000 research reports written by professional research analysts at major investment banking and financial research firms. Reports include financial data and market forecasts on companies and industries.

Investments
Muller Data Corporation, New York, New York

Contains over 50 different data items on corporate and government securities. Includes options, municipals, over-the-counter, and mutual funds. Current and historical data.

The M & A Database
The Hay Group, Philadelphia, Pennsylvania

Includes mergers, buyouts, tender offers, and divestitures valued at $1 million or more. Provides current company information, transaction description, stock price data, and other relevant information.

Market Decision System 7
Bunker Ramo Information Systems, Trumbull, Connecticut

Real-time financial information system includes information on stocks, bonds, options, commodities, currencies, and economic and business news. Also contains historical information and current research reports on 400 widely traded stocks.

Markets Advisory
Markets Advisory, Racine, Wisconsin

Technical analysis information for stocks, industries, market indexes, and more. Includes relative strength, moving averages, momentum, bar charts, point and figure charts, and other relevant information.

Media General Data Base
Media General Financial Services, Inc., Richmond, Virginia

Contains balance sheet, income statement, price, and volume data. Both quarterly and annual financial and trading data are presented.

Mergers and Acquisitions
Securities Data Company, Inc., New York, New York

Covers mergers, tender offers, and self-tender offers since 1981. Provides information on both the target's and acquiror's financial position, specifics of each transaction, price tracking, managers and fees, and geographical location of both the target and the acquiror.

Merlin
Hale Systems, Inc., Remote Computing Division, Roslyn, New York

Contains data on over 12,000 stocks, bonds, rights, warrants, and government issues. Includes both fundamental and technical data. Contains data on options listed on Chicago Board Options Exchange, and the American, Philadelphia, and Pacific stock exchanges. Contains commodities price, volume, and open interest data. Also includes indexes and statistics on the daily or weekly performance of the securities markets.

Merrill Lynch Research Service
Merrill Lynch, Inc., Securities Research Division, New York, New York

Contains summaries of Merrill Lynch's "Weekly Highlights" bulletin. Includes earnings estimates and investment ratings.

Microquote
The Gregg Corporation, Waltham, Massachusetts

Contains trading statistics and descriptive data on over 32,000 stocks, bonds, mutual funds, warrants, and options. Historical prices and data are available for most stocks. Daily, weekly, and monthly data are included.

Munifacts
The Bond Buyer, New York, New York

Contains current news, price, and related information for fixed income instruments. Includes municipals, corporate, and government issues as well as money market instruments. Current prices, key economic data, and market summaries are among the data included.

New Issues of Corporate Securities
Securities Data Company, Inc., New York, New York

Includes all new issues of taxable debt, common stock and preferred stock registered with the SEC since 1970. Provides offering price, coupon, maturity, call and sinking fund provisions, number of shares, earnings growth and other relevant information. Both public and private offering data are available.

New Issues of Municipal Debt
Securities Data Company, Inc., New York, New York

Includes new issues of tax-exempt debt with short and long maturities. Provides information on offering price, maturity, coupon, call and sinking fund provisions, and other relevant information.

Quotron 800
Quotron Systems, Inc., Los Angeles, California

A real-time financial information service with information on stocks, bonds, options, commodities, dividends and earnings, industry performance, and business and economic news. Contains market indicators and statistics as well as information on specific securities.

The Reuter Monitor
Reuters Ltd., New York, New York

Provides 14 services containing financial, securities, commodities, energy and general news information. Services include: Money/financial futures, money markets, grain/livestock, metals, coins, energy, securities, national news, optional news, optional domestic data, optional international data, optional securities quotations, tickers, contributed information.

S & P MarketScope
Standard & Poor's Corporation, New York, New York

Contains descriptive and financial data on over 4600 companies, reports and analyses of the stock, commodities, and municipal bond markets, and financial investment news. Includes earnings and dividend projections, company descriptions and other relevant financial information.

Securities Industry Data Bank (SI Data Bank)
Data Resources, Inc., Washington D.C.

Contains balance sheet and income statement data for twelve sectors of the securities industry. Individual exchange information includes round lot activity, number of shares available and their market value, and volume. Also includes data on credit market debt outstanding, gross proceeds, and number of issues of many types of equity and fixed income securities.

Telerate Financial Information Network
Telerate Systems, Inc., New York, New York

A real-time information service with data on domestic money markets, government securities, international rates, futures, options, stocks, and commercial banking statistics.

Telstat
Telstat Systems, Inc., New York, New York

Contains over 50 different data elements on stocks and bonds from 10 major stock exchanges in the United States and Canada, over-the-counter issues and options. Historical and current data are included. The municipal bond file contains prices, yield data, and other information.

Value Line Data Base II
Arnold Bernhard & Co., New York, New York

Provides compact income statements, balance sheets, sources and uses of funds, key ratios, and forecasts for 1600 companies.

Zacks Fundamentals
Zacks Investment Research, Inc., Chicago, Illinois

Contains earnings data on 3000 companies listed on the New York, American or over-the-counter exchanges for which analysts are making earnings forecasts. Includes 124 data items.

GENERAL INTEREST PERIODICALS

Title	Published
Business Starts	Quarterly
BusinessWeek	Weekly
Cash Flow	Monthly
Chapter 11 Reporter	Monthly
Conference Board Record	Monthly
Conference Board Statistical Bulletin	Monthly
Donoghue's Money Fund Report	Monthly
Dun's	Monthly
Euromoney	Monthly
Fact	Monthly
Finance	Monthly
Financial Executive	Monthly
Financial Planner	Bi-monthly
Financial Review, The	Quarterly
Financial World	Weekly
Forbes	Bi-weekly
Fortune	Bi-weekly
Futures	Monthly
Institutional Investor	Monthly
Investment Dealers' Digest	Weekly
Investment Strategy	Bi-monthly
Japan Stock Journal	Weekly
Market Value Index	Monthly
Mergers & Acquisitions	Quarterly
Money	Monthly
Nation's Business	Monthly
Newsweek	Weekly
OTC Review	Monthly
Stock Market Magazine	Monthly
Time	Weekly
U.S. News & World Report	Weekly
United States Investor	Weekly
Venture Capital	Monthly

RESEARCH AND SCHOLARLY JOURNALS

Title	Published
American Economic Review	Monthly
Bell Journal of Economics	Quarterly
CFA Digest, The (Chartered Financial Analysts)	Quarterly
Financial Analysts Journal	Bi-monthly
Financial Management	Quarterly
Financial Review, The	3 times
Harvard Business Review	Bi-monthly
Journal of Bank Research	Quarterly
Journal of Banking & Finance	Quarterly
Journal of Business	Quarterly
Journal of Cash Management	Bi-monthly
Journal of Commercial Bank Lending	Monthly
Journal of Economic Literature	Monthly
Journal of Finance & Quantitative Analysis	Quarterly
Journal of Finance	5 times
Journal of Financial Economics	Quarterly
Journal of Financial Research	Quarterly
Journal of Futures Markets	Quarterly
Journal of Money, Credit & Banking	Quarterly
Journal of Monetary Economics	Quarterly
Journal of Portfolio Management	Quarterly
Management Science	Monthly
Midland Corporate Finance Journal	Quarterly

NEWSPAPERS

Title	Period
American Banker	Daily
Barron's	Weekly
Bondweek	Weekly
Commercial & Financial Chronicle	Bi-weekly
Credit Markets	Weekly
Daily Commercial News	Daily
Financial Post (Canadian)	Weekly
Financial Times	Daily
Investment Week	Weekly
Investor's Daily	Daily
Japan Economic Journal	Weekly
Journal of Commerce	Daily
M/G Financial Weekly Market Digest	Weekly
Market Chronicle	Weekly
Money Manager	Weekly
National Observer	Weekly

Title	Period
New York Times	Daily
Penny Stock News	Bi-weekly
Pension & Investment Age	Bi-weekly
Wall Street Journal	Daily
Wall Street Transcript	Weekly
Weekly Bond Buyer	Weekly

PUBLICATIONS OF FINANCIAL SERVICES

Arnold Bernhard & Co.

Value Line Investment Survey (weekly)

Covers about 1700 stocks in weekly reports. Three major sections include: (1) commentary and analysis on a select number of issues, (2) summary information on all 1700 stocks, and (3) highlights of recommended purchases and general market information and forecasts. Firms are ranked from highest (1) to lowest (5) in potential.

Value Line New Issues Service (bi-weekly)

Recommends new issues for purchase. Includes pertinent information such as price, number of shares, company descriptions, and so forth.

Value Line OTC Special Situations (bi-weekly)

Contains recommendations for favorable high growth stocks traded over-the-counter. Includes summary information on all issues previously recommended as well as detailed quarterly follow-ups on each recommendation.

Value Line Options & Convertibles (bi-weekly)

Includes information on 585 convertible bonds and preferred stocks, 90 warrants, and 385 options. Provides recommendations, rankings and price analyses. Also includes general information on investing in these types of securities.

Dun & Bradstreet Corporation

Dun & Bradstreet issues the following reports on a regular basis:

Building Permits (quarterly)
Business Expectations (quarterly)
Business Failures (weekly/quarterly)
Business Starts (quarterly)
Monthly Bank Clearings
Weekly Bank Clearings

New Incorporations (monthly)
Wholesale Commodity Price Index (weekly)
Wholesale Food Price Index (weekly)

The reports provide textual and numerical comments, explanations and analyses of current economic situations.

Fitch Investors Service

Ratings Register (monthly)
Includes quality ratings for corporations, commercial paper, preferred stock, and numerous types of bond issues.

Corporate and Industry Research Report (revised periodically)
Includes company descriptions, operations information, financial data and Fitch quality ratings.

Lipper Analytical Distributors, Inc.
Lipper publishes a number of reports evaluating the performance of varying financial instruments and institutions, including:

Annuity & Closed End Survey (performance information)
Mutual Fund Performance Analysis (quarterly rankings by fund objective)
Convertible Analysis Report

Moody's Investors Service

Manuals and News Reports
Moody's publishes seven manuals which cover more than 20,000 U.S. and foreign corporations, and over 15,000 municipal and government entities. Includes industrial, OTC industrial, transportation, public utility, bank and finance, municipal and government, and international manuals. Contains a wide variety of information including company history, financial performance, and much more. Frequent news reports and up-to-date information are provided.

Bond Record (monthly)
Publication providing ratings and other financial data on over 32,000 issues. Includes convertibles, government and municipal issues, commercial paper, preferred stocks, and more.

Bond Survey (weekly)
Provides information on recent corporate bond offerings, ratings of bonds, commercial paper and preferred stock, yield averages, business and market comments, and more.

Dividend Record (twice weekly)

Provides information on new dividends, dividend changes, stock dividends and splits, and more. Includes key dates and amounts for over 11,000 issues.

Handbook of Common Stocks (quarterly)

Contains complete business/financial history, stock price charts, analysis of recent developments, and Moody's outlook for leading companies.

Handbook of OTC Stocks (quarterly)

Similar to the *Handbook of Common Stocks*, but concentrating on stocks traded Over-the-counter.

Investors Fact Sheets Industry Review (bi-annually)

Contains comparative statistics for each of 143 industries and data on all companies in that industry. Includes rankings of each company in an industry by key operating and investment criteria.

National Quotation Bureau

National Bond Summary (monthly)

Summary of quotes and other relevent information on bond transactions.

National Stock Summary (monthly)

Summary of quotes, shares outstanding, dividends, business changes, public offerings, price ranges. Includes six months of information.

Standard & Poor's Corporation (S & P)

Analyst's Handbook (annual with monthly updates)

Provides composite per share data for 67 industries and 15 transportation, financial, and utility groups. Allows for company versus industry, industry versus industry, and company or industry versus the S & P 400 comparisons.

Bond Guide (monthly)

Contains 41 items of descriptive and statistical data on approximately 5500 U.S. and Canadian corporate bonds. Also includes data on convertible and foreign bonds. Quality ratings are given for corporate bonds and all important state and municipal general obligation and revenue bonds.

Called Bond Record (twice weekly)

Includes call notices, prepayment notices, changes in conversion privileges, bond and stock tenders asked, defaults, and more.

Commercial Paper Ratings Guide (monthly)

Contains information on over 800 issues of commercial paper. Includes commercial and long-term debt ratings, bank line policy, and rating rationale.

Corporation Records (revised periodically)

Provides descriptions of general operations, plant locations, subsidiaries, financial structure and securities for 7900 large corporations. Also contains more concise coverage on 2000 corporations next in importance. Daily news section assures that information is always current.

CreditWeek (weekly)

Analyzes ratings, trends, and the outlook for fixed income securities, including corporate and municipal bonds and commercial paper. Detailed analysis of new issues.

Credit Week International (quarterly)

Supplement to CreditWeek. Includes eurobonds, yankee bonds and commercial paper.

Dividend Record (daily, weekly, or quarterly)

Provides dividend information on over 10,000 stocks.

Earnings Forecaster (weekly)

Provides current earnings estimates on 1600 companies. Includes source of estimate, previous year earnings, current price and estimate of future earnings.

Handbooks (semi-annual)

Each handbook focuses on a particular area of interest: growth stocks, high-tech stocks, oil and gas stocks, S&P 500, OTC, American Stock Exchange, and options. Includes feature articles, charts, graphs, and S&P Stock Reports for each area.

Industry Surveys

Economic and business information on 22 industries. Financial data on 1300 companies is included. The *Basic Survey* is published annually for each industry, and is periodically updated by the *Current Survey*. Two other monthly publications, *Trends & Projections*, and *Earning Reports* complete the package.

New Issues Investor (monthly)

Includes recommendations and important information on companies making their initial public offerings of common stock. Provides follow-up reports on previous recommendations and interim updates.

Outlook (weekly)

Comprehensive investment advisory service. Commentary on current market trends, individual stock recommendations for various investment strategies, industry discussions, and general economic analyses.

Daily Stock Price Record (quarterly)

Three volumes of day-by-day accounts of price histories on over 7300 issues listed on the New York, American, and over-the-counter exchanges. Over-the-counter volume includes almost 600 mutual funds.

Register of Corporations, Directors & Executives (annual, with quarterly supplements)

Provides titles and duties of all leading officers and executives, department heads, and technical personnel for over 45,000 nationally known companies.

Stock Guide (monthly)

Statistical summary of investment data on over 5300 common and preferred stocks and 400 mutual funds. 48 data items on each stock are included. Contains forecasts, ratings, rankings, and current financial and market information.

Stock Reports (updated continuously)

Profiles of stock performance and financial history of over 4400 widely traded companies. Includes background information on each company, as well as selected financial data.

Stock Summary (monthly)

Includes 40 data items for each of 1920 stocks. Price, earnings, dividend, and other selected financial information is included.

Statistical Service (bi-annually and monthly)

Consists of three separate publications: the *Security Price Index Record, Business and Financial Statistics*, and *Current Statistics* (published monthly).

Index Services (weekly, monthly, and quarterly)

A variety of reports covering stock price indexes. Provides continuous updating and current information on these indexes.

The Blue List (daily)

Contains information on municipal bond offerings, grouped into 13 categories.

Trendline

Daily Action Stock Charts (weekly)

Charts 754 stocks on a daily basis. Each chart shows 12 months of price and volume history. Includes earnings estimates and rankings, growth rates, relative strength ratios and other information. Includes reports on 44 popular indexes.

Current Market Perspectives (monthly)

Charts 1476 stocks on a weekly basis. Each chart shows four years of price and volume history. Includes price, earnings, and performance information similar to that of the *Daily Action Stock Charts*.

OTC Chart Manual (bi-monthly)

Covers 800 stocks on a weekly basis. Includes earnings, dividend and financial information and estimates, as well as information on technical indicators.

MISCELLANEOUS PUBLISHERS

Title	Publisher
AMEX Data Book	American Stock Exchange
Commodity Chart Service	Commodity Research Bureau
Commodity Year Book	Commodity Research Bureau
Dow Jones Investor's Handbook	Dow Jones
Credit Decisions	Duff & Phelps
Fixed Income Services	Duff & Phelps
The Dun & Hargitt Commodity Service	Dun & Hargitt, Inc.
Financial Stock Guide Service	Financial Information Service
A Half Century of Returns on Stocks and Bonds	Fisher & Lorie
Mutual Fund Fact Book	Inv. Company Institute
Mutual Fund Directory	Inv. Dealers' Digest
Over-the-Counter Growth Stocks	John S. Herold, Inc.
KV Convertible Fact Finder	Kalb, Voorhis & Co.
Credit Critiques	McCarthy, Crisante & Maffier
MCM Rating Summaries	McCarthy, Crisante & Maffier
Rating Watch	McCarthy, Crisante & Maffier
The Stock Picture	M.C. Horsey
NASDAQ/OTC Market Fact Book	National Association of Security Dealers

Title	Publisher
Corporate Affiliations	National Reg. Publishing Company
Nelson's Directory of Wall Street Research	Nelson
Fact Book	New York Stock Exchange
R.H.M. Survey of Warrants, Options & Low Priced Stocks	R.H.M. Associates, Inc.
Yearbook	Securities Industry Association
United Business & Investment Reports	United Business Service
Guide to Bank Trust Portfolios	Vickers Associates, Inc.
Guide to College Endowment Portfolios	Vickers Associates, Inc.
Guide to Insur. Co. Portf. (common stocks)	Vickers Associates, Inc.
Vicker's Investment Company Portfolios	Vickers Associates, Inc.
Investment Companies	Weisenberger
Daily Graphs Stock Option Guide	William O'Neill & Co.

TELEVISION SHOWS

Name	Channel
Network Shows:	
Adam Smith's Money World	PBS
Nightly Business Report	PBS
Strictly Business	NBC
Wall Street Journal Report	Local
Wall Street Week	PBS
Window on Wall Street	PBS
Cable Shows:	
BizNet News Today	USA
Business Times	ESPN
Business Today	FNN
Inside Business	CNN
Marketwatch	FNN
Moneyline	CNN
Moneytalk	FNN
Moneyweek	CNN
Wall Street Final	FNN
Your Money	CNN

GOVERNMENT PUBLICATIONS

Title	Publisher	Frequency
Annual Report of the SEC	SEC	Annual
Annual Statistical Digest	Federal Reserve	Annual
Business Conditions Digest	Dept. of Commerce	Monthly

Title	Publisher	Frequency
Business Statistics	Dept. of Commerce	Bi-annually
Economic Indicators	Council of Economic Advisors	Monthly
Economic Report of the President	Office of the President	Annual
Federal Reserve Bank Reviews	Federal Reserve	Monthly
Federal Reserve Bulletin	Federal Reserve	Monthly
Federal Reserve Monthly Chart Book	Federal Reserve	Monthly
Finance & Development	IMF & World Bank	Quarterly
Flow of Funds	Federal Reserve	Quarterly
International Financial Statistics	International Monetary Fund	Monthly
Money Stock Measures & Liquid Assets		Weekly
Quarterly Financial Report, The	Federal Trade Commission	Quarterly
Statistical Bulletin	SEC	Monthly
Survey of Current Business	Dept. of Commerce	Monthly
Treasury Bulletin	Department of Treasury	Monthly

USEFUL INDEXES

- *Business Periodicals Index*
- *Public Affairs Information Service*
- *Wall Street Journal Index*
- *F & S Index of Corporations and Industries*
- *Predicasts*
- *F & S Index of Corporate Ghange*
- *Disclosure Journal*

COMPANY PROVIDED INFORMATION

All publicly traded companies are required to file certain documents with the SEC. These include the following:

- Annual Report
- Security Prospectus
- 8-K
- 9-K
- 10-K

These reports can be obtained through the SEC, your local library, or the company's shareholder relations department.

INDEX